W9-ADQ-862

THE COMPLETE BOOK OF
COLLECTIBLE CARS

BLUE CHIP AUTO INVESTMENTS
70
YEARS
OF
1930 - 2000

BY RICHARD M. LANGWORTH
AND THE AUTO EDITORS OF CONSUMER GUIDE

Publications International, Ltd.

SPECIAL THANKS TO THE FOLLOWING FOR CONTRIBUTIONS:

Mirco DeCet
David Gooley
Hartford Heritage Auto Museum
Land Rover North America, Inc.
Bruce McPherson
Graham Robson
Brooks Stevens
Jairus Watson

ACKNOWLEDGMENTS

The editors gratefully acknowledge the following photographers whose photographs appear in this book.

Scott Baxter; Ken Beebe; Derek Bell; Les Bidrawn; Mark Bilek; Joe Bohovic; Jan Borgfeldt; Arch Brown; Rob Burrington; Chan Bush; Gary Cameron; Thom Cannell; Bob Cavallo; Fred Chamberlain; Bill Coby; Mirco DeCet; Neil Doherty; Gavin Farmer; Steen Fleron; Roland Flessner; Jim Frenak; Mitch Frumkin; Alex Gabbard; Thomas Glatch; Ed Goldberger; Winston Goodfellow; David Gooley; Gary Greene; Sam Griffith; Mike Hastie; Jerry Heasley; Don Heiny; Fergus Hernandes; Alan Hewko; Bill Hill; Ron Hussey; Bert E. Johnson; Harvey Johnson; Jeff Johnson; Bud Juneau; Tim Kerwin; Milton Kieft; Bill Kilborn; Rick Lenz; Ed Lobit; Randy Lorentzen; Dan Lyons; Vince Manocchi; Mark McMahon; Doug Mitchel; Ron Moorhead; Mike Mueller; David

Newhardt; Neil Nissing; Morton Oppenheimer; Nina Padgett-Russin; David Patryas; Jay Peck; Frank Peiler; Phillips Camera House; Chris Poole; Rick Popely; Rob Reaser; D. Randy Riggs; Jeff Rose; Allan Rosenberg; Scott Rosenberg; William J. Schintz; Andy Selvaggio; Tom Shaw; Mike Slade; Gary Smith; Robert Sorgatz; Richard Spiegelman; Steve Statham; Rick Stiller; Ned H. Stokes; Matt Stone; Tom Storm; David Talbot; Denis L. Tanney; David Temple; Bob Tenney; Rithea Tep; Jim Thompson; Phil Toy; Kris Trexler; Gary Versteege; W.C. Waymack; Joseph H. Wherry; White Eagle Studio; Hub Wilson; Nicky Wright; Franco Zagari; Zoom Photographic.

The editors gratefully acknowledge the following owners whose cars appear in this book.

ACD Museum; George Adams; Noel Adams; Frederic L. Aibel; Martin Allard; George Alleger; Allen County Motors; Andrew Alphonso; Mark Alter; Steve Ames; Barrie Aquailino; David Arent; Ross P. Armijo; Dr. Barbara Atwood; George Augeston; John Augustine; Lynn Augustine; Jeffrey Baker; Michael Bancroft; Raymond & Carole Banicki; Bank of America; Rex Barrett; Tom Barrett; Dave Bartholomew; Frank Baumann; Nancy L. Beauregard; Carl J. Beck; Clarence Becker; Buzz & Fran Beckman; John W. Beebe; Robert Beechy; Chuck Beed; Jim & Joyce Belardi; Larry Bell; Bell and Colville Lotus Dealer; Kevin R. Benham; John Bentz; Don Bergman; Bill & Kathy Berks; Chuck Bernecker; Edward R. Bernstein; TW Bernstein; Michael L. Berzenye; J.R. Betson, Jr.; Ed Bettine; Leslie A. Billib; Rob Bilott; Blackhawk Auto Collection; Jim Blanchard; Frank R. Bobek; Pete Bogard; Rex Bond;

Ray B. Bowersox; Bob Bowkowsky; Ron Bransky; Bob Briggs; David Brodsky; Eugene W. Brotzman; James J. Brown; Scott Brubaker; Judy Bruggenthies; Rodney Brumbaugh; Barb & Tom Bruns; George A. Buchinger; William Buetel; Joe Burke; Frank Burnham; Virginia P. Burns; Bob Bychowski; J. Kim Callahan; Jerry Capizzi; Harvey Caplin; Bonnie Carey; Robert Carlson; Richard Carpenter; Donnie Carr; Dale & Roxanne Carrington; James H. Carson; Dean & Wanda Casey; Mr. & Mrs. Benjamin R. Caskey, Jr.; June Cecil; Bob Chandler; Brad Chandler; Laura Chandler; Otis Chandler; Bernie Chase; Jim Chernock; Chevs N' Vettes Inc. of Scottsdale; Chicago Car Exchange, Inc.; Marty Chung; Gary Clark; Jim Clark; Classic Car Center; Classic Showcase; Jerry Cinotti; Gordon & Dorothy Clemmer; Mick Cohen; John Coleman; Mike Coleman; James E. Collins; Secondo J. Colombero; Dr. Steven Colsen; Fred Comlossy; Community Trading Center; Dennis & Erin Conly; Contemporary & Investment Automobiles; Continental Motors; John Cook; Harry Cornelius; Dave Couling; Mike Cowles; John Cox; Crawford Collection/Western Reserve Historical Society; Briggs S. Cunningham; Cunningham Auto Museum; Donald W. Curtis; Raymond E. Dade; Ted Dahlmann; Arthur & Suzanne Dalby; Richard Daly; Brad Damico; John Danell; Dan Darling; Bill Daubney; Hans Davidson; Jim Davidson; Ted Davidson; Charles Davis; Chris Davis; Don & Linda Davis; Gene Davis; Myron Davis; Sherwood H. Davis; Wayne Davis Restoration; W.E. Davis; Nigel Dawes; Russell & Shirley Dawson; Deer Park Car Museum; Harry DeMenge; Thomas Derro; John J. Deving; The Domino's Collection; Domino's Rearview Museum; Robert Dongara; Orville Dopps; Robert Dowd; Michael Doyle; Stanley & Phyllis Dumes; Pete Dunkel; Maurice Durall; Tim Dusek; Jim Dworschack; John & Mary Dwyer; Jay Dykes; Tom Easterday; Roger Eberenz; Joseph J. Eberle; Al Eichelberger; Glenn Eisenhamer; Donald & Sue Eller; Gunnar Elmgren; Mike Elward; Jerry Emery; John M. Endres; Fred Engers; Fred Engle; Robert English; Roger & Carol Erickson; Esther Day Candies Corp.; Fairway Chevrolet; Vic & Cathy Falcone; Gordon Farqumarson; Russel Farris; Franz Fechner; David L. Ferguson; Mark E. Figliozzi; Don Figone; Peter L. Fino, Jr.; John T. & Jeanne C. Finster; Hudson D. Firestone; Colin Fitzgerald; Burt Van Flue; John Fobair; Steve Foley Rolls-Royce, Inc.; Joseph B. Folladori; Richard Foster; Bob French; Stan Fritzinger; Terry Gale; Don & Becky Galeziewski; Ruben J. Garcia; Paul Garlick; Jack & Jan Garris; P. Garvey; Kenneth Geiger; Charles P. Geissler; Ralph Geissler; Joseph D. Geist; Cliff Gentle; Bob Getsfried; Gary Gettleman; Emain Glassad; William Goodsell; Irvin H. Gordon; Roger & Connie Graeber; Wayne R. Graefen; Dave Graham; Jack Gratzianna; Mary Gray; Michael S. Gray; Neil Greener; Jim D. Gregorio; Tom Griffith; Mike Grippo; Anthony J. Gullatta; Ed Gunther; Wanda Habenicht; Ronald & Sonja Halbauer; George Hamlin; David Hans; Jack Harbaugh; John F. Hare; Ralph Harms; Harrah's National Auto Museum; Jay Harrigan; Billy & Dorothy Harris; Henry Hart; Jerry Hathaway; Dennis J. Hauke; Michael R. Hausman; Ken Havekost; Maurice B. Hawa; William T. Hayes & Sons; Harvey Hedgecock; Duane Hedke; John & Helen Heist; Dennis Helferich; Ross Helko; Steve Hendricks; Jim Hendrix; Dr. Ernie Hendry; Bill Henefelt; Ed Henning; Roy Herbener; James Herman; Edward L. Hess; Jules Heumann; Bud Hicks; Bill Hill; Bob Hill; David Hill; James Hill; Mel R. Hill; Brad & Barb Hillick; Scott Hiss; Holly Hollenbeck; Thomas Hollfelder; David Holls; Andrew Holmes; Tim Holsapple; Bill & Berta Honey; Weston Hook; Lester H. Hooley; David D. Horn; John H. Horning; Bob & Joan Houillon; Dick Hoyt; Dennis Huff; Jeff Hughes; Melvin R. Hull; Lewis H. Hunter; Charlene & Duane Hyatt; Robert Ingold; Chris Jakubowski; Pete Jakubowski; Roger A. James; George Jarmusz; Norman T. Jarrett; Robert M. Jarrett; Donald Jensen; Gerta Orla Jensen; Tom Jervis; George S. Jewell; Tim John; Anthony Johnson; Dick Johnson; Jerry Johnson; Terry Johnson; Albert A. Jones; Bill Jones; Bud Juneau; John Kaelin; Press & Janet Kale; Rick Kamen; T. Donald Kamm; Thomas L. Karkeiwicz; Craig Karr; Roger Kash; W.P. Keeler; James Keller; Kelley Classics; Joe Jelly; John & Minnie Keys; Knox Kershaw; Royce & Clydette Kidd; W. Michael King; William Kipp; John R. Kissinger; Gary J. Kistinger; Larry Klein; Frank Kleptz; Robert Kleptz; George Kling; Kevin Kloubec; Bill Knudson; Steven Knutsen; Philomena Konco-Kohan; William W. Kramer; Ron Kroel; Everett A. Kroeze; Hank Kubicki; Darvin & Becca Kuehl; Richard and Linda Kughn; Phil Kuhn; Jim Labertew; Ron & Debbie Ladley; Jim Lahti; Larry K. Landis; Wesley C. Lantz; Chris Lapp; William Lauer; Ron Laurie; James R. Lauzon; Tony Law; William H. Lawer; Ken Leaman; John D. Lebold; Steve Lefevre; Harold Lehman; Dr. R. Leia; Ken Leighton; Jack Lenhart; Dr. William H. Lenharth; Danny Letner; Dennis Levine; Bob Lewis; Libertyville Lincoln-Mercury, Inc.; Mitch Lindahl; Ronald Ray Lipang; Klaus Lischer; Phillip & Sandy LoPiccolo; Michael J. Lotwis; Robert Loudon; Terry Lucas; Tony Luther; Thomas E. Lyon; Dennis & Cheri Macdonald; Dennis Machul; Bob Macy; John Madison; Larry Maisel; Joe Malta; Mr. Mandarano; Sam & Emily Mann; Bud Manning; Commander Marr; David Marshall; Larry Martin; Richard & Madeline Martindale; Mr. & Mrs. Masson-Styrron; Cliff Mathos; Richard Matzer; Gerard & Lorraine May; Raymond L. May; Lloyd & Martha Mayes; Steve Maysonet; Cecil McCall; Jim McCann; Barry McCaw; Bryan McGilvray; Paul McGuire; W.A. McKnight; Dr. Milt McMillen; Bruce McPherson; Keith W. Meiswinkel; Tom Meleo; Ray Menefee; Michael Mennela; Marty and Jacque Metzgar; Bruce Meyer; Don Micheletti; Charles Michelson; Jack C. Miller; S. Ray Miller Auto Museum; Amos Minter; Albert Mitchell; Thomas Mittler; Thom Moerman; Clay Mollman; Charlie Montano; Bob Montgomery; Mr. & Mrs. Ken Mooney; Bob Moore; Jack E. Moore; Guy Morice; Michael Morocco; Dean J. Moroni; Rod Morris; Harvey Moyses; William R. Muni; Rebecca Munk; Don Myracle; Ken Myracle; M. Randall Mytar; National Motor Museum at Beaulieu; Gerald & Katherine Nell; Bill Nelson; Ken Nelson; Wayne Nelson; Carol Nesladek; Walter Neumayer; David C. Newkirk; Roger Nichols; Jim Noel; Duffy & Kelly Nopenz; Barry Norman; Tom Null; Steve Nye; Dan J. Obele; Jim & Linda O'Dell; Douglas A. Olgilvie; Alan Oman; Edward E. Ortiz; John Otto; Russ Owens; Ann Page; Robert W. Paige; Samuel Pampenella, Jr.; John E. Parker; Patricia & Rexford Parker; Richard T. Parker; Jack Passey, Jr.; Glen & Barbara Patch; Bob Patrick; Thomas J. Patterson; Lawrence Pavia; Greg Pawluk; Thomas & Christine Payne; A.J. Pegno; Gene Peliter; Jim Perrault; Tony Perrett; Peters Motor Cars; Donald W. Peters; Marshall & Ellie Peters; Jeff Peterson; Edsel H. Pfabe; Edward Pfabe; David Piangerelli; Joseph F. Piccione; Joseph Pieroni; Richard Pietizuska; A. La Rue Plotts, Jr.; Thomas E. & Carol A. Podemski; Robert J. Pond Automobile Collection; Lee Pontius; John Poochigian; Bob Porter; Graham Porter; Bernard Powell; Jeff Powell; Merle Preinflak; John Prokop; Glen & Janice Pykiet; Hilary Raab, Jr.; Ted & Jo Raines; Jim Ramage; Ramshead Auto Collection; Ken Rathke; Les Raye; Art Raymo; L. Joe Redford; Don Reel; Robert Reeves; David Reidy; Jim Reilly; Bill Reinhardt; Glen & Vera Reints; Steve Rhodes; Jerry Richman; John Richter; John & Judy Riordan; Richard Rivoir; David L. Robb; Conrad W. Roellchen; Ben Rose; Bob Rose; Dennis D. Rosenberry; Jack Rosenzweig; Chris Ross; Don Ross; Jim Ross; Joseph Rotar; Fred Roth; Herb Rothman; Tony & Anne Marie Rowland; Glyn-Jan Rowley; Jim Rudolph; Vince Ruffolo; Lily Rusnak; Robert Russell; Arthur J. Sabin; Glenn Sager; Darryl A. Salisbury; Bruce Sansone; Robert Sauenschell; Christopher Savill; Al Schaefer; Allen Scherer; Paul Schinnerer; Gary Schneider; Ron & Eleanor Schneider; Rick & Miki Schug; Sam H. Scoles; Kenneth Scotland; Larry & Judy Scott; John Segedy; Robert N. Seiple; Rosemary & Duane Sell; Mike Shafsnitz; Bob & Frances Shaner; Bob & Roni Sue Shapiro; Dana P. Shatts; Carroll Shelby; John W. Siebel; Raymond Silva, Jr.; Duane & Carol Silvius; Roy Sklarin; Henry Smith; Karl W. Smith; Marvin O. Smith; Tracy Snell; John Sobers; Sheryl Sommers; Mike Spaziano; Walt Sprague; Vince & Helen Springer; Richard Staley; H. Robert & Kathryn Stamp; Danny L. Steine; Brooks Stevens Museum; David Stevens; Jack & Holly Stewart; Kurt Stier; John F. Stimac, Jr.; C.A. Stoddard; Ned H. Stokes; M.J. Strumpf; A.J. Sutton; Scott Swaydrak; Brad & Bev Taffs; Emily Tax; Phil Taxman; Adrian Thompson; Eric Thompson; Hubert Thompson; Ken Thompson; Robert Thorton; Eric M. Thurstone; Steven Tillack; Steven & Joyce Toms; Ernest J. Toth, Jr.; Jeff Tranberg; Jerry Tranberger; Thomas Traynor; Kris Trexler; Samuel G. Tribble; June Trombley; Greg Turley; Alan Uejo; Kenneth Ugolini; Dean Ullman; Bill Ulrich; Dennis A. Urban; Bruce Valley; Charles A. Vance; Neil Vedder; Charles Vickery; Carlos & Sherry Vivas; Tony Voiture; Harold VonBrocken; Ron Voyles; Barry Waddell; Jeff Wade; Ron Wakefield; Robert & Christine Waldock; Bob & Wendi Walker; Phil Walker; Robert Walker; Wilmer & Lila Walker; Jeff Walther; Bruce Wanner; Alois Peter Warren II; Bill Warren; Heath Washburn; Charles & Charlotte Watons; Larry Webb; Al Webster; Lewis Weinstein; Anthony Wells; John Wells; Bruce Wennertrom; James W. West; Odus West; Tom West; William E. Wetherhost; Edward J. Wey; H.H. Wheeler; John White; Jim Wickel; Bobby Wiggins; Len Wilby; Al Wilkiewicz; Evelyn & John Willburn; Bryan Williams; Jay Williams; Steve Williams; Dennis G. Wise; Richard Witer; David W. Witt; Patrick Wnek; Bill Woodman; Harry Woodnorth; Harry Wynn; Dennis Yauger; Jerry Yonker; Andrew & Phyllis Young; William Young; Marvin E. Yount, Jr.; Robert Zaitlin; Urs Zangger; Michael Zaworski.

TABLE OF CONTENTS

TABLE OF CONTENTS

TABLE OF CONTENTS

TABLE OF CONTENTS

INTRODUCTION

Welcome to the latest edition of a book that testifies to America's deep and abiding love affair with old cars. Richard Langworth's and Graham Robson's original *Complete Book of Collectible Cars 1940-1980* appeared nearly 20 years ago as the first book of its kind, a fact that figured in its high success as much as the sharp rise in collector car enthusiasm—and prices—that began about the same time. In 1987, responding to the inevitable need for updates to keep pace with changing market trends and vehicle values, the authors added a decade's worth of pre-1940 collectibles and revised a plethora of existing information to create *The New Complete Book of Collectible Cars 1930-80.* Another reason for that update was that we'd expanded Richard Langworth's highly acclaimed *Encyclopedia of American Cars* to cover that same significant half-century, which made similar chronology for this companion volume logical and worthwhile.

Now we've done it again with this new edition that adds another 10 years of coverage at the more recent end of the spectrum. It's prompted in part by the advent of our encyclopedia-like *50 Years of American Automobiles 1939-1989.* Moreover, we've revised the format to make pricing data more meaningful to investors as well as old-car hobbyists in general.

In that 1987 edition we said there were probably a half-million people who acquire, restore, and exhibit older cars, up from a quarter-million seven years before, and still not counting the thousands more in the specialized service industries that support collectors with everything from reproduction parts to books like this. We won't hazard a guess about the hobby's population today, but it has undoubtedly gone up significantly in the interim despite—or maybe because of—the sudden price fallout of the early 1990s.

Conversely—and a happy thing it is for collectors—old car values have generally gone down. Like other investments in the '80s, some old-car values climbed to outrageous heights, freezing out many collectors of more modest means, forcing them to settle for cars of somewhat lower status. A big contributing factor in all this was plenty of willing, available money—some of it foreign—that only encouraged still-higher prices by speculators hoping to make a killing, combined by a growing number of uninformed and over-eager. Today, the col-

lector body is better educated and more experienced.

Though bona fide blue-chips like Duesenberg Js, original Ferrari GTOs, and '60s Corvette Sting Rays have returned to saner levels, the speculative fever of the '80s has rendered certain '50s and '60s Detroit convertibles, hardtop coupes, and muscle cars much scarcer and costlier than they once were. Persistent reports suggest that a good many of those machines went to Europe and Japan, perhaps never to return. The flip side is that next-to-topline models and variations like hardtop sedans and pillarless wagons have, of necessity, come to the fore after years of little or no collector interest, a phenomenon reflected in the contents of this book. Likewise, some of the relatively neglected makes have seen strong value increases—check for example the percentage gains among '60s Plymouths compared to their higher priced onetime rivals from Ford and Chevy.

The number of old-car enthusiasts may be greater than ever, but it encompasses no less variety in the way of backgrounds and personal interests. Some collectors amass old cars—and commercial vehicles, too—the way others gather up antique furniture or old coins, owning five, 10, or more. Some diligently search only for particular models, often those remembered from their youth. Still others concentrate on rare or obscure makes and models or a particular type—'30s Classics or '60s muscle cars, for example. As ever, aficionados pore over newspaper classifieds, advertisements in a wide array of hobby publications, on the fringes of used-car lots, in junkyards, at auctions, and in spots like the proverbial old barns where, says the universal dream, lurks anything from a Packard to a Pacer, ready to be snapped up for a song from some hapless owner ignorant of the treasure he possesses.

But that's just the beginning. Collectors typically want to restore their prizes, perhaps even drive them regularly. Much depends on the car in question, how old or rare it is, its condition, and owner aims. For some, the object may simply be to get the thing running again. Others may settle for nothing less than a ground-up restoration involving tons of money, considerable time tracking down replacement parts (whether reproductions or "new old stock" leftovers), locating specialists for various jobs and, finally, deciding where to keep

the like-new beauty—and how much it's worth to insure. This is an increasingly complicated undertaking, since government at all levels is far more intrusive now than it was even ten years ago: freon for air conditioners has been banned, along with leaded and truly high-test gasoline; some states and municipalities are considering "clunker laws" that will make it all but impossible to register even well-maintained older cars. The collector hobby is just beginning to fight these intrusions—and it had better.

Like fans of most any stripe, car collectors band together in clubs to share their enthusiasm through regular meetings, social gatherings, and shows. And it doesn't take much to encourage many owners to enter their cars in general "open" meets, where they vie for trophies and plaques, public approval (in "people's choice" balloting), and often cash. There are mixed opinions about prizes. Some collectors disdain them, saying they are in this hobby for the fun of it; but prizes bestowed by respected national car clubs also attest to a car's individual "pedigree." Veteran collector and restorer Bob Turnquist, of Hibernia Auto Restoration in New Jersey, says, "a national first prize attests that you are not the only one who thinks you have a great car."

Of course, it's ever true that not every old car is worth collecting or even preserving. Deciding which are and which aren't can be a highly subjective business, since most anything can become "collectible" if it's rare enough due to attrition or original scarcity. But there *are* standards on which knowledgeable car folk can agree and that can be applied with fair consistency and objectivity.

That's the purpose of this book. Like its predecessors, *The Complete Book of Collectible Cars 1930-2000* has been compiled by The Auto Editors of CONSUMER GUIDE in association with an expert in the field, Richard M. Langworth, author of 40 books and 2000 articles about vintage cars, founding editor of AUTOMOTIVE INVESTOR, and longtime contributor to COLLECTIBLE AUTOMOBILE.

Entries again follow the popular CONSUMER GUIDE new-car format, but are more numerous than before—over 1,000 in all—and listed in a single alphabetic form without regard to country of origin. Continued from past editions is a capsule history of the model or models covered in a given entry, plus a summary of characteristics **For** and **Against** collectibility. Where applicable, we cite recognition as a Classic by the Classic Car Club of America (CCCA) or as a Milestone by the Milestone Car Society (MCS). Also continuing are brief **Specifications** and available **Engines**, plus original **Production** broken down where possible by model year, body style, engine, or other pertinent factors.

Original production is one indicator of current availability, and hence value. On that subject, each entry again contains a **Prices** section showing typically asked value ranges for three condition classes: Fair (labeled "Restorable" in earlier editions), Good, and Fine (formerly "Excellent"). Concluding each entry is a **Fine Example Price History** with typical as-traded values for top-condition models over the years since 1982, the compound annual rate of **Return** on investment during 1982-2000, and a 10-year percentage value projection (replacing previous editions' five-year forecast). These changes allow you to see not only where a car is likely to go price-wise, but also where it's been, which should help you better peg prices when you buy or sell.

There's little else you need to know before diving in. However, three areas deserve some explanatory words: the factors involved in the selections, the way prices/projections were determined, and notes on technical data.

SELECTION CRITERIA

All entries, again the product of considerable culling and thought, are arranged alphabetically by make and chronologically by initial production or model year. Historical and technical data are drawn from contemporary accounts, latterday "standard works," and the seasoned judgments of the authors and editors.

Of course, no two people will agree on the full roster. There are doubtless some models you'll think we should have included—and some you'll think we should have left out. To paraphrase the old adage, one person's "classic car" is another's junkpile. There's also no accounting for taste, nor for what one writer has termed the "oddball factor."

Because this work is aimed mainly at American readers, original availability in that market was a first consideration. However, some models and foreign marques not widely known in the U.S. are included because various other factors make these cars too significant and/or valuable to ignore.

One factor that weighed heavily was whether a given model had been recognized as a Milestone car. This citation, created in 1972 with the founding of the Milestone Car Society, has become a widely accepted indicator of historical significance, and this has inevitably had its influence on values. To be a Milestone, a car must be judged superior to its contemporaries in at least two of five categories: styling, engineering, performance ("roadability" as well as acceleration or top speed), innovation (in concept or through some pioneering feature), and craftsmanship.

This broad umbrella can cover a multitude of automobiles. Cars like the Mercedes-Benz 300SL "Gullwing" or Continental Mark II would arguably qualify in all five areas. Others, like the Rolls-Royce Silver Dawn or Frazer Manhattan, barely make it in two—and one of those is Craftsmanship.

We also considered the similar list of Classics set up in the 1950s by the Classic Car Club of America, which was especially important in narrowing down the many possible choices among prewar models. (Though Classic car eligibility runs through 1948, very few postwar cars are Classics.) Though we've noted most Milestones and Classics within the appropriate entries, complete lists of both can be found at the back of this book. Be aware, however, that these lists are not static—cars are added from time to time.

Classics and Milestones were only starting points. High collector interest helped us single out many other important cars not on those lists. In some cases we've included an entire model line, noting individual versions of special merit. These typically comprise, but are not limited to, the body styles enthusiasts traditionally favor: convertible coupes and sedans, wood-body station wagons, hardtop coupes, and some hardtop sedans and hardtop wagons. "Across the board" endorsements are relatively few; those cited reflect collector interest in a make for a given period that is strong enough to render distinctions among models, body types, engines, and so on more or less meaningless. This applies as much to 1930-38 Duesenberg Js as to 1955-57 Chevys.

Limited editions and special packages were obvious candidates, and you'll find a great many here, including some that may surprise you. We also "looked around" them to see if any linemates satisfied the basic MCS criteria. In some cases, they did. Thus, for example, are listed the low-volume, Milestone-certi-

fied 1956-58 Plymouth Furys, and—in a separate entry—their more common, but still worthy, convertible and hardtop companions in the standard Belvedere series.

A final word on selections: Although we do not list customized cars, we've begun to list some light trucks, since they now command highly devoted enthusiast followings.

PRICES

You may be in for a few more surprises here. Unlike periodic "old-car price guides," we do not make hairline distinctions between individual models, body styles, or equipment except where the market makes them or the gulf is obviously wide. Nor have we set up a complex grading system for condition or equipment (and certainly not mileage). Instead, you'll find a more reasoned approach involving just three condition classes:

Fair: This is what collectors mean by a car that's "all there." It has a body, chassis, engine, even an interior, but it may not run, and it will need considerable restoration work (including parts). This definition does *not* encompass "basket cases" that are clearly unsalvageable. To be restorable, a car must have enough of its original "self" left so an owner can bring it back to life, even if it breaks a bank account. Then again, sufficient new and original-stock parts exist for cars like the Ford Model A that you could probably build a new one—but that's cheating.

More notorious are the so-called "assembled cars": latterday body swaps and "reproduction" coachwork often involving, but not at all limited to, Classic chassis such as Auburn, Duesenberg, Packard, and Pierce-Arrow. Such "forgeries" typically aim to turn some relative sow's ear into a priceless silk purse, and are to be avoided as much as deplored. As one stellar example, there are now more open Duesenbergs around than were originally built, which not only deprives us of worthy closed models, but likely means that some poor soul paid a king's ransom for a bogus car. And it's reported that some 1960 Ford convertibles have been "converted" into '60 Edsel ragtops, of which only 76 originals were built. So, like buying a new car, the more you know, the better off you are—but always *caveat emptor*. Or as collectors say, make sure all the numbers match (body, chassis, engine, etc.).

Good: This is either a "stock" original or an older restoration that is fully driveable and serviceable in its present state, but needs obvious mechanical and/or cosmetic attention. Not a show winner by any means, it may need paint, new chrome, interior work, and mechanical ministerings—but not a whole *new* engine or interior. This description also fits a combination of, say, amateur mechanical work and a professional body rebuild.

Fine: Here we mean a car in excellent original or restored condition, capable of scoring at least 85 out of 100 points in typical show judging. Everything on it works as intended, and nothing major needs attention, though there may be a small thing or two that isn't completely right (as there usually is).

The range of **Prices** shown for each condition class is sometimes wide. You may also see some gaps or overlaps between categories, so that a particular specimen you might be interested in buying could fall between them. Obviously, it's an imperfect world. The **2000-2010 Return** projection is based on estimates from past performance and factors like the degree to which a car has stabilized in value; but it does *not* consider general economic forces like the onset of a deep recession.

The rationale for this pricing system is that it's simply impossible to peg collector cars as close to the mark as ordinary used cars. There, values can be quoted down to $10 and $50 increments based on equipment (like air, radio, and automatic), age, and total mileage. Now, common sense would suggest that a 1954 Cadillac with factory air would be worth more than one without, because it's an early example of an option that was uncommon at the time even among Cadillacs. By contrast, A/C won't affect, say, a 1967 Lincoln Continental, because it was standard.

"Interest value," the aforementioned "oddball factor" or "character", also enters into collector-car pricing, but not used-car worth. Few enthusiasts would lust after, say, a 1983 Ford Escort, but a Thunderbird Turbo Coupe is something else, which is why the latter is included here, but not the former. In a few cases, we've dared to suggest future, if long-distant collector potential *primarily* on the basis of "interest value," even though asking prices are still rock-bottom and the market has yet to take any notice. But again, these are "judgment calls." And who's to say we're wrong? After all, there was a time when Auburn Speedsters went cheap.

But the main reason we cannot draw razor-sharp price distinctions is that they just don't exist. Compared to ordinary used cars, even those 10 or more years old, collector cars change hands far less often. Used-car guides like the famous *Kelley Blue Book* track hundreds of thousands of sales over a few months, and can thus average prices with high accuracy. Collector-car guides cover far fewer transactions that may occur over a year or more, and thus can't be anywhere near as precise.

This isn't to deny the value of old-car price guides, which are highly useful in recording these longer-term value trends, thus suggesting changes in demand (or lack thereof) for specific models. A Porsche partisan, for instance, can get a clear idea of what a vintage 911S is worth by following it in a reliable price guide for a few years. But that doesn't necessarily mean that you'd be able to buy such a car at those prices at auction or from a private seller, or even a dealer, where almost any car over 10 years old is too often hyped as a "classic," especially if it's in good condition. Then again, you might snare that 911 for less depending on when and where you buy. As most of us know, convertibles are always worth more in spring than in the dead of winter.

Our purpose is more limited in a way, but also more realistic. The ranges shown are merely guides. You have to take it from there, factoring in your own knowledge of current local market conditions and the car in question. Car clubs can be helpful here.

NOTES ON SPECIFICATIONS

Besides the development and technical background in the History section, each entry provides brief **Specifications** important to enthusiasts. These include overall length, wheelbase (longitudinal distance between front and rear wheel centers), vehicle weight (manufacturer's stated curb weight with base equipment), and original selling price in contemporary U.S. dollars. Multiple figures and/or ranges are shown in cases covering several models and/or years.

Note that **Price (new)** means contemporary base price. For some foreign entries, lack of information on prevailing exchange rates made it impossible to calculate dollar equivalents. To the extent possible, actual or estimated prices are shown for foreign models not officially exported to the U.S. or those sold on a "gray market" basis. For "official" exports, the reader should assume advertised list price at U.S. port of entry unless otherwise stated.

Following the **Specifications** section is one listing the available **Engines.**

Each is shown with its displacement in cubic inches (cid) or cubic centimeters (cc), as appropriate (often both). Type tells you whether the engine's an inline six (I-6) or V-8, etc., with valvetrain type and/or head configuration (sv for side valve, F for F-head [overhead inlet valves, side exhaust valves], ohv for overhead-valve, ohc for single overhead cam, dohc for dual-overhead-cam etc.). Also supplied are rated horsepower and years available. Unless otherwise noted, the reader should assume *SAE gross* horsepower for models through 1971, and *SAE net* ratings thereafter. The two are distinguished in entries that bridge '71. DIN denotes *Deutsche Industrie Normen,* the standard by which virtually all German engines are rated, though it has also been used by other European makers. DIN horsepower is closer to the "truth" than an SAE gross rating, though a shade more flattering than SAE net. A simple "net" bhp refers to a European measurement of horsepower developed at the flywheel with most engine accessories installed. However, this is not the same as SAE net. Similarly, European gross horsepower is a bit more realistic than SAE gross figures.

Foreign automakers sometimes have not—and some still don't—observed formal model years like American producers. Instead, they made styling and mechanical alterations as running changes within a model's life span without regard to the calendar or selling period. Most Detroit manufacturers "saved" these for the following year's models, which usually went on sale a few months before the new calendar year, a practice that gained acceptance in the '30s. Therefore, headings and engine availability for American entries most always reflect *model year* production. Assume *calendar year* for non-U.S. cars unless otherwise noted. Chronology will be evident from each entry's **History** section.

A FINAL WORD

The authors and editors thus warmly welcome your comments, corrections, and additions, of which some from the earlier versions of this work are reflected herein. Address: *The Complete Book of Collectible Cars 1930-2000,* c/o CONSUMER GUIDE Publications, 7373 N. Cicero Avenue, Lincolnwood, IL, USA 60712, e-mail: jstewart@pubint.com

Richard M. Langworth and *The Auto Editors of CONSUMER GUIDE®*

1953-63
AC ACE

1955 Ace roadster

Superlative forerunner of the fabulous Cobra, designed by John Tojeiro with not a little inspiration from the contemporary Ferrari Barchetta. One of the classic postwar English roadsters: all-independent suspension, spartan leather upholstered cockpit, full instrumentation, four-speed gearbox, lithe and lean lines. Minimal weather protection in the English tradition. Excellent performance: 100-plus mph, 0-60 mph in 11.5 seconds. Prominent in production-car racing in both Europe and America in its day, but considered an "exotic" even when new.

✚ FOR Magnificent styling • High performance • High investment potential • Cheaper than a Cobra • Low-production appeal

▬ AGAINST Hard-to-restore aluminum body • Some parts now scarce • Limited U.S. club activity

PRODUCTION
225

SPECIFICATIONS
Length (in.)	149.5
Wheelbase (in.)	90.0
Weight (lbs)	1680
Price (new)	$4000-5500 (U.S.)

ENGINES
cc/type (cid)	bhp	years
1991/ohc I-6 (121)	85/90/103	1954-63

PRICES
FAIR	$25,000-30,000
GOOD	$30,000-35,000
FINE	$35,000-48,500

FINE EXAMPLE PRICE HISTORY
1982 $10,000	**1990** $80,000
1994 $80,000	**1998** $60,000
1982-2000 RETURN 10%	
2000-2010 10%	

1954-63
AC ACECA

1955 Aceca coupe

A smooth GT version of the Ace roadster. One of the great design triumphs, with lines that are faultless from any angle. Composite steel-tube-and-ash body construction was coupled with thick insulation, roll-up windows, and walnut and leather interior.

✚ FOR Landmark styling, even more beautiful than the Ace • Other points as for 1954-63 Ace

▬ AGAINST As for 1954-63 Ace

PRODUCTION
154

SPECIFICATIONS
Length (in.)	149.5
Wheelbase (in.)	90.0
Weight (lbs)	1680
Price (new)	$4000-5500 (U.S.)

ENGINES
cc/type (cid)	bhp	years
1991/ohc I-6 (121)	85/90/103	1955-63

PRICES
FAIR	$15,000-22,000
GOOD	$22,000-28,000
FINE	$28,000-35,000

FINE EXAMPLE PRICE HISTORY
1982 $7500	**1990** $80,000
1994 $60,000	**1998** $40,000
1981-94 RETURN 10%	
2000-2010 15%	

1957-64
AC ACE- AND ACECA-BRISTOL

The AC Bristol began AC's long-running tradition of ACs with an engine transplant. To provide more power, racing driver and engine specialist Ken Rudd suggested AC fit the Bristol 100D2 engine, which yielded a 115-mph top speed and a 0-60 mph time of 8.5 seconds. Rudd later developed three higher stages of tune, with the top Stage 4 producing 148 bhp. The clean and nimble Ace-Bristols dominated their class in Sports Car Club of America racing, and an Aceca took the 2.0-liter GT class win at Le Mans in 1958.

✚ FOR The ultimate version of the Ace/Aceca, with great performance for a 2.0-liter sports car • High appreciation potential

▬ AGAINST Very costly now • Engine parts increasingly scarce • Others as for standard Ace

PRODUCTION
Ace: 463; **Aceca:** 172

SPECIFICATIONS
Length (in.)	149.5
Wheelbase (in.)	90.0
Weight (lbs)	1700
Price (new)	$4700-6000 (U.S.)

1959 Ace-Bristol roadster

ENGINES

cc/type (cid)	bhp	years
1971/ohv I-6 (120)	105-148	1957-64

PRICES

Ace

FAIR	$20,000-35,000
GOOD	$35,000-45,000
FINE	$45,000-60,000

Aceca: deduct 10-15% from above prices

FINE ACE PRICE HISTORY

1982 $12,000		**1990** $110,000	
1994 $90,000		**1998** $70,000	

1982-2000 RETURN 10%
2000-2010 10%

1962-68
AC/SHELBY COBRA 260/289 & AC 289

1964 Cobra 289 roadster

The first of the high-powered transatlantic hybrids created by Texas ex-race car driver Carroll Shelby. Ford's light, efficient small-block V-8 was a natural for the low and lean AC Ace roadster, and was accommodated with only a modest lengthening of the nose. AC's Thames-Ditton premises shipped body and chassis to California where Shelby American dropped in the engine and completed assembly. Like the Ace/Aceca, used a sturdy tubular chassis with all-independent transverse leaf spring suspension—very hard but superbly controllable. Immense performance at low cost. The first 75 production models had the 260-cid engine; others used the 289. AC also built 29 "late" examples with the wider, fender-flared 427 body developed for the big-block version of the Cobra that was produced starting in 1965. These "AC 289s" were sold only in Europe.

FOR Flashing acceleration • Rarity and consequent high desirability • American-made mechanicals • Strong club support

AGAINST Flimsy light-alloy body • Thirsty • British-made parts in short supply • Costs a bundle • Skimpy weather protection • Has almost disappeared from the market

PRODUCTION

654 (including 75 260-cid models, 39 competition roadsters, 6 coupes)

SPECIFICATIONS

Length (in.)	158.0
Wheelbase (in.)	90.0
Weight (lbs)	2315
Price (new)	$5995 (1962 U.S. base)

ENGINES

cid/type	bhp	years
260/ohv V-8	164	1962
289/ohv V-8	260/271/306	1962-65

PRICES

FAIR	$75,000-100,000
GOOD	$100,000-120,000
FINE	$120,000-160,000

FINE ROADSTER PRICE HISTORY

1982 $25,000		**1990** $250,000	
1994 $175,000		**1998** $150,000	

1982-2000 RETURN 12%
2000-2010 10%

1965-67
AC COBRA 427

1967 Cobra 427 roadster

The fastest street sports car ever produced, with mind-boggling acceleration courtesy of Ford's big-inch 427 mill slotted into the light AC Ace roadster. Off the showroom floor, this speed demon was capable of 0-100-0 mph in 14 seconds. Similar to the Cobra 289 except for a beefed-up frame to handle the engine's huge torque output, plus coil springs in place of leaves and fatter tires and wheels residing under the bulgier fenders needed to accommodate them. More exclusive than the 289 model, and also a sure-fire investment, provided you can find one and have the considerable "scratch" it takes to purchase it. Not for unskilled drivers, and a real handful even for an expert, but there's just nothing to touch it for sheer speed and excitement.

FOR As for 1962-65 Cobra 289, but more of it

AGAINST As for 1962-65 Cobra 289, but even costlier and rarer • Extremely thirsty

PRODUCTION

348 (numbered chassis)

SPECIFICATIONS

Length (in.)	158.0
Wheelbase (in.)	90.0
Weight (lbs)	2600 (approx.)
Price (new)	$7000 (approx.)

ENGINES

cid/type	bhp	years
427/ohv V-8	345/425	1965-67

PRICES

FAIR	$80,000-165,000
GOOD	$165,000-200,000
FINE	$200,000-275,000

FINE EXAMPLE PRICE HISTORY

1982 $40,000		**1990** $425,000	
1994 $300,000		**1998** $250,000	

1982-2000 RETURN 12%
2000-2010 15%

1990-2000
ACURA NSX/NSX ZANARDI EDITION

1991 NSX coupe

This striking, mid-engine 2-seater sold in the U.S. in very small numbers only—at first in the thousands, and finally in the hundreds—not surprising because NSX prices began at $60,000 in 1990 and rose to $84,000-$88,000 by the time of the 2000 models. Its 3.0- to 3.2-liter sixes were not large for what is a legitimate supercar, but Honda/Acura engineers wrung out horsepower ratings over the decade that ranged from 270 to 290. The Alex Zanardi edition bowed for '99 and had a firmer suspension, mandatory 6-

speed (other NSX's had available automatics), manual steering, reduced weight, and special trim. NSX was extremely capable but seemed rather too polite and refined for the company it kept (Viper, Porsche 911, Toyota Supra, Chevy Corvette).

FOR Smooth, ripping acceleration • Precise steering and handling • Build quality • Finish, inside and out

AGAINST Thirst • Rear visibility • Stiff ride • Japanese origins

PRODUCTION
1990-2000 approx. 15,000

SPECIFICATIONS
Length (in.)	172.2-173.4
Weight (lbs)	2850-3204
Wheelbase (in.)	99.6
Price (new)	$60,000-88,000

ENGINES
cid/type	bhp	years
181/dohc V-6	252	1990-97
182/dohc V-6	270	1998-2000
194/dohc V-6	290	1998-2000

PRICES
FAIR	$25,000-30,000
GOOD	$30,000-40,000
FINE	$40,000-60,000
2000-2010 RETURN 50%	

1997 Integra Type R coupe

1997-98

ACURA INTEGRA TYPE R

With a planned production of just 2000 worldwide, this street-racer Integra will certainly be rare. Well, plenty of Japanese cars are rare but few are genuinely collectible. Okay, how does a 110-cid four that produced 195 bhp sound?—That's 1.77 bhp per cubic inch, which made this deceptively discreet-looking coupe a factory-made street racer. Handsome in that rather anonymous Honda/Accord mode of the late Nineties, the Type R was built for

speed and speed alone: A/C was an option for '97, and the car left the factory without insulation on floor or dash. Think of it as a '64 Ford Thunderbolt for Generation X.

FOR High-winding engine that gives—and then gives some more • Outstanding brakes • Crisp handling and roadholding • Surprising comfort • A curiosity that doesn't look like one

AGAINST For the moment, of collector interest mainly to the very young, and mostly on the West Coast • A curiosity that doesn't look like one

PRODUCTION[1]
1997 318	**1998** 997	**1999** 263

[1]U.S. Calendar year sales

SPECIFICATIONS
Length (in.)	172.4
Weight (lbs)	2529
Wheelbase (in.)	101.2
Price (new)	$23,500

ENGINES
cid/type	bhp	years
109/ohc I-4	195	1997
110/dohc I-4	195	1998

PRICES (GS-R)
FAIR	$13,000-15,500
GOOD	$15,500-16,500
FINE	$16,500-18,500
2000-2010 RETURN 50%	

1938 6C2300 coupe

1934-39

ALFA ROMEO 6C2300

Replacement for the long-running and successful 1500/1750/1900 range. The "volume" Alfa of these years. Not as fast, yet more civilized, than the firm's contemporary eight-cylinder monster. Styling was strictly derivative of other Alfas and concurrent Italians, though many sedans had distinctly U.S. lines. Early models had beam front axles. Coil spring independent front suspension from 1935 (a

first for Alfa) allied to swing-axle (Alfa said "Porsche type") independent rear. Twincam engines, but no "blowers" now that racing regulations had changed, so top speed less than 80 mph in most cases. Many wheelbase, power, and body style variations. Gave rise to the 6C-2500 of postwar fame.

FOR Less complex than 8C • Good choice of body styles • Still a feasible rebuild bet • Not too rare

AGAINST Not a fashionable Alfa • Disappointing performance • Sedans' stodgy looks • Bodies rot badly and no parts exist

PRODUCTION
1606

SPECIFICATIONS
Length (in.)	160.0-175.0
Wheelbase (in.)	115.0/118.0/128.0
Weight (lbs)	2820-3450 (approx.)
Price (new)	NA

ENGINES
cc/type (cid)	bhp	years
2309/dohc I-6 (141)	68-95	1934-39

PRICES
Roadster	
FAIR	$40,000-65,000
GOOD	$65,000-90,000
FINE	$90,000-150,000
Coupe	
FAIR	$15,000-40,000
GOOD	$40,000-60,000
FINE	$60,000-80,000

FINE ROADSTER PRICE HISTORY
1982 $40,000	**1990** 250,000
1994 $150,000	**1998** $150,000
1982-2000 RETURN 10%	
2000-2010 10%	

1950 6C2500 convertible

1945-52

ALFA ROMEO 6C2500

Last of the coachbuilt Alfas, descended from the Vittorio Jano-designed prewar 2300/2500. Featured light-alloy detachable cylinder heads, double overhead cams, hemispherical combustion chambers, plus four-speed all-synchro transmission. Most models would do 95 mph, the SS 10 mph more. Styles included the SS three-seat coupe, the Sports cabriolet, the lovely Freccia d'Oro (Golden Arrow) coupe (one was blown up in *The Godfather*), and a Sports sedan offered in later years. SS coachwork was by Carrozzeria Touring; others were built by Alfa, though a few were bodied by Farina, Ghia, and others. Three Competizione coupes were built in 1950.

➕ FOR Usually good styling • Reasonable performance • Quality construction • Unique even in Alfa Romeo circles

➖ AGAINST Chancy parts supplies • Fuel thirst • Tricky aluminum bodywork • Unreliable electrics • Some dumpy-looking bodies

PRODUCTION

1947 486 **1948** 451 **1949** 414 **1950-53** approx. 100 (calendar year production)

SPECIFICATIONS

Length (in.)	NA
Wheelbase (in.)	118.0 (SS: 106.0)
Weight (lbs)	3000-3500
Price (new)	NA

ENGINES

cc/type (cid)	bhp	years
2443/dohc I-6 (153)	90/105	1946-52

PRICES

Open models	
FAIR	$20,000-40,000
GOOD	$40,000-65,000
FINE	$65,000-95,000

FINE CABRIOLET PRICE HISTORY

1982 $20,000		**1990** $250,000	
1994 $120,000		**1998** $95,000	
1982-2000 RETURN 2%			
2000-2010 5%			

(Closed model prices vary widely; a best buy is the "Freccia d'Oro" currently running at about half the level of open cars; other closed cars range down to as little as $15,000.)

1 9 5 0 - 5 8
ALFA ROMEO 1900

Alfa's first new postwar generation pioneered a number of firsts for the Italian automaker: unit steel construction, a twincam four-cylinder engine, and engineering specifically with quantity production in mind. Most built were four-door sedans, but Sprints (to 1953) and Super Sprints (from 1953 on) were

1953 1900 Sprint coupe

offered in Touring coupe and Pinin Farina convertibles. Less exclusive than previous Alfas, but cheaper and simpler to buy and operate. The TI versions of the sedan would top 100 mph, the special-bodied models were even faster. These were also the first Alfas to reach North America in significant numbers.

➕ FOR Rugged, high-class Italian twincam engineering • Simple layout • Not too highly tuned

➖ AGAINST Some parts nearly unobtainable now • Little factory support • Bodies rust badly • Few survivors

PRODUCTION

21,304 (includes 949 Sprints, 854 Super Sprints)

SPECIFICATIONS

Length (in.)	Variable with body style
Wheelbase (in.)	98.5
Weight (lbs)	2205 (coupe), 2425 (convertible)
Price (new)	NA

ENGINES

cc/type (cid)	bhp[1]	years
1884/dohc I-4 (115)	100[2]	1950-53
1975/dohc I-4 (121)	115[3]	1953-58

[1]Net [2]Sprint [3]Super Sprint

PRICES

Sedan	
FAIR	$4000-5000
GOOD	$5000-9000
FINE	$9000-12,000
Touring/Pininfarina	
FINE	to $25,000
Zagato	
FINE	to $35,000

FINE TOURING PRICE HISTORY

1982 $5000		**1990** $21,000	
1994 $21,000		**1998** $25,000	
1982-2000 RETURN 6%			
2000-2010 5%			

1 9 5 4 - 6 5
ALFA ROMEO GIULIETTA

The first "small" Alfa, and phenomenally successful. Offered as a conventional four-door sedan styled by Alfa, plus the pretty Sprint coupe from Bertone and the Spider convertible by Pinin Farina

1962 Giulietta Veloce convertible

(Pininfarina from 1961). There were also short-wheelbase, special lightweight models, the Bertone-styled SS, and the SZ by Zagato. Specifications and engine tune were altered to suit the various applications. All Giuliettas had a twincam four-cylinder engine with wet liners, plus four- or five-speed gearboxes and an excellent-handling chassis. Successful in racing and rallying, and sold in the U.S. in huge numbers by Alfa standards. A typically raspy Italian exhaust note made them sound faster than they were, though the Sprints were capable of a genuine 100 mph, and the lightweight specials could see the right side of 120 mph.

➕ FOR Matchless styling (except sedans) • Sturdy engine • Great gearbox • Fine handling • Lots of model variations • No real problems with mechanical parts or rebuilds

➖ AGAINST Rust-prone Italian bodies • Little factory service or parts support • Overly complex mechanicals for the performance

PRODUCTION

177,690 (incl. 27,142 Sprint, 17,096 Spider, 1576 special Sprint)

SPECIFICATIONS

Length (in.)	153.5-162.2
Wheelbase (in.)	93.7 (Spider and SS/SZ: 88.6)
Weight (lbs)	1700 (SZ), 2015 (sedan)
Price (new)	NA

ENGINES

cc/type (cid)	bhp	years
1290/dohc I-4 (79)	80/90/100	1954-65

PRICES

Sprint	
FAIR	$4000-12,000
GOOD	$12,000-20,000
FINE	$20,000-30,000
Spider	
FAIR	$7000-15,000
GOOD	$15,000-28,000
FINE	$28,000-33,000
Sprint Veloce	
FAIR	$5000-15,000
GOOD	$15,000-23,000
FINE	$23,000-30,000
Spider Veloce	
FAIR	$8500-15,000
GOOD	$15,000-22,000
FINE	$22,000-35,000

FINE SPIDER PRICE HISTORY

1982 $4000		**1990** $18,000	
1994 $13,000		**1998** $30,000	
1982-2000 RETURN 13%			
2000-2010 10%			

1 9 5 8 - 6 2
ALFA ROMEO 2000

Successor to the long-running 1900 range, available in sedan, convertible (Spider), and coupe (Sprint) body types. Retained the 1975cc double overhead-cam four from the last of the 1900s, but housed it in a new unit body/chassis. Sedans were built by Alfa, Sprints by Bertone, Spiders by Touring. The faster versions were capable of 110 mph, but these models were overshadowed by the smaller Giuliettas for performance and overall value. Replaced in 1962 by the six-cylinder 2600 series that used the same bodies.

➕ **FOR** Fashionable Italian looks • Rugged engine • Simple chassis

➖ **AGAINST** No factory service support any more • Parts difficult to find • Rust-prone • Spartan trim, furnishings • Somewhat heavy

PRODUCTION

4d sedan 2804 **2d Spider convertible** 3443 **2d Sprint coupe** 700

SPECIFICATIONS

Length (in.)	185.6 (sedan), 180.3 (Sprint), 177.2 (Spider)
Wheelbase (in.)	107.0 (sedan), 101.6 (Sprint), 98.5 (Spider)
Weight (lbs)	2600-2955
Price (new)	NA

1964 2600 Sprint coupe

ENGINES

cc/type (cid)	bhp	years
1975/dohc I-4 (121)	115	1958-62

PRICES

Sprint	
FAIR	$6000-10,000
GOOD	$10,000-14,000
FINE	$14,000-17,000

FINE SPRINT PRICE HISTORY

1982 $3000		**1990** $11,000	
1994 $16,000		**1998** $17,000	
1982-2000 RETURN 11%			
2000-2010 10%			

(Prices are for coupes. Add 40% for special coachwork or spiders. Deduct 20% from prices above for sedan models.)

1 9 6 2 - 6 8
ALFA ROMEO 2600

Continuation of the previous 2000 series as the "senior" Alfa offerings, now with a twincam 2.6-liter six-cylinder engine. Same styling, but more performance and higher sales in these years. Performance boosted to the 120-mph level in some versions. New to the range was a special lightweight coupe styled and built by Zagato, of which only 105 were built.

➕ **FOR** As for 1958-62 2000, but better performance • Zagato's rarity

➖ **AGAINST** As for 1958-62 2000, but engine is rarer and thus more difficult to rebuild

PRODUCTION

4d sedan 2092 **2d Sprint coupe** 6999 **2d Spider convertible** 2255 **2d SZ coupe** 105

SPECIFICATIONS

Length (in.)	185.0 (sedan), 180.3 (Sprint), 177.2 (Spider), 173.2 (SZ)
Wheelbase (in.)	106.7 (sedan), 101.6 (Sprint), 98.4 (Spider, SZ)
Weight (lbs)	2690-2998
Price (new)	NA

ENGINES

cc/type (cid)	bhp	years
2584/dohc I-6 (158)	130	1962-68

PRICES

Sprint	
FAIR	$5000-8000
GOOD	$8000-13,000
FINE	$13,000-18,000

FINE SPRINT PRICE HISTORY

1982 $3500		**1990** $14,000	
1994 $16,000		**1998** $18,000	
1982-2000 RETURN 10%			
2000-2010 10%			

(Add 40% to price for special coachwork or Spiders.)

1 9 7 1 - 7 5
ALFA ROMEO MONTREAL

1972 Montreal coupe

The production version of Alfa Romeo's "dream car" first seen at Expo '67 in Montreal. Distinctive, Bertone-designed body sat on a Giulia floorpan and suspension. Besides its looks, a 2.6-liter twincam V-8—a detuned version of Alfa's 3.0-liter racing unit—made this a very special machine. Not quite in the supercar class—top speed was 137 mph in European trim—it was nevertheless as fast as a Porsche 911, its main price competitor. Not heavily promoted, and not a profit-maker for a firm that was beset by financial and labor troubles at the turn of the decade. All models were equipped with a ZF five-speed gearbox, and the engine was tuned to 200 bhp only. There were no other variations, and Alfa didn't even bother to replace this unique top-of-the-line model after production quietly ended.

⚏ FOR Unique styling • Excellent performance • Low-production appeal • Sturdy Giulia underpinnings • Not that expensive now for what it is

⚏ AGAINST Complex engine nearly hand-built, parts now very scarce, rebuilds tricky • Bodyshell quite rust-prone • Suspension doesn't match straight-line performance • Little importer interest

PRODUCTION

3925

SPECIFICATIONS

Length (in.)	156.0
Wheelbase (in.)	92.5
Weight (lbs)	2830
Price (new)	NA

ENGINES

cc/type (cid)	bhp	years
2593/dohc V-8 (158)	200[1]	1971-75

[1]DIN

PRICES

FAIR	$9000-12,000
GOOD	$12,000-18,000
FINE	$18,000-23,000

FINE EXAMPLE PRICE HISTORY

1982 $12,000		1990 $27,500	
1994 $23,000		1998 $23,000	
1982-2000 RETURN 4%			
2000-2010 5%			

1975-79
ALFA ROMEO ALFETTA GT/ GTV/SPRINT VELOCE

1975-79 Alfetta GTV coupe

Fastback 2+2 derived from Alfa's mid-'70s Alfetta sedan; about 1.5 inches shorter overall on a 4.5-inch shorter wheelbase. Completely different coupe styling—credited to Giorgio Giugiaro—clothed identical chassis boasting five-speed de Dion rear transaxle (with Watt linkage) and a torsion-bar front suspension by lower A-arm, upper transverse arm, and longitudinal link. Standard all-disc power brakes, but manual rack-and-pinion steering. Sold in America only with the 2000cc version of Alfa's legendary all-aluminum twin-cam four, but available elsewhere with 1570- and 1779cc engines. Well liked—mainly for handling—but sales limited by odd dash with the tach dead-ahead and other gauges in the center, plus Alfa's usual fast rusting and poor reliability. Somewhat tidied up through 1979 in evolutionary GTV and Sprint Veloce models, but real improvement would await the V-6-powered GTV-6. Prime pick here may be the special Mario Andretti Signature Edition with rear spoiler, free-flow Ansa exhaust, Koni shocks, autographed dash plaque—and loud red carpeting.

⚏ FOR It's an Alfa • Not costly • Fine handling • Good mileage (20 mpg) • Interesting chassis • Distinctive styling

⚏ AGAINST It's an Alfa • Not that quick (0-60: 12-14 secs) • Not that quiet • Vague shifter • Shoulda been a hatchback • Dumb dash • Italian straight arm driving stance • Usual tinworm and mechanical worries

PRODUCTION

NA

SPECIFICATIONS

Length (in.)	171.0
Wheelbase (in.)	94.5
Weight (lbs)	2200-2660
Price (new)	$8200-$10,495

ENGINES

cc/type	bhp	years
1570/dohc I-4	109[1]	1975-79
1779/dohc I-4	122[1]	1975-79
1962/dohc I-4	111-129[2]	1975-79

[1]DIN [2]SAE net (U.S. model)

PRICES

FAIR	$2400-5000
GOOD	$5000-8000
FINE	$8000-12,000

FINE EXAMPLE PRICE HISTORY

1990 $8000		1994 $10,000	
1998 $12,000		1990-2000 RETURN 4%	
2000-2010 RETURN 5%			

1981-86
ALFA ROMEO GTV-6

Evolutionary replacement for the four-pot Alfetta GT/GTV/Sprint Veloce. Same basic 2+2 coupe design with detail styling differences and V-6 power. Aluminum 60-degree engine

1986 GTV-6 coupe

(from the never-liked, Europe-only "big" Alfa 6 sedan) featured wet liners, hemispherical combustion chambers (like Alfa's veteran four), Bosch L-Jetronic fuel injection, and unusual valvetrain with intakes actuated directly by the cam, exhaust valves by rockers and short pushrods. Not the smoothest V-6 around, but shaved 3-5 seconds off 0-60 times. Improved shifter (from 1985) and more conventional dash, but neither was up to the standards of newer rivals—mostly Japanese models that cost the same or less, thus stealing this Alfa's thunder again. Callaway Engineering of Old Lyme, Connecticut, turned out a small batch of twin-turbo conversions for the U.S. with 66 more horses and 6.1-sec 0-60 ability (vs. 8.5 sec, both according to Road & Track). These may be especially prized by leadfoots, but have so far shown no value advantage for collectors.

⚏ FOR As for Alfetta GT/GTV/Sprint Veloce, plus better performance and ergonomics

⚏ AGAINST As for Alfetta GT/ GTV/Sprint Veloce

PRODUCTION

NA

SPECIFICATIONS

Length (in.)	171.0
Wheelbase (in.)	94.5
Weight (lbs)	2850
Price (new)	$16,500-19,000

ENGINES

cc/type	bhp	years
2492/ohc V-6	154[1]	1981-86

[1]SAE net; U.S. model

PRICES

FAIR	$3000-4000
GOOD	$4000-6000
FINE	$6000-9000

FINE EXAMPLE PRICE HISTORY

1990 $7000		1994 $7500	
1998 $9000			
1982-2000 RETURN 3%			
2000-2010 5%			

1 9 4 6 - 4 9
ALLARD K1

1946-49 K1 convertible

The first series-built British Allard, not counting the limited-production, 100-inch-wheelbase J1. Like the J1, a two-seat sports roadster, but on a 106-inch wheelbase. Like all early Allards, rode a special box-section chassis with transverse leaf spring suspension front and rear. Wheel location was provided by swing axles in front and by a torque tube/beam axle at the rear. The Allard-built body was constructed of wood framing overlaid with steel paneling, and featured a full-width nose with the characteristic waterfall-style grille. A few K1s were sold without engines, mainly in the U.S., but the majority were equipped with British Ford or Canadian Mercury flathead V-8s. Not very refined, and expensive new—but there was no mistaking its individual personality.

🔲 FOR Mechanical simplicity • Lively performance • Rarity

🔲 AGAINST Bodies deteriorate badly • Crude detailing • Except for engine, parts very hard to find

PRODUCTION
151

SPECIFICATIONS
Length (in.)	168.0
Wheelbase (in.)	106.0
Weight (lbs)	2460
Price (new)	NA

ENGINES
cc/type (cid)	bhp	years
3622/sv V-8 (221)	85/95	1946-49
3917/sv V-8 (239.4)	95/100	1946-49

PRICES
FAIR	$10,000-20,000
GOOD	$20,000-30,000
FINE	$30,000-50,000

FINE EXAMPLE PRICE HISTORY
1982 $10,000	**1990** $50,000
1994 $50,000	**1998** $50,000
1982-2000 RETURN 12%	
2000-2010 5%	

1 9 5 0 - 5 1
ALLARD J2

1951 J2 roadster

Stark, two-seat open sports car built with U.S. export in mind by the small English concern headed by former racing driver Sydney Allard. Simple box-section frame had coil spring and swing-axle front suspension, de Dion rear suspension. Light-alloy, cigar-shape body design (somewhat similar to the Healey Silverstone's), with separate cycle-type front fenders. No full-width windshield provided unless you insisted; no weather protection or heater, either. Often supplied without engine or gearbox, which owner would then have installed. The fastest J2s were fitted with Cadillac's new overhead-valve V-8, others with contemporary Ford V-8s or the flathead Lincoln V-12. A high power-to-weight ratio made the J2 quite a stormer, but it was a short-lived model even so. Replaced by the J2-X.

🔲 FOR Performance • Simple mechanical layout • U.S. mechanicals • Active club • Very rare

🔲 AGAINST Crude in detail • Little in the way of comfort • No weather protection • British-made parts very scarce • Are there any left on the market?

PRODUCTION
90

SPECIFICATIONS
Length (in.)	148.0
Wheelbase (in.)	100.0
Weight (lbs)	2500 (depending on engine)
Price (new)	NA

ENGINES
cid/type	bhp	years
331/ohv V-8[1]	160	1950-51
239.4/sv V-8[2]	100	1950-51
292/sv V-12[3]	125	1950-51

[1]Cadillac [2]Ford [3]Lincoln

PRICES
FAIR	$20,000-40,000

GOOD	$40,000-70,000
FINE	$70,000-87,000

FINE EXAMPLE PRICE HISTORY
1982 $15,000	**1990** $95,000
1994 $80,000	**1998** $87,000
1982-2000 RETURN 13%	
2000-2010 10%	

(Add up to 200% to prices for competition models, especially with verified racing history.)

1 9 5 0 - 5 2
ALLARD K2

1952 K2 roadster

Running mate to the J2 of these years, and basically similar to its K1 predecessor. Still with Ford-style transverse leaf spring rear suspension design, but front suspension now by coil springs. Unchanged in appearance except for a smaller grille replacing the K1's "waterfall."

🔲 FOR As for 1946-49 K1

🔲 AGAINST As for 1946-49 K1

PRODUCTION
119

SPECIFICATIONS
Length (in.)	168.0
Wheelbase (in.)	106.0
Weight (lbs)	2460
Price (new)	NA

ENGINES
cc/type (cid)	bhp[1]	years
3622/sv V-8 (221)	85/95	1950-52
3917/sv V-8 (239.4)	95/100	1950-52

[1]gross

PRICES
FAIR	$20,000-30,000
GOOD	$30,000-40,000
FINE	$40,000-50,000

FINE EXAMPLE PRICE HISTORY
1982 $10,000	**1990** $50,000
1994 $40,000	**1998** $50,000
1982-2000 RETURN 12%	
2000-2010 5%	

1952 - 54
ALLARD K3

Another of Sydney Allard's low-production series sports roadsters, retaining many components from the K2. Revised chassis now with tubular construction, similar to that of the J2-X in most respects. De Dion linkage was used for the rear suspension. A major restyle brought a simple, slab-sided, full-width body an oval grille with horizontal slats; a vee'd windshield; and better-quality trim and fittings. Like all production Allards, it was built at the firm's small London workshops. Offered with a choice of Ford or Mercury V-8s. Some visual similarity with the Palm Beach (see entry), but very different mechanically.

✚ FOR As for 1946-49 K1, 1950-52 K2

◼ AGAINST As for 1946-49 K1, 1950-52 K2

PRODUCTION
62

SPECIFICATIONS

Length (in.)	177.0
Wheelbase (in.)	100.0
Weight (lbs)	2580
Price (new)	NA

ENGINES

cc/type (cid)	bhp	years
3622/sv V-8 (221)	85	1952-54
3917/sv V-8 (239.4)	100/110	1952-54

PRICES

FAIR	$10,000-20,000
GOOD	$20,000-30,000
FINE	$30,000-45,000

FINE EXAMPLE PRICE HISTORY

1982 $10,000		**1990** $50,000	
1994 $40,000		**1998** $45,000	

1953 K3 roadster

1982-2000 RETURN 14%
2000-2010 5%

1952 - 54
ALLARD J2-X

1952 J2-X roadster

A re-engineered derivative of the J2, and perhaps the best remembered of Allard's transatlantic hybrids. Powered by Cadillac's modern, high-compression, 331-cid overhead valve V-8 set seven inches further back in the tubular chassis than J2 engines. Otherwise, little changed from its predecessor, with the same cigar-style body shape, separate cycle-type front fenders, and sparse creature comforts. More rigid yet lighter frame, however, so roadholding was improved to match the higher performance potential of the Caddy engine.

✚ FOR As for 1950-51 J2, but more thoroughly engineered

◼ AGAINST As for 1950-51 J2

PRODUCTION
83

SPECIFICATIONS

Length (in.)	148.0
Wheelbase (in.)	100.0
Weight (lbs)	2500
Price (new)	NA

ENGINES

cid/type	bhp	years
331/ohv V-8	160	1952-54

PRICES

FAIR	$50,000-60,000
GOOD	$60,000-80,000
FINE	$80,000-100,000

FINE EXAMPLE PRICE HISTORY

1982 $25,000		**1990** $250,000	
1994 $110,000		**1998** $100,000	

1982-2000 RETURN 8%
2000-2010 10%
(Exceptional examples may sell for more; pedigreed racing examples sell for still more.)

1952 - 59
ALLARD PALM BEACH

1958 Palm Beach convertible

Allard's unsuccessful try at a smaller, lighter, cheaper model to replace its V-8-powered roadsters. Built around a tubular frame and a shorter 96-inch wheelbase. The body was much like the K3's, a full-width roadster style with a one-piece windshield and oval grille. Offered initially with British Ford four- and six-cylinder powerplants. Looking in many ways like the Swallow Doretti, the Palm Beach proved no more popular than that car. A redesign was accordingly instituted for 1956, bringing a more shapely form reminiscent of the Austin-Healey. Ford, Jaguar, and even Chrysler V-8 engines were listed, but only seven of these Mark II cars were built. Never a high-volume manufacturer, Allard had already peaked in the early '50s. The company closed its doors in 1959.

✚ FOR Mechanical simplicity • Neat styling

◼ AGAINST Very few built • No parts available • Crude and less lively compared with concurrent Austin-Healeys and Triumph TRs

PRODUCTION

1.5 Litre 8 **2.2 Litre** 65 **Mark II** 7

SPECIFICATIONS

Length (in.)	156.0
Wheelbase (in.)	96.0
Weight (lbs)	1850/1950
Price (new)	NA

ENGINES

cc/type (cid)	bhp[1]	years
508/ohv I-4 (92)	47	1952-59
2262/ohv I-6 (138)	68	1952-59

[1]gross

PRICES

FAIR	$5000-10,000
GOOD	$10,000-18,000
FINE	$18,000-30,000

FINE EXAMPLE PRICE HISTORY

1982 $7500	**1990** $45,000
1994 $28,000	**1998** $30,000
1982-2000 RETURN 12%	
2000-2010 10	

1952-53 ALLSTATE

1952 A-230 coupe

Sears, Roebuck's version of the Henry J, built by Kaiser-Frazer, and powered by a 80-bhp L-head six or a 68-bhp L-head four from Willys. Sold nationwide through the Sears catalog, but confined to the Southeast in actual promotion. The Allstate features were styled by Alex Tremulis: a more distinctive front end than the Henry J's, special Allstate ornamentation, and many Sears-produced components such as tires, battery, spark plugs. Lack of public response caused Sears to drop the car in early 1953, thus ending the first and last Sears automobile experiment since 1912. *(See also Henry J.)*

FOR More unique and desirable than Henry J • Definite rarity • Quality interior • Good performance (six) • Oustanding gas mileage, up to 25 mpg (four)

AGAINST Indifferent styling • no performance (four) • Distinctively Allstate body parts (grilles, hood ornaments, badges, etc.) now in very short supply

PRODUCTION

1952 four 900 (est.) **1952** six 666 **1953** four 425 (est.) **1953** six 372 (est.)

SPECIFICATIONS

Length (in.)	176.6
Wheelbase (in.)	100.0
Weight (lbs)	2300-2455
Price (new)	$1395-1785

ENGINES

cid/type	bhp	years
134/sv I-4	68	1952-53
161/sv I-6	80	1952-53

PRICES

Four:	
FAIR	$2000-4500
GOOD	$4500-7500
FINE	$7500-10,000
Six:	
FAIR	$3000-5500
GOOD	$5500-8000
FINE	$8000-11,000

FINE SIX EXAMPLE PRICE HISTORY

1982 $3500	**1990** $8500
1994 $9000	**1998** $11,000
1982-2000 RETURN 8%	
2000-2010 5%	

1971-85 ALPINE-RENAULT A310

1974 A310 coupe

The last of Jean Redele's sporting Renault-powered coupes before *La Regie* bought his Dieppe-based specialist firm after the 1973-74 energy crisis, thus saving it. Did not immediately replace the 1957-vintage A108/A110 (continued through the late '70s), but was the same formula, though larger and more spacious: two-seat fiberglass body on a steel backbone chassis with rear engine, all-coil/wishbone suspension, and many Renault components elsewhere.

Initially sold only with tuned Renault fours, but offered from fall '76 with "Douvrin" or "PRV" (Peugeot-Renault-Volvo) V-6, which gave the best performance. Not officially exported Stateside, but "gray market" examples are around at reasonable prices—owing to scant American interest.

FOR A sort of French Porsche 911, but more exclusive

AGAINST Quirky 911-type handling • Spotty parts and service here • Spotty workmanship

PRODUCTION

1.6-liter 2334 **V-6** NA

SPECIFICATIONS

Length (in.)	164.6
Wheelbase (in.)	89.4
Weight (lbs)	2075/2240 (1.6/V-6)
Price (new)	NA

ENGINES

cc/type	bhp[1]	years
1289/ohv I-4	68	1971-75
1605/ohv I-4	126	1971-75
1647/ohv I-4	95	1976-77
2664/ohc V-6	150	1976-85

[1]DIN

PRICES

FAIR	$5000-10,000
GOOD	$10,000-17,500
FINE	$17,500-25,000

FINE EXAMPLE PRICE HISTORY

1994 $25,000	**1998** $25,000
1982-2000 RETURN 2%	
2000-2010 5%	

(Add to prices above: Competition models, 25-50%.)

1985-90 ALPINE-RENAULT GTA

1985-90 GTA coupe

Slightly larger replacement for the A310, but designed by Renault with a firm eye on Porsche 911. Retained its predecessor's rear-engine layout and steel backbone chassis (albeit with standard power steering), but chassis now unitized with a new low-drag fiberglass body (Cd: 0.28). Offered solely with the uprated 2.8-liter "Douvrin/PRV" V-6 (from the big Renault 25 sedan) in 200-bhp Turbo and 160-bhp non-turbo models, both with manual five-speed transaxles (automatic was again conspicuously absent). Quick, especially the Turbo—6.3 seconds 0-60 mph, 150 mph tops—but on-limit handling still tricky. Better ergonomics and more room, too, but still no world-beater GT. Slated for U.S. sale through AMC/Renault for 1987, but canceled when Renault folded its American tent after AMC was sold to Chrysler, which already had a $30,000 sportster in Chrysler's TC by Maserati. Yankee enthusiasts must thus settle for what few private-import specimens exist here—or make a trip to France.

FOR Interesting Porsche 911 challenger with many of the same attributes

AGAINST Also many of the same drawbacks, plus difficult parts and service support

PRODUCTION
NA

SPECIFICATIONS

Length (in.)	170.5
Wheelbase (in.)	92.1
Weight (lbs)	2650
Price (new)	approx. $30,000

ENGINES

cc/type	bhp[1]	years
2849/ohc V-6	160	1985-90
2849/ohc V-6	185/200[2]	1985-90

[1]DIN [2]catalyst/non-catalyst

PRICES

FAIR	$3000-7000
GOOD	$7000-9000
FINE	$9000-10,000

FINE EXAMPLE PRICE HISTORY
Still depreciating

1958-62
AMC METROPOLITAN

Continuation of the 1954-57 Nash/Hudson Metropolitan (see entries) under the AMC badge. Still powered by the Series 56 1500cc Austin overhead-valve four. The tiny "Met" hit its all-time peak of 22,309 units imported in 1959, after which Detroit's compacts overwhelmed it in

1957 Metropolitan hardtop

the economy-car market and sales plummeted drastically. In mid-1959, AMC added an opening trunklid for the first time, along with more comfortable seats, vent wings, and tubeless tires.

FOR The most refined Met • Very economical

AGAINST Dumpy styling, in colors reminiscent of Neapolitan ice cream • A serious ruster

PRODUCTION
1958 13,128 **1959** 22,309 **1960** 13,103 **1961** 853 **1962** 412 (based on shipments from England)

SPECIFICATIONS

Length (in.)	149.5
Wheelbase (in.)	85.0
Weight (lbs)	1850-1890
Price (new)	$1626-1697

ENGINES

cid/type	bhp	years
90.9/ohv I-4	52	1958-62

PRICES

FAIR	$2000-4000
GOOD	$4000-5500
FINE	$5500-9000

FINE EXAMPLE PRICE HISTORY

1982 $3500	1990 $5500
1994 $6000	1998 $9000

1982-2000 RETURN 6%
2000-2010 5%

1967-69
AMC AMBASSADOR DPL & SST 2-DOORS

Successor to the straight-edge 1965-66 Ambassador, with swoopy lines by the late AMC design director Dick Teague in the then-popular "Coke bottle" mode—helped by a two-inch wheelbase stretch. Three series each year: 880/990/DPL for '67, base/

1967 Ambassador DPL convertible

four-door sedans and wagons, but the obvious collectibles here are semi-fastback hardtop coupes and the '67-only DPL convertible. DPL (don't call it "Diplomat") typically furnished with fussy pseudo-brocade upholstery; SST was sportier yet more restrained. Front consoles available in both lines. Small-block V-8s give good performance, the base six good economy; both are sturdy and easily serviced. Other pluses include AMC's usual all-coil suspension with a new Hotchkiss-drive rear (replacing torque-tube), plus a low-profile top stack on the convert. Most of these were likely built with three-speed automatic (either Shift Command, with manual gear-hold, or conventional Flash-O-Matic, both basically Chrysler TorqueFlite), but three-speed, three-speed/OD, and four-speed manuals were available, and are as desirable and rare now as the front disc brake option, especially with V-8. Underrated cars all, and the ragtop DPL is one of the last "undiscovered" '60s convertibles. Post-'69 Ambassadors might also be collected one day, but are omitted here as longer and more ornate—to no good effect.

FOR Pleasant styling • Good performance/economy blend • Rugged engines • Still cheap • Ragtop's rarity and one-year status

AGAINST Mushy handling • Overdone DPL interiors • Rust-prone • Very scarce body panels and soft trim

PRODUCTION
1967 DPL 2d hardtop 12,552 conv 1269 **1968 DPL 2d hardtop** 3696 **SST 2d hardtop** 7686 **1969 DPL 2d hardtop** 4504 **SST 2d hardtop** 8998

SPECIFICATIONS

Length (in.)	202.5
Wheelbase (in.)	118.0
Weight (lbs)	3395-3566
Price (new)	$2958-3622

ENGINES

cid/type	bhp	years
232/ohv I-6	155	1967-69
290/ohv V-8	200	1967-69
343/ohv V-8	235/280	1967-69
390/ohv V-8	315	1968-69

PRICES

Convertible

FAIR	$2000-3000
GOOD	$3000-4500
FINE	$4500-7500

FINE CONVERTIBLE PRICE HISTORY

1982 $3500	**1990** $8500
1994 $8500	**1998** $7500

1982-2000 RETURN 3%
2000-2010 5%

1 9 6 6 - 6 7
AMC MARLIN

1966 Marlin fastback coupe

Continuation of the 1965 Rambler Marlin, which was marketed under the AMC badge for these two years. An attempt to cash in on the temporary boom in fastbacks, the Marlin was based on the mid-size Rambler Classic chassis and claimed "3+3" seating. Its swooping roofline was styled by AMC design chief, the late Richard A. Teague, though he had intended it for the smaller Rambler American. Luxuriously furnished with vinyl bucket seats and deep carpeting, it was billed as a sports car, which it definitely wasn't. For 1967 the car was switched to the longer Ambassador platform, which better suited the long roof. Though it offered some sporty options such as 4-speed shift, tach-ometer, and up to 280 bhp, the Marlin never enjoyed the success of the Big Three ponycars, and was accordingly dropped to make way for AMC's entry in that field, the Javelin.

FOR Has status as a lost cause • Unique looks • Smooth V-8 power • Rarity

AGAINST Unique looks • Limited appreciation potential • Visible, but not distinctive

PRODUCTION

1966 4547 **1967** 2545

SPECIFICATIONS

Length (in.)	195 (1966), 201.5 (1967)
Wheelbase (in.)	112 (1966), 118 (1967)

Weight (lbs)	3050 (1966), 3342 (1967)
Price (new)	$2601 (1966), $2963 (1967)

ENGINES

cid/type	bhp	years
232/ohv I-6	145/155	1966-67
287/ohv V-8	198	1966
327/ohv V-8	250/270	1966
290/ohv V-8	200	1967
343/ohv V-8	235/280	1967

PRICES

FAIR	$1500-2000
GOOD	$2000-3600
FINE	$3600-5500

FINE EXAMPLE PRICE HISTORY

1982 $3000	**1990** $5500
1994 $5500	**1998** $5500

1982-2000 RETURN 4%
2000-2010 3%

1 9 6 8 - 7 0
AMC AMX

1969 AMX 2-passenger coupe

Short-wheelbase two-seater cleverly produced by carving a foot out of the Javelin body. Introduced in mid-1968, it brought AMC's new 390 V-8 (boasting forged steel crankshaft and connecting rods) as an option. Crisp, if chunky, styling coupled with taut suspension, comprehensive instruments (with optional Rally Pak), reclining bucket seats, and optional four-speed gearbox made it a genuine sports car. Saw some success in competition. The AMX name was applied to all manner of post-1970 AMC sporty models from Javelins to Concords to Spirits, and was thereby diluted. The 1968-70 models are the "true" AMXs, and thus have the greatest collector appeal.

FOR Exciting performance • No-nonsense, two-seats-only layout • Still relatively inexpensive • Good parts sources • Active club

AGAINST 390 version has more engine than the chassis can handle • Tends to rust unless given care • Spotty construction quality

PRODUCTION

1968 6725 **1969** 8293 **1970** 4116

SPECIFICATIONS

Length (in.)	177.2 (1968-69), 179.0 (1970)
Wheelbase (in.)	97.0
Weight (lbs)	3097-3126
Price (new)	$3245-3395

ENGINES

cid/type	bhp	years
290/ohv V-8	225	1968-69
343/ohv V-8	280	1968-69
360/ohv V-8	290	1970
390/ohv V-8	315/340	1968-70

PRICES

FAIR	$4000-6000
GOOD	$6000-7500
FINE	$7500-11,000

FINE EXAMPLE PRICE HISTORY

1982 $4100	**1990** $16,000
1994 $16,000	**1998** $14,000

1982-2000 RETURN 6%
2000-2010 5%

1 9 6 8 - 7 0
AMC JAVELIN

1970 Javelin SST hardtop coupe

Dick Teague styled this still under-rated answer to the Mustang and Camaro, a beautifully sculpted, clean lined ponycar. With the standard six, Javelin could cruise effortlessly at 70 mph; with one of the optional V-8s it was capable of much higher cruising speeds and a top end of around 110. Optional "Go Package" with four-barrel 343 V-8, dual exhausts, power front disc brakes, heavy-duty suspension, and wide tires quite desirable. A minor facelift for '69 was followed by more radical sheetmetal surgery for 1970, but the original 1968 edition strikes us as the cleanest Javelin. The same bodyshell was continued through 1974, but clothed in more bulbous, less attractive sheetmetal. Despite the aura of competition success (the Penske/Donohue Trans-Am effort) and big-inch engines, the later Javelins are less desirable.

FOR A bargain compared to contemporary Mustangs and Camaros, offering the same kind of style and spirit • Good mileage with the six • Reasonable blend of performance and economy from the V-8s

AGAINST Most of them have rusted away • Limited appreciation potential • Not much of a following among collectors, who prefer the AMX

PRODUCTION

1968 56,462 **1969** 40,675 **1970** 28,210

SPECIFICATIONS

Length (in.)	182.2 (1968-69),191.0 (1970)
Wheelbase (in.)	109.0
Weight (lbs)	2826-3340
Price (new)	$2482-3995

ENGINES

cid/type	bhp	years
232/ohv I-6	145/155	1968-70
290/ohv V-8	225	1968-69
343/ohv V-8	280	1968-69
390/ohv V-8	315/325/340	1968-70
304/ohv V-8	210	1970
360/ohv V-8	245/290	1970

PRICES

FAIR	$2500-5000
GOOD	$5000-5500
FINE	$5500-9500

FINE EXAMPLE PRICE HISTORY

1982 $3500	**1990** $8000
1994 $6500	**1998** $9500

1982-2000 RETURN 6%
2000-2010 5%

1968-70
AMC REBEL SST HARDTOP & CONV.

1970 SST hardtop coupe

Launched as the Rambler Rebel in 1967 to replace the staid Classic as AMC's mid-size line (see entry). Shared some styling points with the larger Ambassador. AMC badge substituted for '68, when the Rebel was the only AMC series still offering a convertible. The SST was the sportiest Rebel, with a standard "Typhoon" 290

V-8, and many were equipped with bucket seats. In addition, many handling and performance options along Javelin lines were also available. Though it has yet to achieve significant "collectibility," the '68 convertible should gain in importance as the last of AMC's ragtops. Wagons and sedans joined the SST hardtop for 1968-70, but the two-doors are the only models with any collector appeal.

FOR Very low prices • Reasonable availability • Excellent performance and good economy with small-block V-8

AGAINST Little collector recognition • Dwindling parts supplies • Rust tendencies • Clean but mundane styling

PRODUCTION

1968 hardtop 9876 **conv** 823 **1969 hardtop** 5405 **1970 hardtop** 6573

SPECIFICATIONS

Length (in.)	197.0 (1968-69), 199.0 (1970)
Wheelbase (in.)	114.0
Weight (lbs)	3140-3375
Price (new)	$2598-2999

ENGINES

cid/type	bhp	years
290/ohv V-8	200	1968
343/ohv V-8	235/280	1968-69
390/ohv V-8	315/325/340	1968-69
232/ohv I-6	145/155	1969-70
304/ohv V-8	210	1970
360/ohv V-8	245/290	1970

PRICES

FAIR	$1900-2500
GOOD	$2500-4000
FINE	$4000-6500

FINE HARDTOP PRICE HISTORY

1982 $1750	**1990** $6000
1994 $6500	**1998** $6500

1982-2000 RETURN 16%
2000-2010 10%
(Add 30% to prices for 1968 convertible.)

1969
AMC RAMBLER SC/RAMBLER

A limited-edition hardtop, mid-model year addition to the AMC Rambler line (the "American" part of the name was dropped for 1969) built under the aegis of the Hurst shifter people. The fastest car ever produced with the Rambler name, it packed AMC's 390

1969 SC/Rambler hardtop coupe

V-8 and a Borg-Warner four-speed gearbox with (naturally) Hurst linkage. Outlandishly adorned with a bold functional hood scoop; red, white, and blue paint job; tri-color headrests; styled steel wheels and wider tires; and hood lock pins. One magazine clocked the "Scrambler" at just over six seconds in the 0-60 mph sprint, with the quarter-mile timed at a hair over 14 seconds at better than 100 mph. Only a few were made—a dozen more in fact than the 1957 Rambler Rebel—and this plus its high performance makes this pretentious little stormer a nice collectible that's also reasonably affordable.

FOR High performance • Limited production • Budget collectible

AGAINST Tacky "hi-po" add-ons ruin a clean basic shape • Thirsty • Rust-prone

PRODUCTION

1512

SPECIFICATIONS

Length (in.)	181.0
Wheelbase (in.)	106.0
Weight (lbs)	3160
Price (new)	$2998

ENGINES

cid/type	bhp	years
390/ohv V-8	315	1969

PRICES

FAIR	$5000-6700
GOOD	$6700-9000
FINE	$9000-13,000

FINE EXAMPLE PRICE HISTORY

1982 $3750	**1990** $12,000
1994 $12,000	**1998** $13,000

1982-2000 RETURN 7%
2000-2010 8%

1970
AMC REBEL MACHINE

Successor to the '69 SC/Rambler as AMC's factory hot rod. Based on the intermediate Rebel, and offered only for 1970. Standard hardware

1970 Rebel Machine hardtop coupe

included AMC's 390 V-8 with 340 bhp, a 4-speed manual transmission with Hurst shifter, and 3.54:1 rear axle ratio. Body decor comprised a Ram-Air hood scoop; special red, white, and blue paint; and 15-inch magnesium alloy wheels with raised white-letter tires. An 8000-rpm tach, dual exhausts, low back-pressure mufflers, and a definite front end rake completed the package. Though first shown at the NHRA World Championship Drag Finals, it was too heavy to be competitive in that kind of racing, or any other.

✚ **FOR** Increasing interest and price as early ponycars become more expensive • Blistering straight-line performance • Distinctive appearance • Rarity

➖ **AGAINST** "Greasy kid car" styling • Shocking fuel consumption • Indifferent fit and finish • Rust potential • Limited parts supply

PRODUCTION
2326

SPECIFICATIONS
Length (in.)	199.0
Wheelbase (in.)	114.0
Weight (lbs)	3650
Price (new)	$3475

ENGINES
cid/type	bhp	years
390/ohv V-8	340	1970

PRICES
FAIR	$5000-6500
GOOD	$6500-8000
FINE	$8000-12,500

FINE EXAMPLE PRICE HISTORY
1982 $4000	1990 $9000
1994 $10,000	1998 $12,500

1982-2000 RETURN 6%
2000-2010 10%

1971
AMC HORNET SC/360

1971 Hornet SC/360 coupe

Short-lived performance version of American Motors' new compact Hornet introduced for 1970. Offered only as a two-door sedan, the SC/360 was named for its 360-cid derivative of AMC's 343 V-8 (this an enlargement of the 290 V-8). With its standard two-barrel carb it pumped out 245 horses, while a four-barrel option yielded 285. Both versions ran on regular gas. A large hood scoop was provided to assist the hotter engine's breathing, and both models were decked out with tape striping, a heavy-duty handling package, styled steel wheels, and fat tires. An optional four-speed gearbox with Hurst linkage was offered. Not very well accepted by AMC's traditional economy-oriented clientele, it went against the "economy experts" image the company was trying to re-establish as the performance market waned in the early '70s. Though becoming a bona fide collectible now, it's also a spirited little car that can serve as a

good daily-driver for enthusiasts looking for something different.

✚ **FOR** Neat if innocuous styling • Good performance and handling balance • Low-production appeal • Fairly cheap to buy

➖ **AGAINST** Difficult to find • Thirsty • Unit-construction rust propensity

PRODUCTION
784

SPECIFICATIONS
Length (in.)	184.9
Wheelbase (in.)	108.0
Weight (lbs)	3105
Price (new)	$2663

ENGINES
cid/type	bhp	years
360/ohv V-8	245/285	1971

PRICES
FAIR	$2500-3500
GOOD	$3500-5500
FINE	$5500-8000

FINE EXAMPLE PRICE HISTORY
1982 $2000	1990 $5500
1994 $8500	1998 $8000

1982-2000 RETURN 9%
2000-2010 10%

1971-74
AMC JAVELIN

1971 Javelin AMX hardtop coupe

The restyled second-generation AMC ponycar. Longer, lower, wider, and slightly more aerodynamic than its 1968-70 predecessor. Rode a 1-inch-longer wheelbase, though basic inner body structure was unchanged. The more curvaceous styling featured marked bulges over the front wheel arches, something like the then-current Corvette's. The AMX badge was transferred to the Javelin line as the new top model, with base and SST versions continuing as before. Inside was a new dash that curved inward in the middle to give a "cockpit" feel for the driver. Engine choices ran from mild-mannered sixes to AMC's largest-ever V-8, a new 401-cid enlargement of the 343/390 version, rated at 330 horses. It would be the last AMC mill to require premium gas. By now, the performance and ponycar markets were on the downturn, so the Javelin's days were numbered. The base model was deleted for 1972, and the big-block V-8 detuned to run on regular. Still, the 401 was available right on through the last of the line, the '74s, unlike some other ponycars that lost their big-inch options. Limited production makes the AMX versions the most desirable models in this bunch, though none of these Javelins have yet to achieve a significant collector following.

✚ FOR Penske/Donohue race-image rub-off • Last of the line • High performance • Unique styling • Relatively cheap • Nice interior

▬ AGAINST Less graceful than earlier Javs • Hard to find in pristine condition • Thirsty with big-inch engines • Rust-prone

PRODUCTION

1971 26,866 (incl. 2054 AMX) **1972** 32,850 (incl. 3220 AMX) **1973** 26,782 (incl. 4635 AMX) **1974** 27,536 (incl. 4980 AMX)

SPECIFICATIONS

Length (in.)	192.3
Wheelbase (in.)	110.0
Weight (lbs)	2900-3350
Price (new)	$2890-3400 (approx.)

ENGINES

cid/type	bhp	years
232/ohv I-6	145	1971-74
304/ohv V-8	210	1971-74
360/ohv V-8	245/290	1971-74
401/ohv V-8	330[1]	1971-74

[1]Rated 255 bhp SAE net from 1972 on; approx. 270-280 bhp gross

PRICES

FAIR	$2100-4000
GOOD	$4000-5500
FINE	$5500-7500

FINE EXAMPLE PRICE HISTORY

1982 $2700		**1990** $7500	
1994 $8000		**1998** $7500	
1982-2000 RETURN 7%			
2000-2010 8%			

1974-78 AMC MATADOR COUPES

Pillared replacement for the true hardtop coupe in AMC's mid-'70s mid-size line (changed from Rebel to Matador for '71). Built on the same chassis with a shorter wheelbase.

1978 Matador Barcelona II coupe

Hulking semi-fastback styling not one of Dick Teague's better efforts, but had some aerodynamic benefit for AMC's short-lived fling with stock-car racing at the time—which was the main idea. Offered in several trim levels each year. Best for enthusiasts are the sportier "X"-package models with standard body stripes, black grille, styled wheels, etc., plus options like bucket seats and V-8 (small-blocks up to and including AMC's '74-only 401). Still, no Matador is a "driver's car," so the various "designer editions" merit collector interest, too. These include Oleg Cassini (1974-75), Barcelona (1976), and Barcelona II (1977-78), the last with padded vinyl top and (ugh) "opera" windows. More "cheap wheels" than bona fide collectibles now, but they're not being saved, so who knows? At the very least, an interesting low-cost oddball.

✚ FOR Dirt cheap • Minor NASCAR connection • Can't be many '74 401s left • "Distinctive" styling

▬ AGAINST "Distinctive" styling • Tinworm-susceptible • Tough to find in good nick • Tough to restore • No appreciation potential

PRODUCTION

NA, but probably no more than 30 percent of total Matador model-year output. Those figures are: **1974** 99,992 **1975** 59,582 **1976** 41,510 **1977** 30,847 **1978** 10,576; **1974 Cassini** 6165 **1975 Cassini** 1817

SPECIFICATIONS

Length (in.)	209.3
Wheelbase (in.)	114.0
Weight (lbs)	3562-3916
Price (new)	$3096-$4989

ENGINES

cid/type	bhp	years
258/ohv I-6	90/98/110	1974-78
304/ohv V-8	126/150	1974-78
360/ohv V-8	130-195	1974-78
401/ohv V-8	255	1974

PRICES

FAIR	$1200-1500
GOOD	$1500-3000
FINE	$3000-3800

1982 $1600		**1990** $4000	
1994 $4000		**1998** $3800	
1982-2000 RETURN 6%			
2000-2010 Even			

1975-80 AMC PACER

1976 Pacer DL coupe

The "first wide small car." Designed around GM's once-and-future Wankel rotary engine aborted in the first energy crisis, leaving AMC to substitute the one suitable engine it had, an ordinary—and heavy—six. The result was an overweight subcompact long on room but short on pep, workmanship, and—most said—eye appeal. Figuring on the light, compact Wankel led the late AMC design chief Dick Teague to give the initial three-door hatchback a stubby nose and lots of glass, but the latter only contributed weight while the former helped make for what one wag termed "a raindrop in overalls." (It was called worse.) For all that, sales were brisk in the first year, but would never go higher despite the addition of a slightly elongated three-door wagon from 1977 and, to improve performance, a V-8 option for '78-'79. The latter was accompanied by a more "formal" grille, which didn't help, either. Offered in guises from plain DL to fancy Limited and with sporty options like tachometer and styled wheels. Still, no Pacer seems destined to be a high-value keepsake for a long time—if ever.

✚ FOR Oozes '70s character • Dirt cheap • Attrition may work in its favor • Edsels and Corvairs weren't collected once, either

▬ AGAINST Oozes '70s character • Compromises everywhere, but it seemed like a good idea at the time

PRODUCTION

1975 72,158 **1976** 117,244 **1977 3d htchbk sdn** 20,265 **3d wgn** 37,999 **1978 Six** 18,717 **V-8** 2514 **1979 Six** 9201 **V-8** 1014 **1980** est. 2500

SPECIFICATIONS

Length (in.)	172.1/177.0 (sdn/wgn)
Wheelbase (in.)	100.0
Weight (lbs)	2995-3482
Price (new)	$3299-6589

ENGINES

cid/type	bhp	years
232/ohv I-6	90/100/110	1975-80
258/ohv I-6	110/120	1975-80
304/ohv V-8	125/130	1978-79

PRICES

FAIR	$1100-1800
GOOD	$1800-2800
FINE	$2800-3800

FINE EXAMPLE PRICE HISTORY

1994 $4000 **1998** $3500
Depreciated throughout the 1990s.
2000-2010 RETURN 3%

1981-83
AMC EAGLE SX/4 & KAMMBACK

AMC's Eagle was an intriguing 4-wheel-drive offshoot of its late-'70s compact Concord and subcompact Spirit, respectively derived from the 1970-vintage Hornet and its truncated Gremlin sister. Notchback two-door, four-door, and five-door "sportwagon" (all internally dubbed "Eagle 30") arrived for 1980 on a 109.3-inch wheelbase, followed by short-chassis SX/4 and Kammback ("Eagle 50"). SX/4 shared pretty hatch coupe styling with the new-for-'79 Spirit liftback; Kammback was an updated Gremlin. All Eagles employed AMC's innovative "Select Drive" full-time 4WD with vis-

1981 Eagle Kammback coupe

cous-coupling center differential that allowed switching between two- and four-wheel operation from within the vehicle "on the fly." Flared fenders and slightly elevated ride height were the main visual distinctions from rear-drive counterparts. Though senior Eagles may also be collected, the "Eaglets" look to "go platinum" sooner. Smaller size makes them nicer to drive and look at, and fewer were built over fewer years—the big ones ran through 1987. Choose the six over the base Pontiac-supplied four-cylinder engine and an SX/4 over a Kammback (unless rarity counts: the slow-selling Kammback vanished after '82). Also look for desirable features like five-speed manual shift, sliding sunroof, and foglamps.

⊞ FOR Neat idea • Fairly scarce • SX/4's pretty shape • Kammback's rarity • 4WD's bad-weather traction advantages

▬ AGAINST Dull performance • "Trucky" ride • Indifferent workmanship • Seating 2+2 at best • Meager cargo space

PRODUCTION

1981 SX/4 17,340 Kammback 5603 **1982** SX/4 10,445 Kammback 520 **1983** SX/4 2259

SPECIFICATIONS

Length (in.)	166.6
Wheelbase (in.)	97.2
Weight (lbs)	2919-3225
Price (new)	$5995-8319

ENGINES

cid/type	bhp	years
151/ohv I-4	82	1981-83
258/ohv I-6	110	1981-83

PRICES

FAIR	$2000-3000
GOOD	$3000-4500
FINE	$4500-5800

FINE EXAMPLE PRICE HISTORY

1994 $3000 **1998** $5800
Still depreciating in the 1990s.
2000-2010 RETURN 3%

1930-34
AMERICAN AUSTIN

1930 Model A roadster

Produced in Butler, Pennsylvania by Sir Herbert Austin. An early attempt at tariff-busting via local assembly, prefiguring today's U.S. Japanese transplant operations. Based on the British Austin Seven design and powered by a two-main-bearing L-head four. Offered in roadster, runabout, cabriolet, and coupe models, of which the first three are far more desirable. The American Austin failed because of the depression and because Americans didn't really take to cars this tiny. Though few survive today, those that do are increasingly collected. Continued as the American Bantam (see next entry).

⊞ FOR As whimsical and cute as a 1930s car ever got • Low purchase and operating costs • Parts usually inexpensive

▬ AGAINST Underpowered and underbraked • Parts increasingly scarce, particularly sheetmetal

PRODUCTION

1930 8558 **1931** 1279 **1932** 3846 **1933** 4725 **1934** 1300 (est.) (calendar year figures)

SPECIFICATIONS

Length (in.)	105.0
Wheelbase (in.)	75.0
Weight (lbs)	1020-1175
Price (new)	$275-550

ENGINES

cid/type	bhp	years
46/sv I-4	13/14	1930-34

PRICES

FAIR	$3800-5500
GOOD	$5500-9800
FINE	$9800-15,000

1933 Model A coupe

FINE EXAMPLE PRICE HISTORY

1982 $10,000		**1990** $20,000	
1994 $15,000		**1998** $15,000	
1982-2000 RETURN 2%			
2000-2010 3%			

(Open models are at the high end of the price scale.)

1938-41
AMERICAN BANTAM

1938 60 roadster

American Austin built in Butler, Pennsylvania, under Roy S. Evans. Abandoned for Jeep production during World War II and never revived afterward. Evans hired racing engineer Harry Miller to consult with his own engineers, and Alexis de Sakhnoffsky, who designed a new body with a smooth hood, rounded grille, and curvy fenders. He charged Evans a mere $300 and the line was retooled for only $7000! The Bantam I-head engine had full-pressure lubrication, the cars had a new three-speed transmission and cam-and-lever steering. Engines boasted three main bearings after 1939, making the 1940-41 models the best of Butler mechanically. These last cars also had improved brakes, Monroe shocks, Goodyear "air-form" seat cushions (deluxe models), and headlamps mounted in the fenders.

➕ FOR Cute and attractive • Outstanding operating economy • A more deveoped version of the American Austin

➖ AGAINST Still underpowered • Parts problems • Engine durability questionable through 1939

PRODUCTION[1]

1936 under 500 **1937** 3500 (est) **1938** 2000 (est) **1939** 1229 **1940** 800 **1941** 138
[1]Recorded from industry sources. Factory produced no cars in 1935-36; these may have been leftovers or assembled from parts. 1939-41 figures are calendar year.

SPECIFICATIONS

Length (in.)	105.0
Wheelbase (in.)	75.0
Weight (lbs)	1130-1434
Price (new)	$399-565

ENGINES

cid/type	bhp	years
46/sv I-4	20	1938-39
50.1/sv I-4	22	1940-41

PRICES

FAIR	$3500-6000
GOOD	$6000-11,000
FINE	$11,000-16,000

FINE EXAMPLE PRICE HISTORY

1982 $10,500		**1990** $21,000	
1994 $20,000		**1998** $15,000	
1982-2000 RETURN 3%			
2000-2010 5%			

(The Speedster is at the high end of the price scale.)

1961-68
AMPHICAR

Superb neither on water nor land, but nonetheless the world's only amphibious passenger car. Designed by Hans Trippel and powered by a Triumph Herald four-cylinder engine, it did what its maker claimed: run on the road (68 mph tops), sail on water (7 knots maximum) without sinking (rubber gaskets sealed the doors; a bilge pump could be actuated if the scupperlevel rose). A transfer case handled the drive to twin props, and water navigation was via the steering wheel, with the front wheels acting as rudders. It was the sure cure for marina fees, yacht club sharks, and people who wanted to borrow your boat.

➕ FOR Absolutely unique • Engine parts readily available • Perfect for antique boat meets or drive-in pool parties

➖ AGAINST Underpowered and cramped as a car • Drippy '50s styling cliches • A serious ruster (if only it were fiberglass!) • Body parts in short supply

PRODUCTION

3500 (approx.)

SPECIFICATIONS

Length (in.)	157.5
Wheelbase (in.)	83.0
Weight (lbs)	2292
Price (new)	$3395

ENGINES

cc/type (cid)	bhp[1]	years
1147/ohv I-4 (66)	43	1961-68

[1]net

PRICES

FAIR	$5000-7500
GOOD	$7500-10,000
FINE	$10,000-15,000

FINE EXAMPLE PRICE HISTORY

1982 $5000		**1990** $15,000	
1994 $13,250		**1998** $15,000	
1982-2000 RETURN 9%			
2000-2010 5%			

1963-65
APOLLO 3500/5000GT

A sleek, beautiful American gran turismo. The 3500 was powered by light, efficient Buick engines, the vast majority the aluminum-block 3.5-liter

1962 Amphicar convertible

1965 Apollo 500GT coupe

V-8 from the early-'60s Special. The 5000 used bigger LeSabre engines. While the 3500 would do 0-60 in 8.9 seconds and had 130 mph on tap, the 5000GT cut the 0-60 sprint time by 1.5 seconds to 2.0 seconds, and offered another 15-20 mph. The 5000 gained Bendix power front disc brakes to cope with the extra power. The body, styled by Ron Plescia, was bolted to a simple ladder-type frame with modified Buick suspension and a Borg-Warner T-10 four-speed gearbox (also used on the Corvette). Apollo founder Milt Brown set up assembly facilities at Pasadena, California. Bodies were supplied by Frank Reisner's Intermeccanica firm in Turin, Italy. A convertible version, styled by Scaglione, numbered 11 in all, of which 10 were called Vetta Ventura.

➕ FOR Smoother, more nimble than Corvette • Very high performance (5000) • Real exclusivity • Familiar mechanical components • Strong appreciation potential

➖ AGAINST Variable assembly quality, though it improved as production progressed • Not quite as quick as a Corvette off the line

PRODUCTION

Coupes (incl. 5000 GT) 39 **Convertibles** 1 (1964)
An additional 5 cars were built later with leftover bodies. In addition, 17 coupes and 10 convertibles were constructed as Vetta Venturas, of which 14 were completed; 10 bodies were left over.

SPECIFICATIONS

Length (in.)	177.0
Wheelbase (in.)	97.0
Weight (lbs)	2485 (3500)
Price (new)	$6797-8950

ENGINES

cid/type	bhp	years
215/ohv V-8	200	1963-65
300/ohv V-8	250	1964-65

PRICE

3500	
FAIR	$4000-7500
GOOD	$7500-12,500
FINE	$12,500-19,000
5000	
FAIR	$4000-10,000
GOOD	$10,000-18,000
FINE	$18,000-25,000

FINE 5000 PRICE HISTORY

1982 $5500	**1990** $11,000
1994 $17,000	**1998** $25,000
1982-2000 RETURN 13%	
2000-2010 10%	

1954-61
ARNOLT-BRISTOL

1961 Bolide roadster

A hybrid sports car created especially for the North American market by Chicago foreign car entrepreneur Stanley H. "Wacky" Arnolt. Combined the rolling chassis of the British Bristol 404 with a sleek, two-seat body styled by Nuccio Bertone of Italy. Mechanically not a "pure" 404—the transmission and brakes were from the earlier 403—but had a tuned version of Bristol's BS1 Mark II engine with more power than the 404. The sturdy box-section chassis had transverse-leaf front suspension and a carefully located live rear axle. Light weight gave a

good power-to-weight ratio, and acceleration was quick: 0-60 mph in 8.7 seconds, a top end of 110 mph. Offered in three versions: a starkly outfitted "Bolide" roadster, a more completely equipped DeLuxe roadster, and a fixed-roof coupe with roll-up windows (only three of the last were built). Excellent weight distribution and fine road manners made the A-B a racing natural, and it competed with distinction at Sebring in 1955 and '56. Of the total number built, five were aluminum-bodied semi-racers; another four were fitted with 283-cid Corvette V-8s. Expensive now, but body and engine parts are still available through Arnolt's son.

➕ FOR High-quality Bristol engineering • Great handling/roadholding • Punchy, tuneable engine • Low-production exclusivity

➖ AGAINST Engine parts running out now • Rust-prone • Not cheap to restore or maintain • Spartan furnishings • A rarity on the market

PRODUCTION

142 (130 sold; 12 lost to warehouse fire)

SPECIFICATIONS

Length (in.)	168.0
Wheelbase (in.)	96.0
Weight (lbs)	2050-2315
Price (new)	$3995-5995

ENGINES

cc/type (cid)	bhp[1]	years
1971/ohv I-6 (120)	130	1955-61

[1]net

PRICES

FAIR	$7500-15,000
GOOD	$15,000-25,000
FINE	$25,000-45,000

FINE EXAMPLE PRICE HISTORY

1982 $7500	**1990** $35,000
1994 $35,000	**1998** $45,000
1982-2000 RETURN 10%	
2000-2010 10%	

1930-39
ASTON MARTIN 1½-LITRE/2-LITRE

The famous series engineered by Augustus C. Bertelli, introduced in 1927. Built at Feltham—Aston's home at the time, in Middlesex near the then-small Heathrow airport—and powered by Aston's contemporary overhead-

1935 Ulster roadster

cam four. Vintage British, with willowy chassis, skimpy wood-framed bodywork, cycle-type fenders, and a noble radiator. Very sporting. Enjoyed a measure of racing success through several financial crises and management regimes. Four distinct series with various power ratings and model names; most famous among the last are International, Le Mans and, Ulster. No functional connection with the first postwar Astons built under another new owner.

FOR Great "vintage" character • A sports car above all • Super engine • Fine roadholding

AGAINST Seldom traded these days • Parts very difficult • Cramped cockpits • Minimal weather protection • Little U.S. expertise available

PRODUCTION
599

SPECIFICATIONS

Length (in.)	144-168
Wheelbase (in.)	102/120 (1 1/2); 99/116 (2.0)
Weight (lbs)	2000-3100
Price (new)	NA

ENGINES

cc/type (cid)	bhp[1]	years
1495/ohc I-4 (91.2)	56-85	1930-35
1950/ohc I-4 (118.9)	98/110	1936-39
[1]net		

PRICES

FAIR	$25,000-30,000
GOOD	$30,000-50,000
FINE	$50,000-75,000
Ulster	
FAIR	$50,000-80,000
GOOD	$80,000-100,000
FINE	$100,000-125,000

FINE ULSTER PRICE HISTORY

1982 $15,000	**1990** $90,000
1994 $80,000	**1998** $125,000
1982-2000 RETURN 12%	
2000-2010 10%	

1948-50
ASTON MARTIN DB1

1948-50 DB1 convertible

The first Astons built under the aegis of David Brown, the British tractor and transmission magnate who bought the Feltham firm as "a bit 'o fun" in 1947. A complete break with prewar Astons with multi-tubular chassis, trailing-link independent front suspension, hydraulic brakes, and pushrod engine. Most wore florid two-seat convertible coachwork designed by Frank Feeley, formerly of Lagonda (which Brown would also acquire); but one sparse, lightweight racer won the '48 Belgian 24-hour race at Spa, piloted by "Jock" Horsefall and Leslie Johnson. A technical and stylistic dead end, it paved the way for more exciting Astons.

FOR Super scarce • Historical significance • Period British character

AGAINST Expensive for what it is • Rarely traded • Parts impossible

PRODUCTION
15 (some sources list 14)

SPECIFICATIONS

Length (in.)	NA
Wheelbase (in.)	108.0
Weight (lbs)	2240
Price (new)	est. $5000

ENGINES

cc/type (cid)	bhp[1]	years
1970/ohv I-4 (120)	90	1948-50
[1]net		

PRICES

Drophead	
FAIR	$10,000-20,000
GOOD	$20,000-40,000
FINE	$40,000-60,000

FINE EXAMPLE PRICE HISTORY

1982 $15,000	**1990** $80,000
1994 $60,000	**1998** $60,000
1982-2000 RETURN 10%	
2000-2010 10%	

(Deduct 20-25% from above prices for 2/4-seater models.)

1950-53
ASTON MARTIN DB2

A millionaire British industrialist's "bit of fun" that started a long and famous line of sports cars. David Brown's inspired amalgamation of a stillborn Aston Martin chassis design with a twincam six-cylinder engine developed by W.O. Bentley for the by-then bankrupt Lagonda concern. Multi-tubular frame, independent front suspension, and 100-mph performance from a 2.6-liter engine. Prototypes raced with honor in 1949 and '50, and later production models continued to benefit from race-proved improvements. Two-seater fastback coupe and convertible were offered, both with light-alloy bodywork. Unmistakable styling, great charisma, and excellent road manners all add up to a fine automotive collectible.

FOR Racing pedigree • Impeccable road manners • Flexible engine • Not as common as contemporary Jaguar XK120

AGAINST Mechanical parts hard to come by, but still around • No body parts any more • Construction quality not as high as you'd think • Not as quick, either (early Triumph TRs and Austin-Healeys beat it)

PRODUCTION
410

SPECIFICATIONS

Length (in.)	169.5
Wheelbase (in.)	99.0
Weight (lbs)	2660
Price (new)	NA

ENGINES

cc/type (cid)	bhp[1]	years
2580/dohc I-6 (157)	105/125	1950-53
[1]net		

1948 DB2 coupe

PRICES

Coupe

FAIR	$12,000-25,000
GOOD	$25,000-40,000
FINE	$40,000-50,000

Drophead

FAIR	$15,000-30,000
GOOD	$30,000-50,000
FINE	$50,000-85,000

FINE DROPHEAD PRICE HISTORY

1982 $12,000		**1990** $85,000	
1994 $80,000		**1998** $85,000	
1982-2000 RETURN 11%			
2000-2010 10%			

1953-57
ASTON MARTIN DB2/4

1955 DB2/4 coupe

Revised version of the DB2, with 2+2 seating and an early form of hatchback coupe body, now supplied by Mulliner (the convertible by Tickford). Engine capacity increased to 2922cc in 1954, giving a needed gain in power and torque to move these heavier models. The small rear seat made the car more versatile and therefore more attractive to a wider number of buyers, and construction quality was notably better in these years.

➕ **FOR** As for 1950-53 DB2, plus greater practicality

➖ **AGAINST** As for 1950-53 DB2, except for improved construction quality

PRODUCTION

763

SPECIFICATIONS

Length (in.)	169.5
Wheelbase (in.)	99.0
Weight (lbs)	2730
Price (new)	NA

ENGINES

cc/type (cid)	bhp[1]	years
2580/dohc I-6 (157)	125	1953-54
2922/dohc I-6 (178)	140	1954-57

[1]net

PRICES

As for 1950-53 DB2.

1957-59
ASTON MARTIN DB MARK III

Last and best version of the original DB2 design. Offered in the same 2+2 hatchback style as the DB2/4, but given a restyled nose, more power, and—on most examples—front disc brakes. Overshadowed from 1958 on by the new and larger DB4. Model designation here was used to avoid confusion with the 1952 sports-racing DB3. The best quality and fittings of any of the early so-called "W.O." Astons.

➕ **FOR** As for 1953-57 DB2/4 but more so, plus good disc brakes and 120-mph performance

➖ **AGAINST** As for 1953-57 DB2/4

PRODUCTION

550

SPECIFICATIONS

Length (in.)	169.5
Wheelbase (in.)	99.0
Weight (lbs)	2800
Price (new)	NA

ENGINES

cc/type (cid)	bhp[1]	years
2922/dohc I-6 (178)	162/178/195	1957-59

[1]net

PRICES

As for 1950-53 DB2.

1958-63
ASTON MARTIN DB4

The first all-new Aston Martin since the David Brown regime took over in 1950. Offered as a full four-seater coupe with Superleggera (super-light) construction by Touring of Italy. There was also a new platform-style frame and a splendid light-alloy twincam six of great power. Not an easy car to drive well, but very quick—140 mph with the standard engine—and reassuringly solid on the road. Convertible and hardtop derivatives were also built. The DB4 went through five distinct "series" in these years, each faster, better equipped, and more luxurious than the last. A five-speed manual and three-speed automatic transmissions were listed by 1963, along with a choice of two engine tunes.

➕ **FOR** Very fast Italian-style coupe (who needs a Ferrari?) • Magnificent engine and splendid chassis—if properly maintained • Solid and safe—if cared for • A real thoroughbred

➖ **AGAINST** Very rust-prone • Heavy steering • Fuel thirst • Parts available, but costly • Not cheap to buy • High maintenance costs

PRODUCTION

1119

SPECIFICATIONS

Length (in.)	176.0
Wheelbase (in.)	98.0
Weight (lbs)	2885
Price (new)	NA

ENGINES

cc/type (cid)	bhp[1]	years

3670/dohc I-6 (224)   240/266   1958-63
[1]net

PRICES

Coupe
FAIR	$7500-20,000
GOOD	$20,000-35,000
FINE	$35,000-55,000

Drophead
FAIR	$35,000-55,000
GOOD	$55,000-85,000
FINE	$85,000-110,000

FINE DROPHEAD PRICE HISTORY

1982	$15,000	1990	$125,000
1994	$110,000	1998	$110,000

1982-2000 RETURN 12%
2000-2010 10%

1959-61
ASTON MARTIN DB4GT & ZAGATO

Short-wheelbase, two-seat derivatives of the DB4, with lightweight construction for possible racing duty. The GT looked much like the standard DB4, right down to its faired-in headlamps. The Zagato had a more distinctive appearance, with a rounded fastback body and the curious combination of curves and angles associated with this Italian coachbuilder's styling. Less weight, arguably superior aerodynamics, and careful engine tuning all contributed to improved performance, and these Astons were quite fast by any standard. Two more highly sought-after, if prohibitively expensive, collectibles from Newport Pagnell.

FOR Fast (Zagato runs to 150 mph) • Prime investment • Others as for 1958-63 DB4

1960 DB4GT coupe

AGAINST Very flimsy Zagato aluminum body • Highly tuned engine demands much care and attention • Others as for 1958-63 DB4

PRODUCTION

GT 75 **Zagato** 25

SPECIFICATIONS

Length (in.)	171.8 (GT), 168.0 (Zagato)
Wheelbase (in.)	93.0
Weight (lbs)	2705 (approx.)
Price (new)	NA

ENGINES

cc/type (cid)	bhp[1]	years
3670/dohc I-6 (224)	302/314	1959-61

[1]net

PRICES

GT
FAIR	$35,000-60,000
GOOD	$60,000-80,000
FINE	$80,000-95,000

FINE GT PRICE HISTORY

1982	$15,000	1990	$125,000
1994	$90,000	1998	$95,000

1982-2000 RETURN 12%
2000-2010 10%
No recent Zagato pricing available. Zagatos sold for as much as $1.5M at peak ten years ago, but that bubble has burst.

1963-65
ASTON MARTIN DB5

1965 DB5 Vantage coupe

Successor to the DB4, but retained its chassis, basic running gear, and bodyshell, the last with a minor styling update. A bore increase brought displacement of Aston's twincam six to near 4 liters. As with the last DB4s, a choice of engine tunes was available, either 282 or 325 bhp, depending on how much the customer thought he or she could handle. Four transmission choices were offered, including 5-speed ZF manual and Borg-Warner automatic. A much-modified DB5 put this model on the map when it was used as James Bond's spy car in the film *Goldfinger*.

FOR As for 1958-63 DB4

AGAINST As for 1958-63 DB4

PRODUCTION

1187

SPECIFICATIONS

Length (in.)	180.0
Wheelbase (in.)	98.0
Weight (lbs)	3235
Price (new)	$13,200 U.S. in 1964

ENGINES

cc/type (cid)	bhp[1]	years
3995/dohc I-6 (224)	282/325	1963-65

[1]net

PRICES

As for 1958-63 DB4

1965-71
ASTON MARTIN DB6

Reworked replacement for the DB5, with a longer wheelbase, more rear seat space, Kamm-style spoilered tail, and greater weight. Not as fast as earlier DBs, but more practical. Fastback coupe and two-door convertible—called Volante—body styles continued as before. Beginning at the end of 1969 a Mark II version was offered with DBS-type wheels and tires, flared wheel openings, and an optional fuel injection system. Normal engine tune delivered a 140-mph maximum speed, the Vantage version 148 mph.

FOR As for DB4 and DB5, plus more interior room

AGAINST As for DB4 and DB5 • Fuel injection troublesome and best avoided

PRODUCTION

1753

SPECIFICATIONS

Length (in.)	182.0
Wheelbase (in.)	101.7

Weight (lbs)	3250
Price (new)	$15,400 U.S. list in 1966

ENGINES

cc/type (cid)	bhp	years
3995/dohc I-6 (244)	282/335	1965-71

PRICES

As for 1958-63 DB4.

1 9 6 7 - 7 3

ASTON MARTIN DBS & VANTAGE

1968 DBS 6-cylinder coupe

Newly styled four-seat GT supplement to the DB6, revealed in 1967. Designed expressly for a new V-8 engine, but powered initially by Aston's well-tried twincam six. Chassis design was a wider and longer development of the DB6 platform, but fitted with de Dion rear suspension. Dramatically handsome fastback styling by William Towns (then working for AM). British to the core, and literally hand-built at Newport Pagnell, but looked and sounded Italian. Available in normal and 325-bhp Vantage tune (in which form the car would nudge 150 mph). Somewhat bulky, and handling ponderous unless optional power steering was ordered, but very desirable. After a change of company ownership—David Brown sold his Aston Martin Lagonda interests in 1969—the designation was changed to Aston Martin Vantage and minor styling changes, including a switch from quad to dual headlamps, were instituted. The model continued in V-8 form into the 1980s. At one time, a long-wheelbase sedan derivative of this design was rumored for the Lagonda badge, and a prototype was built and widely shown in the British press. However, the revived Lagonda that ultimately emerged was a far different machine, though again styled by Towns.

FOR Proven powertrain and chassis • Solid, reassuring road manners

• Great performance • Six cheaper and easier to maintain than later V-8 • Clean styling • Traditional British GT appointments

AGAINST Steel understructure rusts badly if neglected • Costly to restore • Overshadowed for sheer speed by DBS V-8

PRODUCTION

899, incl. 3 estate cars and 70 Vantage models

SPECIFICATIONS

Length (in.)	180.5
Wheelbase (in.)	102.8
Weight (lbs)	3760
Price (new)	$12,650 FOB factory list in 1969

ENGINES

cc/type (cid)	bhp	years
3995/dohc I-6 (244)	282/325	1967-73

PRICES

Coupe	
FAIR	$12,000-22,000
GOOD	$22,000-30,000
FINE	$30,000-40,000

Volante: Up to and sometimes over $100,000 for fine examples.

FINE COUPE PRICE HISTORY

1982	$10,000	**1990**	$80,000
1994	$45,000	**1998**	$40,000
1982-2000 RETURN 9%			
2000-2010 5%			

1 9 6 9 - 8 9

ASTON MARTIN DBS/AM V-8/ VOLANTE/ VANTAGE

Aston's Italianette GT with its originally intended V-8; did not immediately replace six-cylinder DBS. All-aluminum twin-cam engine designed by Tadek Marek. Horsepower never quoted (*á la* Rolls-Royce), but most British writers estimated near 400 (SAE gross). Available with either five-speed manual or three-speed automatic transmissions. Blistering performance (160+ mph), this despite bulky heft. Otherwise similar to six-cylinder sister, but silkier and more refined, though still a beast. Demise of David Brown's empire prompted Aston Martin V8 name from 1973, when headlamps went from four to two and performance improved via a quartet of two-barrel Weber carbs, replacing Bosch fuel injection. New special-order Vantage companion from spring 1977 with 40-percent more claimed power and 175-mph capability, plus deep front spoiler, blanked-off grille, uprated chassis with wider rolling stock, and manual shift only. Standard-spec Volante convertible offered from mid-1978. Detail revisions then made to coupes, and all specs effectively frozen through the end of production in late 1989, when the successor Virage was ready (see entry). Ultimate expression of this concept was a run of 50 coupes and 25 convertibles built in 1986-88 with tuned engines and special coachwork by Italian specialist Zagato, by then part-owned by Aston chairman Victor Gauntlett.

FOR As for 1967-73 DBS, but even more performance • Parts no problem for now • Zagato specials' rarity • Should always find buyers

AGAINST Gas guzzlers • High insurance premiums • Injection engine finicky to keep in tune • Parts/service very costly • Limited U.S. expertise • Zagato convertible for Europe-only • Others as for 1967-73 DBS

PRODUCTION

DBS V-8 405 (1969-72) **AM V-8** est. 2200

1973 Vantage coupe

AM V-8 **Vantage** 100+ V-8 **Volante** 100-200
Zagato coupe 50 (1986-87) **Zagato convertible**
25 (1988)

SPECIFICATIONS

Length (in.)	180.5-183.7
Wheelbase (in.)	102.8
Weight (lbs)	3800-3900
Price (new)	$16,550-$100,000

ENGINES

cc/type (cid)	bhp[1]	years
5340cc/dohc V-8 (326)	375-408	1969-89

[1]net

PRICES

1988 DBS Coupe

FAIR	$20,000-30,000
GOOD	$30,000-40,000
FINE	$40,000-60,000

1989 Volante conv

FAIR	$30,000-50,000
GOOD	$50,000-75,000
FINE	$75,000-100,000

FINE 1989 VOLANTE PRICE HISTORY

1990 $55,000   **1994** $40,000
1998 $100,000
1990-98 RETURN 8%
2000-2010 10%
(Add 10-15% to above prices for Vantage.)

1990-2000
ASTON MARTIN VIRAGE

1990 Virage coupe

Evolutionary replacement for the DB/AM V-8, the first model offered after Aston's 1987 takeover by Ford U.S. Unveiled as a 2+2 coupe at Birmingham in late '89, a Volante convertible followed in 1993. Virage exports to the U.S. ended the next year. A 550-horsepower Vantage was introduced in 1992, but was never exported to the U.S. Same basic format as predecessor, but 5.3-liter all-aluminum engine modified by Callaway Engineering in the U.S. for a new four-valve cylinder head, intake manifold, and Weber-Marelli electronic management system. Front suspension still by twin wishbones, rear by Watt linkage and de Dion tube, but the last now square-section aluminum. Sleeker body, still aluminum-paneled, with integral spoilers at each end, plus flush headlamps and side glass—all for lower drag coefficient, down to a claimed 0.34. Modernized dash and even more luxury features than late AM V-8s, including heated windshield, rear window, and front seats; trip computer; and remote infrared alarm system. Very expensive, but low planned production—300 yearly at most.

⧉ FOR Great "modern vintage" charm • Exclusivity • High performance (around 6 seconds 0-60 mph, 155 mph all-out) • Svelte styling

▬ AGAINST High purchase and running costs • U.S. parts/service backup remains limited even for an "exoticar" • Still "fuelish" • Appreciation potential unclear now

PRODUCTION

NA

SPECIFICATIONS

Length (in.)	186.4
Wheelbase (in.)	102.8
Weight (lbs)	3950
Price (new)	$150,000-$258,648 (U.S.)

ENGINES

cc/type (cid)	bhp[1]	years
5341/dohc V-8 (326)	330/349	1990-00
5341/dohc V-8 (326)[2]	550	1992-00

[1]SAE net
[2]Supercharged

PRICES

Collector market not yet established.

1995-2000
ASTON MARTIN DB7/DB7 VANTAGE

Aston's DB series dates to 1948, but the designation was dropped in 1972 following the company's sale. The company changed hands more than once in the Eighties, and Ford assumed a 75-percent stake in Aston in 1987. The DB name was wisely revived for a new model based on Jaguar components. The DB7 (de-signed by Aston's Ian Callum) and its uplevel variant, the Vantage, were built at a dedicated plant located at Bloxham, England. The Vantage (the name dates to 1953) is the top of the Aston line, combining elegant yet brutish good looks with quite muscular performance: a '99 Vantage whipped through the 0-100 kph sprint (0-62 mph) in just 5.0 seconds with a 6.0-liter, 420 bhp V-12. Non-Vantage models got 335 bhp from a supercharged straight six, and ran the same sprint in 5.7 seconds. Although underwritten by Ford, these cars represented the summit of British automaking.

⧉ FOR Limited production • Neck-snapping performance • Handling characteristics • Top-notch materials, inside and out • Excellent ergonomics • Cachet that comes with a great name

▬ AGAINST Initial expense • Costly maintenance • Limited storage space

PRODUCTION

1995 698 **1996** 699 **1997** 175 **1998** 572 **1999** 36
1999 Vantage 400 (approx.)

SPECIFICATIONS

Length (in.)	182.9-184.7
Weight (lbs)	3640-4210
Wheelbase (in.)	102.0
Price (new)	$125,000-150,000

ENGINES

cid/type	bhp	years
224/dohc I-6[1]	335	1995-2000
362/dohc V-12	420	1999-2000

[1]Supercharged

PRICES

Collector market not yet established

2000 DB7 Vantage coupe

1 9 3 1 - 3 6
AUBURN EIGHT

A glamorous era was ushered in by the sleek, long Auburn Eights of 1931 with their big 268.6-cid Lycoming engines, bored to 280 cid for 1934. Capable of nearly 90 mph with the lighter open bodies, terrific for the time. A truncated speedster (not the later supercharged model) was available in 1931-33. The most expensive range was the 1933 Salon (Series 8-105) with dual ratio rear axle and a more luxurious interior. The restyled body of 1934 was not liked by Auburn management. Body stylist Gordon Buehrig was brought in from Duesenberg to design the '35 Auburn line. Buehrig's absolutely splendid design was a budget package based on the '34 body, but all new and glamorous from the cowl forward, with an impressive new grille and longer hood. Auburn Eights had a reputation for size, luxury, and performance far beyond their price: the most expensive Custom Eight Dual Ratio in 1932 cost only $1005. Auburn finally collapsed in 1936, one of the saddest deaths in auto history.

✚ FOR Like the Twelve, a CCCA Classic • Superb roadability and performance • Still a good buy among CCCA-listed Classics

▬ AGAINST Traditionally a wallflower compared to the 1935-36 Speedsters and Twelves • Closed models slow to appreciate • High operating costs

PRODUCTION
1931 36,148 **1932** 6000¹ **1933** 4000¹ **1934** 3500¹
1935-36 3000¹
¹Estimated from reported factory production by calendar year

SPECIFICATIONS
Length (in.)	NA
Wheelbase (in.)	127.0, 136.0
Weight (lbs)	3320-4125
Price (new)	$945-1448

ENGINES
cid/type	bhp	years
268.6/sv I-8	98/100	1931-33
280.0/sv I-8	100/115	1934-36

PRICES
Speedsters	
FAIR	$40,000-65,000
GOOD	$65,000-100,000
FINE	$100,000-150,000
Other open	
FAIR	$30,000-60,000
GOOD	$60,000-80,000
FINE	$80,000-140,000
Closed	
FAIR	$11,000-15,000
GOOD	$15,000-25,000
FINE	$25,000-40,000

FINE MODEL SPEEDSTER PRICE HISTORY
1987 $120,000		**1994** $125,000	
1998 $150,000			
1987-2000 RETURN 2%			
2000-2010 5%			

1936 852 Cabriolet

1 9 3 2 - 3 4
AUBURN TWELVE

1932 V-12 Cabriolet

The least expensive V-12 ever at $975 for the Standard coupe and $1275 for the top-of-the-line Custom Speedster. Power by Lycoming (part of Errett Lobban Cord's empire) in a huge double-braced frame. Custom Twelves had a Columbia dual-ratio rear axle with 3.04 and 4.55 gearing, interchangeable under 40 mph. The magnificent V-12 boattail Speedsters, so rare today, were the finest expressions of Classic-era styling. Unfortunately for Auburn, its unprecedented value didn't impress a public adamant for economy cars, and the firm scrubbed all its Twelves after 1934.

✚ FOR One of the most balanced and best engineered 1930s Classics • Stunning design, especially open models • Values still appreciating

▬ AGAINST Prices already formidable • Operating costs and parts commensurately expensive • Lacks "blue chip" aura of Cord and Duesenberg stablemates

PRODUCTION
Under 2000 for the three years; 305 Salon Twelves for 1933

SPECIFICATIONS
Length (in.)	NA
Wheelbase (in.)	133.0
Weight (lbs)	4135-4870
Price (new)	$975-1745

ENGINES
cid/type	bhp	years
391.6/sv V-12	160	1932-34

PRICES
Speedster	
FAIR	$54,000-80,000
GOOD	$80,000-120,000
FINE	$120,000-160,000
Other open	
FAIR	$40,000-65,000
GOOD	$65,000-100,000
FINE	$100,000-150,000
Closed	
FAIR	$15,000-25,000
GOOD	$25,000-40,000
FINE	$40,000-55,000

FINE V-12 SPEEDSTER HISTORY
1982 $65,000		**1990** $125,000	
1994 $135,000		**1998** $160,000	
1982-2000 RETURN 6%			
2000-2010 5%			

1931 8-98 Speedster

1935-36

AUBURN SUPERCHARGED 851/852

1935 851 Speedster

One of the quintessential recognized Classics, with prices and demand to suit. Styling by the late Gordon Buehrig, engineering by August Duesenberg, both directed by Auburn-Cord-Duesenberg president Harold T. Ames. Supercharged Auburns were identified by outside exhaust on the left side of the hood. The speedster returned after being discontinued in '34 and all were supercharged. Speedsters featured beautiful pontoon fenders and a boattail influenced by one of Buehrig's Duesenberg designs. Duesenberg's engine was an extension of the 1934 eight, but with 150 bhp courtesy its Schwitzer-Cummins blower. Speedsters claimed an honest 100 mph off the showroom floor and were among the most breathtakingly beautiful automobiles of all time, yet in 1935 they sold for just $2245. Most Classic enthusiasts wish they had a time machine for cars like these.

FOR Speedster among the top blue chip Classics • Stunning looks and great vintage performance • A legend among motorcars

AGAINST Price, price, and price • High operating costs • Rarity

PRODUCTION

Approx. 500

SPECIFICATIONS

Length (in.)	NA
Wheelbase (in.)	127.0
Weight (lbs)	3565-3729
Price (new)	$1445-2245

ENGINES

cid/type	bhp	years
280.0/sv I-8[1]	150	1935-36

[1] Supercharged

PRICES

Speedsters
FAIR	$60,000-90,000
GOOD	$90,000-115,000
FINE	$115,000-165,000

Other open
FAIR	$40,000-70,000
GOOD	$70,000-100,000
FINE	$100,000-130,000

Closed
FAIR	$15,000-22,000
GOOD	$22,000-35,000
FINE	$35,000-46,000

FINE 851 SPEEDSTER PRICE HISTORY

1982 $59,000	1990 $110,000
1994 $110,000	1998 $165,000
1982-2000 RETURN 6%	
2000-2010 5%	

1981-87

AUDI COUPE/COUPE GT

Fastback 2+2 coupe derived from Audi's 1978-87 third-generation 80/90 junior sedan series, "4000" in the U.S. Combined the basic bodyshell of concurrent all-wheel-drive Quattro coupe (see entry) with conventional 80/90 front-wheel drivetrain with five-cylinder inline engines. Few changes save a minor facelift—for model-year '85 in U.S., accompanied by GT suffix—and interim displacement increases. Surprisingly roomy for a coupe, and pleasant, though not exciting, to drive. Nicely equipped, too, and late-'87 U.S. versions received added standard items including a manual steel sunroof, formerly an option. A long-shot collector's item in the U.S., but scarce enough to be increasingly desired by at least a handful of enthusiasts as time goes by.

FOR Solid German construction • Decent performance and economy • Secure, agile handling • Nice ride • Practical four/five-seater • Affordable

AGAINST Mediocre over-the-shoulder vision • Throbby post-'83 engines • Will always be overshadowed by Quattro Turbo • Limited appreciation potential in U.S.

PRODUCTION[1]

1981 2553	1982 4236
1983 3358	1984 3520
1985 3586	1986 2846
1987 2268	

[1](U.S. calendar-year sales)

SPECIFICATIONS[1]

Length (in.)	177.0
Wheelbase (in.)	99.8
Weight (lbs)	2510
Price (new)	$11,895-18,895

[1]U.S. models

ENGINES

cc/type	bhp	years
2144/ohc I-5	100	1981-83
2226/ohc I-5	110	1984-87
2309/ohc I-5	130	1987

PRICES

Subject to used car market, for fine examples presently up to $4000. No appreciation noted to date.

1980-91

AUDI QUATTRO COUPE

The first series-production car with full-time all-wheel-drive since the rare late-'60s Jensen FF, and a prelude to many future AWD Audis. Bowed in Europe during 1980, in America two years later. Front suspension and sheetmetal shared with contemporary 80/90 sedans ("4000" in U.S.), but unique fastback coupe bodywork behind the cowl, plus a rear sus-

1986 Coupe GT

1984 Quattro coupe

pension with essentially duplicate front-end components: struts and coil springs, plus fixed "steering arms." Sold mostly with a five-speed manual transmission teamed to a turbo-charged, air-to-air intercooler version of the 2.1-liter inline five from the senior Audi 100/200 series ("5000" in U.S.); a normally aspirated 2.2 was available in certain markets from the mid-'80s. All-wheel drive (with center and locking rear differentials) made this a nearly unbeatable European rally car for several years, but a lightweight, short-wheelbase "homologation special" actually had less success than the stock models. Began the worldwide industry craze for high-performance all-drive road cars—including other Audis, one reason it was dropped from the U.S. after 1985 (though limited production continued for Europe all the way through 1990). But that historical significance, plus relative rarity and technical appeal, would seem to ensure its place as a future collectible.

FOR As for 1981-87 Coupe/Coupe GT plus successful, pioneering concept • Spirited performance (8 seconds 0-60 mph, up to 130 mph max.) • Great poor-weather traction • Rally-winner appeal • Not costly

AGAINST Exact appreciation potential unclear now • Some parts bound to be scarce in a few years • Audi image still tarnished in U.S.

PRODUCTION[1]
1982 287 **1983** 240 **1984** 65 **1985** 73 **1986** 1
[1]U.S. calendar-year sales

SPECIFICATIONS[1]
Length (in.)	178.2
Wheelbase (in.)	99.5
Weight (lbs)	3055-3115
Price (new)	$35,000

[1]U.S. models

ENGINES
cc/type	bhp	years
2144/ohc I-5[3]	160/200[1]	1980-91
2226/ohc I-5	136[2]	1987-91

[1]net bhp U.S./European models [2]European models only [3]Turbocharged

PRICES
Subject to used car market, varying between $4000 and $10,000 for clean examples.
2000-2010 RETURN not predicted

1985-91
AUDI 5000CS TURBO QUATTRO/ 200 QUATTRO

1991 200 Quattro sedan

The senior late-'80s Audi in top-line turbocharged trim with Quattro all-wheel drive. Called 5000 CS Turbo Quattro in U.S. through 1988, then 200 Quattro (The 200 badge, previously used elsewhere, was substituted and non-turbo 5000s became 100s.) Always sold in the sedan and 5-door "fasthatch" wagon styles of the second-series 100/200, launched in Europe during 1982 (model-year '84 U.S. debut)—then the most aerodynamic cars of their kind, thanks to low-drag shape with features like flush side glass. Alas, U.S. demand for all Audis was severely hurt by the late-'80s "sudden acceleration" controversy involving 1978-86 5000 models. Though Audi was subsequently cleared, U.S.

business has yet to return to "pre-crisis" levels. Lack of available automatic transmission further limited American interest in these big Quattros, but the standard manual five-speed gave far better performance anyway. Minor facelift and revised dash with 200-series; 2.2-liter turbo-intercooled engine little changed. Also standard antilock brake system throughout; Audi was first, in fact, to offer electronic ABS with fulltime all-wheel drive. The most collectible of recent big Audis for obvious reasons, though values shouldn't start rising for a good while yet.

FOR Brilliant marriage of style and technology • Safety of all-wheel drive and ABS • Big and luxurious • Fairly scarce • U.S. prices still depressed

AGAINST U.S. collector interest depressed • New-generation 100/200 (for 1992), so dwindling parts and service in future

PRODUCTION
1985 451[1] **1986** 3,400[1] **1987** 3245[1] **1988** 1457 **1989** 1334 **1990** 1243
[1]incl. wagon model; others: sedan only

SPECIFICATIONS[1]
Length (in.)	192.7
Wheelbase (in.)	105.8
Weight (lbs)	3350-3450
Price (new)	$29,950-36,930

[1]U.S. models

ENGINES
cc/type	bhp	years
2226/ohc I-5[1]	158-162	1985-90

[1]Turbocharged

PRICES
Subject to used car market, varying widely but most are around $7500 for fine late model examples.
2000-2010 RETURN Not predicted

1989-95
AUDI V-8 QUATTRO

1990 V-8 Quattro sedan

Top-line sedan from Bavaria's other automaker (in Ingolstadt), introduced for 1990 with Audi's first modern V-8 and first four-speed automatic transmission, and the only one offered. Appearance close to that of existing five-cylinder 100/200, and full-time Quattro all-wheel drive similar, but completely different body panels and more prominent grille. Fuel-injected 32-valve four-cam V-8 essentially a pair of Volkswagen 1.8-liter fours, gave performance slightly behind rival Mercedes and BMWs. A strong "ultra-luxury" bid nonetheless, with contemporary "musts" like antilock brakes, driver's airbag, leather interior, and high-power sound system. Collectibility slightly dimmed by five-speed manual alternative for '91 and a 4.2-liter engine with 30 more horses for '92.

FOR All-wheel-drive with ABS safety • Smooth styling • Plentiful amenities • Pleasant to drive • Solid, rust-resistant construction

AGAINST Performance not in BMW /Mercedes class • Stiffish ride • Unseemly road noise • Low marque snob-appeal • Uncertain collector-market prospects

PRODUCTION[1]
1989 889 **1990** 1934
[1]U.S. calendar-year sales

SPECIFICATIONS[1]
Length (in.)	191.9
Wheelbase (in.)	106.4
Weight (lbs)	3950
Price (new)	$47,450

[1]U.S. model

ENGINES
cc/type (cid)	bhp	years
3562/dohc V-8 (217)	240	1990
4200/dohc V-8 (NA)	276	1992-95

PRICES
As above.
Fine examples can be up to $10,000.
2000-2010 RETURN Not predicted

2000
AUDI TT

2000 TT coupe

A genuine novelty and a small masterpiece of design, the sloped-roofed, TT coupe shared its platform with the Audi A4 and the Volkswagen New Beetle, Golf, and Jetta. It rode a considerably more stiff suspension than any of those, and produced grin-inducing performance that existed at about the middle of the pack for its class (0-60 mph in 7.4 seconds) with a 1.8-liter turbocharged inline four rated at 180 bhp. The tight cockpit, though claustrophobic, was practical as well as beautiful, with smartly designed instruments and gauges, and a postmodern circle motif expressed in bodyshape and interior aluminum accents. The driver's biggest challenge was backing up because over-the-shoulder visibility was nil.

FOR Top materials and sensational, concept-car styling, inside and out • High-revving engine and potent performance • Handling and roadholding • Braking • Front-seat comfort • Excellent ergonomics • Available AWD

AGAINST Poor visibility • 2+2 seating in name only • Stiff ride

PRODUCTION
NA

SPECIFICATIONS
Length (in.)	151.9
Weight (lbs)	2910
Wheelbase (in.)	95.4
Price (new)	$30,500

ENGINES
cid/type	bhp	years
107/dohc I-4	180[1]	2000

[1]Turbocharged

PRICES
Subject to used car market for next few years, but in our opinion a good bet to stop depreciating before 2010.

1953-56
AUSTIN-HEALEY 100

1955 100 (BN2) roadster

First of the smooth-lined British roadsters designed by Donald Healey. Based on running gear from the Austin A90 sedan, and adopted by British Motor Corporation (BMC) for quantity production. Rugged ladder-style chassis with steel-and-alloy body welded up to it. Beautiful, and mostly practical for a two-seat open sports car, but let down by comparatively scant ground clearance (the exhaust being the main culprit) and excessive engine heat seeping into the cockpit. The first BN1 models used the A90 four-speed gearbox with low simply blanked off, but a Laycock overdrive brought the forward speeds back to four. The later BN2s had a normal four-speed, plus the overdrive. Well received in the U.S., where enthusiasts found it offered everything contemporary MGs didn't, including a good deal more speed. The early models were predictably the lightest, capable of 0-60 mph in 10.3 seconds and 111 top. Later models were heavier—but more civilized and better equipped. The A-H quickly earned a reputation for being virtually unbreakable in anything short of a complete crack-up. Styling wore well, and evolved with remarkably few changes through the six-cylinder Healey 3000s of the '60s.

FOR Simple, rugged mechanicals • Easy to service and restore • Most parts still available • Styling • Open-air allure

AGAINST Bodies rot badly in wet climates • Minimal ground clearance • Cockpit heat (no cure) • Rather basic equipment

PRODUCTION
BN1 10,688 **BN2** 3924

SPECIFICATIONS
Length (in.)	151.0
Wheelbase (in.)	90.0

Weight (lbs)	2015-2150
Price (new)	NA

ENGINES

cc/type (cid)	bhp[1]	years
2660/ohv I-4 (162)	90	1953-56

[1]net

PRICES

FAIR	$8500-12,000
GOOD	$12,000-18,000
FINE	$18,000-24,000

FINE EXAMPLE PRICE HISTORY

1982 $7500	1990 $32,000
1994 $20,000	1998 $24,000

1982-2000 RETURN 7%
2000-2010 7%

1955
AUSTIN-HEALEY 100S

Racing derivative of the first-series BN1 Austin-Healey. Differences from the mass-production version included a different cylinder head and internal engine modifications for more power, plus a light-alloy bodyshell, four-speed gearbox without overdrive, and standard Dunlop disc brakes on all four wheels. Not as practical for daily driving as the tamer four-cylinder Healeys, but a worthwhile collectible for its rarity and mechanical specification, which provided 0-60-mph sprints in 7.8 seconds and a top speed of 126 mph.

FOR As for 1953-55 BN1, plus rarity (yet reasonably affordable despite that) and strong appreciation potential

AGAINST More fragile than production models • Engine parts mostly gone • Aluminum body restoration difficult • Seldom seen on the market

1955 100S Roadster

PRODUCTION

50

SPECIFICATIONS

Length (in.)	151.0
Wheelbase (in.)	90.0
Weight (lbs)	1925
Price (new)	NA

ENGINES

cc/type (cid)	bhp[1]	years
2660/ohv I-4 (162)	132	1955

[1]net

PRICES

FAIR	$15,000-20,000
GOOD	$20,000-35,000
FINE	$35,000-50,000

FINE EXAMPLE PRICE HISTORY

1994 $45,000	1998 $50,000

1992-2002 10%

1956-59
AUSTIN-HEALEY 100-6

1957 100-6 (BN4) 4-seat roadster

The revised and expanded Healey series of the late '50s, with svelte styling similar to the original's. A longer wheelbase allowed BMC to offer a choice of two-seat (BN6) or four-seat (BN4) layouts, and a detachable hardtop was offered as a new factory accessory. The main item of interest

was a new 2.6-liter six-cylinder engine. This gained a more efficient cylinder head for greater power and performance in November 1957. All BN6s had it, as this model was introduced after the BN4, following customer requests for the return of the "pure" two-seat Healey. Early 100-6s were built in Austin's Longbridge plant, later edition in MG's Abingdon works, the latter incorporating a number of engine improvements including the better cylinder head, revised camshaft, and larger valves. Not the favorite Austin-Healey with collectors, it did 0-60 in an average 11.2 seconds and topped out at 111 mph.

FOR As for 1953-56 BN1/BN2 100 models, plus more readily available spare parts

AGAINST As for 1953-56 BN1/BN2 100 models, but 300 pounds heavier and thus less lively despite bigger engine • Some compromises on original styling, including bodyside two-toning

PRODUCTION

BN4 10,246 **BN6** 4150

SPECIFICATIONS

Length (in.)	157.5
Wheelbase (in.)	92.0
Weight (lbs)	2435
Price (new)	NA

ENGINES

cc/type (cid)	bhp[1]	years
2639/ohv I-6 (161)	102/117	1956-59

[1]net

PRICES

FAIR	$9500-15,000
GOOD	$15,000-20,000
FINE	$20,000-28,000

FINE EXAMPLE PRICE HISTORY

1982 $7200	1990 $30,000
1994 $18,000	1998 $28,000

1982-2000 RETURN 7%
2000-2010 7%

1958-61
AUSTIN-HEALEY SPRITE

The Healey family's follow-up to successful collaboration with British Motor Corporation (BMC) on the Healey 100. This new low-priced sports car featured unitized steel construction on tiny overall dimensions. Running gear and front suspension were borrowed from the Austin A35 sedan. Rear suspension was by cantilever quarter-elliptic springs support-

1961 Sprite roadster

ing a solid axle, about as simple as could be. The original plan to give the Sprite hidden headlamps was abandoned for cost reasons, which resulted in fixed lamps that gave the rounded front end a quaintly cute "frog-eye" appearance. The entire front sheet-metal section, including the fenders, was hinged at the front, and lifted up for superb engine access. At the opposite end of the car, there was no trunk-lid, and only modest storage space in the tail, which was accessible only from behind the hinged front seat backrests. Performance was less than expected—0-60 mph in 23-24 seconds and a top speed of only 80 mph—but handling was predictably sprightly and fuel economy great. Assembly was actually carried out at MG's Abingdon factory, which may explain why a Midget version followed with the Sprite's Mark II restyle. Equipment was very basic initially, with rubber floor mats and clip-on side curtains, but loads of extras were available from the factory and various accessory and performance-parts makers. The Sprite proved enormously popular and, when hotted up, it could top 100 mph.

✚ FOR Mechanical simplicity • Great character • Light and frugal • Parts (except body) still in good supply • Cheap to buy • Fun to drive • Easy to work on

▬ AGAINST Rudimentary ride and equipment • Rusts out easily • Worn chassis prone to oversteer handling behavior

PRODUCTION
48,999

SPECIFICATIONS

Length (in.)	137.2
Wheelbase (in.)	80.0
Weight (lbs)	1460
Price (new)	NA

ENGINES

cc/type (cid)	bhp[1]	years
948/ohv I-4 (58)	43	1958-61

[1]net

PRICES

FAIR	$2500-5000
GOOD	$5000-7000
FINE	$7000-12,000

FINE EXAMPLE PRICE HISTORY

1982 $5500		**1990** $9000	
1994 $9000		**1998** $12,000	
1982-2000 RETURN 4%			
2000-2010 3%			

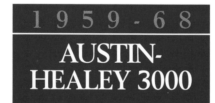

1959-68
AUSTIN-HEALEY 3000

1964-68 3000 Mark III Convertible

Final development of the Austin-Healey theme. Basic layout of the previous 100-6 retained, but with enlarged engine capacity and standard front disc brakes. The Mark II series gained more power and a new "Convertible" model, with the same basic styling plus fold-away top and roll-up door windows. The final Mark III versions had more power still, plus a restyled wood-covered dash, revised rear suspension incorporating radius arms for better axle location, and a less vulnerable exhaust system. These last Healeys also had 120-mph capability. A factory detachable hardtop was available for all 3000s, though few Convertibles were so equipped. All Convertibles had 2+2 seating, but Mark I and II were offered as two-seaters as well. Mark II introduced in spring 1961, the Convertible in summer 1962, and Mark III in spring 1964. Impending U.S. safety and emissions regulations scheduled to take effect after the 1967 model year effectively killed the big Healey in its biggest export market. To continue, it would have had to be redesigned at prohibitive cost. A few leftover '67s may have been sold here as '68s. BMC attempted to fill the gap in both the U.S. and Europe with the six-cylinder MGC, which proved a marketing disaster. Donald Healey would make one more try at building a well-balanced two-seat roadster, the short-lived Jensen-Healey of the early '70s. As our prices indicate, the Mark IIIs have a slight lead on the collector market as the last of the A-Hs and because of their more complete equipment and the best Healey performance (0-60 in 9.8 seconds).

✚ FOR Performance gets better on successive versions • Better braking than 100/6 • Better equipment, too • Same rugged chassis and rugged good looks • Parts easier to obtain now than for earlier models • Last of the breed • Mark III's better ground clearance and equipment

▬ AGAINST As for 1953-56 BN1/BN2

PRODUCTION

Mark I 13,650 **Mark II** 5450 **Mark II Convertible** 6113 **Mark III** 17,712

SPECIFICATIONS

Length (in.)	157.5
Wheelbase (in.)	92.0
Weight (lbs)	2460-2550
Price (new)	$3565 U.S. in 1966

ENGINES

cc/type (cid)	bhp[1]	years
2912/ohv I-6 (178)	124/132/148	1959-67

[1]net

PRICES

FAIR	$8500-16,000
GOOD	$16,000-21,000
FINE	$21,000-30,000

FINE EXAMPLE PRICE HISTORY

1982 $7000		**1990** $20,000	
1994 $24,000		**1998** $30,000	
1982-2000 RETURN 10%			
2000-2010 10%			

1 9 6 1 - 7 1

AUSTIN-HEALEY SPRITE
(& MG MIDGET)

1967 Austin Healy Sprite roadster

Restyled successor to the Mark I "bug-eye" Sprite, with a squared-up nose and tail grafted onto the original main body section. Retained diminutive 80-inch-wheelbase chassis and suspension of its predecessor, though rear springing was changed from quarter- to half-elliptics beginning in spring 1964. Also at that time BMC changed from sliding sidescreens to proper wind-up windows for the doors. The lift-up nose section and lidless tail on early models gave way to a conventional hood and opening trunklid. Engines progressed through several displacements, but all were based on BMC's rugged A-series four-cylinder unit that had been around since the war. Trim and equipment were gradually upgraded over the years. Following the end of Donald and Geoff Healey's association with BMC, their name was removed from the last 1971 models, known simply as Austin Sprite. Also sold with the MG badge as the near-identical Midget, which continued beyond the end of Sprite production through 1979 with a total of 226,526 built. A very basic sports car, the Sprite taught a lot of young Americans what British-style motoring was all about. It's still enjoyable as economical everyday transport, providing you can put up with its very cramped cockpit, hard ride, and crude controls. Offsetting these drawbacks are nimble handling, open-air flair, and sturdy mechanicals just right for novice mechanics. The 1961-67 cars are preferred as federal safety and emissions controls robbed later models of some power and, to an extent, agility.

⊞ FOR Better equipped, more practical than "frog-eye" • Progressively better, though always modest, performance (0-60 in 15-20 seconds, top speed 85-100 mph) • Cheap to buy and run • Parts still relatively plentiful

⊟ AGAINST Cramped accommodations • Low-geared, buzzy engine • Rust-prone • Oxcart ride

PRODUCTION

Mark II 31,665 **Mark III** 25,905 **Mark IV** 22,793

SPECIFICATIONS

Length (in.)	137.5
Wheelbase (in.)	80.0
Weight (lbs)	1550-1650
Price (new)	$2000-3000 (U.S.)

ENGINES

cc/type (cid)	bhp	years
948/ohv I-4 (58)	46	1961-65
1098/ohv I-4 (67)	56/59	1965-68
1275/ohv I-4 (78)	65	1968-71

PRICES

FAIR	$2000-5000
GOOD	$5000-8500
FINE	$8500-10,000

FINE EXAMPLE PRICE HISTORY

1982 $4000		**1990** $7000	
1994 $4550		**1998** $10,000	
1982-2000 RETURN 6%			
2000-2010 5%			

1 9 6 5 - 8 2

AVANTI II

Continuation of Studebaker's 1963-64 Avanti (see entry). Mostly handbuilt in a corner of the old South Bend plant under former dealers Leo Newman and Nathan Altman, who resurrected Stude's would-be salessparker. Retained the Lark convertible chassis, but was altered with a small-block Chevy Corvette V-8, a higher hoodline to accommodate it, reduced-radius wheel openings and less front-end rake for a tidier appearance, and "Avanti II" badges. Offered with "stock" paint colors and interior trims, but could be done in virtually anything the customer wanted—Altman loved pleasing clients this way. A great buy early on, and only a bit less so through the '70s despite steady price escalation, mostly due to inflation. Workmanship deteriorated over time, especially after Altman's untimely death in 1976, but low production almost guarantees collectibility regardless of year.

⊞ FOR Smooth performance • Ubiquitous engines easily serviced • Sensational styling still snares stares • Individual • Out of production (as of 1991)

⊟ AGAINST Poor finish post-1975, especially paint and chrome • Gas mileage falls off in '70s • Poorer investment than original Avanti

PRODUCTION

1965 45 **1966** 98 **1967** 60 **1968** 89 **1969** 103 **1970** 111 **1971** 107 **1972** 127 **1973** 106 **1974** 123 **1975** 125 **1976** 156 **1977** 146 **1978** 165 **1979** 142 **1980** 168 **1981** 200 **1982** 200

SPECIFICATIONS

Length (in.)	192.5
Wheelbase (in.)	109.0
Weight (lbs)	3150-3570
Price (new)	$6550-23,000

ENGINES

cid/type	bhp	years
327/ohv V-8	300[1]	1966-69
350/ohv V-8	300	1969-72
400/ohv V-8	180/245	1973-76
350/ohv V-8	180	1977-80
305/ohv V-8	155	1981-83

[1]SAE gross bhp; all other figures SAE net

PRICES

FAIR	$5800-9500
GOOD	$9500-16,000
FINE	$16,000-22,000

FINE 1970 MODEL PRICE HISTORY

1982 $14,500		**1990** $28,000	
1994 $20,000		**1998** $22,000	
1982-2000 RETURN 3%			
2000-2010 5%			

1981 coupe

1983-90

AVANTI

1984 coupe

The last "coachbuilt" Avantis, built under three different owners. First was Washington, D.C., realtor Steve Blake, who purchased Avanti Motor Corporation from the Altman estate in late 1982 and brought in optional body-color bumpers and black trim, square headlights, a Pontiac Grand Prix dash, and an injected 302 Chevy Camaro V-8. Most of these "updates" appeared in a small run of special 20th Anniversary 1983 models. Financial problems precluded a planned new chassis with an independent rear end designed by Herb Adams, and Blake was forced to sell to Texas ethanol king Michael Kelly in early '85. Operations were shifted from South Bend to a new Youngstown, Ohio, plant, and Kelly's renamed Avanti Motor Corp. took up production of the familiar coupe as well as a new Blake-devised convertible. A 117-inch-wheelbase Luxury Sport Coupe, 123-inch Touring Sedan, and even a 174-inch limo were all promised, but apparently never went beyond prototypes, though a handful of 250-bhp Paxton-supercharged standard coupes evidently did. Questionable business dealings forced Kelly to sell out in 1988 to shopping-mall developer J.J. Cafaro, who continued existing models and announced a 116-inch-wheelbase sedan molded from Raymond Loewy's discarded mockup for a 1966 line of "Avanti-styled" standard Studebakers. Unfortunately, Cafaro's Avanti Automotive Corp. was doomed by a sharp recession and filed for bankruptcy in 1991.

⚡ FOR As for 1965-82 Avanti II, plus arguably better workmanship than on late Altman cars • Kelly/Cafaro convertible • Cafaro sedan very rare

◼ AGAINST Some Blake/Kelly cosmetic changes spoil original Loewy design

PRODUCTION

1983 NA **1984** 287 **1985-87** NA, but limited **1988** 150 **1989-90** est. 300

SPECIFICATIONS

Length (in.)	193 (sedan: 200)
Wheelbase (in.)	109.0 (sedan: 116)
Weight (lbs)	3550-4000
Price (new)	$25,000-50,000

ENGINES

cid/type	bhp	years
305/ohv V-8	170/250[1]	1984-90

[1]SAE net, normal/supercharged (s'chgd. est.)

PRICES

FAIR	$8000-15,000
GOOD	$15,000-23,000
FINE	$23,000-30,000

FINE EXAMPLE PRICE HISTORY

1994 $30,000 **1998** $30,000
1994-2000 RETURN 0%
2000-2010 Even

1933-37

BENTLEY 3½ LITRE

The first Bentley after the original "W.O." firm crashed in 1931 and was taken over by Rolls-Royce. Modified Rolls-Royce 20/25 engine and entirely new chassis were featured. Compared with earlier Bentleys, this was the "Silent Sports Car," softer in character, more refined, and even better built. Really a quasi-Rolls; many now call it a "Rolls-Bentley." Power outputs unstated, and a synchro gearbox with right-hand gearchange restated the pedigree. Built at Derby, not Cricklewood, as a rolling chassis only, so bodies came from outside coachbuilders. Though capable of more than 90 mph in fine style and comfort, the car was still backward, with leaf springs and beam axles front and rear, plus very British styling.

⚡ FOR Great elegance and style • Rolls-Royce build quality • High performance for the period • Sporting but comfortable

◼ AGAINST Very costly to buy • Even more costly to restore • Wood-body rot • Few parts • 1930s UK styling?

PRODUCTION

1177

SPECIFICATIONS

Length (in.)	174.0
Wheelbase (in.)	126.0
Weight (lbs)	3400-3500
Price (new)	NA

ENGINES

cc/type (cid)	bhp	years
3669/ohv I-6 (224)	NA	1933-37

PRICES

Vanden Plas tourer	
FAIR	$65,000-85,000
GOOD	$85,000-100,000
FINE	$100,000-125,000
Other open	
FAIR	$35,000-60,000
GOOD	$60,000-85,000
FINE	$85,000-100,000
Sports salon	
FAIR	$12,000-20,000
GOOD	$20,000-40,000
FINE	$40,000-70,000

(Add 50% to salon price for Freestone & Webb razoredge models.)

FINE VANDEN PLAS TOURER PRICE HISTORY

1982 $30,000 **1990** $180,000
1994 $180,000 **1998** $125,000
1982-2000 RETURN 9%
2000-2010 9%

1936 3½ Litre 2-door convertible

1936-39
BENTLEY 4¼ LITRE

1937 4¼ Litre hardtop coupe

Lineal descendant of the 3½-Litre, with the same chassis, suspension, and choice of custom bodies. Larger engine's extra power and torque—neither ever revealed—made up for the heavier coachwork and equipment that always came along. As before, a Rolls-Royce with a Bentley badge and 90+ mph performance, but no independent front suspension. From late 1938, an "overdrive" transmission with geared-up top was fitted to make the car better suited to fast roads. Many with Park Ward bodies, now without wooden framing, so they've lasted better.

✚ FOR A real aristocrat • Top-drawer build quality • Comfortable, dignified, yet sporting • Parts supply still OK

■ AGAINST Costly to buy, very costly to run • Wood bodies still rot • Inferior to contemporary Americans in ride • Styling a bit traditional

PRODUCTION
1234

SPECIFICATIONS
Length (in.)	192.0
Wheelbase (in.)	126.0
Weight (lbs)	3750
Price (new)	NA

ENGINES
cc/type (cid)	bhp	years
4257/ohv I-6 (260)	NA	1936-39

PRICES
As for 3¼ litre.

1946-52
BENTLEY MARK VI

The first postwar Bentley of Rolls-Royce design, powered by a new six-cylinder F-head engine (overhead intake, side-mounted exhaust valves). Also the first Bentley with standard, factory-designed bodywork (built by Pressed Steel Co.), reflecting a change in Rolls-Royce policy from strictly hand-built to "standardized" bodies that could be produced in greater numbers at the firm's new factory at Crewe. Like prewar Bentleys, the Mark VI was large, stately, and impressive. It rode a massive separate chassis featuring coil-spring independent front suspension, quite an advance for the marque in this period. Most Mark VI cars were the "standard" four-door sedan with semi-traditional lines including separate front fenders. However, a number were built with custom sedan and convertible (drophead) coachwork by such R-R specialists as H.J. Mulliner, Park Ward, and James Young.

✚ FOR Cachet of Rolls ownership • Mechanical parts still readily available • Extensive club interest and restoration assistance

■ AGAINST Standard bodies rot-prone • Custom body replacement panels unobtainable • Costly to maintain, acquire, and restore

PRODUCTION
4946

SPECIFICATIONS
Length (in.)	204.0
Wheelbase (in.)	120.0
Weight (lbs)	4090 (standard sedan)
Price (new)	NA

ENGINES
cc/type (cid)	bhp[1]	years
4256/F I-6 (260)	120/130	1946-52

[1]estimated net; actual output not quoted

PRICES
Saloon	
FAIR	$8000-17,000
GOOD	$17,000-25,000

FINE	$25,000-35,000
Drophead	
FAIR	$30,000-48,000
GOOD	$48,000-66,000
FINE	$66,000-90,000

FINE DROPHEAD PRICE HISTORY
1982 $20,000	**1990** $100,000
1994 $80,000	**1998** $90,000
1982-2000 RETURN 9%	
2000-2010 8%	

1952-55
BENTLEY R-TYPE

1952 2-door coupe by Abbott

Revised version of the Mark VI with greater engine displacement and a longer tail for the standard-body sedan. Offered with optional Rolls-Royce/GM Hydra-Matic automatic transmission beginning in 1952, which became instantly more popular than the manual gearbox. Styling and mechanical changes parallel those made to the look-alike Rolls-Royce Silver Dawn. Maximum speed now over 100 mph, but not that much faster than the Mark VI.

✚ FOR More luggage space than Mark VI • Optional automatic-shift convenience • Others as for 1946-55 Mark VI

1952 Mark VI sedan

◩ **AGAINST** As for 1946-55 Mark VI

PRODUCTION

2320

SPECIFICATIONS

Length (in.)	210.0
Wheelbase (in.)	120.0
Weight (lbs)	4200
Price (new)	NA

ENGINES

cc/type (cid)	bhp[1]	years
4566/F I-6 (279)	130	1952-55

[1]Actual output not quoted; estimated net bhp

PRICES

As for 1946-52 Mark VI.

1952-55
BENTLEY R-TYPE CONTINENTAL

1953 R-Type Continental coupe

Perhaps the most exciting Bentley of the postwar period. A sensationally styled, lightweight fastback coupe built on the R-Type sedan chassis, but some grumble to this day that it aped GM's 1949 fastback look. Only a small number were built, all two-door four-seaters, most with bodywork by H.J. Mulliner. Originally powered by the Bentley six as fitted to the sedans, but a larger-capacity 4887cc version was specified beginning in 1954. A true GT with handling that belied its massive size and still considerable weight. Just the thing for blasting across the continent at easy three-figure speeds of up to 115 mph. Rare, but worth seeking out, and a modern classic even among Bentleys.

➕ **FOR** Distinctive fastback styling • Rot-free light-alloy body • Higher top speed than other R-Types • Others as for Mark VI and R-Type

◩ **AGAINST** Body panel replacements hopeless • Rare and costly to buy • Others as for R-Type

PRODUCTION

208

SPECIFICATIONS

Length (in.)	206.5
Wheelbase (in.)	120.0
Weight (lbs)	3740
Price (new)	NA

ENGINES

cc/type (cid)	bhp[1]	years
4566/F I-6 (279)	145	1952-53
4887/F I-6 (298)	155	1954-55

[1]Actual output not quoted: estimated net bhp

PRICES

FAIR	$70,000-100,000
GOOD	$100,000-150,000
FINE	$150,000-185,000

FINE EXAMPLE PRICE HISTORY

1982 $30,000	1990 $150,000
1994 $125,000	1998 $150,000
1982-2000 RETURN 12%	
2000-2010 10%	

1955-65
BENTLEY S-TYPE

Essentially a "grille-engineered" version of the concurrent Rolls-Royce Silver Cloud of these years, sharing the same all-new chassis, suspension design, and styling of the standard sedan body. Most of those built were the "factory" four-doors, but a few limousine types were also built on a 4-inch-longer wheelbase. As before, chassis were supplied to approved coachbuilders, who created custom sedan and convertible bodies. Powered by the carryover 4.9-liter straight six from the R-Type through the fall of 1959 (Series I or S1), after which Rolls-Royce's new light-alloy, short-stroke 6.2-liter V-8 (said to have been cribbed from the 1949 Cadillac design) took over for the Series II (S2). A restyled

Series III (S3) was announced in the autumn of 1962 and was mostly unchanged mechanically. It was marked by quad headlamps and a lower hood-line—as was the parallel Cloud III, much to the consternation of traditionalists. Replaced in 1965 by the unit-construction Rolls-Royce Silver Cloud and its T-Type Bentley equivalent.

➕ **FOR** Superb luxury • Rolls construction quality • Dignified styling with loads of snob appeal • Excellent club support • Body and mechanical parts still available • Good V-8 performance • Many had GM automatic transmission • Cheaper than a new one

◩ **AGAINST** Not very fast with the six • Rust-prone • Costly to maintain and restore • Low mpg

PRODUCTION

S1 3107 (incl. 35 limousine) **S2 V-8** 1954 **S3 V-8** 1286 (S2/S3, incl. 89 limousine)

SPECIFICATIONS

Length (in.)	212.0 (limo: 216.0)
Wheelbase (in.)	123.0 (limo: 127.0)
Weight (lbs)	4480-4650 (limo: 4650-4815)
Price (new)	NA

ENGINES

cc/type (cid)	bhp[1]	years
4887/F I-6 (298)	NA	1955-59
6230/ohv V-8 (380)	NA	1959-65

[1]Rolls-Royce/Bentley did not quote horsepower

PRICES

Saloon	
FAIR	$10,000-15,000
GOOD	$15,000-25,000
FINE	$25,000-35,000
Flying Spur	
FAIR	$42,000-60,000
GOOD	$60,000-74,000
FINE	$74,000-90,000

FINE SALOON PRICE HISTORY

1982 $5000	1990 $140,000

1957 S1 coupe by Park Ward

1994 $30,000   1998 $35,000
1982-2000 RETURN 15%
2000-2010 5%

1955-65
BENTLEY S-TYPE CONTINENTAL

Continuation of the sporting special-bodied Bentleys aimed at the gentleman-enthusiast, but on the more modern S-Type/Silver Cloud chassis. As with the preceding R-Type models, custom light-alloy bodies were available mainly from H.J. Mulliner and Park Ward. Two-door coupes accounted for most of the very limited production, but a few convertibles were built along with a new four-door sedan dubbed "Flying Spur." Mechanical and appearance changes were the same as for concurrent S-Type sedans, including adoption of the new Rolls-Royce V-8 for Series II models and the "mod" quad-headlamp front end for the Series III. Virtually all Continentals in this period had the R-R/GM Hydra-Matic transmission, which allowed a top speed in the area of 100-115 mph. Conspicuously absent from the specification was disc brakes.

✚ FOR As for R-Type Continental, plus new four-door and more performance • Others as for S-Type sedans

▬ AGAINST As for R-Type Continental and S-Type sedans

PRODUCTION
S1 431 **S2 V-8** 388 **S3 V-8** 312

SPECIFICATIONS
Length (in.)	210.5
Wheelbase (in.)	123.0

Weight (lbs)	3980-4450
Price (new)	NA

ENGINES
cc/type (cid)	bhp[1]	years
4887/F I-6 (298)	NA	1955-59
6230/ohv V-8 (380)	NA	1959-65

[1]Rolls-Royce/Bentley did not quote horsepower

PRICES
Coupe
FAIR	$15,000-25,000
GOOD	$25,000-60,000
FINE	$60,000-75,000

Convertible
FAIR	$50,000-100,000
GOOD	$100,000-150,000
FINE	$150,000-200,000

FINE COUPE PRICE HISTORY
1982 $25,000   1990 $100,000
1994 $80,000   1998 $60,000
1982-2000 RETURN 7%
2000-2010 7%

1982-91
BENTLEY MULSANNE TURBO & TURBO R

1989 Turbo R sedan

The first "blower Bentley" in 50 years. Original Turbo announced two years behind the Bentley Mulsanne/Rolls-Royce Silver Spirit on which it was based, but wasn't sold with them in America.

Differed from normal Mulsanne chiefly in more potent, turbocharged version of Crewe's 6.75-liter aluminum V-8 with well over 300 estimated horsepower—Bentley/R-R continued its policy of not quoting engine outputs. Replacement Turbo R, introduced to Europe in 1985 and to the U.S. for 1989, boasted uprated chassis with stiffer shocks, higher-rate front/rear anti-roll bars and rear self-leveling system, and a new Panhard rod in back. The result was roadholding—thus the R?—to equal the beast's amazing go: 0-60 in 7 seconds or less, top speed near 130 mph despite its barn-bluff shape. Also: revised instrumentation with tachometer and slightly more "buckety" front seats. Adopted from 1990 was Automatic Ride Control, variable-rate shock absorbers computer-managed to driving conditions, which restored some ride comfort lost to the beefed-up suspension. Both versions offered solely with a GM three-speed automatic. This should be the most collectible of the Spirit generation, and the quickest, most distinctive Bentleys since the S-type Continental, with the Turbo R having the edge in esteem thanks to its more capable handling.

✚ FOR The usual Bentley/R-R attractions plus thrilling yet civilized performance • Turbo R's surprising agility

▬ AGAINST Staid styling • Mechanical complexity • Bound to be overshadowed in glamour (and investment potential?) by a slick new 1992 Continental R coupe

PRODUCTION
NA, but limited

SPECIFICATIONS
Length (in.)	207.4
Wheelbase (in.)	120.5
Weight (lbs)	5215
Price (new)	$150,000-167,400

ENGINES
cc/type (cid)[2]	bhp[1]	years
6750/ohv V-8 (412)	315-350	1982-90

[1]Estimated [2]Turbocharged

PRICES
Current prices range from a low of $30,000 to a high of $70,000 for the 1990 Turbo R. Presently the used car market determines value.
2000-2010 RETURN 3%

1998-99
BENTLEY AZURE

Bentley's 4-passenger convertible was one of the world's most striking examples of top-down motoring, with

1962-65 S3 Continental coupe

1998-99 Azure convertible

great mass, enormous showroom prices, and a 6.8-liter turbo V-8 (385-horsepower and 550 lb/ft torque) that produced exhilarating acceleration. Highway/city mileage of 11/16 was terrible, but those who could afford the price of admission never cared. The Azure handled surprisingly well for a car of its size. The adaptive suspension firmed-up the shocks absorbers in fast turns and returned to softer settings for most situations.

✦ **FOR** Muscular performance • Hand-crafted details • Sheer presence

▪ **AGAINST** Enormous price • Great bulk • General air of overkill

PRODUCTION
NA

SPECIFICATIONS

Length (in.)	210.3
Weight (lbs)	5400
Wheelbase (in.)	120.5
Price (new)	$326,500-347-645

ENGINES

cid/type	bhp	years
412/ohv V-8[1]	385	1995-1999

[1]Turbocharged

PRICES
NA

1998-2000
BENTLEY CONTINENTAL

The ultimate expression of high luxury and brute performance from this British marque owned by VW. Appearing at once squarish and racy, the Continental offered all the hand-crafted touches a buyer with $300,000 expected (and probably deserved), plus the thrill of acceleration provided by a torquey, 6.75-liter V-8. A flared

1998 Continental T coupe

and air-dammed SC variant (co-styled by Pininfarina) that arrived in mid-1998 had AiResearch turbocharged V-8, good for 0-60 times in the mid-sixes—impressive for a yacht that weighed about 5400 pounds.

✦ **FOR** Exclusivity • Enormous power and torque • Top-flight cabin materials • Sheer presence

▪ **AGAINST** Price • Thirst • Weight • Tendency to understeer

PRODUCTION
NA

SPECIFICATIONS

Length (in.)	206.3-210.3
Weight (lbs)	4500-5400
Wheelbase (in.)	116.5-120.5
Price (new)	$303,000-330,000 (est.)

ENGINES

cid/type	bhp	years
412/ohv V-8[1]	385-420	1998-2000

[1]Turbocharged

PRICES
NA
2000-2010 No appreciation

1930
BLACKHAWK

One of the several junior makes launched in the heady late Twenties and quietly dropped shortly after the Wall Street crash. Introduced in 1929 as a companion to Stutz and based on the 1928 Model BB. Offered

with an advanced 85-bhp overhead-cam six or a more conventional L-head straight eight by Continental. First-year production was a disappointing 1310 units. Although sixes were listed for 1930, it is believed that only eights were actually built. Priced in the $2000-2800 range and thus an upper-medium car, though one wonders how it came to be rated a Classic. No relation to the famous Stutz Black Hawk (two words) speedster.

✦ **FOR** Solid, four-square Classic styling, recognizably Stutz up front • Wide range of body types including three Weymann styles each model • CCCA Classic status • Rare

▪ **AGAINST** Leisurely performance from the fairly modest powerplants • Parts dicey • High operating costs

PRODUCTION
280 (calendar year)

SPECIFICATIONS

Length (in.)	NA
Wheelbase (in.)	127.5
Weight (lbs)	NA
Price (new)	$2000-2800

ENGINES

cid/type	bhp	years
241.5/ohc I-6	85	1930
268.5/sv I-8	90	1930

PRICES (1929-30)

Speedster	
FAIR	$20,000-40,000
GOOD	$40,000-60,000
FINE	$60,000-80,000
Weymann bodies	
FAIR	$10,000-15,000
GOOD	$15,000-25,000
FAIR	$25,000-40,000
Closed	
FAIR	$8000-12,000
GOOD	$12,000-20,000
FINE	$20,000-30,000

FINE SPEEDSTER PRICE HISTORY

1982 $28,000		**1990** $50,000	
1994 $80,000		**1998** $80,000	
1982-2000 RETURN 8%			
2000-2010 5%			

1963-71
BMC MINI-COOPER S

Inspired "homologation special" based on British Motor Corporation's front-drive minicar designed by Alex Issigonis. Main differences between this production hot rod and the more basic Minis were higher Cooper-tuned versions of the BMC A-series four, beefed-up driveline components, front

1963-68 Mini-Cooper S coupe

disc brakes, and discreet exterior emblems. Offered initially in 1071cc form, a modified version of the Formula Junior engine provided to Cooper. There were also 970cc and 1275cc versions listed from 1964 aimed at 1.0- and 1.3-liter racing classes. Retained the regular Mini's wheel-at-each-corner box-body, only 120 inches long, with full four-seat accommodation. Coopers had slightly better instrumentation and a more businesslike interior. The Mini, but not the Cooper, was in production for more than 40 years and due for replacement in 2001. With the right equipment, the little engine could pump out at least 50 percent more power. The Cooper S carried BMC's rally colors in the early '60s, and did quite well against larger, more powerful opposition. Minis of any kind were never sold widely in the U.S., and the advent of federal emissions and safety standards banned the Cooper S from our market after 1967. Some were sold in Canada until the new Leyland regime dropped the model in 1971.

FOR Cheeky charm unmatched by other cars • Still rare in North America • Wonderfully nimble front-drive handling • Many nonmechanical parts still available • Not expensive

AGAINST Engine parts in short supply • Undercarriage (especially subframe) rust-prone • Noisy • No match for Detroit iron in traffic • Make sure you fit

PRODUCTION
45,442

SPECIFICATIONS

Length (in.)	120.2
Wheelbase (in.)	80.0
Weight (lbs)	1440
Price (new)	NA

ENGINES

cc/type (cid)	bhp	years
970/ohv I-4 (59)	65	1964-65
1071/ohv I-4 (65)	70	1963-64
1275/ohv I-4 (78)	76	1964-71

PRICES

FAIR	$6000-8000
GOOD	$8000-10,000
FINE	$10,000-12,000

FINE EXAMPLE PRICE HISTORY

1982 $3000	**1990** $12,500
1994 $10,000	**1998** $12,000
1982-2000 RETURN 10%	
2000-2010 10%	

1937 328 roadster

Based on the six-cylinder 315/319 of 1934-37, the 328 was a sleek, efficient, two-seat sports roadster with a tubular frame and transverse-leaf-spring independent front suspension. The engine was the cleverly detailed straight six from the 326, with opposed valves and cross-pushrod valvegear. Offered 90+ mph flat out, and its great style and comfort rendered most other middle-price sports cars crudely old-fashioned. The longer, wider, and heavier 327 coupe and convertible fol-

lowed with less power but simpler inline valvegear, plus genuine four-passenger capacity. Appearance of all remarkably similar (aped by the postwar Bristol 400), with trademark "twin-kidney" grille, recessed headlamps, and flowing lines. The 327 was also available with the 328 engine in 1937-41 as the confusingly named 327/28. Up to anything produced by Italy or the U.S. in this period, and likely more sought-after now than they were then.

FOR The most charismatic prewar Bimmers • Advanced chassis • Fine handling • Good performance (328) • Period styling • Durability

AGAINST 328s very expensive • Restoration difficult

PRODUCTION
327 461 **328** 1396

SPECIFICATIONS

Length (in.)	176.0 (327), 156.0 (328)
Wheelbase (in.)	108.3 (327), 94.5 (328)
Weight (lbs)	2425/1830
Price (new)	NA

ENGINES

cc/type (cid)	bhp	years
1971/ohv I-6 (120)	55	1937-41
1971/ohv I-6 (120)	80	1936-40

PRICES

FAIR	$15,000-30,000
GOOD	$30,000-60,000
FINE	$60,000-80,000

FINE DROPHEAD PRICE HISTORY

1982 $18,000	**1990** $125,000
1994 $125,000	**1998** $80,000
1982-2000 RETURN 11%	
2000-2010 5%	

1956-59
BMW 503

The first postwar sporting car from Bavarian Motor Works. Based on the Type 502 sedan box- and tubular-section chassis, and also shared its 3.2-liter V-8 engine. Offered in sleek coupe or cabriolet (convertible) body styles designed by Count Albrecht Goertz, both with 2+2 accommodations. An expensive indulgence, but a great image builder for BMW, which was still recovering from wartime damage and facing many financial problems in these years. Relatively heavy, in the German manner, so performance was limited to about 118 mph maximum. Offered a civilized interior and assured (if not nimble) handling. The four-speed manual gearbox was mounted remotely on early models, as on the 502, but was placed in unit with

1956-59 503 coupe

the engine from late 1957. The original steering column gearchange gave way to a floor-mounted mechanism on later examples.

+ FOR Exclusive '50s BMW • Robust chassis and engine • Rarity • Good appreciation

■ AGAINST Parts impossible to obtain nowadays • Overshadowed by 507, and not as nice to drive • Hard to find • Expensive if you do

PRODUCTION
412

SPECIFICATIONS

Length (in.)	187.0
Wheelbase (in.)	111.6
Weight (lbs)	3310
Price (new)	NA

ENGINES

cc/type (cid)	bhp[1]	years
3168/ohv V-8 (193)	140	1956-59
[1]net		

PRICES

Conv	
FAIR	$8000-16,000
GOOD	$16,000-25,000
FINE	$25,000-40,000
Coupe	
FAIR	$6,000-12,000
GOOD	$12,000-20,000
FINE	$20,000-30,000

FINE CONVERTIBLE PRICE HISTORY

1982 $8000	1990 $45,000
1994 $40,000	1998 $40,000
1982-2000 RETURN 10%	
2000-2010 10%	

1956-59 507 convertible

Two-seat running mate to the Type 503 in this period. Sensational styling, again by Albrecht Goertz, was years ahead of its time, and unrivaled by any other European of the day. It was notable for the lack of BMW's traditional "twin kidney" grille treatment. Running gear was shared with the 503, but higher tune gave the V-8 engine 10 more horsepower, good for a top speed of nearly 130 mph. Basic chassis design was also shared, except for the two-seater's shorter wheelbase. Lighter and better-handling than the 503, the 507 was virtually handbuilt at Munich, and therefore much too expensive for all but a small number of Europeans. Offered in both coupe and cabriolet (convertible) body styles, and brought into the U.S. in very small numbers. That plus its fine engineering and still eye-catching looks makes this probably the most desirable collector

BMW of all.

+ FOR Exclusive and charismatic • Sensational looks • Performance • Beautiful engineering • Rare and highly coveted • Strong club support • High-appreciation investment

■ AGAINST Body and engine parts virtually extinct • Little factory back-up • Expensive

PRODUCTION
253

SPECIFICATIONS

Length (in.)	172.4
Wheelbase (in.)	97.6
Weight (lbs)	2935
Price (new)	NA

ENGINES

cc/type (cid)	bhp[1]	years
3168/ohv V-8 (193)	150	1956-59
[1]net		

PRICES

FAIR	$40,000-85,000
GOOD	$85,000-140,000
FINE	$140,000-220,000

FINE EXAMPLE PRICE HISTORY

1982 $50,000	1990 $450,000
1994 $225,000	1998 $220,000
1982-2000 RETURN 9%	
2000-2010 10%	

1962 3200CS coupe

Interim sporting BMW bridging the gap between the Type 503/507 of the '50s and the 2000/2800CS of the '60s. A close-coupled four-seat coupe based on the Type 503 chassis, sharing the same wheelbase, suspension layout, and powertrain. Styling was courtesy of Bertone of Italy, which also supplied finished bodies to BMW for final assembly in Munich. In overall appearance, the 3200CS was similar to the later 2000/2800CS, particularly the thin-section roof, notched rear side window shape, and slim B-pillars, indicating that Bertone probably influenced BMW's own designers through this model. The Germans' trusty V-8 was tweaked once again to produce 160 bhp, sufficient to give this car a 125-mph top speed. Like the 503/507, mostly hand-built and quite costly as a result. However, an aging chassis and running gear rendered it behind the times almost as soon as it was introduced.

✚ FOR Fast, sturdy, and nicely furnished • Pleasant Bertone styling • Good accommodations • Rarity (especially in U.S.)

▬ AGAINST Quite rust-prone • Scarce body and engine parts • Heavy and thirsty

PRODUCTION
603

SPECIFICATIONS

Length (in.)	190.0
Wheelbase (in.)	111.6
Weight (lbs)	3310
Price (new)	NA

ENGINES

cc/type (cid)	bhp[1]	years
3168/ohv V-8 (193)	160	1962-65

[1]DIN

PRICES

FAIR	$5000-11,000
GOOD	$11,000-17,000
FINE	$17,000-19,000

FINE EXAMPLE PRICE HISTORY

1982 $5000		1990 $18,000	
1994 $12,000		1998 $19,000	
1982-2000 RETURN 9%			
2000-2010 5%			

1965-68
BMW 2000CS COUPE

Coupe derivative of BMW's successful "comeback" early-'60s sedan series designed around the firm's new overhead-cam inline four. Shared under-pan and running gear with the 2000 four-door, but wore a distinctive pillarless hardtop body built by Karmann and incorporating BMW's then-current styling themes. Its only flaw was a snubbed snout that awkwardly tried to blend BMW's trademark kidney grille into a rounded shape accentuated by wide wraparound headlamp/parking light units. Offered in two versions, a lower-powered automatic model and a faster manual car capable of 110 mph. Not space efficient—only passable 2+2 seating in a package longer than the sedan—but was intended more to lend some sportiness to the lineup than to be strictly practical. With new sheetmetal ahead of the cowl and a brilliant six-cylinder engine, the 2000CS would be transformed into the much nicer-looking and more capable 2800CS.

✚ FOR Unique model • Powerful and reliable ohc engine • Fine handling • German craftsmanship • Good appreciation potential • Not costly • Strong club support

▬ AGAINST Beware of unit body/chassis rust • Body parts now hard to acquire • Overshadowed in collector circles by 2800CS • Front end spoils otherwise pleasant styling

PRODUCTION
11,720

SPECIFICATIONS

Length (in.)	178.3
Wheelbase (in.)	100.4
Weight (lbs)	2630
Price (new)	$5185 U.S. in 1966

ENGINES

cc/type	bhp[1]	years
1990/ohc I-4	100/120	1965-68

[1]DIN

1967 2000CS coupe

PRICES

FAIR	$2500-4500
GOOD	$4500-6500
FINE	$6500-9000

FINE EXAMPLE PRICE HISTORY

1982 $4000		1990 $15,000	
1994 $8000		1998 $9000	
1982-2000 RETURN 5%			
2000-2010 5%			

1966-75
BMW 1600

1971 1600 convertible

The second new mass-production BMW sedan of the '60s, slightly smaller than the earlier four-doors and wrongly called "Coupe" in some markets. Production for Europe lasted a decade, with convertibles (conversions by Baur) and a three-door "Touring" hatchback offered in addition to the basic two-door notchback. However, only the two-door 1600 made it to the U.S., and was replaced here after 1970 by the 2002 and its various derivatives mainly to satisfy performance buyers in the face of the strangling effects of emissions and safety rules. The cars covered here were powered by the 1573cc version of BMW's neat overhead-cam four introduced in the early '60s, and which survives today. Thoroughly practical four-seat interior, 100-mph performance, typical Teutonic thoroughness in engineering and construction, and nimble handling made it a hit here and abroad. It also brought the pleasures of owning a Bimmer within reach of a greater range of buyers than ever before.

✚ FOR Straightforward mechanical layout • Sedan practicality with sports-car verve • Reasonably good parts supplies even now • Familiar to U.S. BMW dealers and many specialists • Strong club support • Bargain prices; may be undervalued at present

▬ AGAINST Unitized, so rust a worry • Plain styling, interior decor • Good-condition examples hard to find • Parts expensive • Overshadowed in performance and collector interest by 2002s

PRODUCTION

277,320

SPECIFICATIONS

Length (in.)	164.5
Wheelbase (in.)	98.4
Weight (lbs)	2070
Price (new)	$2658 U.S. list price in 1967

ENGINES

cc/type (cid)	bhp[1]	years
1573/ohc I-4 (96)	85/105	1966-75

[1]DIN; standard/TI models, respectively

PRICES

FAIR	$2500-4500
GOOD	$4500-6500
FINE	$6500-8000

FINE EXAMPLE PRICE HISTORY

1982 $3500		**1990** $18,000	
1994 $8000		**1998** $8000	
1982-2000 RETURN 5%			
2000-2010 Even			

1 9 6 8 - 7 7
BMW 2800CS/3.0CS/ 3.0CSI

Brilliant evolution of the Wilhelm Hofmeister-styled four-cylinder 2000CS coupe, made possible by the remarkably smooth and eager new sohc inline six launched earlier in the upmarket 2500/2800/Bavaria sedan series. Shared the 2000CS body/chassis aft of the firewall, but had a longer front end to accommodate the six, plus revised front suspension and a neat new four-lamp face. Performance was predictably much higher. Bodies still supplied by Karmann, and trimmed neatly—if not luxuriously—with quality materials in the German manner. The original 2.8 engine was enlarged to 3.0 liters in 1971, then given Bosch D-Jetronic fuel injection (3.0CSi) for still more power. At the same time, a detrimmed CSL, with weight-saving aluminum instead of steel for many body panels, was devised for European touring-car competition. This went through two successive versions; the last was sometimes seen with an eye-catching rear wing between shark-shape tailfins, front-fender strakes, and a front airdam. At the other extreme was the 2.5CS, a response to the first "energy crisis" (not officially exported to U.S.). Long a "comer" in Europe and increasingly collected Stateside as the best-looking, best-performing Bimmers since the legendary 507.

FOR Near-timeless looks • Delightful engines • Superb tourers • Brisk-to-vivid performers (exc. 2.5CS) • Good coupe accommodations • Strong club interest • Not too costly now • Mechanical parts still readily available • Bound to appreciate in value

AGAINST As for 2000CS, but trickier rear semi-trailing-arm handling due to greater power • Tends to rust if neglected • Prone to squeaks, rattles, and air leaks • Many examples badly thrashed

PRODUCTION

2800CS 9399 (1968-71) **3.0CS** 11,063 (1971-75, some sources list 10,088) **3.0CSi** 8199 (1971-75) **3.0CSL** 1039, some sources list 1096 **2.5CS** 844 (1974-77)

SPECIFICATIONS

Length (in.)	183.4
Wheelbase (in.)	103.3
Weight (lbs)	2775-3085
Price (new)	approx. $7500-13,000 in U.S.

ENGINES

cid/type	bhp[1]	years
2788/sohc I-6	170	1968-71
2985/sohc I-6	180/200[2]	1971-75
2985/sohc I-6	206	1971-72[3]
3003/sohc I-6	206	1972-73[3]
3153/sohc I-6	206	1972-73
2494/sohc I-6	150	1974-77

[1]DIN [2]3.0CS/CSi [3]3.0CSL

PRICES

FAIR	$3000-5000
GOOD	$5000-10,000
FINE	$10,000-13,000

FINE EXAMPLE PRICE HISTORY

1982 $9000	**1990** $20,000
1994 $9000	**1998** $13,000
1982-2000 RETURN 2%	
2000-2010 Even	

1 9 6 8 - 7 6
BMW 2002

The well-loved and highly successful 2.0-liter version of BMW's smaller sedan, unchanged in dimensions or basic appearances from the original 1600. Offered variously in three different stages of engine tune, not all of which were available in the U.S. because of then-current emissions regulations. Also not available here were custom targa convertible conversions carried out by the Baur coach-works of Stuttgart or the neat "Touring" hatchback derivative of this bodyshell. Carbureted standard and ti models were offered through 1974, the fuel-injected tii beginning for 1972. The mainstay of BMW's American and European lineups in these years, and remarkably little changed. Quite fast—110 mph standard, 120 mph tii in European trim—for such a practical design that included full four-seat capacity, a roomy trunk, well-chosen driving stance, and great outward visibility. Yet, it could beat the socks off many a so-called sports car in a handling duel. Its most oft-criticized shortcomings were no provision for fresh-air ventilation and steadily escalating prices. Replaced by the more refined, more expensive 3-series based on similar mechanicals and suspension, but to many BMW fans the 2002 is the best car ever to come from Munich.

FOR Gutsy character • Great performance • Surprising mileage • High demand item • Others as for 1966-75 1600

AGAINST As for the 1966-75 1600, plus detrimental effects of U.S. emissions controls compared to European versions

PRODUCTION

2d sdn 339,084 **2d cabrio by Baur** 4199 **2d ti sdn** 16,448 **2d tii sdn** 38,703 **3d Touring sdn** 11,488

1971 2800CS coupe

1971 2002Ti coupe

SPECIFICATIONS

Length (in.)	166.5 (1968-73), 176.0 (1974-76)
Wheelbase (in.)	98.4
Weight (lbs)	2150-2450
Price (new)	$5500-8500 (U.S.)

ENGINES

cc/type (cid)	bhp	years
1990/sohc I-4 (121)	100-130[1]	1968-76
1990/sohc I-4 (121)	113-140[2]	1971-76

[1]DIN; European models [2]SAE net, U.S. models

PRICES

FAIR	$3000-7000
GOOD	$7000-9000
FINE	$9000-12,000

FINE EXAMPLE PRICE HISTORY

1982	$4000	1990	$15,000
1994	$8500	1998	$10,000

1982-2000 RETURN 6%
2000-2010 Even

1 9 7 6 - 9 0

BMW 6-SERIES

1985 635CSi coupe

Well-liked, long-lived successor to the "Hofmeister line." Bowed at Geneva in March 1976 as essentially a pillared coupe derivative of BMW's recently launched mid-range 5-Series sedan, albeit with handsome low-waisted styling by Paul Bracq. It introduced BMW's trademark "Cockpit Design" curved-dash motif. Fairly spacious for a coupe, though still more a 2+2 than a practical four-seater. Offered with progressively larger, more potent engines, all variations of Munich's "big six." All U.S. models were fuel-injected; early European types used carburetors. Pre-1982 transmissions were a four-speed Getrag manual or three-speed ZF automatic, then five-speed manual and four-speed auto (the latter with electronic control after '85). Handling improved over 1983 via rear suspension "Trac Link" bushings and "double-pivot" front control arms. Standard antilock brakes from '86 in the U.S. Replaced by the V-12 850i for 1991. While any 6-Series is desirable, the prime picks for enthusiasts are the high-performance M635CSi introduced to Europe in 1978 and its North American M6 cousin (from 1983) built by BMW's Motorsport arm and powered by the 24-valve twin-cam six from the mid-engine M1 Group 4 racer (see entry), linked to a close-ratio five-speed.

✝ FOR Good looks • Spirited BMW performance, handling • Smooth, refined, luxurious • Plenty on the market • Ample parts, service • High collectibility quotient • Early models now very affordable

◾ AGAINST M-models not so affordable yet

PRODUCTION

630CS/CSi 32,932[1] **Others** NA
[1]1978-82 calendar-year sales

SPECIFICATIONS

Length (in.)	187.2/192.7 (European/U.S. models)
Wheelbase (in.)	103.4
Weight (lbs)	3195-3570
Price (new)	$24,000-56,000 in U.S.

ENGINES

cc/type	bhp	years
2985/sohc I-6	185[1]	1976-79
2985/sohc I-6	176[2]	1977
3210/sohc I-6	176-181[2]	1978-84
2788/sohc I-6	184[1]	1980-87
3430/sohc I-6	182[2]	1978-87
3453/dohc I-6	256[2]	1983-88
3430/sohc I-6	208[2]	1988-90

[1]DIN [2]SAE net

PRICES

Values are governed by the used car market. High prices ranged from $9000 for a 1977 CSi to $15,000 for a 1989 version in 1999.
2000-2010 RETURN Still depreciating

1 9 7 8 - 8 7

BMW 7-SERIES

1985 735i sedan

The Bavarian automaker's first foray into the German four-door luxury market previously dominated by the mid- and top-range Mercedes, and its most ambitious car since the V-8-powered 501/502 "Baroque Angels" of the early '50s. Typically BMW in appearance, suspension (front MacPherson struts, rear semi-trailing arms, all-round coil springs), and motive power, the last supplied by a largish single-cam straight six in various displacements. Introduced to Europe in 1977 with 2.8- and 3.0-liter carbureted engines, to America with a fuel-injected 3.2 (733i), later supplanted by a slightly more potent 3.4 (735i). Manual and automatic transmissions available throughout. Though we concentrate here on the American 733i/735i, you may run into "gray market" 728s/730s, which are fine as collector cars but create some added problems for collectors stemming from their "unauthorized status" Stateside. They are easily spotted by closer-fitting bumpers, one of the few major differences from their American cousins. Significant for successfully taking BMW's "sports sedan" ethic upmarket. It made way for the sleeker, much-improved new-generation 7 Series of 1987-88.

✝ FOR Creamy engines • Fine handling for size • Spacious • Handsomely appointed • Available stick shift unusual for this sort of car

◾ AGAINST Not as quick or agile as second-series 7s • Still more "used cars" than sure-fire collector's items • Ratty examples can cost a bundle to restore • Engines need lots of TLC to hold up

PRODUCTION

NA

SPECIFICATIONS

Length (in.)	191.3/197.4 (European/U.S.)
Wheelbase (in.)	110.0
Weight (lbs)	3375-3770
Price (new)	$23,575-42,500 in U.S.

ENGINES

cc/type	bhp[1]	years
3210/ohc I-6	177	1978-84
3430/ohc I-6	182	1984-87
[1]SAE net		

PRICES

Values are governed by the used car market. High prices for the 733-735 sedan ranged from $5000 for a '78 to $20,000 for a '90 in 1999.
2000-2010 RETURN Depreciating slowly

1978-81

BMW M1

BMW's first—and so far only—mid-engine car, an attempt at a Porsche-beating sports-racer. Concept harked to Munich's 1972 gullwing Turbo experimental, styled by Paul Bracq, but the more conventional M1 was shaped by Ital Design/Giorgio Giugiaro. Engineering was contracted to Lamborghini save for a special 24-valve twin-cam version of BMW's big six, which mounted longitudinally to team with the usual five-speed ZF rear transaxle. Fiberglass bodyshell clothed a light multi-tube chassis with twin wishbones, a coil spring, and a big disc brake at each corner. Sant'Agata's mid-decade financial crisis forced BMW to take over the project itself and delayed introduction to October '78, at Paris. Seeking to recoup some of its mounting losses—and generate some of the favorable publicity originally intended—BMW sponsored an all-M1 race series as warmups to various Grands Prix, a kind of European International Race of Champions called Procar. But this only demanded development of a 470-bhp version to Group 4 specs; a similar Group 5 racer with a reduced-capacity 3.2-liter turbo engine was also built. Procar quickly fizzled and the M1 was promptly abandoned, leaving us with a unique and rare BMW with obvious high collector appeal.

✚ **FOR** A true exotic, yet well-equipped and civilized • Low production • Very high performance (160 mph tops, 5.5 seconds 0-60) • Engine parts supply still good • Can only become more valuable

▬ **AGAINST** Styling clunky from some angles • Seldom traded • Not cheap to buy, and won't get any cheaper

PRODUCTION

450 Including Group 4 and 5 competition types

SPECIFICATIONS

Length (in.)	171.7
Wheelbase (in.)	100.8
Weight (lbs)	2865-3120
Price (new)	$53,000 in U.S.

ENGINES

cc/type	bhp[1]	years
3453/dohc I-6	277	1978-81
[1]DIN		

PRICES

Value ranges in 1999 were $90,000 to $145,000.
2000-2010 RETURN 2%

1987-90

BMW M3

A special high-performance edition of BMW's smallest sedan. Designed for Group A of the European Touring Car Championship, which it won its first year out. Essentially the second-generation 3-Series two-door powered by a unique twin-cam, 2.3-liter four-cylinder engine devised by Munich's competition division, BMW Motorsport, hence the "M" designation. Uprated five-speed manual transmission only, plus standard all-disc antilock brakes, limited-slip differential, and fortified suspension. Easily distinguished from ordinary 3s by big deck-lid spoiler, flared fenders, "skirted" rocker panels, front airdam, bonded windshield, and faired-in backlight—all the better for racetrack aerodynamics. Ultimate collectibility questionable now, but should achieve at least minor distinction—perhaps major distinction, given low original production and higher-than-normal attrition.

1987 M3 coupe

✚ **FOR** Scarce in America • Relatively fast (7 seconds 0-60 mph) • Sports-car handling • Family-sedan practicality • Race-winning image

▬ **AGAINST** Noisy, throbby big four lacks low-speed torque • High-effort clutch and shifter • "Boy racer" looks • May be eclipsed by successor based on third-generation "aerodynamic" 3-Series of 1992

PRODUCTION[1]

1987 1121 **1988** 1675 **1989** 979 **1990** 764
[1]U.S. calendar-year sales

SPECIFICATIONS

Length (in.)	171.1
Wheelbase (in.)	100.9
Weight (lbs)	2865
Price (new)	$35,000 (in U.S.)

ENGINES

cc/type	bhp[1]	years
2305/dohc I-4	192	1987-90
[1]SAE net		

PRICES

Values are governed by the used car market. The range in 1999 was $8000 to $20,000.
2000-2010 RETURN 2%

1987-89

BMW M5

Another BMW Motorsport exercise, this time on Munich's second-series mid-size four-door, new in 1982. Identical with lesser 5s save the usual

1979 M1 coupe

1987 M5 sedan

chassis uprating to cope with the high-performance M-88 six as used in the mid-engine M1 and M635CSi/M6 (see entries). A short-timer, and thus few in number, owing to advent of all-new "aerodynamic" 5-Series for 1989—with a new M5 from early '90. Slicker styling may ultimately render the replacement more collectible, but the first M5 is still one of the more rewarding late-model BMWs.

➕ FOR Goes, stops, and handles like few other four-doors • Solid, burly feel • Room for four • Lots of niceties • Not long out of production, so parts and service still good

➖ AGAINST Values have yet to hit bottom • Dull, boxy styling

PRODUCTION[1]

1987 403 **1988** 243 **1989** 547
[1]U.S. calendar-year sales

SPECIFICATIONS

Length (in.)	189.0
Wheelbase (in.)	103.3
Weight (lbs)	approx. 3400
Price (new)	$45,500 in (U.S.)

ENGINES

cc/type	bhp	years
3453/dohc I-6	256	1987-89

PRICES

Values are governed by the used car market.
The range in 1999 was $9000 to $14,000.
2000-2010 RETURN 2%

1988-95
BMW 750IL

BMW's ambitious V-12 flagship four-door. Launched in Europe with other new second-generation 7-Series models about a year ahead of 1988 model-year U.S. debut. Sold Stateside only with the shared, long-wheelbase

1988 750iL sedan

body/chassis of the six-cylinder 735iL, though Europeans also got a standard 111.5-inch wheelbase 750i. Chief distinction was the superbly engineered single-cam aluminum V-12 with dual electronic engine-management systems, including fuel injection "computers"—one for each cylinder bank. The only transmission was a 4-speed electronically controlled ZF with three shift programs: Economy, Sport, and Manual. Other standards included antilock brakes, ZF Servotronic power steering (not universally admired), driver's airbag, leather interior, and the unusual conveniences like road-speed-dependent variable-rate windshield wipers and external closing of windows and sunroof from the front door locks. Suspension followed BMW tradition, providing superb handling allied to great smoothness and silence in a car that scarcely betrayed its two-ton heft. Highly desirable new, and should remain so some years from now when it's "rediscovered" on the collector market.

➕ FOR Space • Grace • Pace (7.1 seconds to 60 mph, 155 mph maximum) • Abundant luxury

➖ AGAINST Thirsty • Bulky • Complex electricals subject to failure gremlins

PRODUCTION
NA

SPECIFICATIONS

Length (in.)	197.8

Wheelbase (in.)	116.0
Weight (lbs)	4235
Price (new)	$70,000-83,950

ENGINES

cc/type	bhp[1]	years
4988/ohc V-12	296	1988-95

[1]SAE net

PRICES

Values are governed by the used car market.
The range in 1999 was $8,000 to $20,000.
2000-2010 RETURN Even

1987-90
BMW Z1

1988-91 Z1 convertible

A treat mainly for Europe: BMW's first open two-seater since the handsome late-'50s 507. Conceived in 1986 by BMW Technik, the Munich automaker's research and development arm, as a testbed for new materials and production processes. Enthusiastic public interest prompted a limited run, though deliveries didn't commence until January 1989. It was powered by the small six from the contemporary 325i sedan, linked to a five-speed manual gearbox. Conventional front suspension and coil springs were found all-round, but the rear featured a new "Z-axle" design with trailing arm, upper lateral link, and lower diagonal link giving geometry á la the "Weissach axle" of Porsche's 928. A steel monocoque inner structure sported bonded/bolted-on fiberglass/polyurethane panels. High rocker panels, for rigidity, necessitated novel drop-down doors instead of side-hinged portals. A folding soft top stowed behind the cockpit beneath a hard cover. Many other innovations and classic sports-car character were there, but the Z1 was more an image-leader than a profit-maker. In fact, BMW made no money on any Z1 sold, and maybe even lost some. It was never certified for U.S. sale, so it's a compliance hassle for would-be American owners, though a few Z1s have undoubtedly made it over as private imports. It's significant for what it may portend for future BMWs that will come Stateside, but highly desirable as a fascinating charmer in its own right.

⊞ **FOR** A virtual "factory dream car" with everyday practicality • Top-down allure • Purposeful looks • Smooth "2.5i" six • Zippy (8 seconds 0-60) • Nippy handler • Solid for a ragtop • Carefully built

◼ **AGAINST** A likely trip to Germany to buy • An argument with Customs to keep it when you return

PRODUCTION

NA, but likely no more than 4000

SPECIFICATIONS

Length (in.)	154.4
Wheelbase (in.)	96.3
Weight (lbs)	2750
Price (new)	$46,000 in Germany

ENGINES

cc/type	bhp	years
2494/sohc I-6	168	1987-90

PRICES

No U.S. prices available.

1991-97
BMW 8-SERIES

BMW's shapely and elegant luxury coupe was introduced for 1991 as successor to the 635CSi. Rear-drive in the classic performance-car mold, the 8-Series offered power and smart luxury in equal measure. The 296-bhp V-12 from BMW's 750iL sedan eventually offered as much as 372 horsepower in the top-of-the line 8-Series CSi model. Other iterations of the V-12, plus a V-8, also were available elsewhere in the Series. The cars' very high 1991 prices (a well-appointed CSi could top $90K) were not well received in that recession year, and sales never recovered.

1991 850i hardtop coupe

⊞ **FOR** Relative rarity • Acceleration • Steering and roadholding • Luxury appointments • Safety features • Unique status in BMW line

◼ **AGAINST** Fuel economy • Passenger room

PRODUCTION

29,650

SPECIFICATIONS

Length (in.)	188.2
Weight (lbs)	4123-4288
Wheelbase (in.)	105.7
Price (new)	$69,900-94,700

ENGINES

liter/type/(cid)	bhp	years
5.0/ohc V-12 (304)	296	1991-93
5.6/ohc V-12 (304)	372	1994-95
4.0/dohc V-8 (243)	282	1994-95
4.4/dohc V-8 (268)	282	1996-97
5.4/ohc V-12 (328)	322	1996-97

PRICES

governed by the used car market, $20,000-65,000 in 1999.

1991-99
BMW M3

1995 M3 coupe

The '91 BMW M3—the performance car of the entry-level 3-Series—was a carryover of the 1987-90 generation. For 1992, this race-bred small

---

sedan (the "M" denoted the company's competition division, BMW Motorsport) sported a new, more rounded body and improved weight balance. By 1995, the M-3 had a mandatory 5-speed, firmed suspension, 17-inch wheels, and Z-rated tires for speeds above 149 mph—an attainable velocity given the car's 240-horse 3.0-liter inline six. A 3.2-liter six and increased torque appeared for '96, and by 1999 the M3 offered upgraded brakes and limited-slip differential. Power seats and cruise control were deleted. A fascinating combination of playfulness and dead-serious aggressiveness

⊞ **FOR** Acceleration • Agile steering and handling • Braking • Driver room and comfort • Visibility

◼ **AGAINST** Choppy ride • Fuel economy • Tire hum

PRODUCTION

coupe 17,184 **cabrio** 786

SPECIFICATIONS

Length (in.)	170.3-175.2
Weight (lbs)	2811-2990
Wheelbase (in.)	101.2-106.3
Price (new)	$34,950-45,900

ENGINES

liter/type/(cid)	bhp	years
2.3/dohc I-4 (NA)	192	1991
2.5/dohc I-6 (152)	189	1992-94
3.0/dohc I-6 (183)	240	1995
3.2/dohc I-6 (192)	240	1996-99

PRICES

governed by the used car market, $10,000-38,000 in 1999.

1996-2000
BMW Z3

Built on BMW's 3-Series chassis, the Z3 2-seat roadster debuted with an adequate 1.9-liter inline four producing 138 bhp. By 2000, a coupe had been added and the four was history, and Z3 offered a trio of inline sixes: 2.5-liter, 2.8, and 3.2, with horsepower rated at 170, 193, and a thumping 240, respectively. With its rounded, Sixties-look styling cues and base prices that remained reasonable, the Z3 found many buyers among sports car lovers who desired more muscle than what a Mazda Miata could provide.

⊞ **FOR** Acceleration • Crisp steering and handling • Good range of engine choices • Voluptuous, sexy bodyshape

◼ **AGAINST** Noise • Choppy ride (M variant) • Wet-weather grip • Cramped cockpit • Awkward coupe styling

1996 Z3 roadster

PRODUCTION

1996 45,212 **1997** 62,943 **1998** 54,802

SPECIFICATIONS

Length (in.)	158.5
Weight (lbs)	2690-2701
Wheelbase (in.)	96.3
Price (new)	$28,750-42,700

ENGINES

liter/type/(cid)	bhp	years
1.9/dohc I-4 (116)	138	1996-98
2.8/dohc I-6 (170)	189	1997-98
2.5/dohc I-6 (152)	170	1999-2000
2.8/dohc I-6 (170)	193	1999-2000
3.2/dohc I-6 (192)	240	1999-2000

PRICES

governed by the used car market. 1997 convertibles $19,000-35,000 in 1999

2001
BMW Z8

2001 Z8 roadster

Dutch designer Adrian van Hooydonk gave the rear-drive Z8 roadster (based on BMW's Z07 concept car) the shapely, retro curves that recalled BMW's 507 roadster of 1956-59. Available as coupe or cabrio, the Z8 boasted a powerful 5.0-liter V-8, shared with BMW's M5 and rated at 400 bhp. A good driver experienced with the car's mandatory 6-speed stick could rip through the 0-60 mph sprint in

about 4.2 seconds. Top speed of this lightweight car (about 2970 pounds, thanks partly to an aluminum space frame) was electronically limited to 156 mph. The Z8 was on prominent display in the 1999 James Bond thriller, *The World is Not Enough*.

FOR Low production • Supercar performance that challenged Porsche's 911 and Ferrari's F355 • Deft, sticky handling • Nostalgic, retro styling

AGAINST Heavy price tag when new • Possible mechanical touchiness

PRODUCTION

Fewer than 500

SPECIFICATIONS

Length (in.)	173.4
Weight (lbs)	2970
Wheelbase (in.)	98.9
Price (new)	$128,000

ENGINES

liter/type/(cid)	bhp	years
5.0/dohc V-8 (302)	400	2000

PRICES

governed by the used car market.

1953 - 55
BRISTOL 403

1953 403 COUPE

The Bristol Aeroplane Company of England got into automobile pro-

duction after WWII using BMW designs purloined as "war reparations" to create its Type 400 and Touring of Italy styled Type 401. The engine was a development of the pre-war BMW 328 inline six. With its hemispherical head and unusual cross-pushrod valve arrangement, it offered creditable performance for its time. Chassis was also BMW derived and offer excellent handling and roadholding. Bristol's standards for quality control and materials were at least as good, and probably higher than, Roll-Royce. The 403 was a mildly revised version of the Type 401, with improved chassis details and greater power and performance (top speed up to 106 mph). Styling was unchanged from the 401, and no convertible body style was offered following demise of the 402.

FOR Individuality • Hand-built quality • Fine chassis and road manners • Club interest, especially in Britain • Better performance than previous models

AGAINST Body parts unavailable • Engine parts neary extinct • Cramped interior • Limited outward visibility • Hard to find

PRODUCTION

300

SPECIFICATIONS

Length (in.)	190.0
Wheelbase (in.)	114.0
Weight (lbs)	2670
Price (new)	NA

ENGINES

cc/type (cid)	bhp[1]	years
1971/ohv I-6 (120)	100	1953-55

[1]Net

PRICES

FAIR	$5000-10,000
GOOD	$10,000-15,000
FINE	$15,000-20,000

FINE EXAMPLE PRICE HISTORY

Not available.
2000-2010 RETURN 5%

1953 - 56
BRISTOL 404

A short-wheelbase two-seat coupe based on the familiar Bristol chassis design. This 96-inch-wheelbase platform was also used for the Italian-styled Arnolt-Bristol sports car. Sleek fastback styling earned the Type 404 the nickname Businessman's Express, but only very rich executives could afford it, which helped keep sales

1953-56 404 coupe

extremely low. Besides, most Bristol customers wanted something more than two-passenger seating. The 404's basic lines, however, would later be applied to the longer and more practical Type 405 sedan. The familiar 2.0-liter inline six-cylinder engine from the '40s continued with yet another horsepower boost—up to 125 bhp in the higher of the two available tunes.

✚ **FOR** Unique (to Bristol) short-wheelbase chassis • Nice styling • Fine performance • Very exclusive • High appreciation • Others as for the 1953-55 Type 403

▬ **AGAINST** Body corrosion • Limited interior room • Rather costly • Where do you find one?

PRODUCTION
40

SPECIFICATIONS

Length (in.)	171.2
Wheelbase (in.)	96.0
Weight (lbs)	2265
Price (new)	NA

ENGINES

cc/type (cid)	bhp[1]	years
1971/ohv I-6 (120)	105/125	1954-56

[1]Net

PRICES

FAIR	$4000-8000
GOOD	$8000-12,000
FINE	$12,000-20,000

FINE EXAMPLE PRICE HISTORY

1982 $7000	**1990** $25,000
1994 $20,000	**1998** $20,000

1982-2000 RETURN 7%
2000-2010 5%

1 9 5 4 - 5 8

BRISTOL 405

The replacement for the Type 401/403, and the only four-door

1954-58 405 sedan

Bristol ever built. Styling derived from the neat 96-inch-wheelbase Type 404 Coupe on the original 114-inch-wheelbase chassis. Sedan bodywork was designed and made by Bristol, but a rare convertible model with coachwork by Abbotts of Farnham was also offered in these years.

✚ **FOR** As for the 1953-55 Type 403, but better entry/exit and interesting styling

▬ **AGAINST** Body rots easily if neglected • Limited performance despite sleek looks • Others as for the 403

PRODUCTION
340 (incl. 43 convertibles)

SPECIFICATIONS

Length (in.)	185.2
Wheelbase (in.)	114.0
Weight (lbs)	2675
Price (new)	$10,000 U.S. equivalent in 1954

ENGINES

cc/type (cid)	bhp[1]	years
1971/ohv I-6 (120)	105	1954-58

[1]Net

PRICES

FAIR	$5000-9000
GOOD	$9000-12,000
FINE	$12,000-18,000

FINE EXAMPLE PRICE HISTORY

1982 $5500	**1990** $22,500
1994 $18,000	**1998** $18,000

1982-2000 RETURN 7%
2000-2010 5%

1 9 5 8 - 6 1

BRISTOL 406

1958-61 406 coupe

A further revision of the basic Type 401/403/405 chassis, this time with an enlarged version of the Bristol straight six and all-disc brakes. The firm reverted to two doors for an all-new notchback coupe body, which set the style for succeeding models of the '60s and '70s. By now, the aging chassis and excess curb weight of what was basically prewar engineering were catching up with Bristol, and its comparatively poor performance was becoming a distinct drawback. That would be rectified with the 407. Cars were still a sideline operation for this aircraft manufacturer, so production was as meager as in previous years, a reflection of the painstaking, handbuilt construction methods employed. Most 406s were built by Bristol, but a handful featured special coachwork—and somewhat bizarre looks—by Zagato of Italy.

✚ **FOR** As for the 1954-58 Type 405, plus crisper appearance and better brakes • Also, surprisingly affordable

▬ **AGAINST** Too heavy • Disappointing performance • Others as for the 405

PRODUCTION
300

SPECIFICATIONS

Length (in.)	198.0
Wheelbase (in.)	114.0
Weight (lbs)	3010
Price (new)	$8400 (U.S.)

ENGINES

cc/type (cid)	bhp[1]	years
2216/ohv I-6 (135)	105/130	1958-61

[1]Net

PRICES

As for the 1954-58 Bristol 405.

1 9 6 5 - 6 7

BRISTOL 409

An updated continuation of the Type 407/408—which adopted Chrysler Hemi V-8 power and TorqueFlite auto-

1966 409 coupe

matic transmission—with fairly extensive (for Bristol) mechanical modifications. These included a larger Chrysler V-8 with the same power as the previous 313-cid unit, plus softer suspension settings and Girling, instead of Dunlop, disc brakes. Cars built from the autumn of 1966 were available with ZF power steering as an optional extra. These were the last Bristols that could be legally imported into the U.S. before the advent of Federal emissions controls, though few actually were.

⊞ FOR Very fast • Well-known Detroit drivetrain • Neat lines • Body durability better than before • Top-flight construction, materials • Chassis parts still available • Not costly for a low-production item

▭ AGAINST Expensive to rebuild (except drivetrain) and run • Not easy to find in the U.S., and not much restoration help available • Modest appreciation

PRODUCTION
300 (est.)

SPECIFICATIONS

Length (in.)	193.5
Wheelbase (in.)	114.0
Weight (lbs)	3528
Price (new)	NA

ENGINES

cc/type (cid)	bhp[1]	years
5211/ohv V-8 (318)	250	1965-67

[1]SAE Gross

PRICES

FAIR	$5000-9000
GOOD	$9000-12,000
FINE	$12,000-15,000

FINE EXAMPLE PRICE HISTORY

1982 $5000	**1990** $18,000
1994 $15,000	**1998** $15,000
1982-2000 RETURN 5%	
2000-2010 8%	

---

1 9 3 0 - 3 1
BUGATTI TYPE 43/43A

Ettore Bugatti's cars had been around since 1910, and by the mid-1920s had become famous in European competition. Built at Molsheim in eastern France, all "Bugs" had a flexible chassis, rock-hard suspensions, and either four- or eight-cylinder engines. Generally considered one of Bugatti's four greatest creations, the straight-eight Type 43 offered a 100-mph top speed, but MGA/Triumph TR3 acceleration. Really a long-chassis Type 35/38 with a larger supercharged engine. Most were built with narrow torpedo-style sports bodies, but some four-seat roadsters are known. The 43A had American-style rumble-seat bodywork.

⊞ FOR Impeccable vintage racing pedigree • Eight-cylinder smoothness • High-quality design • Charisma • A CCCA Classic

▭ AGAINST Rock-hard ride • Crude suspension • Floppy chassis • Few creature comforts • Very costly to buy and restore

PRODUCTION
approx. 150 (began 1927)

SPECIFICATIONS

Length (in.)	154.0
Wheelbase (in.)	117
Weight (lbs)	approx. 2300
Price (new)	NA

ENGINES

cc/type (cid)	bhp	years
2262/ohc I-8 (138)	115	1930-31

PRICES

FAIR	$75,000-125,000
GOOD	$125,000-175,000
FINE	$175,000-250,000

FINE EXAMPLE PRICE HISTORY

Prices vary widely depending on condition and racing pedigree. Highest prices reached were $500,000 a decade ago.

1 9 3 0 - 3 4
BUGATTI TYPE 49

1930-34 Type 49 roadster

The last—and best—of the single-cam eight-cylinder Bugattis. A larger engine made a more flexible, refined tourer than the Type 43. Bodies tended to be bigger, plusher, and more civilized as well. Alloy or wire wheels were specified. "Only" 80 mph allied to Bugatti's habitually hard suspension, but pinpoint-accurate controls and great French character. Practical and versatile by Bugatti standards and not really intended for competition.

⊞ FOR Bugatti engineering with a measure of reliability • Character • Relatively well-known "Bug" • Styling • CCCA Classic status

▭ AGAINST Function before luxury • Hard ride • "Traditional" detailing • Expensive to buy and run • High restoration costs

PRODUCTION
470

SPECIFICATIONS

Length (in.)	165.0
Wheelbase (in.)	127.0
Weight (lbs)	approx. 3000
Price (new)	NA

ENGINES

cc/type (cid)	bhp	years
3257/ohc I-8 (199)	NA	1930-34

PRICES

FAIR	$30,000-60,000
GOOD	$60,000-90,000
FINE	$90,000-125,000

FINE EXAMPLE PRICE HISTORY

No data available

1930-34
BUGATTI TYPE 50

A "derivative" Bugatti built on a scaled-down Type 46 Royale chassis. Gearbox in unit with the rear axle. Up front was the new, large twin-cam eight allegedly patterned on the U.S. Miller racing unit. This was a direct replacement for the Type 46, and big and luxurious by any standards. There was a choice of two wheelbases and several sumptuous bodies. It sold in small numbers because of Rolls-Royce prices, spine-numbing ride, lots of engine noise, and definite "mechanical" character. A very desirable Bugatti for the sportsman rather than the sybarite.

FOR Peerless Bugatti character • Trend-setting twincam eight • Big and impressive • Easy to drive • It's a CCCA Classic

AGAINST Expensive to buy and restore • Mechanically complex • Not many around today • Lacks refinement

PRODUCTION
65

SPECIFICATIONS
Length (in.)	178.0+
Wheelbase (in.)	122/138
Weight (lbs)	4000+
Price (new)	NA

ENGINES
cc/type (cid)	bhp	years
4972/dohc I-8 (303.5)	200[1]	1930-34

[1]Net

PRICES
Coupe	
FAIR	$150,000-200,000
GOOD	$200,000-300,000

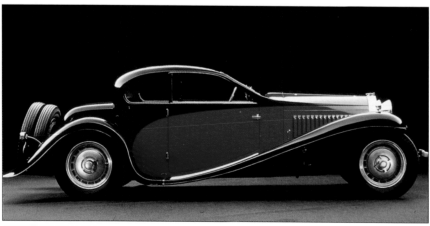

1932 Type 50 coupe

FINE	$300,000-400,000
Tourer	
FAIR	$150,000-200,000
GOOD	$200,000-300,000
FINE	$300,000-400,000

FINE TOURER PRICE HISTORY
1982	$120,000	1990	$650,000
1994	$400,000	1998	$400,000

1982-2000 RETURN 7%
2000-2010 5%

1932-35
BUGATTI TYPE 55

1933 Type 55 roadster

A very exclusive roadgoing version of the small-engined, supercharged Type 51 Grand Prix car. Expect the fierce character of a blown twincam eight and a chassis almost exactly the same as that of the GP car. It was like the Type 43 in many ways, yet considerably faster: some say the standard-bodied two-seat roadster could exceed 112 mph when new, comparable to Ferrari Boxer/Lam-borghini Countach performance today. It offers all of the usual joys and heartaches of a true thoroughbred Bugatti plus greater exclusivity.

FOR High performance • Grand Prix heritage • Styling, of course • "Animal" charm • Rarity • It's a Classic

AGAINST Ludicrous prices • Extremely expensive to own • Chassis old fashioned even for the mid-'30s • Are there any left to find?

PRODUCTION
35

SPECIFICATIONS
Length (in.)	162.0
Wheelbase (in.)	108.0
Weight (lbs)	2050
Price (new)	NA

ENGINES
cc/type	bhp	years
2262/dohc I-8	135[1]	1932-35

[1]Net; supercharged

PRICES
To $1.2M

FINE EXAMPLE PRICE HISTORY
No reliable figures available.

1934-40
BUGATTI TYPE 57/57C

1934 Type 57 convertible coupe

The final statement of Bugatti's design philosophy, combining a fine, modern engine with an uncompromisingly "vintage" chassis and a great variety of startlingly styled bodywork. Still no independent front suspension or synchronized gearbox, but hydraulic brakes from 1938. Splendidly detailed center-lock wire wheels are worth $10,000 just to look at! The supercharged 57C (*Compresseur*) of 1937-39 could easily best the 57 in top speed, 110 versus 95 mph. Pure 1930s supercar apart from the old-fashioned road manners and immensely desirable now.

FOR Magnificent engine • Performance, especially 57C • Styling, especially coupes and cabriolets • Character and sound • Good value today compared with other Bugattis • A CCCA Classic

AGAINST Complex and costly to restore • Archaic handling/roadholding

• Not readily available

PRODUCTION

630

SPECIFICATIONS

Length (in.)	172.0
Wheelbase (in.)	130.0
Weight (lbs)	approx. 3000
Price (new)	NA

ENGINES

cc/type (cid)	bhp[1]	years
3257/dohc I-8 (199)	135/160[2]	1933-40

[1]Net [2]Supercharged (1937-39)

PRICES

C Atlanta	
FAIR	$150,000-200,000
GOOD	$200,000-300,000
FINE	$300,000-400,000
Cabrio	
FAIR	$100,000-150,000
GOOD	$150,000-225,000
FINE	$225,000-300,000
Cpe	
FAIR	$40,000-60,000
GOOD	$60,000-90,000
FINE	$90,000-175,000

FINE CABRIO PRICE HISTORY

1982 $150,000	1990 $500,000
1994 $300,000	1998 $300,000

1982-2000 RETURN 4%
2000-2010 10%

1936-38
BUGATTI TYPE 57S/57SC

1937-39 Type 57SC Atlantic coupe

Even better than the Type 57; this was the more sporting short-chassis version. Sold with the same normally aspirated (S) or supercharged (SC) engines with dry-sump lubrication and a higher state of tune for more power. Mechanically the same otherwise. Quite startling coachwork, still with the unmistakable "horseshoe" radiator. Irresistible to the very rich then as now. The best 57SCs could top 135 mph, unbelievable by late-1930s standards. Today, very few are ever bought or sold.

FOR Very high performance • Styling, especially coupes • Mechanical elegance • Sexy charisma •

Classic status

AGAINST Archaic chassis • Noisy to drive fast • Enormously costly to buy, run, and restore

PRODUCTION

approx. 40

SPECIFICATIONS

Length (in.)	159.0
Wheelbase (in.)	118.0
Weight (lbs)	approx. 2700
Price (new)	NA

ENGINES

cc/type (cid)	bhp[1]	years
3257/dohc I-8 (199)	175/200[2]	1935-38

[1]Net [2]supercharged (1937-38)

PRICES

As for 1934-40 Type 57/57C.
2000-2010 RETURN 10%

1991-95
BUGATTI EB 110/112

Mid-engine, carbon-fiber supercar from an ambitious Nineties revival headed by South Tyrol businessman Romano Artioli. Two-seat snugness plus a 550-bhp V-12 with four Japanese IHI turbos and 443 pounds/feet of torque added to the neck-snapping fun. Zero to 60 mph came up in 3.7 seconds; claimed top speed approached 210. Advance orders at $400,000 apiece were taken as early as 1992, but 1991-95 production amounted to just 139 units. VW bought the rights to the marque in 1998, and by late 1999 an 18-cylinder Bugatti EB 18/4 "Veyron" began to tour the international auto-show circuit.

FOR Blistering performance • Surprising comfort • A credible, if extreme-

seeming, revival of a grand old marque • Extreme scarcity

AGAINST Stratospheric prices • Little chance of one changing hands, and when one does it will do so privately • Quality control of early examples an unknown quantity

PRODUCTION

approx. 139 (1991-95)

SPECIFICATIONS

Length (in.)	172.4
Weight (lbs)	3235
Wheelbase (in.)	100.4
Price (new)	$400,000 (1991-95)

ENGINES

cc/type	bhp	years
3499 /dohc V-12[1]	550	1991-95
6000 (approx)/dohc V-12	460	1993

[1]Turbocharged

PRICES

2000-2010 RETURN Unpredictable

1931-35
BUICK EIGHT

Increasing scarcity and high fluctuation in values among a wide variety of models make it difficult to supply hard and fast guidelines for pre-1936 Buicks. All Series 90s from 1931 on are recognized Classics; no other models are, although individual custom bodies may be certified. Open styles in all series are worth up to $50,000 or more in perfect show condition. Restorable examples will rarely be priced below $4000 if they can be found at all. Closed models run about half that much. The usual rule that open cars far surpass closed models in value applies; likewise, coupes are more sought-after than sedans. Prices remain more moderate among 1934-

1993 EB 110 coupe

1932 Series 60 sedan

35 Buicks. The most desirable models are undoubtedly the Series 90 convertible coupe and phaeton ($55,000 maximum in top condition).

✚ **FOR** Straight-eight smoothness • Senior models' posh and panache • 90 Series models are CCCA-recognized Classics

▬ **AGAINST** Open models' scarcity • Lack of status for all but Series 90s

PRODUCTION

1931 138,695 **1932** 56,790 **1933** 46,924 **1934** 71,009 **1935** 53,249

SPECIFICATIONS

Length (in.)	NA
Wheelbase (in.)	132.0 (1931); 134.0 (1932); 138.0 (1933); 136.0 (1934-35)
Weight (lbs)	4010-4876
Price (new)	$1610-2175

ENGINES

cid/type	bhp	years
344.8/ohv I-8	104-116	1931-35

PRICES

Open	
FAIR	$12,000-20,000
GOOD	$20,000-35,000
FINE	$35,000-50,000
Closed	
FAIR	$7600-17,000
GOOD	$17,000-26,000
FINE	$26,000-35,000

FINE 1932 SPORT PHAETON PRICE HISTORY

1982 $36,000		**1990** $50,000	
1994 $38,000		**1998** $45,000	
1982-2000 RETURN 2%			
2000-2010 4%			

1936-42
BUICK SERIES 60 CENTURY

With remarkably low production for models other than the conventional four-door sedan and coupes, the

1936 Century sedan

Century appeared in 1936 as part of a whole new line with all-steel "Turret-Top" construction. Always powered by the 320-cid ohv straight-eight, which gained 45 horsepower in seven years. The Century's traditional combination of light body and big-Buick power was established during this period. Among the more desirable body styles are the 1937-38 two-door sedans and the sleek fastback sedanet of 1941-42, which vie in popularity with the rare open phaetons and convertibles. Many bare chassis (1936-39) were fitted with custom coachwork and can thereby qualify as CCCA Classics. One of the best all-around Buicks of the period.

✚ **FOR** Good styling • Reasonable parts supplies • Fine straight-line performance • Higher appreciation potential than comparable lower-line Buicks • Good club support

▬ **AGAINST** Undistinguished handling • Fairly thirsty • Not a certified Classic

PRODUCTION

1936 4d sdn 18,203 conv cpe 766 spt cpe 1078 spt cpe R/S 1018 victoria cpe 3799 chassis 1115 **1937** 4d sdn 25,911 conv cpe 843 spt cpe 2873 chassis 1026 2d sdn 4015 phaeton 425 **1938** 4d sdn 14,189 conv cpe 694 spt cpe 2030 chassis 762 2d sdn 1393 phaeton 219 **1939** 4d sdn 18,783 conv cpe 850 spt cpe 3470 chassis 518 phaeton 269 **1940** 4d sdn 8708 bus cpe 44 conv cpe 550 spt cpe 96 phaeton 203 **1941** 4d sdn 15,136 bus cpe 222 sedanet 5547 **1942** 4d sdn 3319 sedanet 1232

SPECIFICATIONS

Length (in.)	NA
Wheelbase (in.)	122.0 (1936); 126.0 (1937-42)
Weight (lbs)	3195-4065

Price (new)	$1035-1620

ENGINES

cid/type	bhp	years
320.2/ohv I-8	120-165	1936-42

PRICES

Open	
FAIR	$14,000-25,000
GOOD	$25,000-35,000
FINE	$35,000-45,000
Closed	
FAIR	$8400-11,000
GOOD	$10,000-20,000
FINE	$20,000-27,000

FINE 1939 PHAETON PRICE HISTORY

1982 $23,090		**1990** $40,000	
1994 $36,000		**1998** $43,000	
1982-2000 RETURN 4%			
2000-2010 4%			

1936-41
BUICK SERIES 70/80 ROADMASTER

Born with the redesign of 1936, the Roadmaster went on to become the most prestigious Buick after the Limited was dropped following World War II. Big and luxurious, it was the ultimate owner-driver Buick of the period. Also well styled and solidly engineered, and still a smooth highway-driver. Aside from the four-door sedan, the production figures speak for themselves: all the other body styles are highly collectible. Not a Classic, except for the odd custom body from 1936-39 production.

✚ **FOR** Luxury and grace • Strong club and parts support • Smooth if not vivid performance

▬ **AGAINST** Thirsty on gas • Lacks Classic status

PRODUCTION

1936 conv phaeton 1230 4d sdn 15,328 chassis 534 **1937** conv phaeton 1155 4d sdn 14,981 chassis 606 formal sdn 489 **1938** conv phaeton 411 4d sdn 4704 chassis 223 formal sdn 296 spt sdn 466 **1939** conv phaeton 367 4d sdn 5619 chassis 143 formal sdn 340 spt sdn 20 **1940** conv phaeton 238 4d sdn 13,733 conv cpe 612 **1941** conv phaeton 326 4d sdn 10,553 conv cpe 1869 spt cpe 2834

SPECIFICATIONS

Length (in.)	NA
Wheelbase (in.)	131.0 (1936-37); 133.0 (1938-39), 126.0 (1940), 128.0 (1941)
Weight (lbs)	3990-4469
Price (new)	$1255-1983

ENGINES

cid/type	bhp	years
320.2/ohv I-8	120-165	1936-41

1938 Roadmaster sedan

1948 Roadmaster convertible

PRICES

Add 5-10% to 1936-42 Century prices; maximum for open cars $55,000.

FINE 1941 PHAETON PRICE HISTORY

1982 $26,000	**1990** $46,000
1994 $40,000	**1998** $55,000
1982-2000 RETURN 6%	
2000-2010 7%	

1 9 3 6 - 4 2
BUICK SERIES 80/90 LIMITED

1940 Limited sedan

Cadillac didn't like the idea of Buick's 1930s prestige models with Brunn custom bodies, so Flint dropped them and put all its luxury emphasis on the long-wheelbase Limited from 1936 on. A smaller Series 80 Limited appeared on a shorter 133-inch wheelbase for 1940 only. Production was low, the cars were huge, and quality and workmanship were exceptional. All Series 90s are recognized Classics. Fully restyled with pontoon fenders for 1942, but only a handful were built. The Limited was revived in 1958, but merely as a glorified Roadmaster that lasted only one year.

➕ **FOR** Luxurious interiors • Outstanding craftsmanship, quality

• 90 Series models are CCCA Classics

➖ **AGAINST** Ponderous road manners (the six-passenger sedan is an exception) • High operating costs.

PRODUCTION

All body styles under 1000 per year except 1936-37 sedans and 1941 sedan; 1942 production extremely low: 365 sedans, 250 limousines, 85 formals. Series 80 Limited (1940 only): 3898 sedans, 270 formals, 250 phaetons, 28 "Streamlined" models (of which 7 were open).

SPECIFICATIONS

Length (in.)	NA
Wheelbase (in.)	138.0 (1936-37); 140.0 (1938-40); 139.0 (1941-42); 133.0 (1940 Series 80)
Weight (lbs)	4400-4765
Price (new)	$1695-2545

ENGINES

cid/type	bhp	years
320.2/ohv I-8	120-165	1936-42

PRICES

Add 10-15% to 1936-42 Century prices; maximum for open cars about $48,000.

FINE 1940 FASTBACK PHAETON PRICE HISTORY

1982 $28,000	**1990** $50,000
1994 $40,000	**1998** $46,000
1982-2000 RETURN 3%	
2000-2010 5%	

1 9 4 2 - 4 8
BUICK ROADMASTER

Buick's luxury standard bearer, and especially attractive in these years. The Harley Earl styling was distinguished by long, tapering pontoon front fenders; a wide, vertical-bar grille; and a "gunsight" hood ornament for the postwar models. The convertible is the most prized body style, but the sleek Sedanet is a better buy. The partially wood-bodied Estate Wagon is also

very rare and desirable.

➕ **FOR** Large and luxurious, a fine touring car • Dynaflow automatic available on '48s

➖ **AGAINST** A hefty armful to drive • High fuel consumption • Sluggish acceleration with Dynaflow

PRODUCTION

1942 4d sdn 5418 **conv** 511 **Sedanet** 2475 **1946 4d sdn** 20,864 **conv** 2587 **Sedanet** 8292 **1947 4d sdn** 47,152 **conv** 12,074 **Sedanet** 19,212 **4d wgn** 529 **1948 4d sdn** 47,569 **conv** 11,503 **Sedanet** 20,649 **4d wgn** 350

SPECIFICATIONS

Length (in.)	217.5
Wheelbase (in.)	129.0
Weight (lbs)	4075-4460
Price (new)	$1395-3433

ENGINES

cid/type	bhp	years
320.2/ohv I-8	144/165	1942-48

PRICES

Conv	
FAIR	$16,000-18,000
GOOD	$18,000-35,000
FINE	$35,000-44,000
Wgn	
FAIR	$14,000-20,000
GOOD	$20,000-28,000
FINE	$28,000-36,000
Closed	
FAIR	$8500-12,000
GOOD	$12,000-18,000
FINE	$18,000-24,000

FINE CONVERTIBLE PRICE HISTORY

1982 $12,500	**1990** $30,000
1994 $30,000	**1998** $44,000
1982-2000 RETURN 8%	
2000-2010 10%	

1 9 4 9
BUICK ROADMASTER RIVIERA

The Milestone designation for this model stems mainly from its two-door "hardtop convertible" body style, which was also pioneered by the '49 Cadillac Coupe de Ville and Oldsmobile Holiday. Also significant for col-

1949 Roadmaster Riviera hardtop coupe

lectors is its quality, leather-accented interior, bright color schemes, and clean, streamlined styling. The big Roadmaster straight eight gives vivid performance for a standard-size car of this period. Hardtop styling gives the Riviera a slight edge over the Roadmaster convertible as the most desirable '49 Buick.

FOR Pioneer hardtop • Clean styling • Very posh • Fine road car • Milestone car status

AGAINST Some body parts increasingly hard to find • Limited availability • High prices if you find one

PRODUCTION
4343

SPECIFICATIONS
Length (in.)	214.1
Wheelbase (in.)	126.0
Weight (lbs)	4420
Price (new)	$3203

ENGINES
cid/type	bhp	years
320.2/ohv I-8	150	1949

PRICES
FAIR	$8000-12,000
GOOD	$12,000-21,000
FINE	$21,000-30,000

FINE EXAMPLE PRICE HISTORY
1982 $11,000		**1990** $30,000	
1994 $20,000		**1998** $30,000	
1982-2000 RETURN 6%			
2000-2010 10%			

1953
BUICK SKYLARK

An exciting, limited-production convertible in the Roadmaster series. Styled by Harley Earl, it prefigured

1953 Skylark convertible

some appearance features of later production Buicks. It was essentially a cut-down version of the standard convertible with a sectioned windshield and body-sides. Though it lacked Buick's trademark portholes, it rode on standard Kelsey-Hayes chrome wire wheels. It also boasted the hottest Buick V-8, tinted glass, "Selectronic" radio with power antenna, and whitewall tires. One of the all-time great Buicks.

FOR Limited production • Ultra-clean, distinctive styling • Performance • Luxury • Built in Buick's Golden Anniversary year • Milestone car status • Prices have held steady for ten years

AGAINST Expensive, even in 2000 dollars • Some Skylark-only parts scarce • Wire wheels can cost $2500 a set

PRODUCTION
1690

SPECIFICATIONS
Length (in.)	207.6
Wheelbase (in.)	121.5
Weight (lbs)	4315
Price (new)	$5000

ENGINE
cid/type	bhp	years
322/ohv V-8	188	1953

PRICES
FAIR	$20,000-30,000
GOOD	$30,000-40,000
FINE	$40,000-58,000

FINE EXAMPLE PRICE HISTORY
1982 $15,000		**1990** $55,000	
1994 $45,000		**1998** $58,000	
1982-2000 RETURN 8%			
2000-2010 3%			

1954
BUICK SKYLARK

1954 Skylark convertible

The Skylark became a separate Buick model this year, but because so few were sold owing to the high price, it was discontinued for 1955. Unlike the '53 model, the '54's body wasn't sectioned, but wheel wells were still full cutouts, ornamentation was unique, and touches like rear fender sculpturing and large chrome tailfins set the Skylark apart from other '54 Buicks.

FOR Alternative to the '53 Skylark • Unique styling features • Performance • Quite rare (not many survive) • Milestone car status

AGAINST Less distinguished than its predecessor • Styling dated now

PRODUCTION
836

SPECIFICATIONS
Length (in.)	206.3
Wheelbase (in.)	122.0
Weight (lbs)	4260
Price (new)	$4483

ENGINES
cid/type	bhp	years
322/ohv V-8	200	1954

PRICES
FAIR	$16,000-28,000
GOOD	$28,000-40,000
FINE	$40,000-50,000

FINE EXAMPLE PRICE HISTORY
1982 $14,000		**1990** $48,000	
1994 $47,500		**1998** $50,000	
1982-2000 RETURN 8%			
2000-2010 10%			

1954-57
BUICK CENTURY

The return of Buick's prewar "factory hot rod." These sportier models

1956 Century convertible

remain reasonably affordable collector's items, though perhaps not much longer, as prices have escalated recently. Century's traditional formula of a big Buick engine in the shorter, lighter Buick platform worked well in these years, particularly 1954-55. Styling is good despite massive size; construction and quality also good except 1957, when it deteriorated. Very fast despite bulk—genuine 100-mph cruisers. A cheaper alternative to a Skylark for '50s Flint fanciers, and superb on the highway. Underrated '57s are included here mainly for styling (a sleeker interpretation of Buick's basic mid-'50s look) and that rare novelty, the Caballero hardtop wagon. Be aware, though, that they're bigger, heavier, and less rewarding to drive.

FOR Still relatively affordable • Outstanding performance • Quite maneuverable (1954-56 particularly so) • Readily available • Nice period styling

AGAINST High fuel (and, some say, oil) consumption • Future price appreciation cloudy • '57 workmanship, roadability

PRODUCTION

1954 conv 2790 **Riviera htp cpe** 45,710 **1955 conv** 5588 **Riviera htp cpe** 80,338 **Riviera htp sdn** 55,088 **1956 conv** 4721 **Riviera htp sdn** 33,334 **Riviera htp sdn** 20,891 **Riviera Deluxe htp sdn** 35,082 **1957 conv** 4085 **Riviera htp cpe** 17,029 **Riviera htp sdn** 26,589 **Caballero 4d htp wgn** 10,186

SPECIFICATIONS

Length (in.)	206.3 (1954), 206.6 (1955), 205.5 (1956), 208.5 (1957)
Wheelbase (in.)	122.0
Weight (lbs)	3795-4230
Price (new)	$2530-3600

ENGINES

cid/type	bhp	years
322/ohv V-8	200/236/220/255	1954-56
364/ohv V-8	300	1957

PRICES

2d htp	
FAIR	$7200-10,000
GOOD	$10,000-13,000
FINE	$13,000-16,000
Conv	
FAIR	$14,500-16,000
GOOD	$16,000-25,000
FINE	$25,000-40,000

FINE CONVERTIBLE PRICE HISTORY

1982 $6500	1990 $45,000
1994 $38,000	1998 $40,000
1982-2000 RETURN 9%	
2000-2010 10%	

1958
BUICK LIMITED

1958 Limited convertible

All the styling excesses of the decade are wrapped up in this bloated, overdecorated kitsch-wagon. It thus has a sort of reverse snob appeal for some; for example, a Detroit stylist commutes to work in a pink convertible. Fine craftsmanship and high-quality interiors. Relatively immune to rust, though chrome plating bills will be high if all that brightwork ever needs attention. Not for everyone, but there's no bigger or flashier example of the best and worst in late-'50s American cars.

FOR One-year-only styling and series • Powerful V-8, smooth automatic

AGAINST Dreadful styling • High thirst • Gargantuan size • Barge-like handling • Limited appreciation potential

PRODUCTION

2d htp 1026 **4d htp** 5571 **conv** 839

SPECIFICATIONS

Length (in.)	227.1
Wheelbase (in.)	127.5
Weight (lbs)	4603-4710
Price (new)	$5002-5125

ENGINES

cid/type	bhp	years
364/ohv V-8	300	1958

PRICES

2d htp	
FAIR	$9000-11,000
GOOD	$11,000-16,000
FINE	$16,000-18,000
Conv	
FAIR	$24,000-30,000
GOOD	$30,000-38,000
FINE	$38,000-41,000

FINE CONVERTIBLE PRICE HISTORY

1982 $8000	1990 $50,000
1994 $52,000	1998 $41,000
1982-2000 RETURN 11%	
2000-2010 7%	

1959-60
BUICK ELECTRA & INVICTA 2-DOORS

The best of the "Buicks so new even the names had to be new!" The '59s were a sharp break with Flint's recent past—along with other '59 GM cars, which comprised a hasty response to Chrysler's instant-hit '57s. The Buicks were longer, wider, and much lower, but also shapelier and less glittery. Hardtops had Chrysler-like thin-section rooflines, and Buick's huge canted tailfins were tasteful, if startling. The latter were rounded off on the clumsier-looking '60s. Invicta picked up from Century as the "hot Buick"; Electra/Electra 225 were what Roadmaster/Limited had been. Engineering advances ran to a lower-riding K-brace frame (ousting the '57-vintage X-member affair), a V-8 enlarged to 401 cubes (low-line LeSabres retained a 364), and two '58 options: "Flight-Pitch" or Triple-Turbine Dynaflow automatic (an alternate to the Twin-Turbine unit standard on Invicta/Electra) and "Air Poise" suspension, a troublesome $188 extra

1959 Electra hardtop sedan

that vanished after 1960. Models not included here have also begun rising in collector esteem, but we think these two-doors have better investment potential.

➕ FOR Wild '59 styling epitomizes tailfin era • Smooth, no-sweat performance • Comfy • Still very affordable • Low original production of some models

➖ AGAINST Big, clumsy, and thirsty • Workmanship way down from mid-'50s Buicks • Hammed-up '60 styling • Not considered "great" Buicks

PRODUCTION

1959 Invicta htp cpe 11,451 **conv** 5447 **Electra htp cpe** 11,216 **Electra** 225 **1960 Invicta htp cpe** 8960 **conv** 5236 **Electra htp cpe** 7416 **Electra** 225 **conv** 6746

SPECIFICATIONS

Length (in.)	217.4/217.9 (1959/60 Invicta), 220.6/221.2 (Electra), 225.4/225.9 (Electra 225)
Wheelbase (in.)	123.0 (Invicta), 126.3 (Electras)
Weight (lbs)	4275-4570
Price (new)	$3447-$4192

ENGINES

cid/type	bhp	years
401/ohv V-8	325	1959-60

PRICES

Conv	
FAIR	$9000-13,000
GOOD	$13,000-18,000
FINE	$18,000-25,000
2d hardtops	
FAIR	$4000-6000
GOOD	$6000-9000
FINE	$9000-13,000

1960 Invicta hardtop coupe

FINE CONVERTIBLE PRICE HISTORY

1982 $5500		**1990** $32,000	
1994 $24,000		**1998** $25,000	
1982-2000 RETURN 8%			
2000-2010 8%			

FINE HARDTOP PRICE HISTORY

1982 $3400		**1990** $8000	
1994 $7500		**1997** $13,000	
1982-2000 RETURN 8%			
2000-2010 5%			

1961-62 BUICK ELECTRA 225 & INVICTA 2-DOORS

1961 Electra hardtop coupe

More underappreciated big Buicks. Standard Electra was canceled for '62, so its hardtop coupe became a "deuce and a quarter," and the Invicta was soon supplanted as the "performance Buick" by the Wildcat line, perhaps because buyers liked that name better. GM's '61 cars were the first to fully reflect the influence of Bill Mitchell, Harley Earl's successor as corporate design chief. Buick fared as well as any GM division, losing dogleg windshields and needless bulk while becoming simpler and more dignified. The '62s were arguably cleaner still, if more visually massive. A novelty that year was "convertible-look" ribbing for

hardtop coupe rooflines. As in 1959-60, Buick four-door hardtops and sedans offered four- or six-window styling, though not in every series, but collectors covet the two-doors. They're the best of this Buick bunch save the bucket-seated '62 Wildcat (see entry).

➕ FOR As for 1959-60 Invicta/Electra, but more tasteful appearance • Somewhat better economy • Improved workmanship • Huge gains in value over past decade

➖ AGAINST Plenty of interest value but questionable appreciation • Still overshadowed by Buicks before and after

PRODUCTION

1961 Invicta htp cpe 6382 **conv** 3953 **Electra htp cpe** 4250 **Electra** 225 **conv** 7158 **1962 Invicta htp cpe** 10,335 **conv** 13,471 **Electra** 225 **htp cpe** 8922 **conv** 7894

SPECIFICATIONS

Length (in.)	213.2/214.1 (1961/62 Invicta), 219.2/220 (Electra)
Wheelbase (in.)	123.0 (Invicta), 126.0 (Electra 225)
Weight (lbs)	4100-4400
Price (new)	$3447-4366

ENGINES

cid/type	bhp	years
401/ohv V-8	325	1961-62

PRICES

FAIR	$2500-10,000
GOOD	$10,000-15,000
FINE	$15,000-24,000

FINE EXAMPLE PRICE HISTORY

1982 $2500		**1990** $9000	
1994 $17,000		**1997** $24,000	
1982-2000 RETURN 14%			
2000-2010 7%			

1961-63 BUICK SPECIAL SKYLARK

Highly underrated pioneer of the sporty compact idea. Ideal transportation now for those collectors who'd prefer to drive a pleasant everyday car that can be sold later for more than they paid for it. Values should keep pace with the rate of inflation, and may even exceed it slightly. Convertibles are naturally more desirable than the coupes, and more expensive. Buick's aluminum V-8 gives decent go. An efficient V-6 was available for 1962-63, and delivers good economy. Quality and luxury surprisingly good, with great attention paid to soundproofing for that big-car feel so

1962 Special Skylark convertible

beloved by Detroit. Still quite contemporary compared to much newer designs.

✚ **FOR** Attractive, if busy, styling • Good gas mileage • Compact size • Posh—look for optional leather bucket seats

▬ **AGAINST** Just beginning to be recognized as collectible • Some susceptibility to body rot • Body parts now scarce

PRODUCTION

1961 sport cpe 12,683 **1962 sport cpe** 34,060 **conv** 8913 **1963 sport cpe** 32,109 **conv** 10,212

SPECIFICATIONS

Length (in.)	188.4 (1961-62) 192.1 (1963)
Wheelbase (in.)	112.0 (1961) 112.1 (1962-63)
Weight (lbs)	2687-2871
Price (new)	$2621-3012

ENGINES

cid/type	bhp	years
215/ohv V-8	155/185/200	1961-63
198/ohv V-6	135	1962-63

PRICES

FAIR	$3300-6800
GOOD	$6800-9700
FINE	$9700-17,000

FINE EXAMPLE PRICE HISTORY

1982 $4000		**1990** $16,000	
1994 $16,000		**1997** $17,000	
1982-2000 RETURN 8%			
2000-2010 5%			

1 9 6 2 - 6 4
BUICK WILDCAT

F lint's first full-size buckets-and-console car. Bowed during '62 as a solitary hardtop coupe in the mid-range Invicta line, then expanded to supplant it entirely by '64. The name harked back to three mid-'50s Motorama

1963 Buick Wildcat hardtop coupe

showmobiles; the body/chassis package was shared with low-line LeSabre. Extra tinsel and standard vinyl roof marked the debut model, still arguably the most desirable of these Wildcats if for no other reason than low production. But 1963-64 convertibles were hardly abundant. Buick styling was more crisply tailored in these years, and bigger V-8s gave better performance despite some added mass. As with other Detroit collectibles, the hardtop sedans here are possible "comers" because so many ragtops and pillarless two-doors have been spoken for. Wildcats became fat cats after 1964 and de-emphasized sporty features—two reasons for sticking with these three model years.

✚ **FOR** Handsome • Potent, unstressed V-8s • Snazzy interiors • Comfortable long-haul touring ability • '62's rarity

▬ **AGAINST** Fuel thirst • Rather big to be practical around town • Less exclusive 1963-64s not high-return investments (and forget the 4d sedan)

PRODUCTION

1962 htp cpe 2000 **1963 htp cpe** 12,185 **htp sdn** 17,519 **conv** 6021 **1964 htp cpe** 22,893 **htp sdn** 33,358 **conv** 7850 **4d sdn** 20,144

SPECIFICATIONS

Length (in.)	214.1/215.7/222.8 (1962/63/64)
Wheelbase (in.)	123.0
Weight (lbs)	4025-4230
Price (new)	$3927-$3961

ENGINES

cid/type	bhp	years
401/ohv V-8	325	1962-64
425/ohv V-8	340/360	1964

PRICES

Htp	
FAIR	$2000-4000
GOOD:	$4000-6000
FINE	$6000-8000
Conv	
FAIR	$5000-10,000
GOOD	$10,000-13,000
FINE	$13,000-18,000

FINE CONVERTIBLE PRICE HISTORY

1982 $4700		**1990** $20,000	
1994 $18,000		**1998** $18,000	
1982-2000 RETURN 6%			
2000-2010 5%			

1 9 6 3 - 6 5
BUICK RIVIERA

1964 Riviera hardtop coupe

B ill Mitchell's magnificent anti-Thunderbird, offered as a hardtop coupe only. Originally intended for Cadillac as a new LaSalle, but awarded to a flagging Buick Division as it neared production. One of the outstanding GM designs of the '60s, respected by an army of industrial designers. Has already gained high repute among collectors for its beautiful lines, personal-luxury character, and smooth performance. Definitely one of the big guns among collectible Sixties Buicks, and high on the list of every serious investor in the marque. Hidden headlights the main styling change for '65. The 1963 original seems to have a slight lead in collector preference.

✚ **FOR** Landmark design one of the best of the 1960s • Milestone car status • Outstanding construction quality • Buckets-and-consoles appeal • Performance

▬ **AGAINST** Bulk • Fuel consumption

PRODUCTION

1963 40,000 **1964** 37,658 **1965** 34,586

SPECIFICATIONS

Length (in.)	208.0
Wheelbase (in.)	117.0

Weight (lbs)	3988-4036	
Price (new)	$4333-4408	

ENGINES

cid/type	bhp	years
401/ohv V-8	325	1963-65
425/ohv V-8	340/360	1964-65

PRICES

FAIR	$4000-6000
GOOD	$6000-8000
FINE	$8000-15,000

FINE EXAMPLE PRICE HISTORY

1982 $4500	**1990** $16,000
1994 $15,000	**1998** $15,000
1982-2000 RETURN 6%	
2000-2010 5%	

1965-67

BUICK SKYLARK GRAN SPORT

1965 Skylark Gran Sport hardtop coupe

Buick's mid-size hot rod of the mid-'60s. Introduced as an option package for the Skylark coupe, hardtop, and convertible, then graduated to separate-series status for 1966. Power in the first two years came from the big-block 401 V-8 from the full-size Buicks, the pentroof engine that dated from Buick's original 1953 "Fireball" ohv V-8. For 1967, an all-new block arrived with semi-wedge heads, and the model designation changed to GS400. That same year, Buick introduced a junior muscle car, the GS340, powered by an enlarged version of its small-block V-8, and front disc brakes were added to the options list. All Gran Sports were built on the heavier convertible chassis, and had a heavy-duty suspension and the requisite scoops, stripes, and bulges as battle dress. Quite quick (0-60 mph came up in as little as 6.0 seconds flat according to one contemporary road test), the GS was also one of the better-handling performance machines of the era, and had Buick's customary luxury and solid construction quality. Prices escalated during the '80s, making this a good alternative to an Olds 4-4-2 or Pontiac GTO. The low-production convertibles are naturally the

most desirable models.

➕ **FOR** Fast • Very roadable • Not over-sized for today • Solid Buick quality • Handsome furnishings • Deft styling

➖ **AGAINST** Very thirsty (requires high octane gas) • Juvenile "go-faster" add-ons • Body parts supplies have dried up

PRODUCTION

1965 2d cpe 11,877 **2d htp** 47,034 **conv** 10,456
1966 2d cpe 1835 **2d htp** 9934 **conv** 2047 **1967**
2d cpe 1014 **2d htp** 10,659 **2d conv** 2140

SPECIFICATIONS

Length (in.)	203.4 (1965), 204.0 (1966), 205.0 (1967)
Wheelbase (in.)	115.0
Weight (lbs)	3283-3505
Price (new)	$2845-3167

ENGINES

cid/type	bhp	years
340/ohv V-8	260	1967
401/ohv V-8	325/340	1965-66
400/ohv V-8	340/360	1967

PRICES

Conv	
FAIR	$4000-8000
GOOD	$8000-11,000
FINE	$11,000-16,000
(Deduct 30% for htp and cpe)	

FINE 1967 GS400 CONVERTIBLE PRICE HISTORY

1982 $3200	**1990** $14,000
1994 $14,000	**1998** $16,000
1982-2000 RETURN 8%	
2000-2010 10%	

1966-67

BUICK RIVIERA

Rarely does Detroit follow one design triumph with another, but the second-generation Riviera was an exception. Larger than the original 1963-65 series, it

was nonetheless deftly executed, with flowing lines that also managed to incorporate the traditional British "razor edge" school exemplified by Hooper-bodied Rolls-Royces. Particularly desirable is the GS (Gran Sport), a package option that included Positraction rear axle, cast aluminum rocker covers, chrome air cleaner, whitewalls, road wheels, and special trim.

➕ **FOR** Less costly than 1963-65 Riviera • Beautiful styling • Milestone car status • Quickness • Roadability (GS)

➖ **AGAINST** Extreme thirst (down to single digits at times) • Too large for its four-passenger capacity

PRODUCTION

1966 45,348 **1967** 42,799

SPECIFICATIONS

Length (in.)	211.3
Wheelbase (in.)	119.0
Weight (lbs)	4180-4190
Price (new)	$4424-4469

ENGINES

cid/type	bhp	years
401/ohv V-8	340	1966
430/ohv V-8	360	1967

PRICES

FAIR	$2500-4500
GOOD	$4500-7500
FINE	$7500-11,000

FINE EXAMPLE PRICE HISTORY

1982 $4200	**1990** $8500
1994 $9500	**1998** $11,000
1982-2000 RETURN 4%	
2000-2010 5%	

1968-72

BUICK GS

Continuation of Buick's mid-size stormer, with all-new styling on GM's split-wheelbase—112 inches on two-doors, 116 on four-doors—A-body

1966 Riviera hardtop coupe

1970 GSX hardtop coupe

platform. A slight bore increase on the Buick small-block V-8 turned the previous GS340 into the GS350. The GS400 continued as before, augmented at mid-1968 model year by the hot Stage I option for the big-block, which included a high-lift cam, reworked carb, and free-flow exhaust system. For 1970, GM rescinded its unwritten ban on intermediates with less than 10 pounds per horsepower, so Buick bolted in its big-car 455 V-8. The GS350 became just plain GS. A mid-season arrival was the GSX, an $888 package option featuring front and rear spoilers, striping, hood-mounted tach, and four-speed manual transmission. Power began to be watered down starting in 1971, but a Stage 1 455 could still scamper from rest to 60 mph in 6.5 seconds. The GSX was dropped for 1972, but the 455 carried on, now rated in SAE net horsepower figures. A new-generation Buick intermediate, the Century, debuted for '73. The GS reverted to being a package option, convertibles disappeared, and appearance was more subdued, but it was still fairly hot. However, we think the desirable Buick muscle cars end with the '72s. The low-production convertibles became much sought-after during the Eighties.

FOR Handsome looks • Great performance • Capable handling • Ragtops' rarity • Atypical models for Buick

AGAINST As for 1965-67 Skylark Gran Sport

PRODUCTION
1968 GS350 2d htp 10,530 **GS400 2d htp** 10,743 **GS400 conv** 2454 **1969 GS350 2d htp** 4933 **GS400 2d htp** 6456 **GS400 conv** 1776 **1970 GS 2d htp** 9948 **GS455 2d htp** 8732 **GS455 conv** 1416 **1971 GS 2d htp** 8268 **conv** 902 **1972 GS 2d htp** 7723 **conv** 852

SPECIFICATIONS
Length (in.) 200.7 (1968-70), 203.3 (1971-72)

Wheelbase (in.)	112.0
Weight (lbs)	3375-3700
Price (new)	$2926-5350

ENGINES

cid/type	bhp	years
350/ohv V-8	280	1968-72
400/ohv V-8	340/360	1968-69
455/ohv V-8	315-360[1]	1970-72

[1]rated at 250 bhp SAE net in 1972; Stage I rated at 270 bhp net

PRICES

Htp	
FAIR	$3500-7000
GOOD	$7000-9000
FINE	$9000-12,000
Conv	
FAIR	$5000-8500
GOOD	$8500-12,000
FINE	$12,000-18,000

FINE GS400 CONVERTIBLE PRICE HISTORY

1982 $3700		**1990** $16,000	
1994 $18,000		**1998** $18,000	
1982-2000 RETURN 9%			
2000-2010 7%			

1971-73
BUICK RIVIERA

1973 Riviera hardtop coupe (non-standard fender vents)

Buick's third generation personal-luxury car, with controversial "boat-tail" styling for these three years. Tapered fastback roof evoked memories of '30s Auburn Speedsters, and reflected a penchant for "classic

design" motifs that afflicted GM styling chief Bill Mitchell late in his career. Gerald Hirshberg ultimately took credit—and blame—for the basic shape. Far more sculptured but far more massive than earlier Rivs, but only a little less popular. Less a "driver's car" too, making the $200 GS performance package—wide tires, uprated suspension, shorter final drive, tighter Turbo Hydra-Matic transmission—as worthwhile now as then. Other interesting extras were automatic climate control and anti-spin "Max Trac," an embryonic traction-control system. Not exactly slow at under 10 seconds 0-60, but power fell after '71 with stricter emissions tuning. Abbreviated boattail and ugly front "safety" bumper for '73, then an ordinary squared-up roofline and little distinction until the handsome front-drive '79 Riv. Mentioned mainly for "oddball value," but these cars are being saved and could well become truly collectible, though probably not for some time.

FOR That styling • Big and plush • Great highway cruiser • Fairly cheap

AGAINST That styling • Too big and plush for some • Erratic build quality • Not a quick-return investment

PRODUCTION
1971 33,810 **1972** 33,728 **1973** 34,080

SPECIFICATIONS

Length (in.)	217.4/218.3/223.4 (1971/72/73)
Wheelbase (in.)	122.0
Weight (lbs)	4325-4490
Price (new)	$5149-5253

ENGINES

cid/type	bhp	years
455/ohv V-8	330[1]	1971
455/ohv V-8	250/260/270[2]	1972-73

[1]SAE gross [2]SAE net

PRICES

FAIR	$2000-4000
GOOD	$4000-6000
FINE	$6000-8000

FINE EXAMPLE PRICE HISTORY

1982 $3000		**1990** $6500	
1994 $6500		**1998** $8000	
1982-2000 RETURN 6%			
2000-2010 5%			

1982
BUICK GRAND NATIONAL

Regal-based trim package created to exploit Buick's success on the NASCAR circuit. Silver-gray and charcoal-gray two-toning, plus stripes and

1982 Grand National coupe

other accents, were eye-catching but this Grand National looked meaner that it really was. A 4.1-liter V-6 produced a mild 125 bhp—sufficient to make the GN a reasonably brisk performer, but one easily outclassed by the relatively mild Camaros and Firebirds of the day, and even by its less flashy sibling, the turbocharged Regal T-Type. Still, the '82 Grand National was a great-looking car, and the fact that just 215 were built for the model year would seem to make collectibility obvious.

⊞ **FOR** Low production • Striking good looks • Easy to repair and maintain

◼ **AGAINST** More show than go • Neither as fast nor as desirable as Grand Nationals that came later in the decade

PRODUCTION
215

SPECIFICATIONS

Length (in.)	200.6
Weight (lbs)	3152
Wheelbase (in.)	108.1
Price (new)	$9728

ENGINES

liter/type/(cid)	bhp	years
4.1/ohv V-6 (252)	125	1982

PRICES

FAIR	$3000-5000
GOOD	$5000-7500
FINE	$7500-11,000
2000-2010 5%	

1982-85
BUICK RIVIERA CONVERTIBLE

Flint's first "factory" drop-top following a seven-year hiatus, though technically a conversion, by American Sunroof Corp. in Lansing also the first

1983 Riviera convertible

top-down Riviera. Based on the first front-drive Riv, one of three downsized 1979 E-body models (along with Cadillac's Eldorado and Oldsmobile's Toronado). Convertible shared appearance, appointments, and most mechanicals with closed 1982-85 Rivs, but few if any were built with the turbocharged V-6 from the sporty T-type coupe. Among standards were power top with heated glass backlight, leather interior, know-nothing dash, the usual full power kit, and four-speed overdrive Turbo Hydra-Matic transaxle. Coupe's body-on-frame construction made conversion straightforward, but structural flex was only on a par with late-'60s ragtops. A rather mushy handler, too. Dropped with the 1986 switch to yet another downsized Riviera, which proved too small to make into a ragtop with a decently wide back seat.

⊞ **FOR** Pleasant and practical latter-day convertible • Big, smooth, and luxurious • Easy to live with

◼ **AGAINST** Dull performance • Roly-poly handling • Mediocre mileage • Prone to many squeaks and rattles • A "distant classic" at best

PRODUCTION
1982 1248 **1983** 1750 **1984** 500 **1985** 400

SPECIFICATIONS

Length (in.)	206.6
Wheelbase (in.)	114.0
Weight (lbs)	3980
Price (new)	$23,995-$26,797

ENGINES

cid/type	bhp	years
231/ohv V-6[1]	190	1982-85
252/ohv V-6	125	1982-84
307/ohv V-8	140	1982-85

[1]Turbocharged

PRICES

FAIR	$3000-6000
GOOD	$6000-8000
FINE	$8000-10,000

FINE EXAMPLE PRICE HISTORY

1994 $6,000
1998 $10,000
1994-2000 RETURN 5%
2000-2010 3%

1985-87
BUICK REGAL GRAND NATIONAL & GNX

1987 Regal GNX coupe

Buick's brief but glorious mid-'80s return to late-'60s muscle. Like its GS forebears, the Grand National started with a mid-size Buick: the 1978-vintage Regal coupe in turbo V-6 T-type form. Initially differed mostly in suspension tuning and full blackout exterior, but further development, including more precise sequential fuel injection, ultimately produced 245 horsepower and 0-60 times of under 5 seconds. More potent still was the derivative 1987 GNX, a joint Buick-McLaren Engines-American Sunroof effort with an alleged 300 bhp—later proved to be 276 actual—thanks in part to a "smarter" engine-computer chip. That one did 0-60 in 4.7 seconds by one account, the standing quarter-mile in 13.5 seconds at 102 mph, this despite a still-mandatory four-speed automatic transmission. For tire-smoking thrills, only a Corvette could touch these blocky bombs. But their days were soon numbered by Buick's retreat from overt performance toward "premium" cars like the 1988 front-drive Regal, though a handful of GNs—not GNXs—were built after other rear-drive Regals departed. GNX's low announced production started a bidding frenzy among would-be owners, and the same supply/demand factor will make it the most coveted of Flint's final factory hot rods.

FOR Spectacular acceleration • Rarity • Buick's last muscle cars • Still-favorable parts/service situation

AGAINST Darth Vader outside, Roseanne Barr inside • Chassis overwhelmed by engine torque • Stiff ride • Spotty workmanship • Bound to have been thrashed by first owners

PRODUCTION

1985 2102 **1986** 5512 **1987** 20193 **1987 GNX** 547

SPECIFICATIONS

Length (in.)	200.6
Wheelbase (in.)	108.1
Weight (lbs)	3250-3545
Price (new)	$13,315-29,290

ENGINES

cid/type	bhp	years
231/ohv V-6[1]	200/235/245/276	1985-87

[1]Turbocharged

PRICES

GRAND NATIONAL	
FAIR	$6000-10,000
GOOD	$10,000-17,500
FINE	$17,500-22,500
GNX	
FAIR	$7500-19,000
GOOD	$19,000-26,000
FINE	$26,000-34,000

FINE GNX PRICE HISTORY

1994 $16,000   **1998** $33,000
1994-2000 RETURN 14%
2000-2010 10%

1988-91
BUICK REATTA

Flint's reply to the Mercedes SL and, more pointedly, the Cadillac Allante—a bid for the luxury two-seat convertible market. Essentially a 1986-generation Riviera with unique coupe styling on a shortened wheelbase, but with the same front-wheel drivetrain with a transverse-mounted V-6 pulling a four-speed automatic transaxle, all-disc brakes—and almost the same length and weight. Also shared Riv's digi-graphic instruments and never-liked Graphic Control Center touch-sensitive "TV screen" for climate control/audio/trip computer adjustments, plus trouble readouts. The 1990s had a more rational panel (also applied to the Riv) with conventional controls and analog gauges. Buick's usual firmed-up Gran Touring suspension was available—and recommended, as handling was flaccid with stock calibrations. Companion convertible, planned all along but delayed by development bothers (mostly with its manual folding top) finally appeared for '90. But by then it was clear the Reatta experiment had failed. Another 1313 coupes and just 305 convertibles were built for '91 before Buick pulled the plug. Production over four years of 21,850 units was only equal to the more optimistic initial estimate for a single year, and that's why the Reatta died.

FOR A pleasant, refined tourer for two • Tidy styling • Gadgets abound • Convertible's rarity and likely strong appreciation • Parts/service still widely available • "Failed experiment" appeal for some

AGAINST No sports car • No Mercedes SL, either • Uninspiring performance • Values won't rise for some years yet

PRODUCTION

1988 cpe 4708 **1989 cpe** 7009 **1990 cpe** 6383
1990 conv 2132 **1991** 2304

SPECIFICATIONS

Length (in.)	183.5
Wheelbase (in.)	98.4

Weight (lbs)	3400-3560
Price (new)	$25,000-$34,995

ENGINES

cid/type	bhp	years
231/ohv V-6	165	1988-90

PRICES

Convertible	
FAIR	$8000-12,000
GOOD	$12,000-17,500
FINE	$17,500-21,000

Coupe: 50% convertible prices

FINE 1991 CONVERTIBLE PRICE HISTORY

1994 Still depreciating
1998 $15,000
2000-2010 5%

1995-99
BUICK RIVIERA/SILVER ARROW

1995 Riviera coupe

Declining sales and a general lack of buyer interest in larger coupes prompted Buick to announce in September 1998 that Riviera production would cease, just four model years after a redesign that was longer and heavier than its predecessor. Acceleration from available V-6s was brisk, and better than that of coupes costing thousands more. Body design successfully blended aggressiveness with Buick-style conservatism. Interior design was less successful. Still, this was a better-than-competent car that celebrated its demise with 200 copies of a paint-and-trim variant called Silver Arrow.

FOR Overall competence and good looks • Limited production (standard Riviera) • Minuscule production (Silver Arrow) • Ride and handling • Used-car prices

AGAINST Mediocre dash design and ergonomics • "Factory collectibles" (Silver Arrow) are seldom collectible

PRODUCTION

NA

1991 Reatta coupe

SPECIFICATIONS

Length (in.)	207.2
Weight (lbs)	3742
Wheelbase (in.)	113.8
Price (new)	$27,632-32,500

ENGINES

liter/type/(cid)	bhp	years
3.8/ohv V-6 (231)	205	1995-97
3.8/ohv V-6 (231)[1]	225	1995
3.8/ohv V-6 (231)[1]	240	1996-99

[1]Supercharged

PRICES

Used car market determines current value.
2000-2010 RETURN Still depreciating

1930-35
CADILLAC EIGHT

1932 V-8 convertible coupe

Certified CCCA Classics and the high point of Cadillac luxury and design in the prewar years, although the Depression caused production to drop drastically after 1932. Not numerous enough now to establish firm price guidelines for individual models. The 353-cid V-8 was based on the 341-cid L-head unit introduced in 1928, one of the great eights of the golden age. Square-rigged styling began to disappear in 1932 and was entirely late-'30s streamlined by 1934. Notable engineering feats peppered this period: "Syncro-Mesh" transmission in 1929, helical-cut synchronized gears in 1932, "No-Draft Ventilation" and vacuum-assisted brakes in 1933, independent front suspension in 1934, all-steel bodies in 1935. Aside from a switch to a new L-head eight in 1936, there were other quality downgrades that have prevented post-1935 models from being cited as Classics across-the-board. In all, very fine cars—connoisseurs' pieces through 1933—but only for the wealthy today.

◧ FOR CCCA Classic status • Superb styling through 1933, excellent through 1935 • 353-cid V-8 one of the great Classic powerplants • High appreciation potential

◪ AGAINST Extremely expensive,

especially open models • Costly to restore • Hard to find even if you have the money

PRODUCTION

1930 11,005 **1931** 10,709 **1932** 2693 **1933** 2906 **1934** 5080 **1935** 3209

SPECIFICATIONS

Length (in.)	NA
Wheelbase (in.)	140.0 (1930) ;134.0, 140.0 (1931-33); 128.0 Series 10, 136.0 Series 20, 146.0 Series 30 (1934-35)
Weight (lbs)	4355-5650
Price (new)	$2645-5695

ENGINES

cid/type	bhp	years
353.0/sv V-8	95/130	1930-35

PRICES

Closed	
FAIR	$7500-17,000
GOOD	$17,000-33,000
FINE	$33,000-50,000
Open	
FAIR	$15,000-40,000
GOOD	$40,000-80,000
FINE	$80,000-140,000

(Fleetwood bodies: add 10-20%)

FINE 1930 ALL-WEATHER FLEETWOOD IMPERIAL LIMOUSINE PRICE HISTORY

1982 $60,000		**1990** $90,000	
1994 $120,000		**1998** $140,000	

1982-2000 RETURN 5%
2000-2010 5%

1930-37
CADILLAC SIXTEEN

The all-time great among Cadillacs, with a gem of an overhead-valve V-16 engine producing 165 bhp and 320 lbs/ft torque. Initially available in 33 different models, sub-models, or trim variations, it returned eight miles

1930 V-16 convertible coupe

per gallon and would do 90 mph. The division used its longest wheelbases and most elaborate bodies and accoutrements for the Sixteens, which sold for $4700 and up—usually far up. Cadillac described its performance fairly accurately as "a continuous flow...constantly at full-volume efficiency...flexible...instantly responsive."

◧ FOR A great locomotive of a car and avidly admired • Very high investment and appreciation potential • Scarcity of all body styles makes each car a rarity • CCCA Classic status

◪ AGAINST Towering purchase price and running costs • Restorations should not be undertaken unless the individual model is very special

PRODUCTION

1930-31 3250 **1932** 296 **1933** 125 **1934** 60 **1935** 50 **1936** 52 **1937** 49

SPECIFICATIONS

Length (in.)	NA
Wheelbase (in.)	148.0 (1930-31); 143.0, 149.0 (1932-33); 154.0 (1934-37)
Weight (lbs)	5115-6450
Price (new)	$4695-9250

ENGINES

cid/type	bhp	years
452.0/ohv V-16	165	1930-37

PRICES

Closed	
FAIR	$20,000-80,000

1934 V-16 coupe by Fleetwood

GOOD	$80,000-150,000
FINE	$150,000-250,000
Open	
FAIR	$40,000-150,000
GOOD	$150,000-250,000
FINE	$250,000-375,000

(Madam X add 25%; Fisher bodies deduct 10%; Post-1934 deduct 30% from above prices.)

FINE 1930 MADAM X ALL-WEATHER PHAETON PRICE HISTORY

1982 $150,000   **1990** $400,000
1994 $450,000   **1998** $375,000
1982-2000 RETURN 6%
2000-2010 8% (closed models, 5%)

1930-37
CADILLAC TWELVE

1932 V-12 All Weather Phaeton

A multi-cylinder companion to the Sixteen and announced nine months later. Basically the overhead-valve V-16 with four fewer cylinders and commensurately less power in smaller bodies mounted on a chassis shared with the Eights. Though not as fast as the Sixteen, the free-revving Twelve was well known for its smooth, even power, and it cost considerably less. The light roadster—$3945 in 1930—would approach 85 mph with the standard rear axle and can still cruise a modern Interstate at 70. As with the Sixteen, sales never recovered from the Depression, and the Twelve lingered on in diminishing volume until it was scrubbed from the Cadillac line in 1938.

➕ **FOR** Full CCCA Classic status • Elegant, luxurious body styles • High investment value

➖ **AGAINST** Expensive to buy and own • Not quite a Sixteen, and always takes a back seat in comparisons—unfairly

PRODUCTION

1930-31 5725 **1932** 1709 **1933** 952 **1934** 683 **1935** 377 **1936** 901 **1937** 474

SPECIFICATIONS

Length (in.) NA
Wheelbase (in.) 140.0, 143.0 for 7P (1930-31);

134.0 for rdstr, cpe, conv cpe; 140.0 for others (1932-33); 146.0 (1934-35); 131.0, 138.0 (1936-37)
Weight (lbs) 4800-6040
Price (new) $3145-6495

ENGINES

cid/type	bhp	years
368.0/ohv V-12	135/150	1930-37

PRICES

1930-33
Open	
FAIR	$23,000-100,000
GOOD	$100,000-160,000
FINE	$160,000-230,000
Closed	
FAIR	$12,000-60,000
GOOD	$60,000-100,000
FINE	$100,000-145,000

(Fisher bodies deduct 10%. Post-1931 deduct 20%)

1934-37
Open	
FAIR	$15,000-40,000
GOOD	$40,000-70,000
FINE	$70,000-100,000
Closed	
FAIR	$8000-16,000
GOOD	$16,000-30,000
FAIR	$30,000-50,000

(Fisher bodies deduct 10%)

FINE 1931 SERIES 370 ALL-WEATHER PHAETON PRICE HISTORY

1982 $86,000   **1990** $235,000
1994 $300,000   **1998** $230,000
1982-2000 RETURN 6%
2000-2010 8% (closed models 5%).

1938-41
CADILLAC SERIES SIXTY SPECIAL

A motoring masterpiece with watershed styling by young William L. Mitchell, who later relieved Harley Earl as GM design chief. Ranked by Cadillac enthusiasts as the marque's leading design accomplishment of the late '30s. Aimed at owner-drivers and sweepingly modern with pontoon fenders, and *sans* running boards and nonfunctional ornamentation. The distinct delineation of the lower body from the greenhouse using elegant, thin-frame side windows was notable. And thanks to the low-revving, high-torque L-head eight, the Sixty Special was a smooth performer. It was handsomely facelifted for 1941 on a revised chassis with more power and newly optional Hydra-Matic Drive. A fixture at Cadillac through the early '70s, it was much less special after '41.

➕ **FOR** One of the late-1930s greats • All are CCCA-rated Classics • A historic styling tour de force that looks as lovely as ever today • Still a fine investment

➖ **AGAINST** Very expensive and still climbing • High operating costs • More expensive to repair/restore than other models of the same year

PRODUCTION

1938 3703 **1939** sdn 5219 **sunroof sdn** 225 **sunroof Imperial** 55 **chassis** 7 **1940** sdn 4472 **division sdn** 110 **Town Car** 15 **1941** sdn 3878 **division sdn** 220 **Town Car** 1 **chassis** 1

SPECIFICATIONS

Length (in.) 208.8 approx.
Wheelbase (in.) 127.0 (1938-40); 126.0 (1941)
Weight (lbs) 4070-4485
Price (new) $2090-3820

ENGINES

cid/type	bhp	years
346.0/sv V-8	135	1938-40
346.0/sv V-8	150	1941

PRICES

FAIR	$7500-15,000
GOOD	$15,000-35,000
FINE	$35,000-50,000

FINE 1940 TOWN CAR PRICE HISTORY

1982 $16,000   **1990** $44,000

1940 Series 60 Special sedan

1941 Series 60 Special sedan

1994 $60,000 **1998** $50,000
1982-2000 RETURN 7%
2000-2010 5%

CADILLAC SERIES 90 SIXTEEN

1938 Series 90 V-16 limousine

Sixteen production was never more than a few hundred per year after 1933. Both the V-12 and original V-16 engines were dropped after 1937, but Cadillac offered a new L-head V-16 for three more model years. At 431 cid and 185 bhp, this powerplant was smaller and lighter but more powerful than the earlier jewel-like engine, but it's never received collector acclaim. The advent of precision-insert con rod bearings helped eliminate the traditional knock and engine wear of eights and sixes, which had occasioned multi-cylinder engines. Cadillac found it uneconomical to continue this

Sixteen past 1940 even though it shared its wheelbase and many body styles with the Series Seventy-Five. Few open models were built, most being Imperial and formal sedans.

➕ FOR Despite lesser reputation, flathead V-16 was smooth and near silent • All models have full Classic status • Luxury, refinement • Good roadability • A bit easier to acquire than pre-1938 models

➖ AGAINST Still very expensive • Extremely hard to find • Colossal restoration costs

PRODUCTION

1938 311 **1939** 136 **1940** 61

SPECIFICATIONS

Length (in.)	NA
Wheelbase (in.)	141.3
Weight (lbs)	4830-5330
Price (new)	$5140-7175

ENGINES

cid/type	bhp	years
431.O/sv V-16	185	1938-40

PRICES

Open	
FAIR	$20,000-45,000
GOOD	$45,000-80,000
FINE	$80,000-120,000
Closed	
FAIR	$15,000-40,000
GOOD	$40,000-70,000
FINE	$70,000-95,000

FINE 1939 CONVERTIBLE SEDAN PRICE HISTORY

1982 $70,000		**1990** $110,000	
1994 $120,000		**1998** $120,000	
1982-2000 RETURN 3%			
2000-2010 5%			

CADILLAC SERIES SEVENTY-FIVE

1949 Series Seventy-Five limousine

A long-running design—because of low production—but happily so good in the first place that nobody felt any need for change. The Seventy-Five remained basically in its prewar form for two years after the rest of the Cadillac line was restyled for 1948. Very well-built, solid cars with all the luxury one expects in a long-wheelbase limousine or formal sedan. Offered in a wide variety of body types, though most of those produced were variations of the seven-passenger sedan. A "Godfather" car for collectors who like their machines high, wide, handsome, and heavy.

➕ FOR Conservative design for the period • Quality • Luxury • Models through 1948 are CCCA-recognized Classics • Postwar models are Milestone cars

➖ AGAINST Too much bulk for many garages • High running costs

PRODUCTION

1941 cars **1949** chassis 155 **1942 cars** 1100 chassis 426 **1946 cars** 635 chassis 1292 **1947 cars** 2410 chassis 2626 **1948 cars** 1260 chassis 2069 **1949 cars** 1501 chassis 1861

SPECIFICATIONS

Length (in.)	225.8
Wheelbase (in.)	136.0 (chassis: 163.0)
Weight (lbs)	4750-4959
Price (new)	$2895-5199

ENGINES

cid/type	bhp	years
346/sv V-8	150	1942-48
331/ohv V-8	160	1949

PRICES

FAIR	$5000-12,000
GOOD	$12,000-20,000
FINE	$20,000-30,000

1982 $8300	**1990** $29,000
1994 $27,500	**1998** $30,000
1982-2000 RETURN 8%	
2000-2010 5%	

1 9 4 8 - 4 9
CADILLAC SERIES SIXTY-TWO CONVERTIBLE/SEDANET

1948 Series 62 Convertible

Elegantly beautiful Cadillacs, part of the first postwar redesign, and among the most graceful cars of the era. The fastback sedanet—also known as the club coupe—had the aura of the Classic "boattail" about it. The significant mechanical difference between the two model years was engines: the '48s ran with the last of the 346-cid flathead V-8s, while the '49s had the first of the pioneering 331-cid overhead-valve, high-compression units. Some collectors prefer the earlier engine, saying it is smoother and quieter, though the ohv unit provided more power and returned better mileage. Both years were almost identical in styling, though the '49 looked a little heavier in front. The '48 possessed a fine one-year-only drum-style instrument cluster; the '49 dash was more conventional.

+ FOR One of the great postwar American designs • High-demand item • Widely recognized for excellence

– AGAINST Fairly high running costs • Uninspired interiors

PRODUCTION
1948 conv 5450 **Sedanet** 4764 **1949 conv** 8000 **Sedanet** 7515

SPECIFICATIONS
Length (in.)	213.9
Wheelbase (in.)	126.0
Weight (lbs)	4125-4449
Price (new)	$2912-3442

ENGINES
cid/type	bhp	years
346/sv V-8	150	1948
331/ohv V-8	160	1949

PRICES
Conv	
FAIR	$9000-22,000
GOOD	$22,000-32,000
FINE	$32,000-38,000
Sedanet	
FAIR	$4000-8000
GOOD	$8000-13,000
FINE	$13,000-20,000

FINE CONVERTIBLE PRICE HISTORY
1982 $15,000	**1990** $42,000
1994 $40,000	**1998** $38,000
1982-2000 RETURN 5%	
2000-2010 5%	

1 9 4 8 - 4 9
CADILLAC SERIES SIXTY-ONE SEDANET

Slightly detrimmed (no front splash guard, for instance) parallel line to the Series Sixty-Two, originally priced about $200 lower and lacking a convertible. The Sixty-One Sedanet had the same fine styling attributes of its upper class cousin, and it carries Milestone car status.

+ FOR Somewhat rarer than the Sixty-Two Sedanet • A bit less costly on today's collector market • Lightest and fastest of the 1948-49 Cadillacs • Milestone-rated model

– AGAINST Slightly less flashy than the Sixty-Two (though some might consider that a plus) • Interior very plain for a Cadillac

1948 Series 61 Sedanet

PRODUCTION
1948 3521 **1949** 6409

SPECIFICATIONS
Length (in.)	213.9
Wheelbase (in.)	126.0
Weight (lbs)	3838-4068
Price (new)	$2728-2788

ENGINES
cid/type	bhp	years
346/sv V-8	150	1948
331/ohv V-8	160	1949

PRICES
FAIR	$4000-7500
GOOD	$7500-12,000
FINE	$12,000-18,000

FINE EXAMPLE PRICE HISTORY
1982 $6000	**1990** $21,000
1994 $20,000	**1998** $18,000
1982-2000 RETURN 6%	
2000-2010 5%	

1 9 4 9
CADILLAC SERIES SIXTY-TWO COUPE DeVILLE

A rare and highly desirable Milestone car that shares honors with the '49 Buick Roadmaster Riviera and Oldsmobile 98 Holiday as the first "hardtop convertibles." Lavishly upholstered in leather and vinyl, with bright metal strips on the headliner simulating convertible top bows. The 1950 and later models are collectible, too, but only the '49 holds Milestone status. Also, post-1949 Cadillacs were more ornate, especially in front.

+ FOR Pioneer hardtop • Loads of luxury • Rarity and consequent desir

1949 Series Sixty-Two Coupe DeVille

ability • Modern ohv V-8 • Milestone status

■ AGAINST Pricey and getting pricier • Hard to find now

PRODUCTION

2150

SPECIFICATIONS

Length (in.)	213.9
Wheelbase (in.)	126.0
Weight (lbs)	4033
Price (new)	$3497

ENGINES

cid/type	bhp	years
331/ohv V-8	160	1949

PRICES

FAIR	$7000-12,000
GOOD	$12,000-19,000
FINE	$19,000-25,000

FINE EXAMPLE PRICE HISTORY

1982 $9500	1990 $30,000
1994 $22,500	1998 $25,000
1982-2000 RETURN 5%	
2000-2010 5%	

1953
CADILLAC SERIES SIXTY-TWO ELDORADO

1953 Series Sixty-Two Eldorado convertible

Like the contemporary Buick Riviera and Oldsmobile Fiesta, a limited-production show car, and widely sought after because of this. Fortunately, quite a few have survived in proportion to the small number built. Cut-down body and "Panoramic" windshield, metal convertible boot, ultra-luxurious upholstery, and chrome plated wire wheels made it the sportiest Cadillac ever. Created quite a stir despite an eye-opening price.

■ FOR Historical importance • Exclusive styling features • Very desirable in Cadillac circles • High performance • Milestone car status

■ AGAINST Heavier-looking than the smooth 1948-49 models • Many body parts now virtually unobtainable • High price on today's market

PRODUCTION

532

SPECIFICATIONS

Length (in.)	215.8
Wheelbase (in.)	126.0
Weight (lbs)	4800
Price (new)	$7750

ENGINES

cid/type	bhp	years
331/ohv V-8	210	1953

PRICES

FAIR	$33,000-45,000
GOOD	$45,000-65,000
FINE	$65,000-80,000

FINE EXAMPLE PRICE HISTORY

1982 $16,000	1990 $90,000
1994 $95,000	1998 $80,000
1982-2000 RETURN 10%	
2000-2010 10%	

1954-55
CADILLAC ELDORADO

Continuation of the successful limited-production 1953 Eldorado, but

1955 Series Sixty-Two Eldorado convertible

priced quite a bit less and built in greater quantity. Like the 1954 Buick Skylark, far less "custom" in these years, sharing the basic Sixty-Two convertible body, but sporting an exclusive shark-fin rear end and round taillights. For 1955, the standard engine was a special high-performance version of the Cadillac V-8, offered on no other model that year. It had twin four-barrel carbs and 270 horsepower.

■ FOR More affordable than the '53 • Lots of luxury • Comparative rarity • Good investment • Parts not normally a problem • Milestone car status

■ AGAINST Larger and thirstier than the '53, too • Also less unique in appearance and engineering

PRODUCTION

1954 2150 **1955** 3950

SPECIFICATIONS

Length (in.)	223.4
Wheelbase (in.)	129.0
Weight (lbs)	4809-4815
Price (new)	$4738-6286

ENGINES

cid/type	bhp	years
331/ohv V-8	230/270	1954-55

PRICES

FAIR	$12,000-20,000
GOOD	$20,000-40,000
FINE	$40,000-55,000

FINE EXAMPLE PRICE HISTORY

1982 $12,000	1990 $80,000
1994 $50,000	1998 $55,000
1982-2000 RETURN 10%	
2000-2010 10%	

1956-58
CADILLAC ELDORADO BIARRITZ

Revised editions of the Eldorado convertible that didn't sell particularly well. Biarritz designation was new for '56 because there was now also a companion hardtop, the Seville (see

1957 Series Sixty-Two Eldorado Biarritz convertible

entry). Cadillac's 331 V-8 was bored out to 365 cubes for 1956, with a special tuned version reserved for Eldorados (twin four-barrel carbs for 1956-57, triple two-throat units for 1958). Comments on mechanical and design features of the Seville also apply here. After 1960, the Seville was dropped from the Eldorado line, which had been separated from the Series Sixty-Two the year before. The 1956-57 models were once considered the last highly collectible Eldorado convertibles through 1971. But the '58 version, a chrome-plated monster, and the '59, which took tailfins to a new level of absurdity, are highly sought out now, particularly the '59. Styling was gradually improved on the early-'60s models, but they were never as "special" as the 1953-57 cars.

⊞ FOR Unique rear-end appearance • Smooth, high-speed performance • Luxurious interiors • Somewhat rare, esp. the '58 • Milestone car status

▣ AGAINST Heavy gas drinker • Less interesting than 1953-55 Eldos • '58 generally considered less desirable

PRODUCTION
1956 2150 **1957** 1800 **1958** 815

SPECIFICATIONS
Length (in.)	222.2 (1956), 222.1 (1957-58)
Wheelbase (in.)	129.0 (1956), 129.5 (1957-58)
Weight (lbs)	4880-5070
Price (new)	$6556-7500

ENGINES
cid/type	bhp	years
365/ohv V-8	305/325/335	1956-58

PRICES
FAIR	$10,000-18,000
GOOD	$18,000-30,000
FINE	$30,000-40,000

FINE EXAMPLE PRICE HISTORY
1982 $12,000   **1990** $55,000

1994 $50,000   **1998** $40,000
1982-2000 RETURN 8%
2000-2010 5%

1956-58
CADILLAC SERIES SIXTY-TWO ELDORADO SEVILLE

1957 Series Sixty-Two Eldorado Seville hardtop coupe

A variation of the Eldorado format in an expensive limited-edition spin-off of the standard Sixty-Two hardtop. The Seville name, it might be noted, was simultaneously used by DeSoto for one of its four-door hardtops, but only for '56. As with the 1954-55 Biarritz convertibles, the '56 Seville shared the basic Sixty-Two body-shell adorned with prominent—and unique—tailfins. For 1957, the whole Cadillac line was redesigned. Eldorados gained softer lines up front, a cigar-shaped rear end with even more prominent shark fins, and a lower stance. Specially tuned V-8s were again exclusive to Eldorados in these years.

⊞ FOR Sedan comfort with hardtop styling • Cadillac amenities and fur-

nishings • Better than average performance • Milestone car status

▣ AGAINST A symbol of Cadillac's mid-'50s preference for flamboyance over taste • Very thirsty

PRODUCTION
1956 3900 **1957** 2100 **1958** 855

SPECIFICATIONS
Length (in.)	222.2 (1956), 222.1 (1957-58)
Wheelbase (in.)	129.0 (1956), 129.5 (1957-58)
Weight (lbs)	4665-4810
Price (new)	$6556-7500

ENGINES
cid/type	bhp	years
365/ohv V-8	305/325/335	1956-58

PRICES
FAIR	$6000-12,000
GOOD	$12,000-24,000
FINE	$24,000-35,000

FINE EXAMPLE PRICE HISTORY
1982 $7500   **1990** $40,000
1994 $30,000   **1998** $30,000
1982-2000 RETURN 8%
2000-2010 5%

1957-58
CADILLAC SERIES SEVENTY ELDORADO BROUGHAM

1958 Series Seventy Eldorado Brougham sedan

Cadillac's four-door response to the Continental Mark II coupe, and at $13,074 priced even higher in the stratosphere (equivalent to more than $80,000 today). While the Mark II stressed conservative looks and engineering, the Brougham was radical: center-opening doors, brushed stainless steel roof, quad headlights (a 1957 first shared with Nash), Caddy's highest-horsepower V-8s, and a problem-laden air suspension. Because of severe leaks, the air suspension was often replaced with conventional coil springs by disgruntled owners, making original Broughams fairly scarce today. Full of high-roller accoutrements, right down to a matched set of silver tumblers and special lipstick and cologne.

➕ **FOR** One-of-a-kind concept • Advanced engineering • The ultimate in luxury • Fine road manners with or without air suspension • a Milestone car

➖ **AGAINST** Very expensive on today's market • Many body and component parts (like those silver tumblers) now impossible to find • High running costs

PRODUCTION

1957 400 **1958** 304

SPECIFICATIONS

Length (in.)	216.3
Wheelbase (in.)	129.0
Weight (lbs)	5315
Price (new)	$13,074

ENGINES

cid/type	bhp	years
365/ohv V-8	325	1957-58

PRICES

FAIR	$12,000-20,000
GOOD	$20,000-29,000
FINE	$29,000-36,000

FINE EXAMPLE PRICE HISTORY

1982 $12,000	1990 $32,500
1994 $30,000	1998 $34,000
1982-2000 RETURN 7%	
2000-2010 5%	

1959-60 CADILLAC ELDORADO BROUGHAM

1959 Eldorado Brougham hardtop sedan

After limited success with the 1957-58 original—and Continental's departure from the super-luxury market—Cadillac farmed out Eldorado Brougham production to Pinin Farina in Italy. PF handled body styling (a mild modification of standard 1959-60 lines marked by less outlandish tailfins) and assembly (using stock Cadillac components) in Turin. Though the 1959-60 Brougham was

more closely related to the standard Cadillacs, price remained the same as for previous models, and sales were few. Name and high status make these models collectible now, though they lack the prestige and interest value of the 1957-58. They did, however, point the way toward the styling of the '61 standard Cadillacs.

➕ **FOR** Priced less than 1957-58 Broughams on today's market • One-upmanship value of Pinin Farina badges • High luxury

➖ **AGAINST** Less different from ordinary Cadillacs than earlier Broughams • Much lower appreciation potential than 1957-58 models • High running costs

PRODUCTION

1959 99 **1960** 101

SPECIFICATIONS

Length (in.)	225.0
Wheelbase (in.)	130.0
Weight (lbs)	NA
Price (new)	$13,075

ENGINES

cid/type	bhp	years
390/ohv V-8	345	1959-60

PRICES

FAIR	$10,000-18,000
GOOD	$18,000-27,000
FINE	$27,000-34,000

FINE EXAMPLE PRICE HISTORY

1982 $11,000	1990 $28,000
1994 $30,000	1998 $32,000
1982-2000 RETURN 7%	
2000-2010 5%	

1959-60 CADILLAC

Depending on your taste, the most outlandish or magnificent of all tailfinned Detroiters, beloved and

despised by equally large and vociferous armies of collectors. There's more unanimity over the powerplant, the new-for-'59 390 being among Cadillac's better V-8s. Glitzy chrome trim, especially on the Eldorado Seville and Biarritz, and lavish color-keyed interiors with a jukebox dash made this the epitome of late-'50s kitch. Tailfins never grew larger even on Chrysler products, but Cadillac cropped them significantly for 1960. By 1965, they'd vanished. A big, powerful highway cruiser with better economy and more competent handling than you'd expect.

➕ **FOR** Distinction—one way or the other • Smooth performance • '59s now icons of their age

➖ **AGAINST** Controversial '59 styling • Workmanship not to earlier Caddy standards • Tends to rust • Eldos and Series Sixty-Two ragtops scarce and expensive now • Costly body/interior restoration (go for a good original)

PRODUCTION

1959 Series 62 htp sdn 6W 23,461 **htp cpe** 21,947 **htp sdn 4W** 14,138 **conv** 11,130 **Series 63 de Ville htp sdn 6W** 19,158 **htp cpe** 21,924 **htp sdn 4W** 12,308 **Eldorado Seville htp cpe** 975 **Biarritz conv** 1320 **Series 60 Special htp sdn 6W** 12,250 **1960 Series 62 htp sdn 6W** 26,824 **htp cpe** 19,978 **htp sdn 4W** 9984 **conv** 14,000 **Series 63 de Ville htp sdn 6W** 22,579 **htp cpe** 21,585 **htp sdn 4W** 9225 **Eldorado Seville htp cpe** 1075 **Biarritz conv** 1285 **Series 60 Special htp sdn 6W** 11,800

SPECIFICATIONS

Length (in.)	225.0
Wheelbase (in.)	129.5
Weight (lbs)	4670-5060
Price (new)	$4892-$7401

ENGINES

cid/type	bhp	years
390/ohv V-8	325/345[1]	1959-60
[1]Standard/Eldorado		

PRICES

Series Sixty-Two de Ville 2d htp

1959 Series Sixty-Two convertible

FAIR	$4000-8500	
GOOD	$8500-17,000	
FINE	$17,000-24,500	
Series Sixty-Two conv		
FAIR	$9500-18,000	
GOOD	$18,000-37,000	
FINE	$37,000-50,000	
Eldorado 2d htp		
FAIR	$8000-15,000	
GOOD	$15,000-20,000	
FINE	$20,000-30,000	
Eldorado conv		
FAIR	$17,000-33,000	
GOOD	$33,000-50,000	
FINE	$50,000-70,000	

Note: Eldorado convertibles were selling at six figures in 1989, have since dropped dramatically, but have still gained strongly in value over the long term.

FINE 1959 ELDORADO CONVERTIBLE PRICE HISTORY

1982 $15,000		**1990** $98,000	
1994 $85,000		**1998** $72,000	
1982-2000 RETURN 10%			
2000-2010 10%			

1960 Coupe de Ville

1961-64
CADILLAC ELDORADO BIARRITZ

Cadillac's top-line specialty convertible, rather less special than in prior years and bereft of its companion Seville hardtop. The '61 benefited from GM's swing to slightly smaller and lighter big cars, as well as from new design chief Bill Mitchell's less flamboyant approach to Cadillac styling. The '62s were even tidier, while the restyled 1963-64s were crisper and more massive-looking. Tailfins were progressively lowered each year—by '64 mere vestiges of the outlandish '59 examples. That same year brought an all-new 429 V-8 boasting improved reliability and even greater refinement. The 1961-63s used the standard Caddy 390 with a single four-barrel carb and, unlike prior years, no extra horsepower. Bucket seats, a no-cost Biarritz option, are worth looking for today. A six-position tilt steering wheel and AM/FM radio became available for '63, "Twilight Sentinel" and automatic climate control for '64, when the Eldo's traditional rear fender skirts were deleted. Dual-circuit "safety" brakes were adopted for '62. Not the line-leader it had been, but a mighty worthy collectible, as all Caddys of this period are becoming. Also far fewer in number than the "everyday" Series Sixty-Two ragtops.

✚ FOR Still the sportiest "standard" Caddy • Fairly rare • It's a convertible • The usual Cad attractions • Long underappreciated, so prices reasonable

▬ AGAINST Much more similar to lesser linemates than earlier Biarritzes • Relatively slow value appreciation, though that's changing

PRODUCTION

1961 1450 **1962** 1450 **1963** 1825 **1964** 1870

SPECIFICATIONS

Length (in.)	222.0
Wheelbase (in.)	129.5
Weight (lbs)	4600-4650
Price (new)	$6477-6630

ENGINES

cid/type	bhp	years
390/ohv V-8	325	1961-63
429/ohv V-8	340	1964

PRICES

FAIR	$6000-12,000
GOOD	$12,000-20,000
FINE	$20,000-28,500

FINE EXAMPLE PRICE HISTORY

1982 $5500	**1990** $40,000
1994 $37,500	**1998** $30,000
1982-2000 RETURN 8%	
2000-2010 5%	

1965-66
CADILLAC ELDORADO BIARRITZ

1966 Eldorado Biarritz convertible

The final rear-drive Eldorados, and among the best of the breed. Wholesale 1965 redesign (save for the big Series Seventy-Five) brought handsome new curved-sided styling, even tidier detailing, a strong new full-perimeter frame (replacing the old '57-vintage X-member affair) with better engine mounts, a new four-link rear suspension, and improved Turbo Hydra-Matic Drive. Result: two of Cadillac's best sales years ever; '65, in fact, saw a new all-time division record. New styling, mercifully little changed for '66, marked by straight-top rear fenders, virtually finless, and stacked quad headlamps. New '65 options included tilt/telescope steering wheel; '66s offered electric "bun warmer" front seat and standard hazard warning flashers. Alas, the drop-top Biarritz, again firmly in the bucks-up Fleetwood line, was still not all that different from standard convertible (now a de Ville) and thus sold only a bit better than earlier '60s models. Long overshadowed by its front-drive successor, but increasingly appreciated today as a rare-ish, top-line collectible from two vintage Cadillac years.

✚ FOR As for 1961-64 Eldorado Biarritz plus arguably better styling and numerous technical improvements

▬ AGAINST Still "less an Eldorado" than '50s forebears owing to continued

1962 Eldorado Biarritz convertible

similarity to other Caddys • Styling too clean for a Cad?

PRODUCTION

1965 2125 **1966** 2250

SPECIFICATIONS

Length (in.)	224.0
Wheelbase (in.)	129.5
Weight (lbs)	4500-4660
Price (new)	$6630-6738

ENGINES

cid/type	bhp	years
429/ohv V-8	340	1965-66

PRICES

FAIR	$5000-8000
GOOD	$8000-12,000
FINE	$12,000-20,000

FINE EXAMPLE PRICE HISTORY

1982 $6000	1994 $30,000
1998 $20,000	
1982-2000 RETURN 6%	
2000-2010 5%	

1968 Fleetwood Eldorado hardtop coupe

One of the more interesting cars of the late '60s, essentially Cadillac's heavily re-engineered version of Oldsmobile's front-wheel-drive Toronado. An exceptional road machine considering its size, with outstanding handling and surprising get-up-and-go. Finely honed body styling in the Cadillac idiom, though somewhat less radical and aggressive than the Toronado's. Growing collector interest in all front-wheel-drive Eldorados means that "collectibility" doesn't end with the 1970 models, though the boom demand for 1976's "last convertible" petered out several years ago. The first-generation cars (coupes only) are still the best investment and the most satisfying to drive.

FOR Engineering excellence • A big luxurious car that can really go, stop

(front discs optional '67-68), and handle • Graceful styling has aged well

AGAINST Driveability problems progressively worse on post-'67 models as emission controls tightened • High running costs

PRODUCTION

1967 17,930 **1968** 24,528 **1969** 23,333 **1970** 28,842

SPECIFICATIONS

Length (in.)	220.0 (approx.)
Wheelbase (in.)	120.0
Weight (lbs)	4500-4630
Price (new)	$6277-6903

ENGINES

cid/type	bhp	years
429/ohv V-8	340	1967
472/ohv V-8	375	1968-69
500/ohv V-8	400	1970

PRICES

FAIR	$2500-4500
GOOD	$4500-7000
FINE	$7000-12,000

FINE EXAMPLE PRICE HISTORY

1982 $3000	1990 $12,000
1994 $10,000	1998 $12,000
1982-2000 RETURN 6%	
2000-2010 5%	

Judged "a dubious collectible at best" by earlier editions of this book, but looks better now that process have settled with dimming memories of 1976's "last convertible" farce. Though big and impressive, Cadillac's second series of personal-

luxury front drivers suffers against its 1967-70 forebearer for hulkier styling and no-progress mechanicals. Still, not appreciably heavier despite appearances, and always outsold the first generation. The convertible, the first open-air Eldo since '66, boasted an easy-as-pie power top that stowed beneath the traditional rigid cover. With the possible exception of the genuine, all-white "last-convertibles" (only 199 built, plus one that Cadillac kept)—the ones bid to absurd levels when new—a '76 has no real edge over a 1971-75 either in monetary or interest value; indeed, the '71 may ultimately be the most desired of these cars as first of the line and fewest in number. But collectors won't likely take any of these cars very seriously for some years yet, though interest is growing.

FOR Minor historical interest • As big and luxurious as they come • In reasonable supply yet

AGAINST Very high running costs • Hardly a great Cadillac

PRODUCTION

1971 6800 **1972** 7975 **1973** 9315 **1974** 7600 **1975** 8950 **1976** 14,000

SPECIFICATIONS

Length (in.)	220.0-224.1
Wheelbase (in.)	126.3
Weight (lbs)	4730-5167
Price (new)	$7751-14,000

ENGINES

cid/type	bhp[1]	years
500/ohv V-8	190-235	1972-76

[1]SAE net; 365 gross bhp in 1971

PRICES

FAIR	$3500-6000
GOOD	$6000-10,000
FINE	$10,000-17,000

FINE EXAMPLE PRICE HISTORY

1982 $12,000	1990 $18,000
1994 $20,000	1998 $20,000
1982-2000 RETURN 2%	
2000-2010 3%	

1975 Fleetwood Eldorado convertible

1976-79
CADILLAC SEVILLE

1978 Seville sedan

First-generation "baby" Cadillac, often described as "international size," and the division's smallest car since the last LaSalle of 1940. Partly a trial balloon for General Motors' revolutionary downsizing program that began in earnest with its 1977 full-size cars. As such, it stood as a complete reversal of Detroit's time-honored notions about size and price—it was the smallest Caddy in living memory, yet costlier than any other model in the line save for the big Series Seventy-Five sedans and limos. A heavy rework of the corporate X-body four-door compact (Chevy Nova, *et al*), with a typical GM rear-drive chassis and front-coil/rear-leaf suspension, but crisper, more formal styling on a 3.3-inch longer wheelbase, Cadillac-assembled Olds engine with exclusive electronic fuel injection system, and full-house standard equipment. A very successful transformation aesthetically, mechanically, and commercially, and still with us in a smaller fifth-generation guise. Four-wheel disc brakes were standard from 1977, but avoid the extremely trouble-prone 1978-79 Oldsmobile-built diesel V-8 option.

⊞ FOR A '70s sleeper • Cadillac cachet and equipment • Clean lines • Good go (10-11 seconds 0-60 mph) • Decent economy • Handy size • Widely available • Very affordable • Parts still plentiful

⊟ AGAINST Not widely recognized yet • A Jag/M-B/BMW rival in size, but not status • Tight cabin • Dismal diesel engine • Humble design origins

PRODUCTION
1976 60,127 **1977** 45,060 **1978** 56,985 **1979** 53,487

SPECIFICATIONS

Length (in.)	204.0
Wheelbase (in.)	114.3
Weight (lbs)	4179-4232
Price (new)	$12,479-14,710

ENGINES

cid/type	bhp	years
350.0/ohv V-8	170/180[1]	1976-79
350.0/ohv V-8	125[2]	1978-79

[1]SAE net, electronic fuel injection [2]Olds-built diesel

PRICES

FAIR	$2000-3000
GOOD	$3000-4500
FINE	$4500-7000

FINE EXAMPLE PRICE HISTORY

1982 $8000		1990 $9500	
1994 $9000		1998 $7000	

1982-2000 RETURN 0%
2000-2010 Even
Note: Squareback Sevilles were bringing huge prices in 1990, but have since leveled off considerably.

1982-85
CADILLAC ELDORADO CONVERTIBLE & TOURING COUPE

The two nicest models in the third front-drive Eldorado series introduced for 1979. Touring Coupe, new for '82, started with the firmed-up "Touring Suspension" option, then tilted more toward the stringback-driving-gloves crowd with a buckets-and-console interior and a subdued exterior with black instead of chrome in many places. It even lacked a vinyl roof and stand-up hood ornament. Color choices expanded for '83, when an extra 10 horsepower made performance more sporting. One disgruntled buyer of a 1976 "last convertible" sued over 1984's reborn Eldo soft-top, a conversion engineered by ASC, Inc., and thus not strictly "factory-built." But it had Cadillac's blessing—and most every convenience, including uplevel Biarritz trim, a power top with glass rear window and full headliner, and rear side windows that raised and lowered with the roof. It wasn't cheap, one reason so few were built. The further-down-sized fourth generation (from 1986) ultimately continued a Touring Coupe (see entry) but was too small to make a practical ragtop, hence that model's second demise. Both too new for strong value appreciation yet, but likely to be gathered in some distant year as the last and best Eldorados in traditional "Cadillac style."

⊞ FOR Handsome, dignified styling • Size nicely balances image and practicality • Pleasant drivers (esp. TC) • Parts/service support still excellent • Relatively inexpensive

⊟ AGAINST Long-shot collectibles right now • So-so handling (esp. Biarritz) • Ditto performance

PRODUCTION
1982 TC 1700 **1983 TC** 1197 **1984 TC** 815 **Biarritz conv** 3,300 **1985 TC** 585 **Biarritz conv** 2,300

SPECIFICATIONS

Length (in.)	204.5
Wheelbase (in.)	114.0
Weight (lbs)	3735-3930
Price (new)	$18,720-22,105

ENGINES

cid/type	bhp	years
249/ohv V-8	125-135	1982-85

PRICES

Depreciating for their first 12-15 years, these Eldorados have lately started up in price. In 2000, convertibles were selling for up to $20,000, coupes for up to $10,000.
2000-2010 RETURN Even

1984 Eldorado convertible

1987-93
CADILLAC ALLANTE

1987 Allante convertible

Clark Avenue's first postwar production two-seater, the sportiest Caddy since the last LaSalle, and a bid to give the "Standard of the World" new luster in the "ultra-luxury" market (over $55,000)—chiefly against the Mercedes SL. Combined a shortened 1986-generation front-drive Eldorado chassis with firm suspension and a tuned version of Cadillac's iron-head/aluminum-block pushrod V-8 with conservative convertible styling, mostly by Italy's Pininfarina. PF also built and trimmed the bodies, and mounted them to platforms air-freighted to Turin via Alitalia 747s—the "Allante Airbridge," Cadillac called it. Assemblies returned by the same means for driveline installation and final assembly at GM's highly automated Poletown plant in suburban Detroit. Few changes in these years. Originally standard lift-off hardtop made optional after 1989 to achieve a lower advertised price. Also a larger, more potent engine and auto-adjusting shock absorbers for '89, no-cost needle gauges from '88 (in lieu of vacuum-fluorescent representations), standard traction control system and driver's airbag for '90, steadily revised soft-top mechanism, and progressively better build quality. In January of '93, the Allante introduced Cadillac's dohc V-8 Northstar engine with 95 more horsepower than the previous V-8. Always very road-capable, but sales ever slow. Seems a definite future collectible, though when and for how much is uncertain.

✚ FOR First Cadillac production sports car • The most roadable, too • Pininfarina panache • Good looks • Standard antilock brakes

▬ AGAINST Nightmarish ergonomics • Not all that peppy with 249-cid/4.1-liter V-8 • Difficult top and variable workmanship through 1989

PRODUCTION
1987 3363 **1988** 2569 **1989** 3298 **1990** 3101 **1991** 2500 **1992** 1931 **1993** 4670

SPECIFICATIONS
Length (in.)	178.6
Wheelbase (in.)	99.4
Weight (lbs)	3500
Price (new)	$51,500-57,000

ENGINES
cid/type	bhp	years
249/ohv V-8	170	1987-88
273/ohv V-8	200	1989-92
279/dohc V-8	295	1993

PRICES
Used car market value, ranging in 2000 from $17,000 for the best early models up to $30,000 for late models
2000-2010 RETURN 2%

1990-91
CADILLAC ELDORADO TOURING COUPE

A good idea revived after five years. Based on the new-for-'86 fourth-generation Eldo that suffered huge sales losses in that second downsizing, winding up too small for most buyers. Sales improved some for '88 with a return to crisp fenderlines, a rear end lengthened three inches, new "power dome" hood, and a bored-out V-8 whose 25 extra horses trimmed 0-60 times from 12.5 seconds to a sprightlier 9.9. GM/Teves anti-lock brakes served safety that year as a new $925 option. The 1990s gained 35 bhp more by switching from throttle-body injection to more efficient multiport, plus a standard driver's airbag. As before, the Touring Coupe, a mid-year addition, sported a deftly dechromed exterior, Cadillac's handling-oriented Touring Suspension package, performance tires on alloy road wheels, and buckets-and-console interior, but the seats now boasted 10-way power adjustment. Computer Command Ride (auto-adjusting shock absorbers) was included, and a special 3.33:1 final drive ratio brought 0-60 times well below 10 seconds. Like other Eldos, offered only with overdrive four-speed automatic transaxle. The Touring Coupe, which carried over into 1991 with only detail changes, was the most athletic Cadillac of its day other than the Allante, making it a good bet to become at least a minor collector's item in future.

✚ FOR Handy size • Smooth and peppy • Comfy, luxurious tourer • Antilock brakes and airbag

▬ AGAINST Mediocre mileage (14.5 mpg) • Workmanship not "Standard of the World" • Few gauges • Too many dashboard buttons • Surprisingly sparse rear-seat space • Not likely to be a high-return investment

PRODUCTION
NA

SPECIFICATIONS
Length (in.)	191.4
Wheelbase (in.)	108.0
Weight (lbs)	3500
Price (new)	$33,545

ENGINES
cid/type	bhp	years
273/ohv V-8	200	1990

PRICES
Used car market value. Best examples bringing up to $12,000 in 2000.
2000-2010 RETURN Still depreciating

1990 Eldorado Coupe (Touring Coupe similar)

CADILLAC SEVILLE STS

1991 Cadillac STS

A Seville option package since late 1988, STS became a separate model in 1990. As with the Eldorado Touring Coupe (which shared the same platform), the STS offered better handling and less chrome than the base model. Automatic-adjustable shock absorbers firmed the suspension at highway speeds and during fast cornering, but offered a comfortable ride at other times. Anti-lock brakes were standard on the STS. A 1990 change to multi-point from single-point fuel injection added 35 horses for a total of 180 horsepower. For '91 a displacement increase from 4.5 to 4.9-liters upped horsepower to 200. Handling and performance compared well with the imports the STS was meant to battle. A luxurious wood and leather interior was marred by a digital instrument panel. Front seat room was good, but the back seat was lacked leg room. In '91 the rear center console was dropped to allow three-across seating. Most prefer the styling of later Sevilles, but the smaller size of this generation made the STS more nimble.

FOR Ride and handling • Performance • Interior

AGAINST Squared-off styling • Back seat leg room • Digital gauges

PRODUCTION
NA

SPECIFICATIONS

Length (ins.)	190.8
Wheelbase (ins.)	108.0
Weight (lbs.)	3570
Price (new)	$36,320-37,395

ENGINES

cid//type	bhp	years
273/ohv V-8	180	1990
300/ohv V-8	200	1991

PRICES

Still depreciating. Current value $9000-12,000
2000-2010 RETURN 0%

CADILLAC SEVILLE STS

1993 Seville STS sedan

The 4-door Seville, like its 2-door sibling, the Eldorado, was restyled for 1992, with three inches added to wheelbase and a full foot added to overall length. Requisite luxury was complemented by a more rounded and aggressive body, with an eye toward competition from Japanese luxury make Lexus. STS (Seville Touring Sedan) had a monochromatic exterior treatment, quicker steering, and thicker stabilizer bars than base Sevilles. Also, the STS spurned the base model's digital gauges for analog readouts, and came with leather seats standard. By 1993, the 4.6-liter, 200-horse V-8 of '92 had been supplanted by a 4.6-liter eight, rated at 300 bhp.

FOR Acceleration • Smooth automatic transmission • Roadholding • Interior materials

AGAINST Thirst • Rear visibility

PRODUCTION
NA

SPECIFICATIONS

Length (in.)	201.0-204.1
Weight (lbs)	3648-3900
Wheelbase (in.)	111.0-112.2
Price (new)	$37,975-48,480

ENGINES

liter/type/(cid)	bhp	years
4.9/ohv V-8 (300)	200	1992
4.6/dohc V-8 (279)	295	1993-94
4.6/dohc V-8 (279)	300	1995-2000

PRICES

Depreciating; governed by the used car market. Late models presently selling for up to $34,000.
2000-2010 RETURN Depreciating

CADILLAC ELDORADO ETC

With a new platform shared by Seville and Eldorado in 1992, the ETC was ready for the competition. The electronic suspension control continued to get more sophisticated as time went by. Starting in 1998 Cadillac's StabiliTrak antiskid system made the ETCs safer in emergency maneuvers on slick roads. For a large coupe, handling was sharp and stable, but not at the expense of the luxury ride. The 200-horsepower ohv V-8 was replaced by the Northstar engine in '93. With dual overhead cams and 295 horsepower, this engine was world class in smoothness and performance. Crisp lines distinguished the Eldorado from the rounded cars of the nineties—although the rear roof pillars blocked rear vision. Eldorados were bigger with more back seat room, even though Eldos kept the 108-inch wheelbase of the previous series, while Sevilles got

1996 Eldorado ETC coupe

an 111-inch wheelbase. In 1998 the Seville was redesigned, while the Eldorado carried on with only detail improvements. For 2000 OnStar navigation and roadside assistance was made standard. As the luxury coupe market dwindled in the nineties, Eldorado ETCs became rarer.

FOR Performance • Handling • Antiskid system

AGAINST Rear visibility • Mediocre mileage • Back seat entry/exit

PRODUCTION
NA

SPECIFICATIONS

Length (ins.)	202.2
Weight (lbs.)	3604-3843
Wheelbase (ins.)	108.0
Price (new)	$34,800-43,695

ENGINES

cid/type	bhp	years
300/ohv V-8	200	1992
279/dohc V-8	295-300	1993-2000

PRICES
Depreciating; governed by the used car market. Late models presently selling for up to $33,000.
2000-2010 RETURN Depreciating

1932-36 CHEVROLET OPEN MODELS

All Chevys of this period are collectible, but the open models are, as usual, more collectible than the others. Topless cars were fast going out of fashion in the threadbare '30s as all-steel bodies began to appear around mid-decade, so the above production figures are not as astonishing as they may at first appear. Top-notch styling arrived with the '32s, reminiscent of Harley Earl's earlier LaSalles. Streamlining began with the '33s, then became more radical on the '34s. Desirability isn't as high on the 1936-40 models. All Chevys from 1932 on had the long-lived and reliable "Blue Flame" six. Open cars began shifting to the Standard series for 1934. The longer-wheelbase DeLuxe versions are more desirable, but the trick is to find one.

FOR Simple to fix, relatively easy to restore • Excellent parts situation

AGAINST Doesn't rival early-30s Ford V-8s among enthusiasts, thus relatively lower investment potential • Hard to find • Easy to over-restore

1935 Standard roadster

PRODUCTION
1932 DeLuxe rdstr 8552 **DeLuxe phaeton** 1000[1] **Standard rdstr** 1118 **Standard phaeton** 600[1] **1933 DeLuxe rdstr** 2876 **DeLuxe phaeton** 543 **DeLuxe cabriolet** 4276 **1934 DeLuxe rdstr** 1974 **DeLuxe cabriolet** 3276 **Standard rdstr** 1038 **Standard phaeton** 234 **1935 Standard rdstr** 1176 **Standard phaeton** 217 **1936 Standard cabriolet** 3629
[1]Estimates

SPECIFICATIONS

Length (in.)	NA
Wheelbase (in.)	109.0 (1932); 110.0 (1933); 107.0/112.0 (1934); 107.0 (1935); 109.0 (1936)
Weight (lbs)	2380-2815
Price (new)	$445-640

1932 DeLuxe phaeton

ENGINES

cid/type	bhp	years
194.0/ohv I-6	60	1932
181.0/ohv I-6	60/74	1933-35
206.8/ohv I-6	65/80	1933-36

PRICES

FAIR	$5000-10,000
GOOD	$10,000-15,000
FINE	$15,000-34,000

(1932-34 models are at the high end of the above ranges.)

FINE 1932 MODEL PRICE HISTORY

1982 $20,000		**1990** $25,000	
1994 $32,000		**1998** $27,000	

1982-2000 RETURN 3%
2000-2010 2%

1941 CHEVROLET SPECIAL DELUXE

1941 Special DeLuxe convertible coupe

A "classic" prewar Chevy, though not a designated Classic. This was an elegant refinement of the 1940 design, with a special Fleetline sedan with more formal styling added to the line-up. Well-proportioned and solidly built, the '41s are prized among Chevrolet fanciers. The top-of-the-line Special DeLuxe commands naturally greater attention than the cheaper Masters. Typically, the rarer body styles are more desirable; the Fleetline receives good marks for its stylish blind rear roof quarters.

FOR Good styling • Construction quality • A vintage Chevy year • Unbreakable six

AGAINST No performance versus Ford V-8 • Very common

PRODUCTION
2d Town Sedan 288,458 **business cpe** 17,602 **cpe** 155,889 **conv** 15,296 **4d Sport Sedan** 148,661 **4d wgn** 2045 **4d Fleetline sdn** 34,162

SPECIFICATIONS

Length (in.)	196.0
Wheelbase (in.)	116.0

| Weight (lbs) | 3040-3410 |
| Price (new) | $769-995 |

ENGINES

cid/type	bhp	years
216.5/ohv I-6	90	1941

PRICES

Closed	
FAIR	$2500-6000
GOOD	$6000-11,000
FINE	$11,000-16,000
Open & wagon	
FAIR	$7000-14,000
GOOD	$14,000-25,000
FINE	$25,000-35,000

FINE CONVERTIBLE PRICE HISTORY

1982 $12,500	**1990** $29,000
1994 $23,000	**1998** $28,000

1982-2000 RETURN 7%
2000-2010 5%

1942 CHEVROLET FLEETLINE

Buyer acceptance of the 1941 Special DeLuxe Fleetline led to this offshoot of the '42 Fleetmaster line. Curiously, only the two-door Aerosedan continued the fastback styling from '41; the Sportmaster was a more conventional notchback. Both models were distinguished by stylish triple chrome bands on the front and rear fenders.

✛ FOR Aerosedan relatively easy to find (highest production of any '42 Chevy) • Top-of-the-line trim • Sleek styling • Bulletproof six

▬ AGAINST Not much go

PRODUCTION

2d Aerosedan 61,885 **4d Sportmaster sdn** 14,530

1942 Fleetline 2-door Aerosedan

SPECIFICATIONS

Length (in.)	196.0
Wheelbase (in.)	116.0
Weight (lbs)	3105-3165
Price (new)	$880 (Aerosedan); $920 (Sportmaster)

ENGINES

cid/type	bhp	years
216.5/ohv I-6	90	1942

PRICES

FAIR	$2500-5000
GOOD	$5000-8500
FINE	$8500-10,500

FINE EXAMPLE PRICE HISTORY

1982 $4000	**1990** $9500
1994 $10,000	**1998** $10,500

1982-2000 RETURN 7%
2000-2010 5%

1942 CHEVROLET SPECIAL DELUXE

1942 Special DeLuxe convertible coupe

A further development of the pretty 1941 styling, with extended front fenders similar to those on the more expensive GM makes. Production halted by February 1942 to make way for defense work, which makes the rarer '42 marginally more desirable than the '41. Only a handful of convertibles and wagons were built; the two-passenger coupe is also extremely scarce. No major mechanical changes from 1941.

✛ FOR Rarity, desirability • Surprising body parts availability today • Others as for '41 models

▬ AGAINST Low production models impossible to find • Plodding performance

PRODUCTION

2d Town Sedan 39,421 **2P cpe** 1716 **4d Sport Sedan** 31,441 **conv** 1182 **5P coupe** 22,187 **4d wgn** 1057

SPECIFICATIONS

Length (in.)	196.0
Wheelbase (in.)	116.0
Weight (lbs)	3070-3425
Price (new)	$815-1095

ENGINES

cid/type	bhp	years
216.5/ohv I-6	90	1942

PRICES

As for 1941 Special Deluxe; no premium in this case for scarce 1942 model year.
2000-2010 RETURN 5%

1946-48 CHEVROLET FLEETLINE

1948 Fleetline Sportmaster sedan

Chevy's top-line fastback and formal notchback sedans in warmed-over postwar guise. As with other models, grille became full width for 1947 and more "important" looking for '48 because of a large vertical bar. Production increased dramatically each year. The 1947-48 Aerosedan is still easy to find and swoopy-looking despite its age. A handful had wood side panels á la Chrysler Town & Country and Nash Suburban of the same years. However, this was not factory equipment; rather, it was a dealer installation.

✛ FOR Not too hard to find • Extremely popular with collectors • Aerosedan's dramatic styling (more

so with wood paneling)

AGAINST Sportmaster's chunky looks • Both types fairly slow to appreciate

PRODUCTION

1946 2d Aerosedan 57,932 **4d Sportmaster sdn** 7501 **1947 2d Aerosedan** 159,407 **4d Sportmaster sdn** 54,531 **1948 2d Aerosedan** 211,861 **4d Sportmaster sdn** 64,217

SPECIFICATIONS

Length (in.)	197.8
Wheelbase (in.)	116.0
Weight (lbs)	3100-3240
Price (new)	$1249-1492

ENGINES

cid/type	bhp	years
216.5/ohv I-6	90	1946-48

PRICES

As for 1941 Special DeLuxe less 10%.

1946-48
CHEVROLET FLEETMASTER

Postwar continuation of the basic 1942 design. Grille went to full width for 1947, became more ornate for '48. Because of its wide availability, attractive styling, and use of precision-type engine main bearings (formerly rough cut), the '48 is clearly more popular than the 1946-47 models. The styling was beginning to age, but these well-built Chevys were no less the quality cars they were in 1942.

FOR Relatively plentiful • Wide availability of body and mechanical parts • Strong club activity and interest

AGAINST Commonplace by any yardstick • Slower to appreciate than

1947 Fleetmaster convertible

the 1941-42 models

PRODUCTION

1946 4d sdn 73,746 **2d sdn** 56,538 **cpe** 27,036 **conv** 4508 **4d wgn** 804 **1947 4d sdn** 91,440 **2d sdn** 80,128 **cpe** 59,661 **conv** 28,443 **4d wgn** 4912 **1948 4d sdn** 93,142 **2d sdn** 66,208 **cpe** 58,786 **conv** 20,471 **4d wgn** 10,171

SPECIFICATIONS

Length (in.)	197.8
Wheelbase (in.)	116.0
Weight (lbs)	3090-3465
Price (new)	$1212-2013

ENGINES

cid/type	bhp	years
216.5/ohv I-6	90	1946-48

PRICES

As for 1941 Special Deluxe

1947-55
CHEVROLET PICKUP

1949 Chevrolet 3100 Series pickup

The first new post-war vehicle from General Motors wasn't a car, but the Chevrolet truck. Arriving in showrooms in mid-1947, the "Advance Design" pickups were well in advance of the new cars that weren't built until 1949 model year. With a wide grille and headlights molded into the fenders, it was a good looking truck that

would look up to date until production ended in early 1955. A new grille and one piece windshield in 1954 were the only major changes to the original styling. The cab was roomier with three across seating and column shift. Chevrolet improved interior ventilation and called it "the cab that breathes". Glass area was greater than before—especially with optional rear corner windows. The bullet-proof Chevy six provided the power. Initially 216 cubic-inches with 90 horsepower, it grew to 235 inches with 108 horsepower in 1953 (112-horsepower in '54).

FOR Pleasing styling • Durable • Handles well for a truck

AGAINST Interior noise • Hard ride

PRODUCTION

1947 NA **1948** 389,690[1] **1949** 201,537[2] **1950** 265,515[2] **1951** 215,175[2] **1952** NA **1953** 203,242[2] **1954** 170,824[2] **1955** NA
[1]Total truck production [2]Half-ton production

SPECIFICATIONS

Length (in.)	191.3-196.6
Weight (lbs)	3100-3215
Wheelbase (in.)	116.0
Price (new)	$1180-1419

ENGINES

cid/type	bhp	years
216/ohv I-6	90/92	1948-52
235/ohv I-6	108/112	1953-54

PRICES

FAIR	$3000-4500
GOOD	$4500-7500
FINE	$7500-12,000
2000-2010 RETURN 2%	

1949-52
CHEVROLET FLEETLINE DELUXE

Here's a car almost everybody's missed, the last of the "torpedo" Chevys. Look at one from the rear three-quarters and you may do a double-take, for there is a close similarity here to the fabulous Bentley R-Type Continental. Or was the '52 Continental a copy of the Chevy? We doubt it, but some buffs insist it was. In any case, both the 2- and 4-door models are truly elegant, but have been overlooked by collectors and so could be an inexpensive yet worthy addition to your garage. Built with all the Swiss-watch quality for which Chevy was noted at the time, and trimmed with the

1949 Fleetline DeLuxe 4-door sedan

best the make had to offer. If you have a choice, the '51 two-door with its more nicely integrated grille would be the one to take.

✚ FOR Low asking prices • Fine construction quality • Rakish good looks

▬ AGAINST A "sleeper"—slow appreciation seems certain • A sleeper on the road, too, especially with Powerglide automatic

PRODUCTION
1949 4d sdn 130,323 **2d sdn** 180,251 **1950 4d sdn** 124,187 **2d sdn** 189,509 **1951 4d sdn** 57,693 **2d sdn** 131,910 **1952 2d sdn** 37,164

SPECIFICATIONS
Length (in.)	197.0-197.8
Wheelbase (in.)	115.0
Weight (lbs)	3095-3155
Price (new)	$1482-1707

ENGINES
cid/type	bhp	years
216.5/ohv I-6[1]	90/92	1949-52
235.5/ohv I-6[2]	105	1950-52

[1]Manual shift [2]Powerglide automatic

PRICES
FAIR	$2000-4500
GOOD	$4500-7000
FINE	$7000-9000

FINE EXAMPLE PRICE HISTORY
1982 $1000		**1990** $7500	
1994 $7500		**1998** $9000	

1982-2000 RETURN 13%
2000-2010 2%

CHEVROLET STYLELINE DELUXE

Harley Earl and company attended to Chevrolet's first postwar restyle after all other GM cars except Pontiac, so these two makes used prewar shells through 1948. But when change

1949 Styleline DeLuxe convertible

did come it was dramatic—the '49 Chevys were some of the best looking GM products ever, and were precision built as well. Power finally went up for 1950 with arrival of the Powerglide two-speed automatic, for which the Chevy six was given increased displacement and 15 percent more horsepower, which was badly needed for the new slushbox. Mundane then and now, the '49s nevertheless make a good choice for routine transportation, and a good, clean original will never lose its value.

✚ FOR Wide availability • 1949 production includes 3342 very desirable wood-body wagons, the last of this type • High construction quality

▬ AGAINST Slow to appreciate in value • Ordinary by any standard

PRODUCTION
1949 4d sdn 191,357 **2d sdn** 147,347 **cpe** 78,785 **conv** 32,392 **4d wgn** 9348 **1950 4d sdn** 316,412 **2d sdn** 248,567 **cpe** 81,536 **conv** 32,810 **4d wgn** 166,995 **1951 4d sdn** 380,270 **2d sdn** 262,933 **cpe** 64,976 **conv** 20,172 **4d wgn** 23,586 **1952 4d sdn** 319,736 **2d sdn** 215,417 **cpe** 36,954 **conv** 11,975 **4d wgn** 12,756

SPECIFICATIONS
Length (in.)	197.0-197.8
Wheelbase (in.)	115.0
Weight (lbs)	3065-3485
Price (new)	$1482-2297

ENGINES
cid/type	bhp	years
216.5/ohv I-6[1]	90/92	1949-52
235.5/ohv I-6[2]	105	1950-52

[1]Manual shift [2]Powerglide automatic

PRICES
Conv	
FAIR	$7000-12,000
GOOD	$12,000-17,000
FINE	$17,000-23,000
Wgn	
FAIR	$2000-12,000
GOOD	$12,000-20,000
FINE	$20,000-27,000
Other	
FAIR	$1500-4000
GOOD	$4000-6500
FINE	$6500-9000

FINE CONVERTIBLE PRICE HISTORY
1982 $6000	**1990** $25,000
1994 $25,000	**1998** $23,000

1982-2000 RETURN 8%
2000-2010 5%

CHEVROLET STYLELINE DELUXE BEL AIR

1951 Styleline DeLuxe Bel Air hardtop coupe

Due to styling priorities favoring higher-priced GM makes, Chevy was a Johnny-come-lately to the hardtop ranks, though it beat both Ford and Plymouth by a year. The smoothly executed Bel Air had the standard GM treatment: a convertible-like deluxe interior and simulated top bows on the headliner. And despite a price just shy of the real convertible's, buyers loved the new hardtop Chevy. Sales shot up in 1951, only to drop when the industry lost momentum during the Korean War's opening stages.

✚ FOR The best-looking, most interesting Chevy of these years • Very high quality for its class • Available Powerglide automatic

▬ AGAINST Not much movement on the collector market • Poor performance, especially with Powerglide

PRODUCTION
1950 76,662 **1951** 103,356 **1952** 74,634

SPECIFICATIONS

Length (in.)	197.5-197.8
Wheelbase (in.)	115.0
Weight (lbs)	3215-3225
Price (new)	$1741-2206

ENGINES

cid/type	bhp	years
216.5/ohv I-6[1]	92	1950-52
235.5/ohv I-6[2]	105	1950-52

[1]Manual shift [2]Powerglide automatic

PRICES

FAIR	$2500-4000
GOOD	$4000-7500
FINE	$7500-11,500

FINE EXAMPLE PRICE HISTORY

1982 $4000		**1990** $11,000	
1994 $11,000		**1998** $11,000	
1982-2000 RETURN 7%			
2000-2010 5%			

1953-54

CHEVROLET BEL AIR HARDTOP/ CONVERTIBLE

1953 Bel Air convertible

Another group of Chevys for the budget-minded collector. The 1953-54 models had transitional styling that was not as expertly drawn as that of 1949-52. Chevrolets grew shorter, wider, and taller, while lacking their predecessor's purity of line. However, they were as well built as ever. Color started to enter the picture—two-tones were commonplace, the contrasting color applied to a sweep panel on the rear fenders and, on hardtops, to the roof. Engine power took a jump in each year, though no V-8 would be offered until 1955.

+ FOR Easy on the wallet • Fairly easy to come by as a good number have survived • More colorful paint and interiors than before

– AGAINST Little collector interest • Less integrated styling

PRODUCTION

1953 conv 24,047 **Bel Air htp** 99,028 **1954 conv** 19,333 **Bel Air htp** 66,378

SPECIFICATIONS

Length (in.)	195.0-195.5
Wheelbase (in.)	115.0
Weight (lbs)	3310-3470
Price (new)	$2051-2185

ENGINES

cid/type	bhp	years
235.5/ohv I-6	105/115	1953
235.5/ohv I-6	115/125	1954

PRICES

Htp	
FAIR	$3500-7500
GOOD	$7500-11,000
FINE	$11,000-18,000
Conv	
FAIR	$6000-17,500
GOOD	$17,500-23,000
FINE	$23,000-29,000

FINE CONVERTIBLE PRICE HISTORY

1982 $6000		**1990** $32,000	
1994 $31,000		**1998** $29,000	
1982-2000 RETURN 10%			
2000-2010 10% (conv), 3% (htp)			

1953-55

CHEVROLET CORVETTE

The first of Chevrolet's fiberglass-bodied sports cars. Disappointing sales for these years nearly killed it after 1954. It was helped tremendously in performance and sales appeal by the new V-8 option for 1955—fewer than a dozen six-cylinder models were built that year. Styling was done by GM Art & Colour under Harley Earl: a toothy grille, stone guards over inset headlamps, "twin pod" rear fenders, "rocketship" taillights. Powerglide two-speed automatic came standard; a 3-speed manual wasn't offered until late in '55. The first-generation cars were considered boulevardiers, though they did handle reasonably well, and the modified "Stovebolt" six delivered good power for its size.

+ FOR Very scarce, for obvious reasons • High collector demand, with extremely strong appreciation potential • Large club following • Historical interest

– AGAINST Expensive • Mixed reputation among non-Corvette owners • Questionable styling • Indifferent quality

PRODUCTION

1953 300 **1954** 3640 **1955** 700

SPECIFICATIONS

Length (in.)	167.0
Wheelbase (in.)	102.0
Weight (lbs)	2650-2705
Price (new)	$2799-3513

ENGINES

cid/type	bhp	years
235.5/ohv I-6	150	1953-55
265/ohv V-8	195	1955

PRICES

1953	
FAIR	$12,000-40,000
GOOD	$40,000-70,000
FINE	$70,000-100,000
1954-55	
FAIR	$9000-20,000
GOOD	$20,000-36,000
FINE	$36,000-58,000

FINE 1954 MODEL PRICE HISTORY

1982 $12,000		**1990** $60,000	
1994 $60,000		**1998** $70,000	
1982-2000 RETURN 10%			
2000-2010 10%			

1953 Corvette roadster

1954 Corvette roadster

1955-57
CHEVROLET BEL AIR (EXC. WAGONS)

1955 Bel Air convertible

Top-of-the-line "classic Chevy," and the most desirable standard Chevrolets on today's market. Outstanding styling, high-performance potential, and fine build quality have created a huge collector following. As with the downmarket models, Bel Air values vary considerably with year. The 1955s and '57s are more in demand than the '56s. Interest apparently relates to original sales, and 1956 was not a record year for Detroit. Stylewise, the 1955 is the purest and finest; the '56 has a reasonable if ordinary facelift; the '57 is the boldest—a quality collectors either despise or applaud. All mid-'50s Bel Airs are still very hot items, so time is of the essence. If you find one for sale and don't take it, rest assured someone else quickly will.

✚ FOR One of the most desirable collector cars around, and the most collectible Chevy passenger car • Classic styling • Great V-8 performance • Tremendous investment

▬ AGAINST Strong buyer competition for good ones, so expect steep asking prices

PRODUCTION
1955 4d sdn 345,372 **2d sdn** 168,313 **2d htp** 185,562 **conv** 41,292 **1956 4d sdn** 269,798 **2d sdn** 104,849 **4d htp** 103,602 **2d htp** 128,382 **conv** 41,268 **1957 4d sdn** 254,331 **2d sdn** 62,751 **4d htp** 137,672 **2d htp** 166,426 **conv** 47,562

SPECIFICATIONS
Length (in.)	195.6 (1955), 197.5 (1956), 200.0 (1957)
Wheelbase (in.)	115.0
Weight (lbs)	3140-3409
Price (new)	$1888-2511

ENGINES
cid/type	bhp	years
235.5/ohv I-6	123/136/140	1955-57
265/ohv V-8	162-225	1955-56
283/ohv V-8	185-283	1957

PRICES
Sdns	
FAIR	$4000-7000
GOOD	$7000-11,000
FINE	$11,000-17,500
2d htp	
FAIR	$9000-12,000
GOOD	$12,000-18,000
FINE	$18,000-28,000
Conv	
FAIR	$17,000-25,000
GOOD	$25,000-35,000
FINE	$35,000-50,000

FINE CONVERTIBLE PRICE HISTORY
1982 $12,000		**1990** $48,000	
1994 $36,000		**1998** $41,000	
1982-2000 RETURN 9%			
2000-2010 10%			

Add 10% for air conditioning, 5% for Power-Pack V-8, 40% for authenticated factory-installed fuel injection (1957); deduct 20% for six-cylinder.

1955-57
CHEVROLET BEL AIR NOMAD

The prettiest station wagon ever, and among the least practical. Only two doors and raked B-pillars made interior access clumsy, especially to the rear. Slanted tailgate was subject to rain leaks and consequent rust. Sales never lived up to expectations, partly because of high prices, and Nomad lost its exclusive styling after 1957. But there's no way to fault the superb looks, especially in 1955 form.

Low production guarantees the Nomad's continued collector appeal and high appreciation potential.

✚ FOR Perhaps the most desirable 1955-57 Chevy • Large following in National Nomad Club • Sure-fire appreciation • Show car styling • Performance

▬ AGAINST Expensive to buy now; some reproduction Nomad-only parts now available, but are quite costly (same for used and NOS) • Leaks and rust around tailgate

PRODUCTION
1955 8530 **1956** 8103 **1957** 6534

SPECIFICATIONS
Length (in.)	197.1 (1955), 200.8 (1956), 202.8 (1957)
Wheelbase (in.)	115.0
Weight (lbs)	3285-3465
Price (new)	$2471-2757

ENGINES
cid/type	bhp	years
235.5/ohv I-6	123/136/140	1955-57
265/ohv V-8	162-225	1955-56
283/ohv V-8	185-283	1957

PRICES
FAIR	$9000-11,500
GOOD	$11,500-17,000
FINE	$17,000-27,000

Note: 1957s are at high end of range, '56s at low end, '55s in middle.

FINE 1957 PRICE HISTORY
1982 $15,000		**1990** $24,000	
1994 $25,000		**1998** $27,000	
1982-2000 RETURN 6%			
2000-2010 5%			

Add 10% for air conditioning, 5% for Power-Pack V-8, 40% for authenticated factory-installed fuel injection (1957); deduct 20% for six-cylinder.

1956 Bel Air Nomad wagon

1955-57
CHEVROLET ONE-FIFTY
(EXCEPT WAGONS)

1957 150 Utilty sedan

Bottom-of-the-line doesn't mean undesirable when it comes to mid-'50s Chevys. Excellent styling and V-8 engines offering up to 1 hp per cubic inch by 1957 make even the plain-Jane One-Fiftys definite collector's items. But you've got to have the "right" equipment, which usually means a hairy engine and stick shift. Chevrolet offered a wide assortment of engine tunes and two different V-8 displacements, and even the milder versions provided sparkling performance. All Chevys in these years are the right size, too—not too small for six passengers, not too big to get out of their own way. The two-door Utility sedan is too bare, the four-door too "practical." We'd take the standard 1957 two-door with a 283 V-8, a leadfoot's temptation if ever there was one.

FOR Priced less than corresponding Two-Tens and Bel Airs • Broad powerplant choice • Exceptional styling • Readily available parts

AGAINST Spartan interiors • Minimal flash (though that's not all bad)

PRODUCTION
1955 4d sdn 29,898 **2d sdn** 66,416 **Utility sdn** 11,196 **1956 4d sdn** 51,544 **2d sdn** 82,384 **Utility sdn** 9879 **1957 4d sdn** 52,266 **2d sdn** 70,774 **Utility sdn** 8300

SPECIFICATIONS
Length (in.)	195.6 (1955), 197.5 (1956), 200.0 (1957)
Wheelbase (in.)	115.0
Weight (lbs)	3070-3236
Price (new)	$1593-2048

ENGINES
cid/type	bhp	years
235.5/ohv I-6	123/136/140	1955-57
265/ohv V-8	162-225	1955-57
283/ohv V-8	185-283	1957

PRICES
FAIR	$2000-4500
GOOD	$4500-7000
FINE	$7000-8500

FINE EXAMPLE PRICE HISTORY
1982 $4000		**1994** $8000	
1990 $7500		**1998** $8500	

1982-2000 RETURN 5%
2000-2010 5%
Add 10% for air conditioning, 15% for Power-Pack V-8, 50% for authenticated factory-installed fuel injection (1957); deduct 10% for six-cylinder.

1955-57
CHEVROLET PICKUP

Workhorse of the 1955-57 Chevy pickup line was the Series 3100, with a traditional "stepside" bed design but little else that was traditional. Indeed, the designs of these trucks were considerably more forward-looking than anything offered by their competitors. Because pickups were used more frequently for personal transportation by this time, and as rolling advertisements for businesses, a market for style existed. Chevy obliged with car-inspired wraparound windshields, eggcrate grilles, and hooded headlamps. Chevy's new 265-cid V-8 produced 145 bhp for '55, and 140 for 1956. The "Trademaster" V-8, new for '56, produced 155 horses. Jewel of the 3100 Series was the Cameo Carrier, a smartly slab-sided beauty with the car-style cues described above, full-width rear window, smooth-sided cargo bed, and two-tone upholstery.

FOR Good looks • Creature com-forts • Excellent performance with six and V-8 • Restoration costs reasonable • One of the most significant American pickups (Cameo) • High future values (Cameo) • Lots of survivors to choose from (base 3100) • Good parts supplies (base 3100)

AGAINST Relatively common (base 3100) • Susceptible to rust • Over-priced on collector market (Cameo) • Some hardware very scarce (Cameo)

PRODUCTION
1955 219,805 **1956** 194,015 **1957** 198,535

SPECIFICATIONS
Length (in.)	NA
Weight (lbs)	3210-3217
Wheelbase (in.)	114.0
Price (new)	$1519-1800

ENGINES
cid/type	bhp	years
235.ohv 5 I-6	123	1955
265 ohv V-8	145	1955
235.ohv 5 I-6	140	1956-57
265 ohv V-8	155	1956-57

PRICES
FAIR	$7000-11,000
GOOD	$11,000-16,000
FINE	$16,000-22,500
Other	
FAIR	$3000-5500
GOOD	$5500-9000
FINE	$9000-11,000

2000-2010 RETURN 3%

1955 Cameo Carrier pickup

1956 3100 Series pickup

1955-57
CHEVROLET TWO-TEN (EXCEPT WAGONS)

1957 210 Sport hardtop coupe

Midrange series in the enormously popular 1955-57 Chevy lineup, boasting a higher trim standard than the One-Fifty, but less sparkle than the Bel Air. The latter had more appeal when new, and does today. The sporty Two-Tens are more affordable than their Bel Air counterparts, however, and offer the same attractive styling, features, and performance. Fewer were sold new, so fewer are around now. Though Chevy's full range of engines was available, most Two-Tens were equipped for workaday duty.

✚ **FOR** Cheaper than Bel Air • Hardtops quite rare • Lovely looks • Parts plentiful • Reasonable appreciation potential

▬ **AGAINST** Far behind Bel Air in collector esteem • Few equipped with performance engines or exotic accessories (though it's easy to add both)

PRODUCTION

1955 4d sdn 317,724 **2d sdn** 249,105 **2d htp** 11,675 **Delray cpe** 115,584 **1956 4d sdn** 283,125 **2d sdn** 205,545 **4d htp** 20,021 **2d htp** 18,616 **Delray cpe** 56,382 **1957 4d sdn** 260,401 **2d sdn** 162,090 **4d htp** 16,178 **2d htp** 22,631 **Delray cpe** 25,644

SPECIFICATIONS

Length (in.)	195.6 (1955), 197.5 (1956), 200.0 (1957)
Wheelbase (in.)	115.0
Weight (lbs)	3130-3320
Price (new)	$1775-2270

ENGINES

cid/type	bhp	years
232.5/ohv I-6	123/136/140	1955-57
265/ohv V-8	162-225	1955-57
283/ohv V-8	185-283	1957

PRICES

Htp

FAIR	$4000-9000
GOOD	$9000-13,500
FINE	$13,500-19,000
Others	
FAIR	$1000-5000
GOOD	$5000-7500
FINE	$7500-10,000

Add 10% for air conditioning, 5% for Power-Pack V-8, 50% for authenticated factory-installed fuel injection (1957); deduct 20% for six-cylinder.

FINE HARDTOP PRICE HISTORY

1982 $10,000		**1990** $20,000	
1994 $12,500		**1998** $18,000	
1982-2000 RETURN 4%			
2000-2010 6%			

1956-57
CHEVROLET CORVETTE

A dramatic improvement on the previous 'Vette. More rakish, better integrated styling featured concave bodyside coves, semi-frenched taillights, an optional hardtop, and a neater front end. Chevy made the V-8 engine standard, and had various optional stages of tune ranging up to the 283-bhp fuel-injected 283 for '57. Fine performance and aggressive good looks literally saved Corvette from an early demise, so this is a historic car apart from its other virtues.

✚ **FOR** Prime investment, especially the fuelie • Good all-around roadability on straights or curves • Better weather protection • Roll-up windows and hardtop • Styling • Rust-free body

▬ **AGAINST** Expensive today • High-performance models can cost a bundle to maintain • Can be overpowered and underbraked, depending on equipment

PRODUCTION

1956 3467 **1957** 6339

SPECIFICATIONS

Length (in.)	168.0
Wheelbase (in.)	102.0
Weight (lbs)	2730-2764
Price (new)	$3149-3465

ENGINES

cid/type	bhp	years
265/ohv V-8	225	1956
283/ohv V-8	220-283	1957

PRICES

FAIR	$13,000-25,000
GOOD	$25,000-35,000
FINE	$35,000-55,000

Add $2000 for two tops, $2000 for twin-4-bbl carbs, $5000+ for 1957 fuel injection

FINE 1957 PRICE HISTORY

1982 $25,000		**1990** $50,000	
1994 $65,000		**1998** $55,000	
1982-2000 RETURN 4%			
2000-2010 8%			

1958
CHEVROLET BEL AIR IMPALA

The 1958 Chevrolets used an all-new, one-year-only bodyshell shared with Pontiac (body sharing with other GM divisions began with the 1959 model year). The '58s were longer, lower, wider, and heavier than the 1955-57s. Styled in the Harley Earl idiom, they were "round" where their predecessors had been "straight." Though not as important as the "classic" Chevys, they expressed commendable restraint in an era of tailfin excesses, and were solidly built. The limited-production Impala, a package option for the Bel Air hardtop and convertibles, featured special trim, deluxe interiors, and the steepest price in the

1957 Corvette convertible

1958 Bel Air Impala hardtop coupe

lineup. A good reception caused Chevy to expand Impala offerings into a separate series for '59.

⊞ FOR Smooth if somewhat bulky styling • Good performance • Luxurious for a Chevy

▬ AGAINST Far less recognition than 1955-57 models • 348 V-8 addicted to gasoline • Handling sacrificed to smooth ride

PRODUCTION

2d htp 43,000 **conv** 17,000 (approx.)

SPECIFICATIONS

Length (in.)	209.1
Wheelbase (in.)	117.5
Weight (lbs)	3458-3523
Price (new)	$2586-2841

ENGINES

cid/type	bhp	years
235.5/ohv I-6	145	1958
283/ohv V-8	185/230/250	1958
348/ohv V-8	250/280/315	1958

PRICES

Conv	
FAIR	$12,000-20,000
GOOD	$20,000-30,000
FINE	$30,000-43,000
Hardtop deduct 50%	

FINE CONVERTIBLE PRICE HISTORY

1982 $10,000	1990 $55,000
1994 $45,000	1998 $40,000
1982-2000 RETURN 9%	
2000-2010 5%	

CHEVROLET CORVETTE

A bulkier extension of the 1956-57 Corvette design, with rather more ornate styling based on previous themes. Increased use of aluminum was featured on the 1960 models,

1959 Corvette convertible

which also received a new rear anti-sway bar to improve handling. A Corvette running under the Briggs Cunningham colors finished eighth overall at the 1960 Le Mans 24-Hour race. A washboard hood (simulated louvers) and twin decklid chrome strips identified the '58; the '59 and '60 were shorn of these doo-dads, and look almost identical to one another. A redesigned cockpit sported a new dash with all gauges grouped in a cluster directly ahead of the driver plus a passenger grab bar.

⊞ FOR Good value appreciation • Somewhat less expensive than 1956-57 models • Sizzling performance • Much improved handling

▬ AGAINST Busy styling (the quad lights don't look happy) • Needless chrome on the '58

PRODUCTION

1958 9168 **1959** 9670 **1960** 10,261

SPECIFICATIONS

Length (in.)	177.2
Wheelbase (in.)	102.0
Weight (lbs)	2793-2840
Price (new)	$3631-3934

ENGINES

cid/type	bhp	years
283/ohv V-8	230-315	1958-60

PRICES

FAIR	$13,000-22,000

GOOD	$22,000-30,000
FINE	$30,000-43,000

(Add $2000 for two tops, $2000 for twin-4-bbl carbs, $5000+ for fuel injection.)

FINE EXAMPLE PRICE HISTORY

1982 $15,000	1990 $40,000
1994 $55,000	1998 $48,000
1982-2000 RETURN 7%	
2000-2010 5%	

CHEVROLET PICKUP

1958 Cameo pickup

In the fifties pickups were getting more stylish and car-like. Chevrolet added integral front fenders to all trucks in 1955 and integral rear fenders on the expensive Cameo Carrier the same year. The Cameo was a deluxe trimmed pickup that used a fiberglass bed and rear fenders. Realizing a slab-sided pickup at reasonable price would be a big seller, Chevy added its Fleetside in 1958. The Feetside used a double walled steel bed, instead of the Cameo's fiberglass, to achieve the slab-sided look. Quad headlights were also added the same year. Also introduced in '58 was the Apache, a trim level with upgraded interior and more exterior chrome. The Cameo was no longer needed and discontinued for 1959. To go with the new car-like styling were available convenience features such as power steering, power brakes, and automatic transmissions. For those who took their trucks off the boulevards, 4-wheel drive was available. Buyers had a choice of Chevy's venerable six or new small-block V-8. In spite of progress in other areas, these pickups still rode on beam axles with leaf springs at each end. All Chevrolet pickups of these years are stylish, but the low production Cameo Carrier is the most collectible.

⊞ FOR Car-like styling • Available 4-wheel drive • Available V-8

▬ AGAINST Crude suspension

• Cameo Carriers hard to find

PRODUCTION

NA

SPECIFICATIONS

Length (in.)	193.6-206.3
Weight (lbs)	3260-3565
Wheelbase (in.)	114.0-127.0
Price (new)	$1,884-2,231

ENGINES

cid/type	bhp	years
235/ohv I-6	135/145	1958-60
283/ohv V-8	160	1958-60

PRICES

1958-60	
Fair	$5000-12,000
Good	$12,000-20,000
Fine	$20,000-30,000
Cameo	
Fair	$5000-12,000
Good	$12,000-20,000
Fine	$20,000-30,000
2000-2010 RETURN 3%	

1959-60
CHEVROLET IMPALA SPORT COUPE & CONVERTIBLE

The most glamorous of the "All New, All Over Again" Chevys and their less radical 1960 continuations. Like other '59 GM'ers, Chevys were longer (by two inches), lower (by one inch) and wider (by three inches outside, five inside). Curvier too, with vast new glass areas and thin-section roof-lines—a reply to Chrysler's "Forward Look" 1957 models. Chevy was the wildest of the GM bunch save for Cadillac, flaunting "bat wing" rear fenders, "cat's eye" taillamps, and a decklid "big enough to land a Piper Cub," as "Uncle

Tom" McCahill of Mechanix Illustrated quipped. Drivetrains were little changed, as was the new-for-'58 X-member chassis with four-link rear suspension. Optional "Level Air" suspension was retained, but still not popular and dropped after '60. Impala, a more successful '58 development, branched from a Bel Air subseries convertible and two-door hardtop Sport Coupe into a new top-line series encompassing a four-door sedan and a four-door hardtop Sport Sedan. Engines and appearance were somewhat tamer for 1960, the former for economy, the latter for sales, though demand remained about the same. Super-tune 348 big-block power available from mid-season '59, but as seldom seen today as "fuelie" small-blocks. These Impalas have finally achieved collector status, with the '59s enjoying an edge for their way-out styling. All remain reasonably priced. Comparable Impala and Bel Air Sport Sedans go for even less, but have many of the same appealing qualities and are definite collector "comers."

✚ FOR Unique styling • Reliable, well-known engines still easily maintained today • Affordable and readily available

▬ AGAINST Brakes tend to overheat and fade • Rust-prone • Slow manual steering (avoid it) • Dull performance with six • Far less wieldy than "classic" 1955-57 models

PRODUCTION

Coupe 182,520 **conv** 72,765 **1960 Sport Coupe** 204,467 **conv** 79,903

SPECIFICATIONS

Length (in.)	210.9
Wheelbase (in.)	119.0
Weight (lbs)	3570-3650
Price (new)	$2595-2970

ENGINES

cid/type	bhp	years
235.5/ohv I-6	135	1959-60
283/ohv V-8	170/185/230	1959-60

| 283/ohv V-8 | 250/290[1] | 1959 |
| 348/ohv V-8 | 250/320/335 | 1959-60 |

[1] fuel injected

PRICES

Htp	
FAIR	$4000-7000
GOOD	$7000-10,000
FINE	$10,000-17,000
Conv	
FAIR	$9000-12,000
GOOD	$12,000-18,000
FINE	$18,000-28,000

FINE CONVERTIBLE PRICE HISTORY

1982 $8000	1990 $32,000
1994 $33,000	1998 $25,000
1982-2000 RETURN 8%	
2000-2010 10%	

(Projection is for convertible only; hardtop, 5%)

1959 Impala Sport hardtop coupe

1960-64
CHEVROLET CORVAIR MONZA

1964 Corvair Monza coupe

Introduced midway through the 1960 model year, the sporty Monza coupe pushed Corvair sales upward dramatically. Before then, Chevy's compact with the air-cooled rear-mounted flat six had not sold well against the very conventional Ford Falcon. Monza quickly revealed an untapped market for bucket-seat compacts with deluxe interiors and, preferably, stick shifts. Chevrolet quickly brought out a convertible version, and began offering performance options such as better brakes, handling packages, and more horsepower. A solid hit, Monza was the best-selling Corvair by 1961, and would remain so right up to the end in 1969.

1960 Impala convertible

⊞ FOR Trend setter • Affordable today • Nice styling • Deluxe interiors • A Milestone car

⊟ AGAINST Twitchy handling on pre-1963 models (tire pressures critical) • Oil leaks • Tends to rust • Indifferent assembly quality

PRODUCTION

1960 cpe 11,926 **1961 cpe** 109,945 **4d sdn** 33,745
1962 cpe 144,844 **conv** 13,995 **4d sdn** 48,059
1963 cpe 117,917 **conv** 36,693 **4d sdn** 31,120
1964 cpe 88,440 **conv** 31,045 **4d sdn** 21,926

SPECIFICATIONS

Length (in.)	180.0
Wheelbase (in.)	108.0
Weight (lbs)	2280-2555
Price (new)	$2238-2492

ENGINES

cid/type	bhp	years
140/ohv flat 6	80/95	1960
145/ohv flat 6	80/98	1961-63
164/ohv flat 6	95/110	1964

PRICES

Cpe	
FAIR	$1500-3500
GOOD	$3500-5500
FINE	$5500-8000
Conv	
FAIR	$2000-4500
GOOD	$4500-7500
FINE	$7500-9500

FINE COUPE PRICE HISTORY

1982 $2500		**1990** $5500	
1994 $8000		**1998** $8000	
1982-2000 RETURN 6%			
2000-2010 6% (Conv 8%)			

1961-62
CHEVROLET CORVETTE

The 1958-60 Corvette, mildly "facelifted" with Bill Mitchell's ducktail rear end first shown on the racing Stingray and the XP-700 show car. Increased performance from the new 327 V-8 for the '62, which also deemphasized the bodyside cove sculpture

1961 Corvette convertible

and had a blacked-out grille. Both models retained quad headlamps but used a simplified mesh grille without previous 'Vettes' trademark teeth. Corvette won the Sports Car Club of America's A-production championship in 1962.

⊞ FOR Neater rear end styling • Significant performance boost on '62s • Last of the first-generation design

⊟ AGAINST Same bulky frontal look • Fuel thirst

PRODUCTION

1961 10,939 **1962** 14,531

SPECIFICATIONS

Length (in.)	176.7
Wheelbase (in.)	102.0
Weight (lbs)	2905-2925
Price (new)	$3934-4038

ENGINES

cid/type	bhp	years
283/ohv V-8	230-315	1961
327/ohv V-8	250-360	1962

PRICES

FAIR	$13,000-20,000
GOOD	$20,000-30,000
FINE	$30,000-40,000

(Add $5000 for fuel injection or 360-bhp 327; $3000 for 340 bhp; $2000 for two tops.)

FINE NORMAL ENGINE EXAMPLE PRICE HISTORY

1982 $15,000		**1990** $35,000	
1994 $48,000		**1998** $48,000	
1982-2000 RETURN 7%			
2000-2010 8%			

1961
CHEVROLET CORVAIR 500 LAKEWOOD

The stripped version of the Corvair wagon, with the same general qualities of the midrange 700-series model but a plainer, cheaper interior.

The only year for the wagon in this trim level. Like 700 models, wagon styling was derived from that of the original Corvair sedans.

⊞ FOR As for 700 Lakewood, plus rarity and one-year model status

⊟ AGAINST As for 700 Lakewood • Low collector interest

PRODUCTION

5591

SPECIFICATIONS

Length (in.)	180.0
Wheelbase (in.)	108.0
Weight (lbs)	2530
Price (new)	$2266

ENGINES

cid/type	bhp	years
145/ohv flat 6	80/98	1961

PRICES

FAIR	$1000-2500
GOOD	$2500-3500
FINE	$3500-5000

FINE EXAMPLE PRICE HISTORY

1982 $2000		**1990** $6000	
1994 $6000		**1998** $5500	
1982-2000 RETURN 5%			
2000-2010 3%			

1961-62
CHEVROLET CORVAIR 700 LAKEWOOD WAGON

1961 Corvair 700 Lakewood wagon

Before the Monza coupe started selling so spectacularly, Chevy's marketing plan for Corvair called for practical vehicles for the second model year. That included these wagons (called Lakewood only for 1961). The Monza's image rubbed off on this little hauler, making it a sort of sport wagon. With a stick shift and various aftermarket performance and handling accessories, it could be exactly that. The pancake six allowed a flat, though high, cargo bed, and the basic Corvair styling suited the wagon body style well. Not important historically, but a car with great character and potential appeal to collectors, especially those who need something distinctive for carrying loads to flea markets.

⊞ FOR Good looks • Scarcity • Very affordable • Low operating costs

⊟ AGAINST The usual early Corvair problems: oversteer (tire pressures critical), oil leaks, rust • Mundane interior • Dropped before the advent of factory performance options

PRODUCTION
1961 20,451 **1962** 3716

SPECIFICATIONS
Length (in.)	180.0
Wheelbase (in.)	108.0
Weight (lbs)	2555-2590
Price (new)	$2331-2407

ENGINES
cid/type	bhp	years
145/ohv flat 6	80/98	1961-62

PRICES
FAIR	$1200-2750
GOOD	$2750-4000
FINE	$4000-5500

FINE EXAMPLE PRICE HISTORY
1982 $2200		**1990** $6500	
1994 $6500		**1998** $6000	
1982-2000 RETURN 5%			
2000-2010 3%			

1961-64
CHEVROLET IMPALA SUPER SPORT V-8

The sporty compact concept applied to the full-size Chevrolet, and it worked remarkably well. Sixes were available for 1962-64, though not many were built. SS equipment, intro-duced mid-1961, was available only for the top-line Impala. The V-8 hardtop and convertible are the center of collector interest today. The Chevy 283/327 offered a good combination of power and efficiency, while the big-block—348 in 1961, 409 in 1961-64—provided neck-snapping performance. The typical SS also had handling and brake options and a 3- or 4-speed manual gearbox besides regular items like bucket seats, console, and deluxe interior. Big, but more competent on twisty back roads than many sports car drivers suspect.

⊞ FOR Still relatively inexpensive • Perhaps the next hot collector items after 1955-57 • Crisp styling • High performance • Reproduction parts available

⊟ AGAINST All the faults with which big cars have been cursed for so long • Fuel thirst • Indifferent construction quality

PRODUCTION
1961 453 **1962** approx. 100,000 **1963** 153,271 **1964** 185,325 with 409 engine: **1961** 142 **1962** 15,091

SPECIFICATIONS
Length (in.)	209.3-210.4
Wheelbase (in.)	119.0
Weight (lbs)	approx. 3500-3800
Price (new)	approx. $3000 (1961), $3200 (1964) with base engines

ENGINES
cid/type	bhp	years
283/ohv V-8	170-195	1962-64
327/ohv V-8	250/300	1962-64
348/ohv V-8	205/340/350	1961
409/ohv V-8	340-425	1961-64

PRICES
Htp	
FAIR	$5000-8000
GOOD	$8000-10,000
FINE	$10,000-17,000
Conv	
FAIR	$8000-10,000
GOOD	$10,000-20,000

1961 Impala Super Sport hardtop coupe

FINE	$20,000-27,500

SS409: add 25% to above prices.

FINE SS CONVERTIBLE PRICE HISTORY
1982 $7500		**1990** $20,000	
1994 $30,000		**1998** $30,000	
1982-2000 RETURN 8%			
2000-2010 5% (SS409 10%)			

1962-64
CHEVROLET CORVAIR MONZA SPYDER

1964 Corvair Monza Spyder convertible

Chevy's "other" sports car in the early '60s, with a big increase in power over other Corvairs from a carefully engineered turbocharger. Strong performance, multi-gauge instrumentation set in a brushed aluminum panel, numerous handling and sports accessories, and a choice of coupe or convertible made the Spyder an ideal domestic alternative to the cramped and uncomfortable low-buck foreign sports cars of the period. Unfortunately, it was introduced right as Corvair sales peaked, and its relatively high base price and mechanical complexity kept sales modest.

⊞ FOR The most desirable pre-1965 Corvair (especially the convertible) • Good parts supplies (except for blower) • Outstanding performance and handling

⊟ AGAINST Not the "poor man's Porsche" some claimed it to be • Difficult to find in an unmodified state • Blower parts may prove scarce

PRODUCTION
1962 cpe 6894 **conv** 2574 **1963 cpe** 11,627 **conv** 7472 **1964 cpe** 6480 **conv** 4761

SPECIFICATIONS
Length (in.)	180.0
Wheelbase (in.)	108.0
Weight (lbs)	2440-2650
Price (new)	$2589-2811

ENGINES

cid/type	bhp	years
145/ohv flat 6	150[1]	1962-63
164/ohv flat 6	150[1]	1964

[1]Turbocharged

PRICES

Htp	
FAIR	$2000-4000
GOOD	$4000-6000
FINE	$6000-7500
Conv	
FAIR	$3000-5000
GOOD	$5000-7500
FINE	$7500-11,000

FINE CONVERTIBLE PRICE HISTORY

1982 $6000	1990 $8000
1994 $12,000	1998 $12,000

1982-2000 RETURN 5%
2000-2010 5%

1962 CHEVROLET CORVAIR MONZA WAGON

1962 Corvair Monza wagon

The most desirable—and scarcest—Corvair wagon. It sported the full Monza treatment: carpeting, bucket seats, color-keyed upholstery. Most often found with automatic transmission, sad to say, which makes manual models that much more highly prized. Like most sporty wagons, it wasn't very popular new, as indeed was the case for all Corvair wagons, which lived for only two model years.

➕ FOR The best buy and highest investment potential among Corvair wagons • Others as for 1961-62 700 models • Monza trim and equipment

➖ AGAINST Extremely rare • Likely to command a fairly stiff price if the owner knows it • Serious oversteer (tire pressures critical)

PRODUCTION

2362

SPECIFICATIONS

Length (in.)	180.0
Wheelbase (in.)	108.0
Weight (lbs)	2590
Price (new)	$2569

ENGINES

cid/type	bhp	years
145/ohv flat 6	80/102	1962

PRICES

FAIR	$1500-2500
GOOD	$2500-4000
FINE	$4000-7000

FINE EXAMPLE PRICE HISTORY

1982 $2500	1990 $7000
1994 $7500	1998 $7000

1982-2000 RETURN 5%
2000-2010 5%

1963-67 CHEVROLET CHEVY II NOVA SUPER SPORT

The compact Falcon-beater wasn't immediately seen as a candidate for the SS treatment, but with the rapid expansion in high-performance small cars Chevrolet offered a bucket-seat SS package for the 1963 Chevy II Nova. These were all six-cylinder cars; a factory V-8 didn't appear until 1964. The latter made this humdrum compact quite a stormer, and won it enthusiastic, if limited, appreciation by performance buyers in its day. Unfortunately, Chevy couldn't get this act completely together. The convertible disappeared after 1963, before the factory V-8 was offered, and some thought the 1966-67 redesign clumsy. Nevertheless, the V-8 versions in the last two years of this generation are highly prized today.

➕ FOR Low-priced • 1963 and 1966-67 models in fairly good supply at present • Still contemporary in size • Light and fast

➖ AGAINST Not yet a prime collectible • Fit and finish debatable • Big-engine models overpowered for brakes, suspension

PRODUCTION

1963 42,432 **1964** 10,576 **1965** 9100 **1966** 21,000 **1967** 10,100

SPECIFICATIONS

Length (in.)	183.0-184.7
Wheelbase (in.)	110.0
Weight (lbs)	approx. 2600-2870
Price (new)	$2430-2487 (six); approx. $2500 (base V-8 hardtop)

ENGINES

cid/type	bhp	years
194/ohv I-6	120	1963-67
230/ohv I-6	140/155	1964-66
250/ohv I-6	155	1967
283/ohv V-8	195/220	1964-67
327/ohv V-8	250-350	1964-67

PRICES

FAIR	$4000-6000
GOOD	$6000-10,000
FINE	$10,000-17,000

Add 30% for 350-bhp V-8.

FINE EXAMPLE PRICE HISTORY

1982 $4000	1990 $6500
1994 $12,000	1998 $13,000

1982-2000 RETURN 9%
2000-2010 5%

1963 Chevy II Nova Super Sport convertible

1963-67
CHEVROLET CORVETTE STING RAY COUPE

1964 Corvette Sting Ray coupe

A genuine grand touring car in every sense of the word, nicely hung together with a vast range of drivetrain options. One of the best styling efforts of the decade, the '63 in particular by virtue of its split rear window (stylist Bill Mitchell felt that deleting it on the '64 "spoiled the whole car"). No changes to the engine lineup for 1963, but the rear suspension was now a three-link independent setup with a single transverse leaf spring. Styling became generally cleaner in successive years. The shortest-lived Corvette design, and probably the most sought-after apart from the 1953-57 models.

FOR One of Chevrolet's greats, with high historical significance • Tremendous investment potential • Outstanding ride, handling, performance

AGAINST Commands high prices, though not as high as they once were

PRODUCTION

1963 10,594 **1964** 8304 **1965** 8186 **1966** 9958 **1967** 8504

SPECIFICATIONS

Length (in.)	approx. 175.5
Wheelbase (in.)	98.0
Weight (lbs)	2859-3000
Price (new)	$4252-4353

ENGINES

cid/type	bhp	years
327/ohv V-8	250-365	1963-67
396/ohv V-8	425	1965
427/ohv V-8	390-435	1966-67

PRICES

1963	
FAIR	$12,000-18,000
GOOD	$18,000-27,000
FINE	$27,000-38,000
1964-67	
FAIR	$12,000-17,000
GOOD	$17,000-25,000
FINE	$25,000-35,000

Add 35% for 396/427 V-8s, 20% for factory fuel injection, $4000 for air conditioning and $3500 for factory knock-off wheels.

FINE 1963 MODEL PRICE HISTORY

1982 $15,000		**1990** $43,000	
1994 $55,000		**1998** $38,000	
1982-2000 RETURN 6%			
2000-2010 5%			

1963-67
CHEVROLET CORVETTE STING RAY CONVERTIBLE

Convertible counterpart to the Sting Ray coupe, with the same stunning appearance and blistering performance. Larger and more powerful engines including the big-block Mark IV unit beginning with 1965, which was the last year for the fuel-injection small-block V-8. Offered like earlier Corvette roadsters with optional lift-off hardtop. Shares Sting Ray coupe's independent rear suspension and interior design with interesting "twin cowl" dash.

FOR Less important than coupe, but still highly desirable • Open-air allure with Sting Ray looks, go • Roadability

AGAINST Expensive now, like the coupe

PRODUCTION

1963 10,919 **1964** 13,925 **1965** 15,376 **1966** 17,762 **1967** 14,436

SPECIFICATIONS

Length (in.)	175.5
Wheelbase (in.)	98.0

Weight (lbs)	2881-3020
Price (new)	$4037-4141

ENGINES

cid/type	bhp	years
327/ohv V-8	250-375	1963-67
396/ohv V-8	425	1965
427/ohv V-8	390-435	1966-67

PRICES

FAIR	$12,500-22,000
GOOD	$22,000-28,000
FINE	$28,000-42,000

Add 35% for 396/427 V-8s, 20% for factory fuel injection, $4000 for air conditioning and $3500 for factory knock-off wheels.

FINE EXAMPLE PRICE HISTORY

1982 $18,000		**1990** $40,000	
1994 $58,000		**1998** $39,000	
1982-2000 RETURN 5%			
2000-2010 5%			

1964-67
CHEVROLET CHEVELLE MALIBU SS V-8

1964 Malibu SS hardtop coupe

Chevrolet's attractive intermediate Super Sport, introduced with the new 1964 Chevelle line as a special series of six-cylinder (not widely collected) and V-8 hardtop coupes and convertibles. GM policy at the time prohibited engines over 400 cubes from being used in anything smaller than

1967 Corvette Sting Ray convertible

standard-size cars save Corvettes, but the 396 option for 1966 and the maximum-power 327s before it gave dazzling pickup in the lighter Chevelle shell.

✚ **FOR** Crisp, clean styling • Reasonable overall size • Less costly than comparable Impala SS • Excellent roadability

▬ **AGAINST** Limited collector recognition until recently • Some body parts scarce now • Big-engine models predictably gas-hungry

PRODUCTION

1964 76,860 **1965** 101,577 (201 SS396s) **1966** 72,300 (all SS396) **1967** 63,000 (all SS396) (Figures include sixes)

SPECIFICATIONS

Length (in.)	197.0
Wheelbase (in.)	115.0
Weight (lbs)	3000-3485
Price (new)	$2646-3033 (with base V-8)

ENGINES

cid/type	bhp	years
283/ohv V-8	195/220	1964-65
327/ohv V-8	250/300/350	1964-65
396/ohv V-8	325-375	1966-67

PRICES

Htp:	
FAIR	$4500-8000
GOOD	$8000-12,500
FINE	$12,500-21,000
Conv:	
FAIR	$6500-11,000
GOOD	$11,000-17,000
FINE	$17,000-26,000
(Add 30% for S396.)	

FINE CONVERTIBLE PRICE HISTORY

1982 $5000		**1990** $24,000	
1994 $29,000		**1998** $26,000	
1982-2000 RETURN 11%			
2000-2010 15% (SS396); 10% (others)			

1965-66
CHEVROLET CORVAIR CORSA

Corsa offers all the good points of the 1962-64 Monza Spyder, plus the sensational styling of the second Corvair generation, and even more horsepower. The standard unblown 140-bhp flat six delivered fine getaway, but the turbocharged version was now up 20 percent in output, and could deliver 115 mph top speed and an 18-second quarter-mile time. In its day, this was perhaps the most sophisticated—certainly one of the most ambitious—cars ever to have come from Detroit: lightweight, world-class han-

1965 Corvair Corsa hardtop coupe

dling, and looks that simply couldn't be improved upon.

✚ **FOR** The most desirable Corvair • High appreciation guaranteed

▬ **AGAINST** As for Monza

PRODUCTION

1965 2d htp 20,291 **conv** 8353 **1966 2d htp** 7330 **conv** 3142

SPECIFICATIONS

Length (in.)	183.3
Wheelbase (in.)	108.0
Weight (lbs)	2475-2720
Price (new)	$2519-2665

ENGINES

cid/type	bhp	years
164/ohv flat 6	140	1965-66
164/ohv flat 6[1]	180	1965-66
[1]Turbocharged		

PRICES

Htp	
FAIR	$2000-3000
GOOD	$3000-6500
FINE	$6500-8500
Conv	
FAIR	$3000-5000
GOOD	$5000-7500
FINE	$7500-11,000

FINE CONVERTIBLE PRICE HISTORY

1982 $6000		**1990** $8000
1994 $12,000		**1998** $11,000
1982-2000 RETURN 2%		
2000-2010 2%		

1965-69
CHEVROLET CORVAIR MONZA

A design triumph from the Bill Mitchell era. Ironically, the Corvair brand was destined to slip away because of too-strong competition from the conventional, but very attrac-

1966 Corvair Monza convertible

tive Mustang, and because of bad publicity about handling problems of the 1960-62 Corvairs. This was the first postwar American car (other than the Corvette) with fully independent rear suspension. These later Corvairs had upper and lower control arms and coil springs (even Corvette lacked the latter), which banished handling ills completely. It remains underappreciated and underrated today, but it's certain to be regarded more highly in the future. This was the kind of car we should have had in the 1970s.

✚ **FOR** Styling • Sophisticated ride and roadability from all-independent suspension • Still affordable • Great fun to drive

▬ **AGAINST** Post-1967 models, though rare, suffer driveability problems as stiffer emission controls took effect • Rust-prone

PRODUCTION

1965 2d htp 88,954 **4d htp** 37,157 **conv** 26,466 **1966 2d htp** 37,605 **4d htp** 12,497 **conv** 10,345 **1967 2d htp** 9771 **4d htp** 3157 **conv** 2109 **1968 2d htp** 6807 **conv** 1386 **1969 2d htp** 2717 **conv** 521

SPECIFICATIONS

Length (in.)	183.3
Wheelbase (in.)	108.0
Weight (lbs)	2440-2770
Price (new)	$2347-2641

ENGINES

cid/type	bhp	years

164/ohv flat 6   95/110/140   1965-69

PRICES

Htp
FAIR	$2000-3000
GOOD	$3000-5500
FINE	$5500-7000

(Deduct 10% for four-door hardtop.)

Conv
FAIR	$2800-4300
GOOD	$4300-6500
FINE	$6500-8000

FINE CONVERTIBLE PRICE HISTORY

1982 $4500		**1990** $7000	
1994 $9000		**1998** $8000	

1982-2000 RETURN 2%
2000-2010 2%

1965-69
CHEVROLET IMPALA SUPER SPORT V-8

The SS edition of the larger, more ponderous full-size Chevy introduced for 1965. The separate Impala SS series vanished for 1968-69, and the equipment reverted to option status, just as in 1961. The 1969 model was officially designated the Impala SS427. As with earlier models, interest centers mainly on the V-8 cars. Six-cylinder versions were offered through '68, but were really a contradiction in terms. "Hi-po" big Chevy production tapered off rapidly after 1965, and was only a fraction of division output by the end of the decade.

FOR Less costly than pre-1965 models • Later editions quite rare • High performance for the period • Luxury interior • SS427 may be a sleeper

AGAINST Bulky, big, and (to many eyes) indifferently styled • Low mileage

1969 Impala Super Sport convertible

• Limited collector recognition

PRODUCTION

1965 243,114 **1966** 119,314 **1967** 76,055 (2124 SS427) **1968** 38,210 (1778 SS427) **1969** 2455 (all SS427)

SPECIFICATIONS

Length (in.)	213.2 (1966-67), 214.7 (1968), 215.9 (1969)
Wheelbase (in.)	119.0
Weight (lbs)	3570-3835
Price (new)	$2950-3650 (base engine)

ENGINES

cid/type	bhp	years
283/ohv V-8	195/200	1965-67
307/ohv V-8	200	1968
327/ohv V-8	250-350	1965-68
396/ohv V-8	325	1966-69
427/ohv V-8	385/390/425	1966-69

PRICES

Conv
FAIR	$4000-8500
GOOD	$8500-13,000
FINE	$13,000-20,000

Htp
FAIR	$2000-4500
GOOD	$4500-8000
FINE	$8000-14,000

(1965-66 models are at the high end of above ranges, 1967-69 at the low end.)

FINE 1965 CONVERTIBLE PRICE HISTORY

1982 $7500		**1990** $15,000	
1994 $24,000		**1998** $20,000	

1982-2000 RETURN 6%
2000-2010 5%

1967 Impala Super Sport hardtop coupe

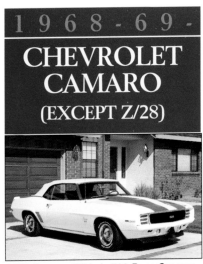

1968-69-
CHEVROLET CAMARO
(EXCEPT Z/28)

1969 Camaro SS Indy 500 Pace Car convertible

Chevrolet's answer to the Ford Mustang—virtually the same formula, in fact, right down to wheelbase, chassis specs, and general powerteam availability. Like Mustang it was derived from a compact, the second-generation 1968 Chevy II/Nova, and marketed with numerous options. Practical size and clean styling—GM's somewhat swoopier version of the long-hood/short-deck Mustang theme—in hardtop coupe or convertible. Heavily facelifted for 1969; continued into calendar 1970 owing to delays with second-generation replacement. High production and the plethora of extra-cost equipment makes hunting for a specific model time-consuming but fun. The exception is the limited-edition high-performance Z/28. Prime picks among early "standard" Camaros include those with the SS or RS option packages—or both. The former delivered firm suspension and small-block V-8s, the latter mainly cosmetic touches including, most notably, hidden headlamps.

FOR A sure investment with V-8, though value increases have eased off lately • Strong collector and club interest • Good V-8 performance • Handy size • Many reproduction parts available

AGAINST Inconsistent assembly quality • Cramped in back • Meager trunk space

PRODUCTION

1967 Six 58,808 **V-8** 162,109[1] **1968 Six** 50,937 **V-8** 184,178[1] **1969 Six** 65,008 **V-8** 178,087[1]
[1]Includes Z/28 (see separate entry)

SPECIFICATIONS

Length (in.)	184.7 (1967-68), 186.0 (1969)
Wheelbase (in.)	108.1
Weight (lbs)	2770-3295

Price (new) $2466-4500

ENGINES

cid/type	bhp	years
230/ohv I-6	140	1967-68
250/ohv I-6	155	1967-69
327/ohv V-8	210/275	1967-69
350/ohv V-8	255/295/300	1967-69
396/ohv V-8	325	1968-69
427/ohv V-8	425	1969

PRICES

Htp	
FAIR	$2500-5000
GOOD	$5000-9500
FINE	$9500-14,000
Conv	
FAIR	$3500-7000
GOOD	$7000-13,000
FINE	$13,000-19,000

To the above prices: Add 10% for RS, 10% for SS, 20% for RS/SS, 25% for SS350. Indy Pace Car (1969) ranges from low of $4600 to high of $23,000 at present.

FINE CONVERTIBLE RS/SS PRICE HISTORY

1982 $8000		**1990** $18,000	
1994 $19,000		**1998** $19,000	
1982-2000 RETURN 6%			
2000-2010 8%			

1967-69
CHEVROLET CAMARO Z/28

This is the Camaro created to beat the Mustang in Sports Car Club of America Trans-Am racing—which it did, winning the championship in 1968 and '69. A package option for the Camaro coupe and the brainchild of Chevy marketing/competition whiz Vince Piggins, the Z/28 had as its heart a specially crafted 302 V-8 (the 327-cid block with the short-stroke 283 crank) rated at 290 horsepower, though actual bhp was closer to 400. Also included: F-41 heavy-duty suspension, front-disc brakes, metallic-lined rear drums,

1967 Camaro Z/28 hardtop coupe

quick steering, 15 x 6 Corvette wheels and 7.75-15 performance tires, special hood with working air intake, close-ratio four-speed gearbox, "ducktail" trunklid spoiler, and broad dorsal racing stripes—all for about $400 list and $800 actual (the four-speed and front discs being "mandatory options"). All-disc brakes became a "service option" during '68, along with a special twin four-barrel manifold ($500), five-leaf rear springs, and additional over-the-counter racing components. The facelifted '69 boasted a rear-facing "Cowl Induction" hood air intake, six-inch-wide rims with E70 tires, and four-bolt main bearings. Production figures imply a '67 is the collector's choice among these Zs, but all are highly coveted today as race-winning muscle/ponycars from the golden age of Detroit performance.

FOR As for 1967-69 Camaro plus lightning-quick performance • Race-track handling prowess • Rarity • Race-winner image

AGAINST As for 1967-69 Camaro, but stratospheric asking prices now • High-octane thirst (11.0:1 compression) • Clean, unmodified originals tough to find

PRODUCTION

1967 602 **1968** 7199 **1969** 19,014

SPECIFICATIONS

Length (in.) 184.7 (1967-68), 186.0 (1969)
Wheelbase (in.) 108.1
Weight (lbs) approx. 3000
Price (new) approx. $5000 delivered

ENGINES

cid/type	bhp	years
302/ohv V-8	290[1]	1967-69

[1]Nominal SAE gross bhp; actual bhp estimated at 400

PRICES

FAIR	$7000-15,000
GOOD	$15,000-20,000

FINE $20,000-25,000

FINE 1968 MODEL PRICE HISTORY

1982 $7000		**1990** $22,000	
1994 $24,000		**1998** $22,000	
1982-2000 RETURN 10%			
2000-2010 8%			

1968-72
CHEVROLET CHEVELLE SS396/SS454

The hairiest of the intermediate Super Sport Chevelles, marketed despite increasingly stringent government regulations that diluted muscle cars—and the muscle-car market—by 1972. Hung on for a few years afterward, but with diminished performance that makes those models far less collectible now. Subjects here employed GM's new-for-'68 "split-wheelbase" A-body platform that put two-door models on a four-inch shorter wheelbase than four-doors. Styling followed Chevy trends in being bulkier and more "sculptured" than in earlier years, but deluxe bucket-seat interiors and flashy paint/striping treatments set the Super Sports apart. For 1971-72, the Super Sport option was extended to any Chevelle V-8 right down to the base 307, and the name changed to Chevelle SS. These are less desirable than the big-block 1968-70 models, though they still pack a sizeable wallop.

FOR Very high 1968-70 performance • Manageable size • Styling still holds up reasonably well

AGAINST Piggish at the pump • Lower appreciation potential than earlier mid-size SS Chevs, especially post-1970s, though still good muscle-car prospects

PRODUCTION

1968 62,785 **1969** 86,307 **1970** 53,599 (SS454: 3733) **1971 SS454** 19,293

SPECIFICATIONS

Length (in.) 197.1-200.9
Wheelbase (in.) 112.0
Weight (lbs) approx. 3550-3700
Price (new) approx. $2900-3500 delivered

ENGINES

cid/type	bhp	years
396/ohv V-8	325/350/375	1968-69
402/ohv V-8[1]	350/375	1970
402/ohv V-8[1]	240/300[2]	1971-72
454/ohv V-8	360/425/450	1970-71
454/ohv V-8	270[3]	1972

[1]Advertised as "396" [2]SAE net/gross [3]SAE net

1971 Chevelle SS hardtop coupe

PRICES

SS396 htp
FAIR	$4000-6900
GOOD	$6900-9500
FINE	$9500-13,500

SS396 Conv
FAIR	$8000-10,500
GOOD	$10,500-17,000
FINE	$17,000-26,000

Add $3500 for 375-bhp 396 V-8.

SS454 htp
FAIR	$5000-8500
GOOD	$8500-13,000
FINE	$13,000-21,000

SS454 Conv
FAIR	$6000-10,000
GOOD	$10,000-19,000
FINE	$19,000-28,000

(Add 60% for LS6 engine.)

FINE SS396 CONVERTIBLE PRICE HISTORY

1982 $5500		**1990** $40,000	
1994 $23,000		**1998** $24,000	
1982-2000 RETURN 10%			
2000-2010 5%			

1 9 6 8 - 7 0

CHEVROLET CHEVY II/ NOVA SS

1968 Chevy II SS 396 coupe

Engineered alongside the 1967 Camaro, Chevrolet's second-series compact (the Chevy II name was offi-cially dropped in favor of Nova after 1968) was offered with some of its hefty engines, including the big 396 with up to 375 bhp. But the Super Sport was reduced to an option package in these years, and was not the separate series it had been previously. The Nova SS continued to be listed as late as 1976, though as with Chevy's other performance models it was not the hell-for-leather machine we knew in the late '60s. Clean, if somewhat anonymous, styling in the then-current GM mold bore a familial relationship to the contemporary Chevelle. Modest production numbers make these high-powered coupe/sedans likely climbers on the collector-car value scale in the future.

FOR A definite "comer" • Still afford-able • Fairly scarce • Zip • Sedan prac-ticality

AGAINST Undistinguished sedan styling • Overpowered • Thirsty • Indifferent construction quality

PRODUCTION

1968 5571 **1969** 17,564 **1970** 19,558

SPECIFICATIONS

Length (in.)	189.4
Wheelbase (in.)	111.0
Weight (lbs)	2995-3048
Price (new)	approx. $2600 (350 V-8)

ENGINES

cid/type	bhp	years
350/ohv V-8	295/300	1968-70
396/ohv V-8	325/350/375	1968-69
402/ohv V-8[1]	350/375	1970

[1]Advertised as "396"

PRICES

FAIR	$4000-6000
GOOD	$6000-8000
FINE	$8000-9000

FINE EXAMPLE PRICE HISTORY

1982 $2500		**1990** $9000	
1994 $7000		**1998** $6500	
1982-2000 RETURN 9%			
2000-2010 3%			

1 9 6 8 - 7 2

CHEVROLET CORVETTE STINGRAY

1970 Corvette LT-1 coupe

Long-lived successor to the 1963-67 Sting Ray in its first five years. Often called the "Shark" owing to all-new styling previewed by 1965 Mako Shark II show car. Production design by Henry Haga's studio under then-Chevy styling director David Holls—and the ever-watchful eye of GM design chief Bill Mitchell, who always considered the Corvette his "pet." Chassis and initial engine choices pretty much '67 carryovers. No model designation at first, but came back as one word—Stingray—from 1969. More begadgeted than 1963-67 (pop-up wipers, fiber-optic light monitors, etc.) and thus heavier. Europeans, curious-ly, liked it more than Americans. Visi-bility, driving position, and cabin/cargo space also suffered. But the new notchback T-top coupe was predictive and popular, outpolling the top-selling convertible for the first time in 1969, and total sales kept trending up (save strike-plagued 1970). Somewhat freer-breathing engines give 1968-70s a slight value edge over 1971-72s, though big-blocks and tuned small-blocks persisted throughout.

FOR Show car style and gadgetry • Tremendous go, especially with big-blocks • Rot-free body (but not chas-sis) • Most every Corvette made is a collectible

AGAINST Generally less desired than 1963-67 Sting Rays • Bulkier, less sporting to drive, too • Fuelishness • Cramped cabin • Inconsistent work-manship • Often trashed by first owners

PRODUCTION

1968 cpe 9936 **conv** 18,630 **1969 cpe** 22,154 **conv** 16,608 **1970 cpe** 10,668 **conv** 6648 **1971**

cpe 14,680 conv 7121 **1972 cpe** 20,486 **conv** 6508

SPECIFICATIONS

Length (in.)	182.5
Wheelbase (in.)	98.0
Weight (lbs)	3055-3215
Price (new)	$4320-5475

ENGINES

cid/type	bhp	years
327/ohv V-8	350	1968
350/ohv V-8	300/350/370	1969-70
350/ohv V-8	200/210/255/275[1]	1971-72
427/ohv V-8	400/430/435	1968-69
454/ohv V-8	390/460	1970
454/ohv V-8	270/285/325[1]	1971-72

[1]SAE net; all others SAE gross

PRICES

Conv	
FAIR	$9000-18,000
GOOD	$18,000-32,000
FINE	$32,000-50,000
Cpe	
FAIR	$7500-24,000
GOOD	$24,000-30,000
FINE	$30,000-46,000

Special engines price range: L88 +400%, L89 +75%

FINE CONVERTIBLE PRICE HISTORY

1982 $9000		**1990** $25,000	
1994 $35,000		**1998** $30,000	
1982-2000 RETURN 11%			
2000-2010 10%			

1970
CHEVROLET CAMARO

A stunning rework of the Chevrolet ponycar, and so good that this second generation would last a dozen years. Sad to say, the convertible body style was dropped; it would have looked stunning. Collector interest in Camaros thus far has generally been

1970 Camaro Z28 coupe

in the 1967-69s, but the 1970 and newer examples are certain to gain in appeal. At what model year the detuned engines of the '70s will take its toll on collectibility is unclear, but post-1970 cars were certainly not in the same performance league with earlier Camaros. Styling didn't suffer as much as on many other cars of the '70s, due to soft-nose facelifts (1974 and '78) that were skillfully blended with the basic 1970 body lines. As the first of the breed, however, the '70 is the one to have.

✚ **FOR** Still reasonably inexpensive • Landmark styling • High appreciation potential (particularly the Z/28)

▬ **AGAINST** Bulkier than 1967-69 • High operating costs with big engines • Not half as roadable as it looks without proper suspension and brake options

PRODUCTION

Sixes 12,566 **V-8s** 112,323 (including 8733 Z/28s)

SPECIFICATIONS

Length (in.)	188.0
Wheelbase (in.)	108.1
Weight (lbs)	3076-3300 (approx.)
Price (new)	$2749-5000+; average V-8: $3500

ENGINES

cid/type	bhp	years
250/ohv I-6	155	1970
307/ohv V-8	200	1970
350/ohv V-8	250/300/360	1970
396/ohv V-8	350/375	1970

PRICES

RS/SS 350	
FAIR	$2500-5000
GOOD	$5000-8000
FINE	$8000-15,000

(Deduct 30% for non-RS/SS 350 models.)
SS 396

FAIR	$6000-8000
GOOD	$8000-13,000
FINE	$13,000-16,000

FINE SS350 PRICE HISTORY

1982 $2500		**1990** $8000	
1994 $17,000		**1998** $15,000	
1982-2000 RETURN 7%			
2000-2010 6%			

1970-71
CHEVROLET MONTE CARLO SS454

1970 Monte Carlo SS454 hardtop coupe

Chevy's fling at a red-hot personal-luxury car. Introduced for 1970, the Monte Carlo was based on the intermediate Chevelle platform, but had a different roofline and the longest hood ever put on a Chevy. Equipped with the mild 307 and 350 V-8s, it offered luxury and smoothness, and was a solid sales hit. A few buyers checked RPO Z20 on the order form, however, and got the 360-bhp 454 big-block V-8, square-tip dual exhausts, and a chassis fortified with automatic-level-control rear shocks, stiffer-than-stock front shocks, and power front disc brakes. Only discreet SS454 badges and thin black rocker panel accents gave a clue as to what was under the hood. Acceleration was vivid: 0-60 mph in 7.7 seconds, the quarter-mile in 16.2 seconds at 90-plus mph. A handful of nonstandard options found their way onto SS Montes, too, such as the 450-bhp LS-6 engine and M-series four-speed manual gearbox (Turbo Hydra-matic was standard). The '71 rendition was little changed except for slightly bolder ornamentation and eye-catching Rally wheels. Altogether, a rare and interesting Chevy from the twilight years of the performance age.

✚ **FOR** A different sort of Chevy: an adult hot rod • Very fast • Subdued good looks • Good roadability • Cushy cabin • Low-production appeal • Sure-fire appreciator

AGAINST A gas hog • Difficult to find • Indifferent construction quality

PRODUCTION
1970 3823 **1971** 1919

SPECIFICATIONS
Length (in.)	205.8
Wheelbase (in.)	116.0
Weight (lbs)	approx. 3600
Price (new)	approx. $3543-3757

ENGINES
cid/type	bhp	years
454/ohv V-8	360/425/450	1970-71

Prices
FAIR	$4500-6000
GOOD	$6000-10,000
FINE	$10,000-13,000

FINE EXAMPLE PRICE HISTORY
1982 $3500	**1990** $12,000
1994 $15,000	**1998** $16,000
1982-2000 RETURN 8%	
2000-2010 5%	

1971-72
CHEVROLET CAMARO Z/28

Continuation of Chevy's beautifully styled second-generation ponycar in its sportiest guise. Little changed from the "1970½" version, except for new high-back bucket seats and various mechanical changes that marked the start of the performance decline going on throughout Detroit. Because the Camaro wasn't spared GM's self-imposed, corporate-wide drop in compression ratios for '71 (along with the Corvette and Pontiac's Firebird), output of the Z's 350 V-8 tumbled from 360 to 330 bhp gross. The following year, use of SAE net horsepower figures made for a more dramatic apparent drop, down to 255. Still, this was one mean machine, offering taut, assured handling combined with very brisk straight-line pickup and nearly flawless appearance. The main reason these particular Camaros warrant inclusion is their low production. The '72s are particularly scarce, reflecting a strike that shut down the Norwood, Ohio, plant for 174 days.

FOR As for 1970 Camaro, plus greater exclusivity

AGAINST As for 1970 Camaro, plus lower Z/28 performance in these years

PRODUCTION
1971 4862 **1972** 2575

SPECIFICATIONS
Length (in.)	188.0
Wheelbase (in.)	108.1
Weight (lbs)	3300
Price (new)	approx. $4000

ENGINES
cid/type	bhp	years
350/ohv V-8	275/255[1]	1971-72

[1]SAE net; rated at 330 bhp gross in 1971

PRICES
FAIR	$5500-7500
GOOD	$7500-10,000
FINE	$10,000-15,000

FINE EXAMPLE PRICE HISTORY
1982 $4000	**1990** $15,000
1994 $17,500	**1998** $13,000
1982-2000 RETURN 8%	
2000-2010 8%	

1973-74
CHEVROLET CORVETTE

The third-generation "Shark" in the years of the first energy crisis and a two-stage transitional facelift. The '73 is unique among 'Vettes for combining a smooth body-color nose with the original '68-vintage "Kamm" tail; the '74 rear was restyled to match the front and for the same reason: Washington's then-new mandate for 5-mph bumpers. Engines further detuned for cleaner air, with the mighty 454 breathing its last for '74. A good many other "lasts" that year, including genuine dual exhausts. Generally simplified over 1968-72 (rear hood extension to conceal wipers instead of pop-up panel, fixed coupe backlight instead of removable). Also improved, with standard radial tires, more efficient Turbo Hydra-Matic option, combined lap/shoulder belts, etc. Besides final big-blocks, collectors should look out for the RPO FE7 Gymkhana Suspension (high-rate springs/shocks for only $7) and the similar Z07 option (with heavy-duty brakes).

FOR As for 1968-72, plus fewer gimmicks • Better workmanship • More rational performance/economy balance • Arguably smoother fore/aft styling

AGAINST As for 1968-72, but down on performance and thus lower potential value return

PRODUCTION
1973 cpe 24,372 **conv** 6093 **1974 cpe** 32,028 **conv** 4629

SPECIFICATIONS
Length (in.)	184.5/185.5 (1973/74)
Wheelbase (in.)	98.0
Weight (lbs)	3325-3390
Price (new)	$5399-$6082

ENGINES
cid/type	bhp[1]	years
350/ohv V-8	190/195/250	1973-74
454/ohv V-8	270/275	1973-74

[1]SAE net

PRICES
Conv	
FAIR	$8000-11,000
GOOD	$11,000-15,000
FINE	$15,000-22,000
Cpe	
FAIR	$5000-8000
GOOD	$8000-12,000
FINE	$12,000-20,000

FINE CONVERTIBLE PRICE HISTORY
1982 $7500	**1990** $17,000
1994 $26,000	**1998** $26,000
1982-2000 RETURN 7%	
2000-2010 5%	

1974 Corvette convertible

1975-77

CHEVROLET CORVETTE STINGRAY

1977 Corvette coupe

The last Stingray "Sharks," though not called Stingray for '77. Same basic styling as '74 save small black-rubber bumper pads and, after 1975, no rear-deck air-extractor vents on coupe. Power now solely 350 small-block in standard and optional higher-output tune. Outputs hit bottom for '75, then climbed slightly with higher compression made possible by newly adopted catalytic converter. Once-mainstay convertible dropped after '75 due to waning sales and a threatened government rollover standard that never materialized. But this was not destined to be the last open-air 'Vette. Few notable changes in these years, but electronic ignition (1975), four-spoke steering wheel (1976), and revamped controls and center console, standard leather upholstery, and no-cost power steering/brakes (1977).

✚ FOR As for 1973-74, but even better performance/economy balance

▬ AGAINST As for 1973-74, but more "used car" than collectible right now, though that's changing

PRODUCTION

1975 cpe 33,836 **conv** 4629 **1976 cpe** 46,558 **1977 cpe** 49,213

SPECIFICATIONS

Length (in.)	185.5
Wheelbase (in.)	98.0
Weight (lbs.)	3430-3450
Price (new)	$6537-8648

ENGINES

cid/type	bhp[1]	years
350/ohv V-8	165/205	1975
350/ohv V-8	180/210	1976-77

[1]SAE net

Prices

Conv	
FAIR	$9000-11,500
GOOD	$11,500-17,000
FINE	$17,000-22,000
Cpe	
FAIR	$4500-6000
GOOD	$6000-10,000
FINE	$10,000-14,000

Add $1000 for air conditioning, $500 for 205-bhp V-8 (1975).

FINE CONVERTIBLE PRICE HISTORY

1982 $8000		**1990** $20,000	
1994 $22,000		**1998** $24,000	
1982-2000 RETURN 5%			
2000-2010 5%			

1975-76

CHEVROLET COSWORTH-VEGA

An unsuccessful try at shoring up the sagging image of the economy Vega. "CosVeg's" attraction was its engine, a destroked version of the regular aluminum-block, 2.3-liter (140-cid) Vega four with a twincam, 16-valve aluminum head designed by Cosworth Engineering in England. Bendix electronic fuel injection fed the cylinders, actuated by a glovebox-mounted computer. Chevy had originally planned to introduce the Cosworth engine as an option for 1974, but problems in meeting emissions standards pushed back the actual launch to April 1975. The result was somewhat disappointing: only 21 more horsepower than the "cooking" Vega (111 versus the 150 bhp rumored earlier) and a total price of well over $6000. The engine package was available only for the hatchback in only one color—black. It included special gold bodyside striping and cast aluminum wheels, wider radial tires, full instrumentation set in an engine-turned dash applique, anti-roll bars front and rear, specific gear ratios for the four-speed manual transmission, free-flow exhaust system, quick steering, and a special vehicle identification plate on the dash. Alas, the Cosworth engine didn't make the Vega into a BMW or Alfa beater. The problem was too little power for too much weight. Despite a planned production run of 5000 units annually, Chevy built less than half that number in 1975. The model continued into the 1976 season, available in any standard Vega color and offered with an optional five-speed gearbox. Many of the cars were still unsold at model year's end. The Vega itself would die after 1977, the victim of a poor reliability/ durability record.

✚ FOR Technical interest • Very rare • Fine handling • Decent performance (0-60 mph in 9 seconds) • Neat looks

▬ AGAINST The premature rusting common to all Vegas • Difficult to find in good condition • Little collector interest at present

PRODUCTION

1975 2061 **1976** 1447

SPECIFICATIONS

Length (in.)	175.4
Wheelbase (in.)	97.0
Weight (lbs)	2523
Price (new)	approx. $6000

ENGINES

cid/type	bhp[1]	years
122/dohc I-4	111	1975-76

[1]SAE net

PRICES

FAIR	$2500-3500
GOOD	$3500-5500
FINE	$5500-7000

FINE EXAMPLE PRICE HISTORY

1982 $5000		**1990** $6500	
1994 $8000		**1998** $8000	
1982-2000 RETURN 2%			
2000-2010 2%			

1975 Cosworth-Vega coupe

1 9 7 7 - 8 1
CHEVROLET CAMARO Z28

1977 Camaro Z28 coupe

Sporty Camaro emphasized handling finesse over straight-line go. Restored to the lineup for mid-'77 after a two-year hiatus to cash in on Camaro's publicity as car of the International Race of Champions (IROC), but also to counter the unbroken sales success of the rival Pontiac Firebird Trans Am in a performance market then reviving after the doldrums of gas-short 1973-74. Engineer Jack Turner decreed tighter springs, thicker front anti-roll bar, a more flexible rear bar, and the obligatory upsized wheel/tire package—all wrapped in bold exterior graphics and bright colors that admirably suited Camaro's basic 1970 body as facelifted from '74. Camaro was facelifted again for '78, and Z28 remained the performance leader until the second generation was retired after 1981. Appearance and equipment changes were evolutionary. Power exclusively 350 V-8s (with electronic control for '81). Turbo Hydra-Matic always available (with a lockup torque converter for '81), but four-speed manual only through 1980.

✚ FOR As for 1971-72 Camaro Z28 plus arguably better ride/handling balance • '77's rarity among second-generation Camaros • Quite affordable • Strong club support

▬ AGAINST Second-generation Camaro vices, including heavy thirst, shoebox-size trunk • Hard to find clean and unmodified • "Greaser" image • Still more "used car" than blue-chip collectible

PRODUCTION
1977 14,349 **1978** 54,907 **1979** 84,877 **1980** 45,137 **1981** 43,272

SPECIFICATIONS

Length (in.)	195.4 (1977), 197.6 (1978-81)
Wheelbase (in.)	108.0
Weight (lbs)	3350-3700
Price (new)	$5170-8265

ENGINES

cid/type	bhp[1]	years
350/ohv V-8	170	1977
350/ohv V-8	175/185	1978
350/ohv V-8	170/175	1979
350/ohv V-8	165/190	1980
350/ohv V-8	175	1981

[1]SAE net

PRICES

FAIR	$2000-3000
GOOD	$3000-4000
FINE	$4000-7000

FINE EXAMPLE PRICE HISTORY
1987 $2500   **1994** $8000
1998 $8000
1987-2000 RETURN 7%
2000-2010 2%

1 9 7 8
CHEVROLET CORVETTE PACE CAR REPLICA

One of two limited editions issued on 'Vette's 25th birthday. This facsimile of the Indy 500 pace car was decked out with a black upper body and silver-metallic lower body, plus the nice-looking alloy wheels and fat Goodyear tires worn by the Silver Anniversary model. The Pace Car Replica also carried front and rear spoilers. A novel touch was that the identifying "Pace Car" decals were supplied separately so the owner could apply them if desired. Upholstery was the buyer's choice of silver leather or a silver leather/grey cloth combination. The seats were a new design scheduled for all '79 Corvettes. Standard equipment included power windows, electric rear window defroster, air conditioning, sport mirrors, and other features, which boosted the Pace Car's price over $4000 above that of the standard Corvette. Because of the announced limited production run, however, the Replicas fetched upwards of $28,000 as would-be collector's items when new. This tempted some owners of standard 'Vettes to paint their cars to match to pass them off as "factory" Pace Cars. All this created much anguish for dealers and buyers alike. In fact, it still does. More than with any other factory special, it will pay to make sure that a '78 Corvette Pace Car is, in fact, the genuine article. The clue is the seats: similar to, but not exactly the same as, the ones used in production '79s. Chevrolet would remember this experience when it issued the Collector Edition 1982 model to mark the last of the third generation 'Vettes. The '78 Replicas came with the L-48 or L-82 V-8. Thus, apart from those seats, about the only way to tell a bogus car from the real thing is by serial number (numbers 900001-906502).

✚ FOR Uniqueness • The Corvette's usual performance and sex appeal • Fine handling • More luggage space than earlier fifth-generation models

▬ AGAINST Verifying authenticity takes more than usual effort • Not easily found • Quite thievable • Costs a mint to insure

PRODUCTION
6502

Corvette Pace Car Replica coupe

SPECIFICATIONS

Length (in.)	185.2
Wheelbase (in.)	98.0
Weight (lbs)	3500
Price (new)	$13,653

ENGINES

cid/type	bhp[1]	years
350/ohv V-8	185/220	1978
[1]SAE net		

PRICES

FAIR	$10,000-13,500
GOOD	$13,500-17,500
FINE	$17,500-23,000

FINE EXAMPLE PRICE HISTORY

1982 $13,000	1990 $25,000
1994 $27,000	1998 $23,000
1982-2000 RETURN 3%	
2000-2010 3%	

1978
CHEVROLET CORVETTE SILVER ANNIVERSARY EDITION

"America's Only True Sports Car" was 25 years old in 1978, and Chevy observed the milestone by fitting special commemorative emblems to all Corvettes that year. In one sense, all '78s can be considered "Silver Anniversary Editions," but one special option makes some more collectible today than others. This was the "25th

Anniversary Paint," option B2Z. It was described in the catalog as "a distinctive two-tone silver paint treatment... Upper body color is silver metallic with charcoal silver on lower body. Pin stripes accentuate front upper profiles, wheel openings, front fender vents, hood, and rear license cavity. Available aluminum wheels and dual sport mirrors required..." All Corvettes got a new fastback roofline with a large, wrap-around backlight for '78. Four-speed manual shift was reinstated as standard, and a higher-output 350 V-8 was optional.

✚ FOR As for 1978 Corvette Pace Car Replica

▬ AGAINST As for 1978 Corvette Pace Car Replica

PRODUCTION

15,283

SPECIFICATIONS

Length (in.)	185.2
Wheelbase (in.)	98.0
Weight (lbs)	3400 (approx.)
Price (new)	approx. $9600

ENGINES

cid/type	bhp[1]	years
350/ohv V-8	175/185/220	1978
[1]SAE net		

PRICES

FAIR	$7000-9000
GOOD	$9000-13,000
FINE	$13,000-20,000

FINE EXAMPLE PRICE HISTORY

1982 $10,500	1990 $17,500
1994 $26,500	1998 $23,000
1982-2000 RETURN 3%	
2000-2010 3%	

1978 Corvette Silver Anniversary Edition coupe

1982-92
CHEVROLET CAMARO Z28 & IROC-Z

1988 Camaro IROC-Z coupe

Modern muscle/ponycars of the third Camaro generation introduced for 1982. Handsome styling (directed by Jerry Palmer) not greatly changed throughout, nor basic chassis specs—including new-to-Camaro all-coil suspension with front MacPherson struts, plus rack-and-pinion steering. Traditional Z28 sport coupe joined for 1985 by still-sportier IROC-Z companion inspired by the Camaros then featured in the International Race of Champions; hallmarks were fortified chassis, bigger rolling stock, unique trim, and a 4-barrel, 190-horsepower 305 V-8 with five-speed manual shift or 215-bhp throttle-body-injected engine with Turbo Hydra-Matic. Optional port-injected 350 V-8 arrived for '87 IROCs, along with Z28 and IROC convertibles, the first open-air Camaros since 1969. Increasingly popular IROC replaced the Z28 entirely after 1987, but the Z28 ousted it after 1990, when Chevy's supplier contract with the IROC event expired. Reborn convertible was engineered and converted by ASC, Inc; top manual but convenient, stowing beneath power-latched metal boot. Year-to-year changes too numerous to detail, but all these Camaros shape up as eminently worthy future collectibles, with 350-cid IROCs and all drop-tops likely to see stronger value gains sooner.

✚ FOR '60s-style performance with '80s-style economy • Sharp handling • Convertibles' relative rarity and ever-green allures • Muscle-car character

▬ AGAINST Styling somewhat dated after a decade • Limited cabin/cargo space • Crowded driving position • Patchy ergonomics • Generally indifferent workmanship

PRODUCTION

1982 Z28 spt cpe 63,563 **1983 Z28 spt cpe** 62,100 **1984 Z28 spt cpe** 100,416 **1985 Z28 spt cpe** 47,022 **IROC-Z spt cpe** 21,177 **1986 Z28 spt cpe** 38,547 **IROC-Z spt cpe** 49,585 **1987 Z28/IROC-Z spt cpe** 52,863 **Z28/IROC-Z conv** 744 **1988 IROC-Z spt cpe** 24,050 **IROC-Z conv** 3761 **1989 IROC-Z spt cpe** NA **conv** NA **1990 Z28 spt cpe** NA **conv** NA

SPECIFICATIONS

Length (in.)	192.0
Wheelbase (in.)	101.1
Weight (lbs)	2870-3350
Price (new)	$9700-20,500

ENGINES

cid/type	bhp	years
305/ohv V-8	150/165/190[1]	1982-86
305/ohv V-8	175/230[1]	1982-92
350/ohv V-8	225/245[2]	1987-92

[1]4-bbl. carb [2]Fuel injection

PRICES

IROC-Z Conv

FAIR	$3000-6000
GOOD	$6000-9000
FINE	$9000-11,000

IROC-Z Cpe

FAIR	$2500-3500
GOOD	$3500-5000
FINE	$5000-8000

Z/28

FAIR	$1500-2500
GOOD	$2500-4000
FINE	$4000-6000

FINE 1982 Z28 PRICE HISTORY

1994 $7500   **1998** $5000
1982-2000 RETURN 0%
2000-2010 Even

1982 CHEVROLET CORVETTE COLLECTOR EDITION

1982 Corvette Collector Edition coupe

Low-volume third-generation fare-well. Combined Corvette's more integrated post-'79 styling with a new 200-bhp version of the venerable 350 V-8 boasting "Cross-Fire" twin-throttle-body fuel injection—the L83 engine destined for the fourth generation. Sold, like other '82s, only with Turbo Hydra-Matic (no more manual four-

speed alternative) and featured 1980-81 weight-reducing measures like thinner window glass and a transverse rear leaf spring made of fiberglass. Unique features included tinted-glass T-tops, functional lift-up "glasshatch" (which Chevy considered including with Corvette's '78 facelift), metallic silver-beige paint (set off with lower-body "shadow" striping), color-keyed leather interior, fine-spoke cast-aluminum wheels like those optional on '60s Sting Rays, and special cloisonne emblems. Unlike earlier 'Vette commemoratives, the Collector was built as needed, not as a fixed portion of production, which by now had transferred from St. Louis to a modern new plant in Bowling Green, Kentucky. Arguably the best late-model "Shark" and, for now, the one real collectible among them, though the rest seem certain to become coveted in time.

⊡ FOR As for earlier third-generation models, plus unique features and limited production • The best "Shark" mileage • Good performance, all things considered (under 8 seconds 0-60 mph)

◨ AGAINST Not instantly distinguishable from other '82s • All the inherent "Shark" vices • Workmanship still far from world-class

PRODUCTION

6759

SPECIFICATIONS

Length (in.)	185.3
Wheelbase (in.)	98.0
Weight (lbs)	3233
Price (new)	$22,538

ENGINES

cid/type	bhp	years
350/ohv V-8	200	1982

PRICES

FAIR	$8500-11,000
GOOD	$11,000-17,000
FINE	$17,000-22,000

FINE EXAMPLE PRICE HISTORY

1982 $23,000   **1990** $22,000
1994 $26,000   **1998** $25,000
1982-2000 RETURN 0%
2000-2010 Even

1983-88 CHEVROLET MONTE CARLO SS

Interesting performance offshoot of Chevy's 1980s personal-luxury coupe. Basic design harked to the downsized 1978 G-body Malibu/Monte Carlo, given slight "aero" styling improvements for '81. Monte SS, a mid-'83 arrival, went further with an eggcrate "droop snoot" and decklid spoiler, plus dechromed exterior *sans* available vinyl covering. Even wilder was the Aerocoupe, a low-volume derivative announced in early 1986 with a huge compound-curve "bubble-back" rear window designed expressly for higher top speeds in NASCAR racing, where Chevy got it approved. Street SS Montes carried a 180-horsepower 305 V-8 with high-lift cam and free-flow exhaust, plus automatic transmission (a three-speed through '83, then four-speed overdrive) and the expected firming up of a very orthodox chassis. Standard interior bench-seat was plain, but buckets were optional from '84. The Aerocoupe was dropped

1987 Monte Carlo SS Aerocoupe

after '87, followed by other Montes a year later, this to make way for front-drive Luminas.

+ FOR Not that common, but still readily available, as are parts • Good go • Nifty looks • "Used car" affordability

■ AGAINST Not a '60s SS by a long shot • Numb steering • Unwieldy off the straight and narrow • Uninspired dash • Spotty build quality

PRODUCTION

1983 4714 **1984** 24,050 **1985** 35,484 **1986** spt cpe 41,164 **Aerocoupe** 200 **1987** spt cpe NA **Aerocoupe** 6052 **1988** spt cpe 16,204

SPECIFICATIONS

Length (in.)	200.4
Wheelbase (in.)	108.0
Weight (lbs)	3350-3525
Price (new)	$10,700-14,320

ENGINES

cid/type	bhp	years
305/ohv V-8	180	1982-88

Prices

FAIR	$2500-3500
GOOD	$3500-5000
FINE	$5000-8000

2000-2010 RETURN 2%, **Aerocoupes** 5%

1983-86
CHEVROLET EL CAMINO SS

Chevy introduced El Camino for 1959 as a car-based pickup, dropped it after 1960, then resurrected it for '64 as a Chevelle variant. El Camino's subsequent glory days of hot performance followed the curve of Sixties' muscle cars, and the vehicle was restyled for 1968, '73, and '78. By 1983 El Camino was closely related to the Monte Carlo, running with Chevy's small-block 305 V-8, rated at 150 bhp and 240 pounds/feet of torque. Monte Carlo's smooth, NASCAR-inspired

1986 El Camino SS pickup

snout announced the El Camino, and "dress-up" options were legion: SS decals, protective side moldings, hood-top air extractor, non-functional side pipes, chrome pickup-box side rails, and cast-aluminum wheels. A dozen body-color choices plus two-toning was available. Given all this gaudiness, it's a relief to report that the El Camino SS was a pretty capable performer: The 0-60 mph sprint took about 10 seconds—not too bad for the period. Positraction limited-slip differential was a popular option.

+ FOR Poised handling • Not-bad performance • Car-like comfort • Last of its breed • Versatility

■ AGAINST Collector interest limited (but growing) • Boy-racer doodads on many examples

PRODUCTION

NA

SPECIFICATIONS

Length (in.)	201.6
Weight (lbs)	approx. 3500
Wheelbase (in.)	117.1
Price (new)	$10,784 (1986 price)

ENGINES

cid/type	bhp	years
305 V-8	150	1983-86
262 (4.3 liter) V-6	130	1985

Prices

FAIR	$2200-3500
GOOD	$3500-5000
FINE	$5000-6000

1984-85
CHEVROLET CORVETTE

The first two seasons for the long-awaited fourth iteration of "America's only true sports car." Planned for '83, but certified as an '84, thus skipping Corvette's 30th birthday.

1985 Corvette coupe

Customary "front/mid-engine" layout, but little lighter than late Sharks despite being slightly shorter on a two-inch tighter wheelbase. No less sleek, though, thanks to modern—if rather conservative—new Jerry Palmer styling that improved aerodynamics. Utility improved, too, via a lift-up glass hatch, "Targa-type" roof with single lift-off section (replacing dual T-tops), more cockpit and luggage space, and front-hinged "clamshell" hood/front fenders. The last gave superb access to a mostly carryover L83 V-8, which was muscled-up to become 1985's L98 via higher compression and substituting Tuned Port Injection for dual-throttle-body "Cross Fire." Other new features included a more sophisticated five-link rear suspension, strong "bird-cage" inner body unitized with a Lotus-style backbone chassis, extensive use of lightweight materials (notably in suspension and brakes) and, after some delay, electronically controlled "4+3 Overdrive" manual transmission. That gearbox actually hindered performance and was thus dubious progress; so, too, the busy dashboard with digital and graphic displays. Still, a good performer in the 'Vette tradition, and the optional Z51 handling package delivered race-car cornering at the expense of an even stiffer ride. Not the best of this breed, but merits consideration as the first of a new Corvette line.

+ FOR More sophisticated than previous Corvettes • More practical, too • Performance still exciting • Still reasonably priced

■ AGAINST Needlessly gimmicky in places • Hard ride • Too prone to squeaks and rattles • Unpleasant "4+3 Overdrive" manual gearbox • Workmanship quite inconsistent

PRODUCTION

1984 51,547 **1985** 39,729

SPECIFICATIONS

Length (in.)	176.5
Wheelbase (in.)	96.2
Weight (lbs)	3200
Price (new)	$21,800-24,873

ENGINES

cid/type	bhp	years
350/ohv V-8	205	1984
350/ohv V-8	230	1985

PRICES

FAIR	$4500-6000
GOOD	$6000-8000
FINE	$8000-12,000

FINE EXAMPLE PRICE HISTORY

Depreciating during the 1990s.
2000-2010 RETURN 2%

1 9 8 6 - 9 0
CHEVROLET CORVETTE "L98" COUPE

1986 Corvette coupe

The fourth-generation Corvette with evolutionary improvements. A revived convertible made 1986 news (see entry), but coupes also benefited from a standard Bosch antilock brake system (ABS), more secure anti-theft provisions, and careful weight-paring that included big-port aluminum cylinder heads (replacing iron), though horsepower was unchanged. A high-mount center stoplamp also appeared, per federal decree. Lower-friction roller-bearing valve lifters added 10 horses for '87, when a Z52 handling package, essentially a softened Z51, joined the options list. The '88s offered new extra-cost 17-inch wheels with high-speed Z-rated tires. Both were standardized for '89 along with Z52 chassis tuning and the convertible's fortified front-end structure. Additional engine massaging for 1990 elevated the L98 V-8 by five horses, and a new low-restriction sport-muffler option added five more. Also that year, the never-liked "4+3 Overdrive" manual gave way to a more manageable new ZF six-speed from the super-performance ZR-1 (see entry), the original '84 dash was replaced by an even busier new design mixing digital and analog gauges, the ABS was improved. Further, the ZR-1's FX3

"Selective Ride Control"—basically auto-adjusting shock absorbers—became optional for manual-shift Z51 cars. For all this, sales declined. Still, these terrific 'Vettes were steadily improved during this period and are bound to see future value appreciation. Low-volume 35th Anniversary 1988 coupes could well "go platinum" first.

⊞ FOR As for 1984-85, plus steadily upgraded equipment and somewhat better quality control • Standard ABS • ZF six-speed manual (1990)

⊟ AGAINST Bound to be overshadowed by the ZR-1 • 35th Anniversary '88 not that "special"

PRODUCTION

1986 27,794 **1987** 20,007 **1988** 15,382[1] **1989** 16,663 **1990** 23,646[2]
[1]includes 2050 35th Anniversary coupes
[2]includes convertibles & ZR-1 models

SPECIFICATIONS

Length (in.)	176.5
Wheelbase (in.)	98.2
Weight (lbs)	3200
Price (new)	$27,027-31,979

ENGINES

cid/type	bhp	years
350/ohv V-8	230/240	1986-89
350/ohv V-8	245/250	1990

PRICES

FAIR	$6000-9000
GOOD	$9000-12,000
FINE	$12,000-16,000

FINE EXAMPLE PRICE HISTORY

Depreciating during the early 1990s.
2000-2010 RETURN 5%

1 9 8 6 - 9 0
CHEVROLET CORVETTE CONVERTIBLE

The ragtop 'Vette reborn—in time to pace the 1986 Indy 500. Chevy regarded all '86 Corvette convertibles as "Indy Pace Car Replicas," supplying regalia decals for owner application, but the actual pacers were bright yellow, whereas production models could be had in any standard color. The fourth generation had been designed with a drop-top in mind, so differences from the coupe were limited to the usual structural strengthening, retuned suspension (midway between base and Z51 package), and a third stoplamp nestled neatly in the back panel instead of clumsily in a roof pod. The top was manual but manageable, and 1989 brought a revived lift-off hardtop (at $1500) retrofittable to 1986-88 models. Other year-to-year changes as per coupes.

⊞ FOR As for 1984-85 and 1987-90 Corvette coupes, plus greater rarity and timeless top-down appeal • A virtual can't-lose investment

⊟ AGAINST Exact investment potential unclear now (as for coupes) • Others as for 1984-85 and 1987-90 Corvette coupes

PRODUCTION

1986 7264 **1987** 10,625 **1988** 7407 **1989** 9749 **1990** 7630

SPECIFICATIONS

Length (in.)	176.5
Wheelbase (in.)	98.2
Weight (lbs)	3265
Price (new)	$33,172-37,264

ENGINES

cid/type	bhp	years
350/ohv V-8	230/240	1986-89
350/ohv V-8	245/250	1990

Prices

FAIR	$7500-11,000
GOOD	$11,000-15,000
FINE	$15,000-18,500
2000-2010 RETURN	
Even	

1986 Corvette convertible

1987 1/2 - 88
CHEVROLET CAMARO IROC-Z CONVERTIBLE

Camaro's top-performing IROC-Z gained a ragtop as a "1987 1/2" offering, and could be had with a 5.0-liter V-8 rated at 215 bhp (220, with manual trans, for '88), or a detuned version of Corvette's 5.7-liter V-8, exclusive to IROC Camaros and producing 225 bhp (230 for '88) and 330 pounds/feet of torque. Even with the regrettably mandatory automatic transmission, the 5.7 made the IROC potent enough to challenge a 225 horse 305 Ford Mustang—great news for Camaro enthusiasts, who had been promised the 5.7 for '86 and failed to get it. Although heavy and claustrophobic with the top up, this crisply styled Camaro has many of collectibility's hallmarks, and is growing in popularity.

✚ **FOR** Convertible allure • Acceleration • Sticky roadholding and taut handling

▬ **AGAINST** Thirst • Road and engine noise • Body flex • Punishing ride • Awful dash design • Engine apt to be tired on all but pristine examples • Mandatory automatic transmission with 5.7 V-8

PRODUCTION
1987 1/2 4000 **1988** NA

SPECIFICATIONS
Length (in.)	192.0
Weight (lbs)	3430 (coupe)
Wheelbase (in.)	101.0
Price (new)	$15,063-18,015

ENGINES
liter/type (cid)	bhp	years
5.7/ohv V-8 (350)	225	1987 1/2
5.7/ohv V-8 (350)	230	1988

1988 Camaro IROC-Z convertible

PRICES
NA

1988 - 89
CHEVROLET BERETTA GTU

1988 Chevrolet Beretta GTU

Built to homologate its Beretta IMSA GTU race car, the production GTU was little more than an appearance package for the Beretta GT. The standard GT had competent handling. The addition of larger wheels (16-inch versus 15-inch) made a huge improvement—even Chevy was surprised. Chevrolet claimed lateral gs rose from .83 to .92. Steering feel and response also improved. The boy racer body cladding suggested high performance, but the GTU was no faster than normal V-6 Barettas.

✚ **FOR** Unexpected good handling • Adequate performance

▬ **AGAINST** Styling hasn't aged well • Poor build quality • Rough ride

PRODUCTION
NA

SPECIFICATIONS
Length (in.)	187.2
Weight (lbs)	2608
Wheelbase (in.)	103.4
Price (new)	$14,893

ENGINES
cid/type	bhp	years
173/ohv V-6	130	1988-89

PRICES
FAIR	$1500-2000
GOOD	$2000-2500
FINE	$2500-3500
2000-2010 RETURN Depreciating		

1988 - 89
CHEVROLET CAVALIER Z24 CONVERTIBLE

1988 Cavalier Z24 convertible

Certainly the sole collectible in the vast fleet of Chevy's front-drive J-car subcompacts launched for 1982. A blend of two good ideas: the convertible Cavalier, new for '83; and the driver-oriented Z24 option, first offered on 1986 notchback and "fasthatch" coupes. Ragtop Z24 arrived with a major Cavalier restyle, but the package continued with 60-degree V-6 power, standard five-speed manual transaxle (designed by Germany's Getrag), optional three-speed automatic, lower-body "aero" skirting, and Special Sport Suspension with quick-ratio steering and the usual chassis upgrades. Color-keyed power top, tinted glass, power door locks, and deck-lid luggage rack all standard. High price and strong competition conspired to do it in after 1989, but decent performance (0-60 in under 10 seconds with manual), comparative rarity, and top-down fun augur well for long-term value appreciation, though Chevy didn't help by selling a redesigned version from '92 to 2000.

✚ **FOR** Open-air fun • Brisk performance • Quick to the helm • Practical daily driver • Parts no problem

▬ **AGAINST** Improved 1992-2000 dims collector prospects for the 1988-89s • Limited trunk and back-seat space • Prone to cowl shake

PRODUCTION

1988 8745 **1989** 13,075

SPECIFICATIONS

Length (in.)	178.7
Wheelbase (in.)	101.2
Weight (lbs)	2665
Price (new)	$15,990-16,615

ENGINES

cid/type	bhp	years
173/ohv V-6	130	1988-89

PRICES

FAIR	$2500-3000
GOOD	$3000-4000
FINE	$4000-5000

2000-2010 RETURN Even

1 9 9 0 - 9 5
CHEVROLET CORVETTE ZR-1

1990 Corvette ZR-1 coupe

First year of the once-rumored "King of the Hill" Corvette, the most potent Chevrolet sports car since the early-'70s big-block Stingrays. Though delayed from a scheduled 1989 debut, allegedly due to last-minute engine problems, it was worth the wait (and officially listed as an option package). This was essentially a fourth-generation Corvette coupe powered by an entirely new all-aluminum 350 V-8 (called LT5) with four overhead cams, 32 valves, a tuned dual-stage intake system (with a "valet" mode that limited power to about 150 bhp), "Direct Fire" all-coil ignition, Tuned Port Injection, and other premium features. Only bore centers and nominal displacement were shared with the iron-block L98. To handle the LT5's rousing 375 horses and 370 pounds/feet torque, Chevy widened the rear fenders three inches to accept huge P315/35ZR17 tires; the suspension was also suitably beefed up and auto-adjusting variable-rate shock absorbers were installed—the FX3 option also available on lesser

'Vettes. The ZR-1 was sold exclusively with the six-speed ZF manual gearbox newly offered on those models. Other specifications and features were as for L98s, including the redesigned 1990 Corvette dash. Ferocious acceleration (4.3 seconds 0-60 according to Chevy and under 5.0 in most road tests), blinding top speed (near 175), and promised limited production prompted the predictable bidding war for early examples, but that fizzled once Chevy gave base-model '91 'Vettes a rounded rump and squared taillamps—the ZR-1's main visual distinctions. Still, it's an obvious collector car, with the 1990 enjoying added status both as the debut ZR-1 and the only one with the original 1984 front-end styling.

➕ **FOR** Stupefying performance • Formidable handling/roadholding (more than 0.9 g on the skidpad) • High technoid appeal • Exclusive • First of a kind

➖ **AGAINST** Bone-jarring ride • Cheesy, overdone dash • Looks too much like lesser 'Vettes?

PRODUCTION

1990 3,049 **1991** 2,044 **1992** 502 **1993** 448 **1994** 448 **1995** 448

SPECIFICATIONS

Length (in.)	176.5
Wheelbase (in.)	96.2
Weight (lbs)	3465
Price (new)	$58,995 (incl. the $31,683 ZR-1 option package)

ENGINES

cid/type	bhp	years
350/dohc V-8	375/405	1990-95

PRICES

1990 Model	
FAIR	$15,000-20,000
GOOD	$20,000-25,000
FINE	$25,000-35,000
1995 Model	
FAIR	$25,000-35,000
GOOD	$35,000-40,000
FINE	$40,000-50,000

2000-2010 RETURN Even

1 9 9 0 - 9 3
CHEVROLET C1500 SS 454

By the nineties Chevrolet's big-block 454-inch V-8 was only used in one-ton trucks. In it's battle against the Ford F-Series, Chevy dropped the big motor into its 2WD half-ton regular cab for a limited-production, hot rod pickup. With 230 horsepower and 385 pounds/feet torque, 0-60 came in less than eight seconds. Initially, the only transmission was a three-speed automatic. All SS 454s had air conditioning, bucket seats, power windows and door locks, cruise control, and Performance Handling Package. The Performance Handling Package (Bilstein shock absorbers, fast-ratio steering, and big 275/60R15 tires) gave amazing agility for a full-sized pickup. For 1991 and later, SS trucks had a true dual exhaust that raised horsepower to 255. Also new for '91, a 4-speed automatic transmission with overdrive improved acceleration and provided more relaxed highway cruising. EPA highway mileage gained only 1 MPG for a still thirsty 12 MPG. Low production and high horsepower—the 454 SS can't help but be collectible.

➕ **FOR** Tire-shredding torque • Good handling • Low production

➖ **AGAINST** Fuel economy • Hard ride • 1990s are high-revving on the highway

PRODUCTION

1990 13,748 **1991-1993** NA

SPECIFICATIONS

Length (in.)	199.4
Weight (lbs)	4073
Wheelbase (in.)	117.5
Price (new)	$18,295-21,240

1990 C1500 454SS pickup

ENGINES

cid/type	bhp	years
454/ohv V-8	230/255	1990-91

PRICES

FAIR	$7000-8500
GOOD	$8500-10,000
FINE	$10,000-14,000

2000-2010 RETURN Depreciating

1 9 9 3 - 2 0 0 0
CHEVROLET Z28 & SS

1995 Camaro Z28 convertible

Camaro Z28 perhaps offered the most performance per buck of any car in the nineties. The cast iron 5.7-liter V-8 engine borrowed from the Corvette put out 275-horsepower initially, but rose to 305 horses in '98 when both Corvette and Camaro switched to a new engine with an aluminum block. Handling and braking were in keeping with that performance. With stiffer bodies and revised suspension, the new for '93 Camaros rode better than the previous generation, but weren't as comfortable as rival Mustang. A convertible was added in 1994 which was also more rigid than the previous generation. The SS Package first offered on '97 Z28s included sport suspension with larger tires, functional hood scoop, and free-flow exhaust system. The first SS packed 305-horsepower, but rose to 320-horsepower in '98. Also new for '98 was new front end styling that improved both looks and headlight performance on all Camaros. The Camaro's future production is uncertain at the time of writing, but with its brute power, it is certain to be collectible.

FOR 0 to 60 times under 6 seconds • Handling • Low price when new

AGAINST Rough ride for day to day driving • Interior room • Fuel economy

PRODUCTION
NA

SPECIFICATIONS

Length (in.)	193.5
Weight (lbs)	3306-3605
Wheelbase (in.)	101.1
Price (new)	$16,779-32,315

ENGINES

cid/type	bhp	years
350/ohv V-8	175/305	1993-97
346/ohv V-8	305/320	1998-00

PRICES

FAIR	$18,000-20,000
GOOD	$20,000-22,000
FINE	$22,000-24,000

Prices subject to used car market.

1 9 9 4 - 9 6
CHEVROLET IMPALA SS

For 1991 the venerable Caprice was given its first complete restyle in 14 seasons. (Chassis, however, was the one used since 1977, and the car remained body-on-frame.) Interesting aero styling could not disguise the rear-drive car's enormous bulk, particularly its bulging flanks and tremendous rear overhang. Some thought it resembled a Step-down Hudson that had eaten too much. Mid-year 1994 brought a resurrection of a grand Chevy nameplate, Impala SS, which appeared on Caprices modified with sharper steering, tighter suspensions, plus a blacked-out grille, leaping-impala emblem, and other appropriately aggressive design mods. A new 5.7-liter V-8, detuned to 260 bhp from the 300 available in its Corvette iteration, came standard on the SS. Caprice/Impala were killed at the end of 1996 so that Chevy could convert its plant to the manufacture of trucks.

FOR Fierce acceleration • Responsive steering • Aggressive presence • Bargains to be had

1995 Impala SS sedan

AGAINST 4-door configuration • Thirst • Bulk • So-so handling • Modest collector interest at present

PRODUCTION
NA

SPECIFICATIONS

Length (in.)	214.1
Weight (lbs)	4036-4061
Wheelbase (in.)	115.9
Price (new)	$22,495-24,905

ENGINES

liter/type/(cid)	bhp	years
5.7 liter/ohv V-8 (350)	260	1994-96

PRICES

FAIR	$12,000-17,000
GOOD	$17,000-20,000
FINE	$20,000-24,000

Prices subject to model year and used car market.
2000-2010 RETURN Depreciating

1 9 9 6
CHEVROLET CORVETTE GS

The final year of the fourth-generation 'Vette was noted with a 1000-unit run of GS models, which replaced the ZR-1 option package as the model's performance king. All GS Corvettes had blue paint with a wide white stripe, red "hash marks" on the left front fender, and special seat trim. Production consisted of 810 coupes and 190 convertibles. Standard GS engine was the LT4, a new 330-horsepower 5.7-liter V-8. In keeping with the true performance spirit, the LT4 was available only with a 6-speed manual transmission. Dual air bags, traction control, and anti-lock 4-wheel disc brakes were standard. An electronic, self-leveling suspension—Selective Real Time Damping—was optional.

FOR It's a Corvette • A special-edition variant of the last of a design gen-

1997 Corvette coupe

1996 Corvette Grand Sport coupe

eration • Acceleration • Handling & roadholding • Available convertible body style • Used-car pricing

■ AGAINST Self-proclaimed "collectible" • Garish paint and other trim • Thirst • Harsh ride • Far too soon for significant collector interest or return on investment

PRODUCTION

1000

SPECIFICATIONS

Length (in.)	178.5
Weight (lbs)	3298 (coupe) 3360 (convertible)
Wheelbase (in.)	96.2
Price (new)	$40,475 (coupe) $47,940 (convertible)

ENGINES

cid/type	bhp	years
350/ohv V-8	330	1996

Prices

FAIR	$20,000-25,000
GOOD	$25,000-30,000
FINE	$30,000-33,000

Prices subject to used car market.
2000-2010 RETURN Depreciating

1997
CHEVROLET CAMARO SS 30TH ANNIVERSARY

One of the better anniversary cars, the 30th Anniversary Edition Camaro was available on all Z28s, but the most collectible were the based on the SS. In addition to the usual SS Package sport suspension and more powerful engine, was a special white and orange striped paint job reminiscent of the '69 Indy Pace Car replicas. Also included was a special interior with white and black houndstooth upholstery, embroidered 30th Anniversary

1997 Camaro SS 30th Anniversary conv.

logos, commemorative dash plaque, and special key fobs. SS 30th Anniversary production was limited to one thousand. Of that thousand, one hundred were built with the 330-horsepower engine also used in '96 Corvette Grand Sport.

■ FOR Rarity • Performnance • Appreciation of other Camaro specials

■ AGAINST Hard to find • Color combination not for everyone

PRODUCTION

NA

SPECIFICATIONS

Length (in.)	193.2
Weight (lbs)	3455
Wheelbase (in.)	101.1
Price (new)	$31,594-38,000 (aprox.)

ENGINES

cid/type	bhp	years
350/ohv V-8	305/330	1997

PRICES

FAIR	$18,000-20,000
GOOD	$20,000-22,000
FINE	$22,000-24,000

Prices subject to used car market.
2000-2010 RETURN Depreciating

1997-2000
CHEVROLET CORVETTE C5

Fifth-generation 'Vette (hence the unofficial "C5" designation) offered improved build quality, better ergonomics (notably circular analog gauges instead of the previous

digital hodgepodge), improved entry/exit, and 345-bhp and 350 pounds/feet of torque from a 5.7-liter V-8. Fiberglass body and rear-wheel drive were retained, maintaining a link to Corvettes past in a car that clearly was looking to the future. A convertible joined the hatchback coupe for 1998. One year later, Chevy introduced the performance-oriented C5 hardtop. Essentially a convertible with a non-removeable fiberglass roof, the hardtop was lighter and slightly more rigid than than the coupe and convertible. It was the least expensive of the line, despite having standard instead of optional six-speed transmission and Z-51 performance suspension.

■ FOR It's a Corvette, and arguably the best so far • Available convertible body style • Acceleration • Handling and roadholding

■ AGAINST Thirst • Prices still high, so a return on investment is years away

PRODUCTION

1997 coupe 9,752 **1998 coupe** 19,235 **1998 convertible** 11,849 **1999 coupe** 18,078 **1999 convertible** 11,161 **1999 hardtop** 4,031

SPECIFICATIONS

Length (in.)	179.7
Weight (lbs)	3218-3245 (coupe) 3246 (convertible)
Wheelbase (in.)	104.5
Price (new)	$37,495-45,320

ENGINES

liter/type/(cid)	bhp	years
5.7 liter/ohv V-8 (350)	345	1997-98
5.7 liter/ohv V-8 (346)	345	1999-2000

PRICES

Subject to used car market
2000-2010 RETURN Depreciating

1998
CHEVROLET CORVETTE PACE CAR

The 1998 Indianapolis 500 was paced by a '98 Corvette convertible. To commemorate the event—and

1998 Corvette Pace Car convertible

to sell ready-made "collectibles" to folks who go for such gewgaws—Chevy produced 1158 Pace Car replicas. Of that number, some were slated to go overseas, others to VIPs, leaving only about 1000 for Chevy dealers in the U.S. The replicas lacked the steel roll bars, rear-facing strobe lights, and other race-only features of the genuine Pace Car, but shared that car's factory-stock 345-bhp V-8 and suspension. Essentially a graphics package, then, the replica was painted bright purple and gussied up with stripes, decals, and wheels in combinations of yellow, red, and white, plus "CORVETTE" in yellow block-letters at the top of the windshield (just in case you forgot what you were driving). Seats were black-and-yellow. In all, a rather silly and quite needless dress-up of a terrific, world-class sports roadster.

⊞ FOR It's a Corvette • It's a convertible • Minuscule production • Acceleration • Handling and roadholding

⊟ AGAINST Factory "collectibles" always questionable investments • Gaudy • Initial investment will not appreciate for years

PRODUCTION
1158

SPECIFICATIONS

Length (in.)	179.7
Weight (lbs)	3245 (coupe) 3246 (convertible)
Wheelbase (in.)	104.5
Price (new)	$47,790

ENGINES

liter/type/ (cid)	bhp	years
5.7 liter/ohv V-8 (350)	345	1998

PRICES
Subject to used car market.
2000-2010 RETURN Depreciating

1931-33
CHRYSLER IMPERIAL SERIES CG/CH/CL

1932 Imperial Series CH speedster

All Imperials of this period are full Classics except for the 1933 Series CX (why it isn't mystifies us). However, it's not hard to understand why the others are classics. These were Chrysler's most magnificent cars of the golden era, massive, built on the longest wheelbases, powered by the largest engines, often fitted with custom bodywork. Powered by nine-bearing straight eights, these 2½-ton giants could hit over 95 mph and rack up 0-60 mph in 22 seconds. Despite all this, it was the styling that makes them so memorable: long, low, gracefully curved, and with a rakish grille reminiscent of Duesenberg's. Many were fitted with available coachwork from the cream of the custom houses: Locke, Derham, Murphy, Waterhouse, and LeBaron. They were flawless in

every way for their time and the most beautiful Chryslers ever built, bar none.

⊞ FOR Magnificent cars and widely respected • All rated Classic by the Classic Car Club of America

⊟ AGAINST Formidable prices • Hard to come by, when they change hands it's usually seldom, and without any advertising fanfare

PRODUCTION
1931 3228 (CG) **1932** 1402 (CH) **1932** 220 (CL) **1933** 151 (CL)

SPECIFICATIONS

Length (in.)	NA
Wheelbase (in.)	145.0 (1931), 146.0
(1932-33 CL), 135.0	(1933 CH)
Weight (lbs)	4480-5330
Price (new)	$1925-3995

ENGINES

cid/type	bhp	years
384.8/sv I-8	125/135	1931-33

Prices

closed bodies	
FAIR	$6000-24,000
GOOD	$24,000-43,000
FINE	$43,000-62,000
Custom open bodies	
FAIR	$50,000-100,000
GOOD	$100,000-200,000
FINE	$200,000-300,000
Custom closed bodies	
FAIR	$13,000-40,000
GOOD	$40,000-70,000
FINE	$70,000-100,000
FINE	
Custom convertible sedan	
1982	$125,000
1990	$350,000
1994	$325,000
1998	$340,000
1982-2000 RETURN 5%	
2000-2010 5%	

1934-37
CHRYSLER AIRFLOW

Chrysler's unsuccessful bid to steal the styling initiative was historically significant for pioneering construction and engine placement in the modern sense. Looks failed to catch on, and the company put more emphasis on conventional models the year following the Airflow's debut. Wind tunnel tests suggested the shape: a teardrop altered to allow for a hood and windshield. Solidly built and an excellent performer with Chrysler straight-eight engines that gave it remarkable speed for a car weighing up to two tons.

⊞ FOR Unique concept • Relatively

1936 Airflow coupe

available • Reasonable operating costs • Good club support

AGAINST An "ugly duckling" reputation has followed it since birth • Limited appreciation potential • No open body styles

PRODUCTION

1934 Eight (CU) 8389 **Imperial** (CV) 2277 **Custom Imperial** (CX) 106 **1935 Eight** (C-1) 4996 **Imperial** (C-2) 2598 **Custom Imperial** (C-3) 125 **1936 Eight** (C-9) 4500 **Imperial** (C-10) 1700 **Custom Imperial** (C-11) 75 **1937 Eight** (C-17) 4600

SPECIFICATIONS

Length (in.)	NA
Wheelbase (in.)	123.0 (CU, C-1, C-9); 128.0 (CV, C-2, C-10, C-17), 137.5 (CX, C-3, C-11)
Weight (lbs)	3823-6000
Price (new)	$1245-2575

ENGINES

cid/type	bhp	years
298.7/sv I-8	122	1934[1]
323.5/sv I-8	115/138	1934-37

[1]CU

PRICES

FAIR	$10,000-15,000
GOOD	$15,000-25,000
FINE	$25,000-37,500
1934 Custom Imperial	
FAIR	$9000-24,000
GOOD	$24,000-45,000
FINE	$45,000-66,000

FINE STANDARD WHEELBASE EXAMPLE PRICE HISTORY

1982 $10,000		**1990** $26,000	
1994 $35,000		**1998** $47,000	
1982-2000 RETURN 8%			
2000-2010 8%			

1934-36
CHRYSLER CUSTOM IMPERIAL AIRFLOW SERIES CW

1937 Custom Imperial Airflow limousine

The only Airflows rated as Classic and the most opulent of the company's senior models converted to this controversial styling for 1934. All are sedans and limousines on the longest wheelbase. Conceived by engineer Carl Breer and designed by Oliver Clark, the highly advanced Airflows had ultra-wide seats, vast interior space, a forward-mounted engine, and solid construction in addition to their "aero" styling. Though the public didn't take to it, it was interesting and predictive for the period.

FOR The longest and thus prettiest Airflow • CCCA Classic status • Novel and worth owning despite history's bum rap • Opulent interiors • Progressive engineering

AGAINST Remains the 1930's Edsel for many • Very scarce • No open body styles

PRODUCTION

1934 22 **1935** 32 **1936** 10

SPECIFICATIONS

Length (in.)	NA
Wheelbase (in.)	146.0 (1934); 146.5 (1935-36)
Weight (lbs)	4750-6250
Price (new)	$5000-5145

ENGINES

cid/type	bhp	years
384.8/sv I-8	150	1934-35
323.5/sv I-8	130	1936

PRICES

FAIR	$21,000-42,000
GOOD	$42,000-74,000
FINE	$74,000-138,000

FINE EXAMPLE PRICE HISTORY

1982 $35,000	**1990** $70,000
1994 $80,000	**1998** $145,000
1982-2000 RETURN 6%	
2000-2010 6%	

1940-42
CHRYSLER NEW YORKER HIGHLANDER

1941 New Yorker Highlander convertible

Chrysler revamped its cars for 1940, and there are many collectible two-door models in this design generation, which lasted into 1949. By far the most interesting are the special-trim two-door (and, rarely, the occasional four-door) New Yorker models with Scottish plaid cloth and leatherette upholstery. This option cost $20-25 extra, and cars so equipped carried "Highlander" script, although Chrysler listed a distinct Highlander model in 1940 only. On convertibles, the plaid fabric was also used for the top boot.

Highlander plaid has been reproduced for restorers.

+ FOR Eye-catching interior • Smooth ride • Comfort

– AGAINST Nondescript styling (though rear fender skirts help) • Drunkardly thirst • Fluid Drive transmission may prove troublesome to maintain

PRODUCTION

Not available, but no more than 1000 per year.

SPECIFICATIONS

Length (in.)	216.0
Wheelbase (in.)	128.5 (1940),127.5 (1941-42)
Weight (lbs)	3570-4033
Price (new)	$1255-1548

ENGINES

cid/type	bhp	years
323.5/sv I-8	135/137/140	1940-42

PRICES

FAIR	$5400-10,800
GOOD	$10,800-18,500
FINE	$18,500-22,000

FINE EXAMPLE PRICE HISTORY

1982 $5000		**1987** $8500	
1990 $14,000		**1994** $20,000	
1982-2000 RETURN 9%			
2000-2010 5%			

1940-42
CHRYSLER NEW YORKER NAVAJO

1942 New Yorker Navajo convertible

Even more exclusive and unusual than the Highlander, this trim option consisted of broadcloth upholstery woven to simulate the design of Navajo Indian blankets. Vertical stripes on 1941s, horizontal with a "Thunderbird" motif on '42s.

+ FOR Rarity and high desirability • Others as for Highlander

– AGAINST As for Highlander

PRODUCTION

Not available; rare model

SPECIFICATIONS

Length (in.)	216.0
Wheelbase (in.)	127.5
Weight (lbs)	3570-4033
Price (new)	$1255-1548

ENGINES

cid/type	bhp	years
323.5/sv I-8	135/137/140	1940-42

PRICES

As per New Yorker Highlander but add 200% for convertible, if extant.
2000-2010 RETURN 10%

1940-42
CHRYSLER WINDSOR HIGHLANDER

The Highlander trim package applied to the smaller six-cylinder Chrysler. Higher production makes this version somewhat more plentiful today.

+ FOR As for New Yorker Highlander

– AGAINST Lower collector demand (convertibles are the best buys) • Others as for New Yorker Highlander

PRODUCTION

Not available; no more than 1500 per year.

SPECIFICATIONS

Length (in.)	210.0
Wheelbase (in.)	122.5 (1940), 121.5 (1941-42)
Weight (lbs)	3135-3661
Price (new)	$1020-1420

ENGINES

cid/type	bhp	years
241.5/sv I-6	108/112	1940-41
250.6/sv I-6	120	1942

1941 Windsor Highlander convertible

PRICES

As per 1940-42 New Yorker Highlander; among Highlanders the upholstery is more important than the model.

1941-42
CHRYSLER WINDSOR TOWN AND COUNTRY

1941 Town and country wagon

A significant step toward the modern station wagon and away from the boxy woody. Somewhat sedan-like in appearance, with a streamlined steel roof and tailgate doors that opened like a clam shell via outboard hinges. The concept was floated by Chrysler Division general manager David Wallace, who was also noted for the "Superfinish" engine process. With Chrysler's L-head six and semi-automatic Fluid Drive, performance was leisurely, but fit, finish, and fittings were top-drawer.

+ FOR High appreciation potential • Unique body style

– AGAINST '41 almost impossible to find • Wood structure difficult, though critical, to maintain

PRODUCTION

1941 9-pass 797 **6-pass** 200 **1942 9-pass** 849
6-pass 150

SPECIFICATIONS

Length (in.)	210.0
Wheelbase (in.)	121.5
Weight (lbs)	3540-3699
Price (new)	$1412-1685

ENGINES

cid/type	bhp	years
241.5/sv I-6	112	1941
250.6/sv I-6	120	1942

PRICES

FAIR	$7000-14,000
GOOD	$14,000-29,500
FINE	$29,500-37,500

FINE EXAMPLE PRICE HISTORY

1982 $18,000		**1990** $26,000	
1994 $27,500		**1998** $37,500	
1982-2000 RETURN 5%			
2000-2010 5%			

1 9 4 6 - 4 8
CHRYSLER CROWN IMPERIAL

1948 Crown Imperial limousine

The largest and most impressive of the "harmonica-grille" postwar Chryslers. Built to the high fit-and-finish standard expected at the price, which was close to $5000 new, quite a bit of dough in those days. Every bit the luxury cars the big Packard Customs and Cadillac Series Seventy-Fives were. All Crowns in this period offered eight-passenger seating, two extra persons were accommodated on fold-down jump seats. Plentiful room for all thanks to the long wheelbase.

FOR Chrysler's highest luxury in this period • Beautifully built, formal cars • Smooth L-head straight eight

AGAINST Ponderous road manners, so no picnic to drive • Fuel thirst • Too long for many garages (and some parking spaces)

PRODUCTION

Sdns 750 **Limos** 650

SPECIFICATIONS

Length (in.)	234.8
Wheelbase (in.)	145.5
Weight (lbs)	4814-4875
Price (new)	$3875-4767

ENGINES

cid/type	bhp	years
323.5/sv I-8	135	1946-48

PRICES

FAIR	$3500-7000
GOOD	$7000-12,000
FINE	$12,000-17,000

FINE EXAMPLE PRICE HISTORY

1982 $4000		**1987** $9000	
1990 $16,000		**1994** $15,000	
1982-2000 RETURN 11%			
2000-2010 6%			

1 9 4 6 - 4 8
CHRYSLER TOWN AND COUNTRY

These are the "classic" Town and Country models most people associate with the name. The eight-cylinder convertible built on the New Yorker chassis is the most common. The postwar T&C applied wood trim on a conventional steel bodies in the "glamor" class with Chrysler's big top-line convertibles and sedans. The mahogany-veneer panels gave way to Di-Noc decals in late 1947 but the white birch framing remained. The eight-cylinder sedan was discontinued early, and its six-cylinder counterpart departed at mid-year 1948. A few 1948 convertibles were reserialed as part of Chrysler's stopgap "first series" 1949 lineup.

FOR High collector recognition • Prime investment, especially now that prices have subsided from the mid-1990s • Striking looks

AGAINST Difficulty of wood maintenance and restoration • High asking prices • Sporty to look at, not to drive

PRODUCTION[1]

1946 6-cyl sdn 124 **8-cyl sdn** 100 **8-cyl. conv** 1935 **1947 6-cyl sdn** 2651 **8-cyl conv** 3136 **1948 6-cyl sdn** 1175 **8-cyl conv** 3309
[1]Figures do not include 1946 factory prototypes

SPECIFICATIONS

Length (in.)	221.8 (6-cyl sdn), 216.8 (8-cyl models)
Wheelbase (in.)	121.5 (6-cyl sdn), 127.5 (8-cyl models)
Weight (lbs)	3917-4332
Price (new)	$2366-3395

ENGINES

cid/type	bhp	years
250.6/sv I-6	114	1946-48
323.5/sv I-8	135	1946-48

PRICES

Conv	
FAIR	$23,000-43,000
GOOD	$43,000-57,500
FINE	$57,500-82,000
Sdn	
FAIR	$10,000-27,000
GOOD	$27,000-34,000
FINE	$34,000-45,000

FINE CONVERTIBLE PRICE HISTORY

1982 $25,000		**1990** $80,000	
1994 $60,000		**1998** $40,000	
1982-2000 RETURN 7%			
2000-2010 10%			

1 9 4 9 - 5 4
CHRYSLER IMPERIAL

With the new boxy body style for 1949, Chrysler decided to field a

1946 Town and Country hardtop coupe (factory prototype)

1952 Imperial sedan

line of "owner-driver" Imperials. The sedan came first, followed briefly by a convertible and club coupe. The Newport hardtop arrived to stay for 1951. These were the top of the Chrysler line—beautifully built and thoroughly engineered, but drably designed and dull on the road. Then as now, they appealed mainly to those who liked Chryslers in general. Though they were an engineering match for Cadillac and Lincoln, especially with the advent of the Hemi V-8 for 1951, they were not as well styled—and styling was almost everything in those years. Sales lagged accordingly. (See also "Imperial," the separate make launched for 1955.)

+ FOR Engineering excellence • Craftsmanship • Luxury • Chrysler's fabled Hemi V-8 beginning in 1951 • Relative rarity

■ AGAINST Underwhelming looks • Fuel thirst • Some body parts in short supply now

PRODUCTION

1949 4d sdn 50 **1950 4d sdn** 9500 **DeLuxe 4d sdn** 1150 **1951 4d sdn** 13,678[1] **clb cpe** 2226[1] **2d htp** 749[1] **conv** 650 **1952 4d sdn** 8033[1] **clb cpe** 1307[1] **2d htp** 440[1] **1953 4d sdn** 7793 **2d htp** 823 **limo** 243 **1954 4d sdn** 4324 **2d htp** 1249 **conv** 1 **limo** 85
[1]Estimated 1951-52 breakdown

SPECIFICATIONS

Length (in.)	212.5 (1949), 213.6 (1950), 212.6 (1951-52), 219.0 (1953-54)
Wheelbase (in.)	131.5 (1949-52), 133.5 (1953-54; '53 hardtop: 131.5)
Weight (lbs)	4220-5295
Price (new)	$3055-7044

ENGINES

cid/type	bhp	years
323.5/sv I-8	135	1949-50
331.1/ohv V-8	180/235	1951-54

PRICES

Sdn
FAIR	$2500-5000
GOOD	$5000-9000
FINE	$9000-11,000

Limo & htp
FAIR	$2500-4000
GOOD	$4000-8000
FINE	$8000-13,000

Conv
FAIR	$10,000-18,000
GOOD	$18,000-27,000
FINE	$27,000-34,000

FINE CONVERTIBLE PRICE HISTORY

1982 $9000		**1990** $22,500
1994 $22,000		**1998** $28,000
1982-2000 RETURN 6%		
2000-2010 10%		

1949
CHRYSLER TOWN AND COUNTRY

1949 Town and Country convertible

A continuation of the T&C idea, but confined strictly to a New Yorker-based convertible, the highest-priced T&C yet. (A Newport hardtop was also planned, but not produced.) As before, the wood trim with Di-Noc "mahogany" inserts adorned doors, rear bodysides (above the fenders), and trunk deck, but only the latter was structural. Craftsmanship was as good as ever, and the Town and Country was still the best-looking Chrysler by a long way.

+ FOR As for previous models • Prices have stabilized

■ AGAINST Fairly scarce now • Less

investment potential than 1946-48 convertibles

PRODUCTION

1000

SPECIFICATIONS

Length (in.)	212.5
Wheelbase (in.)	131.5
Weight (lbs)	4630
Price (new)	$4665

ENGINES

cid/type	bhp	years
323.5/sv I-8	135	1949

PRICES

FAIR	$15,000-28,000
GOOD	$28,000-39,000
FINE	$39,000-52,000

FINE EXAMPLE PRICE HISTORY

1982 $12,000	**1990** $60,000
1994 $60,000	**1998** $60,000
1982-2000 RETURN 9%	
2000-2010 5%	

1950
CHRYSLER TOWN AND COUNTRY NEWPORT

1950 Town and Country Newport hardtop coupe

The final year for a non-wagon T&C (until the Eighties). Chrysler now went the other way, abandoning the ragtop for a pillarless hardtop, still powered by the long-in-the-tooth L-head straight eight. A noteworthy mechanical feature was a type of four-wheel disc brakes, among the first applications for a production model. Unlike conventional disc brakes, these brakes consisted of two discs expanding inside a drum. Frontal styling was cleaned up somewhat over '49, and there were tidier taillights, too. A very pretty car, nicely upholstered, comfortable on the highway, and beautifully constructed.

+ FOR The last of the breed: after 1950, the T&C was a wagon only

- Quite rare, then and now • Prices, which peaked in 1990, are still attractive

AGAINST Wood upkeep difficult • Disc brake problems • Few now left • Prices are on the rise again

PRODUCTION
700

SPECIFICATIONS

Length (in.)	222.5
Wheelbase (in.)	131.5
Weight (lbs)	4670
Price (new)	$4003

ENGINES

cid/type	bhp	years
323.5/sv I-8	135	1950

PRICES

FAIR	$11,000-20,000
GOOD	$20,000-30,000
FINE	$30,000-41,000

FINE EXAMPLE PRICE HISTORY

1982 $3500	1990 $50,000
1994 $40,000	1998 $40,000

1982-2000 RETURN 16%
2000-2010 10%

1951
CHRYSLER SARATOGA CLUB COUPE

1952 Saratoga sedan (1951 club coupe similar)

We cite the club coupe as the sportiest and most collectible of this historically important model. The Saratoga was the lightest Chrysler series available with the revolutionary new V-8 with hemispherical combustion chambers, then in its first year of production. But the Hemi alone isn't enough to qualify the whole series as collector items. Regrettably, Chrysler decided not to offer Saratoga hardtops or convertibles this year, although one experimental Newport hardtop was built. The look-alike 1952 Saratoga would be an alternative, though it lacks "first year" status for the Hemi. For those who like the smoother 1953-54 models, there's the Windsor DeLuxe, which took over for the Saratoga in that period.

FOR Chrysler's "hot rod," with the lighter Windsor body and the powerful Hemi V-8 instead of a six

AGAINST Limited collector interest • Dowdy styling detracts from a brilliant powerplant

PRODUCTION
5355 (est.)

SPECIFICATIONS

Length (in.)	207.8
Wheelbase (in.)	125.5
Weight (lbs)	3948
Price (new)	$3348

ENGINES

cid/type	bhp	years
331.1/ohv V-8	180	1951

PRICES

FAIR	$1500-3000
GOOD	$3000-5000
FINE	$5000-12,000

FINE EXAMPLE PRICE HISTORY

1982 $2000	1990 $11,000
1994 $10,000	1998 $13,000

1982-2000 RETURN 12%
2000-2010 3%

1955-56
CHRYSLER NEW YORKER HARDTOP/ CONVERTIBLE

If you can't afford a 300, these handsome Virgil Exner creations may be just the ticket. The '55 had that "Hundred Million Dollar Look": a split eggcrate grille and tall, chrome-encased "Twin Tower" taillights, plus attractive cloth-and-vinyl interiors and the ever-potent Hemi V-8.

The 1956 acquired a more massive and unified grille and more prominent, though still conservative, tailfins housing large vertical taillights. New that year was the Newport hardtop sedan, which offered four-door practicality with pillarless construction. PowerFlite two-speed automatic was standard (three-speed TorqueFlite became available for mid-'56), controlled by a menacing chrome wand jutting from the dash on '55s and by the famous pushbuttons on '56s. The plushly trimmed St. Regis two-door proved quite popular. Bargain hunters, but not serious collectors, might also consider the less expensive Windsor equivalents, which had their own distinct front and rear styling for '56.

FOR Attractive styling and still reasonably priced • Fast • Luxurious

AGAINST Slower to appreciate than 300s • A bit heavy on the chrome • Big, heavy and thirsty, but if you're reading this entry you don't care

PRODUCTION

1955 Newport 2d htp 5777 **St. Regis 2d htp** 11,076 **conv** 946 **1956 Newport 2d htp** 4115 **St. Regis 2d htp** 6686 **conv** 921 **Newport 4d htp** 3599

SPECIFICATIONS

Length (in.)	218.6 (1955), 220.4 (1956)
Wheelbase (in.)	126.0
Weight (lbs)	4125-4360
Price (new)	$3652-4243

ENGINES

cid/type	bhp	years
331.1/ohv V-8	250	1955
354/ohv V-8	280	1956

PRICES

Conv	
FAIR	$6000-12,000
GOOD	$12,000-20,000
FINE	$20,000-27,500
Htp	
FAIR	$2500-6000
GOOD	$6000-8000
FINE	$8000-12,000

1955 New Yorker Newport hardtop coupe

1956 New Yorker St Regis hardtop coupe

1958 300-D convertible

FINE 1955 CONVERTIBLE PRICE HISTORY

1982 $4500	1990 $20,000
1994 $22,500	1998 $30,000
1982-2000 RETURN 11%	
2000-2010 5%	

1955-56
CHRYSLER C-300/300-B

1956 300-B hardtop coupe

The first of what writer Karl Ludvigsen called the "Beautiful Brutes," and two of the most memorable performance cars ever made. Unabashedly created for NASCAR (National Association for Stock Car Auto Racing), which they dominated until U.S. manufacturers shied away from factory competition support in early 1957. Powered by the most potent Hemi V-8s yet, the 1955 C-300 (as it was officially designated) and 1956 300-B had Virgil Exner's fine body styling, a New Yorker Newport hardtop body with an Imperial eggcrate grille. Though primarily a showroom attention-getter, off the track the big 300 was more than just performance. It also offered luxurious accommodations (including leather upholstery), though it was naturally harder-riding and noisier than a New Yorker.

✚ FOR One of the very important Milestone cars • Prime investment • Very fast • Satisfying to drive

▬ AGAINST Scarcity • High prices • Fuel thirst (and a taste for high-octane gas now hard to come by)

PRODUCTION

1955 1725 **1956** 1102

SPECIFICATIONS

Length (in.)	218.6 (1955), 220.4 (1956)
Wheelbase (in.)	126.0
Weight (lbs)	4005-4145
Price (new)	$4110-4419

ENGINES

cid/type	bhp	years
331.1/ohv V-8	300	1955
354/ohv V-8	340/355	1956

PRICES

FAIR	$6000-12,000
GOOD	$12,000-20,000
FINE	$20,000-33,000

FINE 1955 MODEL PRICE HISTORY

1982 $7500	1990 $35,000
1994 $27,500	1998 $36,000
1982-2000 RETURN 8%	
2000-2010 8%	

1957-58
CHRYSLER 300-C/300-D

Restyled, even more potent extensions of Chrysler's brawny hot rod. The 1957 300-C and 1958 300-D were the last of the Hemi-powered letter series, and were sold in hardtop or new convertible form. On 9.25:1 compression, the '57 Hemi delivered 375 bhp, and 390 bhp (maybe more) was available with special 10:1 compression heads. Three-speed TorqueFlite automatic or manual transmission was offered. The 300 shared its new tor-

sion-bar front suspension with the New Yorker—and other Chrysler products—but had beefier bars. Quality control declined, but the leather-trimmed interior now had individual seats. For 1958, the optional "hi-po" engine was a fuel-injected 392, conservatively rated at 390 bhp. The only differences in Virgil Exner's dramatic styling between the two models are minor: shorter taillights that didn't entirely fill the fin, and a modified windshield header for the 300-D.

✚ FOR The best-looking tailfin Mopars ever • High appreciation potential • Great long-haul road car

▬ AGAINST As for 1955-56 300s, plus definitely susceptible to rust

PRODUCTION

1957 2d htp 1918 **conv** 484 **1958 2d htp** 618 **conv** 191

SPECIFICATIONS

Length (in.)	219.2 (1957) 220.2 (1958)
Wheelbase (in.)	126.0
Weight (lbs)	4235-4475
Price (new)	$4929-5603

ENGINES

cid/type	bhp	years
392/ohv V-8	375/380/390	1957-58

PRICES

Conv	
FAIR	$17,000-30,000
GOOD	$30,000-45,000
FINE	$45,000-55,000
Htp	
FAIR	$9500-15,000
GOOD	$15,000-24,000
FINE	$24,000-35,000

FINE 1958 CONVERTIBLE PRICE HISTORY

1982 $7500	1990 $52,000
1994 $50,000	1998 $49,000
1982-2000 RETURN 13%	
2000-2010 10%	

1957-59
CHRYSLER NEW YORKER HARDTOPS/ CONVERTIBLES

Chrysler's standard top-liners from the golden age of Virgil Exner

1958 New Yorker hardtop coupe

1959 300-E hardtop coupe

styling. The '57s still look best, with ultra-clean lines that were modestly hammed-up on the '58s and lost entirely with the reskinned '59s. Wheelbase unchanged from 1955-56, but all models were longer overall, wider, and up to five inches lower in hardtop form. Much lower beltlines and vastly increased glass areas improved visibility and worked wonderfully with Exner's dart-like profile, defined by soaring tailfins. The '57s introduced those now-famous engineering advances of "Torsion-Aire Ride" (torsion-bar front suspension plus retuned live-axle rear end) and three-speed TorqueFlite automatic transmission. Both were so well-received that they'd be Chrysler Corporation mainstays for over 20 years. As always, New Yorkers offered Chrysler Division's most luxurious trim and appointments, as well as the best performance short of the limited-edition 300s. The redoubtable Hemi V-8 was replaced for '59 by a wedge-head unit that was cheaper to make and no less potent, but Hemi-power is still magic for collectors. Much poorer workmanship in these years contributed to early rusting, one reason relatively few Highland Park cars from this period survive today.

⊞ FOR '57s' great period styling • Smooth, powerful performers • Exemplary handling for the times • Spacious, airy interiors • Some models quite rare • In greater collector demand than ever

▬ AGAINST Compromised 1958-59 styling • Easy tinworm victims, so not that many survivors now • Some body parts and soft trim very hard to find

PRODUCTION
1957 2d htp 8863 **4d htp** 10,948 **conv** 1049 **1958 2d htp** 3205 **4d htp** 5227 **conv** 666 **1959 2d htp** 2435 **4d htp** 4805 **conv** 286

1959 New Yorker convertible

SPECIFICATIONS
Length (in.)	219.2/220.2/220.9 (1957/58/59)
Wheelbase (in.)	126.0
Weight (lbs)	4205-4350
Price (new)	$4202-$4890

ENGINES
cid/type	bhp	years
392/ohv V-8	325/345	1957-58
413/ohv V-8	350	1959

PRICES
Conv	
FAIR	$8000-14,000
GOOD	$14,000-20,000
FINE	$20,000-25,000
Htp	
FAIR	$1500-5000
GOOD	$5000-10,000
FINE	$10,000-14,000

FINE HARDTOP PRICE HISTORY
1982 $5000		**1990** $20,000	
1994 $18,000		**1998** $16,000	
1982-2000 RETURN 7%			
2000-2010 3%			

1959
CHRYSLER 300-E

The fifth edition of the letter-series 300. Basically the same car as the 1958 300-D, but sported a horizontal-bar grille instead of the previous eggcrate and a 413-cid wedgehead V-8 instead of the fabled Hemi. The E's reputation for slug-

gishness is undeserved: most contemporary road tests pegged it a good second quicker than the D up to 60 mph and up to three seconds faster to 90 mph. Rear-end styling was altered in line with other '59 Chryslers. A difficult sales year for the industry as a whole limited production, making this model a real find today.

⊞ FOR Rarer than other 300s • Styling (still good) • Performance • Roadability • Magnificent mile-eater • Interior luxury

▬ AGAINST A "bum rap" for "doing in the Hemi" • Magnificent fuel-eater • Rust-prone

PRODUCTION
2d htp 550 **conv** 140

SPECIFICATIONS
Length (in.)	220.6
Wheelbase (in.)	126.0
Weight (lbs)	4290-4350
Price (new)	$5319-5749

ENGINES
cid/type	bhp	years
413/ohv V-8	380	1959

PRICES
Conv	
FAIR	$16,000-25,000
GOOD	$25,000-37,500
FINE	$37,500-53,500
Htp	
FAIR	$8000-12,000
GOOD	$12,000-19,000
FINE	$19,000-32,000

FINE HARDTOP PRICE HISTORY
1982 $5000		**1990** $32,500	
1994 $32,500		**1998** $35,000	
1982-2000 RETURN 11%			
2000-2010 5%			

1960-62
CHRYSLER NEW YORKERS HARDTOPS/ CONVERTIBLES

The best standard Chryslers from one of the worst periods in Chrysler Corporation history. Wheelbase again measured 126 inches, but all-new

1960 New Yorker convertible

1961 300-G hardtop coupe

"Unibody" construction and somewhat more dynamic styling were touted for 1960. The latter, marked by a big inverted-trapezoid grille and canted fins with wedgy taillamps, was shared by that year's high-performance 300-F, which couldn't have hurt New Yorker sales as much as the optional dummy spare-tire outline for decklids, a needless "classic" fillip often called the "toilet seat." The frontal trapezoid was flipped over for the somewhat more angular '61s, allowing for canted quad headlights, and fins were abruptly shaved off for '62 (Exner later called the result "plucked chickens"). The New Yorker also lost its convertible and hardtop coupe to a new non-letter 300 series (covered elsewhere). Pushbutton TorqueFlite automatic mated to wedge-head 413 V-8s throughout, with the '62 engine was detuned 10 horses for economy reasons. Also shared by all these Chryslers was the striking "Astra-Dome" semispherical gauge cluster with then-pioneering indirect lighting. Still not the most desirable of Chryslers, but pleasant, affordable cars that are now attracting some long-overdue collector interest.

➕ **FOR** Burly wedgehead V-8 • Relaxed, refined performance • Surprisingly good handlers • Still affordable • Last convertible New Yorkers

➖ **AGAINST** Workmanship still mediocre, rust tendency still marked • More hard-to-find body panels and trim pieces

PRODUCTION
1960 2d htp 2835 **conv** 556 **4d htp** 5625 **1961 2d htp** 2541 **conv** 576 **4d htp** 5862 **1962 4d htp** 6646

SPECIFICATIONS
Length (in.)	219.6/215.3 (1960-61/62)
Wheelbase (in.)	126.0
Weight (lbs)	4005-4185
Price (new)	$4263-$4875

1961 New Yorker hardtop coupe

ENGINES
cid/type	bhp	years
413/ohv V-8	350/340	1960-62

PRICES
Conv	
FAIR	$6000-14,000
GOOD	$14,000-20,000
FINE	$20,000-30,000
Htp	
FAIR	$1500-3000
GOOD	$3000-8000
FINE	$8000-14,000

FINE CONVERTIBLE PRICE HISTORY
1982 $6000		**1990** $15,000	
1994 $17,500		**1998** $12,000	
1982-2000 RETURN 10%			
2000-2010 5%			

1960-62
CHRYSLER 300-F/300-G/300-H

Despite styling generally seen as retrograde, the '60 300-F offered some important improvements: unit construction, optional 400-bhp ram-manifold wedgehead V-8, standard bucket seats and center console front and rear, optional Pont-a-Mousson four-speed manual gearbox (fitted to no more than 15 examples), and a choice of axle ratios from 2.93 to 3.73. The embossed decklid "spare tire" was

deleted on the tidier 1961 300-G, which introduced an upside-down trapezoid grille and canted, vertical quad headlights. A heavy-duty three-speed manual was reinstated as an option to replace the French four-speeder, and the 300 reverted to 15-inch wheels for the first time since 1956. The 1962 300-H rode a 4-inch-shorter wheelbase, but retained the same basic look aside from being shorn of its fins.

➕ **FOR** Less costly now than earlier 300s • Aggressive good looks • 300-H's finless rear • Improved assembly quality • Speedy and well-furnished as ever

➖ **AGAINST** Definite ruster • Very thirsty • Requires high octane

PRODUCTION
1960 2d htp 964 **conv** 248 **1961 2d htp** 1280 **conv** 337 **1962 2d htp** 435 **conv** 123

SPECIFICATIONS
Length (in.)	219.7 (1960-61), 215.3 (1962)
Wheelbase (in.)	126.0 (1960-61), 122.0 (1962)
Weight (lbs)	4010-4315
Price (new)	$5090-5841

ENGINES
cid/type	bhp	years
413/ohv V-8	375-405	1960-62

PRICES
Conv	
FINE	$13,000-19,000
GOOD	$19,000-48,000
FINE	$48,000-75,000
htp	
FAIR	$10,000-15,000
GOOD	$15,000-20,000
FINE	$20,000-40,000

FINE 300-H CONVERTIBLE PRICE HISTORY
1982 $6000		**1990** $30,000	
1994 $55,000		**1998** $60,000	
1982-2000 RETURN 16%			
2000-2010 12%			

1962-64
CHRYSLER 300

First of the mid-range Chryslers inspired by the letter-series 300. Introduced as a '62 "plucked chicken,"

1964 "Silver" 300 hardtop coupe

then adopted the "crisp, clean custom look" of 1963-64. Replacing Windsor, this 300 combined letter-series styling with smaller, thriftier standard engines and much lower prices—a winning formula, though sales might have been even better had Chrysler Corporation not been in one of its periodic, self-induced financial spasms. Available with optional front bucket seats that furthered the impression you were in a "real" 300. Prime collector picks here are the handful of 1962-63 models with ram-induction 413/426 wedgeheads (there couldn't have been many); the limited-edition 1963 Pace Setter convertible and hardtop coupe (an open-air 300 paced that year's Indy 500); and the '64 "Silver 300," a "spring special" two-door hardtop with black leather/vinyl interior, matching "Landau" vinyl roof, and silver paint. Pillared 300 sedans show up in factory production tallies, but they never showed up in catalogs and were likely export items; finding one now would be a feat. Again, not the greatest Chryslers ever, but hardly the worst, and some remain quite rare. All have high interest value if not especially high value appreciation potential.

➕ FOR Possible "sleepers" • Torsion-bar suspension, TorqueFlite, great V-8s • Fairly low production of some models

➖ AGAINST Not widely saved, so body/trim parts harder than usual to find • Styling not universally liked • Indifferent workmanship

PRODUCTION
1962 2d htp 11,341 **conv** 1848 **4d htp** 10,030 **4d sdn** 1801 **1963 2d htp** 9423 **Pace Setter 2d htp** 306 **conv** 1535 **Pace Setter conv** 1861 **4d htp** 9915 **4d sdn** 1625 **1964 2d htp** 18,379[1] **4d htp** 11,460 **conv** 1401 **4d sdn** 2078
[1]Incl. special "Silver 300" model

SPECIFICATIONS
Length (in.)	214.9/215.3 (1962/63-64)
Wheelbase (in.)	122.0
Weight (lbs)	3750-4120

Price (new)	$3323-4129

ENGINES
cid/type	bhp	years
383/ohv V-8	305	1962-64
413/ohv V-8	365/380/405	1962
413/ohv V-8	360/365	1963-64
426/ohv V-8	373/385/413/421	1962
426/ohv V-8	373/425/425	1963

PRICES
Conv	
FAIR	$4000-6000
GOOD	$6000-9000
FINE	$9000-14,000
2d htp	
FAIR	$2000-4000
GOOD	$4000-6000
FINE	$6000-9000
4d htp	
FAIR	$2000-3700
GOOD	$3700-4500
FINE	$4500-5500

FINE CONVERTIBLE PRICE HISTORY
1982 $4000		**1990** $14,000	
1994 $15,000		**1998** $14,000	
1982-2000 RETURN 8%			
2000-2010 5%			

1963-64
CHRYSLER
300-J/300-K

1964 300-K hardtop coupe

All-new styling by Virgil Exner characterized Chryslers of this period, billed as having "the crisp, clean custom look." Whether it was good or not is debatable, but the 300 letter-series was the cleanest of the range, with a blacked-out grille and conservative side treatment. The 1963 300-J (Chrysler skipped the letter "I" in the alphabetical sequence) was offered as a hardtop only, and in just one state of tune, and it lacked the traditional emblem and bright spear that had graced 300 rear fenders since 1957. Few '63s were sold. Sales rebounded with the 1964 300-K to set a record. The convertible was reinstated, and a choice of two power stages was offered, including a ram-induction 413 boasting 390 bhp.

➕ FOR Even more affordable than earlier 300s • 300-Ks in good supply • Higher-than-average performance • Low-production appeal

➖ AGAINST Bulky, controversial styling • Rust-prone

1963 300-J hardtop coupe

PRODUCTION
1963 2d htp 400 **1964 2d htp** 3022 **conv** 625

SPECIFICATIONS
Length (in.)	215.5
Wheelbase (in.)	122.0
Weight (lbs)	3965-4000
Price (new)	$4056-5184

ENGINES
cid/type	bhp	years
413/ohv V-8	360/390	1963-64

PRICES
Conv	
FAIR	$6500-12,500
GOOD	$12,500-22,500
FINE	$22,500-32,000
Htp	
FAIR	$5500-10,000
GOOD	$10,000-18,000
FINE	$18,000-25,000

Fine Hardtop Price History
1982 $4500		**1987** $12,500	
1990 $22,500		**1994** $25,000	
1982-2000 RETURN 11%			
2000-2010 8%			

1963-64
CHRYSLER
NEW YORKER
SALON

Fascinating throwback to the glory days of coachbuilt Chryslers,

1963 New Yorker Salon hardtop sedan

though the more impressive Imperial might have been a better venue. New Yorkers were certainly less impressive in these years, demoted from the usual 126-inch wheelbase to the 122-inch junior span to reduce tooling costs at a cash-short time in Chrysler's up-and-down history. Still, the more tailored Virgil Exner styling (one of his final jobs for Chrysler) was at least tasteful if not timeless, and New Yorkers wore it well, announced by unique split grilles both years. The Salon was basically a luxury package for the regular New Yorker hardtop sedan comprising a premium interior with a reclining front passenger's seat, landau-style black-vinyl roof cover, and most every convenience in Chrysler's book—hence its advertised boast as "the world's most complete car." But at $5860 it cost as much as some Imperials, which limited demand and caused Chrysler to abandon the idea after just two years.

✚ FOR As for 1962-64 Chrysler 300, plus "oddball value"

▬ AGAINST As for 1962-64 Chrysler 300, but parts-finding even more nightmarish

PRODUCTION

1963 593 **1964** 1621

SPECIFICATIONS

Length (in.)	215.3
Wheelbase (in.)	122.0
Weight (lbs)	4290
Price (new)	$5860

ENGINES

cid/type	bhp	years
413/ohv V-8	340	1963-64

PRICES

FAIR	$1500-2500
GOOD	$2500-4000
FINE	$4000-6500

FINE EXAMPLE PRICE HISTORY

1982 $2000		**1990** $5500	
1994 $5000		**1998** $7500	
1982-2000 RETURN 7%			
2000-2010 2%			

CHRYSLER 300 2D HARDTOP/ CONVERTIBLE

1966 300 hardtop coupe

Sportiest of the first Chryslers styled by Elwood Engel, who replaced Virgil Exner as Highland Park design chief in 1962 and repeated many of the design hallmarks he'd used at Ford—mainly squarish contours and chrome-edged fenderlines. The non-letter 300 was the mid-range series as before, offering a hardtop sedan and a (likely export-only) pillared four-door in addition to the customary convertible and hardtop coupe. Like other Chryslers, they were longer and heavier than in 1963-64, but reverted from 413 V-8s to the smaller, corporate-mainstay 383. When the letter-series departed after '65, these two-door 300s became the sportiest of all Chryslers, acquiring standard front bucket seats (previously optional) and a somewhat busy, minor facelift.

✚ FOR Period Chrysler virtues, plus nicer styling, especially '65 • Convertibles very rare • Excellent club support • Still somewhat undervalued

▬ AGAINST Likely long-term return on investment • More Chryslers not wide-

ly saved, so trim and body panels just as difficult

PRODUCTION

1965 2d htp 11,621 **conv** 1418 **1966 2d htp** 24,103 **conv** 2500

SPECIFICATIONS

Length (in.)	218.2/222.0 (1965/66)
Wheelbase (in.)	124.0
Weight (lbs)	3940-4085
Price (new)	$3551-$3936

ENGINES

cid/type	bhp	years
383/ohv V-8	315/325/360	1965-66

PRICES

2dr htp	
FAIR	$2250-4000
GOOD	$4000-5500
FINE	$5500-7500
Conv	
FAIR	$3000-7000
GOOD	$7000-9000
FINE	$9000-15,000

FINE CONVERTIBLE PRICE HISTORY

1982 $4000		**1990** $14,000	
1994 $15,000		**1998** $17,000	
1982-2000 RETURN 6%			
2000-2010 5%			

CHRYSLER 300-L

1965 300-L convertible

Last gasp for the letter-series 300 until the all-new (and much higher production) 300M of 1999. The "L" shared Elwood Engel's new styling with other '65 Chryslers, but was more a trim option than a separate model in its own right. Handling and performance were only marginally better than on other Chryslers, and it was hardly the stormer its predecessors had been because only a single 360-bhp powerplant was offered. After 1965, Chrysler abandoned the big-car performance market, and the letter-series was dropped. The non-letter 300, which had replaced the Windsor in the 1962 line, continued on into the 1970s.

✚ FOR More distinctive than other '65 Chryslers • 300 designation

■ AGAINST Little that makes it a thoroughbred • Questionable assembly quality • Thirsty • Big

PRODUCTION

2d htp 2405 **conv** 440

SPECIFICATIONS

Length (in.)	218.2
Wheelbase (in.)	124.0
Weight (lbs)	4170-4245
Price (new)	$4153-4618

ENGINES

cid/type	bhp	years
413/ohv V-8	360	1965

PRICES

Conv	
FAIR	$5000-8000
GOOD	$8000-12,000
FINE	$12,000-18,000
Htp	
FAIR	$3000-5000
GOOD	$5000-7000
FINE	$7000-12,500

FINE CONVERTIBLE PRICE HISTORY

1982 $4500	1990 $22,500
1994 $20,000	1998 $18,000
1982-2000 RETURN 9%	
2000-2010 3%	

1 9 6 7 - 6 8
CHRYSLER 300 2D HARDTOP/ CONVERTIBLE

Continuation of the non-letter 300 series, with new styling (also applied to linemates) on the basic 1965-66 platform (wheelbase and overall length were unchanged). All '67-'68 Chryslers sported sharpened lines and concave bodysides, but 300s still stood apart with the traditional "cross-hair" grille motif and, for '68, hidden headlamps. Two-door hardtops

1967 300 hardtop coupe

used the wide-quarter "fast-top" treatment seen on Dodge/Plymouth counterparts. Power switched to the new corporate 440 big-block V-8 introduced on '66 New Yorkers and Imperials, here packing 350 standard horsepower, 375 with the "TNT" performance option, and sold exclusively with TorqueFlite automatic. Sales remained good, though not great, as buyers were turning in droves from sporty full-sizers to midsize "muscle cars." The companion 300 hardtop sedan, baseline Newport convertible, and Newport/Newport Custom hardtop coupes may also be collected one day, but the two-door 300s look like far better investments, though they'll probably never be blue chips.

✚ FOR Effortless big-block power • TorqueFlite still peerless • Big and roomy, yet a touch sporty • Few convertibles built (again) • Relatively cheap

■ AGAINST Next to no interest yet • Styling more contrived than 1965-66

PRODUCTION

1967 2d htp 11,556 **conv** 1594 **1968 2d htp** 16,953 **conv** 2161

SPECIFICATIONS

Length (in.)	219.0
Wheelbase (in.)	124.0
Weight (lbs)	3985-4105
Price (new)	$3936-4337

ENGINES

cid/type	bhp	years
440/ohv V-8	350/375	1967-68

PRICES

Conv	
FAIR	$3500-5000
GOOD	$5000-7000
FINE	$7000-10,000
Hdtp	
FAIR	$2000-3000
GOOD	$3000-4000
FINE	$4000-6000

FINE CONVERTIBLE PRICE HISTORY

1982 $4000	1990 $14,000
1994 $12,000	1998 $10,000
1982-2000 RETURN 4%	
2000-2010 3%	

1 9 6 9 - 7 1
CHRYSLER 300 2D HARDTOP/ CONVERTIBLE

1969 300 convertible

The final 300s with a direct line to the 1955 original, though few could see their coming demise in 1969, when Chrysler shifted to rounded "fuselage styling" marked by bulged bodysides, diminished glass areas, and very obvious extra length (up 5.5 inches overall). Wheelbases were again unchanged, however, and curb weights were up but fractionally despite the more massive appearance. Chrysler Division thought one of its '69s would be "your next car," but sales were flat and would fall sharply through 1971. The 300s retained unique hidden-headlamp grilles that looked good within the big "loop" bumpers of these years. But though nameplates now read "Three Hundred," there was also writing on the wall, and the series was terminated after '71 owing to continued buyer preference for the cheaper but only slightly less spartan Newports. (The start of new corporate difficulties didn't help.) The 300 convertible didn't last that long, canceled along with its Newport Custom sister after 1970.

✚ FOR Smooth, effortless road cars • Spacious interiors • Huge trunks • Becoming more collectible, especially the convertible

■ AGAINST Debateable styling • Assembly quality takes a big turn for the worse • Didn't take turns like earlier 300s • Collector interest still not high

PRODUCTION

1969 2d htp 16,075 **conv** 1933 **1970 2d htp** 9,583 **conv** 1077 **1971 2d htp** 7256

SPECIFICATIONS

Length (in.)	224.7
Wheelbase (in.)	124.0
Weight (lbs)	3965-4246
Price (new)	$4105-4610

ENGINES

cid/type	bhp	years
440/ohv V-8	350/375	1969-70
440/ohv V-8	335/370	1971

PRICES

Conv	
FAIR	$2000-4000
GOOD	$4000-6000
FINE	$6000-10,000
Htp	
FAIR	$1000-2000
GOOD	$2000-3500
FINE	$3500-5000

FINE CONVERTIBLE PRICE HISTORY

1982 $3000	1990 $10,000
1994 $11,000	1998 $13,000

1982-2000 RETURN 5%
2000-2010 3%

1970
CHRYSLER 300-HURST

Not a return of the fabled letter-series 300s, but a specially produced non-letter 300 hardtop built by Hurst Performance Products and sold through Chrysler dealers. Features included special road wheels, wider-than-stock tires, the 375-bhp version of Chrysler's big-block 440 V-8, heavy-duty suspension, and, of course, a Hurst shifter for the standard TorqueFlite automatic. The exterior was dressed up by a snazzy gold and white paint job, twist-lock hood tiedowns, a subtle scoop at the rear of the hood near the cowl, and a loop-type rear spoiler.

1970 300-Hurst hardtop coupe

FOR Rarity • Good performance • Clean styling

AGAINST Heavy and thirsty • Rust-prone unless looked after

PRODUCTION

Htp 500 conv 1

SPECIFICATIONS

Length (in.)	224.7
Wheelbase (in.)	124.0
Weight (lbs)	4135 (approx.)
Price (new)	$4400 (approx.)

ENGINES

cid/type	bhp	years
440/ohv V-8	375	1970

PRICES

FAIR	$3500-6000
GOOD	$6000-8000
FINE	$8000-12,000

FINE HARDTOP PRICE HISTORY

1982 $3500	1990 $18,000
1994 $18,000	1998 $13,000

1982-2000 RETURN 7%
2000-2010 2%

1979-82
CHRYSLER CORDOBA "300" 1979 & LS

Desperate attempt at recapturing letter-series 300 glory with rather mundane cars. The '79, appearing in the fifth and final year for Chrysler's first-generation personal-luxury Cordoba coupe, was basically a $2040 option package comprising an all-white exterior with special emblems and traditional "cross-hair" 300-style grille, red leather interior with engine-turned dash appliqué, handling suspension with G60-15 tires and "firm-feel" power

1979 Cordoba 300 coupe

steering, and a four-barrel 360 V-8 pulling a shorter rear-axle ratio through the obligatory TorqueFlite automatic. A similar exterior package was devised for the downsized 1980 Cordoba, which was based on the Dodge Aspen/Plymouth Volare compacts, but the official name was LS, fortified underpinnings cost extra, and there were no special engines, just the lowly standard Slant Six and optional 318 V-8. It's mentioned here mainly for interest value. We think the '79 could become a minor collectible in the distant future, but LS prospects seem slim to non-existent at this time.

FOR Dirt cheap • Traditional 300 styling cues

AGAINST Sad reminders of "The Old Chrysler Corporation" • Even clubs look down on them • Patchy workmanship • '79 very rust-prone • Anemic six-cylinder 1980-82 performance

PRODUCTION

1979 est. 2500 **1980 est.** 5000 **1981** 7315 **1982** 3136

SPECIFICATIONS

Length (in.)	215.8/210.1 (1979/80-82)
Wheelbase (in.)	114.9/112.7 (1979/80-82)
Weight (lbs)	4210/3300-3500 (1979/80-82)
Price (new)	$9175 (1979), $7200-8360 (1980-82)

ENGINES

cid/type	bhp[1]	years
225/ohv I-6	85	1980-82
318/ohv V-8	130/165	1980-82
360/ohv V-8	195	1979-80

[1]SAE net

PRICES

FAIR	$1000-2000
GOOD	$2000-4000
FINE	$4000-6000

FINE EXAMPLE PRICE HISTORY

Depreciation during their first two decades has probably turned around for the best examples.
2000-2010 RETURN 3%

1982 Cordoba LS hardtop coupe

1983-86
CHRYSLER LEBARON MARK CROSS T&C CONVERTIBLE

1986 LeBaron Mark Cross T&C convertible

Another Chrysler nod to past glories, this time the late-'40s Town & Country convertible. Essentially, this was a blend of two trim options for the front-drive LeBaron convertible announced with coupe and sedan models for 1982—all based on Highland Park's 1981 Dodge Aries/Plymouth Reliant K-car platform. It was much like those do-or-die compacts in appearance and technical makeup, with different taillamps and a more formal grille the main distinctions. Slightly facelifted for '86. The K-car's 2.2-liter/135-cid "Trans-4" was always standard, with an optional turbo version from '84. The original alternative engine was a Mitsubishi "balancer" four, supplanted for '86 by a Trans-4 stroked to 2.5 liters (153 cid). A five-speed manual transaxle was offered through '84, when the previously optional TorqueFlite became standard. The ragtop Town & Country differed from the normal LeBaron convertible in wood-look plastic side trim (shared with a T&C wagon); the Mark Cross added lush hide upholstery adorned with the leathermaker's logos. Alas, a Mark Cross option was also available in other body styles, which dilutes the T&C ragtop's collector appeal. Then again, this wasn't the most common of Chrysler's reborn '80s ragtops, which should work for it in the future—though perhaps not all that much.

✚ FOR "Used car" prices • Excellent parts/service availability • Practical size • Top-down appeal • Turbo quite peppy • Low production

▬ AGAINST Not that exciting • Tacky bodyside "wood" • Turbo engine rough and boomy • Mediocre manual shift • Prone to cowl/body shake

PRODUCTION
1983 est. 1500 **1984** 1105 **1985** 595 **1986** 501

SPECIFICATIONS
Length (in.)	179.8
Wheelbase (in.)	100.3
Weight (lbs)	2600-2775
Price (new)	$15,595-17,595

ENGINES
cid/type	bhp	years
135/ohc I-4	95-99	1983-86
135/ohc I-4[1]	142-146	1984-86
153/ohc I-4	100	1986
156/ohc I-4	93-101	1983-85
[1]Turbocharged		

PRICES
FAIR	$1200-2800
GOOD	$2800-5000
FINE	$5000-7000

FAIR EXAMPLE PRICE HISTORY
Clean originals are now appreciating.
2000-2010 RETURN 3%

1983-86
CHRYSLER LIMOUSINE/ EXECUTIVE SEDAN

Literal stretches of the early-'80s front-drive LeBaron—the first "carriage trade" Chryslers since the last Stageway Imperial limos of 1970. Though not badged as LeBarons, they looked like what they were: LeBaron coupes with 24 or 31 inches spliced in the middle. The Executive Sedan offered roomy seating for five, while the longer Limousine had a pair of rear jump seats for carrying up to seven; it also sported the customary division 'twixt passenger and chauffeur's compartments. Both featured leather rear seating, TorqueFlite, and the largest available K-car engines—which weren't nearly large enough to move these cars with much gusto. Though bought mainly by companies and airport limousine operators as handier, thriftier "executive transport" than traditional full-size limos, there weren't enough buyers for the idea to endure beyond three years. Little-known then or now, but small enough to be practical daily-drivers for collectors seeking something different. Oddball proof of how Chrysler sailed through the '80s with seemingly endless permutations of the humble K-car.

✚ FOR Oddity value • Fits where "stretch" Caddys and Lincolns won't • Few built, especially the Executive Sedan

▬ AGAINST Still basically K-cars • Anemic performance • Conversions, so some detail workmanship rough • Value appreciation looks minimal

PRODUCTION
1983 est. 500 (both models) **1984 Executive Sedan** 196 **Limo** 594 **1985 Limo** 759 **1986 Limo** 138

SPECIFICATIONS
Length (in.)	203.8/210.8 (Executive/Limo)
Wheelbase (in.)	124.0/131.0 (Executive/Limo)
Weight (lbs)	2950-3250
Price (new)	$18,900-27,500

ENGINES
cid/type	bhp	years
156/ohc I-4	93-101	1983-85
153/ohc I-4	100	1986

PRICES
FAIR	$1000-2500

1985 Limousine

GOOD	$2000-4000
FINE	$4000-5500

FINE EXAMPLE PRICE HISTORY

Not available
2000-2010 RETURN 5% for best examples.

1985 1/2 - 86
CHRYSLER LASER XT

K-car-based, liftback sports coupe that, if properly equipped, offered brisk performance and outstanding handling. Sharply raked windshield and slope nose were highlights of slick, laudably restrained styling. Top model, the XT, ran with a special handling suspension and 2.2-liter turbo four that produced 142/146 horsepower. With this engine and 5-speed manual trans, an XT Laser could manage the 0-60 mph sprint in a hair over eight seconds (add a full second for automatic). Quartermile came up in about 16 seconds with terminal speed in the mid-80s. Top speed about 115. Turbo lag was modest and mid-range response was good. Fully equipped XTs had a slew of high-tech options, including "Electronic Navigator." Total XT production amounted to little more than 10,400.

✚ FOR Novel, latter-day Chrysler-nameplate performance car • Low production numbers • Turbo-powered acceleration • Sticky handling • Mucho luxury and gadgetry • Clean good looks

▬ AGAINST Humble underpinnings • Turbo examples may be tired • "Voice-alert" warning system and other electronic gadgets may have gone wonky with age • Exhaust drone

PRODUCTION

1985 1/2 3452 **1986** 6989

1986 Laser XT coupe

SPECIFICATIONS

Length (in.)	175.0
Weight (lbs)	2665-2695
Wheelbase (in.)	97.0
Price (new)	$11,854

ENGINES

cid/type	bhp	years
135 ohc I-4[1]	146	1985-86

[1]Turbocharged

PRICES

FAIR	$1000-1500
GOOD	$1500-2500
FINE	$2500-3500

2000-2010 RETURN 2% for top condition cars

1987 - 89
CHRYSLER CONQUEST TSi

1987 Conquest TSi

A Mitsubishi Starion sold by Chrysler, the Conquest filled Chrsyler's need for a sport coupe after dropping the Laser. A big four with an intercooled turbocharger provided good performance for the time. In spite of ballance shafts, it was never a smooth running engine. Rear wheel drive and full independent suspension gave good grip and handling on dry pavement. Like some other performance rear-wheel drive cars, the Conquest could be tricky in the wet. Never considered a sophisticated car, the Conquest was quick and fun to drive. Rising prices during the Starion/Conquest's last years kept sales down. The Chrysler version is the rarer of the two.

✚ FOR Strong performance with little turbo lag • Good handling • Rarity

▬ AGAINST Rough engine • Gimicky styling

PRODUCTION

NA

SPECIFICATIONS

Length (in.)	173.2
Weight (lbs)	2822
Wheelbase (in.)	100.5
Price (new)	$17,174-18974

ENGINES

cid/type	bhp	years
156/ohc I-4[1]	176/188	1987-89

[1]Turbocharged

PRICES

FAIR	$2000-3000
GOOD	$3000-3750
FINE	$3750-4500

2000-2010 RETURN Even

1988
CHRYSLER LEBARON LIMITED EDITION GTC CONVERTIBLE

1988 LeBaron Limited Edition GTC convertible

White-bodied, turbo-four convertible released as a spring 1988 model to attract the coveted "young, upscale buyer" to the Chrysler nameplate. Note, please, that this LeBaron was a variant of the J-body LeBaron coupe and convertible that debuted for 1987; those cars were stretched versions of the old Dodge Daytona/Chrysler Laser platform. Other '88 LeBarons were based, variously, on the venerable K-car platform and the H-body Dodge Lancer. Chrysler was clearly fond of the (by now meaningless) LeBaron name, but the fact remained that in whichever version, LeBaron was a creation of the parts bin. The Limited Edition GTC convertible (2754 built) was a mid-year introduction that mated the 2.2 turbo to a 5-speed stick (automatic trans was optional). Firmed-up suspension and all-season performance tires on 15-inch cast aluminum wheels were the GTC's other major features. A loaded GTC ragtop could run some $20,000, but depreciation hit these cars hard.

⊞ FOR Convertible body style • Acceleration • Handling • Low production • Available luxury amenities

⊟ AGAINST Parts-bin heritage • Questionable workmanship • Turbo may be tired • Still a used car

PRODUCTION
2754

SPECIFICATIONS

Length (in.)	184.9
Weight (lbs)	2590
Wheelbase (in.)	100.3
Price (new)	$21,707

ENGINES

cid/type	bhp	years
135 /ohc I-4[1]	146	1988
[1]Turbocharged		

PRICES

FAIR	$2500-3500
GOOD	$3500-4500
FINE	$4500-6000
2000-2010 RETURN Even	

1988-95
CHRYSLER LEBARON GTC

Most exciting of the second-series front-drive LeBaron coupes and convertibles first seen for 1987. Basic K-car chassis, moderately updated,

but handsome new droop-snoot bodywork by Chrysler Design under Thomas C. Gale. The GTC bowed as a mid-1988 "Limited Edition" sporting an all-white exterior (including wheels and most body trim), handling suspension, comprehensive equipment, and Chrysler's 2.2-liter/135-cid "Turbo II" four-cylinder engine with standard five-speed manual or optional TorqueFlite transaxles. The '89s were reruns save a newly intercooled engine with 28 more horses, bright-finish lacy-spoke wheels (instead of white), and a choice of paint colors. The formula repeated again for 1990, but there was a more modern new "ergonomic" dash (by ex-Citroën designer Trevor Creed), the automatic option was deleted, manual shift action was greatly improved, and the engine was treated to Chrysler's new Variable Nozzle Turbo system (VNT), which enhanced driveability by enhancing torque (up 10 pounds/feet to 210). The GTC continued through 1995, which makes it fairly common, so these early ones won't likely start appreciating for some years—if ever. Assuming they do, convertibles will have the usual value edge over coupes.

⊞ FOR Nice lines • Brisk performance • Capable handling • Used-car pricing

⊟ AGAINST No mystique or pedigree • Appreciation potential diminished by mass of lesser linemates

PRODUCTION
1988 cpe 2943 **conv** 2754 **1989** NA **1990** NA

SPECIFICATIONS

Length (in.)	184.9
Wheelbase (in.)	100.3
Weight (lbs)	approx. 2800-3000
Price (new)	$13,995-20,406

ENGINES

cid/type	bhp	years
135/ohc I-4[1]	146	1988

135/ohc I-4[1]	174	1989-92[2]
181/ohc V-6	144	1993-95
[1]Turbocharged [2]Turbo II 1989; Turbo IV 1990		

PRICES

Conv

FAIR	$2000-3000
GOOD	$3000-3750
FINE	$3750-4500

Coupe prices running 50% below convertible.
2000-2010 RETURN 1%

1989-90
CHRYSLER TC BY MASERATI

1989-90 TC by Maserati convertible

Bungled late-'80s Highland Park stab at a semi-exotic flagship. Much like the rival Cadillac Allante in concept, but workaday front-drive K-car chassis with a shorter wheelbase and a smooth two-seat convertible body styled and built by Chrysler. Maserati engineered a new 16-valve twincam cylinder head to replace the eight-valve single-cam cap on Chrysler's 2.2-liter turbo-four. But the resulting 200 horses teamed only with a manual five-speed transaxle; with automatic you got the 160-bhp single-cam engine. Many other components were lifted from corporate bins, but the TC had unique leather interior trim, full power equipment and a liftoff hardtop with Thunderbird-style porthole windows. Maserati handled final assembly in Milan, but numerous problems delayed deliveries until December 1988. Interest had cooled by then, and production ceased by late 1990. No interim changes occurred, save an airbag steering wheel and a 141-bhp non-turbo Mitsubishi V-6 (ousting the 160-bhp four) in the final year.

⊞ FOR Nice (if not original) idea • Interesting background • Practical for a two-seater • Handsome leather upholstery • Manageable manual soft top • Still serviceable by most any Chrysler dealer

⊟ AGAINST K-car pretending to be a Maserati • Unfortunate resemblance to

1989 LeBaron GTC coupe

1987 and later LeBaron convertible • Some rough details • Frustrating turbo lag (especially with automatic)

PRODUCTION

approx. 7000

SPECIFICATIONS

Length (in.)	175.8
Wheelbase (in.)	90.0
Weight (lbs)	3200
Price (new)	$30,000-33,000

ENGINES

cid/type	bhp	years
135/ohc I-4[1]	160	1989
135/dohc I-4[1]	200	1989-90
181/ohc V-6	141	1990

[1]Turbocharged

PRICES

FAIR	$5000-8000
GOOD	$8000-11,000
FINE	$11,000-14,000
2000-2010 RETURN	Still depreciating

1947-52
CISITALIA TYPE 202 GRAN SPORT

1948 Type 202S cabriolet

The car best remembered for its critically acclaimed Pinin Farina styling, one of the designer's landmarks. The brainchild of wealthy Italian industrialist Piero Dusio, Cisitalia started by building single-seat racing cars. The Type 202 was a road-going version of that design, and like it was based on contemporary Fiat 1100 (Type 508) mechanical components. The complex multi-tubular chassis was the product of Dr. Dante Giacosa of Fiat. While the drivetrains were cheap and familiar, the coachbuilt bodies were not. Cisitalia was soon overtaken by cheaper and more modern competitors, and the firm ran out of funds before a Grand Prix race car project was completed. Dusio moved his operations to Argentina, but the cars built there under the Cisitalia name were far different. In 1950, production of the Type 202 was supposed to resume in

Italy under new ownership, but though a few cars were built through 1965, they appeared sporadically. Most were simply cobbled-up amalgamations of mass-produced chassis and drivetrains with special bodies. The trend-setting 202 Gran Sport is the only truly collectible model. A convertible version was offered in addition to Farina's beautifully contoured coupe, which has since been enshrined in New York's Museum of Modern Art.

⊞ FOR Timeless Pinin Farina styling • Unique chassis design • Simple running gear • Very rare, highly prized • A Milestone car

⊟ AGAINST Virtually none left • Not quick (maybe 80 mph tops) • Chassis difficult to restore • Fragile, light-alloy bodywork • Body and mechanical parts extinct

PRODUCTION

approx. 170, incl. 60 cabriolets

SPECIFICATIONS

Length (in.)	NA
Wheelbase (in.)	NA
Weight (lbs)	1760
Price (new)	$6800 U.S. list price

ENGINES

cc/type (cid)	bhp[1]	years
1089/ohv 14 (66)	51-70	1947-52

[1]Gross

PRICES

FAIR	$50,000-80,000
GOOD	$80,000-100,000
FINE	$100,000-120,000

FINE EXAMPLE PRICE HISTORY

1982 $25,000		1987 $75,000	
1990 $160,000		1994 $120,000	
1982-2000 RETURN 12%			
2000-2010 10%			

1934-57
CITROËN "TRACTION AVANT"

The French mass-production pioneer of front drive and all-steel unit construction, the latter encouraged—and tooled—by America's Budd Body Company. It boasted many advances including pushrod ohv engines, removable wet cylinder liners, independent front suspension, and four-wheel torsion-bar springing. The driveline put a three-speed manual gearbox ahead of the differential and engine. This layout influenced the U.S. Cord 810/812. The shifter poked through the dash and worked "backwards," an artifact of Andre Citroën's aborted plan for automatic transmission. Styling, now long world-famous, was low-slung—just 60 inches high, some 18 inches below the contemporary norm—emphasized by omitting running boards. Wheels at the extreme corners made for exceptional interior space, a smooth ride, and—with fairly broad track dimensions—high stability. There were progressive improvements and more powerful four-cylinder engines, plus a six-cylinder alternative from 1938. Mainstay models were four-door sedans: four-seat *legere* ("light"), stretched five/six-seat *normale*, and longer seven/nine-passenger *familiale*. The last had a lift-up rear-end panel—an early hatchback—and was also sold with removable seats as a *commerciale*. A 2+2 coupe

1950 Traction Avant sedan

and convertible were built for a time, as was a low-volume five-seat *coupe de ville*. Not fundamentally changed postwar, but it saw further improvements and, from '53, "trunkback" styling. Starting in 1954, some 3000 Sixes received the radical new oleopneumatic suspension system from the forthcoming 1955 DS19, though Traction assemblies didn't stop until July 1957.

➕ FOR History-makers all • Great character • Unmistakable "French connection" styling • Roomy and smooth-riding

➖ AGAINST Not that common in U.S. • Ditto parts/service/restoration expertise • Ditto club support • Leisurely performance • Established Citröen's reputation for quirkiness

PRODUCTION[1]
4-cyl 708,339 **6-cyl** 50,518
[1]Includes prewar British-built models.

SPECIFICATIONS
Length (in.)	184 (7CV/11 legere); 191 (15/Six and 11 normale); 198.5 (11 familiale/commerciale)
Wheelbase (in.)	114.5 (7CV, 11 legere); 121.5 (15/Six and 11 normale); 129.0 (11 familiale/commerciale)
Weight (lbs)	2650-2950
Price (new)	$1798-2686 (1955 U.S. POE)

ENGINES
cid/type	bhp[1]	years
79.5/ohv I-4	32	1934
93.3/ohv I-4	35	1934
99.3/ohv I-4	36	1934-41
116.6/ohv I-4	45/56	1934-57
175.0/ohv I-6	77	1938-57

[1]Net

PRICES
FAIR	$4000-7000
GOOD	$7000-10,000
FINE	$10,000-15,000

(Add 50% for drophead coupe.)

FINE SALOON PRICE HISTORY
1982 $5000		**1987** $10,000	
1990 $15,000		**1994** $15,000	
1982-2000 RETURN 8%			
2000-2010 8%			

1955-75
CITROËN DS 19/20/21/23

Futuristic design from French pioneer of front-wheel drive, and still quite advanced next to most competitors when it was replaced 20 years later by the long-running CX series. This was the mainstay of the Citröen line for many years, and the "Goddess" was the first car reflecting the firm's

interest and expertise in the art of aerodynamics. The monocoque body/chassis featured fully detachable skin panels; the car could even be driven in "skeleton" form. The DS also introduced Citröen's unique hydraulic (actually gas/oil) all-independent suspension system run from an engine-driven pump that also provided assistance for steering and brakes. The suspension incorporated a variable height adjustment that could be used for clearing road hazards, fording streams, or even jacking up the car when changing a flat. (U.S. advertising touted this as the only car you could ride going up and down.) The low-drag body put the wheels at the "corners" of the car, resulting in a spacious interior. Model designations reflect engine size. Through 1966, the DS used Citröen's ancient four-cylinder engine, but this was replaced by a more modern design in later models. A confusing succession of tuning and equipment changes marked this series through the years, but while it sold fairly well in Europe, the DS was never a high-volume item in the U.S. Most of the ones sold here were four-door sedans, but an even longer wagon was also sold in modest numbers. The hydraulic suspension gave a cloud-like ride that made the DS unmatched in this area by almost any other car, although certain surface irregularities would upset the car strangely. Leech-like roadholding was another virtue, but the performance wasn't. The engines were considered under-powered for really brisk standing-start acceleration, although top speed was high, a benefit of the slippery body. Not the sort of car that stood up well to American driving conditions and owner habits, but a fairly rare and distinctive collectible with the advantage that the long production should make parts easier to come by. The lesser-priced ID models are also worthy of consideration.

➕ FOR Unique design in all respects • Ride and handling still up to current standards • Parts still available from overseas • Budget buy • High appreciation potential • 1955-64 DS and ID 19 are Milestone cars

➖ AGAINST Mechanically complex, so expect restoration and maintenance headaches • Disappointing acceleration • Strange dash and minor control layout • Brakes demand driver practice • Rust-prone

PRODUCTION
1,456,115 of all types

SPECIFICATIONS
Length (in.)	190.5/198.0 (sdn/wgn)
Wheelbase (in.)	123.0
Weight (lbs)	2690-3100
Price (new)	NA

ENGINES
cc/type (cid)	bhp[1]	years
1911/ohv 14 (117)	60	1955-66
1985/ohv 14 (121)	103	1966-75
2175/ohv 14 (133)	115	1968-75
2347/ohv 14 (143)	125	1971-75

[1]DIN

PRICES
FAIR	$3000-4000
GOOD	$4000-6500
FINE	$6500-10,000

FINE EXAMPLE PRICE HISTORY
1982 $2500	**1990** $6000
1994 $7500	**1998** $8500
1982-2000 RETURN 8%	
2000-2010 5%	

1970 DS 21 sedan

CITROËN CHAPRON DS 19/20/21/23
1957-75

1967 DS 21 Chapron Cabriolet

Rare and expensive convertible conversion of the front-drive Citroën DS-series sedans carried out by the French coachbuilder Henri Chapron. Built in very small numbers to customer order mostly for very wealthy private buyers and the French government. Most had two-door bodywork, but some four-door convertible sedans were also built. Chapron continued to carry out this work on the replacement CX models, but like these earlier DS examples most were not exported. Thus, finding a DS ragtop in the U.S. will be akin to the old needle-in-a-haystack exercise.

✚ FOR As for DS19/20/21/23 plus convertible appeal and great scarcity • Milestone status

➖ AGAINST As for DS19/20/21/23, but few body parts available, and body not as rigid

PRODUCTION
approx. 100 per year

SPECIFICATIONS
Length (in.)	190.5
Wheelbase (in.)	123.0
Weight (lbs)	approx. 3200
Price (new)	NA

ENGINES
cc/type (cid)	bhp[1]	years
1911/ohv 14 (117)	60	1955-56
1985/ohv 14 (121)	103	1966-75
2175/ohv 14 (133)	115	1968-75
2347/ohv 14 (143)	125	1971-75

[1]DIN

PRICES
FAIR	$9000-17,000
GOOD	$17,000-24,000
FINE	$24,000-30,000

FINE EXAMPLE PRICE HISTORY
1982 $5000		1990 $25,000	

1994 $27,500		1998 $27,500	
1982-2000 RETURN 12%			
2000-2010 10%			

CITROËN SM
1972-74

The most spectacular postwar Citroën, and a car with strong collector potential despite its mechanical complexity and attendant reliability problems. The SM was the result of a temporary corporate marriage between the French concern and Maserati. It was powered by a four-cam V-6 engine designed by the Italians, and which also found its way into the mid-engine Maserati Merak. Styling was recognizably Citroën and quite stunning, a sort of sports interpretation of DS-series themes. It undoubtedly had good aerodynamics—long a Citroën passion—as the car's 135-mph top speed suggested. Like the DS, the SM used Citroën's fully pressurized hydraulics for brakes and as a suspension medium, but here it also powered the steering, which was lightning quick—two turns lock-to-lock—and would self-center without any driver assist with the car at rest. Another novel touch on European models was a six-headlamp system with the inboard units linked to the steering so they'd turn in the same direction as the front wheels—shades of Tucker! Unfortunately, the SM bowed almost on the eve of the first energy crisis, which made fast tourers like this almost unsalable in Europe and put both Citroën and Maserati in serious financial trouble. Citroën withdrew from the American market after 1974. SM production limped along for about another year, then ceased following Peugeot's acquisition of the firm. Named "one of the ten best cars in the world" in 1971 by *Road & Track* magazine, a debatable accolade, perhaps, in view of subsequent events. Not a strong collector comer at present, but unique design and comparative rarity should start to tell further down the road.

✚ FOR Unique design • Splendid performance • Citroen ride • Rarity

➖ AGAINST Engines subject to cam-drive problems • Parts supplies dicey • Hydraulics a bear if something breaks

PRODUCTION
NA, but probably no more than 5000 total. Years shown are for U.S. importation only.

SPECIFICATIONS
Length (in.)	160.6
Wheelbase (in.)	95.0
Weight (lbs)	2130
Price (new)	$9000 U.S. in 1972

ENGINES
cc/type (cid)	bhp[1]	years
2965/dohc V-6 (181)	190	1972-74

[1]SAE net

PRICES
FAIR	$4000-8000
GOOD	$8000-10,000
FINE	$10,000-14,000

FINE EXAMPLE PRICE HISTORY
1982 $7000		1990 $18,000	
1994 $14,000		1998 $14,000	
1982-2000 RETURN 4%			
2000-2010 5%			

1972 SM coupe

1956
CLIPPER CUSTOM CONSTELLATION

When James J. Nance became Packard president in 1952, one of his immediate marketing objectives was to divorce the Packard marque from the medium-priced field, which had hindered the luxury Packards' sales performance since the war. Nance reinvoked the Clipper name as a Packard model in 1953, then registered Clipper as a separate make for 1956. But by then it was too late—the Clipper "make" lasted only a year, though the name was applied one more time to Packards in 1957. The Constellation hardtop is the flashiest and easily the most desirable '56 Clipper, nicely trimmed and finished, and offered with Packard's innovative Torsion-Level suspension. (For pre-1956 models, see "Packard.")

FOR Good styling (compromised by bizarre two-toning) • Fine ride • Adequate performance • Historical interest

AGAINST A low-profile collectible • Thirsty

PRODUCTION
1466

SPECIFICATIONS
Length (in.)	214.8
Wheelbase (in.)	122.0
Weight (lbs)	3860
Price (new)	$3164

ENGINES
cid/type	bhp	years
352/ohv V-8	275	1956

PRICES
FAIR	$3200-6000
GOOD	$6000-10,000
FINE	$10,000-15,000

FINE EXAMPLE PRICE HISTORY
1982 $4250	1990 $13,000
1994 $15,000	1998 $15,000
1982-2000 RETURN 6%	
2000-2010 5%	

1956-57
CONTINENTAL MARK II

1956 Mark II hardtop coupe

Mid-'50s successor to the original Continental of the '40s. Magnificently styled by a team including John Reinhart, William Clay Ford, and Gordon Buehrig. Engineer Harley Copp's unique "cowbelly" frame dipped low to permit high seating without a tall body. With Multi-Drive three-speed automatic and a balanced, individually tested Lincoln V-8, the Mark II was marketed as an image leader intended to steal Cadillac's thunder in the ultra-luxury class. Despite beautiful styling, it didn't sell well, probably because its price was so close to the (then) breathtaking $10,000 mark. Ford had not originally seen the Mark II as a profit-maker, yet because the firm lost $1000 on each one sold, the urge to cheapen the car for 1958 proved irresistible. A Mark II cabriolet was contemplated, but never actually produced on a series basis.

FOR A famous postwar car • Timeless, elegant styling • High-quality materials • Strong club support

AGAINST Not nearly as elegant a driver as it is a looker • Interiors rather plain for this class of car • High operating costs

PRODUCTION
1956 1325 **1957** 444

SPECIFICATIONS
Length (in.)	218.5
Wheelbase (in.)	126.0
Weight (lbs)	4800-4825
Price (new)	$9695-9966

ENGINES
cid/type	bhp	years
368/ohv V-8	285/300	1956-57

PRICES
FAIR	$7500-12,000
GOOD	$12,000-20,000
FINE	$20,000-28,000

FINE EXAMPLE PRICE HISTORY
1982 $15,000	1990 $30,000
1994 $30,000	1998 $30,000
1982-2000 RETURN 4%	
2000-2010 5%	

1958
CONTINENTAL MARK III

1958 Mark III convertible

Successor to the upper-crust Mark II, but far less exclusive. Essentially a high-line version of 1958's new unit-body Lincoln, with a finer eggcrate grille texture, repeated on the rear panel, which also featured triple-element taillight clusters. A Mercury cost expert had been brought in during the

1956 Clipper Custom Constellation hardtop coupe

Mark III's early planning stages, and the price was cut by 40 percent compared to the Mark II in order to pick up more sales. The line was expanded to include pillared and pillarless sedans and a convertible. Horsepower increased 25 percent. Greatly enlarged and completely different in concept from the Mark II, the Mark III had contemporary styling that would quickly become dated. There was liberal use of bright metal, plus prominent tailfins and canted quad headlamps. Continued for 1959-60 as the Mark IV and V, both of which were officially tagged Lincolns following the demise of the separate Continental Division.

✚ **FOR** More affordable than a Mark II • Powerful • Luxurious • Impressive size

■ **AGAINST** Controversial styling • Prone to mechanical and electrical failures • Very heavy • Gargantuan proportions • Extremely thirsty

PRODUCTION

4d sdn 1283 **2d htp** 2328 **conv** 3048 **Landau 4d htp** 5891

SPECIFICATIONS

Length (in.)	229.0
Wheelbase (in.)	131.0
Weight (lbs)	4800-5040
Price (new)	$5825-6283

ENGINES

cid/type	bhp	years
430/ohv V-8	375	1958

PRICES

4d	
FAIR	$2600-5000
GOOD	$5000-7000
FINE	$7000-9500
2d	
FAIR	$2700-5500
GOOD	$5500-8500
FINE	$8500-12,500
Conv	
FAIR	$7500-12,000
GOOD	$12,000-19,000
FINE	$19,000-30,000

FINE CONVERTIBLE PRICE HISTORY

1982	$5200	1990	$30,000
1994	$30,000	1998	$35,000
1982-2000 RETURN 10%			
2000-2010 5%			

1930-32
CORD
L-29

Errett Lobban Cord's front-drive masterpiece. Designed by Harry Miller and Cornelius Van Ranst, but underpowered with its adopted Auburn

1931 L-29 phaeton sedan

L-head straight-eight engine. A three-speed sliding-pinion transmission was sandwiched between the engine and differential. Brakes (inboard at front) were hydraulics, shocks Houdaille-Hershey all around, and the front half-shafts used Cardan constant-velocity joints—all very advanced. But the result was tail-heavy for a front-driver, so handling could be skittish in certain conditions and the U-joints wore out with fervor. Al Leamy designed the beautiful cowl-forward ensemble, which announced some of the most stunning styling of the day. High initial price limited sales in a competitive field, so Cord cut it drastically in 1931—but it didn't help. Sadly, the L-29 could have been a wonderful car with enough development time, but time wasn't on its side.

✚ **FOR** Some of the most majestic bodywork among full Classics • Novel, predictive engineering • The magic of a name

■ **AGAINST** High price • Extreme scarcity • Complicated mechanicals

PRODUCTION

1930 1700• **1931** 1433 **1932** 335[1]
[1]Registrations—total production about 5000, began in 1929

SPECIFICATIONS

Length (in.)	NA
Wheelbase (in.)	137.5
Weight (lbs)	4300-4560
Price (new)	$2395-3295

ENGINES

cid/type	bhp	years
298.6/sv I-8	115[1]	1930-31
322.0/sv I-8	125	1932

[1]Actual output. Cord advertised output as 125.

PRICES

Open	
FAIR	$35,000-70,000
GOOD	$70,000-120,000
FINE	$120,000-175,000
Closed	

FAIR	$16,000-33,000
GOOD	$33,000-60,000
FINE	$60,000-85,000

FINE 1932 PHAETON PRICE HISTORY

1982	$110,000	1990	$160,000
1994	$165,000	1998	$175,000
1982-2000 RETURN 3%			
2000-2010 5%			

1936-37
CORD
810/812

1937 812 Supercharged cabriolet

One of the most important automobiles of all time. Predictive "coffin nose" styling by Gordon Buehrig, Dale Cosper, Dick Roberson, and Paul Laurenzen. Powered by a Lycoming V-8 connected to a four-speed electric pre-selector gearbox (set the next gear, then stab the clutch to shift). A more compact engine set relatively farther forward in the chassis gave better fore/aft weight balance than the L-29, and the front suspension was independent. Handling was revolutionary for an American car of its time. Offered with a supercharger option in 1937 that yielded 0-60 mph in 11-13 seconds and 110 mph maximum. Design now world famous: wrapped radiator louvers, exposed pipes on the blown 812, turned-metal dash, and concealed headlights (a first). Westchester and

Beverly sedans plus a cabriolet and phaeton were joined by long-wheelbase Custom sedans in 1937. Cheap when first introduced at $2195 tops. Prices then went up and have hardly ever depreciated since.

✚ FOR Perhaps the most recognized single model in history • Design and engineering brilliance • Fine road manners • "Can't miss" investment • CCCA Classic status

▬ AGAINST Mechanically unreliable • High operating costs • Rarely offered for sale, costs a fortune when one is

PRODUCTION

Said to be nearly 3000 by some sources; reported registrations were only 1174 in 1936 and 1146 in 1937.

SPECIFICATIONS

Length (in.)	NA
Wheelbase (in.)	125.0; 132.0 Custom
Weight (lbs)	3715-4170
Price (new)	$1995-3575

ENGINES

cid/type	bhp	years
288.6/sv V-8	115	1936-37
288.6/sv V-8	190[1]	1937

[1]Supercharged

PRICES

Open	
FAIR	$27,000-55,000
GOOD	$55,000-95,000
FINE	$95,000-138,000
Closed	
FAIR	$11,000-24,000
GOOD	$24,000-43,000
FINE	$43,000-65,000

FINE CABRIOLET (SUPERCHARGED) PRICE HISTORY

1982 $75,000		**1990** $115,000	
1994 $110,000		**1998** $138,000	
1982-2000 RETURN 4%			
2000-2010 6%			

1939-42 CROSLEY CONVERTIBLE

1939 convertible

First of the low-cost minis from Cincinnati radio/refrigerator maker Powel Crosley, Jr. It bucked conventional

wisdom by being the nation's tiniest car, not counting American Bantam, and using an air-cooled twin (versus Bantam's water-cooled four). But it was also America's cheapest car and, boasted Powel, the stingiest at over 50 mpg. Alas, its Waukesha engine gave trouble, which was cured by destroking after '39. Most other components also came from outside. Debut soft-top coupe and sedan (with framed sliding windows) were joined for 1940 by a wood-body wagon and semi-open "Parkway" delivery, followed by a panel delivery, pickup, and "Covered Wagon" pickup for '41—all two-doors. Numerous interim modifications severely limited 1940 production (sales were mostly through Crosley appliance stores) and betrayed a somewhat cynical attitude: "It's just another product," Powel said. Offerings for war-shortened '42 were cut to just the wagon, the two convertibles, and a new steel-top "Liberty" sedan, though the catalog showed eight models. Cutesy "toy car" styling was unchanged through '42, marked by a prow front and freestanding headlamps. Very spartan (no gas gauge, optional rear seat), crude (Hawley mechanical brakes, beam-axle/leaf-spring suspension at each end), and slow (45-50 mph tops), but it was the next best thing to an "A" coupon for the wartime gas rationing to come. An encouraged Powel would try more ambitious Crosleys postwar.

✚ FOR A cute job • Interesting artifact • Perfect size for your living room • Very uncommon now • Low prices

▬ AGAINST Near-zero performance • A restorer's nightmare • Collector interest seemingly peaked long ago

PRODUCTION[1]

1939 2,017 **1940** 422 **1941** 2,289 **1942** 1,029

[1]Calendar year, all models.

SPECIFICATIONS

Length (in.)	120.0
Wheelbase (in.)	80.0
Weight (lbs)	925-950
Price (new)	$299-339

ENGINES

cid/type	bhp	years
39.8/sv flat 2	13.5	1939
35.3/sv flat 2	12	1940-42

PRICES

FAIR	$1200-3000
GOOD	$3000-4500
FINE	$4500-6500

FINE EXAMPLE PRICE HISTORY

1982 $2000	**1990** $4000
1994 $4500	**1998** $6000
1982-2000 RETURN 7%	
2000-2010 2%	

1947-48 CROSLEY CONVERTIBLE & WAGON

The first postwar Crosleys, still on an 80-inch wheelbase but more than two-feet longer and looking more "grownup" with new flush-fender styling. Production commenced June 1946, but cars built that year—convertibles and sedans only—were technically '47s. A new-design woody wagon, pickup, and panel delivery went on sale during '47. Big news was a new water-cooled engine with twice the cylinders and double the power of the prewar twin—the five-main-bearing copper-brazed "CoBra" four used in wartime machines from refrigerators to

1947 convertible

Mooney Mite airplanes. Alas, its copper-steel block was prone to chemical corrosion that necessitated early rebuilds (most before 60,000 miles), so a near-identical CIBA unit (Cast-Iron Block Assembly) was substituted in early 1949, though many 1947-48 cars have this retrofitted. The initial divided mesh grille was replaced at mid-1948 by dual bright horizontal bars below a chrome "spinner." Still pretty basic, but sales were better than ever. In fact, Crosley scored record one-year production in 1948—some 10 times better than its prewar best. From then on, though, it was all downhill. The convertible is singled out here for the obvious reasons, the wagon for its utility and "cheeky" air.

✚ FOR More "adult" than prewar models • Better performance (now only marginal) • Thrifty • Wagon's utility • Convertible's sportiness and scarcity • Club support

◼ AGAINST Troublesome CoBra engine (where CIBA not installed) • Top-heavy, thus tippy in corners • Where to find parts? • Limited value appreciation now

PRODUCTION[1]

1947 conv 4017 **2d wgn** 1249 **1948 conv** 2485 **2d wgn** 23,489
[1]Calendar year; 1947 incl. 12 1946 convertibles

SPECIFICATIONS

Length (in.)	145.0
Wheelbase (in.)	80.0
Weight (lbs)	1150-1305
Price (new)	$899-949

ENGINES

cid/type	bhp	years
44.0/sv I-4	26	1947-48

PRICES

FAIR	$1200-2500
GOOD	$2500-5000
FINE	$5000-7000

FINE EXAMPLE PRICE HISTORY

1982 $2850	**1990** $5000
1994 $4600	**1998** $5300
1982-2000 RETURN 6%	
2000-2010 6%	

1 9 4 9 - 5 2
CROSLEY CONVERTIBLE & WAGON

Last years of what author Stan Grayson called "the car for the forgotten man," increasingly forgotten by shoppers in the bigger-is-better men-

tality of the early '50s. Styling was revamped yet again for '49, with "speed line" fenders and a "spinner" grille remarkably like that of the all-new '49 Ford. Overall length was also increased another three inches, "amenities" like wind-up windows and electric wipers were available, and there were more deluxe Super-trim versions of the mainstay sedan, wagon, and convertible. But none of this seemed to help any more than the advent of the winsome Hotshot/Super Sport roadsters (see entries)—or ads that insisted Crosley was "a FINE car." Sales continued sliding, and Powel Crosley belatedly abandoned his dream of an "American Volkswagen" in 1952. The problem, as Grayson observed, was that "the 'forgotten man' for whom the car had been built didn't want to be remembered for driving a Crosley."

✚ FOR As for 1947-48, plus arguably better styling, more reliable CIBA engine, and "failed marque" appeal

◼ AGAINST As for 1947-48 except engine

PRODUCTION

1949 conv 645 **2d wgn** 3803 **1950 conv/Super conv** 478 **2d wgn/Super wgn** 4205 **1951 Super conv** 391 **2d wgn/Super wgn** 4500 **1952 Super conv** 146 **2d wgn/Super wgn** 1355

SPECIFICATIONS

Length (in.)	148.3
Wheelbase (in.)	80.0
Weight (lbs)	1320-1480
Price (new)	$916-1450

ENGINES

cid/type	bhp	years
44.0/sv I-4	26	1949-52

PRICES

As per 1947-48 convertible and wagon.

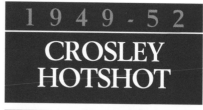

1 9 4 9 - 5 2
CROSLEY HOTSHOT

1949 Hotshot roadster

The open version of Powel Crosley, Jr.'s economy car, and one of the outstanding early postwar sports cars. It could do about 85 mph right off the showroom floor despite its little 44-cid cast-iron four, which was more than adequate for the tiny 1300-pound curb weight. Semi-elliptic/coil front and quarter-elliptic rear suspension gave very nimble handling. Set up for racing, it was even better: a Hotshot won the Index of Performance at Sebring in 1951, and fared well in many road races. But in an age of horsepower and cubic inches, it was overwhelmed in the marketplace, and the company quit the car business in 1952.

✚ FOR Vastly underrated Milestone

1950 convertible

car • Outstanding performance and handling • Easy on fuel • Not difficult to restore

■ **AGAINST** Spot-disc brakes subject to freeze-ups due to dirt • Fair ability to rust • Some parts now in very short supply

PRODUCTION

1949 752 **1950** 742 **1951** 646 **1952** 358 (incl. Super Sports 1950-52)

SPECIFICATIONS

Length (in.)	137.0
Wheelbase (in.)	85.0
Weight (lbs)	1175-1240
Price (new)	$849-952

ENGINES

cid/type	bhp	years
44/sv I-4	25.5/26.5	1949-52

PRICES

FAIR	$1500-3000
GOOD	$3000-5500
FINE	$5500-7500

FINE EXAMPLE PRICE HISTORY

1982 $3000	**1990** $6000
1994 $6000	**1998** $7500
1982-2000 RETURN 6%	
2000-2010 8%	

1950-52
CROSLEY SUPER SPORTS

A more deluxe version of the Hotshot, with built-in doors (auxiliary doors were available as an option for the Hotshot). Better trimmed, but otherwise the same.

➕ **FOR** As for Hotshot

1950 Super Sport roadster

■ **AGAINST** As for Hotshot

PRODUCTION[1]

1950 742 **1951** 646 **1952** 358
[1]Figures include Hotshot

SPECIFICATIONS

Length (in.)	137.0
Wheelbase (in.)	85.0
Weight (lbs)	1175-1240
Price (new)	$925-1029

ENGINES

cid/type	bhp	years
44/sv I-4	25.5/26.5	1950-52

PRICES

As per 1949-52 Crosley Hotshot.

1953-55
CUNNINGHAM C-3

1953 C-3 coupe

Briggs S. Cunningham conceived his original C-1 sports car in 1951 with racing in mind, and his later models were definite contenders. The C-4R finished fourth at Le Mans '52; the following year a C-5R was third, outclassed (and outbraked) by a pair of Jaguars. The C-3, elegantly styled by

Giovanni Michelotti of Carrozzeria Vignale in Turin, was Cunningham's "production" model, high-priced and blindingly fast with its Chrysler Hemi V-8 engine. It was one of two American cars (the other was the '53 Studebaker Starliner) named among the world's ten best designs by Arthur Drexler of the New York Museum of Modern Art. Cunningham lost money on every car he built, however, and halted C-3 production after two years.

➕ **FOR** One of the great American sporting cars, a thoroughbred by any yardstick • Tremendous Hemi power • Fine handling

■ **AGAINST** Cost • Body parts now very scarce

PRODUCTION

coupe 19 **convertible** 9

SPECIFICATIONS

Length (in.)	168.0
Wheelbase (in.)	107.0 (105.0 on first coupe built)
Weight (lbs)	3500 (approx.)
Price (new)	$10,000; $11,000 in 1955

ENGINES

cid/type	bhp	years
331.1/ohv V-8	220-235	1953-55

PRICES

FAIR	$20,000-30,000
GOOD	$30,000-40,000
FINE	$40,000-60,000

FINE EXAMPLE PRICE HISTORY

1982 $15,000	**1987** $30,000
1990 $45,000	**1994** $50,000
1982-2000 RETURN 8%	
2000-2010 10%	

1959-64
DAIMLER SP250

1961-64 SP250 roadster

Daimler's second stab at a sporting model, approved following a company shake-up in the mid-'50s. Ex-motorcycle engine designer Edward Turner became managing director, and laid out a splendid new pushrod V-8 that was first seen in this two-seat roadster. The SP250 chassis and suspension were much like those of the Triumph TR3A (even some parts were shared), as was the gearbox. Styling for the fiberglass body was instantly recognizable: a broad, oval, eggcrate grille; sloping domed hood; curved character lines on front and rear fenders; and even modest fins. It was originally displayed at the New York Auto Show as the Dart, but Dodge complained, so the designation was changed to reflect engine capacity (in ccs divided by 10). Performance was good (120 mph-plus top speed), but it suffered from rather loose body construction (not cured until 1963) and a high price. Some cars were equipped with a Borg-Warner automatic, and a few fixed-roof hardtops were also built. The 2.5-liter V-8 was also used in Daimler's version of the Jaguar Mark II sedan through 1969.

➕ **FOR** Efficient engine and high performance • Reasonable economy • Simple-to-maintain chassis • Rust-free, easy-to-repair fiberglass body

➖ **AGAINST** Spare parts are gone except for TR3A-shared chassis pieces • Looks like a vacuum cleaner • Flimsy body (early models)

PRODUCTION
2465

SPECIFICATIONS
Length (in.)	160.5
Wheelbase (in.)	92.0
Weight (lbs)	2220
Price (new)	$3842 in the U.S., 1960

ENGINES
cc/type (cid)	bhp[1]	years
2548/ohv V-8 (156)	140	1959-64

[1]Net

PRICES
FAIR	$7000-9000
GOOD	$9000-12,000
FINE	$12,000-15,000

1968 1600 roadster (nonstandard wheels)

FINE EXAMPLE PRICE HISTORY
1982 $3500	1990 $7500
1994 $6000	1987 $14,000

1982-2000 RETURN 9%
2000-2010 8%

1961-69
DATSUN 1500 SPORTS/1600/ 2000

Successful British-style '60s sports cars from Nissan, then mostly doing business as Datsun. Replaced the firm's first such car of 1959-60. Styling rather like that of contemporary MGB, which it predated by a full year, and workmanship about on the same par. Engineering orthodox, featuring cruciform-braced box-section frame, coil-and-wishbone front suspension, live rear axle on leaf springs, drum brakes. Drivetrain also ordinary but new: a 71-bhp 1500-cc four mated to four-speed gearbox. There was also a sideways third seat (dropped by '63), but what sold this model (internally designated SP310) was fair pricing that included unexpected sports-car niceties like wind-up windows, radio, heater, and snap-on tonneau. Rapidly improved, starting in '63 with 10 extra horses (via dual Hitachi-built SU carbs), followed in September 1964 by an uprated 1600 model (CSP311) with 96 bhp, genuine 100-mph capability, all-synchro transmission with diaphragm-spring clutch, and front-disc brakes. May 1965 brought a five-main-bearing crankshaft for a refined version, the SPL311, sold in the U.S. as the Datsun 1600. The final evolution was the 1967 2000 SR311, with a new 135-bhp overhead-cam 2.0-liter four and standard five-speed gearbox. That one could reach

115 mph. None of these Datsuns are widely appreciated here, but they're significant in paving the way for the much-loved 240Z and are thus among the few Japanese cars worthy of collector interest.

➕ **FOR** Nice MGB clone with the usual inherent allures, but more exclusive • Decent go, and 2000 is quick (0-60 in 10 seconds) • Still successful in club racing • Very affordable

➖ **AGAINST** Being Japanese a negative for some • Little interest in U.S. • Some parts hard to find • Serious ruster

PRODUCTION
approx. 40,000 total

SPECIFICATIONS
Length (in.)	155.6
Wheelbase (in.)	89.9
Weight (lbs)	2030-2110
Price (new)	$2995 (1969 2000)

ENGINES
cid/type	bhp	years
90.8/ohv I-4	71/81	1961-64
97.3/ohv I-4	96	1964-69
121/ohc I-4	135	1967-69

PRICES
FAIR	$1200-2500
GOOD	$2500-4200
FINE	$4200-7000

FINE EXAMPLE PRICE HISTORY
1982 $3500	1990 $7000
1994 $6500	1998 $7700

1982-2000 RETURN 4%
2000-2010 4%

1970-73
DATSUN 240Z

The first Japanese car with definite collectibility apart from the extremely rare Toyota 2000GT, Datsun's hot-selling Z-car commands a large and fanatical following. It was a sensation when it hit the market at an astoundingly low $3526 base price, with a combination of style, performance, and equipment that sent auto writers into gales of praise and buyers streaming into Datsun showrooms. Though the original bodyshell would be continued through larger engine displacements as the 260Z and 280Z, these first 2.4-liter models are the ones to have. They're less affected by emissions and safety rules than the 1974-77 Zs, and Datsun's fine overhead cam six was never smoother or freer-revving. Handling, too, was better than

1971 240Z coupe (nonstandard wheels)

in later years when clumsy and heavy bumpers added extra weight, particularly to the front end, and made power steering almost mandatory. In all, a marvelous blend of Jaguar E-Type styling and a character not unlike that of the late, lamented Austin-Healey 3000.

✚ FOR Reasonably priced (though values fluctuate) • Great blend of performance, rugged engineering, decent mileage • Well equipped • Still looks great • Fine road manners • Parts supplies still ample

◼ AGAINST Rust-prone, especially lower fenders and rockers • Most were driven hard • Many modified with juvenile add-ons • '73s prone to vapor lock • No convertible

PRODUCTION[1]
1970 16,215 **1971** 33,684 **1972** 52,658
[1]U.S. calendar year sales; total U.S. exports 1970-73: 130,000+.

SPECIFICATIONS
Length (in.)	161.3
Wheelbase (in.)	90.7
Weight (lbs)	2355
Price (new)	$3526 (original U.S. P.O.E.)

ENGINES
cc/type (cid)	bhp	years
146/ohc I-6 (2393)	139-151[1]	1970-73

[1]SAE net

PRICES
FAIR	$2250-5000
GOOD	$5000-8000
FINE	$8000-10,000

FINE EXAMPLE PRICE HISTORY
1982 $3500	**1990** $8000
1994 $6000	**1998** $8500

1982-2000 RETURN 7%
1994-2004 5%

1974 DATSUN 260Z

1974 260Z coupe (nonstandard wheels)

Continuation of Nissan's knock-'em-dead first-generation Z-car with enlarged engine and assorted minor changes (new steering wheel, electronic ignition) mainly for U.S. market. Another nod to America was the long-wheelbase 2+2 derivative that arrived Stateside during 1974; though less graceful than the original two-seater, it carved its own market niche much like Jaguar's E-Type 2+2 had done. Main exterior distinction in this period was bumpers moved slightly away from the body and fitted with little rubber pads to meet Washington's 5-mph impact rule. As noted, less desirable than 240 because of lower, emissions-mandated horsepower, but weight not up alarmingly (about 130 pounds) and lovely styling (by BMW 507-designer Albrecht Goertz) relatively unaffected (save 2+2). Still available with a choice of four-speed manual or three-speed automatic transmissions. Contemporary magazine road tests of the 240

showed a 0-60 time of about 10 seconds and a top speed of 115 mph.

✚ FOR As for 1970-73 240Z, plus somewhat better engine manners

◼ AGAINST As for 1970-73 240Z, but weaker appreciation potential, esp. 2+2

PRODUCTION[1]
1974 cpe 49,172 **2+2** 9499
[1]U.S. sales

SPECIFICATIONS
Length (in.)	173.2 (2-seater), 180.9 (2+2)
Wheelbase (in.)	90.7 (2-seater), 102.6 (2+2)
Weight (lbs)	2665-2855
Price (new)	$4995-5750

ENGINES
cid/type	bhp[1]	years
157/ohc I-6	139	1974-early 75

[1]SAE net

PRICES
FAIR	$1350-3000
GOOD	$3000-4500
FINE	$4500-7000

2000-2010 RETURN 5%

1975-78 DATSUN 280Z

1978 280ZX 2+2 coupe

Last years of Nissan's first-generation Z, introduced in the U.S. in March 1975. A still-larger 2753cc engine (bigger bore), adoption of a catalytic converter, and a switch from twin carbs to Bosch L-Jetronic fuel injection helped bring performance and mileage closer to 1970 levels. A 0-60 run in a '75 280Z now took 9.4 seconds according to *Road & Track*, and gas mileage came in at 19.5 mpg. Styling and handling were more compromised thanks to heavier, more protruding bumpers; wider standard tires prompted some to ask for power steering (not available yet); and some quirks (axle noise, lift-throttle driveline clunking) were not cured. But a retuned suspension provided a better ride, some interior materials were upgraded in appearance and quality, and even the optional air conditioning was improved. All in all, very desirable modern GTs then and now.

⊞ **FOR** As for 1973-75 260Z, plus even better economy and engine driveability • More composed ride

⊟ **AGAINST** As for 1973-75 260Z, but steering heavier • Safety bumpers sully styling

PRODUCTION[1]

1975 cpe 40,216 **2+2** 9499 **1976 cpe** 45,766 **2+2** 13,792 **1977 cpe** 54,954 **2+2** 16,065 **1978** NA
[1]U.S. sales

SPECIFICATIONS[1]

Length (in.)	173.2 (2-seater), 180.9 (2+2)
Wheelbase (in.)	90.7 (2-seater), 102.6 (2+2)
Weight (lbs)	2765-2925
Price (new)	$6285-8000 [1]U.S. model

ENGINES

cid/type	bhp[1]	years
168/ohc I-6	149	1975-78

[1]SAE net

PRICES

FAIR	$1250-3000
GOOD	$3000-5000
FINE	$5000-7500
2000-2010 RETURN 5%	

1935-50
DELAHAYE TYPE 135

Delahaye's fine, modern grand touring car, which took over from Delage in the hearts of sporting drivers. Powered by a very refined truck engine and, like the Delage, distinguished by a variety of typical French shapes. Most were built with sedan and sporting two-door bodywork, but a few serious competition cars were also completed. The chassis was strictly conventional apart from independent front suspension and a synchromesh gearbox, though with supple and advanced road behavior and 100-mph performance. Some cars were fitted with the Cotal electromagnetic gearbox, a real French specialty.

⊞ **FOR** High performance • Excellent roadholding • Styling of sports versions • Simple to maintain • CCCA Classic status

⊟ **AGAINST** Obsolete now, so no parts • No restoration expertise • Few bodies have survived intact • Not widely appreciated in U.S.

PRODUCTION

approx. 200

SPECIFICATIONS

Length (in.)	180.0+
Wheelbase (in.)	116.0
Weight (lbs)	2800+
Price (new)	NA

ENGINES

cc/type (cid)	bhp[1]	years
3237/ohv I-6 (198)	130	1935-36
3557/ohv I-6 (217)	160[2]	1935-39

[1]Gross [2]Competition model only

PRICES

Closed	
FAIR	$20,000-35,000
GOOD	$35,000-50,000
FINE	$50,000-70,000
Open	
FAIR	$40,000-70,000
GOOD	$70,000-95,000
FINE	$95,000-120,000

Special Corse: $200,000+

FINE CABRIOLET PRICE HISTORY

1982 $22,500		**1987** $40,250	
1990 $120,000		**1994** $100,000	
1982-2000 RETURN 11%			
2000-2010 5%			

1936 Type 135 coupe by Figoni et Falaschi

1981-82
DELOREAN "DMC-12"

1981 DMC-12 coupe

Most notorious car since the Tucker, not so much for its abundant faults as the scandal involving its creator: former Pontiac engineer, Pontiac/Chevrolet chief John Z. DeLorean. Initiated in 1974 as an "ethical sports car," design by Bill Collins, another one-time Pontiac engineer. Lotus of England eventually reworked the entire concept, which emerged as a $25,000 rear-engine two-seat coupe with gullwing doors, steel X-member backbone chassis á la Lotus, all-independent suspension, and fiberglass inner body with stainless-steel outer panels. Many proprietary components—notably French "PRV" V-6 and five-speed transaxle. It was assembled at a new purpose-built factory in Northern Ireland. It was promoted to the skies, but sales never met estimates. Numerous assembly problems forced costly fixes, and the firm's finances were both complex and evidently shady. The *coupe d'grace* was DeLorean's 1982 indictment on drug charges. He was later cleared of allegations that he bilked some of his investors, including the British government, which had bankrolled the plant. DeLorean Motor Company went bankrupt in late '82, forcing some 1200 late-production cars to be sold at some $6000 off list by a Columbus, Ohio, liquidator. A planned sedan and turbo conversion were left stillborn. Today, the DeLorean seems an honest if flawed car. And unlike Preston Tucker, John Z. built more than a token few. Still, a classic case of a swinger's ego overpowering common sense.

⊞ **FOR** A controversial modern failure • Decent performance (under 10 seconds 0-60) • Small but enthusiastic owners group • More "finished" than a Bricklin (though that's not saying much) • Some glitches already rectified on some cars • Some cars painted post-purchase

AGAINST Tail-happy rear-engine handling • Mediocre drivetrain • Vision astern nearly nil • Next to no luggage space • Tight cockpit • Inconvenient "mail-slot" door windows • Awkward gullwing doors • Quality still highly variable despite owner fixes

PRODUCTION

approx. 8500

SPECIFICATIONS

Length (in.)	168.0
Wheelbase (in.)	94.8
Weight (lbs)	2840
Price (new)	$25,000

ENGINES

cid/type	bhp	years
174/ohc V-6	130	1981-82

PRICES

FAIR	$8000-10,000
GOOD	$10,000-15,000
FINE	$15,000-21,500

FINE EXAMPLE PRICE HISTORY

Stable in the early 1990s. Slowly appreciating.
2000-2010 RETURN 2%

1934-36
DESOTO AIRFLOW

1936 S2 coupe

Smaller, less expensive running mate to Chrysler's Airflow, and even less saleable. Only one series with fewer body styles and six-cylinder power. Production varied widely, so the figures below indicates which models are most desirable. DeSoto mainly built conventional cars from 1935 on, with Airflows diminishing through the end of this design in 1936. Built on a shorter wheelbase, so it wasn't as nice-looking as its Chrysler counterparts.

FOR Aerodynamics pioneer • Good workmanship and materials • Relatively inexpensive to own and operate

AGAINST Styling as lumpy and controversial as ever • Not a great deal of collector recognition • Low appreciation potential

PRODUCTION

1934 cpe 1584 **brghm** 522 **4d sdn** 11,713 **Town Sedan** 119 **chassis** 2 **1935 cpe** 418 **4d sdn** 6269 **Town Sedan** 40 **bus cpe** 70 **1936 cpe** 250 **4d sdn** 4750

SPECIFICATIONS

Length (in.)	NA
Wheelbase (in.)	115.5
Weight (lbs)	3323-3400
Price (new)	$995-1095

ENGINES

cid/type	bhp	years
241.5/sv I-6	100	1934-36

PRICES

FAIR	$2500-7000
GOOD	$7000-12,000
FINE	$12,000-14,000

FINE EXAMPLE PRICE HISTORY

1982 $9500	**1990** $11,000
1994 $10,000	**1998** $14,000

1982-2000 RETURN 4%
2000-2010 3%

1942
DESOTO CUSTOM

One styling feature makes the '42 DeSoto collectible: hidden headlights. This gimmick, probably inspired by earlier Cords, was unique for 1942 and was far ahead of the "eyelid" styles in the 1960s. DeSoto called them Airfoil headlamps, and they added a new dimension to the cars' styling, allowing the entire grille to be carried smoothly below. Also new for 1942 was the streamlined lady hood mascot, a trademark DeSoto would retain until 1950.

FOR Solid construction • High qual-

ity • Relatively affordable • Hidden headlamps

AGAINST Very ordinary apart from the headlamps • Hard to find now

PRODUCTION

4d sdn 7974 **clb cpe** 2236 **Town Sedan** 1084 **2d sdn** 913 **conv cpe** 489 **bus cpe** 120 **7-pass sdn** 79 **7-pass limo** 20

SPECIFICATIONS

Length (in.)	206.0
Wheelbase (in.)	121.5 (139.5 on 7-pass models)
Weight (lbs)	3205-3820
Price (new)	$1046-1580

ENGINES

cid/type	bhp	years
236.6/sv I-6	115	1942

PRICES

Conv	
FAIR	$5000-11,000
GOOD	$11,000-18,000
FINE	$18,000-26,000
Others	
FAIR	$2500-6000
GOOD	$6000-10,000
FINE	$10,000-15,000

FINE CONVERTIBLE PRICE HISTORY

1982 $11,000	**1990** $25,000
1994 $27,500	**1998** $25,000

1982-2000 RETURN 2%
2000-2010 5%

1942
DESOTO DELUXE

The lower-priced and less elaborately trimmed DeSoto series for '42, also distinguished by the unusual Airfoil hidden headlamps.

FOR As for 1942 Custom

AGAINST As for 1942 Custom, plus less deluxe furnishings

1942 Custom coupe

1942 S10 DeLuxe business coupe

PRODUCTION

4d sdn 6463 **clb cpe** 1968 **2d sdn** 1781 **bus cpe** 469 **Town Sedan** 291 **conv cpe** 70 **7-pass sdn** 49

SPECIFICATIONS

Length (in.)	206.0 (exc. 7-pass)
Wheelbase (in.)	121.5 (139.5 on 7-pass models)
Weight (lbs)	3190-3705
Price (new)	$1010-1455

ENGINES

cid/type	bhp	years
236.6/sv I-6	115	1942

PRICES

As per 1942 DeSoto Custom closed models less 10%.

1 9 4 6 - 4 8

DESOTO CUSTOM SUBURBAN

The most expensive of the 1946-48 DeSoto line was the Custom Suburban. This 139.5-inch-wheelbase, eight-passenger sedan was also equipped with a fold-down rear seat, and no trunk partition. A favorite of livery services for hauling a great deal of luggage along with their passengers. Fine wood trim (and wood grain) was found inside, and wood combined with metal in the standard roof rack.

1948 Custom Suburban sedan

✚ FOR One of the more unique DeSotos, and among the more interesting early-postwar models • Well built

▬ AGAINST Dowdy styling • Hard to find on the collector market

PRODUCTION

7500

SPECIFICATIONS

Length (in.)	225.3
Wheelbase (in.)	139.5
Weight (lbs)	3974-4012
Price (new)	$2093-2631

ENGINES

cid/type	bhp	years
236.6/sv I-6	109	1946-48

PRICES

FAIR	$2500-5000
GOOD	$5000-9500
FINE	$9500-13,500

FINE EXAMPLE PRICE HISTORY

1982 $5900		**1990** $9500	
1994 $11,000		**1998** $11,500	
1982-2000 RETURN 5%			
2000-2010 8%			

1 9 5 0

DESOTO CUSTOM SPORTSMAN

Although Chrysler built seven experimental Town and Country hardtops for 1946, mass-produced pillarless Mopars didn't begin until the 1950 model year. DeSoto's version was the Sportsman upholstered to convertible standards and built with all the integrity that distinguished Chrysler products of this period. Of the several interesting DeSotos from the 1950-51

1950 Custom Sportsman hardtop coupe

generation, the Sportsman hardtop is the most important historically.

✚ FOR Pioneer DeSoto hardtop • Robust construction • Not prone to rust

▬ AGAINST Lackluster six-cylinder performance • Underwhelming looks

PRODUCTION

4600

SPECIFICATIONS

Length (in.)	207.0
Wheelbase (in.)	125.5
Weight (lbs)	3735
Price (new)	$2489

ENGINES

cid/type	bhp	years
236.6/sv I-6	112	1950

PRICES

FAIR	$3500-6000
GOOD	$6000-12,000
FINE	$12,000-17,000

FINE EXAMPLE PRICE HISTORY

1982 $4500		**1990** $9000	
1994 $11,000		**1998** $14,000	
1982-2000 RETURN 8%			
2000-2010 6%			

1 9 5 5 - 5 6

DESOTO FIREFLITE

1956 Fireflite Sportsman hardtop coupe

The first DeSotos completely styled by Virgil Exner, and among the division's most striking cars. Featured lush upholstery and trick design features like a "gullwing" dash and a toothy grille. Performance more than ample from Hemi V-8 engines. Buyers had a choice between solid and wild two-tone colors, the latter with contrasting color in a chrome trimmed bodyside sweepspear. (See also Fireflite Coronado, Pacesetter, and Adventurer.)

⊞ FOR Good styling for the period • Quality construction • Performance

⊟ AGAINST Limited collector appeal • Debatable design details

PRODUCTION

1955 4d sdn 26,637 **2d Sportsman htp** 10,313 **conv** 775 **1956 4d sdn** 18,207 (incl. Coronado) **2d htp** 8475 **conv** 1385 (incl. Pacesetter) **4d htp** 3350

SPECIFICATIONS

Length (in.)	217.9
Wheelbase (in.)	126.0
Weight (lbs)	3890-4075
Price (new)	$2727-3615

ENGINES

cid/type	bhp	years
291/ohv V-8	200	1955
330.4/ohv V-8	255	1956

PRICES

Conv	
FAIR	$5500-10,000
GOOD	$10,000-20,000
FINE	$20,000-25,000
2d htp	
FAIR	$3500-5000
GOOD	$5000-8000
FINE	$8000-12,000
4d models	
FAIR	$1500-3000
GOOD	$3000-5000
FINE	$5000-8000

FINE CONVERTIBLE PRICE HISTORY

1982 $6800		**1990** $27,500	
1994 $23,000		**1998** $25,000	

1982-2000 RETURN 9% **2000-2010** 10%, **others** 5%

1955 Fireflite Coronado sedan

SPECIFICATIONS

Length (in.)	217.9
Wheelbase (in.)	126.0
Weight (lbs)	3940
Price (new)	$3500 (est.)

ENGINES

cid/type	bhp	years
291/ohv V-8	200	1955

PRICES

FAIR	$2500-4000
GOOD	$4000-7000
FINE	$7000-10,000

FINE EXAMPLE PRICE HISTORY

1982 $5300		**1990** $8500	
1994 $9000		**1998** $10,000	

1982-2000 RETURN 1% **2000-2010** 5%

1956
DESOTO FIREFLITE ADVENTURER

1956 Fireflite Adventurer hardtop coupe

The first of DeSoto's supercars, the Division's equivalent to the Chrysler 300. Part of the Fireflite series in this first year, and offered only as a hardtop. Equipped with a specially tuned version of the DeSoto Hemi and firm suspension as standard, it was the fastest DeSoto yet. It was also one of the most visible, with a stock gold-and-white paint job and anodized-gold

blade-type wheel covers.

⊞ FOR Perhaps the most desirable postwar DeSoto • Tremendous performance • Rarity

⊟ AGAINST Busy styling • Expensive to operate • Some Adventurer-only parts now in short supply

PRODUCTION

996

SPECIFICATIONS

Length (in.)	217.9
Wheelbase (in.)	126.0
Weight (lbs)	3870
Price (new)	$3728

ENGINES

cid/type	bhp	year
341.4/ohv V-8	320	1956

PRICES

FAIR	$4000-7500
GOOD	$7500-13,000
FINE	$13,000-19,000

FINE EXAMPLE PRICE HISTORY

1982 $6800		**1990** $15,000	
1994 $15,000		**1998** $16,000	

1982-2000 RETURN 6% **2000-2010** 5%

1955
DESOTO FIREFLITE CORONADO

A springtime trim option offered for the Fireflite four-door sedan. Marked by an arresting three-tone paint job—black top, turquoise body, white color sweep—and an interior to match. Identified by small "Coronado" labels under the Fireflite script on the front fenders. Soon abandoned, although DeSoto had produced a less collectible Coronado package for 1954 as well.

⊞ FOR As for other 1955-56 Fireflites • Striking paint • Rarity

⊟ AGAINST Extremely scarce now

PRODUCTION

500 (est.)

1956
DESOTO FIREFLITE PACESETTER

A near replica of the Fireflite convertible that paced the Indy 500 this year. Had a stock Fireflite drivetrain, but a firmer suspension. It wore Adventurer-style finned wheel covers and its color scheme, and offered many standard features, including power seat and windows.

⊞ FOR Low production, so a sought-

1956 Fireflite Pacesetter convertible

1960 Adventurer hardtop coupe

after rarity • Others as for 1955-56 Fireflite

■ AGAINST Gaudiness • Scarcity • Others as for 1955-56 Fireflite

PRODUCTION

100 (est.)

SPECIFICATIONS

Length (in.)	217.9
Wheelbase (in.)	126.0
Weight (lbs)	4070
Price (new)	$3615

ENGINES

cid/type	bhp	years
330.4/ohv V-8	255	1956

PRICES

FAIR	$7500-13,000
GOOD	$13,000-22,000
FINE	$22,000-29,000

FINE EXAMPLE PRICE HISTORY

1982 $7500	1987 $15,000
1990 $26,500	1994 $25,000
1982-2000 RETURN 10%	
2000-2010 10%	

1957-59
DESOTO ADVENTURER

1957 Adventurer hardtop coupe

DeSoto's limited-edition performance series, now separate from the Fireflite. A declining market cut hard into Adventurer production and DeSoto sales as a whole. As a result, collector demand for these fast, aggressive-looking, heroically tailfinned cars is fast outstripping supply, as the production figures suggest. It continued to offer exceptional performance, and boasted the hottest V-8s available from DeSoto (two power choices were offered for 1958). Like Chrysler, DeSoto switched to a wedgehead V-8 for 1959. Road manners were also very capable. Of the three model years, the '57 is arguably the nicest in appearance.

✚ FOR Very desirable • Good appreciation potential • Fine performance • Great on the highway

■ AGAINST The first in a long line of Mopar rusters • Many body parts now hard to find • High operating costs

PRODUCTION

1957 2d htp 1650 **conv** 300 **1958 2d htp** 350 **conv** 82 **1959 2d htp** 590 **conv** 97

SPECIFICATIONS

Length (in.)	218.0-221.1
Wheelbase (in.)	126.0
Weight (lbs)	3980-4235
Price (new)	$3997-4749

ENGINES

cid/type	bhp	years
345/ohv V-8	345	1957
361/ohv V-8	345/355	1958
383/ohv V-8	350	1959

PRICES

Conv	
FAIR	$6800-13,500
GOOD	$13,500-29,000
FINE	$29,000-40,000
Htp	
FAIR	$3200-10,000
GOOD	$10,000-17,500
FINE	$17,500-25,000

FINE CONVERTIBLE PRICE HISTORY

1982 $5200	1990 $25,000
1994 $25,000	1998 $30,000
1982-2000 RETURN 10%	
2000-2010 10%	

1960
DESOTO ADVENTURER

DeSoto's upper series for 1960, and a kissin' cousin to that year's midrange Chrysler. Both shared a new unitized bodyshell and similar styling with a more integrated trapezoidal grille and sweeping, flared tailfins. The Adventurer was no longer a limited edition, and pushed the former top-line Fireflite down the price-and-prestige ladder. The medium-priced Firedome line vanished, as did the Dodge-based low-line Firesweep series. As "standard" cars, the '60 Adventurers used a milder engine than before, and were in no way related to the hot models of yore. If it has any significance, it is that the Adventurer was the best DeSoto had to offer in its last full model year.

✚ FOR Affordable • Strong engine • Decent "period" styling

■ AGAINST Severe rust problems • Fuel thirst • Limited appreciation potential

PRODUCTION

4d sdn 5746 **2d htp** 3092 **4d htp** 2759

SPECIFICATIONS

Length (in.)	217.0
Wheelbase (in.)	122.0
Weight (lbs)	3895-3940
Price (new)	$3579-3727

ENGINES

cid/type	bhp	years
383/ohv V-8	305	1960

PRICES

2d	
FAIR	$2500-5500
GOOD	$5500-9500
FINE	$9500-12,000
4d	
FAIR	$2000-4000
GOOD	$4000-7000
FINE	$7000-9000

FINE 2D HARDTOP PRICE HISTORY

1982 $3600	1990 $8500
1994 $10,000	1998 $12,000
1982-2000 RETURN 7%	
2000-2010 5%	

DESOTO

1961 hardtop sedan

1969 Mangusta coupe

The token, end-of-the-line models from Chrysler's traditional medium-priced make, a victim of a changed market by the turn of the decade. For 1961, the DeSoto line was whittled down to just two offerings, neither of which bore a series name. A clumsy facelift on the 1960 bodyshell brought a grotesque two-tier grille—neither of which related to the other—curious side sculpturing, and heavy taillights. Production was halted before the end of calendar 1960, almost exactly a year after another medium-priced casualty, the Edsel. It was a sad finale for a make that, though perhaps not among the greats, had always stood for quality—and occasionally performance.

➕ **FOR** Last of the marque • Rarity • Good engine

➖ **AGAINST** Ugly • Thirsty • Rust-prone

PRODUCTION
4d htp 2123 **2d htp** 911

SPECIFICATIONS
Length (in.)	215.8
Wheelbase (in.)	122.0
Weight (lbs)	3760-3820
Price (new)	$3102-3167

ENGINES
cid/type	bhp	years
361/ohv V-8	265	1961

PRICES
As per 1960 DeSoto Adventurer.

DETOMASO MANGUSTA

A striking Italian supercar, the first serious production car effort from motorcycle magnate Alejandro De Tomaso. The mid-engine layout tied a small-block Ford V-8 to a ZF transmission within a steel backbone chassis not unlike Lotus. Chunky, muscular styling by Ghia, then recently acquired by de Tomaso. This was very much a detuned sports-racing car, with considerable rear weight bias, very little luggage space, accommodations for two only, and superb performance. A top speed of 155 mph was claimed, but handling could be tricky, particularly in poor weather when the limited visibility afforded by the low-slung body didn't help matters. The Mangusta was built in very small numbers, and therefore sold to only a fortunate few. It was great for rushing along twisty back roads on sunny days, though, and an admirable piece of sculpture standing still.

➕ **FOR** Performance • Styling • Familiar Detroit iron • Mid-engine panache • Rarity

➖ **AGAINST** Cramped interior, poor ventilation • Suspect wet-road handling • Rust-prone body • Expensive now

PRODUCTION
approx. 400, plus 1 prototype Spider

SPECIFICATIONS
Length (in.)	168.0
Wheelbase (in.)	98.4
Weight (lbs)	3050
Price (new)	$11,150 U.S. 1969 list price

ENGINES
cid/type	bhp	years
302/ohv V-8	230[1]	1967-71

[1]DIN

PRICES
FAIR	$18,000-25,000
GOOD	$25,000-35,000
FINE	$35,000-45,000

FINE EXAMPLE PRICE HISTORY
1982 $18,500	**1990** $65,000
1994 $60,000	**1989** $76,000
1982-2000 RETURN 4%	
2000-2010 5%	

DETOMASO PANTERA

1972 Pantera coupe

Another midships design and dimensionally similar to earlier Mangusta, but new Ghia styling (by American Tom Tjaarda) and a tuned 351 "Cleveland" V-8. Also, new unit-steel understructure plus the usual four-wheel disc brakes and coil/wishbone suspension. More practical than the Mangusta, though a tight cabin, excess cockpit heat, and "Italian straight armed" driving position annoyed some. Black-rubber 5-mph "safety bumpers" were added for 1973-74 "impact" rules, but tougher '75 regs necessitated a full redesign that could not be justified against the meager sales, thus ending U.S. imports. Production continued elsewhere, though at reduced levels. Reintroduced to U.S. on a limited basis in 1981 by the private "Panteramerica" concern. Remarkably little changed save a switch to a Ford of Australia engine (once Dearborn dropped the 351), improved "special-order" quality, and two higher-powered derivatives: mid-'70s 350-bhp GTS and beskirted 1980-replacement GT5, a 300-bhp reply to Lamborghini's Countach. The GT5 lost its "ground effects" in 1983, but went to 330 bhp as the GT5S.

1986 Pantera GT5S coupe

Europe's own environmental movement soon forced power cuts to 212 for the basic Pantera L and 247 for the S. Later built again by a family-owned DeTomaso Automobili as the GT5S, facelifted by Marcello Gandini, with tidier front bumper/spoiler, functional hood ducts, odd "winglet" at the base of windshield, and bulged rear flanks with Ferrari F40-style loop spoiler and integrated under-bumper tray mating with reshaped rocker skirts. Power was the U.S. Ford 302 with port electronic fuel injection, catalytic converter, and new intake manifolding, cams, cylinder heads, valves, and pistons. Also featured were big 17-inch wheels, huge Z-rated tires, larger racing-type Brembo brakes with four-piston aluminum calipers, and longer wishbones all-round.

➕ FOR High performance • Reliable engines • Strong club interest • Great looks, 150-mph performance, and Italian brio add up to one of the most exciting—and hardiest—"world cars" ever powered by Ford

➖ AGAINST Indifferent assembly (1971-74) • Innate mid-engine short-comings • Rust-prone body/chassis (esp. 1971-74) • Parts expensive • Newer models less pure, more "boy racer"

PRODUCTION
1971-74 5629[1] **1975-80** approx. 200 per year **1981-90** approx. 50 per year
[1]U.S. sales; Lincoln-Mercury lists 6091

SPECIFICATIONS
Length (in.)	168.0
Wheelbase (in.)	99.0
Weight (lbs)	3100-3300
Price (new)	$10,295-112,000

ENGINES
cid/type	bhp[1]	years
351/ohv V-8[2]	212-350	1971-89
302/ohv V-8	305	1990

[1]SAE net [2]Engine sourcing changed from Ford

U.S. to Ford Australia circa 1975; U.S. 302 adopted from 1990

PRICES
FAIR	$16,500-25,000
GOOD	$25,000-36,000
FINE	$36,000-60,000

FINE EXAMPLE PRICE HISTORY
1982 $15,000		**1990** $65,000	
1994 $60,000		**1998** $65,000	

1982-2000 RETURN 9%
2000-2010 10%

1940
DODGE DELUXE CONVERTIBLE

Dodge doesn't enjoy the large following of Ford or Chevrolet, so the money-minded collector must pick and choose models more carefully. The obvious ones in the 1940-48 styling generation are the convertibles—and good ones can command staggering prices. This body design was mainly the work of Raymond H. Dietrich, who had left Chrysler by the time it was in production. The flathead Dodge six was no performance engine, but it was known for its reliability and longevity. Accompanying the new rounded styling were sealed beam headlamps (with parking lights in the bezels) and a delete-option running board.

➕ FOR Open-air appeal • Solid construction • Quality leather interior

➖ AGAINST Little styling distinction • Limited collector recognition

PRODUCTION
2100

SPECIFICATIONS
Length (in.)	203.0

Wheelbase (in.)	119.5
Weight (lbs)	3190
Price (new)	$1030

ENGINES
cid/type	bhp	years
217.8/sv I-6	87	1940

PRICES
FAIR	$5000-10,000
GOOD	$10,000-18,000
FINE	$18,000-26,000

FINE EXAMPLE PRICE HISTORY
1982 $15,000		**1990** $25,000	
1994 $25,000		**1998** $25,000	

1982-2000 RETURN 3%
2000-2010 3%

1941-42
DODGE CUSTOM CONVERTIBLE

1942 Custom convertible

A facelift on the 1940 body, featuring a more massive divided grille. The distinctive Dodge ram mascot was now unrecognizable. No-cost Custom features included foam seat cushions, dual electric wipers, and a passenger's door armrest. For 1942, the dull six was stroked to 230.2 cubic inches, a size that would be continued at Dodge all the way up through 1959.

➕ FOR As for the 1940 convertible, and more affordable

➖ AGAINST As for the 1940 convertible • '42 is scarce

PRODUCTION
1941 3554 **1942** 1185

SPECIFICATIONS
Length (in.)	203.3
Wheelbase (in.)	119.5
Weight (lbs)	3384-3476
Price (new)	$1162-1245

ENGINES
cid/type	bhp	years
217.8/sv I-6	91	1941
230.2/sv I-6	102	1942

PRICES
As per 1940 convertible.

1946-49

DODGE CUSTOM CONVERTIBLE

1946 Custom convertible

Postwar continuation of the Dietrich-styled bodywork. Lasted through the spring of 1949, at which point Dodge's restyled "second series" '49s appeared, along with its Chrysler Corporation companion lines. Mechanically and bodily unchanged in these years. A mild facelift of the '42 styling featured an eggcrate grille (slightly heavy on the chrome) incorporating square parking lights.

✚ FOR   Priced lower than prewar counterparts (higher production) • Open-air fun

▬ AGAINST   Very ordinary by any standard

PRODUCTION
9500

SPECIFICATIONS
Length (in.)	204.6
Wheelbase (in.)	119.5
Weight (lbs)	3461
Price (new)	$1649-2189

ENGINES
cid/type	bhp	years
230.2/sv I-6	102	1946-49

PRICES
As per 1940 DeLuxe convertible.

1949

DODGE WAYFARER ROADSTER

An intriguing Dodge, part of the first all-new postwar series. Sort of Detroit's farewell to the genuine roadster, with removable plastic side curtains instead of conventional roll-up

1949 Wayfarer roadster

glass. The Wayfarer's interest value belies its unassuming nature, and despite its economy format it's the most sought-after '49 Dodge. Roll-up windows and wing vents replaced the side curtains during the model year but some purists prefer the original style, suggesting it may be worth marginally more than the later version.

✚ FOR   Strong collector interest • Novelty • Good construction quality • Scarcity

▬ AGAINST   Ho-hum styling • Minimal performance

PRODUCTION
5420

SPECIFICATIONS
Length (in.)	196.0
Wheelbase (in.)	115.0
Weight (lbs)	3145
Price (new)	$1727

ENGINES
cid/type	bhp	years
230.2/sv I-6	103	1949

PRICES
FAIR	$5000-10,000
GOOD	$10,000-17,500
FINE	$17,500-25,000

FINE EXAMPLE PRICE HISTORY
1982 $7500	**1990** $14,000
1994 $23,000	**1998** $23,000
1982-2000 RETURN 7%	
2000-2010 8%	

1950

DODGE CORONET DIPLOMAT

Dodge's first pillarless hardtop and apart from that there's little to rec-

1950 Coronet Diplomat hardtop coupe

ommend it as a collectible. The boxy '49 bodyshell was facelifted for 1950 with a cleaner grille featuring two strong horizontal bars with round parking lights at each end and a Dodge crest in the center, topped by a curved grille-surround trim piece. The hardtop added a natural sportiness to this otherwise conservative design. The low-suds Dodge six provided sedate pickup at best. Fluid drive was standard with four-speed Gyro-Matic optional. Slow, but well-built.

✚ FOR   Pioneer hardtop • Robust construction • Sturdy engine

▬ AGAINST   The same crashing boredom that characterized the entire 1950 line

PRODUCTION
3600

SPECIFICATIONS
Length (in.)	202.9
Wheelbase (in.)	123.5
Weight (lbs)	3515
Price (new)	$2233

ENGINES
cid/type	bhp	years
230.2/sv I-6	103	1950

PRICES
FAIR	$3000-6000
GOOD	$6000-10,000
FINE	$10,000-15,000

FINE EXAMPLE PRICE HISTORY
1982 $3900	**1990** $9500

1950

DODGE CORONET WOODY WAGON

Although the all-steel Sierra wagon is rarer (only 100 built), Dodge's last woody wagon is better-looking and far more sought-after by collectors. Quality birch framing was used on doors and superstructure; the "mahogany" graining on the doors was not veneer but merely a decal.

✚ FOR Wood-body looks • Fine carpentry • Last of a type

▬ AGAINST Wood's susceptibility to rot and surface wear • Dull styling

PRODUCTION

600

SPECIFICATIONS

Length (in.)	197.4
Wheelbase (in.)	123.5
Weight (lbs)	3850
Price (new)	$2865

ENGINES

cid/type	bhp	years
230.2/sv I-6	103	1950

PRICES

FAIR	$3000-6500
GOOD	$6500-11,000
FINE	$11,000-15,000

FINE EXAMPLE PRICE HISTORY

1982 $5700	1990 $12,000
1994 $12,000	1998 $13,000
1982-2000 RETURN 6%	
2000-2010 8%	

1949 Coronet wagon (1950 similar)

1950-51

DODGE WAYFARER SPORTABOUT

1951 Wayfarer Sportabout roadster

A continuation of the 1949 roadster with its own special name. Shared somewhat cleaner styling with other 1950-51 Dodge models. Should have sold better than it did at the low price, but remember that just another $100 bought a much more rakish Chevy convertible in these years.

✚ FOR As for the 1949 Wayfarer roadster, plus low production

▬ AGAINST As for the 1949 Wayfarer roadster

PRODUCTION

1950 2903 1951 1002

SPECIFICATIONS

Length (in.)	196.3
Wheelbase (in.)	115.0
Weight (lbs)	3155-3175
Price (new)	$1727-1924

ENGINES

cid/type	bhp	years
230.2/sv I-6	103	1950-51

PRICES

FAIR	$5000-9000
GOOD	$9000-17,000
FINE	$17,000-24,000

FINE EXAMPLE PRICE HISTORY

1982 $7600	1990 $18,000
1994 $21,000	1998 $23,000
1982-2000 RETURN 7%	
2000-2010 8%	

1953

DODGE CORONET EIGHT CONVERTIBLE

1953 Coronet Eight convertible

The collectible soft-top model in the series that ushered in Dodge's first V-8. The famous Red Ram was essentially a scaled-down version of the Chrysler Hemi, with smooth manifolding and porting, jumbo valves set well apart, excellent thermal efficiency, and considerable high-performance potential. The '53 Dodge line was restyled by Virgil Exner (who'd come to Chrysler from Studebaker in 1949), and looked lighter and less stodgy than earlier models. The V-8 cars performed well, yet offered good economy. One returned 23.4 mpg in the 1953 Mobilgas Economy Run, while other Red Rams were in the process of breaking 196 North American stock car speed records at Bonneville.

✚ FOR First V-8 • Top-down allure • Acceptable styling • High performance • Reasonable price

▬ AGAINST Slow to gain collector recognition • Modest appreciation potential

PRODUCTION

4100

SPECIFICATIONS

Length (in.)	189.6
Wheelbase (in.)	114.0
Weight (lbs)	3438
Price (new)	$2494

ENGINES

cid/type	bhp	years
241.3/ohv V-8	140	1953

PRICES

FAIR	$4500-9000
GOOD	$9000-16,000
FINE	$16,000-21,000

FINE EXAMPLE PRICE HISTORY

1982 $6000		1990 $17,500	
1994 $20,000		1998 $19,000	
1982-2000 RETURN 8%			
2000-2010 5%			

1954 DODGE ROYAL 500 CONVERTIBLE

A pretty and quite desirable Dodge that was a package model fashioned after the Royal convertible that paced the 1954 Indianapolis 500. Not a separate model, but a special derivative of the standard Royal ragtop, which numbered 2000 in all. The 500 package included Kelsey-Hayes chrome plated wire wheels, an exterior spare tire mount, special trim, and a 150-bhp version of Dodge's Red Ram V-8. For a little more money, an Offenhauser manifold and special carburetion that raised output to an estimated 200 bhp was available as a dealer option.

FOR Very desirable • Good styling • Outstanding performance • Indy Pace Car heritage

AGAINST One of the most expensive collector Dodges of the 1950-70 era

PRODUCTION
701

1954 Royal 500 Pace car Replica convertible

SPECIFICATIONS

Length (in.)	196.0
Wheelbase (in.)	114.0
Weight (lbs)	3575
Price (new)	$2632

ENGINES

cid/type	bhp	years
241.3/ohv V-8	150	1954

PRICES

FAIR	$5000-9500
GOOD	$9500-16,000
FINE	$16,000-24,000

Pace Car Replica convertible add 15%; hardtop deduct 25%.

FINE CONVERTIBLE PRICE HISTORY

1982 $7600		1990 $18,500	
1994 $25,000		1998 $24,000	
1982-2000 RETURN 7%			
2000-2010 8%			

1954-56 DODGE PICKUP

1956 C-3 pickup

The only all new vehicle from Chrysler in 1954 was the Dodge truck. The cab was lower and the front fenders were higher. The split windshield of previous models was replaced by a curved one-piece windshield. In '55 the windshield would get a "dog leg" bend for a wraparound effect popular in the Fifties. Also avail-

able in '55 was a wraparound rear window. In spite of the modern frontal styling, the hood still opened from the sides. Under the hood was an L-head six or the first V-8 available in a Dodge truck. In 1955, a fully-automatic transmission was available for the first time. A semi-automatic had been available previously. Cabs were more comfortable and better equipped than before and came in three trim levels: Standard, Deluxe, and Custom. In '55 a Custom Regal topped the line.

FOR Good performance with available V-8 • Smooth ride and good handling • Solidly built • Excellent visibility when equipped with wraparound rear window

AGAINST Steering both slow and heavy • Manual transmission hard to shift

PRODUCTION

1954 35,862 **1955** NA **1956** NA

SPECIFICATIONS

Length (in.)	198.5
Weight (lbs)	2975-3525
Wheelbase (in.)	108.0-116.0
Price (new)	$1331-1525

ENGINES

cid/type	bhp	years
218/sv 1-6	100	1954
230/sv I-6	110/115	1954-56
241/ohv V-8	145	1954
259/ohv V-8	169	1955-56

PRICES

FAIR	$2000-3000
GOOD	$3000-5000
FINE	$5000-7000
2000-2010 RETURN 3%	

1955-56 DODGE CUSTOM ROYAL 2D-MODELS

1955 Custom Royal Lancer hardtop coupe

Dodge's top-line two-door hardtop and convertible, part of Chrysler

Corporation's company-wide redesign in these years, the one that turned its fortunes around after the lean early-50s period. Styling, evolved by Exner lieutenant Murray Baldwin, featured a bold divided grille and flashy side trim. The '55 Custom Royal prefigured 1956 Chrysler products in having small, chrome-plated bolt-on fins. A neat asymmetrical dash and plush interior were also provided. Lancer hardtops shared another new idea with the '55 DeSoto Coronado—three-tone paint jobs. A four-door Custom Royal hardtop also dubbed Lancer was added for 1956, but the two-doors have the edge in collector appeal.

✚ **FOR** Distinctive looks • Fine performance from standard the V-8 • Higher D-500 power options available

▬ **AGAINST** A certain flashiness that some say hasn't worn well

PRODUCTION
1955 2d htp 30,499 **conv** 3302 **1956 2d htp** 26,000 (est.) **conv** 2900 (est.)

SPECIFICATIONS
Length (in.)	212.1
Wheelbase (in.)	120.0
Weight (lbs)	3480-3630
Price (new)	$2543-2913

ENGINES
cid/type	bhp	years
270.1/ohv V-8	183/193	1955
315/ohv V-8	218/260	1956

PRICES
Conv	
FAIR	$5000-10,000
GOOD	$10,000-17,500
FINE	$17,500-24,000
Htp	
FAIR	$3000-6500
GOOD	$6500-9000
FINE	$9000-14,000

FINE HARDTOP PRICE HISTORY
1982 $4800		**1990** $15,000	
1994 $12,000		**1998** $14,000	
1982-2000 RETURN 8%			
2000-2010 8%			

1956 Custom Royal Lancer LaFemme hardtop coupe

option for the Custom Royal Lancer hardtop in the spring of 1955. It included a pink and white color scheme, special color-keyed upholstery, and a raft of interior accessories like a cosmetic kit, raincoat and cap, and umbrella that were housed in special storage compartments behind the front seat. The '56 edition strutted about in two-tone lavender.

✚ **FOR** Unique limited edition • Others as for 1955-56 Custom Royal Lancer

▬ **AGAINST** Ask Patricia Ireland

PRODUCTION
1000 (est.)

SPECIFICATIONS
Length (in.)	212.1
Wheelbase (in.)	120.0
Weight (lbs)	3480-3505
Price (new)	$2843-2993

ENGINES
cid/type	bhp	years
270.1/ohv V-8	183/193	1955
315/ohv V-8	218/260	1956

PRICES
FAIR	$5000-8000
GOOD	$8000-11,000
FINE	$11,000-17,000

FINE EXAMPLE PRICE HISTORY
1982 $5280		**1990** $17,000	
1994 $15,000		**1998** $16,500	
1982-2000 RETURN 10%			
2000-2010 8%			

1956 Custom Royal D-500 sedan

tings. Most D-500s were based on the Custom Royal, but a few Coronets were ordered this way by racers, and were definitely wolves in sheep's clothing.

✚ **FOR** Terrific performance for the period • Rare

▬ **AGAINST** High operating costs

PRODUCTION
2500 (est.)

SPECIFICATIONS
Length (in.)	212.1
Wheelbase (in.)	120.0
Weight (lbs)	3250-3630
Price (new)	$2200-3000 (approx.)

ENGINES
cid/type	bhp	years
315/ohv V-8	260	1956

PRICES
For hardtops and convertibles add 30% to 1955-56 Custom Royal prices. For other models, approximately the same as for Custom Royal hardtop.
2000-2010 RETURN 10%

1955-56
DODGE CUSTOM ROYAL LANCER LAFEMME

What the male chauvinists at Dodge thought women would die for in the mid-'50s. Appeared as a trim

1956
DODGE D-500

Not a distinct model, but a performance package available for any '56 Dodge V-8, Coronet, Royal, or Custom Royal. Consisted mainly of a 260-bhp version of the Dodge 315 V-8, plus appropriately stiffer suspension set-

1957-58
DODGE CUSTOM ROYAL 2-DOORS

Dodge's top-line convertible and hardtop coupe in the "Swept-

1958 Custom Royal convertible

Wing" era, a reference to the bold fins and glittery front end highlighting Virgil Exner's dramatic, all-new '57 styling. Though "busier" than other Chrysler Corporation products that year, Dodges were still graceful and fairly well integrated. But a modest '58 facelift was followed by more swollen and garish '59s which, perhaps as a consequence, have only now started garnering collector interest—other than those with the hot D-500 option (see below). Dodge naturally shared in Chrysler's new-for-'57 torsion-bar front suspension, optional three-speed pushbutton TorqueFlite automatic, and much more rakish new thin-pillar bodyshells. The last featured greatly lowered beltlines and vastly increased glass areas, including a compound-curve windshield on the convertible and all '58 hardtops. A flash recession cut heavily into '58 sales and rendered quite rare a "Spring Special" Custom Royal two-door hardtop dubbed Regal Lancer, basically the standard article with minor trim alterations. Though Customs are preferred, current scarcity suggests considering a hardtop sedan, the mid-line Royal hardtops, and the low-line Coronet hardtops and convertible. All have many of the same good (and bad) qualities and are thus nice alternatives, if not the best dollar-return investments.

FOR Decisively improved roadability • Performance • Great '50s flash

AGAINST Seriously rust-prone • Sloppy workmanship • Some trim and body parts now hard to find

PRODUCTION
1957 htp cpe 32,000 **conv** 4000 (est.) **1958 htp cpe** 9500 (est.) **conv** 2000 (est.) **Regal Lancer htp cpe** 1163

SPECIFICATIONS
Length (in.)	212.2 (1957), 213.8 (1958)
Wheelbase (in.)	122.0
Weight (lbs)	3670-3810
Price (new)	$2920-3298

ENGINES
cid/type	bhp	years
325/ohv V-8	245/285	1957
350/ohv V-8	295	1958

PRICES
Conv:	
FAIR	$7000-12,000
GOOD	$12,000-20,000
FINE	$20,000-28,000
Htp:	
FAIR	$4000-8000
GOOD	$8000-12,000
FINE	$12,000-16,000

Note: 1957s are at the higher end of the price scales, 1958s at the lower end.

FINE 1957 CONVERTIBLE PRICE HISTORY
1982 $6000	**1990** $29,000
1994 $20,000	**1998** $30,000
1982-00 RETURN 9%	
2000-2010 5%	

1957-59 DODGE D-500

1957 D-500 hardtop coupe

Continuation of Dodge's high-performance package in the late '50s, with a choice of conventional carburetor or fuel injection. Top horsepower ranged from 333-345, usually with two four-barrel carbs, but in 1958 the top 333-bhp rating came via fuel injection,

which was quickly withdrawn because it proved so troublesome. These cars were extremely fast, and could be quite colorful, too, but some feel they're less distinctive than the 1956 D-500. They're also comparatively scarcer, however.

FOR As for 1957 Custom Royal Lancer • Sensational go • Rarity

AGAINST More expensive to run than the standard Custom Royal • '59 styling • Others as for 1957 Custom Royal Lancer

PRODUCTION
3000 (est.)

SPECIFICATIONS
Length (in.)	212.2 (1957), 213.8 (1958), 217.4 (1959)
Wheelbase (in.)	122.0
Weight (lbs)	3444-4000
Price (new)	$2200-3500 (approx.)

ENGINES
cid/type	bhp	years
325/ohv V-8	285/310	1957
354/ohv V-8	340	1957
361/ohv V-8	320/333[1]	1958
383/ohv V-8	320/345	1959

[1]333 bhp with FI

PRICES
For Custom Royal, add 30% to hardtop and convertible prices (see 1957-58 Dodge Custom Royal). On other models, approximately the same as for Custom Royal hardtop.
2000-2010 RETURN 5%

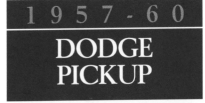

1957-60 DODGE PICKUP

1958 D100 Sweptside pickup

Dodge pickups were redesigned numerous times in the Fifties, most notably for 1957, when a "Forward Look" front end was adopted; and for '58, which brought quad headlamps, reworked horizontal-bar grille, and numerous two-tone paint combinations. The D100 ("100" designating ½-ton) Sweptside had bowed for 1957 as a prestige item to answer Chevy's slow-selling but gorgeous Cameo

Carrier. The Sweptside, with its station-wagon flanks, continued for 1958, when it was joined by the better-selling Sweptline, which eschewed the Sweptside's car-like fins for a large, square bed that was as wide as the cab. Model-year 1959 brought a new grille and, more significantly, a hard-pulling 318-cid V-8 rated at 205 bhp and 290 pounds/feet of torque. The final year of the series, 1960, offered little new beyond a mesh grille. Apt to be overlooked is the 1/2-ton Power Wagon, with modern wraparound windshield and available 4-wheel-drive.

✚ FOR Not collected nearly as fervently as they should be, so examples can be had at reasonable prices • Representative of a significant styling interlude • Hardy and practical as well as good-looking

▬ AGAINST Questionable parts availability • Susceptibility to rust

PRODUCTION
1958 24,563 **1959** NA **1960** 33,454

SPECIFICATIONS
Length (in.)	NA
Weight (lbs)	3225-3475
Wheelbase (in.)	108/116
Price (new)	$1714-2189

ENGINES
cid/type	bhp	years
230.2/sv 1-6	120	1958-59
314.6/ohv V-8	204	1958-59
318/ohv V-8	205	1959

PRICES
Half-ton	
FAIR	$1900-3000
GOOD	$3000-4800
FINE	$4800-6600
2000-2010 RETURN 3%	

1 9 6 2
DODGE LANCER GT

Chevy's Corvair Monza proved that bucket seats, floorshift, high-trim interiors, and sporty styling made compacts much more saleable than low-line economy small cars, and everybody rushed to copy it. At Dodge this meant a tricked-up version of the compact Lancer, introduced for 1961 as a badge-engineered divisional sibling of the Plymouth Valiant. Based on 1961's new two-door hardtop, the Lancer GT for '62 was hardly a grand tourer in the accepted sense, but it was a pleasant little car, and shared Virgil Exner's

1962 Lancer GT hardtop coupe

interesting Valiant styling. In basic design and appointments it paralleled the '62 Valiant Signet hardtop. For its 1963 compacts Dodge discarded the Lancer name in favor of Dart, making this a one-year-only model.

✚ FOR Rugged Slant-Six engine, with a 225-cid "big-block" available • Hop-up equipment was available • Right size for today's driving • Cheap

▬ AGAINST Styling a bit bulgy • Rust-prone • Indifferent fit and finish

PRODUCTION
13,683

SPECIFICATIONS
Length (in.)	188.8
Wheelbase (in.)	106.5
Weight (lbs)	2560
Price (new)	$2257

ENGINES
cid/type	bhp	years
170/ohv I-6	101	1962
225/ohv I-6	145	1962

PRICES
FAIR	$1200-2500
GOOD	$2500-4000
FINE	$4000-7000

FINE EXAMPLE PRICE HISTORY
1982 $1750		**1990** $6800	
1994 $8000		**1998** $7000	
1982-2000 RETURN 8%			
2000-2010 4%			

1 9 6 2 - 6 4
DODGE POLARA 500 2-DOORS

Sporty bucket-seat top-liners in the years of smaller full-size Dodges, built solely with V-8s. Chrysler design chief Virgil Exner thought the public

1962 Polara 500 hardtop coupe

would take to "downsized" big Dodges (and Plymouths) with styling drawn from his Valiant/Lancer compacts. He was wrong—1962 was a sales disaster. It would have been worse for Dodge had the division not rushed out a true full-sizer, the '62 Custom 880, which was really a replacement for the recently departed DeSoto. Elwood Engel, Exner's successor, managed to improve things considerably for '63—save the grille, still pretty weird. Stretching the wheelbase three inches to a true "full-size" span helped Dodge (but not Plymouth). Engel made looks all but conventional for '64, the exceptions being the grille (again) and the hardtop coupe roofline, the latter going from Thunderbird rectilinear to a rakish V-shape. Polara 500s were the brightest and most colorful of these "intermediate" Dodges, and offered a wide array of wedge-head V-8s up to 413s and 426s with both short and long ram-induction manifolds and truly stupendous power. These were the engines that, in the lighter low-line models, made Dodge a force on stock-car ovals and dragstrips alike. Dodge's mid-size platform was nicely "recycled" into 1965's mid-size Coronet line, again with bucket-seat "500" models (see entry).

✚ FOR Performance, esp. with big-block V-8s • Size still practical today • Good handling • Superb TorqueFlite automatic on most examples • Many engine parts still obtainable • Strong club support

◼ AGAINST Scarce then, more so now • Early rust-out one reason • Oddball styling another reason (esp. '62) • Some trim and body panels difficult to obtain • Value appreciation still slow

PRODUCTION

1962 12,268[1] **1963** 7256 **1964** 17,787[1]
[1]Includes htp sdns

SPECIFICATIONS

Length (in.)	202.0 (1962), 208.2 (1963), 209.8 (1964)
Wheelbase (in.)	116.0 (1962), 119.0 (1963-64)
Weight (lbs)	3315-3455
Price (new)	$2960-3227

ENGINES

cid/type	bhp	years
318/ohv V-8	230	1964
361/ohv V-8	310	1962
383/ohv V-8	305-335	1963-64
413/ohv V-8	365-410	1962
426/ohv V-8	365-425	1963-64

PRICES

Conv	
FAIR	$3000-6500
GOOD	$6500-9000
FINE	$9000-12,500
Htp	
FAIR	$1500-4000
GOOD	$4000-6500
FINE	$6500-9500

FINE HARDTOP PRICE HISTORY

1982 $2000		**1990** $7500	
1994 $7500		**1998** $10,000	
1982-2000 RETURN 12%			
2000-2010 5%			

1963-66
DODGE DART GT

Successor to the Lancer GT as Dodge's sporty compact. Slightly upsized with a new body. Styling by Elwood Engel has a minimum of fussiness (except maybe grilles) that has worn well. The GTs offered the most deluxe Dart trim and several sporty mechanical options. From 1964, Chrysler's fine 273-cid V-8 (from which the revised 1967 318 was derived) was listed as an option. Up to 235 bhp was available for '65, making this one of the hotter compacts around. The same basic package was continued for 1966 in a rather effective facelift with more squared-off lines.

◻ FOR Affordable • Wide powerteam choice • Available as hardtop and convertible • Attractive styling • Decent road manners

◼ AGAINST Limited collector interest • Limited appreciation potential • Body-rot tendency: dangerous in uni-body cars

PRODUCTION

1963 Sixes 34,227 **1964 Sixes** 37,660 **V-8s** 12,170 **1965 Sixes** 35,000[1] **V-8s** 10,000[1] **1966 Sixes** 20,000[1] **V-8s** 10,000[1]
[1]Estimated

SPECIFICATIONS

Length (in.)	196.4
Wheelbase (in.)	111.0
Weight (lbs)	2670-2995
Price (new)	$2289-2828

ENGINES

cid/type	bhp	years
170/ohv I-6	101	1963-66
225/ohv I-6	145	1963-66
273.5/ohv V-8	180/235	1964-66

PRICES

FAIR	$1500-3500
GOOD	$3500-5000
FINE	$5000-9000

(Convertibles are at high end of above range.)

FINE CONVERTIBLE PRICE HISTORY

1982 $2200		**1990** $9500	
1994 $10,000		**1998** $10,000	
1982-2000 RETURN 7%			
2000-2010 3%			

1965 Dart GT convertible

1965-66
DODGE CORONET 500

1965 Coronet 500 hardtop coupe

Most exciting mid-size Dodges of the early muscle-car years. Coronet 500 succeeded the Polara 500 as the top-line bucket-seat convertible and hardtop coupe for '65, when styling was fully revamped. The '66s got redesigned bodyshells and styling akin to that of the new Charger fastback (see entry), which was planned for a mid-'65 debut. The series was watered down by making a six standard and V-8s optional—and by the addition of a four-door sedan, one reason for higher '66 production. A special lightweight Hemi-Charger version of the 2-door Coronet sedan was offered for '65. It had radically-relocated front and rear axles for more rearward weight distribution, and was built to order strictly for drag racing. Power came from a hemi-head 426 V-8, conservatively rated at 425-bhp (actual horsepower is estimated at close to 500). Also included in the package were heavy-duty suspension, bigger front anti-roll bar, four-speed gearbox, and "police" brakes. Hemi-Chargers were hard to buy, as most were snapped up by pros. But those that could get one were treated to impressive performance, with seven-second 0-60 mph times and a top speed of 120 mph. Specially-prepared drag versions reigned supreme during 1965. For '66, the 425-bhp Hemi was offered in all versions of the Coronet, replacing the wedge-head 426.

◻ FOR Clean styling • Coronet's good handling and plush interior • Hemi-Charger's rarity, uniqueness, and gobs of power

◼ AGAINST Not high-status collectible • Hemi-Chargers very costly to keep and restore

PRODUCTION

1965 Coronet 500 32,745 **1965 Hemi-Charger** est. 500 **1966 Coronet 500** 55,683

1965 Hemi-charger coupe

SPECIFICATIONS

Length (in.)	202.0-203.0 (Coronet), 200.0 (Hemi-Charger)
Wheelbase (in.)	117.0 (Coronet), 115.0 (Hemi-Charger)
Weight (lbs)	3115-3345
Price (new)	$2674-2921

ENGINES

cid/type	bhp	years
225/ohv I-6	145	1966
273/ohv V-8	180	1965-66
318/ohv V-8	230	1965-66
361/ohv V-8	265	1965-66
383/ohv V-8	325	1965-66
426/ohv V-8	365/425[1]	1965[1]

[1]1965 Hemi-Charger only; "425" bhp advertised (est. 500 actual)

PRICES

Coronet 500 Conv (318)	
FAIR	$3000-5500
GOOD	$5500-8000
FINE	$8000-10,000
Hemi Charger Htp	
FAIR	$10,000-16,000
GOOD	$16,000-22,000
FINE	$22,000-28,000

FINE HEMI-CHARGER PRICE HISTORY

1982	$8000	1990	$38,000
1994	$32,000	1998	$30,000
1982-2000 RETURN 8%			
2000-2010 5%			

1965-66
DODGE MONACO/ MONACO 500

1965 Monoco hardtop coupe

Limited-edition luxury hardtop coupe in the big-Dodge line reconstituted for '65 on a 121-inch wheelbase. The debut Monaco shared new squared-up Elwood Engel styling with companion Polara and Custom 880 series, but boasted a special buckets-and-console interior with wicker-look trim. The corporate-mainstay 383 V-8 was standard, along with TorqueFlite automatic; engine options ranged up to a wedge-head 426. The '66 was basically a facelifted repeat available with fewer engine choices, but was tagged "500" to separate it from that year's new standard Monaco line, which replaced the Custom 880. Not yet a high-demand collector's item, but worth seeking out as a pleasant car that's fairly uncommon. Not considered here, but equally worthy, are the parallel Polara 500 convertible and hardtop coupe of these years, which are likely even rarer (no exact production breakouts available), yet just as sporty.

FOR Unique, short-lived model • Nice looks • Proven, capable drivetrains • Spacious • Good big '60s Ford/Chevy alternative

AGAINST Little collector interest • Trim and body panels scarce • Not much exterior distinction from lesser linemates

PRODUCTION

1965 13,096 **1966** 10,840

SPECIFICATIONS

Length (in.)	213.3
Wheelbase (in.)	121.0
Weight (lbs)	3895-4000
Price (new)	$3355-3604

ENGINES

cid/type	bhp	years
383/ohv V-8	270/315/325	1965-66
413/ohv V-8	340	1965
426/ohv V-8	365	1965
440/ohv V-8	350	1966

PRICES

Htp	
FAIR	$1000-2500
GOOD	$2500-4500
FINE	$4500-8000
(Deduct 45% for sedan models.)	

FINE HARDTOP PRICE HISTORY

1982	$2000	1990	$7500
1994	$7100	1998	$7600
1982-2000 RETURN 9%			
2000-2010 5%			

1966-67
DODGE CHARGER

This was Dodge's response to the fastback fad started by Plymouth's Barracuda and the Mustang 2+2, but on a larger scale. Launched at mid-model year 1966, but originally scheduled for introduction to preview the '66 Coronet, with which it shared most sheetmetal below the beltline. Because it was an intermediate like the Rambler Marlin, the Charger could have been an aesthetic disaster, but long side windows prevented its sweeping roof from looking too heavy. Unique touches included hideaway headlamps, a standard V-8, and a split fold-down rear seatback with trunk partition *á la* Barracuda. Power options ran from the 361 and 383 V-8s up to the 440 Magnum and the legendary 426 Hemi. Manual three- and four-speed transmissions and the stiffened Rally suspension were also available. With automatic and the 383, the car timed out at 9 seconds in the 0-60 mph dash, and could reach 110 mph, or more with longer gearing. Not a big sales winner in these years, but the fuselage-shaped '68 design would change all that.

FOR Handsome in its way (better looking than a Marlin) • Wide powerteam choices (but 383 or Hemi fidgety for the street) • Cargo-carrying versatility • Busy but fully instrumented dash

AGAINST Quirky styling • Mediocre

1966 Charger hardtop coupe

build quality • High running costs with big V-8s

PRODUCTION

1966 37,344 **1967** 15,788

SPECIFICATIONS

Length (in.)	208.0
Wheelbase (in.)	117.0
Weight (lbs)	3480-3499
Price (new)	$3122-3130

ENGINES

cid/type	bhp	years
318/ohv V-8	230	1966-67
361/ohv V-8	265	1966
383/ohv V-8	325	1966-67
426/ohv V-8	425	1966-67
440/ohv V-8	375	1967

PRICES

FAIR	$2500-6000
GOOD	$6000-10,000
FINE	$10,000-14,000

(Add 100% for Hemi)

FINE EXAMPLE PRICE HISTORY

1982 $5800	**1990** $15,000
1994 $11,000	**1998** $14,000
1982-2000 RETURN 5%	
2000-2010 5%	

1967-70 DODGE CORONET R/T

1968 Coronet R/T convertible

Offered in two-door hardtop or convertible form, the R/T—for Road/ Track—version of the mid-size Dodge was a crisply styled, luxurious, high-speed machine. It packed the "Magnum" 440 V-8 as standard, and offered the 426 Hemi as an option. Features included heavy-duty suspension, bucket seats, special identification, and Dodge's bumblebee tail striping. A vast styling improvement occurred for 1968, and this design continued through the final Coronet R/T of 1970. For 1971, the Coronet became more mundane, and Dodge performance buyers had to look to other models.

FOR Good styling (very good from 1968 on) • Outstanding performance

• Prices are well down from early 1990s

AGAINST Fuelishness • Mediocre quality control

PRODUCTION

1967 10,000 (est.) **1968** 10,849 **1969** 7238 **1970** 2615

SPECIFICATIONS

Length (in.)	209.2
Wheelbase (in.)	117.0
Weight (lbs)	3530-3721
Price (new)	$3199-3785

ENGINES

cid/type	bhp	years
426/ohv V-8	425	1967-69
440/ohv V-8	375/390	1967-70

PRICES

Conv	
FAIR	$7000-10,000
GOOD	$10,000-15,000
FINE	$15,000-21,000
Htp	
FAIR	$4000-6500
GOOD	$6500-9000
FINE	$9000-14,000

(Add 35% for Hemi)

FINE 1969 CONVERTIBLE PRICE HISTORY

1982 $2800	**1990** $30,000
1994 $32,000	**1998** $25,000
1982-2000 RETURN 13%	
2000-2010 5%	

1968-70 DODGE CHARGER R/T

All-new notchback replacement for Dodge's fastback sports/specialty mid-size model. It was a styling sensation then, and still looks great today. The R/T was the more sporting of the two versions initially offered, identified by its "Scat Pack" bumblebee-striped tail, and comprehensively equipped for grand touring American-style. The usual plethora of powerplants was available, including the Hemi. In these cars Dodge achieved a combination rare in Detroit: classic lines, outstanding performance, and better-than-average quality control. It was a good one. Unfortunately, it wouldn't last long. Styling deteriorated, and more emphasis was placed on luxury than performance after 1970, a reflection of sky-high insurance rates and dwindling customer demand for hot cars. The name continued through the '70s until it was completely watered down for Dodge's personal-luxury duplicate of the Chrysler Cordoba, then for a "performance" version of the front-drive 024 (Omni) coupe.

FOR Styling • Performance • Prices have come down so much that the R/T is definitely undervalued

AGAINST Only its basic character— high-compression, high-octane engines don't cope well with today's low-calorie gas

PRODUCTION

1968 20,000 (est.) **1969** 20,057 **1970** 10,337 (includes Daytona model)

SPECIFICATIONS

Length (in.)	208.0
Wheelbase (in.)	117.0
Weight (lbs)	3575-3610
Price (new)	$3506-3711

ENGINES

cid/type	bhp	years
318/ohv V-8	230	1968-70
383/ohv V-8	290/330/335	1970
426/ohv V-8	425	1968-70
440/ohv V-8	375/390	1968-70

PRICES

FAIR	$4000-7000
GOOD	$7000-10,000

1968 Charger R/T hardtop coupe

FINE $10,000-15,000
(Add 100% for Hemi)

FINE EXAMPLE PRICE HISTORY

1982 $4100	1990 $36,000
1994 $20,000	1998 $18,000
1982-2000 RETURN 12%	
2000-2010 5%	

1968-70

DODGE CORONET SUPER BEE

1969 Coronet Super Bee hardtop coupe

The budget version of the Coronet R/T, much in the mold of the Plymouth Road Runner. It packed the Mopar 383 V-8 as standard. Available as a pillared coupe in its first year like Road Runner, it added a two-door hardtop alternative for 1969 and '70. However, unlike Plymouth, Dodge never offered a convertible version of its low-bucks muscle car. Roughly comparable in interior appointments to the Coronet 440, and marked externally by the bumblebee tail striping Dodge used in those years on all its hotter models, which formed the "Scat Pack." In its final season, the Super Bee was listed with the big Hemi V-8 as an option, as well as the 390-bhp 440 "Six-Pack" V-8 with three two-barrel carbs.

✚ FOR   As for Coronet R/T

◼ AGAINST   As for Coronet R/T

PRODUCTION

1968 20,000 (est.) **1969** 27,846 **1970** 15,506

SPECIFICATIONS

Length (in.)	209.2
Wheelbase (in.)	117.0
Weight (lbs)	3200-3535
Price (new)	$3027-3138

ENGINES

cid/type	bhp	years
383/ohv V-8	335	1968-70
426/ohv V-8	425	1970
440/ohv V-8	390	1970

PRICES

FAIR	$3500-5500

GOOD	$5500-8000
FINE	$8000-14,000

(Add 100% for Hemi, 55% for Magnum 440.)

FINE EXAMPLE PRICE HISTORY

1982 $3300	1990 $22,500
1994 $13,000	1998 $18,000
1982-2000 RETURN 9%	
2000-2010 5%	

1968-69

DODGE DART GTS

1968 Dart GTS hardtop coupe

Dodge's answer to the Chevrolet Nova SS, and based on the rebodied 1967 design by Elwood Engel. Darts in general have yet to achieve collector status, with one exception: the hot GTS, with a standard 340-cid V-8, or Chrysler's potent 383 offered optionally. Available as a hardtop or convertible, both luxuriously and comprehensively equipped. At about 3000 pounds, these were tremendously powerful—and often greatly underrated by opponents on the dragstrip.

✚ FOR   Low-cost performance • Neat styling

◼ AGAINST   Indifferent quality • Growing parts scarcity • Low appreciation

PRODUCTION

1968 8745 **1969** 6702

SPECIFICATIONS

Length (in.)	195.4
Wheelbase (in.)	110.0
Weight (lbs)	3065-3210
Price (new)	$3189-3419

ENGINES

cid/type	bhp	years
340/ohv V-8	275	1968-69
383/ohv V-8	300/330	1968-69

PRICES

Conv	
FAIR	$3500-7000
GOOD	$7000-13,000
FINE	$13,000-19,000

(Hardtop deduct 25%.)

FINE CONVERTIBLE PRICE HISTORY

1982 $3000	1990 $20,000
1994 $15,000	1998 $19,000
1982-2000 RETURN 12%	
2000-2010 8%	

1969

DODGE CHARGER DAYTONA

This was an aerodynamic weapon to help Dodge take the NASCAR title away from Ford, and built by Creative Industries in Detroit. It featured a smooth droop-snoot (with hidden headlights) bolted to the front frame members and a huge rear stabilizer wing supported by struts mounted from inside the trunk. "Street" Daytonas scored 14.5-second quarter-mile times at around 95 mph when equipped with the Mopar 440 V-8. The Daytona won 80 percent of the races it entered, and helped Dodge take 22 Grand Nationals, four less than Ford. Dodge built only enough to qualify it for NASCAR, and production ceased after 1969. Instead, a Daytona performance version of the 1970 Charger R/T was

1969 Charger Daytona hardtop coupe

fielded, while Plymouth's Superbird took up where Dodge "Winged Warrior" left off.

⊡ FOR An important contributor to performance and racing history • Wild looks • Outstanding performance • Prices still down from 1990s

⊡ AGAINST Nervous in daily use • Slack quality control • Cop-baiting appearance • Probably won't have been pampered • Prices have started up again

PRODUCTION

Between 501 and 507 (factory figure 505)

SPECIFICATIONS

Length (in.)	220.0
Wheelbase (in.)	117.0
Weight (lbs)	approx. 3900
Price (new)	approx. $4000

ENGINES

cid/type	bhp	years
440/ohv V-8	375	1969
426/ohv V-8	425	1969

PRICES

FAIR	$14,000-37,000
GOOD	$37,000-52,000
FINE	$52,000-65,000

FINE EXAMPLE PRICE HISTORY

1982 $9000	1990 $60,000
1994 $60,000	1998 $54,000
1982-2000 RETURN 13%	
2000-2010 10%	

1 9 7 0 - 7 4
DODGE CHALLENGER COUPES

The closed versions of Dodge's belated answer to the Ford Mustang and Chevrolet Camaro; convertibles offered only through 1971

1971 Challenger R/T hardtop coupe

(see entry). A near-cousin to Plymouth's third-generation Barracuda apart from outer body panels and two-inch longer wheelbase. Too late to do Dodge much good in a declining pony-car market, but rapid sales fall-off after first year has left some very rare— and now very sought-after—Challengers. Prime picks are the low-volume R/T and its even sportier 1970-only T/A offshoot, created for SCCA Trans-Am racing and roughly equivalent to the AAR 'Cuda. It featured a tuned 340 "Six Pak" V-8, hood scoop, rear spoiler, tape stripes, and louvered backlight. Wide engine choice through '71, including the fabled Hemi and big-block 440; optional small-block V-8s and standard sixes thereafter, when a Rallye coupe—an option package after '72—ousted the R/T as the enthusiast's Challenger. Big-block models tend to garner the highest collector prices today, but the sportier small-blocks are more practical and nicer to drive because the big engines simply overwhelmed the chassis. SE (Special Edition) coupes with wide-quarter/small-backlight vinyl roof and luxury interior are as rare as ragtops and just as worth seeking out.

⊡ FOR Uncommon ponycar • Muscle models' high performance • Smooth styling (probably nicest on the '70s) Strong club support and collector interest

⊡ AGAINST Poor materials/construction quality • Rust-prone • Heavy and thirsty • Real room only for two • Clean, well-maintained originals hard to find • Value appreciation leveling off now, though still climbing

PRODUCTION

1970 base 53,337 **SE** 6584 **R/T** 12,747 **R/T SE** 3979 **T/A** 2142 **1971 base** 23,088 **R/T** 4630 **1972 base** 18,535 **Rallye** 8123 **1973** 32,596[1] **1974** 16,437[1]

[1]incl. Rallye option

SPECIFICATIONS

Length (in.)	191.3
Wheelbase (in.)	110.0
Weight (lbs)	3028-3495
Price (new)	$2851-3498

ENGINES

cid/type	bhp[1]	years
225/ohv I-6	110/145	1970-72
318/ohv V-8	150/230	1970-74
340/ohv V-8	240/275	1970-73
360/ohv V-8	245	1974
383/ohv V-8	275/335	1970-71
426/ohv V-8	425	1970-71
440/ohv V-8	375/390	1970-711

[1]SAE gross

PRICES

FAIR	$3000-7000
GOOD	$7000-10,000
FINE	$10,000-20,000

(Add 80% for Hemi, 60% for 440)

FINE 1971 R/T PRICE HISTORY

1982 $2900	1990 $25,000
1994 $11,000	1998 $18,000
1982-2000 RETURN 12%	
2000-2010 8%	

1 9 7 0 - 7 1
DODGE CHALLENGER CONVERTIBLES

1970 Challenger R/T convertible

Short-lived open version of Dodge's too-late Mustang/Camaro-fighter, dropped after only two years due to meager demand in a withering ponycar market. Shared basic Bill Brownlie styling with Challenger coupes, and offered the same wide engine array, but sporty R/T model available for 1970 only. So many engines, trim options, and colors that some combinations are probably near one-of-a-kind. Pace car for the '71 Indy 500, but no replicas were made for the public.

⊡ FOR As for 1970-74 Challenger coupes, plus convertible allure, even greater exclusivity, and superior investment potential

⊡ AGAINST As for 1970-74 Challenger coupes, but much harder to find and restore

PRODUCTION

1970 3173 **R/T** 1070 **1971** 2165

SPECIFICATIONS

Length (in.)	191.3
Wheelbase (in.)	110.0
Weight (lbs)	3103-3470
Price (new)	$3120-3535

ENGINES

cid/type	bhp[1]	years
225/ohv I-6	110/145	1970-71
318/ohv V-8	150/230	1970-71
340/ohv V-8	240/275	1970-71
383/ohv V-8	275/335	1970-71
426/ohv V-8	425	1970-71
440/ohv V-8	375/390	1970-71
[1]SAE gross		

PRICES

FAIR	$4000-8000
GOOD	$8000-15,000
FINE	$15,000-25,000
(Add 100% for Hemi, 80% for 440 or Six-Pak)	

FINE EXAMPLE PRICE HISTORY

1982 $2600		**1990** $17,500	
1994 $18,000		**1998** $22,000	
1982-2000 RETURN 15%			
2000-2010 10%			

1971-72
DODGE DEMON 340

Arguably the one collectible Dodge compact after the 1968-69 Dart GTS. Much the same idea, but the big 383 V-8 was replaced by Chrysler's winning 340 small-block, an extension of the late-'60s 273/318. The body shifted from hardtop coupe to the pillared two-door fastback first seen as the 1970 Plymouth Duster (offered in a similar 340 model), with the wheelbase cut three inches from that of other Darts. The Demon name, accompanied by little cartoon "devil" decals, caused an uproar among some religious groups, and was

thus changed to Dart Sport after '72. Besides the tuned engine with dual exhausts, the 340 added upgraded chassis and rolling stock, bodyside striping, top-trim interior, and a matte-black hood with twin air scoops to the basic economy Demon coupe. All but the special hood was retained for the facelifted replacement Sport, which sold much better and carried on through 1975 with a more emissions-controllable 360 engine. While there's nothing wrong with a Sport, the Demon 340 is more desirable owing to "short-timer" status, lower resulting production, and less-restricted engines. The '71 is preferred for its higher gross horsepower over the detuned '72.

✚ **FOR** Svelte performance compact • Nice enough looks • Not that many built • Ready parts/service support • Cheap

▬ **AGAINST** Seriously rust-prone • Soft-trim supplies dwindling • Not a high value appreciator now

PRODUCTION

1971 10,098 **1972** 8750

SPECIFICATIONS

Length (in.)	192.5
Wheelbase (in.)	108.0
Weight (lbs)	3165-3210
Price (new)	$2656-$2721

ENGINES

cid/type	bhp[1]	years
340/ohv V-8	240/275	1971-72
[1]SAE gross		

PRICES

FAIR	$1000-3000
GOOD	$3000-3500
FINE	$3500-8000

FINE EXAMPLE PRICE HISTORY

1982 $3000		**1990** $7500	
1994 $8000		**1998** $8000	
1982-2000 RETURN 6%			
2000-2010 5%			

1971 Demon 340 hardtop coupe

1978-79
DODGE MAGNUM XE

1978 Magnum XE coupe

A more handsome version of Dodge's late-'70s Charger, which had switched from the wildly curvy "fuselage" look of 1971-74 to the more formal, squarish lines of Chrysler's new personal-luxury 1975 Cordoba—to no good sales effect. In essence, this was the sportier 1976-77 Charger Daytona package with a sloped three-bar body-color grille, headlamps behind flip-up glass covers, and bulged front/rear fenders. Serious drivers chose the Grand Touring option which added larger tires, stiffer suspension and deleted the opera window slats. Options included leather buckets and a T-bar roof with removable panels. Chrysler's time-honored torsion-bar front suspension was still employed, but engines were strictly economy- and emissions-conscious "lean-burn" V-8s, linked with proven TorqueFlite automatic. By no means a performance Dodge in the '60s mold, but good looks give it some distant potential as a minor collector's item.

✚ **FOR** Understated period styling • Reliable drivetrains • "Used car" cheap

▬ **AGAINST** A dubious collectible at best • Usual 1970s car worries and sloppy workmanship • Relatively tepid performance

PRODUCTION

1978 55,431 **1979** 30,354

SPECIFICATIONS

Length (in.)	215.8
Wheelbase (in.)	114.9
Weight (lbs)	3785-3886
Price (new)	$5448-5709

ENGINES

cid/type	bhp[1]	years
318/ohv V-8	140/155	1978-79
360/ohv V-8	155/170	1978-79
400/ohv V-8	190/195	1978-79
[1]SAE net		

PRICES

FAIR	$1500-2500
GOOD	$2500-5000
FINE	$5000-7500

FINE EXAMPLE PRICE HISTORY

Depreciating or flat in 1980s-90s; just beginning to appreciate.
2000-2010 RETURN 2%

1980-83
DODGE MIRADA

1980 Mirada hardtop coupe

Personal-luxury Dodge spinoff of the second-generation 1980 Chrysler Cordoba, replacing the previous Charger/Magnum. Sales withered quickly despite clean, sharp-edged styling announced by a Magnum-like nose with a "Cord-type" slat grille. Part of the effort to reestablish Dodge as Chrysler's "performance" division, but only first-year models with the optional 360 V-8 could claim any sort of go. Shared the long-wheelbase Dodge Aspen/Plymouth Volare compact platform used for the contemporary mid-size Dodge Diplomat/Chrysler LeBaron, with rather sloppy ride and handling from odd suspension with transverse front torsion bars. CMX appearance option available throughout added fancy wheels and cloth convertible-style roof cover with blind sail panels. Has minor interest as the last rear-drive Dodge with any connection to the grand late-'60s Charger, and as one of the old-line models saved in Chrysler's 11th-hour financial rescue by Lee Iacocca and Congress.

✛ **FOR** Handsome • Good performance with 360 V-8 • Nice interior • Better workmanship than earlier Magnum/Charger • Yours for a song

▬ **AGAINST** "Nautical" ride and handling • Dull performer without 360 V-8 • Scant interest even among clubs • Little hope for value appreciation in the next 15 years

PRODUCTION

1980 32,746 **1981** 11,899 **1982** 6818 **1983** 5597

SPECIFICATIONS

Length (in.)	209.5
Wheelbase (in.)	112.7
Weight (lbs)	3230-3380
Price (new)	$6645-9011

ENGINES

cid/type	bhp	years
225/ohv I-6	85-90	1980-83
318/ohv V-8	130/165[1]	1980-83
360/ohv V-8	130/185	1980
[1]2/4-bbl.		

PRICES

FAIR	$1500-2000
GOOD	$2000-2500
FINE	$2500-3000

FINE EXAMPLE PRICE HISTORY

Depreciating in 1980s-90s.
2000-2010 RETURN 2%

1982-84
DODGE RAMPAGE/ PLYMOUTH SCAMP

Mini-El Caminos, these sharp little half-ton pickups were created by shortening the roof of the Charger L-body and adding a doubled-walled, galvanized cargo box. A longer wheelbase than the Charger gave a better ride and the styling was sweet. Upgraded, sporty models—Rampage Sport (1982), Rampage 2.2 (1983-84) and Plymouth Scamp—boasted rorty exhaust, 14" wheels, low-profile tires, special trim, instruments, deluxe interior and (in 1983-84) a five-speed transaxle. Sales slumped early, for they were neither pure truck nor pure car. Scamp lasted only a year and is extremely rare. Rampage received a

1982 Rampage pickup

nice facelift for 1984 but production that year was almost as low as Scamp.

✛ **FOR** Slick styling • Rarity • The only front-wheel-drive pickups besides VW's stodgy Rabbit • Long-lived engine • Fuel economy • Brisk performance

▬ **AGAINST** No collector interest • Specific body parts virtually extinct • No separate frame like most pickups, so rust attacks non-galvanized portions of unibody—don't buy one with serious tinworm

PRODUCTION

Rampage: 17,576. Model year est.: **1982** 17,000 **1983** 7500 **1984** 3000 **Scamp: 1983** 2129

SPECIFICATIONS

Length (in.)	183.6
Wheelbase (in.)	104.2
Weight (lbs)	2295-2400
Price (new)	$6698-7315

ENGINES

cid/type	bhp	years
135/ohc I-4	110	1982-84

PRICES

FAIR	$1500-2000
GOOD	$2000-3000
FINE	$3000-4500

FINE EXAMPLE PRICE HISTORY

Depreciating in 1980s/90s; clean rust-free examples have now stabilized in price.
2000-2010 RETURN Even

1983-87
DODGE SHELBY CHARGER

First of the modern performance Dodges created by Carroll Shelby in a second collaboration with friend

1987 Shelby Charger coupe

Lee Iacocca, recalling their original '60s Cobra and GT Mustang projects at Ford. Appeared during 1983 as a heated-up new-wave Charger, which had bowed for 1979 as the 024 (along with Plymouth's TC3, later Turismo), a "fasthatch" coupe based on the front-drive 1978 Dodge Omni/Plymouth Horizon subcompacts. First-year production ran a tuned version of the K-car 2.2-liter "Trans-4" linked to a manual five-speed transaxle, and had a much stiffer chassis to suit. Also included were wider "Swiss cheese" cast-aluminum wheels, front and rear spoilers, skirted rocker panels, a special interior with Shelby logos, and silver or blue paint set off by broad silver or blue stripes. A turbo 2.2, equal-length half-shafts, and gas-charged shocks were substituted from about mid-1985; there were also larger brakes and tires, an uprated cooling system, more supportive seats, and alternative exterior colors. Little changed for '86 save for required high-mount third stoplamp, then carried on into early '88, when this Charger series was discontinued to make room for the new Dodge Shadow/Plymouth Sundance line. A long-term collectible, but Shelby connection, limited volume, and "fun factor" should eventually work in its favor.

FOR Turbo speedy (about 8 seconds 0-60) • Tight handling • Hatchback versatility • Very affordable • Plentiful parts/service support

AGAINST Loud • Rough-riding • Abundant torque-steer in hard take-offs • So-so assembly quality • Juvenile image • Not ever likely to be a high-return investment

PRODUCTION
1983 8251 **1984** 7552 **1985** 7709 **1986** 7669 **1987** 2011

SPECIFICATIONS
Length (in.) 174.8

Wheelbase (in.) 99.1
Weight (lbs) 2330-2480
Price (new) $8290-9360

ENGINES
cid/type	bhp	years
135/ohc I-4	110	1984
135/ohc I-4[1]	146	1985-87
[1]Turbocharged		

PRICES
FAIR	$1500-2000
GOOD	$2000-2500
FINE	$2500-4000

FINE EXAMPLE PRICE HISTORY
Depreciating in 1980s/90s; clean rust-free examples have now stabilized in price.
2000-2010 RETURN 1%

1984-86
DODGE 600ES TURBO CONVERTIBLE

1984 600 ES Turbo convertible

Sporty, low-volume turbocharged edition of the front-drive K-car convertible that bowed as a Dodge 400 for 1982, along with companion Chrysler LeBarons. Combined the then-most potent version of Chrysler's 2.2-liter "Trans-4" engine with the "sport/handling" package featured on other ES Dodges; chassis upgrades comprised thicker front and rear sway bars, "high-control" shocks, "firm-feel" quick-ratio

power steering, and beefy performance tires on multi-hole cast-alloy wheels. It had the same exterior styling as the non-turbo 600 ragtop, but less chrome and standard black-finish decklid luggage rack. Always sold with TorqueFlite automatic transaxle, except for a manual five-speed available in 1984 only. The interior was standard K-car in 600/LeBaron dress, save for a three-spoke sport steering wheel; it had the same unfortunate, hard-to-read digi-graphic instrumentation and, for a time, annoying "voice" warnings for everything from "low oil pressure" to "door is ajar." Power top had a glass backlight and separate rear-quarter windows. Dropped with the end of this mid-size Dodge convertible after '86.

FOR Top-down fun • Quick—0-60 in under 9 seconds • 20+ mpg • Agile and front-drive grippy • Inexpensive • Practical size

AGAINST Collector prospects dim and distant • Throttle lag, excess underhood heat, and similar turbo bothers • Prone to cowl/body shake • Mickey Mouse dash • Mother-in-law vocal warning system

PRODUCTION
1984 est. 2000 **1985** 5621 **1986** 4759

SPECIFICATIONS
Length (in.)	180.7
Wheelbase (in.)	100.3
Weight (lbs)	2650
Price (new)	$12,895-14,856

ENGINES
cid/type	bhp	years
135/ohc I-4[1]	146	1984-86
[1]Turbocharged		

PRICES
FAIR	$1250-2500
GOOD	$2500-4300
FINE	$4300-6200

FINE EXAMPLE PRICE HISTORY
Depreciating in 1980s/90s; clean rust-free examples have now stabilized in price.
2000-2010 RETURN 1%

1984-90
DODGE DAYTONA TURBO Z & SHELBY Z

Hottest of Dodge's late-'80s G-24 front-drive sports coupes, riding a platform shared with Chrysler's near-

1984 Daytona Turbo Z coupe

identical 1984-86 Laser. Called Turbo Z for its 1984 debut, Shelby Z for 1987-88, then Daytona Shelby—the latter two for Chrysler performance consultant Carroll Shelby. Its much-modified K-car chassis featured all-round coil springs, front MacPherson struts, trailing-arm rear beam axle, and power rack-and-pinion steering topped by a husky 2+2 "fasthatch" body with design overtones of the Chevy Camaro and Porsche 928. The Turbo/Shelby powertrain was always a transverse turbocharged 2.2-liter four (initially the 146-bhp "Turbo I") teamed with a manual five-speed or optional three-speed automatic trans-axle. Horsepower was upped on the '87 "Turbo II" engine (manual-shift only) via an intercooler and higher boost pressure; internals were strengthened, too. The new 1990 "Turbo IV" had better driveability (mainly less throttle lag) with a new VNT blower (Variable Nozzle Technology). All Daytonas were facelifted for '87 with a hidden-headlamp "droop snoot" and revamped tail. Upgrades included a standard driver's airbag for '88, no-cost all-disc brakes from '89, a new dash and cockpit-adjustable variable-rate shock absorbers for '90. Confusingly, a C/S Competition Package was optionally available for base models from 1988 and delivered most Shelby goodies—racy exterior add-ons, fortified chassis, hot engine—with less weight. Still, the later Shelby-badged models look the best collector bets, with Turbo Zs trailing. None, however, should start being gathered in for a good while yet.

➕ **FOR** Purposeful looks • Good go (8-9 seconds 0-60) • Grippy, agile front-drive handling

➖ **AGAINST** Some body and cockpit trim juvenile • Stiff ride • Noisy • Clunky manual shifter • Marked torque-steer • Hazy collector prospects

PRODUCTION

1984 Turbo Z est. 5000 **1985 Turbo Z** 8023 **1986 Turbo Z** 17,595 **1987 Shelby Z** 7152 **1988 Shelby Z** 7580 **1989 Shelby Z** NA **1990 Shelby Z** NA

SPECIFICATIONS

Length (in.)	175.0
Wheelbase (in.)	97.1
Weight (lbs)	2650-2950
Price (new)	$11,495-13,295

ENGINES

cid/type	bhp	years
135/ohc I-4[1]	146	1984-86
135/ohc I-4[1]	174	1987-90
156/ohc I-4[1]	150	1990
[1]Turbocharged		

FINE EXAMPLE PRICE HISTORY

Depreciating in 1980s/90s; clean rust-free examples have now stabilized in price.
2000-2010 RETURN 2%

1988-90 DODGE LANCER SHELBY

Sporty low-volume offshoot of Dodge's late-'80s front-drive Lancer sedan, the H-body five-door hatchback also sold as the Chrysler LeBaron GTS. Not to be confused with the contemporary Shelby Lancer (see entry), a still-sportier confection built by Shelby Automobiles in California, not Chrysler in Michigan. Lancer Shelby started with the sporty production ES model and added a monochrome exterior (first in red or white, then black, too), lower-body "aero" skirts, low-profile rear-roof spoiler, and a leather interior, plus an uprated "handling" chassis and intercooled 174-horsepower "Turbo II" engine—with manual five-speed only; the optional automatic transaxle required the 146-bhp "Turbo I" engine. Air conditioning and a power driver's seat were standard. At best, an iffy collector's item for the distant future due to Shelby-built cousin's greater mystique, higher power, and even lower production. Still, an interesting newer factory flyer that's quite practical day-to-day. Dropped with other Lancers after 1989.

➕ **FOR** Roomy • Hatchback versatility (fold-down rear seat) • Good performance and economy • "Used car" cheap • Rare

➖ **AGAINST** Collectibility far from certain • Mediocre fit and finish • Usual manual-shift clunkiness and Chrysler turbo-four boominess

PRODUCTION

1988 279 **1989** NA **1990** NA

SPECIFICATIONS

Length (in.)	180.4
Wheelbase (in.)	103.1
Weight (lbs)	2850
Price (new)	$17,395

ENGINES

cid/type	bhp	years
135/ohc I-4[1]	146/174[2]	1988-90
[1]Turbocharged[2]manual/automatic transaxle		

FINE EXAMPLE PRICE HISTORY

Depreciating in 1980s/90s; clean rust-free examples have now stabilized in price.
2000-2010 RETURN 2%

1989-1990 DODGE DAKOTA SPORT CONVERTIBLE

Genuine novelty characterizes this 3000-unit convertible pickup truck from Dodge—the first vehicle of its kind since Ford's roadster-pickup of 1934. By the late Eighties, many own-

1989 Lancer Shelby sedan

1989 Dakota Sport convertible pickup

ers of compact Japanese pickups were chopping the roofs to create custom drop-tops. Dodge's structurally sound variant with manually operated vinyl top was created in conjunction with Automobile Specialty Company, a division of ASC, Inc. Only one model, the uplevel "Sport," was available, though 2- and 4-wheel-drive Dakotas were offered. Standard drivetrain was a 3.9-liter, 125 bhp V-6 mated to a 5-speed stick. A 6.5-foot cargo bed brought a measure of practicality. Appealing then and now.

✚ **FOR** Novelty • Small production run • Plentiful parts • Comfortable and, for its day, refined • Competent off-road (with 4WD)

▬ **AGAINST** Scarcity, as most went to California and Florida • Slow off the line • Wind noise with top down

PRODUCTION
approx. 3000

SPECIFICATIONS

Length (in.)	185.9
Weight (lbs)	2885
Wheelbase (in.)	111.9
Price (new)	$17,500 (est)

ENGINES

cid/type	bhp	years
239/ohv V-6	125	1989-90

PRICES

FAIR	$2000-4000
GOOD	$4000-6000
FINE	$6000-8000
2000-2010 RETURN: Depreciating	

1 9 9 1 - 9 2
DODGE SPIRIT R/T

Billed by Dodge as "one of the world's fastest production sedans",

1991 Spirit R/T sedan

the Spirit R/T had a 0-60 time of less than seven seconds, but looked like a plain wrapper sedan. The base Spirit was a solid and competent, though uninspiring sedan. The R/T added a hot engine, stiffer suspension, and larger wheels. These components produced an entertaining sport sedan with family car room. The turbocharged engine with Lotus designed head put out 224-horsepower from only 2.2-liters. Ballance shafts allowed the motor to pull smoothly to its 6500-RPM redline. A 5-speed manual was the only transmission. The chassis generated good grip, but pitched and rolled while doing it. Limited production and high performance should make the R/T collectible.

✚ **FOR** Performance • Interior room • Short stopping distances with anti-lock brakes • Low production

▬ **AGAINST** Plain looks • Lack of refinement • Lots of plastic in the interior

PRODUCTION
NA

SPECIFICATIONS

Length (in.)	181.2
Weight (lbs)	3089
Wheelbase (in.)	103.5
Price (new)	$17,280-18,674

ENGINES

cid/type	bhp	years
135/dohc I-4[1]	224	1991-92

[1]Turbocharged

PRICES

FAIR	$2000-3500
GOOD	$3500-5000
FINE	$5000-6500
2000-2010 RETURN Still depreciating	

1 9 9 1 - 9 2
DODGE STEALTH R/T TURBO

1991 Stealth R/T Turbo coupe

Dodge variant of the somewhat more aggressive-appearing but essentially identical Mitsubishi 3000GT; both of those were stretched versions of Mitsubishi's Eclipse platform. Three Stealth models shared a 3.0-liter V-6, variously rated at 164, 222, and (for the Turbo) 300 bhp. Standing-start acceleration was very quick, less than 5 seconds, but the turbo was slow to kick in and the car's steering felt numb and artificial. 2+2 seating was more a concession to insurance rates than to practicality, and removed the Stealth from the ranks of "pure" sports cars.

✚ **FOR** Acceleration • Handling and roadholding • Quiet for the class

▬ **AGAINST** Fuel economy • Turbo lag • Numb steering

PRODUCTION
NA

SPECIFICATIONS

Length (in.)	179.1
Weight (lbs)	3793
Wheelbase (in.)	97.2
Price (new)	$29,267-30,855

ENGINES

cid/type	bhp	years
181/dohc V-6[1]	300	1991-92

[1]Turbocharged

PRICES

FAIR	$3000-4500
GOOD	$4500-8000
FINE	$8000-12,500
2000-2010 RETURN Still depreciating	

1992
DODGE DAYTONA IROC R/T

1992 Daytona IROC R/T coupe

The 224-horsepower motor from the Dodge Spirit R/T was too good to be used in just one car. In '92 Dodge dropped it in the Daytona IROC. Turbo charging, dual overhead cams, and a head designed by Lotus raised power output to 100-horsepower per liter. That power in a 3,134 pound car produced sub-15 second quarter mile times. Using that power was tricky. That much power in a light front-wheel drive car produced large amounts of torque steer and wheel spin. The standard Daytona suspension was stiffened. While that produced high cornering grip on smooth roads, the ride was punishing. For those who wanted to feel as if they were driving a race car from the International Race of Street Champions, the IROC R/T was just the thing. For most people it was a hard car to live with on daily basis. The Daytona had been around since 1984 and would go out of production after '93. The IROC R/T was its final glory.

FOR Fast • Rare • Hatchback convenience

AGAINST Harsh ride • Torque steer • Poor traction in rain and snow

PRODUCTION

NA

SPECIFICATIONS

Length (in.)	179.8
Weight (lbs)	3134
Wheelbase (in.)	97.2
Price (new)	$18,532-19,215

ENGINES

cid/type	bhp	years
135/dohc I-4[1]	224	1992-93

[1]Turbocharged

PRICES

FAIR	$2000-3000
GOOD	$3000-4000
FINE	$4000-5500
2000-2010 RETURN Still depreciating	

1992-2000
DODGE VIPER RT/10

1992 Viper RT/10 roadster

Although it offered increasing levels of creature comforts over the years, the limited-production Viper (only 200 in its debut year) remained true to its original role: a brutish, gorgeous, nasty sports car designed to keep pace with the world's best. Viper never was as refined as its supercar counterparts, but because it cost a mere fraction of a Lamborghini Diablo or a Ferrari F-40, few buyers complained. In fact, most reveled in the car's noisy, cranky nature and its blatant refusal to be polite. Heart-stoppingly quick, thanks to an 8.0-liter V-10 rated at 400 bhp when introduced and uprated to 450 by the time of the 2000 model; torque rating for the latter model was a prodigious 490 pounds/feet. Six-speed stick was mandatory from the beginning. Drop-dead gorgeous GTS fastback coupe variant bowed for '96.

FOR Neck-snapping acceleration • Handling and roadholding • Sheer presence • Relative rarity

AGAINST Noise • Fuel economy • Tiring to drive • Insurance costs

PRODUCTION

1992 200 **1993** 300 (approx.)

SPECIFICATIONS

Length (in.)	175.1
Weight (lbs)	3445-3487
Wheelbase (in.)	96.2
Price (new)	$50,000-67,225

ENGINES

cid/type	bhp	years
488/ohv V-10	400	1992-95
488/ohv V-10	415	1996
488/ohv V-10	450	1997-2000

PRICES

FAIR	$20,000-30,000
GOOD	$30,000-45,000
FINE	$45,000-60,000

Used car market and model year determines actual value within these ranges.
2000-2010 RETURN Depreciating slowly

1996
DODGE RAM INDY 500 EDITION

Most automakers issue commemorative editions of their Indianapolis 500 pace cars. Dodge issued a special edition of the Indy official service truck instead. The Dodge Viper GTS (pace car for 1996), was already a limited-production special edition to begin with. The "big-rig" inspired styling introduced on the '94 Ram lifted Dodge from an invisible player in the full-size truck market to major force. For the Indy special Dodge painted its short-bed regular cab Brilliant Blue with twin white stripes. A dealer-installed decal kit came with each truck. The decals could be used to duplicate the look of

1996 Ram Indy pickup

the actual speedway service truck—or be left off all together. All Indy 500 Special Edition commemorative trucks started with top-line Laramie SLT package with 5.9-liter V-8 and 4-speed automatic transmission. In normal tune the 5.9-liter put out 230-horsepower. The Indy version was modified to produce 245 horses. The Indy 500 models also added chrome-tipped sport tuned exhaust, Dodge graphic across the top of the windshield, and wide 275/60R17 tires on alloy wheels. The Dodge Ram was a desirable truck to start with. The Indy special edition package and extra horses should make it more desirable.

☐ FOR Well-executed Indy 500 graphics • Good looking truck to begin with • Has extra power to go with graphics

☐ AGAINST Not as rare as some special editions • Poor gas mileage

PRODUCTION

6000 (approx.)

SPECIFICATIONS

Length (in.)	204.1
Weight (lbs)	4009
Wheelbase (in.)	118.7
Price (new)	$20,233

ENGINES

cid/type	bhp	years
360/ohv V-8	245	1996

PRICES

Determined by used car market
2000-2010 RETURN Still depreciating

1997-2000
DODGE VIPER GTS

1997 Viper GTS coupe

A coupe version of the RT/10 roadster, the GTS offered many refinements. The hardtop made the Viper more rigid and quieter. Unlike the roadster, the GTS was weatherproof. A more powerful engine, improved suspension, adjustable pedals, and roll-up windows were later carried over to the

RT/10. The styling was inspired by the Shelby Cobra Daytona and was more aerodynamic than the roadster. Top speed rose to 185. In '99 an ACR (American Club Racer) package was available for those who wanted to race their Vipers on weekends. The package included racing tires and suspension, 5-point seat belt harness, ACR nameplates and graphics, and deleted the air conditioning, radio, and fog lights. About 400 ACR Vipers were sold in '99 and production 250-500 was planned for 2000.

☐ FOR Quieter and more weatherproof than the roadster • Curvacious styling

☐ AGAINST Same as RT/10 roadster

PRODUCTION

1999 400 (approx.)

SPECIFICATIONS

Length (in.)	176.7
Weight (lbs)	3380-3460
Wheelbase (in.)	96.2
Price (new)	$66,000-69,725

ENGINES

cid/type	bhp	years
488/ohv V-10	450	1997-00

PRICES

FAIR	$35,000-45,000
GOOD	$45,000-55,000
FINE	$55,000-65,000

Used car market and model year determines actual value within these ranges.
2000-2010 RETURN Depreciating but slowly.

1956-58
DUAL-GHIA

Conceived by auto transport contractor Eugene Casaroll, who formed Dual Motors in Detroit to build this limited-production convertible based on

Virgil Exner's Dodge Firebomb/Firearrow show cars of the early '50s. When Chrysler decided not to put the basic design into production, Casaroll bought the original Firebomb show car, had it reengineered, and contracted to buy complete Dodge chassis, including the hot D-500 V-8. The plan was to build 150 Dual-Ghias per year. Chassis were shipped to Turin, Italy, where the Ghia coachworks hammered out the steel bodies by hand over aluminum dies. Designer Paul Farago had added extra passenger and cargo space to enhance liveability. Quality was the watchword: body moldings were held in place with chrome-plated brass clips, while the interiors were swathed in genuine Connolly hides. Ghia fitted body to chassis, and the completed assembly was returned to Detroit where Dual Motors installed the drivetrain and the interior trim. Despite all its custom craftsmanship, the D-G was priced less than a contemporary Cadillac Eldorado and Continental Mark II. Hollywood personalities—notably Frank Sinatra, Peter Lawford, and other members of the "Rat Pack"—vied with one another to get on the waiting list. But mounting costs combined with Casaroll's refusal to compromise quality lost the company money on every car. Distinctive and quite fast, it had a top speed of 120 mph according to a contemporary road test. The first-generation D-G venture wound down in 1958.

☐ FOR Exclusivity • Handsome good looks • Strongly built • Excellent performance

☐ AGAINST Very costly now • Body hardware extinct • Multi-piece Italian body seriously rust-prone

PRODUCTION

117 (includes 13 prototypes; two cars were converted to hardtops)

1957 convertible

SPECIFICATIONS

Length (in.)	203.0
Wheelbase (in.)	115.0
Weight (lbs)	3800
Price (new)	$7741

ENGINES

cid/type	bhp	years
315/ohv V-8	230-285	1956-58

PRICES

FAIR	$15,000-25,000
GOOD	$25,000-40,000
FINE	$40,000-55,000

FINE EXAMPLE PRICE HISTORY

1982 $15,000	1987 $30,000
1990 $55,000	1994 $55,000
1982-2000 RETURN 11%	
2000-2010 10%	

1961-63
DUAL-GHIA L6.4

A comeback attempt by Casaroll and company. Built only as a glassy two-door hardtop with new styling by Ghia, though the frontal appearance was quite similar to that of the earlier Dual-Ghia. The model designation relates to the displacement, in liters, of the Chrysler 383-cid wedgehead V-8, but there were fewer Mopar components—including the separate chassis, which was now a special design as Chrysler had switched to unit construction for all its cars except Imperial in 1960. It was twice as costly as its predecessor, and faster but softer riding, with handling not as taut as that of the earlier cars. But svelte good looks made up for a lot, and everybody who was anybody wanted one. Again, however, incredibly high overhead costs plagued the project, and Casaroll called it quits after a mere handful of cars were built. He would go on to play a role in the project that led to a new Stutz, born out of Virgil Exner's proposal for a modern Duesenberg.

+ FOR As for 1956-58 Dual-Ghia, and even more desirable

– AGAINST As for 1956-58 Dual Ghia, but even costlier and harder to find

PRODUCTION

26

SPECIFICATIONS

Length (in.)	210.0
Wheelbase (in.)	115.0
Weight (lbs)	4200
Price (new)	$13,500

ENGINES

cid/type	bhp	years
383/ohv V-8	335	1961-63

PRICES

As per 1956-58 Dual-Ghia.

1930-37
DUESENBERG MODEL J/SJ/SSJ/JN

The undisputed "King of the Classics," announced in 1928 by E.L. Cord and engineered by Fred Duesenberg. It was powered by an exquisite 32-valve Lycoming straight eight with at least 200 horsepower—ads claimed 265—and capable of 90 mph in second gear and about 115 mph in top. Aided by extensive use of weight-saving materials, these mammoths were surprisingly light. Bodywork was anything the customer desired—and could afford—so "standard" examples were few. The supercharged SJ bowed in 1932 with 320 bhp or, with August Duesenberg's "ram's horn" manifolds, a smashing 400 bhp. A stock SJ could hit 104 mph in second and 140 flat-out, and racing great Ab Jenkins recorded 160 mph on one trial lap. Tremendous in size and presence, Duesies nevertheless had balance, precision, and finesse, and were remarkably docile at low speeds. Two short-chassis SJ roadsters, designated SSJ, were built for and purchased by actors Gary Cooper and Clark Gable. The lithe LeGrand bodywork was symbolic more of Gable's personality than Coop's. Both cars have survived. The comparatively plain Model JN appeared in 1935 as a last gasp. An attempt to give a more modern look to an aging design, the JN

was equipped with smaller 17-inch-diameter wheels, skirted fenders, and bullet shaped taillights. E.L. Cord built "the world's finest motor car" with no real plan to make money, and Duesenberg didn't. What killed it, however, was not the Depression but the collapse of Cord's business empire in 1937.

+ FOR Everything (to quote Ken Purdy: "With his mind and his two good hands [Fred Duesenberg] had created something new and good and, in its way, immortal.")

– AGAINST The near-impossible odds of owning one

1935 SSJ roadster (Gary Cooper car)

PRODUCTION

470, incl. 36 Model SJ, 2 Model SSJ, 10 Model JN; total engines: 480 (began late 1928)

SPECIFICATIONS

Length (in.)	NA (variable with body)
Wheelbase (in.)	142.5, 153.5 (JN, lwb J), 125.0 (SSJ)
Weight (lbs)	4800-5200
Price (new)	from $11,000; average $15,000-18,000 depending on body (J chassis $8500)

ENGINES

cid/type	bhp	years
420.0/dohc I-8	265	1930-37
420.0/dohc 1-8[1]	320/400	1932-37

[1] Supercharged

PRICES

Each Model J Duesenberg was custom-bodied and thus different; the cars do not therefore submit to any generalizations about value. The best

1930 J Torpedo Convertible Berline by Murphy

open bodied SJs hit $3.5 million in 1989, while the top closed bodies reached $2 million, but prices have since dropped back by as much as 60%. Caution: owing to complete body replication, there are now more open-bodied Duesenbergs than were built originally, and many of these replica bodies are built to a very high order. This does not disqualify them from consideration, but the origins of any open body should be investigated if not authenticated by the seller. Though Duesenberg prices are (happily) not soaring as they were, they are still blue chip investments.
2000-2010 10%

1958 Citation convertible

The brightest and the best in the debut year of what would turn out to be a flop. The most interesting and luxurious of the '58 Edsel line, it wasn't cheap when new. Despite considerable size and weight, it was quite speedy thanks to a torquey big-block V-8. Sharing its chassis and bodyshell with the '58 Mercury, it also featured a full array of late-'50s gadgetry: "Teletouch" automatic transmission with pushbuttons in the steering wheel hub, a rotating drum speedometer that changed color as speed rose (a throwback to the '30s), and every power accessory then known to the civilized world. The Citation convertible would be the most expensive Edsel ever built, and was also the second lowest in production this year, making it a highly coveted commodity. In all, the Edsel showed that even the best market research can mislead if you don't ask the right questions. "Do we really need another medium-priced car?" was the one Ford should have asked in the first place.

⊞ FOR Looks like no other car on the road • Power • Luxury • Large club following • "Lost cause" panache • Better quality control than on smaller Ford-based Edsels

▣ AGAINST Retains its "loser" image to this day • Styling more panned than praised • Gulps gas • Electrical maladies (particularly those pushbuttons)

PRODUCTION
4d htp 5112 **2d htp** 2535 **conv** 930

SPECIFICATIONS
Length (in.)	218.9
Wheelbase (in.)	124.0
Weight (lbs)	4136-4311
Price (new)	$3535-3801

ENGINES
cid/type	bhp	years
410/ohv V-8	345	1958

PRICES
Conv	
FAIR	$8000-14,000
GOOD	$14,000-19,000
FINE	$19,000-26,500
2d htp	
FAIR	$4000-7000
GOOD	$7000-11,000
FINE	$11,000-14,500
4d htp	
FAIR	$2500-5500
GOOD	$5500-7500
FINE	$7500-10,000

FINE CONVERTIBLE PRICE HISTORY
1982 $7500	**1990** $30,000
1994 $25,000	**1998** $30,000
1982-2000 RETURN 8%	
2000-2010 5%	

1958
EDSEL CORSAIR

This was the first step down on the Edsel price-and-luxury ladder for '58, a slightly detrimmed version of the Citation. Aside from front fender script, it was marked externally by absence of the contrasting color insert used on the Citation's concave rear fender scallop, or "spear" as some prefer to describe it. There was no convertible offered, but the Corsair was based on the same Mercury platform and powered by the larger of Edsel's two V-8s.

⊞ FOR As for 1958 Citation, but more affordable

▣ AGAINST As for 1958 Citation

PRODUCTION
4d htp 5880 **2d htp** 3312

SPECIFICATIONS
Length (in.)	218.9
Wheelbase (in.)	124.0
Weight (lbs)	4134-4235
Price (new)	$3346-3425

ENGINES
cid/type	bhp	years
410/ohv V-8	345	1958

PRICES
2d htp	
FAIR	$3000-5500
GOOD	$5500-8000
FINE	$8000-12,000
4d htp	
FAIR	$2500-4500
GOOD	$4500-6500
FINE	$6500-9500

FINE 2D HARDTOP PRICE HISTORY
1982 $3600	**1990** $12,500
1994 $13,000	**1998** $14,000
1982-2000 RETURN 7%	
2000-2010 7%	

1958
EDSEL PACER

The more expensive and better equipped of Edsel's two junior series for '58, based on the 118-inch-wheelbase (116 for wagons) platform introduced with the 1957 Ford. Shared basic styling—including the much maligned "toilet-seat grille"—and interior design with the Citation and Corsair, but had a notably lighter "greenhouse." The lineup included the Bermuda wagon with simulated wood side trim *á la* Ford's Country Squire; the

1958 Corsair hardtop coupe

166

1958 Pacer convertible

nine-passenger version was the rarest of the '58 Edsels. Like the cheaper companion Ranger series, it was available only with a 361 V-8 based on Ford's FE-series Y-Block engine, and—with its light body—was probably the most agile Edsel. Also like the Ranger, it was built alongside Fords, mainly at the firm's Louisville assembly plant where quality control was more lax than on the senior cars built by Lincoln-Mercury.

⊞ FOR Cheaper than Citation/Corsair • Speedy • "Distinctive" looks

⊟ AGAINST "Distinctive" looks • Less power and sheer luxury than the bigger models • Somewhat thirsty • Construction quality bordered on slipshod

PRODUCTION

2d htp 6139 **4d sdn** 6083 **4d htp** 4959 **conv** 1876 **Bermuda 6P wgn** 1456 **Bermuda 9P wgn** 779

SPECIFICATIONS

Length (in.)	213.1 (wagons: 205.5)
Wheelbase (in.)	118.0 (wagons: 116.0)
Weight (lbs)	3773-3919
Price (new)	$2375-3247

ENGINES

cid/type	bhp	years
361/ohv V-8	303	1958

PRICES

Conv	
FAIR	$6000-12,000
GOOD	$12,000-18,000
FINE	$18,000-24,000
(Deduct 60% for 2d htp, 65% for 4dr htp.)	

FINE CONVERTIBLE PRICE HISTORY

1982 $6600		1990 $22,500	
1994 $20,000		1998 $25,000	
1982-2000 RETURN 8%			
2000-2010 8%			

1958 EDSEL RANGER

The bottom end of the '58 Edsel line, it used the shorter wheelbase and smaller—though still plenty big

1958 Ranger coupe

enough—engine of the Pacer. It had the same basic styling, but simplified side trim and interior decor. Body styles unique to this series were the two-door sedan and Roundup wagon.

⊞ FOR Affordable—and likely to remain so • Others as for other 1958s

⊟ AGAINST The slowest appreciation rate among '58 Edsels • The least exciting, too

PRODUCTION

4d sdn 6576 **2d htp** 5546 **2d sdn** 4615 **4d htp** 3077 **Villager 6P wgn** 2294 **Villager 9P wgn** 978 **Roundup 2d wgn** 963

SPECIFICATIONS

Length (in.)	213.1 (wagons: 205.5)
Wheelbase (in.)	118.0 (wagons: 116.0)
Weight (lbs)	3729-3900
Price (new)	$2519-2990

ENGINES

cid/type	bhp	years
361/ohv V-8	303	1958

PRICES

2d htp	
FAIR	$2250-4500
GOOD	$4500-6000
FINE	$6000-9500
(Deduct 20% for 4d htp, 40% for sdns.)	

FINE 2D HARDTOP PRICE HISTORY

1982 $3500		1990 $12,000
1994 $12,000		1998 $12,000
1982-2000 RETURN 6%		
2000-2010 6%		

1959 EDSEL CORSAIR

1959 Corsair convertible

The uppermost series for the second year of Dearborn's million-dollar baby. Now based exclusively on the Ford chassis and bodyshell, the Edsel lineup was consolidated around three series—Ranger, Corsair, and wagons—the last now broken out separately. The pre-ordained facelift was shared by all: a more unified grille still dominated by the central "horse collar" motif, restyled taillights, and revised side trim. As a result, the '59s looked chromier than the '58s. Meanwhile, prices were slashed in an effort to attract customers back into near-deserted showrooms. The costliest model, the Corsair convertible, listed at just $3072, versus the $3801 price tag of the more-or-less comparable '58 Citation. Ford's 332 V-8 was standard for the Corsair, with the 361-cid unit from the 1958 smaller models optional across the board (the 410 was gone). There was also a reduction in gimmickry, such as the replacement of the "Cyclops-Eye" speedometer and the troublesome Tele-Touch transmission pushbuttons by a conventional column lever control.

⊞ FOR Less unique appearance than the '58, but possibly more successful • Most models still in good supply

⊟ AGAINST Less distinctively "Edsel" than the '58s • Won't ever appreciate as much, either, though convertibles aren't all that cheap now

PRODUCTION

4d sdn 3301 **2d htp** 2315 **4d htp** 1694 **conv** 1343

SPECIFICATIONS

Length (in.)	210.9
Wheelbase (in.)	120.0
Weight (lbs)	3696-3790
Price (new)	$2812-3072

ENGINES

cid/type	bhp	years
332/ohv V-8	225	1959

361/ohv V-8	303	1959

PRICES

A third less than 1958 Edsel Corsair.

1959 EDSEL RANGER HARDTOPS

1959 Ranger hardtop coupe

The '59 Ranger four-door sedan set the Edsel production record for a single model—12,814 units. This, of course, makes it comparatively plentiful today. But it's the scarcer hardtops that should concern the collector. Less elaborately trimmed and equipped than the Corsairs, they were available with a delete-option six, Ford's well-known 223-cid unit, as well as a standard 292 V-8. The Corsair's standard 332-cid powerplant and the carryover 361 V-8 were also offered, though seldom ordered. Most comments for the '59 Corsair also apply here.

✛ FOR As for '59 Corsair, but priced less

▬ AGAINST As for '59 Corsair, but slower to appreciate and less luxurious

PRODUCTION

2d htp 5474 **4d htp** 2352

SPECIFICATIONS

Length (in.)	210.9
Wheelbase (in.)	120.0
Weight (lbs)	3591-3682
Price (new)	$2691-2756

ENGINES

cid/type	bhp	years
223/ohv I-6	145	1959
292/ohv V-8	200	1959
332/ohv V-8	225	1959
361/ohv V-8	303	1959

PRICES

As per 1958 Edsel Ranger hardtops.
2000-2010 RETURN 5%

1960 EDSEL RANGER

The last of the Edsels, and obviously even more closely related to this

1960 Ranger convertible

year's Ford, with which it shared a brand-new bodyshell. Though much more conventional in appearance, the '60 was short-lived—by now it was too late to save the Edsel. Production ceased after only 3000 units had been built, making the '60s the rarest—and therefore the most desirable—Edsels, at least to some. The Ranger was one of two series, Villager wagons the other. Front-end styling abandoned the much-joked-about "Olds-sucking-a-lemon" vertical grille motif in favor of a horizontal split grille, entirely too similar to the '59 Pontiac's, though this was purely a coincidence. Heavy chrome accents appeared on a full-length crease along the upper bodysides, and a drooping thinner chrome molding was used below. At the rear, twin vertical oval pods housed taillights and backup lamps on either side (also seen on the mid-1960 Mercury Comet in a canted position), and looked distinctive if a bit out of place on a rear panel clearly designed for the Ford's horizontal half-moon units. The six was still a no-cost extra, while a 352 V-8 was a $58 extra above the 292 V-8.

✛ FOR Last of the line • Very rare • Strong appreciation

▬ AGAINST Little real distinction • Certain parts in short supply • Beware convertible "reproductions" based on the '60 Ford Sunliner ragtop—there's more than a few out there

PRODUCTION

4d sdn 1288 **2d sdn** 777 **2d htp** 295 **4d htp** 135 **conv** 76

SPECIFICATIONS

Length (in.)	216.4
Wheelbase (in.)	120.0
Weight (lbs.)	3601-3836
Price (new)	$2643-3000

ENGINES

cid/type	bhp	years
223/ohv I-6	145	1960
292/ohv V-8	185	1960
352/ohv V-8	300	1960

PRICES

Conv
FAIR	$7500-13,000
GOOD	$13,000-19,000
FINE	$19,000-27,000

2d htp
FAIR	$3000-5500
GOOD	$5500-8000
FINE	$8000-12,000

Sdns & 4d htp: Deduct 50% from 2d htp prices.

FINE CONVERTIBLE PRICE HISTORY

1982 $7000		**1990** $25,000	
1994 $22,500		**1998** $28,000	
1982-2000 RETURN 8%			
2000-2010 8%			

1960 EDSEL VILLAGER WAGONS

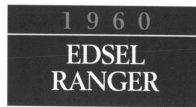

1960 Villager wagon

Edsel wagons are not as desirable as other body styles, but these two 1960 Villagers are so rare as to be an exception. With less than 300 built, they are hot in Edsel circles, and probably undervalued. They shared basic styling and mechanicals with the '60 Ranger models (and '60 Fords), so comments about them also apply here.

✛ FOR Rarity • Interesting styling (a

Ford that took pep pills?) • Others as for 1960 Ranger

◼ AGAINST As for 1960 Ranger

PRODUCTION

6P 216 **9P** 59

SPECIFICATIONS

Length (in.)	214.8
Wheelbase (in.)	120.0
Weight (lbs)	4029-4046
Price (new)	$2989-3072

ENGINES

cid/type	bhp	years
223/ohv I-6	145	1960
292/ohv V-8	185	1960
352/ohv V-8	300	1960

PRICES

FAIR	$1800-3000
GOOD	$3000-4500
FINE	$4500-7000

FINE EXAMPLE PRICE HISTORY

1982 $3100 **1990** $8500
1994 $10,000 **1998** $10,000
1982-2000 RETURN 5%
2000-2010 5%

1 9 6 5 - 6 9
EXCALIBUR
SERIES I

First, most successful, and longest-lived of the American "neoclassics" that started cropping up in the '60s, and thus the only one worthy of collector interest. Conceived by Brooks Stevens as the Studebaker SS—a "contemporary classic" on a Lark Daytona convertible chassis shown at the 1964 New York Auto Show. When faltering Studebaker withdrew its endorsement at the last minute, Stevens showed the SS himself and was inundated with orders, hence his

decision to proceed with independent production that he eventually turned over to sons David and William. Initial two-seat SSK roadster was a handsome brute in the image of the late-'20s Mercedes SSK, one of Brooks' favorite cars. A bulkier standard roadster and a four-seat phaeton were added in 1966, when power was switched to Chevrolet's 327 small-block V-8. Fiberglass bodies would be a feature on all Excaliburs; Series I cars continued with a modified Lark chassis, like the showmobile. Among the fastest and best handling of the Excalibur breed, but traffic-stopping style is why first owners included many rich-and-famous.

➕ FOR Exhilarating performance (0-60 in under 5 seconds) • High fun quotient • Tasteful, crowd-pleasing looks • Competent handling • SSK a magnificent replica, though not line-for-line exact • Small but devoted club

◼ AGAINST Rather spartan • Collector bias against "replicars" • Parts/service support iffy now (see 1987-97 Series V)

PRODUCTION

1965 SSK rdstr 56 **1966 rdstr/SSK rdstr** 87 **phaeton** 3 **1967 rdstr/SSK rdstr** 38 **phaeton** 33 **1968 rdstr/SSK rdstr** 37 **phaeton** 20 **1969 rdstr/SSK rdstr** 47 **phaeton** 44

SPECIFICATIONS

Length (in.)	170.0
Wheelbase (in.)	109.0
Weight (lbs)	2100-2600
Price (new)	$7250-10,000

ENGINES

cid/type	bhp[1]	years
289/ohv V-8	290	1965
327/ohv V-8	300-435	1966-69
[1]SAE gross		

PRICES

SSK	
FAIR	$12,000-15,000
GOOD	$15,000-19,000
FINE	$19,000-28,000
Others	
FAIR	$7000-11,000
GOOD	$11,000-16,000
FINE	$16,000-24,000

FINE SSK PRICE HISTORY

1982 $20,000 **1990** $35,000
1994 $25,000 **1998** $29,000
1982-2000 RETURN 2%
2000-2010 5%

1 9 7 0 - 7 4
EXCALIBUR
SERIES II

Continuation of Brooks Stevens' "contemporary classic," now under the auspices of his two sons operating as SS Automobiles, Inc. The major change for Series II was David Stevens' new purpose-designed box-section frame with a central X-member, two-inch longer wheelbase, plus suspension components and all-disc brakes borrowed from the contemporary Corvette. The earlier 327 Chevy V-8 was replaced by its more emissions-amenable 350 enlargement, and Turbo Hydra-Matic was newly offered in addition to the four-speed manual. Model choices were unchanged and the basic styling left intact, but equipment was far more complete, running to heating/air conditioning, tilt steering wheel, power steering and brakes, Positraction, leather upholstery, chrome wire wheels and luggage rack, AM/FM stereo, even air horns and twin sidemount spares. Prices were hiked to suit, but the Excalibur remained a relative bargain. Sales were little changed, not for want of demand, but because the Stevenses desired to limit production so as not to dilute their market.

➕ FOR As for 1965-69 Series I, plus superior ride and handling • Much better equipped

◼ AGAINST As for 1965-69 Series I save equipment

PRODUCTION

1970 rdstr/SSK rdstr 11 **phaeton** 26 **1971** 0 **1972 rdstr** 13 **phaeton** 52 **1973 rdstr** 22 **phaeton** 100 **1974 rdstr** 26 **phaeton** 92

SPECIFICATIONS

Length (in.)	172.0
Wheelbase (in.)	111.0
Weight (lbs)	2750-3000
Price (new)	$12,000-17,000

ENGINES

cid/type	bhp[1]	years

1965 Series I roadster

350/ohv V-8	300	1970-74
[1]SAE gross		

PRICES

FAIR	$8000-12,000
GOOD	$12,000-17,000
FINE	$17,000-27,000

FINE EXAMPLE PRICE HISTORY

1982 $12,000		**1990** $25,000
1994 $22,300		**1998** $24,500
1982-2000 RETURN 5%		
2000-2010 5%		

1975-79
EXCALIBUR SERIES III

1975-79 Series III phaeton.

The last Excaliburs directly descended from Brooks Stevens' 1964 Studebaker SS. Still the same great echo of a late-'20s Mercedes SSK, save for new intregral "clamshell" fenders on both roadster and phaeton. Chassis as per Series II, except for an inch-longer wheelbase and a new bolt-on front sub-frame devised by David Stevens for simpler, cheaper accident repair. Tightening emissions limits prompted another switch in Chevy engines, this time to the big-block 454, though 1978's added fuel-economy mandates necessitated a return to the small-block 350 for valedictory '79 models. The Series III would prove the

most popular Excalibur, with the more practical four-seat phaeton handily outselling the two-seat roadster, as usual. Standard equipment level still very high, performance still decent despite less real horsepower, handling still good despite the much heavier engine.

➕ **FOR** As for Series I and II, plus more readily available

➖ **AGAINST** As for Series I and II, but higher numbers, so prices slightly depressed

PRODUCTION

1975 rdstr 8 **phaeton** 82 **1976 rdstr** 11 **phaeton** 173 **1977 rdstr** 15 **phaeton** 222 **1978 rdstr** 15 **phaeton** 248 **1979 rdstr** 27 **phaeton** 340

SPECIFICATIONS

Length (in.)	175.0
Wheelbase (in.)	112.0
Weight (lbs)	4350
Price (new)	$18,900-28,600

ENGINES

cid/type	bhp[1]	years
454/ohv V-8	215	1975-78
350/ohv V-8	180	1979
[1]SAE net		

PRICES

As per 1970-74 Excalibur Series II plus 10%.

1980-86
EXCALIBUR SERIES IV

The first new-design Excaliburs since the original: much longer, heavier, and more luxury tourers than "classic sports cars." The two-seat roadster and four-seat phaeton were as before, but with first-ever roll-up windows, power soft-tops, and optional liftoff hardtops; the roadster also

gained a raffish rumble seat. Sleek new David Stevens styling paralleled the evolution of the Mercedes SS/SSK, which had inspired earlier models, into the late-'30s 500/540K. The chassis was scaled up to match the bigger bodies—wheelbase grew more than two feet—but emissions and fuel-economy concerns dictated using Chevy's small 305 V-8, linked to a converter-lockup automatic transmission, which combined with the much-increased weight for much-reduced performance. That, plus the start of a severe recession, depressed sales even as inflation forced higher prices, yet the Stevenses faced burdensome new overhead costs from a heavy revamping of their suburban Milwaukee plant to improve quality. The result was a steadily worsening situation that forced the brothers to file for bankruptcy in mid-1986. Ironically, this came just after Excalibur marked its 20th Anniversary with its first commemorative models: 50 roadsters and 50 phaetons bearing two-tone exteriors with chrome sweepspears and pewter plaques, plus Connolly leather interiors with wood trim. Happily, the firm was soon sold, enabling production of similar Series V models. Unhappily, this salvation would prove only temporary.

➕ **FOR** Still a great ego trip • Smoother, quieter, and more luxurious than earlier Excaliburs • Workmanship somewhat better, too

➖ **AGAINST** Weighty extra bulk • Tepid acceleration • Ponderous handling • Limited rear-seat and cargo space • Makeshift engineering solutions in places

PRODUCTION

1980 phaeton 93 **1981 phaeton** 199 **rdstr** 36 **1982 phaeton** 152 **rdstr** 60 **1983-86** NA

SPECIFICATIONS

Length (in.)	202.0
Wheelbase (in.)	125.0
Weight (lbs)	4300-4400
Price (new)	$37,700-62,000

ENGINES

cid/type	bhp[1]	years
305/ohv V-8	155	1980-87
[1]SAE net		

PRICES

FAIR	$17,000-22,000
GOOD	$22,000-30,000
FINE	$30,000-42,000

FINE EXAMPLE PRICE HISTORY

Depreciated through the 1990s; prices presently stable.
2000-2010 RETURN 3%

1980-84 Series IV phaeton

1987-97
EXCALIBUR SERIES V

1989 Series V phaeton

The most recent Excaliburs—and the last. Built under the auspices of Henry Warner, president of the Acquisition Company of Illinois, who bought the Excalibur Automobile Corporation from the Stevens brothers and reorganized it as Excalibur Marketing Corp (EMC). By early 1987, Series IV roadsters and phaetons were again trickling out of Excalibur's Milwaukee-area plant as Series V models differing chiefly in a more powerful 350 Chevy V-8 option to redress the weak performance of the standard 305. At midyear, EMC revealed a new 144-inch-wheelbase four-door Touring Sedan at the elevated $65,650 base price applied to both open Series Vs, with which it shared frontal styling. Also announced was an even more extravagant 204-inch-wheelbase "grand limousine," conceived earlier, along with the Sedan, by David Stevens as a sales-building line extension. At least one of each was built. But none of this served to attract the capital needed to offset mounting debts in an economy again gone slack, nor did a three-year, $9-million lease deal with a Chicago concern involving some 150 cars. As a result, Excalibur went bankrupt a second time, and production ceased in June 1990. The firm was later sold amid charges of odometer fraud, installing some used parts, and failure to meet federal passive-restraint requirements. In 1991, Michael Timmer, who had purchased the firm for $1.33 million in November 1991 and spent about $1 million on plant improvements. The firm was bankrupt before production could resume. Udo and Jens Geitlinger bought the firm and started production in 1993. A revised Series III, called the Limited Edition, was also produced. Car production ended in 1997, although the firm continued with other projects.

FOR As for 1980-86 Series IV, plus even greater scarcity • Better potential performance with the optional 350 V-8

AGAINST As for 1980-86 Series IV

PRODUCTION

1993 4 **1994** 2 **1995** 3

SPECIFICATIONS

Length (in.)	204.0 (rdstr, phaeton), 224 (Touring Sedan)
Wheelbase (in.)	124.0 (rdstr, phaeton), 144.0 (Touring Sedan)
Weight (lbs)	4400-4800
Price (new)	$65,650-104,595

ENGINES

cid/type	bhp[1]	years
305/ohv V-8	170	1988-90
350/ohv V-8	225[2]	1988-90
[1]SAE net	[2]estimated	

PRICES

Depreciation slowed in late 1990s.
2000-2010 RETURN even

1954-59
FACEL VEGA FVS & FV

Classy Franco-American hybrid GT. Power by Chrysler, designed and built by Facel Metallon, previously known as a body supplier to other manufacturers. Styling was probably influenced by the Simca Sport and other cars built by Facel in the late '40s and early '50s. Engineered in limited-production Italian style, with a large-tube fabricated chassis carrying independent front suspension and a conventional live axle rear end. The separate bodyshells were built by Facel. Costly, but very fast thanks to Chrysler Hemi-head V-8s, which were supplied with increased displacement in 1956 and again in '58. Top speed was at least 130 mph, more on later models with the larger engines. Usually recognized by a distinctive "face" with a vertical eggcrate grille flanked by oval head/parking lamp clusters, and usually rode on wire wheels. Most FVs were thin-pillar two-door coupes, but a few convertibles were also constructed.

FOR Individual French styling • Performance • Reliable Detroit engines • Low-production appeal

AGAINST Heavy and thirsty • Few parts available now • Drum brakes • Only modest appreciation

PRODUCTION

352 (incl. 11 conv)

SPECIFICATIONS

Length (in.)	179.0-181.0
Wheelbase (in.)	103.5/104.7
Weight (lbs)	3585-4105
Price (new)	$7000 U.S. (Vega); $7500/9750 (FV)

ENGINES

cc/type (cid)	bhp[1]	years
4528/ohv V-8 (276)	170	1954-55
4768/ohv V-8 (291)	180	1954-55
5407/ohv V-8 (330)	250	1956-57
5801/ohv V-8 (354)	325	1958-59
[1]SAE gross		

PRICES

FAIR	$8000-15,000
GOOD	$15,000-25,000
FINE	$25,000-35,000

FINE EXAMPLE PRICE HISTORY

1982 $7500		**1987** $30,000	
1990 $50,000		**1994** $35,000	
1982-2000 RETURN 11%			
2000-2010 5%			

1957 FVS hardtop coupe

1 9 5 7 - 6 4
FACEL VEGA EXCELLENCE

1959 Excellence hardtop sedan

A long-wheelbase four-door hardtop derivative of the FV-series coupe, with standard automatic transmission and Chrysler V-8 power. Styling was an interesting blend of then-current Detroit and European themes, including the formal Facel "face," wraparound windshield, and rear-hinged back doors. A very heavy car both in appearance and on the scale. Engine displacement and output were generally the same as for other Facel models of the period. Another very low-production, almost limousine-type model intended more as a car of state than a private owner-driver vehicle.

FOR As for 1954-59 FVS, plus greater rarity and unique body style

AGAINST As for 1954-59 FVS, plus trouble-prone bodywork

PRODUCTION
156

SPECIFICATIONS

Length (in.)	207.0
Wheelbase (in.)	125.0
Weight (lbs)	4315
Price (new)	NA

ENGINES

cc/type (cid)	bhp[1]	years
5407/ohv V-8 (330)	250	1957
5801/ohv V-8 (354)	325	1958-59
6276/ohv V-8 (383)	360	1959-64

[1]SAE gross

PRICES

FAIR	$5000-10,000
GOOD	$10,000-15,000
FINE	$15,000-25,000

FINE EXAMPLE PRICE HISTORY

1982 $7500	**1987** $22,500
1990 $32,500	**1994** $25,000
1982-2000 RETURN 9%	
2000-2010 8%	

1 9 5 9 - 6 2
FACEL VEGA HK500

1959 HK500 hardtop coupe

A rebodied version of the original FV-series Facel Vega with a larger Chrysler V-8 engine. Notable for having a full wraparound windshield in the best Detroit style, but otherwise quite Italian looking. More massive and impressive than the FV, and probably more controllable due to standard power steering and four-wheel Dunlop disc brakes. The HK500 engine was Chrysler's wedgehead 383-cid unit, able to push this hefty GT to a top speed of 140 mph. Chrysler's TorqueFlite automatic transmission was offered as an option to the French Pont-a-Mousson four-speed manual gearbox (also offered as an option on the 1960 Chrysler 300-F). Identification points include HK500 script on the trunklid and stacked quad headlamps.

FOR As for 1954-59 FVS

AGAINST As for 1954-59 FVS, but better brakes

PRODUCTION
490

SPECIFICATIONS

Length (in.)	181.0
Wheelbase (in.)	105.0
Weight (lbs)	4035
Price (new)	NA

ENGINES

cid/type	bhp[1]	years
383/ohv V-8	360	1959-62

[1]SAE gross

PRICES

FAIR	$8000-15,000
GOOD	$15,000-25,000
FINE	$25,000-35,000

FINE EXAMPLE PRICE HISTORY

1982 $7500	**1987** $30,000
1990 $50,000	**1994** $35,000
1982-2000 RETURN 11%	
2000-2010 5%	

1 9 6 2 - 6 4
FACEL VEGA FACEL II/III

1962 II hardtop coupe

The second complete restyle on the original FV-series Facel chassis, and successor to the HK500. Tubular chassis construction, a live rear axle, four-wheel disc brakes, and the Chrysler 383 V-8 were all continued. The more square-cut body lines were set off by vertical quad headlamps covered by bulging lenses. A taller, non-wrapped windshield and slimmer roof pillars were also featured. Top speed was now up to about 150 mph, making this a real Ferrari competitor in its day. However, Facel went bankrupt during 1964, a result of too-few sales and high tooling costs for the smaller four-cylinder Facellia model that didn't prove successful.

FOR As for FVS and HK500 models, plus last of the line, most developed, probably the best looking • Great rarity

AGAINST As for FVS and HK500 models

PRODUCTION
180

SPECIFICATIONS

Length (in.)	185.5
Wheelbase (in.)	105.0
Weight (lbs)	4035
Price (new)	NA

ENGINES

cid/type	bhp	years
383/ohv V-8	355/390[1]	1962-64

[1]SAE gross, automatic/manual transmission

PRICES

FAIR	$7000-18,000
GOOD	$18,000-28,000
FINE	$28,000-45,000

FINE EXAMPLE PRICE HISTORY

1982 $8500	**1990** $75,000
1994 $45,000	**1998** $45,000
1982-2000 RETURN 11%	
2000-2010 10%	

PRICES

See remarks under 1948-51 Ferrari 166.
2000-2010 RETURN 10%

1951-55
FERRARI TYPE 340/342/375 AMERICA

1953 342 America coupe

A new Ferrari combination: Type 166/195/212 chassis engineering plus the more massive long-block V-12 engine designed by Aurelio Lampredi and first raced in 1950. Very fast, and built in extremely limited quantity with custom Italian bodywork. The top speed capability on most examples was in the region of 140 mph.

FOR As for 166/195/212

AGAINST As for 166/195/212, plus virtually unobtainable parts for "Lampredi" engines

PRODUCTION

Type 340 22 **Type 342** 6 **Type 375** 12

SPECIFICATIONS

Length (in.)	approx. 170.0 (variable with body style)
Wheelbase (in.)	104.3 (Type 340/342);

1948-51
FERRARI TYPE 166

1950 Type 166 MM Barchetta roadster

Ferrari's first road car following the 166 Sports of 1947, and the model that established the firm's design pattern for the next 10 years. Major highlights included an oval-section large-tube chassis, independent front suspension, live rear axle, and the first of the legendary "Colombo" single-cam V-12 engines. Bodywork was supplied to order by Italian coachbuilders such as Vignale, Ghia, and Pinin Farina, never Ferrari itself, on a choice of two wheelbases. At this time, the firm wasn't really interested in selling road cars, so all these 166s were essentially hand-built, and not far removed from Ferrari's racing machines. Rarity, Italian style, and status as Ferrari's first "production" series are the main attractions for collectors.

FOR Rarity • First "production" Ferrari • Simplest type of Ferrari engineering • High club and collector interest • Strong appreciation

AGAINST Body parts no longer available, most other parts nearly gone • Less performance than expected • Very expensive • Hard to find

PRODUCTION

38

SPECIFICATIONS

Length (in.)	146.2 (variable with body)
Wheelbase (in.)	98.4/103.1 (per customer choice)
Weight (lbs)	2000 (average)
Price (new)	NA

ENGINES

cc/type (cid)	bhp	years
1995/sohc V-12 (122)	110	1948-51

PRICES

General note: The purchase of a Ferrari requires expert assistance and exacting market advice; prices change so rapidly as to be obsolete from the moment of publication—and they don't always go up. For latest pricing information two sources are outstanding: the Ferrari Market Letter, telephone (770) 381-1993; and the CPI Value Guide, telephone (301) 317-4228.
2000-2010 RETURN 10%

1948-53
FERRARI TYPE 195/212

1950 195S Italy coupe

Larger-engine derivatives of the 166 Inter offered in a greater array of coachbuilt body styles. Most were created for touring or sports-racing use, and all were two-seaters. Typical top-end speed was 110 mph for the 195s and 120 for the 212s.

FOR As for 1948-51 Type 166, though not the first road-going Ferraris

AGAINST As for 1948-51 Type 166

PRODUCTION

195 Series 25 **212 Series** 80 (est.)

SPECIFICATIONS

Length (in.)	146.2 (variable with body)
Wheelbase (in.)	98.4/103.1 (per customer choice)
Weight (lbs)	approx. 2100
Price (new)	NA

ENGINES

cc/type (cid)	bhp	years
2340/ohc V-12 (143)[1]	130[2]	1948-53
2562/ohc V-12 (156)[3]	140/170[3]	1948-53

1952 212 Export roadster

Weight (lbs)	110.2 (Type 375) 2650 (average)
Price (new)	NA

ENGINES

cc/type (cid)	bhp[1]	years
4101/ohc V-12 (250)[2]	220	1951-55
4522/ohc V-12 (276)[3]	300	1951-55

[1]Net [2]Type 340/342 [3]Type 375

PRICES

See remarks under 1948-51 Ferrari 166.
2000-2010 RETURN 10%

1954-55
FERRARI TYPE 250 EUROPA

1955 250 SWB Europa coupe

The final development of the Type 166 platform, this time with a smaller version of the big Lampredi engine, the only Ferrari 250 to use this type. With suitable gearing, top speed could be as high as 130 mph. Again, Italian coachbuilders provided sleekly styled bodies. Pinin Farina supplied most in the form of a high-waisted semi-fastback coupe, but some cabriolets came from Vignale. Nearly all Europas were sold in the U.S.

✚ **FOR** As for Type 166/195/212, plus distinctive bodywork and more performance

▬ **AGAINST** As for Type 166/195/212

PRODUCTION

21

SPECIFICATIONS

Length (in.)	170.0
Wheelbase (in.)	110.2
Weight (lbs)	2650
Price (new)	NA

ENGINES

cc/type (cid)	bhp[1]	years
2963/ohc V-12 (181)	200	1954-55

[1]Net

PRICES

Ferraris from the mid-1950s to mid-1960s have remained more stable than the others during the market upheavals of the late 1980s and early 1990s. Most cars put up for sale are reasonably good restorations and the "fair" example is seldom seen. For latest price evaluations we strongly recommend the Ferrari Market Letter, telephone (770) 381-1993 and CPI Value Guide, telephone (301) 317-4228).
2000-2010 RETURN 8%

1954-64
FERRARI TYPE 250GT

1959 250GT spyder

Ferrari's first true "production" series, Enzo's standard products that continued successfully for 10 years. All shared the same large diameter tube frame, coil-spring independent front suspension, and live rear axle, plus the delightful and powerful 3.0-liter Colombo V-12 engine, with power progressively increased as the years went on. Disc brakes were added to the specification in 1959. There were several distinct series or families based primarily on body type, all with two-passenger seating. As before, all bodies were built and designed by Italian coachwork suppliers, never at the Maranello factory. The Pinin Farina (Pininfarina from 1961) coupes of 1958-60 are well known, as is the sleek Berlinetta Lusso of 1962-64, probably the prettiest of the group. The series also includes the mean GTO (Gran Turismo Omologato), Ferrari's inter-pretation of the dual-purpose race-and-ride sports car, plus Farina's handsome Spyder California roadsters. Some competition 250GTs were also built, equipped with five-speed gearboxes. Despite careful hand construction, workmanship on these cars was variable and not always satisfactory. But there was no mistaking what would come to be frequently described as the banshee wail of the Ferrari V-12 or the thrilling performance it delivered (up to 130-140 mph). Despite limited numbers, this is a diverse group, so collector prices span a wide range.

✚ **FOR** Best-known thoroughbred Ferrari two-seaters • Fierce performance • Some mechanical parts still available along with restoration help • Limited-production appeal • Period italian styling

▬ **AGAINST** No body parts around, and construction quality spotty • Corrosion a severe problem generally • Very costly to acquire and restore • Limited number on the market • May be expensive to insure

PRODUCTION

Approx. total 2500 **GTB (Berlinetta)** 80 **GTO** 42 **Spyder California** 104 **Lusso** 350

SPECIFICATIONS

Length (in.)	185.0 (GTB: 164.0; GTO: 173.2)
Wheelbase (in.)	102.3 (94.5 Spyder California, GTB, GTO)
Weight (lbs)	2100-2815
Price (new)	Variable

ENGINES

cc/type (cid)	bhp[1]	years
2953/ohc V-12 (180)	220-300	1956-64

[1]Net; output variable depending on application and state of tune

PRICES

2000 price ranges for good to fine examples:
1958-60 Pininfarina coupe $36,500-56,900
1959-62 Cabriolet $107,000-137,000

1962 250 GTO coupe

1956-58 Boano-Ellena $88,000-145,000
1958-59 California Spyder long wheelbase
$368,000-470,000
1962 California Spyder short wheelbase
$450,000-605,000
For latest price evaluations we strongly recommend the Ferrari Market Letter, telephone (770) 381-1993 and CPI Value Guide, telephone (301) 317-4228)
2000-2010 RETURN 8%

1 9 5 6 - 5 9

FERRARI TYPE 410 SUPER AMERICA

1957 410 Superamerica coupe

A further refinement of the "ultimate street Ferrari" concept initiated with the 340/342/375 America. The chassis was modified by the coil-spring front suspension design from the concurrent 250GT series. Like its predecessors, the Superamericas were monstrously powerful and blindingly fast—up to 165 mph in top tune. The aggressively styled bodies were almost always executed by Pininfarina and were offered in open and closed form. The wheelbase initially was 110.2 inches, later shortened to 102.3. A very desirable group of cars even among Ferraris.

⊞ FOR As for all early Ferraris, plus phenomenal speed and power • Great exclusivity • Wonderful styling

◼ AGAINST As for earlier Ferraris, but brakes not really up to the performance • Indifferent construction quality

PRODUCTION
Series I 15 **Series II** 8 **Series III** 15

SPECIFICATIONS
Length (in.)	175.0 (variable with coachbuilder)
Wheelbase (in.)	110.2/102.3 (1956/1957-59)
Weight (lbs)	2400-2500
Price (new)	NA

ENGINES
cc/type (cid)	bhp[1]	years
4961/ohc V-12 (393)	340/400	1956-59

[1]Net; Series I & II/Series III

PRICES
For latest price evaluations we strongly recommend the Ferrari Market Letter, telephone (770) 381-1993 and CPI Value Guide, telephone (301) 317-4228)
2000-2010 RETURN 10%

1 9 6 0 - 6 6

FERRARI TYPE 400 SUPER-AMERICA/ TYPE 500 SUPERFAST

Final developments of the earlier America/Superamerica series. Still two-seaters with custom-crafted bodywork styled and built by Pininfarina, mostly two-door coupes. Powered by the largest of Ferrari's then-current single cam V-12s. The main difference between the two types (apart from bodywork) was in engine displacement and output, wheelbase, and overall length—the Type 500 being longer, heavier, and more powerful than the 400. During its production life, the Type 400 chassis was shortened by seven inches. Both series also used more powerful disc brakes instead of the drums on earlier models.

⊞ FOR As for Type 410 Superamerica, plus better (disc) brakes

◼ AGAINST As for Type 410 Superamerica

1964 500 Superfast coupe

PRODUCTION
Type 400 48 **Type 500** 37

SPECIFICATIONS
Length (in.)	172.0/190.0 (Type 400/500 depending on body
Wheelbase (in.)	95.3/102.3 (Type 400); 104.3 (Type 500)
Weight (lbs)	2860/3100 (Type 400/500)
Price (new)	NA

ENGINES
cc/type (cid)	bhp[1]	years
3967/ohc V-12 (242)[2]	340	1960-66
4961/ohc V-12 (303)[3]	400	1960-66

[1]Net [2]Type 400 [3]Type 500

PRICES
For latest price evaluations we strongly recommend the Ferrari Market Letter, telephone (770) 381-1993 and CPI Value Guide, telephone (301) 317-4228)
2000-2010 RETURN 12%

1 9 6 0 - 6 8

FERRARI TYPE 250/330GT 2+2

Ferrari's first four-seaters. Built on the 250GT chassis from the late '50s with coil-spring front suspension and a live rear axle. Wheelbase remained as before (about 102 inches), but pedals and front floorboard were moved forward along with the front seats, leaving a marginal but still useful rear seat area. Sold initially as the 250GTE 2+2 with twin headlamps and notchback two-door coupe bodywork, later offered as the 330GT

1963 330GT 2+2 coupe

"America." Another 330 variant had four headlamps at first, then reverted to twin lights and acquired a new jutting snout. The 3.0-liter 250s were equipped with a four-speed-plus overdrive transmission, the 4.0-liter 330s with a five-speed gearbox. Like Ford's Thunderbird, it proved to be much more popular than Ferrari's two-seat models.

⊞ **FOR** Traditional Ferrari virtues • More practical accommodations • Good supply (by Ferrari standards) • Most mechanical parts still available • Active club

▭ **AGAINST** Bodies rust badly • Early overdrive transmissions troublesome • Heavier and slower than two-seaters • Body parts gone • Mechanical parts cost a mint • Not very strong appreciation

PRODUCTION

250GT 2+2 950 **330GT** 1000

SPECIFICATIONS

Length (in.)	185.0
Wheelbase (in.)	102.4
Weight (lbs)	2820-3040
Price (new)	$14,200 U.S. in 1967

ENGINES

cc/type (cid)	bhp[1]	years
2953/ohc V-12 (180)[2]	240	1960-68
3967/ohc V-12 (242)[3]	300	1960-68
[1]Net	[2]250GT 2+2	[3]330GT 2+2

PRICES

Current range for good to fine examples
$25,000-45,000.
See notes under previous entry.
2000-2010 RETURN 5%

1963-65
FERRARI TYPE 250/275LM

The first mid-engine Ferrari road car, though actually more of a racing machine. Derived from the 250P racing prototype, with the usual type of Ferrari multi-tube chassis, "Colombo" engine mounted aft of the driver, and all-independent coil-spring suspension. The

1964 250LM coupe

two-seat closed coupe body was built by Scaglietti, and a few open versions were also seen in racing. Very fast, indeed—170 mph with the proper gearing. All but the first example had the 3.3-liter Ferrari V-12. Extremely rare and desirable, and not really related to any other roadgoing Ferrari. That it ever got off the track at all was probably because the firm wanted to qualify it for production-class events.

⊞ **FOR** Very exclusive and exotic • Superb roadholding and agility • Race-level performance from well-known "street" components • Unmistakable styling • Great Ferrari club interest

▭ **AGAINST** Not on the market much and very costly • No spare parts available • Too high-strung for everyday traffic • Cramped accommodation

PRODUCTION

40

SPECIFICATIONS

Length (in.)	161.0
Wheelbase (in.)	95.0
Weight (lbs)	1880
Price (new)	NA

ENGINES

cc/type (cid)	bhp[1]	years
3286/ohc V-12 (200)	320	1963-65
[1]Net		

PRICES

For latest price evaluations we strongly recommend the Ferrari Market Letter, telephone (770) 381-1993 and CPI Value Guide, telephone (301) 317-4228)
2000-2010 RETURN 8%

1964-68
FERRARI TYPE 275GTB & GTB/4

An important forerunner of several later '60s Ferraris because of its rear transaxle (gearbox in unit with the final drive). The chassis was the usual multi-tube affair with the by-now customary all-independent suspension. Power was supplied by the 3.3-liter Ferrari V-12, initially with single-cam head. From the fall of 1966, however, a new twincam head was applied for the derivative GTB/4. The GTB had the famous "rope drive" propshaft, a very slim unit carried in center bearings, while the GTB/4 had engine, propshaft cover, transmission, and differential all bolted up in one solid unit. Bodywork was by Scaglietti as on the concurrent LM, all two-seat coupes with long-hood/short-deck proportions. A convertible version called GTS (for Spyder) was also available.

⊞ **FOR** More modern handling than other Ferraris of the period • Great performance (155 mph for GTB/4) • Chassis/suspension components still available • Great club backup

▭ **AGAINST** Overshadowed by its Daytona successor • Styling not as popular as on earlier or later models • Very costly to buy, restore, and run

PRODUCTION

GTB 450 **GTB/4** 280 **GTS (conv)** 200

SPECIFICATIONS

Length (in.)	171.3
Wheelbase (in.)	94.5

1965 275GTB/C (competition) coupe

| Weight (lbs) | 2490 |
| Price (new) | $14,500 U.S. in 1966 |

ENGINES

cc/type (cid)	bhp[1]	years
3286/ohc V-12 (201)[2]	280/300	1964-68

[1]DIN bhp; GTB [2]dohc on GTB/4 and GTB/4

PRICES

Current range for good to fine examples:
275GTB $175,000-225,000
275GTB/4 $275,000-350,000
We recommend two authoritative sources for up to the minute pricing: Ferrari Market Letter, telephone (770) 381-1993; CPI Price Guide, telephone (301) 317-4228.
2000-2010 RETURN 10%

1966-70
FERRARI TYPE 330/365 GTC & GTS

1968 365 GTS convertible

These are essentially larger-engine versions of the 275GTB/GTS powered by single-cam V-12 engines of 3967cc (330 cid) or 4390cc (365 cid). The Spyder convertible was mostly the same as the corresponding 275GTS. The 330/365GTCs shared a new, but less rakish, two-seat coupe bodyshell designed by Pininfarina. All models in this series featured a front engine/rear transaxle drivetrain arrangement plus all-independent suspension.

✚ **FOR** As for 1964-68 275 series, plus more performance

▬ **AGAINST** As for 1964-68 275 series, plus GTC styling more pedestrian

PRODUCTION

330GTC 600 **330GTS** 100 **365GTC** 200 **365GTS** 20

SPECIFICATIONS

Length (in.)	173.2
Wheelbase (in.)	94.5
Weight (lbs)	2650-3195
Price (new)	NA

ENGINES

cc/type (cid)	bhp[1]	years
3967/ohc V-12 (242)[2]	300	1966-68
4390/ohc V-12 (268)[3]	320	1968-70

[1]Net [2]330GTC/GTS [3]330GTC/GTS

PRICES

Recent price ranges for good to fine examples:
330 GTC $58,000-78,000
330 GTS $145,000-180,000.
See notes under previous entry.
2000-2010 RETURN 10%

1967-71
FERRARI TYPE 365GT 2+2

Almost all of Ferrari's then-current GT ideas wrapped up in one package, a replacement for the 330GT 2+2. Carried the firm's typical multi-tubular chassis design, but with new all-independent suspension. Engine was the big-displacement V-12 mated to a front-mounted gearbox and 275GTB-type rigid driveline. Had the distinction of being Ferrari's largest car to date, with long, classically refined styling by the masterful house of Pininfarina. Despite fairly hefty weight and size, could top 150 mph. Criticized at the time for limited rear seat room for so large a package, but who ever said a Ferrari must meet the standards applied to lesser cars? Early-production examples ran on disc wheels with knock-off hubs, but later cars had Daytona five-spoke alloy wheels. Not the most famous Ferrari of the '60s, but one of the most numerous and one of the easiest to acquire today.

✚ **FOR** As for 1960-68 330GT 2+2

▬ **AGAINST** As for 1960-68 300GT 2+2

PRODUCTION

800

SPECIFICATIONS

Length (in.)	196.0
Wheelbase (in.)	104.2
Weight (lbs)	3500
Price (new)	$18,900 U.S. in 1969

ENGINES

cc/type (cid)	bhp[1]	years
4390/ohc V-12 (268)	320	1967-71

[1]DIN

PRICES

Current range for good to fine examples:
$30,000-90,000, varying widely with condition and venue (auctions vs. private sellers).For latest price evaluations we strongly recommend the Ferrari Market Letter, telephone (770) 381-1993 and CPI Value Guide, telephone (301) 317-4228)
2000-2010 RETURN 8%

1967-69
FERRARI DINO 206GT

Another landmark Ferrari—Maranello's first car with the Dino twin-cam V-6, and the first with a transverse mid-engine layout. The all-alloy engine was actually built by Fiat, however, and was aimed at Formula Two racing. The Dino also marked Ferrari's attempt at starting a companion marque. The model did not wear the famous prancing horse badge, and the factory referred to it strictly as a Dino. But nobody was fooled: this was a true Ferrari, even if it didn't have 12 cylinders. It certainly acted and sounded like one: same delightful exhaust snarl, plus extremely deft handling thanks to the balanced weight distribution made possible by the mid-engine placement. It was even styled by Ferrari's by-now favored design house, Pininfarina.

1967-69 365GT 2+2 coupe

177

1969 Dino 206GT coupe

Curvaceous yet compact, the body was marked by headlights set back deeply in the front fenders, plus a short, sloping nose and an upright back window set in between flowing rear quarters or flying buttresses. Not much luggage room, but who cared? This car was—and still is—for enthusiasts who just can't resist the temptation to tear along a winding two-lane blacktop when nobody's looking.

✚ FOR Small and nimble, a delight to drive • Still in good supply despite low production • Parts still available • Great performance (140 mph tops) from 2.0-liter engine • You're welcome at Ferrari meets

▬ AGAINST Rust-prone body • Limited accommodation • Pricey parts and service • Not cheap to buy

PRODUCTION
150

SPECIFICATIONS

Length (in.)	165.0
Wheelbase (in.)	90.0
Weight (lbs)	2380
Price (new)	NA

ENGINES

cc/type (cid)	bhp[1]	years
1987/dohc V-6 (121)	180	1967-69

[1]DIN

PRICES

Recent price range for fine examples: $45,000-60,000.
2000-2010 RETURN 5%

1968-74
FERRARI TYPE 365GTB/4 DAYTONA

The last, greatest, and most popular of the front-engine, two-seat pro-duction Ferraris. Arguably the prettiest, too, with sensational fastback coupe styling by Pininfarina. Scaglietti built the bodies, including some Spyder convertibles, which rested on the basic 275GTB/4 chassis. Suspension and mechanical layout were also similar, but the Daytona had a near-new 4.4-liter twin-cam V-12 that gave phenomenal performance for a road car—up to 175 mph if you were brave enough. European models sported a full-width plastic lens with the headlights mounted outboard behind it; since this was illegal in the U.S., cars imported here were given hidden headlights (later used in other markets, too). Competed successfully and with surprising effectiveness. Perhaps the ultimate in sex appeal aside from the later mid-engine Berlinetta Boxer. Unfortunately, you won't find one for sale every day. Some coupes have been turned into roadsters by aftermarket conversion companies, a point to keep in mind if authenticity is of prime importance.

1969 365GTB/4 Daytona Spyder

✚ FOR Everything: mind-boggling speed, great looks, superb road manners • Parts and service still available • Active Ferrari club support • Relatively good U.S. supply

▬ AGAINST Not cheap, and expensive to own • Our 55/65-mph speed limit; where could you really drive it? • Body rot worries • Real thief-bait • Can you afford the insurance?

PRODUCTION
cpe 1285 **Spyder** 127

SPECIFICATIONS

Length (in.)	174.0
Wheelbase (in.)	94.5
Weight (lbs)	3530
Price (new)	$19,500 U.S. in 1970

ENGINES

cc/type (cid)	bhp[1]	years
4390/dohc V-12 (268)	362	1968-73

[1]DIN

PRICES

Recent price ranges for good to fine examples:
365 GTB/4 Spyder $110,000-170,000
cpe $100,000-160,000.
2000-2010 RETURN 5%

1969-73
FERRARI DINO 246GT/GTS

1972 Dino 246GT coupe

A re-engineered successor to the Dino 206, now with a more reliable 2.4-liter iron-block V-6 engine and—from 1972—a new targa-top Spyder (GTS) alternative. Built in greater numbers, but otherwise mostly the same as the 206GT in styling and mechanical specifications. Replaced by the 3.0-liter Dino 308 V-8 series beginning in 1973.

✚ FOR As for 1967-69 Dino 206GT, but more reliable and more available

▬ AGAINST As for 1967-69 Dino 206GT

PRODUCTION
GT 2732 **GTS** 1180

SPECIFICATIONS

Length (in.)	165.0
Wheelbase (in.)	90.0
Weight (lbs)	2380
Price (new)	approx. $15,000 U.S. in 1972

ENGINES

cc/type (cid)	bhp[1]	years
2418/dohc V-6 (148)	195	1969-73

[1]DIN

PRICES

Recent price ranges for good to fine examples:
cpe $37,000-60,000
Spyder $60,000-90,000
2000-2010 RETURN 10%

1 9 7 4 - 8 5

FERRARI 365GT4 BB & 512BB/BBi

Maranello's first big "middie," successor to the front-engine Daytona as Ferrari's "deluxe" sports car. Followed tradition with 12 cylinders and Pininfarina-designed and built body. Very different otherwise, from horizontally opposed, longitudinally mounted midships engine to curvy, menacing styling, to new chassis of square and rectangular tubing. Fiberglass lower body panels, finished in black, were another new wrinkle. All-disc brakes, five-speed rear transaxle, and four-wheel double-wishbone coil-spring suspension like the Daytona, but the double springs at each back wheel and all hardware were new. Though heavy for its size, the Berlinetta Boxer ("Boxer" for flat-opposed engine) was startlingly fast: up to 175 mph and around 7 seconds 0-60. Even faster was the 512BB with a larger engine (still with six two-throat Weber carbs) that was nonetheless more tractable at low speeds. Top speed rose to near 190 mph, 0-60 fell to about 5.5 seconds. Subtle styling changes included functional NACA ducts on lower bodysides, modest chin spoiler, four taillights instead of six, and 1.5 extra inches in tail length. Bosch K-Jetronic fuel injection adopted in late '81 for replacement 512BBi, which was slower (less power) but cleaner at the tailpipe.

■ **FOR** Singular sensation: shattering performance with enormous presence • First Ferrari of its kind • A high-inter-

est collectible like most every Ferrari • Good parts/service availability • Active Ferrari club support

■ **AGAINST** Manual steering heavy for parking (but perfect for three-figure speeds) • A strict two-seater with limited passenger and luggage space • Costly to buy • Costly to maintain/ restore

PRODUCTION

365GT4 BB approx. 400 **512 BB/BBi** NA

SPECIFICATIONS

Length (in.)	171.7
Wheelbase (in.)	98.4
Weight (lbs)	3420-3620
Price (new)	$NA

ENGINES

cid/type	bhp[1]	years
267.8/dohc flat 12	344	1974-76
302/dohc flat 12	340/360[2]	1976-81

[1]DIN [2]injected/carbureted

PRICES

2000 price ranges for good to fine examples
365 GT4BB $70,000-88,000
512BB $60,000-85,000
512 BBi $66,000-95,000.
2000-2010 RETURN 8%

1 9 7 5 - 8 5

FERRARI 308/308I GTB/GTS

Beautiful mid/V-8 replacement for the V-6 Dino 246GT, unveiled at Paris in 1975. Chassis and drivetrain from the Dino/Ferrari 308GT4 2+2 of 1973. Four-cam 90-degree engine (with toothed-belt cam drive) rode transversely ahead of rear axle and drove through the usual dry-plate clutch to a manual five-speed transaxle. Pininfarina styling taut and mus-

1980 308 GTB coupe

cular, yet smooth and sensuous—one of autodom's all-time greats. Concave wedges in upper bodysides leading to functional air intakes would appear on future Ferraris. Initially only a closed coupe (berlinetta, GTB); Targa-style spyder (GTS), with louvered rear side windows and removable roof panel, added for 1977. Both retagged 308i in 1981 to denote Bosch K-Jetronic fuel injection, replacing the original four Weber carbs for easier emissions control. (There was also a 208 GTB/GTS for the tax-burdened Italian market, with a 2.0-liter V-8 that was turbocharged in '81.) For 1982, a new four-valve cylinder head restored most of the interim power loss for 308i models wearing Quattrovalvole badges, as well as body-color bumpers (previously black), hood louvers between the still-hidden headlamps, and a small trailing-edge roof spoiler. The most popular Ferrari so far, and one of the best known. Not widely collected yet, but its time will come.

■ **FOR** Peerless shape, one of PF's best • Fine performance (as little as 6 seconds 0-60) • Exemplary handling

■ **AGAINST** Tight two-seat cockpit • The usual notchy mid-engine shifter • Styling restricts outward vision (especially on Spyder) • Little baggage space

PRODUCTION

308 (1975-80) 3665 (including 208) **308i** (1980-85) NA

SPECIFICATIONS

Length (in.)	166.5/172.4 (European/U.S. models)
Wheelbase (in.)	92.1
Weight (lbs)	3085-3250
Price (new)	$28,500-52,640 (U.S. East Coast POE)

ENGINES

cid/type	bhp[1]	years
179/dohc V-8	240/205/230[2]	1975-85

[1]SAE net[2]Carbureted(308)/injected (308i)/injected 4-valve (Quattrovalvole)

PRICES

2000 price range for good to fine examples:
$17,000-$45,000, varying widely depending on model year and condition.
2000-2010 RETURN 5%

1983 512BBi (Berlinetta Boxer injection) coupe

1985 288 GTO coupe

First race-and-ride Ferrari since the last 250 GTO of 1964, but somewhat plusher—more so with $1800 option package comprising air conditioning, electric windows, and AM/FM/cassette stereo. Looked like a modified 308 GTB, but had a 4.3-inch longer wheelbase to accommodate longitudinal, not transverse, engine. That engine was different, too: still a four-cam V-8 but slightly smaller (2855 vs. 2927cc) and breathing through twin turbochargers and intercoolers to develop considerably more power. Like the original GTO, it was engineered for a racing class—here FISA Group B, which required that at least 200 be built for homologation (omologato, the "O" in GTO). Ferrari complied, but did not certify the car for U.S. sale, though a few found their way Stateside anyway. Called 288 for its nominal cc displacement per cylinder—a Ferrari tradition—and to distinguish it from the hallowed 250. Unfortunately, the 288 had little chance to distinguish itself in competition, as Group B was canceled after two tragedy-plagued seasons (1985-86), but already a first-rank collectible that can only become more valuable in

the future.

✚ FOR   Virtual no-lose investment • Unique even among Ferraris • Purposeful competition character, performance, and road manners • Typical Maranello style, charisma, and interest value

◼ AGAINST   Costs a mint • Specialized design costly and difficult to fix • Scarce in U.S. • All Ferrari values currently in flux, so future dollar return uncertain

PRODUCTION
200

SPECIFICATIONS
Length (in.)	168.9
Wheelbase (in.)	96.5
Weight (lbs)	2555
Price (new)	$83,400 in U.S.

ENGINES
cid/type	bhp[1]	years
174/dohc V-8[2]	400	1984-87

[1]DIN [2]turbocharged, 32 valves

PRICES
2000 price range for good to fine examples: $250,000-300,000
2000-2010 RETURN 5%

FERRARI 328 GTB/GTS
1985-89

Improved evolution of the 308i Quattrovalvole, with 32-valve four-cam V-8 bored and stroked to near 3.2 liters, good for an additional 30 horsepower in U.S. form. Retained Bosch K-Jetronic injection, but Marelli electronic ignition switched from Digiplex to the more sophisticated Multiplex system. Other distinctions included a wheelbase stretched an insignificant 0.4-inch, a dash revamped for better legibility and ergonomics, recontoured

1986 328 GTS coupe

seats, a grille reworked for more efficient radiator airflow, and uprated brakes and air conditioning. Supplanted for 1990 by the rebodied, still-larger-displacement 348tb/ts (see entry).

✚ FOR   As for 1975-85 308-series, plus worthy detail improvements

◼ AGAINST   As for 1975-85 308-series, but too new for collector-market trends to be established

PRODUCTION
NA

SPECIFICATIONS
Length (in.)	168.7-169.[1]
Wheelbase (in.)	92.5
Weight (lbs)	3140-3350[1]
Price (new)	$58,400-$71,900 [1]U.S. models

ENGINES
cid/type	bhp[1]	years
194/dohc V-8	260	1985-89

[1]SAE net

PRICES
2000 price ranges: 328GTSi $45,000-65,000; **328GTS** $32,000-61,000; **1988 328GTB Quattrovalvole** $40,000-60,000
2000-2010 RETURN 5%

FERRARI TESTAROSSA
1985-91

1988 Testarossa coupe

The mid-engine big Ferrari, successor to the Berlinetta Boxers. Much like them in basic format, but slightly larger, though lighter (thanks to aluminum instead steel body panels save roof and doors). New twin radiators, flanking the midships V-12, prompted distinctive bodyside "strakes"—channels that ducted cooling air in more efficiently. Engine an improved 512BBi unit; chassis also held over save wider tracks and two-inch longer wheelbase. Spectacular Pininfarina styling. Overall 77.8-inch beam makes it one of today's widest production cars. Performance easily matches looks:

over 180 mph maximum, 5.3 seconds 0-60. Only the aging Lamborghini Countach had the TR's measure, and it was far less wieldy or accommodating. Very civilized, if a bit clumsy in traffic (39.4-foot turning circle), but unbeatable for ground-level flying.

✚ FOR Unique styling • Thrilling performance • Relatively luxurious • Supercar road manners • A sure-fire future collectible

▬ AGAINST Purchase price and running costs may demand you mortgage your house • Limited baggage space • Possibly overexposed in media

PRODUCTION

NA

SPECIFICATIONS

Length (in.)	176.6
Wheelbase (in.)	100.4
Weight (lbs)	3660
Price (new)	$100,000+

ENGINES

cid/type	bhp	years
302/dohc flat 12	380	1985-90

PRICES

2000 price range:$49,000-83,000 depending on condition and to a lesser extent model year.
2000-2010 RETURN even

1 9 8 7 - 9 1
FERRARI F40

High-tech, cost-no-object successor to the race-and-ride 288 GTO, introduced to celebrate the Ferrari firm's 40th birthday. Also historic as the last new Ferrari unveiled by founder Enzo Ferrari, who died in 1988. That unveiling came in 1987, but the car wasn't genuinely available until 1990

1990 F40 coupe

('91 in the U.S.). Looks like a heavily modified 288, and wheelbase is identical, but F40 is visibly larger, especially its 78-inch width and overall length just 2.2 inches short of the big Testarossa's. Steel space-frame chassis with 288-style suspension topped by body of mostly carbon-fiber and Kevlar composites; nose and tail sections hinged, racing-style. More potent engine, evolved from the 288's four-cam, 32-valve turbo/intercooled V-8, packs 471 standard horsepower; an option package with different turbos and cam profiles adds 200 bhp. GTO's rear five-speed manual transaxle pulls rangier final drive (2.73 vs. 2.90:1) for over 200-mph top speed, yet acceleration is fierce: under 4 seconds 0-60. To cope with this performance are wide Pirelli "P Zero" tires on equally massive five-spoke wheels, plus a three-position ride-height control that automatically lowers the car at speed by 20mm to reduce drag. All this plus deliberately limited production and a sky-high price have already made the F40 a gilt-edge collectible.

✚ FOR No-lose investment (if you can afford it) • Race-caliber performance, dynamic behavior • A singular event in Ferrari history • Just as exclusive (only 200 slated for U.S. sale)

▬ AGAINST Only millionaires with racing licenses need apply • Spartan (no carpeting, wind-up windows, etc.) • Noisy (what race car isn't?)

PRODUCTION

1000

SPECIFICATIONS

Length (in.)	174.4
Wheelbase (in.)	94.5
Weight (lbs)	2980
Price (new)	$415,000 (U.S.)

ENGINES

cid/type	bhp[1]	years

179/dohc V-8[2]	478	1987-91

[1]SAE net [2]Turbocharged

PRICES

Insufficient data, though recent sales range between $250,000 and 300,000.
2000-2010 RETURN not calculable

1 9 9 0 - 9 5
FERRARI 348TB/TS

1990 348tb coupe

Replacement for the 328 GTB/GTS as the "volume" Ferrari. A similar rear/mid-engine concept, but rounded new Testarossa-like Pininfarina styling riding a four-inch longer wheelbase and measuring 6.5-inches wider (though slightly shorter overall). Main technical difference is five-speed gearbox turned from longitudinal to transverse—*transversale*, hence "t" in the model names—and mounted beneath an engine resituated "north-south" (instead of "east-west" as on 308/328). Result is a more compact powertrain that opens up more cockpit and trunk space, as well as lowering the center of gravity, the latter more than offsetting the inherently greater tail-heaviness. Engine a bored-and-stroked upgrade of Ferrari's four-cam 32-valve V-8. Standard antilock brakes, new for Maranello. Interior fully redesigned and competitively ergonomic. Furnishings plush for a Ferrari, with no-cost air conditioning, electric windows and mirrors, and a central-locking system; audio optional.

✚ FOR As for 1985-89 328-series, but a tad quicker (6 seconds 0-60, 170 mph all-out) • Handling less twitchy, more forgiving • Shifter more manageable • Safe, powerful ABS brakes • More "professional" finish and detail design

▬ AGAINST As for 1985-89 328-series, but lift-throttle oversteer still lurks • Limited luggage room • Costly • Too new to establish exact value trends (though surely a future collectible)

PRODUCTION

NA

SPECIFICATIONS

Length (in.)	166.7
Wheelbase (in.)	96.5
Weight (lbs)	3270
Price (new)	$94,800-135,000

ENGINES

cid/type	bhp[1]	years
208/dohc V-8	300	1990

[1]SAE net

PRICES

2000 prices ranged from $43,000 up depending on condition and model year.
2000-2010 RETURN not calculable

1995-2000

FERRARI F355

1996 F355 Spyder

The F355 was the least expensive Ferrari and was also considered the most fun to drive. Replacing the 348, the F355 was subtlely improved in almost every way. It had a 40-valve V-8 that produced over 100-horsepower per liter and loved to rev. The Berlinetta (coupe) had a top speed of 183 mph and a 0-60 time below five seconds. A six-speed manual trasnsmission replaced the previous 5-speed. In '98 Ferrari made its Formula 1 paddle shifter available for road cars. Two steering-wheel mounted paddles (one for upshifts, one for downshifts) controlled the gearbox and also worked clutch. Handling was more balanced—especially in the wet. Power steering was available for the first time in Ferrari 2-seater as a no-cost option. Styling was similar to 348, but cleaner, with better areodynamics. In '96 the Berlinetta was joined by a targa and a Spyder (convertible). The spyder stayed in production for 2000, when the hardtops had been replaced by the 360 Modena.

+ FOR Wonderful engine • Excellent handling with comfortable ride • Build quality still improving

– AGAINST Costly to buy and maintain • Limited head room

PRODUCTION

NA

SPECIFICATIONS

Length (in.)	167.2
Weight (lbs)	3150-3390
Wheelbase (in.)	96.5
Price (new)	$130,000-147,615

ENGINES

cid/type	bhp	years
213/dohc V-8	375	1995-00

PRICES

2000 prices ranged from $85,000 up depending on condition and model year.
2000-2010 RETURN not calculable

1996-2000

FERRARI 456GT/456M

Exciting grand touring car from Modena, Italy, with 2+2 seating, shapely yet understated styling by Pininfarina, and a hairy 5.5-liter V-12 that produced 436 bhp. The 0-60 sprint was accomplished in a hair over 5 seconds; the quarter mile in about 13.5. Top speed exceeded 185 mph. Predictably, mileage—10 city, 16 highway—suffered, but if you could afford the 1999 base price of $218,000, you didn't care. Smart 51/49 front/rear weight distribution gave flat, neutral handling. GTA variant ("A" for "automatic") ran with a capable 4-speed automatic, and put up performance figures a shade slower than the manual 6-speed GT. 456M ("M" for "modified") had a revised grille and reworked instrument panel.

+ FOR Ferrari mystique • Acceleration • Handling and road-holding • Beauty

– AGAINST Initial cost • Thirst

PRODUCTION

NA

SPECIFICATIONS

Length (ins.)	186.2
Weight (lbs)	3725
Wheelbase (in.)	102.4
Price (new)	$207,000-229,950

ENGINES

cid/type	bhp	years
334/dohc V-12	436	1996-2000

PRICES

2000 prices ranged from $150,000 to $200,000
2000-2010 RETURN not calculable

1997-2000

FERRARI 550 MARANELLO

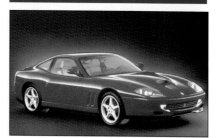

1997-00 550 Maranello coupe

A Testarossa replacement without the outrageous styling, but with outrageous performance. The factory claimed a 199-mph top speed and 0-

1999 456M GT coupe

60 took only 4.3 seconds. Based on the grand touring 456 platform, the 550 was shortened and lightened. The V-12 was tweaked to produce 485-horsepower. In spite of these modifications, the Maranello was still spacious, comfortable, and quiet for a supercar. Good aerodynamics and a 50/50 weight distribution ensured stable handling—even at maximum speed. The combination of refinement and blistering performance was amazing even at the $200,000-plus price.

FOR Race car performance • Stable handling makes the performance safe to use • Unexpected luxury and refinement

AGAINST Look don't match performance • Purchase price

PRODUCTION
NA

SPECIFICATIONS

Length (in.)	179.1
Weight (lbs)	3725
Wheelbase (in.)	98.4
Price (new)	$200,000(est)-212,000

ENGINES

cid/type	bhp	years
334/dohc V-12	485	1997-00

PRICES
2000 prices ranged from $200,000 to $225,000
2000-2010 RETURN not calculable

1952 - 54
FIAT 8V

1952-54 8V coupe by Zagato

A classic case of engineers "thinking aloud", and a very specialized product from a firm whose main business is mostly four-cylinder economy models. Typical limited-production Italian sports car usable on the road, but really intended for "production" racing. The chassis featured all-independent suspension, as well as some transmission components borrowed from the four-wheel-drive Fiat Campagnola. The narrow-angle (70-degree) V-8 was never used in any other Fiat. Neither were the narrow, hand-built two-seat bodies (supplied by Fiat, Ghia, and Zagato), often with staggered seats to leave sufficient working room for the driver. Though the 8V enjoyed some competition success against Alfa Romeo, it was never intended for volume sale. Expensive when new, and its limited-production nature means that replacement parts of all kinds are virtually unobtainable today, as is the car itself.

FOR Unique design • Distinctive styling • Rapid for its day • Very rare • High appreciation

AGAINST Parts virtually extinct • Survivors very rust-prone • Factory would rather not remember it • Almost impossible to find

PRODUCTION
114

SPECIFICATIONS

Length (in.)	158.6
Wheelbase (in.)	94.5
Weight (lbs)	2340
Price (new)	NA

ENGINES

cc/type (cid)	bhp[1]	years
1996/ohv V-8 (122)	105/115	1952-54

[1]Net

PRICES

FAIR	$6000-12,000
GOOD	$12,000-20,000
FINE	$20,000-30,000

FINE EXAMPLE PRICE HISTORY

1982 $25,000		**1990** $50,000	
1994 $40,000		**1998** $35,000	
1982-2000 RETURN 1%			
2000-2010 3%			

1953 - 62
FIAT 1100TV

The sporty, higher-power version of Fiat's small-to-medium market family sedan line of these years, with 53 bhp instead of the base 36-bhp 1100cc engine. The "TV" designation stands for "Touring Veloce"—lively touring car. Many variations were tried through the series' decade of production. Most were based on the boxy, upright four-door sedan bodyshell, but there was also a quaintly styled open two-seat roadster, which is the body style to have today. Stark trim and equipment, but very sporting road manners made the 1100TV a natural in its day as a platform for rally use. Sedans featured an identifying "cyclops" auxiliary center headlight in the grille. The basic 1100 design continued to be built in other countries after its phaseout in Italy. These included India, where production lasted until the mid-'70s.

FOR No-nonsense engineering • Quite lively • Unbreakable engine if cared for • Some parts still available

AGAINST Unexciting styling, even on roadster • Monocoque construction rust worries • Limited performance (80 mph tops) • Not very refined

PRODUCTION
NA

SPECIFICATIONS

Length (in.)	148.0

1957-63 1100TV roadster

Wheelbase (in.)	92.0
Weight (lbs)	1865
Price (new)	NA

ENGINES

cc/type (cid)	bhp[1]	years
1089/ohv I-4 (66)	53	1953-62

[1]Gross

PRICES

FAIR	$1000-2000
GOOD	$2000-3500
FINE	$3500-6000

FINE EXAMPLE PRICE HISTORY

1982 $2000		1990 $4500	
1994 $4500		1998 $5500	
1982-2000 RETURN 6%			
2000-2010 5%			

1 9 5 9 - 6 6

FIAT 1200/1500/ 1500S/1600S CABRIOLET

Fiat's first high-volume in-house sports car, based on mass-production components. Its steel monocoque body was engineered by Fiat, but styled by Pinin Farina, with square, sleek lines reminiscent of the contemporary Innocenti Spyder (the rebodied, license-built Italian version of the Austin-Healey Sprite). The suspension and manual gearbox (no automatic available) were borrowed initially from the Fiat 1200 sedan. Offered in base form with an overhead-valve four and as the faster, more expensive "S" with an OSCA-designed twincam unit. Both versions acquired more displacement and power in 1963. The twincam was as good as any Alfa engine of the day, but was never used in any other Fiat. Practical two-seaters all—and the true forerunners of the even more successful 124 Sport Spyder.

✚ FOR Neat, timeless styling • Good road manners • Simple engine and mechanical equipment • Much easier top conversion than contemporary Brit roadsters • Twincam models' brisk performance

▬ AGAINST Ohv models' limited top speed (90 mph at best) • No factory support or interest now • Not a "fashionable" collector's item • Twincam engine parts extinct • Latin rust habit

PRODUCTION

43,000

SPECIFICATIONS

Length (in.)	159.0

1963-65 1500 cabriolet

Wheelbase (in.)	92.0
Weight (lbs)	approx. 1985-2000
Price (new)	NA

ENGINES

cc/type (cid)	bhp[1]	years
1221/ohv I-4 (75)	63	1959-63
1491/dohc I-4 (91)	90	1959-63
1481/ohv I-4 (90)	80	1963-66
1568/dohc I-4 (96)	100	1963-66

[1]Gross

PRICES

FAIR	$2500-5000
GOOD	$5000-8000
FINE	$8000-12,500

FINE 1500S PRICE HISTORY

1982 $3000		1990 $6500	
1994 $6500		1998 $8500	
1982-2000 RETURN 9%			
2000-2010 5%			

1 9 6 1 - 6 8

FIAT 2300S

1961-68 2300S coupe

Here's a remarkable case of a silk purse being made from a sow's ear. Began life as a one-off design study that was then adopted by Fiat as a regular model. The neat four-seat semi-fastback coupe styling was from the house of Ghia, which also supplied finished bodyshells to Fiat for mounting on chassis from the firm's 2300 sedan. The complicated six-cylinder engine developed 150 bhp—good for a top end of 120 mph—and four-wheel disc brakes were unique to this specification at Fiat. Also produced in base (non-S) form with a 117-bhp version of the same engine. This was the firm's sporting flagship in these years until the advent of the Ferrari-engine Fiat Dinos of 1967-68. Styling was typical of Ghia coupes in this period, with a high grille and tail, reverse-slant C-pillar, and a wraparound backlight with two chrome vertical divider bars forming triangular-shaped outer sections.

✚ FOR Ghia styling • Fine performance • Four-seat accommodation • Good appreciation • Not expensive

▬ AGAINST Very rust-prone • Few mechanical parts now available • Replacement body panels extinct • Not plentiful in U.S. • Dubious collector merit

PRODUCTION

NA

SPECIFICATIONS

Length (in.)	182.0
Wheelbase (in.)	104.3
Weight (lbs)	2790
Price (new)	NA

ENGINES

cc/type (cid)	bhp[1]	years
2279/ohv I-6 (139)	117/150	1961-68

[1]Gross

PRICES

Spyder	
FAIR	$1000-2000
GOOD	$2000-3000
FINE	$3000-5000
(Cpe deduct one third)	

FINE SPYDER PRICE HISTORY

1982 $2000		1987 $2500	
1990 $4000		1994 $4000	
1982-2000 RETURN 5%			
2000-2010 3%			

1 9 6 5 - 7 4
FIAT 850 COUPE & SPYDER

1965-74 850 Sport Coupe

Two more special-bodied Fiat sports cars based on mundane sedan components. In this case, the basis was the rear-engine 850, which donated its floorpan, drivetrain, and all-independent suspension to a neat little Fiat-designed four-seat fastback coupe and a Bertone-bodied two-seat roadster. Not quick by any means—85-90-mph top speed—and quite noisy and cramped, but great fun to drive (except perhaps in a strong crosswind) because of Lilliputian size and light weight. Both models were popular in the U.S., at least by European sales standards, particularly the Spyder, which was seen as the Italian entry in the basic sports car market against such traditionalists as the Triumph Spitfire and A-H Sprite/MG Midget. Engine size was increased to 903cc for 1969, partly to compensate for U.S. emissions rules, but 1968 American-spec models used an even smaller 817cc engine to get under the minimum displacement limit for desmogging. Safety laws also took their toll, particularly on the Spyder, which lost its covered headlights in favor of a more "frog-eye" look with exposed units. It also acquired heavier, more ungainly bumpers. The Spyder continued longer than the coupe, and was eventually succeeded by the mid-engine X1/9. The Italian tuning firm Abarth offered hotted up versions of both models, some with twincam engines, but only a relative few made it to the U.S., where most were used for racing in SCCA and similar events. Notable for being the last of Fiat's rear-engine sports models.

⊞ **FOR** Styling (especially early Spyders) • Simple chassis • Great character • Sprightly handling

⊟ **AGAINST** Parts now difficult to obtain, especially for body • Fiat's well-known tinworm propensities • Cramped • Noisy • Indifferent construction quality

PRODUCTION
Cpe 342,873 **Spyder** 124,660

SPECIFICATIONS
Length (in.)	149.0/141.0 (Spyder/cpe)
Wheelbase (in.)	80.0
Weight (lbs)	1620/1610 (Spyder/cpe)
Price (new)	approx. $2500 (U.S. POE)

ENGINES
cc/type (cid)	bhp[1]	years
843/ohv I-4 (51)	54	1965-68
903/ohv I-4 (55)	60	1969-74

[1]Gross

PRICES
Spyder	
FAIR	$1500-3500
GOOD	$3500-6000
FINE	$6000-9500

(Cpe deduct one third.)

FINE SPYDER PRICE HISTORY
1982 $2000		**1990** $4000	
1994 $4000		**1998** $6000	

1982-2000 RETURN 10% **2000-2010** 10%

1 9 6 8 - 7 2
FIAT 124 SPORT

The most successful of the Fiat sports cars, based on the suspension and running gear of the 124 sedan introduced in 1966. The dohc Fiat-designed four-cylinder engine, derived from the pushrod sedan unit, was built in huge numbers, and survived into the '80s. So did the Pininfarina-bodied Spyder, which outlasted the factory-styled four-seat coupe, which was dropped after 1974. As with Fiat's other volume sports cars, these were built on shorter wheelbases, and had less space but better handling and performance than their sedan cousins. Engine displacement was increased to 1608cc for 1971, later to 1756cc and then to 1995cc in the face of tighter U.S. emissions controls and added weight from our impact-protection rules as the decade progressed. We have arbitrarily limited "collectibility to these five model years as these cars are least affected by our regulations. However, later Spyders will almost certainly achieve high desirability in the future. The Spyder was later produced by Pininfarina, with remarkably little styling change.

⊞ **FOR** Styling • Simple engineering • Spirited performance (100 mph) • Good U.S. supply • Most parts still available • Spyder's convenient soft top mechanism • Italian brio • Good trunk space for sports cars • Good appreciation • Not costly to buy • Good mileage

⊟ **AGAINST** Premature rust-out • Dubious mechanical and electrical reliability

PRODUCTION
1.4/1.6-liter Spyder 60,233 **1.8-liter Spyder** 69,208 **2.0-liter Spyder** 48,998 **cpe** 279,672

SPECIFICATIONS
Length (in.)	156.0/162.0 (Spyder/cpe)
Wheelbase (in.)	89.8/95.3 (Spyder/cpe)
Weight (lbs)	2100/2005 (Spyder/cpe)
Price (new)	$2924-3694 (original U.S. base prices 1968-72)

ENGINES
cc/type (cid)	bhp[1]	years
1438/dohc I-4 (88)	96	1968-70
1608/dohc I-4 (98)	104	1971-72

[1]Net

1974 124 Spyder 1000 (similar to 1972)

PRICES

FAIR	$1500-3000
GOOD	$3000-5000
FINE	$5000-7000 (1972 Spyder up to $11,000)

FINE EXAMPLE PRICE HISTORY

1982 $1500		1990 $3000	
1994 $4000		1998 $5000	

1982-2000 RETURN 9%
2000-2010 4%

1 9 6 7 - 7 3

FIAT DINO SPYDER & COUPE

An exciting collaboration between Fiat and Ferrari, and mutually beneficial. The former gained a glamorous line leader; the latter was able to qualify its twincam Dino V-6 for Formula Two through Fiat, which built the engines for this application. A mass-production effort for Ferrari, which took over assembly toward the end of the run; a low-volume sideline for Fiat. Offered as a clean-lined two-door fastback styled by Bertone and as a roadster designed by Pininfarina. Both coachworks also built the monocoque body/chassis, though the engineering was Fiat's. Cars built up to late 1969 had a 2.0-liter displacement and a live rear axle; after this, capacity was boosted to 2.4 liters (with iron replacing aluminum for the block) and independent rear suspension. The coupe had four seats and a longer wheelbase than the two-seat Spyder. Later models are preferred for their bigger engine, better suspension, five-speed ZF gearbox, and more "practiced" construction. Never officially sold as part of the U.S. Fiat line; most were brought in privately before government regulations made such things difficult.

FOR Panache of Ferrari-designed engine • High performance • Simpler in design than equivalent Ferraris and much cheaper

AGAINST Limited U.S. availability • Notorious body corrosion • Crude rear suspension (2.0-liter models) • Body parts no longer stocked • Running gear difficult to rebuild and maintain

PRODUCTION

2000 Spyder 1163 **cpe** 3670 **2400 Spyder** 420 cpe 2398

SPECIFICATIONS

Length (in.)	161.7/177.7 (Spyder/cpe)
Wheelbase (in.)	88.8/100.4 (Spyder/cpe)
Weight (lbs)	2600/2825 (Spyder/cpe)
Price (new)	NA

ENGINES

cc/type (cid)	bhp[1]	years
1987/dohc V-6 (121)	160	1967-69
2418/dohc V-6 (148)	180	1969-73

[1]DIN

PRICES

Spyder	
FAIR	$17,000-20,000
GOOD	$20,000-25,000
FINE	$25,000-30,000

(Cpe deduct 50%)

FINE SPYDER PRICE HISTORY

1982 $12,000		1990 $60,000	
1994 $18,000		1998 $24,000	

1982-2000 RETURN 6%
2000-2010 5%

1 9 7 2 - 8 9

FIAT/BERTONE X1/9

Low-cost "parts bins" sports car with rear/mid-engine format and wedgy

1973 X1/9 coupe

Targa-style two-seat bodywork designed and supplied by Bertone. Mechanicals from Fiat's front-drive 128 line, transplanted between a snug cockpit and a small rear trunk; a second, even smaller cargo hold lived in front. Small but well-planned, with space-saving all-independent coil/strut suspension. Four-speed manual transaxle through 1980, when the original 1.3-liter ohc four was replaced by a 1.5-liter unit that partly made up for interim power losses to U.S. emission controls; standard five-speed manual gearbox from 1981. Performance further improved the following year via Bosch L-Jetronic fuel injection, replacing the carburetor. Fiat decided to abandon sports cars soon afterwards, and turned the X1/9 over to its coachbuilder, who sold it as a somewhat more luxurious "Bertone" in diminishing numbers through early 1989, when production was halted. Few other changes during a long run, but clumsy U.S.-inspired "safety" bumpers from early '70s added length and weight.

FOR Nimble, mid-engine handling • Open-air fun • Econocar mileage • Practical for size and concept • Cost still low

AGAINST The usual Fiat foibles: ready rust-out, slapdash workmanship, buzzy, unreliable engines • Cockpit tight for six-footers • Rather commonplace • No great U.S. collector interest at present

PRODUCTION

approx. 180,000

SPECIFICATIONS

Length (in.)	150.5-158.5
Wheelbase (in.)	86.7
Weight (lbs)	2150-2250
Price (new)	$3500-13,000

ENGINES

cc/type (cid)	bhp[1]	years
1298/ohc I-4 (78.7)	75	1972-79
1498/ohc I-4 (91.4)	67	1980-81
1498/ohc I-4 (91.4)	75	1982-89

[1]SAE net

PRICES

FAIR	$1500-2500
GOOD	$2500-3500
FINE	$3500-5000

FINE EXAMPLE PRICE HISTORY

Depreciating or flat in 1990s
2000-2010 RETURN 2%

1967-73 Dino Spyder

1930-31
FORD MODEL A

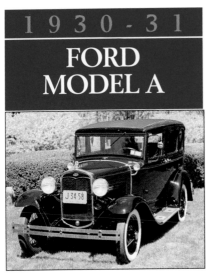

1931 Model A sedan

Superficially the same as the early 1928-29 models, but considerably altered in detail. Changes included lower, wider fenders, higher hoodline, stainless-steel instead of nickel-plated radiator and headlamp shells, smaller-diameter wheels, a higher steering ratio, and standard vacuum wipers and balloon tires. New body styles comprised DeLuxe two-door phaeton and, from autumn 1930, a Victoria coupe. The Model As packed more value for the money than just about any other car on the road, and the public responded: Ford again led Chevrolet in production for 1929-31. Though its transverse-leaf suspension was basically the same as that of the long-lived Model T, the Model A was superior in every way, and far more sophisticated. It would do 65 mph (some optimistically claimed 70), had a modern electrical system and three-speed gearbox, plus it stopped much better with its four- (instead of two-) wheel mechanical brakes. It was also so ruggedly constructed that hundreds of thousands of them were still plying the roads of America in the late Fifties.

➕ FOR For years the most popular single collector car • Strong support from two large clubs • Supply of both mechanical and structural parts almost endless (many reproduction) • Wide variety of body styles, most of which are readily available • Reasonable prices

➖ AGAINST Indifferent and inaccurate restorations common • Tends to be over-restored • Prices are beginning to pick up

PRODUCTION
1930 1,261,053 **1931** 626,579 (some sold through April 1932)

SPECIFICATIONS
Length (in.)	NA
Wheelbase (in.)	103.5
Weight (lbs)	2155-2462
Price (new)	$430-660

ENGINES
cid/type	bhp	years
200.5/sv I-4	40-50	1930-32

PRICES
Open	
FAIR	$5000-11,000
GOOD	$11,000-18,000
FINE	$18,000-28,000

(Deluxe phaeton is at high end of these ranges, roadster at low end.)

Closed	
FAIR	$2500-6000
GOOD	$6000-11,500
FINE	$11,500-17,000

FINE DELUXE PHAETON PRICE HISTORY
1982 $10,000		**1990** $22,000	
1994 $20,000		**1998** $28,000	
1982-2000 RETURN 7%			
1982-2005 5%			

1932-33
FORD MODEL B/C

Extension of the Model A, sharing the new 1932 Model 18 V-8 body, except for badging. The V-8's strong public reception prompted Ford to abandon four-cylinder cars after 1934, resulting in extreme scarcity of certain models today, particularly Model Cs.

➕ FOR Worth collecting; the Model C must be one of the few 1930s "sleepers" left—extremely scarce • Priced no more than comparable Model As, and as a result—in our opinion—underpriced

➖ AGAINST Very difficult to find a '32, even the far more common Tudor and Fordor sedans • Try to find a '33 or '34 four-cylinder • Everybody wants the V-8 anyway

PRODUCTION
1932 Model B 75,945 **1933 Model C** 7560 For 1932, about 56,000 units were **Tudor coupes/sedans**, 10,000 were **Fordors/DeLuxe Tudors**, and 3719 were **DeLuxe roadsters**. Other styles were under 1000 units each. For 1933, 5000 were **Standard 5-Window coupes** or **Tudors**; others were under 1000 each. Fewer than 30 units each of the **Cabriolet, DeLuxe coupe**, and **Victoria** were built for 1933. A very few '34 Fords were also built as fours.

SPECIFICATIONS
Length (in.)	NA
Wheelbase (in.)	106.5
Weight (lbs)	2021-2505
Price (new)	$410-600

ENGINES
cid/type	bhp	years
200.5/sv I-4	50	1932-33

PRICES
As per the Model A, except all open models up to $32,000 in fine condition.
2000-2010 5%

1932-38
FORD V-8 OPEN MODELS & WAGONS

All of these Ford V-8s are collectible, and the general remarks applied to open cars and wagons apply. Typically, however, the former are the ones to look for. Hoping to leap-frog Chevy's six, Ford brought out the wonderful little V-8 only four years after the Model A debuted, and it was a tremendous buy for the money. The cast-iron flat

1932 Model B DeLuxe Tudor sedan

1934 V-8 DeLuxe roadster

1940 V-8 DeLuxe coupe

head gave at least 78 mph. Streamlining began with the much swoopier 1933 models, which also had a longer wheelbase. Horsepower was 85 by 1934, the cars even sleeker. A much smaller V-8 choice was added beginning with 1937, when styling took another turn, now very rounded and smooth indeed. The early V-8 years brought fairly swift change by Ford standards, with body design evolving dramatically (all-steel by 1937), engines growing in power, and time-honored body styles like the roadster and convertible sedan being phased out.

⚑ **FOR** Open models and the beautiful woody wagons are among the most desirable standard production cars of the 1930s • Plentiful parts original and repro

◼ **AGAINST** Some V-8 experts say open models like phaeton and convertible sedan are grossly overpriced; investment potential is less than previously • Later Fordors very dowdy

1938 V-8 wagon

PRODUCTION

1932 2d DeLuxe rdstr 6893 **2d Standard rdstr** 520 **4d DeLuxe phaeton** 923 **4d Standard phaeton** 483 **cabriolet** 5499 **conv sdn** 842 **1933 2d DeLuxe rdstr** 4223 **2d Standard rdstr** 126 **4d DeLuxe phaeton** 1483 **4d Standard phaeton** 232 **cabriolet** 7852 **wgn** 1654 **1934 4d DeLuxe phaeton** 3128 **4d Standard phaeton** 373 **cabriolet** 14,496 **wgn** 2905 **1935 2d DeLuxe rdstr** 4896 **4d DeLuxe phaeton** 6073 **cabriolet** 17,000 **conv sdn** 4234 **wgn** 4536 **1936 2d DeLuxe rdstr** 3862 **4d DeLuxe phaeton** 5555 **cabriolet** 4616 **conv sdn** 5601 **3/5P conv** 4616 **wgn** 7044 **1937 2d DeLuxe rdstr** 1250 **4d DeLuxe phaeton** 3723 **cabriolet** 18,184 **conv sdn** 4378 **wgn** 9304 **1938 4d DeLuxe phaeton** 1169 **conv sdn** 2703 **3/5P conv** 7405 **wgn** 6944

SPECIFICATIONS

Length (in.)	varies
Wheelbase (in.)	106.5 (1932); 112.0 (1933-38)
Weight (lbs)	2217-2543 (1932); 2337-3020 (1933-38)
Price (new)	$425-900

ENGINES

cid/type	bhp	years
221.0/sv V-8	65/85	1932-38
136.0/sv V-8	60	1937-38

PRICES

Open	
FAIR	$5000-15,000
GOOD	$15,000-27,000
FINE	$27,000-39,000
Wgns	
FAIR	$4000-12,000
GOOD	$12,000-20,000
FINE	$20,000-30,000

1932 PHAETON PRICE HISTORY

1982 $24,000		**1990** $28,000	
1994 $29,000		**1998** $32,000	

1982-2000 RETURN 3%
2000-2010 3%
Note: Prewar Ford V-8s through 1938 have not appreciated much in the last two decades. Collectors enjoy them for characteristics other than investment. The most desirable body styles and years may be arrayed in this order: cabriolets and convertibles, woody wagons, roadsters. Preferable years for these in order are 1939, 1936, 1933-34, 1932. Next come convertible sedans (1932, 1936, 1935, 1939, 1937), phaetons (1934, 1933, 1936, 1935, 1932), and convertible coupes (1932, 1934, 1933, 1936, 1935).

A mong the prettiest Fords ever built, thanks to deft design work by Bob Gregorie and the keen aesthetic sense of Edsel Ford. The legendary '40s have been favored by many enthusiasts for three generations. Our choice would be the 1940 85-bhp convertible, but the serious investor would want to look for the scarce '39 convertible sedans—and the woodies are hardly common. The 1939-40 Standard series offered the same body styles except for convertibles, but were somewhat dumpier in appearance because they carried less bright trim, plainer interiors, and were based on the year-earlier DeLuxe styling (a curious Ford practice from 1938-40).

⚑ **FOR** Superb styling • Vast following and club support • Good performance • Fine construction

◼ **AGAINST** Increasingly expensive • Open models almost overpriced now

PRODUCTION

1939 conv cpe 10,422 **conv sdn** 3561 **cpe** 37,326 **Tudor sdn** 144,333 **wgn** 6155 **Fordor sdn** 90,551 **1940 conv cpe** 23,704 **cpe** 27,919 **Tudor sdn** 171,368 **wgn** 8730 **Fordor sdn** 91,756 **bus cpe** 20,183

SPECIFICATIONS

Length (in.)	195.0
Wheelbase (in.)	112.0
Weight (lbs)	2752-3262
Price (new)	$702-947

ENGINES

cid/type	bhp	years
221/sv V-8	85	1939-40

PRICES

Open	
FAIR	$7000-15,000
GOOD	$15,000-26,000
FINE	$26,000-38,000
Wgns	
FAIR	$5500-11,000
GOOD	$11,000-16,000
FINE	$16,000-28,000

Other	
FAIR	$2250-4750
GOOD	$4750-8500
FINE	$8500-21,000

FINE CONVERTIBLE SEDAN PRICE HISTORY

1982 $22,000		**1990** $35,000	
1994 $35,000		**1998** $35,000	
1982-2000 RETURN 3%			
2000-2010 5%			

1941-42
FORD V-8 SUPER DELUXE

1942 Super DeLuxe wagon

An all-new Ford arrived for 1941 on a two-inch-longer 114-inch wheelbase, but it lacked the clean-lined beauty of the '40. It was heavier and bigger all-around, especially inside. The top-line series was now designated Super DeLuxe, and came in much the same body styles as the previous DeLuxe. There was even a third series this year, the spartan bottom-line Special. And—heresy to old Henry for sure—a 90-bhp L-head six was introduced to replace the underpowered 60-bhp V-8 of 1937-40; it was available in all three series. A more integrated, more massive-looking grille and new one-piece fenders were the main appearance changes for '42, the model year that ended by early February as Ford—like the other automakers—shifted to defense production.

✚ FOR Popular • Well-built • Good performance

▬ AGAINST Very ordinary in appearance and feel • Modest appreciation

PRODUCTION
1941 350,000 **1942** 80,000 (est.)

SPECIFICATIONS
Length (in.)	198.2
Wheelbase (in.)	114.0
Weight (lbs)	2969-3419
Price (new)	$777-1013

ENGINES
cid/type	bhp	years
221/sv V-8	85/90	1941-42

PRICES
Conv & Wgn	
FAIR	$5500-13,000
GOOD	$13,000-22,000
FINE	$22,000-32,000
Other	
FAIR	$2000-8000
GOOD	$8000-12,000
FINE	$12,000-20,000

FINE 1941 CONVERTIBLE PRICE HISTORY

1982 $18,000		**1990** $28,000	
1994 $29,000		**1998** $32,000	
1982-2000 RETURN 4%			
2000-2010 3%			

1946-48
FORD V-8 SUPER DELUXE SPORTSMAN

A convertible in the mold of Chrysler's Town and Country, with wooden framing and mahogany or birch inserts helping to jazz up what was basically a prewar design. Essentially fielded as a showroom traffic-builder, as was the T&C and the Nash Suburban. This was the most expensive Ford in these years, and as such not too saleable. Collectors have changed all that though, not to mention boosting asking prices. A very pretty car despite its outmoded styling, and it packed traditional Ford V-8 performance.

✚ FOR Good performance • Nice looks • Rarity • It's a convertible • Milestone car status

▬ AGAINST Pricey today • Structural wood demands periodic maintenance

PRODUCTION
1946 1209 **1947** 2250 **1948** 28

SPECIFICATIONS
Length (in.)	198.2
Wheelbase (in.)	114.0
Weight (lbs)	3340-3366
Price (new)	$1982-2282

ENGINES
cid/type	bhp	years
239.4/sv V-8	100	1946-48

PRICES
FAIR	$11,000-22,000
GOOD	$22,000-37,500
FINE	$37,500-55,000

FINE EXAMPLE PRICE HISTORY

1982 $27,500		**1990** $60,000	
1994 $50,000		**1998** $55,000	
1982-2000 RETURN 4%			
2000-2010 5%			

1948-52
FORD PICKUP

Buyers interested in good performance and rugged good looks could hardly do better than Ford's "Bonus Built" truck series that debuted for 1948. The line encompassed half- to 3-ton models highlighted by a "Million Dollar Cab" with "Living-Room" comfort. These were higher and wider than earlier Ford light-duty trucks, and could be had with a useful variety of Ford sixes and V-8s. Stylistically, these are transitional vehicles, with flatter hoods that suggested the increasingly car-like truck styling that would follow.

1947 Super DeLuxe Sportsman convertible

1948 F-1 pickup

A "Five Star Extra" interior brought an insulated headliner, thicker sound deadeners, foam padded seat, door locks, dome light, and twin horns. By late in the series' run, available body colors included the likes of Alpine Blue and Sea Island Green. For 1953, Ford Motor Company's 50th anniversary year, Bonus Builts were replaced by the F-100 line.

✚ FOR Relatively large supply, so prices are low • Progressive styling • Performance (V-8 models) • Reasonable supply of most parts

➖ AGAINST Plenty of 'em, so investment return is limited • Some parts in short supply

PRODUCTION

1948 108,006[1] **1949** 104,803[1] **1950** 148,956 **1951** 117,414 **1952** 81,537
[1]Total 1/2 ton truck production.

SPECIFICATIONS

Length (in.)	188.8
Weight (lbs)	2990-3211
Wheelbase (in.)	114
Price (new)	$1232-1361

ENGINES

cid/type	bhp	years
226/sv I-6	95	1948-51
215/ohv I-6	101	1952
239/sv V-8	100/106	1948-52

PRICES

F100	
FAIR	$2000-5000
GOOD	$5000-8000
FINE	$8000-12,000

Add 30% for the 236 V8 [1954-55] and 272 [1956].
2000-2010 RETURN 3%

1 9 4 9

FORD CUSTOM V-8 (EXC. SEDANS)

1949 Custom convertible

This should be a Milestone car because of its adroit styling—albeit in part the work of moonlighting Studebaker people—and traditional V-8 performance (the engine was much improved this year, though the horsepower rating didn't change). It also receives kudos for a contemporary chassis with independent front suspension and parallel leaf springs in back, even though old Henry would never have approved of dumping his beloved transverse-spring suspension. Solid construction was also a keynote, though workmanship on the early '49s left something to be desired. This gradually improved during the model year, however, and was excellent in 1950.

The wagon this year was a two-door model, and a partial woody with more steel construction. All in all, the new Ford was great stuff for '49, good enough to rejuvenate the firm's failing corporate health. The company's success in the '50s was made possible largely by the basic excellence of this car, the first all-new Ford in a very long time. We single out the non-sedan body styles as having more than average collector interest and especially good styling.

✚ FOR Historical importance • Fine styling • Improved V-8 • Engineering improvements, finally bringing Ford in line with its competitors • Good driver's cars

➖ AGAINST Moderately rust-prone • Early assembly quality problems • Nobody wants the sixes, which were also available on most Customs

PRODUCTION

clb cpe 150,254 **conv** 51,133 **wgn** 31,412

SPECIFICATIONS

Length (in.)	196.8
Wheelbase (in.)	114.0
Weight (lbs)	2948-3543
Price (new)	$1511-2119

ENGINES

cid/type	bhp	years
239.4/sv V-8	100	1949

PRICES

Conv	
FAIR	$5000-10,000
GOOD	$10,000-18,000
FINE	$18,000-26,000
Wgn	
FAIR	$4000-8000
GOOD	$8000-14,000
FINE	$14,000-20,000
Others	
FAIR	$3000-6000
GOOD	$6000-10,000
FINE	$10,000-15,000

FINE WAGON PRICE HISTORY

1982 $12,000		**1990** $25,000	
1994 $19,000		**1998** $19,000	

1982-2000 RETURN 3%
2000-2010 5%

1 9 5 0 - 5 1

FORD CUSTOM CRESTLINER

A gussied-up version of the regular Tudor sedan added late in the 1950 model year, this model was designed to fill in for a true "hardtop convertible" pending the arrival of the

1951 Custom Crestliner 2-door sedan

Victoria for 1951. After all, Chevy already had the Bel Air hardtop for 1950, and Powerglide automatic, too. Styling by Gordon Buehrig featured a contrasting "Duesenberg" color sweep panel on the bodysides and a padded top. Arresting two-tone paint jobs were offered with black as the main color. It was priced $200 upstream of the Custom Tudor, which may explain why sales were not impressive. The '51 was a bit less individualistic, but still different enough to warrant serious consideration. This model is perhaps the most interesting of the 1950-51 Fords, and well worth considering.

+ FOR Unique, in spite of minor historical significance • Others as for 1949 Custom, including improved quality

− AGAINST Not a true hardtop • Still no automatic • Individual trim pieces hard to find • As for 1949 Custom

PRODUCTION
1950 17,601 **1951** 8703

SPECIFICATIONS
Length (in.)	196.7 (1950), 197.3 (1951)
Wheelbase (in.)	114.0
Weight (lbs)	3050-3065
Price (new)	$1711-1595

ENGINES
cid/type	bhp	years
239.4/sv V-8	100	1950-51

PRICES
FAIR	$3000-6500
GOOD	$6500-12,000
FINE	$12,000-17,000

FINE EXAMPLE PRICE HISTORY
1982 $6100	**1990** $10,000
1994 $12,000	**1998** $14,500
1982-2000 RETURN 6%	
2000-2010 5%	

1951
FORD CUSTOM VICTORIA

1951 Custom Victoria hardtop coupe

Ford's first hardtop, offered only in V-8 guise. It appeared in the last year of the 1949 styling generation—and a bit late at that. Still, it proved immensely popular, outselling Chevrolet's Bel Air by about 7000 units this year. The pillarless superstructure was styled by Gordon M. Buehrig (of Auburn-Cord-Duesenberg fame), who had come to Dearborn after leaving the Loewy team at Studebaker. Despite exceptionally clean lines, a relatively posh interior, and good performance from the reliable flathead V-8, the first Victoria used to be somewhat overlooked by collectors, but in the last decade has become more desired. A plus for this top-line model was the debut of Ford's optional self-shift Ford-O-Matic this year, giving it an advantage over Chevy's two-speed Powerglide. Enthusiasts will probably prefer the overdrive gearbox.

+ FOR Historical significance • One of the best-looking 1949-51 Fords • Reasonable parts supplies • Decent performance from the sturdy V-8 engine

− AGAINST As for 1950-51 Custom Crestliner

PRODUCTION
110,286

SPECIFICATIONS
Length (in.)	197.3
Wheelbase (in.)	114.0
Weight (lbs)	3188
Price (new)	$1925

ENGINES
cid/type	bhp	years
239.4/sv V-8	100	1951

PRICES
FAIR	$3000-6000
GOOD	$6000-11,000
FINE	$11,000-15,000

FINE EXAMPLE PRICE HISTORY
1982 $5500	**1990** $11,000
1994 $9500	**1998** $15,500
1982-2000 RETURN 8%	
2000-2010 6%	

1953-56
FORD F-100 PICKUP

1953 F-100 pickup

Ford celebrated its golden anniversary with a new truck in 1953. The F-100 styling was clean and modern, but it had more. It looked like a truck: tough, solid, practical, ruggedly handsome. That might explain its sucess when new, and also its almost cult-like following as a collector vehicle. Also helping the F-100's appeal was a well designed cab with comfortable driving position and convenient controls. The '54 F-100s weren't that powerful. The 101-horsepower six and 110-horsepower flathead V-8 were carried over from previous years. That changed in '54 when the old flathead was replaced by a new overhead-valve V-8 putting out 130-horsepower. Later versions of the new V-8 generated up to 176-horsepower. Power for the six also continued to rise. By 1956, the six cylinder's power was up to 137 horses. The Ford trucks that followed in 1957 were lower and more car-like. Many still prefer the truck-like 1953-56 generation.

✚ FOR Looks like a truck • Powerful engines (after 1953) • Handles well for a fifties truck

▬ AGAINST Rough ride for those used to modern trucks • Generally not as fast, either • Prices have escalated—it's much harder to find a bargain

PRODUCTION

1953 F-100 116,437 **1954 F-100** 101,202 **1955 F-100** 124,842 **1956 F-100, short bed** 137,581 **1956 F-100, long** bed 25,122

SPECIFICATIONS

Length (in.)	189.1-203.2
Weight (lbs)	3102-3325
Wheelbase (in.)	110.0-118.0
Price (new)	$1,330-1,611

ENGINES

cid/type	bhp	years
215/ohv I-6	101	1953
223/ohv I-6	115/137	1954-56
239/sv V-8	110	1953
239/ohv V-8	130	1954
272/ohv V-8	162/176	1955-56

PRICES

F100 FAIR	$2000-5000
GOOD	$5000-8000
FINE	$8000-12,000

Add 30% for the 236 V8 [1954-55] and 272 [1956].

2000-2010 RETURN 3%

1954
FORD CRESTLINE SKYLINER

The first of Ford's production "bubbletops"—along with that year's Mercury Sun Valley equivalent—featuring a green-tinted transparent Plexiglas forward roof section. An idea of designer L. David Ash, it predicted modern counterparts in today's sunroof and flip-up sunroofs. A sunshade was offered to keep interior heat levels reasonable on bright days, and though Ford claimed that interior heat was increased only slightly without it, others insisted that it was needed. Otherwise, the Skyliner wasn't much different from the regular hardtop. Despite only a $109 price premium over the regular Victoria hardtop, it

1954 Crestline Skyliner hardtop coupe

scored but a fourth of that model's sales. Most came with Ford's first overhead-valve V-8, the new Y-Block introduced for '54, which gave better performance than the venerable flathead. The see-through roof continued as an option for the 1955-56 Fairlane Crown Victoria, but sales were again minuscule compared to the steel-topped version. The Skyliner name was revived for Ford's retractable hardtop of 1957-59, another model altogether (see entry).

✚ FOR Interesting and ahead of its time • Good construction quality • Decent performance • Clean—if somewhat bland-styling • A good example of Ford's seeming obsession with greenhouse styling in the '50s • A Milestone car

▬ AGAINST A sweatbox in summer according to some owners • Some rust tendencies

PRODUCTION

13,344

SPECIFICATIONS

Length (in.)	198.3
Wheelbase (in.)	115.5
Weight (lbs)	3265
Price (new)	$2164

ENGINES

cid/type	bhp	years
223/ohv I-6	115	1954
239/ohv V-8	130	1954

PRICES

FAIR	$4000-8000
GOOD	$8000-14,000
FINE	$14,000-20,000

FINE EXAMPLE PRICE HISTORY

1982 $5500		**1990** $14,000	
1994 $12,000		**1998** $20,000	

1982-2000 RETURN 8%
2000-2010 8%

1955-56
FORD FAIRLANE

1956 Fairlane Crown Victoria coupe

In all the hoopla about mid-'50s Chevys over the years, most people seemingly had forgotten these Fords, which were pretty nice, too. The Fairlane—named for Henry Ford's Fair Lane mansion in Dearborn—was the new top-of-the-line series for 1955, equivalent to the Chevy Bel Air, and came in six flavors; a four-door Victoria hardtop was added for '56. All featured fine styling with the rakish "Fairlane stripe" side trim and optional flashy two-tone paint, and were solidly designed (though sometimes sloppily assembled), and quick in top V-8 form. Low production makes the plastic-top Crown Victoria the most collectible model in this group, with the Sunliner ragtop and the steel-top Crown Victoria hardtop following in importance and desirability.

✚ FOR Clean, colorful styling • Good performance • Solidly built (though assembly quality sometimes lagged, especially on the '55s) • Has become a hot collector item over the last decade; appreciation still looks good

■ **AGAINST** Despite fine design, not the solid investment a 1955-56 Chevy is • Generally not as fast, either • Prices have escalated—it's much harder to fine a bargain

PRODUCTION

1955 2d Club Sedan 173,311 **4d Town Sedan** 254,437 **Victoria 2d htp** 113,372 **Crown Victoria** 33,165 **Crown Victoria (plastic top)** 1999 **Sunliner conv** 49,966 **1956 2d Club Sedan** 142,629 **4d Town Sedan** 224,872 **Victoria 2d htp** 177,735 **Victoria 4d htp** 32,111 **Crown Victoria 2d sdn** 9209 **Crown Victoria (plastic top)** 603 **Sunliner conv** 58,147

SPECIFICATIONS

Length (in.)	198.5
Wheelbase (in.)	115.5
Weight (lbs)	3155-3315
Price (new)	$1914-2272

ENGINES

cid/type	bhp	years
223/ohv I-6	120/137	1955-56
272/ohv V-8	162/182	1955-56
292/ohv V-8	200	1956
312/ohv V-8	215/225	1956

PRICES

Conv:	
FAIR	$7000-15,000
GOOD	$15,000-26,000
FINE	$26,000-35,000
Crown Vic:	
FAIR	$5500-10,000
GOOD	$10,000-19,000
FINE	$19,000-27,000
(Add $3000 for plexiglas top)	
2d htp:	
FAIR	$3500-8000
GOOD	$8000-14,000
FAIR	$14,000-23,000
Others:	
FAIR	$2250-5000
GOOD	$5000-10,000
FINE	$10,000-17,000

FINE CONVERTIBLE PRICE HISTORY

1982 $9500		**1990** $35,000	
1994 $30,000		**1998** $33,000	
1982-2000 RETURN 8%			
2000-2010 5%			

1955-57
FORD THUNDERBIRD

O ne of the earliest collectibles among postwar cars, the two-seat T-Bird has, if anything, gained in popularity as the years have passed (as the planned 2001 model suggests). Its original sales triumph over the Chevrolet Corvette was the result of clean styling, creature comforts, and V-8 refinement rather than Corvette's novel fiberglass construction and sports-car

1957 Thunderbird 2-passenger convertible

starkness. Even so, sales volume didn't impress Ford's then- conservative management (headed by Robert S. McNamara). A four-seat replacement was in the works for 1958 even as the first 'birds rolled off the line, thereby making them collector's items almost immediately. To many eyes, the heavily facelifted '57 is the most desirable because of its arguably more "together" styling. It's also the most numerous owing to an extended model year, and was offered with the widest array of powerteams. Most surviving two-seaters were spoken for long ago, however, so acquiring one now will require a hefty bank account—and a lot of patient looking.

■ **FOR** Outstanding styling; still looks great • Good performance • Beginning to gain back value it lost in the 1990s • Large club support • Two-seat mystique

■ **AGAINST** Handling uninspired • Pricey • Some rust susceptibility

PRODUCTION

1955 16,155 **1956** 15,631 **1957** 21,380

SPECIFICATIONS

Length (in.)	175.3 (1955-56), 185.2 (1957)
Wheelbase (in.)	102.0
Weight (lbs.)	2980-3145
Price (new)	$2944-3408

ENGINES

cid/type	bhp	years
292/ohv V-8	193-212	1955-57
312/ohv V-8	215-340	1956-57

PRICES

FAIR	$11,000-23,000
GOOD	$23,000-32,000
FINE	$32,000-45,000

The 1957 model is at the higher end of these scales.
Add 50% for supercharged F-Bird, 1957; add $2000 for hardtop.

FINE 1957 MODEL PRICE HISTORY

1982 $19,000	**1990** $55,000

1994 $42,000		**1998** $45,000
1982-2000 RETURN 7%		
2000-2010 10%		

1957-58
FORD FAIRLANE 500

1958 Fairlane 500 Club Victoria hardtop coupe

F ord's new top-line series in these feast-then-famine years. Shared a new 118-inch wheelbase platform with standard Fairlane hardtops and sedans, two inches longer than that of junior Custom/Custom 300 models and a newly separate Station Wagon line. Longer, lower, and wider in '50s fashion, with many styling elements from the 1955 Mystere show car. Bigger, weightier new bodies matched by lower-profile "cowbelly" frame with dropped rear floorpan and kicked-up aft siderails permitting a two-inch reduction in overall height. The suspension was improved via swept-back front lower control arms and longer rear leaf springs. All '57 engines were basically '56 units tuned for more power (in the usual ways). Facelifted '58s looked more elaborate: quad headlamps above a '58 Thunderbird-style bumper/grille, broader side trim, scalloped rear deck, four oval taillamps, and longitudinal roof ribs (to strengthen those panels, a '57 weakness). Main mechanical advances were new "big-block" 332/352 V-8s and a more sophisticated three-speed Cruise-O-Matic self-shift transmission. Ford beat Chevy in '57 model-year production, then suffered much lower sales in 1958's flash recession, as did most everyone else. Not as well built as earlier Fords (early rust-out was common) and not widely recognized among collectors until lately, so relatively scarce now. Still, well worth searching for. (See separate entry on gimmicky new Skyliner "retractable," included in Fairlane 500 series through 1959.)

✚ FOR Tasteful '57 flash • V-8 performance brisk to bombshell • Smooth ride • Roomy • Less costly now than comparable Chevys

▭ AGAINST • Debatable '58 styling ('57s generally priced higher) • Build quality down on 1955-56 • Rust-prone • Still not the investment a comparable Chevy is

PRODUCTION

1957 Victoria htp sdn 68,550 **4d Town Sedan** 193,162 **Victoria htp cpe** 183,202 **2d Club Sedan** 93,756 **Sunliner conv** 77,726 **1958 Victoria htp sdn** 14,713 **4d Town Sedan** 105,698 **Victoria htp cpe** 80,349 **2d Club Sedan** 34,041 **Sunliner conv** 35,029

SPECIFICATIONS

Length (in.)	207.2/207.5 (1957/'58)
Wheelbase (in.)	118.0
Weight (lbs)	3346-3556
Price (new)	$2235-2650

ENGINES

cid/type	bhp	years
223/ohv I-6	144	1957-58
272/ohv V-8	190/205	1957-58
292/ohv V-8	212	1957
312/ohv V-8	245/270[1]	1957
332/ohv V-8	240/265[1]	1958
352/ohv V-8	300	1958

[1] 2/4-bbl. carb

PRICES

Conv	
FAIR	$4500-12,000
GOOD	$12,000-18,000
FINE	$18,000-30,000
2d htp	
FAIR	$3000-6000
GOOD	$6000-12,000
FINE	$12,000-19,000
Others	
FAIR	$1500-4000
GOOD	$4000-10,000
FINE	$10,000-15,000

FINE 1957 CONVERTIBLE PRICE HISTORY

1982 $6500		**1990** $27,500	
1994 $24,000		**1998** $28,000	
1982-2000 RETURN 10%			
2000-2010 10% **(closed models** 5%)			

1957-59
FORD FAIRLANE 500 SKYLINER

The world's first production retractable hardtop-convertible. It seemed like a good idea at the time (and a typically '50s one at that), but proved to be a complicated beast with a lot to go wrong. It was also expensive, $400 more than the conventional Sunliner soft top. Both factors put the crimp in sales. Stylists did the best they could to provide enough room for that big roof to slide back into the trunk area. But even though the roof was shorter than on other models and its front section hinged for more compact storage, the Skyliner still ended up with a higher, longer rear deck and bulgier "bustle" rear panel. It also differed from other Fords in having a standard V-8, a relocated gas tank (behind the back seat instead of under the trunk floor), and little luggage space with the top down. Heavily restyled and re-engineered for 1959, and officially part of that year's new top-line Galaxie series though it continued to wear Fairlane 500 script. An interesting car, and a reminder of that age when Detroit thought it could do anything.

✚ FOR Technical fascination • A crowd-pleaser • Good appreciation potential • Less troublesome than most people think • Milestone car status

▭ AGAINST Mechanical/electrical gremlins • Clumsy rear styling • Shares

a great deal with ordinary Fords

PRODUCTION

1957 20,766 **1958** 14,713 **1959** 12,915

SPECIFICATIONS

Length (in.)	210.8/208.1 (1957-58/1959)
Wheelbase (in.)	118.0
Weight (lbs)	3916/4069/4064 (1957-59)
Price (new)	$2942/3163/3346

ENGINES

cid/type	bhp	years
272/ohv V-8	190	1957
292/ohv V-8	200/205/212	1957-59
312/ohv V-8	245	1957
332/ohv V-8	225/240/265	1958-59
352/ohv V-8	300	1958-59

PRICES

FAIR	$6000-12,000
GOOD	$12,000-22,000
FINE	$22,000-37,000

FINE EXAMPLE PRICE HISTORY

1982 $7000		**1990** $32,500	
1994 $29,000		**1998** $35,000	
1982-2000 RETURN 11%			
2000-2010 8%			

1958-60
FORD THUNDERBIRD

The first of the four-seat Thunderbirds, and nicknamed "Squarebird" because of its boxy lines and wide-pillar roof—which would be applied to other Ford models from Galaxies to Falcons in the '60s, and plenty of competitors, too. A slow starter in collector circles, it has come of age now, and enjoys a fairly wide following. Underrated for years because of its two-seater predecessors, this T-Bird series was, in fact, quite interesting:

1957 Fairlane 500 Skyliner retractable convertible coupe

1958 Thunderbird convertible

unit construction, low build, and the pioneering bucket-seats-and-console interior established the personal-luxury concept. A retractable hardtop had been planned, but was shelved because of the Skyliner experience and the Bob McNamara regime at Ford took a high-profit approach to design. Prize picks are the '58 convertible (rare because of initial production delays), the special "Golden Edition" 1960 hardtop, and a limited-production 1960 hardtop with the country's first postwar sliding steel sunroof (about 2500 built). There were few mechanical changes in these years apart from the Lincoln 430 V-8, which was added as an option for 1959-60.

FOR Luxurious • Reasonably compact • Strong club support • Nice looks • Personal-luxury pathfinder • Great highway cruiser • Milestone car

AGAINST Rusts easily • Heavy • Thirsty • Variable construction quality • Clumsy handling

PRODUCTION

1958 2d htp 35,758 **conv** 2134 **1959 2d htp** 57,195 **conv** 10,261 **1960 2d htp** 78,447 [1] **conv** 11,860 **"Gold Top" 2d htp** 2536
[1] Incl. approx. 2500 sunroof models

SPECIFICATIONS

Length (in.)	205.3
Wheelbase (in.)	113.0
Weight (lbs)	3799-3944
Price (new)	$3631-4222

ENGINES

cid/type	bhp	years
352/ohv V-8	300	1958-60
430/ohv V-8	350	1959-60

PRICES

FAIR	$4600-10,000
GOOD	$10,000-25,000
FINE	$25,000-35,000

Add 30% for the 430 engine.
(Convertibles are at the high end of these ranges, hardtops at the low.)

FINE CONVERTIBLE PRICE HISTORY

1982 $7500		1990 $31,000	
1994 $25,000		1998 $33,000	
1982-2000 RETURN 10%			
2000-2010 5%			

1959 FORD GALAXIE/ FAIRLANE 500 VICTORIA & SUNLINER

1959 Galaxie Sunliner convertible

Ford's most glamorous '59s (excluding the Skyliner "retrac"), with a complete reskin of the basic 1957-58 design. Noticeably squared-up lines (shared with lesser models) featured bigger windshields, "gullwing" headlamp brows, and a "Flying-V" back panel cradling large round taillamps. Boastfully billed as "The World's Most Beautifully Proportioned Cars," the '59 actually won a design award at the Brussels World's Fair. Still, it looked quite conservative next to Chevy's "batfin" '59s, though that—and a strike at GM—probably helped Ford eke out another production triumph. The Galaxie appeared midyear as a pair of Fairlane 500 hardtops with rectilinear, wide-quarter Thunderbird-style rooflines. They sold exceptionally well, thus establishing a Ford styling hallmark that would persist

for the next several years and be widely copied. The Fairlane 500 Sunliner convertible (and the "retrac") gained Galaxie script at the same time. V-8s, slightly detuned as a sop to buyers, were made economy-conscious by the '58 recession. Suspension tweaks improved ride at the expense of handling, but workmanship improved, and durability was served by no-wax "Diamond Lustre" enamel paint and long-life aluminized mufflers. Lower original production argues for the wrapped-backlight Fairlane 500 hardtops as the preferred collectibles here, but the Galaxies are preferred as the first-of-a-kind, while the Sunliner is in a class by itself.

FOR As for 1957-58 Fairlane 500, plus improved workmanship and durability • A little easier on gas

AGAINST As for 1957-58 Fairlane 500, but sloppier handling • Less appreciated by collectors than '57s

PRODUCTION

Sunliner conv 45,868 **500 Victoria htp sdn** 9,308 **500 Victoria htp cpe** 23,892 **Galaxie Victoria htp sdn** 47,728 **Galaxie Victoria htp cpe** 121,869

SPECIFICATIONS

Length (in.)	208.1
Wheelbase (in.)	118.0
Weight (lbs)	3416-3578
Price (new)	$2537-2839

ENGINES

cid/type	bhp	years
223/ohv I-6	145	1959
292/ohv V-8	200	1959
332/ohv V-8	225	1959
352/ohv V-8	300	1959

PRICES

Sunliner	
FAIR	$5000-10,000
GOOD	$10,000-19,000
FINE	$19,000-27,000
Victoria	
FAIR	$3000-6000
GOOD	$6000-11,000
FINE	$11,000-16,000

FINE SUNLINER PRICE HISTORY

1982 $6500		1990 $25,000	
1994 $22,500		1998 $27,000	
1982-2000 RETURN 9%			
2000-2010 5%			

1960-61 FORD GALAXIE STARLINER & SUNLINER

Raciest of Ford's bigger-than-ever early-'60s big cars. The all-new 1960s were some six inches longer,

1960 Galaxie Sunliner convertible

almost five inches wider, and nearly 200 pounds heavier. Graceful styling helped hide the heft, however: sloped hood, simple grille, straight A-pillars, clean chrome-edged fenderlines, and modest horizontal tailfins (nodding to Chevy's '59 "batwings"). Sunliner again led the top-line Galaxie group, but the Starliner was a real surprise: a pillarless semi-fastback two-door hardtop replacing 1959's highly popular square-roof version. It looked ready to race—and did. It also sold well, though evidently not well enough to suit Ford. A conventional hardtop coupe was reinstated for '61, and Starliner sales nose-dived; the model would not return. All '61 "standard" Fords (a needed new distinction with the advent of compacts) were slightly shorter and lighter, and tastefully made over with a concave grille, reshaped hood, more rounded bodysides, and a return to large round taillamps. Ford began moving toward "Total Performance" in these years with 1960's "Interceptor 360" version of the 352 V-8, then with 1961's enlarged 390 big-block offering up to 401 bhp. Both were very low-volume options, making them very desirable today. As are these cars, which are finally getting the collector notice they deserve.

FOR Swoopy styling • Big and spacious • Smooth V-8 powerteams • Lush ride • Still fairly inexpensive, but growing in popularity • Ample club support • Moving up strongly in value

AGAINST Good-condition originals not plentiful • Some trim and body parts scarce now • Still "in-betweeners" with less value appreciation potential than some earlier and later big Fords

PRODUCTION
1960 Starliner htp cpe 68,461 **Sunliner conv** 44,762 **1961 Starliner htp cpe** 29,669 **Sunliner conv** 44,614

SPECIFICATIONS
Length (in.)	213.7 (1960), 209.8 (1961)
Wheelbase (in.)	119.0
Weight (lbs)	3617-3791
Price (new)	$2599-2860

ENGINES
cid/type	bhp	years
223/ohv I-6	135/145	1960-61
292/ohv V-8	175/185	1960-61
352/ohv V-8	300/360	1960-61
390/ohv V-8	375/401	1961

PRICES
Sunliner	
FAIR	$3500-8000
GOOD	$8000-15,000
FINE	$15,000-22,000
Starliner	
FAIR	$3000-6000
GOOD	$6000-10,000
FINE	$10,000-15,000

FINE 1960 SUNLINER PRICE HISTORY
1982 $5200		**1990** $27,500	
1994 $15,500		**1998** $17,000	
1982-2000 RETURN 10%			
2000-2010 10%			

1961-63
FORD FALCON FUTURA

1962 Falcon Futura coupe

This was Ford's contender in the bucket-seat compact market opened up by the Chevrolet Corvair Monza. It debuted as a two-door sedan only for 1961. A choice of two rooflines—regular and T-Bird style—was offered for '62. For '63, the Futura was expanded into a separate series, with a four-door sedan, two-door hardtop, and convertible added, and you could get much the same interior treatment on the Squire wagon as well. It was limited to two six-cylinder engines until the lively V-8 Sprint arrived for mid-1963. The '63 was probably the prettiest of the Falcons, as only minor grille and ornamentation changes were made to the clean simplicity of the original 1960 styling. The '63 convertibles and "slantback" hardtops are especially attractive and easily the most desirable models in this group.

FOR Low-bucks collectible • Handsome interior • Styling • Surprising ride and roadability • Good V-8 performance

AGAINST Rust prone • Only fair assembly quality • Sedate performance (avoid the underpowered 144 six)

PRODUCTION
1961 2d sdn 44,470 **1962 2d sdn** 17,011 **1963 2d sdn** 27,018 **2d htp** 28,496 **conv** 31,192 **4dr sdn** 31,236

SPECIFICATIONS
Length (in.)	181.1
Wheelbase (in.)	109.5
Weight (lbs)	2308-2645
Price (new)	$2116-2470

ENGINES
cid/type	bhp	years
144.3/ohv I-6	85	1961-63
170/ohv I-6	101	1961-63
260/ohv V-8	164	1963

PRICES
2drs	
FAIR	$1800-4000
GOOD	$4000-7000
FINE	$7000-11,000
Add 30% for convertibles, deduct 30% for 4d sdns.

FINE 1963 2D HARDTOP PRICE HISTORY
1982 $3100		**1990** $8500	
1994 $8000		**1998** $11,000	
1982-2000 RETURN 6%			
2000-2010 6%			

1961-63
FORD THUNDERBIRD

The third-generation Thunderbird, successor to the 1958-60 "Squarebird." Chassis design remained much as before, but was reworked slightly for a smoother ride and better handling.

1963 Thunderbird hardtop coupe

An all-new bodyshell featured a severely pointed front "prow," modest fins above huge renditions of Ford's traditional round taillights, and softer roof contours on hardtops. The cowl was shared with the new Lincoln Continental, and some similarity in grille styling is evident, particularly the quad headlamps recessed in oblong housings. The interior design featured a dash that curved at its outboard ends to blend in with the door panels, and had the first "Swing-Away" steering wheel. Great attention to quality control and soundproofing made this the most comfortably quiet T-Bird to date. Ford's burly 390 V-8 was the only engine offered for '61, but a higher-output "M" unit was cataloged for 1962-63. A new Landau hardtop with simulated top irons on its rear roof pillars introduced a T-Bird styling gimmick that would be retained for several years. The models to look for are the M-engine versions and 1963's Limited-Edition Landau with special trim.

FOR Good styling • High quality • Smoothness • Refinement

AGAINST Rust problems • Thirst

PRODUCTION

1961 2d htp 62,335 **conv** 10,516 **1962 2d htp** 69,554[1] **conv** 7030 **1963 2d htp** 42,806 **conv** 5913 **Landau 2d htp** 14,139
[1]Incl. Landau hardtop

SPECIFICATIONS

Length (in.)	205.0
Wheelbase (in.)	113.0
Weight (lbs)	3958-4370
Price (new)	$4172-4912

ENGINES

cid/type	bhp	years
390/ohv V-8	300/340	1961-63

PRICES

Conv	
FAIR	$6000-12,000
GOOD	$12,000-21,000
FINE	$21,000-30,000

Htp	
FAIR	$4000-8500
GOOD	$8500-14,500
FINE	$14,500-21,000

FINE CONVERTIBLE PRICE HISTORY

1982 $7000		**1990** $30,000	
1994 $22,500		**1998** $28,000	
1982-2000 RETURN 9%			
2000-2010 8%			

1962-64
FORD GALAXIE 500XL

1963 Galaxie 500XL convertible

The first of the big performance Fords, with bucket seats, console, and posh interior trim. Introduced for mid-1962 as one of the "Lively Ones," a subseries in the Galaxie 500 lineup (named after the 500-mile NASCAR races in which Ford was doing so well). Numerous drivetrain options were available from the start, including a four-speed manual transmission and up to 425 bhp. At mid-season 1963, the XL hardtop gained a sloping semi-fastback roofline (shared with equivalent Mercurys), and a four-door version was added. For 1964, styling was more sculptured and busier than the straight-lined 1962-63 models. De-emphasized as a performance car after Ford's winningest NASCAR year ever, 1965, in which the division's full-size cars cleaned up on the super-

tracks against smaller, lighter intermediate competition. However, the XL remained part of the Ford line through 1970, though engines were progressively detuned to comply with federal emissions mandates. Quality control was a strong point on these cars, particularly the '64s.

FOR Historical interest • Race image rub-off • Straight-line performance • Luxury • Refinement • Robust construction

AGAINST Fuelishness • A handful in corners

PRODUCTION

1962 2d htp 28,412 **conv** 13,183 **1963 2d htp** 134,370 **conv** 29,713 **4d htp** 39,154[1] **1964 2d htp** 58,306 **conv** 15,169 **4d htp** 14,661
[1]Incl. non-XL Galaxie 500s

SPECIFICATIONS

Length (in.)	209.0/210.0 (1962-63/1964)
Wheelbase (in.)	119.0
Weight (lbs.)	3672-3722
Price (new)	$2268-3495

ENGINES

cid/type	bhp	years
289/ohv V-8	195	1963-6
292/ohv V-8	170	1962
352/ohv V-8	220	1962-64
390/ohv V-8	300/330	1962-64
406/ohv V-8	385/405	1962
427/ohv V-8	410/425	1963-64

PRICES

Conv	
FAIR	$3500-8000
GOOD	$8000-15,000
FINE	$15,000-22,000

Htp	
FAIR	$2500-6000
GOOD	$6000-10,000
FINE	$10,000-16,000

FINE CONVERTIBLE PRICE HISTORY

1982 $4625		**1990** $16,000	
1994 $12,000		**1998** $21,000	
1982-2000 RETURN 10%			
2000-2010 5%			

1962-63
FORD THUNDERBIRD SPORTS ROADSTER

A gesture toward buyers pining for the two-seat Thunderbird in the early '60s. A fiberglass tonneau cover, designed by Bud Kaufman, fit over the rear seat area of the normal four-seat convertible to give the appearance of a two-seater with a very long rear deck.

1963 Thunderbird Sports Roadster convertible coupe

Twin headrests at the cover's forward edge fit over the regular front bucket seats, and were raised so as to flow back to the rear, thus avoiding a too-flat appearance. The cover was designed so as not to interfere with the convertible top's operation. Kelsey-Hayes chrome-plated wire wheels were standard, and the stock rear fender skirts were deleted to provide clearance for their knock-off centers. Offered by the factory for these two years only, but a few tonneau covers found their way onto the restyled '64 convertible (minus the wire wheels) at the dealer level. In all, a clever idea (usually attributed to Lee Iacocca), but it didn't take hold, probably because the cover was cumbersome to remove or replace and the price was high. Rarity and distinctive good looks make this the prime collectible among T-Birds of these years.

FOR Attractiveness • Unique equipment • Rarity • Others as for 1961-63 Thunderbird • Strong appreciation lately

AGAINST Body rust • Fuel thirst • Tonneau won't fit the trunk • Wire wheels costly to fix and replacements are scarce

PRODUCTION
1962 1427 **1963** 455

SPECIFICATIONS
Length (in.)	205.0
Wheelbase (in.)	113.0
Weight (lbs)	4471-4396
Price (new)	$5439-5563

ENGINES
cid/type	bhp	years
390/ohv V-8	300/340	1962-63

PRICES
FAIR	$8000-13,000
GOOD	$13,000-23,000
FINE	$23,000-34,000

FINE EXAMPLE PRICE HISTORY
1982 $12,000	**1990** $35,000
1994 $32,500	**1998** $31,000

1982-2000 RETURN 7%
2000-2010 10%

1963-65
FORD FALCON FUTURA SPRINT V-8

1964 Falcon Sprint V-8 hardtop coupe

Easily the most important collector Falcon. Introduced for mid-1963, and quite successful in a short international rally career that was part of Ford's Total Performance competition program in the '60s. Available with the outstanding 260-cid small-block V-8 as an option for 1963-64, and a very lively performer. The Sprint also featured a slightly tweaked suspension, bucket-seats-and-console interior from the base Futura, and more complete instrumentation including a tachometer. A four-speed manual gearbox was listed at extra cost. Continued as part of the Futura series for 1964, when all Falcons were reskinned with bulkier, more sculpted sheetmetal. Only a handful were built in its final year, when the 260 was replaced by the 289-cid version of the small-block V-8. The '65s are worth looking for because of low production, but the '63s are the nicest looking.

FOR Fine handling and perfor-mance • Fun to drive • Not too gas-greedy '63 styling '65's rarity

AGAINST Variable construction quality • Rust-prone • Manual steering

PRODUCTION
1963 2d htp 10,479 **conv** 4602 **1964 2d htp** 13,830 **conv** 4278 **1965 2d htp** 2806 **conv** 300

SPECIFICATIONS
Length (in.)	181.1 (1963), 181.6 (1964-65)
Wheelbase (in.)	109.5
Weight (lbs)	2438-3008
Price (new)	$2320-2671

ENGINES
cid/type	bhp	years
260/ohv V-8	164	1963-64
289/ohv V-8	200	1965

PRICES
FAIR	$2200-5000
GOOD	$5000-10,000
FINE	$10,000-15,000

Convertibles are at the high end of these ranges.

FINE 1963 CONVERTIBLE PRICE HISTORY
1982 $4400	**1990** $15,000
1994 $12,000	**1998** $15,000
1982-2000 RETURN 8%	
2000-2010 8%	

1963-70
FORD (GB) LOTUS-CORTINA

The brilliant "homologation special" based on Ford of England's mass-market Cortina sedan, created by Colin Chapman for racing and rallying duty. Main difference between the bread-and-butter models and this "pro-duction" flyer (offered only in two-door form) was the engine, a conversion of the sturdy Ford GB four-cylinder unit with a Lotus-designed twincam cylinder head. Lightweight body panels and a rather complicated rear suspension (which proved unreliable and was later simplified) were also featured. The first-generation "Mark 1" models were assembled by Lotus with Ford-supplied components, and retained the current Cortina's angular styling. The situation was reversed beginning with the restyled Mark II Cortina introduced in 1967, and the Lotus variant was put together at Dagenham with far fewer special components. Both series were identified by a black grille, Lotus emblems, distinctive green bodyside striping against white body paint, a lower ride height, and wider-than-stock wheels and tires. The interiors were basically the same as for concurrent

1963-66 Lotus-Cortina Mark I coupe

Cortina GTs, with full instrumentation, bucket seats, and all-black color scheme, but a wood-rimmed, Lotus-badged steering wheel was fitted to most examples. The Lotus-Cortina was quite fast for a 1.6-liter sedan of the '60s (105 mph top speed), and was Ford's main weapon on the international rally circuit until it was succeeded by the smaller Escort Twin-Cam in 1969. The Mark I model was sold in limited numbers through Ford import dealers in the U.S. The Mark II was never officially brought in, but a few may have sneaked across our borders before the regulatory curtain fell on cars that couldn't meet federal emissions and safety standards.

✚ FOR Pocket-rocket performance • Lotus image rub-off • Terrific handling • Many body parts and some mechanical pieces still available • Active Lotus club • Race history • High appreciation potential • Pretty rare in U.S. • Not expensive

◼ AGAINST Very ordinary production body • Non-aluminum body panels rust badly • Engine demands careful tuning • Mark I models fragile • Mark II models less distinctive • Limited U.S. availability • Hard to find in good, unmodified condition

PRODUCTION
"Mark I" 2927 **"Mark II"** approx. 4000 (Ford-built)

SPECIFICATIONS
Length (in.)   168.0
Wheelbase (in.) 98.0
Weight (lbs.) 1820 (Mark 1), 2010 (Mark II)
Price (new) $2548 U.S. equivalent in 1964

ENGINES
cc/type (cid)	bhp[1]	years
1558/dohc 14 (95)	105/110	1963-70

[1]net bhp, Mark I/Mark II

PRICES
FAIR	$5000-7500
GOOD	$7500-10,000
FINE	$10,000-15,000

FINE EXAMPLE PRICE HISTORY
1982 $3500   **1987** $15,400
1994 $18,000
1982-92 RETURN 7%
2000-2010 5%

1965-66
FORD GALAXIE 500XL

1965 Galaxie 500XL convertible

Continuation of the sporty Galaxie 500 sub-series in the first new big-Ford generation since 1960. The '65s boasted more angular styling (announced by stacked quad headlamps), a sturdier new frame derived from stock-car racing experience, Ford's first-ever coil-spring rear suspension, stronger front suspension hardware, and tighter rear-axle location via twin control arms, a single lateral member, and a Panhard rod. Bodies were stronger, too, and fewer attachment points reduced noise. That led Ford to advertise its '65s as "quieter than a Rolls-Royce," a claim made mainly for the new limousine-like LTD hardtop sedan. Even so, Ford's big '65 stockers gave the division its best-ever NASCAR season, winning 48 of the 55 scheduled

Grand National events. XLs retained a sporty buckets-and-console interior *a la* 1962-64, and offered power options up to a 410-horse 427; the new free-revving small-block "Challenger 289" was standard. A manual four-speed was still available with the big mills, but most XLs continued to be built with the trusty 3-speed Cruise-O-Matic. The mildly facelifted '66s gained "7-Litre" companions, the name referring to metric displacement of their standard "428" V-8. This engine was actually closer to 427 cid, but it was designed for low-speed torque, not high-rpm performance, and was thus named to avoid confusion. Despite two-ton heft, these Fords could be quite fast, and were rewarding to drive in most any form. Their declining popularity in these years reflects less on their abilities than the market's growing preference for the even speedier mid-size muscle machines then appearing. More long-overlooked Fords that are worthy of collector esteem.

✚ FOR Handsome • Big, smooth, and quiet • Go-power ample to astounding • Lush, sporty interiors • Relatively scarce (esp. with the 427 V-8) yet still cheap • Many parts still in good supply • Growing club support

◼ AGAINST Not "mature" collectibles yet, though fast becoming so • Far from agile • Require plenty of premium petrol

PRODUCTION
1965 htp cpe 28,141 **conv** 9849 **1966 htp cpe** 25,715 **conv** 6360 **7-Litre htp cpe** 8705 **7-Litre conv** 2368

SPECIFICATIONS
Length (in.)   210.0
Wheelbase (in.) 119.0
Weight (lbs)   3497-4059
Price (new) $3233-3872

ENGINES
cid/type	bhp	years
289/ohv V-8	195/200	1965-66
352/ohv V-8	250	1965-66
390/ohv V-8	275/300/315	1965-66
428/ohv V-8	345	1966
427/ohv V-8	410/425	1965-66

PRICES
Conv
FAIR	$2500-6000
GOOD	$6000-9000
FINE	$9000-15,000

Fastback: Deduct 20%

FINE CONVERTIBLE PRICE HISTORY
1982 $3800   **1990** $12,000
1994 $15,000   **1998** $13,000
1982-2000 RETURN 9%
2000-2010

1 9 6 5 - 6 6

FORD MUSTANG

1965 Mustang convertible

Ford's biggest success of the '60s, and originator of the "ponycar" concept. Essentially a sporty compact with long-hood/short-deck proportions based on Falcon and Fairlane chassis and drivetrain components. Phenomenally successful a generation ago, it is still avidly pursued by collectors today, many of whom grew up with the car and are now reaching their peak earning years. Introduced in April 1964 as '65 models, the early cars are often called '64¹/₂s. The fastback was added six months after launch, at which time some engine and equipment shuffling took place. Modest appearance and options alterations marked the carry-over '66 version. Despite cramped rear seat accommodations, It's still a practical everyday car for the '80s, particularly with one of the thrifty sixes. A plethora of available factory accessories and option packages mean there's no "typical" example of the breed, but cars with the "hi-po" 289 V-8, manual shift, the GT package, or all three are worth searching for. Unfortunately, they're also in greater demand than tamer models, and bring correspondingly higher asking prices.

FOR Vast following • Good styling • Fine V-8 performance • Good six-cylinder economy • Practical size • GT & GT/A are Milestone cars

AGAINST Indifferent quality control • Some rust problems • Wildly fluctuating • Values seem to us overstated ($18,000 for a hardtop?)

PRODUCTION

1965 2d htp 501,965 **conv** 101,945 **fstbk** 77,079 **1966 2d htp** 499,751 **conv** 72,119 **fstbk** 35,698

SPECIFICATIONS

Length (in.)	181.6
Wheelbase (in.)	108.0

Weight (lbs)	2583-2650
Price (new)	$2372-2653

ENGINES

cid/type	bhp	years
170/ohv I-6	101	1965
200/ohv I-6	120	1965-66
260/ohv V-8	164	1965
289/ohv V-8	200/225/271	1965-66

PRICES

Conv	
FAIR	$5000-11,000
GOOD	$11,000-21,000
FINE	$21,000-30,000
Fstbk	
FAIR	$4500-10,000
GOOD	$10,000-18,000
FINE	$18,000-25,000
Htp	
FAIR	$3500-7500
GOOD	$7500-13,000
FINE	$13,000-18,000

(Add 10% for Pony interior and GT package; 30% for high-performance 271 bhp engine.)

FINE CONVERTIBLE PRICE HISTORY

1982 $6500		**1990** $18,500	
1994 $20,000		**1998** $27,000	
1982-2000 RETURN 10%			
2000-2010 3%			

1 9 6 6 - 6 7

FORD FAIRLANE 500XL GT

Sportiest of the mid-size Fords of the mid-'60s. It shared the normal XL's bucket-seats-and-console interior and distinguishing exterior striping, but had a standard 315-bhp 390 V-8 with a 335-bhp option for blistering straight line go. Ford's mighty 427 V-8 was also listed as an option starting at mid-model-year 1966, though it's likely only a few found their way into these models. Appearance was notably leaner and tauter in these years compared to previous Fairlanes. Cars with automatic were designated GT/A on exterior emblems. The small-block 289 V-8 became the standard GT powerplant for '67, but 270- and 320-bhp versions of the big-block 390 were intermediate power options just below the 427. Far less numerous than the base XLs, but only modest appreciation potential despite this, except for the ragtops.

FOR Sensible size • High performance • Good construction quality • Nice lines

AGAINST Thirsty • Some body parts becoming scarce • Convertibles are hard to come by

PRODUCTION

1966 2d htp 33,015 **conv** 4327 **1967 2d htp** 18,670 **conv** 2117

SPECIFICATIONS

Length (in.)	197.0
Wheelbase (in.)	116.0
Weight (lbs)	3070-3607
Price (new)	$2843-3068

ENGINES

cid/type	bhp	years
289/ohv V-8	200	1967
390/ohv V-8	270-335	1966-67
427/ohv V-8	410/425	1967

PRICES

Conv	
FAIR	$2500-6000
GOOD	$6000-10,000
FINE	$10,000-16,000

(Hardtop: deduct 40%)

FINE CONVERTIBLE PRICE HISTORY

1982 $3100		**1990** $12,000	
1994 $10,000		**1998** $14,000	
1982-2000 RETURN 10%			
2000-2010 5%			

1966 Fairlane 500XL convertible

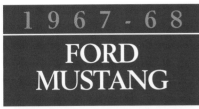

1968 Mustang Fastback coupe

FORD MUSTANG
1967-68

The heavily facelifted continuation of Ford's 1965-66 ponycar design. The main styling changes for 1967 were bulkier sheetmetal below the beltline, a more aggressive grille, a concave tail panel (with the three-element taillight clusters now separated), and a full fastback roofline for that body style. The big-block 390 V-8 was available for the first time as the top power option. It gave strong acceleration, but made the car a piggish handler. Chassis engineers tweaked suspension attachment bushings for reduced noise, vibration, and harshness. The '68s were marked by a simpler grille and side trim, and the hulking 427 V-8 was made available on a very limited basis. Overwhelming collector interest right now is in the 1965-66 Mustang, but comparable 1967-68 models can be had at half the price. However, the prospect of strong value appreciation is unclear at the moment. An interesting Shelbyesque derivative, the 1968 California Special hardtop, may be the exception because of limited production.

FOR More affordable than 1965-66s, and much the same qualities • The '67 GT & GT/A are Milestone cars

AGAINST As for 1965-66 Mustang, plus the first emissions controls on '68s and poor handling with big-inch engines

PRODUCTION
1967 2d htp 356,271 **conv** 44,808 **fstbk** 71,042
1968 2d htp 249,447 **conv** 25,376 **fstbk** 42,581

SPECIFICATIONS
Length (in.)	183.6
Wheelbase (in.)	108.0
Weight (lbs)	2568-2745
Price (new)	$2461-2814

ENGINES
cid/type	bhp	years
200/ohv I-6	115/120	1967-68
289/ohv V-8	195-271	1967-68
302/ohv V-8	230	1968
390/ohv V-8	320/325	1967-68
427/ohv V-8	390	1968

PRICES
Conv	
FAIR	$3500-6000
GOOD	$6000-18,000
FINE	$18,000-26,000
Fstbk	
FAIR	$3000-6000
GOOD	$6000-13,000
FINE	$13,000-19,000
Htp	
FAIR	$2500-5000
GOOD	$5000-9500
FINE	$9500-16,000

(See 1965-66 Ford Mustang for special equipment considerations.)

FINE CONVERTIBLE PRICE HISTORY
1982 $4000	**1990** $15,000
1994 $18,000	**1998** $22,000
1982-2000 RETURN 12%	
2000-2010 3%	

FORD TORINO GT
1968-69

Ford's sporting intermediates in these years, part of the newly named upper series in the restyled Fairlane line. The usual buckets-and-console interior treatment and a more muscular chassis continued to set these GTs apart from the "family" Torinos and Fairlanes just like the previous Fairlane 500XLs. New this year was a sleek fastback two-door hardtop that proved very slippery—and very successful—in long-distance stock car races. Restyled for 1970 with sleeker-looking lines that actually proved less aerodynamic on the supertracks.

FOR As for 1966-67 Fairlane 500XL GT • Convertible rarity • Neat if not timeless styling

AGAINST Spotty assembly quality • Thirsty with performance engines

PRODUCTION
1968 2d fstbk 74,135 **2d htp** 23,939 **conv** 5310
1969 2d fstbk 61,319 **2d htp** 17,951 **conv** 2552

SPECIFICATIONS
Length (in.)	201.0
Wheelbase (in.)	116.0
Weight (lbs)	3173-3356
Price (new)	$2747-3090

ENGINES
cid/type	bhp	years
302/ohv V-8	210/220/230	1968-69
351/ohv V-8	250/290	1969
390/ohv V-8	265/335	1968-69
427/ohv V-8	390	1968
428/ohv V-8	335	1969

PRICES
Conv	
FAIR	$2500-5000
GOOD	$5000-9000
FINE	$9000-14,000
Others	
FAIR	$1800-4000
GOOD	$4000-7000
FINE	$7000-11,000

FINE CONVERTIBLE PRICE HISTORY
1982 $2800	**1990** $8000
1994 $12,000	**1998** $14,000
1982-2000 RETURN 10%	
2000-2010 5%	

FORD MUSTANG BOSS 302/429
1969-70

The Boss 302 was Ford's purpose-built contender for the Sports Car Club of America's Trans-Am sedan road racing series, and was similar in concept to Chevy's Camaro Z/28 pack-

1969 Torino GT fastback coupe

1969 Mustang Boss 429 fastback hardtop coupe

age. Exciting design work by ex-GM stylist Larry Shinoda, including back-light louvers, a front under-bumper lip spoiler, trunklid wing spoiler, and distinctive bodyside striping, marked this near race-ready version of the Mustang fastback. Underneath were a stiff suspension, four-speed gearbox, power front disc brakes, wide tires, and a much-fortified, high-winding 302 V-8. From mid-1969, a plainer looking very limited-production Boss 429 was also available, created mainly to homologate the Boss 429 engine for NASCAR competition. The Bosses have tremendous appeal because of "factory racer" exclusivity, but are a rare bird on today's market.

➕ **FOR** Tremendous performance • Handling/roadholding • Rarity • Milestone car status

➖ **AGAINST** Not very tractable for street use • High running costs • Hard to find in original condition • Expensive

PRODUCTION

1969 302 1934 **429** 858 **1970 302** 6318 **429** 498

SPECIFICATIONS

Length (in.)	187.4
Wheelbase (in.)	108.0
Weight (lbs)	3210-3227
Price (new)	$3588-3720

ENGINES

cid/type	bhp	years
302/ohv V-8	290	1969-70
429/ohv V-8	360	1969-70

PRICES

302	
FAIR	$6500-14,000
GOOD	$14,000-24,000
FINE	$24,000-35,000
429	
FAIR	$11,000-23,000
GOOD	$23,000-40,000
FINE	$40,000-58,000

FINE BOSS 429 PRICE HISTORY

1982 $6000	1990 $60,000
1994 $48,000	1998 $52,000
1982-2000 RETURN 15%	
2000-2010 8%	

1969-70
FORD MUSTANG MACH 1/ CONVERTIBLE/ GRANDE

The best collector bets among regular production models in the second Mustang generation. Prime pick is the performance-leading Mach 1, replacing the previous GT for '69. Basically the normal "SportsRoof" fastback with matte-black hood, hood locks, I.D. bodyside striping, special trim, and a firmed-up chassis. Base power was a 250-horsepower 351 V-8, but options went all the way to a 335-bhp 428 Cobra Jet—complete with protruding "shaker" hood scoop. The Grande hardtop coupe, also new for '69, emphasized luxury with extra sound insulation, color-keyed vinyl top, wire-wheel covers, beltline paint striping, various bright exterior moldings, and good simulated teak interior accents—all for about $230 over the standard hardtop. A lowly six was standard for both the Grande and the ever-desired Mustang convertible, but options extended to a 300-bhp 351. Wheelbase was unchanged in these years, but the styling was huskier, simplified for '70 by a return to dual head-lamps (previously quads) and tidier detailing throughout.

➕ **FOR** Mach 1's performance • Grande's luxury • Convertible's usual attractions • Very strong club support • Plentiful NOS and reproduction parts • Appreciation potential good to excellent

➖ **AGAINST** Less sought-after than earlier Mustangs • Little demand for six-cylinder models (get a V-8) • Less practical styling

PRODUCTION

1969 Mach 1 72,458 **conv** 14,746 **Grande htp cpe** 22,182 **1970 Mach 1** 40,970 **conv** 7673 **Grande htp cpe** 13,581

SPECIFICATIONS

Length (in.)	187.4
Wheelbase (in.)	108.0
Weight (lbs)	2873-3240
Price (new)	$ 2849-3271

ENGINES

cid/type	bhp[1]	years
200/ohv I-6	115	1969-70
250/ohv I-6	155	1969-70
302/ohv V-8	220	1969-70
351/ohv V-8	250/300	1969-70
428/ohv V-8	335/365	1969-70[2]
429/ohv V-8	375	1970[2]
[1]SAE gross	[2]Optional Mach 1 only	

PRICES

FAIR	$3000-6500
GOOD	$6500-12,000
FINE	$12,000-18,000

FINE EXAMPLE PRICE HISTORY

1982 $3200	1990 $16,000
1994 $16,000	1998 $17,000
1982-2000 RETURN 12%	
2000-2010 3%	

1969
FORD TORINO COBRA & TALLADEGA

A pair of mid-size muscle Fords with somewhat different aims. The no-frills Torino Cobra replied to Plymouth's popular '68 Road Runner, and was

1970 Mach 1 fastback hardtop coupe

1969 Torino Cobra fastback coupe

1969 Talladega fastback coupe

actually an option package on the new-for-'68 Torino notchback and fastback SportsRoof hardtop coupes. Production isn't available because it was folded in with Fairlane 500 models, but most were probably built as fastbacks. Standards comprised a 335-bhp 428 V-8, four-speed manual shift, heavy-duty suspension, six-inch-wide wheels, F70 x 14 wide-oval tires, and a taxicab-plain interior. Tail and front fenders wore small, cartoon snakes—decals at first, emblems later. Options included several axle ratios, Cruise-O-Matic, Ram-Air induction with a broad hood scoop, buckets, console, tach, power front-disc brakes, and limited-slip differential. It proved its mettle on the dragstrips; typical standing quarter-mile time was 14.5 seconds; 0-60 mph took six seconds flat. The Talladega, named for the 2.66-mile Alabama superspeedway that opened in '69, aimed to put Torino back in the NASCAR hunt against the slicker, faster Mercury Cyclones and Dodge Chargers. Developed in the wind tunnel, it was a Torino fastback given an extended front end (by six inches) that gently curved to a flush Cobra grille. The result was less drag and higher top speed with no more horsepower. Street versions, all with white bodies and flat-black hoods, were built to meet production minimums. Equipment was much like the Cobra's save for mandatory Cruise-O-Matic, power steering and brakes (with front discs), and a competition suspension. The Talladega accomplished its mission, helping Ford to 26 NASCAR Grand National wins and the 1969 championship.

➕ FOR Muscle-car performance and mystique • Talledega's rarity and purpose-built character • Terrific enthusiasm for this genre

➖ AGAINST Few sound, sanitary originals left • Collector prices have been volatile • Not much fun to drive except in a straight line • Variable workmanship

PRODUCTION

Cobra NA (option package) Talladega 754 (incl. prototypes)

SPECIFICATIONS

Length (in.)	200.1 (Cobra), 206 (Talladega)
Wheelbase (in.)	116.0
Weight (lbs)	3490-3600
Price (new)	Cobra, $3164-3189; Talladega, NA

ENGINES

cid/type	bhp	years
428/ohv V-8	335	1969

PRICES

Talladega	
FAIR	$3500-8000
GOOD	$8000-12,000
FINE	$12,000-20,000
Torino Cobra	
FAIR	$3000-6500
GOOD	$6500-10,500
FINE	$10,500-16,500

FINE TORINO COBRA PRICE HISTORY

1982 $4200		**1990** $14,000	
1994 $14,000		**1998** $16,000	
1982-2000 RETURN 9%			
2000-2010 5%			

1970-71
FORD TORINO GT & COBRA

Early-'70s continuations of Ford's late-'60s bucket-seat mid-sizers and their high-performance Cobra cousin. Inch-longer wheelbases and curvy new styling "shaped by the wind," though the latter actually made the cars slower on NASCAR's super-tracks. No notchback GT or Cobra hardtops here, just semi-fastbacks. Drivetrains were much as before for '70, but some engines were detuned for emissions, mileage, and insurance reasons. Downgrading in standard engines occurred for '71: the GTs from a V-8 to a six, the Cobra from a 428 big-block to a four-barrel "Cleveland" small-block, though both could still be ordered with a 429 in four versions with up to 370 horsepower. By that time, though, performance was being legislated away, and the all-new '72 Torino mirrored the market by being still-bigger, heavier, more luxury-oriented—and minus both Cobra and convertibles. The GT hardtop held on, but only as a shadow of its former self. All this explains why the 1970-71 GTs and Cobras are included here, though they aren't likely to ever be high-status collectibles.

➕ FOR Last of their kind • Swoopy styling • Sporty • Performance still high with the right options • Used-car cheap

➖ AGAINST Still little collector interest • Workmanship mixed • Driveability bothers crop up • Cobra less special than in '69

PRODUCTION

1970 GT htp cpe 56,819 **GT conv** 3939 **Cobra htp cpe** 7675 **1971 GT htp cpe** 31,641 **GT conv** 1613 **Cobra htp cpe** 3054

SPECIFICATIONS

Length (in.)	206.2
Wheelbase (in.)	117.0
Weight (lbs)	3287-3490
Price (new)	$3105-3525

1970 Torino GT convertible

ENGINES

cid/type	bhp[1]	years
250/ohv V-6	145	1971
302/ohv V-8	220/250	1970-71
351/ohv V-8	285/300	1970-71
429/ohv V-8	360/370/375	1970-71

[1]SAE gross

PRICES

GT coupe

FAIR	$1800-4000
GOOD	$4000-8000
FINE	$8000-12,000

GT conv

FAIR	$2500-5800
GOOD	$5800-9000
FINE	$9000-14,500

GT Cobra

FAIR	$4000-7500
GOOD	$7500-13,000
FINE	$13,000-19,000

FINE GT COBRA PRICE HISTORY

1982 $4300	**1990** $13,000
1994 $15,000	**1998** $19,000
1982-2000 RETURN 9%	
2000-2010 5%	

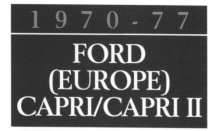

1970-77 FORD (EUROPE) CAPRI/CAPRI II

1972-73 Mercury Capri coupe

European ponycar built by Ford's subsidiaries in both England and Germany, where it proved as popular (comparatively speaking) as the original Mustang. Introduced in 1969, the Capri was brought to the U.S. in late 1970 under the Mercury nameplate, though it never bore that badge. While European customers could choose from a vast array of power and trim options (the personalizing with options concept that had proved so successful here), U.S. buyers initially got a German-built coupe in one state of trim, powered by the British Ford 1600cc crossflow "Kent" engine as used in the Cortina. There were reasons for this: German construction quality was superior and the Cortina four was already emissions-legal. Buyers took to the Capri in sufficient numbers to encourage Ford to broad-

en power and trim choices. Thus, a larger 2.0-liter four was added shortly (along with more complete engine instrumentation), followed by a V-6. In 1974, the car was treated to a mild frontal redo and a new dashboard, then was extensively redesigned with revised outer panels and a hatchback rear as the Capri II, introduced late in the 1975 model year and officially designated a '76. Base, luxury Ghia, and sporty "S" models were listed, the last available with a striking black-and-gold color scheme reminiscent of the John Player Lotus Grand Prix cars. Unfavorable currency exchange rates were rendering German goods quite costly by 1977, by which time Ford was well along with a more civilized domestic ponycar to replace the modestly successful Mustang II. It was decided to give Mercury a Capri version of this car for 1979, and imports of "the sexy European" were halted. Production ceased in 1987. Collectibility still arguable at this point, but the potential is there.

➕ FOR Easy parts connections via Lincoln-Mercury • Nice performance/economy balance • Good handler • Inexpensive to buy and maintain

➖ AGAINST Seriously rust-prone • Indifferent body and interior trim quality • V-6 valvetrain and oil leak problems • Little collector interest at present

PRODUCTION

Capri I 1,169,088 **Capri II** 404,169 through 1977

SPECIFICATIONS

Length (in.)	167.8 (1970) to 174.8 (1977)
Wheelbase (in.)	100.8
Weight (lbs.)	2150 (1970) to 2571 (1977 Ghia)
Price (new)	$2445 (1970) to $4373 (1977); $4585 (1977 Ghia)

ENGINES

cc/type (cid)	bhp	years
1599/ohv I4(98)	64	1971-72
1993/ohc I4(122)	85	1971-74
2550/ohv V6 (156)	107/120	1972-73
2792/ohv V6 (171)	119/110	1974-77

Note: Not officially imported for 1975 model year and after 1977.

PRICES

FAIR	$1500-3000
GOOD	$3000-5000
FINE	$5000-7500

FINE EXAMPLE PRICE HISTORY

Prices, depressed for years, are beginning to pick up, but mainly in England.
2000-2010 RETURN 2%

1971 FORD MUSTANG BOSS 351

Effective replacement for the Boss 302 in the first year of the "fat" Mustang generation, though much less unique than its forebears and never actively raced. Not much more than a Mach 1 with different side striping, Boss-type front spoiler, and a standard 330-horsepower 351 V-8 instead of a 210-bhp 302. However, its $856 price premium did include the Mach's special "competition" suspension option (high-rate front springs/shocks, staggered rear shocks, stabilizer bars at each end). Canceled at mid-model year for lack of buyers in a rapidly withering performance market, it's included here mainly for keeping alive the "Trans-Am Mustang" notion, even if not very well or for very long.

➕ FOR Racy looks • Fine go for the period (under 6 seconds 0-60) • Low

1971 Mustang Boss 351 fastback hardtop coupe

original production • Some collector interest now • Plentiful owner support from many excellent clubs

⬛ **AGAINST** Far less "special" than Boss 302 *vis-a-vis* Mach 1 • Suffers as much as other Mustangs from '71 upsizing • Few good-condition originals left

PRODUCTION
est. 1800

SPECIFICATIONS

Length (in.)	187.5
Wheelbase (in.)	109.0
Weight (lbs)	3220
Price (new)	$3268

ENGINES

cid/type	bhp[1]	years
351/ohv V-8	330	1971

[1]SAE gross

PRICES

FAIR	$6000-11,000
GOOD	$11,000-15,000
FINE	$15,000-25,000

FINE EXAMPLE PRICE HISTORY

1982 $4050	**1990** $22,500
1994 $25,000	**1998** $30,000
1982-2000 RETURN 12%	
2000-2010 3%	

1 9 7 1 - 7 3
FORD MUSTANG CONVERTIBLES & MACH 1

The prime standard-model picks from one of the least-collectable eras of early Mustang. However, despite being bigger, heavier, and more "styled," the 1971-73s weren't nearly as bad as the press painted them, as handling, roadholding, and even steering precision were all improved. So, too, was interior space, the main reason for the "more ponycar" approach taken during the design's late-'60s gestation. But these Mustangs were born to a changing, troubled market, and fast-tightening emissions controls took a big performance toll after 1971 (no more big-block V-8, just detuned small-blocks and six). Ford didn't help by demoting the Mach 1 fastback to a standard 302, nor by offering its front-end look on lesser Mustangs in an Exterior Decor Group and, for 1972, a Sprint Decor Option with big patches of blue on an otherwise white body, plus red pinstripes,

five-spoke styled wheels, and U.S.A. stars-and-stripes decals. But all these cars looked racy, the '71s offered some semblance of genuine muscle-car power, and Mustang's body-color bumper covers coped handsomely with 1973's new 5-mph impact standard while adding less than five inches to overall length. Not the best Mustangs in most people's view, but quite worthy of being saved and savored.

➕ **FOR** Unique in Mustang history • Sleek lines • Mustang charisma • V-8 performance acceptable to exhilarating • Roomier cabins (though still pretty tight) • More sought-after now • Club support as ardent as for any Mustang

⬛ **AGAINST** Less exciting and not as sought-after as earlier models • Price appreciation still weak • Top-condition originals tough to find

PRODUCTION
1971 Mach 1 36,499 **conv** 6121 **1972 Mach 1** 27,675 **conv** 6401 **1973 Mach 1** 35,440 **conv** 11,853

SPECIFICATIONS

Length (in.)	189.5 (1971-72), 193.8 (1973)
Wheelbase (in.)	109.0
Weight (lbs)	3050-3220
Price (new)	$3015-3268

ENGINES

cid/type	bhp	years
250/ohv I-6	95/100/145[1]	1971-73
302/ohv V-8	210[1]	1971
302/ohv V-8	136[2]	1972-73
351/ohv V-8	240/285[2]	1971
351/ohv V-8	168/255/275[2]	1972
351/ohv V-8	155[2]	1973
429/ohv V-8	370[1]	1971

[1]SAE gross [2]SAE net

PRICES

Mach 1	
FAIR	$3000-7000
GOOD	$7000-12,000
FINE	$12,000-14,000

Conv	
FAIR	$3500-7000
GOOD	$7000-13,000
FINE	$13,000-16,000

FINE CONVERTIBLE PRICE HISTORY

1982 $4200	**1990** $9000
1994 $11,500	**1998** $18,000
1982-2000 RETURN 8%	
2000-2010 5%	

1 9 7 8
FORD MUSTANG II KING COBRA

1978 Mustang King Cobra fastback coupe

An interesting low-production "paint-on performance" edition of Ford's pudgy little subcompact ponycar in its last season. It was designed under the auspices of Ford styling chief Eugene Bordinat, and given impetus by the sales success of the earlier Cobra II option package. Available only as a three-door fastback, the King Cobra had almost every racy styling touch a kid could want. There was a giant snake decal and bold scoop on the hood and tape stripes on the roof, rear deck, rocker panels, around the windshield and wheel arches, and on the deep front air dam that was also part of

1971 Mustang Mach 1 fastback hardtop coupe

the package. The words "King Cobra" appeared on each door and on the standard decklid spoiler. A black-finished grille, window moldings, headlamp bezels, and wiper arms, plus a brushed aluminum instrument panel applique completed the cosmetics. Functionally, the King Cobra was built around the Mustang II's optional small-block V-8, bolstered by standard power steering, "Rallye" handling package, and Goodrich raised white-letter 70-series radial tires. Capable of 17 second quarter-mile times—not high performance like in the '60s, but good for an emissions-throttled, safety-certified 1970s car. Much less numerous than the Cobra II models (which earned hoots of derision from Shelby Mustang lovers), but it seems likely to remain a low-appreciation item on the collector market for some time yet.

⊞ FOR "Macho" appearance features • Good performance/economy balance • A decent handler • Hatchback practicality • Cheap-to-buy, sensible daily driver

▭ AGAINST Muscle-car doodads look silly on this scale to some eyes • Collectibility questionable at present

PRODUCTION

5000 (est.)

SPECIFICATIONS

Length (in.)	175.0
Wheelbase (in.)	96.2
Weight (lbs)	approx. 2950
Price (new)	$5075

ENGINES

cid/type	bhp	years
302/ohv V-8	140[1]	1978

[1]SAE net

PRICES

FAIR	$2500-3000
GOOD	$3000-6000
FINE	$6000-7500

FINE EXAMPLE PRICE HISTORY

1994 $7000   **1998** $8250
Depreciating through most of the 1990s, now stable.
2000-2010 RETURN 2%

1979
FORD MUSTANG PACE CAR REPLICA

Ford's totally redesigned third-generation ponycar was chosen to pace

1979 Mustang Pace Car replica coupe

the 1979 Indianapolis 500, just as the original Mustang had done 25 years earlier. A few weeks before the race, Ford issued these pace-car replicas, which introduced styling features adopted the following year for the optional Cobra package. While the one-off '79 pace car was powered by a much-modified 302 V-8 and had a T-bar roof (which caused a few construction headaches), the replicas were offered with either the stock-tune V-8 or Ford's interesting turbocharged 2.3-liter four-cylinder engine. Everything else was the same, though: distinctive pewter and black paint treatment with orange and red tape striping, aerodynamic slatted grille above a deep chin spoiler, special hood scoop, plus multi-adjustable Recaro racing-type bucket front seats. The usual pace car regalia adorned the bodysides, and included a multi-image running horse logo. All the replicas were the three-door hatchback equipped with a four-speed manual shift and flip-up glass sunroof. A very nice limited edition of a well-balanced, stylish, latterday ponycar.

⊞ FOR Fairly exclusive • Tasteful performance-look styling • Fine handling • Nice interior • Basic body and mechanical pieces still as close as your local dealer

▭ AGAINST Not that much different mechanically from stock '79s • Watch

out for bogus replica conversions of standard Mustangs • Too recent to be a high-demand item yet

PRODUCTION

11,000

SPECIFICATIONS

Length (in.)	179.1
Wheelbase (in.)	100.4
Weight (lbs)	2800 (approx.)
Price (new)	NA

ENGINES

cid/type	bhp[1]	years
140/ohc I-4[2]	140	1979
302/ohv V-8	140	1979

[1]SAE net [2]Turbocharged

PRICES

FAIR	$2500-3500
GOOD	$3500-5500
FINE	$5500-7000

FINE EXAMPLE PRICE HISTORY

1982 $6000	**1990** $7500
1994 $5000	**1998** $6600

1982-2000 RETURN 1%
2000-2010 2%

1983-93
FORD MUSTANG GT CONVERTIBLE

The reborn Mustang convertible in its sportiest, most potent, and thus most collectible form. After a long absence, both the GT and open-air models returned during 1983, when Ford's evergreen ponycar received its first facelift since the third-generation 1979 redesign. There was also a GT version of the mainstay hatchback coupe and a less sporty LX convertible, but when '80s Mustangs become

1986 Mustang GT convertible

prime collectibles—as they eventually will—the GT ragtop will be one of the first. Most GTs in these years were built with the veteran 302 small-block V-8, which saw progressive power increases and an induction change from four-barrel carb (1983-85) to fuel injection (1986 on); all teamed with standard manual five-speed, or optional automatic (which shifted from three-speed to overdrive four-speed starting with 1985). Uprated "handling" suspension was always included, with firm springs/ shocks and bigger-than-stock wheels/ tires. A second makeover for 1987 brought "aero" body addenda that made GTs "boy-racer" busy, and Ford diluted potential sales by offering a V-8 package for LXs. Still, Mustang remained true to its original '60s concept, and the convertible was quite practical with its easy-fold power top and glass backlight. Too new and numerous to show any price appreciation yet, but almost bound to later. Possible "sleepers" here are the 4508 paint-and-tape "GT-350" hatchbacks and convertibles built in Mustang's 20th Anniversary year.

FOR Great small-block scoot (8 seconds or less 0-60 mph) • Sporty, top-down fun • "Modern nostalgia" • Best-built ragtop Mustangs ever • Still current, so plentiful parts/service • Depreciation has bottomed out; values will now improve

AGAINST Old-fashioned handling • Tight back seat • Small trunk • Structure a bit "willowy" • Debatable post-1986 styling

PRODUCTION

1983 12,000 **1984** 10,000 **1985** 10,000 **1986** 18,000 **1987** 20,238 **1988** 15,000 **1989-90** 20,000 (all figures estimated except 1987)

SPECIFICATIONS

Length (in.)	179.6
Wheelbase (in.)	100.4
Weight (lbs)	2850-2975
Price (new)	$13,050-10,848

ENGINES

cid/type	bhp	years
302/ohv V-8	165/175	1983-84
302/ohv V-8	180/210	1985
302/ohv V-8	200	1986
302/ohv V-8	205-225	1987-93

PRICES

FAIR	$2500-4000
GOOD	$4000-6000
FINE	$6000-8000

FINE EXAMPLE PRICE HISTORY

1982 $6000		**1990** $7500	
1994 $5000		**1998** $6600	

1982-2000 RETURN 3%
2000-2010 2%

1983-84
FORD MUSTANG TURBO GT

Unsuccessful next-to-last attempt at force-feeding the market a force-fed ponycar. Mustang had continued in its 1979 third generation with a standard Pinto/Fairmont 2.3-liter ohc four, but also offered a new turbo version—usually with a performance-minded Cobra option package. It offered the hottest available engine, but driveability bothers proved chronic, prompting Ford to withdraw it after 1981. Meantime, a sluggish national economy revived in time for 1982's reborn Mustang GT with a high-output 302 V-8, and a new "horsepower war" was on. But Ford still thought some buyers wanted near-V-8 power with greater fuel efficiency, so an improved turbo 2.3 was offered for '83 with port-electronic fuel injection instead of a carburetor, plus a "blow through" turbo system (replacing the previous "draw down" plumbing)—the same engine used in that year's new Thunderbird Turbo Coupe. For Mustang, Ford wisely tied it to the GT-equipped "fasthatch" coupe, but the bottom line was $386 above a comparable V-8 GT, and automatic shift wasn't available. Worse, the blown four was peakier and less torquey, so the car was slower. A Turbo GT convertible was added for '84, but sales didn't improve and the idea was abandoned for '85. The similar but more specialized Mustang SVO would meet the same fate a year later.

FOR Interesting modern Mustang • Relatively rare, especially the convertible • Adroit handling • Coupe hatchback practical

AGAINST Only Mustang fans care • Engine noisy and torqueless

PRODUCTION

Approx. 3600 (incl. approx. 600 convertibles)

SPECIFICATIONS

Length (in.)	179.6
Wheelbase (in.)	100.4
Weight (lbs)	2950-3050
Price (new)	$9714-13,245

ENGINES

cid/type	bhp	years
140/sohc I-4[1]	142/145	1983-84

[1]Turbocharged

PRICES

FAIR	$1500-2500
GOOD	$2500-3000
FINE	$3000-4000

FINE EXAMPLE PRICE HISTORY

Depreciating until recently.
2000-2010 RETURN 2%

1983-88
FORD THUNDERBIRD TURBO COUPE

The sportiest "personal" Ford since the supercharged F-Birds of 1957. Announced with the 1983 "aero-styled" 10th generation, slightly smaller than the Fairmont-based 1980-82s and far more radical in appearance but on a similar chassis. The Turbo Coupe came with the just-improved turbocharged version of Ford's 2.3-liter

1983 Mustang Turbo GT coupe

1984 Thunderbird Turbo coupe

ohc four (hence the name), plus black exterior accents, contoured bucket seats, and a firm suspension featuring four rear shock absorbers ("Quadra-Trac"), two sited horizontally to resist axle tramp. Only a five-speed manual was offered for '83, but an optional three-speed automatic (at some power penalty) was listed for 1984-86, after which a four-speed automatic took over. Progressively improved in other ways through '86—more instruments, water-cooled turbo center bearing, larger wheels/tires—before getting a heavy facelift and the more powerful intercooled engine of the recently defunct Mustang SVO for 1987. Also new that year were standard all-disc brakes and variable-rate shock absorbers. Much of the Turbo Coupe package was eventually offered with the 302 V-8 in LX models that sold as well or better, and didn't suffer the TC's "on/off" power quirks. How this will affect Turbo Coupe collectibility remains to be seen.

✚ FOR Good performer, all things considered (0-60 in 10 seconds or less) • Agile handler, too • Sporty demeanor • 1983-86 styling • Well-equipped • Relatively luxurious •Cheap

▬ AGAINST Throttle lag, exhaust boom, and other nasty engine traits • Jekyll-and-Hyde ride • Visibility not great • Little, if any, value appreciation prospects for foreseeable future

PRODUCTION

NA; total series: **1983** 121,999 **1984** 170,533

1985 151,851 **1986** 163,965 **1987** 128,135 **1988** 147,243

SPECIFICATIONS

Length (in.)	197.6 (1983-86), 202.1 (1987-88)
Wheelbase (in.)	104.0
Weight (lbs)	3075-3415
Price (new)	$11,790-17,250

ENGINES

cid/type	bhp	years
140/ohc I-4[1]	142/145/155	1983-86
140/ohc I-4[1]	150/190	1987-88

[1]Turbocharged

PRICES

FAIR	$1250-2000
GOOD	$2000-3000
FINE	$3000-4500

FINE EXAMPLE PRICE HISTORY

Depreciating until recently.
1982-2000 RETURN 0%
2000-2010 2%

1984-85
FORD LTD LX

Dearborn's short-lived nod to the growing mid-'80s "Eurosedan" market, though more a "four-door Mustang" answering similar concoctions from domestic rivals. Based on the new-for-'83 "little" LTD cloned from the 1978-vintage Fairmont compact. Mustang had used a shortened Fairmont chassis since '79, so creating this LX was a matter of substituting appropriate components (most developed for an LTD Police Package) and adding the requisite "blackout" exterior. Specifics included a throttle-body-injected 302 V-8, four-speed automatic, "Traction Lok" rear axle, high-rate gas-filled shocks, stiff springs, a larger front anti-roll bar, and Eagle GT performance tires. Power brakes, steering, and windows were standard along with front buckets, center shift console, a

special gauge cluster with tach, six-way power driver's seat with adjustable lumbar support, and gray cloth upholstery. Colors were silver, charcoal, and light blue, with a grille to match. Much livelier than four- and six-cylinder LTDs, and genuinely fun to drive. In retrospect, though, a sports-sedan stand-in pending the slick new 1986 Taurus and, perhaps as a result, not heavily promoted. Production ended after only some 18 months.

✚ FOR Brisk pickup (9 seconds 0-60) • Refined drivetrain • Capable handling • Good brakes • Roomy enough for four • Above-average fit-and-finish • Inexpensive

▬ AGAINST Dowdy looks • Weak value appreciation at best

PRODUCTION

3260

SPECIFICATIONS

Length (in.)	196.5
Wheelbase (in.)	105.5
Weight (lbs)	2950
Price (new)	$11,100

ENGINES

cid/type	bhp	years
302/ohv V-8	165	1984-85

PRICES

FAIR	$1500-2200
GOOD	$2200-3200
FINE	$3200-5000

FINE EXAMPLE PRICE HISTORY

Depreciating until recently.
1982-2000 RETURN 0%
2000-2010 2%

1984-86
FORD MUSTANG SVO

1985 Mustang SVO coupe

Last of the force-fed Fords, with initials standing for Dearborn's then-new Special Vehicle Operations unit that conceived this package for the Mustang hatchback comprising special appearance touches and a high-output

1984 LTD LX sedan

intercooled version of the blown 2.3-liter Turbo GT/Thunderbird Turbo Coupe four. Unique grilleless nose, "biplane" rear spoiler, and wheelwell fairings reflected Ford's new turn to "aero" design, and a large hood scoop fed the water-to-air intercooler. The SVO also sported two headlamps (instead of four), a front airdam with integral foglamps, fat V-rated tires on cast-aluminum wheels, and a performance chassis with stiff springs, Koni adjustable shocks, thick front stabilizer bar, quick-ratio high-effort power steering, enlarged front disc brakes, and matching rear discs (replacing drums). Inside were multi-adjustable Turbo Coupe seats and pedals repositioned for easier heel/toe maneuvers with the mandatory five-speed manual transmission. The result was a sophisticated screamer (only about 7.5 seconds 0-60) that excited "buff books" but not buyers. The reason was the V-8 Mustang GT, which delivered a similar wallop for $6000 less. An air-to-air intercooler added 30 horses for '85, when flush "composite" headlamps appeared. But the market had spoken and the SVO was dropped after '86. An honest try for a more "European" Mustang, but failed because its concept was a contradiction in terms.

✚ FOR Another short-lived modern Mustang, and more specialized • Good acceleration • Delightful "light-footed" handling feel • A roomy, practical 2+2 • Relatively luxurious • Special-interest value

◼ AGAINST All-or-nothing power delivery • Gimmicky "split-level" rear spoiler • Valued mainly by Mustangers now • Not likely to be widely coveted for some time yet

PRODUCTION
1984 4508 **1985** 1954 **1986** 3382

SPECIFICATIONS
Length (in.)	179.6
Wheelbase (in.)	100.4
Weight (lbs)	2995-3140
Price (new)	$14,521-15,596

ENGINES
cid/type	bhp	years
140/ohc I-4[1]	175-205	1984-86

[1]Turbocharged

PRICES
FAIR	$2500-4500
GOOD	$4500-6500
FINE	$6500-9500

FINE EXAMPLE PRICE HISTORY
Depreciating until recently, now moving back up.
1982-2000 RETURN 0%
2000-2010 2%

1989-91
FORD TAURUS SHO

Performance version of Ford's "Eurostyle" family four-door, new for '86. SHO meant a "Super High Output" 3.0-liter V-6—a.k.a. "Shogun"— the everyday overhead-valve "Vulcan" unit reengineered by Yamaha to be almost completely new. Prime changes: 24-valve twincam cylinder head with pent-roof combustion chambers; two-stage induction system with 12 individual runners. To avoid unwanted torque-steer with front-wheel drive, Ford installed equal-length halfshafts, recalibrated suspension, added performance tires and rear disc brakes (to match the fronts). Exterior distinctions were subtle (some said too subtle): perimeter rocker skirts, more aggressive lower front facia, and a thin air slot below the Ford "navel" emblem in the nose. The interior was standard save for contoured, multi-adjustable front seats, center console, and analog gauges. Available only with a somewhat balky, Mazda-supplied manual five-speed because Ford didn't have an automatic transaxle strong enough for the Shogun's torque—the main factor in yearly sales that were only half of what Ford expected.

✚ FOR Faster than a similar vintage BMW 535i 0-60 (under 7.5 seconds) • Revvy yet tractable engine with strong mid-range pull and primo sounds • Secure, stable front-drive handling and grip • Roomy • Plenty of amenities

◼ AGAINST Too new to predict ultimate collectibility • Heavy-handed five-speed • Low-buck metal dash/door trim

---

PRODUCTION[1]
1989 12,000 **1990** est. 7000
[1]Calendar-year sales

SPECIFICATIONS
Length (in.)	188.4
Wheelbase (in.)	106.0
Weight (lbs)	approx. 3100
Price (new)	$19,739-21,633

ENGINES
cid/type	bhp	years
182/dohc V-6	220	1989-90

PRICES
FAIR	$2000-3000
GOOD	$3000-4500
FINE	$4500-6000
2000-2010 RETURN Even		

1989-95
FORD THUNDERBIRD SUPER COUPE

1990 Thunderbird Super Coupe

Successor to the Turbo Coupe as the hotshot T-Bird in 1989's new 11th generation. Still a closed five-seater, but broader of beam, five inches longer in wheelbase, and some 300 pounds heavier. Old 2.3-liter turbo four junked for a newly supercharged 3.8 V-6 with 20-60 more horsepower. Manual five-speed and automatic four-speed transmissions, all-disc antilock brakes, auto-adjusting shock absorbers, and

1989 Taurus SHO sedan

uprated rolling stock as before, but independent rear suspension a first for T-Bird. Styling simpler and more graceful, made racier on the SC via perimeter lower-body skirts, twin-venturi front bumper, and debossed I.D. lettering on both bumpers. Cabin plusher than ever, enhanced by new low-profile dash. Criticized by road-testers and admitted by Ford as too heavy for real agility, but lots of cornering "stick" and smooth, rapid acceleration. Not a super-seller in the troubled late-'80s market, but low volume plus many laudable qualities argue for it as a future collectible. A handful of special 35th Anniversary 1989 models may have a slight value edge.

➕ FOR An American BMW 6-Series • Fast mover (under 8 seconds 0-60) • Secure, "beefy" steering/handling • ABS brakes • Luxurious

➖ AGAINST Heavy and thirsty • Manual shift a chore • Trunk and back-seat space limited • Some interior trim tacky

PRODUCTION
NA

SPECIFICATIONS

Length (in.)	198.7
Wheelbase (in.)	113.0
Weight (lbs)	approx. 3600
Price (new)	$20,000-23,000

ENGINES

cid/type	bhp	years
232/ohv V-6[1]	210-230	1989-95
[1]Supercharged		

PRICES

FAIR	$2000-6000
GOOD	$6000-8000
FINE	$8000-11,500

Price range depends on model year and is subject to used car market.
2000-2010 RETURN Even

FORD THUNDERBIRD 35TH ANNIVERSARY EDITION

The final "heavy-coupe" Thunderbird generation produced this 5000-unit anniversary model, which was a gussied-up Super Coupe, the supercharged and intercooled apex of the T-Bird line. Performance buffs liked the

1990 Thunderbird 35th Anniversary Edition coupe

SC's 210-horse blown V-6, which ran the 0-60-mph sprint in 7.5 seconds with 5-speed manual, and the quarter-mile in the mid-15-second range at just under 90 mph. Although heavy at 3581 pounds, this rear-driver was reasonably poised, and was big fun in straight-line travel. Regrettably, the Anniversary Edition brought nothing to the SC party beyond special upholstery, wheels, an accent stripe, badging, and black-and-platinum body paint.

➕ FOR Performance • Aggressive, slab-sided design • Limited production

➖ AGAINST Still a "used car" • A cosmeticized "factory collectible," and thus not likely to excite great collector interest

PRODUCTION
1990 5000 (aprox.)

SPECIFICATIONS

Length (in.)	198.7
Weight (lbs)	3581
Wheelbase (in.)	113.0
Price (new)	$22,253

ENGINES

cid/type	bhp	years
232/ohv V-6[1]	210	1990
[1]Supercharged		

PRICES

FAIR	$2000-6000
GOOD	$6000-8000
FINE	$8000-11,500

Price range depends on model year and is subject to used car market.
2000-2010 RETURN Even

FORD TAURUS SHO

Restyled in 1992, the SHO still looked and drove much the same as its predecessor. For the first time the SHO had front end styling that differed from the other Taurus'. Though that difference was subtle. The biggest change was the availability of a 4-speed automatic transmission in '93. Ford did more than just drop in an automatic transaxle. The automatic SHO had a slightly larger engine than the manual version. The extra torque of the larger engine mated better with the automatic tansmission. The suspension was also slightly softer for the automatic cars. Automatic or 5-speed, the SHO was still one of America's best sport sedans.

➕ FOR As for 1989-91 • Available automatic transmission

➖ AGAINST As for 1989-91

PRODUCTION
NA

SPECIFICATIONS

Length (in.)	192.0
Weight (lbs)	3131-3118
Wheelbase (in.)	106.0
Price (new)	$23,889-25,140

ENGINES

cid/type	bhp	years
182/dohc V-6	220	1992-95
195/dohc V-6	220	1993-95

PRICES

Fair	$5000
Fine	$14,000

1993 Taurus SHO sedan

1993 FORD MUSTANG COBRA

1993 Mustang Cobra coupe

A "factory collectible" that really will be collected, because the things that set it apart from other '93 Mustangs were genuine, significant performance upgrades: tweaked suspension and handling, and an uprated version of the GT's 5.0-liter V-8, cranking 245 bhp as opposed to the GT's 205. Visual cues unique to the Cobra were kept to a tasteful minimum: dual exhausts, rocker panel extension moldings, rear bumper fascia, and a rear spoiler with built-in center brake light. A modest Cobra snake emblem was positioned behind each front wheel-arch. Production amounted to only about 5000, which adds to the Cobra's allure. Still a used car, but prices will rise before it's ten years old.

FOR Acceleration • Roadholding & handling • Limited production • The real article, not a prettied-up fake

AGAINST Still a "used car" • Thirst

PRODUCTION
1993 4993

SPECIFICATIONS
Length (in.)	179.6
Weight (lbs)	3225
Wheelbase (in.)	100.5
Price (new)	$19,900

ENGINES
cid/type	bhp	years
302/ohv V-8	245	1993

PRICES
FAIR	$10,000-13,000
GOOD	$13,000-15,000
FINE	$15,000-19,000

Prices governed by used car market.
2000-2010 RETURN Depreciating

1994 FORD MUSTANG COBRA

All 1994 Mustang Cobra convertibles were Indy Pace Car replicas, although it was up to owner's discretion (or lack of it) to apply the decals. As with the '93, it the Cobra bits that make it more collectible than regular Mustangs. An extra 25-horsepower, upgraded suspension and brakes separatred Cobras from the GTs. Exterior differences were subtle. A smoother front fascia with fog lights and small snakes on the front fenders were the most obivious changes. The interior was distinguished by leather seats and white-faced gauges. All Mustangs were redesigned for '94 with better styling and improved suspensions. Convertibles were stiffer than before, but still had some flex on rough roads. Only 1,000 Cobra convertibles were built in 1994, but almost the same car was available in '95—hurting its collectibilty.

FOR Performance • Low production • Easier to drive daily than a Camaro Z28

AGAINST Not as fast as a Camaro • Body more flexible than it should be

PRODUCTION
1994 1000

SPECIFICATIONS
Length (in.)	181.5
Weight (lbs)	3500
Wheelbase (in.)	101.3
Price (new)	$23,535

ENGINES
cid/type	bhp	years
302/ohv V-8	240	1994

PRICES
Convertible	
Fair	$18,000
Good	$21,300
Fine	$27,275

1995 FORD MUSTANG COBRA R

1995 Mustang Cobra R coupe

A true collector's item rather than a "factory special," the Cobra R was produced mainly for race enthusiasts. The purpose-built engine was the first Mustang 5.8-liter (351 cid) since 1973, and it was worth the wait: 300 bhp and a thumping 365 pounds/feet of torque. A stout, Tremec 5-speed manual trans was mandatory. Stiffened suspension and a "rally bar" linking the tops of the front shock towers to the firewall aided handling and structural rigidity. Weight-saving was accomplished in Draconian fashion: no sound-deadening or insulation material; no back seat; lightweight front buckets from the base Mustang; a 20-gallon Kevlar bladder rather than a standard metal fuel tank. And you could forget about AC, power windows and locks, radio, and similar weight-adding features. The R's Spartan character was a big part of its appeal, and although it was no treat as a daily driver, it never was intended to

1994 Mustang Cobra Pace Car convertible (with 1964 Mustang Pace Car)

fill that role, anyway. Only about 250 were made, and buyers had to show a valid competition license and documented racing history.

◼ FOR Street-legal and race-ready • Outstanding handling & roadholding • Understated good looks • Minuscule production

◼ AGAINST Many examples were raced, and thus will be tired • Noticeable lack of creature comforts • Noise • Thirst • Pricey from the get-go

PRODUCTION
1995 250

SPECIFICATIONS
Length (in.)	181.5
Weight (lbs)	3326
Wheelbase (in.)	100.5
Price (new)	$22,253

ENGINES
cid/type	bhp	years
351/ohv V-8	300	1995

PRICES
FAIR	$20,000-25,000
GOOD	$25,000-30,000
FINE	$30,000-35,000

Prices governed by used car market.
2000-2010 RETURN Depreciating

1 9 9 6 - 9 9
FORD TAURUS SHO

1996 Taurus SHO sedan

The first generation SHO was available with only a manual transmission. The last version had only an automatic. That seemed symbolic of the softening of Ford's sport sedan. The new dual overhead cam V-8 was developed and built with Yamaha—as was the V-6 it replaced. The V-8 wasn't much faster, but it was more relaxed. The SHO had firmer suspension with adjustable shock absorbers and more precise steering than the normal Taurus. All Tauruses had new aerodynamic bodies for '96. The SHO styling cues were always subtle, but with the new design, SHOs stood out even

less. With the 2000 Taurus restyling the SHO was gone.

◼ FOR Sharp handling • Low production • Engine unique to car

◼ AGAINST Styling not universally loved • Not as exciting as previous versions • Harsh ride

PRODUCTION
NA

SPECIFICATIONS
Length (in.)	198.3
Weight (lbs)	3510
Wheelbase (in.)	108.5
Price (new)	$25,930-29,000

ENGINES
cid/type	bhp	years
207/dohc V-8	235	1996-99

PRICES
Subject to used car market

1 9 9 8
FORD NASCAR F-150 PICKUP

Ford's ¹/₂-ton F-150 pickup was America's best-selling vehicle—again—in 1998, and hardly needed a special edition to spur sales. But because the 50th anniversary years of the F-Series and NASCAR happened to coincide, a 3000-unit F-truck was tricked out and sent to showrooms. Lowered ride height and unique tires and wheels were the major changes from an XL F-150 with optional V-8. The only available engine was the smaller of Ford's two V-8s, the 4.6-liter Triton rated at 220 bhp and 290 pounds/feet of torque at 3250 rpm. Five-speed manual stick was standard; 4-speed automatic was an extra-cost option. Other features were cosmetic: a low front air dam with

color-keyed (mandatory black) grille surround, checkered-flag graphics, NASCAR decals and badging, plus NASCAR-logo floormats and headrests. All told, a capable hauler in gaudy dress.

◼ FOR NASCAR/F-150 connection • Limited production

◼ AGAINST Mainly a trim package • Collector appeal likely to be regional

PRODUCTION
1998 3000

SPECIFICATIONS
Length (in.)	202.2
Weight (lbs)	4028
Wheelbase (in.)	119.9
Price (new)	$19,995

ENGINES
cid/type	bhp	years
281/ohc V-8	220	1998

PRICES
Prices governed by used car market.
2000-2010 RETURN Depreciating

1 9 9 8 - 0 0
FORD SVT CONTOUR

One of the nicer driving American sport sedans, the Contour SVT was based on Ford's slow selling compact sedan. The Special Vehicle Team (SVT) massaged the standard V-6 to produce an extra 25-horsepower and a pleasant growl. A crisp-shifting 5-speed manual was the only transmission available. The suspension was modified for crisper handling, but not at the expense of comfort. All SVTs had comfortable leather seats, though back seat room was tight. The exterior gained fog lights, some body cladding, and larger alloy wheels. This well

1998 F-150 NASCAR Edition pickup

1998 Contour SVT sedan

equipped sedan offered only two options—sunroof and CD player. All this was priced at $22,365. In spite of this value, sales were below expectations. Maybe the collector market will be kinder to the SVT.

⊞ FOR Sharp handling • Sweet engine • Well equipped

⊟ AGAINST Cramped interior • Looks like a Contour • Lacks prestige name of some other sport sedans

PRODUCTION
1998 6535 **1999** 2760

SPECIFICATIONS
Length (in.)	183.9
Weight (lbs)	3055
Wheelbase (in.)	106.5
Price (new)	$22,365-22,715

ENGINES
cid/type	bhp	years
155/dohc V-6	195-200	1998-00

PRICES
Subject to used car market.

1999
FORD MUSTANG 35TH ANNIVERSARY

Every 1999 Mustang was a 35th anniversary model (complete with 35th anniversary badging), so this cosmetically enhanced ponycar was as good as the '99 GT that it really was—which is to say: aggressively handsome (all Mustangs got a "New Edge" restyle for the model year) and pleasingly quick with its 260 bhp 4.6-liter V-8). The $2695 anniversary option

1999 Mustang 35th Anniversary convertible

reserved for just 5000 cars offered next to nothing: black-and-silver leather on seats and door panels; birthday logo floormats; black, back-panel appliqué; and a short black stripe leading from the forepart of the hood and culminating in a raised dummy scoop. The package was available with the GT coupe and convertible, and it's the latter, of course, that will be the more collectible of the two. But a considerably better bet for future collectibility is the '99 Cobra. Come to that, a standard '99 GT will be valued virtually as highly as this empty dress-up package.

⊞ FOR It's a Mustang • Available convertible body style • Acceleration • Handling & roadholding • Limited production

⊟ AGAINST A "factory collectible," and a weak one at that • Many years of depreciation ahead before a slow climb to "collectible" status and value • Easy to counterfeit

PRODUCTION
1999 5000

SPECIFICATIONS
Length (in.)	183.2
Weight (lbs)	3069-3211
Wheelbase (in.)	101.3
Price (new)	$23,565-27,565

ENGINES
cid/type	bhp	years
282/ohc V-8	260	1999
2000-2010 RETURN Depreciating		

1932-34
FRANKLIN SUPERCHARGED TWELVE

1933 Series 17-A Supercharged Twelve sedan

While all the Franklins are historic and collectible, the great Supercharged Twelve represented the company's finest hour and is easily the most significant model of its later years. At nearly 400 cubic inches, this engine was the largest in Franklin history, and with traditional air cooling and aluminum construction it was unique and technically fascinating. Coachwork was hand-built by Franklin itself in Syracuse to a LeBaron design, distinguished by a sharply vee'd grille and a long, shapely hood extending back to a rakishly angled windshield. Imposingly beautiful but, like so many of its ilk, it just didn't sell in the depressed market of the day.

⊞ FOR Spectacular engineering to a unique specification • Magnificent coachwork • CCCA Classic status, yet not too pricey for its class

⊟ AGAINST Scarcity of available models • Significant parts shortage • High maintenance/operating costs • No open body styles

PRODUCTION
Approx. 400

SPECIFICATIONS
Length (in.)	NA
Wheelbase (in.)	144.0
Weight (lbs)	5515-5900
Price (new)	$2885-3185

ENGINES
cid/type	bhp	years
398.0/sv V-12[1]	150	1932-34
[1]Supercharged		

PRICES
FAIR	$5000-12,000
GOOD	$12,000-18,000
FINE	$18,000-40,000

FINE EXAMPLE PRICE HISTORY
1982 $41,000		**1987** $31,000	

1990 $50,000   1994 $50,000
1982-2000 RETURN 0%
2000-2010 2%

1947 Manhattan sedan

Top-of-the-line Kaiser-Frazer product, the first entirely new postwar body style, and a never before equalled array of interior and exterior colors are points that distinguish these Howard Darrin-designed four-door sedans. The bulbous body and long wheelbase gave enormous interior space, and combined with an economical six-cylinder engine to provide smooth highway travel with surprising gas mileage. Colors and fabrics were selected by designer Carleton Spencer, a genius whose efforts predicted industry-wide practice.

✚ FOR Historical importance: the first straight-through fenderlines and advanced color/trim combinations • High quality • Parts supplies still good • A Milestone car

━ AGAINST Underwhelming styling • Engine subject to cooling problems, enjoys blowing head gaskets

PRODUCTION
1947 32,655 **1948** 18,591

SPECIFICATIONS
Length (in.)	203.0
Wheelbase (in.)	123.5
Weight (lbs)	3375
Price (new)	$2712-2746

ENGINES
cid/type	bhp	years
226.2/sv I-6	112	1947-48

PRICES
FAIR	$2200-4500
GOOD	$4500-7000
FINE	$7000-10,000

FINE EXAMPLE PRICE HISTORY
1982 $3000   1990 $7500
1994 $9000   1998 $10,000
1982-2000 RETURN 9%
2000-2010 5%

The first Frazers were built by Graham-Paige Motors under a worksharing agreement with Kaiser-Frazer. Costs of operations proved more than G-P could bear, so the firm sold its interests to K-F. Standard (non-Manhattan) Frazers bearing serial numbers up to F47-009940 (1001 was the first number) are G-P products, and bear the nameplates of that old-line company. That historical aspect plus rarity puts these models in a class apart from K-F-built Frazers this year.

✚ FOR Extremely rare • Historical interest • New styling for the time

━ AGAINST Not pretty • Mundane interiors • Almost impossible to find, yet not a high-potential investment

PRODUCTION
8940

SPECIFICATIONS
Length (in.)	203.0
Wheelbase (in.)	123.5
Weight (lbs)	3340
Price (new)	$2295

ENGINES
cid/type	bhp	years
226.2/sv I-6	100	1947

PRICES
FAIR	$2000-4000
GOOD	$4000-7000
FINE	$7000-8500

FINE EXAMPLE PRICE HISTORY
1982 $2000   1990 $6500
1994 $8500   1998 $10,000
1982-2000 RETURN 9%
2000-2010 2%

The last Frazer authorized by Joseph W. Frazer before he was replaced as K-F president by Edgar Kaiser. These cars retained the previous bodyshell, spruced up with a new—and more attractive—honeycomb grille and large vertical taillamps. The convertibles required a heavily reinforced X-braced frame to provide torsional stiffness for the roofless body, which was virtually handbuilt from the sedan shell. This wasn't a true ragtop in the sense that the window frames and the little B-pillar window didn't retract.

✚ FOR Same good qualities of 1947-48 • More glittery look • Posh interior • Unusual postwar convertible sedan style, scarce and desirable • Milestone car status

━ AGAINST As for 1947-48 Manhattan • Convertible trim, particularly interior, nearly impossible to find

PRODUCTION[1]
4d sdn 9950 **4d conv sdn** 70
[1]Figures approximate; includes some reserialed 1949s sold as 1950 models

SPECIFICATIONS
Length (in.)	207.5
Wheelbase (in.)	123.5
Weight (lbs)	3391-3726
Price (new)	$2595-3295

ENGINES
cid/type	bhp	years
226.2/sv I-6	112	1949-50

PRICES
Sdn	
FAIR	$2500-4500
GOOD	$4500-7000
FINE	$7000-10,000

1947 4-door sedan

1949 Manhattan convertible sedan

Conv	
FAIR	$8000-15,500
GOOD	$15,500-23,000
FINE	$23,000-35,000

FINE CONVERTIBLE PRICE HISTORY

1982 $9000	1990 $28,500
1994 $25,000	1998 $41,000
1982-2000 RETURN 8%	
2000-2010 5%	

1951
FRAZER MANHATTAN

1951 Manhattan hardtop sedan

The last of the Frazers. Marked by an extreme facelift from the cowl forward by K-F stylist Herb Weisinger, who also raised the rear fenders and gave them shallow, faired-in taillights. Also new was Hydra-Matic transmission, "imported" from General Motors, as standard. Despite styling that generally provoked an all-or-nothing reaction, more '51s could have been sold than were built, but the main reason for offering them at all was to use up leftover Kaiser convertible and hardtop bodies. When they were gone (by mid-1951), so was the Frazer.

FOR Scarce and desirable • High-quality materials and body construc-

tion • Last of the marque • Value spurted in late 1990s

AGAINST Debatable styling • Body parts in short supply • Same engine drawbacks as other 226-cid K-F models

PRODUCTION

4d htp sdn 152 **4d conv sdn** 131

SPECIFICATIONS

Length (in.)	211.4
Wheelbase (in.)	123.5
Weight (lbs)	3771-3941
Price (new)	$3075 (either model)

ENGINES

cid/type	bhp	years
226.2/sv I-6	115	1951

PRICES

Htp	
FAIR	$2400-4600
GOOD	$4600-7000
FINE	$7000-10,000
Conv	
FAIR	$8000-16,000
GOOD	$16,000-24,000
FINE	$24,000-33,000

FINE HARDTOP PRICE HISTORY

1982 $5000	1990 $18,000
1994 $21,000	1998 $30,000
1982-2000 RETURN 11%	
2000-2010 5%	

1951
FRAZER (STANDARD MODEL)

The base series in Frazer's last model year, with the same styling as the '51 Manhattan. Includes the intriguing Vagabond utility sedan, a carryover of the 1949-50 Kaiser model

1951 4-door sedan

featuring a double rear hatch and fold-down rear seatback that opened up an enormous load bed. The Vagabond was K-F's halfway solution to the problem of how to offer wagon-like cargo carrying capacity and versatility without the tooling expense for a separate wagon body. The regular sedan was more luxurious than previous base Frazers, being trimmed to 1949-50 Manhattan levels.

FOR Good quality • Smooth road cars • Vagabond's versatility, unusual design

AGAINST As for 1951 Manhattan

PRODUCTION

9931 (incl. approx. 3000 Vagabond 4d utility sdns)

SPECIFICATIONS

Length (in.)	sedan: 211.4; Vagabond: 207.7
Wheelbase (in.)	123.5
Weight (lbs)	3456-3556
Price (new)	$2359-2999

ENGINES

cid/type	bhp	years
226.2/ I-6	115	1951

PRICES

Both models	
FAIR	$2000-4000
GOOD	$4000-6500
FINE	$6500-9000

FINE VAGABOND PRICE HISTORY

1982 $2750	1990 $8500
1994 $9500	1998 $10,500
1982-2000 RETURN 7%	
2000-2010 3%	

1930-39
FRAZER NASH CHAIN-DRIVE MODELS

The Frazer Nash marque grew out of the GN design, and was always related in philosophy to the HRG (see entry). FN's claims to fame were a simple chassis with a cart-spring suspension and chain-drive (one chain for

1930-39 chain-drive roadster

each gear) transmission. They were characterized by stark vintage-style bodies with cycle-type fenders that gave them an uncompromisingly sporty nature. Traction (with no differential) was remarkable, as was the animal-like handling response, but creature comforts and accommodation were nearly nonexistent. Maximum speeds ranged from 70 to 90 mph depending on engine and coachwork. Over the years, a variety of 1½-liter four- and six-cylinder engines were used. Specifications are for the popular Meadows-engine TT (Tourist Trophy) Replica model.

FOR Prewar Brit sports car appeal • Handling • Rugged durability • Active (UK) club • Simple to rebuild • CCCA Classic status for some upon application

AGAINST Poor weather protection • Frail transmission (but easy to repair) • Very hard suspension • Cramped interiors • Not well known in the U.S.

PRODUCTION
350

SPECIFICATIONS
Length (in.)	150.0
Wheelbase (in.)	102.0
Weight (lbs)	1800
Price (new)	NA

ENGINES
cc/type (cid)	bhp[1]	years
1496/ohv I-4 (91)	62	1931-39

[1]Gross

PRICES
Infrequent sales over a broad variety of models make generalities unwise in the case of Frazer

Nash. Continuing demand for chain-driven Frazer Nashes has exerted upward pressure on prices despite the market fall-out of the 1990s. British quotes were running upwards of $60,000 for most models.
2000-2010 RETURN 5%

1948-56
FRAZER NASH

1948-56 LeMans Replica roadster

A hand-built British sports car of the old school, powered by the contemporary Bristol six-cylinder engine based on prewar BMW engineering. A variety of body styles from closed coupe to single-seat Formula 2 racer was available for the tubular ladder-style chassis featuring independent front suspension and a live rear axle. All bodies were made of aluminum. Several engine tunes were also offered, with output ranging from 105 to 130 bhp. In fact, there was no such thing as a "standard"

Frazer Nash, as the production total suggests, each one being made to special order. The best-known models were the cycle-fender High Speed/Le Mans Replicas. Envelope-body cars included the colorfully named Mille Miglia, Targa Florio, Sebring, and Fast Tourer. They were costly when new despite minimal trim and equipment, mostly because of expensive, painstaking construction techniques. A thoroughbred driving machine all the way, with no concessions to comfort or modern engineering.

FOR Excellent handling • High performance (up to 120 mph) • Very rare • Rustproof body

AGAINST Supply restricted, to say the least • Very expensive to buy • Few outside UK • No body, chassis parts now • Expensive to restore and maintain

PRODUCTION
95

SPECIFICATIONS
Length (in.)	150.0 (variable with body)
Wheelbase (in.)	96.0
Weight (lbs)	1800-1950
Price (new)	NA

ENGINES
cc/type (cid)	bhp[1]	years
1971/ohv I-6 (120)	105-130	1948-56

[1]Net

PRICES
Recent prices include the following: **Le Mans replica**, $198,000; **Mille Miglia (1949-54)**, $100,000; **drophead cpe**, $70,000; **Targa Florio**, $70,000; **1952 rdstr**, $50,000; **1953 LeMans cpe** $45,000; **Sebring**, $60,000.
2000-2010 RETURN 5%

1963-68
GLAS 1300/1700/1600 GT

1963 1300 GT 2+2 coupe

A brave attempt at a sporting product by an old-line German independent in its final years. All are 2+2 fastback coupes with unit construction and shapely styling by Frua of Italy, which also built a few convertibles with similar lines beginning in 1965. Model designations reflect displacement of the sohc four-cylinder engines. The 1300 and (from 1965) 1700 units were Glas' own, borrowed from its "volume" sedans and notable for the first cogged belt for the cam drive. The 1700 GT was briefly offered in the U.S. before Glas was absorbed by BMW, which attempted to boost sales by substituting the engine, transmission, and rear suspension from its 1600ti sedan.

FOR Distinctive Italian-inspired styling • Advanced Glas engine (1300/1700) • More powerful and reliable BMW engine (1600) • Very rare in U.S.

AGAINST Parts of all kinds are gone • BMW can't help much • Very rust-prone • Serious handling flaws on 1300/1700

PRODUCTION
1300/1700 GT (1963-67) approx. 800 **BMW 1600GT (1967-68)** 1255

SPECIFICATIONS
Length (in.)	161.4
Wheelbase (in.)	91.4
Weight (lbs)	2010/2115 (1700/1600)
Price (new)	$3695, '66 1700 GT in U.S.

ENGINES
cc/type (cid)	bhp[1]	years
1289/ohc I-4 (79)	75	1963-67
1682/ohc I-4 (103)	100	1965-67
1573/ohc I-4 (96)	105	1967-68

[1]DIN

PRICES
FAIR	$2500-4000
GOOD	$4000-6000
FINE	$6000-8000

FINE 1600 GT PRICE HISTORY
1982 $3000		**1987** $6000	
1990 $10,000		**1994** $8000	
1982-2000 RETURN 10%			
2000-2010 3%			

1965-68
GLAS 2600/3000 GT

A last desperate move by Glas to change its image as a maker of stodgy family cars. Italian stylist Pietro Frua designed the conservative but clean semi-fastback four-seat coupe body, which rested on a special platform chassis with de Dion rear suspension. Power was supplied by a V-8, effectively two four-cylinder units from the 1300 GT on a common crankcase, and a surprisingly successful piece of

quick production engineering. Following the takeover of Glas by BMW in 1966, engine size was uprated to 3.0 liters for 1967 in an attempt to broaden the model's market appeal. It also acquired circular blue-and-white BMW logos on the hood, trunklid, and hubcaps. Styling had much in common with the Frua-designed Maseratis of the period, though there was also some family resemblance to the smaller 1300/1700 GT. The front end was marked by a fussy grille with large, high-set square headlamps.

FOR Interesting styling • U.S. rarity • Effective engine and performance (125 mph maximum)

AGAINST Few built • Engine, chassis components unavailable • Hard to find now

PRODUCTION
NA

SPECIFICATIONS
Length (in.)	182.0
Wheelbase (in.)	98.4
Weight (lbs)	2485
Price (new)	NA

ENGINES
cc/type (cid)	bhp[1]	years
2576/dohc V-8 (157)	140	1965-66
2982/dohc V-8 (182)	160	1967-68

[1]DIN

PRICES
FAIR	$5000-7500
GOOD	$7500-9000
FINE	$9000-15,000

FINE 2600 GT PRICE HISTORY
1982 $7000		**1987** $12,000	
1990 $18,000		**1994** $15,000	
1982-2000 RETURN 5%			
2000-2010 3%			

1955-57
GMC SUBURBAN

1955 S-100 Suburban pickup

GMC's version of Chevrolet's Cameo pickup was initially called Town & Country. The name was changed to Suburban to avoid trouble with Chrysler, but was probably confused with the Suburban wagon. The Suburban shared the same smooth styling of the Cameo, but the GMC had the advantage of bigger, more powerful engines than Chevrolet. The six was an GMC design, while the V-8 was borrowed from Pontiac. While Chevrolet built the Cameo as a low-production model, GMC used the Suburban as a promotional piece to draw showroom traffic. Suburbans are therefore much rarer than Cameos.

FOR Trend-setting style • Rarity • Better performance than a Cameo

AGAINST Even harder to find than a Cameo • Parts also hard to find

1967 3000GT coupe by Frua

PRODUCTION

NA

SPECIFICATIONS

Length (in.)	198
Weight (lbs)	3645
Wheelbase (in.)	114.0
Price (new)	$1,923[1]

[1]1955 price

ENGINES

cid/type	bhp	years
248/ohv I-6	125	1955
269/ohv I-6	130	1956-57
287/ohv V-8	155	1955
316/ohv V-8	180	1956
347/ohv V-8	206	1957

PRICES

Fair	$3300
Good	$5675
Fine	$10,450

1992 Syclone pickup

1991-92
GMC SYCLONE

GMC's S-15 compact pickup was named "Sonoma" for 1991, and because GMC wanted to establish a distinct corporate identity, about 3000 copies of the Sonoma were fitted with a 4.3-liter EFI Vortec V-6 with a turbocharger that increased horsepower from 160 to 280; torque came in at 350 pounds/feet at a relatively low 3600 rpm. Sole transmission was a 4-speed Hydra-Matic with a high-capacity cooling system. A lowered, beefed-up suspension and full-time AWD helped keep the Syclone planted on the pavement. Sole body-color choice was a "two-tone" gloss black/matte black scheme. Lower body cladding and alloy wheels contributed to an unmistakable but laudably restrained "muscle" look. GMC claimed 0-60 times of less than 5 seconds, and quarter-mile runs of 13.4 seconds. From 0-100 mph, the Syclone was well-nigh unbeatable. This was Corvette ZR-1 and Ferrari 348ts territory—and for just $25,500.

✚ FOR Supercar-style acceleration • Exclusive to GMC—no other GM variant • Darkly sinister good looks • High level of comfort • Novelty

▬ AGAINST It's a truck • Thirst • Exhaust racket

PRODUCTION

NA

SPECIFICATIONS

Length (in.)	180.5
Weight (lbs)	3600
Wheelbase (in.)	108.3
Price (new)	$25,970-26,995

ENGINES

cid/type	bhp	years
262/ohv V-6[1]	280	1991-92

[1]Turbocharged

PRICES

FAIR	$11,000-12,000
GOOD	$12,000-18,000
FINE	$18,000-21,500
2000-2010 RETURN	Depreciating

1992-93
GMC TYPHOON

1993 Typhoon 2-door wagon

Sharing a drivetrain with the GMC Syclone, the Typhoon used the heavier body of the GMC Jimmy 2-door. A slight loss in performance was more than made up for with practicality of 4-passenger seating and covered cargo area. All Typhoons had leather seats and were well equipped. With its sophisticated 4-wheel drive system and wide tires, the Typhoon handled well. The antilock brakes were also extremely effective for a truck. The truck origins made themselves known on rough pavement. The lowered ride-height ruled out leaving the pavement for off-roading. The market for a truck with supercar performance was limited when new, but low production and high performance has always been a safe bet in the collectors market.

✚ FOR Almost as fast as a Syclone • More practical than a Syclone • Sinister good looks

▬ AGAINST A truck that can't haul much • Rough ride

PRODUCTION

NA

SPECIFICATIONS

Length (in.)	170.3
Weight (lbs)	3800
Wheelbase (in.)	100.5
Price (new)	$28,995-29,320

ENGINES

cid/type	bhp	years
262/ohv V-6[1]	280-285	1992-93

[1]Turbocharged

PRICES

FAIR	$13,000-16,000
GOOD	$16,000-22,000
FINE	$22,000-24,500

1964-66
GORDON-KEEBLE GK1 & GKIT

A feeble attempt to combine Chevrolet V-8 power with British chassis engineering and Bertone styling. This smart, close-coupled four-seat coupe featured a fiberglass body set on a separate multi-tubular chassis. It was very fast thanks to the 300-bhp Chevy 327 V-8, and also offered good handling and running refinement. The Bertone styling dated from 1960, and was a more elegant forerunner of

1965 GK1 coupe by Bertone

the Iso Rivolta shape. The G-K was distinguished by a four-headlamp front end, with the lamps mounted in slant-eye formation. Considered as desirable as a Ferrari at the time, it nonetheless lacked the cachet of a famous name. Ultimately, the Gordon-Keeble was a commercial failure because it was underpriced. It's a very sought-after car today because of its rot-free body, but not common or widely known outside its home country.

FOR Rustproof fiberglass body • High performance from easily serviced Detroit iron • Styling • Exclusivity • Active British club

AGAINST No chassis or body parts any more • Extremely costly to buy • Not as refined as equivalent Ferrari • Are there any in the States?

PRODUCTION

GK1 80 **IT** 19

SPECIFICATIONS

Length (in.)	189.5
Wheelbase (in.)	102.0
Weight (lbs)	3165
Price (new)	NA

ENGINES

cc/type (cid)	bhp[1]	years
5355/ohv V-8 (327)	300	1964-66

[1]Gross

PRICES

FAIR	$7500-12,000
GOOD	$12,000-20,000
FINE	$20,000-30,000

(Deduct 20% for fiberglass instead of steel body.)

FINE GK1 PRICE HISTORY

1982 $9000	1987 $18,000
1990 $30,000	1994 $25,000
1982-2000 RETURN 8%	
2000-2010 5%	

GRAHAM SUPERCHARGER

The remarkable, radical "Spirit of Motion," better known as the "sharknose" Graham. Introduced for recession-plagued 1938, it underwhelmed the market. First offered only as a four-door sedan in two trim levels, but expanded to include a two-door coupe and sedan for 1939-40 in Standard and Custom versions. The Graham-built centrifugal supercharger was the only blower available in a popular-priced car and boosted horsepower on the Continental six from about 90 to 116 for 1938-39 and 120 for 1940. It was quietly dropped in 1940 in favor of the Hollywood, which was based on the Cord 810 dies. A year later, Graham-Paige abandoned the car business altogether for $20 million worth of defense contracts. Joseph W. Frazer gained control of G-P in 1944 and briefly returned to the field with the 1946 Frazer, but soon sold its automotive interests to Kaiser-Frazer Corporation.

FOR Exotic, if bizarre, styling • Good performance • Rarity

AGAINST Body parts very scarce • Good examples hard to find

PRODUCTION

1938 2410 **1939** 2479 **1940** under 1000

SPECIFICATIONS

Length (in.)	NA
Wheelbase (in.)	120.0
Weight (lbs)	3250-3370
Price (new)	$1070-1295

ENGINES

cid/type	bhp	years
217.8/sv I-6[1]	116-120[1]	1938-40

[1]Supercharged

PRICES

FAIR	$4000-6000
GOOD	$6000-9000
FINE	$9000-15,000

FINE EXAMPLE PRICE HISTORY

1982 $7500	1987 $9000
1990 $10,000	1994 $12,000
1982-2000 RETURN 8%	
2000-2010 5%	

1938 Custom Supercharger sedan

GRAHAM HOLLYWOOD

1941 Hollywood sedan

Companion to the Skylark from Hupp, part of a last-ditch comeback attempt by two moribund automakers trying to survive together instead of singly. Both cars were based on a modified version of the 1936-37 Cord sedan body, but with rear-wheel drive instead of front drive and a different front-end treatment that shaved several inches from the Cord's overall length. The Hollywood was powered by Graham's own supercharged six-cylinder engine with an offset carburetor and air cleaner to clear the low Cord hoodline. Horsepower was increased slightly for 1941 (mostly by the stroke of a pen), when an unblown version was also listed. The complexity of the old Cord dies delayed Hollywood/Skylark production, and the project never really got off the ground. The main appeal here is for "underdog" fans interested in the uncommon.

FOR Pretty • Pretty unusual • Cheaper than a Cord • Historical interest

AGAINST A challenge to restore because of body complexity • Expect rust • Body parts (especially those unique to these models) very scarce • Not plentiful

PRODUCTION

1959 (some sources list 1597)

SPECIFICATIONS

Length (in.)	190.0
Wheelbase (in.)	115.0
Weight (lbs)	2915-2965
Price (new)	$968-1250

ENGINES

cid/type	bhp[1]	years
217.8/sv I-6	93-124	1940-41

[1]124 supercharged

PRICES

FAIR	$5000-8000
GOOD	$8000-12,000
FINE	$12,000-20,000

FINE EXAMPLE PRICE HISTORY

1982 $9000		1987 $12,000	
1990 $14,000		1994 $17,500	
1982-2000 RETURN 5%			
2000-2010 5%			

1946-54
HEALEY

These were Donald Healey's initial offerings as an independent manufacturer in Warwick, England. The models here were all built on the same newly designed box-section chassis featuring a trailing-arm type of independent front suspension. Up to the early '50s, Healey specified the 2.4-liter Riley four-cylinder engine and corresponding transmission, but some 25 cars were equipped with the 3.0-liter Alvis six-cylinder engine from 1951 to '54. Roadster and coupe bodies for both "series" were supplied by various English coachbuilders. The open models were known as Westland, Sportsmobile, Abbott, and Alvis-Healey; the closed versions had bodywork by Elliott, Duncan, and Tickford. The Tickford coupe was perhaps the most stylish of the lot, but the Silverstone (named after the famous British automobile race course) was undoubtedly the most romantic, with a stark roadster body, freestanding cycle-type fenders, headlamps mounted behind a tall vertical grille, low-cut windscreen, and large slotted-disc wheels. By 1950, Donald Healey had become involved with Nash, and most of his firm's efforts went into the Nash-Healey hybrid. Then in 1953, he became more closely involved with British Motor Corporation in design and production of the BMC-built Austin-Healey 100. As a result, few of his "independent" products were built

in these years or sold outside England.

⊞ FOR Famous name • Hand-built appeal • Relatively fast (100-105 mph) • Good road manners • Silverstone's stark functionalism, Milestone status • Not difficult to rebuild or maintain

▬ AGAINST Body and chassis parts are no more • Poor body quality • Styling of some models • Not a high-demand collectible despite current steep values

1952 Tickford sedan

PRODUCTION

Silverstone 105 Tickford 225 Elliott 101 conv 25 Total 781

SPECIFICATIONS

Length (in.)	174.0 (average, depending on body style)
Wheelbase (in.)	102.0
Weight (lbs)	2400-3000
Price (new)	NA

ENGINES

cc/type (cid)	bhp[1]	years
2443/ohv I-4 (149)	104	1946-51[2]
2993/ohv I-6 (183)	106	1951-54[2]

[1]Gross [2]Approximate calendar years, based on extant vehicles

PRICES

Silverstone	
FAIR	$20,000-30,000
GOOD	$30,000-40,000
FINE	$40,000-60,000
Others	
FAIR	$10,000-15,000
GOOD	$15,000-17,500
FINE	$17,500-22,500

1950 Silverstone roadster

1982 $10,000		1987 $50,000	
1990 $100,000		1994 $50,000	
1982-2000 RETURN 10%			
2000-2010 5%			

1951
HENRY J DELUXE

1951 Deluxe fastback coupe

Pioneer American compact, the attempt by tycoon Henry J. Kaiser to reach less affluent buyers who could only afford a used car. A good idea messed up with dumpy styling (selected over several better-looking proposals, including one by Howard Darrin with a familial relationship to the stunning '51 Kaiser), very plain interior decor, sparse standard equipment, and a steep price (not much less than that of a full-size Chevy, Ford, or Plymouth). Total model year production was 81,942 units, with the six-cylinder DeLuxe slightly leading the four-cylinder standard version.

⊞ FOR Surprising performance and handling • Reliable engine • Low operating costs

▬ AGAINST Low-buck finish inside and out • Rust-prone • Dumpy styling

PRODUCTION

43,400 (est.)

SPECIFICATIONS

Length (in.)	174.5
Wheelbase (in.)	100.0
Weight (lbs)	2341
Price (new)	$1499

ENGINES

cid/type	bhp	years
161/sv I-6	80	1951

PRICES

FAIR	$2000-3500
GOOD	$3500-5500
FINE	$5500-8000

FINE EXAMPLE PRICE HISTORY

1982 $3000	1990 $6500
1994 $8000	1998 $8000

1982-2000 RETURN 90%
1992-2002 3%

1951
HENRY J
STANDARD

1951 Standard fastback coupe

Four-cylinder running mate to the Henry J DeLuxe, intended for the bottom end of the market. Same comments apply here except for the engine, which sacrificed performance for remarkable fuel economy (up to 35 mpg when driven conservatively).

+ FOR Mileage • Easy on the collector's budget • Others as for 1951 DeLuxe

– AGAINST Underpowered • Heavy steering • Choppy ride • Others as for 1951 DeLuxe

PRODUCTION

38,500 (est.)

SPECIFICATIONS

Length (in.)	174.5
Wheelbase (in.)	100.0
Weight (lbs)	2293
Price (new)	$1363

ENGINES

cid/type	bhp	years
134.2/sv I-4	68	1951

PRICES

As the 1951 Henry J Deluxe less 10%.

1952
HENRY J
VAGABOND

An interim version of Kaiser's compact, actually a leftover '51 fitted with a "continental" outside spare tire and a slightly upgraded interior. Available with both four- and six-cylinder engines, and identified by appropriate front fender script.

+ FOR The outside spare did a little for the dumpy looks • Others as for 1951 models

– AGAINST Otherwise, it was the same package • Others as for 1951 models

PRODUCTION

7017

SPECIFICATIONS

Length (in.)	179.4
Wheelbase (in.)	100.0
Weight (lbs)	2365-2385
Price (new)	$1407-1552

ENGINES

cid/type	bhp	years
134.2/sv I-4	68	1952
161/sv I-6	80	1952

PRICES

As per 1951 Henry J DeLuxe, plus 5%.

1952-54
HENRY J
CORSAIR

1953 Corsair fastback coupe

As before, the four-cylinder companion to the DeLuxe, and sharing the same improvements. Also see 1951 Henry J standard.

+ FOR As for 1952-54 Corsair DeLuxe, but with better economy and poorer performance

– AGAINST As for 1952-54 Corsair DeLuxe

PRODUCTION

1952 7600 **1953** 8500 **1954** 800 (all est.)

SPECIFICATIONS

Length (in.)	181.5
Wheelbase (in.)	100.0
Weight (lbs)	2370-2405
Price (new)	$1399-1517

1952 Vagabond fastback coupe

ENGINES

cid/type	bhp	years
134.2/sv I-4	68	1952-54

PRICES

FAIR	$1700-2500
GOOD	$2500-5000
FINE	$5000-7500

FINE EXAMPLE PRICE HISTORY

1982 $3000		**1990** $7000	
1994 $8500		**1998** $7500	
1982-2000 RETURN 5%			
2000-2010 3%			

1952-54
HENRY J CORSAIR DELUXE

1953 Corsair Deluxe fastback coupe

An attempt to improve the Henry J's sales appeal. Marked externally by a full-width grille and taillamps set into the tips of the little rear fender fins. Interiors became a bit less spartan, the dash was revised slightly, and prices were higher, though they were reduced a little as time went on. As before, DeLuxe signified the six-cylinder engine. None of this was enough to halt the sales downslide. Total production—including the four-cylinder versions—was 23,658, 16,672, and 1123 for these model years, respectively.

FOR Better looking (but not much) • Improved workmanship • Good economy • Sprightly performance (0-60 mph in 16 seconds)

AGAINST The same dull styling

PRODUCTION

1952 8900 **1953** 8100 **1954** 300 (all est.)

SPECIFICATIONS

Length (in.)	181.5
Wheelbase (in.)	100.0
Weight (lbs)	2405-2455
Price (new)	$1566-1664

ENGINES

cid/type	bhp	years
161/sv I-6	80	1952-54

PRICES

FAIR	$2000-3000
GOOD	$3000-6000
FINE	$6000-8500

FINE EXAMPLE PRICE HISTORY

1982 $3200		**1990** $6000	
1994 $9000		**1998** $8000	
1982-2000 RETURN 5%			
2000-2010 3%			

1930-34
HISPANO-SUIZA H6C

A massive six-cylinder machine from the renowned Franco-Spanish concern and one of its best. It was built in both France and Spain like most "Hissos," and like Rolls-Royce offered only as a rolling chassis. French specialists supplied most of the coachwork. High weight limited top speed to 90 mph for all except the very rare short-chassis Boulognes. All French-built examples had right-hand drive. Strictly vintage-style chassis engineering with beam axles on leaf springs at both ends. The engine was the jewel in this particular crown, and the name did the rest. Like a vintage Bentley, you bought it for what it said about you rather than what it was—plus, of course, its locomotive-like reliability.

FOR Advanced engine • Very high build quality • French coachbuilt elegance • Performance (short-chassis models) • CCCA Classic status

AGAINST Old-fashioned chassis for the '30s • Expensive to buy and restore • Rather truck-like • No new parts anymore

PRODUCTION

264 (began 1924)

SPECIFICATIONS

Length (in.)	165.0/178.0
Wheelbase (in.)	133.5/146
Weight (lbs)	approx. 4000
Price (new)	NA

ENGINES

cc/type (cid)	bhp[1]	years
7982/ohc I-6 (487)	150	1930-34

[1]Gross

PRICES

Prices vary with bodies. Some recent price ranges quoted by dealers and collectors: **six-light saloon**, $40,000-80,000; **Kellner & Castagna coupes**, $180,000-375,000; **Fernandez Sedanca de Ville**, $150,000-250,000; **dropheads and roadsters**, $250,000-350,000, **phaeton**, $250,000-400,000.
2000-2010 RETURN 5%

1931-38
HISPANO-SUIZA J12

Hispano-Suiza brought together Swiss design, Spanish capital, and French production facilities to create what many consider the world's best automobile of the mid-1930s, Rolls-Royces and the Grosser Mercedes notwithstanding. Offered only as a rolling chassis, with massive construction and a choice of four wheelbases. The huge "square" V-12 (long stroke engine optional) was an engineering masterpiece, but burned fuel as rapidly as you'd expect in an enormously heavy car. Still it could move the car 0-60 in 12 seconds and on past 100. Bodywork, of course, was to customer choice, and most examples carried every luxury and convenience feature imaginable at the time. A very few were built with sporty styles, those by Saoutchik being the most memorable and striking. A genuine international

1928 H6C boattail roadster

1933 J12 cabriolet

Classic of interest today only to a very fortunate few.

✚ **FOR** Exclusivity • Magnificent V-12 performance • Styling • Hispano quality and snob appeal • It's a Classic

▬ **AGAINST** Too costly for mere mortals • Old-fashioned chassis • Parts nearly impossible • Very thirsty

PRODUCTION
120

SPECIFICATIONS

Length (in.)	192+
Wheelbase (in.)	135/146/150/158
Weight (lbs)	4900-6500
Price (new)	NA

ENGINES

cc/type (cid)	bhp[1]	years
9424/ohv V-12 (575)	220	1931-38
1131/ohv V-12 (690)	250	1935-38

[1]Gross

PRICES

Prices vary with bodies. Few change hands, but the most pedigreed sporting bodies can command up to $500,000, while closed bodies bring up to $150,000 in prime condition.
2000-2010 RETURN 5%

1979-82
HONDA PRELUDE

Who better to build a practical sports car than Honda? Well-built, reliable, and economical—the Prelude was also a fun-to-drive little car. The 1.8-liter overhead-cam four from the Accord was dropped into a 91.3-inch wheelbase notchback coupe. This smooth engine provided brisk, but not blinding performance. With rack pinion steering and fully independent suspension, the Prelude was an nimble handler. Styling was

1979 Prelude coupe

pleasant, rather than flamboyant. The break with conservatism was the dashboard. The tachometer was mounted inside the circular speedometer. In '81 the concentric speedometer/tach combination was replaced by normal parallel round gauges. A solid Prelude will appreciate, but a car needing restoration will never return your investment.

✚ **FOR** Fun and practical • Good mileage • Standard sunroof

▬ **AGAINST** Rust prone • Optional automatic transmission saps performance • Cramped back seat

PRODUCTION[1]
1979 39,831 **1980** 50,676 **1981** 43,450 **1982** 37,872
[1]U.S. calendar year sales.

SPECIFICATIONS

Length (in.)	161.4
Weight (lbs)	2130
Wheelbase (in.)	91.3
Price (new)	$6,445-8,445

ENGINES

cid/type	bhp	years
91/ohc I-4	72-75	1979-82

PRICES

FAIR	$750-1000
GOOD	$1000-1500
FINE	$1500-2550

1983-87
HONDA PRELUDE

Bigger and better than the first generation, the new for '83 Prelude had

1983 Prelude coupe

a lower nose for a more sporting look and improved aerodynamics. A new double-wishbone suspension made possible a lower hood-line and also helped make the Prelude one of the best handling front-drivers available at the time. In '84 discs replaced the rear drum brakes. The 1.8-liter four-cylinder engine with dual carbs was carried over from the previous car. In late 1985 the Si joined the base model. The Si added a fuel-injected 2-liter engine, alloy wheels, and upgraded interior. The new engine offered better drivability and felt stronger than its 10-horse increase suggested.

✚ **FOR** Handling • Well-built • Smooth-running engine (Si)

▬ **AGAINST** Handling comes at the price of a rough ride • Lacks excitement • Too plain to be noticed by the collector's market in the near future

PRODUCTION[1]
1983 41,188 **1984** 66,924 **1985** 75,938 **1986** 79,841 **1987** 72,708
[1]U.S. calendar year sales.

SPECIFICATIONS

Length (in.)	168.9-172.0
Weight (lbs)	2266-2379
Wheelbase (in.)	96.5
Price (new)	$9,987-15,475

ENGINES

cid/type	bhp	years
112/ohc I-4	100	1983-87
120/ohc I-4	110	1985-87

PRICES

FAIR	$1050-2000
GOOD	$2000-3000
FINE	$3000-4700

1984-87
HONDA CIVIC CRX

CRX, Motor Trend"s "1984 Import Car of the Year," appeared simultaneously with the third-generation Civic wagon and hatchback, and heralded a significantly more aggressive marketing strategy. The 2-door CRX, a

1984 Civic CRX hatchback coupe

hatchback variant, ran with a 12-valve 1.5-liter four that developed 78 horsepower or an 8-valve engine that developed less power, but returned record fuel economy figures. CRX established the long hood/stubby deck look that defined Civic coupes for a decade. More significantly, it suggested that Honda created fun as well as transportation. The car was a sales success and spawned other, sportier cars.

✚ **FOR** Very much a budget buy • Good workmanship • Handling & roadholding

▬ **AGAINST** Little collector interest at the moment • Not particularly quick • Tiny four may be pooped • Japanese origins

PRODUCTION[1]

1984 48,445 **1985** 57,152 **1986** 64,106 **1987** 48,355
[1]U.S. calendar year sales

SPECIFICATIONS

Length (in.)	144.6
Weight (lbs)	1713
Wheelbase (in.)	86.6
Price (new)	$6149-8475

ENGINES

cid/type	bhp	years
81/ohc I-4	60	1984
91/ohc I-4	58/76	1984-87

PRICES

FAIR	$1000-1500
GOOD	$1500-2250
FINE	$2250-3000
2000-2010 RETURN 0%	

1985-87
HONDA CIVIC CRX SI

A full model year after the introduction of the Civic CRX, Honda

1986 Civic CRX Si hatchback coupe

upped the ante with the CRX Si, the archetypal "pocket rocket" which, although not a sports car, offered sportive performance and handling. Roomier than the competing Pontiac Fiero and Toyota MR2, the Si slipped through the gears quickly while sipping fuel. Programmed Fuel Injection wrung 91 bhp and 93 pounds/feet of torque from the 1.5-liter four. The Si was at its best above 5000 rpm. Performance below 3000 was tepid, and owners learned to spend as little time there as possible.

✚ **FOR** Willing, high-winding engine • Butter-smooth shifter and clutch • Go-kart handling • Workmanship • Seminal "pocket rocket "

▬ **AGAINST** Heavy steering • Torque steer • Japanese origins

PRODUCTION[1]

1985 19,763 **1986** 23,637 **1987** 17,652
[1]U.S. calendar year sales

SPECIFICATIONS

Length (in.)	144.6
Weight (lbs)	1713
Wheelbase (in.)	86.6
Price (new)	$8279-9395

ENGINES

cid/type	bhp	years
91/ohc I-4	91	1985-87

PRICES

FAIR	$1200-1800
GOOD	$1800-2800
FINE	$2800-3800
2000-2010 RETURN 0%	

1988-91
HONDA PRELUDE

1988 Prelude Si 4WS coupe

The third generation Prelude was a lot like the second. Styling and engineering changes were evolutionary rather than revolutionary, with one exception—four-wheel-steering. Honda was the first to offer what was once thought to be the next big thing. Parking maneuvers were much easier with tighter turning circle made possible with all four wheels steering. On the road, the car had to be pushed hard to notice an advantage from 4-wheel steering. Most buyers chose not to spend the $1,300 to steer all four wheels. The old carbureted engine soldiered on through 1990. The fuel-injected 2.0-liter gained dual-overhead-cams and power rose to 135-horsepower. A 2.1-liter 140-horsepower engine was added in 1990. The extra power was needed because the Prelude was gaining weight with each redesign.

✚ **FOR** Oddity value of available four-wheel-steering • Still pleasant to drive with either steering system • Honda dependability

▬ **AGAINST** Four-wheel-steering might be hard to repair • Softer and heavier than previous Preludes • Still unexciting

PRODUCTION

1988 52,541 **1989** 42,882 **1990** 37,814 **1991** 27,672

SPECIFICATIONS

Length (in.)	175.6
Weight (lbs)	2840
Wheelbase (in.)	101.0
Price (new)	$13,495-19,200

ENGINES

cid/type	bhp	years
119/ohc I-4	104-105	1988-90
119/dohc I-4	135	1988-91
125/dohc I-4	140	1990-91

PRICES

FAIR	$2175-4500
GOOD	$4500-6000
FINE	$6000-8000

1992-95

HONDA PRELUDE

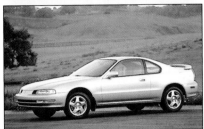

1995 Prelude SE coupe

The 1992 Prelude looked different from the previous model, but performed nearly the same. That wasn't a bad thing. Preludes always had agile handling and brisk acceleration. Four-wheel-steering returned, but was an electronic rather than mechanical system. The $2,500 premium for 4ws discouraged most buyers. Honda abandoned the system after '94. In 1994 the Honda VTEC engine with varible valve timing was added. This 190-horsepower engine lacked low end grunt, but came alive above 5,000 RPM. All Prelude engines were smooth running, but the VTEC was especially sweet.

✚ FOR Smooth, free-reving engines • Performance (VTEC) • Good handling and brakes

▬ AGAINST Gimicky dashboard with hard to read gauges • Unexciting styling • Cramped back seat

PRODUCTION
1992 36,040 **1993** 22,540 **1994** 15,467 **1995** 12,517

SPECIFICATIONS
Length (in.)	174.8
Weight (lbs)	2885
Wheelbase (in.)	174.8
Price (new)	$17,000-25,620

ENGINES
cid/type	bhp	years
132/ohc I-4	135	1992-95
138/dohc I-4	160	1992-95
132/dohc I-4	190	1994-95

1993-97

HONDA DEL SOL

Honda dropped the Civic-based CRX hatchback for '93 and

1995 del Sol VTEC coupe

replaced it with the del Sol, a Civic-based, 2-seat semi-convertible notchback with a lift-off roof panel and motorized drop-down rear window. Initially rolled out in California, it was available nationwide soon after. Although not a sports car in the Mazda Miata sense, nor a 2+2 like Toyota's Celica, the del Sol was generally capable and amusing. By the end of its run, three iterations of a 1.6-liter overhead-cam inline four were available; the top engine produced a rousing 160 bhp, and stirring performance.

✚ FOR Acceleration (Si and VTEC) • Steering • Roadholding • Fuel economy

▬ AGAINST Body flex • Engine and tire noise • Visibility • Japanese origins

PRODUCTION[1]
1993 25,748 **1994** 21,075 **1995** 14,021 **1996** 8,489 **1997** 5,603
[1] U.S. calendar year sales

SPECIFICATIONS
Length (in.)	157.3
Weight (lbs)	2301-2396
Wheelbase (in.)	93.3
Price (new)	$13,200-19,600

ENGINES
cid/type	bhp	years
91/ohc I-4	102	1993-95
97/ohc I-4	106/125	1993-97
97/dohc I-4	160	1994-97

PRICES
Governed by used car market. Maximum in 2000: $10,000
2000-2010 RETURN Depreciating

1935-56

HRG 1100/ 1500

Stark, hard-riding vintage British sports car, continued with few changes into the postwar world. The cramped two-seat cockpit featured creature comforts notable by their absence. Except for the unsuccessful envelope-body "Aerodynamic" model (of which only 30 were built in 1946-48), all HRGs had the same styling, including the traditional vertical radiator, cycle-type front fenders, and Bugatti-type exposed front quarter-elliptic leaf springs. It was powered by a choice of two four-cylinder engines from the Singer Motor Company of Coventry. The HRG was slower than it looked (73 mph tops for the 1100, 83 mph for the 1500), but very nimble. A real driver's car, and quite reliable for rallying and other competition, but incredibly uncomfortable. Like a cold shower, invigorating but painful.

✚ FOR Low-production appeal • British "trad" style • Strong, simple • More exclusive than a postwar MG • Active British club

▬ AGAINST Very hard suspension • No parts available now • Little weather protection • Prewar engineering • Virtually unknown in the U.S.

PRODUCTION
240

SPECIFICATIONS
Length (in.)	144.0
Wheelbase (in.)	99.5/103.5
Weight (lbs)	1510-1750
Price (new)	NA

ENGINES
cc/type (cid)	bhp[1]	years

1948 HRG 1500 roadster

1074/ohc I-4 (65)	40	1935-56
1496/ohc I-4 (91)	61	1935-56
[1]Net		

PRICES

An almost total absence of known sales makes it impossible to quantify HRG prices. Dealers suggest $25,000 for an average two-liter Sports; show winners will cost much more.
2000-2010 RETURN No prediction

1 9 3 0 - 3 3

HUDSON EIGHT

Coupled with the closure of the famous Biddle & Smart coachbuilders, the Depression severely hurt sales of Hudson's premium models, and none are rated Classics after 1929. Perhaps some should be. Hudson Eights were often luxurious, and usually smooth, effortless performers, thanks to the firm's new 1930 L-head engine, which would run through 1952. The Greater Eight and Major Eight lines of 1931-33 offered a number of stylish open body types, including speedsters, roadsters, and phaetons with coachwork by LeBaron, Murray, and Briggs. Designer Frank Spring began his long Hudson career with the pretty '32s, whose beautiful vee'd grille and flowing fenderlines carried over on the 1933s. Four-square styling was then abandoned for Hudson's new generation of 1934.

✚ FOR Strong club support • Handsome styling • Snob appeal of the occasional custom body • Good tourers

■ AGAINST A mite underpowered

• Parts problems

PRODUCTION

1930 85,407 **1931** 22,156 **1932** 8000 (est) **1933** 1890

SPECIFICATIONS

Length (in.)	NA
Wheelbase (in.)	119.0, 126.0 (1930-32); 119.0 (1933); 132.0 (1932-33 Major)
Weight (lbs)	2675-3650
Price (new)	$735-1595

ENGINES

cid/type	bhp	years
213.5/sv I-8	80	1930
233.7/sv I-8	87	1931
254.0/sv I-8	101	1932-33

PRICES

Open	
FAIR	$8500-18,000
GOOD	$18,000-33,000
FINE	$33,000-48,000
Closed	
FAIR	$2500-7000
GOOD	$7000-10,000
FINE	$10,000-19,000
FINE	

1931 GREATER EIGHT SPORT PHAETON PRICE HISTORY

1982 $35,000		**1990** $50,000	
1994 $45,000		**1998** $45,000	
1982-2000 RETURN 2%			
2000-2010 2%			

1931 8 boattail speedster

1932 Greater 8 coupe

1 9 3 5 - 3 8

HUDSON CUSTOM EIGHT

1936 Custom 8 convertible coupe

After a series of shorter, smaller Eights in 1934, Hudson released the big Custom for 1935, with a new all-steel body in brougham and sedan styles on an extra-long wheelbase. Chassis spans varied from 120 to 129 inches on an expanding line of bodies through 1938, during which time Hudson gradually evolved toward more enveloping, curvy bodywork. Styling was all-new for 1936, but not as radical as most of the competition's. These are big, handsome cars that deserve a close look, if you can find one in good shape.

✚ FOR Innovative and contemporary for the time • Handsome styling, more streamlined in each successive year • Solidly built • Good performance

■ AGAINST Not many open bodies available • Relatively high operating costs • Parts supplies short, so consider only top-condition examples

PRODUCTION

1935 NA **1936** NA **1937** 6926 **1938** NA

SPECIFICATIONS

Length (in.)	NA
Wheelbase (in.)	124.0 (1935); 120.0/127.0 (1936); 122.0/129.0 (1937-38)
Weight (lbs)	2950-3275
Price (new)	$845-1299

ENGINES

cid/type	bhp	years
254.5/sv I-8	113-128	1935-38

PRICES

Open	
FAIR	$7500-13,000
GOOD	$13,000-23,000
FINE	$23,000-35,000
Closed	
FAIR	$2500-5000
GOOD	$5000-8000
FINE	$8000-15,000

1 9 3 9 - 4 0

HUDSON EIGHT

1940 Eight convertible coupe

Handsomely restyled for 1939 and extensively facelifted for 1940, these Hudsons shared the sharp-nosed look of concurrent Fords and Studebakers and are among the nicest-looking Detroit cars of these years. Called Country Club (the Big Boy name appeared on two long-wheelbase 1940 models), the top-of-the-line Eights used Hudson's longest chassis, carried its highest prices, and were the most lavishly equipped cars ever to bear the White Triangle logo. Except for larger displacement, the company's big, smooth-running L-head eight continued largely unchanged from its original 1930 form. Total 1939 production is not available but was probably a shade lower than the 1940 figure.

⊞ FOR Slick styling • Excellent go off the line • Good roadability

⊟ AGAINST Rust-prone • Somewhat clumsy handling • Thirsty

PRODUCTION

1939 9000 (est.) **1940** 10,620

SPECIFICATIONS

Length (in.)	NA
Wheelbase (in.)	122.0/129.0 (1939); 118.0/125.0 (1940)
Weight (lbs)	3003, 3400
Price (new)	$860-1430

ENGINES

cid/type	bhp	years
254.5/sv I-8	122-128	1939-40

PRICES

As per 1935-38 Hudson Custom Eight.

---

1 9 4 1 - 4 2

HUDSON COMMODORE EIGHT

Continuation of the smooth-performing big Eights. Hudson facelifted again for these last prewar models, and changed wheelbase lengths. A wide range of body styles was catalogued: convertible sedans (an estimated 200 and 100 built) and wagons (80 built). Appearance changes for 1942 included hiding the running boards and lowering and cleaning up the grille.

⊞ FOR Pleasing good looks • Solid construction • Good performance • Avid club support

⊟ AGAINST Heavy handling • Thirsty • Somewhat rust-prone

PRODUCTION

1941 9718 **1942** 6592

SPECIFICATIONS

Length (in.)	NA
Wheelbase (in.)	121.0
Weight (lbs)	3110-3400
Price (new)	$1071-1451

ENGINES

cid/type	bhp	years
254/sv I-8	128	1941-42

PRICES

Wagon	
FAIR	$6500-11,000
GOOD	$11,000-19,000

---

1 9 4 6 - 4 7

HUDSON COMMODORE EIGHT

1946 Commodore Eight sedan

The top-line series in Hudson's early postwar lineup. It shared its bodyshell and most design features with other models; all were holdovers of the 1941-42 offerings. Available as a four-door sedan, club coupe, and Brougham convertible coupe. Ragtops were few, probably not exceeding 500 units for both model years here. The big eight gave the Commodore strong performance, and you also got nicer trim than in the Super Six. A companion Super Eight series with slightly less luxurious fittings was also offered in sedan or club coupe body styles only.

⊞ FOR Construction quality • Luxury

1941 Commodore Eight long wheelbase sedan

- Enthusiastic club • Top-line models
- Fine performance

◨ AGAINST Not a styling masterpiece
- Heavy steering • Clumsy handling

PRODUCTION

1946 8193 **1947** 12,593

SPECIFICATIONS

Length (in.)	204.5
Wheelbase (in.)	121.0
Weight (lbs)	3235-3435
Price (new)	$1760-2196

ENGINES

cid/type	bhp	years
254/sv I-8	128	1946-47

PRICES

Conv	
FAIR	$5500-11,000
GOOD	$11,000-19,000
FINE	$19,000-28,000
Others	
FAIR	$2500-5500
GOOD	$5500-9000
FINE	$9000-13,500

FINE CONVERTIBLE PRICE HISTORY

1982 $13,000	**1990** $27,500
1994 $32.000	**1998** $28,000
1982-2000 RETURN 5%	
2000-2010 5%	

1 9 4 6 - 4 7
HUDSON SUPER SIX

The best-selling Hudsons in the early postwar years, and the most readily available today. Body choices were two- and four-door sedans, coupe, club coupe, and convertible. Soft-top production was about 2500 units for the two years. Styling was a little busier than in 1940-42, but was still based on the prewar bodyshell. Three transmissions were offered: overdrive, Drive-Master, and Vacumotive Drive. The last was a semi-

1947 Super Six convertible

automatic clutch, while Drive-Master combined semi-automatic clutch and shift functions. A Commodore Six sedan and club coupe were also available in these two model years.

⊞ FOR Relatively easy to find • Strong club support • Solid construction

◨ AGAINST Busy styling • Heavy steering • Plain interiors

PRODUCTION

1946 61,787 **1947** 49,276

SPECIFICATIONS

Length (in.)	204.5
Wheelbase (in.)	121.0
Weight (lbs)	2950-3750
Price (new)	$1481-2021

ENGINES

cid/type	bhp	years
212/sv I-6	102	1946-47

PRICES

As per 1946-47 Commodore Eight less 10%.

1 9 4 8 - 4 9
HUDSON COMMODORE EIGHT

1949 Commodore Eight sedan by Derham

Hudson's top-of-the-line series, offered in three body styles including a convertible. It proved more popu-

lar than previous incarnations because of trend-setting "Step-down" design and scored close to 60,000 sales for these two model years, during which no styling or specification changes were made. Smooth and ground-hugging in appearance, and more roadable by far than virtually any other full-size American car because of its low center of gravity.

⊞ FOR Luxury • Performance • Robustness • Roadability • Good appreciation potential

◨ AGAINST Thirsty • Priciest of the 1948-49s

PRODUCTION

1948 35,315 **1949** 28,687

SPECIFICATIONS

Length (in.)	207.5
Wheelbase (in.)	124.0
Weight (lbs)	3600-3800
Price (new)	$2448-3198

ENGINES

cid/type	bhp	years
254/sv I-8	128	1948-49

PRICES

As per 1946-47 Commodore Eight, plus 35%.

1 9 4 8 - 4 9
HUDSON COMMODORE SIX

1949 Commodore Six convertible

Costlier (about $200 more) companion series to the Super Six, available as a Brougham convertible as well as two- and four-door sedan body types in these years. Chief difference from the Super Six was a more lushly appointed interior with such amenities as fold-down armrests and a chrome-plated steering column.

⊞ FOR As for 1948-49 Super Six

◨ AGAINST As for 1948-49 Super Six, but somewhat heavier, so performance poorer

PRODUCTION

1948 27,159 **1949** 32,715

SPECIFICATIONS

Length (in.)	207.5
Wheelbase (in.)	124.0
Weight (lbs)	3540-3780
Price (new)	$2374-3057

ENGINES

cid/type	bhp	years
262/sv I-6	121	1948-49

PRICES

As per 1946-47 Super Six, plus 30%.

1948-49
HUDSON SUPER EIGHT

The cheaper of Hudson's two eight-cylinder series in this period, both running with a 254-cid L-head straight eight. It was offered only in four-door sedan and two-door club coupe guise. Though rarer than other 1948-49 models, the lack of top-line status makes it less desirable despite that.

➕ FOR The great Step-down design, plus eight-cylinder performance

➖ AGAINST Scarce; hard to find • No "sporty" body styles

PRODUCTION

1948 5338 **1949** 6365

SPECIFICATIONS

Length (in.)	207.5
Wheelbase (in.)	124.0
Weight (lbs)	3495-3550
Price (new)	$2245-2343

ENGINES

cid/type	bhp	years
254/sv I-8	128	1948-49

PRICES

FAIR	$2500-5000

1949 Hudson Super Six sedan (externally same as Super Eight)

GOOD	$5000-9000
FINE	$9000-13,500

FINE CLUB COUPE PRICE HISTORY

1982 $5000		**1990** $8000	
1994 $10,000		**1998** $13,500	
1982-2000 RETURN 6%			
2000-2010 5%			

1948-49
HUDSON SUPER SIX

1949 Super Six Business coupe

One of the truly significant new designs of the early postwar years, the "Step-down" Hudson was low and sleek. It even looks pretty good today. Unit body/chassis construction featured a dropped floorpan (hence the nickname) surrounded by massive chassis girders for a very safe, solid structure. Big instrument dials on a businesslike dash and armchair-comfortable seats marked the exceptionally roomy interior. The result of all this was soaring sales, with the low-priced Super Six again leading the four-series Hudson line. The same five body styles from 1946-47 were again fielded. Super Six convertible production is estimated at 88 and 1870 for these two years, respectively. There were no body or mechanical changes for '49.

➕ FOR Design merit • Excellent roadability • Solid construction

➖ AGAINST Very little—one of the greats

PRODUCTION

1948 49,388 **1949** 91,333

SPECIFICATIONS

Length (in.)	207.5
Wheelbase (in.)	124.0
Weight (lbs)	3460-3750
Price (new)	$2053-2836

ENGINES

cid/type	bhp	years
262/sv I-6	121	1948-49

PRICES

Conv	
FAIR	$6500-12,000
GOOD	$12,000-22,000
FINE	$22,000-32,000
Others	
FAIR	$2000-4500
GOOD	$4500-8000
FINE	$8000-12,000

FINE CONVERTIBLE BROUGHAM PRICE HISTORY

1982 $11,000		**1990** $25,000	
1994 $25,000		**1998** $32,000	
1982-2000 RETURN 7%			
2000-2010 5%			

1951-53
HUDSON HORNET

The most remembered Hudson of the postwar years, one of the industry's all-time greats. Virtually unbeatable in stock-car racing through 1954, it continued to compete with some success even after the Step-down line came to an end with the Nash-based '55 Hudsons. Amazingly, this racing success was achieved with a six-cylinder engine—the last performance six before Pontiac's late '60s overhead-cam engine. "Twin-H Power" arrived for 1953 (twin carbs and dual manifold induction) and the 210-bhp 7-X racing engine late that same year were early examples of factory "prodifying" that helped the likes of Marshall Teague and Herb Thomas dominate NASCAR and AAA tracks against ostensibly much more potent machinery. Positioned just below the top-line Commodore Eight series for 1951-52, it moved to the top for '53. The Hornet's legendary performance prowess gives it a big edge in collector appeal over the basically similar Pacemaker, Super Six, and Wasp models of this period.

➕ FOR One of the great postwar landmarks—a true champion • Fine performance • Surprising handling • Quality • Luxury

🔲 **AGAINST** Step-down design looking dated by '51 • Interior and some exterior details clumsily executed • Thirsty

1952 Hornet sedan

PRODUCTION

1951 43,656 **1952** 35,921 **1953** 27,208 (**Conv** estimates: 550, 360, 150; **Hollywood 2d htp** estimates: 2100, 2160, 910)

SPECIFICATIONS

Length (in.)	208.3/208.5 (1951-52/1953)
Wheelbase (in.)	124.0
Weight (lbs)	3530-3780
Price (new)	$2543-3342

ENGINES

cid/type	bhp	years
308/sv I-6	145/160/170	1953

PRICES

Conv	
FAIR	$8000-15,000
GOOD	$15,000-27,000
FINE	$27,000-40,000
Htp	
FAIR	$4000-8000
GOOD	$8000-14,000
FINE	$14,000-$20,000
Others	
FAIR	$3000-6000
GOOD	$6000-10,000
FINE	$10,000-15,000
FINE	

CONVERTIBLE BROUGHAM PRICE HISTORY

1982 $10,500		**1990** $30,000	
1994 $32,000		**1998** $42,000	
1982-2000 RETURN 8%			
2000-2010 8%			

1952-54
HUDSON WASP

An attractively upgraded version of the short-wheelbase 1950-52 Pacemaker, with the larger Commodore six for

---

1952 Wasp Hollywood hardtop coupe

improved performance. A full line of sedans, club coupe, hardtop and convertible body styles was offered in the 1952 debut series, then became the Super Wasp offerings for 1953-54. Just three closed bodies were listed for the standard Wasp in those years. For continuation of convertible and hardtop see 1953-54 Super Wasp.

➕ **FOR** A bit more compact, easier-to-handle Step-down • Overshadowed by the mighty Hornet, so less expensive • Quality construction and materials

🔲 **AGAINST** Lower appreciation than Hornet • Not too many around now

PRODUCTION

1952 21,876 **1953** 17,792 **1954** 11,603 (incl. 1953-54 Super Wasp)

SPECIFICATIONS

Length (in.)	201.5
Wheelbase (in.)	119.0
Weight (lbs)	3340-3635
Price (new)	$2209-3048

ENGINES

cid/type	bhp	years
232/sv I-6	112/126	1953-54
262/sv I-6	127	1952-53

1951 Hornet Hollywood hardtop coupe

PRICES

1952 Conv	
FAIR	$7000-14,000
GOOD	$14,000-25,000
FINE	$25,000-35,000
Others	
FAIR	$2500-6000
GOOD	$6000-10,000
FINE	$10,000-14,000

FINE HARDTOP PRICE HISTORY

1982 $4000	**1990** $7000
1994 $10,000	**1998** $14,000
1982-2000 RETURN 9%	
2000-2010 5%	

1953-54
HUDSON JET

1953 Hudson Jet sedan

Hudson's ill-starred attempt to save itself with a compact at a time when demand for such cars was quite limited and what market there was belonged mainly to Rambler. Solidly built with traditional Hudson engineering integrity, but the styling was dowdy and the price uncomfortably close to that of the standard Ford, Chevy, and Plymouth. Production failed to break 40,000 during two model years, and the Jet certainly hastened Hudson's demise as a fully independent automaker. This basic version appeared as a four-door sedan only. A two-door was added the following year, along with a stripped "Family Club" two-door late in the season.

FOR Good quality • Decent performance • Excellent roadability

AGAINST Dull • Barren interior • Rust-prone

PRODUCTION
1953 11,000 **1954** 7000 (both estimated)

SPECIFICATIONS
Length (in.)	180.7
Wheelbase (in.)	105.0
Weight (lbs)	2650-2715
Price (new)	$1621-1858

ENGINES
cid/type	bhp	years
202/sv I-6	104/106/114	1953-54

PRICES
FAIR	$1500-3500
GOOD	$3500-6500
FINE	$6500-9000

FINE EXAMPLE PRICE HISTORY
1982 $3500		**1990** $6500	
1994 $9000		**1998** $9000	
1982-2000 RETURN 6%			
2000-2010 3%			

1953-54
HUDSON
SUPER JET

1953 Super Jet sedan

The upper-class version of Hudson's ho-hum compact, though no different bodily or mechanically from the plain Jet. Offered from the first in two- and four-door sedan styles, with the scrunched-up proportions that gave the Jet the look of a big Hudson—or 1952 Ford—that had shrunk at the cleaners.

FOR As for 1953-54 Jet, but nicer

furnishings and easier to live with

AGAINST As for 1953-54 Jet

PRODUCTION
1953 10,000 **1954** 6000 (both estimated)

SPECIFICATIONS
Length (in.)	180.7
Wheelbase (in.)	105.0
Weight (lbs)	2695-2725
Price (new)	$1933-1954

ENGINES
cid/type	bhp	years
202/sv I-6	104/106/114	1953-54

PRICES
As per 1953-54 Hudson Jet plus 5%.

1953-54
HUDSON
SUPER WASP

This was a luxury expansion of the shorter-wheelbase, full-size Hudson series. A full line including convertible and Hollywood hardtop. As in previous years, there were no Step-down wagons, which would have helped the firm's sales—they declined each year the design continued without significant change. One of the problems was that the Step-down was difficult and very expensive to alter. Hudson did manage a fairly extensive reskinning operation for the Step-down's final year, however, with a more contemporary square-sided look that did away with the very '40s "torpedo" lines. The Super Wasp was distinguished from the regular Wasp by an air-vent hood orna-

1953 Super Wasp coupe

ment and appropriate script on the glovebox door, trunklid, and front fenders above the bodyside moldings. The '54 models had a more powerful version of the Hudson six with slightly greater displacement.

FOR As for 1952-54 Wasp

AGAINST As for 1952-54 Wasp

PRODUCTION
See 1953-54 Wasp (combined production; no separate figures available) Est. **1953 conv** 50 **Hollywood 2d htp** 590

SPECIFICATIONS
Length (in.)	201.5
Wheelbase (in.)	119.0
Weight (lbs)	3455-3680
Price (new)	$2413-3048

ENGINES
cid/type	bhp	years
262/sv I-6	127	1953
262/sv I-6	140	1954

PRICES
As per 1952-54 Hudson Wasp.

1954
HUDSON
HORNET

Hudson's legendary race winner in the last year of the by-now aged Step-down design. It featured the most radical facelift to be carried out on the original 1948 body, with raised rear fenders carrying fender-tip taillights and a more aggressive full-width grille. The usual Hornet sedan, coupe, Hollywood hardtop, and convertible

1954 Hornet Brougham convertible

were supplemented during the model year by the Hornet Special two- and four-door sedans and club coupe. All were powered by the 160-bhp version of the famous Hornet six. But the buying public was V-8 crazy, and despite Hudson's continued race track successes sales dropped appreciably. Temporary salvation came with the Nash-Kelvinator merger on May 1, 1954.

FOR Milestone car status • As for 1951-53 Hornet

AGAINST As for 1951-53 Hornet, but styling less distinctive

PRODUCTION

24,833

SPECIFICATIONS

Length (in.)	208.5
Wheelbase (in.)	124.0
Weight (lbs)	3620-3800
Price (new)	$2742-3288

ENGINES

cid/type	bhp	years
308/sv I-8	160/170	1954

PRICES

As per 1951-53 Hudson Hornet.

1954-55 HUDSON ITALIA

1954 Italia coupe

Built by Italy's Carrozzeria Touring on the chassis and mechanicals of the compact Jet, this grand touring coupe styled by Frank Spring might have been the basis for a whole new model line had Hudson remained independent. Advanced styling features included a wraparound windshield, doors cut into the roof, functional fender-mounted air scoops, flow-through ventilation, and form-fitting leather-covered bucket seats. Powered by the higher-output 114-bhp Jet six, the Italia was not fast despite its "Superleggera" (lightweight) construction and aluminum bodywork, but would have undoubtedly been swifter had it been built in mass-production quantity. A tall $4800 price tag put the kabosh on sales, and the Nash/Hudson merger—actually a Nash takeover—ended whatever chance it had for inspiring Hudson's own models for 1955 and beyond.

FOR Rare and desirable • Advanced styling and design features • Good road car • Not a Milestone, but should be

AGAINST Styling gimmicky in places • Flimsy construction • Body parts now unobtainable

PRODUCTION

25, plus one prototype coupe and one prototype four-door (X-161)

SPECIFICATIONS

Length (in.)	200.0
Wheelbase (in.)	105.0
Weight (lbs)	2710
Price (new)	$4800

ENGINES

cid/type	bhp	years
202/sv I-6	114	1954-55

PRICES

FAIR	$6000-12,000
GOOD	$12,000-20,000
FINE	$20,000-30,000

FINE EXAMPLE PRICE HISTORY

1982 $15,000		**1990** $25,000	
1994 $40,000		**1998** $30,000	
1982-2000 RETURN 4%			
2000-2010 5%			

1954 HUDSON JET-LINER

Certainly the model to look for if a Hudson Jet turns you on. This was the top-line offering in the car's second—and final—year, with a choice of two- or four-door sedans. The interior decor featured duotone vinyl trim. Most Jet-Liners had the optional 114-bhp version of Hudson's small L-head six-cylinder engine, which actually had been tooled from the old Commodore eight. Designer Frank Spring's proposed styling was much prettier than the shape that finally emerged, the Jet's kiddy-car proportions being fostered mainly by Hudson president Edward Barit.

FOR The best of the Jets • Moderately luxurious • Good performance • Fine roadability

AGAINST As for 1953-54 Jet and Super Jet • Not too many around

PRODUCTION

2000 (est.)

SPECIFICATIONS

Length (in.)	180.7
Wheelbase (in.)	105.0
Weight (lbs)	2740-2760

1954 Jet-Liner sedan

Price (new)	$2046-2057	

ENGINES

cid/type	bhp	years
202/sv I-6	104/106/114	1954

PRICES

As per 1953-54 Hudson Jet.

1955-57
HUDSON HORNET

Unflatteringly referred to nowadays as the "Hash," the predictable result of the American Motors merger. Now built as a reskinned Nash on the Kenosha, Wisconsin, assembly lines instead of in Hudson's old Detroit factory. Styling was individual, but in most eyes became progressively worse. The '55 was the cleanest model of this trio, with a broad eggcrate grille and distinctive two-toning. For 1956 there was "V-Line Styling" that attempted to put Hudson's traditional triangle logo shape in every nook and cranny, blindingly accented by tacky anodized aluminum appliqués. The last Hudsons appeared for '57, even more gaudy than before. The Hornet's legendary six, with and without Twin-H Power, was offered through 1956, Packard's 320 V-8 in 1955 and the first half of '56, and AMC's new 327-cid V-8 in 1957. A late 1956-only Hornet Special came with Kenosha's new 250 V-8 and a lower price. A companion Wasp series was also fielded for 1955-56 based on the shorter wheelbase Nash Statesman platform and with less ornate trim.

It was replaced by the Hornet Super for '57, while the more deluxe version was called Hornet Custom.

✚ **FOR** The comfy Nash body • Hudson's great six or new V-8s • Good performance • Not too expensive • Appreciating faster lately

▬ **AGAINST** Dreadful 1956-57 appearance • Thirsty • Rusts easily • Body parts supplies spotty or nonexistent • Not a true Hudson

PRODUCTION

1955 4d sdn 10,010 **Hollywood 2d htp** 3324
1956 4d sdn 6512 **Hollywood 2d htp** 1640
1957 3876 (combined total)

SPECIFICATIONS

Length (in.)	209.3
Wheelbase (in.)	121.3
Weight (lbs)	3467-3826
Price (new)	$2405-3159

ENGINES

cid/type	bhp	years
308/sv I-6	160/170	1955
308/sv I-6	165/175	1956
320/ohv V-8	208	1955-56
250/ohv V-8	190	1956
327/ohv V-8	255	1957

PRICES

Htp	
FAIR	$3000-9500
GOOD	$9500-14,000
FINE	$14,000-19,000

Sdns: deduct 30% from hardtop prices.

FINE HARDTOP PRICE HISTORY

1982 $5500		**1990** $9000	
1994 $15,000		**1998** $18,000	
1982-2000 RETURN 10%			
2000-2010 8%			

METROPOLITAN
See 1955-57 Nash

1940-41
HUPMOBILE SKYLARK CUSTOM

1941 Skylark Custom sedan

Last gasp of the old Hupp Company in the auto business, after which it became a component supplier to other carmakers. Like the Graham Hollywood—the result of a Hupp-Graham accord—it was based on the old dies from the front-drive 1936-37 Cord sedan, but 5.5 inches shorter overall and with rear-wheel drive. Appearance differed only slightly from the Hollywood's, and the Skylark's engine was Hupp's four-main-bearing L-head six, about midway in performance between the supercharged and unsupercharged versions of the Graham engine. The complexity of the Cord dies and other problems delayed production start-up until May 1940, by which time most of the sizeable number of initial orders had been cancelled. The Skylark was thus even less successful than the Hollywood.

✚ **FOR** Almost as pretty as a Cord • Rare and increasingly desirable • Good performance • Uniqueness

▬ **AGAINST** Spare parts (especially body pieces) very limited

PRODUCTION

319 (some sources list 371), plus 35 prototypes constructed in 1939

SPECIFICATIONS

Length (in.)	190.0
Wheelbase (in.)	115.0
Weight (lbs)	3000
Price (new)	$895-1145

ENGINES

cid/type	bhp	years
245/sv I-6	101	1940-41

PRICES

FAIR	$3000-5500
GOOD	$5500-9500
FINE	$9500-15,000

1955 Hornet sedan

FINE EXAMPLE PRICE HISTORY

1982 $8500 **1987** $9000
1990 $9500 **1994** $15,000
1982-2000 RETURN 2%
2000-2010 5%

1955-56
IMPERIAL

1955 Newport hardtop coupe

Chrysler's best car, spun-off as a separate make beginning with the 1955 models, which were terrific. Styled by Virgil Exner along the lines of his 1954 Parade Phaeton show cars. A big split eggcrate grille was used up front, distinctive gunsight taillights adorned the rear, and sculpted, flowing body lines with fully radiused rear wheel openings appeared in between. The '56s gained modest tailfins plus slightly longer wheelbase and length. Power was supplied by Chrysler's Hemi V-8, with a displacement and power boost for '56. Also that year a four-door hardtop sedan was added to the line in common with other Chrysler divisions.

FOR Fine styling • Good quality control • Great road car • One of the more affordable luxury Milestones

AGAINST Thirsty • Handling and braking not up to the horsepower

PRODUCTION

1955 4d sdn 7840 **Newport 2d htp** 3418 **1956 4d sdn** 6821 **Southampton 2d htp** 2094 **Southampton 4d htp** 1543

SPECIFICATIONS

Length (in.) 223.0 (1955), 226.0 (1956)
Wheelbase (in.) 130 (1955), 133.0 (1956)
Weight (lbs) 4565-4680
Price (new) $4483-5225

ENGINES

cid/type	bhp	years
331/ohv V-8	250	1955
354/ohv V-8	280	1956

PRICES

FAIR	$4000-6500
GOOD	$6500-10,000
FINE	$10,000-18,000

(Hardtops are at the high end of the above range.)

FINE HARDTOP PRICE HISTORY

1982 $4700 **1990** $15,000
1994 $16,500 **1998** $18,000
1982-2000 RETURN 5%
2000-2010 5%

1955-56
CROWN IMPERIAL

A continuation of the long Imperials of the early '50s, with Exner styling and sybaritic furnishings. They were the last cars of their type built in Detroit, after which Chrysler farmed out assembly to Ghia in Turin, Italy. These eight-passenger models replaced all the previous long-wheelbase offerings bearing Dodge, DeSoto, and Chrysler nameplates. Styling and mechanical changes paralleled those made to the standard Imperials of these years.

FOR As for 1955-56 Imperial, but less roadable because of the extra size and weight

AGAINST Thirsty • Large and cumbersome • Body parts unique to these models now very scarce • Won't fit in most garages • Depreciating lately

PRODUCTION

1955 4d sdn 45 **limo** 127 **1956 4d sdn** 51 **limo** 175

SPECIFICATIONS

Length (in.) 242.5
Wheelbase (in.) 149.5
Weight (lbs) 5145-5205
Price (new) $6973-7737

ENGINES

cid/type	bhp	years
331/ohv V-8	250	1955
354/ohv V-8	280	1956

PRICES

FAIR	$4000-7000
GOOD	$7000-9000
FINE	$9000-11,000

FINE EXAMPLE PRICE HISTORY

1982 $5500 **1990** $14,000
1994 $17,500 **1998** $13,000
1982-2000 RETURN 4%
2000-2010 2%

1957-59
IMPERIAL CROWN

1957 Crown convertible

Midrange series in Chrysler's expanded, late-'50s flagship line, given a new bodyshell for '57 with soaring "Forward Look" styling. Offerings included the first open Imperials since 1953, the only series with this body style. Featured, like divisional siblings, Chrysler's new torsion-bar front suspension that greatly improved ride and handling. Besides Virgil Exner's heroically sized tailfins, styling was highlighted by complicated grillework, Imperial's trademark "gunsight" taillamps, and a large, compound-curve windshield. The Hemi V-8 was replaced by a larger, less complicated wedgehead V-8 for 1959. The '57s recorded what would prove to be Imperial's best one-year sales.

1956 Crown Imperial limousine by Ghia

◆ FOR Luxurious and majestic • Comfortable road car

▬ AGAINST Not as well-built as 1955-56 models • Easy ruster • Thirsty

PRODUCTION

1957 4d sdn 3642 **Southampton htp sdn** 7843 **Southampton htp cpe** 4199 **conv** 1167 **1958 4d sdn** 1240 **Southampton htp sdn** 4146 **Southampton htp cpe** 1939 **conv** 675 **1959 4d sdn** 1335 **Southampton htp sdn** 4714 **Southampton htp cpe** 1728 **conv** 555

SPECIFICATIONS

Length (in.)	226.3
Wheelbase (in.)	129.0
Weight (lbs)	4730-4915
Price (new)	$5269-5774

ENGINES

cid/type	bhp	years
392/ohv V-8	325/345	1957-58
413/ohv V-8	350	1959

PRICES

Conv	
FAIR	$10,000-17,000
GOOD	$17,000-23,000
FINE	$23,000-33,000
2d htp	
FAIR	$3500-7000
GOOD	$7000-11,000
FINE	$11,000-16,000
4d models	
FAIR	$2500-5000
GOOD	$5000-8000
FINE	$8000-11,000

FINE CONVERTIBLE PRICE HISTORY

1982 $8000	**1990** $25,000
1994 $30,000	**1998** $30,000
1982-2000 RETURN 9%	
2000-2010 5%	

1957-65
CROWN IMPERIAL BY GHIA

Low demand sent Chrysler calling on Ghia of Italy to build its long-wheelbase limousines starting in 1957. Chrysler sent over a two-door hardtop body mounted on the more rigid convertible chassis. Ghia then cut the car apart, added 20.5 inches to the wheelbase, reworked the superstructure, and applied posh upholstery and interior accouterments. Each of these custom Crowns took a month to build, and at $15,075 in 1957 (up to $18,500 by 1965) not many were sold. One problem was that the Imperial lacked Cadillac's prestige among heads of state, funeral directors, and corporate executives. Though quite luxurious and having the Ghia name's snob appeal, they just didn't compete well

with the Standard of the World's Series Seventy-Five limos. Styling generally followed model year changes for the standard Imperial line.

◆ FOR Very rare • Ride • Luxury • Smooth performance

▬ AGAINST Enormity • Thirst • Rust threat • Scarce body parts • Mixed construction quality

1964 Crown Imperial limousine by Ghia

PRODUCTION

1957 36 **1958** 31 **1959** 7 **1960** 16 **1961** 9 **1962** 0 **1963** 13 **1964** 10 **1965** 10

SPECIFICATIONS

Length (in.)	248.0 (average)
Wheelbase (in.)	149.5
Weight (lbs)	5960-6100
Price (new)	$15,075-18,500

ENGINES

cid/type	bhp	years
392/ohv V-8	325	1957-59
413/ohv V-8	340/350	1960-65

PRICES

FAIR	$3500-7000
GOOD	$7000-18,000
FINE	$18,000-25,000

FINE EXAMPLE PRICE HISTORY

1982 $7500	**1990** $18,000
1994 $25,000	**1998** $25,000
1982-2000 RETURN 8%	
2000-2010 2%	

1957-59
IMPERIAL LEBARON

1959 LeBaron Southampton hardtop sedan

Imperial's premium series, introduced with the expanded 1957 line and named after the great '30s coachworks that did some of its best work on Imperial chassis. Only two identically priced four-door models—pillared sedan and pillarless Southampton hardtop— pitched $400-500 above comparable Crowns and thus not very popular when new, but worth seeking out now for that, as well as somewhat greater luxury. (LeBaron was Chrysler's answer to the Cadillac 60 Special.) Bodily and mechanically the same as less costly contemporaries.

◆ FOR Rarity • Luxury • Comfort • Tasteful "ultra-car" styling for the period

▬ AGAINST Fuelishness • Rust-prone • Hard to find nowadays

PRODUCTION

1957 4d sdn 1729 **Southampton htp sdn** 911 **1958 4d sdn** 501 **Southampton htp sdn** 538 **1959 4d sdn** 692 **Southampton htp sdn** 622

1959 Crown Imperial limousine by Ghia

SPECIFICATIONS

Length (in.)	226.3
Wheelbase (in.)	129.0
Weight (lbs)	4765-4940
Price (new)	$5743-6103

ENGINES

cid/type	bhp	years
392/ohv V-8	325/345	1957-58
413/ohv V-8	350	1959

PRICES

FAIR	$2500-5000
GOOD	$5000-7500
FINE	$7500-20,000

FINE SOUTHAMPTON PRICE HISTORY

1982	$5400	1990	$14,000
1994	$14,000	1998	$18,000
1982-2000 RETURN 8%			
2000-2010 7%			

1960-63
IMPERIAL CROWN

1962 Crown convertible

The last Exner-styled Imperials. All shared a new 1960 bodyshell and retained separate frames even though other Chrysler products switched to "Unibody" construction after '59. Initially swollen fins, florid front, and simulated rear-deck spare tire outline, then facelifted with throwback "classic era" freestanding headlamps (in pods on short stalks within pocketed fenders) and gull-like rear "wings." The last were plucked for '62 and 1956-style "gunsight" taillamps appeared on the straight-top fenders. Elwood Engel, Exner's successor, put taillights back in the fenders on the (again) mildly refurbished '63s, and the previous year's split grille was replaced by a group of little rectangles. Chrysler's wedgehead 413 used all years, and few mechanical or chassis changes from 1957-59. Interiors continued to be luxurious, set off by a commanding but gimmick-laden dash awash in pushbuttons for transmission (standard TorqueFlite automatic), heating/air conditioning, etc.

⊞ FOR Cheaper than pre-1960 Crowns • High luxury • Surprisingly roadable

⊟ AGAINST Questionable 1960-61 styling • Still rust-prone • Thirsty • Spotty fit and finish

PRODUCTION

1960 4d sdn 1594 **Southampton htp sdn** 4510 **Southampton htp cpe** 1504 **conv** 618 **1961 Southampton htp sdn** 4769 **Southampton htp cpe** 1007 **conv** 429 **1962 Southampton htp sdn** 6911 **Southampton htp cpe** 1010 **conv** 554 **1963 Southampton htp sdn** 6960 **Southampton htp cpe** 1067 **conv** 531

SPECIFICATIONS

Length (in.)	228.0 (1960), 227.1 (1961-62), 227.8 (1963)
Wheelbase (in.)	129.0
Weight (lbs)	4720-4865
Price (new)	$5403-5782

ENGINES

cid/type	bhp	years
413/ohv V-8	340/350	1960-63

PRICES

Conv	
FAIR	$6000-11,000
GOOD	$11,000-18,000
FINE	$18,000-32,000
Others	
FAIR	$3500-6000
GOOD	$6000-10,000
FINE	$10,000-13,500

FINE 1960 CONVERTIBLE PRICE HISTORY

1982	$6100	1990	$18,000
1994	$25,000	1998	$26,000
1982-2000 RETURN 10%			
1992-2002 5%			

1960-63
IMPERIAL LEBARON

Again the priciest standard Imperials. Series shorn of pillared four-door after 1960, leaving a single Southampton hardtop sedan. Costlier and more luxurious than comparable Crowns, but otherwise the same.

⊞ FOR As for 1960-63 Crown, plus greater rarity

⊟ AGAINST As for 1961-63 Crown

PRODUCTION

1960 4d sdn 692 **Southampton htp sdn** 999 **1961 Southampton htp sdn** 1026 **1962 Southampton htp sdn** 1449 **1963 Southampton htp sdn** 1537

SPECIFICATIONS

Length (in.)	228.0 (1960), 227.1 (1961-62), 227.8 (1963)
Wheelbase (in.)	129.0
Weight (lbs)	4725-4875
Price (new)	$6318-6434

ENGINES

cid/type	bhp	years
413/ohv V-8	340/350	1960-63

PRICES

FAIR	$3500-6000
GOOD	$6000-10,000
FINE	$10,000-15,000

1961 LeBaron hardtop coupe

FINE 1960 SOUTHAMPTON 4D HARDTOP PRICE HISTORY

1982 $4200	**1990** $10,000
1994 $12,000	**1998** $12,000
1982-92 RETURN 9%	
2000-2010 5%	

1964-70

IMPERIAL CROWN

The base Imperial series in these years, and more popular than the LeBaron up through 1968. Chrysler's new head stylist, ex-Ford designer Elwood Engel, favored crisp, conservative lines instead of Virgil Exner's baroque curves, and the 1964-66 Imperials are similar in overall theme to Engel's square-cut 1961 Lincoln Continental. To provide extra quietness and road noise isolation in its flagship models, Chrysler retained separate body/frame construction through 1966. Imperial was then redesigned around a unit body/chassis and a shorter wheelbase. It was, in fact, quite similar to then-current Chryslers except for its less sculptured outer body panels. The similarity increased on the "fuselage-styled" '69s, by which time Imperial was on the decline as a major luxury-market competitor despite a sizeable drop in prices. The trend continued into the '70s, until Imperial ceased as a separate make after 1975. The '76 was nothing more than a Chrysler New Yorker with Imperial nameplates. The name was then dormant until 1981, when it was revived for a high-roller personal-luxury coupe based on the mid-size Chrysler Cordoba/LeBaron platform.

FOR Good supply • Convertible's strong appreciation potential • Smooth highway performance

AGAINST Indifferent fit and finish • Very gas-hoggish • Too big for some

1967 Crown convertible

PRODUCTION

1964 2d htp 5233 **4d htp** 14,181 **conv** 922 **1965 2d htp** 3974 **4d htp** 11,628 **conv** 633 **1966 2d htp** 2373 **4d htp** 8977 **conv** 514 **1967 2d htp** 3225 **4d htp** 9415 **conv** 577 **4d sdn** 2193 **1968 2d htp** 2656 **4d htp** 8492 **conv** 474 **4d sdn** 1887 **1969 2d htp** 224 **4d htp** 823 **4d sdn** 1617 **1970 2d htp** 254 **4d htp** 1333 **4d sdn** 1617

SPECIFICATIONS

Length (in.)	227.8 (1964-66), 224.7 (1967-68), 229.7 (1969-70)
Wheelbase (in.)	129.0 (1964-66), 127.0 (1967-70)
Weight (lbs)	4555-5345
Price (new)	$5374-6497

ENGINES

cid/type	bhp	years
413/ohv V-8	340	1964-65
440/ohv V-8	350/360	1966-70

PRICES

As per 1960-63 Imperial Crown less 50%.

1964-70

IMPERIAL LEBARON

1965 LeBaron hardtop sedan

Imperial's small-volume (except for the bumper 1969 season) upper-class line, still a more luxurious version of the less expensive models. Offered only as a four-door hardtop through 1968, it was then joined by a two-door companion. Priced $600-800 upstream of the comparable Crowns, it boasted more standard accessories and more lavish interior appointments. A half-dozen cars were converted into limousines by the Stageway Coaches company in Arkansas, Chrysler's attempt to keep alive the spirit of the earlier Ghia Crowns. Predictably, comments for 1964-70 Crown models also apply here.

FOR Reasonably good supply • A daily-driver for big-car collectors • High-grade interior • Power assists galore

AGAINST Fuel thirst • Bulk • Quality control slipped after '68 • Depreciating lately

PRODUCTION

1964 2949 **1965** 2164 **1966** 1878 **1967** 2194 **1968** 1852 **1969 4d htp** 14,821 **2d htp** 4592 **1970 4d htp** 8426 **2d htp** 1803 **Limo 6 in 1967 and 1968,** 6 (est.) 1969 and 1970

SPECIFICATIONS

Length (in.)	227.8 (1964-66), 224.7 (1967-68), 229.7 (1969-70), 260.7 (1967-68 limo), 265.7 (1969-70 limo)
Wheelbase (in.)	129.0 (1964-66), 127.0 (1967-70), 163.0 (limo)
Weight (lbs)	4610-5090, 6300-6500 (limo)
Price (new)	$5898-6596, $15,000-18,500 (limo)

ENGINES

cid/type	bhp	years
413/ohv V-8	340	1964-66
440/ohv V-8	350/360	1966-70

PRICES

FAIR	$1000-3000

1964 Crown hardtop coupe

| GOOD | $3000-4500 |
| FINE | $4500-6500 |

FINE EXAMPLE PRICE HISTORY

1982 $2200		**1990** $7500	
1994 $8500		**1998** $7000	
1982-2000 RETURN 7%			
2000-2010 8%			

1 9 8 1 - 8 3
IMPERIAL

Short-lived and cynical resurrection of Chrysler's luxury make: actually a clever reskin of the long-wheelbase 1976-vintage M-body platform used for the Dodge Aspen/Plymouth Volare compacts, among other things. Marked by chiseled, "formal" lines, stand-up grille, hidden headlamps, razor-edge roofline, and "bustle" trunk. The last looked to be a copy of Cadillac's similar treatment on the new 1980 second-generation Seville four-door, but was purely accidental and, arguably, nice-looking. Drivetrain comprised the veteran 318 V-8 (injected) and TorqueFlite. Orthodox rear-drive chassis save odd transverse front torsion bars, inherited from lesser M-body models, and old-fashioned rear leaf springs Frank Sinatra sang "It's time for Imperial" in TV commercials, and a (give-us-a-break) 1982-83 "Sinatra Edition" included tapes of his songs. Neither this nor fully equipped "one price" marketing stimulated much interest in a difficult market then doubtful of Chrysler's ability to survive. Imperial was revived yet again for 1990, this time as a four-door that was even less special than this coupe.

➕ **FOR** Interesting, low-volume modern Chrysler • Luxurious leather-lined cabin • Power everything • Smooth and quiet, except for those Sinatra tapes • Used-car cheap

➖ **AGAINST** Roly-poly handling • Numb steering • Overassisted brakes • Quality not as originally advertised • Not very interesting even to MoPar mavens

PRODUCTION
1981 7225 **1982** 2329 **1983** 1427

SPECIFICATIONS

Length (in.)	213.3
Wheelbase (in.)	112.7
Weight (lbs)	3945-4020
Price (new)	$18,311-20,988

ENGINES

cid/type	bhp	years
318/ohv V-8	140	1981-83

PRICES

FAIR	$1200-2500
GOOD	$2500-4500
FINE	$4500-6000

FINE EXAMPLE PRICE HISTORY

No information
2000-2010 RETURN 0%

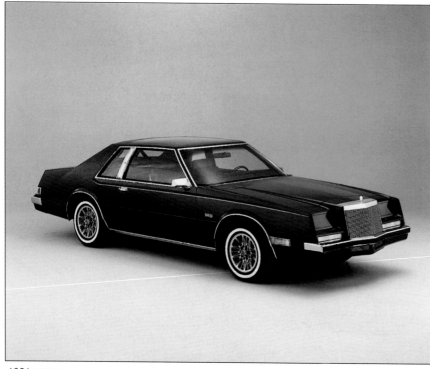

1981 coupe

1 9 9 1 - 9 2
INFINITI M30 CONVERTIBLE

1992 M30 convertible

The Q45 needed a companion, so the Japanese-market Nissan Leopard was rebadged and sent to American Infiniti showrooms. A coupe arrived first and the convertible joined it a year later. The conversion was well done. The body was admirably stiff. Both top and windows went down with touch of a button. The rear drive, six-cylinder convertible provided adequate performance and handling. Styling was conservative or dull depending on your point of view. Never a big seller, the M30 convertible lasted only two years.

➕ **FOR** Rarity • It's a convertible • Well equipped

➖ **AGAINST** Cramped back seat • Rear visibility

PRODUCTION[1]
1991 6311 **1992** 3749
[1]U.S. coupe and convertible sales.

SPECIFICATIONS

Length (in.)	188.8
Weight (lbs)	3576
Wheelbase (in.)	103.0
Price (new)	$31,000-33,700

ENGINES

cid/type	bhp	years
182/ohc V-6	162	1991-92

PRICES

FAIR	$8400-10,000
GOOD	$10,000-12,000
FINE	$12,000-13,800

1 9 6 1 - 7 0
INNOCENTI SPIDER/COUPE

One of several products resulting from the linkup between British Motor Corporation (BMC) and Italy's

1964 spider

Innocenti. Essentially the Austin-Healey Sprite/MG Midget platform rebodied by Ghia; production by OSI, near Milan. More stylish, expensive, and exclusive than the "Spridget," but a little heavier. Mechanical changes parallel those of British relatives, and basic chassis was unaltered. These Innocentis had roll-up door windows years before the Spridgets.

■ **FOR** More attractive and civilized than the BMC product • Familiar and sturdy chassis, mechanicals

■ **AGAINST** Heavier than equivalent Sprite/Midget • No body parts available now • Serious ruster • Little expertise and interest in U.S.

PRODUCTION
NA

SPECIFICATIONS
Length (in.)	135.0
Wheelbase (in.)	80.0
Weight (lbs)	1595 (Spider), 1700 (Coupe)
Price (new)	$2900 in U.S. in 1964

ENGINES
cc/type (cid)	bhp[1]	years
948/ohv I-4 (58)	45/56	1961-67
1098/ohv I-4 (67)	59	1968-70
1275/ohv I-4 (78)	65	1970-71

[1]net

PRICES
FAIR	$3500-6500
GOOD	$6500-8000
FINE	$8000-12,000

FINE EXAMPLE PRICE HISTORY
No recent sales records available.
2000-2010 RETURN 2%

1963-70
ISO RIVOLTA

An Italo-American hybrid from a company whose main business was refrigerators. Power was supplied by the familiar Chevrolet 327 V-8 mounted in a steel platform chassis designed by ex-Ferrari engineer Giotto Bizzarrini. The steel notchback coupe body was styled by Bertone, and offered full four-passenger seating. A very roadable machine thanks partly to the de Dion rear suspension, and quite fast—up to 142 mph. Some models were fitted with a ZF five-speed gearbox, others with the Chevy four-speed manual or three-speed automatic. Rather "soft" for a high-performance Latin, designed with an eye to American sales, which were never high. Not as sleek as contemporary Ferraris, but roomier. It's a more practical proposition for mechanical rebuilds and routine servicing on this side of the Atlantic, too, due to mass-production drivetrains. Replaced by the S4 Fidia sedan at the end of the decade.

■ **FOR** Simple, sturdy Detroit powertrains • Fine chassis • Cheaper than other Italian exotics • Prices have fallen off since the crazy times • Nice Bertone styling

■ **AGAINST** Lacks pedigree of a Ferrari or Maserati • Rust-prone • No body/chassis parts can be found

PRODUCTION
NA, but very limited

SPECIFICATIONS
Length (in.)	187.4
Wheelbase (in.)	106.0
Weight (lbs)	3420
Price (new)	approx. $9200 (U.S.)

ENGINES
cid/type	bhp[1]	years
327/ohv V-8	300/335	1962-70

[1]Gross

PRICES
FAIR	$10,000-12,000
GOOD	$12,000-17,500
FINE	$17,500-25,000

FINE EXAMPLE PRICE HISTORY
1982 $9000		**1990** $40,000	
1994 $28,000		**1998** $24,000	

1982-2000 RETURN 6%
2000-2010 5%

1965-74
ISO GRIFO

1971-74 Iso Grifo coupe

A short-wheelbase, two-seat fastback derivative of the Iso Rivolta. The handsome, muscular styling was again by Bertone, with a low greenhouse and large windshield and backlight. Four headlamps were used at the outer ends of a split grille. Some cars had a hood bulge to provide clearance for the air cleaners of the Chevy-built V-8 engines, offered variously in 327- and 427-cid sizes. Late in the model run, the nose was modified to look more Ferrari-like, and hooded headlamps were adopted. Built in very limited numbers.

■ **FOR** Detroit powertrain with performance and distinctive styling • Prices well down from the heights • Cheaper than Italian exotics

■ **AGAINST** Lacks pedigree of a Ferrari or Maserati • Rust-prone • No

body/chassis parts can be found

PRODUCTION

NA, but very limited

SPECIFICATIONS

Length (in.)	175.0
Wheelbase (in.)	98.5
Weight (lbs)	3180-3520
Price (new)	NA

ENGINES

cid/type	bhp[1]	years
327/ohv V-8	300/335	1965-74
427/ohv V-8	385/400	1968-74

[1]Gross

PRICES

FAIR	$10,000-20,000
GOOD	$20,000-30,000
FINE	$30,000-45,000

FINE EXAMPLE PRICE HISTORY

1982 $12,500		1990 $65,000	
1994 $40,000		1998 $42,500	

1982-2000 RETURN 8%
2000-2010 5%

1 9 6 7 - 7 4
ISO S4 FIDIA

Four-door successor to the Rivolta coupe, using the same basic chassis design on a six-inch longer wheelbase. Styling by Ghia featured a blunt nose with quad square headlamps, a fairly short tail, and flowing "coke-bottle" fender lines. The plain but well-appointed interior featured standard air conditioning, an impressively instrumented dash, center console, and front bucket seats. Big and heavy, but quite quick with a top speed in excess of 130 mph.

FOR As for previous Isos, plus bet-ter equipment and four-door prac-ticality

AGAINST As for previous Isos

PRODUCTION

NA, but very limited

SPECIFICATIONS

Length (in.)	195.7
Wheelbase (in.)	112.2
Weight (lbs)	3700
Price (new)	$14,300, U.S. 1969 base price

ENGINES

cid/type	bhp[1]	years
327/ohv V-8	300	1967-74

[1]Gross

PRICES

As for 1965-74 Grifo.

1 9 8 3 - 8 6
ISUZU IMPULSE

Called the Piazza, was a sensation at the 1979 Geneva Auto Show, and again when it reappeared there in 1981. Little wonder, for its smooth, unbroken lines had been penned by Giorgetto Giugiaro, with flush glass, hidden body seams, and no brightwork other than badge and aluminum wheels. Underneath, though, was a humble, Chevette-based platform that dated back to a GM/Isuzu business arrangement of the early Seventies. The Piazza bowed in Japan for 1981 and was introduced, as the Impulse, in the U.S. for '83. A 1.9-liter ohc four put out 90 horse-power and 108 pounds/ feet of torque—good only for 0-60 times of about 13.2 seconds with 5-speed stick. A Turbo arrived as a late 1985 model, and brought far better perfor-mance capability: 140 bhp and 166 pounds/feet of torque; 60 mph came up from a stop in about 8.5 seconds. Inside, key controls were grouped on pods that snugged close to each side of the steering wheel.

FOR Italian design virtually unchanged from show-car iteration • Acceleration (Turbo) • Novel, practical ergonomics • Fuel economy

AGAINST Chevette underpinnings • Listless acceleration (non-Turbo models) • Engine thrashy above 3000 rpm • Jittery over bumps • Questionable build quality • Parts likely to be scarce • Japanese nameplate

PRODUCTION

1983 8855		1884 12,806	
1985 14,173		1986 12,864	

U.S. calendar year sales

SPECIFICATIONS

Length (in.)	172.6
Weight (lbs)	2734
Wheelbase (in.)	96.0
Price (new)	$10,498-13,499

ENGINES

cid/type	bhp	years
119/ohc I-4	90	1983-86
122/ohc I-4[1]	140	1985-86

[1]Turbocharged

PRICES

FAIR	$1000-1500
GOOD	$1500-2000
FINE	$1800-2200

2000-2010 RETURN 0%

1 9 4 5 - 4 8
JAGUAR MARK IV

1948 Mark IV 3.5 Litre sedan

Jaguar's first cars after World War II, essentially continuations of the 1938-39 models. Most were four-door sedans and shared the same bodyshell, but the 1.5 Litre model rode a six-inch shorter wheelbase and had a four- instead of six-cylinder engine made by the Standard Motor Car

1983 Impulse hatchback coupe

Company. Appearance was marked by a long hood, upright radiator capped by the Jaguar mascot, large freestanding headlamps, flowing separate front fenders, and a narrow, close-coupled body. An archaic—even by the late '40s—leaf-spring/live-axle suspension was used both front and rear. High-quality interior furnishings included a traditional British wood dash with large, plainly marked dials. Top speed for the 1.5 Litre was about 70 mph; the 3.5 Litre could reach a bit over 90 mph. Most Mark IVs were built with right-hand drive for the British market as Jaguar's export drive didn't begin in earnest until a few years later.

FOR Classic lines • CCCA Classic status • Rugged simplicity • Rare in U.S. • Convertibles very desirable • Prices have recently retreated to realistic levels

AGAINST Parts supplies dried up long ago • Limited performance • Poor body quality • Old-fashioned chassis

PRODUCTION

1.5 Litre 5761 **2.5 Litre** 1861 **3.5 Litre** 4420 **Conv** 104 (2.5 Litre), 560 (3.5 Litre)

SPECIFICATIONS

Length (in.)	173.0 (1.5), 186.0 (2.5/3.5)
Wheelbase (in.)	112.5 (1.5), 120.0 (2.5/3.5)
Weight (lbs)	2970 (1.5), 3585 (2.5), 3670 (3.5)
Price (new)	NA

ENGINES

cc/type (cid)	bhp[1]	years
1776/ohv I-4 (108)	65	1945-48
2663/ohv I-6 (163)	105	1945-48
3485/ohv I-6 (213)	125	1945-48

[1]Gross

PRICES

Open	
FAIR	$15,000-30,000
GOOD	$30,000-45,000
FINE	$45,000-60,000

(Deduct one-third for closed models.)

FINE DROPHEAD PRICE HISTORY

1982 $12,500		**1990** $80,000	
1994 $60,000		**1998** $55,000	
1982-2000 RETURN 10%			
2000-2010 5%			

1948-51
JAGUAR MARK V

The first true postwar Jaguars, with an all-new chassis featuring independent front suspension. This platform would be used for the later Mark VII sedans and, in shortened form, for the pace-setting XK sports cars begin-

ning in 1948. Styling was an updated version of the Mark IV, still with a traditional vertical radiator and sweeping separate fenders, but headlamps were now partially integrated into the fenders. Roomy four-door saloons (sedans) were most common, but many 3.5 Litre chassis were built with dignified two-door drophead (convertible) coupe bodywork, and are considerably more collectible today. Engines were essentially holdovers of the prewar six-cylinder units. Like all such Jaguars, they were fast for the period (more than 90 mph for the 3.5 Litre models), and trimmed with lots of real wood cappings and plush upholstery.

FOR As for 1945-48 Mark IV, plus better handling • Dropheads have Milestone car status • Has mainly held onto its 1990s inflated values

AGAINST As for 1945-48 Mark IV • Pricey, maybe overvalued

PRODUCTION

2.5 Litre Saloon 1661 **2.5 Litre Drophead** 29 **3.5 Litre Saloon** 7831 **3.5 Litre Drophead** 972

SPECIFICATIONS

Length (in.)	187.0
Wheelbase (in.)	120.0
Weight (lbs)	3700/3860 (sdn/conv)
Price (new)	NA

ENGINES

cc/type (cid)	bhp[1]	years
2663/ohv I-6 (163)	105	1948-51
3485/ohv I-6 (213)	125	1948-51

[1]Gross

PRICES

Open	
FAIR	$19,000-30,000
GOOD	$30,000-40,000
FINE	$40,000-55,000
Closed	
FAIR	$5000-10,000
GOOD	$10,000-15,000
FINE	$15,000-25,000

FINE DROPHEAD PRICE HISTORY

1982 $25,000		**1990** $65,000	
1994 $65,000		**1998** $58,000	
1982-2000 RETURN 5%			
2000-2010 3%			

1948-54
JAGUAR XK120

1949 XK120 roadster (alloy body)

One of the most important Milestones from either side of the Atlantic, a trend-setting sports car that became a legend in its own time. A modern envelope body with integral fenders was new for Jaguar, and was mounted on a massive, newly designed chassis with torsion bar front suspension. The sleek, flowing lines were created by Jaguar's William Lyons, and would have wide industry influence. A vee'd windshield rode above a long hood that tapered to a narrow, oval grille flanked by large headlamps nestled in the "catwalk" areas between the fender tops and the grille. Delicate-looking bumpers front and rear were connected by curvaceous, perfectly proportioned fenders. This was the car that introduced the remarkable XK-series twincam six, which would prove amazingly adapt-

1950 Mark V convertible

able and long-lived. The XK120 (the designation stemmed from the top speed recorded by prototypes) was offered as an open roadster, drophead (convertible), and fixed-head (steel top) coupe. Bodies were constructed initially of light alloy, then switched to conventional pressed steel. Incredible value for the money when new, and amazingly successful despite heavy handling and marginal brakes (later improved). It still commands a huge and loyal following nearly 30 years after it went out of production.

FOR Classic styling • Legendary performance • Rugged, long-life engine • Most mechanical parts still available • Active club support • A Milestone car • Prices at bargain levels compared to a decade ago

AGAINST Body rusts badly if neglected • Heavy steering • Dodgy brakes • Poor driving position • Not cheap

PRODUCTION

Roadster 7631 **cpe** 2678 **conv** 1769

SPECIFICATIONS

Length (in.)	174.0
Wheelbase (in.)	102.0
Weight (lbs)	2855-3080
Price (new)	approx. $3500 in 1951

ENGINES

cc/type (cid)	bhp[1]	years
3442/dohc I-6 (210)	160/180	1948-54
[1]Gross		

PRICES

Open	
FAIR	$17,000-30,000
GOOD	$30,000-40,000
FINE	$40,000-65,000
Cpe	
FAIR	$9000-15,000
GOOD	$15,000-22,000
FINE	$22,000-28,000

FINE ROADSTER PRICE HISTORY

1982 $18,000		1990 $72,500	
1994 $60,000		1998 $78,000	
1982-2000 RETURN 8%			
2000-2010 8%			

1950-57
JAGUAR MARK VII/VIIM

Hot on the heels of the stunning XK120 sports car came Jaguar's first all-new postwar sedan, combining the previous Mark V chassis with the magnificent XK twincam six. The bulbous envelope body retained a distinctive Jaguar vertical grille and a trace of

1952 Mark VII sedan

the traditional separate fenderlines. The leading front fender tips, rear fenders, roof, tail, and side window shapes were all gently rounded. Roomy compared to previous Jaguars, it still came with all the usual wood and leather fittings. This was also the first car from Coventry offered with an optional automatic transmission, supplied by Borg-Warner. The Mark VII had 160 bhp and foglamps recessed into the front fender valences. The Mark VIIM replaced it in 1954 with a 190-bhp version of the XK six and freestanding fog lights. All models were equipped with drum brakes, and power steering was not available. Succeeded by the Mark VIII series in 1957.

FOR Six passenger room combined with near XK120 performance • Graceful "period" styling • Not too expensive for a collectible • Both series are Milestone cars

AGAINST Rust-prone • Body parts no longer around • Marginal brakes • Construction quality doesn't match looks

PRODUCTION

Mark VII 20,939 **Mark VIIM** 9261

SPECIFICATIONS

Length (in.)	196.5
Wheelbase (in.)	120.0
Weight (lbs)	3865
Price (new)	approx. $4000-4600 (U.S.)

ENGINES

cc/type (cid)	bhp[1]	years
3442/dohc I-6	160/190	1950-57
[1]Gross		

PRICES

FAIR	$3500-9000
GOOD	$9000-12,000
FINE	$12,000-17,000

FINE EXAMPLE PRICE HISTORY

1982 $9000		1990 $16,000
1994 $20,000		1998 $20,000
1982-2000 RETURN 4%		
2000-2010 3%		

1951-53
JAGUAR C-TYPE

A very specialized car developed by Jaguar primarily for racing, but it could also be used on the road—as indeed many were. It borrowed many XK120 components (twincam engine, gearbox, rear axle), but had its own multi-tubular chassis and distinctive aerodynamic light-alloy open roadster body. Styling was unmistakably Jaguar, with a touch of the XK120's lines in profile, but the oval, vertical bar grille was shorter and wider. No concession was made to weather protection or comfort. There was no heater and little in the way of exhaust muffling or sound deadening; they would have only added weight, undesirable in a racing machine. A successful competitor at Le Mans (scoring outright wins in 1951 and '53), with a top speed comfortably over 140 mph.

FOR Significance to Jaguar racing history • Rugged reliability • Restoration help still available • Low-production scarcity

1951 C-Type competition roadster

■ AGAINST A sunny-days-only machine • Flimsy body • A noisy extrovert • Exorbitant asking prices • Virtually off the market

PRODUCTION

43 (plus 11 race versions)

SPECIFICATIONS

Length (in.)	157.0
Wheelbase (in.)	96.0
Weight (lbs)	2075
Price (new)	approx. $6000 U.S. equivalent

ENGINES

cc/type (cid)	bhp[1]	years
3442/dohc I-6 (210)	200	1951-53

[1]Gross

PRICES

At market peak, C-types with documented competition history were bringing $750,000 to over $1 million; though street Jaguars have taken a heavy beating in the collector market for the last few years, racing cars have been less affected, and most experts now expect a documented example to sell for close to these levels.
2000-2010 RETURN 8%

1954-57
JAGUAR D-TYPE & XKSS

The D-Type succeeded the C-Type as Jaguar's "factory racer" in these years, but was less practical as a road car. The XKSS was essentially a street version of it, with minimal bumpers, two opening doors (instead of one), a full windshield, and a rudimentary folding top. A disastrous fire at the Jaguar plant cut short production, which was never resumed afterward. The aerodynamic shape of these cars predicted the styling of the production E-Type (XKE in the U.S.) introduced in 1961. A small oval front air intake, highly arched fenders, and considerable bodyside tuck-under were comple-

1955 D-Type competition roadster

mented on some cars by a faired-in headrest for the driver, and a few had a vertical fin trailing from this. Power was supplied by a race-tuned XK engine hooked to an all-synchromesh gearbox. A complex multi-tubular front frame was used, with separate monocoque center and tail sections. A dozen factory racers were built in 1955-56 with long noses and integral tailfins. Top speed was over 150 mph with suitable gearing. The XKSS was built only in 1957.

■ FOR The ultimate in "macho" • Sturdy production Jaguar components • High-performance • Predictive styling

■ AGAINST Impractical on the road • Terrifically expensive today • Expensive to restore, maintain • None really left on the market • Appeal diluted by modern replicas

1957 XKSS roadster

PRODUCTION

D-Type 71 (incl. 18 team race cars) **XKSS** 16

SPECIFICATIONS

Length (in.)	154.0
Wheelbase (in.)	90.6
Weight (lbs)	1930 (D-Type), 2015 (XKSS)
Price (new)	approx. $5600 (XKSS), $9900 (D-Type) in U.S.

ENGINES

cc/type (cid)	bhp[1]	years
3442/dohc I-6 (210)	250	1954-57

[1]Gross

PRICES

At market peak, D-type short-nose racers were at $750,000 to $1 million, while long-nose versions were at $900,000 to $1.2 million. Interest in certified competition Jaguars continues strong despite market hiccups at the lower end, and all D-types are still worth in excess of $600,000. The XKSS has probably surpassed seven figures, too.
2000-2010 RETURN 8%

1954-57
JAGUAR XK140

1956 XK140 roadster

A re-engineered version of the XK120 intended specifically for the increasingly important North American export market. Styling was basically the same except for a "wide stripe" grille. The fixed-roof coupe and soft top convertible models now offered +2 rear seating. Mechanical changes included an improved cooling system and steering (now rack-and-pinion), and sturdier bumpers. Automatic transmission became available late in the model run except for the roadster.

■ FOR As for XK120, plus better performance and sturdier body • Milestone status

■ AGAINST As for XK120, except for improved brakes and handling

PRODUCTION

Roadster 3347 **cpe** 2797 **conv** 2740

SPECIFICATIONS

Length (in.)	176.0
Wheelbase (in.)	102.0
Weight (lbs)	3135-3250
Price (new)	approx. $3600 U.S. in 1955

ENGINES

cc/type (cid)	bhp[1]	years
3442/dohc I-6 (210)	190/210	1954-57

[1]Gross

PRICES

Prices 5-10% more than 1948-54 Jaguar XK120. Though purists cavil, there is little market difference now between the original 120 and its successor.
1992-2002 RETURN 10%

JAGUAR MARK VIII

1956-59

Slightly heavier replacement for the Mark VII/VIIM sedans. It featured minor styling changes and more power, but was otherwise the same. Identification points include a one-piece instead of split windshield, two-tone paint, a bolder grille, reshaped seats, and more luxurious interior trim. Output of the XK twincam six was boosted from 190 to 210 bhp for this application, about one horsepower per cubic inch. Still with drum brakes, however. Most examples were fitted with Borg-Warner automatic transmission.

FOR As for 1950-57 Mark VII/VIIM • Another Milestone Jag

AGAINST As for 1950-57 Mark VII/VIIM

PRODUCTION

6332

SPECIFICATIONS

Length (in.)	196.5
Wheelbase (in.)	120.0
Weight (lbs)	4030
Price (new)	approx. $5000 U.S.

ENGINES

cc/type (cid)	bhp[1]	years
3442/dohc I-6 (210)	210	1956-59

[1]Gross

PRICES

FAIR	$3500-10,000
GOOD	$10,000-17,000
FINE	$17,000-25,000

FINE EXAMPLE PRICE HISTORY

1982 $8600	1990 $25,000
1994 $22,500	1998 $25,000

1982-2000 RETURN 7%
2000-2010 3%

1957-58 Mark VIII sedan

JAGUAR XK150

1957-61

1958 XK150 coupe

The final derivative of the XK120, but more "matronly" in appearance. The basic XK120/140 bodyshell was substantially restyled with higher front fenders, a wider grille, and a curved, one-piece windshield. The heavier look was matched by a gain in curb weight, though it didn't spoil the good overall balance of previous models. The basic XK chassis was retained, updated with Dunlop disc brakes at each wheel. The 210-bhp version of the 3.4-liter twincam inline six was standardized, and beginning in the fall of 1959 a 3.8-liter bored-out enlargement with 20 extra horses was offered as an optional extra. Many were sold with the Borg-Warner automatic transmission. Replaced by the sensational E-Type during 1961.

FOR As for 1954-57 XK140, plus better brakes and more restful performance • Milestone status

AGAINST As for 1954-57 XK140, but less pleasant lines and extra weight

PRODUCTION

3.4 Litre rdstr 1297 **3.4 Litre cpe** 3445 **3.4 Litre conv** 1903 **3.8 Litre rdstr** 42 **3.8 Litre cpe** 656 **3.8 Litre conv** 586

SPECIFICATIONS

Length (in.)	177.0
Wheelbase (in.)	102.0
Weight (lbs)	3220-3520
Price (new)	approx. $4500-5200 U.S.

ENGINES

cc/type (cid)	bhp	years
3442/dohc I-6 (210)	210	1957-61
3781/dohc I-6 (231)	230	1959-61

PRICES

During the seller's market of the early 1990s the less elegant but more civilized and reliable XK150 met the XK120's value across the boards, since then it has tailed off slightly, and now runs about $10,000 less, model for model, in similar condition.
2000-2010 RETURN 8%

JAGUAR XK150S

1958-61

1959 XK150S roadster

The fiercest of all the early XKs thanks to a more highly tuned twincam engine with a different cylinder head and three SU carburetors. Not available with automatic transmission, the "S" version boasted a top speed of well over 135 mph. Identified from the outside by discreet badges and from under the hood by the triple carburetors.

FOR As for 1957-61 XK150, plus more performance and greater rarity • A Milestone car, of course

AGAINST As for 1957-61 XK150, but more difficult to find

PRODUCTION

3.4 Litre rdstr 888 **3.4 Litre cpe** 199 **3.4 Litre conv** 104 **3.8 Litre rdstr** 36 **3.8 Litre cpe** 150 **3.8 Litre conv** 89

SPECIFICATIONS

Length (in.)	177.0
Wheelbase (in.)	102.0
Weight (lbs)	3220-3520

Price (new)   approx. $5600 U.S. in 1958

ENGINES

cc/type (cid)	bhp[1]	years
3442/dohc I-6 (210)	250	1958-61
3781/dohc I-6 (231)	265	1959-61

[1]Gross

PRICES

Rdstr	
FAIR	$30,000-45,000
GOOD	$45,000-60,000
FINE	$60,000-80,000

(Other models at commensurate premiums compared to standard XK150s.)

FINE EXAMPLE PRICE HISTORY

1982 $14,000	1990 $90,000
1994 $75,000	1998 $75,000

1982-2000 RETURN 11%
2000-2010 10%

1959-61
JAGUAR MARK IX

The last of the original 1950 Mark VII design, now with four-wheel disc brakes, power steering, and the bored-out 3.8-liter twincam engine as standard equipment. Virtually all were equipped with Borg-Warner automatic transmission. The only appearance change of note compared to the previous Mark VIII was a change in the identifying nameplate on the trunklid.

FOR As for Mark VII/VIIM and Mark VIII, plus better brakes • More affordable than it's been in a long time

AGAINST As for Mark VII/VIIM and Mark VIII • Lately depreciating

PRODUCTION

10,005

SPECIFICATIONS

Length (in.)	196.5
Wheelbase (in.)	120.0
Weight (lbs)	4000
Price (new)	approx. $6500 U.S. in 1961

ENGINES

cc/type (cid)	bhp[1]	years
3781/dohc I-6 (231)	220	1959-61

[1]Gross

PRICES

FAIR	$4500-9500
GOOD	$9500-12,000
FINE	$12,000-17,500

FINE EXAMPLE PRICE HISTORY

1982 $8600	1990 $24,000
1994 $22,500	1998 $20,000

1982-2000 RETURN 4%
2000-2010 Even

1961 Mark IX sedan

1960-69
JAGUAR MARK II

1960 Mark II sedan

The restyled and more attractive successor to Jaguar's smaller sedan line ("Mark I") introduced in 1956. The monocoque bodyshell was given a more open greenhouse and minor exterior trim changes, but stayed dimensionally the same. Powered by the workhorse XK twincam six in a choice of three displacements and power ratings, and available with both manual and automatic transmission. Numerous other extra-cost items were listed, including overdrive and handsome knock-off-center wire wheels. All these are good-handling cars and, in the case of the 3.8-liter versions, quick (up to 135 mph maximum). This series had a live-axle rear suspension, unlike later models that had an independent setup. Sold fairly widely in the U.S. through 1967, after which the 3.8-liter engine was dropped to make room in the lineup for the new XJ6 and the remaining models were renamed 240 and 340.

FOR Compact size • Fine handling • Legendary XK performance • Wide choice of specs • Many parts still available • Conservative British appearance

• 3.4- and 3.8-liter "small sedans" 1957-64 are Milestone cars

AGAINST Unit construction rust problem • Limited performance (2.4 liter) • Not as much room as you'd think

PRODUCTION

2.4 Litre 25,173 **3.4 Litre** 28,666 **3.8 Litre** 30,141 **240** 4446 **340** 2800

SPECIFICATIONS

Length (in.)	181.0
Wheelbase (in.)	107.4
Weight (lbs)	3200-3360
Price (new)	$4800 U.S. for 3.8-Litre in 1960

ENGINES

cc/type (cid)	bhp[1]	years
2443/dohc I-6 (149)	120	1960-69
3442/dohc I-6 (210)	210	1960-69
3781/dohc I-6 (231)	220	1960-67

[1]Gross

PRICES

FAIR	$4000-8000
GOOD	$8000-14,000
FINE	$14,000-21,500

FINE EXAMPLE PRICE HISTORY

1982 $8000	1990 $14,000
1994 $17,500	1998 $20,000

1982-2000 RETURN 6%
2000-2010 5%

1961-71
JAGUAR E-TYPE (XKE)

Jaguar's sensational '60s sports car, successor to the XK150 but sharing a good many styling and technical details first seen on the racing D-Type. Like that car, the E-Type's construction used a multi-tube front end bolted to a "bathtub" steel bodyshell. The long, low hood and front fenders were one assembly, and hinged at the front to lift up for almost unrestricted engine

1963 E-Type coupe

1963 Mark X sedan

access. The 3.8-liter version of the venerable twincam XK engine was marketed first, along with a manual gearbox with non-synchro first gear. Independent suspension and disc brakes were found at each wheel, and the E-Type quickly earned fame for its terrific roadability matched with brisk performance. Beginning in 1965, the larger 4.2-liter engine and an all-synchro transmission were specified, which improved low-speed driving ease. Initial body styles were the traditional two-seat roadster and a sleek new fastback coupe with a side-hinged rear door. These were joined in 1966 by a stretched-wheelbase coupe with 2+2 seating and somewhat less lithe appearance. U.S. models were sold as the XKE, and differed little from British-market versions through 1967. After that, styling suffered due to federal safety standards, which brought side marker lights, clumsy bumpers, and more upright exposed headlights (previously mounted behind smoothly shaped plastic covers). The basic design continued into the early '70s in much-modified form with Jaguar's then-new V-12. That ultimately gave way to the XJS, which was more a GT than a true sports-car successor. The E-Type is still a head-turner today, and one of the most desirable collector's items you can own. Roadster prices skyrocketed during the late '80s and are still holding on.

FOR Great collectible • Fantasy styling still looks good • Performance (140+ mph) • Parts and service plentiful • Handling • Milestone status for 1961-67 models • Strong club support

AGAINST Bodies attract tinworm • Costly to restore and maintain • Limited cockpit, luggage space • Marginal cooling capacity for warm weather areas • English electrical gremlins • Expensive, but not as much as a few years ago

PRODUCTION

3.8 Litre rdstr 7820 **3.8 Litre cpe** 7670 **4.2 Litre rdstr** 18,180 **4.2 Litre cpe** 12,630 **4.2 Litre 2+2 cpe** 10,930

SPECIFICATIONS

Length (in.)	175.0/184.5 (2-seaters/2+2)
Wheelbase (in.)	96.0/105.0 (2-seaters/2+2)
Weight (lbs)	2690-2800/3100 (2-seaters/2+2)
Price (new)	approx. $5600-6500 U.S.

ENGINES

cc/type (cid)	bhp[1]	years
3781/dohc I-6 (231)	265	1961-65
4235/dohc I-6 (258)	265	1965-71

[1]Gross

PRICES

Conv	
FAIR	$15,000-25,000
GOOD	$25,000-35,000
FINE	$35,000-48,500
Cpe	
FAIR	$7000-12,000
GOOD	$12,000-17,000
FINE	$17,000-23,000

FINE CONVERTIBLE PRICE HISTORY

1982 $11,000	**1990** $40,000
1994 $55,000	**1998** $57,000
1982-2000 RETURN 9%	
2000-2010 8%	

1961-65
JAGUAR MARK X

The largest Jaguar sedan ever, completely different from its Mark IX predecessor in styling and chassis design. Body-on-frame construction was replaced by a massive unitized structure with coil-spring independent rear suspension like that of the E-Type. Offered in these years with the 3.8-liter version of the famous twincam XK engine, and came equipped with power steering and Borg-Warner automatic transmission. It was almost as large as some full-size American cars of the period, but managed to look smaller because of the traditionally graceful Jaguar styling. Its appearance was much more modern than the Mark IX's, too, with straight-through fenders (no hint of separate "wings" remained), a tapering tail, and a sloping front end with a shallower grille. The interior had all the usual Jaguar accouterments: wood-faced dash bristling with switches and dials and comfy seats upholstered in genuine leather. A few Mark Xs were fitted with a division window and sold as limousines. Despite its size, this big cat could reach 120 mph, though it wasn't terribly quick off the line. Not many were sold in the U.S.

FOR Roomy, comfortable highway car • Nice blend of modern and traditional styling • Lovely XK engine • Well-equipped • Handling (despite size) • Not too costly to buy • Milestone status

AGAINST Rusts easily • Trim and body parts in short supply • Poor mileage • Underpowered for give-and-take traffic • May be too large for some • Depreciating lately, to virtual bargain status

PRODUCTION

12,977

SPECIFICATIONS

Length (in.)	202.0
Wheelbase (in.)	120.0
Weight (lbs)	4175
Price (new)	Approx. $7000 (U.S.)

ENGINES

cc/type (cid)	bhp[1]	years
3781/dohc I-6 (231)	265	1961-65

[1]Gross

PRICES

FAIR	$4000-9000
GOOD	$9000-11,000
FINE	$11,000-14,000

FINE EXAMPLE PRICE HISTORY

1982 $8100	**1990** $23,000
1994 $20,000	**1998** $18,000
1982-2000 RETURN 3%	
2000-2010 Even	

1963-69
JAGUAR S-TYPE/420

1967 420 sedan

Literal extensions of Jaguar's original Mark II sedan series first seen in 1956. The S-Type, introduced for 1963, featured a longer, Mark X-like tail grafted onto the original unitized body/chassis structure. To go with it, Jaguar added a coil-spring independent rear suspension similar to that of the E-Type. In 1967, to provide even closer family resemblance with the Mark X, which was renamed 420G that year, Jaguar announced the 420. This was an S-Type with a squared-up Mark X nose including a square grille and four headlamps. By this time, there was little of the original 2.4-liter Mark II left. All these models carried the by-now familiar twincam XK engine, with model designation reflecting displacement (3.4S, 3.8S, 420). Typical Jaguar interior appointments were featured, and both manual and automatic transmissions were available. Each version was slightly heavier and less nimble than the one before it. The 420 was capable of 125 mph, and was also sold in England as the badge-engineered Daimler Sovereign with a traditional fluted grille and different trim details. This series can be considered the direct predecessor of the sterling XJ6, which arrived for the 1969 model year.

✚ FOR As for 1960-69 Mark II series, plus better ride and handling and more luggage space

▬ AGAINST As for 1960-69 Mark II series, but mileage hurt by increasing weight

PRODUCTION
3.4S 10,036 **3.8S** 15,135 **420** 9801

SPECIFICATIONS
Length (in.)	187.0
Wheelbase (in.)	107.7
Weight (lbs)	3585-3700
Price (new)	$6300 U.S. for 3.8S in 1964;

$7000 for 420 in 1967

ENGINES
cc/type (cid)	bhp[1]	years
3442/dohc I-6 (210)	210	1963-66
3781/dohc I-6 (231)	220	1963-66
4235/dohc I-6 (258)	245	1966-69

[1]Gross

PRICES
FAIR	$6000-9500
GOOD	$9500-12,500
FINE	$12,500-16,000

FINE 1967 420 PRICE HISTORY
1982 $6000	**1990** $19,000
1994 $19,000	**1998** $20,000
1982-2000 RETURN 6%	
2000-2010 5%	

1965-70
JAGUAR MARK X & 420G

Continuations of Jaguar's larger sedan, now with the larger 4.2-liter version of the faithful dohc six specified for the E-Type beginning in 1965. Though a manual gearbox was available, most of these cars had Borg-Warner's three-speed automatic. The standard power steering system was also revised. There were no visual changes compared to the "Series 1" Mark X. The result was a more torquey and flexible limousine-like Jaguar. The model was renamed 420G beginning in 1967 to bring nomenclature into line with that of the smaller 240/340/420 sedans based on the Mark II platform. Appearance changes were confined to thin chrome side moldings and a more formal upright grille. After 1967, the 420G was effectively withdrawn from the U.S. market (though it continued overseas until about 1970), leaving Jaguar without a prestige offering until the arrival of the XJ6, which replaced both the Mark X and the compact S-Type/420 series.

✚ FOR As for 1961-64 Mark X, but greater low-end torque for easier city driving • Mark X a Milestone car

▬ AGAINST As for 1961-64 Mark X

PRODUCTION
Mark X 5680 **420G** 5554

SPECIFICATIONS
Length (in.)	202.0
Wheelbase (in.)	120.0
Weight (lbs)	4300
Price (new)	NA

ENGINES
cc/type (cid)	bhp[1]	years
4235/dohc I-6 (258)	265	1965-70

[1]Gross

PRICES
FAIR	$3500-8000
GOOD	$8000-10,000
FINE	$10,000-13,000

FINE EXAMPLE PRICE HISTORY
1982 $8000	**1990** $20,000
1994 $18,000	**1998** $16,000
1982-2000 RETURN 3%	
2000-2010 Even	

1969-73
JAGUAR XJ6/XJ12

Superb single replacement for both the 420G/Mark X and S-Type/Mark II. Sized between those earlier Jaguar "saloons," but all-new styling—supervised as always by Sir William Lyons—was uncommonly graceful and pretty for a four-door. Initially sold with 2.8- and 4.2-liter versions of Coventry's veteran twin-cam XK six (only the larger one came to America, from late '69),

1967 420G sedan

1969 XJ6 sedan

but also designed to accept the twin-cam V-12 from the stillborn mid-engine XJ13 experimental racer. A single-cam V-12, first in the Series E-Type, was offered from 1972 in the XJ12. Sold mostly with three-speed Borg-Warner automatic, but sixes were also available with a four-speed manual. Offered outside the U.S. in companion Daimler models, the six-cylinder Sovereign and 12-cylinder "Double Six" (respective production: 15,139 and 879), with that make's trademark "fluted" grille, plus more lavish interiors. Jaguar refined its sedan chassis with anti-dive/anti-squat geometry and new purpose-designed tires. The results were a fine and silky ride, plus great silence thanks to a stronger new unitized structure. More XJs would follow, but these early cars are the purest of the line and the least compromised by later U.S. requirements (though the design also took account of those), and thus arguably the most collectible now.

➕ **FOR** Grace, pace • Luxurious wood-and-leather cabin • Silken engines • Good performance (0-60: 10.5 seconds, XJ6; 8.5, XJ12) • Super sedan handling • Full power assists • XJ12's rarity • All versions still relatively inexpensive

➖ **AGAINST** Not much space • Jaguar's usual reliability and rust worries • "Vintage" ergonomics • Avoid ratty specimens—there are lots of them

PRODUCTION[1]

1969 XJ6 8085 **1970 XJ6** 17,525 **1971 XJ6** 23,546 **1972 XJ6** 14,885 **XJ12** 326 **1973 XJ6** 14,850 **XJ12** 2894
[1]Regular fiscal-year production

SPECIFICATIONS

Length (in.)	189.5
Wheelbase (in.)	108.8
Weight (lbs)	3885 (XJ6), 3950 (XJ12)
Price (new)	XJ6, $7600; XJ12, $11,000 (introductory U.S. POE)

ENGINES

cc/type (cid)	bhp	years
2792/dohc I-6 (171)[1]	140	1969-72
4235/dohc I-6 (258)	245/186[2]	1969-72
5343/sohc V-12 (326)	265/241[2]	1972-73

[1]Not sent to U.S. [2]European/U.S. models

PRICES

FAIR	$2000-4500
GOOD	$4500-6500
FINE	$6500-8500

FINE EXAMPLE PRICE HISTORY

1982 $4500	**1990** $6500
1994 $9000	**1998** $9000
1982-2000 RETURN 4%	
2000-2010 Even	

1971-75
JAGUAR E-TYPE SERIES III V-12

A continuation of Jaguar's '60s sports car, but considerably hammed up by size increases, safety bumpers, and emissions equipment. The main attraction was Jaguar's powerful—but thirsty—new V-12 engine, which was also offered in the XJ sedan. To accommodate the longer power-plant, Jaguar adopted the 9-inch longer wheelbase previously used for the Series I/II 2+2 coupe. Body modifications included a wider track, wider tires mounted on slotted wheels adorned with disc wheel covers (wire wheels optional), crosshatch grille insert, and more ungainly bumpers. Offered only as a convertible (many still prefer to call it a roadster) and 2+2 coupe, effectively replacing all six-cylinder E-Types. Quite fast (0-60 mph in 7.5 seconds and a 15.4-second quarter mile were reported by *Road & Track* magazine), and the least expensive 12-cylinder sports cars on the market. Ultimately doomed by the energy crisis because of its fuelishness, as well as buyer preference for GT-like refinement and safety. Jaguar obliged with the XJS four-seat coupe in 1976.

➕ **FOR** Traditional E-Type looks • Plush yet all-business cockpit • Electrifying getaway • Mechanical parts still available • Last of the breed

➖ **AGAINST** Thirsty • Mechanically unreliable • Expensive to fix • Very rust-prone • Prices well down since early 1990s

PRODUCTION

9382 (U.S. sales only)

SPECIFICATIONS

Length (in.)	184.4/189.6 (1972-74/1975)
Wheelbase (in.)	104.7
Weight (lbs)	3380-3450
Price (new)	Cvt: $6950 (1972)-$9200 (1975)

ENGINES

cc/type (cid)	bhp[1]	years
5343/ohc V-12 (326)	244-272	1972-75

[1]SAE net

PRICES

Conv	
FAIR	$12,500-25,000
GOOD	$25,000-32,500
FINE	$32,500-45,000
Cpe	
FAIR	$10,000-14,000
GOOD	$14,000-17,500
FINE	$17,500-22,000

FINE CONVERTIBLE PRICE HISTORY

1982 $15,000	**1990** $70,000
1994 $60,000	**1998** $50,000
1982-2000 RETURN 7%	
2000-2010 5%	

1974 XKE Series III

1973-79

JAGUAR XJ6/XJ12 SERIES II

1978 XJ12

Improved follow-ups to the brilliant "Series I" XJ sedans, announced for Europe in October 1973, for the U.S. in 1974. Initial changes involved stronger, higher-set bumpers (the front one prompting an abbreviated grille) and updated instrument panel with all gauges grouped in front of the driver and a large center vent for the improved air conditioning. Late '74 brought four additions to the line: six- and 12-cylinder XJC hardtop coupes (see separate entry below) and a similar pair of "L" (long) sedans with the wheelbase stretched four inches for additional rear leg room. The latter sold so well that they eventually supplanted the original standard-wheelbase sedans entirely. Few other year-to-year changes save switching the automatic transmission from the outmoded Borg-Warner to a more modern GM Turbo Hydra-Matic during 1976. Both V-12 and XK six retained dual carburetors (fuel injection for American cars in 1978-79) and power ratings close to Series I levels, even on emissions-tuned American models. The XJ6 2.8 remained a tax-beating "economy special" mainly for Europe. Equivalent Daimler Sovereign and Double Six continued (respective total production: 20,075 and 4292), but again not for the U.S.

✛ FOR As for 1969-73 Series I, plus tidier dash and even lower asking prices today

▬ AGAINST As for 1969-73 Series I, but front end slightly "chubbier" • Workmanship even spottier

PRODUCTION[1]

1973 XJ6 1656 **XJ12** 168 **1974 XJ6** 18,270 **XJ12** 4744 **1975 XJ6** 14,229 **XJ12** 2239 **1976 XJ6** 15,440 **XJ12** 3283 **1977 XJ6** 10,956 **XJ12**

1913 **1978 XJ6** 15,422 **XJ12** 3284 **1979 XJ6** 1528 **XJ12** 429
[1]Jaguar fiscal-year production; FY=calendar year after 1975

SPECIFICATIONS

Length (in.)	194.8 (L: 198.8)
Wheelbase (in.)	108.8 (L:112.8)
Weight (lbs)	3950-4300
Price (new)	$10,300-20,000 (in U.S.)

ENGINES

cc/type (cid)	bhp	years
2792/dohc I-6 (171)[1]	140	1973-75
3442/dohc I-6 (210)	161	1975-79
4235/dohc I-6 (258)	245/162-186	1973-79
5343/ohc V-12 (326)	265/244[2]	1973-79

[1]Mainly for Europe [2]European/U.S. models

PRICES

XJ6	
FAIR	$2500-5000
GOOD	$5000-9000
FINE	$9000-12,000
XJ12	
FAIR	$3500-6500
GOOD	$6500-10,000
FINE	$10,000-13,500

FINE XJ12 PRICE HISTORY

Depreciated in 1980s and 1990s, now leveled off.
2000-2010 RETURN Even

1975-78

JAGUAR XJC

A neat-looking hardtop derivative of the superlative Jaguar XJ sedan, built only on the original short-wheelbase Series I platform. Called "the corporate sports car" by Jaguar's U.S. advertising agency, and "the corpulent sports car" by one agency wag. Originally scheduled to be launched along with the Series II sedans in late 1973, but actual production was considerably delayed because of structural rigidity bothers. This was a rival

in concept for the "New Generation" Mercedes-Benz hardtops of the day, but it didn't sell well, perhaps because of its restricted rear seat space, the very thing that led to adoption of a longer wheelbase for the sedans. Plush leather and walnut interior, neat styling, and smooth, powerful engines (your choice of the traditional dohc six or the new V-12) combine with low production to make the XJC a high-potential collectible. One of the few cars of the '70s that looked great and performed beautifully despite safety and emissions regulations. UK production continued through 1978, after which the "C" was dropped and the sedans updated to Series III specifications.

✛ FOR Low-production appeal • High investment potential long term • Luxury and full amenities • Scintillating to sizzling performance • Unique body style • Mechanical parts still plentiful, especially for the six

▬ AGAINST The usual Jag reliability headaches • Expensive to repair and maintain • Somewhat rust-prone

PRODUCTION

Six 1794 **V-12** 686 (U.S. sales only)

SPECIFICATIONS

Length (in.)	195.0
Wheelbase (in.)	108.8
Weight (lbs)	4195
Price (new)	$17,000 U.S. in 1976

ENGINES

cc/type (cid)	bhp[1]	years
4235/dohc I-6 (258)	162	1975-78
5343/ohc V-12 (326)	244	1976

[1]SAE net

PRICES

FAIR	$4000-8000
GOOD	$8000-11,000
FINE	$11,000-14,000

1975 XJ6C hardtop coupe

FINE EXAMPLE PRICE HISTORY

Depreciating in the early 1980s but turned strongly up, posting returns of over 20% on purchase price between 1988 and 1990. Leveled since, and again a bargain: look at those low production figures!
2000-2010 RETURN 8%

1975-95
JAGUAR XJ-S

1993 XJ-S convertible

1980 XJ-S coupe (European version)

Ostensible "sports car" replacement for the E-Type, but built on a shortened XJ sedan chassis and thus bigger, heavier, quieter, and plusher—really a 2+2 GT. Initially powered by the E-Type Series III V-12, but Lucas fuel injection replaced carburetors to ease U.S. emissions cleanup. Economy never great, but improved by a claimed 20 percent via high-swirl, high-compression May "Fireball" cylinder head from 1982, signified by "H.E." badges— for "High Efficiency." Born during the "committee think" years of Jaguar's British Leyland ownership, reflected in styling somewhat compromised from that laid down by Sir William Lyons and his longtime collaborator, aerodynamicist Malcolm Sayer (the last full-time Jaguar design project for both). Complex nose, equally odd back panel and "flying buttress" roofline all criticized, but overall appearance bucked the mid-'70s "tab A into slot B" Italian approach by being curvy, low, and distinctively Jaguar. Built mostly with self-shift GM Turbo Hydra-Matic through 1982, when a six-cylinder companion with standard five-speed manual became available for Europe, powered by the new twin-cam 24-valve AJ6 engine destined for the second-generation XJ6 (XJ40). Introduced with it were AJ6 and V-12 Cabriolets: two-seat semi-convertibles with a fold-down rear roof section and a T-bar structure with removable roof panel above the seats. V-12 XJ-SC came to the U.S. in 1986. Full convertibles replaced the Cabriolets in 1988, initially coupe conversions (by

Karmann for Europe, Hess & Eisenhardt for the U.S.), full factory-built models by late '89. Facelifted for '92, the XJ-S was produced through '95. In 1993 Tom Walkinshaw's JaguarSport (builder of Jaguar's LeMans winners of 1988 and 1990) built 100 examples of the XJR-S with firmer suspension and a 6-liter V-12 putting out 318-horsepower. In '94 a 278-horsepower version of the 6-liter was available in the standard XJ-S. Though Jaguar breeding and low volume imply collectibility, it's too early to predict the XJ-S's ultimate place on the value scale, though the short-lived Cabriolets may be imminent "sleepers."

✚ **FOR** Opulent and refined high-speed GT • V-12's technical and snob appeals • Not that common, yet readily available • Plentiful parts/service • Active club support

▬ **AGAINST** Styling? • Dash cheap-looking in early period • Complicated, so upkeep costly and time-consuming

PRODUCTION

1975-85 5.3 manual coupe 352 **1975-85 5.3 automatic coupe** 29,378 **1983-84 3.6 coupe** 554 **1983-84 3.6 Cabriolet** 189 **1985**[1] 3784 **1986**[1] 4885 **1987**[1] 5380 **1988**[1] 4783 **1989**[1] 4458 **1990**[1] 4715
[1]U.S. calendar-year sales; otherwise worldwide calendar-year production

SPECIFICATIONS

Length (in.)	191.7-200.5
Wheelbase (in.)	102.0
Weight (lbs)	3830-4015
Price (new)	$19,600-81,000

ENGINES

cc/type (cid)	bhp	years
5343/ohc V-12 (326)	244	1975-81
5343/ohc V-12 (326)	262	1982-92
5993/ohc V-12 (366)	278/318	1993-95
3590/dohc I-6 (219)	225[1]	1984-95
[1]DIN		

PRICES

Prices are still governed mainly by the used car market, and range from a low of $5000 for a good 1976 coupe to a high of $28,000 for a 1995 6.0 convertible. At the moment there appear

more than enough used examples to meet the demand.
2000-2010 RETURN Generally depreciating

1979-86
JAGUAR XJ6 SERIES III

1986 XJ6 sedan

Final evolution of the original XJ sedan concept, but more extensively modified with an airier superstructure (with help from Pininfarina) that added 1.5 inches to overall height. Minor styling changes elsewhere, plus detail interior and technical revisions. All models now on the "L" wheelbase— XJC coupes and short-wheelbase sedans dropped. XJ12, with "high efficiency" May head from 1982, continued for Europe through '92, but withdrawn from the U.S. in light of new federal fuel economy standards that Jaguar had trouble meeting even with the mainstay XJ6. Later Series III XJs somewhat better-built, especially with the end of British Leyland ownership, fresh infusions of British government money, and the arrival of a tough but effective new leader in John Eagan. The Series III actually resulted from delays in finalizing its Project XJ40 successor, but it stayed around somewhat longer than planned due to a sudden strong sales surge (beginning with the general 1982 economic recovery) that rendered an immediate replacement unnecessary. Still, the XJ40 disappointed in several ways, and some marque fanciers prefer these Series IIIs as the last XJ6s with genuine Jaguar style and character. Derivative Daimler Sovereign and Double Six continued for Europe (respective production through 1984: 16,740 and 5049). In America, a Sovereign-like XJ6 Vanden Plas (named for the old-line British coachbuilder) was offered from 1982, boasting more standard features and interior wood trim.

✚ **FOR** As for Series I/II, plus workmanship improved each year • Somewhat more head room • Plush Vanden Plas available • Still subject to used-car pricing

▬ **AGAINST** As for Series I/II, but won't really be collectible for some years yet

PRODUCTION

1979 XJ6 6146 **XJ12** 937 **1980 XJ6** 9836 **XJ12** 814 **1981 XJ6** 10,216 **XJ12** 457 **1982 XJ6** 14,422 **XJ12** 518 **1983 XJ6** 17,412 **XJ12** 341 **1984 XJ6** 19,758 **XJ12** 1509 **1985-86** NA

SPECIFICATIONS

Length (in.)	191.7/200.5
	(European/U.S. models)
Wheelbase (in.)	113.0
Weight (lbs)	3860-4065
Price (new)	$25,000-40,100 in U.S.

ENGINES

cc/type (cid)	bhp	years
3442/dohc I-6 (NA)	161[1]	1979-86
4235/dohc I-6 (258)	300/176[2]	1979-86
5343/ohc V-12 (326)	295/299[1]	1979-86

[1]DIN (not available U.S.)[2]European/U.S. models

PRICES

Standard models in 2000 ranged from $2500 to $7000, Vanden Plas models about 50% higher. Still governed in part by the used car market, but the best examples have stopped depreciating.
2000-2010 RETURN 0%

1987-94

JAGUAR XJ6

The oft-postponed successor to the original XJ sedan line, developed as Project XJ40. Introduced to Europe in 1986, as a 1988 U.S. model in early '87. Basically the same successful concept with squarer styling; simplified design for more consistent, higher-quality assembly; standard antilock brakes; and a wholly new drivetrain. The last combined the "AJ6" 3.6-liter 24-valve inline six (first test-marketed in the European XJ-S) and a new four-speed ZF automatic transmission with a

1990 XJ6 sedan

unique "J-gate" selector providing manual-override capability. As quiet and smooth-riding as any previous XJ6, but lackluster performance prompted higher compression for 1988, producing small gains in horsepower and torque. Performance further improved via a stroked 4.0-liter replacement for 1990, when a revamped instrument panel appeared with analog minor gauges instead of vacuum-fluorescent bargraphs. Always sold in America in base and ritzy Vanden Plas forms, joined for 1990 by an in-between Sovereign model with Euro-style square headlamps (also applied to the V-P) and a new top-line Majestic with Daimler-style fluted grille. European offerings included 2.9- and later 3.4-liter entry-level models (with available with manual transmission) as well as derivative Daimlers, but there would be no new-generation XJ12 until 1993. Reason: the XJ40 was deliberately designed not to accept the Jaguar V-12, one result of a political dispute during the waning days of Leyland ownership.

✚ **FOR** Smooth and quiet • Few peers for ride comfort • All the expected modern amenities • Wood-and-leather opulence • ABS brakes • Best-built Jag sedan ever • Still current

▬ **AGAINST** 3.6-liter relatively torqueless at low rpm • 4.0-liter not as refined as it might be • Handling not that sporty • Not that roomy for size • Quirky details • Iffy collector's investment now

PRODUCTION[1]

1987 17,539 **1988** 15,944 **1989** 14,509 **1990** 14,013
[1]U.S. calendar-year sales

SPECIFICATIONS[1]

Length (in.)	196.4
Wheelbase (in.)	113.0
Weight (lbs)	3905-4015

Price (new)	$43,500-59,400

[1]U.S. models

ENGINES[1]

cc/type (cid)	bhp	years
3590/dohc I-6 (219)	189/195	1987-89
3980/dohc I-6 (243)	223	1990

[1]U.S. models

PRICES

Prices range in 2000 from $8400 to $26,000, Vanden Plas and 1990 Sovereigns $2000-3000 higher.
2000-2010 RETURN Depreciating

1995-2000

JAGUAR XJR

1998 XJR sedan

The first redesigned Jag XJ sedan under Ford ownership had more than 2000 new or retooled components, and was available in base XJ6, Vanden Plas, XJR, and XJ12 guises. The collectible bet, the XJR, ran with a 322-horse supercharged 4.0-liter six; it was the first engine in Jaguar history that was not naturally aspirated. The supercharged six was refined but gave out with a pleasing growl and brisk, smooth acceleration. In 1998 Jaguar brought out its first V-8 engine. The XJR gained a supercharged version of that engine. With 50 more horsepower than the six,

0-60 times fell below six seconds. Although nearly silent at idle, the new V-8 still had a pleasant growl when pushed.

➕ FOR First supercharged Jag • Acceleration • Good ergonomics • Civilized ride • Steering • Handling • FoMoCo reliability

➖ AGAINST Thirst • Brick-like aerodynamics • Possible collector stigma because of FoMoCo connection

PRODUCTION

1995 2,913 **1996** 2,006 **1997** 989 **1998 6-cylinder** 47 **1998 V-8** 4,155 **1999** 3,128

SPECIFICATIONS

Length (in.)	197.8
Weight (lbs)	4075-4215
Wheelbase (in.)	113.0
Price (new)	$65,000-68,550

ENGINES

cid/type	bhp	years
243/dohc I-6[1]	322	1995-98
244/dohc V-8[1]	370	1998-00

[1]Supercharged

PRICES

Governed entirely by the used car market. 1995-98 models in 2000 ranged from $28,000 to $60,000, later models higher.
2000-2010 RETURN Depreciating

1999 XK8 coupe

Weight (lbs)	3709-3962
Wheelbase (in.)	101.9
Price (new)	$64,900-71,200

ENGINES

cid/type	bhp	years
244/dohc V-8	290	1997-00

PRICES

1997 Coupe:	
FAIR	$35,000-45,000
GOOD	$45,000-50,000
FINE	$50,000-55,000
1997 Convertible:	
FAIR	$40,000-48,000
GOOD	$48,000-55,000
FINE	$55,000-60,000

2000-2010 RETURN Depreciating.

1997-2000

JAGUAR XK8

The XK8 replaced the twenty year old XJS and shared its floorpan. Everything else was new—including the first V-8 in Jaguar's history. This impressively smooth engine could push the XK8 to sixty in less than seven seconds. Although too big to be a sports car, it still handled better than a two-ton car had a right to. The styling recalled the Jaguar E-Type with its rounded lines and oval grille. Inside was the expected walnut dashboard and leather seats. Convertibles outsold the better-looking coupes by over seven to one. Fast, comfortable, and beautiful—either coupe or convertible will be collectible.

➕ FOR Gorgeous styling • Plush interior • Fast •

➖ AGAINST Almost useless back seat • Rear visibility

PRODUCTION

1997 coupe 1021 **1997 convertible** 5843 **1998 coupe** 677 **1998 convertible** 5184 **1999 coupe** 439 **1999 convertible** 5237

SPECIFICATIONS

Length (in.)	187.4

2000

JAGUAR XKR

2000 XKR coupe

4-passenger luxury sports car was stunning in "base" XK8 form, and quite superb in uplevel, supercharged XKR variant. Blown 4.0-liter V-8 made 370 horsepower and 387 pounds/feet of torque, and could dash from 0-60 mph in less than 6 seconds—quick for a heavy car. The R's computer controlled shock absorbers and 18-inch wheels improved handling with little harm to the XK's absorbent ride. Functional hood louvers and mesh grille were subtle clues that the Jaguar was supercharged. One of the great grand touring cars of its time.

➕ FOR Acceleration • Good ergonomics • Build quality • Luxury appointments • Available convertible, with power top and glass backlight • Agreeable ride • Relatively limited production

➖ AGAINST Awkward entry/exit • Claustrophobic cabin

SPECIFICATIONS

Length (in.)	187.4
Weight (lbs)	3785-4021
Wheelbase (in.)	101.9
Price (new)	$76,800-81,800

ENGINES

cid/type	bhp	years
244/dohc V-8[1]	370	2000

[1]Supercharged

PRICES

Governed by the used car market
2000-2010 RETURN Depreciating

1967-73

JEEP JEEPSTER COMMANDO

1967 Jeepster Commando convertible

An interesting reprise of the 1948-51 Willys Jeepster concept, also designed by Milwaukee-based Brooks Stevens. Really a stretched Jeep CJ, with the same trademark face and simple basic chassis, but more car-like styling aft of the cowl; 4-wheel drive optional. Offered as a two-door wagon, pickup, convertible, and roadster to battle the Ford Bronco and Chevy Blazer in the embryonic "personal" RV market. Two-seat roadster had a manual half-top and open cargo area where the convertible had a standard back seat, plus a full-length top with optional power operation. The ragtop got a better top for '68, plus a hinged tailgate (as on the wagon and pickup) and full doors with roll-down windows. Engines were initially Jeep's mainstay "Hurricane 4" and optional "Dauntless" V-6, the latter acquired from Buick's early-'60s Special compact; Buick promptly bought it back once American Motors took over Kaiser-Jeep in 1970. Only AMC engines were offered by 1972—including a peppy 304 V-8— when the wheelbase was stretched three inches (for improved stability), tracks widened (same reason), load capacities raised (via higher-rate springs), front fenders squared, a blunt mesh grille applied, the convertible canceled and, curiously, the Jeep name removed from I.D. Killed after 1973 due to declining sales in the face of stiff Big Three competition. Of interest to collectors are two 1971 wagon "package models:" the Hurst/Jeepster Special with Hurst shifter (manual or automatic), hood-scoop-mounted tach, wide tires, and hood stripes; and the V-6 SC-1 with a white top, gold body, "rally" stripes, and special trim.

■ **FOR** Fun vehicles all, especially open models • Good V-6/V-8 performance • Rugged versatility • Jeep cachet • Very low cost • Enthusiastic club support

■ **AGAINST** Clean originals hard to find • Rust-prone • Anemic 4-cylinder performance • Not likely to see high value appreciation

PRODUCTION
NA

SPECIFICATIONS
Length (in.)	168.5 (1967-71), 174.5 (1972-73)
Wheelbase (in.)	101.0 (1967-71), 104.0 (1972-73)
Weight (lbs)	2700-3050
Price (new)	$2465-3456

ENGINES
cid/type	bhp	years
134/ohv I-6	75	1967-71
225/ohv V-6	160	1967-71
232/ohv I-6	100	1972-73
258/ohv I-6	110	1972-73
304/ohv V-8	150	1972-73

PRICES
FAIR	$1200-2000
GOOD	$2000-3500
FINE	$3500-6000

FINE EXAMPLE PRICE HISTORY
1982	$2000	1990	$4000
1994	$6200	1998	$5000
1982-2000 RETURN 6%			
2000-2010 4%			

1 9 6 2 - 6 6
JENSEN CV8

Low-production Anglo-American hybrid built by the small, West Bromwich coachworks run by Richard and Alan Jensen, successful purveyors of custom bodies for various British chassis in the '30s. The CV8 was the last—and regrettably the ugliest—of Jensen's own fiberglass-body production models descended from the original 541 design first seen in 1953. The four-seat, close-coupled coupe body rested on a very strong tubular chassis, with the tubes sealed to act as vacuum reservoirs for the brakes. The styling, which had evolved through several previous models, was marked by a controversial front end with slant-eye quad headlamps flanking a jutting, eggcrate grille. Wheel openings were accented with sharp horizontal creases above, and the gently curved tail had three small circular lights. Power was supplied by contemporary Chrysler wedgehead V-8s, initially 361 cid, then 383. The Mark I became the Mark II in 1963, followed by the Mark III in 1965. More aerodynamic than it looked, the CV8 could reach 130 mph, and was fairly quick from standstill. Almost all examples had right-hand drive, and few were sold in the U.S. Expensive when new, mostly a func-

tion of Jensen's small production capacity and semi-handbuilt construction methods.

■ **FOR** Torquey, reliable Chrysler power • Rot-free fiberglass body • Very low production • Mechanical parts plentiful yet • Low cost high performance

■ **AGAINST** Love-it-or-leave-it styling • Burly handling • Fuel thirst • Modest rear-seat accommodation • Body parts becoming scarce • Prices have bombed since early 1990s.

PRODUCTION
Mark I/II 314 **Mark III** 182

SPECIFICATIONS
Length (in.)	184.5
Wheelbase (in.)	105.0
Weight (lbs)	3360-3515
Price (new)	NA

ENGINES
cid/type	bhp[1]	years
361/ohv V-8	305	1962-63
383/ohv V-8	330	1963-65
[1]Gross		

PRICES
FAIR	$3000-6000
GOOD	$6000-9000
FINE	$9000-12,000

FINE EXAMPLE PRICE HISTORY
1982	$8000	1990	$25,000
1994	$12,000	1998	$12,000
1982-2000 RETURN 5%			
2000-2010 2%			

1 9 6 6 - 7 6
JENSEN INTERCEPTOR

The handsome successor to the CV8, reviving a name first used in

1965 CV8 coupe

1975 Interceptor convertible

1949. Retained its predecessor's sturdy tubular chassis with conventional A-arm/coil-spring front suspension, live axle/leaf-spring rear suspension, and a Chrysler drivetrain mounted well back for good weight distribution. The brutish but clean all-steel body was designed by Touring of Italy, but built by Vignale, then Jensen itself. The smart two-door coupe featured square-cut lines except for a gently rounded tail with an enormous wraparound window that doubled as a luggage compartment hatch. No serious U.S. import efforts were made before the 1971 Series III models. The Series II, announced in 1969, differed from the Series I mainly in having standard power steering and minor trim and mechanical alterations. San Francisco sports car baron Kjell Qvale became involved in Jensen's management in the early '70s, and it was through him that the Interceptor was officially certified for U.S. sale. At that point, the previous 383-cid Chrysler engine gave way to the 440 unit, and a reworked dashboard was slotted in. Also new was a convertible version sold in very low quantity. A special SP model was offered on the British market, with a three-carburetor version of the Series III power unit, which delivered a top end of about 140 mph. A very exclusive executive express of enduring style, the Interceptor was ultimately doomed by Jensen's collapse in 1976 following the ill-fated Jensen-Healey sports car project.

➕ **FOR** Italian grace • American pace • Fairly plentiful, yet has low-production appeal • Ubiquitous, easily serviced drivetrains • Some body parts still available in UK • Very affordable now

➖ **AGAINST** Change to steel construction brings rust worries • Very heavy on fuel • Only modest appreciation potential

PRODUCTION

6387

SPECIFICATIONS

Length (in.)	186.0
Wheelbase (in.)	105.0
Weight (lbs)	3500-4000
Price (new)	$15,500 (U.S. 1973 list price)

ENGINES

cid/type	bhp[1]	years
383/ohv V-8	325/330	1966-71
440/ohv V-8	350/385	1971-76

[1]Gross

PRICES

Cpe	
FAIR	$5000-7500
GOOD	$7500-10,000
FINE	$10,000-15,000
1974-76 conv	
FAIR	$10,000-17,000
GOOD	$17,000-23,000
FINE	$23,000-30,000

FINE 1976 CONVERTIBLE PRICE HISTORY

1982 $7000		**1990** $45,000	
1994 $35,000		**1998** $30,000	
1982-2000 RETURN 9%			
2000-2010 2%			

1966-71
JENSEN FF

A trail-blazing high-performance GT closely related to the contemporary Interceptor, but featuring Ferguson Formula four-wheel drive and a Dunlop "Maxaret" anti-skid braking system. It differed from the Interceptor in appearance only in a four-inch longer wheelbase (all ahead of the cowl) and an extra vertical cooling louver in the front fenders. Very complex, and very expensive to build—too costly, in fact, to be continued once the Interceptor was reworked to Series III specifications. Offered only with Chrysler TorqueFlite automatic transmission and power steering. The FF drive system worked via a center differential, and was full-time. Never officially sold in the U.S., though a few early examples were likely imported privately. Built on an as-needed basis, which along with the unique specification guarantees collectibility. However, finding one won't be easy.

➕ **FOR** Unique concept (the world's first 4WD supercar) • Real exclusivity • Terrific traction • Others as for 1966-76 Interceptor

➖ **AGAINST** FF drivetrain parts in short supply, as are longer hood and fenders • Limited appreciation • Restoration costly and complex

PRODUCTION

318

SPECIFICATIONS

Length (in.)	191.0
Wheelbase (in.)	109.0
Weight (lbs)	4030
Price (new)	NA

ENGINES

cid/type	bhp[1]	years
383/ohv V-8	325/330	1966-71

[1]Gross

PRICES

FAIR	$7000-10,000
GOOD	$10,000-18,000
FINE	$18,000-22,500

FINE EXAMPLE PRICE HISTORY

1982 $10,000		**1990** $35,000	
1994 $18,000		**1998** $18,000	
1982-2000 RETURN 7%			
2000-2010 3%			

1966-71 FF coupe

1972-77

JENSEN-HEALEY & JENSEN GT

1974 Jensen-Healy roadster (with hardtop)

The brainchild of Jensen's U.S. distributor, Kjell Qvale, this two-seat sports car was seen as a way for the small British manufacturer to crack the mass market and return to profitability in the face of declining demand for its large Interceptor. Launched after a protracted gestation period, the J-H was either a challenge to the trends of the '70s or an answer to a question nobody asked, depending on your point of view. In an age of closed GTs, it was a traditional open roadster; at a time when the mid-engine layout was all the rage, it had a conventional front-mounted engine—and a live rear axle and rear drum brakes. The general styling was suggested by the indomitable Donald Healey, and was clean but certainly not eye-catching. Handling was good, but cowl shake and a clumsy-to-put-up soft top were throwbacks to the good/bad old days. The engine was a dohc four supplied by Lotus, a development of a Vauxhall (British GM) unit. Suspension pieces and steering were also borrowed from Vauxhall, the four-speed all-synchro gearbox from Chrysler UK's Sunbeam Rapier HK120. Engine problems surfaced early, and along with the uninspired design kept sales far below expectations. Donald Healey disassociated himself from the venture, which is why a 2+2 coupe derivative was called Jensen GT. It didn't help. Production ground to a halt in early 1977. Because the company had so much of its assets tied up in the project, the J-H's demise effectively spelled the end of Jensen as well. The J-H will never rank with its Austin-Healey predecessor among the truly great British sports cars, but it's been finding greater desirability with collec-

tors as time passes.

✚ FOR Sprightly performance (up to 125 mph) and reasonable economy (24 mpg) • Traditional sports car virtues in a newer package • Rarity interest

▬ AGAINST Parts supplies variable • Still a questionable investment • Little organized club support at present • Rust-prone

PRODUCTION

1972 705 **1973** 3846 **1974** 4550 **1975** 1301 **1976** 51 **U.S. imports** 7709

SPECIFICATIONS

Length (in.)	162-166
Wheelbase (in.)	92.0
Weight (lbs)	approx. 2200/2400 (rdstr/GT cpe)
Price (new)	$4795 original U.S. list price

ENGINES

cc/type (cid)	bhp	years
1973/dohc I-4 (120)	140	1973-77

PRICES

FAIR	$3000-5000
GOOD	$5000-6000
FINE	$6000-8000

FINE EXAMPLE PRICE HISTORY

1982 $3000	1990 $8000
1994 $7000	1998 $7000

1982-2000 RETURN 6%
2000-2010 3%

1930-31

JORDAN MODEL 8G/90

Last gasp of a famous company. These big eight-cylinder cars rode the firm's two longest wheelbases and were almost as glorious as Ned Jordan's famous ads had tried to paint their much

less impressive forebears in the '20s. A phaeton, convertible, and roadster were offered in the 1930 8G line. The following year's Model 90 series included a 125-inch-wheelbase Speedboy sport phaeton and the last of the famous Playboy roadsters, on the 131-inch chassis. Jordan filed for receivership in April 1931. Though always "assembled" cars with proprietary engines and other mechanicals, Jordans remained a cut above the norm even in these final years. Curiously, they have yet to be recognized as Classics.

✚ FOR Last-of-the-line status • Exclusivity • Beautiful styling • Relatively affordable • The timeless mystique of Ned Jordan's great ads

▬ AGAINST Extreme scarcity of all models, open ones particularly • Almost impossible parts situation

PRODUCTION

No more than 2000

SPECIFICATIONS

Length (in.)	NA
Wheelbase (in.)	125.0 (8G), 131.0 (90)
Weight (lbs)	3700-5000
Price (new)	$2395-2995

ENGINES

cid/type	bhp	years
268.5/sv I-8	85	1930-31

PRICES

Closed	
FAIR	$5000-10,000
GOOD	$10,000-20,000
FINE	$20,000-30,000
Open	
FAIR	$12,000-18,000
GOOD	$18,000-30,000
FINE	$30,000-50,000
	(Add 25% for 1931 Series 2)

FINE EXAMPLE PRICE HISTORY

No recent sales data available. The Model Z Speedway Ace sedan and Sportsman roadster were additional models in the 8G line, but only one roadster is known to exist.

1931 Series Z Sportsman

1947-48
KAISER CUSTOM

This was a more luxurious, top-of-the-line model among early Kaisers, and also more desirable now, though built in smaller quantities and not as easily found. Its price premium over the basic Special was largely due to its more plush, color-keyed interior. Exterior trim was much the same on both models, though Customs did carry identifying fender script.

FOR Very rare • Smooth riding road car • Significant styling for its time

AGAINST Slab-sided design now looks old • Engine not known for reliability • Interior restoration expensive

PRODUCTION
1947 5412 **1948** 1263

SPECIFICATIONS
Length (in.)	203.0
Wheelbase (in.)	123.5
Weight (lbs)	3295
Price (new)	$2456-2466

ENGINES
cid/type	bhp	years
226.2/sv I-6	100/112	1947-48

PRICES
FAIR	$2000-4500
GOOD	$4500-7000
FINE	$7000-9500

FINE EXAMPLE PRICE HISTORY
1982 $4300		**1990** $7500	
1994 $8000		**1998** $10,500	
1982-2000 RETURN 5%			
2000-2010 4%			

1947 Custom sedan

1949-50
KAISER DELUXE

DeLuxe sedan

The DeLuxe was Kaiser's renamed upper series for these years. It shared the 1949 facelift with the cheaper Specials, and '49 leftovers were reserialed—but otherwise unchanged—for 1950. The DeLuxe lineup included three interesting models. The Vagabond was a spiffier version of the Special Traveler. Both were sedans with a double-hatch rear end and fold-down back seat, giving Kaiser a station wagon-type model without the expense of tooling up for a separate body. The four-door convertible sedan had a counterpart in the Frazer Manhattan line. Both were literally hand-built from sedan bodies—aided by the cutting torch—and mounted on heavier-than-stock frames to preserve some semblance of body rigidity. The Virginian was a fixed-roof convertible with either a painted or padded vinyl top. This trio exemplified Kaiser's innovative thinking in trying to broaden its market. Little fixed-position framed windows substituted for B-pillars on the convertible and Virginian, and both also had fixed side window frames, thus detracting from the "open-air" feeling.

FOR Unique body styles • Good quality • Lots of color inside and out

AGAINST Underpowered • Underbraked • Clumsy handling • Thirstier than earlier Kaisers • Severely rust-prone

PRODUCTION
4d sdn 38,250 **Vagabond 4d util sdn** 4500 **Virginian 4d htp sdn** 946 **4d conv** 54 (all est.)

SPECIFICATIONS
Length (in.)	206.5
Wheelbase (in.)	123.5
Weight (lbs)	3341-3726
Price (new)	$2195-3195

ENGINES
cid/type	bhp	years
226.2/sv I-6	112	1949-50

PRICES
Sdn	
FAIR	$2000-4500
GOOD	$4500-7000
FINE	$7000-9500
Conv	
FAIR	$8000-16,000
GOOD	$16,000-24,000
FINE	$24,000-32,000
Virginian	
FAIR	$2500-5000
GOOD	$5000-7500
FINE	$7500-10,000

FINE CONVERTIBLE PRICE HISTORY
1982 $9000		**1990** $28,500	
1994 $25,000		**1998** $40,000	
1982-2000 RETURN 8%			
2000-2010 3%			

1949-50
KAISER SPECIAL TRAVELER

1949 Special Traveler utility sedan

Basic version of the DeLuxe Vagabond, more affordable for collectors, and possibly just the thing for your flea marketing. It sold in reasonable numbers when new, and offered station wagon-style cargo carrying flexibility. Though it looked just like a conventional Kaiser sedan, it had rear double-hatch doors and a flip-down back seat that opened up to give an impressive nine-foot load platform.

✚ FOR More available and affordable than the Vagabond • Others as for 1949-50 DeLuxe

■ AGAINST Lacks Milestone status • Lower appreciation than a Vagabond • Others as for 1949-50 DeLuxe

PRODUCTION

22,000 (est.)

SPECIFICATIONS

Length (in.)	206.5
Wheelbase (in.)	123.5
Weight (lbs)	3456
Price (new)	$2088

ENGINES

cid/type	bhp	years
226.2/sv I-6	100	1949-50

PRICES

FAIR	$2000-4000
GOOD	$4000-6000
FINE	$6000-8500

FINE EXAMPLE PRICE HISTORY

1982 $3600	1990 $8000
1994 $11,000	1998 $11,000
1982-2000 RETURN 5%	
2000-2010 5%	

1951 KAISER DELUXE

The DeLuxe was the top-line series in Kaiser's all-new second-generation lineup. A daring and successful styling departure for its day, it featured the lowest beltline and greatest glass area in the industry—a distinction it would retain until Virgil Exner's '57 Chrysler products appeared. It was designed largely by Howard "Dutch" Darrin, assisted by Duncan McRae, with detail trim applied by Herb Weissinger. The wheelbase was shortened five inches, and the unique Traveler utility sedan/wagon model was continued, bolstered by a two-door running mate. Unfortunately, power continued to be the Kaiser L-head six, which was already becoming increasingly old-hat as other makes had or were adopting modern V-8s. Kaiser never would get one, though, and this was one factor that caused sales to spiral downward, leading eventually to the death of the Kaiser marque.

✚ FOR Beautiful styling, perhaps the best among early-'50s domestics • Good quality • Smooth highway performance

■ AGAINST Can rust, particularly rocker panels and fenders • Vapor lock a constant problem • Other engine quirks, including overheating • Lack of hardtop and convertible models

PRODUCTION

Traveler 2d util sdn 10,000 **4d sdn** 70,000 **2d sdn** 11,000 **4d Traveler util sdn** 1000 **2d clb cpe** 6000 (estimated breakdowns; total model year production including Specials: 139,452)

SPECIFICATIONS

Length (in.)	210.4
Wheelbase (in.)	118.5
Weight (lbs)	3111-3345
Price (new)	$2275-2433

ENGINES

cid/type	bhp	years
226.2/sv I-6	115	1951

PRICES

FAIR	$2000-4000
GOOD	$4000-7000
FINE	$7000-10,000

FINE EXAMPLE PRICE HISTORY

1982 $3000	1990 $6560
1994 $11,000	1998 $15,000
1982-2000 RETURN 8%	
2000-2010 3%	

1951 DeLuxe Traveler sedan

1951 KAISER DRAGON

1951 Golden Dragon sedan

A special-trim version of the Kaiser DeLuxe created by K-F's brilliant color and upholstery specialist Carleton Spencer. The initial models were all called Golden Dragon, and had two-tone paint, embossed "dragon" vinyl, rolled and pleated upholstery, and a smooth vinyl headliner. A second series with padded tops and "dinosaur" vinyl upholstery was offered as the Golden (yellow paint/black upholstery), Silver (grey/maroon), Emerald (dark green/light green), and Jade (metallic green/straw) Dragon. Any Dragon is quite rare and hard to come by today, but these were the most spectacular and desirable of the '51 Kaisers.

✚ FOR Very luxurious • Good appreciation • Others as for 1951 DeLuxe

■ AGAINST As for 1951 DeLuxe

PRODUCTION

approx. 1000, mostly 4d sdns

SPECIFICATIONS

Length (in.)	210.4
Wheelbase (in.)	118.5
Weight (lbs)	3111-3345
Price (new)	$2400-2560

ENGINES

cid/type	bhp	years
226.2/sv I-6	115	1951

PRICES

FAIR	$2500-6000
GOOD	$6000-9000
FINE	$9000-12,000

FINE EXAMPLE PRICE HISTORY

1982 $4000	1990 $9500
1994 $13,000	1998 $12,000
1982-2000 RETURN 7%	
2000-2010 5%	

1952
KAISER VIRGINIAN DELUXE

This was the upper-priced series in Kaiser's interim 1952 line, announced at the start of the model year. Composed of leftover '51s with new serial numbers and badges, it was withdrawn after the "genuine" '52s were ready. Most came with a standard "continental" exterior-mount spare tire.

➕ FOR As for 1951 DeLuxe, plus scarcity

➖ AGAINST As for 1951 DeLuxe

PRODUCTION

Approx. 3500; total production incl. Virginian Special: 5579

SPECIFICATIONS

Length (in.)	215.7
Wheelbase (in.)	118.5
Weight (lbs)	3111-3345
Price (new)	$2095-2241

ENGINES

cid/type	bhp	years
226.2/sv I-6	115	1952

PRICES

FAIR	$2000-3500
GOOD	$3500-6500
FINE	$6500-9000

FINE EXAMPLE PRICE HISTORY

1982 $3500		**1990** $7500	
1994 $11,000		**1998** $10,000	
1982-2000 RETURN 6%			
2000-2010 3%			

1952-53
KAISER MANHATTAN

The trend-setting '51 Kaiser got a newly named top-line series for 1952: Manhattan. A pleasant facelift included a heavier bumper/grille combination, smooth teardrop taillights, and little chrome rear fender fins on the '53s. Color was strongly featured for '52, and reemphasized for '53 with attractive upholstery combinations of boucle cloth and straw-pattern vinyl. These are among the nicest Kaisers to drive, very roomy, and remarkably frugal with gas.

➕ FOR Exceptional styling • Low running costs • Smooth road cars

➖ AGAINST The tinworm likes rocker panels and floorpans • Cloth upholstery hard to duplicate • Optional hyper-fast power steering needs constant driver correction

PRODUCTION

1952 4d sdn 16,500 **2d sdn** 2000 **2d clb cpe** 500 **1953 4d sdn** 15,450 **2d sdn** 2500 (Breakdowns estimated. Total 1952 production, including DeLuxe models: 26,552; **1953 Manhattan:** 17,957. **One Traveler 2d util sdn found;** no volume production.)

SPECIFICATIONS

Length (in.)	208.5 (1952), 211.1 (1953)
Wheelbase (in)	118.5
Weight (lbs.)	3185-3371
Price (new)	$2601-2654

ENGINES

cid/type	bhp	years
226.2/sv I-6	115/118	1952-53

PRICES

FAIR	$2000-5000
GOOD	$5000-7500
FINE	$7500-11,000

FINE EXAMPLE PRICE HISTORY

1982 $4500		**1990** $8800	
1994 $11,000		**1998** $16,000	
1982-2000 RETURN 6%			
2000-2010 3%			

1953
KAISER "HARDTOP" DRAGON

1953 Dragon sedan

No Dragons were built for 1952 but in 1953 the luxury Kaiser reappeared with a unique interior by designer Carleton Spencer, now a separate model. It featured 14-carat gold-plated hood ornament, exterior emblem, fender script, and glovebox nameplate. Thick carpeting was found inside, along with "Bambu" vinyl upholstery, combined with boucle-grained vinyl (if you got the canvas top), or "Laguna" cloth (with the "bambu" vinyl top). Standard equipment included automatic transmission, radio, heater, trunk carpeting, and extra sound insulation, plus power steering late in the production run. Even though it wasn't a true hardtop, as the name implied, this was the most luxurious Kaiser ever built. And well it should have been—it listed at $258 more than a Cadillac Series Sixty-Two four-door sedan.

➕ FOR Desirability, appreciation both high • Very comfortable long-haul tourer • Sharp looks • Distinctive luxury furnishings

➖ AGAINST Gold plating expensive to restore • Bambu vinyl difficult to match or replace • Laguna cloth extinct • Twitchy power steering • Still just a six-cylinder sedan underneath

PRODUCTION

1952 Manhattan sedan

SPECIFICATIONS

Length (in.)	211.1
Wheelbase (in.)	118.5
Weight (lbs)	3320
Price (new)	$3924

ENGINES

cid/type	bhp	years
226.2/sv I-6	118	1953

PRICES

FAIR	$2500-6000
GOOD	$6000-10,000
FAIR	$10,000-15,000

FINE EXAMPLE PRICE HISTORY

1982 $3400	1990 $11,000
1994 $15,000	1998 $15,000

1982-2000 RETURN 8%
2000-2010 5%

1·9·5·4
KAISER-DARRIN DKF-161

1954 Darrin roadster (with hardtop)

Howard "Dutch" Darrin's dramatic sliding-door sports car utilized a Willys F-head engine under a fiberglass body laid over the Henry J chassis. Features included an unusual "kiss me" grille, sliding doors, three-position "landau" top, full instrumentation, and a floorshift (with overdrive a common option). More a boulevardier than an outright sports car, the Darrin could nevertheless do 0-60 mph in about 13 seconds and approach the 100-mph mark. But at its steep price, few were sold. Darrin purchased about 100 leftovers and fitted some with Cadillac V-8 engines. The vast majority of Darrins are still around; most have been traced by enthusiasts.

◩ FOR Swoopy styling • Unique sliding doors • Rare and hotly sought-after • A guaranteed show-stopper

◩ AGAINST Fiberglass bodywork subject to stress cracks • Hardware and windshields extremely scarce • Not cheap • No performance

PRODUCTION

435

SPECIFICATIONS

Length (in.)	184.1
Wheelbase (in.)	100.0
Weight (lbs)	2175
Price (new)	$3668

ENGINES

cid/type	bhp	years
161/F I-6	90	1954

PRICES

FAIR	$7500-15,000
GOOD	$15,000-23,000
FINE	$23,000-34,000

FINE EXAMPLE PRICE HISTORY

1982 $13,500	1990 $32,500
1994 $32,000	1998 $35,000

1982-2000 RETURN 6%
2000-2010 6%

1·9·5·4-55
KAISER MANHATTAN

An astonishingly successful facelift on Dutch Darrin's 1951 design, performed by K-F stylist Herb Weissinger. All-new sheetmetal forward of the cowl featured a concave oval grille reminiscent of the Buick XP-300 show car (which Henry Kaiser liked) and curvy front fenders with headlights and parking lights set in chrome-encircled teardrops, again borrowed from Buick. At the rear were large "Safety-Glo" taillights with illuminated lenses running atop the fenders, and the rear window was fully wrapped around. The redesigned dash was given large, aircraft-like toggle lever controls. Exclusive to these top-line Kaisers was a McCulloch super-

charged version of the staid old L-head six, boasting 22 more horsepower. The blower freewheeled economically when not in use. None of this was enough to save Kaiser, however, and production ceased before the end of the model year. The design was salvaged, though, and built in Argentina as the Kaiser Carabela through the early '60s—a tribute to an excellent design.

◩ FOR Last of the line • Advanced styling, interior design • High comfort levels • Quick for a standard-size six-cylinder car

◩ AGAINST Heavy front end, heavy steering without assist • Supercharger was too much for the engine and reliability suffered • Still no V-8 or hardtop

PRODUCTION

1954 4d sdn 3860 **2d sdn** 250 (est. breakdown; total 1954 production: 4110) **1955 4d sdn** 226 **2d sdn** 44 (does not include 1021 export 1955 4d sdns)

SPECIFICATIONS

Length (in.)	215.6
Wheelbase (in.)	118.5
Weight (lbs)	3265-3350
Price (new)	$2334-2670

ENGINES

cid/type	bhp	years
226.2/sv I-6	140[1]	1954-55

[1]Supercharged

PRICES

FAIR	$2500-5000
GOOD	$5000-8000
FINE	$8000-12,000

FINE EXAMPLE PRICE HISTORY

1982 $5200	1990 $10,000
1994 $12,000	1998 $13,000

1982-2000 RETURN 5%
2000-2010 5%

1954 Manhattan sedan

1954
KAISER SPECIAL

1954 (early) Special sedan

The junior Kaiser for 1954 came in two versions. "Early" models were leftover '53 Manhattan on the inside, with the new '54 front clip and oversize '54 "Safety-Glo" taillights, but no wrap-around rear window. "Late" Specials were true '54s, with a revised, aircraft-inspired dash and wrapped backlight, but less luxurious interior fittings than the top-line Manhattans. Special was not offered with the supercharger, so power output was the same as in 1953—an uninspiring 118 horsepower. Both Specials are desirable today because so few were made. Of the two, the early ones are preferred for their more "classic" cabin appointments and the famous "bambu" vinyl, plus easier handling and steering. Both Specials were offered in two- and four-door sedan form; the two-door is much rarer (one for every six four-doors), and now command a small price premium.

➕ FOR Less costly than the '54 Manhattan • Early Special's interior and Early handling ease • Rarity

➖ AGAINST Later Special's rather plain trim • No supercharger means lack of interest value (but a more reliable engine)

PRODUCTION
Early: 3500; **late:** 929

SPECIFICATIONS
Length (in.)	215.6
Wheelbase (in.)	118.5
Weight (lbs)	3235-3305
Price (new)	$2334-2389

ENGINES
cid/type	bhp	years
226.2/sv I-6	118	1954

PRICES
As per 1954-55 Kaiser Manhattan.

1930-31
KISSEL WHITE EAGLE

The grand last hurrah for a long-running company that got its start in back in 1907. Sporty models were favored by film stars, gangsters, politicians, and high-flyers until a deepening Depression wiped out the Hartford, Wisconsin, automaker. The later Kissels had a Lycoming-based eight (early engines were Kissel-made), at least 132 inches between wheel centers, and a price topping $3000. A plethora of gorgeous closed "custom" (they really weren't) and open bodies officially comprised the 8-126 series. They have the distinction of being the only Kissels rated as Classics by the Classic Car Club of America, and rightly so.

➕ FOR Beautiful bodywork • Rakish styling • Smooth performance • Exclusivity • Appreciation potential • CCCA classic status • Hartford Heritage (Kissel) Museum in the make's hometown of Hartford, Wisconsin

➖ AGAINST Extremely scarce (more built in 1929, however) • Ditto parts • Try to find one

PRODUCTION
Not more than 50

SPECIFICATIONS
Length (in.)	NA
Wheelbase (in.)	132.0, 139.0
Weight (lbs)	4000-5000
Price (new)	$3185-3885

ENGINES
cid/type	bhp	years
296.8/sv I-8	100	1930-31

PRICES
Open	
FAIR	$10,000-20,000
GOOD	$20,000-40,000
FINE	$40,000-60,000
Closed	
FAIR	$10,000-18,000
GOOD	$18,000-25,000
FINE	$25,000-33,000

FINE EXAMPLE PRICE HISTORY
No available sales data.
2000-2010 RETURN 5%

1948-49
KURTIS

1949 convertible

This was famed race-car builder Frank Kurtis' interesting postwar sports car. The 100-inch-wheelbase chassis was integral with a two-seater body made mainly of aluminum. Power was supplied by a supercharged Studebaker Champion six, though some cars ran with a Ford flathead V-8. Only a few were built—estimates vary on the precise number—when Kurtis sold out to super-salesman Earl "Madman" Muntz, who continued the concept in somewhat altered form as the Muntz Jet (see entry).

➕ FOR Rare and unique • Sprightly,

1930 White Eagle speedster

though not amazingly quick • Ubiquitous engines

■ **AGAINST** You'll pay plenty to own one • Bodywork hard to restore, impossible to replace

PRODUCTION

20-34

SPECIFICATIONS

Length (in.)	169.0
Wheelbase (in.)	100.0
Weight (lbs)	2300
Price (new)	$5000

ENGINES

cid/type	bhp	years
169.6/sv I-6	105[1]	1948-49
239.4/sv V-8	110	1948-49

[1]Supercharged

PRICES

FAIR	$10,000-18,000
GOOD	$18,000-28,000
FINE	$28,000-45,000

FINE EXAMPLE PRICE HISTORY

1982 $12,000		**1990** $27,500	
1994 $40,000		**1998** $43,000	
1982-2000 RETURN 9%			
2000-2010 5%			

1 9 3 8 - 3 9
LAGONDA V-12

The second-generation "Bentley," produced under the aegis of W.O. Bentley after he joined Lagonda in 1935. It was bred in the same heroic mold as his earlier cars, but with a magnificent single-cam 60-degree V-12. Features included a solid separate chassis, torsion-bar independent front suspension, and a huge choice of bodies from tourers to limousines. Though the engine is a problem for today's restorers—parts for it simply don't exist anymore—this was one of the '30s fastest British cars, with a brave and well-executed basic concept that made it altogether more sporting and exciting than a contemporary Rolls/Bentley. Silky smooth performance up to a 105-mph top speed in a 5000-pound car was—and is—formidable.

✚ **FOR** High performance from splendid engine • Rarity • Smooth and sophisticated • Styling • A CCCA Classic

■ **AGAINST** Engine parts not available • Complex to maintain • Heavy and thirsty • Ownership costs very high • Little U.S. interest

PRODUCTION

189

SPECIFICATIONS

Length (in.)	200.0-212.0
Wheelbase (in.)	124.0-138.0
Weight (lbs)	4400-5000
Price (new)	NA

ENGINES

cc/type (cid)	bhp[1]	years
4480/ohc V-12 (273)	180	1938-39

[1]Gross

PRICES

Rapide	
FAIR	$100,000-150,000
GOOD	$150,000-200,000
FINE	$200,000-300,000
Other Open	
FAIR	$35,000-50,000
GOOD	$50,000-75,000
FINE	$75,000-90,000

Closed: Deduct 50% from above.

FINE OPEN EXAMPLE PRICE HISTORY

1982 $80,000		**1990** $100,000	
1994 $100,000		**1998** $100,000	
1982-2000 RETURN 6%			
2000-2010 5-10%			

1939 V-12 convertible

1 9 4 9 - 5 8
LAGONDA 2.6/3.0 LITRE

1949-58 Lagonda 3.0-litre sedan by Tickford

The first postwar Lagonda, designed under W.O. Bentley but produced by David Brown of Aston Martin, Lagonda's new owner. Its engine was the same as used in Aston Martin DB2 and DB2/4. A rigid cruciform chassis with independent rear suspension was clothed in semi-classical sedan and convertible bodywork by Tickford. Top speed of the 2.6 was only 90 mph, but the 3.0 could reach the magic "ton" (100 mph). These were handbuilt cars aimed at the wealthy and priced accordingly.

✚ **FOR** Aston Martin powertrain • Many mechanical parts still available • Advanced chassis for the period

■ **AGAINST** Limited performance (2.6) • Old-fogey styling • Body parts extinct • Bodies deteriorate rapidly • Not plentiful in the U.S.

PRODUCTION

2.6 Litre (1949-53) 550 **3.0 Litre (1953-58)** 420

SPECIFICATIONS

Length (in.)	188.0/196.0 (2.6/3.0)
Wheelbase (in.)	113.5
Weight (lbs)	3345/3410 (2.6 sdn/conv), 3615/3660 (3.0 sdn/conv)
Price (new)	NA

ENGINES

cc/type (cid)	bhp	years
2580/dohc I-6 (158)	105[1]	1949-53
2922/dohc I-6 (178)	140[2]	1953-58

[1]Net (2.6 Litre) [2]Gross (3.0 Litre)

PRICES

FAIR	$5000-8000
GOOD	$8000-15,000
FINE	$15,000-22,000

FINE 2.6 LITRE PRICE HISTORY

1982 $8000		**1990** $35,000	
1994 $15,000		**1998** $22,000	
1982-2000 RETURN 5%			
2000-2010 5%			

1961-64
LAGONDA RAPIDE

1961-64 Rapide sedan

After a three-year hiatus, the Lagonda marque returned on a high-performance sedan as Aston Martin again tried the four-door GT formula. The Rapide used a longer-wheelbase version of the DB4 platform, with a de Dion rear suspension and the same dohc six in a lower state of tune. Sleek body styling was spoiled by a clumsy front-end treatment, with four headlamps (two large and two small) and an unfortunate Edsel-like vertical grille. More massive than the DB4, too much so to qualify as an Aston Martin product in the mind of prospective buyers, though the car lived up to its name with a top speed of approaching 130 mph. Production was an on-again, off-again proposition, and virtually all the handful of cars actually completed remained in England.

FOR Very rare • Aston performance with four-door convenience • Many mechanical parts still stocked • Nice lines despite front end

AGAINST Where do you begin to look? • Big, heavy, and thirsty • Body parts extinct

PRODUCTION
55

SPECIFICATIONS
Length (in.)	195.5
Wheelbase (in.)	114.0
Weight (lbs)	3780
Price (new)	NA

ENGINES
cc/type (cid)	bhp[1]	years
3995/dohc I-6 (244)	236	1961-64

[1]Net

PRICES
FAIR	$7500-12,500
GOOD	$12,500-17,500
FINE	$17,500-25,000

FINE EXAMPLE PRICE HISTORY
No sales reports available.
2000-2010 RETURN No prediction

1976-90
LAGONDA

This radically styled Lagonda, built at the rate of no more than one per week, was a four-door sedan with severely angular styling by William Towns, which was somewhat rounded off after 1986. The chassis was the familiar AM platform-type with all-independent suspension by double wishbones fore, de Dion axle with Watt linkage aft, but also with rear-self-leveling. Powered by the 5.3-liter dual-cam V-8 from the DBS/AM V-8 coupe (see entry), linked to Chrysler's TorqueFlite automatic. Power steering, windows and seats were standard, along with big all-disc brakes. A snug four-place cabin with British-traditional wood and leather trim was dominated by a gadgety instrument panel, somewhat simplified from 1983 but always with digigraphic displays. Digital fuel injection was adopted in 1986, though the effect on engine output wasn't precisely known, owing to Aston's policy of not quoting horsepower/torque (á la Rolls-Royce). There was more than adequate muscle, however, despite weighty heft, with 0-60 typically averaging 8-9 seconds, top speed around 140 mph. Handbuilt and thus a very rare bird, especially in the U.S.

FOR Head-turner • One of the world's fastest four-doors • Rare • Opulent

AGAINST Gas guzzler • Fit/finish disappoints in spots • Cramped rear entryways • Seating really too snug • Gimmicky dash • Ultimate collector status unclear

PRODUCTION
est. 500

SPECIFICATIONS
Length (in.)	208.0
Wheelbase (in.)	114.0
Weight (lbs)	4550
Price (new)	$50,000-187,500

ENGINES
cid/type	bhp[1]	years
326/dohc V-8	289/263	1976-90

[1]Estimated net bhp for European/U.S. models

PRICES
Early models
FAIR	$25,000-40,000
GOOD	$40,000-55,000
FINE	$55,000-70,000

Late models are at the upper end of these ranges.

FINE EXAMPLE PRICE HISTORY
Depreciated throughout the 1990s.
2000-2010 RETURN Depreciating.

1964-68
LAMBORGHINI 350/400 GT

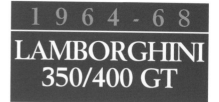

The first of the Ferrari-fighting high-performance GTs backed by Italian tractor king Ferruccio Lamborghini. The engine and chassis design was mostly the work of ex-Ferrari engineer Giotto Bizzarrini. The former was an intricate, jewel-like four-cam V-12. The

1976-85 sedan

latter was a typical low-volume Italian tubular frame with an all-independent coil-spring suspension system. The 350 GT was a two-seater notchback coupe with a 3.5-liter engine. The 400 GT was basically the same car with +2 rear seating shoehorned in and a larger 4.0-liter displacement. Styling was curiously rounded, and though it had the right proportions it lacked the grace and panache of Maranello's Pininfarina-shaped cars in these years. Significant as the progenitor of the later and more famous Lamborghinis. Replaced by the Islero in 1968.

✚ FOR First edition Italian exotic • 150-mph-plus performance • Magnificent engine

▬ AGAINST Styling • Poor body construction • Body panels aren't to be found • Expensive to restore, run, and insure • Most survivors already spoken for

PRODUCTION
380

SPECIFICATIONS

Length (in.)	184.5
Wheelbase (in.)	100.4
Weight (lbs)	2650/3200 (350 GT/400 GT)
Price (new)	$14,250 U.S. for a 1966 400 GT

ENGINES

cc/type (cid)	bhp[1]	years
3464/dohc V-12 (211)	280	1964-68
3929/dohc V-12 (240)	330	1964-68
[1]DIN		

PRICES

350	
FAIR	$20,000-40,000
GOOD	$40,000-60,000
FINE	$60,000-70,000

FINE 350 GT PRICE HISTORY

1982 $22,000	1990 $175,000
1994 $115,000	1998 $105,000
1982-2000 RETURN 7%	
2000-2010 5%	

1966-73 LAMBORGHINI MIURA

The sensational mid-engine Lamborghini that started life as a dream car, and was "forced" into production by public demand. Apart from the Ferrari 275LM, this was the first production mid-engine exotic: powered by Lamborghini's renowned 4.0-liter quad-cam V-12 mounted just aft of the two-seat cabin and situated trans-

versely instead of longitudinally as in the front engine Lamborghinis. Taking drive to the rear wheels was a five-speed manual gearbox, the only one offered. The separate chassis was big and brawny but light, and boasted the all-independent suspension expected in cars of this class. The aggressive, low-slung body was styled by Bertone, and consisted of a steel structure overlaid with unstressed aluminum panels. Body contours were curvy and sensual. When not in use, the exposed headlamps reclined into recesses in the front fenders. The front fenders/hood and engine/wheel/tail cover lifted up as complete assemblies for service access. No Spyder version was officially sold, though a few of the closed cars may have been converted, and an open car was seen briefly at auto shows. Sold in three forms throughout its life: the P400, the higher-powered 400S in 1970, and the ultra-rapid Miura SV from 1971. It was billed as the fastest production car in the world at the time, and the SV's claimed 180-mph top speed seemed to back that up. Not for those to whom considerations like luggage space and noise control are important, but surely one of the fastest ways to travel on land short of a surface-to-surface missile.

✚ FOR Unique styling • Monstrous performance • Technical interest • Trend-setter • Prices have tumbled (but they're still high)

▬ AGAINST Costly to buy and run • Highly impractical • Rust-prone • Body parts hard to find

PRODUCTION
760

SPECIFICATIONS

Length (in.)	171.5
Wheelbase (in.)	98.5
Weight (lbs)	2850

Price (new)	$19,250 U.S. in 1969

ENGINES

cc/type (cid)	bhp[1]	years
3929/dohc V-12 (240)	350-385	1966-73
[1]DIN		

PRICES

FAIR	$60,000-85,000
GOOD	$85,000-95,000
FINE	$95,000-115,000

FINE EXAMPLE PRICE HISTORY

1982 $28,000	1990 $200,000
1994 $100,000	1998 $110,000
1982-2000 RETURN 9%	
2000-2010 5%	

1968-78 LAMBORGHINI ESPADA

1975 Espada coupe

The long-lived four-seat Lamborghini with styling inspired by Bertone's Marzal show car of 1966. The magnificent 4.0-liter V-12 engine was front-mounted in a steel platform chassis with all-independent suspension, and drove the rear wheels through a five-speed gearbox or (on some mid-'70s specimens) a Chrysler TorqueFlite automatic. The same basic chassis layout was also used in short-wheelbase form for the Jarama 2+2 coupe. The Espada looked like no other car on the road: a low, wide front

1968 Miura coupe

end with quad headlamps flanking a simple blacked-out grille; large inset hood scoops; huge windshield; a low beltline kicked up at the rear, and a near-horizontal fastback roofline terminating in a chopped tail with a glass panel between the taillights to assist rearward vision. A large and heavy car, it offered marginal four-place seating and a top speed of "only" 150 mph. One of the most exotic of the limited-production Latin flyers, and surprisingly practical despite that.

✚ **FOR** One-of-a-kind styling • Near four-seat layout • Delectable engine • All the amenities you could want • Low-production snob appeal

▬ **AGAINST** Hardly cheap today • Costly to restore and run • Most survivors have rusted badly • Body parts have vanished • Gas guzzler • A rare commodity

PRODUCTION
1000 (est.)

SPECIFICATIONS
Length (in.)	184.0
Wheelbase (in.)	104.5
Weight (lbs)	3750
Price (new)	$21,000 U.S. in 1969

ENGINES
cc/type (cid)	bhp[1]	years
3929/dohc V-12 (240)	325-365	1968-78

[1]DIN

PRICES
FAIR	$10,000-20,000
GOOD	$20,000-28,000
FINE	$28,000-34,000

FINE MODEL PRICE HISTORY
1982 $26,000	1990 $60,000
1994 $40,000	1998 $40,000

1982-2000 RETURN 2%
2000-2010 2%

1968-70
LAMBORGHINI ISLERO

The rebodied replacement for the original 350GT/400GT. It used the same chassis, but was offered only with the 4.0-liter version of the quad-cam V-12. The more angular body styling was the work of Marazzi of Milan, but paled next to the Bertone-designed Espada and mid-engine Miura sold alongside it. Seating was still strictly 2+2, and the Islero was quite fast—more than 140 mph available. It was replaced as the least exotic Lambo by the Jarama in 1970.

1968 Islero coupe

✚ **FOR** As for 1964-68 350GT/400GT, plus neater (if more bland) looks • Affordable for a Lambo

▬ **AGAINST** Undistinguished for a supercar • Others as for 1964-68 350GT/400GT

PRODUCTION
225

SPECIFICATIONS
Length (in.)	178.0
Wheelbase (in.)	100.4
Weight (lbs)	2795
Price (new)	approx. $18,000 U.S.

ENGINES
cc/type (cid)	bhp[1]	years
3929/dohc V-12 (240)	330	1968-70

[1]DIN

PRICES
FAIR	$15,500-26,000
GOOD	$26,000-35,000
FINE	$35,000-45,000

FINE EXAMPLE PRICE HISTORY
1982 $18,000	1990 $140,000
1994 $45,000	1998 $45,000

1982-2000 RETURN 7%
2000-2010 5%

1970-78
LAMBORGHINI JARAMA 400GT/GTS

The last member of Lamborghini's 400GT series, successor to the short-lived Islero. The Jarama was essentially the same mechanical package (front-mounted quad-cam V-12 driving the rear wheels through a five-speed gearbox) wrapped in a newly designed, very angular 2+2 coupe bodyshell styled by Bertone. Unlike its

1970 Jarama coupe

predecessors, though, the Jarama featured unit-steel construction instead of a separate tubular chassis. Wheelbase was even shorter than on the original 350GT, but clever use of interior space allowed Lamborghini to claim marginal 2+2 seating, even if the rear passengers had to adopt the lotus position to fit. Suspension was the same at both ends: unequal-length A-arms, coil springs, and antiroll bar. A terrific performer in a straight line (100 mph was only 18 seconds away from standstill), the Jarama was also a delightful handler, no doubt due as much to its ultra-wide tires and low center of gravity as to the suspension. Not the most practical Lambo from the standpoint of packaging and interior design, but the aggressive styling has aged well. It fell victim to Lamborghini's roller-coaster financial fortunes in the mid- to late-'70s. Most of those brought to the U.S. were 1972-spec models (sold through the 1974 model year), though some later versions, including the similar GTS may have been brought in and certified privately.

✚ **FOR** Supercar performance • Bertone styling • Sumptuous appointments • Pedigree road manners • Half the price it was a decade ago

▬ **AGAINST** Thirsty • Expensive to run • Limited accommodations • Erratic construction quality

PRODUCTION

NA

SPECIFICATIONS

Length (in.)	176.5
Wheelbase (in.)	93.5
Weight (lbs)	approx. 3600
Price (new)	$23,500 U.S. in 1972, rising to $28,000 in 1975

ENGINES

cc/type (cid)	bhp[1]	years
3929/dohc V-12 (240)	350	1970-78

[1]Net

PRICES

FAIR	$10,000-20,000
GOOD	$20,000-30,000
FINE	$30,000-40,000

FINE PRICE HISTORY

1982 $30,000	1990 $105,000
1994 $70,000	1998 $50,000
1982-2000 RETURN 2%	
2000-2010 5%	

1975 Urraco coupe

Lamborghini's reply to Ferrari's V-6 Dino, not a successor to the mighty Miura. It was powered by a brand-new all-aluminum V-8 with "only" one overhead camshaft per cylinder bank, mounted crosswise behind a nominal four-place cockpit and driving the rear wheels through a five-speed gearbox. Unit construction with all-independent MacPherson-strut suspension (aided by transverse arms and anti-roll bars) gave the leech-like handling/roadholding expected in a "midi." A low and wide 2 + 2 coupe by Bertone, it was marked by Miura-like slats over the fastback rear window, plus a short, pointy front, and large wheels and tires. Initially sloppy dash design improved as production progressed, but not the oft-criticized Italian straight-armed driving position. Offered with three different engine displacements, but the 2.0-liter version was a home-market "tax dodge" not sold in the U.S.

Effectively replaced by a restyled targa-top derivative called Silhouette, which in turn led to the Jalpa powered by the basic Urraco engine.

◧ FOR A supercar in everything but size • Delightful engine • Superb road manners • Quick • Parts expensive when available

◨ AGAINST Unit-construction rust worries • Limited passenger and luggage space • Odd driving stance Messy dash • Rather piggish (about 13 mpg) • Spotty parts/service support

PRODUCTION

P250 520 P300 190 P200 66

SPECIFICATIONS

Length (in.)	167.3
Wheelbase (in.)	96.3
Weight (lbs)	2420-2820
Price (new)	$22,500 U.S. in 1975 (P250), $24,150 in 1977 (P300)

ENGINES

cc/type (cid)	bhp[1]	years
2463/ohc V-8 (152)	220[2]	1970-76
2996/ohc V-8 (183)	265[3]	1975-79
1994/ohc V-8	182[2]	1075-77

[1]Net [2]P250 [3]P300 [3]P200

PRICES

FAIR	$10,000-18,000
GOOD	$18,000-27,000
FINE	$27,000-32,500

FINE EXAMPLE PRICE HISTORY

1982 $32,000	1990 $45,000
1994 $30,000	1998 $32,000
1982-2000 RETURN 0%	
2000-2010 3%	

The wildest-looking supercar yet and successor to the Miura.

Premiered as LP5000 Countach show car in 1971; modified production model not available until late '73. Unusual midships drivetrain put quad-cam V-12 longitudinally (versus Miura's transverse) with a five-speed shift linkage ahead. Drive to the rear wheels via a power takeoff through the sump to a ZF limited-slip differential. Body, by Bertone's Marcello Gandini, almost pyramidal in shape. Wide "beetle-wing" doors hinged at the front to swing upwards, though access clumsy to the wide but very low and snug cockpit dominated by a large central tunnel and aircraft-like dash. Advanced tubular space-frame chassis clothed by aluminum panels (initially just a millimeter thick). Suspension by unequal-length A-arms, coil springs, and anti-roll bar fore; aft by upper lateral links, A-arms, upper and lower trailing arms, twin coil springs and shocks, and anti-roll bar. Evolutionary Countach S (LP400S) announced in 1978 with revised geometry to accommodate superwide wheels and tires; tack-on fender flares were added for the same reason, along with front spoiler and an optional rear wing. Carburetion revised, though still six Webers and no change in rated power. Engine enlarged to keep pace with emissions tuning for 1982 LP5000, then stroked, given new 4-valve heads, and Bosch KE-Jetronic fuel injection for the ultimate LP5000 Quattrovalvole of 1985, which also rode a slightly longer wheelbase. Americans unwilling to truck with "gray market" importers missed out on the Countach from the mid-Seventies through 1982, a reflection of Lamborghini's periodic financial crises of that period. The firm was bought by Chrysler Corporation in 1987 and Countach production wound down about two years later to make room for the replacement Diablo (see entry).

1975 LP400 Countach coupe

➕ **FOR** Exotic looks, specifications • Fantastic performance (at least 170 mph) • Great charisma ensures collectibility

➖ **AGAiNST** Costs a mint • So does upkeep • Outward vision impossible • Cramped cabin • Trucky ride and manual steering • Ultimate collector values yet to be established

PRODUCTION

LP400 150 (1974-78) **LP400S** 466 (1978-82) **LP500S** 323 (1982-85) **LP5000S QV** approx. 500 (1985-89)

SPECIFICATIONS

Length (in.)	163.0 (1974-84), 165.4 (1985-89)
Wheelbase (in.)	96.5 (1974-84), 98.4 (1985-90)
Weight (lbs)	2915-3285
Price (new)	$52,000-120,000 (U.S.)

ENGINES

cid/type(cc)	bhp[1]	years
239.8/dohc V-12 (3929)	375	1974-82
290/dohc V-12 (4754)	375[2]	1982-85
315.3/dohc V-12 (5167)[3]	455	1985-89

[1]DIN [2]325 SAE net in U.S. [3]Quattrovalvole (4 valves/cylinder)

PRICES

FAIR	$55,000-74,000
GOOD	$74,000-80,000
FINE	$80,000-87,000

1989 Anniversary model: present range in good to fine condition $82,000-102,000.

FINE EXAMPLE PRICE HISTORY

1990 $175,000		**1994** $145,000	
1998 $100,000			
1982-2000 RETURN 5%			
2000-2010 5%			

1976-77
LAMBORGHINI SILHOUETTE

1976 Silhouette coupe

Sant'Agata's first open-air production car, essentially the mid-engine P300 Urraco with "Targa-style" semiconvertible bodywork. Bodies were designed and supplied by Bertone, as before. Lift-off roof panel apart, Urraco appearance was updated by bulging flat-top wheelarches, a deeper front spoiler incorporating oil-cooler and front-brake air ducts, "five-hole"

wheels lifted from those on the Bravo show car, and a "tunnelback" rear window/engine cover that gave a slightly different . . . silhouette. Inside was a tidier dash, but no more "+2" rear seating. Predictably, the Silhouette was much like the P300 Urraco in other respects, including performance—and also indifferent workmanship and suspect reliability. That plus more Lamborghini financial problems rendered Silhouette a mere two-year venture. Only a few came to the U.S. It was effectively replaced in late 1982 by yet another evolution, the P350 Jalpa (see entry).

➕ **FOR** As for 1972-79 Urraco, plus more ergonomic dash • Open-air appeal • Production much more limited

➖ **AGAINST** As for 1972-79 Urraco, but some body parts harder to find

PRODUCTION

54 (some sources list 52)

SPECIFICATIONS

Length (in.)	168.5
Wheelbase (in.)	95.5
Weight (lbs)	2750
Price (new)	approx. $30,000 in U.S.

ENGINES

cid/type (cc)	bhp[1]	years
183/dohc V-8 (2996)	265	1976-77

[1]SAE net

PRICES

FAIR	$20,000-25,000
GOOD	$25,000-27,500
FINE	$27,500-40,000

FINE EXAMPLE PRICE HISTORY

1987 $30,000		**1990** $100,000	
1994 $45,000		**1998** $40,000	
1987-2000 RETURN 3%			
2000-2010 3%			

1982-1989
LAMBORGHINI JALPA

The junior Lamborghini of the '80s: essentially an updated Silhouette issued after a four-year hiatus to rejoin the battle with Ferrari's similar 308-series. Major changes involved a quad-cam V-8 stroked to 3.5 liters for easier emissions tuning, plus somewhat more aggressive styling (mainly in bodyside treatment), again conceived and executed by Bertone. Still a Targa-style two-seater with a carbureted engine mounted transversely amidships, plus a five-speed rear transaxle and fully independent suspension, all as per Urraco/Silhouette. But it was little quicker owing to slightly less horsepower—for cleaner air—and somewhat more weight—thanks to added amenities for more civilized touring. Production was both limited and sporadic, reflecting Lamborghini's continuing financial woes, which looked to be solved with the 1987 takeover by Chrysler Corporation. Also, Jalpa output tended to be sacrificed to that of its brutish, futuristic big brother, the Countach, which earned a bigger per-unit profit. Production was terminated by 1990.

➕ **FOR** As for Urraco and Silhouette, plus somewhat better workmanship

➖ **AGAINST** As for Urraco and Silhouette, but newer and thus less certain a collector car • Still fairly expensive

1982 Jalpa coupe

PRODUCTION

NA

SPECIFICATIONS

Length (in.)	166.0
Wheelbase (in.)	95.5
Weight (lbs)	3300
Price (new)	approx. $54,000 in U.S.

ENGINES

cc/type (cid)	bhp	years
3485/dohc V-8 (213)	250	1982-89

PRICES

Fine examples $34,500-43,500.
2000-2010 RETURN 3%

1990-2000
LAMBORGHINI DIABLO

The much-anticipated replacement for the almighty Countach and first and last of the "Chrysler Lamborghinis". Chrysler sold Lamborghini in 1994 to an Indonesian firm. Unveiled in 1990, but not really available until '91. Chrysler allegedly softened the original sharp-edged lines of Countach designer Marcello Gandini, leading to a well-publicized "feud" that was ultimately patched up. But the end product was still striking in the extreme: less brazen than Countach, but no less menacing. Wheelbase increased by 5.9 inches, overall length by 10.2 inches, height by 1.4 inches, and width by 1.6 inches (to a fat 80.3), resulting in a slightly roomier two-place cockpit with ergonomics and outward vision no Countach owner ever knew. Alas, weight also ballooned—by some 300 pounds—despite hood, engine cover, rocker panels, bumpers, and transmission tunnel of light carbon-fiber; the roof was steel, other outer panels of heavier-gauge aluminum than Countach used. The chassis was basically carryover, as was a "back-to-front" quad-cam V-12

with a five-speed transmission run forward, but the structure was a new-design square-tube latticework, the short driveshaft taking power rearward now nestled beside the sump instead of running through it, and the 48-valve engine was enlarged some 40 cubic inches for truly prodigious horsepower and torque. Early road tests showed eye-popping performance of 4.5 seconds 0-60 and over 200 mph flat out, plus surprisingly benign handling for a big tail-heavy car and racetrack-level roadholding (over 0.90 g). No antilock brakes, but fine stopping ability with huge all-round vented discs. An all-wheel-drive roadster was offered in '99. For 2000 the coupe was also equipped with all-wheel-drive. The exotic hand-built nature and quarter-million-dollar asking price ensure exclusivity and, doubtless, an "instant" collector's item for a rich, fortunate few.

⊞ FOR One-of-a-kind looks • Ferrari F40 its only peer for performance, roadability, exclusivity, "Oh, wow!" value • Relatively plush • Easier to drive and live with than any Countach

▣ AGAINST That price! • Relatively noisy (but glorious sounds!) • Complex, so costly to maintain (but if you have to ask. . . .)

PRODUCTION

Limited

SPECIFICATIONS

Length (in.)	175.6
Wheelbase (in.)	104.3
Weight (lbs)	3620-3950
Price (new)	$239,000-286,500

ENGINES

cc/type (cid)	bhp	years
5707/dohc V-12 (348)[1]	492/530	1990-2000

[1] 4 valves/cylinder

PRICES

2000 asking prices for 1990 model $100,000-112,000. More recent cars priced higher, depending on market.
2000-2010 RETURN Depreciating.

1990 Diablo coupe

1951-58
LANCIA AURELIA COUPE & SPYDER

1955 Aurelia coupe

Hailed by many as the first "true" GT, the Aurelia coupe was a two-door fastback based on the chassis and drivetrain of the Aurelia sedan. Styling by Pinin Farina was distinguished by a proud, distinctively shaped Lancia grille and a smooth, sloping roofline. Like all contemporary Lancias, the coupe had a sliding-pillar front suspension, and shared its V-6 engine and rear-mounted gearbox with the sedan. Two engine sizes were offered through six marginally different "series" in the model's life: 1991cc (1951-53) and 2451cc (1953-58). Available beginning in 1954 was a pretty Farina-styled open roadster (Spyder) on a shorter wheelbase. The first Z40 built had a trendy wraparound windshield and no door windows. After that a conventional windshield and roll-up glass appeared. A major chassis change occurred in 1954, when the semi-trailing-link independent rear suspension was exchanged for a de Dion layout on coupes. Spyders used the de Dion arrangement exclusively.

⊞ FOR Significant modern Lancia • Milestone status • Agile handling • Styling (especially Spyder) • Engineering • Performance

▣ AGAINST Rust-prone • Parts now hard to obtain • Not numerous any more

PRODUCTION

Cpe 3871 **Spyder** 761

SPECIFICATIONS

Length (in.)	172.0/165.4 (cpe/Spyder)
Wheelbase (in.)	104.7/96.5 (cpe/Spyder)
Weight (lbs)	2630/2500 (cpe/Spyder)
Price (new)	approx. $5500 U.S. for 1956

Spyder; $5800 for 1958 GT coupe

ENGINES

cc/type (cid)	bhp[1]	years
1991/ohv V-6 (121)	75/80	1951-53
2451/ohv V-6 (150)	118/122	1953-58

[1]Net

PRICES

Spyder

FAIR	$10,000-20,000
GOOD	$20,000-40,000
FINE	$40,000-60,000

(Deduct 75% for cpe, add 10% for 2.4 liter engine.)

FINE SPYDER PRICE HISTORY

1982 $9000		**1990** $45,000	
1994 $30,000		**1998** $60,000	

1982-2000 RETURN 11%
2000-2010 5%

1959-64

LANCIA FLAMINIA COUPE & SPYDER

Introduced in 1956 as the eventual replacement for the Aurelia, the all-new Flaminia also featured a V-6 engine, though of a different type. It also had a similar rear transaxle but a much more modern coil-spring front suspension. The "volume" model in this series was the Pinin Farina-styled four-seat notchback coupe. There were also various special-bodied coupes and Spyder roadsters offered on a shortened version of the Flaminia sedan chassis designed by the likes of Touring, Zagato, and Ghia. Engine displacement was raised from 2.5 to 2.8 liters in 1963, and four-wheel disc brakes were used from the beginning. By the early '60s, the Flaminia had become overshadowed by the smaller and more saleable Fulvia and Flavia series. The most striking of the coachbuilt cars was probably the Zagato fastback, with sleek Alfa-type lines and headlamps deeply set into housings covered by clear lenses.

FOR Italian brio and style • Fine brakes • Capable road manners • Zagato's distinctive looks • The 1959-64 Zagato and 1961-63 GT coupe/convertible are Milestone cars

AGAINST Body rot problems • Parts difficult to find now • Mediocre styling on Farina notchback coupe

1958-60 Flaminia coupe

PRODUCTION

2.5-Litre cpe 4151 **2.8-Litre cpe** 1133 **2.5-Litre special-bodied units** 2593 **2.8-Litre special-bodied units** 868

SPECIFICATIONS

Length (in.)	184.5/177.0 (cpe/Zagato)
Wheelbase (in.)	108.3/99.2 (cpe/Zagato)
Weight (lbs)	3265/2670 (cpe/Zagato)
Price (new)	approx. $6500 U.S. in 1960

ENGINES

cc/type (cid)	bhp[1]	years
2458/ohv V-6 (150)	119/140	1959-63
2775/ohv V-6 (169)	150	1963-69

[1]Net

PRICES

Spyder

FAIR	$4000-10,000
GOOD	$10,000-18,000
FINE	$18,000-25,000

(Cpe deduct 15%, Zagato add 50%)

FINE SPYDER PRICE HISTORY

1982 $5000		**1990** $30,000	
1994 $20,000		**1998** $20,000	

1982-2000 RETURN 9%
2000-2010 5%

1962-75

LANCIA FLAVIA 2000 COUPE/ CONVERTIBLE/ ZAGATO

The first Italian car with front-wheel drive, and the first Lancia to make use of a horizontally opposed engine. As with other Lancia series, a humdrum sedan (not included here) was introduced first, followed by these more desirable sporty models. These consist of a smart Pinin Farina-styled notchback coupe with four headlamps

1962 Flavia Zagato coupe

and four seats, plus a convertible and an "ugly/beautiful" Zagato fastback with a lightweight body. Engine displacement rose to 1.8 liters in 1963, and the lineup continued mostly unchanged until 1969. At that point, everything but the notchback was dropped. The coupe was given a restyled nose and reintroduced without the Flavia appellation as the 2000, denoting its enlarged 2.0-liter flat four. Fuel injection was offered as well as carburetors during the lengthy model run. Most examples weren't as fast as their styling implied, but the injected Zagato could reach 120 mph given enough space. Production gradually tapered off beginning around 1969, when Fiat took over Lancia.

FOR Lancia prestige and engineering • Neat Pininfarina styling • "Distinctive" Zagato styling • Front-drive pace-setter • Milestone status for the 1962-66 coupe

AGAINST Rust-prone • Drivetrain parts have dried up

PRODUCTION

Flavia 1500 cpe/conv 4449 **Flavia Zagato 1500 Sport** 98 **Flavia 1800 cpe/conv** 16,445 **Flavia Zagato 1800 Sport** 628 **2000 cpe** 6791

SPECIFICATIONS

Length (in.)	176.5/175.6 (cpe/Zagato)
Wheelbase (in.)	97.6
Weight (lbs)	2550-2800/2340 (cpe/Zagato)
Price (new)	NA

ENGINES

cc/type (cid)	bhp[1]	years
1500/ohv flat 4	(92)	1962-63
1800/ohv flat 4	(110)	1963-69
1990/ohv flat 4	(121)	1969-75

[1]90 bhp (net) to 140 bhp (gross) depending on displacement and fuel delivery (injection or carburetors)

PRICES

FAIR	$4000-8000
GOOD	$8000-12,000
FINE	$12,000-17,000

FINE ZAGATO PRICE HISTORY

1982 $5500	1990 $17,500
1994 $15,000	1998 $15,000
1982-2000 RETURN 8%	
2000-2010 5%	

1965-76

LANCIA FULVIA COUPE & ZAGATO

1965-76 Fulvia coupe

The last Lancia wholly designed by the old-line Italian automaker before it was acquired by Fiat, which then took increasing responsibility for engineering and styling of subsequent Lancias. New from end to end, with front-wheel drive and a narrow-angle overhead cam V-4 engine inclined at 45 degrees in the nose. Besides a dull-looking four-door sedan (not considered here), the Fulvia was offered as a deliciously cute 2+2 notchback coupe and as a longer two-seat Sports coupe styled by Zagato in its typical fashion. The latter featured extensive use of aluminum body panels, as did the special high-performance HF coupe. Engine displacement was increased from 1.2 to 1.3 liters in 1967, the last year these cars were legally imported into the U.S. An extensively revised 1.6-liter version of the V-4 was optional for 1969 and later HFs and the last 1971 Zagatos. All models featured four-wheel disc brakes and splendid front-drive handling. The HF earned its stripes in European rallying, and hung around after the Fiat-based Beta series arrived to replace other Fulvia models in the early '70s.

✚ **FOR** Neat styling • Handling • Performance (110 mph for 1.6) • Brakes

▬ **AGAINST** Meager parts supplies • Bodies rust-prone • Most slower than they look • Crowded cabin

PRODUCTION

1.2-Litre cpe 20,436 **1.2-Litre HF cpe** 490 **1.3-Litre Zagato** 202 **1.3-Litre cpe** 113,599 **1.3-Litre HF cpe** 2239 **1.3-Litre Zagato** 6100 **1.6-Litre HF cpe** 3690 **1.6-Litre Zagato** 800

SPECIFICATIONS

Length (in.)	156.0/161.0 (cpe/Zagato)
Wheelbase (in.)	91.7
Weight (lbs)	1975-2110/1820/2060 (cpe/HF/Zagato)
Price (new)	$3520/$4520 (1.3 cpe/1.3 Zagato) in U.S. in 1967

ENGINES

cc/type (cid)	bhp[1]	years
1216/dohc V-4 (74)	80	1965-67
1298/dohc V-4 (79)	90	1967-76
1584/dohc V-4 (97)	115	1969-76

[1]DIN

PRICES

FAIR	$4000-7000
GOOD	$7000-12,000
FINE	$12,000-17,000

(Add 50% for Zagato or HF)

FINE COUPE PRICE HISTORY

1982 $4000	1990 $16,500
1994 $15,000	1998 $15,000
1982-2000 RETURN 8%	
2000-2010 5%	

1974-75

LANCIA STRATOS

A compact "homologation special" built to street-legal specs in sufficient numbers to qualify as a Group 4 production GT for international rallying. It evolved from an even wilder 1970 Stratos show car based on Lancia's rally-winning Fulvia HF (see entry). A midships drivetrain from Ferrari's Dino 246 (see entry) was transplanted to a new unit body/chassis structure designed and built by Bertone with all the expected features—four-wheel double-wishbone/coilspring suspension, all-disc brakes, rack-and-pinion steering. Weight was minimized via a tilting nose and tail sections of fiberglass, plus minimal equipment, though road versions had all the necessities. Aggressive styling was dominated by a radically curved superstructure resembling nothing so much as a driver's helmet. Prototypes began competing in 1972, and one captured the Spanish Rally in April 1973. The 492 roadgoing models were quickly built by September '73, leaving the thus-homologated "production" Stratos to win the World Rally Championship three years straight: 1974-76. Its last major victory came with the 1979 running of the fabled Monte Carlo Rally (a private Monaco entry).

✚ **FOR** Exciting, unique appearance • Quick—6.8 seconds 0-60 mph, 140+ all-out • Sharp, balanced handling • Rare, especially in the U.S. • Highly coveted by a small enthusiast cadre

▬ **AGAINST** Parts supplies impossible • Tight, noisy cockpit • Virtually no baggage space • Poor outward vision • Costly to buy and maintain

PRODUCTION

492 road versions, plus 8-10 factory team cars

SPECIFICATIONS

Length (in.)	146.1
Wheelbase (in.)	85.8
Weight (lbs)	2160
Price (new)	$16,195 in Italy

ENGINES

cc/type (cid)	bhp[1]	years
2418/dohc V-6 (148)	190	1974-75

1974 Stratos coupe

[1]SAE net

PRICES

Price estimates vary widely. The French price guide published by *Auto Passion* raised the Stratos' top value from $50,000 to $100,000 in 1989, but that was at the market peak; *Automotive Investor* reported a sale at only $20,000 in late 1995.
2000-2010 RETURN 5%

1948-85
LAND-ROVER SERIES I-III

This was a British reply to the American Army's go-anywhere four-wheel-drive vehicle that proved so valuable in World War II, but introduced in the early postwar period. It was very different in appearance, with fully enclosed front wheels and severe, angular body lines. Early models had inboard headlamps mounted behind a mesh-screen grille guard. Later models had exposed lamps that ultimately were moved into the front fenders. Offered in a bewildering choice of models—short and long wheelbases, gasoline and diesel engines, various body styles: pickup truck, van, station wagon, special-purpose coachwork. Like most 4x4s, the Land-Rover affords two- or four-wheel drive with high and low ranges, and has front and rear differential locking for the ultimate in traction on low-friction surfaces and difficult terrain. Bodies are made of light alloy to keep weight down. The passenger compartment is spartan but very functional. Never intended to double as a passenger car (the more stylish and luxurious Range Rover introduced in 1970 fills that role),

the Land-Rover is built and sold strictly for hard work in conditions that would stop other vehicles cold. It's still in production today (available with a detuned version of the ex-Buick 3.5-liter aluminum V-8), and remains a mainstay of the British Army, fire departments, and seekers of high adventure from tropical jungles to frozen tundra. It wasn't imported to the U.S. in any significant volume, though not too difficult to find.

✚ **FOR** Rugged durability • Supreme all-terrain capability • Rust-free body • Wide choice of sizes, types, specifications • Still in production, though more civilized now

➖ **AGAINST** Hard springing, mountain-goat ride • Spartan • Not very fast (about 60 mph) • Early body and mechanical parts questionable now

PRODUCTION

761,000 (Series I, II, IIA)

SPECIFICATIONS

Length (in.)	132.0-175.0 (depending on body)
Wheelbase (in.)	80/86/107/109
Weight (lbs)	2500-3600 (depending on specifications)
Price (new)	NA

ENGINES

cc/type (cid)	bhp[1]	years
1596/F I-4 (97)	50	1948-51
1997/F I-4 (122)	52	1952-58
2286/ohv I-4 (140)	77	1958-85
2625/F I-6 (160)	85	1967-85
2052/ohv I-4[2] (125)	55	1958-61
2286/ohv I-4[2] (140)	62	1958-85
3528/ohv V-8 (215)	100[3]	1980-85

[1]Net [2]Diesel [3]Est.

PRICES

FAIR	$2500-4000
GOOD	$4000-10,000
FINE	$10,000-15,000

1971-85 Land Rover Series III wagon

FINE EXAMPLE PRICE HISTORY

The way their price has held up is amazing, though the Land Rover is still considered more utility than collector vehicle. Appreciation has certainly has kept up with inflation, but value varies enormously depending on condition.
2000-2010 RETURN Even

1930-33
LA SALLE

1930 340 convertible coupe

A continuation of the Classic junior Cadillac introduced in 1927, the LaSalle reached its apogee as a luxury car during this post-Great Crash period of rapidly diminishing sales. The '30s were longer, heavier, and costlier than previous LaSalles, and included six Fleetwood offerings. Cost cutting began for 1931 when the Cadillac 353-cid L-head V-8 was specified in a rationalization move, but it was at least as good an engine as the LaSalle 340. Prices were also reduced, by about $500. But Cadillac prices were also coming down, and those few people that could afford cars in this class tended to opt for the more prestigious senior make, which began to catch up to its junior companion in volume. The last CCCA-recognized Classic LaSalle was the '33. Later models were vastly altered for appeal to the medium-priced market.

✚ **FOR** Spectacular styling • Mechanical integrity • 1927-33 models are CCCA Classics

➖ **AGAINST** Expensive • A "junior Cadillac" even in the Classic era

PRODUCTION

1930 14,986 **1931** 10,095 **1932** 3386 **1933** 3482

SPECIFICATIONS

Length (in.)	NA
Wheelbase (in.)	134.0 (1930-31), 130.0/136.0 (1932-33)
Weight (lbs)	4340-5065
Price (new)	$2195-3995

ENGINES

cid/type	bhp	years
340.0/sv V-8	90	1930
353.0/sv V-8	95/115	1931-33

1933 345-C coupe

PRICES

Fleetwood open

FAIR	$20,000-35,000
GOOD	$35,000-65,000
FINE	$65,000-90,000

(Deduct 5% for Fisher open bodies.)

Fleetwood closed

FAIR	$15,000-30,000
GOOD	$30,000-55,000
FINE	$55,000-78,000

(Deduct 5% for Fisher closed bodies.)

FINE 1930 FLEETWOOD "FLEETLANDS" ALL-WEATHER PHAETON HISTORY

1982 $77,000		1990 $120,000	
1994 $110,000		1998 $94,000	
1982-2000 RETURN 1%			
2000-2010 3%			

1934-40
LA SALLE

1937 50 convertible coupe

The tightening grip of the Depression spurred the development of a smaller 119-inch-wheelbase LaSalle powered by an Oldsmobile straight-eight engine for 1934. Model offerings dropped to four, and prices were cut about $600, making this more an upper-medium priced car than a near-luxury model. This basic situation persisted until 1937, when LaSalle borrowed the V-8 from the '36 Cadillac Sixty. At the same time it adopted a four-inch-longer wheelbase. The public responded, sending LaSalle on to an all-time production record. A sharp recession in 1938 crippled sales, however, so the 1939-40 models reverted to a shortened wheelbase, though with excellent styling. The 1940 design would be the last for LaSalle—and one of the year's best. But by that time,

Cadillac no longer really needed a separate nameplate. Though a '41 LaSalle was planned, GM therefore killed the marque in favor of the down-market Series Sixty-One Cadillac.

✚ FOR A well-respected make • Good styling, especially 1940 • Smooth Cadillac V-8s and quality 1937-40

▬ AGAINST Body hardware very scarce • Open models quite pricey • Are there many left to find? • 1934-36 models seen more as senior Oldsmobiles than as junior Cadillacs

PRODUCTION

1934 7195 **1935** 8651 **1936** 13,004 **1937** 32,000 **1938** 14,675 **1939** 21,127 **1940** 24,130

SPECIFICATIONS

Length (in.)	NA
Wheelbase (in.)	119.0 (1934-35), 120.0 (1936), 124.0 (1937-38), 120.0 (1939), 123.0 (1940)
Weight (lbs)	3460-4110
Price (new)	$1175-1895

ENGINES

cid/type	bhp	years
240.3/sv I-8	95/105	1934-36
322.0/sv V-8	125/130	1937-40

PRICES

Open

FAIR	$10,000-20,000
GOOD	$20,000-35,000
FINE	$35,000-50,000

Closed

FAIR	$4000-13,000
GOOD	$13,000-20,000
FINE	$20,000-30,000

FINE 1940 CONVERTIBLE SEDAN PRICE HISTORY

1982 $29,000		1990 $75,000	
1994 $75,000		1998 $57,000	
1982-2000 RETURN 4%			
2000-2010 3%			

1995 SC300 coupe

A graceful coupe that challenged the Mercedes SL at about half the price. The SC 300/400 was developed from Lexus' respected LS 400 sedan. The coupe had well-balanced handling with good grip in tight turns. It was also a quiet and comfortable cruiser. The SC 400's V-8 was turbine smooth and powerful. The SC 300 had an in-line six that was also smooth and almost as quick—for considerably less money. Until 1998 the six was available with either a 5-speed manual or 4-speed automatic transmission. The V-8 was automatic only. Both had plush interiors. Leather was standard in the 400—optional in the 300. The back seat was cramped in both.

✚ FOR Pleasing styling • Well-built • Smooth engines

▬ AGAINST Tight back seat • Fuel economy

1940 52 Torpedo sedan

PRODUCTION[1]

1991 SC 300 2401 **1991 SC 400** 9374 **1992 SC 300** 7982 **1992 SC 400** 12695 **1993 SC 300** 6451 **1993 SC 400** 9624 **1994 SC 300** 4537 **1994 SC 400** 7392 **1995 SC 300** 3356 **1995 SC 400** 4364 **1996 SC 300** 2390 **1996 SC 400** 2557 **1997 SC 300** 2999 **1997 SC 400** 2043 **1998 SC 300** 1766 **1998 SC 400** 1243 **1999 SC 300** 1731 **1999 SC 400** 826
[1]U.S. sales.

SPECIFICATIONS

Length (in.)	191.1
Weight (lbs)	3455-3625
Wheelbase (in.)	105.9
Price (new)	$31,100-55,905

ENGINES

cid/type	bhp	years
183/dohc I-6	225	1991-00
242/dohc V-8	250-290	1991-00

PRICES

FAIR	$9000-15,000
GOOD	$15,000-30,000
FINE	$30,000-42,000

Depends entirely on used car market.
2000-2010 RETURN Depreciating

1930-32
LINCOLN V-8 MODELS L/K/KA

The long-running Model L had been around since Lincoln's founding in 1921, but was a design anachronism even then. Lincoln replaced it in 1931 with a modernized, though dimensionally identical, Model K that had a new chassis with torque-tube drive, floating rear axle, worm-and-roller steering, and hydraulic shocks. The K's V-8 retained the old L engine's "fork-and-blade" rods and three-piece cast-iron block/crankcase assembly. All models rode the same wheelbases, and included a wide variety of semi- and full-custom bodies, the latter supplied by Locke, Judkins, Brunn, LeBaron, Willoughby, Dietrich, and others. Prices ranged as high as $7400, and three long-wheelbase chassis—145/150/155 inches—were offered. The K chassis was given over to the V-12 Series KB of 1932. That year's V-8 Series KA chassis reverted to the L wheelbase but retained the K's improvements.

✚ FOR Recognized CCCA Classics • Superb coachwork, particularly the custom bodies • Noble Lincoln pedigree

■ AGAINST Extremely costly to buy, own, and maintain • Parts problems increasing • Model L not in the same league with some other '30s Classics

PRODUCTION

1930 L 3222 **1931 K** 3556 **1932 KA** 2224

SPECIFICATIONS

Length (in.)	Varies with bodywork
Wheelbase (in.)	136.0 (1930, 1932), 145.0 (1931)
Weight (lbs)	4740-6000
Price (new)	$4200-7400

ENGINES

cid/type	bhp	years
385.0/sv V-8	90-125	1930-32

PRICES

Open	
FAIR	$18,000-50,000
GOOD	$50,000-90,000
FINE	$90,000-125,000
Closed	
FAIR	$10,000-25,000
GOOD	$25,000-45,000
FINE	$45,000-65,000

(Closed bodies: Add 15% for custom bodies)

FINE 1931 MODEL K CUSTOM-BODIED ROADSTER

1982 $70,000		**1990** $100,000	
1994 $125,000		**1998** $115,000	

1982-2000 RETURN 4%
2000-2010 5%

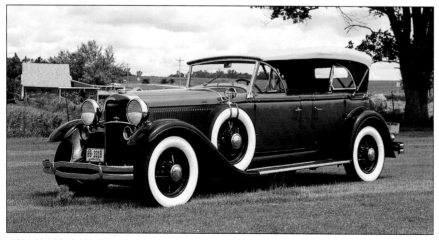
1931 V-8 Model K phaeton

1932-34
LINCOLN V-12 MODELS

1933 Lincoln V-12 Model KB sedan

Lincoln's answer to the multi-cylinder Cadillacs and Packards. The huge KB had more performance than the 1931 Model K, yet actually sold for less initially and was offered with a wider array of bodies. It was magnificent around town and a fast tourer, renowned for good looks, quality, luxury, and performance that defied comparison with most ordinary cars of the day. Greatest of them all was the Murphy dual-cowl sport phaeton, which commands the highest price on today's market. A possible ringer here is the 1933 KA with its smaller one-year-only engine. However, all these V-12s are closely related and do not affect value as much as condition and, of course, body style.

✚ FOR Tremendous presence, grand by any standard • Superb coach-work and "clockwork" • A great touring car even now • Full CCCA Classic status

■ AGAINST Mechanical complexity and resultant headaches • Titanic expense from purchase to sale • As scarce as you'd expect

PRODUCTION

1932 KB 1525 **1933 KA** 1118 **KB** 596 **1934 KA** 1679 **KB** 752

SPECIFICATIONS

Length (in.)	Variable
Wheelbase (in.)	145.0 (1932-34 KB), 136.0 (1933-34 KA)
Weight (lbs)	4719-5990
Price (new)	$2700-7200

ENGINES

cid/type	bhp	years
448.0/sv V-12	150	1932-33 (KB)
381.7/sv V-12	125	1933 (KA)
414.0/sv V-12	150	1934 (KA-KB)

PRICES

As for 1930-32 V-8s, but individual model prices almost impossible to establish owing to scarce sales. Consult auction reports, individual owners, and club sources. Maximum in fine condition: $180,000 for Dietrich convertible sedan. Minimum in fine condition: $50,000 for Model KA sedan. Middling price $130,000 for body 518A dual cowl phaeton (see below).

FINE 1933 DUAL-COWL PHAETON 518A

1982 $75,000		**1990** $140,000	
1994 $130,000		**1998** $120,000	
1982-2000 RETURN 3%			
2000-2010 3%			

1935-40
LINCOLN MODEL K

1939 Model K convertible sedan by LeBaron

The senior Lincoln of the late '30s following the advent of the medium-price Zephyr for 1936 (see entry). All had the K designation and the 414-cid V-12 introduced with the 1934 KA/KB. It was still very costly, so production dwindled as the lean years wore on—as it did for multi-cylinder Packards and Cadillacs. Special-order only 1940 models were built on the 1939 chassis. One of these was the famous 160-inch-wheelbase "Sunshine Special" parade car of Presidents Roosevelt and Truman, which now resides at the Henry Ford Museum in Dearborn. This was officially replaced for '41 by a long-wheelbase Lincoln Custom based on a much-modified Zephyr structure, chassis, and running gear.

⊞ FOR Quality • Performance • The poor man's K, available at much more down to earth prices • CCCA Classic status

⊟ AGAINST Prices likewise reflect the move from four-square styling to streamlining, not handled particularly well compared to, say, Packard or Cadillac • High running costs

PRODUCTION

1935 1434 **1936** 1013 **1937** 977 **1938** 416 **1939** 133 **1940** NA

SPECIFICATIONS

Length (in.)	Variable

Wheelbase (in.)	136.0/145.0
Weight (lbs)	5030-6300
Price (new)	$4200-7400

ENGINES

cid/type	bhp	years
414.0/sv V-12	150	1935-40

PRICES

1935-6 Open	
FAIR	$15,000-45,000
GOOD	$45,000-80,000
FINE	$80,000-115,000
1935-6 Closed	
FAIR	$10,000-25,000
GOOD	$25,000-45,000
FINE	$45,000-65,000

(Add 40-50% for custom bodied closed models; deduct 5% per year after 1936 for open body models.)

1935 LEBARON CONVERTIBLE PHAETON PRICE HISTORY

1982 $51,000		**1990** $135,000	
1994 $100,000		**1998** $105,000	
1982-2000 RETURN 5%			
2000-2010 5%			

1936-48
LINCOLN-ZEPHYR

Zephyr, was Lincoln's response to the Depression. Its predictive and innovative streamlined design was suggested by designer John Tjaarda. Teardrop-inspired styling and unit construction were retained for production, but the original rear-engine layout was discarded as too radical. Though mechanically unique in many ways, especially its new small V-12 derived from the Ford V-8, it was dogged by reliability woes for a time. It offered considerable interior space compared to most rivals, but no hydraulic brakes until 1939. A two-speed Columbia rear axle was an option through 1942.

Structurally revised for 1940, it was heavily facelifted the following year. It returned after the war as a warmed-over 1942 continuation with more glitter and fewer body styles—but without the Zephyr name.

⊞ FOR Unique and pioneering design, the first successful streamliner • Very strong club support • Interesting—and often rare—model and trim variations

⊟ AGAINST Medium-price aura • Few open models built (none 1936-37); many late ones scrapped for Continental restorations • Mechanically somewhat unreliable and prone to overheating • Underpowered, especially convertibles

1942 Lincoln-Zephyr convertible coupe

PRODUCTION

1936 14,994 **1937** 29,997 **1938** 19,111 **1939** 20,905 **1940** 21,536 **1941** 20,094 **1942** 6118 **1946** 16,179 **1947** 19,891 **1948** 6470

SPECIFICATIONS

Length (in.)	NA
Wheelbase (in.)	122.0 (1936-37); 125.0 (1938-48)
Weight (lbs)	3289-4245
Price (new)	$1165-3142

ENGINES

cid/type	bhp	years
267.3/sv V-12	110	1936-39
292.0/sv V-12	120	1940-41
305.0/sv V-12	130	1942
292.0/sv V-12	125	1946-48

1939 Lincoln-Zephyr convertible coupe

PRICES

Open	
FAIR	$8000-22,000
GOOD	$22,000-38,000
GOOD	$38,000-55,000
Closed	
FAIR	$3000-12,000
GOOD	$12,000-21,000
FINE	$21,000-30,000

FINE 1939 CONVERTIBLE SEDAN PRICE HISTORY

1982	$25,000	1990	$55,000
1994	$45,000	1998	$48,000

1982-2000 RETURN 5%
2000-2010 5%

1941 Continental cabriolet

Originally designed as a custom-bodied special for Edsel Ford, Bob Gregorie's "Mark I" Continental seems to look better and better as the years pass. These first models—identical mainly except for pushbuttons instead of handles on the '41 doors—are the cleanest of the breed. Essentially, it was a sportier version of the contemporary Lincoln-Zephyr, powered by the long-stroke V-12 derived from Ford's flathead V-8. This engine had a history of inadequate water passages and poor oil flow before 1940, though these problems were partly corrected by then. The original Continental was one of the first cars recognized as something more than a mere machine—by New York's Museum of Modern Art and the Classic Car Club of America, among others—and one of the finest examples of the automobile as art.

✚ FOR Ageless design • A highly coveted CCCA Classic

▬ AGAINST Questionable mechanical reliability • High running costs • Not cheap and quite rare

PRODUCTION

1940 2d cpe 350 **2d cabrio** 54 **1941 2d cpe** 850
2d cabrio 400

SPECIFICATIONS

Length (in.)	209.8
Wheelbase (in.)	125.0
Weight (lbs)	3740-3890
Price (new)	$2783-2916

ENGINES

cid/type	bhp	years
292/sv V-12	120	1940-41

PRICES

Open	
FAIR	$12,500-25,000
GOOD	$25,000-45,000
FINE	$45,000-65,000
Closed	
FAIR	$9500-19,000
GOOD	$19,000-34,000
FINE	$34,000-50,000

FINE 1941 CONVERTIBLE PRICE HISTORY

1982	$25,000	1990	$52,500
1994	$60,000	1998	$65,000

1982-2000 RETURN 6%
2000-2010 5%

A facelifted version of the 1940-41 Continental, with a somewhat fussier horizontal-bar grille and raised, squared-off rear fenders. New this year was an enlarged version of Lincoln's flathead V-12 that unfortunately proved less reliable than its predecessor. The restyle increased overall length by seven inches, and weight was up, too.

✚ FOR As for the 1940-41 Continental, but not quite as nice-looking • Rarity in abbreviated prewar

1942 Continental cabriolet

model year • A CCCA Classic

▬ AGAINST Expensive now • High running costs

PRODUCTION

2d cpe 200 **2d cabrio** 136

SPECIFICATIONS

Length (in.)	216.8
Wheelbase (in.)	125.0
Weight (lbs)	4000-4020
Price (new)	$3000

ENGINES

cid/type	bhp	years
305/sv V-12	130	1942

PRICES

As per 1940-41 Lincoln Continental.

1947 Continental coupe

Postwar continuation of the prewar Continental based on the 1942 body dies and chassis design, but identified by a massive-looking, two-tier eggcrate grille. Only detail changes occurred in these three model years.

Because of problems with the bored-out 305-cid version, the V-12 reverted to its 1940-41 292-cid displacement, though somehow an extra five horsepower had been found. Plans for a 1949 successor were shelved as Ford sought to gain badly needed sales with its high-volume models. The Mark II had to wait until 1956, when it appeared without the Lincoln nameplate as the product of an entirely distinct Ford Motor Company Continental Division.

⊞ **FOR** As for 1942 Continental, including Classic status • A Milestone car as well

⊟ **AGAINST** As for 1942 Continental, but more plentiful

PRODUCTION

1946 2d cpe 265 **2d cabrio** 201 **1947 2d cpe** 831 **2d cabrio** 738 **1948 2d cpe** 847 **2d cabrio** 452

SPECIFICATIONS

Length (in.)	216.8
Wheelbase (in.)	125.0
Weight (lbs)	4090-4135
Price (new)	$4662-4746

ENGINES

cid/type	bhp	years
292/sv V-12	125	1946-48

PRICES

Open	
FAIR	$13,000-25,000
GOOD	$25,000-45,000
FINE	$45,000-65,000
Closed	
FAIR	$9800-20,000
GOOD	$20,000-35,000
FINE	$35,000-50,000

FINE CONDITION CONVERTIBLE PRICE HISTORY

1982 $25,000	**1990** $47,500
1994 $47,500	**1998** $65,000
1982-2000 RETURN 6%	
2000-2010 5%	

1949-51
LINCOLN COSMOPOLITAN

The upper series in Lincoln's first all-new postwar lineup, part of Ford's company-wide redesign for '49. Though no match for Cadillac in sales or performance, Lincolns were still high-quality luxury cars able to cover long distances quickly and quietly. The '49 Cosmopolitan offerings included both Town and Sport four-door sedans, while the 1950-51 range listed the Capri, a high-spec two-door coupe

with a canvas-covered roof and fine upholstery, intended to fill in for a true pillarless hardtop as a competitor for Cadillac's Coupe de Ville. Styling in these years was similar to Mercury's (the base Lincoln series used the same bodyshell) on a four-inch longer wheelbase. The "bathtub" look then in vogue was accented with frenched head and taillamps, a low grille, and—unique to the 1945-50 Cosmo—heavy chrome moldings on the fender flares. Power was by a larger version of Ford's faithful flathead V-8; overdrive (1949-50) and GM Hydra-Matic (1949-51) were options.

⊞ **FOR** Luxury • Solid build • Smooth performance

⊟ **AGAINST** Gorpy styling • No speedster

PRODUCTION

1949 35,123 **1950 2d cpe** 1824 **4d sdn** 8341 **conv** 536 **1951 2d cpe** 2727 **4d sdn** 12,229 **conv** 857

SPECIFICATIONS

Length (in.)	221.3 (1949-50), 223.5 (1951)
Wheelbase (in.)	125.0
Weight (lbs)	4194-4640
Price (new)	$3186-3950

ENGINES

cid/type	bhp	years
336.7/sv V-8	152/154	1949-51

PRICES

Conv	
FAIR	$6000-12,000
GOOD	$12,000-22,000
FINE	$22,000-32,000
Others	
FAIR	$4000-10,000
GOOD	$10,000-17,500
FINE	$17,500-25,000

FINE CONVERTIBLE PRICE HISTORY

1982 $8500	**1990** $28,000
1994 $25,000	**1998** $29,000
1982-2000 RETURN 8%	
2000-2010 6%	

1952-54
LINCOLN CAPRI

1953 Capri hardtop coupe

Replacement for the Cosmopolitan as Lincoln's top of the line series, offered in three body styles. Both series rode a new 123-inch-wheelbase chassis with newly designed ball joint front suspension, recirculating-ball power steering, and jumbo drum brakes. In the engine room was Ford Motor Company's first overhead-valve V-8, which would be extended to Ford and Mercury (with reduced displacement) for 1954. For 1953, the Lincoln V-8 produced more power per cubic inch (0.64) than any of its competitors. Styling changed completely too, with a more contemporary squared-off look, clean almost to the point of being plain, and again uncomfortably similar to

1951 Cosmopolitan convertible

Mercurys of these years. Extensive sound deadening enhanced refinement, and the optional air conditioning system featured flow-through ventilation. These Lincolns are highly regarded today for their superlative performance in the Carrera Panamericana (Mexican Road Race) in these years.

✚ FOR Clean, handsome looks • Fine fit and finish • Performance • Good handling for the class • Milestone car status

▬ AGAINST Some rust likely • Body hardware scarce now

PRODUCTION

1952 4d sdn 7000 (est.) **2d htp** 5681 **conv** 1191
1953 4d sdn 11,352 **2d htp** 12,916 **conv** 2372
1954 4d sdn 13,598 **2d htp** 14,000 **2d conv** 1951

SPECIFICATIONS

Length (in.)	214.1 (1952-53), 214.8 (1954)
Wheelbase (in.)	123.0
Weight (lbs)	4140-4350
Price (new)	$3331-4031

ENGINES

cid/type	bhp	years
317.5/ohv V-8	160/205	1952-54

PRICES

Conv	
FAIR	$6500-13,000
GOOD	$13,000-23,000
FINE	$23,000-33,000
Htp	
FAIR	$5000-10,000
GOOD	$10,000-19,000
FINE	$19,000-26,000
Sdn	
FAIR	$3000-7000
GOOD	$7000-12,000
FINE	$12,000-17,000

FINE CONVERTIBLE PRICE HISTORY

1982 $8600		**1990** $28,000	
1994 $27,500		**1998** $32,000	
1982-2000 RETURN 8%			
2000-2010 8%			

1955 LINCOLN CAPRI

One of the few makes (others were Kaiser, Studebaker, and Willys) to start 1955 without a wraparound windshield, mainly because this year's design was a facelift of the 1952-54 styling. It came off exceptionally well, however, ultra-clean front to rear, with massive taillights housed in elongated fenders. Solidly built with the best materials. Power and comfort more than ample. Lincoln finally introduced an automatic transmission of its own,

1955 Capri convertible

dubbed TurboDrive. To keep pace in the horsepower race, the ohv V-8 was bored out to 341 cid for an extra 20 bhp. Sales overall were down compared to 1954, again going against industry trends, probably because the restyle didn't come across as "new" enough.

✚ FOR Underrated as a collectible • Clean styling in an ostentatious year • Smooth road performance • Comfort • Luxury • Milestone status

▬ AGAINST Rust can be a bother • Drinks gas greedily

PRODUCTION

4d sdn 10,724 **2d htp** 11,462 **conv** 1467

SPECIFICATIONS

Length (in.)	215.6
Wheelbase (in.)	123.0
Weight (lbs)	4245-4415
Price (new)	$3752-4072

ENGINES

cid/type	bhp	years
341/ohv V-8	225	1955

PRICES

As per 1952-54 Lincoln Capri.

1956-57 LINCOLN PREMIERE

Lincoln's new premium series in these years, relegating Capri to second-class status. The all-new design featured a longer, lower, wider, and heavier body typical of the '50s, a revised chassis on a three-inch-longer wheelbase, and a brand-new "True-Power" V-8 with 285 horses. Styling was right up to date, inspired by the Futura show car: peaked headlamps,

1956 Premiere hardtop coupe

partially covered rear wheel openings, wrapped windshield, and a long rear deck tapering to give the straight-through rear fenders a hint of fins. The 1957 facelift brought stacked quad headlamps, much more prominent fins, and the addition of a four-door hardtop called Landau. A short-lived design, it was replaced by even larger, unit construction models for 1958.

✚ FOR Large and luxurious • Ample power

▬ AGAINST Thirsty • Vague, imprecise handling • Considerable rust threat

PRODUCTION

1956 2d htp 19,619 **4d sdn** 19,465 **conv** 2447
1957 2d htp 15,185 **4d sdn** 5139 **conv** 3676
Landau 4d htp 11,223

SPECIFICATIONS

Length (in.)	222.8 (1956), 224.6 (1957)
Wheelbase (in.)	126.0
Weight (lbs)	4347-4676
Price (new)	$4601-5381

ENGINES

cid/type	bhp	years
368/ohv V-8	285/300	1956-57

PRICES

Conv	
FAIR	$7500-15,000
GOOD	$15,000-27,000
FINE	$27,000-39,000
Htp	
FAIR	$5000-11,000
GOOD	$11,000-19,000

FINE	$19,000-27,000
Sdn	
FAIR	$3000-7000
GOOD	$7000-12,000
FINE	$12,000-18,000

FINE CONVERTIBLE PRICE HISTORY

1982 $8700	**1990** $32,500
1994 $28,000	**1998** $38,000
1982-2000 RETURN 9%	
2000-2010 6%	

1 9 5 8 - 6 0
LINCOLN PREMIERE

1958 Premiere hardtop sedan

The completely redesigned standard Lincoln. Again, priced higher than Capri, but less than the new companion Continental Marks III, IV, and V of these years. About six inches longer and several hundred pounds heavier, which made the new 430-cid big-block "MEL" V-8 a must. Output was progressively reduced, however, in the quest for whatever mileage improvement was possible in these giants. Styling was marked by quad headlights in slanted recesses flanking an enormous grille and huge bumpers front and rear. Convertibles were sent over to the new Continental Mark III companion line, which shared the standard Lincoln's unit body/chassis construction and basic appearance. A minor facelift was ordained for '59, and a more thorough redo—including a reworked greenhouse—was accomplished for '60. Collector opinion is very divided on these cars. Some find them hideous, overly complex, and wallowy, while others think they're just the thing for long-haul cruising in '50s-style comfort. Low sales and less of the "more is better" attitude generally in Detroit led to an all-new downsized Lincoln line for '61.

+ FOR As for 1956-57 Premiere

■ AGAINST As for 1956-57 Premiere, but heavier (with expected consequences for mileage and roadability) • Controversial styling • Not that much

different from concurrent Continentals

PRODUCTION

1958 2d htp 3043 **4d sdn** 1660 **Landau 4d htp** 5572 **1959 2d htp** 1963 **4d sdn** 1282 **Landau 4d htp** 4606 **1960 2d htp** 1364 **4d sdn** 1010 **Landau 4d htp** 4200

SPECIFICATIONS

Length (in.)	229.0 (1958), 227.2 (1959-60)
Wheelbase (in.)	131.0
Weight (lbs)	4798-5064
Price (new)	$5318-5945

ENGINES

cid/type	bhp	years
430/ohv V-8	315-375	1958-60

PRICES

2d	
FAIR	$3500-8000
GOOD	$8000-12,000
FINE	$12,000-18,000
4d	
FAIR	$2500-5000
GOOD	$5000-9000
FINE	$9000-14,000

FINE 2D HTP PRICE HISTORY

1982 $3600	**1990** $11,000
1994 $16,500	**1998** $16,000
1982-2000 RETURN 10%	
2000-2010 8%	

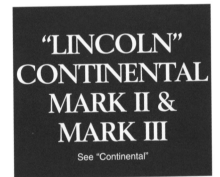

"LINCOLN" CONTINENTAL MARK II & MARK III

See "Continental"

1959 Continental Mark IV hardtop sedan

1 9 5 9
LINCOLN CONTINENTAL MARK IV

A modestly facelifted continuation of the 1958 Continental Mark III, now with the addition of a Town Car (Formal Sedan) and limousine, the latter priced close to the 1956-57 Mark II. Continental officially became a Lincoln again for the first time since 1948 following Continental Division's reabsorption into Lincoln-Mercury—which itself was reconstituted from the previous Mercury-Edsel-Lincoln structure. As on this year's standard Lincoln, the big 430 V-8 lost 25 horsepower to detuning. Styling retained its similarity to that of the lower-line models, except for the sedan and hardtops' reverse-slanted rear roofline with an electrically retractable backlight. The Town Car and limo both had a more conventional roof with blind C-pillars and padded tops. Interiors wore Ford Motor Company's best fabrics and fittings, and most every popular creature assist was standard, as might be expected.

+ FOR As for 1958-60 Lincoln Premiere, plus extra luxury • Non-ragtops are relatively affordable • Mark III, IV, and V Continental convertibles are Milestone cars (and no longer cheap)

■ AGAINST Appeal diluted by similarity to lesser Lincolns • Moderately rust-

prone • Electrical/mechanical gremlins
• High running costs (especially fuel)

PRODUCTION

4d sdn 944 **2d htp** 1703 **conv** 2195 **4d htp** 6146 **4d Formal Sedan** 78 **limo** 49

SPECIFICATIONS

Length (in.)	227.1
Wheelbase (in.)	131.0
Weight (lbs)	4967-5061
Price (new)	$6598-10,230

ENGINES

cid/type	bhp	years
430/ohv V-8	350	1959

PRICES

Conv	
FAIR	$5000-10,000
GOOD	$10,000-18,000
FINE	$18,000-26,000
Sdn	
FAIR	$3000-6000
GOOD	$6000-10,000
FINE	$10,000-15,000
Htps	
FAIR	$3500-8000
GOOD	$8000-14,000
FINE	$14,000-21,000

FINE CONVERTIBLE PRICE HISTORY

1982 $5500		1990 $35,000	
1994 $30,000		1998 $25,000	
1982-2000 RETURN 10%			
2000-2010 5%			

1960
LINCOLN CONTINENTAL MARK V

1960 Continental Mark V convertible

A continuation of the Mark IV, with only detail styling changes and 35 less horsepower from the big-inch Lincoln V-8. Comments for 1958-60 Lincoln Premiere as well as the 1959 Mark IV apply here.

✚ FOR As for 1959 Mark IV

▬ AGAINST As for 1959 Mark IV

PRODUCTION

4d sdn 807 **2d htp** 1461 **conv** 2044 **4d htp** 6604 **Formal Sedan** 136 **limo** 34

SPECIFICATIONS

Length (in.)	227.2
Wheelbase (in.)	131.0
Weight (lbs)	5044-5481
Price (new)	$6598-10,230

ENGINES

cid/type	bhp	years
430/ohv V-8	315	1960

PRICES

As per 1959 Lincoln Continental Mark IV.

1961-63
LINCOLN CONTINENTAL

Among the most handsome large American cars ever produced. Chiseled, classic lines from the pen of Elwood Engel stayed the same through these years except for minor grille insert and rear panel changes. Superbly engineered with a rigid unit body/chassis, extensive sound insulation, very close machining tolerances, and an unprecedented number of long-life service components such as a fully sealed electrical system and thorough factory-applied corrosion protection. The big Lincoln 430 V-8 from previous years was retained in somewhat detuned form. Each car was bench tested at 3500 rpm for three hours before installation (equivalent to nearly 100 mph), and all cars were given individual 12-mile road tests before shipment, reflecting the strong emphasis given quality control. This car also reintroduced the convertible sedan body type, the first since Kaiser-Frazer's 1949-51 model. More compact than its immediate predecessors, this Continental rode the same wheelbase as the very roadable 1952-55 Lincolns.

✚ FOR Styling excellence • High quality • Fast and remarkably agile for the luxury class • Poshness • Convertible sedan's uniqueness, allure • A Mile-

stone car

▬ AGAINST Mechanical complexity • Electrical bothers • Somewhat rust-prone

PRODUCTION

1961 4d sdn 22,203 **4d conv sdn** 2857 **1962 4d sdn** 27,849 **4d conv sdn** 3212 **1963 4d sdn** 28,095 **4d conv sdn** 3138

SPECIFICATIONS

Length (in.)	212.4 (1961), 213.0 (1962), 213.3 (1963)
Wheelbase (in.)	123.0
Weight (lbs)	4927-5370
Price (new)	$6067-6916

ENGINES

cid/type	bhp	years
430/ohv V-8	300/320	1961-63

PRICES

Conv	
FAIR	$5000-9000
GOOD	$9000-16,000
FINE	$16,000-23,000
Sdn	
FAIR	$2500-5000
GOOD	$5000-9000
FINE	$9000-12,000

FINE CONVERTIBLE PRICE HISTORY

1982 $4500		1990 $8000	
1994 $18,500		1998 $18,000	
1982-2000 RETURN 10%			
2000-2010 10%			

1961-67
LINCOLN CONTINENTAL BY LEHMANN-PETERSON

These were Lincoln's custom-built cars of state, converted from standard models by this respected Chicago coachbuilding firm. Division windows,

1962 Continental convertible sedan

jump seats, and similar limousine equipment was offered, available to customer order. Wheelbase was lengthened considerably, and the chassis was reinforced and suspension pieces beefed up to cope with the extra weight. Some sources list production beginning with 1963 models only.

✚ **FOR** Milestone status • Limousine luxury • Pretend you're in the White House

▬ **AGAINST** Oversized • Thirsty • Unique body parts scarce

PRODUCTION

NA (limited)

SPECIFICATIONS

Length (in.)	250.0
Wheelbase (in.)	160.0
Weight (lbs.)	approx. 6000 (variable)
Price (new)	$10,000 and up (variable with equipment)

ENGINES

cid/type	bhp	years
430/ohv V-8	300/320	1961-65
462/ohv V-8	340	1966-67

PRICES

FAIR	$3000-6000
GOOD	$6000-10,000
FINE	$10,000-14,000

FINE EXAMPLE PRICE HISTORY

1982 $4000	1990 $12,000
1994 $10,000	1998 $12,000
1982-2000 RETURN 7%	
2000-2010 3%	

1964-67
LINCOLN CONTINENTAL

After making only detail changes to the Continental through 1963, Lincoln extended the car's wheelbase three inches for '64, but generally left its good looks alone. A two-door hardtop was added for '66, and the unique—but slow-selling—convertible sedan was dropped after 1967. Also for '66, Lincoln's V-8 got its first displacement increase since 1958 and the hood was lengthened. These Continentals continued to emphasize quality furnishings and attention to construction details, and considering their size they were a pleasure to drive. The elegantly understated styling has held up very well.

✚ **FOR** Classy appearance • Quality • Luxury • Fine handling • Others as for 1961-63 Continental, including

1966 Continental hardtop coupe

Milestone status

▬ **AGAINST** As for 1961-63 Continental

PRODUCTION

1964 4d sdn 33,369 **4d conv sdn** 3328 **1965 4d sdn** 36,824 **4d conv sdn** 3356 **1966 4d sdn** 35,809 **4d conv sdn** 3180 **2d htp** 15,766 **1967 4d sdn** 33,311 **4d conv sdn** 2276 **2d htp** 11,060

SPECIFICATIONS

Length (in.)	216.3 (1964-65), 220.9 (1966-67)
Wheelbase (in.)	126.0
Weight (lbs)	5055-5505
Price (new)	$5485-6938

ENGINES

cid/type	bhp	years
430/ohv V-8	320	1964-65
462/ohv V-8	340	1966-67

PRICES

As per 1961-63 Lincoln Continental.

1968-71
CONTINENTAL MARK III

1969 Continental Mark III hardtop coupe

The model that revived Continental as a separate marque in the '60s. Never officially listed as a Lincoln—it was an L-M Division product since there was no separate Continental Division, as there had been in 1956-58. Another of Ford's attempts to upstage Cadillac, the Mark III was aimed squarely at the Eldorado and other large personal-luxury cars. Sales rarely trailed Eldorado's by more than 2000 units, so the Mark III must be considered a success. Handsome if a bit baroque in appearance, the Mark III has lately begun to take hold with collectors, who seem to prefer it to the later Mark IV and V of 1972-79.

✚ **FOR** Crisp, traditional styling • Elegance and luxury • Smooth long-haul road car • A Milestone car • Values soared during the '80s

▬ **AGAINST** Values soared during the '80s • Thirsty • Expensive to restore, so fine a clean one

PRODUCTION

1968 7770 **1969** 23,088 **1970** 21,432 **1971** 27,091

SPECIFICATIONS

Length (in.)	216.1
Wheelbase (in.)	117.2
Weight (lbs)	4739-4762
Price (new)	$6585-7281

ENGINES

cid/type	bhp	years
460/ohv V-8	365	1968-71

PRICES

FAIR	$3000-7000
GOOD	$7000-12,000
FINE	$12,000-17,000

FINE EXAMPLE PRICE HISTORY

1982 $4800	1990 $15,000
1994 $12,000	1998 $14,000
1982-2000 RETURN 8%	
2000-2010 5%	

1972-76

LINCOLN CONTINENTAL MARK IV

Replacement for the Mark III in the reborn line of "personal" Lincolns directly descended—or so said Henry Ford II—from the original 1940 "Mark I" and mid-'50s Mark II (see entries). Like its predecessor, it shared basic chassis and structure with a current Ford Thunderbird (here, the redesigned '72), and was thus larger, heavier, and more massive-looking than the III. Followed Mark form in its stand-up grille and trademark decklid spare-tire hump, but oval rear-quarter "opera windows" cut into the standard vinyl roof were a dubious aesthetic addition. The '72s with their closer-fitting bumpers are arguably the best-looking of these models: later IVs gained mandated 5-mph "battering rams" that added length and visual bulk. Big-block 460 V-8 throughout (still linked to the three-speed SelectShift automatic), with year-to-year horsepower adjustments per prevailing emissions limits; post-'74s with catalytic converter have better driveability. Not a great Mark, but popular when new despite inflation-fueled price escalation, plus piggish thirst underscored by the 1973-74 energy crisis. Collectors should note the 1973-75 "Luxury Group" packages and 1976 "Designer Editions," the former keyed to various color schemes inside and out (Silver, Gold, etc.), the latter allegedly put together by Cartier and Bill Blass.

✚ **FOR** Big, smooth, and cushy • Used-car prices • Parts still plentiful

▬ **AGAINST** Lumpy styling • Lumb-ering road manners • A real gasaholic • Investment potential dim and distant

PRODUCTION
1972 48,591 **1973** 69,437 **1974** 57,316 **1975** 47,145 **1976** 56,110

SPECIFICATIONS
Length (in.)	220.1 (1972), 223.3 (1973), 228.3 (1974-76)
Wheelbase (in.)	120.4
Weight (lbs)	4800-5050
Price (new)	$8640-11,060

ENGINES
cid/type	bhp[1]	years
460/ohv V-8	195-220	1972-76

[1]SAE net

PRICES
FAIR	$3000-6000
GOOD	$6000-10,000
FINE	$10,000-15,000

FINE EXAMPLE PRICE HISTORY
1982 $3800	**1990** $10,000
1994 $9000	**1998** $12,000
1982-2000 RETURN 9%	
2000-2010 8%	

1977-79

LINCOLN CONTINENTAL MARK V

1979 Continental Mark V coupe

Reskinned continuation of the 1972-76 Mark IV, with crisper, sleeker lines and nearly 400 fewer pounds. Weight reduction enabled switching to a standard "small-block" 400 V-8 and making the previous 460 optional, a change anticipating 1978's new fuel-economy mandates that killed the big-block engine for '79. Heavier emphasis on "Designer" models in this period: Cartier, Bill Blass, plus new Pucci and Givenchy packages. Of special interest are 1978's Diamond Jubilee Edition, commemorating Ford Motor Company's 75th birthday, and 1979's "Collector Edition," a subtle late-season tipoff that a downsized Mark VI was due for 1980.

✚ **FOR** As for 1972-76 Mark IV, plus slightly better economy • Handling improved, and not nearly as bad as appearances suggest

▬ **AGAINST** As for 1972-76 Mark IV, but note comments above

PRODUCTION
1977 80,321 **1978** 72,602 **1979** 75,939

SPECIFICATIONS
Length (in.)	230.3
Wheelbase (in.)	120.4
Weight (lbs)	4590-4650
Price (new)	$11,400-13,100

ENGINES
cid/type	bhp[1]	years
400/ohv V-8	159-180	1977-79
460/ohv V-8	208	1977-78

[1]SAE net

PRICES
FAIR	$2500-6000
GOOD	$6000-10,000
FINE	$10,000-14,000

FINE EXAMPLE PRICE HISTORY
1982 $3500	**1990** $8500
1994 $8000	**1998** $10,000
1982-2000 RETURN 9%	
2000-2010 10%	

1984-92

LINCOLN CONTINENTAL MARK VII LSC

The closest thing to the "hot rod Lincoln" celebrated in song. Introduced with standard and "Designer" Mark VIIs, all based on the new aero-look 1983 Thunderbird, but overt performance touches belied LSC's "Luxury Sport Coupe" title. Distinctions included a handling suspension with firm springs/shocks, quick-ratio power steering, performance tires on cast-alloy wheels, foglights, sporty but sub-

1972 Continental Mark IV coupe

1984 Continental Mark VIII LSC coupe

dued bucket-seat interior (with after-thought analog gauges from '85), and a throttle-body-injected 302 V-8. Horses were upped by 20 for '85 via dual exhausts, tube headers, aluminum intake manifold with high-flow throttle body, performance cam, and low-restriction air cleaner. Another 25 bhp was achieved for '88 via new cylinder heads and further-improved induction. Teves anti-lock brakes became optional for '85, standard from 1986. Otherwise, minor trim and equipment changes each year; a driver's side airbag (accompanied by a dash reworked to accommodate it) was a notable safety advance for 1990. Too new to be collectible yet, and maybe too numerous as well: against all odds, the LSC ultimately became the best-selling Mark VII. Still, a very nice newer model with plenty of enthusiast appeal and perhaps some investment appeal down the road.

✚ FOR Smooth and quick (0-60 in well under 9 seconds) • Handling more than decent • Well equipped • Well built • ABS brakes (exc. '84) • Still current

▬ AGAINST No appreciable dollar return for some time yet, if ever • Small cabin for exterior size • Mediocre outward vision

PRODUCTION[1]

1984 33,344 **1985** 18,355 **1986** 20,056 **1987** 15,286 **1988** 38,259 23,184 **1989** 27,030 **1990** 18,000 est.
[1]all Mark VII models

SPECIFICATIONS

Length (in.)	202.8
Wheelbase (in.)	108.6
Weight (lbs)	3625-3775
Price (new)	$23,700-32,156

ENGINES

cid/type	bhp	years
302/ohv V-8	140-180	1984-85
302/ohv V-8	200	1986-87
302/ohv V-8	225	1988-92

PRICES

Prices in 2000 were $7000-10,000 for top examples.
2000-2010 RETURN Even for fine copies

1993-98
LINCOLN MARK VIII

1993 Mark VIII coupe (with 56-57 Mark II)

Combining Lincoln's twin-cam V-8 with the rear drive Thunderbird chassis, the new Mark VIII was well received at its introduction. The V-8 could move the big coupe quite rapidly. The fully independent suspension had sophisticated self-levelling system. The ride was comfortable, but well controlled. The styling was aerodynamically modern, but with a bump on the trunk lid to recall its heritage. In mid-'95 the rather austere interior was improved with a new center console and wood interior trim. Also introduced mid-season was a more sporting LSC version. With more power, less chrome, and a tauter suspension, this was the most desirable Mark VIII.

✚ FOR Performance • Smooth ride • Good handling for a large coupe

▬ AGAINST Rear seat access • In spite of early promise, seemed dated after only five years

PRODUCTION[1]

1993 31,852 **1994** 26,830 **1995** 17,433 **1996** 15,859 **1997** 16,023 **1998** 10,505
[1] U.S. calendar year sales

SPECIFICATIONS

Length (in.)	206.9
Weight (lbs)	3768
Wheelbase (in.)	113.0
Price (new)	$36,640-40,890

ENGINES

cid/type	bhp	years
281/dohc V-8	280-290	1993-98

PRICES

FAIR	$8000-15,000
GOOD	$15,000-20,000
FINE	$20,000-28,000

2000-2010 RETURN Depreciating

1998
LINCOLN MARK VIII COLLECTOR'S EDITION

1998 Mark VIII Collector's Edition coupe

The 1997 model year rang down the curtain on the rear-drive Thunderbird and Mercury Cougar, and observers reasoned that the similar Lincoln Mark VIII would shortly pass away as well. It did. Model-year 1998 was the last for this big (3900-pound), slow-selling coupe, a fate that had already been determined when the Collector's Edition was announced early in 1998. The LSC Mark VIII upon which the Collector's Edition was based had a 4.6-liter 290-bhp V-8 good for 0-60 times of less than 7 seconds. Swoopy good looks gave plenty of presence, but its bulk (overall length 207.2 inches) was considerable, and by the late Nineties the Mark VIII could no longer compete with comparable cars from Cadillac and Lexus, or with sport-utes. The "special" touches on this Collector's Edition were slight: gold badging on doors and deck-lid; a gold Lincoln star affixed to the center of the body-colored grille; extra wood trim; special wheel treatments; two body colors: White Pearlescent and Cordovan. Production was a mere 1294 units.

✚ FOR Performance • Sensual bodywork • Novel, "split-level" dash/instrument panel • Tiny production run

▬ AGAINST Quite large, and an inefficient user of space • Plasticky interior components • "Factory collectibles" often are not

PRODUCTION
1998 1294

SPECIFICATIONS

Length (in.)	207.2
Weight (lbs)	3765
Wheelbase (in.)	113.0
Price (new)	$40,890

ENGINES

cid/type	bhp	years
281/dohc V-8	290	1998

PRICES
Governed by used car market.
2000-2010 RETURN Depreciating

1 9 5 9 - 6 3
LOTUS ELITE

1959-63 Elite coupe

Lotus' first serious road car. It was notable for being a fiberglass, monocoque two-seat coupe with virtually no steel body reinforcement. Smooth styling was marked by a low-set oval air intake, sloping hood, and a neat, cut-off tail. The plexiglass door windows didn't roll down, so they had to be removed and stored elsewhere. Chassis features included fully independent suspension and four-wheel disc brakes. Power was supplied by an all-aluminum overhead-cam four made by Coventry Climax and offered in various states of tune: 71/83/95/105 bhp. A British BMC or German ZF manual transmissions was used. The initial Series I models had a MacPherson-type rear suspension layout, which

Lotus called "Chapman strut," while the Series II had revised lower wishbone geometry, and was built in greater numbers. In the end, this was a somewhat fragile car that was expensive for Lotus to build (it lost money on every one) and for customers to buy, but it gave the firm valuable "volume" production experience. Costly to keep on the road and not all that refined, but it's a high-appreciation investment of ageless beauty.

✚ FOR One of the most beautiful coupes ever built • Technical sophistication • Handling • Performance (up to 120 mph) • Good economy • Prices more affordable now • A Milestone car

▬ AGAINST Engine, suspension breakdowns common • Small and cramped • Fiberglass deteriorates • Noisy • Parts now in short supply

PRODUCTION
988

SPECIFICATIONS

Length (in.)	148.0
Wheelbase (in.)	88.0
Weight (lbs)	1460
Price (new)	$4500 at first, $5244 in 1960

ENGINES

cc/type (cid)	bhp[1]	years
1216/ohc I-4 (74)	71-105	1959-63
[1]Net		

PRICES

FAIR	$13,000-18,000
GOOD	$18,000-23,000
FINE	$23,000-28,000

FINE EXAMPLE PRICE HISTORY

1982 $10,000		**1990** $40,000	
1994 $35,000		**1998** $30,000	
1982-2000 RETURN 6%			
2000-2010 5%			

1 9 5 7 - 8 0
LOTUS SEVEN

The original British "club racer," about as pure a sports car as you'll ever see. Introduced in 1957 as a kit to get around the home market purchase tax, it was later sold by Lotus fully assembled, and then built by Caterham Cars of South London with few changes to the original Colin Chapman design. Intended as a low-cost way to enjoy sporty motoring and/or to go racing, and its kit-car heritage showed in the wide variety of proprietary engines that fit in the lightweight square-rigged body. The Seven was about as spartan as they come—even side curtains and a rudimentary soft top were options—and its tiny size made the cockpit extremely confining for anyone larger than a munchkin. It was like driving a motorized roller skate. Performance depended on what engine/transmission was used, but could have ranged from brisk to sensational. Wonderful on twisty, lightly traveled back roads because of marvelously precise handling and cornering abilities, but worrisome in traffic because the low build made you invisible to most other drivers. The stark, functional styling—freestanding headlamps, flowing and separate front fenders, upright windshield that could be folded flat, a bobtail rear—has been widely imitated. Most Sevens had light-alloy bodies, but the early-'70s Mark IV versions used fiberglass. Lotus relied

1960-70 Seven roadster

most heavily on British Ford engines, including the Chapman-modified dohc unit, which is the one to look for on the collector market. Though we only go up to 1980 here (the Seven continued on), this was an extremely versatile platform that wouldn't die, mainly because it provided only the basics required for high-spirited driving fun.

FOR Handling • Simplicity • Individuality • Entertainment value

AGAINST Somewhat fragile • Lacking in refinement and modern amenities—and proud of it • Not suitable for all-round use

PRODUCTION

S1 242 **S2** 1370 **S3** 350 **S4** approx. 1000 Caterham Seven (S3) 5000+

SPECIFICATIONS

Length (in.)	132.0
Wheelbase (in.)	88.0
Weight (lbs)	1655 (average)
Price (new)	approx. $5500 U.S. in 1970 (variable with drivetrain components specified)

ENGINES

cc/type (cid)	bhp	years

Most examples fitted with four-cylinder Ford of Britain engines of 1000-1600cc. Output ranges from 40 DIN bhp to 125. Valvetrain configurations include side valve, overhead valve, and twin overhead cam (Chapman-modified 1588cc unit only).

PRICES

1958-73

FAIR	$10,000-14,000
GOOD	$14,000-18,000
FINE	$18,000-25,000

FINE EXAMPLE PRICE HISTORY

1982 $5000		1990 $35,000	
1994 $32,500		1998 $25,000	

1982-2000 RETURN 9%
2000-2010 3%

1964 Elan coupe

If the Elite was Lotus' first serious road car, the Elan was the first prac-

tical one. It also introduced what would become a Lotus design trademark, a folded-steel "backbone" chassis. The diminutive fiberglass body was available in open and closed styles, distinguished by neat lines and pop-up headlamps. Power was supplied by the 1558cc twincam Lotus four based on the British Ford pushrod unit. The Elan progressed through five different series, designated S1 to S4 through 1971, followed by the Elan Sprint. Power went from 105 bhp at first to 115 (net), then to 126 (DIN) for the Sprint. Trim and equipment were also steadily upgraded. Tiny size, light weight, all-independent suspension, and fast rack-and-pinion steering made the Elan the standard for sports car handling and roadholding in its day. Passenger and cargo space were both very restricted, but ideal for those young-at-heart types small enough to fit. Quite quick, too—up to 120 mph, excellent zing for a 1.6-liter car. It was imported to the U.S. in relatively small numbers.

FOR Performance • Roadability • Mechanically simple (apart from engine) • Surprising mileage • Neat styling • High fun quotient • Emma Peel's favorite

AGAINST Engine not reliable • Cramped interior • Roadster's old-fashioned top • Very vulnerable to crash damage • Size works against you in heavy traffic • Body parts now impossible to come by

PRODUCTION

9659

SPECIFICATIONS

Length (in.)	145.0
Wheelbase (in.)	84.0
Weight (lbs)	1515
Price (new)	approx. $5600 U.S. for S/E roadster in 1967

ENGINES

cc/type (cid)	bhp[1]	years
1558/dohc I-4 (95)	105-126	1962-73

[1]See text

PRICES

Open	
FAIR	$9000-15,000
GOOD	$15,000-19,000
FINE	$19,000-25,000
Closed	
FAIR	$8000-12,000
GOOD	$12,000-15,000
FINE	$15,000-19,500

FINE ROADSTER PRICE HISTORY

1982 $5000	**1990** $17,500
1994 $19,000	**1998** $20,000

1982-2000 RETURN 9%
2000-2010 10% (cpe 5%)

1967-74 LOTUS ELAN +2

Essentially a stretched version of the Elan, sharing the same chassis layout and drivetrain. As the name suggests, the +2 rode a longer wheelbase that was supposed to provide enough cabin space for an extra pair of passengers, but in reality this was still only a two-seater, albeit less cramped than its smaller sister. The graceful fiberglass bodyshell was styled along similar lines, but was trimmed and equipped to a

1972 Elan +2 coupe

higher standard. Unlike the Elan, the +2 was never available in kit form. Beginning in 1971, a revised model appeared, called the +2S 130, with more horsepower. In the fall of 1972, a five-speed gearbox became available for the +2S 130/5. All models were capable of reaching about 120 mph.

FOR As for 1962-73 Elan, plus roomier interior and greater U.S. rarity • High-value appreciation

AGAINST As for 1962-73 Elan, but harder to find in the U.S.

PRODUCTION

4798

SPECIFICATIONS

Length (in.)	169.0
Wheelbase (in.)	96.0
Weight (lbs)	2085
Price (new)	approx. $6800 U.S. for +2S 130 in 1972

ENGINES

cc/type (cid)	bhp[1]	years
1558/dohc I-4 (95)	115/126	1967-74

[1]Net/DIN

PRICES

FAIR	$4000-6000
GOOD	$6000-7500
FINE	$7500-9000

FINE EXAMPLE PRICE HISTORY

1982 $5000	**1990** $22,500
1994 $20,000	**1998** $10,000
1982-2000 RETURN 4%	
2000-2010 5%	

1·9·6·7·-·7·5
LOTUS EUROPA

Lotus' first mid-engine car, intended as a running mate to the front-engine Elan, and possibly as its eventual successor. It was less expensive to build, however, because of the proprietary drivetrain borrowed from the front-drive Renault 16 sedan. In the Europa, the engine was turned around back-to-front and mounted behind the tiny two-seat cockpit to drive the rear wheels. The separate bodyshell was made of fiberglass as on other Lotus models, but featured broad, high sail panels aft of the doors that earned the nickname "bread van." The front end was reminiscent of the Elite's, with a low nose, small oval air intake, and scooped headlight recesses. The result was a lightweight car with impeccable handling, but the same cramped interior and dubious construction qual-

1969 Europa coupe

ity that were limiting the Elan's market appeal. Because of Lotus' desire to crack the Common Market (one reason for using the Renault drivetrain), all Series I models were sold outside England. The Series II arrived in 1970 with bolt-on, instead of bonded, body attachments and the larger 1565cc version of the Renault four from the 16TS. In 1972, Lotus fitted its own twincam 1558cc four (based on the British Ford ohv "Kent" engine) to produce the Series III, which also got slightly lower sail panels for a marginal visibility improvement. In the U.S., this model was known as the Europa Special, and was equipped with the "Big Valve" Lotus dohc engine. A five-speed gearbox was optional. U.S. imports were sporadic until 1970, when Europa was certified for U.S. sale. Most of the ones you'll find here will be late Series II and Special models.

FOR Technical interest • Marvelous roadability • Good mileage • Fine twincam performance • Lotus pedigree • Strong appreciation

AGAINST Ugly • Dubious spare parts supplies now • Very cramped cockpit • Wicked rear vision • Fragile in a crack-up • Spotty construction quality

SPECIFICATIONS

Length (in.)	156.5
Wheelbase (in.)	91.0
Weight (lbs)	1350
Price (new)	$4695 U.S. in 1969; approx. $6000 U.S. in 1973

ENGINES

cc/type (cid)	bhp	years
1470/ohv I-4 (90)	78[1]	1967-70
1565/ohv I-4 (95.5)	87[2]	1970-72
1558/dohc I-4 (95.1)	113[3]	1973-75

[1]Net [2]SAE net [3]SAE net for U.S. model

PRICES

FAIR	$4000-9000
GOOD	$9000-12,000

FINE	$12,000-15,000

FINE EXAMPLE PRICE HISTORY

1982 $5500	**1990** $16,000
1994 $13,000	**1998** $13,000
1982-2000 RETURN 6%	
2000-2010 5%	

1·9·7·6·-·8·7
LOTUS ESPRIT/ESPRIT TURBO

1976-87 Esprit Turbo coupe

Exciting final legacy of the late Colin Chapman. Began as a 1972 show car by Giorgetto Giugiaro's Ital Design studio; chiseled "flying doorstop" styling went into production three years later with remarkably few changes. Retained Lotus's favored "backbone" chassis and all-independent suspension, but employed fiberglass bodywork (as on other contemporary Lotuses) with impregnated color (by a still closely guarded process). First powered by a longitudinal, midships 2.0-liter 16-valve twincam slant-four (the all-Lotus Type 907 unit first seen in the Jensen-Healey and actually half of a stillborn V-8), linked to five-speed manual transaxle. Though performance was good in European tune, the detoxed U.S.

model was unremarkable at a tick over 9 seconds 0-60. The first version also suffered from marginal cooling and chassis-transmitted mechanical and road noise. These problems were addressed by 1980's new Turbo Esprit with a blown 2.2-liter engine, stronger chassis, modified rear suspension, better brakes, larger wheels, deep front airdam, and "aero" rocker panels. Results were 150 mph all out (versus 135) plus even tighter handling and greater high-speed stability. Interim non-turbo "S2.2" Esprit became an S3 during 1983 with adoption of the Turbo chassis and body. The Turbo switched from carburetors to Bosch fuel injection in 1987. The following year brought new, more rounded outer body panels, plus updated interiors and other improvements. While those newer Esprits will surely be collected one day, the pre-1988 models should see appreciation sooner, both in dollars and enthusiast esteem.

FOR Sharp styling • Performance (esp. Turbo) • Good economy • Rot-free body • Not too costly now • Typically athletic Lotus handling

AGAINST Typically cramped Lotus cockpit • Typically problematic Lotus fit and finish • Limited U.S. parts/service backup

PRODUCTION

S1 (1975-79) 1060 S2 (1979-80) 88 S3/Turbo (1980-87) NA

SPECIFICATIONS

Length (in.)	169.0
Wheelbase (in.)	96.0
Weight (lbs)	2200-2650
Price (new)	$16,000-57,000

ENGINES

cc/type (cid)	bhp[1]	years
1973/dohc I-4 (120.4)	120-140[2]	1976-80
2174/dohc I-4 (132.7)	160	1980-86
2174/dohc I-4 (132.7)[3]	210/215	1980-88

[1]SAE net; all engines 4 valves/cylinder [2]160 DIN in European tune [3]Turbocharged

PRICES

Esprit	
FAIR	$6000-12,000
GOOD	$12,000-17,500
FINE	$17,500-22,000

2000-2010 RETURN 2%

1990-91
LOTUS ELAN

Nifty but controversial British roadster with front-wheel drive and an

1990 Elan convertible

Isuzu 1.6-liter four underwritten by General Motors and developed by Lotus. You can still hear the sound of eyebrows being raised. Available in two flavors: normally aspirated, 130-horse (not available U.S.); and turbo-intercooled 165-bhp. A sophisticated suspension carried on the famed Lotus road manners. The turbo ripped through the 0-60 sprint in 6.7 seconds, and handling was equally as impressive. British journalists loved the Elan; Yank commentators were somewhat less enthusiastic.

FOR Performance • Top handling & roadholding • Quick steering • Non-jarring ride • A Lotus was good enough for Mrs. Peel, so a Lotus is good enough for you

AGAINST Front-drive • Debatable styling • GM held the purse strings • Japanese powerplant

PRODUCTION

470 (approx. U.S. Sales)

SPECIFICATIONS

Length (in.)	152.2
Weight (lbs)	2250
Wheelbase (in.)	88.6
Price (new)	$39,040

ENGINES

cid/type	bhp	years
96.9/dohc I-4	130	1990-91
96.9/dohc I-4[1]	165	1990-91

[1]Turbocharged

PRICES

FAIR	$12,000-17,000
GOOD	$17,000-20,000
FINE	$20,000-24,000

2000-2010 RETURN Depreciating

1996-2000
LOTUS ESPRIT V8

Other supercars had eight or twelve cylinders. Lotus finally joined the

1996 Esprit V-8 coupe

club by replacing its turbocharged four-cylinder with a V-8. Not just any any V-8, but twin-turbo, twin cam, 32-valve howler. Designed for power, not refinement, the Esprit engine put out 350-horsepower and 89 decibels of noise at full throttle. Sixty mph was reached in 4.4 seconds. Top speed was about 175. Because the new engine weighed not much more than the four, the Esprit's excellent handling was unaffected. Build quality also continued to improve with the V-8. Of all the Esprits, this is the most desirable.

FOR Neck snapping performance • Handling • Smooth ride for a performance car

AGAINST Loud • Still the same cramped cockpit

PRODUCTION

1996 260 1997 177 1998 241 1999 250

SPECIFICATIONS

Length (in.)	172.0
Weight (lbs)	3045
Wheelbase (in.)	96.0
Price (new)	$79,325-83,000

ENGINES

cid/type	bhp	years
214/dohc V-8[1]	350	1996-00

[1]Turbocharged

PRICES

1997 Model:	
FAIR	$50,000-55,000
GOOD	$55,000-60,000
FINE	$60,000-65,000

2000-2010 RETURN Depreciating

1931-33
MARMON SIXTEEN

The fabulous, 100-mph grand classic that evidently had more state-of-the-art engineering than any other multi-cylinder motorcar of the day. Remarkably light for its size—bodies used aluminum extensively—and uncommonly elegant. Styled by pioneer industrial designer Walter Dorwin Teague and his son, Walter Jr. A clean vee'd radiator, deep doors, minimal ornamentation, a low roofline, and fender flanges to hide shocks and other chassis bits were common to all models. LeBaron did the standard closed bodies, Waterhouse a couple of tourers, and Hayes a victoria to an Alexis de Sakhnoffsky design; the last cost a formidable $5700. More styles were offered in 1932, but by then the limited demand for multi-cylinder luxury cars had been gobbled up by Cadillac's Sixteen, which had arrived on the market a year earlier than Marmon's. Auto production stopped in 1933. A revival attempt that included Harry Miller (successful Indy car constructor of the Twenties) failed. Truck production continued into the Eighties and the company is still making truck components.

✚ FOR Outstanding performance • Sensational coachwork • A design and engineering paragon that's long been on every knowledgeable historian's "10 Best American Cars" list • A CCCA Classic

▬ AGAINST Extremely scarce • Stratospheric prices

PRODUCTION
350 (est.)

SPECIFICATIONS
Length (in.)	NA
Wheelbase (in.)	145.0
Weight (lbs)	5090-5440
Price (new)	$4825-5900

ENGINES
cid/type	bhp	years
490.8/ohv V-16	200	1931-33

PRICES
Open	
FAIR	$50,000-90,000
GOOD	$90,000-125,000
FINE	$125,000-180,000
Closed	
FAIR	$15,000-35,000
GOOD	$35,000-60,000
FINE	$60,000-80,000

FINE 1933 CONVERTIBLE SEDAN PRICE HISTORY
1982	$65,000	1990	$185,000
1994	$175,000	1998	$175,000
1982-2000 RETURN 6%			
2000-2010 6%			

1946-50
MASERATI A6/1500

1946-50 A6 coupe

The first road-going Maserati, built and sold in extremely small numbers and offered in two-seat closed coupe or open cabriolet body styles designed by Pinin Farina. The front end on both was smooth, marked by a radiator similar to that of Maserati's racing machines. In overall shape, there was a slight resemblance to the Lancia Aurelia coupe. The A6/1500 naturally owed much to the competition "Masers," including its large-diameter-tube chassis with coil-spring independent front suspension and conventional live-axle rear suspension. The engine was an sohc six developed from a late-'30s racing unit. It was very small for a six, and produced only 65 horsepower, so the car was not very fast—the factory claimed only 94 mph tops. It wasn't very exciting to drive, either, and expensive when new, but it's a high-interest collectible as the first of the great Maserati road cars.

✚ FOR Historical interest • Reliable engine • Solid chassis • Rarity

▬ AGAINST Parts nonexistent today • Not very fast • Crudely finished • Difficult to find, and expensive when you do

PRODUCTION
60

SPECIFICATIONS
Length (in.)	160.0
Wheelbase (in.)	100.4
Weight (lbs)	1765
Price (new)	NA

ENGINES
cc/type (cid)	bhp[1]	years
1488/sohc I-6 (91)	65	1946-50

[1]Net

PRICES
Conv	
FAIR	$20,000-40,000
GOOD	$40,000-60,000
FINE	$60,000-75,000
Sports-Racing models to $350,000	

FINE CONVERTIBLE PRICE HISTORY
1982	$35,000	1990	$150,000
1994	$75,000	1998	$75,000
1982-2000 RETURN 4%			
2000-2010 5%			

1951-57
MASERATI AG6 & AG6/2000

Successor to the A6/1500 as Maserati's "production" model, and based on a similar chassis and mechanical layout. Powered initially by a larger single-overhead-cam six, later revised with a dohc engine that was essentially a detuned version of Maserati's sports-racing/Grand Prix unit. All models featured two-seat custom-built bodies. Design work was

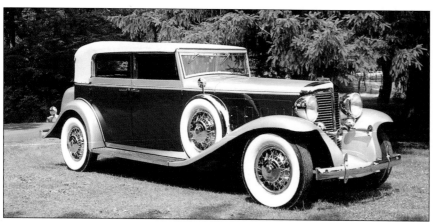
1932 Sixteen convertible sedan

1951-57 AG6 coupe by Zagato

handled by Vignale, Frua, Zagato, Allemano, and—with the sohc engine only—Pinin Farina. Styling differed according to coachbuilder, the only common link being the grille.

➕ FOR As for 1946-50 A6/1500, plus more performance with twincam engine

➖ AGAINST As for A6/1500

PRODUCTION

sohc engine 16 **dohc engine** 59

SPECIFICATIONS

Length (in.)	154.0 average
Wheelbase (in.)	100.4
Weight (lbs)	1900 average
Price (new)	NA

ENGINES

cc/type (cid)	bhp[1]	years
1954/sohc I-6 (119)	100	1951-53
1985/dohc I-6 (121)	150	1953-57

[1]Net

PRICES

Recent prices for very good to fine examples: **Frua cabrios** (5 built) $100,000-200,000; **2000s** by Zagato, Frua, and Allemano $150,000-300,000.

FINE ZAGATO PRICE HISTORY

1982 $50,000	**1990** $450,000
1994 $300,000	**1998** $300,000
1982-2000 RETURN NA	
2000-2010 10%	

1957-64
MASERATI 3500GT/GTI

The first Maserati produced in any significant numbers. Like many Italian exotics of the day, it was built on a simple, robust chassis composed of large-diameter tubes. All bodies were custom made in the Italian tradition, and the maximum production rate was

1963 3500GT coupe

just 10 cars per week. A coupe, supplied mostly by Touring, and a Spyder roadster, by Vignale, were offered. The former was marked by straight-through fenderlines and the characteristic air vents in the front fenders behind the wheel openings. Power was supplied by an enlarged version of Maserati's famous dohc Grand Prix engine of the '50s, with mechanical fuel injection (GTI) from 1962 on. Also at that time, all cars got four-wheel disc brakes. As befits a small specialist manufacturer, no two 3500GTs were exactly the same, customers being able to specify changes from the "standard" spec to suit their individual needs and tastes.

➕ FOR High performance (130 mph maximum) • Strong, reliable engine • Fine brakes • Handsome styling • Roadability • Racing heritage • Milestone status

➖ AGAINST Factory now out of parts • Most survivors have seen hard lives • Injection tricky to service

PRODUCTION

2223

SPECIFICATIONS

Length (in.)	180.0
Wheelbase (in.)	102.3
Weight (lbs)	3400
Price (new)	$11,400 U.S. list price in 1960

ENGINES

cc/type (cid)	bhp[1]	years
3485/dohc I-6 (213)	220/235	1957-64

[1]Net bhp for carbureted/injected engine

PRICES

Cpe	
FAIR	$15,000-25,000
GOOD	$25,000-33,000
FINE	$33,000-40,000
Spyder	
FAIR	$30,000-45,000
GOOD	$45,000-65,000
FINE	$65,000-80,000

FINE COUPE PRICE HISTORY

1982 $12,000	**1990** $85,000
1994 $40,000	**1998** $40,000
1982-2000 RETURN 7%	
2000-2010 7%	

1962-66
MASERATI SEBRING

1964 Sebring Series I coupe

Rebodied, modernized successor to the 3500GTI, sharing the same chassis and drivetrain. Built exclusively with Vignale coachwork, it was a ruggedly styled two-seat notchback coupe marked by quad headlamps and an eggcrate grille incorporating a prominent Maserati trident emblem.

➕ FOR As for 1958-64 3500GT/GTI

➖ AGAINST As for 1958-64 3500GT/GTI

PRODUCTION

Series I 348 **Series II** 98

SPECIFICATIONS

Length (in.)	176.0
Wheelbase (in.)	102.3
Weight (lbs)	3330
Price (new)	NA

ENGINES

cc/type	bhp[1]	years
3485/dohc I-6	235	1962-64
3694/dohc I-6	245	1965-66
4104/dohc I-6	255	1966

[1]Net

PRICES

FAIR	$12,000-20,000
GOOD	$20,000-30,000
FINE	$30,000-40,000

FINE EXAMPLE PRICE HISTORY

1982 $11,500	**1990** $65,000

1994 $35,000   **1998** $35,000
1982-2000 RETURN 8%
2000-2010 8%

MASERATI MISTRAL

A sportier-looking running mate to the Sebring coupe, with sleek styling by Pietro Frua and better performance via extra displacement from Maserati's twincam engine. Both the fastback coupe and Spyder roadster bore Frua's characteristic design themes: long, sloping hood leading down to a blade-like front bumper surmounting the grille; a tall, glassy greenhouse; rounded corners; and a high, short tail. The coupe featured a lift-up wraparound rear window/hatch, and the Spyder was quite close to Frua's later AC 428 in overall appearance. Acceleration was electrifying, yet the Mistral (named for a hot desert wind) was at its best on the open road, which it could devour with prodigious ease.

➕ FOR As for 1962-66 Sebring, plus handsome Frua lines, more go

➖ AGAINST As for 1962-66 Sebring

PRODUCTION

Cpe 828 **Spyder** 120

SPECIFICATIONS

Length (in.)	177.0
Wheelbase (in.)	94.4
Weight (lbs)	approx. 2800
Price (new)	$14,700 U.S. in 1968

ENGINES

cc/type (cid)	bhp[1]	years
3485/dohc I-6 (213)	235	1963

3964/dohc I-6 (225)	245	1964-70
4012/dohc I-6 (245)	255	1966-70

[1]Net

PRICES

Cpe	
FAIR	$12,500-20,000
GOOD	$20,000-30,000
FINE	$30,000-40,000
Spyder	
FAIR	$30,000-55,000
GOOD	$55,000-80,000
FINE	$80,000-100,000

FINE COUPE PRICE HISTORY

1982 $15,000		**1990** $62,500	
1994 $32,500		**1998** $40,000	

1982-2000 RETURN 6%
2000-2010 5%

MASERATI QUATTRO- PORTE

1963-65 Quattoporte sedan

A four-seat Italian supercar with four-door convenience was a rarity in the '60s. It still is, which makes the Quattroporte (Italian for "four doors") an unusual collectible for high-performance enthusiasts. Once again, Maserati gave its styling brief to Pietro Frua, who devised an interesting mix of curves and angles for this very large

GT. As on his Mistral, the sedan's greenhouse was tall, very glassy, and showed noticeable curvature. A jutting "mouth" carrying the Maserati trident was flanked by twin rectangular headlamps, changed to four round units on later European and all U.S. models. The chassis was a combination of tubular and box-section elements, and incorporated disc brakes for all wheels. A de Dion rear suspension was used initially, but was later discarded in favor of a less troublesome, bog-simple live axle on semi-elliptic leaf springs. Power was supplied by a four-cam V-8, essentially a "prodified" version of the mighty 450S racing engine of the late '50s. This would continue as Maserati's main powerplant well into the '70s. For the Quattroporte, it was destroked to 4.2 liters, then upped to 4.7 with the switch in rear suspension. Of the total number built, approximately 500 cars got the larger power unit. Aside from Iso's unsuccessful S4 Fidia, no other producer of high-performance GTs tried the GT sedan idea, though Aston Martin thought about it. Maserati gave up on it for a few years, partly due to financial troubles, but brought out another Quattroporte for the European market in 1979.

➕ FOR Supercar go with four-door convenience • Distinctive design • Sumptuous, spacious cabin • Fast (130 mph) • Reliable engine • Not costly, all things considered

➖ AGAINST Thirsty • Questionable body construction • Trouble-prone de Dion suspension on early examples • Costly to restore and run • Not likely to go up in value very rapidly

PRODUCTION

759

SPECIFICATIONS

Length (in.)	196.0
Wheelbase (in.)	108.0
Weight (lbs)	3810
Price (new)	$15,000 U.S.

ENGINES

cc/type (cid)	bhp[1]	years
4136/dohc V-8 (253)	260	1963-68
4719/dohc V-8 (288)	290	1968-69

[1]Net

PRICES

FAIR	$5500-9000
GOOD	$9000-13,000
FINE	$13,000-17,000

FINE EXAMPLE PRICE HISTORY

1982 $12,000		**1990** $20,000	
1994 $15,000		**1998** $17,000	

1982-2000 RETURN 2%
2000-2010 2%

1963-70 Mistral coupe

1965-68
MASERATI MEXICO

1967 Mexico coupe

A high-style, four-seat notchback coupe built on a short-wheelbase version of the Quattroporte sedan's platform chassis. Styling and body construction were by the Vignale coachworks, marked by a low beltline, slim roof pillars, a broad hood, wide grille, four headlamps, and squared-up rear wheel openings. Fitted exclusively with the Quattroporte's leaf-spring rear suspension, not the earlier de Dion arrangement, and genuine wire wheels. The larger-displacement rendition of Maserati's quad-cam V-8 was tuned to produce 330 bhp in this application. Like the sedan, the Mexico was fitted with ZF five-speed manual transmission.

✚ FOR As for 1963-70 Quattroporte, but rarer, with two doors • Clean looks • Scarcity

◼ AGAINST As for 1963-70 Quattroporte

PRODUCTION
250

SPECIFICATIONS
Length (in.)	187.4
Wheelbase (in.)	103.5
Weight (lbs)	3640
Price (new)	NA

ENGINES
cc/type (cid)	bhp[1]	years
4136/dohc V-8 (253)	260	1965-68
4719/dohc V-8 (288)	330	1965-68
[1]Net

PRICES
FAIR	$7500-12,000
GOOD	$12,000-20,000
FINE	$20,000-30,000

FINE EXAMPLE PRICE HISTORY
1982 $12,750		**1990** $50,000	
1994 $30,000		**1998** $30,000	
1982-2000 RETURN 5%			
2000-2010 5%			

1967-73
MASERATI GHIBLI

R eplacement for the Mistral as Maserati's premium two-seat GT. The most memorable thing about the Ghibli is its styling—masculine yet sensuously curvy, with perfect proportions and adroit detailing courtesy of Giorgetto Giugiaro. The long snout sported flip-up headlamps at its leading edge, and the full-fastback roofline swept right back to a short, cropped tail panel. The low, ground-hugging appearance suggested considerable heft, and the steel-body Ghibli was indeed quite weighty (nearly two tons). Yet, it was capable of up to 160 mph thanks to extra displacement and output from the Maserati four-cam V-8. The chassis was basically the same as that of the Quattroporte/Mexico, still with the leaf-spring rear suspension, but the wheelbase was shorter. It was Maserati's best until it was replaced by the mid-engine Bora, and a rival for Ferrari's 375GTB/4 and the Lambor-ghini Miura in its heyday. Buying, restoring, and then running one will take an understanding banker, but even after two decades a Ghibli is one of the sexiest collectibles you can have in your garage.

✚ FOR Stunner styling (less so on street-legal U.S. models after 1970) • Amazing performance • Fine furnishings • Marvelous Maserati engine • Good appreciation potential • Affordable again after a wild ride in the early 1990s.

◼ AGAINST As for 1965-68 Mexico, plus early rust-out if the body's neglected • Fuelishness • Mixed assembly quality

PRODUCTION
Cpe 1149 **Spyder** 125

SPECIFICATIONS
Length (in.)	180.7
Wheelbase (in.)	100.4
Weight (lbs)	3745
Price (new)	$20,000 (1971 U.S. list price)

ENGINES
cc/type (cid)	bhp[1]	years
4719/dohc V-8 (288)	330	1967-70
4930/dohc V-8 (301)	355	1970-73
[1]Net

PRICES
Cpe	
FAIR	$15,000-25,000
GOOD	$25,000-32,000
FINE	$32,000-40,000
Spyder	
FAIR	$50,000-70,000
GOOD	$70,000-85,000
FINE	$85,000-100,000

FINE COUPE PRICE HISTORY
1982 $6250	**1990** $60,000
1994 $35,000	**1998** $40,000
1982-2000 RETURN 12%	
2000-2010 10%	

Note: many very professional conversions of coupes to Spyders exist. Such cars are not subject to the above price scale for genuine Spyders. Insist on documentation of any Spyder's originality.

1967-69 Ghibli coupe (Quattroporte background)

1973 Indy coupe

1969-74
MASERATI INDY

Replaced the Mexico as Maserati's four-seat GT, and differed from the firm's other front engine V-8 cars in using steel unit body/chassis construction. Styling, by Vignale, was completely different in detail from that of the Ghia-bodied Ghibli, yet the two cars had some familial relationship, particularly in the long, shark-like nose with hidden headlamps. The Indy sported a longer greenhouse with a prominent B-pillar, however, and rode a longer 102.5-inch wheelbase. It was more a 2+2 than a genuine four-seater, yet nonetheless proved popular, and offered the bonus of generous (for the class) luggage space under a large rear hatch. A ZF manual or an optional automatic transmission were offered as on other V-8 Maseratis. The Indy was dropped during an ownership change in 1975-76 when Maserati was taken over (briefly as it turned out) by Citroën.

✚ FOR Neat, trim lines • Four-seat accommodation • High flyer (155 mph) • Engine parts still available

▬ AGAINST Unit-construction rust worries • Body panels very difficult to find • Thirsty • Costly to restore and insure

PRODUCTION
1136

SPECIFICATIONS
Length (in.)	186.6
Wheelbase (in.)	102.5
Weight (lbs)	3640
Price (new)	$18,500 (1970 U.S. list price)

ENGINES
cc/type (cid)	bhp[1]	years
4136/dohc V-8 (253)	260	1969-72
4719/dohc V-8 (288)	330	1972-73
4930/dohc V-8 (301)	355	1973-74

[1]Net

PRICES
FAIR	$10,000-16,000
GOOD	$16,000-23,000
FINE	$23,000-30,000

FINE EXAMPLE PRICE HISTORY
1982 $6000	**1990** $55,000
1994 $32,500	**1998** $32,000
1982-2000 RETURN 10%	
2000-2010 10%	

1971-80
MASERATI BORA

The first evidence of what would be a fairly brief Citroën/Maserati alliance. It was introduced at the 1971 Geneva salon, with production beginning the following year, and unusual in using Citroën's high-pressure hydraulics to power its brakes. The same system also actuated the standard power seats, and unusually the pedals were adjustable as well. Power was provided by Maserati's well-proven quad-cam V-8 mounted longitudinally amidships and driving the rear wheels through a ZF five-speed gearbox. Initially, displacement was 4.7 liters for the European market, but U.S. models used the larger 4.9-liter version as in the Ghibli and, later, the Khamsin. The mid-engine layout afforded a natural rear weight bias that obviated the need for power steering. Aggressively muscular styling by Giorgetto Giugiaro featured a short, pointy nose, bulging bodysides, a full fastback roof tapering to a sharply cut-off tail, neatly upswept door windows, and a squat, powerful-looking stance. Roomy for a mid-engine two-seater, it was also surprisingly refined. Naturally, it was fast, with 0-60 mph coming up in about 7.5 seconds from rest, with a top end of 160 mph available for those who could indulge such things. Maserati's up-and-down financial fortunes in the '70s, aggravated by a sudden drop in the supercar market following the 1973-74 Arab oil embargo, made the Bora a very expensive commodity. Ultimately, high price and high fuel consumption forced the end of production. Not a high-appreciation item at first, but it seems certain to gain in stature.

✚ FOR Powerful looks • Powerful performance • Surprisingly light and easy to drive • Phenomenal roadability • Engine parts still available • Dash like a 747's

1973 Bora coupe

■ AGAINST Easily confused with tamer Merak cousin • Thirsty • Costly to acquire and maintain • Brakes take getting used to

PRODUCTION

571

SPECIFICATIONS

Length (in.)	181.0
Wheelbase (in.)	102.3
Weight (lbs)	approx. 3800
Price (new)	$26,900 U.S. in 1973, rising to $39,900 in 1978

ENGINES

cc/type (cid)	bhp[1]	years
4709/dohc V-8 (287.4)	310	1971-74
4930/dohc V-8 (300.8)	320[2]	1975-80

[1]Net [2]280 U.S.

PRICES

FAIR	$17,500-27,500
GOOD	$27,500-40,000
FINE	$40,000-50,000

FINE EXAMPLE PRICE HISTORY

1982 $18,000		**1990** $120,000	
1994 $60,000		**1998** $52,000	
1982-2000 RETURN 6%			
2000-2010 5%			

1972 - 83
MASERATI MERAK

Very much a little brother to the V-8 Bora, sharing its wheelbase, forward body structure, and mid-engine configuration. But the Merak was arguably more Citroën than Maserati, borrowing the Maserati-designed dohc V-6 engine, five-speed transmission, and even the dashboard from the Citroën SM. The Merak also differed

1979 Merak SS coupe

from the Bora in rear structure, having a flat rear deck and nonstructural "flying buttresses" that carried the roofline down to the tail panel instead of a hatch and glassed-in rear quarters. It also made use of Citroën hydraulics for its all-disc braking system, but lacked the Bora's hydraulically adjustable seats. The 90-degree V-6 was shorter than it was wide, so it was mounted fore/aft instead of transversely as in Ferrari's 308 series. In fact, the Merak used the SM's entire front-wheel-drive package turned around 180 degrees, which left room for a pair of tiny rear seats suitable only for infants. Lighter and a bit more economical than the Bora, but not as fast—0-60 mph in around nine seconds. Meraks sent to the U.S. up to 1977 suffered compared to their Italian counterparts in having unsightly bulges in the rear decklid to provide air cleaner clearance. Following the dissolution of the Citroën/ Maserati "marriage" and Maserati's subsequent takeover by Alejandro de Tomaso, a revised version called the Merak/SS was issued in 1976, which did away with the bulge as well as the SM dash (replaced by fittings from the by-now discontinued Bora). Withdrawn from the U.S. market after 1979, it became a victim of surging fuel prices

and inflation.

☙ FOR Giugiaro styling • Splendid roadability • Marginal +2 seating, unusual for a mid-engine GT • Comfortable, well-appointed cockpit

■ AGAINST Looks outsized now • Not that thrifty with fuel • Same cam-drive problems and hydraulic system worries that plagued the SM • Odd Citroën dash in early models • Modest collector following at present

PRODUCTION

1666

SPECIFICATIONS

Length (in.)	180.0
Wheelbase (in.)	102.3
Weight (lbs)	approx. 3200
Price (new)	$19,975 U.S. in 1974, rising to $40,550 in 1981

ENGINES

cc/type (cid)	bhp[1]	years
2965/dohc V-6 (181)	180-182[2]	1972-83
1999/dohc V-6 (122)	170[3]	1976-79

[1]SAE net [2]190-220 for Europe [3]Italian market only

PRICES

FAIR	$10,000-15,000
GOOD	$15,000-22,500
FINE	$22,500-30,000

FINE EXAMPLE PRICE HISTORY

1982 $15,000		**1990** $40,000	
1994 $30,000		**1998** $30,000	
1982-2000 RETURN 4%			
2000-2010 5%			

1974 - 82
MASERATI KHAMSIN

1977-82 Khamsin coupe

It wasn't easy to follow a styling masterwork like the Ghibli, but Bertone succeeded with its show-stopping successor. Following Maserati's practice of naming its cars after fierce desert winds, it was dubbed Khamsin, and debuted at the 1972 Turin show to replace the Giugiaro-designed car as Maserati's big front-engine GT. Its dashing contours were highlighted by marked tumblehome on a low greenhouse, a very long hood with asymmetrically placed lateral cooling louvers, hidden headlamps, and a Kammstyle tail panel with a glass insert between the taillamps to assist rearward vision in what was a fairly low car. The snug cabin afforded a low seating position up front and occasional rear accommodation on a none-too-comfortable, thinly padded bench. Like its predecessor, the Khamsin utilized a front-engine/rear-drive configuration and the powerful Maserati quad-cam V-8. Unlike the Ghibli, though, it had fully independent rear suspension—A-arms and coil springs—instead of a solid axle on leaf springs. Reflecting Maserati's then-current partnership with Citroën, the Khamsin used the French firm's high-pressure hydraulic system for power assistance to the steering and brakes, and even the clutch. The result was a driving feel unique among Italian supercars. The steering, for instance, required only two turns lock-to-lock, and would automatically self-center with the vehicle at standstill. A ZF five-speed manual gearbox put the power to the road (automatic was optional), which meant about seven seconds to 60 mph for a determined driver and easy three-figure cruising speeds. Withdrawn from the U.S. market after 1979, but produced through 1982 for Europe and other areas.

✛ FOR Sex appeal • High performance, Italian style • Finely balanced handling/roadholding • Light controls • Ride still firm, but more comfortable than Ghibli's

◼ AGAINST Thirsty (12 mpg or so) • Complex mechanicals, so frequent (and costly) service a must • Dealers aren't everywhere • Erratic construction quality

PRODUCTION
421

SPECIFICATIONS

Length (in.)	180.0
Wheelbase (in.)	100.3
Weight (lbs)	approx. 3800
Price (new)	$32,975 U.S. list in 1975; $42,600 in 1978

ENGINES

cc/type (cid)	bhp[1]	years
4930/dohc V-8 (301)	280-315[2]	1974-82

[1]SAE net [2]320 bhp for Europe

PRICES

FAIR	$12,000-16,000
GOOD	$16,000-27,500
FINE	$27,500-35,000

FINE EARLY EXAMPLE PRICE HISTORY

1982 $17,500		1990 $70,000	
1994 $40,000		1998 $40,000	

1982-2000 RETURN 4%
2000-2010 5%

MASERATI KYALAMI

An early result of Maserati's 1975 takeover by Alessandro deTomaso after the breakup of its "marriage" with Citroën. Really a badge-engineered version of DeTomaso's Longchamp, which in turn was a shortened coupe derivative of his earlier Jaguar XJ6-ish Deauville sedan. Shared the Longchamps all-steel unit structure, all-independent suspension, and essential Frua styling, but had dual headlamps, Maserati "trident" grille, and Maser V-8s (instead of small-block Fords). The first 100 Kyalamis (named for the South African Grand Prix circuit) carried the 4.1-liter unit; the senior 4.9-liter became optional from 1978, though slightly detuned from its applications in the mid-engine Bora and front-engine Khamsin (see entries). A ZF five-speed manual transmission was standard, Chrysler TorqueFlite optional (versus the Longchamps' Ford automatic). A low-cost but ultimately unsuccessful attempt at boosting Maserati sales during a difficult time, but a rare and worthy special-interest

semi-exotic with obvious collector-car potential. Genuine Maser power merits its inclusion here instead of the Longchamp (or Deauville). Effectively replaced by the BMW-like Biturbo as the "mass-market" Maserati.

✛ FOR Uncommon, especially in U.S. • Genuine Maserati V-8s • Good performance (minimum top speed 145 mph, 0-60 in under 8 seconds)

◼ AGAINST Lesser-known Maser with half-breed image • Weak parts/service backup in U.S. • So-so workmanship • Not often or widely traded in U.S.

PRODUCTION
150

SPECIFICATIONS

Length (in.)	180.0
Wheelbase (in.)	102.3
Weight (lbs)	3835
Price (new)	est. $30,000 U.S. equivalent

ENGINES

cc/type(cid)	bhp[1]	years
4136/dohc V-8 (252.4)	255	1977-83
4930/dohc V-8 (301)	280	1978-83

[1]SAE net

PRICES

FAIR	$12,000-15,000
GOOD	$15,000-20,000
FINE	$20,000-27,500

FINE EXAMPLE PRICE HISTORY

Depreciating in early 1980s, but turned around later in the decade, then hit $60,000 at the peak of the boom in 1990. Prices have been stable since, and will probably remain so.
2000-2010 RETURN 2%

1977-83 Kyalami coupe

1979-89
MASERATI QUATTROPORTE

1979 Quattroporte sedan

Maserati's second luxury sedan, not counting the aborted Bertone-styled, V-6-powered "Quattroporte II" of 1974 (only five built). Like Kyalami, another early Alessandro de Tomaso idea for putting Maserati back in the black after he took control following the end of Maserati's short-lived "marriage" with Citroën. Apparently difficult to finalize and market, however: the debut came in 1976, but deliveries did not start in earnest until 1981-82. Sized close to Jaguar's XJ6 and even had a similar independent rear suspension, but somewhat heavier owing to robust separate chassis and full-house equipment. Initially offered with the small 4.1-liter version of Maserati's brilliant twin-cam V-8, but the 4.9 option was standardized in 1985 for best performance and because customers had been ordering it. A five-speed manual gearbox was available in Europe, but the three-speed Chrysler TorqueFlite automatic was the sole transmission during an on-again/off-again U.S. sales effort that ended shortly after Maserati announced the smaller, more affordable Biturbo as its mainstay seller. The QP continued elsewhere, though, and 1987 brought slightly more power, extra equipment, and a new name—Royale—before assemblies ceased some two years later.

⊞ FOR Surprising performance (with automatic, 0-60 under 10 seconds, 120+ mph all out) • Fine handling despite size and weight • Leather-lined opulence • Rare everywhere

▣ AGAINST Parts/service support rare, especially in U.S. • Thirsty • Head room slim • Detail finish less than Teutonic • Sedan configuration works against it as a collectible

PRODUCTION

NA, but limited

SPECIFICATIONS

Length (in.)	196.0
Wheelbase (in.)	110.2
Weight (lbs)	4750
Price (new)	$63,000-67,000

ENGINES

cc/type (cid)	bhp[1]	years
4136/dohc V-8 (252)	260	1979-84
4930/dohc V-8 (301)	288	1985-89

[1]SAE net

PRICES

1984-86 Models

FINE	$8000-10,000
GOOD	$10,000-13,000
FINE	$13,000-15,000

2000-2010 RETURN Even

1978-85
MAZDA RX-7

The first affordable small GT since the original Datsun Z-car. Initiated in 1974 as Project X605; Japanese sales commenced in 1978 (as the Savanna), U.S. sales for model-year '79. The design was orthodox apart from a compact two-rotor Wankel engine in "front midships" position—but modern: all-coil suspension with front MacPherson struts and trailing-arm/Watt-linkage live rear axle, front-disc/rear-drums brakes, recirculating-ball steering (with available power assist). Mazda had been perfecting Dr. Felix Wankel's engine since acquiring a license from Germany's NSU, and the RX-7's proved even more reliable than earlier Mazda rotaries, yet no less turbine-smooth. Economy still not great, but only in relation to horsepower, which remained remarkable for the small displacement. This RX-7 was built only as a hatchback coupe in several trim/equipment levels. Americans initially got base S and better-equipped GS models. Both were facelifted inside and out for 1981, when a new GSL arrived with standard rear discs, limited-slip differential, alloy wheels, and power windows. A slightly larger six-port engine with fuel injection powered an even better GSL-SE from 1984. RX-7s dominated sub-2-liter production-class racing in these years, and also did well in rallies. Pert and fun to drive, yet practical, they're among today's few genuinely collectible Asian cars, though significant value appreciation is still a long way off.

⊞ FOR Good go (8.5-9.5 seconds 0-60) • Nimble two-seater handling • Fine ergonomics • Hatchback practicality • Well-built • Near-bulletproof engine • Very affordable

▣ AGAINST Cockpit cramped for six-footers • Not much baggage space • Very rust-prone without special care • Stiffish ride • Tail-happy at times

PRODUCTION

1978 72,692 **1979** 71,617 **1980** 56,317 **1981** 59,686 **1982** 59,686 **1983** 57,684 **1984** 63,959 **1985** 63,105

SPECIFICATIONS

Length (in.)	169.0
Wheelbase (in.)	95.3
Weight (lbs)	2440-2640
Price (new)	$6995-15,295 in U.S.

ENGINES

cid/type	bhp	years
70/2-rotor Wankel	100	1978-85
80/2-rotor Wankel	135	1984-85

PRICES

Still governed by used car market. Ranges from $1200-5000 (1978) to $1300-3000 (1985).
2000-2010 RETURN Even

1984 RX-7 coupe

1986-91
MAZDA RX-7

1990 RX-7 Turbo coupe

Mazda's second-generation rotary sports car. Much like the original in size and format, but some 250 pounds heavier. Styling new but still rather derivative—this time aping Porsche 928 and Chevy Camaro. Bowed with a slightly more potent version of the six-port 13B engine (from the previous GSL-SE) and with an intercooled Turbo II version (new to America but not Japan) delivering a remarkable 182 horses in U.S. trim. Simpler front suspension contrasted with more complex semi-trailing-arm rear-end geometry providing minor toe-in under high lateral loads. Standard all-disc brakes and, for some models, optional two-stage auto-adjusting shock absorbers. Standard five-speed manual gearbox across the board as before; non-turbos also offered with four-speed overdrive automatic (replacing a three-speed). U.S. offerings expanded to include a non-turbo coupe with the "+2" rear seating package previously restricted to Europe and Japan. A Sports Package (firm suspension, power steering, "aero" body add-ons) and a Luxury Package (power sunroof, better trim) were also added. Extra-cost antilock brakes arrived for certain '87 models and became a Turbo standard for 1989, when both engines got power boosts. In between came the first factory-built RX-7 convertible, a non-turbo two-seater. Second generation less popular than the first—mainly due to fast-rising prices in a lackluster economy plus stronger competition—but no less appealing. Replaced by yet another new RX-7 for 1992.

🔃 FOR As for 1978-85, plus more amenities and advent of convertible

▣ AGAINST As for 1978-85, but heavier and not as speedy or nimble

PRODUCTION

1986 72,760 **1987-90** NA

SPECIFICATIONS

Length (in.)	168.9
Wheelbase (in.)	95.7
Weight (lbs)	2625-3030
Price (new)	$11,995-26,530 in U.S.

ENGINES

cid/type	bhp	years
80/2-rotor Wankel	146	1986-89
80/2-rotor Wankel	160	1989-91
80/2-rotor Wankel[1]	182	1986-89
80/2-rotor Wankel[1]	200	1989-91
[1]Turbocharged		

PRICES

Coupe	
FAIR	$1500-4500
GOOD	$4500-6000
FINE	$6000-7500

Still governed by used car market.
2000-2010 RETURN Depreciating

1988-91
MAZDA RX-7 CONVERTIBLE

Handsome, second-generation model of Mazda's innovative rotary-engine sports car was British in character, sophisticated-Japanese in origins and execution. The RX-7 evoked the best of both of those motoring worlds, with slick good looks, capable handling, marvelous cruising attributes, and dependable engineering and quality. Convertible was heavy, and could be had only with a normally aspirated, 80-cid 146-bhp 2-rotor Wankel. The ragtop was no road burner: the 0-60 run was managed in about 10.3 seconds and top speed was 125 mph. (A far more muscular 182-horse Turbo was available with the coupe only.) Drawbacks aside, the RX-7 ragtop was glorious at the 2000-3200-rpm mid-range.

🔃 FOR Precise steering • Flick-of-the-wrist 5-speed stick • Good ergonomics • Easy-to-use convertible top • Still in pretty good supply

▣ AGAINST Acceleration • Japanese nameplate

PRODUCTION

6000 (U.S. sales)

SPECIFICATIONS

Length (in.)	168.9
Weight (lbs)	3003
Wheelbase (in.)	95.7
Price (new)	$21,000-27,715

ENGINES

cid/type	bhp	years
80/2-rotor Wankel	146-160	1988-91

PRICES

1988-91 Models	
FAIR	$4250-7000
GOOD	$7000-9000
FINE	$9000-11,000

2000-2010 RETURN Depreciating

1988 RX-7 convertible

1990-2000

MAZDA MX-5 MIATA (INCLUDING LIMITED EDITIONS)

Japanese "retro" sports car in the MGB/Triumph Spitfire mold, but not a copy of anything old or new, and not a "corporate kit car," either. Idea instigated by American auto writer Bob Hall, and major styling input from Mazda R&D in California (which later hired him), but the engineering work was done in Japan. A front-engine/rear-drive open two-seater of fairly orthodox design, with all-independent coil-spring suspension, twin-cam 16-valve four, all-disc power brakes, rack-and-pinion steering (assisted at extra cost), and a winsome, surprisingly spacious monocoque body with a simple-as-pie manual soft-top. A unique truss-like "Power Plant Frame" with an additional longitudinal stiffening member provided uncommonly good torsional rigidity. Initially offered with a five-speed manual gearbox, but a four-speed automatic option was soon added to the detriment of both performance and economy. Much better performing than most low-cost British sports cars of yore. Better equipped, too (heater, driver's airbag, full carpeting). Extras

ran to a lightweight lift-off hardtop, air, limited-slip differential, and two package options with items like alloy wheels, cruise control, and power windows. Many factory-approved dealer accessories, too. Instant high demand sent prices way above sticker during the first 18 months, but that particular type of "Miata Mania" later quieted down. Other types didn't, including owners who eagerly went club racing and aftermarket vendors who offered all sorts of cosmetic and hop-up items. The factory offered a Limited Edition almost every year of production. Most were color and trim variations of the standard Miata. An exception was the R Package—available from 1994 until '99 when it became the Sport Package. The R Miata was aimed at the weekend "club racer" with track oriented sport suspension and a limited-slip differential. Miatas are still selling briskly (with improvements), so too soon to predict ultimate collectibility, but we'd bet that Miatas will be as coveted tomorrow as Spits and Spridgets are today.

FOR Terrific styling • Terrific open-air fun • Delightfully revvy engine • Decent go (8.6 seconds 0-60) • Practical for a two-seater • Fine ergonomics • Japanese reliability • Still current

AGAINST Anti-Japan bias among some enthusiasts • Too new and numerous for any near-term value appreciation • Tiny trunk

PRODUCTION
approx. 83,000

SPECIFICATIONS
Length (in.)	155.4
Wheelbase (in.)	89.2
Weight (lbs)	2182-2250
Price (new)	$13,800-23,995

ENGINES
cid/type	bhp	years
97/dohc I-4	116	1990-93
118/dohc I-4	128-140	1994-00

PRICES
1991-96 Models
FAIR	$4000-8000
GOOD	$8000-12,000
FINE	$12,000-17,500

Still governed by used car market.
2000-2010 RETURN Depreciating

1993-95

MAZDA RX7

1993 RX-7 coupe

A sports car that should have been more sucessful. After gaining weight with the second generation RX7, Mazda got back to sports car basics with a taut third generation. A more powerful rotary motor could push the bantam-weight two-seater to sixty

1999 MX-5 Miata roadster

in less than six seconds. Handling was even better than performance. Razor sharp steering and tenacious grip made the Mazda a joy on twisting roads. The price for this entertainment was a harsh ride—especially with the firmer suspension of R-1 and R-2 models. The rounded body seemed to be shrink-wrapped around the mechanical components. The tight interior had a comfortable glove-like fit for all but taller drivers. High prices, declining sport coupe market, and reliablity problems comspired to cut short the car's run in the U.S. The RX7 should find the sucess that eluded it while new in the collectors market.

FOR A blast to drive • Unusual rotary motor • Strong brakes

AGAINST Poor quality—especially 1993 models • Hard ride • Turbo lag makes for difficult around town driving

PRODUCTION[1]

1993 5,062 **1994** 2,212 **1995** 1,399
[1]U.S. calendar year sales

SPECIFICATIONS

Length (in.)	168.5
Weight (lbs)	2870
Wheelbase (in.)	95.5
Price (new)	$32,500-37,500

ENGINES

cid/type	bhp	years
81/2 rotor Wankel[1]	255	1993-95

[1]Turbocharged

PRICES

1988-91 Models:

FAIR	$4250-7000
GOOD	$7000-9000
FINE	$9000-11,000

2000-2010 RETURN Depreciating

1994-98
MCLAREN F1

McLaren, the British race car constructor, decided to build a road car. Not surprisingly, it was the fastest car in the world. Top speed was 231 mph and 0-60 took 3.2 seconds. The F1 was a clean-sheet design, with all components except the taillights built specifically for it. These components were light as possible. Cost was no object. Carbon fiber was used for the body panels and understructure. Virtually every mechanical component was of aluminum or magnesium. BMW Motorsports was contracted to design the 48-valve V-12 engine. The 6.1-liter motor developed 627-horsepower. The central driver's seat (placed between the two passenger seats) offered good visability and pedals could be optimally placed without interference from wheel arches. Despite its brute power, the F1 was well mannered on the road. Built for the road, it also proved itself at the track—winning the 1995 LeMans.

FOR Fastest car in the world • Beautiful workmanship • Engine docile a low speeds

AGAINST The most expensive car in the world • No ABS

PRODUCTION

NA

SPECIFICATIONS

Length (in.)	168.8
Weight (lbs)	2425
Wheelbase (in.)	107.0
Price (new)	$810,000-1,000,000 (est)

ENGINES

cid/type	bhp	years
370/dohc V-12	627	1994-98

PRICES

Not calculable from our data.Likely to hold at just under new car prices.Good potential for the future.

1996 F1 coupe

1 9 3 0 - 3 9

MERCEDES-BENZ TYPE 770 GROSSER

1931 Type 770 Grosser limousine (built for King Faisal of Iraq)

D-B's Depression-era flagship, announced four years after the merger between Daimler and Benz. Massive, powerful, and ponderous, it was intended for heads of state and certain political leaders, hence the use of the name "Grand." Smooth and dignified by German standards, and easy to drive slowly as well as quickly. It boasted a newly designed overhead-valve straight eight and supercharger, plus vacuum-servo brakes and an optional Maybach pre-selector gearbox, but ordinary beam axles front and rear and rather undistinguished—though lavishly furnished—bodywork. Some survivors are erroneously billed as the "Hitler Mercedes," though it's doubtful. Hitler had only one as his personal car. Emperor Hirohito of Japan bought seven, which he used into the 1960s.

FOR Period M-B flagship • Exclusivity and rarity • Cost-no-object engineering • A CCCA Classic

AGAINST Heavy styling • No parts for restoration • Very expensive; too much historical hype keeps them that way

PRODUCTION

117

SPECIFICATIONS

Length (in.)	210.0
Wheelbase (in.)	136.0
Weight (lbs)	6000+
Price (new)	NA

ENGINES

cc/type (cid)	bhp[1]	years
7655/ohv I-8 (467)	150/200	1930-37

[1]Net; supercharger out/in

PRICES

FAIR	$75,000-125,000
GOOD	$125,000-250,000
FINE	$250,000-$400,000

(High-end values are for open bodies.)

FINE PULLMAN PRICE HISTORY

1982	$150,000	1990	$500,000
1994	$400,000	1998	$400,000

1982-2000 RETURN 3%
2000-2010 3%

1 9 3 3 - 3 9

MERCEDES-BENZ 380K/500K/540K

Streamlined 1930s follow-up to the massive Porsche-designed S/SS/SSK of the late '20s. It had a supercharged straight eight with clutch-in blower as before, and added all-independent suspension, but it was more touring than sports car in character. The new engine design by Hans Nibel, one of his last works, was progressively enlarged. D-B's Sindelfingen works supplied the vulgar but impressive and comfortable bodies. Top speed was 90 mph for the 380K up to 105 mph+ for the 540K. It was D-B's ultimate in this period apart from the Grossers and priced accordingly, hence the low production. Though ideal for swishing along Hitler's new autobahnen, it took harder work on twisting roads (no power steering, but hydraulic brakes on later cars). Styling was the great selling point, especially on the beautifully streamlined 500/540 Special Roadster. It has the distinction now as being among the most expensive of collector cars.

FOR German period styling • 500/540 performance • Mercedes reliability • Latter-day charisma/value • A true Classic

1939 540K Cabriolet

AGAINST Very expensive to buy and restore • Heavy fuel consumption • Hard work to drive • No body and few mechanical parts to be found

PRODUCTION

380K 114 (1933-34) **500K** 354 (1934-36) **540K** 447 (1936-39)

SPECIFICATIONS

Length (in.)	185-205
Wheelbase (in.)	123.5/129.5 (380K/500 and 540K)
Weight (lbs)	4500-5100
Price (new)	$12,000 U.S. in 1936-39

ENGINES

cc/type (cid)	bhp[1]	years
3823/ohv I-8 (233)	90/120	1933-34[2]
5019/ohv I-8 (306)	100/160	1934-36[3]
5401/ohv I-8 (330)	115/180	1936-39[4]

1936 500K roadster

¹Net; supercharger out/in ²380 ³500 ⁴540

PRICES

Headline-grabbing prices for Classic Mercedes have been broadcast for several decades, and the market remains strong. Ranges for very good to fine examples quoted in 1990-91 dealer publications ranged from $500,000 to $1.5m. Prices have since returned to half or less of those levels. Recent auction prices for cabriolets up to $275,000 (not sold), for TB convertible $185,000 (sold).
2000-2010 RETURN Not predictable

1938-40

MERCEDES-BENZ TYPE 770 GROSSER

Titanic successor to the original Grosser, built largely for the greater glory of the Third Reich. Heavier and more ostentatious, with a slightly more powerful version of the previous straight eight. More up to date, with oval-tube chassis, coil-spring independent front suspension, and de Dion rear suspension, all as per D-B's most recent Grand Prix racers. As with the earlier model, production was strictly to

1938 Type 770 Grosser open limousine

special order. Predictably, most were reserved for Adolf Hitler and his cronies and had gargantuan bodies with armor plating.

✚ FOR Rarity • Presence • More modern styling, engineering • Most of M-B's best in this period • CCCA Classic status

▬ AGAINST As big and heavy as they come—and as impractical • No parts for restoration • Amazingly expensive to buy and own • Little to excite the enthusiast

PRODUCTION
88

SPECIFICATIONS

Length (in.)	246.0
Wheelbase (in.)	155.0
Weight (lbs)	7600-8100
Price (new)	NA

ENGINES

cc/type (cid)	bhp¹	years
7655/ohv I-8 (467)	155/230	1938-40

¹Net; supercharger out/in

PRICES

As for 1930-37 Mercedes-Benz Type 770 Grosser.

1951-62

MERCEDES-BENZ TYPE 300

The first completely new offering from Daimler-Benz following World War II, with the emphasis mainly on engineering. A big car for big occasions, the 300 featured new running gear from end to end, including an overhead-cam 3.0-liter inline six that would later gain fame in the 300SL racing and road-going sports cars. The chassis was an oval-tube affair with independent suspension all around. Rear ride height was electrically adjustable from inside by means of

1951 Type 300 limousine

1957 Type 300Sc convertible

auxiliary torsion bars. Massive for a European car, with "transition" styling that marked M-B's move to more modern full-width envelope body lines. Though it remained in production for a decade, in its last years it was mostly an indulgence for the firm. The design went through four distinct phases. More horsepower, optional automatic transmission, and a higher final drive were offered beginning with the 300c in 1955. The 300d introduced in 1957 was more powerful still. Offered as pillared and pillarless four-door sedans plus a limousine model, all with upright, traditional lines featuring a tall Mercedes grille, semi-integrated front fenders, and a short, rounded rump. Ponderous to drive, but meticulously engineered and beautifully finished.

✚ FOR Solid separate chassis • Thorough, somewhat advanced engineering for the time • "Gothic" styling for those who like it • Spaciousness • Well-equipped • A Milestone car

▬ AGAINST Bulky and tedious in tight spots • Parts impossible to find • Not cheap to restore or maintain • If you bought it at high market, you lost!

PRODUCTION
300/300b 6214 (1951-55) **300c** 1432 (1955-57) **300d** 3077 (1957-62)

SPECIFICATIONS
Length (in.)	195.0 (limo: 204.0)
Wheelbase (in.)	120.0 (limo: 124.0)
Weight (lbs)	3860-4400
Price (new)	NA

ENGINES
cc/type (cid)	bhp	years
2996/ohc I-6 (183)	115/125/160	1951-62

PRICES
Conv	
FAIR	$25,000-47,000
GOOD	$47,000-68,000
FINE	$68,000-90,000
Sdn	
FAIR	$10,000-13,000
GOOD	$13,000-18,000
FINE	$18,000-30,000

FINE CONVERTIBLE PRICE HISTORY
1982 $36,000		**1990** $200,000	
1994 $150,000		**1998** $120,000	
1982-2000 RETURN 5%			
2000-2010 5%			

1952-58
MERCEDES-BENZ TYPE 300S/Sc

Massive but tremendously impressive short-wheelbase derivatives of Mercedes' flagship sedan series, offering greater engine power and even better equipment. The initial 300S had a 150-bhp version of the normal 3.0-liter straight six. The later Sc switched from carburetors to fuel injection (related to the 300SL system) to obtain an extra 50 horses. Styling was very much in the late-'30s mold. Open versions were offered both with and without roll-down windows and folding top, and the fixed-roof coupe had very broad rear quarters and a small rear window.

✚ FOR As for 1951-62 Type 300, plus more power and performance, and more manageable • Milestone status • This is one Merc that has held onto most of its soaring early 1990s value

▬ AGAINST As for 1951-62 Type 300 • Expensive

PRODUCTION
300S: cpe 216 **conv** 203 **rdstr** 141 **300Sc:** cpe 98 **conv** 49 **rdstr** 53

SPECIFICATIONS
Length (in.)	186.0
Wheelbase (in.)	114.0
Weight (lbs)	approx. 3600
Price (new)	NA

ENGINES
cc/type (cid)	bhp[1]	years
2996/ohc I-6 (183)	150/220	1952-58

[1]Gross

PRICES
Open	
FAIR	$70,000-160,000
GOOD	$160,000-195,000
FINE	$195,000-235,000

(Closed models deduct 60%.)

FINE 1955 SC ROADSTER PRICE HISTORY
1982 $38,000		**1990** $200,000	
1994 $230,000		**1998** $200,000	
1982-92 RETURN 12%			
2000-2010 10% (closed models 5%)			

1954-63
MERCEDES-BENZ 300SL

The imposing "panzerwagen" sports car from Germany, a direct devel-

1954 300SL coupe

1956-62 190SL convertible

opment of the racing M-B SL prototypes fielded for GT endurance events starting in 1952. Offered initially as a closed coupe with unique, upward-opening doors that earned it the nickname "Gullwing." In appearance, the 300SL was quite modern compared to other current Mercedes, with a horizontal grille dominated by a big three-pointed star, twin longitudinal bulges in the hood, rounded front fenders and trunklid, prominent eyebrows over the wheel openings, and a heavy ground-hugging look that belied its SL ("super leicht" or "super light") designation. The 300SL was a pioneer of the multi-tube "space frame" approach to chassis construction. All-independent suspension—the rear by treacherous swing axles—and direct fuel injection were other features. The Gullwing's doors left wide, high sills that made clambering in and out a chore for some, but the cockpit was snug and businesslike in the German manner. In 1957, the coupe was replaced by a two-seat roadster with conventional front-hinged, side-opening doors. A detachable steel top was offered as an option. M-B offered a choice of final drive ratios, which allowed a maximum speed of up to 165 mph from the 3.0-liter straight six shared with the flagship 300 sedan models. This was a car that required regular, expensive servicing, but a highly desirable grand tourer then, even more so today. It was replaced by a smaller-engine SL series with more angular styling beginning in 1963.

FOR Timeless, unmistakable looks • Performance aplenty • Thorough Germanic engineering (except rear suspension) • Selling for nearly half a million in 1990, it was predicted by some to double by 2000; but the market came back to reality and today it's a relative bargain for a truly great car

AGAINST Tricky swing-axle handling (though better on roadster) • Costly to

acquire and maintain • Parts hard to come by • Most examples were spoken for long ago

PRODUCTION
1954-57 cpe 1400 **1957-63 rdstr** 1858

SPECIFICATIONS
Length (in.) 180.0
Wheelbase (in.) 94.5
Weight (lbs) 2750/3000 (cpe/rdster)
Price (new) approx. $7300 U.S. in 1956; approx. $11,400 in 1960

ENGINES
cc/type (cid)	bhp[1]	years
2996/ohc I-6 (183)	240/250	1954-63

[1]Gross

PRICES
Gullwing	
FAIR	$100,000-150,000
GOOD	$150,000-180,000
FINE	$180,000-220,000
Rdstr	
FAIR	$70,000-100,000
GOOD	$100,000-150,000
FINE	$150,000-175,000

FINE GULLWING PRICE HISTORY
1982 $120,000	1990 $450,000
1998 $320,000	
1982-2000 RETURN 4%	
2000-2010 5%	

1955-63
MERCEDES-BENZ 190SL

The first high-volume Daimler-Benz sports car, and one of the firm's best-known U.S. models in the '50s. It followed Austin-Healey/Triumph TR practice in using mass-production components, in this case the four-cylinder engine, running gear, and (shortened) floorpan from the Type 180 sedan series. Styling was deliberately cho-

sen for close identification with the exotic 300SL, and featured a similar low grille, long hood, wheel opening eyebrows, and generally rounded contours. Not really intended for competition use and too heavy for its engine anyway, it was a pleasant tourer with a top speed capability of slightly more than 105 mph. Many left the factory with a removable steel top in addition to the normal folding fabric roof. Easier to maintain and cheaper to own than a 300SL then and now, and built with all the solid integrity for which Mercedes had long been famous. Overlooked for many years because of its stolid performance, the 190SL is still reasonably priced on the collector market (or was until the mid- to late Eighties). It's also fairly available because a good many made their way to the States. In all, an unbeatable combination of open-air driving appeal and the magic of the three-pointed star.

FOR Mercedes cachet • Solid construction • Simple engineering means fairly easy upkeep • Some mechanical parts still available • Another Milestone Mercedes

AGAINST Limited performance • Tricky swing-axle handling/roadholding • Rust-prone • Expensive upkeep

PRODUCTION
25,881

SPECIFICATIONS
Length (in.) 169.0
Wheelbase (in.) 94.5
Weight (lbs) 2515
Price (new) $4000 (original U.S. list price)

ENGINES
cc/type (cid)	bhp[1]	years
1897/ohc I-4 (116)	120	1955-63

[1]Gross

PRICES
Conv:	
FAIR	$10,000-17,000
GOOD	$17,000-25,000
FINE	$25,000-32,500

FINE EXAMPLE PRICE HISTORY
1982 $13,000	1990 $35,000
1994 $35,000	1998 $35,000
1982-2000 RETURN 6%	
2000-2010 5%	

1959-71
MERCEDES-BENZ COUPE/ CABRIOLET

Long-lived replacements for the early-'50s 300S/Sc coupe and cabriolet, announced per Mercedes practice about a year behind their new-design "S-class" sedan parent (internally designated W111/112). Basic design with mildly wrapped windshield, straight-through fenderlines, and short-ish rear deck (bereft of the sedans' initial tailfins) would endure through five single-overhead-cam engines—four sixes and a valedictory V-8—offering progressively more horsepower. Typical period M-B chassis with low-pivot rear swing-axles also unchanged throughout, but air suspension on late 300s and V-8 models. Bosch mechanical fuel injection (hence "E," Einspritzung, injection) for all engines save the V-8, which used Bosch's then-new D-Jetronic electronic system. Interiors featured carefully applied quality materials, including leather on some models, and sufficient, if not spacious, accommodations for four. Coupe was a true pillarless hardtop, while its open-air companion had a fully lined folding top in the German cabriolet manner—and was thus rather bulky when lowered. Oddly, no direct successors, though junior "New Generation" coupes of 1968-76 carried

on the tradition. The V-8 280SE 3.5 is the best collector choice for performance, refinement and, possibly, future dollar return.

✚ FOR Nice styling (still looks good) • Mechanicals as for the more numerous counterpart sedans • M-B construction, quality, snob appeal • Key mechanical parts still available • Good club support

▬ AGAINST Some body parts now scarce • Weighty, so mileage nothing special • Swing-axle handling woes • Sixes rather "clattery"

1962 300SE hardtop coupe

PRODUCTION

220SE 16,902 (1959-65) **250SE** 6213 (1965-68) **300SE** 3127 (1962-67) **280SE** 5187 (1967-71) **280SE** 3.5 4502 (1969-71)

SPECIFICATIONS

Length (in.)	192.0
Wheelbase (in.)	108.0
Weight (lbs)	3330-3650
Price (new)	$8900-14,500 in U.S.

ENGINES

cid/type (cc)	bhp[1]	years
134/ohc I-6 (2195)	120/134	1959-65
152/ohc I-6 (2496)	150/170	1965-68
182/ohc I-6 (2996)	160/185	1962-65
182/ohc I-6 (2996)	170/195	1965-67
170/ohc I-6 (2778)	160/180	1967-71
213/ohc V-8 (3499)	200/230	1969-71

[1]DIN/SAE net

PRICES

Cabrio	
FAIR	$12,500-28,000
GOOD	$28,000-45,000
FINE	$45,000-58,000
Coupe	
FAIR	$4000-8000
GOOD	$8000-12,000
FINE	$12,000-24,000

FINE CABRIOLET PRICE HISTORY

1982 $25,000		**1990** $48,000	
1994 $48,000		**1998** $55,000	
1982-2000 RETURN 5%			
2000-2010 5%			

1963-80
MERCEDES-BENZ TYPE 600

1971 600 limousine

The "Grosser" Mercedes—the car of popes, potentates, and pop singers. Crafted only by hand on an as-needed basis, the 600 was notable for its great bulk, unprecedented by European standards and as large as

1959-60 220SE cabriolet

anything Cadillac ever made. Three "production" models were listed, all with Mercedes' four-square styling that related to lesser models of the period. There were a standard-wheelbase four-door, a longer-wheelbase "Pullman" four-door, and an even longer sedan with six doors. A very few were also built with a "landaulette" type of rear passenger compartment, complete with fold-down fabric section, for parades and functions of state. All models featured a division window to separate the chauffeur from his "passengers." The first Mercedes to use the firm's massive 6.3-liter V-8, which later powered the incredibly fast 300SEL 6.3 sedan of 1968. The enormously complex chassis featured air suspension and electro-hydraulic controls. It was surprisingly fast for its size, and not all that bad for handling, either. It was also a direct match for the upper Rolls-Royce models in concept, mechanical sophistication, and equipment, if not in image. Production continued through the end of 1981, by which time the 600 had been left behind by technical advances made to lower-line models. Frequently seen in motion pictures whenever a big, impressive, slightly sinister limo was called for.

➕ FOR Exclusivity • Grandeur • Top-flight engineering and construction quality • Ballroom-size interior • Beautiful ride • The most imposing Mercedes you can own • A Milestone car

➖ AGAINST Too big for most • Hardly economical • Costly to buy • Complex, so parts and service cost a bundle • Demands specialized service knowledge

PRODUCTION
2677

SPECIFICATIONS

Length (in.)	218.0/246.0 (std/Pullman)
Wheelbase (in.)	126.0/153.5 (std/Pullman)
Weight (lbs)	5445/5820 (std/Pullman)
Price (new)	approx. $60,000 U.S. in 1963

ENGINES

cc/type (cid)	bhp[1]	years
6332/ohc V-8 (387)	250	1963-80

[1]DIN

PRICES

FAIR	$14,000-25,000
GOOD	$25,000-37,500
FINE	$37,500-68,000

FINE EXAMPLE PRICE HISTORY

1982 $21,000		**1990** $125,000	
1994 $65,000		**1998** $65,000	
1982-2000 RETURN 7%			
2000-2010 5%			

1963-71
MERCEDES-BENZ 230/250/280SL (W113)

Replacement for both the 300SL and 190SL as Mercedes "sports car" for the '60s. Far slower and less sporting than the former, but more practical. Faster and more advanced than the 190SL, though it also borrowed the floorpan and running gear of a "volume" M-B sedan, in this case the 1959 220S/SE. Unique styling, however, marked by square-cut lines, vertical pod-type headlamps, and typical low SL grille with large tristar emblem. Offered initially with a 2.3-liter version of Mercedes' fuel-injected four-main-bearing dohc six, plus optional automatic transmission and—like the 190SL and 300SL roadster—a liftoff steel hardtop, albeit a new depressed-center design sometimes called the "pagoda roof." Strictly a two-seater, but a small package shelf behind could take two small riders in a pinch. Rear suspension continued M-B's favored low-pivot swing axles. Interim 250SL ran a new seven-main 2.5-liter engine with the same rated horsepower as the 2.3, but with somewhat more torque for superior refinement and driving ease. A bore increase gave the replacement

280SL an extra 20 horses that more than compensated for performance-sapping U.S. safety and emissions regulations while making the car faster and still easier to drive. Fairly common in the U.S., yet collector values remain strong.

➕ FOR M-B engineering • Tidy lines • Open-air allure • Active club interest • Many mechanical parts still available

➖ AGAINST Heavyish and a bit fuelish • Monocoque construction, so rust potential • Modest handling limits • Middling performance (230SL) • Costly parts and service • Engines not as smooth or quiet as you'd think

PRODUCTION
230SL 19,831 (1963-67) **250SL** 5196 (1966-68) **280SL** 23,885 (1967-71)

SPECIFICATIONS

Length (in.)	169.5
Wheelbase (in.)	94.5
Weight (lbs)	2855-2900
Price (new)	$6500-8000 in U.S.

ENGINES

cid/type (cc)	bhp[1]	years
141/dohc I-6 (2308)	150/170	1963-67
152/dohc I-6 (2496)	150/170	1966-68
170/dohc I-6 (2778)	170/180	1967-71

[1]DIN/SAE gross

PRICES

FAIR	$7000-14,000
GOOD	$14,000-20,000
FINE	$20,000-30,000

FINE EXAMPLE PRICE HISTORY

1982 $16,000		**1990** $25,000	
1994 $33,000		**1998** $30,000	
1982-2000 RETURN 4%			
2000-2010 4%			

1968 280SL convertible

1967-72
MERCEDES-BENZ 300SEL 6.3

1969 300SEL sedan

A German-built freeway flyer with electrifying performance. It was created by slotting the big quad-cam V-8 engine from the massive 600 limousine into the smaller, lighter type W109 bodyshell ordinarily propelled by M-B's 3.0-liter six. As in the 600, Bosch timed-flow fuel injection was used, good for a rousing 250 bhp (DIN) and a solid 369 lbs/ft torque. The result, according to factory figures, was 0-100 kph (62.5 mph) in 6.5 seconds and a top end of 130 mph plus, making this the world's fastest luxury sedan. Air suspension with built-in self-leveling was exclusive to the 6.3 among Mercedes' "mass-market" models. Other features included standard air conditioning, leather upholstery, M-B's four-speed automatic transmission, AM/FM radio, and central locking system. Impossible to tell from an ordinary 300 SEL except by the discreet "6.3" badge on the right of the trunklid, and many owners removed that to avoid suspicious glances from the law. A goodly proportion of the deliberately limited production run made its way to the U.S. It was withdrawn in the aftermath of the first energy crisis, and also to make way for the new-generation W116 series S-class sedans introduced for 1973, and was succeeded in the lineup by the 450SEL 6.9 in 1976.

✚ FOR Prestige with punch • Four-door convenience • Superlative construction quality • Solid handling • Rarity

▬ AGAINST Air suspension leak problems • Thirsty • Some mechanical parts in short supply

PRODUCTION[1]
1967 1 **1968** 1094 **1969** 2578 **1970** 1797 **1971** 670 **1972** 386

[1]Calendar year

SPECIFICATIONS
Length (in.)	196.9
Wheelbase (in.)	112.8
Weight (lbs)	4010
Price (new)	approx. $14,500 U.S. in 1969

ENGINES
cc/type (cid)	bhp[1]	years
6332/dohc V-8 (387)	250	1967-72

[1]DIN

PRICES
As per 1963-67 Mercedes-Benz 230SL less 25%.

1968-76
MERCEDES-BENZ 250/280C/CE

The sportiest non-SL Mercedes of this period. All were derived from the square-lined "New Generation" sedan first seen in 1967, differing mainly in a slightly shortened pillarless roof with two-inch-lower overall height. Six-cylinder engines featured throughout, but the U.S. 250C actually used a 2.8-liter unit to maintain power in the face of new performance-sapping federal safety and emissions rules. Bosch electronic fuel injection was fitted to all engines save the 250C (twin carburetors) and the twincam 280C, the latter the U.S. version of the injected European 280CE announced in 1971. Less coveted than earlier "S-class" coupes, but nice newer collector cars with few vices and most all the expected Mercedes virtues.

✚ FOR Mercedes cachet • Pleasant handling • Tight and solid for hardtops • Most parts still readily available

▬ AGAINST Tend to be pricey even as used cars • Styling rather dull for hardtops • Performance not thrilling • Limited back-seat space

PRODUCTION
250C 8824 (1968-72) **250CE** 21,787 (1968-72) **250C** 11,768 ("2.8" 1969-76) **280CE** 11,518 (1971-76)

SPECIFICATIONS
Length (in.)	184.5
Wheelbase (in.)	108.3
Weight (lbs)	3070-3200
Price (new)	$6625-14,700

ENGINES
cid/type (cc)	bhp	years
153/ohc I-6 (2496)	130/146[1]	1968-76
153/ohc I-6 (2496)[2]	150/170[1]	1968-76
170/ohc I-6 (2778)[2]	157[3]	1968-72
168/dohc I-6 (2746)[2]	185/205[1]	1971-76
168/dohc I-6 (2746)[2]	120-180[3]	1972-76

[1]DIN/SAE net [2]Fuel injection [3]SAE net (U.S. version)

PRICES
FAIR	$2000-5000
GOOD	$5000-8000
FINE	$8000-13,000

FINE EXAMPLE PRICE HISTORY
1982 $13,000		**1990** $32,500	
1994 $14,000		**1998** $13,000	
1982-2000 RETURN 0%			
2000-2010 2%			

1970-90
MERCEDES-BENZ SL (R107)

Long-lived successor to the W113 SL series. Much the same concept, but larger, heavier, and plusher. More imposing, too, with lines echoed in

1968 250C hardtop coupe (European version)

1981 380SL convertible

1970s S-class sedans, because Bruno Sacco designed both. Less agile than its lighter predecessor, but still quite capable—and more predictable in corners with M-B's traditional rear swing axles altered to function as semi-trailing arms. Sold only with various V-8s in the U.S., where styling was compromised by quad headlamps (versus single flush units) plus protruding "safety" bumpers from 1974. Remarkably few changes over many years (mostly engines), though a more efficient four-speed automatic was substituted along the way for the original three-speeder; manual shift was available only on six-cylinder models. The later 5.0- and 5.6-liter V-8s are preferred for performance, but there's nothing wrong with the "little" 3.8-liter V-8 of the early '80s—or, for that matter, a six. Finally replaced for 1990 by a far more ambitious SL, the all-new R129.

➕ **FOR** Solid, highly refined touring machines all • Good performance with larger engines • Mercedes cachet • Convertible allure • Not long gone, so parts/service backup still ample

➖ **AGAINST** Not sports-car agile • Mileage disappointing to drunkardly • Rather too common in some locales • Mercedes North America won't help with "gray market" Euro-spec cars

PRODUCTION[1]

350SL 15,304 (1970-80) **450SL** 66,298 (1971-80) **280SL** 22,598 through 1984 (1974-89) **380SL** 45,056 through 1984 (1980-85) **500SL** 6053 through 1984 (1980-86) **300SL** NA (1985-89) **420SL** NA (1985-89) **560SL** NA (1986-89)
[1]Parentheses indicate production years, not model years

SPECIFICATIONS

Length (in.)	172.4-182.3
Wheelbase (in.)	96.7
Weight (lbs)	3390-3880
Price (new)	$10,540-64,230

ENGINES

cc/type (cid)	bhp	years
3499/ohc V-8 (213.5)	230	1970-80
4520/ohc V-8 (275.8)	190-250	1971-80
2746/dohc I-6 (168)	177-180[1]	1974-85
3818/ohc V-8 (233)	218[1]	1980-85
3839/ohc V-8 (234)	155	1980-85
4973/ohc V-8 (305)	231-240	1980-89
2962/ohc I-6 (181)	188[1]	1985-89

4196/ohc V-8 (256)	218[1]	1985-89
5547/ohc V-8 (339)	227	1986-89

[1]DIN (European models); otherwise SAE net

PRICES

1970s SL	
FAIR	$6000-10,000
GOOD	$10,000-16,000
FINE	$16,000-28,000

FINE EXAMPLE PRICE HISTORY

In early 2000, asking prices varied between $16,000 for an early 1970s 350SLC to $32,000 for a 1990 300 SL and $36,000 for a 1990 500 SL. Model year still affects price on late models.
2000-2010 RETURN 2% (early models)

1971-81
MERCEDES-BENZ SLC

A "first"—and so far an "only"—for Mercedes: a four-place offshoot of the two-seat SL, in this case the R107-series design that preceded it to market by about a year. Chief differences were a wheelbase lengthened 14 inches to make room for a nominal back seat, plus a fixed pillarless superstructure above the resulting 2+2 cabin. The result was somewhat ungainly—aggravated, perhaps, by vertical slats on the rear halves of the back side windows that attempted a more "close-coupled" look. Few basic changes over a fairly successful 10-year run other than engine choices, which mostly paralleled shifts for concurrent SLs and involved somewhat thriftier new-generation V-8s starting in the late '70s. A six-cylinder SLC was never part of Mercedes' U.S. line, and virtually all American-spec models carried the earlier 4.5-liter V-8. Later, bespoilered European 450SLC 5.0 and 500SLC models are occasionally seen here as private or "gray market" imports, and may be worth seeking out for their superior performance. However, Mercedes-Benz of North America doesn't provide parts/service backup for such cars, so *caveat emptor*. SLC's successor was the more stylish 380/500/560 SEC, which began appearing in 1982 as hardtop companions to their then-new parents, the W126 "S-class" sedans.

➕ **FOR** Interesting modern Mercedes • Fairly rare, especially in U.S. • Smooth, V-8 performance • M-B's robust construction, high resale values, and high-zoot image

➖ **AGAINST** Awkward styling • Back seat not practical for adults • Not that quick (except 5.0 V-8s) • Less nimble than an SL • Not yet a very high-status Merc collectible

PRODUCTION[1]

350SLC 13,925 (1971-80) **450SLC** 31,739 (1972-80) **280SLC** 10,666 (1974-81) **450SLC 5.0** 2769 (1977-81) **380SLC** 3789 (1980-81) **500SLC** 1299 (1980-81)
[1]Parentheses indicate production years, not model years

SPECIFICATIONS

Length (in.)	186.6-196.4
Wheelbase (in.)	110.8
Weight (lbs)	3200-3500
Price (new)	$15,100-36,600

ENGINES

cc/type (cid)	bhp	years
3499/ohc V-8 (213.5)	200/230[1]	1971-80
4520/ohc V-8 (275.8)	217-225[2]	1971-80
4520/ohc V-8 (275.8)	160-190[3]	1971-80
2746/dohc I-6 (168)	177-185[2]	1974-81
4990/ohc V-8 (305)	240[2]	1977-78
4973/ohc V-8 (304)	231/240[2]	1979-81
3818/ohc V-8 (233)	218[1]	1980-81
3839/ohc V-8 (234)	155[3]	1980-81

[1]DIN/SAE net [2]DIN(European model) [3]SAE net (U.S. model)

PRICES

450SLC	
FAIR	$4000-7500

1979 450SLC hardtop coupe

GOOD	$7500-10,000
FINE	$10,000-15,000
350SLC	
FAIR	$3000-5000
GOOD	$5000-7000
FINE	$7000-10,000

FINE EXAMPLE PRICE HISTORY.

Depreciation has generally stopped for the best examples, but prices have not risen much higher than the above figures for any model year.
2000-2010 RETURN Even

1975-80

MERCEDES-BENZ 450 SEL 6.9

1977 450 SEL 6.9 sedan

Continuation of the big-engine S-class sedan, now built on the W116 platform introduced for 1973. Considerably changed from its 6.3 predecessor, it featured somewhat lower and sleeker lines that were still distinctly Mercedes. A bore increase brought up displacement on the big quad-cam V-8 engine, still related to the original 600 limousine unit, and there were numerous modifications such as Bosch K-Jetronic fuel injection, breakerless electronic ignition, dry-sump lubrication, and hydraulic valve gear actuation. The suspension was shared with lesser-powered S-class models (lower A-arms, upper transverse links, and anti-roll bar in front; semi-trailing arms and anti-roll bar at the rear), but springing was now provided by hydropneumatic oil/nitrogen struts instead of air bags as on the 6.3. As before, rear end self-leveling was incorporated to compensate for a heavy load of luggage or passengers. The revised chassis gave even better handling and roadholding than the already capable 6.3, plus a softer ride. Equipped with most every conceivable luxury feature, the 6.9 was slightly slower than the 6.3 off the line, but had a bit more available in top speed, now about 140 mph. It came only with a three-speed torque-converter automatic transmission, which replaced the

previous four-speed fluid-coupling unit. Fast but thirsty, the 6.9 was launched a good three years after the rest of the W116 range because of Mercedes' sense of propriety in the wake of the 1973-74 Arab oil embargo. When fuel prices "destabilized" again in 1979, U.S. fuel economy standards were in force, which made the 6.9 something of a liability here. Accordingly, the model was dropped after 1979. Still, this was the fastest version of what was widely considered "the best sedan in the world," argument enough for its status as a collectible.

✚ FOR As for 1968-72 300SEL 6.3, plus greater refinement and better ride and handling

▬ AGAINST As for 1968-72 300SEL 6.3, but U.S. versions more affected by desmogging and bumper rules than corresponding 6.3s • Also, very pricey and likely to remain so

PRODUCTION

1816 (U.S. sales incl. European deliveries)

SPECIFICATIONS

Length (in.)	205.5
Wheelbase (in.)	116.5
Weight (lbs)	approx. 4500
Price (new)	$35,000 U.S. in 1976; $50,000 in 1979

ENGINES

cc/type (cid)	bhp[1]	years
6834/dohc V-8 (417)	250	1975-80

[1]SAE net, U.S. model

PRICES

FAIR	$4000-6000
GOOD	$6000-8000
FINE	$8000-15,000

FINE 1975 MODEL PRICE HISTORY

1982 $13,500		**1990** $22,500	
1994 $17,000		**1998** $15,000	
1982-2000 RETURN 1%			
2000-2010 2%			

1983-88

MERCEDES-BENZ 190E 2.3-16

A somewhat unexpected version of Mercedes' entry-level W201 compact sedan—a "factory hot rod" to counter the sportiest small BMWs and to win some business back from aftermarket concerns that had been cashing in by turning ordinary Mercedes into high-performance "sports sedans." Starting with the everyday 190E 2.3, M-B installed a new twin-cam 16-valve version of its four-cylinder injected engine (developed by Cosworth in England), added "aero" rocker skirting and decklid spoiler, upgraded the suspension, enlarged the tires and antilock brakes, and spruced up the cabin with extra gauges, a bucketed two-place back seat, and standard leather trim. The result was a car that could manage 0-60 in under 8 seconds with the five-speed manual (a four-speed automatic was ostensibly optional) and tear through slaloms with balanced, forgiving responses and plenty of stick. Alas, it wasn't cheap—nearly $12,000 more than the ordinary 190E 2.3. That, plus its specialized nature limited sales—so much so in the U.S. that the 2.3-16 was withdrawn after just two years (1986-87). But the concept continued for Europe, first in late 1988 with a replacement 2.5-16 packing 204 horses, followed in 1990 by an even wilder-looking "Evolution II" with 235 bhp. Highly desired by U.S. enthusiasts as a "short-timer" in this market, but those European continua-

1983 190E 2.3-16 sedan

tions ultimately diminish the 2.3-16's collector-car luster—and maybe values, too.

✚ **FOR** Superb acceleration, handling, braking • Quite refined for a "factory hot rod" • Sedan practicality • Easy parts/service even in U.S.

▬ **AGAINST** Some dislike "boy racer" styling • Same small 190-series trunk and back seat • Specialized engine, so repairs costlier than already high M-B norm • Ultimate collector status unclear

PRODUCTION

approx. 5000

SPECIFICATIONS

Length (in.)	174.4
Wheelbase (in.)	104.9
Weight (lbs)	2770-3030
Price (new)	approx. $37,200 in U.S.

ENGINES

cid/type	bhp[1]	years
140/dohc I-4	185/167	1983-88

[1]DIN/SAE net (European/U.S. models)

PRICES

FAIR	$3500-6000
GOOD	$6000-12,000
FINE	$12,000-14,500

FINE EXAMPLE PRICE HISTORY

Depreciated through the 1990s. Top prices for fine examples were around $7500 in Spring 2000 **2000-2010 RETURN** 0%

1991-2000
MERCEDES-BENZ SL

1993 600SL convertible

Mercedes' top-line convertible bowed for 1991 with 300SL and 500SL iterations. These were two-ton cars, which contributed to solidity but that hampered acceleration with the 300's 228-horse 3.0-liter inline 6. The 500's 322-horse 5.0-liter V-8 had considerably more pep. A 389-bhp 6.0 liter V-12 600SL bowed for '93, with a staggering base price of $119,500. By 2000,

only the 500 and 600 remained, priced at $82,600 and $128,950, respectively—rarefied territory. The entry-level 6-cylinder was dropped for '98, leaving the 302-bhp 5.0-liter V-8 and the 389-horse 6.0 liter V-12. Safety-conscious automatic roll bar was a hallmark from the beginning, and materials & finish inside and out were superb.

✚ **FOR** They're convertibles • V-12/convertible combo (600SL) • Acceleration (500SL, 600SL) • Handling • Build quality • Safety features

▬ **AGAINST** Acceleration (300SL) • "Used-car" prices still enormous • Thirst

PRODUCTION[1]

1991 7482 **1992** 4879 **1993** 4828 **1994** 5919 **1995** 6964 **1996** 6856 **1997** 8025 **1998 500** 7232 **1998 600** 577 **1999 500** 7394 **1999 600** 459
[1]U.S. Calendar year sales

SPECIFICATIONS

Length (in.)	176.0-177.1
Weight (lbs)	3605-4473
Wheelbase (in.)	99.0
Price (new)	$72,500-128,950

ENGINES

cid/type	bhp	years
181/dohc I-6	228	1991-93
195/dohc I-6	228	1994-97
303/dohc V-8	315/322	1991-98
303/ohc V-8	302	1999-00
365/dohc V-12	389	1993-00

PRICES

Spring 2000 prices for fine examples ranged between $35,000 (1991 300SL) to $70,000 (1998 600SL) and are governed by the used Mercedes market. **2000-2010 RETURN** Depreciating

1998-2000
MERCEDES-BENZ CLK320/430

Determined to pursue the hot-selling BMW 3-Series, M-B added new features to their C-Class cars for '98, and introduced a sportive coupe variant, the CLK 320 (2.8-liter, 194-bhp V-6) and CLK430 (4.3-liter, 302 bhp V-8, introduced for 1999 model year). The CLK was quick, even with the six, and had the capable road manners typical of Mercedes.

✚ **FOR** Available convertible • Acceleration • Materials and build quality

▬ **AGAINST** Tight interiors • Still used cars, and not inexpensive • Pokey downshifts from automatic transmission

PRODUCTION[1]

1998 320 coupe 6247 **1998 320 convertible** 2384 **1998 430 coupe** 2991 **1999 320 coupe** 5975 **1999 320 convertible** 5142 **1999 430 coupe** 3190 **1999 430 convertible** 2407
[1]U.S. Calendar year sales

SPECIFICATIONS

Length (in.)	180.2
Weight (lbs)	3213-3665
Wheelbase (in.)	105.9
Price (new)	$39,850-55,600

ENGINES

cid/type	bhp	years

2000 CLK320 coupe

195/ohc V-6	215	1998-00
260/ohc V-8	275	1999-00

PRICES

Governed by used Mercedes market.
2000-2010 RETURN Depreciating

1998-2000
MERCEDES-BENZ SLK230

2000 SLK Designo roadster

Mercedes' returned to sports car building with the SLK. European buyers could take their choice of a 2.0-liter naturally aspirated four-cylinder engine or supercharged 2.3-liter four, as well as 5-speed manual or automatic transmissions. All U.S. market cars had the supercharged engine. The manual transmission wasn't available in the states until the '99 model year. The supercharged engine was leisurely off the line, but had plenty of punch at high speeds. Unfortunately the motor sounded coarse and unrefined at all speeds. Handling was secure and stable through the turns. The most unique feature of the car was its folding steel top. Pushing a button transformed the SLK from closed coupe to open convertible in seconds.

FOR Unique retractable top • Solid structure • Curve-hugging handling

AGAINST Coarse engine • Power not always on tap • Lacks steering feel

PRODUCTION[1]

1998 9549 **1999** 8763
[1]North American calendar year sales

SPECIFICATIONS

Length (in.)	157.3
Weight (lbs)	3025
Wheelbase (in.)	94.5
Price (new)	$39,700-41,000

ENGINES

cid/type	bhp	years
140/dohc I-4[1]	185	1998-00

[1]Supercharged

PRICES

In Spring 2000, $40,000 for the best '98 models, more for later models.
2000-2010 RETURN Depreciating

1998-2000
MERCEDES-BENZ ML55/E55/C43 (AMG SPECIALS)

Mercedes' relationship with German-based aftermarket tuner AMG has produced some interesting vehicles over the years, and three of them appeared within the span of the three model years noted above. The ML55 was AMG's variant on M-B's successful M-Class sport-ute, distinguished by exclusive, shapely fender flares and spoilers (designed in California); special wheels; and 342 horsepower from a 5.4-liter V-8. Chassis, brakes, and suspension were beefed up from stock. Pure luxury inside, and 0-60 mph in 6.3 seconds. The AMG E-Class variant, the E55, though boasting the similar engine and horsepower rating as the ML55, was a more subtle creation, marked mainly by black-on-white gauges, enormous tires, twin chrome exhaust pipes, and an "E55 AMG" trunklid badge. Top speed exceeded 170 mph. And then there was AMG's version of M-B's entry-level C-Class, which ran with a 4.3-liter V-8 tuned to 302 bhp. Sixty mph came up from a stop in 5.9 seconds. Five-speed automatic was mandatory on this trio of AMG/Mercedes specials.

FOR Blazing acceleration • Good mid-range response • Handling & road-holding (E55, C43) • Exclusivity

AGAINST Thirst • Mandatory automatic transmissions • High prices, new and used

1999 E55 sedan

PRODUCTION[1]

1998 E5580 **1998 C43** 788 **1999 ML55** 16 **1999 E55** 1024 **1999 C43** 546
[1]U.S. Calendar year sales

SPECIFICATIONS

Length (in.) ML55	182.5
Weight (lbs)	4861
Wheelbase (in.)	111.0
Price (new)	$64,900
Length (in.) E55	189.4
Weight (lbs)	3680
Wheelbase (in.)	111.5
Price (new)	$69,100-69,800
Length (in.) C43	177.4
Weight (lbs)	3448
Wheelbase (in.)	105.9
Price (new)	$52,750-53,000

ENGINES

cid/type ML55	bhp	years
332/ohc V-8	342	2000
cid/type E55		
332/ohc V-8	349	1999-00
cid/type C43		
260/ohc V-8	302	1998-00

PRICES

Governed by used Mercedes market.
2000-2010 RETURN Depreciating

2000 ML55

1999 C43 sedan

307

1 9 3 9 - 4 0
MERCURY

Ford's medium-priced make in its initial incarnation. Shared Bob Gregorie's sharp styling with contemporary Fords. Hallmarks were curvy contours, a clean grille, and flush-mounted headlamps. Only one series for 1939, with four models, including a convertible and a slick Coupe-Sedan with narrow B-pillars and a hardtop look about it. A neat convertible sedan was added for 1940 and is now a very hot collectible. The engine was a slightly larger and more powerful version of the Ford flathead V-8. Excellent sales quickly established Mercury as a permanent gap-filler in the Dearborn stable.

FOR Fine period styling • Good performance • Solid construction

AGAINST Continues to trail the far more numerous 1939-40 Fords in value, despite generally superior specification

PRODUCTION
1939 70,835 **1940** 86,062 (Incl. foreign assemblies)

SPECIFICATIONS
Length (in.)	199.0
Wheelbase (in.)	116.0
Weight (lbs)	2995-3249
Price (new)	$916-1212

ENGINES
cid/type	bhp	years
239.0/sv V-8	95	1939-40

PRICES
Conv	
FAIR	$6000-11,000
GOOD	$11,000-20,000
FINE	$20,000-30,000
Others	
FAIR	$2500-7500
GOOD	$7500-13,000
FINE	$13,000-19,000

FINE CONDITION CONVERTIBLE PRICE HISTORY
1982	$22,000	1990	$32,500
1994	$27,500	1998	$29,000

1982-2000 RETURN 2%
2000-2010 3%

1 9 4 1 - 4 2
MERCURY

Completely restyled for 1941, with a two-inch longer wheelbase and a wider selection of models. New were a two-passenger coupe and a four-door

1942 Tudor sedan

wagon, while the romantic convertible sedan was dropped. Mechanically unchanged, though the flathead V-8 gained five horsepower for '42, when a new clutchless transmission called "Liquamatic" was also briefly offered. The '42 facelift saw a two-tier horizontal grille substituted for the vertically split '41 affair, giving a more massive look. Production halted in early February 1942, making the last prewar Mercs comparatively rare today.

FOR Fit and finish • Good performance

AGAINST Clumsier styling than 1939-40

PRODUCTION
1941 82,391 **1942** 22,816 (both est.)

SPECIFICATIONS
Length (in.)	202.5

1940 DeLuxe convertible

Wheelbase (in.)	118.0
Weight (lbs)	3008-3528
Price (new)	$910-1260

ENGINES

cid/type	bhp	years
239.4/sv V-8	95/100	1941-42

PRICES

Conv & Wgn	
FAIR	$5000-10,000
GOOD	$10,000-20,000
FINE	$20,000-29,000
Others	
FAIR	$2500-6000
GOOD	$6000-10,000
FINE	$10,000-16,000

FINE STATION WAGON PRICE HISTORY

1982	$17,000	1990	$30,000
1994	$27,500	1998	$27,500

1982-2000 RETURN 3%
2000-2010 3%

1946
MERCURY SPORTSMAN

Mercury's counterpart to the wood-bodied Ford Sportsman convertible, produced in very limited numbers for this model year only. Like the Ford, it featured structural wood paneling along the bodysides and on the rear deck, but was otherwise identical with other models. All were basically warmed-over '42s as Ford had neither time nor money for a brand-new design in the early postwar period. Priced a towering $500 above the standard ragtop, it was intended to lure buyers back into newly reopened showrooms and to renew interest in what was by then a rather familiar group of cars pending arrival of the all-new models scheduled for 1949.

✚ **FOR** The most interesting and sought-after (because of low production) early postwar Merc • A Milestone car

➖ **AGAINST** High maintenance and/or restoration costs for wood trim • Extremely scarce and expensive now because of that • Curiously modest appreciation potential

PRODUCTION

205

SPECIFICATIONS

Length (in.)	201.8
Wheelbase (in.)	118.0
Weight (lbs)	3407
Price (new)	$2209

ENGINES

cid/type	bhp	year
239.4/sv V-8	100	1946

PRICES

FAIR	$10,000-18,000
GOOD	$18,000-32,000
FINE	$32,000-46,000

FINE EXAMPLE PRICE HISTORY

1982	$24,000	1990	$60,000
1994	$55,000	1998	$46,000

1982-2000 RETURN 4%
2000-2010 5%

1949-51
MERCURY

1949 Sport sedan

The first all-new postwar Mercurys, the "bathtub" generation popularized by actor James Dean in *Rebel Without a Cause* and beloved of '50s customizers. Four body styles, three shared with contemporary junior Lincolns, though on a three-inch shorter wheelbase. Mercury's structural-wood wagon shifted from four to two doors in these years and shared its bodyshell with Ford's wagon. The familiar flathead V-8 was enlarged from 1946-48, then offered with a new extra-cost self-shifting Merc-O-Matic transmission in 1951. Horsepower was raised by two that same year, when styling was more noticeably changed via a bolder "face" and (wagon excepted) slightly longer rear fenders. Convertibles and the 1950-51 Monterey

1946 Sportsman convertible

pseudo-hardtops (see below) are the prime collector picks for the usual reasons. But wagons are the rarest of all these models and are equally worthy, though there's nothing wrong with a standard coupe or the sedans, the last with their throwback center-opening "suicide" doors.

✚ FOR Good performance • Period "bathtub" styling • Solid construction • Values holding up well

▬ AGAINST Many turned into "lead sleds," so low-volume models now hard to find in good stock condition

PRODUCTION

1949 coupe 120,616 **4d Sport Sedan** 155,882 **conv** 16,765 **2d wgn** 8044 **1950 coupe** 151,489 (includes Monterey) **4d Sport Sedan** 132,082 **conv** 8341 **2d wgn** 1746 **1951 coupe** 142,168 (includes Monterey) **4d Sport Sedan** 157,648 **conv** 6759 **2d wgn** 3812

SPECIFICATIONS

Length (in.)	207.0
Wheelbase (in.)	118.0
Weight (lbs)	3321-3800
Price (new)	$1979-2530

ENGINES

cid/type	bhp	years
255.4/sv V-8	110/112	1949-51

PRICES

Conv & wagon

FAIR	$5000-13,000
GOOD	$13,000-18,000
FINE	$18,000-33,000
Others	
FAIR	$3000-10,000
GOOD	$10,000-17,000
FINE	$17,000-20,000

FINE CONVERTIBLE PRICE HISTORY

1982 $14,500	1990 $25,000
1994 $23,000	1998 $25,000
1982-2000 RETURN 5%	
2000-2010 5%	

1950-51
MERCURY MONTEREY

This was the most exotic model in Mercury's first postwar generation: the "James Dean" design introduced for 1949 that became a favorite of customizers in the '50s. A counterpart to the Ford Crestliner of these years, and intended as a fill-in for a true pillarless hardtop. In essence, it was a standard club coupe with a plusher interior and a roof cover made of either canvas or leather. A stroke increase brought rated power of the FoMoCo flathead V-8 up to 110 bhp for '50 and 112 the following year. Styling was marked by the smooth but bulky "bathtub" look popular in the late '40s. The '51 facelift brought a bolder grille and squared-off rear fenders, as well as the optional three-speed Merc-O-Matic automatic transmission.

✚ FOR Rarity • Luxury • Good performance • Styling

▬ AGAINST Very hard to come by, and not cheap

PRODUCTION

NA; 2000 est.

SPECIFICATIONS

Length (in.)	207.0
Wheelbase (in.)	118.0
Weight (lbs)	3480-3485
Price (new)	$2116-2157

ENGINES

cid/type	bhp	years
255.4/sv V-8	110/112	1950-51

PRICES

FAIR	$6000-13,000
GOOD	$13,000-19,000
FINE	$19,000-24,000

FINE EXAMPLE PRICE HISTORY

1982 $7700	1990 $10,000
1994 $15,000	1998 $20,000
1982-2000 RETURN 7%	
2000-2010 5%	

1951 Monterey coupe

1952-54
MERCURY MONTEREY

1952 Monterey convertible

A standout among early '50s Mercurys for exceptional styling and sound engineering, coupled with solid construction and high-quality fit and finish. Monterey was a top-line subseries in 1952, then became a separate line (with a three-model Custom series further down the price scale) for 1953-54. Ford's flathead V-8 continued in the first two years, with its highest horsepower rating ever in Mercury tune. For 1954, the company's new Y-Block overhead-valve V-8 arrived with a five-main-bearing crankshaft and standard four-barrel carburetor. After being a "little Lincoln" in styling and bodyshell for 1949-51, Mercury again became more of a junior line in these years, with similar styling to Ford but on a three-inch longer wheelbase.

➕ **FOR** Good looks • Quality • Reasonably quick for the period, especially with overdrive

➖ **AGAINST** Slower to appreciate than concurrent Fords • Susceptible to rust in underbody areas

PRODUCTION
1952 4d sdn 30,000 (est.) **2d htp** 24,453 **conv** 5261 **1953 4d sdn** 64,038 **2d htp** 76,119 **conv** 8463 **4d wgn** 7719 **1954 4d sdn** 65,995 **2d htp** 79,553 **conv** 7293 **4d wgn** 11,656

SPECIFICATIONS
Length (in.)	202.2 (1952-53), 206.3 (1954)
Wheelbase (in)	118.0
Weight (lbs.)	3375-3735
Price (new)	$2115-2776

ENGINES
cid/type	bhp	years
255.4/sv V-8	125	1952-53
256/ohv V-8	161	1954

PRICES
Conv	
FAIR	$5500-11,000
GOOD	$11,000-20,000
FINE	$20,000-29,000

Htp	
FAIR	$3000-6000
GOOD	$6000-10,000
FINE	$10,000-15,000
Others	
FAIR	$2500-5000
GOOD	$5000-9000
FINE	$9000-12,000

FINE CONVERTIBLE PRICE HISTORY
1982 $7700	**1990** $22,500
1994 $23,000	**1998** $28,000
1982-2000 RETURN 8%	
2000-2010 conv 7%, **other models** 3%	

1954-55
MERCURY SUN VALLEY

Sharp Mercury version of the "bubbletop" Ford Skyliner/Crown Victoria, with a tinted Plexiglas front roof section and deluxe interior with a clip-in sunshade for hot days. In other respects, however, this was just like the regular steel-topped hardtops. Offered in the top-line series, Monterey for '54 and Montclair for '55. Appearance for '54 was a busier facelift of the original 1952 styling. The following year, the wheelbase was lengthened an inch, and sheet metal became crisper, though more massive. Also for '55, the Mercury ohv V-8 got a displacement boost, which brought output to 188 bhp for Custom and Monterey models or 198 bhp as standard for Montclairs. Despite its greater numbers, the '54 has remained the more popular, and is often found with distinctive yellow paint that contrasts nicely with the dark green plastic top. Unlike the Plexi-top Crown Victoria, the Sun Valley was not carried on into 1956.

➕ **FOR** Novelty value • Handsome styling • Modern ohv V-8 with ample performance • Milestone car status

➖ **AGAINST** A sweat box on hot days • 1955 restyle was different if not for the better • Rust threat in floor, rocker panels, fenders

PRODUCTION
1954 9761 **1955** 1787

SPECIFICATIONS
Length (in.)	204.2 (1954), 206.3 (1955)
Wheelbase (in.)	118.0 (1954), 119.0 (1955)
Weight (lbs)	3535-3560
Price (new)	$2582-2712

ENGINES
cid/type	bhp	years
256/ohv V-8	161	1954
292/ohv V-8	198	1955

PRICES
FAIR	$6000-13,000
GOOD	$13,000-20,000
FINE	$20,000-25,000

The 1954 models are at the upper end of these ranges.

FINE EXAMPLE PRICE HISTORY
1982 $9000	**1990** $25,000
1994 $22,000	**1998** $25,000
1982-2000 RETURN 6%	
2000-2010 1954 model 6%, **1955 model** 3%	

1955 Montclair Sun Valley hardtop coupe

1956 Montclair convertible

1955-56

MERCURY MONTCLAIR HARDTOP/ CONVERTIBLE/ PHAETON

The most collectible offerings—save the "Plexi-roof" Sun Valley hardtop coupe, considered separately above—in Mercury's new-for-'55 premium series, which demoted the former top-line Monterey to mid-range status. Bright new square-shouldered styling on an inch-longer wheelbase implied an all-new design, but the '55s and the even bolder, facelifted '56s were actually artful reskins of Merc's successful 1952-54 platform. Mostly evolutionary engineering changes included factory air as a new '55 option, plus "on-demand" low-gear kickdown for the extra-cost three-speed Merc-O-Matic Drive (which previously started in second). Montclairs predictably offered Mercury's best trim and most complete standard equipment in these years. The '55s sported a slim chrome-edged panel just under the belt-line that keyed to roof color with optional two-toning. The '56 "Big M" story involved larger V-8s with more power, plus new Phaeton hardtop sedans in all series, which expanded down to near

Ford price territory with the addition of cheap Medalist models. Growing collector interest in hardtop sedans is why the Montclair Phaeton is included here, but also note its Sport Sedan companion with the same raking roofline, but slim fixed B-pillars, unique to the '56 Montclair line and fairly rare with only 11,765 built.

✚ **FOR** Burly good looks with just enough period flash • Modern, powerful V-8s • Long underappreciated, so some models fairly scarce

▬ **AGAINST** Collector values now rising fast • Not many saved over the years, so some parts as hard to find as the cars themselves

PRODUCTION

1955 conv 10,668 **htp cpe** 71,588 **1956 conv** 7762 **htp Sport Coupe** 50,562 **Phaeton htp sdn** 23,493

SPECIFICATIONS

Length (in.)	206.3
Wheelbase (in.)	119.0
Weight (lbs)	3490-3725
Price (new)	$2630-2900

ENGINES

cid/type	bhp	years

1956 Montclair Phaeton hardtop sedan

| 292/ohv V-8 | 198 | 1955 |
| 312/ohv V-8 | 225/335 | 1956 |

PRICES

FAIR	$1500-4000
GOOD	$4000-12,000
FINE	$12,000-31,000

FINE EXAMPLE PRICE HISTORY

1982 $9000	**1990** $25,000
1994 $27,500	**1998** $31,000
1982-2000 RETURN 8%	
2000-2010 5%	

1957-58

MERCURY TURNPIKE CRUISER

1957 Turnpike Cruiser convertible (pace car replica)

The top-line offerings in the "dramatic expression of dream car design" cars introduced for 1957. Widely but ineffectually promoted as a separate series for 1957, the Turnpike Cruiser was reduced to a Montclair sub-series for 1958 (minus the convertible), and quietly forgotten for '59. Styling in these years was a direct takeoff of the XM Turnpike Cruiser show car. The production models simply dripped with the latest in gimmickry: "skylight dual curve windshield," air-intakes-cum-radio-aerials in the upper windshield corners, pushbutton "Merc-O-Matic" drive, a "memory seat" adjustable to any one of 49 positions, and a reverse-slanted retractable rear window on hardtops. Engine displacement and rated power went up in both years throughout the Mercury line. No matter—high prices, a sluggish market, and a public shift away from "futuristic" styling and gadgets kept sales way below expectations.

✚ **FOR** Gadgets galore • Flamboyant looks • Good performance and comfort • The Convertible Cruiser was the '57 Indy 500 Official Pace Car

▬ **AGAINST** Very thirsty • A rust bucket • Styling preposterous in the view of many

PRODUCTION

1957 2d htp 7291 **4d htp** 8305 **conv** 1265 **1958 2d htp** 2864 **4d htp** 3543

SPECIFICATIONS

Length (in.)	211.1 (1957), 213.2 (1958)
Wheelbase (in.)	122.0
Weight (lbs)	4015-4230
Price (new)	$3498-3758

ENGINES

cid/type	bhp	years
368/ohv V-8	290	1957
383/ohv V-8	330	1958

PRICE

Closed models

FAIR	$2600-6000
GOOD	$6000-12,000
FINE	$12,000-18,000
	(Add 50% for conv.)

FINE CONVERTIBLE PRICE HISTORY

1982 $6500		**1990** $14,599	
1994 $20,000		**1998** $23,000	

1982-2000 RETURN 6%
2000-2010 5% (convertibles 8%)

1959-60
MERCURY PARK LANE

As big as a "Big M" ever got, the last remnant of Dearborn's overly ambitious mid-'50s expansion plan that also produced jumbo Lincolns and the ill-timed Edsel. The platform was still unique to Mercury, as in 1957-58 (though once also planned for '59 Edsels), but all-new, with husky styling, more massive proportions, and huge compound-curve windshields. All this, plus wider, new-design frames with longer wheelbases and lower floorpans for vast interior space (abetted up front by a more compact dash). The new-for-'58 Park Lane completely took over for the glitzy Turnpike Cruiser as the top-line series, though all hardtops were now called Cruiser. Park Lanes again rode Merc's longest wheelbase and car-ried the huge Lincoln 430 V-8 as standard. A four-barrel carb was featured for '59, but the '60 came with a two-barrel, a faint gesture toward "economy" brought on by the '58 recession. Styling was quieter both inside and out for 1960. A still-depressed medium-price market makes these pricey Park Lanes among the rarest 1959-60 Mercurys, though like so many contemporaries they've since become coveted as big, bright, and brazen. Not included here, but also worthy of collector consideration, are the wood-look Colony Park wagons, trimmed to Park Lane standards and the last of the pillarless big-Merc wagons first seen for '57.

✚ **FOR** Period size and style • Huge interiors • Smooth performance • Still somewhat overlooked and thus cheaper than some rivals

▬ **AGAINST** Moderately rust-prone • Thirsty • Not many preserved, so both cars and some parts now quite scarce

PRODUCTION

1959 Cruiser htp sdn 7206 **Cruiser htp cpe** 4060 **conv** 1257 **1960 Cruiser htp sdn** 5788 **Cruiser htp cpe** 2974 **conv** 1525

SPECIFICATIONS

Length (in.)	222.8 (1959), 219.2 (1960)
Wheelbase (in.)	125.0
Weight (lbs)	4310-4500
Price (new)	$3955-4205

ENGINES

cid/type	bhp	years
430/ohv V-8	345	1959
430/ohv V-8	310	1960

1959 Park Lane convertible

PRICES

Conv
FAIR	$3500-8000
GOOD	$8000-16,000
FINE	$16,000-25,000

2d htp
FAIR	$2000-5000
GOOD	$5000-8000
FINE	$8000-13,000

4d htp
FAIR	$1200-4000
GOOD	$4000-6000
FINE	$6000-10,000

FINE 2D HARDTOP PRICE HISTORY

1982 $3500		**1990** $16,500	
1994 $15,000		**1998** $13,000	

1982-2000 RETURN 6%
2000-2010 3%

1961-63
MERCURY COMET S-22

The S-22 was Mercury's entry in the sporty-compact field of the early '60s, as well as the division's counterpart to the Ford Falcon Futura. It came equipped much the same way, too, with a luxury interior and bucket seats. But the Comet's 4.5-inch longer wheel-base and unique styling helped differentiate it from the Falcon. First introduced as a two-door sedan for mid-1961, the Comet served as an expanded subseries with the addition of a two-door hardtop and convertible for 1963. Offered initially with a small six in two displacements, it also came with a Ford of Europe floorshift manual gearbox as an option. For '63, Ford's outstanding small-block V-8 was offered at extra cost in 221- and 260-cid forms. Overall, the S-22 had decent handling and roadholding, adequate-to-brisk performance depending on the engine, and was quite attractive as a hardtop or convertible.

+ FOR Cheaper to buy than Falcon

1963 Comet S-22 convertible

Futura • Compact size suits today's traffic conditions • Six's good mileage • V-8 go • Hardtop and ragtop body styles for 1963

■ AGAINST A ruster (check your potential purchase carefully underneath) • Limited appreciation potential • Underwhelming styling • Six's lackluster performance (don't even consider the smaller six)

PRODUCTION

1961 2d sdn 14,004 **1962 2d sdn** 7500 (est.)
1963 2d sdn 6303 **2d htp** 5807 **conv** 5757

SPECIFICATIONS

Length (in.)	194.8
Wheelbase (in.)	114.0
Weight (lbs)	2441-2825
Price (new)	$2171-2710

ENGINES

cid/type	bhp	years
144.3/ohv I-6	85	1961-62
170/ohv I-6	101	1961-63
221/ohv V-8	145	1963
260/ohv V-8	164	1963

PRICES

Conv
FAIR	$2000-4000
GOOD	$4000-6000
FINE	$6000-12,000

(Deduct 35% for hardtop & coupe.)

FINE CONVERTIBLE PRICE HISTORY

1982 $3200		**1990** $10,000	
1994 $12,000		**1998** $12,000	

1982-2000 RETURN 7%
2000-2010 3%

1962-63
MERCURY METEOR S-33

This was the sporty buckets-and-console version of the short-lived Mercury cloned from Ford's new-for-'62 mid-size Fairlane. It bowed along

1963 Meteor S-33 hardtop coupe

with the mid-'62 Fairlane 500 Sport Coupe as a pillared two-door; the '63 was a proper hardtop coupe, also available in bench-seat Custom form. Offered with a six and the brilliant "thinwall" 221 and 260 small-block V-8s, the latter introduced with the Fairlane. The 260 would be today's collector's choice for both performance and dollar return, but there can't have been many installed given this model's very low production. The S-33 had more exterior brightwork and better interior trim than lesser Meteors, but all these were very orthodox cars—really just scaled-up Ford Falcon/Mercury Comet compacts—and the Meteor wasn't nearly as popular as the Fairlane despite styling with a faint familial resemblance to that of full-size Mercs. The Meteor was thus abandoned after two years in favor of a more impressive, restyled Comet line with a bucket-seat Caliente and Cyclone models that effectively replaced the S-33.

+ FOR Interesting, short-lived model • Smooth, strong V-8 performance • Good 6-cylinder economy • Bucket-and-console sportiness • A practical daily-driver

■ AGAINST Not many to find • Finish low-buck in spots • Weak 6-cylinder performance • Still little collector interest (though this is gradually changing) • Weak potential value appreciation

PRODUCTION

1962 5900 **1963** 4865

SPECIFICATIONS

Length (in.)	203.8
Wheelbase (in.)	116.0
Weight (lbs)	2960-3030
Price (new)	$2510-2630

ENGINES

cid/type	bhp	years
170/ohv I-6	101	1962-63
221/ohv V-8	145	1962-63
260/ohv V-8	164	1962-63

PRICES

FAIR	$1000-2000
GOOD	$2000-3000
FINE	$3000-6000

FINE EXAMPLE PRICE HISTORY

1982 $2500		**1990** $7500

1994 $6500   **1998** $6000
1982-2000 RETURN 4%
2000-2010 Even

1 9 6 2
MERCURY MONTEREY CUSTOM S-55

1962 Monterey S-55 convertible

First of the big bucket-seat Mercurys introduced in reply to the growing early-'60s interest in sportier cars generally—and to counter Pontiac's hot-selling '62 Grand Prix in particular. Arrived at mid-model year as a hardtop coupe and convertible along with sibling Ford Galaxie 500XLs, and much like them technically. A 300-horse-power 390 V-8 was standard, but Dearborn's new 406 enlargement—"Marauder" in Mercury-speak—was available on a very limited basis with 385 or 405 bhp via free-flow intake and exhaust systems, mechanical lifters, and 10.9:1 compression. Still, most of these S-55s were built with the base engine and Multi-Drive automatic, and emphasized sporty luxury with interiors featuring thin-shell bucket seats, shift console, and plenty of bright metal and mylar trim. Not a sales success in '62, but it would nonetheless carry on for the next several seasons.

+ FOR Strong special-interest value for some collectors • Sporty, luxurious interior • Smooth, potent performance • Still relatively affordable despite rarity and "muscle" image

▬ AGAINST Forgettable styling • Unique body and trim pieces as scarce as the cars • Visual distinctions mainly inside, not outside

PRODUCTION

htp cpe 2772 **conv** 1315

SPECIFICATIONS

Length (in.)	120.0
Wheelbase (in.)	120.0
Weight (lbs)	3800-3900
Price (new)	$3488-3738

ENGINES

cid/type	bhp	years
390/ohv V-8	300	1962
406/ohv V-8	385/405	1962

PRICES

Conv

FAIR	$3000-6000
GOOD	$6000-8500
FINE	$8500-13,000

(Deduct 30% for hardtop; add 100% for 406.)

FINE CONVERTIBLE PRICE HISTORY

1982 $3500   **1990** $12,000
1994 $14,000   **1998** $13,000
1982-2000 RETURN 8%
2000-2010 5%

1 9 6 3 - 6 4
MERCURY S-55 & MARAUDER

As Mercury's cousin to the Ford Galaxie 500XL, these were large luxurious cars. The Marauders usually sported bucket seats, and were offered with a wide assortment of V-8s. The "slantback" two-door hardtop debuted for 1963 ½ as part of the Monterey Custom series, and was also available in sportier S-55 form—a bucket-seat subseries begun in 1962, packing a heavy-duty suspension and a 300-bhp 390 V-8 as standard. S-55s also came as a notchback hardtop and convertible. No S-55 version was offered for 1964, but you could get Marauder fastback styling in all of Mercury's big-car series—Monterey, Montclair, and Park Lane—with either two or four doors. Engine options were extended that year—Mercury's 25th anniversary—to include the mighty 410/425-bhp 427, compared to a 385/405-bhp 406 in 1963. Interestingly enough, there hasn't been a whole lot of collector movement in big-Merc performance models of the early '60s, even the convertibles, which are hardly numerous.

+ FOR Lots of room • Ample, even awesome performance • Brawny looks • Strong runners

▬ AGAINST Drinks a lot of gas • Scarce body parts • Moderately rust-prone

PRODUCTION

1963 S-55 2d formal htp 3863 **S-55 conv** 1379 **S-55 Marauder fstbk htp** 2319 **Marauder fstbk htp** 7298 **1964 Monterey Marauder 2d htp** 8760 **4d htp** 4143 **Montclair Marauder 2d htp** 6459 **4d htp** 8655 **Park Lane Marauder 2d htp** 1052 **4d htp** 4505

SPECIFICATIONS

Length (in.)	215.0 (1963), 215.5 (1964)
Wheelbase (in.)	120.0
Weight (lbs)	3887-4056
Price (new)	$3083-3413

ENGINES

cid/type	bhp	years
390/ohv V-8	250/300/330	1963-64
406/ohv V-8	385/405	1963
427/ohv V-8	410/425	1964

PRICES

Conv

1964 Montclair Marauder hardtop coupe

1963 S-55 Marauder hardtop coupe

FAIR $2500-5000
GOOD $5000-9000
FINE $9000-13,000
(Deduct 30% for htp, including Marauder fastback hardtop; add 40% for Super Marauder engines.)

FINE CONVERTIBLE PRICE HISTORY

1982 $3500	1990 $12,000
1994 $14,000	1998 $13,000
1982-2000 RETURN 8%	
2000-2010 7%	

1964-65
MERCURY COMET CALIENTE 2-DOORS

Sporty top-shelf models in the more expensive "senior compact" Comet line issued to do what the slow-selling mid-size Meteor couldn't. The Comet remained a close Ford Falcon relative in these years, and thus more compact than intermediate. But it was also more heavily facelifted than the restyled 1964-65 Falcons, with busy sheetmetal sculpturing, a complex grille, and extra inches tacked onto to the rear of Falcon bodyshells. Caliente—Spanish for "hot"—offered a square-lined four-door sedan as well as a convertible and hardtop coupe, all with a standard bench front seat and six-cylinder power. What collectors seek are the 2-doors with optional buckets and small-block V-8s. Regardless, they boasted decent handling and fine economy thanks to fairly low weight, this despite pedestrian engineering. Long overshadowed as collector cars by the more overtly sporting 1964-65 Cyclone hardtop, but scarcity of those and increased interest in some lower-line '60s models argues for these Calientes, especially the ragtop.

✚ FOR Still very affordable • Convertibles are fun and uncommon • Terrific small-block V-8s available

▬ AGAINST Rust-prone • Performance dull with sixes • Contrived styling • Clean originals hard to find • Ditto some body/trim parts

PRODUCTION
1964 htp cpe 31,204 **conv** 9039 **1965 htp cpe** 29,247 **conv** 6035

SPECIFICATIONS
Length (in.)	195.1/195.3 (1964/65)
Wheelbase (in.)	114.0
Weight (lbs)	2668-2869
Price (new)	$2375-2664

ENGINES
cid/type	bhp	years
170/ohv I-6	101	1964
200/ohv I-6	120	1964-65
260/ohv V-8	164	1964
289/ohv V-8	210	1964
289/ohv V-8	200/225	1965

PRICES
Conv	
FAIR	$2500-5000
GOOD	$5000-9000
FINE	$9000-13,000
(Deduct 30% for hardtop.)

1965 Comet Caliente convertible

FINE CONVERTIBLE PRICE HISTORY
1982 $3500	1990 $10,000
1994 $11,500	1998 $13,000
1982-2000 RETURN 8%	
2000-2010 5%	

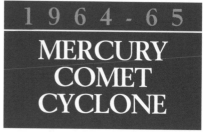

1964-65
MERCURY COMET CYCLONE

1964 Comet Cyclone hardtop coupe

An even sportier offshoot of Comet's top-line 1964-65 Caliente: a hardtop coupe with standard bucket seats and 289 V-8. Distinguished by less exterior brightwork, and simulated chrome-reverse wheels with exposed lug nuts, plus tachometer, three-spoke pseudo-woodgrain steering wheel, special interior trim, dashboard trim with "camera-case" finish, and chrome engine dressup. Like other Comets, the Cyclone acquired stacked headlamps and wider-appearing rear end in a '65 restyle, plus more available V-8 power.

✚ FOR A sporty, bucket-seat Merc with V-8 power at an affordable price

▬ AGAINST Rather confused styling • Spotty quality control • Moderately rapid ruster

PRODUCTION
1964 7454 **1965** 12,347

SPECIFICATIONS
Length (in.)	195.1/195.3 (1964/65)
Wheelbase (in.)	114.0
Weight (lbs)	2860-2994
Price (new)	$2655-2683

ENGINES
cid/type	bhp	years
289/ohv V-8	200/210/225	1964-65

PRICE $8500-13,500
FAIR	$3000-6000
GOOD	$6000-8500

FINE EXAMPLE PRICE HISTORY
1982 $3500	1990 $9000
1994 $11,500	1998 $12,000
1982-2000 RETURN 8%	
2000-2010 5%	

1966-67

MERCURY CYCLONE

Mercury's smallest hot cars in these years, finally moved up to mid-size status with the adoption of the new '66 Ford Fairlane platform. This was a distinct series usually referred to without the Comet handle. The mid-year GT models carried a big 390 V-8 with chrome dress-up, a functional twin-scoop fiberglass hood, and an uprated performance suspension package; others had a standard 289 small-block V-8 and offered the handling mods optionally. All featured bucket-seat interiors and unique styling touches. Optional big-block 427s with up to 425 nominal bhp were added for '67, but they were very rare then, and even more so now.

⬦ FOR Clean, handsome styling • Great performance • Not something you see every day

◼ AGAINST Fair construction quality • Moderately rust-prone • GTs thirsty and now muscle-car costly

PRODUCTION

1966 htp cpe 6889 **conv** 1305 **GT htp cpe** 13,812 **GT conv** 2158 **1967 htp cpe** 2682 **conv** 431 **GT htp cpe** 3419 **GT conv** 378

SPECIFICATIONS

Length (in.)	203.0-203.5
Wheelbase (in.)	116.0
Weight (lbs)	3075-3595
Price (new)	$2700-3295

ENGINES

cid/type	bhp	years
289/ohv V-8	200	1966-67
390/ohv V-8	265-335	1966-67
427/ohv V-8	390/410/425	1967

PRICES

GT/GTA conv	
FAIR	$3500-7500
GOOD	$7500-10,000
FINE	$10,000-13,000

GT/GTA htp	
FAIR	$3000-6000
GOOD	$6000-8500
FINE	$8500-11,500

(Non-GT/GTA models: deduct 15% for convertibles and 20% for hardtops.)

FINE GTA CONVERTIBLE PRICE HISTORY

1982 $3350		**1990** $15,000	
1994 $13,000		**1998** $13,000	
1982-2000 RETURN 8%			
2000-2010 5%			

1966

MERCURY S-55

Mercury's revived big performance car, returning as a separate series after a two-year absence. It featured "Torque Box" construction—frames individually tuned to minimize noise and harshness—a standard 428 big-block V-8, heavy-duty chassis, plus

1966 S-55 convertible

a sporty bucket-seat interior. Styling was square and clean "in the Lincoln Continental tradition," as the ads put it. Few were sold, although Mercury generally had a successful big-car year in 1966.

⬦ FOR Clean looks • Rarity means high appreciation • High performance

◼ AGAINST Low mpg • Some rust potential • Body parts scarce now

PRODUCTION

2d htp 2916 **conv** 669

SPECIFICATIONS

Length (in.)	220.4
Wheelbase (in.)	123.0
Weight (lbs)	4031-4148
Price (new)	$3292-3614

ENGINES

cid/type	bhp	years
428/ohv V-8	345	1966

PRICES

Conv	
FAIR	$3500-6000
GOOD	$6000-8000
FINE	$8000-12,000

(Deduct 25% for hardtop.)

1967 Cyclone GT hardtop coupe

FINE CONVERTIBLE PRICE HISTORY

1967-68
MERCURY COUGAR

Lincoln-Mercury's upmarket pony-car, introduced two years behind the Mustang and based on its basic chassis design and bodyshell, except for a three-inch longer wheelbase and its own sheetmetal. A pretty car with good performance, it could be optioned for fine handling, too. To our eyes, it's at least as desirable as contemporary Mustangs, particularly the XR-7 version with its woodgrain, fully instrumented dash and leather seat facings. Unlike the Mustang, Cougar didn't bother with sixes. FoMoCo's 289 V-8 was standard for base and XR-7 models, while the GT boasted the 390. For 1968, a new GTE version was added, packing the big 427 V-8. A handling package was standard on GT/GTE (necessary with the heavy big-block V-8s), and is an important option to look for on lesser versions.

⊞ FOR Clean long-hood/short-deck styling • Pleasant combination of performance and economy with small-block V-8 • High performance in GT/GTE • XR-7s are Milestone cars

⊟ AGAINST Some electrical headaches • Rocker panel and floorpan rust • GT/GTE thirsty and nose-heavy

PRODUCTION

1967 2d htp 116,260 **GT 2d htp** 7412 **XR-7 2d htp** 27,221 **1968 2d htp** 81,014[1] **XR-7 2d htp** 32,712
[1]Includes GT/GTE

SPECIFICATIONS

Length (in.)	190.3
Wheelbase (in.)	111.0
Weight (lbs)	2988-3174
Price (new)	$2851-3232

ENGINES

cid/type	bhp	years
289/ohv V-8	195/200/225	1967-68
302/ohv V-8	210/230	1968
390/ohv V-8	280/320/325	1967-68
427/ohv V-8	390	1968

PRICES

XR-7	
FAIR	$2500-5000
GOOD	$5000-9000
FINE	$9000-13,000
(Deduct 10% for non-XR-7.)	

1968 Cougar XR-7 hardtop coupe

FINE XR-7 PRICE HISTORY

1967
MERCURY MONTEREY S-55

1967 S-55 hardtop coupe

A continuation of the S-55 package under the Monterey label, it was phased out almost as soon as the model year began, probably because big performance cars were deemed inappropriate for a make with luxury aspirations. Styling was of the new rounded "Coke-bottle" school adopted this year, and somewhat less distinctive than before, though more and more like a Lincoln. Mechanical details were as for the '66 S-55.

⊞ FOR Extremely rare, and above-average investment • Good performance • Reasonable handling for size

⊟ AGAINST As for 1966 S-55

PRODUCTION

2d htp 570 **conv** 145

SPECIFICATIONS

Length (in.)	218.5
Wheelbase (in.)	123.0
Weight (lbs)	3837-3960
Price (new)	$3511-3837

ENGINES

cid/type	bhp	years
428/ohv V-8	345	1967

PRICES

As per 1966 Mercury S-55.

1968-69
MERCURY CYCLONE

1969 Cyclone fastback coupe

Mercury's last '60s muscle cars. Still a separate series, but based on the curvy, somewhat larger new 1968 Comet/Montego. Debuted in formal notchback and sleeker fastback styles, both hardtop coupes, in base and GT trim. Smoother frontal styling gave fastback Cyclones better aerodynamics and thus higher top speeds than Ford's similar Torinos could manage on NASCAR supertracks, and Cyclone quickly established itself as the car to beat. As before, the '68 GT came with a 390 big-block, and all Cyclones offered 427 and 428 power options. Notchbacks were dropped for

'69, but fastbacks were mildly facelifted and a new CJ428 appeared with a 335-bhp 428 Cobra-Jet engine, plus four-speed stick, heavy-duty suspension, and no-charge Ram-Air induction. In January '69 the Cyclone Spoiler appeared with a large rear wing (not approved for NASCAR) and signature fender decals honoring Merc pilots Cale Yarborough and Dan Gurney. There was also a Spoiler II with a flush grille and further aero tweaks á la Ford's concurrent Torino Talladega. Alas, the GT became a mere option package for '69, when the high-winding 427 was deleted and non-CJ Cyclones were downgraded to a standard mildly tuned 302 small-block. Still, the big-inch Cyclones are highly desired as slick, quick machines from the "golden age" of Detroit performance.

➕ **FOR** Aggressive styling • GTs, CJ, and Spoilers all *bona fide* muscle cars in high demand today • Strong NASCAR performance record • Limited production promises strong value retention

➖ **AGAINST** Mediocre fit-and-finish • High running costs • Prone to wheelarch and floor rust • GT/CJ/Spoiler expensive now, and not getting any cheaper • Big price increases lately

1969 Cyclone Spoiler II Cale Yarborough fastback coupe

PRODUCTION

1968 notchback htp cpe 1034 **GT notchback htp cpe** 334 **fastback htp cpe** 6165 **GT fastback htp cpe** 6105 **1969 fastback htp cpe** 5882 **CJ fastback htp cpe** 3261

SPECIFICATIONS

Length (in.)	206.2
Wheelbase (in.)	116.0
Weight (lbs)	3275-3635
Price (new)	$2771-3224

ENGINES

cid/type	bhp	years
302/ohv V-8	210/220/230	1968-69
351/ohv V-8	250/290	1969
390/ohv V-8	320/325/335	1968-69
427/ohv V-8	390	1968
428/ohv V-8	335	1968-69

PRICES

Cyclone	
FAIR	$2000-4000
GOOD	$4000-7000
FINE	$7000-10,000
427	
FAIR	$3500-7000
GOOD	$7000-13,000
FINE	$13,000-19,000
428	
FAIR	$2000-5000
GOOD	$5000-9000
FINE	$9000-13,000

(Deduct 10% for notchbacks.)

FINE 427 FASTBACK PRICE HISTORY

1982 $2800		**1990** $10,000	
1994 $14,000		**1998** $19,000	
1982-2000 RETURN 12%			
2000-2010 8%			

1969-70 MERCURY COUGAR

The second-series Cougar, with a longer, wider body on the same 111.0-inch wheelbase and two new convertible offerings. Styling was similar to 1967-68, but more ordinary, particularly the grille. XR-7s continued to feature a full set of needle gauges and leather-faced seat upholstery as standard, and wore blackout grilles for 1970. The former GT and GTE models were reduced to option packages available with or without XR-7 trim, but continued to pack big-block V-8s. A new variation was the Eliminator package for the hardtop, sporting appropriate tape striping, a rear decklid spoiler, wide wheels and tires, and a 300-bhp version of Ford's 351 V-8. Like concurrent Mustangs, these were the last of the true ponycar Cougars. For 1971, Ford and Mercury both bulked up their ponycars, making them heavier and less agile, though more luxurious, than their predecessors. Styling became more like that of the mid-size Montego, which the Cougar was later based on.

➕ **FOR** As for 1967-68 Cougar

➖ **AGAINST** As for 1967-68 Cougar, but less distinctive styling and somewhat lower appreciation potential

PRODUCTION

1969 2d htp 66,331 **conv** 5796 **XR-7 2d htp** 23,918 **XR-7 conv** 4024 **1970 2d htp** 49,479 **conv** 2322 **XR-7 2d htp** 18,565 **XR-7 conv** 1977

SPECIFICATIONS

Length (in.)	193.8/196.1 (1969/70)
Wheelbase (in.)	111.0
Weight (lbs)	3219-3408
Price (new)	$3016-3692

ENGINES

cid/type	bhp	years
302/ohv V-8	290	1970
351/ohv V-8	250/290/300	1969-70
390/ohv V-8	320	1969
428/ohv V-8	335	1969-70

PRICES

Conv	
FAIR	$2500-5000
GOOD	$5000-9000
FINE	$9000-13,000

(Add 45% for Eliminator, deduct 10% for hardtop, deduct 10% for non-XR-7.)

FINE XR-7 CONVERTIBLE PRICE HISTORY

1982 $3300		**1990** $11,000	
1994 $10,000		**1998** $13,000	
1982-2000 RETURN 9%			
2000-2010 5%			

1969 Cougar Eliminator hardtop coupe

MERCURY MARAUDER
1 9 6 9 - 7 0

1969 Marauder X100 hardtop coupe

Mercury's last fling with full-size fire breathers, issued at the twilight of the performance age. The Marauder was built on a shorter 121-inch-wheelbase chassis (versus 123 for other big Mercs except wagons), which it shared with the Ford XL. Hidden headlights and the grille design were as for the luxury Marquis, while quad taillights and the flying-buttress roof design were exclusive to the Marauder in the Mercury line. The X-100 was the hotter version, boasting the big 429 V-8 and 360 horses. The Marauder changed only in detail for 1970, when production was only about one third of '69 output.

✚ FOR Terrific go • Smooth highway cruiser • Good looks • Well built • Luxury • Comfort • Last of the "sumo"

class hot Mercs • Pretty rare

▬ AGAINST Thirsty • Special trim nearly extinct

PRODUCTION
1969 2d htp 9031 **X-100 2d htp** 5635 **1970 2d htp** 3397 **X-100 2d htp** 2646

SPECIFICATIONS
Length (in.)	219.1/221.8 (1969/70)
Wheelbase (in.)	121.0
Weight (lbs)	3972-4191
Price (new)	$3503-4136

ENGINES
cid/type	bhp	years
390/ohv V-8	265/280	1969-70
429/ohv V-8	360	1969-70

PRICES
X-100	
FAIR	$2000-5000
GOOD	$5000-7000
FINE	$7000-10,000

(Deduct 20% for non-X-100 model.)

FINE X-100 PRICE HISTORY
1982 $1700		**1990** $8000	
1994 $10,000		**1998** $10,000	
1982-2000 RETURN 11%			
2000-2010 8%			

MERCURY CYCLONE
1 9 7 0 - 7 1

Last of the mid-size muscle Mercs, but less collectible than the 1968-69 models. The main reason is more contrived styling with a protruding "gunsight" grille and a semi-fastback hardtop roofline, similar to that on Ford's 1970-71 Torino. Both combined with extra weight, aggravated by an inch-longer wheelbase, to make these less competitive as stock cars—leaving the more aero-efficient '69s to carry Mercury's NASCAR colors for several more seasons. The GT remained a package option for the base Cyclone, and standard power for both was a two-barrel 351 V-8. The Spoiler switched from a 428 to a 429 V-8 packing 370 standard horses, 375 in optional mechanical-lifter "Super CJ" tune. Unfortunately, these engines weren't as strong as they seemed, so the heftier curb weights took a toll in street performance as well. But the muscle market was fast-dwindling anyway, and the Cyclones disappeared for '72 in favor a single new-design Montego GT fastback that was even less special.

✚ FOR Last of their kind • Comparatively rare • Performance still good, though less than before • Mechanical parts still plentiful • Values rising now, if modestly

▬ AGAINST Workmanship declines again • Less unique than earlier Cyclones

PRODUCTION
1970 2d htp 1695 **GT 2d htp** 10,170 **Spoiler 2d htp** 1631 **1971 2d htp** 444 **GT 2d htp** 2287 **Spoiler 2d htp** 353

SPECIFICATIONS
Length (in.)	209.9
Wheelbase (in.)	117.0
Weight (lbs)	3460-3775
Price (new)	$3238-3759

1971 Cyclone Spoiler hardtop coupe

ENGINES

cid/type	bhp	years
351/ohv V-8	250	1970
351/ohv V-8	240/285	1971
429/ohv V-8	360/370/375	1970
429/ohv V-8	370	1971

PRICES

GT
FAIR $2000-4000
GOOD $4000-7000
FINE $7000-10,000
(Deduct 10% for non-GT; add 40% for Spoiler, 428 or 429.)

FINE GT PRICE HISTORY

1982 $3300 **1990** $9000
1994 $8000 **1998** $9500
1982-92 RETURN 7%
2000-2010 5% (8% for 428/429 engines)

1971-73
MERCURY COUGAR

The last Cougar ponycars. They shared an enlarged new body/chassis design with the third-generation Ford Mustangs, but rode a five-inch longer wheelbase. Unlike the Mustang, which still offered overt performance models, Cougar now tilted decisively toward luxury, though to no good sales effect until 1973, when a six-year sales slide finally ended. An unstressed 429 big-block was offered for '71 only; other engines were two- and four-barrel 351 small-blocks, de-

rated after '71 with the industry switch to SAE net horsepower quotes. The Cougar was really less a ponycar in these years than a cousin to the lush mid-size Montego—which it became by shifting to that platform for '74. Still, the 1971-73s aren't as boring as you might think and are worth collector consideration, especially XR-7 hardtops—as nice inside as ever—and the super-rare ragtops, both XR-7 and base.

FOR Last of their kind • Smooth and plush, especially XR-7s • Mechanical and most body parts still available • Good club support • Convertible values drifting up

AGAINST Probably won't ever be a high-status Cougar • So-so workmanship • Rust-prone unless looked after • Clean convertibles tough to find

PRODUCTION

1971 2d htp 34,008 **conv** 1723 **XR-7 2d htp** 25,416 **XR-7 conv** 1717 **1972 2d htp** 23,731 **conv** 1240 **XR-7 2d htp** 26,802 **XR-7 conv** 1929 **1973 2d htp** 21,069 **conv** 1284 **XR-7 2d htp** 35,110 **XR-7 conv** 3165

SPECIFICATIONS

Length (in.)	196.7-199.5
Wheelbase (in.)	113.0
Weight (lbs)	3330-3530
Price (new)	$3289-3903

ENGINES

cid/type	bhp	years
351/ohv V-8	240/285[1]	1971
351/ohv V-8	168/262/266[2]	1972
351/ohv V-8	168/264[2]	1973
429/ohv V-8	370[1]	1971

[1]SAE gross [2]SAE net

PRICES

Conv
FAIR $2000-4000
GOOD $4000-7000
FINE $7000-12,000
(Deduct 15% for hardtop.)

FINE CONVERTIBLE PRICE HISTORY

1982 $3800 **1990** $9500
1994 $8500 **1998** $11,000
1982-2000 RETURN 7%
2000-2010 4%

1984-88
MERCURY COUGAR XR-7

1987 Cougar XR-7 coupe

The return of a truly sporting XR-7 after a decade's absence, though the name decorated some forgettable interim models. It bowed a year behind the redesigned Cougar and the Ford

1971 Cougar XR-7 convertible

Thunderbird Turbo Coupe. The XR-7 shared the T-Bird's new-for-'83 "aero" styling—save for a more formal roofline—firm suspension, four-cylinder turbocharged engine, and standard five-speed manual gearbox. A three-speed automatic was optional through '86, after which all Cougars (and T-Birds) were heavily facelifted to be even more aerodynamic, and the XR-7 parted company by switching to the T-Bird/Cougar/Mustang 5.0-liter V-8, recently updated with fuel injection and teamed with a mandatory four-speed automatic. Nice cars all, with sportier interiors, more aggressive looks, and tauter handling than other concurrent Cougars, but we'd have the V-8 over the turbo-four any day. It may ultimately be less collectible than the T-Bird TC regardless of engine, and was replaced for 1988 by a new-generation XR-7 with 3.8-liter supercharged V-6, a cousin to that year's new Thunderbird Super Coupe (see entry).

✚ **FOR** Good turbo performance (0-60 in about 10 seconds) • V-8 smooth, refined, and torquey • 1983-86 styling • Well-equipped • Pleasant drivers • Not long deceased • Priced like used cars

⊟ **AGAINST** Throttle lag, exhaust boom, and other nasty turbo traits • Visibility not great • Scant chance of significant value appreciation in foreseeable future

PRODUCTION

NA; all models: **1984** 131,190 **1985** 117,274 **1986** 135,909 **1987** 104,526 **1988** 119,162

SPECIFICATIONS

Length (in.)	197.6-200.8
Wheelbase (in.)	104.2
Weight (lbs)	3055-3485
Price (new)	$13,065-16,626

ENGINES

cid/type	bhp	years
140/sohc I-4[1]	142/145/155	1983-86
302/ohv V-8	150/155	1987-88

[1]Turbocharged

PRICES

Depreciating through 1990s. Top price $3500.
2000-2010 RETURN Even

1991-94
MERCURY CAPRI

Not really a sports car. Not a true four-seater. The Mercury Capri fell

1991 Capri XR2 convertible

between the cracks and was never a big seller. Australian-made and based Mazda 323 components, the Capri was an economical 2+2 convertible. Although not intended as a sports car, the Capri was always unfavorably compared to the Mazda Miata. The cars biggest fault was body flex. A soft suspension provided a pleasant ride, but mediocre handling. Performance was adequate with the base 1.6-liter dohc four and more than adequate in the turbocharged XR2 model.

✚ **FOR** It's a convertible • Economical • Fairly rare and Australian

⊟ **AGAINST** Uninspired looks and abilities • Body flex • Back seat almost useless

PRODUCTION[1]

1991 21,200 **1992** 12,557 **1993** 9,723 **1994** 3,948
[1]U.S. Calendar year sales

SPECIFICATIONS

Length (in.)	166.1-167.1
Weight (lbs)	2385-2423
Wheelbase (in.)	94.7
Price (new)	$12,990-17,250

ENGINES

cid/type	bhp	years
97/dohc I-4	100	1991-94
97/dohc I-4[1]	132	1991-94

[1]Turbocharged

PRICES

Spring prices for 1991-92 Turbos ranged up to $6000.
2000-2010 RETURN Generally depreciating

1997
MERCURY COUGAR XR7 30TH ANNIVERSARY EDITION

1997 Cougar XR7 30th Anniversary Edition coupe

By the late Nineties, big, heavy, rear-drive coupes had worn out their welcomes in the American marketplace. At FoMoCo, Cougar's XR7 joined the T-Bird and Lincoln Mark VIII as a casualty of the period. Yet even as these cars prepared for their final bows, Ford found publicity and a few extra consumer dollars with farewell, "collector's editions." A somewhat less sportive variant of the T-Bird, the base XR7 (based on the competent 1989 re-do) was an angularly handsome cruiser that was sluggish with the standard 145-bhp 3.8-liter V-6, but pleasingly quick with an optional 205-bhp 4.6-liter V-8. Creature comforts were in abundance and build quality was good. The anniversary edition (available in dark red only) had upgraded front brakes; sport-tuned suspension (on V-8 models only); sport shocks; uplevel buckets; 16-inch tires on lacy-spoke alloy wheels; and the usual assortment of identifying badges. For all this, this final XR7 never developed "youth appeal," which will not help collectibility.

FOR Acceleration (V-8) • Limited production • Luxury amenities

AGAINST Thirst (V-8) • Acceleration (V-6) • Numb handling • Balky, 4-speed automatic trans • Collectibility, if any, is many years away

PRODUCTION
NA

SPECIFICATIONS

Length (in.)	199.9
Weight (lbs)	3536
Wheelbase (in.)	113.0
Price (new)	$18,325

ENGINES

cid/type	bhp	years
232/ohv V-6	145	1997
281/ohc V-8	205	1997

PRICES
Spring 2000 top value for fine example was $13,000.
2000-2010 RETURN Depreciating

1985-89
MERKUR XR4TI

First in a scheduled squadron of European Fords for Lincoln-Mercury dealers to sell against Mercedes, BMW, and other upmarket imports in the late '80s. This was actually a hybrid: the sporty German-built Sierra XR4i two-door hatchback sedan powered by Dearborn's turbocharged 2.3 "Lima" four (hence the "T") instead of Cologne's 2.8-liter V-6. New Merkur marque ("Mercury" in German) was part of an ill-advised marketing strategy. Most people didn't remember the name, and those who did generally couldn't pronounce it properly (Mair-KOOR). But the car was nifty: about BMW 3-Series size, responsive and, with five-speed manual, quick (0-60 in under eight seconds). But cars with the optional three-speed automatic lost a high-lift cam, 20 horses, and 20 critical pounds/feet of torque (down to 180 total). L-M also bungled initial options availability—too few automatics and leather interiors—and the "jell-o mold" lines, though in step with Ford's emerging "aero look," was controversial, especially the "biplane" rear spoiler. Sales peaked in 1986, the first full year, then fell fast through 1989, when costly new passive-restraint mandates prompted L-M to abandon yet another "captive import." The few interim changes included larger new-style wheels for '87, a single low-profile spoiler, and an optional monochrome exterior for '88.

FOR Unique American-market Eurosedan • "Orphan marque" appeal for some enthusiasts • Good go with manual • Nimble • Roomy rear seat for a sport coupe • Roomy cargo hold • Teutonically solid • Inexpensive

AGAINST Should be "cheap wheels" for a long time • Irritating turbo lag, especially with automatic • Engine buzzy-boomy (though less so than in T-Bird Turbo Coupe) • Styling controversial • L-M dealers won't want to know you

PRODUCTION[1]
1985 8974 **1986** 14,315 **1987** 9123 b5745 **1989** 4017
[1]Calendar-year U.S. sales

SPECIFICATIONS

Length (in.)	178.4
Wheelbase (in.)	102.7
Weight (lbs)	2920
Price (new)	$16,360-19,065

ENGINES

cid/type	bhp	years
140/ohc I-4[1]	150/175	1985-89

[1]Turbocharged

PRICES
Top price at present $3500
2000-2010 RETURN 2% for fine examples, 0% for others

1930-32
MG M-TYPE MIDGET

Abingdon's first small sports car, and now a real collector's item despite running gear borrowed from the contemporary—and more mundane—Morris Minor sedan. It's little overhead-cam engine advanced for the day (the cam drive doubled as the generator drive), but most everything else was cheap and cheerful. In typical period British fashion, this was a narrow two-seater with a flexible chassis, ox-cart springs, and beam axles front and rear. Skimpy wood-framed bodywork, some fabric-covered, sported boattail rear-end styling, a two-piece vee'd windshield, and freestanding cycle-type fenders. A very perky character belied a top speed of no more than 60 mph flat out, this despite low weight. As with so many prewar (and postwar) British sportsters, weather protection was minimal, cockpit appointments spartan. The M-Type was also offered as a close-coupled Sportsman's Coupe, but it's the roadster everyone remembers.

FOR Classic looks • Cheeky character • Small size, great heart • Uncomplicated • Rare nowadays

AGAINST Negligible performance • Tight cockpit • Spindly engineering, build • Parts almost impossible to get anymore • Little value appreciation

PRODUCTION
3235 (began 1928)

1986 XR4Ti coupe

1930 M-Type roadster

SPECIFICATIONS

Length (in.)	123.0
Wheelbase (in.)	78.0
Weight (lbs)	1120
Price (new)	NA

ENGINES

cc/type (cid)	bhp[1]	years
847/ohc I-4 (52)	20/27	1928-32

[1]Net

PRICES

FAIR	$5000-10,000
GOOD	$10,000-15,000
FINE	$15,000-25,000

FINE EXAMPLE PRICE HISTORY

1982 $8000	**1990** $20,000
1994 $22,000	**1998** $25,000
1982-2000 RETURN 7%	
2000-2010 5%	

1 9 3 2 - 3 4
MG J-TYPE MIDGET

Successor to the M-Type and its dumpy four-seat D-Type companion. The basic ohc four was retained, though with a new head that delivered more power. Wheelbase was extended eight inches, too, and there was new body styling that forecast the shape of MGs all the way through the TD of the early Fifties. All J2s were open two-seaters. Early exam-ples had cycle-type fenders, which later gave way to clamshell-type "swept wings." The four-seat J1 was offered in both open and closed form. Cutaway doors and wood-framed bodies were common to both J-Types. The J maintained MG practice with a very hard leaf-spring suspension, solid front and rear axles, non-synchromesh gearbox, and precious little weather protection, but J2 performance was improved to almost 80 mph. A supercharged J3 and super-charged competition J4 were added to the line in late '32.

✚ FOR Sweet, almost feminine character • Creditable go and handy size in a vintage Brit sportster • Rare and valuable

▬ AGAINST Not much value for money in today's terms • Crude "crash-box" • Cramped cockpit • Antediluvian ride, handling

PRODUCTION

J1 380 **J2** 2083

SPECIFICATIONS

Length (in.)	124.0
Wheelbase (in.)	86.0
Weight (lbs)	1260
Price (new)	NA

ENGINES

cc/type (cid)	bhp[1]	years
847/ohc I-4 (52)	36	1932-34
746/ohc I-4 (46)	NA/72[2]	1932-34

[1]Net [2]Supercharged J3/J4

PRICES

J1/J2	
FAIR	$7500-12,000
GOOD	$12,000-18,000
FINE	$18,000-30,000
(J3 add 25%; J4, 65%)	

FINE J1 PRICE HISTORY

1982 $8500	**1990** $35,000
1994 $30,000	**1998** $30,000
1982-2000 RETURN 8%	
2000-2010 5%	

1 9 3 4 - 3 6
MG PA/PB

1934-35 PA Airline coupe

Smoother and marginally more so-phisticated than the J2 it replaced, but still mainly for masochists with nar-row shoulders. It retained MG's unmistakable design hallmarks: proud radiator, freestanding headlamps, classic clamshell fenders, and "slab-back" fuel tank. The PA also retained the existing 847cc displacement, while the PB had a bored-out 939cc version with eight extra horsepower. Three body styles were offered: two-seat roadster (the most sought-after today), a four-seater, and the unusual, gracefully shaped "Airline" fastback coupe. All featured center-lock wire wheels, real leather upholstery, and MG's customary wood-framed body construction, plus fold-down windshields on the open models. The PA/PB was capable of 70+ mph, but a hard ride and lack of gearbox synchronization made this a rugged driving experience.

FOR Last MGs in the original Cecil Kimber mold • Rarity • Small, light, and handy • Excellent club support

AGAINST Performance still limited • Rot-prone bodies • Parts now scarce and pricey • Cramped • Bone-crusher ride • Not an everyday find

SPECIFICATIONS

Length (in.)	131.0
Wheelbase (in.)	87.5
Weight (lbs)	1510
Price (new)	NA

ENGINES

cc/type (cid)	bhp	years
847/ohc I-4 (52)	35[1]	1934-35
939/ohc I-4 (57)	43[1]	1935-36
[1]Net		

PRICES

FAIR	$5000-10,000
GOOD	$10,000-15,000
FINE	$15,000-25,000

FINE EXAMPLE PRICE HISTORY

1982 $7000   **1990** $33,500
1994 $25,000   **1998** $25,000
1982-2000 RETURN 8%
2000-2010 5%

1936-39
MG TA/TB

The TA was Abingdon's first offering after MG merged with the Nuffield organization, and rather different from the superseded P-Types—and less distinctly MG. The transmission (with synchromesh phased in as a running change after the first few months of production) and pushrod engine were both based on Morris Ten components; there were no other important mechan-

1936 TA roadster

ical changes. Styling was very familiar, and similar to the P-Type's, though bodies were longer and a touch wider. The rakish roadster was joined in 1938 by a new drophead (convertible) coupe with full-height doors crafted by Tickford. TA's old-fashioned long-stroke engine was replaced on the 1939-only TB models by the new shorter-stroke (but still markedly undersquare) XPAG unit, which would run into the mid-Fifties. These models were important as the direct ancestors of the romantic postwar TC, which was essentially a carryover TB.

FOR Rarity, especially TB • More space than PB • Simple engineering • Many parts common with TC • 1930s MG appeal • Ample club support

AGAINST Hard ride • Still cramped despite larger bodies • Bodies still rot-prone • Not much go or refinement

PRODUCTION

TA 3003 (1936-39) **TB** 379 (1939 only)

SPECIFICATIONS

Length (in.)	140.0
Wheelbase (in.)	94.0
Weight (lbs)	1960
Price (new)	NA

ENGINES

cc/type (cid)	bhp[1]	years
1292/ohv I-4 (79)	52	1936-39[2]
1250/ohv I-4 (76)	54	1939[3]
[1]Net [2]TA [3]TB		

PRICES

As per 1935-36 MG Type PA/PB.

1945-49
MG TC

1945-49 TC roadster

An archetypal prewar British sports car design carried over into the early postwar period. But the TC was different: somehow it turned Americans onto European sports cars. Its Milestone status derives partly from that, and partly from its classic 1930s lines: freestanding headlamps, upright radiator shell, sweeping front fenders, rakish cutaway doors, fold-down windshield, abbreviated tail (housing the fuel tank and spare tire), and spindly 19-inch-diameter wire wheels (with knock-off hubs, of course). The TC was a very old-fashioned car even before the war, with a flexible ladder-type chassis and crude solid axle suspension front and rear. The TC's ride was jiggly and stiff, but its agility was a revelation to Yankees raised on workaday Fords and Chevys. Not very fast, with a top speed under 80 mph and acceleration to match, but its simple 1250cc four wore like the cast iron it was made of. Despite rumors to the contrary, no left-hand-drive models were built. It's still a cult car, and a prime collectible best reserved for top-down, sunny-days driving.

➕ **FOR** Very desirable even now • Simple, rugged engineering • Huge following • Good number of mechanical and body parts, many reproduction, still available • Milestone status

➖ **AGAINST** Costly now and not appreciating much at present • Dreadful ride • Body rots easily • Cramped accommodations • Appeal diluted now by mass of replicas • Amazing price spread

PRODUCTION

10,000

SPECIFICATIONS

Length (in.)	139.5
Wheelbase (in.)	94.0
Weight (lbs)	1735
Price (new)	$1895 U.S. in 1949

ENGINES

cc/type (cid)	bhp[1]	years
1250/ohv I-4 (76)	54	1945-49

[1]Net

PRICES

FAIR	$5000-9000
GOOD	$9000-16,000
FINE	$16,000-22,000

FINE EXAMPLE PRICE HISTORY

1982 $21,000	1990 $32,500
1994 $21,000	1998 $22,000
1982-2000 RETURN 1%	
2000-2010 2%	

1949-53
MG TD

A more modern version of the TC with the same irresistible charm. The engine and transmission weren't changed, but most everything else was. A new box-section chassis with coil-spring independent front suspension was concealed by a wider, squatter body, still in traditional British-roadster style. The separate headlamps and flowing front fenders were retained, as were the classic TC overall proportions, but the large-diameter wire wheels gave way to smaller steel disc wheels. The TD was built with left-hand drive for the U.S., which eagerly took most exports. It was still a crude car, with a primitive and frustrating folding top and snap-in side curtains. The TD II appeared in 1951 with more standard equipment and detail styling changes. This was followed by a TD "Mark II" with a little more horsepower. TDs were actively raced by Americans learning about things like road courses and rallying, and MG assisted with tuning kits for the little four-cylinder engine. In all, the TD was a much better car than the TC, but not as pure in styling, which may be why it's considered less desirable by some collectors today.

➕ **FOR** Better ride and handling than TC • Simple to work on • Chassis and engine parts still around • Still in great demand • A Milestone car • Recent jump in value compared to TC, which has been static

➖ **AGAINST** Same limited performance as TC • Wood-framed bodies don't hold up well • Body parts very costly now • Horribly old-fashioned, even when new • Is it overpriced today?

SPECIFICATIONS

Length (in.)	145.0
Wheelbase (in.)	94.0
Weight (lbs)	1930
Price (new)	NA

ENGINES

cc/type (cid)	bhp[1]	years
1250/ohv I-4 (76)	54-57	1949-53

[1]Net

PRICES

FAIR	$4000-8000
GOOD	$8000-14,000
FINE	$14,500-20,000

FINE EXAMPLE PRICE HISTORY

1982 $17,000	1990 $23,500
1994 $15,000	1998 $20,000
1982-2000 RETURN 1%	
2000-2010 3%	

1953 TD Mark II roadster

MG

1953-55

MG TF/ TF 1500

A hastily revamped TD, built for less than two years. The most noticeable difference in the TF was its appearance, a kind of streamlined update of the TC/TD. The nose was reworked to accommodate a raked-back radiator shell with dummy screw cap, headlamps were faired into the front fenders, the tail was revised, and instruments were given octagonal housings echoing the MG badge. The drivetrain was taken straight from the TD, but beginning in the autumn of 1954 an enlarged, more powerful four was substituted and the model designation changed to TF 1500.

FOR As for 1950-53 TD plus better styling

AGAINST As for 1950-53 TD and less "classic" appearance • Not a Milestone • A real T-series MG is one with a radiator cap you can unscrew to pour water in

PRODUCTION
9600 total **TF 1500** 3400

SPECIFICATIONS
Length (in.)	147.0
Wheelbase (in.)	94.0
Weight (lbs)	1930
Price (new)	NA

ENGINES
cc/type (cid)	bhp[1]	years
1250/ohv I-4 (76)	57	1953-54
1466/ohv I-4 (89)	63	1954-55

[1]Net

PRICES
FAIR	$5000-10,000
GOOD	$10,000-14,000
FINE	$14,000-22,000

FINE EXAMPLE PRICE HISTORY
1982 $16,000	**1990** $25,000
1994 $19,000	**1998** $20,000

1982-2000 RETURN 2%
2000-2010 3%

1953-58

MG ZA/ZB MAGNETTE

1958 ZB Magnette sedan

British Motor Corporation's mid-'50s sports sedan. It was related to the contemporary Wolseley 4/44, with the same rounded, Italianette styling and coil-spring independent front suspension, but with a traditional MG radiator. Ride height was slightly lower than that of other BMC models on this platform, and the drivetrain previewed that of the forthcoming MGA sports car. Not very quick—only 80-85 mph tops—but the handling was sporty, and nice decorative details helped compensate for the so-so performance. The ZB-series offered more horsepower, a "proper British" wood-faced dash, wraparound rear window, and optional "Varitone" two-color paintwork. It was loved by enthusiasts for its four-seat capacity and talented road moves.

FOR Roomy, four-seat body • Interesting period British design • Drivetrain common with ubiquitous MGA • Handling

AGAINST Limited performance • Rust-prone • Body parts very scarce • Still little known in U.S., so collector interest is limited

PRODUCTION
ZA 12,754 **ZB** 23,846

SPECIFICATIONS
Length (in.)	169.0
Wheelbase (in.)	102.0
Weight (lbs)	2465
Price (new)	$1820 U.S. in 1955-56

ENGINES
cc/type (cid)	bhp[1]	years
1489/ohv I-4 (91)	60/68	1952-58

[1]Net, ZA/ZB

PRICES
FAIR	$3000-5000
GOOD	$5000-7500
FINE	$7500-11,000

FINE EXAMPLE PRICE HISTORY
1982 $6000	**1990** $10,000
1994 $9000	**1998** $10000

1982-2000 RETURN 4%
2000-2010 2%

1955 TF 1500 roadster

327

MGA

1955-62

MG's late-'50s sports car, considered almost shockingly modern compared to its square-rigged T-series predecessors. Styling was sleek and up to date. The long hood terminated in a rounded front end bearing a squat, MG-style radiator/grille. Front fenders were semi-integrated with the envelope body, and swept back and downward into the doors, then kicked up into the curvy rear fenders. The sloping tail was bereft of an outside spare tire. Offered in both the traditional roadster with side curtains and, later, a fixed-roof coupe with a wraparound rear window and (horrors!) roll-up door glass. The wood framing for the body gave way to modern all-steel construction. The initial specification was basically as for the TF 1500. In 1960, the sturdy four was bored out to just under 1.6 liters, and the all-drum brakes were changed to a front-disc/rear-drum system. The 1600 Mark II sported more upright vertical grille bars and a displacement a bit over 1.6 liters for more power. The smooth bodywork aided top speed, which was in the vicinity of 100 mph (slightly more on the Mark II). With this model, MG was firmly estab-

lished as part of the American scene. The MGA is considered by some to be the last MG faithful to "true" sports-car precepts (stark appointments, minimal weather protection), and marked a transition between the "vintage" T-series and "modern" MGB eras for the marque.

FOR Styling • Strong chassis • Mechanically simple, easy to work on • Most parts still available • Open-air fun (roadster) • Good U.S. supply • Still commands intense interest

AGAINST Steel-body rust worries • Limited luggage space

PRODUCTION

1500 58,750 **1600** 31,501 **1600 Mark II** 8719

SPECIFICATIONS

Length (in.)	156.0
Wheelbase (in.)	94.0
Weight (lbs)	1985/2050 (rdstr/cpe)
Price (new)	approx. $2500 U.S. in 1960

ENGINES

1957 MGA coupe

cc/type (cid)	bhp[1]	years
1489/ohv I-4 (91)	72	1955-57
1588/ohv I-4 (97)	80	1957-60
1622/ohv I-4 (99)	86	1961-62

[1]Net

PRICES

Rdstr

FAIR	$4000-7000
GOOD	$7000-10,000
FINE	$10,000-18,000

(Deduct 10% for coupe.)

FINE RDSTR PRICE HISTORY

1982 $7000		**1990** $17,500	
1994 $12,000		**1998** $18,000	

1982-2000 RETURN 6%
2000-2010 5%

MGA TWIN-CAM & DELUXE

1958-62

1959 MGA Twin Cam roadster

An extensively revised version of the MGA, and sold alongside the

1960 MGA roadster

regular models. The main distinction, as the name implies, was its four-cylinder engine with a double-overhead-cam head. This power unit was finicky to tune, and wouldn't tolerate low-grade fuel, but most surviving cars have been modified to run on today's low-calorie stuff. Also equipped with four-wheel disc brakes and steel, center-lock disc wheels. Much faster than the "cooking" MGAs, the Twin-Cam could reach 115 mph, but was quite a bit more expensive and produced in limited numbers primarily for competition duty. It was dropped sometime before the MGA itself, replaced by the "1600 DeLuxe," which retained the all-disc brakes but reverted to the normal 1.6-liter (1588 and 1622cc) pushrod engines from the standard models.

FOR As for 1955-62 MGA, plus more performance and exclusivity

AGAINST Few parts left now for complex dohc engine • Hard to find in reasonable condition • Not as easily found as regular MGA • Others as for 1955-62 MGA

PRODUCTION
2111 (plus 388 "1600 DeLuxe" models)

SPECIFICATIONS
Length (in.)	156.0
Wheelbase (in.)	94.0
Weight (lbs)	2185/2245 (rdstr/cpe)
Price (new)	approx. $3200 U.S. in 1960

ENGINES
cc/type (cid)	bhp[1]	years
1588/dohc I-4 (97)	108	1958-60
1588/ohv I-4 (97)	80	1960
1622/ohv I-4 (99)	86	1961-62

[1]Net

PRICES
Twin Cam
FAIR	$8000-10,000
GOOD	$10,000-18,000
FINE	$18,000-26,000

Deluxe
FAIR	$4000-8000
GOOD	$8000-11,000
FINE	$11,000-22,000

FINE TWIN CAM PRICE HISTORY
1982 $7500		1990 $30,000	
1994 $30,000		1998 $24,000	

1982-2000 RETURN 7%
2000-2010 Twin Cam 10%, **Deluxe** 5%

1962-80
MGB & MGBGT

One of the longest-running models in recent history and, as it would turn out, the last "real" MGs to be built. Introduced in two-seat roadster form, it was then supplemented by a closed 2+2 GT coupe at the start of the 1966 model year. Power came via BMC's sturdy B-series four-cylinder engine, essentially the MGA unit bored out to near 1.8 liters. The 1962-64 models had three-main-bearing engines; five mains were adopted with the '65s. The monocoque bodyshell was cleanly styled, if a bit plain, marked by a wide MG vertical-bar grille and headlamps residing in front fender "scoops." In

British fashion, the roadster's top was still infuriatingly difficult to put up or take down, but purists cringed at the "modern" roll-up door windows and proper heater. A Mark II version arrived for the 1968 model year with an all-synchromesh gearbox (earlier cars had a non-synchro first gear), and automatic transmission was made an extra-cost item. A good many manual cars were fitted with Laycock de Normanville overdrive, a worthwhile extra to look for. Styling and equipment changed little through 1968. After that, however, things got worse, particularly on "federalized" MGBs. Beginning in 1969, BMC took the cheapest and least imaginative ways to meet U.S. safety and emissions requirements, including a hastily contrived padded overlay that hid the normal glovebox and engines that were progressively detuned, dropping in both horsepower and torque every year. U.S. models also got ugly rubber-covered bumpers in the early '70s, then were cranked up on their suspensions to meet headlight height requirements. This was accompanied by a protruding black "bra" that simply ruined the original tidy front end appearance. Already eclipsed by more modern competitors by the late '60s, the B was probably kept on too long (it lasted into the fall of 1980). For us, the most desirable models are the 1962-67 roadsters and the pretty little GT coupes that were sold in the U.S. through 1975.

FOR Parts and service easy (British Heritage will even sell you a complete

1963 MGB roadster

1978 MGB roadster

new roadster body) • Solid engineering • Sturdy and simple to maintain • Fine handling (to 1974) • Extensive club support • Cheap to buy and run • Traditional MG virtues (and vices)

■ AGAINST Too common for high appreciation • Very rust-prone • Slower than it looks (100 mph tops) • GT body panels scarce in U.S. • Typically suspect British construction quality

PRODUCTION

Approximately 515,000, incl. approx. 150,000 GT coupes

SPECIFICATIONS

Length (in.)	153.3
Wheelbase (in.)	91.0
Weight (lbs)	2030-2600/2190 (rdstr/GT)
Price (new)	$2500-8000 U.S.

ENGINES

cc/type (cid)	bhp[1]	years
1798/ohv I-4 (110)	60-95	1962-80

[1]Net

PRICES

MGB	
FAIR	$2500-5000
GOOD	$5000-8000
FINE	$8000-10,000
GT	
FAIR	$2500-4000
GOOD	$4000-7000
FINE	$7000-9000

FINE 1965 MGB PRICE HISTORY

1982 $4100	1990 $8500
1994 $10,000	1998 $12,500

1982-2000 RETURN 5%
2000-2010 3%

1 9 6 7 - 6 9
MGC & MGCGT

1969 MGCGT coupe

A short-lived—and unsuccessful—attempt at making the MGB a successor to the late Austin-Healey 3000. The normal four-cylinder engine was replaced by a 3.0-liter inline six completely different in detail from the Healey unit. Torsion bars were substituted for the B's front coil springs, 15-inch wheels replaced 14-inchers, and the hood grew a prominent bulge to clear the bulkier powerplant. In other respects, the C was much like the B—except in the way it drove. It suffered ponderous understeer, and didn't have as much snap as it should have due to a conspicuous lack of torque. Nevertheless, it was fast in a straight

line (120 mph available) and reasonably economical. The motoring press turned up its collective nose, as did most potential buyers, and the C was withdrawn after only about two years. It was offered in both roadster and GT coupe body styles with standard all-synchromesh manual gearbox or optional automatic. Not very popular in the U.S. for the obvious reasons, including a somewhat steeper price than that of the much more pleasant MGB.

⊞ FOR Most parts still available in UK • Better performance and equipment than the MGB

■ AGAINST Heavy steering and stodgy handling • Engine parts becoming scarce • Poor reputation among non-MG enthusiasts

PRODUCTION

8999 (incl. 4449 GT cpes)

SPECIFICATIONS

Length (in.)	153.2
Wheelbase (in.)	91.0
Weight (lbs)	2460/2610 (rdstr/GT)
Price (new)	approx. $3700 U.S. in 1969

ENGINES

cc/type (cid)	bhp[1]	years
2912/ohv I-6 (178)	145	1967-69

[1]Net

PRICES

MGC	
FAIR	$2500-4500
GOOD	$4500-8000
FINE	$8000-11,500
GT	
FAIR	$2000-3500
GOOD	$3500-6000
FINE	$6000-9000

FINE MGC PRICE HISTORY

1982 $5000	1990 $6500
1994 $10,000	1998 $11,500

1982-2000 RETURN 5%
2000-2010 3%

1 9 7 1 - 7 9
MG MIDGET MARK III/1500

A continuation of the "Spridget," following the departure of the Austin-Healey Sprite in 1970, but still based on the Mark II platform dating back to 1961. Updated by a minor restyle and extra equipment as the Mark III from 1971-74, still powered by the venerable BMC A-series four in 1275cc form. U.S. safety and emissions regulations began adding weight and draining power as the decade wore on, and the new British Leyland regime needed to

1974-79 Midget 1500 roadster

meet even stiffer forthcoming regulations as economically as possible in its biggest export market. The result was the 1500, which arrived for the 1975 model year sporting ugly black "rubber baby buggy bumpers" and the entirely different 1.5-liter engine from corporate stablemate Triumph Spitfire. Despite production economies that dictated relatively crude solutions to meeting the standards, the Midget retained its appeal as a low-cost "learner's" sports car, an old-fashioned machine you could buy new to experience what traditional open-air motoring was all about. It sold in modest numbers until its phase-out after the 1979 season, by which time financially troubled BL had more or less decided to abandon the sports car market. Midget collectibility is still something of a question mark right now, but the car will probably always have its advocates, which means it should hold its value fairly well in coming years.

➕ FOR Inexpensive • Economical • Perhaps the cheapest way to get into topless driving • Others as for 1961-71 Austin-Healey Sprite • Appreciated strongly in last 20 years but probably topped out

➖ AGAINST British construction quality problems • Very cramped cockpit • Noisy at speed • Hard ride • Archaic specs

PRODUCTION

approx. 110,000

SPECIFICATIONS

Length (in.)	137.6/141.0/143.0 (1971-74/1975-76/1977-79)
Wheelbase (in.)	80.0
Weight (lbs)	1560-1826
Price (new)	$2395 U.S. in 1971, rising to $5200 by 1979

ENGINES

cc/type (cid)	bhp[1]	years
1275/ohv I-4 (78)	55-62	1971-74
1493/ohv I-4 (91)	50-55	1975-79

[1]SAE net

PRICES

FAIR	$1500-3000
GOOD	$3000-6000
FINE	$6000-10,000

FINE EXAMPLE PRICE HISTORY

1982	$1000	1990	$4000
1994	$5000	1998	$9500
1982-1994 RETURN 15%			
2000-2010 4%			

1966-77
MONTEVERDI 375-SERIES

Super-exclusive family of ultra-performance GTs assembled in Switzerland under the aegis of Peter Monteverdi. All used American Chrysler drivetrains and a tubular-steel chassis with de Dion rear suspension. The cleanly styled bodies were designed and supplied by Italian carrozzerie Fissore. As with other makes catering to a limited clientele, there was really no "standard" Monteverdi, each car being built more or less to customer taste. But three models were listed: a two-seat 375C coupe and 375S cabriolet, and a 2+2 L coupe. Appearance on all was typical late-'60s supercar: somewhat angular contours, glassy greenhouse with delicate pillars, shapely notchback rear end, broad eggcrate grille with quad headlamps. Most Monteverdis stayed in Europe, but a few were "smuggled" into the U.S. after 1967.

➕ FOR Rare and individual • Sturdy Detroit drivetrains with parts still in good supply • Styling • Performance

➖ AGAINST Build quality erratic • Body parts extinct • How many could there be left?

PRODUCTION

NA, but very limited (approx. 50 per year)

SPECIFICATIONS

Length (in.)	181.1 (two-seaters), 189.0 (L coupe)
Wheelbase (in.)	104.8
Weight (lbs)	3345-3630
Price (new)	approx. $50,000 (U.S. equivalent)

ENGINES

cid/type	bhp[1]	years
440/ohv V-8	380	1966-67

[1]Gross

1970 375-Series coupe

PRICES

Up to $75,000

FINE EXAMPLE PRICE HISTORY

1982 $28,500	**1990** $100,000
1994 $70,000	**1998** $70,000
1982-2000 RETURN 0%	
2000-2010 2%	

MORGAN 4/4 SERIES I

Malvern Link's first four-wheel sports car, introduced after 26 years of building nothing but three-wheelers (with the single wheel at the rear). The 4/4 was very much an extension of the original design, with the same sliding-pillar independent front suspension and Z-section frame side members, both still found on today's "Moggies." Much like the early MG T-Type in concept and character, though it wasn't as fast or agile. Offered in roadster and convertible (full top) body styles, both featured wood-framed bodywork built by Morgan. Early examples carried Coventry-Climax power before Morgan switched to engines from the Standard Motor Car Company, used exclusively post-war. Top speed was only about 70 mph, but that was enough thanks to the spine-jarring ride, lack of creature comforts, and slow-synchro gearbox.

As usual, the two-seat roadsters are more desirable, but all these cars have immense charm.

✠ FOR Period British sports car appeal • Simple to maintain • More exclusive than concurrent MGs • The company's still in business • Good factory and club support

▄ AGAINST Amazingly hard ride • Wood-frame bodies rot badly • Cramped cockpit • Few mechanical parts left and no body items

PRODUCTION

824 prewar, 578 postwar

SPECIFICATIONS

Length (in.)	136.0/139.0 (rdstr/conv)
Wheelbase (in.)	92.0
Weight (lbs)	1625-1735
Price (new)	NA

ENGINES

cc/type (cid)	bhp[1]	years
1098/F I-4 (67)	45	1938-39
1122/F I-4 (68)	34	1936-39
1267/ohv I-4 (77)	40	1939-50

[1]Gross

PRICES

FAIR	$10,000-13,000
GOOD	$13,000-16,000
FINE	$16,000-26,000

FINE POSTWAR EXAMPLE PRICE HISTORY

1982 $7000	**1990** $20,000
1994 $22,500	**1998** $26,000
1982-92 RETURN 8%	
2000-2010 5%	

MORGAN PLUS 4

1952 Plus 4 convertible

Replacement for the 4/4, with the same basic body and chassis engineering on a four-inch longer wheelbase, and still with a sliding-pillar front suspension and separately mounted Moss gearbox. The longer chassis enabled an extra pair of "occasional" seats to be stuffed into the cockpit. Styling and engineering gradually changed over the years, with a sloping nose and faired-in headlamps by the mid-'50s. But even in 1968, a Morgan was still like Morgans always had been—modified 1930s styling, louvered hood, rudimentary equipment, nice handling, and a rock-hard ride. Mechanical changes included adoption of front disc brakes in 1960, a switch to the 1991cc Triumph TR2 engine in

1937 4/4 roadster

1954 (338 built), later the TR3 power-plant (1795 built), then adoption of the 2138cc TR4 powerplant in 1962 (1565 built). A Super Sports version was offered with souped-up TR engines by the British Lawrencetune firm. Most had light-alloy bodies.

⊞ FOR As for 1939-50 4/4 Series I, plus more performance and better mechanical parts availability • Milestone car status

▬ AGAINST As for 1939-50 4/4 Series I

PRODUCTION

3854 total, 2206 exported to the U.S.; **Supersport** 101

SPECIFICATIONS

Length (in.)	144.0
Wheelbase (in.)	96.0
Weight (lbs)	approx. 1915
Price (new)	NA

ENGINES

cc/type (cid)	bhp[1]	years
2088/ohv I-4 (127)	68	1950-54
1991/ohv I-4 (122)	90-100	1954-62
2138/ohv I-4 (131)	100-105	1963-68

[1]Gross

PRICES

FAIR	$10,000-13,000
GOOD	$13,000-18,000
FINE	$18,000-28,000

(Add 50% for Super Sports.)

FINE EXAMPLE PRICE HISTORY

1982 $8000		**1990** $30,000	
1994 $25,000		**1998** $28,000	
1982-2000 RETURN 8%			
2000-2010 8%			

MORGAN 4/4

A reborn 4/4 built on the Plus 4 chassis, still with wood-framed bodies and the odd sliding-pillar front sus-pension that dates back to 1910. Drivetrains now came from Ford Britain, not Triumph. This was still a two-seat roadster, but with a cowled radiator, semi-faired headlamps, and sloped tail of the "modernized" mid-'50s Plus 4. There were few major changes after launch, but Morgan was always quick to adopt the latest available Ford engines (all fours) and associated manual gearboxes—three-speed through 1960, four-speed to 1982, then five-speed. Also, front-disc brakes were adopted in 1960, the "safety-ized" dash from the V-8-powered Plus 8 (see entry) in 1968. A 2+2 roadster was added after the Plus 4's 1968 demise, and both versions were renamed "4/4 1600." A Fiat twin-cam 1.6 was offered from 1982 as an alternative to Ford power, by then the front-drive European Escort "CVH" unit. Three years later, Morgan revived the Plus 4 as a 2.0-liter model, again powered by Fiat. It was always handbuilt, so production was never high: 6-8 in a good week. Beloved, like all Morgans, as defiantly "vintage"—so little changed for so long that its become its own "neoclassic."

⊞ FOR As for 1950-68 Plus 4

▬ AGAINST As for 1950-68 Plus 4, but less performance (depending on engine, 0-60 in 10-10.5 seconds, top speed 92-102 mph)

PRODUCTION

Series II 387 **Series III** 59 **Series IV** 206 **Series V** 639 **4/4 1600** NA

SPECIFICATIONS

Length (in.)	144.0
Wheelbase (in.)	96.0
Weight (lbs)	1570-1700
Price (new)	$1260 U.S. in 1955-56

ENGINES

cc/type (cid)	bhp[1]	years
1172/sv I-4 (71)	36-39	1955-59
997/ohv V-4 (91)	54	1959-61
1340/ohv I-4 (82)	60	1962-63
1498/ohv I-4 (92)	78	1963-68
1598/ohv I-4 (97)	88	1968-82
1598/dohc I-4 (97)	96	1982-87

[1]Net

PRICES

FAIR	$10,000-13,000
GOOD	$13,000-16,000
FINE	$16,000-25,000

FINE POSTWAR EXAMPLE PRICE HISTORY

1982 $7000		**1990** $20,000	
1994 $22,500		**1998** $26,000	
1982-92 RETURN 8%			
2000-2010 5%			

1978 4/4 roadster

1963-66
MORGAN PLUS FOUR PLUS

1965 Plus 4 Plus coupe

A strange bird: the only Morgan with anything close to "modern" styling. Atop an unaltered Plus 4 frame with a 2.2-liter Triumph TR4 engine was a bubble-top fixed-roof coupe body made of fiberglass. The almost bell-shaped roof contrasted with the rather four-square lower body with straight-through fenderlines and a flat rear deck. Seating was strictly for two, and the side windows were fixed. The car wasn't a commercial success, either because Morgan misjudged its customers or the styling didn't appeal to enough people. Today it's a very desirable rarity, though reportedly only 10 were sent to the U.S.

✛ FOR Extreme scarcity • Interesting appearance • Greater comfort and refinement • Others as for 1950-68 Plus 4

◼ AGAINST Impossible to find any more • Body parts extinct • Others as for 1950-68 Plus 4

PRODUCTION
26

SPECIFICATIONS
Length (in.)	152.0
Wheelbase (in.)	96.0
Weight (lbs)	1820
Price (new)	NA

ENGINES
cc/type (cid)	bhp[1]	years
2138/ohv I-4 (131)	100	1963-66

[1]Gross

PRICES
FAIR	$9000-12,000
GOOD	$12,000-18,000
FINE	$18,000-30,000

FINE EXAMPLE PRICE HISTORY
1982 $8500		1990 $25,000	
1994 $21,000		1998 $25,000	

1982-2000 RETURN 9%
2000-2010 8%

1968-00
MORGAN PLUS 8

A continuation of the Plus 4 design, but heavily modified. Morgan's antiquated sliding-pillar front suspension and rugged ladder chassis were retained, but the wheelbase grew by two inches. This setup made for a hard ride, but provided good handling. *Road & Track* managed a "respectable" 0.86g on the skidpad. The rakish two-seat roadster body, still with cutaway doors and a crude folding top, continued to rely on wood framing to support its steel panels. The big change was under the hood. In place of the previous Triumph four was a light-alloy V-8, the 3.5-liter Rover powerplant that British Leyland had acquired from Buick in the early '60s. Despite the awful aerodynamics of the traditional styling, top speed moved up to an impressive 125 mph, with similar gains in acceleration. Some Plus 8s were fitted with light-alloy body panels (19 "Lightweights" according to one source), but all wore cast-alloy wheels. Beginning in mid-1972, the antediluvian Moss gearbox finally gave way to a Rover transmission mounted in unit with the engine. A few cars were converted to run on propane and imported to the U.S. by a California firm. This was before the V-8 was certified for U.S. sale in the Rover 3500 sedan. In 1989 the V-8 (shared with Ranger Rover and later Land Rover Discovery) was increased to 3.9-liter. For 1999, the interior was lengthened by two inches. This provided extra room in the cockpit for the fitting of optional airbags. Production continues at this writing, and there's a long waiting list, so older examples are also much in demand.

✛ FOR The only replicar that never went out of production • Very fast • Lovely ex-GM engine • Traditional roadster appeal • Rare in U.S.

◼ AGAINST Wood still rots • Few

1983 Plus 8 roadster

creature comforts • Unyielding ride • Mechanical parts increasingly difficult to come by outside UK

PRODUCTION

3000+ to date (188 to the U.S. as of mid-1988)

SPECIFICATIONS

Length (in.)	147.0-155.9
Wheelbase (in.)	98.0
Weight (lbs)	1875-2250
Price (new)	$2800 (at factory in 1969)

ENGINES

cc/type (cid)	bhp[1]	years
3528/ohv V-8 (215)	143-155	1968-84
3528/ohv V-8 (215)	190	1984-89
3946/ohv V-8 (241)	190	1989-00

[1]Net

PRICES

1968-82	
FAIR	$12,000-17,500
GOOD	$17,500-22,500
FINE	$22,500-30,000

FINE EXAMPLE PRICE HISTORY

After five years of age, Plus Eights hold their value and will gradually begin to appreciate. Present values for 1990s models to $44,000.
2000-2010 RETURN 5%

1956-71

MORRIS MINOR 1000

The final development of the original 1948 small car designed by the innovative Alex Issigonis, later of Mini fame. It was once considered the car that could have done for Britain what the VW Beetle did for Germany, and more respected now than it ever was when in production. One of the first all-new postwar British models, the Minor was intended to provide low-cost motoring for the masses, and re-mained largely unchanged throughout its long life. Light in weight, it utilized all-steel unit body/chassis construction and an unusual (for the day) torsion bar front suspension. Styling was quaintly rounded, but provided a roomy interior within a fairly short wheelbase. Two- and four-door sedans and a two-door Traveler wagon with "Olde English" wood trim and twin side-hinged rear doors were offered. Intended as a minimal car in keeping with the "less is more" philosophy, so trim and equipment were very basic. The engine was BMC's A-series four, a rugged, almost unbreakable engine was offered variously in two displace-ments. The Minor was far from excit-ing, however (top speed only around 75 mph), but its quick steering and capable chassis made it a surprisingly good-handling car. Although it was supposed to be replaced in the early '60s by the advanced front-drive BMC 1100 family (an Issigonis creation based on Mini design principles), the Minor continued in production due to steady, healthy customer demand. A good deal of its engineering was used in other, later BMC/British Leyland cars, so parts are surprisingly plentiful today through UK sources. A total of 1,582,302 Minors (all engine varia-tions) had been built when production finally ceased in October 1970.

FOR Great character and thor-oughly British • Fine handling • Bullet-proof engines • Engine and chassis parts still around • Easy to work on • Good accommodation for size • A cheap collectible that's cheap to run • Cult status in England

AGAINST Body/chassis very rust-prone • Front suspension often falls apart • Woodie wagon trim a bear to restore • Sparse trim and equipment • Slow by most any standard and not very refined

PRODUCTION

948cc 544,048 **1098cc** 303,443

SPECIFICATIONS

Length (in.)	148.0
Wheelbase (in.)	86.0
Weight (lbs)	1755 (average)
Price (new)	NA

ENGINES

cc/type (cid)	bhp	years
948/ohv I-4 (58)	37	1956-65
1098/ohv I-4 (67)	48	1965-71

PRICES

Conv, van, wgn	
FAIR	$3000-4000
GOOD	$4000-5000
FINE	$5000-7500

(Deduct 25% for pickup, 50% for sdn)

FINE CONVERTIBLE PRICE HISTORY

1982 $2500		**1990** $6500	
1994 $6500		**1998** $6000	

1982-2000 RETURN 7%
2000-2010 5%

1957 Minor Traveller wagon

1954 Jet convertible

1951-54

MUNTZ JET

A much-modified derivative of the Frank Kurtis sports car (see entry) backed by ace huckster and radio king Earl "Madman" Muntz. His Muntz Jet retained the basic Kurtis styling, but had a more fully outfitted interior—complete with a radio mounted in a front center armrest—and full four-passenger seating. A lift-off hardtop was also included. The first 28 cars were built in California with aluminum bodies riding an extended 113.0-inch-wheelbase chassis. All had Cadillac's 331-cid ohv V-8. Production was then shifted to Muntz's home base, Evanston, Illinois, where the wheelbase was increased to 116 inches and power switched to the L-head Lincoln V-8. A numerically lower final drive ratio gave the Jet a higher top speed than the Kurtis, and Muntz claimed a 0-60 mph time of as low as nine seconds. The Jet was much heavier and far less agile, however. Muntz lost about $1000 on every one he sold, the main reason he gave up on the venture after four years.

FOR Rarity • Performance • Decent handling • Strong appreciation • Milestone car status

AGAINST Body parts very scarce • Aluminum body restoration expensive • Steel body rust • Costly on today's market

PRODUCTION

394

SPECIFICATIONS

Length (in.)	182.0/185.0
Wheelbase (in.)	113.0/116.0
Weight (lbs)	approx. 3300
Price (new)	$5000-6000

ENGINES

cid/type	bhp	years
331/ohv V-8	160	1951
336.7/sv V-8	154	1952-54

PRICES

FAIR	$8000-15,000
GOOD	$15,000-20,000
FINE	$20,000-30,000

FINE EXAMPLE PRICE HISTORY

1982 $5000	**1990** $30,000
1994 $25,000	**1998** $27,000
1982-2000 RETURN 8%	
2000-2010 5%	

1930-34

NASH TWIN-IGNITION EIGHT

These were the largest Nashes in a period of sumptuous, beautiful styling and boasting lots of special fea-

1932 981 Twin Ignition Eight Victoria convertible

tures. "Twin-Ignition" meant two sets of plugs/points/condensers/coils operating from a single distributor. The 1930 T-I Eight became the Model 890 in 1931; the same 298.6-cid engine was used on the 1932 Model 990, while that year's 1090 Advanced Eight and Ambassador received a larger bored-out 322-cid version. The latter was adopted for the 1933 Advanced and Ambassador Eights. The 128-inch-wheelbase Advanced Eight was scrubbed during the model rationalization of 1934 (though the name remained on a smaller car). Most often riding wheelbases of 133 and 142 inches, all of these Nashes had outstanding performance and were nicely assembled with quality materials, one of the reasons the CCCA recognizes the 1931 series 890; 1932 series 990, Advanced Eight, and Ambassador Eight; and 1933-34 Ambassador Eight as full Classics. Lesser Twin-Ignition Eights of 240 and 260.8 cid, as well as the T-I Sixes, aren't accorded Classic status, but they're also fine cars worthy of consideration.

✚ **FOR** Underrated and quite affordable; look for open models • Styling • Road manners • Interest value • CCCA Classic status on top models

▬ **AGAINST** Lack of hobby recognition • Mechanical complexity

PRODUCTION

1930 12,801 **1931** 6199 **1932** 5791 **1933** 1590 **1934** 5000 (est.)

SPECIFICATIONS

Length (in.)	Varies
Wheelbase (in.)	124.0/133.0 (1930), 121.0/ 128.0/133.0/142.0 1931-34
Weight (lbs)	3770-4650
Price (new)	$1475-2055

ENGINES

cid/type	bhp	years
240/ohv I-8	88-94	1931-32
260/ohv I-8	100	1932-34
298.6/ohv I-8	100/115	1930-32
322/ohv I-8	125	1932-34

PRICES

Open	
FAIR	$7500-15,000
GOOD	$15,000-35,000
FINE	$35,000-52,000
Closed, long wb	
FAIR	$3000-11,000
GOOD	$11,000-20,000
FINE	$20,000-29,000
Closed, short wb	
FAIR	$2000-6000
GOOD	$6000-15,000
FINE	$15,000-25,000

1932 SERIES 980 CONVERTIBLE SEDAN PRICE HISTORY

1982 $21,000		**1990** $45,000	
1994 $50,000		**1998** $52,000	
1982-2000 RETURN 6%			
2000-2010 5%			

1939-42 NASH AMBASSADOR EIGHT

Nash's best in its final styling generation before the war. Also the firm's last eight-cylinder offerings until 1955. Marked by a striking front-end design plus the traditional Nash valve-in-head engine with nine main bearings for uncommon smoothness and longevity. A variety of closed bodies was offered along with a cabriolet (convertible). The latter was dropped for 1942 when Nash adopted a rather less successful horizontal grille. The 1939-41 models are arguably better-looking.

✚ **FOR** Nice styling • Smooth performance • Quality • Relatively easy on the budget, even convertibles • Good club support

▬ **AGAINST** Limited availability • Parts supplies limited • Rust-prone

PRODUCTION

1939 17,052 **1940-42** 33,000 (est.)

SPECIFICATIONS

Length (in.)	213.2 (1939-40); 210.2 (1941-42)
Wheelbase (in.)	125.0 (1939-40); 121.0 (1941-42)
Weight (lbs)	3260-3820
Price (new)	$1084-1295

ENGINES

cid/type	bhp	years
260.8/ohv I-8	115	1939-42

PRICES

Cabrio	
FAIR	$6000-15,000
GOOD	$15,000-25,000
FINE	$25,000-35,000
Others	
FAIR	$2000-4500
GOOD	$4500-8000
FINE	$8000-12,000

FINE CABRIOLET PRICE HISTORY

1982 $11,000		**1990** $27,500	
1994 $35,000		**1998** $35,000	
1982-2000 RETURN 7%			
2000-2010 5%			

1939-42 NASH AMBASSADOR SIX

1941 Ambassador Six sedan

Six-cylinder counterpart to the Ambassador Eight, though mounted on a four-inch shorter 121-inch wheelbase in 1939-40, which the Eight also adopted for 1941-42. Like the Eight, the Six was powered by a

1941 Ambassador Eight convertible

smooth overhead-valve engine (and also of long-stroke design), and offered in a similar lineup of body styles.

➕ **FOR** As for 1939-42 Ambassador Eight, but even less costly

➖ **AGAINST** As for 1939-42 Ambassador Eight

PRODUCTION

1939 8500 **1940-42** 55,000 (est.)

SPECIFICATIONS

Length (in.)	209.2
Wheelbase (in.)	121.0
Weight (lbs)	3180-3470
Price (new)	$925-1130

ENGINES

cid/type	bhp	years
234.8/ohv I-6	105	1939-42

PRICES

As per 1939-42 Ambassador Eight less 10%.

1941-42
NASH 600

Replacement for the 1940 LaFayette as Nash's low-priced product, and much more popular. This was an important car in that it introduced unit body/chassis construction. Its wheel

1942 600 sedan

base measured nine inches shorter than the Ambassadors' and its light weight yielded astounding gas economy—hence the designation, which stood for 600 miles on a 20-gallon tank. No convertible was offered, but the 600 nevertheless helped Nash-Kelvinator to a $4.6 million profit in 1941.

➕ **FOR** Low running costs • Solid build

➖ **AGAINST** As for 1940-42 Ambassador Eight and Six

PRODUCTION

60,000 (est.)

SPECIFICATIONS

Length (in.)	199.6
Wheelbase (in.)	112.0
Weight (lbs)	2490-2655
Price (new)	$730-918

ENGINES

cid/type	bhp	years
172.6/sv I-6	75	1941-42

PRICES

FAIR	$2500-5000
GOOD	$5000-9000
FINE	$9000-13,000

FINE EXAMPLE PRICE HISTORY

1982 $5150	**1990** $6750
1994 $5500	**1998** $13,000
1982-2000 RETURN 10%	
2000-2010 5%	

1946-48
NASH AMBASSADOR SUBURBAN

The most interesting early postwar Nash, essentially the prewar Ambassador fastback four-door trimmed with wood *á la* Chrysler Town & Country. Not a hot seller, but useful in getting car-hungry customers back into the showrooms and interested again in the holdover prewar design. Offered only with the prewar overhead-valve six as Nash abandoned its straight eight in these years. It's very uncommon today, but a fine example of a maker's attempt to spruce up its image in this period.

➕ **FOR** Scarcity and high appreciation

1947 Ambassador Suburban sedan

potential • Construction quality • Uniqueness

◼ **AGAINST** Only 10-15 known to survive today • Wood trim demands high maintenance • Subject to general underbody and structural rust

PRODUCTION
1946 272 **1947** 595 **1948** 130

SPECIFICATIONS
Length (in.)	209.2
Wheelbase (in.)	121.0
Weight (lbs)	3470-3664
Price (new)	$1929-2239

ENGINES
cid/type	bhp	years
234.8/ohv I-6	112	1946-48

PRICES
FAIR	$6000-10,000
GOOD	$10,000-15,000
FINE	$15,000-24,000

FINE EXAMPLE PRICE HISTORY
1982 $6000	**1990** $19,000
1994 $25,000	**1998** $24,000
1982-2000 RETURN 8%	
2000-2010 8%	

1 9 4 8
NASH AMBASSADOR CUSTOM CABRIOLET

An addition to the 1948 line, this was the first Nash convertible since 1941—and the last, unless you count the Ramblers. The Custom Cabriolet was built using tooling from the pre-war Ambassador Cabriolet, thus inexpensively adding a little glamor to the carryover '48 lineup. It is one of the more desirable Nashs of these years, but only 1000 were built, which also makes it among the scarcest and most valuable.

✚ **FOR** Good appreciation potential • Historical interest • Fine fit and finish • Scarcity

◼ **AGAINST** As for 1946-48 Ambassador Suburban, but no wood trim

PRODUCTION
1000

SPECIFICATIONS
Length (in.)	209.2
Wheelbase (in.)	121.0
Weight (lbs)	3465
Price (new)	$2345

ENGINES
cid/type	bhp	years
234.8/ohv I-6	112	1948

PRICES
FAIR	$5000-12,000
GOOD	$12,000-18,000
FINE	$18,000-25,000

FINE EXAMPLE PRICE HISTORY
1982 $11,000	**1990** $21,500
1994 $25,000	**1998** $25,000
1982-2000 RETURN 5%	
2000-2010 5%	

1948 Custom Cabriolet

1950 Airflyte Ambassador Super sedan

1 9 4 9 - 5 1

NASH AIRFLYTE AMBASSADOR

The best in the first entirely new postwar Nash generation. Design began taking shape under chief engineer Nils Erik Wahlberg during the war; actual styling is claimed by Holden Koto and Ted Pietsch. The production car, dubbed Airflyte, had superior aerodynamics, making it an excellent long-distance road car. But some called its looks unfortunate—the nearest thing to a bathtub on wheels America ever built (partly because of the closed-in front and rear wheel wells). Bulbous lines disguised what was a very good car, notable for its "Uniscope" instrument cluster, superior "Weather-Eye" heating system, and monocoque construction. It was offered in several trim levels each year, variously designated Super, Custom, and Super Special, and received higher, squared-off rear fenders and a vertical-bar grille for 1951. Ambassadors used the longer Nash wheelbase and were more luxuriously trimmed than the lower-priced line, called 600 in 1949 and Statesman in 1950-51.

➕ FOR Not costly at present • A fine road car with high comfort levels • Durable mechanicals

➖ AGAINST Love-it-or-hate-it bulbous styling • Rust potential

PRODUCTION
198,000 (est.)

SPECIFICATIONS
Length (in.)	210.0 (1949-50), 211.0 (1951)
Wheelbase (in.)	121.0
Weight (lbs)	3325-3445
Price (new)	$2039-2501

ENGINES
cid/type	bhp	years
234.8/ohv I-6	112/115	1949-51

PRICES
FAIR	$1000-2500
GOOD	$2500-5000
FINE	$5000-8000

FINE EXAMPLE PRICE HISTORY
1982	$2000	1990	$6500
1994	$6000	1998	$8000
1982-2000 RETURN 7%			
2000-2010 5%			

1 9 5 0 - 5 2

NASH RAMBLER

This was America's most successful early compact. The original Rambler came as a cute convertible (with fixed side window frames) and a two-door wagon (which captured most of the sales). A Country Club hardtop was added for '51. Unit construction made for tightness, relative quiet, and light weight, while a small L-head six

1951 Rambler Custom convertible

provided pleasing thrift and reasonable performance. Rambler rescued Nash's—and later AMC's—fortunes in the '50s, and laid the basis for the company's soaring success in the early '60s.

➕ FOR Pioneer compact • Practicality • Economy that's liveable today • Very affordable

➖ AGAINST Low appreciation • Unit-body rust-out always a threat • Enclosed front wheel wells mean unduly wide turning circle

PRODUCTION
160,000 (est.)

SPECIFICATIONS
Length (in.)	176.0
Wheelbase (in.)	100.0
Weight (lbs)	2420-2515
Price (new)	$1808-2119

ENGINES
cid/type	bhp	years
172.6/sv I-6	82	1950-52

PRICES
Conv

FAIR $2000-4000
GOOD $4000-6500
FINE $6500-9000
(Deduct 25% for other models.)

FINE CONVERTIBLE PRICE HISTORY

1982 $3300   1990 $7000
1994 $7000   1998 $10,000
1982-2000 RETURN 6%
2000-2010 convertibles 5%, others 2%

1951
NASH-HEALEY

The result of an agreement between sports-car builder Donald Healey of England and Nash-Kelvinator president George Mason. The first examples of this short-lived series of Anglo-American hybrids featured a dashing aluminum roadster body powered by an ohv Nash six tuned to deliver 125 bhp. Racing versions finished ninth in class in the Mille Miglia and fourth overall at Le Mans. Styling was in the British mold, with a divided windshield and side curtains, but a vertical bar grille and a prominent badge preserved Nash identity.

✚ FOR One of the most desirable (and among the first) postwar American sports cars • Quick on straights, nimble on curves • High appreciation • Exclusivity • Milestone status

▬ AGAINST Aluminum bodywork flimsy • Body parts scarce now • Expensive

PRODUCTION

104

SPECIFICATIONS

Length (in.)	170.8
Wheelbase (in.)	102.0
Weight (lbs)	2690
Price (new)	$4063 (most built had $96 overdrive option)

ENGINES

cid/type	bhp	years
234.8/ohv I-6	125	1951

PRICES

FAIR	$6500-12,500
GOOD	$12,500-22,000
FINE	$22,000-32,000

FINE EXAMPLE PRICE HISTORY

1982 $13,000   1990 $35,000
1994 $35,000   1998 $32,000
1982-2000 RETURN 6%
2000-2010 5%

1952-54
NASH AMBASSADOR

1954 Ambassador Custom sedan

The much-improved, rebodied successor to the 1949-51 Airflyte, with styling based on Pinin Farina concepts. The new squared-off body design continued the curious skirted front wheel openings, a Nash trademark that found little buyer acceptance and created a huge turning circle for a car of fairly compact dimensions for its day. A "Le Mans" power option based on the Nash-Healey engine was offered for 1953-54, and provided 140 bhp via dual carbs and a high-compression head. An attractive "floating-bar" grille was adopted for '54. Country Club hardtops were offered, but not convertibles. More desirable than the shorter, dumpier Statesman models because of more balanced appearance and a new enlarged version of the big Nash six. Nash continued to pioneer such comfort features as fully reclining front seats and the effective "Weather Eye" heating/ventilation system.

✚ FOR Generally attractive looks • Great long-haul car • PF badges

▬ AGAINST Little collector interest • Parts scarce • Rusts easily • Not many around • Tedious handler

PRODUCTION

150,000 (est.)

SPECIFICATIONS

Length (in.)	209.3
Wheelbase (in.)	121.3
Weight (lbs)	3410-3575
Price (new)	$2521-2735

ENGINES

cid/type	bhp	years
252.6/ohv I-6	120/130/140	1952-54

PRICES

Htp	
FAIR	$2000-4000

1951 Nash-Healey roadster

GOOD	$4000-6500
FINE	$6500-10,000
Others	
FAIR	$750-2500
GOOD	$2500-5000
FINE	$5000-9000

(Add 10% for Le Mans engine.)

FINE COUNTRY CLUB HARDTOP PRICE HISTORY

1982 $2700		**1990** $8500	
1994 $10,000		**1998** $14,000	

1982-2000 RETURN 8%
2000-2010 hardtops 5% (others 2%)

1952-54
NASH-HEALEY

1953 Nash-Healey roadster

A much revised, second-generation Anglo-American hybrid. The body was now made of steel, and shaped by Pinin Farina. Identified by headlamps mounted within a simple bar grille and uplifted rear fenders. Surprisingly, curb weight was about the same as the '51 aluminum-body model. A longer-wheelbase fixed-roof coupe dubbed Le Mans (in honor of the N-H's racing successes) was added for '53, and the roadster dropped for '54. Some leftover '54s were retitled and sold as '55s. The racers continued to do well, particularly at Le Mans 1952 where one finished third overall, led only by two Mercedes. The experimental Rambler Palm Beach might have replaced the N-H as American Motors' sports car for 1956, but very limited sales and tight finances—plus the practical bent of AMC president George Romney—spelled the end of the project.

➕ **FOR** Larger-engine models more rapid • Le Mans roomy; a genuine GT • Fine handling • Thoroughbred pedigree • A Milestone car

➖ **AGAINST** Not cheap • Most survivors are off the market

PRODUCTION

1952 150 **1953** 162 **1954** 90

SPECIFICATIONS

Length (in.)	170.8 (roadster), 177.0 (coupe)
Wheelbase (in.)	102.0 (roadster), 108.0 (coupe)
Weight (lbs)	2750 (cvt), 2990 (cpe)
Price (new)	$4721-5899

ENGINES

cid/type	bhp	years
234.8/ohv I-6	125	1952[1]
252.6/ohv I-6	140	1952-54

[1]Through serial #N2309 and N3000-3023

FINE CONVERTIBLE PRICE HISTORY

1982 $14,000	**1990** $35,000
1994 $38,000	**1998** $40,000
1982-2000 RETURN 6%	
2000-2010 5%	

1953-55
NASH RAMBLER

Nash's sales-winning compact, now restyled more along the lines of the contemporary Pinin Farina senior cars. Model offerings expanded noticeably for '54 with the addition of two- and four-door sedans and a four-door Cross Country wagon—joining the two-door wagon, hardtop, and convertible—plus a new low-priced DeLuxe two-door and returning Custom and Super versions of all body styles. The four-door sedans and Cross Country used a longer 108-inch wheelbase. Rambler was spun off as an individual make for 1956, and later models are found under that heading. The 100-inch-wheelbase two-door sedan and

1955 Rambler Custom Cross Country wagon

wagon from these years would be resurrected with only detail changes for 1958 as the Rambler American.

FOR As for 1950-52 Rambler

AGAINST Slow appreciation • Not as historically significant, but otherwise as for 1950-52 Rambler

PRODUCTION

150,000 (est.)

SPECIFICATIONS

Length (in.)	176.5; 186.4 (4d sdn)
Wheelbase (in.)	100.0; 108.0 (4d sdn)
Weight (lbs)	2400-2685
Price (new)	$1550-2150

ENGINES

cid/type	bhp	years
184/sv I-6	85/90	1953-54
195.6/sv I-6	90/100	1955

PRICES

As per 1950-52 Nash Rambler.

1954-56
NASH METROPOLITAN SERIES 54

Nash president George Mason's idea of the ultimate commuter/ shopping car. Styling was based on the Bill Flajole design for the NXI show car and bore a resemblance to the big Nash, but the scale was tiny:

the Met's wheelbase was shorter than a VW Beetle's. Bodies were built in England by Fisher & Ludlow, and the four-cylinder engines came from Austin, which also did final assembly. A three-passenger convertible and fixed-roof hardtop were offered. Later cars had flashy two-tone paint that reminded one stylist of "Neapolitan ice cream." The Met met with modest success in the U.S., and was continued by AMC even after Nash and Hudson had left the scene—both badges were used on the car so both sets of dealers could sell it. The little 1.2-liter engine was bored out to 1.5 liters during the 1956 model year to produce the Met 1500, and the car would remain basically unaltered until sales ceased in the early '60s.

FOR Low-bucks collectible • Still makes sense for around-town use • A certain charm • Mileage

AGAINST Rusts easily • Unreliable Austin engine • Dumpy styling

PRODUCTION

1954 13,095 **1955** 6096 **1956** 3000 (est.) (Figures based on shipments from Great Britain)

SPECIFICATIONS

Length (in.)	149.5
Wheelbase (in.)	85.0
Weight (lbs)	1803/1843 (conv/coupe)
Price (new)	$1445/1469 (cpe/conv)

ENGINES

cid/type	bhp	years
73.8/ohv I-4	42	1954-56

PRICES

FAIR	$1250-3000
GOOD	$3000-5000
FINE	$5000-9000

FINE EXAMPLE PRICE HISTORY

1982 $3500	**1990** $4500
1994 $6000	**1998** $7000
1982-2000 RETURN 6%	
2000-2010 3%	

1955-57
NASH AMBASSADOR

1956 Ambassador Six Super sedan

Final appearance of the Farina-styled 1952-54 design, with a wraparound windshield, inboard headlamps, concave grille (1955-56), and progressively more garish two-toning and chrome trim. Excellent performance from Packard's 320 V-8 introduced for '55, and AMC's own 250 V-8 on the mid-1956 Special, and a 327-cid

1954 Metropolitan convertible

enlargement for all '57s. Colorful plush interiors continued, so comfort levels were as high as ever. Basic styling was good—better than contemporary Hudsons', though that's not saying much—but details were thoughtless. The '57 pioneered quad headlamps (along with the Cadillac Eldorado Brougham), arranged vertically no less. There were still no wagons, convertibles, or hardtop sedans, however. The Ambassador Six was dropped after '56, but its longer wheelbase and resulting better proportions make it more desirable than the smaller-engine six-cylinder 1955-56 Statesman. Nash disappeared as a make after '57, but the Ambassador name lived on as a stretched, more luxurious Rambler.

FOR Design, preferred over 1955-57 Hudsons • Last of the line • Others as for 1952-54 Ambassador

AGAINST Very rust-prone, so not many left now • Busy styling • Others as for 1952-54 Ambassador

PRODUCTION
Eight 20,000 (est. total) **Six** 15,000 (est. total) **1956 Eight Special** 4154 **1957 Eight (incl. Super/Custom)** 5000

SPECIFICATIONS
Length (in.)	209.3
Wheelbase (in.)	121.3
Weight (lbs)	3538-3839
Price (new)	$2425-3095

ENGINES
cid/type	bhp	years
252.2/ohv I-6	130/140	1955-56
320/ohv V-8	208	1955-56
250/ohv V-8	190	1956
327/ohv V-8	255	1957

PRICES
Htp	
FAIR	$2000-4000
GOOD	$4000-6000
FINE	$6000-11,500
4d sdn	
FAIR	$1000-3000
GOOD	$3000-6500
FINE	$6500-9000

FINE HARDTOP PRICE HISTORY
1982 $3000		**1990** $8500	
1994 $13,000		**1998** $15,000	
1982-2000 RETURN 8%			
2000-2010 5%			

1956-57
NASH METROPOLITAN SERIES 56 1500

A revised version of the Nash economy runabout, introduced mid-

1988 300ZX coupe

1956 Metropolitan convertible

model year 1956. Features included a larger engine and more horsepower, plus a larger clutch, different paint treatment, Z-shaped bodyside moldings, and a new mesh grille bearing either Nash or Hudson emblems according to the selling dealer. The imitation hood scoop of the previous Met was erased. Top speed went from 70 mph to 80, making the Met somewhat more suitable for higher-speed American driving conditions. It continued to be sold by AMC through 1962, though production ended in mid-1960. (See AMC entry for later models.)

FOR Somewhat livelier • Brighter, flashier • Otherwise as for 1954-56 Series 54

AGAINST The same curious looks and doubtful Austin engine (albeit with more robust displacement)

PRODUCTION
1956 6000 (est.) **1957** 15,317

SPECIFICATIONS
Length (in.)	149.5
Wheelbase (in.)	85.0
Weight (lbs)	1803/1843 (conv/cpe)
Price (new)	$1527-1591

ENGINES
cid/type	bhp	years
90.9/ohv I-4	52	1956-57

PRICES
As per 1954-56 Nash Metropolitan Series 54.

1984-89
NISSAN 300ZX

Third-generation Nissan Z, evolved from the bulbous 1978-83 Datsun 280ZX. More GT than light-footed sports car, like its predecessor, but it looked cleaner and meaner, and its new 3.0-liter single-cam V-6 was smoother, quieter, and more potent than the 280's inline six. Wider wheels and tires gave slightly wider tracks, a new four-speed automatic option (with electronic control and three shift modes) gave greater driving flexibility than the previous three-speeder. A revamped cockpit provided more room, better outward vision, and even more features—including gimmicky, extra-cost electronic instruments. Like the 280, the 300 was offered as a two-seat Turbo and non-turbo two-seater and long-wheelbase 2+2, all hatchback coupes. Mainly detail year-to-year changes, but an '87 facelift slicked up appearance, and improved induction added a few horses for 1988-89. All-coil suspension (with front struts and rear semi-trailing arms) and assisted all-disc brakes were standard throughout. A T-roof was standard from '85, but solid-roof non-turbos with lower prices were reinstated from 1986. Far less adventuresome than its 1990 replacement, but nicer to drive and live with than the relatively dull 280ZX. Now a questionable investment for profit-seekers, but it should be at least a minor collector's item in the future.

FOR Smooth, refined, and quick (7.2-9.0 seconds 0-60) • Capable handling • Comfy GT ride • Well built • Used car prices and availability

▇ AGAINST Dubious gadgety options on some models • Slightly "bathtub" driving position • Tame styling becomes ungainly on 2+2

PRODUCTION

NA

SPECIFICATIONS

Length (in.)	170.7 (2-seater), 178.5 (2+2)
Wheelbase (in)	91.3 (2-seater), 99.2 (2+2)
Weight (lbs)	3050-3150
Price (new)	$15,800-24,200

ENGINES

cid/type	bhp	years
181/ohc V-6	160	1984-87
181/ohc V-6	200	1984-87
181/ohc V-6	165	1988-89
181/ohc V-6[1]	205	1988-89
[1]Turbocharged		

PRICES

Top price for the best 2-seater $8000, for the 2+2 $7000, for the 1984 Anniversary Edition $7500.
2000-2010 RETURN Depreciating

1990-96
NISSAN 300ZX TURBO

1990 300ZX Turbo coupe

Twin turbos with twin intercoolers, variable valve timing, dual overhead cams, distributorless ignition, 4-wheel steering, front and rear multi-link independent suspension, anti-lock brakes—the 300ZX Turbo had all the early nineties high-tech features. Fortunately they all worked well. The car was fast: 0-60 in 5.6 seconds, top speed 155. The 4-wheel steering enhanced the responsiveness of the Z's stable handling. Unfortunately for collectors the Turbo was only available as 2-seater coupe—the convertible was never available in Turbo spec.

▣ FOR Performance • Handling • Well built

▇ AGAINST Harsh ride • High-tech features may be expensive to repair

---

PRODUCTION[1]

1990 NA **1991** NA **1992** NA **1993** 1363 **1994** 974 **1995** 515
[1]Total 300ZX production including Turbos

SPECIFICATIONS

Length (in.)	169.5
Weight (lbs)	3480-3540
Wheelbase (in.)	96.5
Price (new)	$33,000-44,879

ENGINES

cid/type	bhp	years
181/dohc V-6 [1]	300	1990-96
[1]Turbocharged		

PRICES

$14,000-30,000 for best examples.
2000-2010 RETURN Depreciating

1993-96
NISSAN 300ZX CONVERTIBLE

Factory-built "basket-handle" convertible that carried on Z-car tradition of speed, style, and roadholding. Top-notch materials and engineering were obvious assets. Normally aspirated 222-bhp 3.0-liter V-6 with manual trans gave 0-60 times of about 7.7 seconds, despite a tendency to bog in first gear. Acceleration in middle gears was impressive. Automatic transmission versions, which sold in far greater numbers, were not as quick.

▣ FOR Acceleration • Quasi-convertible body style • Handling & roadholding • Build quality

▇ AGAINST Quasi-convertible body style • Likely to have been driven hard • Parts may be scarce • Not as quick as similar vintage hatchback-only 300ZX Turbo

---

PRODUCTION

NA

SPECIFICATIONS

Length (in.)	169.5
Weight (lbs)	3432
Wheelbase (in.)	96.5
Price (new)	$36,570-45,579

ENGINES

cid/type	bhp	years
181/dohc V-6	222	1993-96

PRICES

$20,000-30,000 for best examples.
2000-2010 RETURN Deprecaiting

1995-98
NISSAN 200SX SE-R

1996 200SX SE-R coupe

Cheap and fun, the 200SX SE-R was overlooked by most sport coupe buyers. A sweet-revving dual overhead cam four was mated to a precise shifting gearbox. The SE-R was fun to drive on winding roads, but not at the price of ride comfort. Based on the Sentra sedan and sharing its wheelbase, the 200SX had a roomy back seat for a sport coupe. The styling was either plain or Q-ship depending on your point of view.

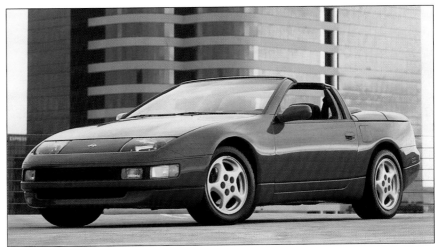

1993 300ZX convertible

✛ **FOR** Fun to drive • Economical to buy • Economical to own

▬ **AGAINST** Plain looks • Not likely to do much better in the collector market than it did in the new car market

PRODUCTION

1996 7205 **1997** 3200 **1998** 3504

SPECIFICATIONS

Length (in.)	170.1
Weight (lbs)	2600
Wheelbase (in.)	99.8
Price (new)	$15,269-17,549

ENGINES

cid/type	bhp	years
122/dohc I-4	140	1995-98

PRICES

$8500-12,000

1963-66
NSU WANKEL SPIDER

The first production car powered by Felix Wankel's rotary engine, produced in limited numbers by this old-line German firm to test public reaction. Unlike the later twin-rotor, front-drive Ro80 sedan, the Wankel Spider used a single-rotor engine mounted in its tail to drive the back wheels. The unit body/chassis was based on that of the ugly little Prinz sedan, but styling was created by Bertone. Accommodation was for two only, and there was no external clue as to the nature of the engine or its loca-

tion. Unfortunately, the Wankel hadn't been completely perfected, and the one-rotor configuration proved less reliable and refined than predicted. Nonetheless, the Spider was quite quick for its displacement (equivalent to a 500cc reciprocating engine), with up to 92 mph at the top end. More a toy than a serious production effort, though it undoubtedly gave NSU valuable experience in manufacturing this new kind of engine and information about how it would stand up to typical owner use.

✛ **FOR** Curiosity value • Historical interest • Cuteness • Comparative rarity • Milestone car status

▬ **AGAINST** Unreliable engine • Indifferent body construction • Not plentiful

PRODUCTION

Approx. 5000

SPECIFICATIONS

Length (in.)	143.0
Wheelbase (in.)	79.0
Weight (lbs)	1545
Price (new)	$2487 U.S. in 1967

ENGINES

cc/type (cid)	bhp[1]	years
500/1-rotor Wankel (30.5)	50	1963-66

[1]DIN

PRICES

FAIR	$1000-2000
GOOD	$2000-3000
FINE	$3000-4000

FINE EXAMPLE PRICE HISTORY

1982	$2500	**1990**	$3500
1994	$3500	**1998**	$3500
1982-2000 RETURN 0%			
2000-2010 2%			

1967-77
NSU RO80

1967-77 Ro80 sedan

A second-generation Wankel-engine car from by-now faltering NSU, and the firm's flagship model. The new twin-chamber engine was linked to a clutchless (semi-automatic) gearbox driving the front wheels. This mechanical package was clothed in a wind-cheating four-door sedan body featuring a very high, curved windshield; low rectangular grille; flowing fender contours; rounded "six light" greenhouse; and a short, high tail. Critically acclaimed when introduced for its advanced engineering, the Ro80 was just as much condemned when its engine proved cantankerously unreliable. Disgruntled owners, especially Britons, often resorted to substituting Ford V-4 or V-6 engines once the Wankel gave up the ghost. Like the Wankel Spider, it was the engine that spoiled an otherwise capable and interesting car. The main problem was

1963-66 Wankel Spider

short-lived rotor tip seals and resulting oil leaks when they wore out, plus chamber-wall distortion and other problems that usually necessitated a replacement engine or a complete rebuild before 30,000 miles. NSU lost its shirt on this car, partly because it tried to bolster the Wankel's reputation by honoring all warranty claims. NSU was absorbed by VW in 1969, which continued the car through 1977, after which it was unceremoniously dropped. By then, production of NSU's tiny rear-engine models had ceased, and the firm was folded in with VW's recently acquired (from Mercedes-Benz) Audi subsidiary, which ultimately took over NSU's Neckarsulm production facilities. It would be left to Toyo Kogyo (Mazda) of Japan to work out the bugs in Felix Wankel's engine, which it eventually did, but not before almost going the same way as NSU.

✚ **FOR** Trend-setter • Unique styling • Smooth road manners • Engine marvelous when it's whole

▬ **AGAINST** Premature rotor tip wear and oil leaks • Engine parts in short supply • Bad body corrosion problems

PRODUCTION

47,400

SPECIFICATIONS

Length (in.)	188.0
Wheelbase (in.)	112.5
Weight (lbs)	2670
Price (new)	NA

ENGINES

cc/type cid	bhp[1]	years
995/2-rotor Wankel (60)	113	1967-72

[1]DIN

PRICES

FAIR	$2000-3500
GOOD	$3500-5000
FINE	$5000-7000

FINE EXAMPLE PRICE HISTORY

1982 $2500		1990 $6500	
1994 $6500		1998 $7000	
1982-2000 RETURN 7%			
2000-2010 3%			

1940 OLDSMOBILE SERIES 90

One of the nicest-looking late prewar Oldsmobiles, and top of the 1940 line. This was the only Olds series this year powered by an eight, an inline L-head developing 110 bhp. Hydra-Matic transmission, pioneered by Olds, was found in most examples. Styling was bold for the times, with semi-flush-mounted headlamps, GM's "Turret-Top" all-steel body construction, and gracefully rounded fenders. A solid car, and one that can still cope with today's traffic conditions, though acceleration is slow.

✚ **FOR** Good styling • Superb workmanship • Fine performance • Open models' rarity

▬ **AGAINST** Relatively low appreciation compared to sister makes like Buick • Body parts now scarce

PRODUCTION

4d sdn 33,075 **2d club cpe** 10,836 **2d conv cpe** 290 **4d conv phaeton** 50

SPECIFICATIONS

Length (in.)	210.0
Wheelbase (in.)	124.0
Weight (lbs)	3440-3750
Price (new)	$1069-1570

ENGINES

cid/type	bhp	years
257.1/sv I-8	110	1940

PRICES

Conv	
FAIR	$10,000-19,000
GOOD	$19,000-33,000
FINE	$33,000-48,000
Others	
FAIR	$3000-6000
GOOD	$6000-11,000
FINE	$11,000-16,000

FINE CONVERTIBLE PRICE HISTORY

1982 $21,000		1990 $40,000	
1994 $38,000		1998 $48,000	
1982-2000 RETURN 5%			
2000-2010 5%			

1941-42 OLDSMOBILE CUSTOM CRUISER 8 & 98

Evolution of the 1940 design, with the same mechanical features and somewhat busier styling. The '41

1940 Series 90 sedan

1941 Custom Cruiser convertible

1942 98 sedan

Custom Cruiser 8 became the '42 98, which received more sweeping pontoon fenders and a two-inch longer wheelbase to go with them. As with other makes, low production makes the '42s—along with the last of Olds' convertible sedans—highly desirable today.

✠ FOR As for 1940 Series 90

▬ AGAINST As for 1940 Series 90

PRODUCTION
1941 club cpe 6305 **4d sdn** 22,081 **2d conv cpe** 1263 **4d conv phaeton** 119 **1942 club cpe** 1771 **4d sdn** 4672 **2d conv cpe** 216

SPECIFICATIONS
Length (in.)	210.0/213.0 (1941/42)
Wheelbase (in.)	125.0/127.0 (1941/42)
Weight (lbs)	3430-3955
Price (new)	$1079-1450

ENGINES
cid/type	bhp	years
257.1/sv I-8	110	1941-42

PRICES
Conv	
FAIR	$12,000-20,000
GOOD	$20,000-34,000
FINE	$34,000-49,000
Others	
FAIR	$2500-6000
GOOD	$6000-11,000
FAIR	$11,000-16,000

FINE CLUB COUPE PRICE HISTORY
1982 $6500		**1990** $13,000	
1994 $14,000		**1998** $16,000	
1982-2000 RETURN 6%			
2000-2010 5%			

1946-47
OLDSMOBILE CUSTOM CRUISER 98

1946 Custom Cruiser 98 sedan

Postwar carryover of Oldsmobile's top-line series on the same long chassis. Mechanical specifications were unchanged. Improved styling, however, especially up front where the complicated prewar grille was replaced by a simpler bar affair.

✠ FOR More available and affordable than prewar models • Fine high-speed cruisers

▬ AGAINST Holdover styling • Body and trim pieces now in short supply

PRODUCTION
1946 2d club sdn 2459 **4d sdn** 11,031 **conv** 874 **1947 2d club sdn** 8475 **4d sdn** 24,733 **conv** 3940

SPECIFICATIONS
Length (in.)	213.0
Wheelbase (in.)	127.0
Weight (lbs)	3680-4075
Price (new)	$1762-2307

ENGINES
cid/type	bhp	years
257.1/sv I-8	110	1946-47

PRICES
Conv	
FAIR	$5500-10,000
GOOD	$10,000-18,000
FINE	$18,000-27,000
Others	
FAIR	$2500-4500
GOOD	$4500-8000
FINE	$8000-11,500

FINE CONVERTIBLE PRICE HISTORY
1982 $10,000		**1990** $25,000	
1994 $25,000		**1998** $27,000	
1982-2000 RETURN 6%			
2000-2010 5%			

1948
OLDSMOBILE FUTURAMIC 98

Oldsmobile's first all-new postwar models, introduced early in calendar 1948. (Early production Dynamic 98s were essentially a continuation of the 1946-47 models.) Fine styling by Harley Earl's Art & Colour Studio was a sensation at the time. Power was still supplied by the familiar Olds straight eight, now up slightly in horsepower.

FOR Superb styling • Often passed over in favor of '48 Cadillacs • Smooth road performance • Solid construction

AGAINST Relatively limited appreciation potential • Outmoded engine

PRODUCTION

2d club sdn 2000 **DeLuxe 2d club sdn** 9000 **4d sdn** 4000 **DeLuxe 4d sdn** 25,000 **DeLuxe conv** 9000 (all est.)

SPECIFICATIONS

Length (in.)	213.5
Wheelbase (in.)	125.0
Weight (lbs)	3645-4035
Price (new)	$2078-2624

ENGINES

cid/type	bhp	years
257.1/sv I-8	115	1948

PRICES

Conv

FAIR	$5500-11,000
GOOD	$11,000-19,500
FINE	$19,500-28,000
Others	
FAIR	$1000-3500
GOOD	$3500-8000
FINE	$8000-12,000

FINE CLUB COUPE PRICE HISTORY

1982 $3700	1990 $8500
1994 $6500	1998 $12,000
1982-2000 RETURN 7%	
2000-2010 5%	

1949
OLDSMOBILE FUTURAMIC 98 HOLIDAY

1949 Futuramic 98 Holiday hardtop coupe

Shares honors with the Buick Riviera and Cadillac Coupe de Ville as the industry's first "hardtop convertible," a deft creation by GM design under the ever-innovative Harley Earl. Widely overlooked today, possibly because of its low production and consequent rarity. It was trimmed to convertible standards, which is to say plush, and featured simulated convertible-top bows on the interior headliner like other early GM hardtops. The year's other big news was shared by other 98s and the new Futuramic 88 series, the now-famous Rocket V-8, a modern high-compression overhead-valve unit, amazingly powerful and efficient for its day.

FOR Historical importance (hardtop and V-8) • Performance • High-quality materials • Craftsmanship • Strong value increase • Milestone car status

AGAINST Guzzles gas • A bit large for some • Body parts scarce today

PRODUCTION

3006

SPECIFICATIONS

Length (in.)	213.0
Wheelbase (in.)	125.0
Weight (lbs)	4000
Price (new)	$2973

ENGINES

cid/type	bhp	years
303.7/ohv V-8	135	1949

PRICES

FAIR	$4500-9000
GOOD	$9000-16,000
FINE	$16,000-23,000

FINE EXAMPLE PRICE HISTORY

1982 $5000	1990 $25,000
1994 $20,000	1998 $21,000
1982-2000 RETURN 10%	
2000-2010 8%	

1948 Futuramic 98 Club Sedan

1950 Futuramic 88 convertible

1949-50

OLDSMOBILE FUTURAMIC 88

Designated a Milestone for its outstanding blend of styling and performance. Can legitimately be considered Detroit's first high-volume "muscle car." A last-minute addition to the 1949 line, the 88 (along with the luxury 98) featured the year's new high-compression overhead-valve V-8. It was lighter than the 98, though (it shared the Chevy/Pontiac bodyshell), and thus a real tiger. It also dominated NASCAR stock-car racing into 1951. Good looks and sparkling pickup were available in a wide range of body styles, offered in standard and fancier DeLuxe trim. Particularly desirable today are the low-production convertibles, the all-steel wagons (with imitation wood trim and the last Olds wagons until 1957), and the Holiday hardtop added for 1950. In 1952, the Super 88 took over the role of the most powerful Olds in the lightest body, gaining more horsepower as the years went by, along with increasingly bulky styling and more weight.

✚ **FOR** Power and performance • Quality • Looks • Good club support • Racing record • Sure-fire investment • Milestone status for the Holiday hardtop and convertible

▬ **AGAINST** Some rust threat • Body and trim parts scarce

PRODUCTION

1949 2d club sdn 28,707 **2d club cpe** 11,591 **conv** 5434 **4d Town Sedan** 5833 **4d sdn** 46,386 **4d wgn** 1355 **1950 2d club sdn** 31,093 **2d club cpe** 21,456 **conv** 9127 **4d sdn** 141,111 **4d wgn** 2382 **2d Holiday htp** 1366 **2d sdn** 50,561

SPECIFICATIONS

Length (in.)	202.0
Wheelbase (in.)	119.5
Weight (lbs)	3455-3780
Price (new)	$1878-3296

ENGINES

cid/type	bhp	years
303.7/ohv V-8	135	1949-50

PRICES

Conv	
FAIR	$7000-14,000
GOOD	$14,000-27,000
FINE	$27,000-34,000
Htp & wgn	
FAIR	$4000-12,000
GOOD	$12,000-22,000
FINE	$22,000-30,000
Others	
FAIR	$1800-4000
GOOD	$4000-8000
FINE	$8000-12,000

FINE CONVERTIBLE PRICE HISTORY

1982 $9500		**1990** $32,500	
1994 $30,000		**1998** $39,000	
1982-2000 RETURN 8%			
2000-2010 5%			

1951-53

OLDSMOBILE SUPER 88

1951 Super 88 sedan

Replacements for the 1949-50 DeLuxe 88s—a separate in-between series introduced along with a substantial '51 Olds restyle. The previous 88 line with its full range of body types (save wagons) was cut to just two standard-trim sedans (called "Deluxe 88" for 1952-53) to make room for the similar group of Supers, which also used the smaller GM B-body and, for '51, the same "Rocket" V-8 that powered all Oldsmobiles. Thereafter, base 88s had less power than Supers or top-line 98s, making the middle series the true successor to the original "Futuramic" 88 as Lansing's hot rod. Though Supers (and 98s) gained 25 horses for 1952-53 (via a higher-lift cam and new "Quadri-Jet" four-barrel carburetor), Olds was eclipsed in NASCAR racing by the surprising six-cylinder Hudson Hornets. But 88 sales kept rising anyway thanks to expanding options—ever-improving Hydra-Matic, power steering for '52, air conditioning and power brakes for '53—plus trendy, if not timeless, styling. Somewhat overlooked by collectors—though we can't imagine why—they're now better appreciated for their fine performance and the solid craftsmanship typical of Olds in these years.

✚ **FOR** Good period go (about 12 seconds 0-60) • Solid workmanship • Fairly plush • Broad model choice • Active club • Still relatively inexpensive

▬ **AGAINST** Appreciating slower than 88s before and after • Some body and trim pieces hard to find

PRODUCTION

1951 club cpe 7328 **Holiday 2d htp** 3914 **Deluxe Holiday 2d htp** 14,012 **Deluxe conv** 4468 **1952 club cpe** 2050 **4d sdn** 70,606 **2d sdn** 24,963 **conv** 5162 **Holiday 2d htp** 15,777 **1953 4d sdn** 119,317 **2d sdn** 36,824 **conv** 8310 **Holiday 2d htp** 36,881

SPECIFICATIONS

Length (in.)	203.8
Wheelbase (in.)	120.0
Weight (lbs)	3579-3895
Price (new)	$2219-2853

ENGINES

cid/type	bhp	years
303.7/ohv V-8	135	1951
303.7/ohv V-8	160-65	1952-53

PRICES

Conv	
FAIR	$5000-11,000
GOOD	$11,000-20,000
FINE	$20,000-29,000
Holiday Htp	
FAIR	$3500-8000
GOOD	$8000-14,000
FINE	$14,000-21,000
Others	
FAIR	$2000-5000
GOOD	$5000-9000
FINE	$9000-12,500

FINE HOLIDAY HARDTOP PRICE HISTORY

1982 $6300		**1990** $17,500	
1994 $15,000		**1998** $14,000	
1982-2000 RETURN 5%			
2000-2010 5%			

1953
OLDSMOBILE
98 FIESTA

A special limited-edition luxury convertible based on the standard 98 bodyshell, one of three GM "show cars for the public" introduced this year (Buick Skylark and Cadillac Eldorado were the others). Predictive styling, with wraparound windshield, spinner hubcaps (widely copied as an aftermarket accessory), and flush-folding top. It cost a lot, but came with a special tuned version of the Rocket V-8, a custom leather-lined interior, and just about every option in the book—including Hydra-Matic, power steering and brakes, and electric windows and seat. More a glamor item than a serious high-volume seller, it was withdrawn after a short production run (Buick and particularly Cadillac were more successful with their snazzy ragtops).

✚ **FOR** Rare, highly prized • Advanced styling features • Hot performer for its day • A Milestone car

▬ **AGAINST** Virtually impossible to find now • Heavy and thirsty • Unique body parts and trim are replacement headaches • Expensive to buy and restore • Widely diverging asking prices

PRODUCTION

458

SPECIFICATIONS

Length (in.)	215.0
Wheelbase (in.)	124.0
Weight (lbs)	4453
Price (new)	$5717

ENGINES

cid/type	bhp	years
303.7/ohv V-8	170	1953

PRICES

FAIR	$9500-19,000
GOOD	$19,000-32,000
FINE	$32,000-48,000

FINE EXAMPLE PRICE HISTORY

1982 $16,000		**1990** $45,000	
1994 $47,000		**1998** $48,000	
1982-2000 RETURN 7%			
2000-2010 5%			

1953 Fiesta convertible

1954 - 56

OLDSMOBILE 98 & SUPER 88

Arguably the best combination of styling, performance, engineering, and craftsmanship seen from Lansing since WWII. The '54s boasted all-new X-member frames with longer wheelbases (longest on 98s), bigger-bore "Rocket" V-8s with more power, and colorful new square-shouldered styling marked by GM's trendy "Panoramic" wraparound windshield. Enthusiastic public response boosted Olds from sixth to fifth in industry production, then to fourth for banner '55. All models were nicely facelifted—flaunting splashy two-toning—and hardtop sedans arrived at mid-season, along with companion Buicks. The '56s received another restyle (announced by a gaping "mouth" grille) and even more power. The Super 88 remained the "performance" line, sharing its higher-power engine with the luxury top-range 98s. In all, a very nice group of collectible cars for all the reasons that made them so desirable when new.

➕ FOR Long underrated, yet still quite affordable • Good performance • Tasteful mid-'50s styling • Solid craftsmanship • Active club • Good investment

➖ AGAINST Still hard to find in good condition (though that's changing) • Some body/trim parts scarce • Overchromed dashboards

PRODUCTION

1954 Super 88 4d sdn 111,326 **2d sdn** 27,882 **conv** 6452 **Deluxe Holiday 2d htp** 42,155 **98 Deluxe 4d sdn** 47,972 **Holiday 2d cpe** 8865 **Deluxe Holiday 2d cpe** 29,688 **Starfire conv** 6800 **1955 Super 88 4d sdn** 111,316 **2d sdn** 11,950 **conv** 9007 **Deluxe Holiday 4d htp** 47,385 **Deluxe Holiday 2d htp** 62,534 **98 4d sdn** 39,847 **Starfire conv** 9149 **Deluxe Holiday 4d htp** 31,267 **Deluxe Holiday 2d htp** 38,363 **1956 Super 88 4d sdn** 59,728 **2d sdn** 31,949 **Holiday 4d htp** 52,239 **Holiday 2d htp** 74,739 **98 4d sdn** 20,105 **Holiday 4d htp** 42,320 **Holiday 2d htp** 19,433 **Starfire conv** 8531

SPECIFICATIONS

Length (in.)	Super 88/98: 205.3/214.3 (1954), 203.3/212.3 (1955-56)
Wheelbase (in.)	122.0 (Super 88), 126.0 (98)
Weight (lbs)	3730-4325
Price (new)	$2410-3740

ENGINES

cid/type	bhp	years
324.3/ohv V-8	195/202/240	1954-56

1956 Super 88 convertible

PRICES

Conv	
FAIR	$7500-15,000
GOOD	$15,000-26,000
FINE	$26,000-38,000
2d htp	
FAIR	$4500-10,000
GOOD	$10,000-18,000
FINE	$18,000-26,000
Others	
FAIR	$2500-5000
GOOD	$5000-9000
FINE	$9000-13,000

FINE CONVERTIBLE PRICE HISTORY

1982 $9000	**1990** $40,000
1994 $35,000	**1998** $38,000

1982-2000 RETURN 9%
2000-2010 10%, **closed models** 5%

1957 - 58

OLDSMOBILE 98 & SUPER 88

The follow-ups to Oldsmobile's two upper series of 1954-56, with a more exaggerated version of the same formula that proved far less salable, though a more difficult market was partly to blame. The lower-riding '57s were fully redesigned with new ground-hugging frames, reworked suspension (but with retrograde rear leaf springs replacing coils), and more rakish styling (though it paled against the knockout '57 Chrysler products). Power rose via an enlarged Rocket

1955 98 Holiday hardtop sedan

1957 98 Starfire convertible

V-8 that could be further muscled up with a new $83 "J-2" tri-carburetor option. There was also a $385 J-2 racing package with special cam, pistons, and other internals, though it was little publicized and thus little known except among racers. Wagons, called Fiesta, returned for the first time since 1950: a pillared 88 four-door and a pillarless Super 88. The '58 story was more of the same, but styling was blockier and dazzlingly overchromed. Sales would likely have fallen even without that year's flash recession. Olds 88s still went stock-car racing in these years, but the few successes achieved—mainly by the Petty family—were peripheral to sales, which now relied on gadgets like 1958's costly and troublesome "New-Matic Ride" air suspension option. Build quality took a tumble, and this plus low original production explains today's relative lack of survivors. Not Oldsmobile's best, but now attracting more collector interest—even the kitschy '58s. Prime picks are the low-volume convertibles, Super 88 Fiestas (really), and any J-2 model.

🕀 FOR Period flash • Plentiful performance, especially J-2s (0-60 under nine seconds) • Luxury, especially 98s • Relative exclusivity

🗕 AGAINST Clean originals scarce, especially J-2s • Poorer workmanship and more rust-prone than 1954-56s • Overdone '58 styling (a plus for some, though)

PRODUCTION
1957 Golden Rocket Super 88 Holiday 2d htp 31,155 **Holiday 4d htp** 39,162 **conv** 7128 **4d sdn** 42,629 **Fiesta 4d htp wgn** 8981 **2d sdn** 2983

Starfire 98 Holiday 2d htp 17,791 **Holiday 4d htp** 32,099 **conv** 8278 **4d sdn** 21,525 **1958 Super 88 Holiday 2d htp** 18,653 **Holiday 4d htp** 27,521 **conv** 3799 **4d sdn** 33,844 **Fiesta 4d htp wgn** 5175 **98 Holiday 4d htp** 11,012 **Holiday 4d htp** 27,603 **conv** 5605 **4d sdn** 16,595

SPECIFICATIONS

Length (in.)	208.2/217 (Super 88/98)
Wheelbase (in.)	122.5/126.0 (Super 88/98)
Weight (lbs)	4000-4390
Price (new)	$2968-4300

ENGINES

cid/type	bhp	years
371.1/ohv V-8	277/300[1]	1957
371.1/ohv V-8	305/312[1]	1958

[1]Standard/J-2 option

PRICES

Conv	
FAIR	$5000-10,000
GOOD	$10,000-20,000
FINE	$20,000-32,000
2d htp & wgn	
FAIR	$2800-8000
GOOD	$8000-12,000
FINE	$12,000-15,000
Others	
FAIR	$2000-4000
GOOD	$4000-7000
FINE	$7000-10,000

FINE VISTA CRUISER WAGON PRICE HISTORY

1982 $5000		**1990** $22,500	
1994 $13,000		**1998** $15,000	
1982-2000 RETURN 7%			
2000-2010 5%, **convertibles** 8%			

1959-60
OLDSMOBILE 98 & SUPER 88

More of Oldsmobile's biggest and brawniest, this time from the

1959 98 Celebrity sedan

"Linear Look" years. Like other GM cars, the '59s resulted from a crash design program responding to the enormously successful '57 Chrysler products that decisively seized industry styling leadership (only to lose it by 1959). They also reflected a new GM body-sharing plan. Olds fared fairly well aesthetically, with the least flamboyant lines of any '59 GMer save Pontiac. It was little heavier than before despite the obvious dimensional increases and much greater glass areas. A stronger new semi-unitized body/frame structure (aft of the cowl) helped. So did a larger Rocket V-8 for Super 88/98, though power wasn't up much due to a slight compression cut, a nod to a newly economy-conscious market. There were many other improvements, too, including "Air Scoop" brakes, "Roto-Matic" power steering, and two-stage "split choke and fast idle mechanism." The Super 88 Fiesta wagon was now a pillared model. Simpler "Balanced Design" styling with new lower-body sheetmetal identified the 1960s, which continued the economy trend (begun in '58) with still lower numerical axle ratios. A 98 convertible paced the 1960 Indy 500. These Oldsmobiles were as long ignored as the 1957-58s, but stronger value appreciation potential now reflects increased collector interest, especially among younger enthusiasts.

✚ FOR Low, wide, and not overdone (especially '60s) • Performance still ample • Built somewhat better than 1957-58s • Big and spacious • Active club • Some models very scarce now, yet prices remain reasonable

➖ AGAINST Ragtops expensive • Still rather rust-prone • No more J-2 option • Supers more like standard 88s • Some body/trim parts difficult to find • Size

PRODUCTION

1959 Super 88 Celebrity 4d sdn 37,024 **Fiesta 4d wgn** 7015 **Holiday SceniCoupe htp** 20,259 **Holiday SportSedan htp** 38,467 **conv** 4895 **98 Celebrity 4d sdn** 23,106 **Holiday SceniCoupe htp** 13,669 **Holiday SportSedan htp** 36,813 **conv** 7514 **1960 Super 88 Celebrity 4d sdn** 35,094 **Fiesta 4d wgn** 7230 **Holiday SceniCoupe htp** 16,464 **Holiday SportSedan htp** 33,285 **conv** 5830 **98 Celebrity 4d sdn** 17,188 **Holiday SceniCoupe htp** 7635 **Holiday SportSedan htp** 27,257 **conv** 7284

SPECIFICATIONS

Length (in.)	Super 88/98: 218.4/223.0 (1959), 217.6/220.9 (1960)
Wheelbase (in.)	123.0/126.3 (Super 88/98)
Weight (lbs)	4135-4390
Price (new)	$3178-4362

ENGINES

cid/type	bhp	years
394/ohv V-8	315	1959-60

PRICES

Conv	
FAIR	$5000-9000

GOOD	$9000-13,000
FINE	$13,000-24,000
2d htp	
FAIR	$2500-6000
GOOD	$6000-10,000
FINE	$10,000-16,000
Others	
FAIR	$1500-3000
GOOD	$3000-6000
FINE	$6000-9000

FINE 2D HARDTOP PRICE HISTORY

1982 $3600		**1990** $12,500	
1994 $12,000		**1998** $16,000	

1982-2000 RETURN 9%
2000-2010: 5%, **convertibles** 8%

1961 Starfire convertible

Oldsmobile's full-size performance cars of the early '60s. Introduced in convertible-only form as a sub-model in the 1961 Super 88 series. It became a separate series from 1962 on, but was always built on Oldsmobile's shorter chassis, not the Ninety-Eight platform, and fitted with the most powerful Olds V-8s through 1965. It's found a niche in today's collector market, the crisply styled 1962-63 models in particular being among the most desirable Oldsmobiles of these years. The rarer convertibles naturally lead the hardtops in value, but all Starfires are eminently collectible for their relatively low production, smooth highway cruising ability, and Ninety-Eight-level luxury interior with bucket seats, console, and high-grade trim.

✚ FOR Big, comfortable road-eater • Luxury • Distinctive styling • Strong performer

➖ AGAINST Thirsty • Starfire-only trim bits scarce now

PRODUCTION

1961 conv 7600 **1962 conv** 7149 **2d htp** 34,839 **1963 conv** 4401 **Holiday 2d htp** 21,148 **1964 conv** 2410 **Holiday 2d htp** 13,753 **1965 conv** 2236 **Holiday 2d htp** 13,024 **1966 Holiday 2d htp** 13,019

SPECIFICATIONS

Length (in.)	212.0 (1961), 213.9 (1962), 214.5 (1963), 215.3 (1964), 216.9 (1965-66)
Wheelbase (in.)	123.0
Weight (lbs)	4013-4334
Price (new)	$3564-4778

ENGINES

cid/type	bhp	years
394/ohv V-8	325/330/345	1961-64
425/ohv V-8	370/375	1965-66

1960 Super 88 convertible

PRICES

1961-63 conv

FAIR	$6000-10,000
GOOD	$10,000-20,000
FINE	$20,000-30,000

1962-64 htp

FAIR	$2500-4500
GOOD	$4500-6500
FINE	$6500-13,000

FINE 1961 CONVERTIBLE PRICE HISTORY

1982 $5600		**1990** $33,500	
1994 $29,000		**1998** $30,000	

1982-2000 RETURN 11%
2000-2010 10% (hardtops 5%)

1 9 6 2 - 6 3

OLDSMOBILE F-85 DELUXE JETFIRE

The most technically interesting and collectible version of Oldsmobile's early '60s F-85 compacts, offered in limited numbers for these two years only. It was based on the bucket-seat Cutlass coupe introduced for 1961, but powered by a turbocharged version of the Buick aluminum V-8 available for the F-85/Skylark at the time. Though the turbo yielded one bhp per cubic inch, it caused reliability problems involving carbon buildup, not fully alleviated by Olds' alcohol-and-water injection, which was standard with the package. The Jetfire was quite rapid

when working properly, however, with 0-60 mph available in 8.5 seconds from standstill and a top speed of 107 mph. But the old axiom "there's no substitute for cubic inches" was still very much in force in Detroit, so Olds abandoned this pocket powerhouse for 1964 in favor of a larger Cutlass with big-inch, conventional cast-iron V-8s.

✚ FOR Technical, historical interest • Good go • Build quality • Practical size • Neat, slightly innocuous looks • Pretty affordable

➖ AGAINST Mechanical woes • Rust can attack undercarriage • Special parts in short supply • Modest appreciation rate

PRODUCTION

1962 3765 **1963** 5842

SPECIFICATIONS

Length (in.)	188.2/192.2 (1962/63)
Wheelbase (in.)	112.0
Weight (lbs)	2739-2774
Price (new)	$3049-3048

ENGINES

cid/type	bhp	years
215.0/ohv V-8	215	1962-63

PRICES

FAIR	$2500-4000
GOOD	$4000-8000
FINE	$8000-8500

FINE EXAMPLE PRICE HISTORY

1982 $3200		**1990** $8000
1994 $8500		**1998** $8500

1982-2000 RETURN 6%
2000-2010 5%

1 9 6 4 - 6 5

OLDSMOBILE F-85 CUTLASS 4-4-2

1964 F-85 Cutlass 4-4-2 hardtop coupe

Oldsmobile's counterpart to the Pontiac GTO in the burgeoning mid-size muscle market. It wasn't a separate model in these years, but an option package usually ordered on the sporty Cutlass two-doors. An outgrowth of the "Police Apprehender Pursuit Package" (option B-09) that was theoretically available on any '64 F-85 or Cutlass. Renamed 4-4-2 to denote four-speed floorshift manual gearbox, four-barrel carburetor, and dual exhausts. The package also threw in heavy-duty suspension, wider wheels and tires, special rear axle and driveshaft, heavy-duty engine mounts/steering gear/frame, front and rear stabilizer bars, 11-inch clutch, 70-amp

1962 F-85 Jetfire convertible

battery, and special nameplates. For 1965, the designation stood for a new standard 400-cid V-8 with four-barrel carb and dual exhausts. The 4-4-2 package could be combined with any trim level from plain to fancy. Exhilarating performance was guaranteed: 0-60 mph came up in 7.5 seconds, the standing-start quarter-mile in 17 seconds, and top speed was around 125 mph. Road manners were a cut above its competitors'.

FOR A stormer from the good old days • Capable handling • Reasonable size • Nice styling • Strong appreciation • Convertibles rare • Milestone car status

AGAINST Thirsty and doesn't like today's low-calorie gas • Not as quick as a GTO

PRODUCTION
1964 Holiday 2d htp 2999 **1965 Holiday 2d htp** 21,535 **conv** 3468

SPECIFICATIONS
Length (in.)	203.0/204.3 (1964/65)
Wheelbase (in.)	115.0
Weight (lbs)	3141-3338
Price (new)	$2700-3200 (base; approx.)

ENGINES
cid/type	bhp	years
330/ohv V-8	310	1964
400/ohv V-8	345	1965

PRICES
Conv	
FAIR	$2500-5500
GOOD	$5500-10,000
FINE	$10,000-15,000

(Deduct 35% for hardtops and coupes.)

FINE CONVERTIBLE PRICE HISTORY
1982 $4875	**1990** $12,000
1994 $12,000	**1998** $14,000
1982-1994 RETURN 7%	
2000-2010 5%	

1964-65
OLDSMOBILE JETSTAR I

Sporty flagship for Oldsmobile's new low-priced Jetstar 88 series, and arrived with it for 1964. Curiously listed as part of the Dynamic 88 series in its debut year, then as a separate model for '65. Essentially, this was the Starfire idea at a more popular price, but offered only as a two-door hardtop. Not as successful, probably because the market was turning to the lighter, more maneuverable intermediates packing similar big-inch engines. Powerplants were the same as Starfire's, but a bit less weight gave the Jetstar I better pickup. The Jetstar 88 series lasted through 1966, then was renamed Delmont.

FOR Very low production; suggests possible appreciation rise • Good performance • Decent styling • Nicely outfitted interiors

AGAINST Not really collectible yet • Low appreciation now • Special trim parts hard to get

PRODUCTION
1964 16,084 **1965** 6552

SPECIFICATIONS
Length (in.)	215.3/216.9 (1964/65)
Wheelbase (in.)	123.0
Weight (lbs)	4019-3982
Price (new)	$3603-3602

ENGINES
cid/type	bhp	years
394/ohv V-8	345	1964
425/ohv V-8	370	1965

PRICES
FAIR	$1700-3500
GOOD	$3500-5500
FINE	$5500-8500

FINE EXAMPLE PRICE HISTORY
1982 $3500	**1990** $10,000
1994 $10,500	**1998** $8500
1982-2000 RETURN 5%	
2000-2010 3%	

1966-67
OLDSMOBILE CUTLASS 4-4-2

Oldsmobile's mid-size muscle machine, listed as a separate series beginning in 1966. It continued with the 115-inch wheelbase and square-rigged styling initiated with the 1964 Cutlass redesign. More flowing body contours and a shorter 112-inch chassis for two-doors arrived for '68, and continued through 1970. Horsepower generally went up in each of

1964 Jetstar I hardtop coupe

1966 Cutlass 4-4-2 convertible

these years, and 1970 brought a big 455 V-8 option following GM's decision to rescind its unwritten rule against cars this size with less than 10 pounds per horsepower. Styling and equipment changes usually paralleled those in the tamer Cutlass models, but beefed-up suspension, air-induction hood, sporty striping, and other performance mods were reserved strictly for the 4-4-2. A rare tri-power option with 360 bhp was listed for '66, then disappeared, making cars so equipped a rare find. There were also various package models with identifying W-30 or W-31 (based on the 350 V-8) decals and special paint. Not included here but surely worth exploring are the special Hurst/Olds conversions that began with a Force-Air 455 model in 1968 packing 380 bhp. Power and performance started to slide with the 1971 models. The 4-4-2 reverted to an option package for '72, and held on as a shadow of its former self for a few years after that.

➕ **FOR** Fast, but never overstressed • Big, easy-revving engines • Good handling • Aggressive looks • Strong appreciation potential • Milestone car status

➖ **AGAINST** Thirsty, of course • Cop-baiting appearance add-ons on some models • Indifferent fit and finish in later years

PRODUCTION

1966[1] **2d cpe** 1430 **2d Sport Coupe** 3937 **Holiday 2d htp** 10,053 **2d htp** 3827 **conv** 2750 **1967**[1] **2d Sport Coupe** 5215 **Holiday 2d htp** 16,514 **conv** 3104 **1968 2d Sport Coupe** 4282 **Holiday 2d htp** 24,183 **conv** 5142 **1969 2d Sport Coupe** 2475 **Holiday 2d htp** 19,587 **conv** 4295 **1970 2d Sport Coupe** 1688 **Holiday 2d htp** 14,709 **conv** 2933

[1](Proportioned from total Cutlass production. Total 4-4-2 production 1966: 21,997 1967: 24,833)

SPECIFICATIONS

Length (in.)	204.2 (1966-67), 201.6 (1968), 201.9 (1969) 203.2 (1970)
Wheelbase (in.)	115.0/112.0 (1966-67/1968-70)
Weight (lbs)	3502-3740
Price (new)	$2604-3567

ENGINES

cid/type	bhp	years
350/ohv V-8	325	1968-70
400/ohv V-8	350/360	1966-67
455/ohv V-8	365/370	1970

PRICES

Conv	
FAIR	$3500-6500
GOOD	$6500-11,000
FINE	$11,000-15,000
Others	
FAIR	$1500-5000
GOOD	$5000-8000
FINE	$8000-12,000

FINE COUPE PRICE HISTORY

1982 $3360		**1990** $10,000	
1994 $10,000		**1998** $12,000	
1982-2000 RETURN 8%			
2000-2010 5%			

1966-67
OLDSMOBILE TORONADO

A bold idea combined with intriguing styling. This was the first attempt to apply front wheel drive to a full-size American car since the mid-'30s Cord, and one of the most desirable Oldsmobiles ever produced. The drive system featured a split transmission with the torque converter behind the V-8 engine and the gearbox located

1966 Toronado hardtop coupe

remotely under its left cylinder bank; the two were connected by a chain drive and sprocket. This arrangement allowed the heavy engine to sit over the front wheels, which resulted in a favorable weight distribution (54/46 percent front/rear) for such a large fwd car. Styling changed only in detail in the Toro's first two years, and was exquisite—every detail beautifully executed by GM design chief William L. Mitchell. Jutting front fenders, hidden headlamps, muscularly flared wheel arches, and a cropped tail trailing a smooth fastback roofline makes the first-generation models unmistakable even now. As it should be, the original '66 is more desirable, but there's nothing wrong with a '67 if you're less concerned about "first of its kind" status.

➕ **FOR** A technological success that's with us yet • It's a Milestone car • Exceptional traction, handling, performance • Distinctive styling (evokes Cord comparisons for some) • Luxury • Comfort • Strong appreciation

➖ **AGAINST** Complicated mechanical restoration • Not cheap to run • Heavy front tire wear • Rust-prone

PRODUCTION

1966 2d htp 6333 **Deluxe 2d htp** 34,630 **1967**

2d htp 1770 **Deluxe 2d htp** 20,020

SPECIFICATIONS

Length (in.)	211.0
Wheelbase (in.)	119.0
Weight (lbs)	4310-4366
Price (new)	$4617-4869

ENGINES

cid/type	bhp	years
425/ohv V-8	385	1966-67

PRICES

FAIR	$2000-4000
GOOD	$4000-6000
FINE	$6000-9000

FINE EXAMPLE PRICE HISTORY

1982 $4000	1990 $13,000
1994 $10,000	1998 $10,000
1982-2000 RETURN 5%	
2000-2010 3%	

1968-71
OLDSMOBILE 442 & W31

These were Lansing's last "golden age" muscle cars. Built on GM's new-for-'68 A-body platform like period divisional siblings, specifically the short-wheelbase version reserved for two-door intermediates. Much swoopier styling with semi-fastback coupe rooflines and Oldsmobile's by-now trademark split grilles. Though the 4-4-2 retained its familiar mechanical/equipment formula in these years, a big-block 455 V-8 replaced the 400

from 1970 to keep pace with performance-sapping emissions tuning. A new W-30 option with cold-air induction gave both engines slightly more power. But there was also a W-31 package with a higher-output 350 small-block available for basic Cutlass two-doors—almost a 4-4-2 in everything but name. Olds also diluted 4-4-2 sales with sporty Cutlass "S" coupes and, for 1970 only, a bright-yellow Rallye 350 option (W-45) that had lots of 4-4-2 show but less go. With all this plus a performance market increasingly besieged by rising insurance rates, even stricter emissions limits, and waning buyer interest, the 4-4-2 series reverted to option status for 1972, then stumbled along as a shadow of its '60s self before being dropped. The name would reappear on mostly cosmetic options for later Cutlasses, but a true revival wouldn't be attempted until the mid-'80s.

➕ **FOR** Fast, but never overstressed • Big, easy-revving engines • Good handling • Aggressive looks • As valued now as any muscle cars

➖ **AGAINST** High collector prices reflect strong demand and limited supply • Thirsty, of course • Cop-baiting appearance • Indifferent fit-and-finish in later years

PRODUCTION

1968 conv 5142 **Sports Coupe** 4282 **Holiday 2d htp** 24,183 **1969 conv** 4295 **Sports Coupe** 2475 **Holiday 2d htp** 24,193 **1970 conv** 2933

Sports Coupe 1688 **Holiday 2d htp** 14,709 **1971 conv** 1304 **Holiday 2d htp** 6285

SPECIFICATIONS

Length (in.)	201.6-203.6
Wheelbase (in.)	112.0
Weight (lbs)	3500-3730
Price (new)	$3087-3743

ENGINES

cid/type	bhp	years
350/ohv V-8	325	1969-71
400/ohv V-8	325/350[1]	1968-69
400/ohv V-8	360[2]	1968-69
455/ohv V-8	365	1970-71
455/ohv V-8	370[2]	1970-71

[1]Manual/automatic transmission [2]W-30 air induction option

PRICES

Conv:	
FAIR	$3500-7000
GOOD	$7000-13,000
FINE	13,000-20,000
Cpe:	
FAIR	$2000-5000
GOOD	$5000-9000
FINE	$9000-15,000

(Pace car edition add 40%.)

FINE CONVERTIBLE PRICE HISTORY

1982 $4550	1990 $27,500
1994 $11,000	1998 $19,000
1982-2000 RETURN 9%	
2000-2010 8%	

1968-72
OLDSMOBILE HURST-OLDS

A series of low-production conversions carried out by Hurst

1968 4-4-2 hardtop coupe

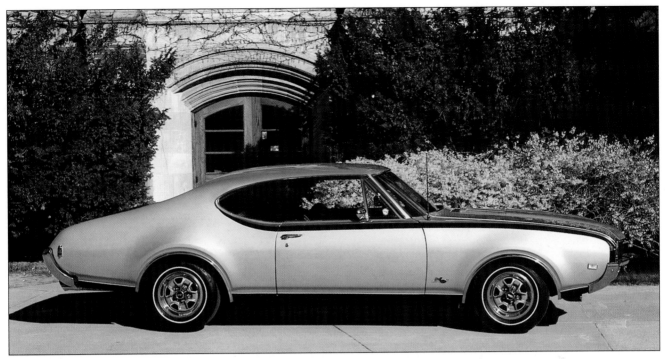

1968 Hurst-Olds hardtop coupe

Performance Products on the contemporary Oldsmobile Cutlass 4-4-2. It began life as a personal car for George H. Hurst, president of Hurst-Campbell, Inc. The main difference between the factory's 4-4-2 and the H/O (Hurst said the initials stood for "Hairy Olds") was in the engine. Until 1970, GM had an unwritten corporate ban against production models smaller than full-size with less than 10 pounds per horsepower. Hurst stepped in where the factory dared not tread, substituting Oldsmobile's big-block 455 V-8 for the top 400-cid unit from the ordinary 4-4-2. To this was added a fiberglass hood with forced-air induction (by means of mean-looking twin hood scoops), special gray and black paint, appropriate emblems, and a modified Turbo Hydra-Matic transmission with Hurst's Dual-Gate floor-mount shifter that allowed full manual hold in any of the three gears. The full range of Cutlass options was available for the H/O. The package proved successful from a promotional standpoint, and returned for 1969 with 10 fewer horses, revised gold and white paint, and a new rear deck spoiler. Most H/Os in these years were two-door hardtops, but a few fixed-pillar coupes may have been given the treatment as well. When Olds offered the 455 as a production option for 1970, the H/O vanished. It then resurfaced in 1972, this time based on the plusher, heavier Cutlass Supreme platform. This package was little more than fancy trim, but it was available in both hardtop and convertible styles, some with Official Pace Car regalia to celebrate the H/O's selection for that year's Indy 500. These cars also had the top W-30 engine, fiberglass hood with functional scoops, and snazzy wheels and tires, but offered no extra performance over a properly optioned factory 4-4-2. The H/Os are desirable today primarily for their high performance and limited-production appeal.

✚ **FOR** As for 1966-70 Cutlass 4-4-2, plus more performance (1968-69 models) and greater rarity

▬ **AGAINST** As for 1966-70 Cutlass 4-4-2, but harder to find, and even thirstier

PRODUCTION

1968 515 **1969** 906 **1972** 629

SPECIFICATIONS

Length (in.)	201.6/201.9/203.6 (1968/69/72)
Wheelbase (in.)	112.0
Weight (lbs)	approx. 3500-3800
Price (new)	$4760 original list price in 1969

ENGINES

cid/type	bhp[1]	years
455/ohv V-8	380/390	1968-69

[1]SAE gross; rated at 300 bhp net for 1972

PRICES

FAIR	$3500-7500
GOOD	$7500-13,500
FINE	$13,500-21,000

1972 Hurst-Olds Pace Car convertible

FINE EXAMPLE PRICE HISTORY

1982 $6000	**1990** $20,000
1994 $23,000	**1998** $21,000
1982-2000 RETURN 7%	
2000-2010 5%	

1 9 6 8 - 7 0
OLDSMOBILE TORONADO

Continuation of Oldsmobile's big front-driver, still on a 119-inch wheelbase. Aside from greater engine displacement, the main difference between these models and the 1966-67 editions is styling, which became progressively more "formal" and therefore less distinctive. The original jutting front fenders were blunted for 1968, and overlaid with a massive divided grille. This face was retained for 1969, but the tail was lengthened and an optional vinyl roof was available to destroy the unbroken line from C-pillar

1969 Toronado hardtop coupe

to lower body. Headlights were exposed for 1970 (some owners complained the headlight doors acted up on earlier models), and the trim was rearranged just for the sake of change. Underneath all the glitter, though, the Toronado was still the same fine car, but it's the retrograde appearance changes that make these versions less desirable now. Toronado would grow to unbelievable proportions for 1971 and beyond, and these are hardly collectible at all.

✚ FOR More affordable • Others as for 1966-67 Toronado

▬ AGAINST Ham-fisted styling alterations and slower appreciation • Others as for 1966-67 Toronado

PRODUCTION
1968 2d htp 3957 **Custom 2d htp** 22,497 **1969 2d htp** 3421 **Custom 2d htp** 25,073 **1970 2d htp** 2351 **Custom 2d htp** 23,082

SPECIFICATIONS
Length (in.)	221.4/214.8/214.3 (1968/69/70)
Wheelbase (in.)	119.0
Weight (lbs)	4316-4386
Price (new)	$4750-5216

ENGINES
cid/type	bhp	years
455/ohv V-8	375/400	1968-70

PRICES
FAIR	$2000-3500
GOOD	$3500-5500
FINE	$5500-9500

FINE EXAMPLE PRICE HISTORY
1982 $3100	**1990** $9000
1994 $10,000	**1998** $10,000
1982-2000 RETURN 6%	
2000-2010 3%	

1974 Hurst-Olds W-30 "Colonade" coupe

Continuation of the specialty midsize Oldsmobiles created and marketed by Hurst, now based on the "Colonnade" bodyshell introduced for 1973. As before, the powertrain was built around the 455 big-block V-8 and Turbo Hydra-Matic with Dual-Gate shifter, embellished with special paint schemes, color-keyed road wheels, radial tires, and special H/O regalia. You had your choice of two colors in '73: white or black with contrasting gold trim. The following year, the H/O was again chosen for Indy Official Pace Car duty, and was issued with appropriate decals for the owner to apply. For the first time, buyers could have either the "W-30" big-block or a smaller 350 V-8 (option code Y-77), a sign of the move away from performance in the wake of the first fuel crisis. Of the year's total production, 1420 units had the smaller V-8. Performance was de-emphasized even more for 1975 in favor a new T-top roof treatment with removable glass panels, a business Hurst was beginning to get into to make up for the sag in its aftermarket speed equipment sales. The '75 was based on the heavier, formal-roof Cutlass Supreme model rather than the semi-fastback Cutlass S used for the 1973-74 H/Os, and the detuned engines necessitated by stiffening emissions controls make these cars less fiery than their predecessors. Nevertheless, they are interesting newer models that attempted to keep the performance spirit of the '60s alive in an age when everything seemed to be working against development and sale of enthusiast cars. This plus low production make the last Hurst-built H/Os possible collector-car comers down the road.

✚ FOR Scarcity • Decent performance for the period • Many amenities • Eye-catching appearance • Last of a type

▬ AGAINST Somewhat fuelish • Collectibility questionable at present • Fewer mechanical differences from stock models than earlier H/Os

PRODUCTION
1973 1097 **1974** 1800 **1975** 2535

SPECIFICATIONS
Length (in.)	207.0/211.5/211.7 (1973/74/75)
Wheelbase (in.)	112.0
Weight (lbs)	approx. 3850
Price (new)	NA

ENGINES

cid/type	bhp[1]	years
350/ohv V-8	200	1974-75
455/ohv V-8	250	1973-75

[1]Est. SAE net

PRICES

FAIR	$3500-5500
GOOD	$5500-8000
FINE	$8000-11,000

FINE EXAMPLE PRICE HISTORY

1982 $3500	1990 $9000
1994 $7000	1998 $9000

1982-2000 RETURN 8%
2000-2010 5%

1977
OLDSMOBILE TORONADO XSR

1977 Toronado XSR coupe

A special version of Lansing's personal-luxury front-driver, offered in the next-to-last year for the outsize second-generation Toronado

design introduced for 1971. Its main distinction was a complex U-shaped rear window recalling Studebaker's wrapped 1947-51 Starlight coupe treatment—an early limited-production tryout for the "hot-wire bent" technology that Chevy would apply to its 1977-79 Impala coupes. Little remarkable otherwise, and a quite forgettable car, styling apart. It's included here mainly for novelty value and as a present-day "cheap wheels" that may show some value appreciation in the distant future.

FOR Unusual looks • T-top's open-air versatility • Big and impressive • Rare, yet dirt cheap

AGAINST Not much power • Big and clumsy • Overdone "boudoir" interior • Graceless styling • Little collector potential

PRODUCTION

2714

SPECIFICATIONS

Length (in.)	227.5
Wheelbase (in.)	122.0
Weight (lbs)	4781
Price (new)	$11,132

ENGINES

cid/type	bhp	years
403/ohv V-8	185	1977

PRICES

FAIR	$2000-3000
GOOD	$3000-5000
FINE	$5000-8000

FINE EXAMPLE PRICE HISTORY

1994 $7000	1998 $7500

2000-2010 RETURN 3%

1983-87
OLDSMOBILE CUTLASS/ HURST & 4-4-2

A late-'80s revival of the mid-size muscle Olds developed by Hurst Performance Products. Issued on the 15th anniversary of the original Hurst/Olds, but marketed by Lansing as an adjunct to the standard Cutlass line. Based on the downsized 1978-vintage A-body Cutlass notchback coupe, and featuring the expected suspension upgrades plus a black-over-silver exterior with red accent stripes, spoilers front and rear, buckets-and-console interior with extra gauges, and tuned four-barrel 307 Olds V-8 driving a four-speed Turbo Hydra-Matic transmission. A novelty was Hurst's "Lightning Rod" transmission selector with no fewer than three sticks: a stubby main lever and one auxiliary wand each for first and second gears. The latter allowed "slam" upshifts for maximum acceleration (recalling Hurst's "Slap Shifter" of the '60s). That acceleration was pretty good—about eight seconds 0-60—but the arrangement

1983 Cutlass/Hurst coupe

confused customers and was discarded for an orthodox single stick when Olds repackaged Hurst's concept as a new 4-4-2 for 1985. This was similar to the H/O, but could be had with a less flashy monotone exterior and most all the luxury extras available on top-line Supreme coupes. Canceled with the advent of a new front-drive Cutlass Supreme for 1988, and production was deliberately limited, but a respectable reminder of the good old big-inch days.

FOR Muscle-car looks • Tire-smoking getaways • Scarce • Parts/service backup still good • Not costly

AGAINST Many examples have been trashed • So-so detail workmanship • Awful velour interior trim • Eclipsed in all-out performance by some other modern muscle cars

PRODUCTION
1983 Hurst 3000 **1984 Hurst** 3500 **1985 Salon 4-4-2** 3500 **1986 est.** 3000 **1987 Supreme 4-4-2** 4210

SPECIFICATIONS
Length (in.)	200.0
Wheelbase (in.)	108.1
Weight (lbs)	approx. 3350
Price (new)	$12,070-14,700

ENGINES
cid/type	bhp	years
307/ohv V-8	170/180	1983-87

PRICES
FAIR	$3000-5000

GOOD	$5000-7500
FINE	$7500-9000

FINE EXAMPLE PRICE HISTORY
Depreciating during 1990s
2000-2010 3%

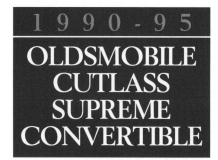

1990-95
OLDSMOBILE CUTLASS SUPREME CONVERTIBLE

A surprising mid-year addition in the third season for Oldsmobile's W-body front-drive Cutlass Supreme line—surprising in that some thought this convertible would be based on the smaller N-body Cutlass Calais. The basic design for Oldsmobile's first rag-top since 1975 was shared with W-body coupes and sedans: all-independent suspension, transverse 3.1-liter V-6, four-speed automatic transaxle, all-disc power brakes with optional antilock control. The convertible, however, came only in mid-level Supreme SL trim, though with a power top and, in lieu of B-pillars, a stiffening hoop above the cockpit, which restored some structural strength and allowed retention of the coupe's "tavern" door handles and shoulder-belt anchors. A

long-shot collectible now, but has distant potential depending on ultimate production and history's judgment.

FOR Nice-enough looks • Not likely to be very numerous

AGAINST Performance and handling dull by modern standards

PRODUCTION
est. 2000

SPECIFICATIONS
Length (in.)	192.3
Wheelbase (in.)	107.5
Weight (lbs)	3500
Price (new)	$19,500-25,470

ENGINES
cid/type	bhp	years
189/ohv V-6	135-160	1990-95

PRICES
Current price range $5500-$8500
2000-2010 RETURN Depreciating

1990-92
OLDSMOBILE TORONADO TROFEO

Although very similar to the slow-selling 1986-89 Toronado, the 1990-92 iteration was a clever reworking, with bolder styling, longer overall

1990 Cutlass Supreme convertible

1991 Toronado Trofeo coupe

length, and a reworked suspension. Gorgeous sheetmetal was sophisticated yet sportive, and the 170-horse 3.8-liter "3800" V-6 was acceptable, though pokey (0-60 in about 9.7 seconds). The Visual Information Center, a dash-mounted video screen designed for touchless control of stereo and climate systems, was an expensive, bothersome option, but a working one may enhance collectibility.

✚ FOR Luxurious appointments • Curvy bodystyle • Toronado heritage

▬ AGAINST Gimmicky dash • Modest performance • Depreciation will continue for many years

PRODUCTION

1990 9426 **1991** 5348 **1992** 5197

SPECIFICATIONS

Length (in.)	200.3
Weight (lbs)	3462
Wheelbase (in.)	108.0
Price (new)	$24,995-27,295

ENGINES

cid/type	bhp	years
231/ohv V-6	165/170	1990-92

PRICES

Current range up to $8500 for fine examples. **2000-2010 RETURN** Depreciating

1969-73
OPEL GT

The curvy little "mini-Corvette" designed by GM's Clare MacKichan while on duty at Opel in Russelsheim, Germany. It was developed from the Opel GT show car of a few years earlier, but wasn't as exciting, mainly because wind tunnel tests decreed a sharper Kamm-style back, less smooth-looking front end, and a rounder profile. Chassis and running gear were shared with the contemporary Kadett, Opel's smallest model line. Bodies were built by Brissonneau & Lotz in France, then shipped to Germany for final assembly. The GT was strictly a two-seater, and like the 1968 Corvette had no external trunklid (cargo had to be wedged in behind the seatbacks and pushed into a small hold, hidden by a simple curtain). The driver sat quite low relative to the belt-line, and faced an impressive-looking dashboard with full instrumentation. The hidden headlights rotated (by means of a manually controlled cockpit lever) upward out of their recesses, giving the car a kind of "frogeye" look. The GT has only recently emerged as a collectible, and examples may still be had for reasonable prices. Offered initially in the U.S. with two engines as in Europe, but it's important to look for the reliable 1900 cam-in-head engine rather than the base 1.1-liter ohv unit. The latter was frugal with gas, but its pistons tended to seek daylight, especially near the redline. Dropped from the U.S. Opel lineup after 1973, but production continued in Europe for a short while.

✚ FOR A bargain price for a notable piece of design • Superb handling • Decent performance with 1900 engine • Styling • Sportiness

▬ AGAINST Seriously rust-prone (check potential buys carefully underneath) • Noisy, underpowered, somewhat questionable 1100 engine • Hard to find in clean, original condition

PRODUCTION[1]

1969 11,880 **1970** 21,240 **1971** 13,696 **1972** 12,055 **1973** 11,693
[1] U.S. calendar-year sales.

SPECIFICATIONS

Length (in.)	162.0

1973 GT 1900 coupe

Wheelbase (in.)	95.7
Weight (lbs)	2105
Price (new)	$3395 (original U.S. list)

ENGINES

cc/type (cid)	bhp	years
1078/ohv I-4 (65.8)	67	1969-70
1897/ohv I-4 (115.8)	75-90	1969-73

PRICES

FAIR	$800-1500
GOOD	$1500-2500
FINE	$2500-4000

FINE 1.9-LITER PRICE HISTORY

1982 $2000	1990 $4500
1994 $5500	1998 $5500

1982-2000 RETURN 4%
2000-2010 3%

1971-75
OPEL 1900/MANTA COUPE/ RALLYE/LUXUS

Smooth Euro-ponycar styled by Chuck Jordan, GM Director of Design. It competed for pizzazz and practicality with the Mustang-like Capri from Ford of Europe, but was larger and not as quick despite less weight.

All U.S. export models carried Opel's robust 1.9-liter cam-in-head four. The coupes were always called Manta in Europe and shared chassis, all-coil suspension, and drivetrain with the more upright Ascona sedans and wagons. All were initially marketed in America (through Buick dealers as per previous Opels from 1958) as the 1900; the Manta name (but not Ascona) was applied from 1973. Rallye version had extra instruments, foglamps, matte-black hood, bodyside striping, stiffer suspension, slotted wheels, and a shorter final drive. Luxus had cord cloth upholstery, four-spoke wheels, and none of the Rallye's "boy-racer" goodies, but was quieter and more comfy. Also, a vinyl-trimmed base coupe was offered all years. "Crash" bumpers arrived for 1974-75, Bosch fuel injection for '75 only. Withdrawn from the U.S. market due to the unfavorable dollar-to-deutsche-mark ratio at the time and resulting price escalation. Not to be confused with the later Isuzu-built "Opels" from Japan, based on the German T-car design also used for the Chevy Chevette. Compression was lowered for 1972-74, so the '71s and '75s have the best go.

FOR Ultra-strong engine • Neat looks, though aging now • Terrific handling • Class-leading passenger/trunk room • German build quality • Cheap

AGAINST Parts tough to find • Driveability problems on '72s • Fuel injection woes on '75s • Original Luxus cloth upholstery doesn't hold up • Undergeared and noisy • No collector potential

PRODUCTION[1]

1971 8378 **1972** 10,647 **1973 Rallye** 8360 **Luxus** 17,536 **1974 Rallye** 7959 **Luxus** 14,026 **1975** 15,118
[1]U.S. sales

SPECIFICATIONS

Length (in.)	162.0
Wheelbase (in.)	95.7
Weight (lbs)	2105-2225
Price (new)	$2490 in 1971, $2800 (Luxus) 1973, $3800 (Manta) 1975

ENGINES

cc/type	bhp	years
1897/ohv I-4	90[1]/70[2]	1971-74
1897/ohv I-4	77[2]	1975

[1]SAE gross [2]SAE net

PRICES

FAIR	$1200-1800
GOOD	$1800-2500
FINE	$2500-3500

FINE RALLYE PRICE HISTORY

1982 $1800	1990 $4000
1994 $4000	1998 $4000

1982-2000 RETURN 4%
2000-2010 2%

1971 1900 Rallye coupe

1930-32
PACKARD EIGHT

The quintessential Classic. Powered by Packard's by-then traditional big inline eights, it was offered with magnificent closed body types plus phaeton, roadster, and convertible styles as well as the exotic Speedster (1930). Individual customs by Dietrich and Packard were available for the 833, 840, and 904 chassis. Styling was strictly evolutionary and bore the same hallmarks, with streamlining increasingly evident as the years passed. Bijur automatic chassis lube and more power arrived in 1931, improved all-synchromesh transmission in 1932.

✚ FOR Nothing less than majestic • Plethora of parts suppliers • Strong club support • CCCA Classic status

▬ AGAINST Expensive • Trucky handling • High operating costs

PRODUCTION

1930 726 15,731 **733** 12,531 **734 Speedster** 113 **740 Custom** 6200 **745 DeLuxe** 1789 **1931 826** 6009 **833** 6096 **840 Custom** 2035 **845 DeLuxe** 1310 **1932 901** 3922 **902** 3737 **903 DeLuxe** 955 **904 DeLuxe** 700

SPECIFICATIONS

Length (in.)	Varies
Wheelbase (in.)	127.5-147.5
Weight (lbs)	3935-5635

1930 DeLuxe Eight phaeton

Price (new)	$2385-7250

ENGINES

cid/type	bhp	years
320.0/sv I-8	90-110	1930-32[1]
384.8/sv I-8	106-120	1930-31[2]
384.8/sv I-8	125-145	1930[3]
384.8/sv I-8	135	1932[4]

[1]Models 726, 733, 826, 833, 900, 901 [2]Models 740, 745, 840, 845 [3]Model 734 [4]Models 903, 904

PRICES

Custom Bodies:	
Open	
FAIR	$25,000-80,000
GOOD	$80,000-200,000
FINE	$200,000-290,000
Closed	
FAIR	$20,000-70,000
GOOD	$70,000-150,000
FINE	$150,000-250,000
Factory bodies:	
Open	
FAIR	$18,000-50,000
GOOD	$50,000-90,000
FINE	$90,000-140,000
Closed	
FAIR	$7000-35,000
GOOD	$35,000-60,000
FINE	$60,000-90,000

FINE 1932 VICTORIA PRICE HISTORY

1982 $60,000		**1990** $150,000	
1994 $145,000		**1998** $150,000	
1982-2000 RETURN 5%			
2000-2010 5%			

1932-33
PACKARD 900 LIGHT EIGHT & 1001 EIGHT

The Light Eight was Packard's first response to the Depression—an attempt to expand volume upward by

1932 900 Light Eight convertible coupe

extending price downward. Built on its own shorter wheelbase, the Light Eight weighed significantly less than the standard Eight but used its engine, and thus had better performance. Priced at the upper end of the medium bracket and a quality car, though not as nice-looking as other Packards. A bargain for customers, it cost almost as much to build as other models and stole some of their sales. The factory hardly broke even, so the Light Eight was dropped after but one year. The 1001 of 1933 was its spiritual successor.

FOR Performance • Club support • Historical importance: first "junior" Packard since the 1921-28 Single Six, preceding Cadillac's downpriced La-Salle by two years, but still a luxury car • CCCA Classic

AGAINST Staid styling • Body parts scarce • Slower to appreciate than senior linemates

PRODUCTION

1932 Series 900 6750 **1933 Series 1001** 1882

SPECIFICATIONS

Length (in.)	NA
Wheelbase (in.)	127.8/127.5 (900/1001)
Weight (lbs)	3930-4115 (900); 4150-4335 (1001)
Price (new)	$1895-1940 (900); $2150-2250 (1001)

ENGINES

cid/type	bhp	years
320.0/sv I-8	110-120	1932-33

PRICES

Rdstr	
FAIR	$12,000-25,000
GOOD	$25,000-45,000
FINE	$45,000-62,000
Others	
FAIR	$5500-12,500

GOOD	$12,500-20,000
FINE	$20,000-30,000

FINE 1933 ROADSTER COUPE PRICE HISTORY

1982 $32,000	1990 $90,000
1994 $55,000	1998 $62,000
1982-2000 RETURN 4%	
2000-2010 2%	

1 9 3 2 - 3 9
PACKARD TWIN SIX/ TWELVE

Initially conceived for a front-drive set-up that never happened, the Twelve had to be massaged to give it superior performance to the Eights, since the original rationale was for a car below their rank. Nevertheless, it was whisper-quiet at 60-70 mph and smoothly refined at all except its flat-out 90 mph. It carried Packard's largest and lushest custom and semi-custom bodies on the longest wheel-bases. Like the Super Eight, it received independent front suspension and conventional (instead of Bijur) lube fittings in 1937, when it also commanded Packard's only wheelbase over 140 inches. Switched to the lighter Super Eight chassis in 1938, it lost the 144-inch chassis entirely. Shelved after 1939, when it was Packard's only custom-bodied line.

FOR Unquestioned all-time Packard great • Smooth, satisfying performance • Outstanding quality, coachwork, engineering • A famous power

1937 Twelve Victoria convertible by Dietrich

plant • Classic status

AGAINST Price • Limited availability • High restoration/operating costs

PRODUCTION

1932 (Twin Six) 549 **1933** 520 **1934** 960 **1935** 721 **1936** 682 **1937** 1300 **1938** 566 **1939** 446

SPECIFICATIONS

Length (in.)	Varies
Wheelbase (in.)	142.5/147.5 (1932); 142.0/147.0 (1933-34); 139.0/144.0 (1935-37); 134.0/139.0 (1938-39)
Weight (lbs)	4950-5950
Price (new)	$3420-8510

ENGINES

cid/type	bhp	years
445.5/sv V-12	160	1932-34
473.0/sv V-12	175	1935-39

PRICES

In our last edition, Twelve prices were pacing that of the Super Eight; today they are well ahead, but not as high as they were a few years ago. The best custom bodies have hit over $350,000 at auction, but today they can often be acquired for $50,000-100,000 less. Early closed Twelves are much cheaper: $50,000 will buy a good sedan, $75,000 a rumble seat coupe. From 1935 Twelves looked much like Super Eights, but you still pay more—up to $150,000 for factory open bodies compared to around $100,000 for Super Eights with the same body. (Closed bodies maximum $60,000 for Twelves). Low end of the

1934 Twelve phaeton by LeBaron

Twelve market is toward the end of the run: a 1939 factory body sedan is at maximum at $50,000. The high end is in the beginning; still a 1934 convertible victoria by Dietrich, one of the most beautiful Packards, is well down from its $400,000 high of ten years ago. These Packards are blue chip long-term investments but don't look for astonishing gains in a few years. **2000-2010 RETURN** 5%.

1 9 3 3 - 3 6
PACKARD SUPER EIGHT

A big, strong, beefy Classic. Shared much of the mighty Twelve's chassis and body componentry through 1936, after which it was reduced to a much smaller, lighter, and more modern design. Gradually outdistanced by the Twelve in price, it thus falls in a grey area among collectors. At the time, Packard increasingly concentrated on the medium-priced field exploited by the One Twenty. Individual customs were offered in 1933-34; wheelbases shrank in 1935 as Packard consolidated its senior models, although the LeBaron-built all-weather cabriolet was continued.

✚ **FOR** The Twelve's great looks for less money • Fine highway tourer • Excellent investment • It's a Classic

➖ **AGAINST** Scarce and increasingly pricey • A lot of car to handle • Sadly, more often trailered than driven

1936 Super Eight phaeton by Dietrich

PRODUCTION
1933 1300 **1934** 1920 **1935** 1392 **1936** 1330

SPECIFICATIONS
Length (in.)	NA
Wheelbase (in.)	135.0/142.0 (1933); 135.0/142.0/147.0 (1934); 132.0/139.0/144.0 (1935-36)
Weight (lbs)	4490-5525
Price (new)	$2750-7065

ENGINES
cid/type	bhp	years
384.8/sv I-8	145-150	1933-36

PRICES
Open	
FAIR	$18,000-75,000
GOOD	$75,000-130,000
FINE	$130,000-185,000
Closed	
FAIR	$7000-32,000
GOOD	$32,000-56,000
FINE	$56,500-80,000

FINE 1934 CUSTOM SPORT PHAETON PRICE HISTORY
1982 $56,000		**1990** $175,000	
1994 $200,000		**1998** $140,000	
1982-2000 RETURN 7%			
2000-2010 5%			

1 9 3 5 - 3 9
PACKARD ONE TWENTY/ EIGHT

Historically the most important Packard of the Thirties. It saved the company at the time, though emphasis on middle-priced products in the postwar years ultimately cost Packard its life. The model sold very well, with traditional styling, straightforward specifications, and a modest but reliable and smooth L-head straight eight. Designated Eight for 1938 only. Interesting models include the post-1935 convertible sedan

1937 One Twenty convertible coupe

(called "Dietrich" but no relation), a wagon, and long-wheelbase sedans and customs (from 1937). Long subject to an unfair press as a "cheap Packard," it nonetheless offered good value for money, excellent performance, and high quality. Without it, the company would have expired by 1936.

✚ FOR The best all-around touring Packard of the 1930s • The most affordable Packard Eight from the same period • Traditional Packard styling • Plenty of parts suppliers • Very popular among collectors

➖ AGAINST Still haunted by the "cheap Packard" label • Lacks Classic status, save custom bodies • Closed models look very ordinary

PRODUCTION
1935 24,955 **1936** 55,042 **1937** 50,100 **1938** 22,624 **1939** 17,647

SPECIFICATIONS
Length (in.)	NA
Wheelbase (in.)	120.0 (1935-36); 120.0/138.0 (1937), 127.0/139.0/148.0 (1938); 127.0/148.0 (1939)
Weight (lbs)	3340-5225
Price (new)	$945-5385

ENGINES
cid/type	bhp	years
257.2/sv I-8	110	1935
282.0/sv I-8	120	1936-39

PRICES
Open	
FAIR	$10,000-25,000
GOOD	$25,000-42,000
FINE	$42,000-55,000
Closed	
FAIR	$5000-18,000
GOOD	$18,000-25,000
FINE	$25,000-35,000

FINE 1939 CONVERTIBLE SEDAN PRICE HISTORY
1982 $27,000		**1990** $50,000	
1994 $55,000		**1998** $55,000	

1982-2000 RETURN 5%
2000-2010 open models 5% (others 2%)

1937-38
PACKARD SUPER EIGHT

Far more successful than concurrent Twelves, probably because it sold for much less, the 1937-38 was vastly downsized from earlier in both seen and unseen places. Independent front suspension, a smaller Eight, grease nipples instead of Bijur lubrication, and hydraulic brakes were featured, and the old "suicide" front doors were eliminated. It was also more streamlined in keeping with current trends (the radiator was raked 30 degrees now) but retained the "Packard look." Weight was cut almost as dramatically as on GM's famous downsizing program of the late 1970s.

✚ FOR Excellent driving machine • Last of the floor-shift Super Eights • Glorious dash with five big dials • Strong club and parts support • Classic status • Almost affordable by mortals

➖ AGAINST No overdrive available • Relatively scarce and tend to be pricey • Not as snooty a model as the earlier Classics

PRODUCTION
1937 5793 **1938** 2478

SPECIFICATIONS
Length (in.)	NA
Wheelbase (in.)	127.0/134.0/139.0
Weight (lbs)	4530-5360
Price (new)	$2335-4945

ENGINES
cid/type	bhp	years
320.0/sv I-8	135	1937
320.0/sv I-8	130	1938

PRICES
Open	
FAIR	$15,000-35,000
GOOD	$35,000-55,000
FINE	$55,000-80,000
Closed	
FAIR	$5000-15,000
GOOD	$15,000-30,000
FINE	$30,000-45,000

FINE 1939 LIMOUSINE PRICE HISTORY
1982 $28,000		**1990** $130,000	
1994 $60,000		**1998** $50,000	

1982-2000 RETURN 5%
2000-2010 open models 5%, **closed** 3%

1940-42
PACKARD CUSTOM SUPER EIGHT 180 BY DARRIN

Howard A. "Dutch" Darrin began building rakish convertibles on the Packard Eight chassis in 1937. These became regular catalog items in the

1937 Super Eight sedan

1940 Custom Super Eight convertible by Darrin

senior series for 1940-42, along with a Sport Sedan offered for 1940 only. A Convertible Sedan was available on the 138-inch wheelbase through 1941, and the 127-inch-wheelbase Convertible Victoria—the most exotic and desirable of these cars—was available in all three years.

✠ FOR One of the great Classics • Splendid styling • Super luxury

▣ AGAINST Formidable prices • Expensive to restore • Structural weaknesses

PRODUCTION

fewer than 200 (est.)

SPECIFICATIONS

Length (in.)	NA
Wheelbase (in.)	127.0/138.0
Weight (lbs)	3920-4121 (Victoria), 4050 (Conv Sdn), 4490 (Sport Sdn)
Price (new)	$4595 (Victoria), 6332 (Conv Sdn), 4795 (Sport Sedan)

ENGINES

cid/type	bhp	years
356/sv I-8	160/165	1940-42

PRICES

Open	
FAIR	probably not available
GOOD	$50,000-90,000
FINE	$90,000-150,000
(Sport Sedan deduct 30%.)	

FINE CONVERTIBLE PRICE HISTORY

1982 $60,000		**1990** $150,000	
1994 $145,000		**1998** $145,000	
1982-2000 RETURN 7%			
2000-2010 5%			

PACKARD CUSTOM SUPER EIGHT

Among the last Packards with custom coachwork—in this case an all-weather cabriolet on the 138-inch wheelbase and a Town Car on the 148-inch wheelbase by the Rollson (formerly Rollston) company. These senior Packards did not adopt the flush-sided Clipper styling in 1942 as did the One Eighty sedans. Their classic lines preserved traditional Packard appearance from the marque's golden age. Among closed Packards from this period, they were the most elegant and luxurious.

✠ FOR Superb workmanship • CCCA Classic status • Rare and desirable

▣ AGAINST Expensive to acquire and maintain

PRODUCTION

fewer than 100

SPECIFICATIONS

Length (in.)	NA
Wheelbase (in.)	138.0/148.0
Weight (lbs)	4050-4075 (cabrio), 4175-4200 (Town Car)

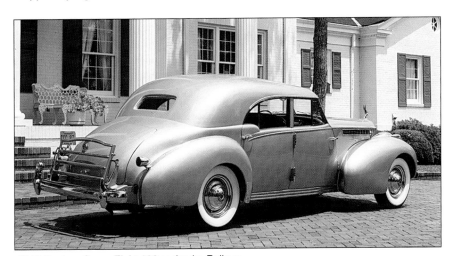

1940 Custom Super Eight 180 sedan by Rollson

Price (new)	$4473-4792 (cabrio), $4599-4889 (Town Car)

ENGINES

cid/type	bhp	years
356/sv I-8	160	1940-41
356/sv I-8	165	1942

PRICES

FAIR	$17,500-45,000
GOOD	$45,000-70,000
FINE	$70,000-90,000

FINE EXAMPLE PRICE HISTORY

1982 $31,500	1990 $95,000
1994 $115,000	1998 $105,000

1982-2000 RETURN 8%
2000-2010 3%

1941 One Twenty convertible coupe

1 9 4 0 - 4 2
PACKARD ONE TEN CONVERTIBLE

This was the most prized model in the six-cylinder companion series of the One Twenty line, built on a five-inch shorter, 122-inch wheelbase. Like the Eights, this convertible coupe retained a traditional upright Packard appearance when other bodystyles went to the more streamlined "Clipper" styling for 1942, though the ragtop was called a "Clipper One Ten" anyway. Unlike the One Twenty series, no convertible sedan was offered.

➕ FOR More affordable than One Twentys • Others as for 1940-42 One Twenty • Overdrive a plus, especially with this engine

➖ AGAINST Far less masterful on the road than the One Twenty • Less impressive to look at, too • Column shift with linkage prone to stick

PRODUCTION

1940 750 **1941** 500 **1942** 500 (all est.)

SPECIFICATIONS

Length (in.)	NA
Wheelbase (in.)	122.0
Weight (lbs)	3200-3315
Price (new)	$1104-1375

ENGINES

cid/type	bhp	years
245.3/sv I-6	100	1940-41
245.3/sv I-6	105	1942

PRICES

FAIR	$6500-15,000
GOOD	$15,000-25,000
FINE	$25,000-37,000

FINE CONVERTIBLE PRICE HISTORY

1982 $16,500	1990 $35,000
1994 $38,000	1998 $37,000

1982-2000 RETURN 5%
2000-2010 3%

1940 One Ten convertible coupe

1 9 4 0 - 4 2
PACKARD ONE TWENTY CONVERTIBLE

The much sought-after open models in Packard's junior series, offered as a standard or DeLuxe convertible coupe and convertible sedan for 1940 and '41. The convertible sedan was dropped the following year. That year, Clipper styling (and name) was applied to most of the Packard line, leaving a DeLuxe convertible as the only small Packard Eight with "traditional" styling, though it was called a "Clipper One Twenty" anyway. The One Twenty was not, as is often assumed, a cheap car; in price it compared most closely with Buick and Chrysler. Its 282-cid straight eight was silky smooth in operation, and the car had performance and roadability of a high order.

➕ FOR The most affordable prewar Packard Eight convertibles • Classic lines that will always be in style • Fine performance • Traditional Packard quality

➖ AGAINST A bit pricey • Lowly reputation among the uninitiated • Column shift with linkage prone to stick

PRODUCTION

1940 1500 **1941** 1000 **1942** 1000 (all est.)

SPECIFICATIONS

Length (in.)	NA
Wheelbase (in.)	127.0
Weight (lbs)	3540-4000
Price (new)	$1277-1753

ENGINES

cid/type	bhp	years

282/sv I-8	120	1940-41
282/sv I-8	125	1942

PRICES

FAIR	$8000-18,000
GOOD	$18,000-30,000
FINE	$30,000-45,000

FINE 1940 CONVERTIBLE SEDAN PRICE HISTORY

1982 $25,000	1990 $50,000
1994 $50,000	1998 $34,000

1982-2000 RETURN 4%
2000-2010 5%

1939-42
PACKARD SUPER EIGHT/ ONE SIXTY CONVERTIBLE

In major change, Super Eight bodies were now shared with the One Twenty, the wheelbase shrank to 127 inches, and the shifter went from floor to steering column, where it was called "Handishift" and soon became notorious for sticking in a gear. But overdrive was now available, and the Super's new engine was a magnificent 356-cid straight eight. Body styles were a convertible coupe and convertible sedan, the latter dropped in 1942. In 1941 both body styles could be had in Deluxe trim featuring wood garnish moldings. Although all One Sixtys are highly desirable,

these open styles naturally generate the greatest interest and command the highest prices. This is a great Packard that many believe combines the best traditional styling with the most modern engineering.

➕ FOR Traditional Packard four-square styling • Powered by what is probably Packard's finest straight eight • Usually found with Overdrive • CCCA Classic status • Sidemounts and runningboards were optional

➖ AGAINST All come with the not-so-handy, column mounted "Handishift" • Plastic dashboard knobs and trim don't hold up • Body looks like a One Twenty... • But don't be fooled, and don't fall for a One Twenty convertible body grafted onto a One Sixty chassis—there are differences and experts should be consulted

PRODUCTION

Fewer than 500 per year.1941: On the basis of high serial numbers covering 85% of production, the Packard Club reports 250 convertible coupes and 200 convertible sedans

SPECIFICATIONS

Length (in.)	NA
Wheelbase (in.)	127.0
Weight (lbs)	3795-4160
Price (new)	$1775-2180

ENGINES

cid/type	bhp	years
356/sv I-8	160	1939-41
356/sv I-8	165	1942

PRICES

FAIR	$14,000-28,000
GOOD	$28,000-45,000
FINE	$45,000-75,000

FINE EXAMPLE PRICE HISTORY

1982 $50,000	1990 $75,000
1994 $75,000	1998 $75,000

1982-2000 RETURN 3%
2000-2010 5%

1941
PACKARD CLIPPER

1942 Clipper 120 sedan (1941 Clipper similar)

The first car to combine modern flush-sided styling with the Packard nameplate, replacing straight lines with curves. The original design seems to have come from Dutch Darrin, but detail development was the work of Packard's own Werner Gubitz. Offered only as a four-door sedan in its debut year on the 127-inch-wheelbase chassis, and was well-received by the public. The following year, most Packards from One Ten to One Eighty acquired similar styling. Convertibles were the notable exceptions (hence their collectibility today as preservers of the

1942 One Sixty convertible coupe

"old order"), along with formal models and certain commercial bodies.

⊞ **FOR** Historical importance • Fine engineering • Good performance • Packard panache • Overdrive, useful with small eight

▬ **AGAINST** Collector recognition still limited • In short supply • No long wheelbase models • That clunky column shifter

PRODUCTION

16,600

SPECIFICATIONS

Length (in.)	203.0
Wheelbase (in.)	127.0
Weight (lbs)	3725
Price (new)	$1420

ENGINES

cid/type	bhp	years
282/sv I-8	125	1941

PRICES

FAIR	$3000-6500
GOOD	$6500-11,000
FINE	$11,000-16,000

FINE EXAMPLE PRICE HISTORY

1982 $7200	1990 $10,000
1994 $15,000	1998 $16,000
1982-2000 RETURN 5%	
2000-2010 3%	

1942
PACKARD CLIPPER ONE EIGHTY

The top of the standard-body prewar Packard line. "Clipper" styling applied to this year's senior One Sixty and One Eighty sedans and club coupes resulted in handsome cars that are still enviable today. The One Eighty sedan was priced at $2196, making it considerably more expensive than its One Sixty linemate and about 50 percent costlier than the '41 Clipper. The interior offered fine carpeting, Bedford cord upholstery, and two types of woodgraining on side panels. The big 356 straight eight was as smooth and powerful as ever.

⊞ **FOR** The most luxurious prewar Packard • Smooth, comfortable tourer • Superb engine • Elegant looks • A CCCA Classic

▬ **AGAINST** Extremely scarce • The Handishift, as usual

PRODUCTION

1942 Clipper One Eighty sedan

600 (est.)

SPECIFICATIONS

Length (in.)	212.0
Wheelbase (in.)	127.0
Weight (lbs)	4010-4030
Price (new)	$2099-2196

ENGINES

cid/type	bhp	years
356/sv I-8	165	1942

PRICES

FAIR	$5000-10,000
GOOD	$10,000-18,000
FINE	$18,000-26,000

FINE EXAMPLE PRICE HISTORY

1982 $9900	1990 $22,000
1994 $35,000	1998 $26,000
1982-2000 RETURN 6%	
2000-2010 5%	

1946-47
PACKARD CUSTOM SUPER CLIPPER

Postwar continuation of the elegant Clipper-based 1942 models at their most luxurious. The 127-inch-wheel-base four-door sedan and club coupe were now joined by a seven-passenger sedan and limousine built for Packard by the Henney body company on the long 148-inch chassis. Though these used basically stock mechanicals, their body panels were somewhat different. Many experts today think this well-balanced design could have carried Packard through to its first complete postwar restyle, which took place for the 1951 model year. Instead, a modified, bloated look replaced it for 1948.

⊞ **FOR** One of the few with both Classic and Milestone status • Timeless design; seems to look better every year • Superb quality • Smooth performance

▬ **AGAINST** Henney body panels in short supply

PRODUCTION

Sdns & cpes 7162 **lwb models** 3081

SPECIFICATIONS

Length (in.)	204.0/225.0
Wheelbase (in.)	127.0/148.0
Weight (lbs)	3384-4090/4870-4920
Price (new)	$2913-3449/$4332-4668

1947 Custom Super Clipper Club Coupe

ENGINES

cid/type	bhp	years
356/sv I-8	165	1946-47

PRICES

FAIR	$5500-12,000
GOOD	$12,000-18,000
FINE	$18,000-25,000

FINE SEDAN PRICE HISTORY

1982 $7000	**1990** $14,000
1994 $16,000	**1998** $22,000
1982-2000 RETURN 8%	
2000-2010 5%	

1 9 4 8 - 5 0
PACKARD CUSTOM EIGHT

Packard's top-line series during the "elephantine" styling era, benefiting greatly in appearance from its long wheelbase. Also the last Packards powered by the venerable 356-cid nine-main-bearing straight eight. A full range of typically Packard appointments was fitted here, including Amboyna burl woodgraining, leather-piped Bedford cord upholstery, Mosstred carpeting from New York's Shelton Looms, a unique fore/aft headliner seams on the Twenty-Second Series 1948-49 (early) models, and "Ultramatic Drive" on the Twenty-Third Series 1949 (late)-1950 cars. Initial 1948 production almost completely met demand, which suggests Packard's market had changed considerably from the luxury-only orientation of prewar times. The long sedans and limousines were dropped from the Twenty-Third Series, as was the fast-back two-door club sedan.

FOR Packard's best in this period • Outstanding construction • Comfort • Smooth performance • Milestone car

AGAINST The ugliest period of Packard's postwar era (though Customs looked better than lesser models)

PRODUCTION

1948 2d/4d sdns 5936 **conv** 1105 **lwb sdn/limo** 230 **chassis** 1941 **1949a 2d/4d sdns** 2990 **conv** 213 **lwb sdn/limo** 50 **1949b 2d/4d sdns** 973 **conv** 68 **chassis** 160 **1950 2d/4d sdns** 707 **conv** 77 **chassis** 244

SPECIFICATIONS

Length (in.)	204.0/225.0
Wheelbase (in.)	127.0/148.0
Weight (lbs)	4110-4530 (lwb: 4860-4880)
Price (new)	$3700-4520 (lwb: $4704/4868)

1950 Custom Eight sedan

ENGINES

cid/type	bhp	years
356/sv I-8	160	1948-50

PRICES

Conv	
FAIR	$10,000-17,000
GOOD	$17,000-25,000
FINE	$25,000-35,000

Others: As per 1946-47 Packard Custom Super Clipper less 10%.

FINE CONVERTIBLE PRICE HISTORY

1982 $14,000	**1990** $40,000
1994 $40,000	**1998** $35,000
1982-2000 RETURN 5%	
2000-2010 convertible 5%, **others** 2%	

1 9 4 8 - 5 0
PACKARD EIGHT STATION SEDAN

An interesting sedan-like station wagon designed along the lines of the streamlined 1941-42 Chrysler

1948 Eight Station Sedan

Town & Country. Sheetmetal was shared with the standard Eight ahead of the firewall, and most of the rear body was metal. Ash framing on the bodysides was decorative, but it did have a structural purpose for the tailgate area. Priced just $300 below the Custom Eight, it didn't sell well. Most Station Sedans built were '48s; those sold through 1950 were simply retitled leftovers.

✚ FOR The most desirable junior Packard of the period • Fine construction quality • Historically important • Not too costly

▬ AGAINST "Pregnant elephant" styling • Expensive to maintain • Not easy to find

PRODUCTION
3864

SPECIFICATIONS
Length (in.)	204.6
Wheelbase (in.)	120.0
Weight (lbs)	4075
Price (new)	$3425-3449

ENGINES
cid/type	bhp	years
288/sv I-8	130/135	1948-50

PRICES
FAIR	$9500-14,000
GOOD	$14,000-20,000
FINE	$20,000-30,000

FINE EXAMPLE PRICE HISTORY
1982 $9000	1990 $35,000
1994 $35,000	1998 $35,000
1982-2000 RETURN 6%	
2000-2010 5%	

1 9 4 9 - 5 0
PACKARD SUPER DELUXE EIGHT

This car was the reason why Custom Eight sales dropped so drastically after 1948. The Super shared the grille style and wheelbase of the costlier Custom, and dealers could even supply its cloisonne-decorated hubcaps. The 1949-50 Customs were not as richly trimmed as the '48s, and the Super Deluxe's 327-cid straight eight was almost as smooth as the big 356 unit. No wonder many buyers saw little reason to pick the Custom and pay $700-900 more.

✚ FOR Custom Eight looks at a lower price still its biggest attraction • Better

1949 Super DeLuxe Eight convertible

performance than heavier Custom despite smaller engine

▬ AGAINST As for 1948-50 Custom Eight

PRODUCTION
1949 2d/4d sdns 3000 (est.) **conv** 685 **lwb sedan/limo** 4 **1950 2d/4d sdns** 2000 (est.) **conv** 600

SPECIFICATIONS
Length (in.)	211.7/225.7
Wheelbase (in.)	127.0/141.0
Weight (lbs)	3855-4260 (lwb: 4600-4620)
Price (new)	$2894-2919 (lwb: $3950-4100)

ENGINES
cid/type	bhp	years
327/sv I-8	150	1949-50

PRICES
Conv	
FAIR	$9600-15,500
GOOD	$15,500-22,500
FINE	$22,500-28,500
Other	
FAIR	$3000-6000
GOOD	$6000-10,000
FINE	$10,000-14,500

(Add 25% to above range for lwb models.)

FINE CONVERTIBLE PRICE HISTORY
1982 $11,000	1990 $32,500

1994 $35,000	1998 $31,000
1982-2000 RETURN 6%	
2000-2010 convertible 5%, others 2%	

1 9 5 1 - 5 4
PACKARD PATRICIAN

Packard's newly named top-line standard sedan in the early '50s. Along with other models, it carried the firm's first complete redesign since the Clipper of a decade earlier. The shape, which designer John Reinhart named "high pockets," didn't wear particularly well, however. There was no criticizing the Patrician's integrity, though—it was beautifully built, comfortable in the Packard tradition, and surprisingly fast. Most buyers thought it dull and uninteresting next to the tailfinned Cadillac V-8s and the very roadable Lincolns of these years, and spent their money accordingly.

✚ FOR Top-of-the-line • Quality • Luxury • Milestone car

1951 Patrician 400 sedan

■ **AGAINST** Rust-prone • 1954 gear-start Ultramatic gave frequent trouble

PRODUCTION

1951 9001 **1952** 3975 **1953** 7456 **1954** 2760

SPECIFICATIONS

Length (in.)	218.0
Wheelbase (in.)	127.0
Weight (lbs)	4100-4190
Price (new)	$3662-3890

ENGINES

cid/type	bhp	years
327/sv I-8	155/180	1951-53
359/sv I-8	212	1954

PRICES

FAIR	$3000-7000
GOOD	$7000-12,000
FINE	$12,000-16,000

FINE EXAMPLE PRICE HISTORY

1982 $6600	**1990** $12,000
1994 $16,000	**1998** $16,000
1982-2000 RETURN 65%	
2000-2010 3%	

1951-54
PACKARD PATRICIAN FORMAL SEDAN BY DERHAM

Longtime Packard body builders Derham and Company of Rosemont, Pennsylvania, answered PMCC president James Nance's call for a Formal Sedan by adapting a leather (occasionally canvas) padded top and a smaller rear window to the basic Patrician sedan. The result was a very "private" four-door that managed to capture the flavor of the old coach-building days before the war.

✚ **FOR** They made so few

■ **AGAINST** And you'll pay accordingly

1954 Patrician Formal Sedan by Derham

1954 Caribbean convertible

PRODUCTION

approx. 25 per year

SPECIFICATIONS

Length (in.)	218.0
Wheelbase (in.)	127.0
Weight (lbs)	4335
Price (new)	$6531

ENGINES

cid/type	bhp	years
327/sv I-8	155/180	1951-53
359/sv I-8	212	1954

PRICES

FAIR	$5000-8000
GOOD	$8000-12,000
FINE	$12,000-18,000

FINE EXAMPLE PRICE HISTORY

1982 $7500	**1990** $14,500
1994 $20,000	**1998** $17,000
1982-2000 RETURN 5%	
2000-2010 5%	

1953-54
PACKARD CARIBBEAN

Packard's answer to the Cadillac Eldorado, both in concept and marketing strategy. A limited-production, ultra-posh convertible styled by Richard A. Teague, who took as his inspiration the Henney-built Pan American show cars of 1952. It was built on the 122-inch-wheelbase chassis and basic convertible body, but with a more rakish appearance thanks to full rear wheel cutouts (for '53 only) and distinctive chrome trim. Powered by Packard's five-main-bearing 327 straight eight initially, it was then switched to the nine-main unit with displacement increased to 359 cid for 1954. These were the most luxurious and sporting Packards in a generation.

✚ **FOR** Dashing looks • Ample comfort • One of the most desirable postwar Packards • Good appreciation potential • Milestone car

■ **AGAINST** Hefty prices, but cheaper than they once were

PRODUCTION

1953 750 **1954** 400

SPECIFICATIONS

Length (in.)	220.3
Wheelbase (in.)	122.0
Weight (lbs)	4265-4660
Price (new)	$5210-6100

ENGINES

cid/type	bhp	years
327/sv I-8	180	1953
359/sv I-8	212	1954

PRICES

FAIR	$10,000-21,000
GOOD	$21,000-30,000
FINE	$30,000-40,000

FINE EXAMPLE PRICE HISTORY

1982 $12,900	**1990** $30,000
1994 $38,000	**1998** $40,000
1982-2000 RETURN 7%	
2000-2010 7%	

1953-54

PACKARD CLIPPER SPORTSTER

This was an interesting member of the lower-priced Packard line that offered hardtop-style appointments (two-tone paint and a nice interior) without the pillarless roof. It came at a reasonable price, only $185 above the basic Clipper DeLuxe club sedan. It was eclipsed in its second year by a true pillarless model, the Panama, in the Clipper Super series.

➕ **FOR** Uncommon • Affordable

➖ **AGAINST** Trim on the plain side • Are there any left?

PRODUCTION

1336

SPECIFICATIONS

Length (in.)	213.3
Wheelbase (in.)	122.0
Weight (lbs)	3595-3720
Price (new)	$2805-2830

ENGINES

cid/type	bhp	years
288/sv I-8	150	1953
327/sv I-8	165	1954

PRICES

FAIR	$4000-8000
GOOD	$8000-11,000
FINE	$11,000-15,000

FINE EXAMPLE PRICE HISTORY

1982 $4800		**1990** $32,500	
1994 $16,000		**1998** $12,000	

1955 Caribbean convertible

1982-2000 RETURN 9%
2000-2010 5%

1955-56

PACKARD CARIBBEAN

A continuation of the posh Packard sporty car, with updated (but not all-new) styling and a revised chassis featuring torsion bar suspension. Also new: Packard's first overhead valve V-8, putting out an impressive 275 bhp from its 352 cid. A bore increase the following year brought output up to a rousing 310 bhp. Ultramatic Drive was improved for greater reliability. The last of the great open Packards, Caribbeans sported flashy three-tone paint jobs, reversible cloth or leather front seat covers (1956), a broad eggcrate grille, and distinctive "cathedral" taillights. Broken out into a separate series for '56, when a companion two-door hardtop was fielded in addition to the usual soft top. Remarkably, in view of the number built, these flashy models are not much costlier today than 1953-54 Caribbeans.

➕ **FOR** High on the want list of postwar Packard fanciers • Satisfying road car • Low-production appeal • High-yield investment • Milestone car status

➖ **AGAINST** Ultramatic and suspension know-how are hard to find • Rust problems • Gaudy styling in the opinion of many

PRODUCTION

1955 500 **1956 2d htp** 263 **conv** 276

SPECIFICATIONS

Length (in.)	218.5
Wheelbase (in.)	127.0
Weight (lbs)	4590-4755

1954 Clipper DeLuxe Sportster coupe

| Price (new) | $5495-5995 | |

ENGINES

cid/type	bhp	years
352/ohv V-8	275	1955
374/ohv V-8	310	1956

PRICES

FAIR	$12,500-20,000
GOOD	$20,000-30,000
FINE	$30,000-44,000

(Deduct 25% for 1956 htp.)

FINE CONVERTIBLE PRICE HISTORY

1982 $10,000	1990 $32,500
1994 $42,500	1998 $42,500

1982-2000 RETURN 9%
2000-2010 7%

1955 Clipper Custom Constellation hardtop coupe

1955
PACKARD CLIPPER CUSTOM CONSTELLATION

An attractive hardtop with the new ohv V-8 and torsion-level suspension from the senior Packards. Engine output was discreetly rated at 15 bhp less, however. Offered this year in the new Clipper Custom series, which then became part of the lineup for the separate Clipper make for '56 (see Clipper). The most desirable of the smaller '55 Packards then and now.

FOR Nice styling • Fine ride • Good performance • Rarity • Strong appreciation potential

AGAINST Thirsty • Some body parts hard to find

PRODUCTION
6672

SPECIFICATIONS

Length (in.)	214.8
Wheelbase (in.)	122.0
Weight (lbs)	3865
Price (new)	$3076

ENGINES

cid/type	bhp	years
352/ohv V-8	245	1955

PRICES

FAIR	$3200-5500
GOOD	$5500-9000
FINE	$9000-14,000

(For 1956 model, see "Clipper.")

FINE EXAMPLE PRICE HISTORY

1982 $4425	1990 $12,000
1994 $15,000	1998 $14,000

1982-2000 RETURN 7%
2000-2010 5%

1955-56
PACKARD FOUR HUNDRED

New two-door hardtop derivative of the Patrician sedan, built on the longer of Packard's two wheelbases in these years. A pillarless roof and more frequent use of two-toning gave it a sportier look. Otherwise identical with the four-door sedan.

FOR As for 1955-56 Patrician, plus hardtop sportiness and stronger appreciation

AGAINST As for 1955-56 Patrician

PRODUCTION
1955 7206 **1956** 3224

1955 400 hardtop coupe

SPECIFICATIONS

Length (in.)	217.8
Wheelbase (in.)	127.0
Weight (lbs)	4080-4250
Price (new)	$3930-4190

ENGINES

cid/type	bhp	years
352/ohv V-8	260	1955
374/ohv V-8	290	1956

PRICES

FAIR	$4000-7500
GOOD	$7500-11,000
FINE	$11,000-16,000

FINE EXAMPLE PRICE HISTORY

1982 $6500	1990 $20,000
1994 $18,000	1998 $17,000

1982-2000 RETURN 5%
2000-2010 7%

1955 Patrician sedan

1955-56
PACKARD PATRICIAN

Packard's top-line four-door, continuing from previous years with a clever facelift by Dick Teague. The result throughout the line was a Packard that managed to look less like the five-year-old design it was and more like the competition. Bold grillework, cathedral taillights, advanced torsion bar suspension with self-leveling, and a new ohv V-8 were shared with the sporty Caribbeans, but exterior and interior trim were appropriately more muted in keeping with the Patrician's upper-class image.

+ FOR Period styling • Smooth performance • Luxury • Widely sought today • Low production • Packard nameplate • Milestone car status

– AGAINST Indifferent assembly quality • Occasionally suffers from rust

PRODUCTION

1955 9127 **1956** 3775

SPECIFICATIONS

Length (in.)	217.4
Wheelbase (in.)	127.0
Weight (lbs)	4045-4275
Price (new)	$3890-4160

ENGINES

cid/type	bhp	years
352/ohv V-8	260	1955
374/ohv V-8	290	1956

PRICES

FAIR	$3000-5000
GOOD	$5000-7000
FINE	$7000-16,000

FINE EXAMPLE PRICE HISTORY

1982 $4300	1990 $12,500
1994 $16,000	1998 $16,000

1982-2000 RETURN 6%
2000-2010 5%

1956
PACKARD EXECUTIVE

New bottom-line series in the senior Packard line, intended to bridge a small price gap created when Clipper became a separate make this year. It was built on the Clipper's shorter 122-inch wheelbase, but had senior front-end styling and decklid treatment. Power was provided by the top engine

1956 Executive hardtop coupe

from '55, the 275-bhp 352 V-8.

⊡ FOR A genuine Packard that's still affordable • Clean period styling • Good performance • Exceptional torsion-level suspension • Strong appreciation potential

⊟ AGAINST Low-line status • Tends to rust • Fuel thirst • Body parts now scarce

PRODUCTION
4d sdn 1784 **2d htp** 1031

SPECIFICATIONS
Length (in.)	214.8
Wheelbase (in.)	122.0
Weight (lbs)	4185 (either model)
Price (new)	$3465/3560

ENGINES
cid/type	bhp	years
352/ohv V-8	275	1956

PRICES
Htp	
FAIR	$3500-6000
GOOD	$6000-8000
FINE	$8000-13,000
Sdn	
FAIR	$1500-3000
GOOD	$3000-5000
FINE	$5000-8000

FINE HARDTOP PRICE HISTORY
1982 $4225		**1990** $13,500	
1994 $11,500		**1998** $18,000	
1982-2000 RETURN 7%			
2000-2010 5%			

1957
PACKARD CLIPPER

The so-called "Packardbaker," based on the concurrent Studebaker President and built alongside it at South Bend, following the decision to close Packard's Detroit factory. These cars were issued partly to meet dealer franchise requirements and partly with the hope that demand for a big, luxury Packard would eventually return. Styling, by Dick Teague, made clever use of traditional Packard "cues" like '56 Clipper taillights, '55 Clipper hubcaps, and a dashboard similar to the 1955-56 dash. Body, chassis, and running gear were pure Studebaker, however. The once broad lineup was thinned to just two models, the four-door Town Sedan and four-door Country Sedan wagon, in an obvious effort to cut production costs. Clipper's interesting powerplant was the familiar Studebaker 289 with 275 bhp courtesy of a McCulloch supercharger, so per-

1957 Clipper Country wagon

formance was respectable despite its humble origins. These were not Packards in the true sense, though they were very good Studebakers.

⊡ FOR An historical footnote • Performance • Better-looking than a lot of rival '57s • Scarce yet affordable

⊟ AGAINST McCulloch supercharger notoriously fickle • Front fender rust • Badge-engineered character • not much investment value

PRODUCTION
4d sdn 3940 **4d wgn** 869

SPECIFICATIONS
Length (in.)	211.8/204.8 (sdn/wgn)
Wheelbase (in.)	120.5/116.5 (sdn/wgn)
Weight (lbs)	3570/3650
Price (new)	$3212/3384

ENGINES
cid/type	bhp	years
289/ohv V-8[1]	275	1957
[1]Supercharged		

PRICES
FAIR	$1200-3000
GOOD	$3000-4500
FINE	$4500-6500

FINE EXAMPLE PRICE HISTORY
1982 $3100	**1990** $6500

1994 $9500	**1998** $10,000
1982-2000 RETURN 5%	
2000-2010 3%	

1958
PACKARD

The three standard models in Packard's last-gasp line, essentially Studebaker-based '57 Clippers with a low-budget facelift by Duncan McRae. Design highlights included swollen tailfins; quad headlamps paired in ugly pods; and a low, wide eggcrate grille that strained to emulate the "fishmouth" of the new Packard Hawk—with a trace of Packard's once-esteemed "ox-yoke" radiator. These Packardbakers were as conventional and aged as their Studebaker parents (whose basic design dated from '53) and offered only the non-supercharged Stude 289 V-8 (unlike the Hawk). Alas, time had run out for Packard, rendering these among the rarest of '50s cars and thus some of the toughest to acquire today. The mainstay sedan led in "volume," but the wagon was scarcest of all, followed by the hardtop

1958 hardtop coupe

coupe with its delicate Chrysler-like roofline (shared with Stude's '58 Starliner). Left stillborn by Studebaker-Packard's fast-failing fortunes in this period was an ambitious "comeback" program for 1957-59 involving clever body-sharing among three distinct makes, including mid-price Clippers and all-new luxury Packards styled along the lines of Dick Teague's 1956 Predictor show car.

✚ FOR Super rare • Last-of-the-line interest value • Club support • As Studebakers they were very good cars

■ AGAINST As rust-prone as the '57s • Jukebox styling • Most body/trim parts virtually impossible now

PRODUCTION

2d htp 675 **4d sdn** 1200 **4d wgn** 159

SPECIFICATIONS

Length (in.)	213.2/209.2/206.2
	(sdn/htp/wgn)
Wheelbase (in.)	120.5 (sdn), 116.5 (wgn/htp)
Weight (lbs)	3480-3555
Price (new)	$3212-3384

ENGINES

cid/type	bhp	years
289/ohv V-8	225	1958

PRICES

Htp	
FAIR	$3000-6000
GOOD	$6000-9000
FINE	$9000-12,000
Sdn & wgn	

FAIR	$1200-3000
GOOD	$3000-4500
FINE	$4500-6500

FINE HARDTOP PRICE HISTORY

1982 $3700	**1990** $9500
1994 $10,500	**1998** $13,000
1982-2000 RETURN 8%	
2000-2010 3%	

1 9 5 8
PACKARD HAWK

The Hawk was the most interesting and collectible of four Studebaker-based models fielded in Packard's last year. Styling, by Duncan McCrae, based on the Studebkaer Hawk, which itself evolved from the original 1953 "Loewy coupe." The bizarre styling was influenced by Roy Hurley of Curtiss-Wright, which had picked up Stude-baker-Packard as a tax write-off but quickly convinced himself he was a car designer. The Hawk had a low jutting "mouth," mylar-adorned tailfins, simu-lated spare tire embossed into the trunklid, and padded armrests out-board of the side windows to simulate a vintage aircraft. The inside was more serious, with fine leather upholstery and a no-nonsense dash with full instrumentation. Power was supplied by the McCulloch-supercharged ver-sion of the Studebaker 289 V-8.

✚ FOR Much better than its exterior styling suggests • Exceptional perfor-mance (the fastest Packard ever) • Luxury • Last of the line • Low-pro-duction appeal • Strong recent appreci-ation

■ AGAINST Studebaker fender rust problem • Vacuum-cleaner frontal styling • Hard to find body and trim parts

PRODUCTION
558

SPECIFICATIONS

Length (in.)	204.6
Wheelbase (in.)	120.5
Weight (lbs)	3470
Price (new)	$3995

ENGINES

cid/type	bhp	years
289/ohv V-8[1]	275	1958

[1]Supercharged

PRICES

FAIR	$4500-9500
GOOD	$9500-16,500
FINE	$16,500-24,000

FINE EXAMPLE PRICE HISTORY

1982 $5700	**1990** $17,500
1994 $17,500	**1998** $24,000
1982-2000 RETURN 9%	
2000-2010 6%	

1958 Hawk hardtop coupe

2000 A.I.V. roadster

1997-2000
PANOZ A.I.V. ROADSTER

Most small production sports cars are made in England or Italy. The Panoz A.I.V. Roadster was made in Hoschton, Georgia. A bare-bones roadster, there was a minimum of bodywork and even less weather protection. The A.I.V. was for fast drives on sunny days. A.I.V. stood for Aluminum Intensive Roadster and it was. Seventy percent (including frame and body) of the Panoz was alloy. Similar to the Plymouth Prowler in its styling and use of aluminum, the A.I.V. went one better by dropping in a 305-horsepower Mustang Cobra V-8. The lightweight roadster was faster to 60 than the Mustang and most other cars. The race car-like suspension gave .97g of grip, but still had a relatively comfortable ride. Unlike some other cottage industry products, the Panoz was well developed, beautifully assembled, and could be serviced at a Ford dealer.

FOR Fast • Purposeful, no unneeded weight or luxuries • Drivetrain parts and service easy to find

AGAINST Handling can tricky at the limit • Lacks exotic appeal of some low production sports cars

PRODUCTION
1997-99 184

SPECIFICATIONS
Length (in.)	159.0
Weight (lbs)	2570-2698
Wheelbase (in.)	104.5
Price (new)	$57,980-62,500

ENGINES
cid/type	bhp	years
281/dohc V-8	305	1997-00

PRICES
2000-2010 RETURN Depreciating

2000
PANOZ ESPERANTE

Race-bred Le Mans-class roadster developed and bankrolled by American racing fanatic and pharmaceutical (patch delivery system) tycoon Don Panoz and son, Danny. Utilizing a Mustang floorpan and other ponycar components, the Esperante has a front-mid-engine configuration (50/50 front/rear weight distribution); rear drive; a 281-cid, 320-bhp Ford V-8; and aluminum body panels sleekly styled á la Aston-Martin. Many of the Panoz's underpinnings were suggest-ed by race-car designer Adrian Reynard and designed by engineer John Leverett. Unlike a lot of would-be sports car manufacturers, Panoz had the financial wherewithal to pull off his dream. A prototype mule driven by buff-book writers during the summer of 1999 looked good and performed well, but revamps, particularly to the interior, were promised. The Ford mill, mated to a 5-speed manual, produced 0-60 times of 5.1 seconds. The quarter-mile run blurred by in 13.7 seconds at 103.5 mph. $80,000 list price (as of 1999) discouraged many buyers, but there's little doubt that the Esperante will develop considerable collector appeal.

FOR Exclusivity and limited production • Acceleration • Handling & roadholding • Full complement of safety features • Racing heritage

AGAINST Considerable initial cost • Future parts availability and manufacturer support are unknown • Purists may object to Ford/Mustang components

2000 Esperante roadster

SPECIFICATIONS

Length (in.)	176.3
Weight (lbs)	2800
Wheelbase (in.)	106.0
Price (new)	$80,000 (est)

ENGINES

cid/type	bhp	years
281/dohc V-8	320	2000

PRICES

2000-2010 RETURN Depreciating

1951-58
PEGASO Z102

A hand-built prestige product of ENASA, the state-owned Spanish truck and bus company. Designed for high-performance grand touring by Wilfredo Ricart, former Alfa Romeo technical director. A semi-monocoque steel underbody was used to mount standard factory-styled or custom bodies from specialist coachbuilders, including some Italian designs. It was powered by a four-cam V-8 variously offered in different displacements and states of tune; the largest version was available with a supercharger at extra cost. In its day, the Z102 was the fastest "production" car in the world, able to beat even contemporary Ferraris. No two were exactly alike, and because cars were only a sideline operation for the factory, there were few agents to handle sales and ser-

1953 Berlinette coupe

vice. The company has since gone out of business.

FOR Very rare and exotic • Fast (140-150 mph) • Engineering • Distinctive appearance

AGAINST Forget restoration: parts are long extinct • Quite expensive

PRODUCTION

110

SPECIFICATIONS

Length (in.)	161.5 (average; variable with body fitted)
Wheelbase (in.)	92.0
Weight (lbs)	2180 (average; variable with body and equipment)
Price (new)	NA

ENGINES

cc/type (cid)	bhp[1]	years
2474/dohc V-8 (151)	140	1951-58
2816/dohc V-8 (172)	180	1951-58
3178/dohc V-8 (194)	210/275[2]	1951-58

[1]Gross [2]Normal/Supercharged

PRICES

FAIR	$15,000-25,000
GOOD	$25,000-50,000
FINE	$50,000-70,000

FINE Z102B PRICE HISTORY

1982	$40,000	1990	$100,000
1994	$70,000	1998	$70,000

1982-2000 RETURN 4%
2000-2010 5%

1989-91
PEUGEOT 405 Mi 16

Peugeot hoped its new 405, the 1988 European Car of the Year, would increase its share of the American market. It didn't. Peugeot withdrew from the U.S. after 1991 sales of less than 4,000. The 405 had

1989 405Mi 16 sedan

pleasant, if unexciting styling by Pininfarina. The Mi 16 model had a 16-valve 4-cylinder putting out 150 horses. Performance was about average for a mid-range sport sedan. Handling was above average, but with the traditional French smooth ride. Reliability was questionable, but Peugeot left behind a good parts supply in the U.S. Prices are cheap, but don't expect a huge return on investment with the Mi. Instead, enjoy a fun to drive car with unique French character.

FOR Ride and handling • Never common • Well equipped

AGAINST Reliability • Noisy • Average looks and performance

PRODUCTION
NA

SPECIFICATIONS
Length (in.)	177.7
Weight (lbs)	2695
Wheelbase (in.)	105.1
Price (new)	$20,700-21,990

ENGINES
cid/type	bhp	years
116/dohc I-4	150	1989-91

PRICES
FAIR	$1500-2500
GOOD	$2500-4000
FINE	$4000-6000
2000-2010 RETURN Depreciating	

1930-38
PIERCE-ARROW EIGHT

Acquired in 1928 by Studebaker, just in time for the Depression, Pierce spent most of the '30s in a rear-guard action for survival, a fight it did not win. The company became independent with Studebaker's early 1933 bankruptcy, but had so heavily invested in the new Twelve that it was caught in a cash-flow vice. Nevertheless, the straight-eight Pierce-Arrow was a fine product, deftly engineered to operate like a Swiss watch, though the bodies were on the ponderous side. The line was restyled and more streamlined in 1934 and again in 1936, but losses continued and production wound down. Pierce declared final bankruptcy in December 1937 and was liquidated the following year.

FOR The panache of a blue-chip nameplate • Excellent support via Pierce-Arrow Society • Finely engineered high-speed touring cars • Strong investment potential • A genuine CCCA Classic

AGAINST Expensive to acquire and operate • Scarce, particularly open models • Engine parts increasingly hard to come by

PRODUCTION
1930 6795[1] **1932** 2284[1] **1933** 1527 **1934** 1358[1] **1935** 523 **1936** 636 **1937** 121 **1938** 12[1]
[1]Est.

SPECIFICATIONS
Length (in.)	NA
Wheelbase (in.)	132.0-144.0 (1930); 134.0-147.0 (1931); 137.0/142.0 (1932); 136.0/139.0 (1933); 136.0/139.0/144.0 (1934-38)
Weight (lbs)	4290-5600
Price (new)	$2495-6400

ENGINES
cid/type	bhp	years
340.0/sv I-8	115	1930-31
366.0/sv I-8	125/135	1930-35
385.0/sv I-8	132/150	1934-38

1936 Eight Model 1601 sedan

1932 Eight Series 54 coupe

PRICES

1931-33 Open
FAIR	$20,000-50,000
GOOD	$50,000-80,000
FINE	$80,000-110,000

1931-33 Closed
FAIR	$9000-28,000
GOOD	$28,000-50,000
FINE	$50,000-70,000

1934-38 Open
FAIR	$13,000-28,000
GOOD	$28,000-50,000
FINE	$50,000-72,000

1934-38 Closed
FAIR	$9,000-25,000
GOOD	$25,000-45,000
FINE	$45,000-65,000

Silver Arrow
FAIR	$25,000-45,000
GOOD	$45,000-80,000
FINE	$80,000-120,000

1931 SPORT TOURER PRICE HISTORY

1982 $100,000		**1990** $120,000	
1994 $110,000		**1998** $106,000	
1982-2000 RETURN 1%			
2000-2010 2%			

1930-38
PIERCE-ARROW TWELVE

Engineered by Pierce's famous Karl M. Wise. The engine was initially offered in two sizes, but the smaller version was quickly dropped owing to its lackluster performance. Enlarged in 1933 for more power (one averaged nearly 113 mph at Bonneville over 24 hours). Greatest

1933 Twelve Silver Arrow sedan

among a flock of fine bodies was the Silver Arrow show car of 1933, of which only five were built. Sales had few good periods after 1931, and Pierce Motor Car Company foundered despite restyling in 1934 and 1936. Production was suspended in 1937 except for show models and spare parts. A 1938 line was announced, but the firm went bankrupt in December 1937 and was liquidated the following May.

✚ FOR The ultimate Classic-era Pierce-Arrow • Smooth performance from a gem of an engine • Posh coachwork of high quality • As fine a Classic as you can buy • Relatively underpriced

▬ AGAINST Costly all the same • Scarcity • Mechanical complexity • High operating expenses

PRODUCTION

1932 199 **1933** 771 **1934** 377 **1935** 204 **1936** 206 **1937** 43 **1938** 12 (Est. by Pierce-Arrow Society)

SPECIFICATIONS

Length (in.)	NA
Wheelbase (in.)	137.0/142.0/147.0 (1932); 136.0/139.0/137.0/142.0/147.0 (1933); 139.0/144.0/147.0 (1934-38)
Weight (lbs)	4620-5780
Price (new)	$2785-7200

ENGINES

cid/type	bhp	years
398.0/sv V-12	140	1932
429.0/sv V-12	150	1932-33
462.0/sv V-12	175/185	1934-38

PRICES

As per 1930-38 Pierce-Arrow Eight.
2000-2010 RETURN 2%

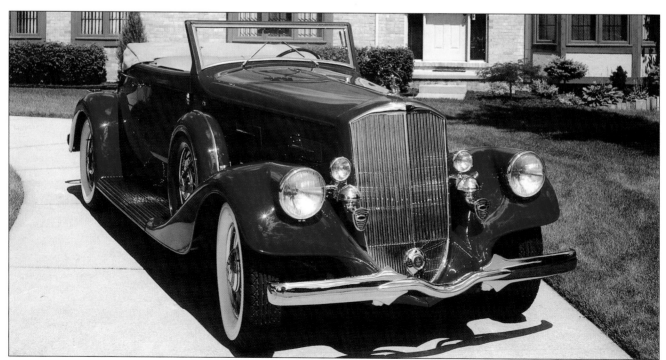

1934 Twelve Model 1240-A convertible coupe

1930-32
PLYMOUTH

Long beloved by collectors (the Plymouth Owners Club was originally devoted only to the four-cylinder models). Good-looking small cars with styling that followed general Chrysler trends, which were excellent in the early '30s. Mechanical features included four-wheel hydraulic brakes, "Floating Power" rubber engine mounts in 1931, and more horsepower in 1932—the four-cylinder Plymouth's final year. There were also some attractive open body styles offered, including the always scarce phaeton.

➕ FOR Easy to acquire, own, and run • Good club support • Parts readily available • Decent investment (open body styles)

➖ AGAINST Not as smooth or mechanically sophisticated as the Chevy six or '32 Ford V-8 • Closed models slow to appreciate

PRODUCTION

1930-31 76,950 (approx. 57% in 1931) **1932** 83,910 **1932** open models (PA & PB): **rdstr** 4843 **4d phaeton** 787 **conv cpe** 7636

SPECIFICATIONS

Length (in.)	NA
Wheelbase (in.)	109.0 (1930 Model U, 1930-31 Model 30U, 1932 PA); 112.0/121.0 (1932 PB)
Weight (lbs)	2280-3075

Price (new)	$495-785

ENGINES

cid/type	bhp	years
175.4/sv I-4	45	1930[1]
196.1/sv I-4	48	1930-31[2]
196.1/sv I-4	56/65	1932[3]

[1]Model U [2]Model 30U [3]Model PA/PB

PRICES

Open	
FAIR	$5000-10,000
GOOD	$10,000-17,500
FINE	$17,500-25,000
Closed	
FAIR	$1500-4000
GOOD	$4000-8000
FINE	$8000-11,500

FINE 1932 SPORT PHAETON PRICE HISTORY

1982	$19,500	**1990**	$25,000
1994	$25,000	**1998**	$23,000
1982-2000 RETURN 2%			
2000-2010 3%			

1941-49
PLYMOUTH SPECIAL DELUXE CONVERTIBLE & WAGON

The most interesting body styles among Forties Plymouths, with unspectacular, rounded styling and the reliable, if ordinary, 87/95-bhp flathead

1941 Special DeLuxe convertible

six. Though quite dull, these cars gave Chrysler a firm hold on third place in industry production. The upper-level Special DeLuxe series replaced the 1940 DeLuxe, and included convertible coupes and woody wagons in all years. Nicely finished with quality materials, they were built in fairly low numbers. The mildly restyled postwar carryovers remained unchanged from 1946 through the first part of the '49 model year, being replaced by the all-new boxy "second series" '49s that spring.

➕ FOR Solid construction • Relatively affordable

➖ AGAINST Ordinary styling and engineering • Not much performance

PRODUCTION

1941 conv cpe 10,545 **4d wgn** 5594 **1942 conv cpe** 2806 **4d wgn** 1136 **1946-49 conv cpe** 15,295 **4d wgn** 12,913

1932 Model PA coupe

1946 Special DeLuxe wagon

SPECIFICATIONS

Length (in.)	196.8
Wheelbase (in.)	117.0
Weight (lbs)	3166-3402
Price (new)	$1007-2068

ENGINES

cid/type	bhp	years
201.3/sv I-6	87	1941
217.8/sv I-6	95	1942-49

PRICES

Conv	
FAIR	$4000-9000
GOOD	$9000-15,000
FINE	$15,000-22,000
Wgn	
FAIR	$4500-9000
GOOD	$9000-16,000
FINE	$16,000-23,000

FINE 1941 CONVERTIBLE PRICE HISTORY

1982 $14,000	1990 $25,000
1994 $20,000	1998 $22,000
1982-2000 RETURN 3%	
2000-2010 3%	

1949
PLYMOUTH DELUXE SUBURBAN

Here's an historically important model you can buy for little money and use as practical transportation to boot. Built on Plymouth's shorter 111-inch-wheelbase DeLuxe chassis, the Suburban pioneered all-steel station wagon construction (based on a passenger-car chassis). In effect, it made this body style more practical and easier to live with. Beautiful though it was, the structural wood used in station wagons up to this time took a lot of work to keep in good condition. And keeping it up was critical for body rigidity. Collectors may bemoan their loss today, but the fact is that woody wagons were already on the way out by the late '40s. The Suburban and the wagons that followed were thus a logical and inevitable step that would make the wagon a permanent—and popu-

1949 DeLuxe Suburban wagon

lar—part of the American automotive scene in the '50s.

➕ FOR Well-built • Historical interest • Practicality • Had a surge in value in the 1990s but...

➖ AGAINST ...the surge is probably over

PRODUCTION

19,220

SPECIFICATIONS

Length (in.)	185.3
Wheelbase (in.)	111.0
Weight (lbs)	3105
Price (new)	$1840

ENGINES

cid/type	bhp	years
217.8/sv I-6	97	1949

PRICES

FAIR	$2000-4000
GOOD	$4000-7000
FINE	$7000-10,000

FINE EXAMPLE PRICE HISTORY

1982 $2700	1990 $8500
1994 $8000	1998 $12,000
1982-2000 RETURN 8%	
2000-2010 3%	

1951-52
PLYMOUTH CRANBROOK BELVEDERE

Plymouth's first "hardtop convertible," introduced in the top-line series, naturally. As was customary in Detroit at the time, the new body style was given its own distinct name. It arrived at about the same time as the Ford Victoria, but a year behind Chevy's Bel Air. Like them, it featured a deluxe convertible-like interior. And for 1952 it sported an interesting two-tone paint job that carried the roof color down and over the rear deck—adding some much needed spice to the very

1952 Cranbrook Belvedere hardtop coupe

conservative design first seen in 1949. You'll have to look closely to tell the two model years apart, and there were no mechanical changes. Chrysler itself quoted only combined production figures for all its lines in these years, perhaps for this reason.

✚ FOR Important in Plymouth history • Solidly built • Big value gains in last decade

▬ AGAINST Odd, uninspired styling • Not much collector following

PRODUCTION

51,266 (combined)

SPECIFICATIONS

Length (in.)	193.9
Wheelbase (in.)	118.5
Weight (lbs)	3182/3105
Price (new)	$2114-2216

ENGINES

cid/type	bhp	years
217.8/sv I-6	97	1951-52

PRICES

FAIR	$4000-7500
GOOD	$7500-13,000
FINE	$13,000-19,000

FINE EXAMPLE PRICE HISTORY

1982 $4500		**1990** $10,000	
1994 $17,500		**1998** $19,000	
1982-2000 RETURN 9%			
2000-2010 3%			

1 9 5 5 - 5 6
PLYMOUTH BELVEDERE CONVERTIBLE & HARDTOP

After years of staid boxiness, Plymouth got a healthy injection of pizzazz with a startlingly new 1955 line, part of Chrysler's wholesale design turnaround that year. Styling, by Virgil Exner's lieutenant Murray Baldwin, was clean and pleasing: peaked front fenders, wrapped windshield, shapely rear fenders. Belvedere, which had become the top-line series the previous year, featured an optional bodyside contrasting color sweep and nicely outfitted interior. Like Chevrolet, Plymouth also got its first V-8 for 1955 in 241- and 260-cid displacements. Hardtops could be had with the familiar L-head six, but the V-8 was standard in the ragtop, and proved more popular in Belvederes by a factor of three. A mild facelift for '56 brought taller finned rear fenders housing slim vertical taillights, plus an eggcrate-center grille, pushbutton controls for the optional two-speed Power-Flite automatic (replacing a wand in the dash), and larger V-8s with power options up to 200 bhp.

✚ FOR Sharp looks • Fine V-8 performance • An attractive buy • Just as good as contemporary Chevys

▬ AGAINST Limited appreciation potential • Lacks broad collector following • Slightly weird symmetrical dash layout

PRODUCTION

1955 2d htp 47,375 **conv** 8473 **1956 2d htp** 24,723 **conv** 6735 **4d htp** 17,515

SPECIFICATIONS

Length (in.)	203.8/204.8 (1955/56)
Wheelbase (in.)	115.0
Weight (lbs)	3261-3585
Price (new)	$2217-2638

ENGINES

cid/type	bhp	years
230.2/sv I-6	117/125/131	1955-56
241/ohv V-8	157	1955
260/ohv V-8	167/177	1955
270/ohv V-8	180	1956
277/ohv V-8	187/200	1956

PRICES

Conv	
FAIR	$5000-10,000
GOOD	$10,000-18,000
FINE	$18,000-26,000

1955 Belvedere convertible

2d htp	
FAIR	$3600-8000
GOOD	$8000-15,000
FINE	$15,000-21,000
4d htp	
FAIR	$2000-4000
GOOD	$4000-7000
FINE	$7000-10,000

FINE CONVERTIBLE PRICE HISTORY

1982 $6500	1990 $20,000
1994 $20,000	1998 $26,000
1982-2000 RETURN 9%	
2000-2010 5%	

1956
PLYMOUTH FURY

First of the limited-edition, high-performance Plymouths, a kind of junior version of the Chrysler 300. Available only as a two-door hardtop, painted off-white and bearing an anodized gold bodyside sweepspear. Standard power was provided by a 303-cid enlargement of Plymouth's "Hy-Fire" V-8 packing 240 horses. Off the showroom floor, the car was capable of 0-60 mph in 10 seconds and 110 mph tops. A specially prepared Fury hit 145 mph in tests on the sands of Daytona Beach.

◆ FOR Rapid • Contemporary good looks • Nicely finished throughout • Not pricey for a low-production item • Strong value rise in 1990s • A Milestone car • Overall, the most satisfying Fury, yet lower priced than

1956 Fury hardtop coupe

1957-58s

◼ AGAINST Styling far from timeless • Rust bothers • No convertible

PRODUCTION

4485

SPECIFICATIONS

Length (in.)	204.8
Wheelbase (in.)	115.0
Weight (lbs)	3650
Price (new)	$2866

ENGINES

cid/type	bhp	years
303/ohv V-8	240	1956

PRICES

FAIR	$5000-9500
GOOD	$9500-16,000
FINE	$16,000-24,000

FINE EXAMPLE PRICE HISTORY

1982 $5500	1990 $20,000
1994 $15,000	1998 $21,000
1982-2000 RETURN 9%	
2000-2010 7%	

1957-58
PLYMOUTH BELVEDERE CONVERTIBLE & HARDTOP COUPE

Plymouth's top-of-the-line models (aside from the limited-production Fury), all-new again for 1957 with "Suddenly It's 1960" styling, longer wheelbase, torsion bar front suspension, and a newly available three-speed TorqueFlite automatic. As before, the convertible came only with a V-8, and there were hairier options available throughout the line, which also included the stripped Plaza and

1957 Belvedere convertible

mid-priced Savoy models. Unfortunately, these dramatic new Plymouths were let down by noticeably poorer quality control, a problem that plagued all Chrysler products in this period and one that damaged the corporation's fine engineering reputation. Styling was modestly revised for 1958, with the then-obligatory four-headlamp front end, horizontal-bar grille, and shorter taillights residing in the '57 fins. Though very rust-prone, these Plymouths have a lot to recommend them as collectibles.

FOR A budget collectible • Important and striking design • Good V-8 performance • Fine handling • Big recent value jumps

AGAINST Rust can be fatal • Much smaller following than Chevy or Ford

PRODUCTION

1957 2d htp 67,268 **conv** 9866 **1958 2d htp** 36,043 **conv** 9941

SPECIFICATIONS

Length (in.)	206.1
Wheelbase (in.)	118.0
Weight (lbs)	3325-3585
Price (new)	$2349-2762

ENGINES

cid/type	bhp	years
230.2/sv I-6	132	1957-58
277/ohv V-8	197/235	1957
301/ohv V-8	215/235	1957
318/ohv V-8	225/250	1958
350/ohv V-8	305/315	1958

PRICES

Conv	
FAIR	$5000-12,000
GOOD	$12,000-20,000
FINE	$20,000-30,000
Htp	
FAIR	$3000-9000
GOOD	$9000-16,000
FINE	$16,000-23,000

FINE HARDTOP PRICE HISTORY

1982 $2900	**1990** $14,000
1994 $12,000	**1998** $22,000
1982-2000 RETURN 13%	
2000-2010 8%	

1957-58
PLYMOUTH FURY

A continuation of Plymouth's high-performance special, now clothed in Virgil Exner's swoopy, low-beltline styling with a thin-section roof and hefty sharkfin rear. Still available only as a hardtop in these years. Standard power came from a 318 V-8. For 1958, a 350-cid unit was offered with 315 bhp courtesy of fuel injection; it proved troublesome and was quickly abandoned. The Fury was very good-looking for its day, and still holding up well despite those fins. Only minor styling changes were seen for '58, confined to quad headlamps, a more unified grille,

and revised taillights. Chrysler's construction quality took a nosedive beginning with the '57s, and its cars developed a reputation for early rust-out. This means good-condition Fury survivors will be even harder to find than the low production figures suggest.

FOR High style • Exceptional performance • Probably undervalued—a good investment • Milestone car status • Big recent jump in value

AGAINST Very thirsty and demands high octane • Seriously rust-prone • Most examples were not pampered

PRODUCTION

1957 7438 **1958** 5303

SPECIFICATIONS

Length (in.)	206.1
Wheelbase (in.)	118.0
Weight (lbs)	3595/3510
Price (new)	$2925/3067

ENGINES

cid/type	bhp	years
318/ohv V-8	290	1957-58
350/ohv V-8	305/315	1958

PRICES

FAIR	$5000-10,000
GOOD	$10,000-17,500
FINE	$17,500-28,000

FINE EXAMPLE PRICE HISTORY

1982 $5000	**1990** $22,000
1994 $17,500	**1998** $24,000
1982-2000 RETURN 11%	
2000-2010 7%	

1957 Fury hardtop coupe

1959 Sport Fury hardtop coupe

1959
PLYMOUTH SPORT FURY

This was the replacement for the Fury as Plymouth's high-performance cars this year (base Fury name was now used for the top-line standard series, pushing Belvedere and Savoy down a notch and knocking out Plaza). Now available as a convertible as well as the usual hardtop coupe. Standard power was a 260-bhp 318 V-8; Plymouth's "Golden Commando" 361 was optional. A heavy facelift on the 1957-58 bodyshell, shared with lesser models, featured a broad eggcrate grille, prominent headlamp eyelids, and longer, higher tailfins. The Sport Fury also wore an embossed spare tire bulge on the trunklid. New for '59 was Chrysler's optional swivel front seats, semi-bucket affairs that turned outward when a door was opened to assist entry/exit. Handling and performance were as good as ever, and assembly quality as bad as ever. Not one of Plymouth's best years, but relative low cost today and spirited acceleration makes the Sport Fury an interesting addition to a car collector's stable.

✠ FOR Fast on straights and curves • Typical '50s gadgetry

◼ AGAINST Pug-ugly compared with the neat 1957-58 • Still too susceptible to early rust-out • Gadget gremlins

PRODUCTION
2d htp 17,867 **conv** 5990

SPECIFICATIONS
Length (in.)	208.2
Wheelbase (in.)	118.0
Weight (lbs)	3475/3670
Price (new)	$2927/3125

ENGINES
cid/type	bhp	years
318/ohv V-8	260	1959
361/ohv V-8	305	1959

PRICES
Conv	
FAIR	$5500-10,000
GOOD	$10,000-18,000
FINE	$18,000-25,000
(Hardtop deduct 30%.)

FINE CONVERTIBLE PRICE HISTORY
1982 $5000	**1990** $15,000
1994 $16,000	**1998** $22,000
1982-2000 RETURN 11%	
2000-2010 7%	

1962-64
PLYMOUTH SPORT FURY

Plymouth's "full-size" buckets-and-console offerings of the early '60s, though really intermediates (like lesser models). Chrysler design chief Virgil Exner applied scaled-up Valiant styling to a shrunken group of standard 1962 Plymouths (and Dodges), believing the public was ready for smaller big cars. It wasn't, and sales suffered drastically. Ex's successor, Elwood Engel, helped turn things around with more conven-

1962 Sport Fury convertible

1962 Valiant V-200 Signet hardtop coupe

tional styling, including Thunderbird-style square hardtop rooflines for '63, then more rakish vee'd C-pillars for '64. Plymouth, unlike Dodge, kept its 116-inch '62 wheelbase in all these years, but offered a similar array of engines. Sport Fury—a name revived from 1959 at mid-'62—came with special trim (including medallions and wheel covers) and only with V-8s, all wedgeheads, with options up to potent ram-induction 413s and 426s. A big-inch Sport Fury of this vintage would be a rare find today; come to that, any of these Plymouths are uncommon owing to early rustout and, no doubt, a basic design that just didn't encourage many people to preserve the cars.

✚ FOR Light weight, handy size • Good V-8 performance • Sporty interiors • Unusual collector cars • Strong club support • Relatively inexpensive

▬ AGAINST Clean originals hard to find • Ditto many body and trim parts • Recent appreciation was probably a fluke

PRODUCTION
1962 2d htp 4039 **conv** 1516 **1963 2d htp** 11,483 **conv** 3836 **1964 2d htp** 23,695 **conv** 3858

SPECIFICATIONS
Length (in.)	202.0 (1962), 205.0 (1963), 206.5 (1964)
Wheelbase (in.)	116.0
Weight (lbs)	3195-3405
Price (new)	$2851-3095

ENGINES
cid/type	bhp	years
318/ohv V-8	230	1963-64
361/ohv V-8	310	1962
361/ohv V-8	265	1963-64
383/ohv V-8	320-335	1962-64
413/ohv V-8	365-410	1962
426/ohv V-8	365-425	1963-64

PRICES
Conv	
FAIR	$3000-7000
GOOD	$7000-12,000
FINE	$12,000-17,000
(Hardtop deduct 15%.)	

FINE CONVERTIBLE PRICE HISTORY
1982 $3500		**1990** $10,000	
1994 $11,500		**1998** $13,000	
1982-2000 RETURN 10%			
2000-2010 5%			

1962
PLYMOUTH VALIANT SIGNET

A bucket-seat hardtop, Signet arrived in the last year of the first-generation Valiant designed by Virgil Exner. The pillarless body style had debuted a year earlier in the V-200 series along with a fixed-pillar two-door sedan and, if anything, enhanced the chunky lines Plymouth's compact wore in these years. Listed as a separate model for '62, the Signet had an even cleaner appearance thanks to a black-painted grille and absence of the previous decklid tire bulge. With its posh appointments it was an obvious rival to the Corvair Monza and Falcon Futura.

It was available only with a six-cylinder engine in a choice of two displacements, but it was a good one—Chrysler's famed ohv Slant Six, which was already renowned for the rugged dependability that would keep it in production for three decades.

✚ FOR Some are still around • Attractive bucket-seat interior • Floorshift available • Good performance with the 225 six • Unburstable engine with parts still as close as your nearest dealer • Cheap

▬ AGAINST Rust-prone unit construction • Underpowered with the 170 six • Limited appreciation potential • Odd styling

PRODUCTION
28,586

SPECIFICATIONS
Length (in.)	184.2
Wheelbase (in.)	106.5
Weight (lbs)	2515
Price (new)	$2230

ENGINES
cid/type	bhp	years
170/ohv I-6	101	1962
225/ohv I-6	145	1962

PRICES
FAIR	$1200-2500
GOOD	$2500-4500
FINE	$4500-6250

FINE EXAMPLE PRICE HISTORY
1982 $1700		**1990** $5500	
1994 $6000		**1998** $6200	
1982-2000 RETURN 8%			
2000-2010 3%			

1966 Barracuda hardtop coupe

1 9 6 4 - 6 6

PLYMOUTH BARRACUDA

"Glassback" derivative of the compact Valiant, launched in early 1964 as part of the Signet 200 series. It appeared about two weeks before Ford's Mustang, which was probably a coincidence, though most observers took it as Plymouth's direct reply to the Dearborn ponycar. Barracuda retained the Valiant's lower body, but used a fastback superstructure with a massive wraparound backlight and stubby trunklid. It came equipped with the Signet's bucket-seat interior, plus a flip-down rear seatback and security panel that opened up the trunk area for carrying long items (the ads liked to show surfboards). Engine offerings were the same as Valiant's, with the 225 Slant Six standard, or a new 273 V-8 optional. Horsepower options ran from 180 to 235 in these years, and a "Rallye" suspension and four-speed gearbox were also listed. Facelifted along with Valiant for '66, but got its own distinct grille. A special Formula S package was available beginning in 1965, and turned the Barracuda into a very capable road machine.

✚ FOR Satisfying V-8 performance • Excellent six-cylinder mileage and durability • "Hatchback" practicality • Affordable • At home in today's traffic • 1965-66 Formula S is a Milestone car

▬ AGAINST Huge rear window cooks interior on sunny days • Indifferent assembly quality • Can rust • Obviously Valiant-based

PRODUCTION

1964 23,433 **1965** 64,596 **1966** 38,029

SPECIFICATIONS

Length (in.)	188.2
Wheelbase (in.)	106.0
Weight (lbs)	2725-2865
Price (new)	$2365-2556

ENGINES

cid/type	bhp	years
225/ohv I-6	145	1964-66
273/ohv V-8	180/235	1964-66

PRICES

FAIR	$1500-3500
GOOD	$3500-5000
FINE	$5000-8000

Formula S add up to 75%

FINE FORMULA S PRICE HISTORY

1982 $3450		**1990** $12,000	
1994 $10,000		**1998** $14,000	
1982-2000 RETURN 5%			
2000-2010 5%			

1 9 6 5 - 6 6

PLYMOUTH SATELLITE & SUPER SPORT

Continuation of the 1962-64 Sport Fury idea, but now a true intermediate with introduction of a genuine big-Fury line as one of Plymouth's "Roaring '65s." The buckets-and-console Satellite was the top series in that year's reconstituted Belvedere brigade, basically the 1962-64 "standard" Plymouth with crisper outer sheetmetal. Engines were again V-8s only, as on previous Sport Furys, but started with a new small-block 273 and ran to the big 426 wedge (as for 1963-64). A unique special-order '65 offering was the Super Sport, a lightened two-door sedan (in the low-line Belvedere I series) on an inch-shorter wheelbase created especially for drag racing and powered by a newly revived Hemi-head V-8 with the same 425 nominal horsepower as the wedge. For 1966, both the wedge and the SS were phased out, and the Hemi was made a full production option, ostensibly for any Belvedere (and Fury), though most were doubtless installed in the light low-end pillared models favored by quarter-mile specialists. Nicer

1965 Satellite convertible

styling and improved workmanship paid off in more Satellites being built than previous Sport Furys. Again, though, these cars are fairly uncommon on today's collector market and have no appreciable value edge over their predecessors, though they're very nice period Plymouths. The Super Sport is much rarer and more valued for all the usual reasons.

✠ FOR As for 1962-64 Sport Fury, plus better quality, nicer looks • Super Sport is rare, rapid and a Milestone car • Hemi prices have plunged and they're affordable again

▬ AGAINST As for 1962-64 Sport Fury, plus Super Sport now almost impossible to find

PRODUCTION

1965 2d htp 23,341 **conv** 1860 **1966 2d htp** 35,399 **conv** 2759 **1965 Super Stock cpe** NA

SPECIFICATIONS

Length (in.)	203.4/200.5 (1965/66)
Wheelbase (in.)	116.0/115.0 (Satellite/SS)
Weight (lbs)	3170-3320
Price (new)	$2649-2910

ENGINES

cid/type	bhp	years
273/ohv V-8	180	1965-66
318/ohv V-8	230	1965-66
361/ohv V-8	265	1965-66
383/ohv V-8	325/330	1965-66
426/ohv V-8[1]	365	1965
426/ohv V-8[2]	425	1965-66

[1]Wedgehead [2]Hemi

PRICES

Conv	
FAIR	$3500-7000
GOOD	$7000-12,500

FINE	$12,500-18,000

(Deduct 30% for hardtop. Add 80% for Hemi, 60% for 426 Commando.)

FINE HEMI HARDTOP PRICE HISTORY

1982 $3200		**1990** $40,000	
1994 $12,500		**1998** $18,000	
1982-2000 RETURN 11%			
2000-2010 7% (non-Hemis 3%)			

1967-69
PLYMOUTH BARRACUDA

Plymouth's sporty compact, now a true ponycar with pretty, well-integrated new styling on a two-inch longer wheelbase. Two V-8s, a 273 and 383, were offered for '67, joined by a 340 unit for 1968-69. All could be coupled with the Formula S package consisting of heavy-duty suspension, tachometer, Wide-Oval tires, and special emblems and war paint. The 225 Slant Six was standard for 1968-69. The original fastback was augmented by a handsome new convertible and a curiously styled notchback hardtop with a curved rear window. Styling changes were limited to grilles and minor trim for 1968-69. All models came with a complete set of engine gauges set in a simple, no-nonsense dash. Collectors should note the production figures. Convertibles stand to become ultra-rare in the future, so their rapid appreciation of the late '80s is likely to continue.

✠ FOR Convertibles' rarity and strong appreciation • Smooth styling • Handy size • Roadability • Overall balance with smaller V-8s • Formula S capability and Milestone status

▬ AGAINST Rust potential • Body and some mechanical parts hard to find • 383's clumsier handling

PRODUCTION

1967 2d htp 28,196 **conv** 4228 **2d fstbk htp** 30,110 **1968 2d htp** 19,997 **conv** 2840 **2d fstbk htp** 22,575 **1969 2d htp** 12,757 **conv** 1442 **2d fstbk htp** 17,788

SPECIFICATIONS

Length (in.)	193.0
Wheelbase (in.)	108.0
Weight (lbs)	2793-2940
Price (new)	$2449-3082

ENGINES

cid/type	bhp	years
225/ohv I-6	145	1968-69
273/ohv V-8	180/235	1967
318/ohv V-8	230	1968
340/ohv V-8	275	1968-69
383/ohv V-8	300/325/330	1967-69

PRICES

Conv	
FAIR	$3000-5000
GOOD	$5000-8000
FINE	$8000-12,000
Others	
FAIR	$2000-4000
GOOD	$4000-7000
FINE	$7000-11,000

(Add 25% for 383 V-8.)

FINE CONVERTIBLE PRICE HISTORY

1982 $3000		**1990** $17,500	
1994 $12,500		**1998** $18,000	
1982-2000 RETURN 9%			
2000-2010 5%			

1967 Barracuda hardtop coupe

1967 Belvedere GTX hardtop coupe

1967
PLYMOUTH BELVEDERE GTX

A more serious Plymouth muscle car, successor to the big-inch Satellite (which continued this year in lower-power form). Like other Belvederes, this was largely a repeat of the handsome 1966 package, but set off with special identification—silver and black grille and trunklid applique, simulated hood air scoops, quick-fill-style fuel cap, dual exhausts—to give plenty of warning to others at stoplights. The standard GTX engine was an enlarged version of Chrysler's wedgehead V-8 with 440 cubes and 375 bhp. The Hemi was the only option, still rated at its customary (and nominal) 425 bhp. Not stark, with full carpeting, vinyl upholstery, bucket seats, and plenty of sparkling interior accents, and offered in both hardtop and convertible body styles. It wasn't a tremendous seller when new, so has a certain status now as a low-volume collectible.

FOR As for 1966 Satellite 426 • 440 V-8 less temperamental • Rarity (especially convertibles and Hemi V-8) • Milestone car • Bucked the trend and rose strongly in value lately

AGAINST As for 1966 Satellite 426

PRODUCTION

2d htp 2000 **conv** 300 (both est.)

SPECIFICATIONS

Length (in.)   200.5

Wheelbase (in.)	116.0
Weight (lbs)	3545/3615
Price (new)	$3178-3418

ENGINES

cid/type	bhp	years
426/ohv V-8	425	1967
440/ohv V-8	375	1967

PRICES

FAIR	$7000-10,000
GOOD	$10,000-15,000
FINE	$15,000-22,000

(Deduct 40% for hardtop,)

FINE CONVERTIBLE PRICE HISTORY

1982	$3500	1990	$20,000
1994	$22,500	1998	$17,000
1982-2000 RETURN	12%		
2000-2010	8%		

1968-70
PLYMOUTH ROAD RUNNER

Plymouth's cleverly named budget bomb based on the intermediate Belvedere. It was aimed squarely at younger buyers interested in high performance, but who couldn't afford a GTX or who thought that model too ritzy. With a base price below $3000, the Runner packed a standard 383 V-8 with 335 bhp, plus four-speed transmission, heavy duty suspension, GTX-like hood bulges, a taxicab-basic interior, little cartoon bird decals on the doors, and a unique "beep-beep" horn. A fixed-pillar coupe with flip-out rear side windows was offered initially, joined during the '68 model year by a hardtop. A soft top version was added for '69, along with dress-up options for those who weren't comfortable with the plain trim. The Road Runner continued as a Plymouth model after 1970, ultimately winding up as a package option for the 1976 Volare compact.

FOR Low-priced new, still so today • Convertibles' rarity and appreciation • High performance and Hemi availability • Milestone car status • Rose rapidly in value lately

AGAINST Indifferent assembly quality • Greasy kid car

1969 Road Runner convertible

PRODUCTION

1968 2d cpe 29,240 **2d htp** 15,359 **1969 2d cpe** 33,743 **2d htp** 48,549 **conv** 2128 **1970 2d cpe** 15,716 **2d htp** 24,944 **conv** 824

SPECIFICATIONS

Length (in.)	202.7
Wheelbase (in.)	116.0
Weight (lbs)	3435-3790
Price (new)	$2896-3313

ENGINES

cid/type	bhp	years
383/ohv V-8	335	1968-70
426/ohv V-8	425	1968-70
440/ohv V-8	375/390	1969-70

PRICES

Conv	
FAIR	$6000-9000
GOOD	$9000-13,000
FINE	$13,000-22,000
Others	
FAIR	$3000-6000
GOOD	$6000-8500
FINE	$8500-14,000

(Add 50% for Hemi, 40% for 440 Six-Pack.)

FINE CONVERTIBLE PRICE HISTORY

1982 $3700		**1990** $30,000	
1994 $26,000		**1998** $22,000	
1982-2000 RETURN 11%			
2000-2010 7%			

1 9 7 0
PLYMOUTH AAR 'CUDA

Highly specialized high-performance limited edition of Plymouth's third-generation Barracuda ponycar, available only for 1970. It was named for Dan Gurney's All-American Racers team, which campaigned it in that season's SCCA Trans-Am series, though with only fair success (Ford's Mustang won the championship). Showroom AARs were identified by a matte-black fiberglass hood with tiedowns and functional air scoop, upper-bodyside "strobe" striping, rear-deck spoiler, and hiked-up tail, the last part of a fortified suspension package that included extra-large G70x15 tires. Power came from Chrysler's 340 small-block V-8 in "Six Pack" form, with three two-barrel carbs on a special Edelbrock aluminum manifold, plus special cylinder heads and valvetrain and a revised exhaust system with large side-exit "trumpet" pipes. Prized today as a rare, small-block muscle machine from the twilight of Detroit's "golden" performance age.

✚ FOR Rarity • Competition connection • Tremendous presence and go-power • Big value jump of late

▬ AGAINST Super-high octane a must • High running costs • Ruster • Sloppy workmanship

PRODUCTION
est. 1500

SPECIFICATIONS

Length (in.)	186.7
Wheelbase (in.)	108.0
Weight (lbs)	approx. 3400
Price (new)	$ NA

ENGINES

cid/type	bhp[1]	years
340/ohv V-8	290	1970

[1]Nominal SAE gross

PRICES

FAIR	$6000-12,000
GOOD	$12,000-16,000
FINE	$16,000-23,000

FINE EXAMPLE PRICE HISTORY

1982 $4200		**1990** $25,000	
1994 $23,000		**1998** $30,000	
1982-2000 RETURN 11%			
2000-2010 5%			

1970 AAR 'Cuda hardtop coupe

1970-71

PLYMOUTH BARRACUDA CONVERTIBLES

The short-lived convertibles in Plymouth's third-generation ponycar line, offered only for these two years. Rebodied like the hardtop models for 1970 with husky yet clean lines to make room for big-block Chrysler V-8s up to the torquey 440 and ferocious 426 Hemi. The performance-oriented 'Cuda became a separate series, offering a standard 375-horsepower 383. But these heavier engines made for piggish handling, and the 'Cudas were a bit overdecorated even for muscle machines. More tasteful were the base and new luxury Gran Coupe series with standard slant six and V-8 options of 318, 340 and 383 cid; the latter provided more than sufficient go. Only detail styling, mechanical and equipment changes were made for '71, but production slipped in a faltering ponycar market. The convertibles were never high-demand items, making them quite rare today. Notchback coupe companions carried on through 1974, after which Barracuda was abandoned, a victim of the first energy crisis.

➕ FOR Quite rare for the period • Small-blocks handle well • Good performance except with six • "Last convertible" appeal • Values trending strongly up

➖ AGAINST Six's poor pickup • Very rust-prone • Slapdash workmanship • Prices escalating rapidly

PRODUCTION

1970 base 1554 **'Cuda** 635 **Gran Coupe** 596
1971 base 1014 **'Cuda** 374

SPECIFICATIONS

Length (in.)	186.7
Wheelbase (in.)	108.0
Weight (lbs)	3071-3200
Price (new)	$3034-$3700

ENGINES

cid/type	bhp[1]	years
225/ohv I-6	110/145	1970-71
318/ohv V-8	150/230	1970-71
340/ohv V-8	240/275	1970-71
383/ohv V-8	275/335	1970-71
426/ohv V-8	425	1970-71
440/ohv V-8	375/390	1970-71

[1]SAE gross

PRICES

FAIR	$3500-6500
GOOD	$6500-9500
FINE	$9500-25,000

(Note: Only a handful of Hemi convertibles were built; although Hemi prices are well down from a premium of at least 100% of above)

FINE EXAMPLE PRICE HISTORY

1982 $4000		**1990** $18,000	
1994 $12,500		**1998** $23,000	
1982-2000 RETURN 12%			
2000-2010 18%			

1970 'Cuda convertible

1971 'Cuda hardtop coupe

1970-74
PLYMOUTH BARRACUDA COUPES

The final closed Barracudas, marked by more aggressive, "more ponycar" notchback styling and a much beefier new basic structure shared with Dodge's concurrent Challenger (see entries). Somewhat more numerous than the short-lived 1970-71 convertibles, though not much in the case of the later performance-oriented 'Cudas. All of these are hardtop models save a fixed-pillar price-leader that was tried to no good sales effect for 1971 only. Base and sporty 'Cuda versions throughout, plus luxury Gran Coupe (with formal vinyl-covered roof, a twin to Challenger SE) for 1970-72. A minor facelift occurred for '71, after which styling was again lightly modified—then frozen. Performance declined along with production, though not as much as horsepower numbers might imply, but big-block engines were cancelled after '71 in deference to rising insurance rates and a consequent waning in buyer interest. Big-blocks command the highest values as collector cars, but most any V-8 example is a fine investment, indicated by asking prices that continue rising with fair speed.

➕ **FOR** As for 1971-72 Barracuda convertibles, but easier to find and somewhat cheaper to buy

➖ **AGAINST** As for 1971-72 Barracuda convertibles

PRODUCTION

1970 base htp cpe 25,651 **Gran Coupe htp** 8183 **'Cuda htp cpe** 18,880 **1971 base pillared/htp cpe** 9459 **Gran Coupe htp** 1615 **'Cuda htp cpe** 6228 **1972 base htp** 10,622 **'Cuda htp cpe** 7828 **1973 base htp cpe** 11,587 **'Cuda htp cpe** 10,626 **1974 base htp cpe** 6745 **'Cuda htp cpe** 4989

SPECIFICATIONS

Length (in.)	186.7
Wheelbase (in.)	108.0
Weight (lbs)	2905-3235
Price (new)	$2764-3252

ENGINES

cid/type	bhp[1]	years
225/ohv I-6	110/145	1970-72
318/ohv V-8	150/230	1970-74
340/ohv V-8	240/275	1970-73
360/ohv V-8	245	1974
383/ohv V-8	275/335	1970-71
426/ohv V-8	425	1970-71
440/ohv V-8	375/390	1970-71

[1]SAE gross

PRICES

FAIR	$2000-5000
GOOD	$5000-12,000
FINE	$12,000-26,000

(See note concerning Hemis under 1970-71 Plymouth Barracuda convertibles.)

FINE EXAMPLE PRICE HISTORY

1982 $2200	**1990** $14,000
1994 $10,000	**1998** $13,000

1982-2000 RETURN 16%
2000-2010 5%

1970-73
PLYMOUTH DUSTER 340

The sporty performance edition of Plymouth's Valiant-based fastback coupe, introduced with standard Dusters for 1970. Name reflected the power source: a tuned dual-exhaust version of Chrysler's high-winding 340 small-block V-8. Underpinnings were fortified to suit, and standard interior appointments were among the best in Plymouth's compact line. Styling and equipment changes were shared with other Dusters in these years, including a heavy frontal facelift for '73, by which time actual horsepower had been slightly downgraded for mileage and emissions reasons. The hot Duster was continued with even less power after '73 as the Duster 360, which may also be collectible one day. But the 340s have definite potential now as late "junior muscle cars" that are not all that common.

1970 Duster 340 coupe

FOR Brisk acceleration • Handy compact size • Adept handling • Room for four • Strong club support • Still quite affordable

AGAINST Rust-prone • Workmanship varies a lot • Values rising but slowly, and probably won't go very high

PRODUCTION

1970 24,817 **1971** 12,886 **1972** 15,681 **1973** 15,731

SPECIFICATIONS

Length (in.)	192.5
Wheelbase (in.)	108.0
Weight (lbs)	3100-3175
Price (new)	$2547-2822

ENGINES

cid/type	bhp	years
340/ohv V-8	275[1]	1970-71
340/ohv V-8	240[2]	1972-73

[1]SAE gross [2]SAE net

PRICES

FAIR	$1000-2000
GOOD	$2000-4000
FINE	$4000-8500

FINE EXAMPLE PRICE HISTORY

1982 $2700		**1990** $6500	
1994 $7000		**1998** $8600	
1982-2000 RETURN 7%			
2000-2010 3%			

1970
PLYMOUTH ROAD RUNNER SUPERBIRD

Plymouth's continuation of the limited-production Dodge Charger Daytona (1969), again offered to the public to satisfy production requirements for stock-car racing. Carried the same "droop snoot" nose with hidden headlamps and the high rear stabilizer wing mounted on tall struts (though details differed). Competition versions could achieve over 220 mph. At the 1970 Daytona 500, Pete Hamilton beat the field with an average speed of nearly 150 mph, and the Superbird went on to take 21 of the 38 Grand National events that year. For the 1971 season, NASCAR changed its rules to bar these "Winged Warriors," leaving the Superbird, like the Charger Daytona before it, a one-year-only special. The "street" model carried the 375-horsepower 440 wedgehead V-8, and the fabled Hemi was optional.

FOR Strong collector following • Special Daytona/Superbird club • Tremendous performance • Unique appearance • Race record • A Milestone car

AGAINST High running costs • Even higher purchase price • Indifferent construction quality • Special body pieces may present restoration problems • Not many around

PRODUCTION

1920

SPECIFICATIONS

Length (in.)	220.0
Wheelbase (in.)	116.0
Weight (lbs)	3785
Price (new)	$4298

ENGINES

cid/type	bhp	years
440/ohv V-8	375	1970
426/ohv V-8	425	1970

PRICES

440

FAIR	$16,000-30,000
GOOD	$30,000-37,000
FINE	$37,000-45,000

1970 Road Runner Superbird hardtop coupe

1970 Sport Fury GT sedan

Hemi

FAIR	$23,000-40,000
GOOD	$40,000-60,000
FINE	$60,000-85,000

FINE 440 PRICE HISTORY

1982 $7000		**1990** $60,000	
1994 $45,000		**1998** $50,000	
1982-2000 RETURN 16%			
2000-2010 7%			

1 9 7 0 - 7 1
PLYMOUTH SPORT FURY GT

Plymouth's somewhat belated attempt at a high-performance full-size model, produced in very low numbers for these two model years only. Though a Sport Fury subseries had been offered previously as the top of Plymouth's big-car line and was available with the division's largest engines, the GT version was even more special. As part of Plymouth's 1970 "Rapid Transit System," this two-door hardtop was decked out with the big-block Super Commando 440 V-8 with a single four-barrel carb, good for 350 horses. A 390-bhp version with Plymouth's Six-Pack carburetion (a trio of two-barrels) was optional. The package also included heavy-duty under-pinnings and bodyside "strobe stripes." For 1970 only, a companion model, the S/23, was also listed, powered by the mild-mannered 318. Horsepower ratings for the basically similar '71 Sport Fury GT were 335 standard and 385 for the six-pot engine. Not an answer to a market trend, nor did it start one, but an interesting newer collectible for those interested in high performance with big-car room and ride.

➕ FOR Exclusivity • Performance • Interior room, luxury • Burly looks • Last of the big performance Plymouths

➖ AGAINST The usual unit-construction rust worries • Very thirsty • Hard to find in good condition • Not in high demand, and not likely to be for awhile yet

PRODUCTION

1970 NA **1971** 375

SPECIFICATIONS

Length (in.)	214.9/215.1 (1970/71)
Wheelbase (in.)	120.0
Weight (lbs)	approx. 3950
Price (new)	$3898

ENGINES

cid/type	bhp	years
440/ohv V-8	335-390	1970-71

PRICES

1970

FAIR	$2000-4000
GOOD	$4000-5500
FINE	$5500-8500

FINE 1970 MODEL PRICE HISTORY

1982 $2800		**1990** $12,000	
1994 $10,000		**1998** $9000	
1982-2000 RETURN 7%			
2000-2010 3%			

1 9 7 1 - 7 5
PLYMOUTH GTX & ROAD RUNNER

A continuation of Plymouth's muscle cars, now with brand-new, handsome styling shared with the ordinary family models (the 115-inch-wheelbase Sebring/Sebring Plus coupes and the 117-inch-wheelbase Satellite sedans and wagons). Convertibles were dropped with the switch in platform, but there was still some semblance of performance for 1971. That year's Road Runner came with a 300-bhp 383 V-8 that ran on regular gas. The GTX was powered by a four-barrel 440 V-8 with 370 bhp. The 425-bhp Hemi and the 440 Six-Pack were

1971 GTX hardtop coupe

optional for both. For 1972, the Hemi was made a dealer option, a victim of tightening emissions controls and—as the production figures suggest—a dramatic drop in demand for high-performance intermediates. The GTX was cancelled, but the Runner lived on, offering a standard 400-cid V-8, with the 440 optional. The Road Runner was continued with progressively less power through 1975, after which the concept was applied to the compact Volare as an option package.

✛ **FOR** Handsome looks • Decent performance for the period • Fairly rare, yet still reasonably available today

◼ **AGAINST** Rust-prone • Performance falls off greatly after '71 • Collectibility not yet firmly established

PRODUCTION
1971 RR 2d htp 14,218 **GTX 2d htp** 2942 **1972 RR 2d htp** 7628 **1973 RR 2d cpe** 19,056 **1974 RR 2d cpe** 11,555 **1975 RR 2d cpe** 7183

SPECIFICATIONS
Length (in.)	203.5
Wheelbase (in.)	115.0
Weight (lbs)	approx. 3300
Price (new)	$3120-3973

ENGINES
cid/type	bhp	years
318/ohv V-8	150/170	1973-75
340/ohv V-8	275/240[1]	1971-73
360/ohv V-8	180/245	1973-75
383/ohv V-8	300	1971
400/ohv V-8	165/260[1]	1972-75
426/ohv V-8	425	1971
440/ohv V-8	370/385[2]	1971-75

[1]SAE gross/net bhp [2]1971 SAE gross bhp; 260-

280 bhp SAE net 1972-75

PRICES
1971 Models:
GTX
FAIR	$3000-9000
GOOD	$9000-13,000
FINE	$13,000-18,000

GTX Hemi
FAIR	$16,000-22,000
GOOD	$22,000-30,000
FINE	$30,000-35,000

RR
FAIR	$2500-9000
GOOD	$9000-13,000
FINE	$13,000-18,000

RR Hemi
FAIR	$16,000-22,000
GOOD	$22,000-30,000
FINE	$30,000-35,000

1972-75 models:
RR
FAIR	$1000-5000
GOOD	$5000-8000
FINE	$8000-12,000

FINE GTX PRICE HISTORY
1982 $2400		**1990** $12,000	
1994 $11,000		**1998** $11,000	
1982-2000 RETURN 13%			
2000-2010 5%			

1971 Road Runner hardtop coupe

1997-2000
PLYMOUTH PROWLER

If the Prowler wasn't a sure fire collectible when it was introduced, phasing out the Plymouth brand sealed its fate. The last car to bear the Plymouth badge, the Prowler was a nineties interpretation of a fifties hot rod. With its cycle front fenders, long hood, chopped convertible top; no car could turn more heads. A real hot rod had a big V-8, stick, and rear wheel drive. The Prowler had rear wheel drive, but made do with a V-6 with 4-speed automatic. Still, performance was brisk in the lightweight roadster. Aluminum was used extensively in the body and mechanical components. AutoStick allowed the driver limited manual shifting. Left on its own, the automatic delivered sharp downshifts at the slightest touch of the accelerator. Cornering was flat at the price of a bumpy ride. The Prowler could get one noticed on the boulevard, then provide entertainment on winding back roads.

⊞ FOR Traffic stopping looks • As fun as it looks • Great collector appeal

⊟ AGAINST Never intended as a daily driver • Trunk barely holds a garment

2000 Prowler roadster

bag • Poor visibility with top up

PRODUCTION[1]
1997 463 **1998** 2,124 **1999** NA
[1]Calendar year production.

SPECIFICATIONS
Length (in.)	165.3
Weight (lbs)	2838-2860
Wheelbase (in.)	113.3
Price (new)	$38,300-42,800

ENGINES
cid/type	bhp	years
215/ohc V-6	214/253	1997-00

PRICES
PRICES Governed by used car market, presently $40,000-55,000

1942-48
PONTIAC STREAMLINER

The last prewar Pontiac and its postwar continuations in the division's upper-priced series. Fresh pontoon-fender styling was changed only in detail during these years. Top-line Chieftain models are the pick among the rare '42s; only 11,041 Eights and 2458 Sixes were built. Choicest of the choice would be the wood-body wagon

1948 DeLuxe Streamliner wagon

and the slick sedan-coupe. The convertible was relegated to the Torpedo line (see entry). Postwar hallmarks were triple chrome fender strips and a full-width grille on '46s, a simpler grille for '47s, and a top-of-the-grille nameplate on '48s. The last appeared with "Silver Streak" chrome script, a term earlier applied to Pontiac styling. DeLuxe versions of the four-door sedan, wagon, and sedan-coupe were offered for '48 only. The '48s were also the first Pontiacs to offer Hydra-Matic automatic transmission.

✚ FOR Solid construction • Quality materials • Among GM's nicer-looking mid-'40s cars • Rarity of some models

➖ AGAINST Solid but stolid engines • '42s hard to find • High maintenance on woody wagons • Indifferent performance • Lacks the appeal of concurrent Chevys

PRODUCTION
1942 Six 12,742 **Eight** 26,506 **1946 Six** 43,430 **Eight** 49,301 **1947 Six** 42,336 **Eight** 86,324 **1948 Six** 37,742 **Eight** 123,115

SPECIFICATIONS
Length (in.)	210.3
Wheelbase (in.)	122.0
Weight (lbs)	3400-3870
Price (new)	$1030-2490

ENGINES
cid/type	bhp	years
239.2/I-6	90	1942-48
248.9/I-8	103	1942-48

PRICES
Wgn

FAIR	$5500-11,000
GOOD	$11,000-19,000
FINE	$19,000-28,000
Others	
FAIR	$2300-6000
GOOD	$6000-10,000
FINE	$10,000-15,000

FINE STATION WAGON PRICE HISTORY
1982 $8400		**1990** $22,500	
1994 $22,500		**1998** $28,000	
1982-2000 RETURN 7%			
2000-2010 5%			

1942-48 PONTIAC TORPEDO CONVERTIBLE

Pontiac's only convertible of the mid-'40s, built on the shorter-wheelbase chassis and available with the familiar six- and eight-cylinder engines like the Streamliners. A more elaborately trimmed DeLuxe soft-top was offered for 1947-48 at about $50 extra. Styling changes parallel those made to Streamliners (see entry). Mechanical changes were almost nil in this period, however.

✚ FOR Convertible allure • Nicely finished inside and out • '42's rarity • Others as for 1942-48 Streamliner

➖ AGAINST As for 1942-48 Streamliner

PRODUCTION
1942 2500 **1946** 5000 **1947** 10,000 **1948** 10,000 (all est.; calendar year production 10,020 in 1947, 15,937 in 1948)

SPECIFICATIONS
Length (in.)	204.5
Wheelbase (in.)	119.0
Weight (lbs)	3525-3605
Price (new)	$1165-2072

ENGINES
cid/type	bhp	years
239.2/sv I-6	90	1942-48
248.9/sv I-8	103	1942-48

PRICES
FAIR	$2000-12,000
GOOD	$12,000-19,000
FINE	$19,000-24,000

FINE EXAMPLE PRICE HISTORY
1982 $10,700		**1990** $25,000	
1994 $22,500		**1998** $22,500	
1982-2000 RETURN 5%			
2000-2010 5%			

1949 PONTIAC CHIEFTAIN DELUXE

The cream of the crop in Pontiac's first new postwar generation. Clean, modern styling was courtesy of Harley Earl's staff, and similar in general concept to that seen on GM's other new model lines this year. All

1947 Torpedo convertible

1949 Chieftain DeLuxe sedan

Pontiacs now rode the same 120-inch-wheelbase chassis. The former top-line Streamliner series moved down to take over for the old Torpedo, while the new Chieftain moved in above it. Both series were offered with the familiar inline flathead engines from earlier years, and there were DeLuxe trim models in each.

⊞ **FOR** Good construction quality • First new postwar design • Good tourer

⊟ **AGAINST** Lackluster engine

PRODUCTION

50,000 (est.)

SPECIFICATIONS

Length (in.)	202.5
Wheelbase (in.)	120.0
Weight (lbs)	3345-3670
Price (new)	$1805-2206

ENGINES

cid/type	bhp	years
239.2/sv I-6	90/93	1949
248.9/sv I-8	104/106	1949

PRICES

Conv	
FAIR	$6000-12,000
GOOD	$12,000-18,000
FINE	$18,000-22,500
Others	
FAIR	$1500-3000
GOOD	$3000-5000
FINE	$5000-7200

FINE CONVERTIBLE PRICE HISTORY

1982 $6800	**1990** $23,000
1994 $19,000	**1998** $21,000
1982-2000 RETURN 7%	
2000-2010 3%	

1 9 4 9
PONTIAC STREAMLINER WOOD-BODY WAGON

Last of the wood-bodied Pontiac cargo haulers, though there was hardly as much wood as before. It was offered as an alternative to a new all-steel wagon this year, though there was little difference in price. Both six- and eight-cylinder versions were available. A standard-trim eight-passenger model was offered, and there was a six-passenger equivalent with DeLuxe trim only.

⊞ **FOR** Well ahead of contemporary all-steel wagons in value • Fine carpentry • Last of the breed

⊟ **AGAINST** Wood care costly, time-consuming • Pricey • Same old engines

PRODUCTION

1000 (est.)

SPECIFICATIONS

Length (in.)	202.5
Wheelbase (in.)	120.0
Weight (lbs)	3730/3835 (Six/Eight)
Price (new)	$2543/2690 (Six/Eight)

1949 Streamliner DeLuxe wagon

ENGINES

cid/type	bhp	years
239.2/sv I-6	90/93	1949
248.9/sv I-8	104/106	1949

PRICES

FAIR	$8600-15,000
GOOD	$15,000-21,000
FINE	$21,000-30,000

FINE EXAMPLE PRICE HISTORY

1982 $5400	**1990** $15,000
1994 $15,000	**1998** $15,500
1982-2000 RETURN 11%	
2000-2010 3%	

1950
PONTIAC CHIEFTAIN CATALINA

1950 Chieftain Catalina hardtop coupe

Pontiac's first pillarless hardtop, the first car to bear what would become one of the division's most familiar names, and introduced along with the Chevrolet Bel Air a year after Buick, Cadillac, and Oldsmobile had broken ground with this body type. It came decked out with convertible-type interior fittings—including chrome headliner strips to simulate a true convertible's top ribs. Offered with either six- or eight-cylinder L-head engines, the Catalina was available in Pontiac's DeLuxe trim or as the even ritzier Super, the only model so designated through 1952. Styling throughout the 1950 line was a mild facelift of the all-new 1949 look. A small bore increase gave the hardy old straight eight a small boost in rated horsepower.

✚ **FOR** Historical interest • Smooth looks • Others as for 1949 Chieftain DeLuxe

▬ **AGAINST** Same dull old engines

PRODUCTION

40,000 est.

SPECIFICATIONS

Length (in.)	202.5
Wheelbase (in.)	120.0
Weight (lbs)	3469/3549 (Six/Eight)
Price (new)	$2000-2127

ENGINES

cid/type	bhp	years
239.2/sv I-6	90	1950
268.4/sv I-8	108	1950

PRICES

FAIR	$3200-5500
GOOD	$5500-8000
FINE	$8000-11,000

FINE EXAMPLE PRICE HISTORY

1982 $5000	**1990** $12,000
1994 $11,000	**1998** $15,000
1982-2000 RETURN 5%	
2000-2010 3%	

1955-57
PONTIAC SAFARI

Pontiac's version of the two-door Chevrolet Nomad wagon, produced only in these years, though the Safari name was applied to Pontiac's conventional four-door wagons beginning with the '58s. It was powered by the Division's excellent new ohv V-8, which increased in displacement and horsepower in each of these years. The exciting blend of hardtop and wagon styling developed at Chevrolet was so fascinating to Pontiac that the Division won permission from GM management (to Chevy's chagrin) to build its own version. Elegantly trimmed inside, flashy outside with bright two-tone paint treatment and chrome accents aplenty. Though built on the shorter 122-inch-wheelbase Chieftain 870 chassis—not the Star Chief's 124—it was usually considered part of that top-line series because it was trimmed and equipped similarly. Interestingly, the 1955-56 wore no identifying series script. Like Nomad, the Safari didn't sell well because of its steep price and lack of full wagon practicality. Not many were made, so asking prices now are on the high side.

✚ **FOR** A Milestone Pontiac • Styling • Good performance • Low-production appeal • High appreciation potential

▬ **AGAINST** Special Safari pieces hard to find • Like Nomad, subject to water leaks and some rust around tailgate

PRODUCTION

1955 3760 **1956** 4042 **1957** 1292

1955 Safari wagon

SPECIFICATIONS

Length (in.)	206.7/207.7 (1955-56/1957)
Wheelbase (in.)	122.0
Weight (lbs)	3636-3750
Price (new)	$2962-3481

ENGINES

cid/type	bhp	years
287.2/ohv V-8	180	1955
316/ohv V-8	227	1956
347/ohv V-8	270/290	1957

PRICES

FAIR	$4000-7000
GOOD	$7000-13,000
FINE	$13,000-20,000

FINE EXAMPLE PRICE HISTORY

1982 $8500	1990 $18,000
1994 $16,500	1998 $19,000
1982-2000 RETURN 5%	
2000-2010 3%	

1955 Star Chief convertible

• Values rising, and more quickly than previously • Good club support

■ **AGAINST** Not cheap to run • Some trim/body parts scarce

PRODUCTION

1955 Catalina htp cpe 99,629 **conv** 19,762 **1956 Catalina htp cpe** 43,392 **Catalina htp sdn** 48,035 **conv** 13,510 **1957 Catalina htp cpe** 33,682 **Catalina htp sdn** 44,283 **conv** 12,789

SPECIFICATIONS

Length (in.)	210.2/212.6/213.8 (1955/56/57)
Wheelbase (in.)	124.0
Weight (lbs)	3566-3860
Price (new)	$2499-3105

ENGINES

cid/type	bhp	years
287.2/ohv V-8	173-200	1955
316.6/ohv V-8	202-227	1956
347.0/ohv V-8	244/270/290	1957

PRICES

Conv	
FAIR	$7500-14,000
GOOD	$14,000-27,000
FINE	$27,000-35,000

FINE EXAMPLE PRICE HISTORY

1982 $8000	1990 $30,000
1994 $29,000	1998 $35,000
1982-2000 RETURN 9%	
2000-2010 convs. 5%, others 3%	

1955-56
PONTIAC STAR CHIEF HARDTOPS & CONVERTIBLE

Pontiac's sportiest mid-'50s models in the top-line series that had bowed for 1953 on a two-inch longer wheelbase than the cheaper Chieftains. All-new styling and Pontiac's first modern V-8 for '55 were followed by larger, more potent engines for the modestly facelifted '56s—which included pillarless hardtop sedans for the first time—and the more substantially restyled '57s. The latter were the first Pontiacs in living memory without the trademark "silver streak" hood trim, a '30s idea of "Big Bill" Knudsen, and abandoned by his son "Bunkie," then Pontiac Division general manager. Overall length increased for 1956-57, but Pontiac never got into the "fin game" in the way some other makes did—including sister Chevrolet, whose bodyshells it continued to share. These Pontiacs featured typical Harley Earl styling, however, with lots of brightwork, colorful two-toning and, '57s excepted, somewhat unattractive blunt noses. Long overlooked, but now recognized as the most collectible period Ponchos other than the contemporary Safari wagons and the first '57 Bonneville (see entries).

■ **FOR** Reasonably plentiful and affordable • Solidly built (though '57s less so) • Good performance • Top-line trim, equipment • Historic V-8 Pontiacs

1957
PONTIAC BONNEVILLE

The fastest "Indian" yet: an image-building limited-edition convertible conceived by performance enthusiast and Pontiac Division chief S.E. "Bunkie" Knudsen. It shared basic body and styling with the '57 Star Chief convertible, but boasted a new mechanical fuel-injection system (similar, but not identical, to Chevrolet's contemporary "Ramjet" setup). "Fuel Injection" front-fender plaques provided external identification along with unique tri-spinner wheel covers and flashy ribbed brushed-aluminum rear-fender gravel guards below applied bright-metal "bombs." Most all these Bonnevilles were painted white. More a sales-promotion tool than serious money-maker, but it did its job well enough to become Pontiac's top-line series from 1958.

■ **FOR** Rare • Big, fast, good-looking

1957 Bonneville convertible

• Still a strong value-appreciator

■ **AGAINST** Almost too scarce and costly now • Demands high-calorie fuel • Are there any originals left?

PRODUCTION
630

SPECIFICATIONS

Length (in.)	213.8
Wheelbase (in.)	124.0
Weight (lbs)	4285
Price (new)	$5782

ENGINES

cid/type	bhp	years
347.0/ohv V-8	300/310	1957

PRICES

FAIR	$19,000-30,000
GOOD	$30,000-45,000
FINE	$45,000-60,000

FINE EXAMPLE PRICE HISTORY

1982 $15,000		**1990** $80,000	
1994 $75,000		**1998** $60,000	
1982-2000 RETURN 11%			
2000-2010 8%			

1958
PONTIAC BONNEVILLE

Continuation of the '57 Bonneville convertible, with a new hardtop coupe companion. They were a counterpart to Chevrolet's new '58 Bel Air Impalas (down to a rear-facing dummy roof scoop on hardtops), and just as much a one-year-only offering (owing to a revised GM body-sharing arrangement for 1959 and beyond). The '58 looked more like other Pontiacs than the '57 had, but the "New Direction" '58 styling was no less glitzy (though more restrained than that year's Olds and Buick). Available with the most Pontiac horses, including 300-bhp Tri-

1958 Bonneville convertible

Power (three two-barrel carbs) and 310-bhp fuel-injected 370-cid V-8s, the basic 1955 engine enlarged for the fourth year in a row. Now built on Pontiac's "junior" chassis with a two-inch-shorter wheelbase than the Star Chief platform, and thus a little lighter and faster than the debut '57 Bonneville. The costly, trouble-prone new "Ever-Level" air suspension option was quite rare on these models—few were ordered across the entire '58 line. Most of the cars that did have it were later converted to conventional coil springs, making that an option worth seeking out today.

■ **FOR** As for 1957 Bonneville, but more readily available and stronger appreciation potential

■ **AGAINST** As for 1957 Bonneville, but somewhat poorer workmanship

PRODUCTION
htp cpe 9144 **conv** 3096

SPECIFICATIONS

Length (in.)	211.7
Wheelbase (in.)	122.0
Weight (lbs)	3710-3925
Price (new)	$3481-3586

ENGINES

cid/type	bhp	years
370/ohv V-8	255-310	1958

PRICES

Conv	
FAIR	$17,000-20,000
GOOD	$20,000-38,000
FINE	$38,000-60,000
Htp	
FAIR	$7500-14,000
GOOD	$14,000-22,000
FINE	$22,000-26,000

(Add 20% for fuel injection.)

FINE CONVERTIBLE PRICE HISTORY

1982 $7000		**1990** $35,000
1994 $38,000		**1998** $55,000
1982-2000 RETURN 14%		
2000-2010 10%		

1959-60
PONTIAC BONNEVILLE HARDTOPS & CONVERTIBLES

The sportiest of the "volume" Bonnevilles that ousted Star Chief as Pontiac's top full-line series for 1959, the year the division intro-

1959 Bonneville hardtop sedan

duced "Wide Track" design and some of Detroit's cleanest styling. It returned to the 124-inch Star Chief wheelbase, however. A broad split grille and "twin-fin" rear fenders were replaced by a vee'd grille and rocket-tube taillights for 1960, but thin-pillar hardtop roof-lines, vast glass areas, and sporty vinyl interiors (with individual "buckety" seats on some two-doors) were featured throughout. Pontiac enlarged its 1955 V-8 yet again, this time to 389 cubes. Fuel injection was gone, but Bonneville offered up to 348 horses with Tri-Power carburetion, a returning and still fairly popular option. Counter-part convertible and hardtops in the low-line, 122-inch-wheelbase Catalina series are equally collectible now—really preferred by performance fans for being lighter—but we single out the Bonnevilles as the biggest, brightest, and best models in the years when number-five Pontiac first staked its lasting claim as Detroit's number-three seller.

FOR Great styling, especially the '59s • Fine performance • Surprisingly good handling • Big, smooth, and impressive • Still available and quite affordable

AGAINST Too big to make practical daily drivers? • Hardtop sedans less in demand than two-doors • Needs plenty of high-octane gas

PRODUCTION

1959 Sport Coupe htp 27,769 **Vista htp sdn** 38,696 **conv** 11,426 **1960 Sport Coupe htp** 24,015 **Vista htp sdn** 39,037 **b** 17,062

SPECIFICATIONS

Length (in.)	220.7
Wheelbase (in.)	124.0
Weight (lbs)	3965-4070
Price (new)	$3257-3478

ENGINES

cid/type	bhp	years
389/ohv V-8	260-348	1959-60

PRICES

Conv	
FAIR	$6000-14,000
GOOD	$14,000-21,000
FINE	$21,000-28,000
Htp	
FAIR	$2000-6000
GOOD	$6000-10,000
FINE	$10,000-15,000

FINE HARDTOP PRICE HISTORY

1982 $3800		**1990** $12,000	
1994 $12,000		**1998** $14,000	
1982-2000 RETURN 8%			
2000-2010 5%			

---

1 9 6 1 - 6 2
PONTIAC CATALINA/ VENTURA/ BONNEVILLE TWO-DOORS

1962 Catalina hardtop coupe

Appealing Pontiacs from the first years of GM styling dictated directly by William L. Mitchell. The handsome, clean-lined '61s were shorter in wheelbase, four inches shorter overall, and many pounds trimmer than the already nice '60s, and featured a revived split-theme grille and a crisp, "extruded" look. The '62s were slightly bulkier both in appearance and in fact, but some prefer them for that reason; hardtop coupe rooflines were remodeled to give the illusion of a convertible with its top up. Pontiac's by-then famous "Wide Track" chassis continued to provide uncommonly good big-car handling, while the division's 389 V-8 was further muscled up to provide uncommon big-car performance. These years also brought the first of the special-order 421 engines that did Pontiac proud in drag racing, though they were typically installed in the lightest Catalina two-door sedans. Catalina-based Ventura models (including hardtop sedan) were offered for '61 only, after which the name graced a Catalina trim option. These cars were once overlooked by collectors, but no more, yet they're still reasonably priced and plentiful. Future value appreciation seems both strong and lasting.

FOR Terrific period styling • Great road cars • Bright, colorful trimmings • Some performance and appearance options quite rare • Available and affordable • Good, if not great, investment

AGAINST Not much, though some body/trim parts predictably scarce now

PRODUCTION

1961 Catalina Sport Coupe htp 14,524 **conv** 12,379 **Ventura Sport Coupe htp** 13,297 **Bonneville Sport Coupe htp** 16,906 **conv** 18,264 **1962 Catalina Sport Coupe htp** 46,024 **conv** 16,877 **Bonneville Sport Coupe htp** 31,629 **conv** 21,582

SPECIFICATIONS

Length (in.)	209.7 (1961 Catalina/Ventura), 211.9 (1962 Catalina), 217.0 (1961 Bonneville), 218.6 (1962 Bonneville)
Wheelbase (in.)	119.0 (1961 Catalina/Ventura), 120.0 (1962 Catalina), 123.0 (Bonneville)
Weight (lbs)	3680-4005
Price (new)	$2766-3570

ENGINES

cid/type	bhp	years
389/ohv V-8	215-348	1961-62
421/ohv V-8	373/405	1961-62

PRICES

conv	
FAIR	$4000-9000
GOOD	$9000-14,000
FINE	$14,000-22,000
Bonneville Sport Coupe	

1961 Ventura hardtop coupe

1962 Bonneville hardtop coupe

FAIR	$2500-6500
GOOD	$6500-9500
FINE	$9500-14,000

FINE CONVERTIBLE PRICE HISTORY

1982 7500	1990 $20,000
1994 $20,000	1998 $17,000

1982-2000 RETURN 7%
2000-2010 5%, htps 3%

1962-64
PONTIAC GRAND PRIX

One of the earliest and most popular personal cars of the '60s, and the first in a long line of posh Pontiacs that continue to this day. Introduced as a single hardtop model in mid-1962, it was built on the 120-inch-wheelbase Catalina platform, Pontiac's shorter big-car chassis. Elegantly decked out with the buckets-and-console interior so popular in those years, it offered cleaner looks than other Pontiacs, plus fine handling. The straight-lined '62 styling was replaced for 1963-64 with more flowing fender contours and an interesting concave rear window exclusive to the GP in the Pontiac line (but shared with the Olds Starfire). Also special to it were the grille treatment and a tail panel with concealed taillights. Grand Prix continued as a full-size car and grew larger and heavier as the years went by. After 1968 it became a long-wheelbase intermediate based on the Tempest/Le Mans series. The "classic" early '60s GPs are

the ones to look for, however. Engine choices in this period were built around the 389 and 421 V-8s, with optional Tri-Power (triple two-barrel carbs) and horsepower as high as 370.

FOR Desirable, collectible standard-size sportster • Crisp good looks • Performance • Posh interior

AGAINST A natural hunger for high-octane gas • Limited appreciation potential, though that's changing

PRODUCTION

1962 30,195 **1963** 72,959 **1964** 63,810

SPECIFICATIONS

Length (in.)	211.9/213.6 (1962/1963-64)
Wheelbase (in.)	120.0
Weight (lbs)	383
Price (new)	$3489-3499

ENGINES

cid/type	bhp	years
389/ohv V-8	303/370	1962-64
421/ohv V-8	350/370	1963-64

PRICES

FAIR	$2000-5000
GOOD	$5000-7500
FINE	$7500-11,000

(Add 10% for Tri-Power, add 30% for 421 V-8.)

FINE 1962 MODEL PRICE HISTORY

1982 $5000	1990 $11,500
1994 $10,000	1998 $10,000

1982-2000 RETURN 5%
2000-2010 3%

1963 Grand Prix hardtop coupe

1 9 6 2 - 6 3

PONTIAC TEMPEST LE MANS

Pontiac's compact, introduced for 1961, was technically interesting. It featured a radical flexible driveshaft and a rear-mounted transmission/differential combination (transaxle) with independent rear suspension. This layout was not shared with the companion Buick Special and Oldsmobile F-85 (introduced the same year and using the same bodyshell as Tempest) or anything else. However, it was advanced, as shown by Porsche's much later adoption of the concept for its 924 and 928. The most sporting of the early Tempests were the Le Mans Sport Coupe and convertible. Introduced as a package option during the '61 model year, it became a full-fledged series from 1963 on (the name would eventually supplant Tempest for Pontiac's intermediate line). In these years, Le Mans meant bucket seats, console, posh interior decor, and exclusive exterior emblems. Power options had graduated to the hot 326 V-8 by 1963. The standard Tempest engine in these years was a four-cylinder unit, basical-

ly half of a 389 Pontiac V-8.

◩ **FOR** Technical interest • Practical size • Sporty looks • Good performance with optional V-8s

◪ **AGAINST** Tricky handling, especially in the wet • Mechanical complexity • Rust-prone • Some mechanical parts becoming scarce

PRODUCTION

1962 2d Sport Coupe 39,662 **conv** 15,559 **1963 2d Sport Coupe** 45,701 **conv** 15,957

SPECIFICATIONS

Length (in.)	189.3
Wheelbase (in.)	112.0
Weight (lbs)	2800-3035
Price (new)	$2294-2794

ENGINES

cid/type	bhp	years
194.5/ohv I-4	110-166	1962-63
215/ohv V-8	185	1962
326/ohv V-8	260	1963

PRICES

Conv	
FAIR	$2300-5000
GOOD	$5000-6000
FINE	$6000-9500
Htp	
FAIR	$1500-3000
GOOD	$3000-5500
FINE	$5500-7000

FINE CONVERTIBLE PRICE HISTORY

1982 $4000		**1990** $11,000
1994 $10,000		**1998** $13,000
1982-2000 RETURN 5%		
2000-2010 5%		

1 9 6 4 - 6 7

PONTIAC CATALINA 2+2

1964 Catalina 2+2 hardtop coupe

A special package option for the mid-'60s Catalina convertible and hardtop coupe, Pontiac's "other" entry in the sporty big-car market uncovered by its Grand Prix. But where the GP emphasized luxury, the 2+2 stressed performance. Though items varied somewhat from year to year, the package always included a hotter mill than Catalina's standard V-8, firmed-up suspension, discreet exterior cues, and a more youthful all-vinyl interior, usually with bucket seats and center console. From there you customized to taste with more power, four-speed manual or three-speed automatic transmission, extra gauges, air, power assists,

1963 Tempest Le Mans convertible

1966 Catalina 2+2 convertible

and all the rest. It's probably a safe bet that 2+2s were mostly built with 389 V-8s, and after peaking in sales in 1965 declined quickly through 1967, after which the option was dropped in light of the mid-size "muscle car mania" then sweeping the performance field. Like other Pontiacs, the 2+2s became larger and swoopier after '64, but they were still among the few truly sporting big cars in the GM stable (not counting Chevy's SS Impalas), and have gradually become coveted as such. Though production break-outs aren't available, the convertible had to be quite rare.

✠ FOR Uncommon sports/luxury cars with bite • Nice period styling • Big, smooth and impressive • Prices still fairly reasonable

▬ AGAINST Value appreciation middling to weak • High-octane a must • Workmanship varies greatly (best on '64s) • Convertibles hard to find

PRODUCTION
1964 7998 **1965** 11,519 **1966** 6383 **1967** 1768

SPECIFICATIONS

Length (in.)	213.6/214.6/218.4 (1964/1965-66/1967)
Wheelbase (in.)	120.0/121.0 (1964/1965-67)
Weight (lbs)	3750-3910
Price (new)	$3160-3664

ENGINES

cid/type	bhp	years
389/ohv V-8	283-330	1964
389/ohv V-8	265-338	1965-66
421/ohv V-8	320-370	1964
421/ohv V-8	338-376	1965-66
428/ohv V-8	360/376	1967

PRICES

Conv	
FAIR	$2500-7500
GOOD	$7500-12,000
FINE	$12,000-16,000
Htp	
FAIR	$1500-5000

GOOD	$5000-8500
FINE	$8500-12,000

FINE CONVERTIBLE PRICE HISTORY

1982 $2500	**1990** $14,000
1994 $13,500	**1998** $18,000
1982-2000 RETURN 12%	
2000-2010 5% (htp 3%)	

1964-65
PONTIAC TEMPEST GTO

Virtual originator of the '60s "muscle car" concept, generally credited to ad man Jim Wangers. Introduced as an interim '64 package option for the newly upsized Tempest Le Mans Sports Coupe, hardtop coupe, and convertible. Initial equipment comprised a three-speed manual floorshift, 389 V-8, quick steering, stiff suspension, dual exhausts, and premium tires—all for about $300. To this you could add four-speed manual or three-speed automatic transmission, sintered-metallic brake linings, heavy-duty cooling, limited-slip differential, and power options destined to go up the scale every year. The GTO shared basic Tempest/Le Mans styling for the most part, but sported unique grille accents, hood scoops, and those all-important badges. All GTOs have long been highly coveted, high-priced collector cars, but some

1964 Tempest GTO coupe

1965 Tempest GTO convertible

prefer these early models as the first and purest of the breed, if not the all-time fastest.

❖ FOR Milestone status • Tremendous go • Fine handling • More rabidly sought-after than ever

◼ AGAINST High operating costs, especially insurance • So-so construction quality

PRODUCTION
1964 Sports Coupe 7384 **htp cpe** 18,422 **conv** 6644 **1965 2d Sports Coupe** 8319 **htp cpe** 55,722 **conv** 11,311

SPECIFICATIONS
Length (in.)	203.0
Wheelbase (in.)	115.0
Weight (lbs)	3000-3565
Price (new)	$2751-3500

ENGINES
cid/type	bhp	years
389/ohv V-8	325-360	1964-65

PRICES
Conv	
FAIR	$6000-10,000
GOOD	$10,000-15,000
FINE	$15,000-21,000
Cpe/htp	
FAIR	$4000-8000
GOOD	$8000-10,000
FINE	$10,000-17,000

FINE COUPE PRICE HISTORY
1982 $6100		**1990** $18,000	
1994 $15,500		**1998** $17,000	
1982-2000 RETURN 6%			
2000-2010 5%			

1965-66
PONTIAC GRAND PRIX

The second iteration of Pontiac's big sports/luxury hardtop coupe.

Still built on the shorter Catalina platform, but larger and weightier than the 1962-64 original, and with the same flowing new "coke-bottle" styling featured on all full-size Poncho's in this period. GP, however, maintained tradition with a somewhat more formal roofline than Catalina two-door hardtops, complete with a concave backlight as in 1963-64. But it was somewhat less distinctive than earlier GPs, which was reflected in much lower sales—the '66 garnered only about half as many as the '64. Still, these follow-ups are worthy alternatives to a first-series GP, with the added bonuses of greater rarity and lower asking prices.

❖ FOR Big, bold and brawny • Ample luxury • Good performance • Still not very costly relative to earlier GPs

◼ AGAINST Still not as good an investment as earlier GPs • Workmanship falls off, too • Handling not in the same league, either

PRODUCTION
1965 58,881 **1966** 36,757

SPECIFICATIONS
Length (in.)	214.6
Wheelbase (in.)	121.0
Weight (lbs)	3940-4015
Price (new)	$3495

ENGINES
cid/type	bhp	years
389/ohv V-8	265-333	1965-66
421/ohv V-8	338-376	1965-66

1966 Grand Prix hardtop coupe

1967 GTO convertible

PRICES

FAIR	$2000-6000
GOOD	$6000-9000
FINE	$9000-10,000

FINE EXAMPLE PRICE HISTORY

1982 $3900		1990 $10,000	
1994 $10,000		1998 $10,000	
1982-2000 RETURN 7%			
2000-2010 3%			

1966-67

PONTIAC GTO

The wildly successful "Goat" in rebodied second-series form. The chassis was essentially unchanged, but pretty new outer sheetmetal conferred a more flowing look, marked by kicked-up rear fenders, an even wider-appearing grille with stacked (versus side-by-side) quad headlamps, and a new "tunneled" rear roofline on closed models. No big mechanical alterations were seen, but power switched from the 389 to a more emissions-tunable 400 enlargement for 1967, a sign that mandatory federal smog standards were on the way.

FOR As for 1964-65 GTO, including Milestone status • Plus more readily available hardtops and lower current asking prices for all models

AGAINST As for 1964-65 GTO, but less in demand and less potential dollar return

PRODUCTION

1966 2d Sports Coupe 10,363 **htp cpe** 73,785 **conv** 12,798 **1967 2d Sports Coupe** 7029 **htp cpe** 65,176 **conv** 9517

SPECIFICATIONS

Length (in.)	206.4/206.7 (1966/67)
Wheelbase (in.)	115.0
Weight (lbs)	3445-3555
Price (new)	$2783-$3165

ENGINES

cid/type	bhp	years
389/ohv V-8	333-360	1966
400/ohv V-8	255-360	1967

PRICES

Conv	
FAIR	$5500-10,000
GOOD	$10,000-14,000
FINE	$14,000-19,000
Htp	
FAIR	$3500-7000
GOOD	$7000-10,000
FINE	$10,000-13,500
(Add 20% for Tri-Power, 20% for Ram Air.)	

FINE CONVERTIBLE PRICE HISTORY

1982 $5000		1990 $25,000	
1994 $25,000		1998 $19,000	
1982-2000 RETURN 8%			
2000-2010 5%			

1967-69

PONTIAC FIREBIRD

Pontiac's slightly more upmarket version of the Chevrolet Camaro, and just as successful. It used the same basic body/chassis design, but wore a distinctly Pontiac divided grille. Offered initially with five different Pontiac engines ranging from a base-tune version of the division's overhead-cam six (introduced in 1966 Tempests) to a 325-bhp 400 V-8. Models designations signaled what was under the hood. The interesting Sprint used a modified 215-bhp six with a Rochester Quadra-Jet carb, hot timing, and other tweaks. There were also Firebird 326s with 250

1968 Firebird hardtop coupe

and, in HO form, 285 bhp. The 326 became a 350 for '68. Styling was virtually unchanged until 1969, when a heavy facelift appeared, along with the first of the mighty Trans Ams (see entry). In all, Pontiac offered a broad and interesting ponycar lineup with something to suit most every collector taste.

⊞ FOR Large following • Pleasant drivers • Lots of variety • Nice styling • Lower-power models still inexpensive (but creeping up) • Value appreciation remains strong

▣ AGAINST Cramped in back • Tiny trunk • High V-8 running costs • Hot models won't likely have been pampered • Early ohc sixes were troublesome

PRODUCTION

1967 htp cpe 67,032 **conv** 15,526 **1968 htp cpe** 90,152 **conv** 16,960 **1969 htp cpe** 76,059 **conv** 11,649

SPECIFICATIONS

Length (in.)	188.4/188.8/191.1 (1967/68/69)
Wheelbase (in.)	108.0
Weight (lbs)	2955-3346
Price (new)	$2666-3045

ENGINES

cid/type	bhp	years
230/ohc I-6	165/215	1967
250/ohc I-6	175/215/230	1968-69
326/ohv V-8	250/285	1967
350/ohv V-8	265/330	1968-69
400/ohv V-8	335/345	1969

PRICES

Conv
FAIR	$3000-6000
GOOD	$6000-9000
FINE	$9000-11,000

Htp
FAIR	$2000-4000
GOOD	$4000-7000
FINE	$7000-9500

(Add 35% for 400 cid V-8, 40% for Ram Air.)

FINE CONVERTIBLE PRICE HISTORY

1982 $2500		**1990** $12,000	
1994 $10,000		**1998** $10,500	
1982-2000 RETURN 9%			
2000-2010 5%			

1967-68
PONTIAC GRAND PRIX

Heavily revamped third version of the big sports/luxury Pontiac, bigger and more massive-looking than ever despite an unchanged wheelbase. A notable '67 announcement was the first-ever Grand Prix convertible wearing the massive new bumper/grille with hidden headlamps that adorned that year's hardtop coupe (still with concave backlight). But ragtops were fast-falling from favor throughout Detroit, and low demand rendered the open-air GP a one-year-only model. GP sales as a whole were waning, too, and 1968's even heavier-looking restyle didn't help. Engines were enlarged for easier emissions tuning with no severe power losses in these years of first-phase federal smog restrictions. First-phase Washington-

mandated safety equipment also featured in these years. Otherwise it was mostly business as usual, but declining GP business prompted Pontiac to rethink the entire car for 1969. The '67 convertible has since become a minor collector's item, but hardtops are worth searching out, though they'll probably never become high-status high-value cars.

⊞ FOR As for 1965-66 Grand Prix, plus rare, one-year-only '67 convertible and lower current asking prices for all models

▣ AGAINST As for 1965-66 Grand Prix, but clumsier styling and even less agile

PRODUCTION

1967 htp cpe 37,125 **conv** 5856 **1968 htp cpe** 31,711

SPECIFICATIONS

Length (in.)	215.6/216.3 (1967/68)
Wheelbase (in.)	121.0
Weight (lbs)	4005-4075
Price (new)	$3549-3813

ENGINES

cid/type	bhp	years
400/ohv V-8	350	1967-68
428/ohv V-8	360-390	1967-68

PRICES

Htp
FAIR	$1300-3500
GOOD	$3500-6500
FINE	$6500-9000

Conv
FAIR	$3000-7000
GOOD	$7000-10,000
FINE	$10,000-15,000

1967 Grand Prix convertible

FINE HARDTOP PRICE HISTORY

1982 $3000		**1990** $8500	
1994 $8000		**1998** $10,000	
1982-2000 RETURN 7%			
2000-2010 5%			

1968-72
PONTIAC GTO

1971 GTO convertible

Third-generation Pontiac supercar. Redesigned on GM's new-for-'68 A-body platform that put two-door intermediates like GTO on a shorter wheelbase than four-door models. Offerings thinned by one with cancellation of the previous pillared Sport Coupe. GTO maintained its family resemblance to contemporary big Pontiacs, particularly in front with a massive bumper/grille proboscis covered in ding-resistant body-color Endura plastic. (One TV commercial showed maniacal "engineers" harmlessly whacking the daylights out of it.) A 1970 facelift modified the appearance á la '69 Firebird, with exposed, separated headlamps and prominent "eyebrows" above the wheelarches. Then came a lower, more protruding snout, though still sheathed in color-matched Endura. Arriving for '69 was "The Judge" option package featuring a 366-horse Ram Air IV V-8, Hurst shifter, front-fender identification decals, and a low decklid spoiler. For 1970, GM rescinded its edict against intermediates with less than 10 pounds/horsepower, and Pontiac duly made its big 455 a GTO option. But horsepower then declined in the face of stiffening emissions controls, rising insurance rates, and falling muscle-car sales. By 1972, the Judge and convertibles were gone, and the GTO was a package option once more. A 310-bhp Super Duty 455 was available in a rebodied '73 model, but the following year saw the option transferred to Pontiac's Ventura compact, after which the great "Goat" disappeared altogether. Pre-1971 models still hold the greatest appeal and highest values as collector cars, with some model/option combinations so rare as to be almost one of a kind. None are cheap today, and can only become costlier as the years roll on.

➕ **FOR** The same qualities as earlier GTOs, plus rarity of convertibles, "Judge" models, and various high-power options • 1968-69 models are Milestone cars

➖ **AGAINST** As for 1966-67 GTO, but asking prices much stiffer than they recently were and are still heading skyward

PRODUCTION

1968 htp cpe 77,704 **conv** 9980 **1969 htp cpe** 58,126 **Judge htp cpe** 6725 **conv** 7328 **Judge conv** 108 **1970 htp cpe** 32,737 **Judge htp cpe** 3629 **conv** 3615 **Judge conv** 3615 **1971 htp cpe** 9497 **Judge htp cpe** 357 **conv** 661 **Judge conv** 17 **1972 htp cpe** 5807

SPECIFICATIONS

Length (in.)	200.7/201.2/202.9 (1968/1969/1970-72)
Wheelbase (in.)	112.0
Weight (lbs)	3506-3700
Price (new)	$3101-4070

ENGINES

cid/type	bhp	years
400/ohv V-8	265-370	1968-71
455/ohv V-8	350/366/370	1970
455/ohv V-8	325/335	1971
455/ohv V-8	220/250[1]	1972

[1]SAE net; other figures SAE gross

PRICES

1968-70 htp	
FAIR	$3000-7000
GOOD	$7000-10,000
FINE	$10,000-14,000
1968-71 conv	
FAIR	$3500-8000
GOOD	$8000-12,000
FINE	$12,000-17,000
1971-72 htp	
FAIR	$2500-6000
GOOD	$6000-10,000
FINE	$10,000-13,500
Judge htp	
FAIR	$5500-9000
GOOD	$9000-13,000
FINE	$13,000-20,000
Judge conv	
FAIR	$6500-12,000
GOOD	$12,000-20,000
FINE	$20,000-32,000

(Add 25% for Ram Air [std on Judge], 10% for 455 V-8.)

FINE JUDGE CONVERTIBLE PRICE HISTORY

1982 $5000		**1990** $25,000	
1994 $35,000		**1998** $35,000	
1982-2000 RETURN 12%			
2000-2010 8% (htp 5%)			

1968 GTO hardtop coupe

1969
PONTIAC FIREBIRD TRANS AM

First of the fire-breathing Firebirds named after the Sports Car Club of America's late-'60s Trans-American racing series for production compact "sedans." It arrived as a mid-season offering in the third year of Pontiac's ponycar. Ironically, a T/A would never win the T-A championship, though "Canadian Firebirds"—really "Pontiacized" Camaros—did race, albeit with little success. Not that any of this mattered, for the Trans Am cast an image-boosting glow over the entire Firebird line. The debut '69, actually a $725 option package announced at the Chicago Auto Show in February, came with a potent Ram-Air 400 V-8; four-on-the-floor; the expected heavy-duty suspension, steering, and brakes; and rear spoiler, simulated front-fender air outlets, functional twin-scoop hood, name decals, and white paint set off by broad, blue, dual dorsal racing stripes. A special tunnel-port 303 small-block engine was allegedly available, but production is doubtful. Output was low anyway (note the mere eight ragtops), and the the first generation T/A was fated to be a one-year-only model. Reconstituted with Firebird's "1970½" second generation, the Trans Am would go on to keep the ponycar flame burning brightly through the '70s almost all by itself.

1969 Firebird Trans Am convertible

✚ FOR First of a great breed • Rare and unique Firebird model, especially convertible • True muscle-car performance • Great handling • Solid, if pricey, investment

◼ AGAINST Almost impossible to find anymore • Costs a mint if you do • Stupendous insurance costs

PRODUCTION
htp cpe 689 conv 8

SPECIFICATIONS
Length (in.)	191.1
Wheelbase (in.)	108.0
Weight (lbs)	approx. 3150-3450
Price (new)	approx. $3550-3750

ENGINES
cid/type	bhp	years
400/ohv V-8	345	1969

PRICES
Cpe

FAIR	$3000-5500
GOOD	$5500-10,000
FINE	$10,000-18,000
Conv	
FAIR	$4500-9000
GOOD	$9000-15,000
FINE	$15,000-25,000

FINE COUPE PRICE HISTORY
1982	$7200	**1990**	$18,000
1994	$15,000	**1998**	$14,000
1982-2000 RETURN 6%			
2000-2010 8%			

1969-72
PONTIAC GRAND PRIX

Pontiac's sports/luxury personal car reconfigured from full-size to intermediate on a new "A-special" platform

1969 Grand Prix Model SJ hardtop coupe

with an exclusive 118-inch wheelbase. Immediate high sales success prompted Chevrolet to offer its similar Monte Carlo from 1970—which perhaps partly explains why GP deliveries declined after debut '69. Still a hardtop coupe, but in two trim levels now, J and SJ (*á la* Duesenberg), the latter with ritzier appointments and, in most years, more standard power. The '69 introduced an innovative curved "cockpit" dash design, and was liked for that as well as for handling much better than any GP since the '62 original, which it closely matched in size. Modestly facelifted for '71 with a crisper, slightly "boattailed" rear deck before being replaced by 1973's new fixed-pillar "Colonnade" generation. Built mostly with Hydra-Matic, but three- and four-speed manuals were offered, and would be rare finds today. Not yet high-status collector's items, but the '69s and, to some extent, the '70s have been moving up in both esteem and dollar value. A rarity to watch for is the 1971 Hurst SSJ, a semi-custom conversion with electric sunroof, gold-colored wheels and, of course, Hurst shifter.

✚ **FOR** Sports/luxury Pontiac in a

1971 Grand Prix Model J hardtop coupe

handier size • Smooth, strong big-block V-8s • Easy and cheap to acquire

◼ **AGAINST** Thirsty • Indifferent workmanship • Mediocre outward vision • Tight back seat • Not a high-return dollar investment at present

PRODUCTION

1969 112,486 **1970** 65,750 **1971** 58,325 **1972** 91,961

SPECIFICATIONS

Length (in.) 210.2/212.9 (1969-70/1971-72)
Wheelbase (in.) 118.0
Weight (lbs) 3715-3900
Price (new) $3866-4472

ENGINES

cid/type	bhp	years
400/ohv V-8	300/350	1969-71
400/ohv V-8	250[1]	1972
428/ohv V-8	370/390	1969
455/ohv V-8	325/370	1970-71
455/ohv V-8	300[1]	1972

[1]SAE net; other figures SAE gross

PRICES

FAIR	$1500-4000
GOOD	$4000-6000
FINE	$6000-10,000

(Add 20% for 428-cid V-8.)

FINE EXAMPLE PRICE HISTORY

1982 $2800		**1990** $6500	
1994 $7000		**1998** $9500	
1982-2000 RETURN 8%			
2000-2010 5%			

1970
PONTIAC FIREBIRD

The second-generation Pontiac pony-car, introduced mid-way through the model year. Beautifully styled under the direction of Division studio chief Bill Porter, it was distinctively Pontiac despite continued bodyshell sharing with Camaro. Increasingly tough Federal emissions and bumper-impact regulations were met successfully in later years without compromising the clean,

1970 Firebird coupe

pure shape too much. But as is often the case with collectible cars, these first-of-the-line models are the most desirable. Offered in four distinct variations of a single coupe body style (a convertible was never contemplated). Two, standard and Esprit, were mild; Formula 400 and the spoilered Trans Am were the wild ones. They're worth having for the styling and performance, and the top models are rapidly gaining the attention of collectors.

➕ FOR One of the best designs anywhere • Great performance • Fine roadability • Formula/Trans Am rarity • Reasonable asking prices, though rising now

➖ AGAINST Big engines thirsty • Sixes anemic • Limited back seat space • Tiny trunk • Performance versions won't have had an easy life

PRODUCTION

Standard 18,874 **Formula 400** 7708 **Esprit** 18,961 **Trans Am** 3196

SPECIFICATIONS

Length (in.)	191.6
Wheelbase (in.)	108.0
Weight (lbs)	3140-3550
Price (new)	$2875-4305

ENGINES

cid/type	bhp	years
250/ohv I-6	155	1970
350/ohv V-8	255	1970
400/ohv V-8	330/345	1970

PRICES

Trans Am
FAIR	$4500-8000
GOOD	$8000-11,000
FINE	$11,000-16,000

400
FAIR	$2000-4000
GOOD	$4000-8000
FINE	$8000-10,000

Others
FAIR	$1500-3500
GOOD	$3500-6000
FINE	$6000-8000

FINE TRANS AM PRICE HISTORY

1982 $5500		**1990** $14,000	
1994 $12,500		**1998** $14,000	
1982-2000 RETURN 7%			
2000-2010 5%			

1971-73 PONTIAC FIREBIRD TRANS AM

Pontiac's rip-snorting ponycar model, a continuation of the new second-generation design launched at mid-model year 1970. Each of these Trans Ams makes our collectibles roster on the basis of low production, particularly the '72s, which were in short supply because of a crippling auto workers strike at GM's Norwood, Ohio, F-car plant that also affected Camaro Z28 output. Styling and equipment remained relatively unchanged from 1970 ½, but the advent of low-compression engines at GM starting with the '71 model year robbed the Trans Am of some of its fire. Nevertheless, it's desirable for macho styling and acceleration to match. The first of what would become known as the "screaming chicken" Firebird hood decals arrived as a $53 option for the '73s, but the once-functional shaker hood scoop was corked up. Trans Am power for 1971-72 was supplied exclusively by Pontiac's 455 H.O. V-8 (factory order code LS-5). For 1973, a detuned version (L-75) became standard, and a new Super-Duty engine (installed in only 252 Trans Ams) was optional.

➕ FOR As for 1970 Firebird, plus Trans Am's performance appeal and greater exclusivity than other models in these years

➖ AGAINST As for 1970 Firebird, plus fuel thirst • Also, difficult to find now in clean, original condition

PRODUCTION

1971 2116 **1972** 1286 **1973** 4802

SPECIFICATIONS

Length (in.)	191.6
Wheelbase (in.)	108.2
Weight (lbs)	approx. 3700
Price (new)	$4103-4557

ENGINES

cid/type	bhp[1]	years
455/ohv V-8	250-310	1971-73

[1]SAE net bhp; rated at 335 bhp gross (305 SAE net) in 1971

PRICES

FAIR	$4000-8000
GOOD	$8000-11,000
FINE	$11,000-15,000

1972 Trans Am coupe

FINE EXAMPLE PRICE HISTORY

1982 $4500   **1990** $13,000
1994 $12,500   **1998** $14,000
1982-2000 RETURN 8%
2000-2010 5%

1973-75

PONTIAC GRAND AM

Pioneering American "Eurosedan," based on the workaday mid-size Le Mans and sharing the new-for-'73 "Colonnade" styling common to all GM intermediates. The name derived from its presumed combination of Grand Prix luxury and Trans Am performance. It was engineered by wizards John Seaton and Bill Collins, who tried to approximate the character and capabilities of comparable Mercedes-Benz and BMW models at a third or half their cost. Ride and handling weren't as good, but the differences were acceptable given the much lower price. The shorter-wheelbase coupe was more able (and popular) than the longer, heavier sedan. Easily distinguished from other Pontiacs by a bulbous nose made of Endura deformable plastic.

✚ FOR Fine roadability and performance • Distinctive styling (especially in white) • Not a hot item now, thus inexpensive

◼ AGAINST Debatable styling to some • Interior strains to ape M-B design • Rust-prone • Body and soft-trim parts drying up; repros seem a long way off • Not much collector recognition now

PRODUCTION

1973 2d cpe 34,443 **4d sdn** 8691 **1974 2d cpe** 13,961 **4d sdn** 3122 **1975 2d cpe** 8786 **4d sdn** 1893

SPECIFICATIONS

Length (in.)	208.0/212.0 (2d/4d)
Wheelbase (in.)	112.0/116.0 (2d/4d)
Weight (lbs)	3992-4073
Price (new)	$4264-4976

ENGINES

cid/type	bhp[1]	years
400.0/ohv V-8	170-225	1973-75
455.0/ohv V-8	200-290	1973-75

[1]SAE net

PRICES

2d cpe	
FAIR	$1500-3000
GOOD	$3000-4500
FINE	$4500-7500
4d sdn	
FAIR	$1500-3000
GOOD	$3000-4500

1973 Grand Am coupe

FINE	$4500-6000

FINE COUPE PRICE HISTORY

Depreciating during 1980s. Fine examples stable now.
2000-2010 RETURN 2%

1976

PONTIAC FIREBIRD LIMITED EDITION TRANS AM

A special version of Pontiac's top ponycar, an outgrowth of an idea suggested by GM styling chief William L. Mitchell and executed by designer John R. Schinella. Introduced to commemorate Pontiac's 50th anniversary, the Limited Edition was mechanically the same as other Trans Ams—but you couldn't miss it on the street. It was all-black, highlighted by gold striping, grille insert and trim, and gold colored, honeycomb pattern polycast wheels. Inside was a gold-anodized instrument panel appliqué, gold steering wheel spokes, and special upholstery. A Hurst T-bar roof with smoke-tinted removable glass panels was offered as an extra, but leak problems led Pontiac to curtail installations to just 643. The deliberately restricted production run quickly sold out, which convinced Pontiac to offer a similar treatment under the name Special Edition for 1977-79. These are far more numerous and hence less desirable from the collector standpoint, though they're immensely desirable cars. The big-block 455-cid V-8 vanished after 1976.

✚ FOR Looks still turn heads • Fine performance • Super handling • Low production appeal

1976 Firebird Limited Edition Trans Am coupe

AGAINST Collector prices not firmly established at present • Very thirsty • Difficult and expensive to insure • Sure-fire thief and cop bait

PRODUCTION

2400

SPECIFICATIONS

Length (in.)	196.8
Wheelbase (in.)	108.2
Weight (lbs)	approx. 3600
Price (new)	$8500

ENGINES

cid/type	bhp[1]	years
400/ohv V-8	185	1976
455/ohv V-8	200	1976

[1]SAE net

PRICES

FAIR	$3000-5000
GOOD	$5000-7500
FINE	$7500-10,000

FINE EXAMPLE PRICE HISTORY

Depreciating in 1980s-90s. Now stable
2000-2010 RETURN 2%

1 9 7 9
PONTIAC 10TH ANNIVERSARY TRANS AM

Another commemorative Firebird, this one marking the first decade of Pontiac's still-successful ponycar. Officially priced at around $10,600, but the announced low production and the model's perceived historical significance created a rash of speculation (classified ads appeared shortly after introduction listing $30,000 asking prices). Equipped

1979 10th Anniversary Trans Am coupe

with power everything, it also featured a distinctive silver and charcoal paint treatment, T-bar roof with silver-tint glass hatches, silver interior with leather upholstery, the heavy-duty WS-6 handling package, and "Turbo Alloy" wheels designed by John Schinella and made by Appliance. The Tenth Anniversary Trans Am (TATA) came with the Oldsmobile built 403 V-8 that was standard in the normal versions, but Pontiac had saved some of its own 400-cid V-8s with higher horsepower just for this special birthday model, even though the engine had been dropped for '79. A very few 400s were teamed with a four-speed manual gearbox, making this the most desirable drivetrain of the lot. Too new to be in wide circulation on the collector market, but a car that's sure to go up in value as the years pass and the brilliant second-generation Firebird becomes a more distant memory.

FOR As for 1976 Firebird Limited Edition Trans Am

AGAINST As for 1976 Firebird Limited Edition Trans Am

PRODUCTION

7500

SPECIFICATIONS

Length (in.)	196.8
Wheelbase (in.)	108.2
Weight (lbs)	approx. 3600
Price (new)	$10,619 base

ENGINES

cid/type	bhp[1]	years
400/ohv V-8	220	1979
403/ohv V-8	185	1979

[1]SAE net

PRICES

FAIR	$2700-5000
GOOD	$5000-7000
FINE	$7000-10,000

FINE EXAMPLE PRICE HISTORY

Depreciating through 1980-90s, fine examples now stable.
1990 $15,000
1994 $8000
2000-2010 RETURN 2%

1 9 8 3 - 8 7
PONTIAC 6000STE

An honest American attempt at a "Euro-style" sports sedan, a

1983 6000STE sedan

response to mid-Eighties "yuppie" demand for same. Based on Pontiac's A-body front-drive 6000 family sedan (new for '82), it boasted a smooth 2.8-liter V-6 instead of a rough "big four," plus no-cost automatic transmission, high-rate suspension, low-key exterior, driver-oriented buckets/console interior, and extra conveniences like a roadside emergency kit and a trunk-mounted air compressor. STE meant "Special Touring Edition," and the car lived up to that name. Replaced by an all-wheel-drive version by 1989. Not likely to be collected for some time yet, but it's an interesting semi-certain long shot prospect.

FOR Fairly uncommon newer Pontiac • Smooth performance • Good handling • Restrained yet sporty appointments • Used-car cheap

AGAINST Little collector interest at present • Acceleration not thrilling • As problem-prone as any period GMer • Gruesome gauge grouping

PRODUCTION
1983 6719 **1984** 19,236 **1985** 22,728 **1986** 26,299 **1987** 8802

SPECIFICATIONS
Length (in.)	188.7
Wheelbase (in.)	104.9
Weight (lbs)	2823-3035
Price (new)	$13,572-18,100

ENGINES
cid/type	bhp	years
173/ohv V-6	135	1983-87

PRICES
Still depreciating. Current range $1500-4000
2000-2010 RETURN 0%

1984-88
PONTIAC FIERO SE & GT

The sportiest of Pontiac's daring but doomed mid-engine two-seater coupes. It became famous—infamous really—for flash engine fires (addressed by a recall) and for pioneering the "driveable space frame" with plastic outer panels adopted by GM's minivans and Saturn subcompacts after Fiero's demise. SE was the original enthusiast's Fiero, with a standard 2.8-liter V-6 (versus lesser models' four), plus uprated suspension. The GT arrived during model-year 1985 with a more aggressive nose (derived from that of the '84 Fiero that paced the Indy 500), plus rear spoiler, mellow exhaust system, and "ground effects" body addenda. This package *sans* V-6 became the '86 SE, while that year's GT switched from notchback to imitation fastback styling via a "flying buttress" roofline, plus a new tail. A close-ratio five-speed transaxle, GM-built to a German Getrag design, became available in June. Fiero belatedly received its own unique suspension hardware for '88, ousting the previous collection of Chevette/X-car parts, plus improved manual shift. But after spending $30 million on this update, GM pulled the Fiero's plug, ostensibly because the car was unprofitable at its lower than projected sales volume. As the best and the last, '88 GTs should "go collectible" first, though perhaps not strongly and not for some time. Earlier V-6 models will take even longer, except possibly for the limited run of replica '84 Indy Pace Cars. Four-cylinder Fieros likely won't make it at all.

FOR Another interesting, semi-successful modern Pontiac • Inexpensive • Good '88 ride and handling

AGAINST Mediocre acceleration (too heavy for this V-6) • Cramped cockpit • Poor driving position and outward vision • Noisy • A rough-rider (except '88) • Workmanship variable and sloppy

PRODUCTION
1984 SE 67,671 **1985 SE** 24,734 **GT** 22,534 **1986 SE** 32,305 **GT** 17,660 **1987 SE** 3875 **GT** 15,968 **1988 GT** est. 5000

SPECIFICATIONS
Length (in.)	162.7
Wheelbase (in.)	93.4
Weight (lbs)	2465-2783
Price (new)	$9599-13,999

ENGINES
cid/type	bhp	years
151/ohv V-6	130-135	1984-88

PRICES
Still depreciating. Current range $1250-7500.
2000-2010 RETURN 0%

1987 Fiero GT

1986-89
PONTIAC SUNBIRD TURBO GT CONVERTIBLE

Likely the one real collector's item in the vast GM army of front-drive J-car subcompacts besides Chevy's V-6 Cavalier Z24 convertible—and then only as liveliest of Pontiac's small open-air models. Those began with a normally aspirated four-cylinder job for 1984; turbo power and sporty GT features were combined two years later. Styling and equipment were updated almost annually in these years—as they had to be to keep this basic 1982 design competitive. But sporty-ish lower-priced Sunbirds stole some of the GT's thunder and, no doubt, some of its sales. The GT Turbo convertible was dropped after 1989, though a turbo coupe and a non-turbo ragtop persisted. A surprisingly rare late-model Poncho, but strictly a long-shot investment for the foreseeable future, though it won't tie up much capital and offers cheap daily-driver fun in the meantime.

✚ FOR Good performance plus reasonable mpg • Top-down allure • Fairly rare yet bargain-priced • Fun to drive • Sunbirds still current, so ample parts/service backup

1986 Sunbird Turbo GT convertible

▬ AGAINST Nasty turbo lag and exhaust boom • So-so convertible rigidity • Not very roomy • Little collector interest • Values won't bottom out for some time

PRODUCTION
1986 1268 **1987** 1505 **1988** est. 2000 **1989** est. 2000

SPECIFICATIONS
Length (in.)	173.7-178.2
Wheelbase (in.)	101.2
Weight (lbs)	2645-2577
Price (new)	$14,399-16,899

ENGINES
cid/type	bhp	years
112/ohc I-4 T[1]	150	1986
121/ohc I-4 T[1]	165	1987-89

[1]Turbocharged

PRICES
Still depreciating. Current range $2000-5000.

1986
PONTIAC 2+2 GRAND PRIX AERO COUPE

A one-year "homologation special" based on the 1978-vintage Grand Prix notchback, with unique styling features intended to make Richard Petty and other Pontiac pilots more competitive in the "aero war" then raging on NASCAR supertracks. Seeking to reduce aerodynamic drag, designer Terry Henline crafted a laid-back twin-nostril grille, huge "bubbleback" rear

1986 2+2 Grand Prix Aero Coupe

# PONTIAC

window, and four-inch-high spoiler on a decklid shortened to match the big backlight. All this helped the racers somewhat, but the 200 street cars built to qualify the model as "production" ran only a mild 5.0-liter V-8 with throttle-body fuel injection, linked to a four-speed automatic transmission. Happily, the street cars also came with gas-filled shocks, high-rate springs, beefier sway bars, and 15x7 Rally wheels with Eagle GT performance tires. Other pluses were fast-ratio power steering, extra gauges, air, cruise control, power windows and door locks, front bucket seats, center console, and a leather-rim tilt steering wheel. A cousin to Chevrolet's similarly styled Monte Carlo SS, the 2+2 was initiated first, but not produced as long. Not really a successor to the brash late-Sixties 2+2s, but a modern semi-custom with obvious collector appeal.

FOR Rarity • "NASCAR connection" • Well equipped • Strong value appreciation possible, though distant

AGAINST Not that pleasant to drive • Acceleration doesn't match "race-car" looks • Semi-handbuilt, and looks it

PRODUCTION
200

SPECIFICATIONS

Length (in.)	201.9
Wheelbase (in.)	108.1
Weight (lbs)	3530
Price (new)	$18,214

ENGINES

cid/type	bhp	years
305/ohv V-8	165	1986

PRICES

FAIR	$3000-4000
GOOD	$4000-6000
FINE	$6000-8000

PRICES

2000-2010 RETURN 0%

1987-92
PONTIAC FIREBIRD TRANS AM GTA

Hottest of the third-generation Firebirds first seen for 1982, introduced as a 1987 package option for the "normal" 5.0-liter Trans Am. A 350 V-8 would have been a small-block 20 years before, but was big muscle in the late '80s. The GTAs arrived with throttle-body fuel injection and 210 horses; a switch to more efficient multiport injection added 15 for '88, and by '91 gained a further 15 via reduced-friction measures. The GTA was always distinguished from regular Trans Ams by special badges and trim and extra standard equipment including the biggest rolling stock in Firebird's arsenal. Limited to four-speed overdrive automatic, but that wasn't a big performance drawback. Year-to-year changes mainly involved equipment, with a driver's airbag a notable addition for 1990.

FOR Modern muscle/ponycar with looks and performance to match • Still current, so no-sweat parts/service • Subject to used-car pricing

AGAINST Fuelish • Ride rock-hard • Patchy detail workmanship • Rather cramped for exterior size • Collectibility far from certain

PRODUCTION
est. 10,000 each year

SPECIFICATIONS

Length (in.)	191.6
Wheelbase (in.)	101.0
Weight (lbs)	3435-3490
Price (new)	$19,300-25,880

ENGINES

cid/type	bhp	years
350/ohv V-8	210-240	1987-92

PRICES

Still depreciating. Current range $4000-10,000
2000-2010 RETURN 1%

1989 Firebird Trans Am GTA coupe

1988-89
PONTIAC 6000STE AWD

All-wheel-drive successor to the front-drive 1983-87 STE, though both were offered during 1988. A new permanently engaged drive system was connected to a stroked 3.1-liter overhead-valve V-6 that gave no more power than the front-driver's 2.8; a pity, because curb weight was somewhat higher. Also on hand were new antilock brakes as standard, plus an enlarged fuel tank and an independent rear suspension (borrowed from the then-new W-body Grand Prix) to replace the previous dead-beam axle. The AWD model took over entirely for 1989, but the front-drive STE was essentially preserved in a mid-line S/E sedan (and wagon). For 1990, the STE label was applied to the top mid-size Grand Prix sedan, and the AWD 6000 became an S/E.

FOR As for 1984-87 STE

AGAINST As for 1984-87 STE

PRODUCTION

NA, but limited

SPECIFICATIONS

Length (in.)	188.7
Wheelbase (in.)	104.9
Weight (lbs)	3100
Price (new)	$22,599

ENGINES

cid/type	bhp	years
191/ohv V-6	135	1988-89

PRICES

Still depreciating. Current value up to $4500.
2000-2010 RETURN 0%

1989 Grand Prix Turbo coupe

1988-90
PONTIAC GRAND PRIX TURBO

A symbol of how Pontiac returned to profitability in the '80s by returning to solid performance. Essentially the W-body front-drive Grand Prix coupe introduced for 1988, with the sportiest SE trim and a turbocharged version of the mainstay 3.1-liter V-6. Engineered in conjunction with the McLaren division of ASC, Inc., and complete with all the expected go-faster goodies including Pontiac's heavy-duty Y99 suspension option, lacy-spoke wheels with high-speed 245/50ZR16 "gatorback" tires, all-disc brakes (with standard antilock control after '88), and aerodynamic lower-body "cladding" in ding-resistant plastic. Also featured were fog lights, gold-tint "Turbo" badges, a busy dash with full instrumentation (and head-up display speed readout after '88), plus air and an ear-blaster stereo system. Leather upholstery and a tilt/slide moonroof were the only options. Rather gimmicky in form and function, but a strong, refined performer with athletic moves. Sufficiently rare to bear watching as a future collectible.

FOR Fine go (7.6 seconds 0-60) • Tenacious cornering • Relaxed high-speed cruiser • Lavishly equipped • Used-car pricing prevails

AGAINST Looks a bit "boy racer" • Dash woefully overstyled • No real collector interest likely before 2010

PRODUCTION

1988 est. 1000 **1989** est. 1000 **1990** est. 1500

SPECIFICATIONS

Length (in.)	193.9
Wheelbase (in.)	107.5
Weight (lbs)	approx. 3400
Price (new)	$26,016-28,000

ENGINES

cid/type	bhp	years
191/ohv V-6	205	1988-90

PRICES

Still depreciating. Current values to $6000.
2000-2010 RETURN 0%

1989 6000STE AWD sedan

1989 20th Anniversary Trans Am coupe

1989
PONTIAC 20TH ANNIVERSARY TRANS AM

Latest in the long string of limited-edition commemorative Trans Ams, this time honoring both the T/A's 20th birthday and the selection of this special model as 1989 Indy 500 Pace Car. Though Pontiac built replicas for the public, it proudly claimed that any of these 'Birds could handle pace-car duty without engine modifications. All the odder, then, that power was not by Pontiac but by the blown Buick V-6 from the late Regal GNX, albeit physically slimmed via different heads (borrowed from a non-turbo version) to fit the T/A's engine bay. Stated horsepower was 250—25 more than the GTA's 5.7-liter V-8—and actual horses were close to 270 by most estimates. Despite a mandatory four-speed overdrive automatic, this Trans Am was capable of well under 6 seconds 0-60, a sub-13-second standing quarter-mile, and over 155 mph flat out. Full-tilt standard equipment abounded, as expected in such cars, including T-top roof, ultra-firm WS6 sport suspension with 16-inch lacy-spoke alloy wheels and wide 245/50 performance tires,

GTA "aero" body addenda, air conditioning, camel-color interior with "articulated" front seats, cruise control, power windows and door locks—and the traditional regalia decals for use at the owner's discretion. Not many were built, and the "race-ready" image could mean astronomical asking prices in the future, so be wary if this is your kind of car.

✚ FOR As for 1987-90 GTA, plus greater exclusivity and higher performance • It looks like prices are back on the rise

■ AGAINST As for 1987-90 GTA, plus unruly "rush acceleration" when turbo kicks in

PRODUCTION
approx. 1500

SPECIFICATIONS

Length (in.)	191.6
Wheelbase (in.)	101.0
Weight (lbs)	3400
Price (new)	$25,000

ENGINES

cid/type	bhp	years
231/ohv V-6[1]	250	1989

[1]Turbocharged

PRICES

FAIR	$10,000-12,000
GOOD	$12,000-15,000
FINE	$15,000-20,000

FINE EXAMPLE PRICE HISTORY

1990 $25,000		**1994** $15,000	

1998 $19,000
2000-2010 RETURN 2%

1991-92
PONTIAC FIREBIRD CONVERTIBLE

1991 Firebird convertible

These were lightly facelifted "interim" models designed to bridge the 1990 Firebirds and the all-new '93s. Ragtops were available in base, Formula, and Trans Am form. Three engines were available: 140-bhp 3.1-liter V-6; 170-bhp 5.0-liter V-8; and a 205-horse 5.0-liter V-8. (Firebird's top engine, a 5.7-liter V-8 producing 240 horsepower, was not available with convertible Firebirds.) Despite its "boy racer" image, Firebird has legions of fans, and although these convertible 'birds are neither flashy nor historically

1993 Firebird Trans Am coupe

significant, they will be collectible.

➕ FOR Acceleration • Convertible body style • Handling & roadholding • Enduring Firebird appeal

➖ AGAINST Thirst • Noise • Ride

PRODUCTION

1991 1505 **1992 base** 950 **1992 Trans Am** 555

SPECIFICATIONS

Length (in.)	195.1
Weight (lbs)	3280
Wheelbase (in.)	101.1
Price (new)	$19,159-23,875

ENGINES

cid/type	bhp	years
191/ohv V-6	140	1991-92
305/ohv V-8	205/230	1991-92

PRICES

Still depreciating. Current range: $5000-8000
2000-2010 RETURN 0%

1993-2000

PONTIAC FIREBIRD

Similar to the Chevrolet Camaro in mechanical specifications and driving feel, the Firebird offered slightly different styling and trim. Firebird's (and Camaro's) base model was initially powered by a 3.4-liter V-6. Mid-year '95 GM's venerable, but excellent, 3.8-liter V-6 was available as an option. In '96 the 3.8 was the base model's standard engine. Smooth running with 200-horsepower, the base V-6 was a good alternative for those not wanting the expense and high insurance premiums of the V-8 Formula and Trans Am models.

➕ FOR As for 1993-00 Chevrolet Camaro SS/Z28

➖ AGAINST As for 1993-00 Chevrolet Camaro SS/Z28

PRODUCTION[1]

1993 26,893 **1994** 45,028 **1995** 42,302 **1996** 32,622 **1997** 32,524 **1998** 31,692
[1]U.S. calendar year sales.

SPECIFICATIONS

Length (in.)	193.3-197
Weight (lbs)	3232-3455
Wheelbase (in.)	101.1
Price (new)	$13,995-30,700

ENGINES

cid/type	bhp	years
207/ohv V-6	160	1993-95
231/ohv V-6	200	1995-00
350/ohv V-8	275-305	1993-97
346/ohv V-8	305-327	1998-00

PRICES

Still depreciating, governed by model year.
Current range $7000 30,000
2000-2010 RETURN 0%

1994

PONTIAC 25TH ANNIVERSARY TRANS AM

Although a less-potent performer than the awesome 20th Anniversary Trans Am of 1989, this 1994 limited edition (1500 units) delivered gruff, American-style muscle in a striking package. A cosmeticized Trans Am GT, the car ran with a 275-bhp detuned

1994 25th Anniversary Trans Am coupe

variant of Corvette's LT1 5.7-liter V-8, running through a 6-speed manual transmission. Four options were available: automatic transmission, CD player, T-top, and traction control. This was a fun car, but "anniversary" decals, badges, and embroidery do not necessarily indicate high future collectibility.

✚ **FOR** Acceleration • Handling & roadholding • Firebird appeal

■ **AGAINST** Thirst • Noise • Ride • Still a used car • Likely to have been driven hard • A "factory collectible," and a half-hearted one at that

PRODUCTION

1994 coupe 1250 (est) **1994 convertible** 250 (est)

SPECIFICATIONS

Length (in.)	197.0
Weight (lbs)	3455-3668
Wheelbase (in.)	101.1
Price (new)	$22,504-27,964

ENGINES

cid/type	bhp	years
350/ohv V-8	275	1994

PRICES

Still depreciating. Current range: $13,000-23,000.
2000-2010 RETURN 0%

1999 PONTIAC FIREBIRD TRANS AM 30TH ANNIVERSARY SPECIAL EDITION

Pontiac celebrated Firebird's 30th year by producing 1065 coupe and 535 convertible Anniversary Special Editions. An anniversary edition is only as good as the car it's based upon. Pontiac used its Trans Am with WS6 Ram Air Perfornmance and Handling Pkg. This car had functional hood scoops that helped up horsepower to 320. Suspension and tires were upgraded to make the most of the extra power. The 30th Anniversary

Pkg added: white paint with blue stripes, blue top (convertible), badging, white leather interior, articulating bucket seats, numbered dashboard plaque, polished alloy wheels with blue clearcoat accents.

✚ **FOR** Ran Air performance • 30th Anniversary more subtle than previous editions

■ **AGAINST** Not for those who don't like white cars

PRODUCTION

1999 coupe 1065 **1999 coupe** 535

SPECIFICATIONS

Length (in.)	193.3
Weight (lbs)	3340-3492
Wheelbase (in.)	101.1
Price (new)	$30985-35055[1]

[1]Includes required option packages.

ENGINES

cid/type	bhp	years
346/ohv V-8	320	1999

PRICES

Depreciating.Current range to $23,000.
2000-2010 RETURN 0%

1999 Firebird Trans Am 30th Anniversary Edition convertible

1950-55
PORSCHE 356

Essentially a sports version of Dr. Ferdinand Porsche's Volkswagen Type 1 (Beetle) design, and the first production model from his independent carmaking firm. Based closely at first on the VW's platform chassis and running gear, including its rear-mounted air-cooled flat-four engine and swing-axle rear suspension. It gradually became more distinct mechanically, stronger, faster, and more versatile. Offered in several body types, of which the 2+2 coupe with squat, stubby, rounded lines was most numerous. A cabriolet and an open roadster, called Speedster, were added later. Early 356s (through late 1951) are identifiable by their divided, slightly vee'd windshield. Generally top-quality construction, but handling was tricky near the limit. High-geared for flat-out cruising like the Beetle.

+ FOR First of the Porsches • Good economy and roadability • Compact and manageable • Fine construction quality • A Milestone car

■ AGAINST Controversial styling (most like it, though) • Tricky handling • Limited performance • Mechanical and body parts now in short supply

PRODUCTION
10,678

1954 356 Speedster

SPECIFICATIONS

Length (in.)	152.0-156.0
Wheelbase (in.)	82.7
Weight (lbs)	1675-1830
Price (new)	$4200 U.S. for 1952 coupe; $4400 for 1954 Super; $3500 for 1955 1500S Speedster

ENGINES

cc/type (cid)	bhp[1]	years
1086/ohv flat 4 (66)	40	1950-54
1286/ohv flat 4 (79)	44	1951-54
1290/ohv flat 4 (79)	55	1953-55
1488/ohv flat 4 (91)	55/70	1952-55

[1]DIN

PRICES

FAIR	$8500-16,000
GOOD	$16,000-30,000
FINE	$30,000-45,000

FINE EXAMPLE PRICE HISTORY

1982 $8000		**1990** $28,000	
1994 $22,900		**1998** $45,000	
1982-2000 RETURN 11%			
2000-2010 8%			

1956-59
PORSCHE 356A

A modified version of the original 356, with a curved one-piece windshield, more specialized Porsche components, and a greater choice of engines. A new powerplant was the race-bred, dohc Carrera unit, intended mainly for competition or flat-out high-speed on-road use.

+ FOR As for Type 356, including Milestone ranking

■ AGAINST As for Type 356

PRODUCTION
20,626

1956 356A coupe

SPECIFICATIONS

Length (in.)	152.0-156.0
Wheelbase (in.)	82.7
Weight (lbs)	1800-2000
Price (new)	approx. $3700-3950 U.S.

for 1600 models; Carrera approx. $6000 in 1956

ENGINES

cc/type (cid)	bhp[1]	years
1290/ohv flat 4 (79)	44/60	1956-57
1582/ohv flat 4 (97)	50/75	1956-59
1498/dohc flat 4 (91)	90/100	1956-58

[1]DIN

PRICES

Cpe	
FAIR	$4000-7500
GOOD	$7500-15,000
FINE	$15,000-22,500
Rdstr	
FAIR	$20,000-26,000
GOOD	$26,000-35,000
FINE	$35,000-40,000
Cabrio	
FAIR	$5000-14,000
GOOD	$14,000-25,000
FINE	$25,000-37,000
Speedster	
FAIR	$17,000-35,000
GOOD	$35,000-42,000
FINE	$42,000-58,000
Carrera	
FAIR	$44,000-55,000
GOOD	$55,000-75,000
FINE	$75,000+

FINE COUPE PRICE HISTORY

1982 $8500		**1990** $30,000	

1994 $21,500		**1998** $22,000	
1982-2000 RETURN 6%			
2000-2010 6%			

1960-65

PORSCHE 356B/356C

Further developments of the original Type 356 design, identified by raised headlights and bumpers. A bit more interior room was found for the 356B by modifying the floorpan. Engine displacement now centered around 1.6 liters, and as before the air-cooled horizontally opposed four was offered in several stages of tune from the standard 60-bhp version on up through the 90-bhp Super 90 model and the dohc 115-bhp Carrera. A larger rear window and suspension refinements were also instituted. A hardtop coupe was briefly offered through 1961. For the 356C, disc brakes were fitted at each wheel, and equipment was again upgraded to keep pace with escalating prices. Top speeds were up to 110 mph for the 90-bhp over-head-valve engine, while the Carrera could see 120 mph. In its final year, the 356 was built alongside its eventual successor, the 911.

FOR As for 1949-55 Type 356 and 1955-59 Type 356A, plus more performance and refinement, better equipment and handling • Milestone status

AGAINST As for 1949-55 Type 356 and 1955-59 Type 356A

PRODUCTION

356B 25,834 (1959-63) **356C** 16,674 (1963-65)

SPECIFICATIONS

Length (in.)	152.0-156.0
Wheelbase (in.)	82.7
Weight (lbs)	1950-2080
Price (new)	approx. $4100-4300

U.S. for "Normal" and Super 90 models

ENGINES

cc/type (cid)	bhp[1]	years
1582/ohv flat 4 (97)	50-95	1960-65
1588/dohc flat 4 (97)	105/115	1960-61

[1]DIN

PRICES

As per 1955-59 Porsche 356A with following ranges for the **Super 90: cpe,** $8000-18,000; **cabrio,** $18,000-32,000; **rdstr** $32,000-46,000.
2000-2010 RETURN 6%

1965 356C coupe

1962-64
PORSCHE CARRERA 2

The special high-performance race-and-rally version of the Type 356B/C, powered by a 2.0-liter enlargement of the dohc Carrera engine, hence the model designation. Very fast, with a top speed of up to 130 mph, and its beefed-up disc brakes helped keep the performance in check. Built with various body types, including some with styling by Zagato of Italy. Noisy, temperamental, and not meant for everyday road use.

FOR As for 1959-65 Type 356B/356C, plus race-car specifications

AGAINST As for 1959-65 Type 356B/356C, but more a racer than a road car and expensive to acquire and maintain

PRODUCTION
Type 356B 1810 (1962-63) **Type 356C** 2134 (1963-65)

SPECIFICATIONS
Length (in.)	152.0-156.0
Wheelbase (in.)	82.7
Weight (lbs)	2230
Price (new)	approx. $7600 U.S. in 1962

ENGINES
cc/type (cid)	bhp[1]	years
1966/dohc flat 4 (120)	130	1962-64

[1]DIN

1963 Carrera 2 356B coupe

PRICES
FAIR	$24,000-48,000
GOOD	$48,000-85,000
FINE	$85,000-120,000

FINE EXAMPLE PRICE HISTORY
1982 $10,000		**1990** $130,000	
1994 $116,000		**1987** $120,000	
1982-2000 RETURN 16%			
2000-2010 10%			

1965-69
PORSCHE 911

The all-new second-generation Porsche, originally announced as the Type 901. It retained the 356-series chassis layout, with all-independent suspension, four-wheel disc brakes, and a rear-mounted air-cooled engine with horizontally opposed cylinders. However, everything was new, including the all-steel monocoque body/chassis construction and thoroughly modern styling marked by a hood sloping down between prominent headlamps, ovoid side window shape, full-fastback roof, and sloping tail. Powered by a six instead of a four, the 911 was initially offered as a 2+2 coupe. For the 1967 model year it was supplemented by the "Targa," with a removable roof panel over the cockpit and take-out rear window that converted it into an open roadster with a fixed rollbar. Also for '67, a more powerful "S" model was added with 160 instead of 130 bhp. A detuned 911T (Touring) appeared the following year with 110 bhp, and the standard 911 was

1969 911S coupe

1965 912 coupe

renamed 911L (Luxe). Much faster than the 356s, with 130 mph available right from the first, more on later versions. The rear seat backrests were split, and could be folded down for additional luggage space, a good thing as there wasn't much in the nose. Noisier but more exciting than its predecessor, the 911 was still plagued by sudden oversteer in tight corners, a function of hanging the engine out back beyond the rear axle centerline. Besides the five-speed manual gearbox, a three-speed semi-automatic (dubbed "Sportomatic") was offered beginning with the '68 models. Updated for 1969 by a slight increase in wheelbase (achieved by moving the rear wheels further back) and adoption of wider wheels and tires to improve handling, which necessitated greater flare for the wheel openings. Mechanical fuel-injection replaced carburetors on the 911L and 911S to meet U.S. emissions requirements, and the 911L was redesignated 911E. The '69s were designated the B-series, superseding the A-series '68s.

FOR Timeless styling • Fast (especially 911S) • Parts no problem • Active Porsche club • Top-class construction and engineering • Wonderful driver's car • Good economy

AGAINST Engine noise • Tricky handling • Minimal storage space

PRODUCTION

36,533

SPECIFICATIONS

Length (in.)	164.0
Wheelbase (in.)	87.0/89.3 (1965-68/1969)
Weight (lbs)	2200-2300
Price (new)	approx. $7000 U.S. base price in 1967

ENGINES

cc/type (cid)	bhp[1]	years
1991/ohc flat 6 (122)	110-180	1965-68

[1]DIN

PRICES

Cpe
FAIR	$3500-6000
GOOD	$6000-9000
FINE	$9000-12,000

(Add 5% for Targa, 25% for 911S, 30% for 911S Targa.)

FINE COUPE PRICE HISTORY

1982 $7000	1990 $10,000
1994 $10,000	1998 $12,000
1982-2000 RETURN 3%	
2000-2010 5%	

PORSCHE 912/912E

Economy version of the 911, with the same basic body/chassis design but simplified furnishings, narrower tires, and two fewer cylinders. Initial late-Sixties models used the powerplant from the final 356C model, the 1600SC, good for over 120 mph given enough room. The 912 then vanished with introduction of the C-series 911 in 1969 and its place in the lineup was taken by the mid-engine VW-powered 914. But the concept was revived

1976 912E coupe

some seven years later as the 912E, this time with the 1971cc fuel-injected engine adopted from the 914, which wasn't selling that well. Curb weight somehow blew up by 400 pounds, but superior torque and a standard five-speed gearbox combined for small gains in acceleration and top speed over the original 912. Alas, unfavorable exchange rates rendered the E too costly for its performance, and Porsche took a very different tack in an "entry-level" car with 1977's new front-engine water-cooled 924.

➕ FOR As for contemporary 911s, plus somewhat simpler engines, better mpg, and lower asking prices now

➖ AGAINST As for contemporary 911s, but slower, and bound to be overshadowed by them

PRODUCTION[1]

1965 6440	**1966** 8700	**1967** 3239	**1968** 11,921
1976 2099

[1]Calendar year; 1968 total includes 1969 models

SPECIFICATIONS

Length (in.)	164.0/168.9 (912/912E)
Wheelbase (in.)	87.1 (1965-68), 89.3 (1969), 89.4 (1976)
Weight (lbs)	2140-2560
Price (new)	$4700-11,000 in U.S.

ENGINES

cc/type (cid)	bhp[1]	years
1582/ohv flat 4 (97)	102	1965-69
1971/ohv flat 4 (120.2)	90[2]	1976

[1]DIN [2]86 bhp SAE net for U.S. model

PRICES

912	
FAIR	$3000-6000
GOOD	$6000-8000
FINE	$8000-12,000
912E	
FAIR	$4000-5500
GOOD	$5500-7500
FINE	$7500-13,000

FINE 912 PRICE HISTORY

1982 $5000		**1990** $11,500
1994 $8500		**1998** $19,000
1982-2000 RETURN 5%		
2000-2010 5%		

1969-71
PORSCHE 911

The "C-series" 911 produced from August 1969. Its main distinction was a larger-bore engine giving a capacity of close to 2.2 liters and somewhat more power across the board. The main benefit, however, was increased torque that made the 911 easier and more relaxing to drive, especially in give-and-take city/suburban conditions. Brakes were also improved, and there were many detail mechanical and equipment changes. A ZF limited-slip differential was added as an option. As before, the low-power 911T used carburetors (now Zeniths instead of the previous Webers, however) while the 911E and S used fuel injection. The Targa body style was still available in each variation. Continued with a 2.4-liter version of the overhead cam flat-six after 1971.

➕ FOR As for 1965-69 911, plus better equipment and easier driveability

➖ AGAINST As for 1965-69 911

PRODUCTION

24,700

SPECIFICATIONS

Length (in.)	164.0
Wheelbase (in.)	89.3
Weight (lbs)	2250-2350
Price (new)	approx. $7000 U.S. list for 911E in 1969

ENGINES

cc/type (cid)	bhp[1]	years
2195/ohc flat 6 (134)	125-180	1969-71

[1]DIN

PRICES

FAIR	$3600-8000
GOOD	$8000-10,000
FINE	$10,000-13,000

FINE EXAMPLE PRICE HISTORY

1982 $7500		**1990** $16,000
1994 $16,000		**1998** $13,000
1982-2000 RETURN 3%		
2000-2010 3%		

1970 911E coupe

1 9 7 0 - 7 6

PORSCHE 914

A semi-successful attempt by Porsche to crack the mass market, marking a return to its early close collaboration with Volkswagen. Designed by Porsche, the 914 was powered by the air-cooled 1.7-liter pushrod flat-four from VW's 411 sedan series. It was mounted just behind the two-seat cockpit ahead of a 911 gearbox, which was turned around 180 degrees for this application. The unit steel body/chassis made some use of 911 pieces for its all-independent suspension, but styling and body panels were unique. Only one body style was offered, a notchback coupe with a lift-off targa-style roof panel. The grille-less front end featured flip-up headlamps. The cabin was wide but rather short, so seating was a bit cramped for larger persons. The interior bore some resemblance to the 911's, but made extensive use of VW bits (instruments, door hardware, and the like). For 1973, the engine was enlarged to 1971cc as on the VW 412, and offered more power and torque for greater low-speed flexibility. The balanced weight distribution from the mid-engine layout provided excellent handling and road-holding, and performance was good

(102 mph initially, 120 mph on later versions). Marketed in Europe as a "VW-Porsche," but sold exclusively as a Porsche in the U.S. Final assembly was done by the Karmann coachworks in Osnabruck, West Germany. Sales never lived up to expectations (though the 914 was popular in the States), perhaps because it was not viewed as a "real" Porsche by potential buyers. It was replaced by the front-engine, water-cooled 924 beginning with the 1976 model year.

✚ FOR Mid-engine layout • Decent sports car stowage space • Road manners • Open-air versatility • Good supply in U.S.

▬ AGAINST Horrible engine access • Middling performance for a Porsche • Limited cabin space • Rust-prone • Engine parts drying up in U.S.

PRODUCTION

115,596

SPECIFICATIONS

Length (in.)	158.0
Wheelbase (in.)	96.5
Weight (lbs)	2100
Price (new)	$3595 original U.S. list, rising to $5300 in 1973

ENGINES

cc/type (cid)	bhp[1]	years
1679/ohv flat 4 (102)	80	1970-73
1971/ohv flat 4 (120)	100	1973-76
1795/ohv flat 4 (110)	75	1974-75
[1]DIN		

PRICES

FAIR	$2000-3500
GOOD	$3500-5000
FINE	$5000-8000

FINE EXAMPLE PRICE HISTORY

1982	$2500	**1990**	$5000
1994	$6000	**1998**	$6000
1982-2000 RETURN 7%			
2000-2010 3%			

1 9 7 0 - 7 6

PORSCHE 914/6

A six-cylinder version of the "VW-Porsche" 914, and built by Porsche at Zuffenhausen. Powered by the 2.0-liter carbureted flat-six from the previous 911T, but mounted amidships. Wider light-alloy wheels and fatter tires were standard equipment to suit the larger engine's greater performance potential. Other differences compared to the four-cylinder model included slightly larger vented disc brakes, deluxe trim, and more complete instrumentation. Priced quite a bit higher than the 914, the 914/6 cost almost as much as a 911T, which had the advantage of "true" Porsche status in the eyes of many, a factor that undoubtedly hurt sales. As a result, it was dropped after only two years.

✚ FOR As for 1970-75 914, plus more performance and better equipment • Much rarer than the 914 in U.S.

▬ AGAINST As for 1970-72 914, plus

1970 914 Targa coupe

1970 914/6 Targa coupe

confused image from "mixed" parentage

PRODUCTION

3351

SPECIFICATIONS

Length (in.)	158.0
Wheelbase (in.)	96.5
Weight (lbs)	2070
Price (new)	approx. $6100 in U.S. in 1970

ENGINES

cc/type (cid)	bhp[1]	years
1991/ohc flat 6 (122)	110	1970-71

[1]DIN; 125 bhp gross in U.S. tune

PRICES

FAIR	$9000-12,000
GOOD	$12,000-16,000
FINE	$16,000-21,000

FINE EXAMPLE PRICE HISTORY

1982 $7500		**1990** $18,000	
1994 $18,000		**1998** $18,500	

1982-2000 RETURN 6%
2000-2010 5%

1972-73 PORSCHE 911

Continuation of Porsche's durable rear-engine sports car design, now with an enlarged (stroked) version of the familiar air-cooled flat six and fuel injection for all models. Length went up slightly for 1973 as Porsche more successfully than most met U.S. bumper impact regu-

lations with comparatively little change to overall appearance. Other changes for '73 included a small under-bumper front spoiler for the E and S models, and a rearranged shift pattern for the 911S 5-speed gearbox. Also offered as the Carrera RS, a street version of the racing Carrera that appeared in 1973, but not legally saleable in the U.S.

➕ **FOR** As for 1969-71 Type 911

➖ **AGAINST** As for 1969-71 Type 911

PRODUCTION

1972 5120 **1973** 5836 (U.S. calendar-year sales)

SPECIFICATIONS

Length (in.)	163.9/168.4 (1972/73)
Wheelbase (in.)	89.4
Weight (lbs)	approx. 2600
Price (new)	$10,160 U.S. for 1973 911S

ENGINES

cc/type (cid)	bhp[1]	years
2341/ohc flat-6 (143)	134-181	1972-73

[1]DIN

PRICES

911T	
FAIR	$3700-6000
GOOD	$6000-8500
FINE	$8500-12,500
911E	
FAIR	$4000-6500
GOOD	$6500-9000
FINE	$9000-14,200
911S	
FAIR	$4500-8000
GOOD	$8000-11,000
FINE	$11,000-16,500

FINE 911T PRICE HISTORY

1982 $10,000		**1990** $13,000	
1994 $13,000		**1998** $15,000	

1982-2000 RETURN 1%
2000-2010 even

1972 911S coupe

1974-77
PORSCHE 911

Again confounding those pundits who thought the 911 should have been retired by the mid-'70s, Porsche successfully updated the model for 1974 by another bore increase and a switch from Bosch mechanical to Bosch electronic fuel injection. The result was a modest gain in horsepower and acceleration with only a small penalty in fuel economy, both achieved while meeting the strictest ever U.S. emissions laws. Bumpers became more prominent starting with the '74s, basically the same style seen for a number of years thereafter. Model offerings were shuffled, with a base 911 replacing the previous T, the 911S substituting for the former mid-range E, and a new Carrera—with wider wheels and tires, modest tail spoiler, and bold bodyside lettering—taking over for the previous 911S. This non-turbocharged Carrera was essentially a U.S. version of the European RS minus its extra performance. For 1975, the line was pared to 911S and Carrera only. After that, only the S remained as Porsche introduced its Type 930 Turbo Carrera (later called simply Porsche Turbo) for 1976. It was still very much the same car it had been in earlier years, but cornering power and handling predictability both gradually improved.

1974 911 Targa coupe

➕ FOR As for 1969-71 Type 911, plus parts and service more easily available

➖ AGAINST As for 1969-71 Type 911

PRODUCTION[1]

1974 5120 (incl. 548 Carrera models) **1975** 5480 (incl. 576 Carrera models) **1976** 6486 (incl. 626 Turbo Carrera) **1977** 6226 (incl. 517 Turbo Carrera)
[1]All figures U.S. calendar-year sales

SPECIFICATIONS

Length (in.)	168.9
Wheelbase (in.)	89.4
Weight (lbs)	approx. 2600
Price (new)	$9950 U.S. in 1974, rising to $14,395 in 1977 for 911S

ENGINES

cc/type (cid)	bhp[1]	years
2687/ohc flat 6 (164)	143-167	1974-77

[1]SAE net

PRICES

911
FAIR	$4500-7500
GOOD	$7500-11,000
FINE	$11,000-15,500

911S
FAIR	$4800-8000
GOOD	$8000-12,000
FINE	$12,000-17,000

FINE EXAMPLE PRICE HISTORY

Depreciating until recently; prices presently stable.
2000-2010 RETURN 2%

1975-88
PORSCHE TURBO CARRERA/930/ 911 TURBO

Exciting, eminently collectible turbocharged version of Porsche's rear-engine 911, so heavily re-engineered as to merit a separate type number.

1976 911 Turbo coupe

Introduced as the Turbo Carrera coupe with markedly flared wheelarches, wide tires (wider still at the rear), and a prominent tray-like rear spoiler that's long been known as the "whale tail" among Porschephiles. Initially powered by the then-current 2.7-liter 911 flat six bored out to near 3.0 liters, fitted with an oil cooler and KKK turbocharger, and mated to a special wide-ratio four-speed gearbox (instead of the close-ratio five-speed to take advantage of the blown engine's prodigious torque curve). The chassis was suitably beefed up with Bilstein gas/oil shocks and other heavy-duty pieces to match the 5.0-second 0-60 mph and sub-14-second standing quarter-mile performance. Equipment was surprisingly lush for a high-performance sports car, so options were initially few (electric-sliding sunroof, limited-slip differential, heavy-duty starter, "Turbo" bodyside graphics). A 1978 name change to just Porsche Turbo was accompanied by a 3.3-liter engine with an air-to-air intercooler, plus cross-drilled four-caliper brakes (discs, of course) from the fabled mid-engine 917 endurance racer. Performance was little changed, with the bigger engine simply keeping pace with U.S. emissions standards and tighter new European limits then being imposed. Withdrawn from the U.S. market after 1979, though sales continued elsewhere. It was then revived for 1986 as the 911 Turbo with interim chassis improvements that made for safer, more predictable cornering; also

offered for the first time in the normal 911's semi-convertible Targa and new-for-'82 full Cabriolet models. "Turbo slant-nose modification option" for 1987 gave you the look of Porsche's late-'70s Type 935 racers for $24,000 (not counting the car!); this became a separate 930S model for 1988. It was revamped yet again for '91 on the much-modified 1990 Carrera 2 platform.

+ FOR Performance thrills aplenty • Surprising luxury and fuel economy • Stands boldly apart from other 911s • Fair rarity

− AGAINST Handling and performance demand respect and quick reflexes • Costly to maintain and restore • Even early models still quite expensive

PRODUCTION
est. 7500

SPECIFICATIONS

Length (in.)	168.9
Wheelbase (in.)	89.4
Weight (lbs)	2700-3850
Price (new)	$26,000-70,975 in U.S.

ENGINES

cc/type (cid)	bhp	years
2993/ohc flat 6[1] (183)	245/234[2]	1975-77
3299/ohc flat 6[1] (201)	265/253[2]	1978-85
3299/ohc flat 6[1] (201)	282[3]	1986-88

[1]Turbocharged [2]DIN (European version)/SAE net (U.S. version) [3]SAE net (U.S.version)

PRICES

FAIR	$13,000-35,000
GOOD	$35,000-42,000
FINE	$42,000-54,000

1978-83
PORSCHE 911SC

A refined evolution of Porsche's ageless rear-engine sports car. The previous 2.7-liter air-cooled flat six was enlarged to near 3.0 liters, essentially a normally aspirated version of the Type 930/911 Turbo powerplant. Also: a catalytic converter for U.S. models, standard front/rear anti-roll bars and power brakes, a new clutch-disc hub that forced moving the engine 30 mm rearward (though with no effect on handling), and cancellation of the never-liked Sportomatic semi-automatic transmission option. U.S. models became quite a bit plusher in this period, receiving standard air conditioning, power windows, and a center console for 1980; headlight washers, leather front seats, and an upgraded audio system for '82. Prices were boosted to suit, aggravated by a second energy crisis, a resulting deep new recession, and more roaring inflation. March 1982 saw introduction (at Geneva) of the long-rumored 911SC Cabriolet, Porsche's first true factory-built convertible since the last 356 model of

1979 911SC coupe

1982 928 coupe

1965, though the Targa semi-convertible was continued. All three body styles were updated to become 911 Carrera models from 1984 (see entry).

✚ FOR As for earlier 911s, plus even easier parts/service availability and somewhat lower prices

▬ AGAINST As for earlier 911s, but more common and somewhat less sought-after

PRODUCTION
NA

SPECIFICATIONS

Length (in.)	168.9
Wheelbase (in.)	89.4
Weight (lbs)	2740-2750
Price (new)	approx. $25,000-32,000 in U.S.

ENGINES

cc/type (cid)	bhp[1]	years
2993/ohc flat 6(183)	172	1978-83

[1]SAE net

PRICES

FAIR	$7400-12,000
GOOD	$12,000-18,000
FINE	$18,000-21,500

FINE EXAMPLE PRICE HISTORY

Depreciating slowly until recently.
1990 $28,000		**1994** $20,000	
1998 $20,000			
2000-2010 RETURN 4%			

1978-95
PORSCHE 928 SERIES

Erstwhile 911 replacement conceived in the early '70s as the first "all-Porsche Porsche," with nothing owed to the marque's beginnings in the humble Volkswagen Beetle. It was about as different from the 911 as it could be, with a front-mounted, water-cooled fuel-injected V-8 connecting to a rear transaxle (five-speed manual or optional Daimler-Benz three-speed automatic) with "Weissach" independent rear suspension (named for the home city of Porsche's research center) featuring "self-correcting" toe control. The rounded, heavy-looking 2+2 coupe body was designed by American Tony Lapine. An all-aluminum V-8 employed linerless silicon-etched bores as on Chevy's old Vega subcompact, though Porsche's construction proved infinitely more reliable. All-disc brakes, novel tilt steering wheel/instrument pod, and comprehensive equipment in all years. The evolutionary 928S bowed for 1980 with fortified suspension and more potent 4.7-liter engine; the latter was denied the U.S. until 1983, when the optional automatic shifted to a four-speed overdrive unit. A bored 5.0-liter V-8 with twin-cam heads and 32 valves arrived for '85, standard antilock brakes for '86. A restyled S4 ("fourth series") appeared for 1987 with a reshaped nose, smoother tail, less aero drag, and still more power. The GTS, introduced in 1993, was the final variation of the 928. The V-8, enlarged to 5.4 liters, put out 345 horsepower. The mildly revised styling was ever controversial, clothing a great modern GT of tremendous ability.

✚ FOR Deceptively fast (0-60: 6.3-7.0 seconds with manual) • Smooth, refined V-8 • Terrific high-speed handling • Solid German craftsmanship • Early models now relatively affordable • Excellent parts/service support

▬ AGAINST Love/hate looks • Thirsty • Choppy ride • Cramped cabin • Frequent electrical and mechanical maladies

PRODUCTION
4.5-liter 17,710 **4.7-liter** 16,777 **Others** NA

SPECIFICATIONS

Length (in.)	175.7-178.1
Wheelbase (in.)	98.3
Weight (lbs)	3300-3505
Price (new)	$26,00-82,260 in U.S.

ENGINES

cc/type (cid)	bhp[1]	years
4474/ohc V-8 (273)	218	1978-82
4644/ohc V-8 (285)	234	1983-84
4957/dohc V-8 (302)	288	1985-86
4957/dohc V-8 (302)	316/326	1987-92
5400/dohc V-8 (329)	345	1993-95

[1]SAE net for U.S. versions

PRICES

Prices range from $4500-10,000 for 1978 models to $19,000-29,000 for 1990 models.
2000-2010 RETURN 2%

1982-91
PORSCHE 944 SERIES

A refined derivative of the late-Seventies 924, and its one-time replacement as the "budget Porsche," though both models were sold for a time. It shared the 924's basic 2+2 "glasshatch" coupe body, all-independent suspension and front-engine/rear-transaxle layout, but used a Porsche-built slant four—effectively half of the big 928's V-8—instead of a 2.0-liter Audi unit. Fairly large four-cylinder displacement prompted adoption of Mitsubishi-licensed contra-rotating "balancer" shafts for smoothness (a feature originated by England's Frederick Lanchester some eight decades before). Wheelarches were "blistered" to contain wider rolling stock, and the cabin upgraded from the 924's rather spartan interior. Combined electronic ignition/fuel injection appeared for '84, a new-design dashboard for 1985 (replacing the inherited 924 panel), a companion Turbo model for 1986 with a more aggressive nose and lower-body styling. The mid-range non-turbo S was added mid-1986 with a twin-cam 16-valve cylinder head, bigger ports, and more efficient manifolding giving extra power over the base eight-valve engine. Antilock brakes became an S/Turbo option for '87, when the Turbo received standard dual airbags; the S offered those optionally, then as no-cost 1988 equipment. ABS became a line-wide standard for '89, when displacement was bumped to 2.7 liters for the base 944 and to 3.0 liters for a 16-valve S2 coupe, which adopted Turbo styling. The Turbo and base 944 then disappeared and a long-delayed 944 cabriolet joined the S2 coupe for 1990. As a lot, the 944 was a much better car than the 924, but still had a fair share of flaws—one reason, perhaps, why Porsche evolved it further into the 968 series of 1992.

⚡ FOR Fine performance/economy balance • Turbo go (about 6.1 seconds typical 0-60) • Go-kart handling, cornering • Terrific brakes (especially with ABS)

▬ AGAINST Cramped cockpit • Heavy manual steering • Build quality erratic and disappointing for a Porsche (actually assembled by Audi, save Turbo) • Successor 968 likely to overshadow 944 in future values and collector interest

PRODUCTION

NA

SPECIFICATIONS

Length (in.)	168.9
Wheelbase (in.)	94.5
Weight (lbs)	2900-3060
Price (new)	$18,450-50,300

ENGINES

cc/type (cid)	bhp[1]	years
2479/ohc I-4 (151)	143/147	1982-85
2479/ohc I-4 (151)	158	1988-89
2479/ohc I-4[2] (151)	217	1986-89
2479/dohc I-4[2] (151)	188	1986-88
2680/ohc I-4 (163.6)	162	1989
2990/dohc I-4 (182.5)	208	1989-91

[1]SAE net for U.S. models [2]Turbocharged

PRICES

Prices range from $3000-5500 for the 1983 model to $11,000-15,500 for the 1990 model and $13,000-19,000 for the 1990 S2 cabriolet.
2000-2010 RETURN even

1983 944 coupe

PORSCHE 911 CARRERA

Final development in the patient, sustained evolution of the classic rear-engine Porsche up to its historic 25th birthday. The main change was another enlargement of the evergreen air-cooled flat six, this time to 3.2 liters and 200 bhp courtesy of Bosch Motronic integrated ignition/fuel injection; further refinements added 14 horses for 1987-89. Still offered in coupe, Targa semi-convertible, and fully open Cabriolet body styles with five-speed overdrive manual transmission only. For 1989, Porsche added a 911-based evocation of the romantic mid-Fifties 356 Speedster with a similar cut-down windshield and side windows, skimpy soft top, restyled "beetle back" rear deck—and a stupendous exoticar price. Other Carrera changes included thicker brake rotors, standard fog lights and, Speedster excepted, a "Turbo Look" appearance option offering the panache and chassis prowess of the awesome 930 at an equally awesome price (over $25,000).

✛ FOR As for 1978-83 911SC, but rare one-year Speedster in a class by itself both as car and investment

◼ AGAINST As for 1978-83 911SC, but Speedsters rarely traded and cost the earth when they are

PRODUCTION
NA

SPECIFICATIONS
Length (in.)	168.9
Wheelbase (in.)	89.4
Weight (lbs)	2750-2950
Price (new)	$31,950-51,250

ENGINES
cc/type (cid)	bhp[1]	years
3164/ohc flat 6 (193)	200	1984-86
3164/ohc flat 6 (193)	214	1987-88

[1]SAE net for U.S. model

PRICES
Price ranges are $13,500-28,500 for the coupe, $14,000-29,000 for the Targa, and $16,500-34,000 for the cabriolet.
2000-2010 RETURN even

PORSCHE 959

The scarce, speedy, sophisticated all-wheel-drive 911 variant conceived for Europe's short-lived Group B "factory experimental" racing series. With wild-looking bodywork over a steel central structure, the 959 looked like an exaggerated 911 Carrera coupe, but was aerodynamically functional and rendered in lightweight materials, including high-tech Kevlar. Massive, low-profile tires wrapped

1988 959 coupe

around large antilock disc brakes were driven from a special short-stroke opposed six with dual KKK turbochargers operating sequentially, plus water-cooled heads, titanium con rods, and other premium internals. The drive system employed a six-speed gearbox with extra-low first—ostensibly for "off-road" use—and a front differential with a multiplate hydraulic clutch functioning as a differential; the normal rear diff was a locking limited-slip type. Front/rear torque apportioning was computer-controlled automatically or by one of four driver-selectable programs: "Traction" (both ends locked for maximum pull), "Ice" (50/50), "Wet" (40/60), and "Dry" (40/60 up to 20/80 in hard acceleration). Suspension departed from 911 tradition with all-around double wishbones and twin coil-over shocks (versus torsion bars, front struts, and rear semi-trailing arms). Shocks, also computer-controlled, offered soft, firm, and automatic damping modes plus three ride heights. Built in fairly plush "Comfort" and detrimmed "Sport" models, the latter lighter by 110-130 pounds. Both offered over 190 mph flat out, 0-60 in about 4 seconds, stupendous handling, and equally impressive low-speed tractability. A competition version, the 961, proved its ability by winning the punishing Paris-Dakar Rally in 1984 and '86.

Strictly a technical flagship, the 959 was never certified for U.S. sale—which only made Americans of means (or at least influence) want it all the more. A few did come Stateside, but most stayed in Europe. Dr. Wolfgang Porsche, youngest son of the firm's founder, got the first, in April 1987; the remainder of the deliberately limited, painstakingly built run was completed about a year later. For all the obvious reasons, this is a modern blue-chip automotive investment of the first rank.

➕ FOR Explosive performance • Safe-as-a-house road prowess • High exclusivity • Superb craftsmanship • Can't-miss investment

➖ AGAINST Stupendous trading prices now • Not readily on the market for quite awhile • No official U.S. parts/service backup

PRODUCTION

approx. 230 including prototypes and Type 961 competition models

SPECIFICATIONS

Length (in.)	168.9
Wheelbase (in.)	89.4
Weight (lbs)	2977/3088 (Comfort/Sport)
Price (new)	$230,000

ENGINES

cc/type	bhp[1]	years
2849/ohc flat 6[2]	450	1986-88

[1]DIN [2]Turbochargers

PRICES

Insufficient data.

1989-98
PORSCHE 911 CARRERA 4

Simplified, more reasonably priced series-production offshoot of the super-sophisticated 959, with a less involved all-wheel-drive system that still provided automatic torque apportioning to fit driving conditions (though with a normal 69-percent rearward bias). Accompanied by yet another enlargement of the traditional air-cooled flat six, this time let out to no less than 3.6 liters—and the first power steering in 911 history (a standard feature). Available in all three 911 body styles, but only with a five-speed manual transmission. Styling looked unchanged at first glance, but subtly reshaped front and rear ends improved aerodynamics, and the inner structure was so fully redesigned (mainly for easier manufacturing) as to have little in common with earlier 911 monocoques. Suspension was also modern-

1989 911 Carrera 4 coupe

1990 Carrera 2 cabriolet

ized with all-around coil-over shocks, front wishbones, and rear semi-trailing arms, ousting torsion bars, and rear swing axles at last. The Carrera 4 arrived with antilock all-disc brakes; standard dual airbags were added for 1990, when the companion rear-drive Carrera 2 models bowed at somewhat lower prices (see below).

✚ FOR Automatic all-wheel-drive traction and stability • Timeless 911 styling and enthusiast appeal • Torquey, tractable 3.6 engine • Traditionally strong 911 resale values

▬ AGAINST Not ever likely to be cheap • Close visual similarity to ordinary late-model 911s • Shift action still 911-vague and sticky • Some interior detailing surprisingly cut-rate for the price

PRODUCTION
NA

SPECIFICATIONS
Length (in.)	167.3
Wheelbase (in.)	89.5
Weight (lbs)	3200-3400
Price (new)	$69,500-78,350

ENGINES
cc/type (cid)	bhp[1]	years
3600/ohc flat 6 (219.7)	247/282	1989-98

[1]SAE net for U.S. models

PRICES
Market price of 1990 model in 2000 was $24,500-34,000 for the coupe and Targa, and $28,000-37,500 for the cabriolet.
2000-2010 RETURN 3%

1990-1996
PORSCHE 911 CARRERA 2

The "classic Porsche" renewed for the start of its second quarter-century. Essentially a rear-drive version of the new all-wheel-drive Carrera 4, with the same modernized suspension, enlarged engine, freshened appearance, and standard power steering. A Carrera 2 exclusive marked another first in 911 history: a fully automatic transmission option. This was called Tiptronic, referring to both its electronic shift control and a secondary gate (beside the main selector) with "+" and "-" positions that permitted "tipping" into higher and lower gears with the speed of a well-shifted manual gearbox. Standard dual airbags and antilock brakes were also per Carrera 4, with more comfort and convenience features than any regular 911 before. But still a genuine rear-engine Porsche, the most tractable ever, yet no less exhilarating to drive. Also the costliest regular 911 in history, though circumstances had by now forced Porsche to give up trying to be a "volume" producer and settle for being a "boutique" producer.

✚ FOR As for earlier 911s, but greater low-speed tractability, so easier to drive every day • Likely to appreciate within a decade

▬ AGAINST As for earlier 911s, but softer character • Tail-heavy handling still ready to surprise the unwary.

PRODUCTION
NA

SPECIFICATIONS
Length (in.)	167.3
Wheelbase (in.)	89.5
Weight (lbs)	3031-3150
Price (new)	$58,500-66,800

ENGINES
cc/type (cid)	bhp[1]	years
3600/ohc flat 6 (219.7)	247	1990

[1]SAE net for U.S. models

PRICES
Market price of 1990 model in 2000 was $23,000-33,000 for the coupe and Targa and $25,000-35,000 for the cabriolet.
2000-2010 RETURN 2%

1 9 9 5 - 9 8

PORSCHE 911 (993 SERIES)

Ferocious yet tractable update of the venerable 911, called "993" internally at Porsche. A new, aluminum-cast rear suspension was a major improvement; others included uprated brakes, quicker-ratio steering, and a traction-control system called Automatic Brake Differential (ABD). The 3.6-liter flat six produced 270 horsepower or up to 424 horsepower in the Turbo S, and the standard manual shift gained one forward speed, to six. The best collectible bet will be the Turbo S of which only 199 were sold in North America. The Turbo S interior gained carbon fiber accents and additional leather. Horsepower jumped from the Turbo's standard 400 to 424—a record for a production Porsche. A benchmark evolution of one of the world's greatest automobiles.

⊞ FOR Acceleration • Handling & roadholding • It's a Porsche • It's a 911

⊟ AGAINST Thirst • Understeer (Carerra 4)

PRODUCTION
1995 5277 **1996** 7254 **1997** 6223 **1998** 7982

SPECIFICATIONS
Length (in.)	167.7
Weight (lbs)	3065-3490
Wheelbase (in.)	89.4
Price (new)	$59,900-150,000

1996 911 Carrera coupe

ENGINES
cid/type	bhp	years
220/ohc flat 6	270/282	1995-98
220/ohc flat 6[1]	400/424	1995-97

[1]Turbocharged

PRICES
Governed by the used car market. Price ranges for 1995 models in 2000 were $38,000-48,000 for Carrera 2 coupe, $43,000-57,000 for Carrera 2 cabirolet, $40,000-50,000 for Carrera 4 coupe, and $45,000-57,000 for Carrera 4 cabriolet.
2000-2010 RETURN Depreciating

1 9 9 9 - 2 0 0 0

PORSCHE BOXTER

Much-anticipated, rear-drive convertible sports car was the new entry-level Porsche, base-priced at "just" $41,000 for 1999, and intended to compete with the Mercedes SLK and BMW Z3. Boxster's 2.5-liter flat six mated to standard 5-speed manual shifter produced lively performance: about 7.0 seconds 0-60 mph. A 5-speed "Tiptronic" shifter was optional. Model-year 1999 brought the noticeably more peppy Boxster S, with a 250-bhp 3.2-liter flat six. Porsche claimed 0-60 times of 5.9 seconds. Road manners of base or S were impeccable, the fun factor enormous.

⊞ FOR Acceleration • Steering & roadholding • Braking • It's a Porsche

⊟ AGAINST Stiff ride • Noise • Plastic rear window

PRODUCTION
1999 base 11909 **1999 S** 772

SPECIFICATIONS
Length (in.)	169.9-171.0
Weight (lbs)	2866-2943
Wheelbase (in.)	95.1
Price (new)	$39,980-49,930

1999 Boxter roadster

ENGINES

cid/type	bhp	years
153/dohc flat 6	201	1999-00
194/dohc flat 6	250	1999-00

PRICES

Current list prices
2000-2010 RETURN Depreciating

1956-57
RAMBLER HARDTOP SEDANS & WAGONS

First of the bigger, square-lined Ramblers from the new American Motors Corporation begat by the 1954 Nash/Hudson merger. They featured unit construction, per Nash tradition, on the 108-inch-wheelbase platform introduced with the first four-door Ramblers of 1954. Power was provided by an updated version of Nash's veteran small six as standard. Neat, if boxy, new styling featured Rambler's

first wrapped windshield and stepped "basket handle" rear roof. Tri-tone paint could be ordered to dress up top-drawer Customs. Strictly four-doors in these years, as the familiar 100-inch two-doors were dropped after '55 (only to be revived as 1958 Rambler Americans). Choices were pillared sedans and Cross Country wagons in Deluxe, Super, and Custom trim, plus a Custom hardtop sedan. All reappeared for '57, but the Custom wagon became a hardtop, plus a nifty small V-8 arrived at extra cost, and minor trim changes included a stylized "R" hood logo in place of Nash and Hudson badges. The last signaled Rambler's new status as a separate make—and the end of Nash and Hudson after '57. Though 1957's V-8 Rebel hardtop sedan remains more collectible than these models (see entry), pillarless Customs were more numerous to begin with and are thus cheaper today. Note, too, the '57 Super four-door hardtop, probably as rare now as that Rebel. Factory "continental kit" exterior spare tire is an option worth looking for on the hardtops.

✚ FOR Interesting, overlooked mid-

'50s hardtops • Cheap to buy, restore, and run • Comparatively scarce • V-8s pretty lively • Sixes thrifty • Fine club support

▬ AGAINST Rust-prone, so not that many around now • Relatively low value appreciation potential

PRODUCTION[1]

1956 79,166 **1957** 91,469
[1]All models; breakdown not available

SPECIFICATIONS

Length (in.)	191.1 (198.9 w/cont kit)
Wheelbase (in.)	108.0
Weight (lbs)	2936-3392
Price (new)	$2208-2630

ENGINES

cid/type	bhp	years
195.6/ohv I-6	120/135	1956-57
250.0/ohv V-8	190	1957

PRICES

FAIR	$875-2000
GOOD	$2000-3500
FINE	$3500-6600

FINE EXAMPLE PRICE HISTORY

1982 $2500	**1990** $5500
1994 $6500	**1998** $9000
1982-2000 RETURN 6%	
2000-2010 4%	

1956 Hudson Rambler Custom sedan

1957
RAMBLER REBEL

1957 Rambler Rebel hardtop sedan

A specially trimmed four-door hard-top in the Custom series, introduced as a mid-1957 offering. It belied Rambler's conservative economy image because of its 327 V-8 (from the last of the Big Nash and Hudson cars) and 9.5:1 compression ratio, good for 255 bhp and a 0-60 mph time of about seven seconds. A beefed-up driveline was matched by heavy-duty Gabriel adjustable shocks. A Bendix electric fuel injection unit was supposed to be offered as an option later, but never materialized. Styling was attractive and sporty, a mild facelift of the all-new '56 look and with a few touches unique to the Rebel. Among them was a chrome bodyside sweepspear filled with gold-colored anodized aluminum—not unlike the Plymouth Fury's, in fact. As a Rambler, this Rebel was a contradiction in terms, however, and went against the grain of George Romney's plans for sensible products. For 1958 all V-8-equipped Ramblers were called Rebel, but the biggest engine listed was a 250. The 327 came only in the longer-wheel-base Ambassador, which sold in limited numbers.

✚ FOR AMC's first performance car • Not yet noticed by much of the hobby, thus still quite affordable • Unique one-year-only model • Low production • Plenty of zip • Good club support

▬ AGAINST Special trim pieces in short supply • Rust-prone unless properly cared for • Not easily found

PRODUCTION
1500

SPECIFICATIONS
Length (in.)	191.1
Wheelbase (in.)	108.0
Weight (lbs)	3353
Price (new)	$2786

ENGINES
cid/type	bhp	years
327/ohv V-8	255	1957

PRICES
FAIR	$1500-3300
GOOD	$3300-5300
FINE	$5300-8800

FINE EXAMPLE PRICE HISTORY
1982 $2500	**1990** $6500
1994 $10,000	**1998** $11,000
1982-2000 RETURN 8%	
2000-2010 5%	

1958-62
RAMBLER AMBASSADOR

A stretched makeover of the 1956-57 Rambler originally intended as the '58 Nash and Hudson, but released as a Rambler, a name deemed better for sales. Styling was even more squared and important-looking than 1956-57: new lower-body sheetmetal with trendy quad headlamps and canted tailfins, all shared with the compan-

1960 Ambassador Custom sedan

ion 108-inch-wheelbase Rambler Six and Rebel series. Ambassadors, however, had nine extra inches between wheel centers—all ahead of the firewall—plus a more complex grille (often a love-it or hate-it affair), spiffier interior trim, and a standard 327 V-8. The last was AMC's own design, first offered in the flashy '57 Rebel and a bored-out cousin to that year's new 250-cid unit, which was continued in '58 Rebels. Detail trim changes attended to 1959, followed by facelifted 1960-61 models with rather odd faces but no semi-dogleg A-pillars. Styling became more conservative for '62, when ever-slow sales prompted AMC to consolidate the Ambassador with the 108-inch Rambler line (by then called Classic). Initial models were Super and Custom sedans and Custom hardtop sedans and wagons. There were also a few low-end Deluxe models for 1959-62, intended mainly for export. Hardtops were dropped after 1960, and the series hierarchy changed to Deluxe, Custom, and top-shelf "400" for 1962. Pillarless models are the obvious choices here, if you can find one, but the wagons appeal to some enthusiasts and all these cars are now rather uncommon. The production chart indicates just how rare some models are, and was supplied by the AMC Rambler Club.

➕ FOR Unusual premium Kenoshans • Fine V-8 engine and (invariably) automatic transmission (with pushbuttons 1958-59) • Not many survivors, yet still cheap

➖ AGAINST Rust-prone • Many parts as scarce as the cars • Styling not the greatest • Road manners aren't either • Ditto investment prospects today

PRODUCTION

1958 Super 4d sdn 2774 **4d wgn** 1051 **Custom 4d sdn** 6369 **4d wgn** 2742 **4d htp wgn** 294 **4d htp sdn** 340 **1959 Deluxe 4d sdn** 155 **Super 4d sdn** 4675 **4d wgn** 1782 **Custom 4d sdn** 10,791 **4d htp wgn** 1447 **4d wgn** 4341 **4d htp wgn** 578 **1960 Deluxe 4d sdn** 302 **Super 4d sdn** 3990 **4d wgn** 1342 **4d wgn 8P** 637 **Custom 4d sdn** 10,949 **4d htp** 1141 **4d wgn** 3849 **4d htp wgn** 435 **4d wgn 8P** 1153 **1961 Deluxe 4d sdn** 273 **Super 4d sdn** 3299 **4d wgn** 1099 **4d wgn 8P** 277 **Custom 4d sdn** 9269 **4d sdn** 831 (bucket seat) **4d wgn** 1099 **4d wgn 8P** 784 **1962 Deluxe 2d clb sdn** 45 **4d sdn** 421 **4d wgn** 77 **Custom 2d clb sdn** 659 **4d sdn** 7398 **4d wgn** 4302 **"400" 2d clb sdn** 459 **4d sdn** 15,120 **4d wgn** 6401 **4d wgn 8P** 1289

SPECIFICATIONS

Length (in.)	200.2/198.5/190.0 (1958-59/1960-61/1962)
Wheelbase (in.)	117.0/108.0 (1958-61/1962)
Weight (lbs)	3250-3595
Price (new)	$2587-3111

ENGINES

cid/type	bhp	years
327/ohv V-8	250/270	1958-62

PRICES

FAIR	$900-2000
GOOD	$2000-3500
FINE	$3500-6500

FINE EXAMPLE PRICE HISTORY

1982 $1200	1990 $5000
1994 $7500	1998 $6100

1982-2000 RETURN 11%
2000-2010 3%

RAMBLER AMERICAN CONVERTIBLE & HARDTOP

Sportiest of the final 100-inch-wheelbase Ramblers and arguably the most desirable now. The '61 Americans were essentially Nash's successful 1950-55 design as revived and updated for 1958, but with completely new outer sheetmetal by American Motors design director Edmund A. Anderson. The reskin did a good job of disguising 10-year-old bodies, but produced unfashionably stubby cars that looked small even for compacts, but they did get away from the old "bathtub" look. Mainstream offerings remained two- and four-door sedans and wagons, but a convertible was offered for the first time since 1954, newly reconfigured with roll-down door glass instead of fixed side-window frames. A hardtop coupe joined it in the top-trim series for '63. The ragtop was initially a Custom, then a "400," and finally a "440." The hardtop came for '63 as a bench-seat 440 and bucket-seat 440-H. All but the last carried AMC's smallest six in 125-horsepower form; the 440-H had the

1963 American convertible

138-bhp version from the intermediate Rambler Classic. Sporty body types notwithstanding, these cars have slim chance of becoming prized collectibles, certainly much less than their better-looking successors, but they merit consideration by budget-minded hobbyists as interesting and fairly uncommon cheap—and fun—wheels.

⊞ FOR Fun on a budget • Easy on gas • Do-it-yourself simple • Convertible's top-down allure • Hardtop's likely rarity • Ample support from two major clubs

◼ AGAINST Pedestrian performance • Rust-prone • Many body/trim parts hard to find • Modest appreciation potential • Boxy (if tidy) styling

PRODUCTION

1961 Custom conv 10,855 **conv** 2063 (bucket seats) **1962 400 conv** 13,497 **1963 440 conv** 4750 **2d htp** 5101 **400-H 2d htp** 9749

SPECIFICATIONS

Length (in.)	173.1
Wheelbase (in.)	100.0
Weight (lbs)	2550-2743
Price (new)	$2136-2369

ENGINES

cid/type	bhp	years
195.6/ohv I-6	125/138	1961-63

PRICES

Conv	
FAIR	$2000-4000
GOOD	$4000-6000
FINE	$6000-9000
Htp	
FAIR	$750-1500
GOOD	$1500-3000

FINE	$3000-5400

FINE CONVERTIBLE PRICE HISTORY

1982 $2500		**1990** $6000	
1994 $7000		**1998** $6700	
1982-2000 RETURN 8%			
2000-2010 5%			

1963-64
RAMBLER AMBASSADOR 880/990 TWO-DOORS

More special-interest AMC products now coming to the collector fore. The '63 Ambassadors, all-new except for drivetrains, remained V-8-only offerings, but lost their usual long chassis to share a trim new 112-inch-wheelbase platform with six- and eight-cylinder Rambler Classics. All featured clean, simple styling by AMC's Ed Anderson marked by curved side glass, plus AMC's usual unit construction with new one-piece "Uniside" door-frame assemblies. Billed as "The New Shape of Quality," the Classic/Ambassador won *Motor Trend's* "Car of the Year" honors, but the Ambassador won far fewer buyers and was duly cut from 10 models (in 880 and 990 series) to a single four-model line for '64. But that foursome included two glamorous new two-door hardtops,

AMC's first since Nash/Hudson days. The buckets-and-console 990-H version is by far the most collectible of these Ambassadors for obvious reasons, but there's nothing wrong with the standard '64 hardtop—or, for that matter, a pillared '63 two-doors, a few of which were fitted with bucket seats and floorshift.

⊞ FOR Trim good looks • Smooth standard V-8 • Fairly posh interiors • Pretty uncommon • Strong, active club support

◼ AGAINST Usual AMC tinworm worries • Many body/trim parts difficult • High dollar return unlikely

PRODUCTION

1963 880 2d clb sdn 41 **880 2d clb sdn** 1042 **990 2d clb sdn** 1764 **1964 990 2d htp** 1464 **990-H 2d htp** 2955

SPECIFICATIONS

Length (in.)	188.8
Wheelbase (in.)	112.0
Weight (lbs)	3110-3255
Price (new)	$2337-2917

ENGINES

cid/type	bhp	years
327/ohv V-8	250/270	1963-64

PRICES

FAIR	$625-2000
GOOD	$2000-3500
FINE	$3500-5700

FINE EXAMPLE PRICE HISTORY

1982 $1200		**1990** $4000	
1994 $7000		**1998** $6000	
1982-2000 RETURN 10%			
2000-2010 3%			

1964 Ambassador 990 hardtop coupe

1964-65
RAMBLER AMERICAN 440 HARDTOP & CONVERTIBLE

AMC's sportiest small two-doors rejuvenated with handsome new styling by Richard A. Teague. This was his first big project after taking over from Ed Anderson as AMC design domo—on a clever downsizing of the award-winning 1963 Classic/Ambassador platform, with the same curved side glass and "Uniside" one-piece door-frame assemblies. The redesign upped wheelbase six inches over 1961-63, but overall length only four, bringing much roomier interiors. Rear-seat width, for instance, increased a full foot. Drivetrains were as before, with higher standard horsepower in the bucket-seat 440-H hardtop coupe (optional elsewhere). Not the ultimate versions of these cars, but arguably the purest and certainly worthy budget collectibles. The American's '64 styling—mildly facelifted for '65—proved popular enough to win Teague a vice presidency, something he was proud of until the day he died.

FOR Elegantly simple lines, trim

1965 American convertible

and clean • Engines peppy yet miserly • Handy compact size • Pretty scarce now, yet still cheap • Enthusiastic club support

AGAINST The usual unibody tin-worm troubles • Some body and trim parts hard to find • Low-rate appreciators (like most AMC cars)

PRODUCTION
1964 440 2d htp 19,495 **440-H 2d htp** 14,527 **440 conv** 8907 **1965 440 2d htp** 13,784 **440-H 2d htp** 8164 **440 conv** 3882

SPECIFICATIONS
Length (in.)	177.2
Wheelbase (in.)	106.0
Weight (lbs)	2596-2750
Price (new)	$2133-2418

ENGINES
cid/type	bhp	years
195.6/ohv I-6	125/138	1964-65

PRICES
FAIR	$750-3000
GOOD	$3000-5000
FINE	$5000-6700

FINE EXAMPLE PRICE HISTORY
1982 $2500	1990 $5500
1994 $7000	1998 $6500

1982-2000 RETURN 6%
2000-2010 3%

1964
RAMBLER CLASSIC TYPHOON

A sporty limited-edition special based on AMC's first mid-size hardtop coupe. It was basically a pro-

1964 Classic Typhoon hardtop coupe

motional showcase for the firm's then-new "Torque Command" six, destined to be a company mainstay for the next 20 years. Equipped with buckets-and-console interior, two-tone exterior (black top over Solar Yellow body), black grille accents, and requisite badges; it was little different from regular Classics otherwise. Listed here as another little-known and overlooked period AMCer with high special-interest value, if not great appreciation potential.

FOR Scarce, special-interest hardtop • Good performance/economy balance • Convenient size for modern motoring

AGAINST Typical unibody rust bothers • Unique trim pieces difficult if not impossible to locate • Not a high appreciator despite rarity

PRODUCTION

2520

SPECIFICATIONS

Length (in.)	190.0
Wheelbase (in.)	112.0
Weight (lbs)	2818
Price (new)	$2985

ENGINES

cid/type	bhp	years
232/ohv I-6	145	1964

PRICES

FAIR	$1000-2100
GOOD	$2100-3800
FINE	$3800-6400

FINE EXAMPLE PRICE HISTORY

1982 $1900		1990 $5500	

1994 $8000		1998 $6500	
1982-2000 RETURN 8%			
2000-2010 3%			

1965-66
RAMBLER AMBASSADOR HARDTOPS & CONVERTIBLES

Reskinned continuation of the 1963-64 Ambassador, restored to a longer wheelbase than mid-range Classics. Badged as a Rambler for '65, as an "AMC" thereafter. Dick Teague's tasteful facelift featured stacked quad headlamps, a wide convex grille, straight chrome-edged fenderlines, and elongated rear decks. Only modest changes were seen for 1966, but hardtop coupes acquired aptly named "crisp-line" rear-roof contours. The '65s, part of AMC's "Sensible Spectaculars" line, offered essentially carry-over V-8s, but base power switched to the firm's new 232-cubic-inch six with 155 standard horsepower, or 145 as a credit option. Ambassador's first convertible, in the top-shelf 990 series, also made news that year. For 1966, the buckets-and-console 990-H hardtop was renamed DPL and stressed snob appeal over sportiness via extra exterior brightwork and luxury houndstooth-fabric interior trim. A bench-seat

990 hardtop was offered both years. Ambassador scored far better 1965-66 sales than in 1963-64, which confirms inherent rightness of this makeover.

FOR Conservative styling has held up pretty well • Smooth V-8 performance • Roomy • Fair rarity • Even the ragtops are cheap

AGAINST Low asking prices reflect limited appreciation prospects • Tinworm troubles • Body and trim parts increasingly scarce

PRODUCTION

1965 990 2d htp 5034 **conv** 3499 **990-H 2d htp** 6382 **1966 htp cpes** NA (total Ambassadors built: 34,222) **conv** 1798

SPECIFICATIONS

Length (in.)	200.0
Wheelbase (in.)	116.0
Weight (lbs)	3198-3462
Price (new)	$2600-2955

ENGINES

cid/type	bhp	years
232/ohv I-6	145/155	1965-66
327/ohv V-8	250/270	1965-66

PRICES

Htp	
FAIR	$800-2000
GOOD	$2000-3500
FINE	$3500-5600

FINE HARDTOP EXAMPLE PRICE HISTORY

1982 $2500		1990 $5000	
1994 $8000		1998 $6000	
1982-2000 RETURN 5%			
2000-2010 3%			

1966 Ambassador 990 convertible

1965 Classic 770 convertible

RAMBLER CLASSIC HARDTOPS & CONVERTIBLE

About the only collectible middle-size Ramblers between 1958 and '67 other than the '64 Typhoon hardtop (see entry), though these, too, are much like contemporary Ambassadors, which are generally more desired. Essentially the 1963-64 design with a rectilinear reskin similar to that of concurrent Ambassadors. The Classic's wheelbase was unchanged, however, so its hood remained shorter, overall proportions a little stumpier. A new convertible in the top-line 770 series for '65 was followed by a sporty '66 hardtop called Rebel, basically the previous year's bucket-seat 770-H model with a new "crisp-line" roof, loud checked upholstery, and special badges. As with the Ambassador, drivetrains were little changed from '64, but more closely shared with the senior line.

✚ **FOR** As for 1965-66 Ambassador, plus slightly better maneuverability and fuel economy • Club support

◼ **AGAINST** As for 1965-66 Ambassador

PRODUCTION

1965 770 2d htp 14,778 **conv** 4953 **770-H 2d**

htp 5706 **1966 770 2d htp** 8736 **conv** 1806 **Rebel 2d htp** 7512

SPECIFICATIONS

Length (in.)	195.0
Wheelbase (in.)	112.0
Weight (lbs)	3060-3169
Price (new)	$2436-2696

ENGINES

cid/type	bhp	years
232/ohv I-6	145/155	1965-66
287/ohv V-8	198	1965
327/ohv V-8	250/170	1965-66

PRICES

As per 1965-66 Rambler Ambassador conv and htp less 10%.

RAMBLER MARLIN

American Motors' attempt to cash in on the sporty fastback craze of the mid-60's. Essentially, it was a re-roofed version of the intermediate Rambler Classic, yielding "3+3" seating. Styling, created by Richard A. Teague, was first seen on a handsome 1964 show car, the Tarpon, based on the smaller Rambler American platform (which would have made it a 2+2). While its sweeping fastback looked good, it did not suit the larger-scale Classic, and was aggravated by that car's nose, which looked too short and stubby in relation. It came out shortly after the Plymouth Barracuda, so comparisons were inevitable. Though the Marlin had a nice optional bucket-seat interior, it lacked the Plymouth's fold-down rear seat. The Rambler nameplate was removed for the carryover '66 version, and for 1967 the Marlin was switched to the longer Ambassador chassis, which yielded more pleasing overall proportions. But it was too late—Marlin never really picked up enough buyer support to warrant continuing it. Besides, AMC had a more attractive

1965 Marlin hardtop coupe

sporty car ready in the '68 Javelin.

FOR Plush, bucket-seat interior • Decent performance with optional drivetrains • Historical oddity • Prices still low

AGAINST Rust a constant worry • "Distinctive" styling • Slow to appreciate

PRODUCTION

10,327

SPECIFICATIONS

Length (in.)	195.0
Wheelbase (in.)	112.0
Weight (lbs)	3234
Price (new)	$3100

ENGINES

cid/type	bhp	years
232/ohv I-6	155	1965
287/ohv V-8	198	1965
327/ohv V-8	270	1965

PRICES

FAIR	$1350-2700
GOOD	$2700-4000
FINE	$4000-5900

FINE EXAMPLE PRICE HISTORY

1982 $3100		**1990** $5500	
1994 $6500		**1998** $6500	
1982-2000 RETURN 4%			
2000-2010 3%			

1 9 6 6 - 6 9
RAMBLER ROGUE

Dick Teague's pretty little Rambler American hardtop in its buckets-and-console trim. It replaced the 1964-65 440-H as AMC's sporty compact for '66. Offered with six-cylinder engines only that year, and afterwards with AMC's efficient 290 V-8 in two stages of tune (2- and 4-bbl set-ups). These nicely trimmed little runabouts didn't change much in these years, though the '68 was the last to use the American badge and the '69 version is even more interesting historically as this was the last year for the Rambler nameplate. A Rogue convertible was offered for one year only, 1967, the last soft top in the American series. It's an extremely rare bird today—and still quite up to date in size, performance, and mileage, and quite affordable. And to our eyes, one of the nicest styling jobs ever done in Kenosha.

FOR Quite affordable • Styling • Sportiness • Mileage and low running costs • Peppy with V-8

AGAINST Unit construction rust worries • Little appreciation potential

PRODUCTION

1966 2d htp 8718 **1967 2d htp** 4249 **conv** 921 **1968 2d htp** 4765 **1969 2d htp** 3543

SPECIFICATIONS

Length (in.)	181.0
Wheelbase (in.)	106.0
Weight (lbs)	2630-2821
Price (new)	$2244-2611

ENGINES

cid/type	bhp	years
199/ohv I-6	128	1966-67
232/ohv I-6	145	1967-69
290/ohv V-8	200/225	1967-69

PRICES

FAIR	$800-1600
GOOD	$1600-2800
FINE	$2800-4700

(Add 33% for '67 conv.)

FINE HARDTOP PRICE HISTORY

1982 $2500		**1990** $5000	
1994 $5500		**1998** $6000	
1982-2000 RETURN 4%			
2000-2010 3%			

1967 Rogue hardtop coupe

1967 Rebel SST hardtop coupe

1967
RAMBLER REBEL SST

Renamed, redesigned replacement for the 1961-66 Classic; continued after '67 as the AMC Rebel (see entry). The Rebel name wasn't new, of course, but the styling was: Dick Teague's tastefully restrained interpretation of the flowing "coke bottle" look then all the rage. The SST convertible and hardtop coupe were the sporty top-liners (bucket seats optional) in a full Rebel range that continued the Classic's role as AMC's intermediate. Appearance was helped by a two-inch longer wheelbase than in 1963-66, but the senior Ambassadors wore Teague's new styling even better due to longer hoods that made proportions more balanced. A wide "venturi" grille, side-by-side quad headlamps, wedgy "delta" taillights and, on SSTs, fake "bullet" air scoops ahead of the rear

wheels distinguished Rebels from Ambassadors. Technical improvements included new 290 and 343 V-8s, the first in a new family of "thinwall" engines that would see wide application in future years, plus optional front-disc power brakes and weight-reducing Hotchkiss drive, ousting AMC's traditional torque-tube setup. Most Rebels were likely built with extra-cost automatic, but floorshift three- and four-speed manuals were available, and would be rare finds today on any SST (a name meant to convey images of that just-announced aeronautical marvel, the SuperSonic Transport). Despite modest production, these cars are not big-dollar appreciators, but they're among the more interesting and satisfying of later AMC models and still very affordable.

✛ FOR Styling pretty and long under-rated • Good six-cylinder economy, fine V-8 go • Handles better than Classics, especially with chassis options • Relatively roomy • Yours for a song • Strong club support

◼ AGAINST The usual AMC rust alert

• Build quality not to Classic standards
• Near-term profit-seekers needn't bother

PRODUCTION
1967 SST 2d htp 15,287 **conv** 1686

SPECIFICATIONS
Length (in.)	197.0
Wheelbase (in.)	114.0
Weight (lbs)	3110-3180
Price (new)	$2604-2872

ENGINES
cid/type	bhp	years
232/ohv I-6	145/155	1967
290/ohv V-8	200	1967
343/ohv V-8	235/280	1967

PRICES
Conv	
FAIR	$1350-3500
GOOD	$3500-4000
FINE	$4000-6900
Htp	
FAIR	$700-1900
GOOD	$1900-3200
FINE	$3200-5000

FINE CONVERTIBLE PRICE HISTORY
1982 $1750		**1990** $4000	
1994 $7000		**1998** $7000	
1982-2000 RETURN 9%			
2000-2010 3%			

RENAULT FLORIDE/ CARAVELLE

1968 Caravelle hardtop coupe

Sporty derivatives of Renault's tiny Dauphine: a close-coupled 2+2 hardtop and convertible. They shared underpan and running gear with the troublesome little rear-engine sedan, as well as its all-independent suspension, but concealed them with much prettier styling, by Italy's Allemano. Bodies and final assembly were handled under contract by Brissonneau & Lotz in France. Floride came first, then gave way in 1962 to the Caravelle with its squared-up nose, longer hardtop roof—and a name more saleable in California. The latter also boasted slightly better back-seat space from a radiator moved rearward. Slightly more performance (though still not much) was provided by a larger and more modern engine, borrowed from the new R8 sedan. A bored-out version from 1964 brought still better performance (top speed went from 75 to 90 mph), as well as a handier all-synchro gearbox. This was really Renault's answer to the VW Karmann-Ghia, just as the Dauphine and R8 battled the Beetle, but was far less successful in the U.S. and was never a big seller anywhere. U.S. imports doubtful after 1967, when the French firm's big Stateside push was the front-drive 16 hatchback sedan.

➕ **FOR** Tidy styling • Rather rare • Cheap • Frugal with gas

➖ **AGAINST** No performance • Tail-heavy, serious oversteer • Running gear not very reliable • Rust-prone • Hard to find • Little known or cared about in U.S.

PRODUCTION

NA

SPECIFICATIONS

Length (in.)	167.7
Wheelbase (in.)	89.0
Weight (lbs)	1680-1780
Price (new)	$2200 U.S. in 1967

ENGINES

cc/type (cid)	bhp[1]	years
845/ohv I-4 (52)	40	1959-62
956/ohv I-4 (58)	51	1962-63
1108/ohv I-4 (68)	55-58	1964-68

[1]Gross

PRICES

Conv	
FAIR	$1200-2000
GOOD	$2000-4500
FINE	$4500-7000
Cpe	
FAIR	$500-1000
GOOD	$1000-3000
FINE	$3000-5000

FINE CONVERTIBLE PRICE HISTORY

1982 $2750		**1990** $2750	
1994 $4500		**1998** $7000	
1982-2000 RETURN 6%			
2000-2010 2%			

RENAULT 8 GORDINI 1100/1300

This was a limited-production "homologation special" based on the mass-market R8 sedan, intended as Renault's race-and-rally competitor against the BMC Mini-Cooper S. The

1964-69 8 Gordini 1300 sedan

rear-mounted, air-cooled engine used the normal R8 block, with a cross-pushrod cylinder head designed by the Amadee Gordini tuning firm. The original 1108cc displacement was boosted to 1255cc in mid-1966. Though it shared the standard R8's boxy, undistinguished four-door body, almost all Gordinis were painted French Racing Blue with white "go faster" tape stripes on hood, roof, and rear deck. The 1300 version had four instead of two headlamps and an auxiliary fuel tank. Like the R8, the Gordini boasted all-independent suspension and four-wheel disc brakes, the latter an unusual feature for a European small car in those days. The 1100s had a four-speed center-control gearbox, replaced by a five-speed Gordini box on 1300s. Noisy and crude, but very eager, with up to 110 mph in normal tune and even more possible with special tuning. Not seriously imported to the States.

FOR Performance • Gutsy character • Gordini engine and brakes • Most body and chassis parts still available • Cheap collectible with high appreciation potential

AGAINST Hard to find in U.S. • Dodgy handling • Rust-prone body • Lacking in refinement

PRODUCTION

NA

SPECIFICATIONS

Length (in.)	157.5
Wheelbase (in.)	89.3
Weight (lbs)	1755/1875 (1100/1300)
Price (new)	NA

ENGINES

cc/type (cid)	bhp[1]	years
1108/ohv I-4 (68)	95	1964-66
1255/ohv I-4 (77)	103	1966-69

[1]Gross

PRICES

FAIR	$1000-2500
GOOD	$2500-3500
FINE	$3500-6000

FINE EXAMPLE PRICE HISTORY

1982	$3500	1990	$5000
1994	$5000	1998	$5000

1982-2000 RETURN 3%
2000-2010 2%

1985-87

RENAULT ALLIANCE CONVERTIBLE

The open-air finale to the mid-'80s alliance that resulted in modified Renault 9 sedans built in Kenosha, Wisconsin, by American Motors. Developed in the U.S. as a derivative of the two-door Alliance notchback in one of Dick Teague's final efforts as head of AMC design. It shared its front-drive subcompact platform with the companion Alliance and derivative Encore hatchback, as well as their transverse 1.7-liter (105-cid) four-cylinder engine, five-speed manual or three-speed automatic transaxle, all-independent suspension, and front-disc power brakes. Initial L and spiffier

DL convertibles, both with no-cost power soft tops, were joined for 1987 by a snappier 2.0-liter (120-cid) GTA version (also offered as a closed two-door), a self-proclaimed "pocket rocket" with racy exterior add-ons, larger wheels and tires, and upgraded suspension. Unfortunately, "Franco-American Motors" was then on the ropes thanks to fast-falling sales of the make-or-break Alliance line. Renault soon left the U.S. market (again), leaving AMC to be absorbed by Chrysler Corporation. Not the world's greatest convertible, but a fairly rare oddball that deserves saving against the dim prospect of even greater scarcity and possible value appreciation in the future. Look for a nice GTA ragtop at a bargain price.

FOR Open-air fun • Practical for a ragtop • GTA tossable • Thrifty engines • Used-car cheap

AGAINST Excess cowl shake • Marginal trunk and back-seat space • Sit-up-and-beg driving stance • Boomy, buzzy engines • Ride often choppy • Workmanship not the best

PRODUCTION

1985 7141 **1986** 2015 **1987** 1991

SPECIFICATIONS

Length (in.)	163.8
Wheelbase (in.)	97.8
Weight (lbs)	2189-2298
Price (new)	$10,295-12,899

ENGINES

cid/type	bhp	years
105/ohc I-4	77	1985-87

1985 Alliance convertible

1931 Royale sedan

120/ohc I-4	95	1987

PRICES

FAIR	$2000-3000
GOOD	$3000-4000
FINE	$4000-5000

FINE EXAMPLE PRICE HISTORY

1990 $5500	1994 $5000
1998 $5000	
2000-2010 RETURN 2%	

1931-34
REO ROYALE

Underrated luxury car styled by Amos Northup, with pioneer streamlined bodywork featuring flowing front fenders, a long hood, and dignified radiator. An immense 152-inch-wheelbase chassis was used for a seven-passenger sedan and limo in the 8-35 range of 1932. With its big nine-bearing straight eight and Northup's glamorous bodies, the Royale was a splendid car, but entirely wrong for the depressed times. The cars we cite are the only Reos ranked as Classics by the CCCA, and every one deservedly so.

FOR Splendid, ahead-of-its-time coachwork • Smooth straight-eight performance • Luxury and quality • Handsome styling • Some good buys still to be found • CCCA Classic status

AGAINST Parts scarce • A bit out of the ordinary and not as well recognized as they should be

PRODUCTION

1931 8-31 707 **8-35** 2711 **1932 8-31** 126 **8-35** 176 (incl. 12 lwb) **Custom** 5128 (incl. 4 lwb) **1933 Eight** 1300 (est.) **Custom Eight** 127 **1934 N-1 Custom Eight & N-2 Eight** NA

SPECIFICATIONS

Length (in.)	Variable
Wheelbase (in.)	131.0/135.0 (1931-34); 152.0 (1932-33)
Weight (lbs)	4310-5075
Price (new)	$1500-3895

ENGINES

cid/type	bhp	years
358.0/sv I-8	125	1931-34

PRICES

Open	
FAIR	$11,000-26,000
GOOD	$26,000-46,000
FINE	$46,000-66,000
Closed	

FAIR	$6200-14,000
GOOD	$14,000-25,000
FINE	$25,000-36,000

FINE CONVERTIBLE PRICE HISTORY

1982 $37,000	1990 $40,000
1994 $45,000	1998 $65,000
1982-2000 RETURN 4%	
2000-2010 3%	

1930-35
ROLLS-ROYCE PHANTOM II

An updated version of the original New Phantom (Phantom I) of 1925, with a new chassis—on two long wheelbases—and a much-modified engine and transmission. Typical of between-the-wars Royces in every

1930-35 Phantom II convertible (owned by Charlie Chaplin)

way. All have stately hand-built coachwork, by Brewster on most left-hand-drive export models. Massive, heavy and predictably expensive. Performance and economy took a back seat to build quality and sumptuous fittings, lending credence to R-R's claim that this was "The Best Car in the World." A lower chassis featured four-wheel hydraulic brakes and more modern Hotchkiss drive and hypoid rear end instead of the torque tube used on the Silver Ghost/Phantom I, but retention of beam-axle suspension front and rear (on semi-elliptic leaf springs) made it somewhat old-fashioned toward the end of the model's life. Numerous changes occurred during these years, including smaller wheel/tire diameter, one-shot lube system, and synchromesh gearing on third and fourth (from 1932) and on second (1935 models). This model was particularly significant as the last R-R designed by Henry Royce. Special Continental models (280 built) are the most coveted today.

FOR R-R panache, prestige • Cost-no-object engineering • Exquisite looks • Restoration still possible from factory parts supplies • Extremely reliable • CCCA Classic status, of course

AGAINST Very expensive • You'll need a mortgage to restore one • Archaic road manners and heavy to drive

PRODUCTION

1672 (some sources list 1767; began 1929)

SPECIFICATIONS

Length (in.)	Variable with body style
Wheelbase (in.)	144.0/150.0
Weight (lbs)	approx. 5000-6500
Price (new)	NA

ENGINES

cc/type (cid)	bhp	years
7668/ohv I-6 (468)	120[1]	1930-35

[1]Not officially quoted

PRICES

Open	
FAIR	$20,000-50,000
GOOD	$50,000-140,000
FINE	$140,000-200,000
Closed	
FAIR	$25,000-35,000
GOOD	$35,000-55,000
FINE	$55,000-85,000

FINE EXAMPLE PRICE HISTORY

1982 $50,000		**1990** $250,000	
1994 $250,000		**1998** $200,000	

1982-2000 RETURN 8%
2000-2010 5%
(Note: Bodies and credentials vary enormously, and figures well in excess of the above have been cheerfully paid for very special coachwork and/or famous associations.)

1930-36 ROLLS-ROYCE 20/25

The second-generation "small" Rolls-Royce, the direct replacement for the original "20." Unlike the Phantom I, there was no Springfield equivalent built in the U.S. As with all such prewar Rolls-Royces, it was offered only as a rolling chassis for coachbuilt bodywork, so a huge variety of styles still exists. Beautifully and carefully crafted, but surprisingly slow even for the period—about 70 mph tops. A synchromesh gearbox was added for 1932, a complete centralized chassis lubrication for 1934. The British at their best, so no excuse needed to buy one.

FOR Magnificent construction • Mechanical parts still available • Silky controls • Luxurious British fittings • A CCCA Classic

AGAINST Very high parts and restoration costs • Stodgy performance • Body restoration difficult

PRODUCTION

3827

SPECIFICATIONS

Length (in.)	average 180.0
Wheelbase (in.)	129.0
Weight (lbs)	approx. 3800
Price (new)	NA

ENGINES

cc/type (cid)	bhp	years
3680/ohv I-6 (224)	65[1]	1930-36

[1]Not officially quoted

PRICES

Open	
FAIR	$20,000-50,000
GOOD	$50,000-80,000
FINE	$80,000-100,000
Closed	
FAIR	$10,000-20,000
GOOD	$20,000-35,000

1936 20/25 sedanca coupe

FINE $35,000-40,000

FINE DOCTOR'S COUPE PRICE HISTORY

1982 $15,000	**1990** $95,000
1994 $80,000	**1998** $40,000
1982-2000 RETURN 11%	
2000-2010 5%	

1 9 3 5 - 3 9
ROLLS-ROYCE PHANTOM III

R-R's response to the multi-cylinder giants from America and Europe, and the first Royce with a V-type engine. It was complex and released before it was fully developed, so it was not entirely successful. Much more modern than the PII, it came with a GM-type coil-spring independent front suspension. The long-stroke, seven-main-bearing V-12 featured hydraulic valve lifters, twin-coil ignition, triple-pressure lubrication, wet liners, and marine-type conrods. Unfortunately, the interesting iron/alloy construction was corrosion-prone, which led to cooling problems. Shorter than the PII in wheelbase and overall length, but only a little lighter, it was nonetheless surprisingly rapid. Incomparable specialist coachwork on all examples, mostly limousines and sedans. Survival rates have not been high, as many engines suffered neglect in middle age. Arguably the world's best prewar car. A high-status item today, but best tackled only by serious collectors.

1937 Phantom III limousine by Inskip

☒ **FOR** Advanced V-12 engineering • High-quality period coachwork • Smooth, silent, serene, dignified • Marque and model magic • Another CCCA Classic

▬ **AGAINST** Extremely expensive to buy and restore • Nightmarish body rebuilds • More for passengers than drivers • Hard to find now, as is restoration expertise

PRODUCTION

710

SPECIFICATIONS

Length (in.)	191.0 (average)
Wheelbase (in.)	142.0
Weight (lbs)	approx. 5800
Price (new)	NA

ENGINES

cc/type (cid)	bhp	years
7338/ohv V-12 (448)	165-180[1]	1935-39
[1]Not officially quoted		

PRICES

Open	
FAIR	$50,000-100,000
GOOD	$100,000-150,000
FINE	$150,000-200,000
Closed	
FAIR	$20,000-40,000
GOOD	$40,000-70,000
FINE	$70,000-95,000

FINE SEDANCA PRICE HISTORY

1982 $30,000	**1990** $120,000
1994 $120,000	**1998** $95,000
1982-2000 RETURN 9%	
2000-2010 5%	

1 9 3 6 - 3 8
ROLLS-ROYCE 25/30

Interim replacement for the 20/25 (see entry) as the "small" R-R, with a larger engine and more modern late-prewar styling. As before, solid-axle front suspension and a wide choice of coachbuilt body styles. A tad quicker than the 20/25, though weights rose almost as quickly as horsepower in this

1936-38 25/30 coupe

period. A "junior edition," but every inch a Rolls-Royce and built with infinite care.

⊞ FOR As for 1930-36 Model 20/25 • CCCA Classic status, as with all 1925-48 Rolls-Royces

■ AGAINST Stodgy performance • Not that expensive, but costly to restore • Less status than senior models

PRODUCTION

1201

SPECIFICATIONS

Length (in.)	180.0 (average)
Wheelbase (in.)	132.0
Weight (lbs)	approx. 4000
Price (new)	NA

ENGINES

cc/type (cid)	bhp	years
4257/ohv I-6 (260)	85[1]	1936-38

[1]Not officially quoted

PRICES

As for 1930-36 Rolls-Royce 20/25.

1938 Wraith sedan

1938-39
ROLLS-ROYCE WRAITH

The last and most modern junior Royce of the prewar period, taking over for the 25/30 (see entry). Wheelbase was extended four inches over that of its predecessor for a chassis thoroughly revised along Phantom III lines, featuring GM-like independent front suspension with enclosed coil springs. A semi-elliptic leaf-sprung solid rear axle and servo-assisted four-wheel hydraulic brakes were as before. More graceful though still very stately bodywork was supplied by specialists, as per R-R tradition. Most were sedans with razor-edge lines, but a few, more flowing coupes and convertibles were also completed. Development was cut off by the outbreak of World War II, and the model would not be revived postwar, making this effectively a two-year-only offering and thus among the rarest prewar Royces today. It bears no mechanical relationship with post-1945 models.

⊞ FOR High-quality build • Pleasant, up-to-date handling • Magnificent furnishings and detailing • Marque's customary snob appeal • Exclusivity • CCCA Classic status

■ AGAINST Generally "heavier" styling than earlier R-R juniors • Still not fast (about 80 mph tops) • Costly to buy and restore • Rot-prone wood-frame bodywork a real headache

PRODUCTION

491

SPECIFICATIONS

Length (in.)	Variable with body
Wheelbase (in.)	136.0
Weight (lbs)	approx. 5200
Price (new)	NA

ENGINES

cc/type (cid)	bhp	years
4257/ohv I-6 (260)	90[1]	1938-39

[1]Est.—not officially quoted.

PRICES

As for 20/25 and 25/30 models (see entries).

1946-59
ROLLS-ROYCE SILVER WRAITH

The custom-bodied Rolls-Royce series in the postwar years, continuing a famous name of the '30s. R-R built the chassis, essentially a stretched-wheelbase version (127 or

1947-48 Silver Wraith sedan by James Young

1949-55 Silver Dawn sedan

133 inches) of the contemporary 120-inch Silver Dawn/Bentley Mark VI platform, with the same suspension design and drivetrains. Bodywork was supplied by traditional R-R specialists—Park Ward, H.J. Mulliner, Hooper, and others—most with wood framing and light-alloy or steel panels. Many had "classic" lines, with freestanding headlamps, separate front fenders, division window between passengers and chauffeur, and the characteristic Rolls-Royce "parthenon" grille. Complete luxury equipment was expected, and interiors were decked out with leather upholstery, wood trim, and, in a few cases, cut-glass ornaments. Displacement of R-R's F-head six was increased to 4.5 liters in 1951, then 4.9 liters in 1955; otherwise, few mechanical changes were seen in these years. In this era there was no doubt: these were "The Best Cars in the World."

FOR Handcrafted bodies, individual detailing • Superb workmanship • Opulence on a grand scale • Unbeatable Rolls-Royce cachet and exclusivity • Strong club support • Classic status through 1948 • Milestone status for all years

AGAINST Limited performance • Thirsty • Ponderous to drive • Body parts extinct • Now very costly to buy, restore, and own

PRODUCTION

127-in. wb 1144 **133-in. wb** 639

SPECIFICATIONS

Length (in.)	200.0-206.0
Wheelbase (in.)	127.0/133.0
Weight (lbs)	4735-5405
Price (new)	NA

ENGINES

cc/type (cid)	bhp[1]	years
4257/F I-6 (260)	NA	1947-51
4566/F I-6 (279)	NA	1951-55
4887/F I-6 (298)	NA	1955-59

[1]NA; Rolls-Royce customarily did not quote power or torque output

PRICES

Open	
FAIR	$20,000-40,000
GOOD	$40,000-60,000
FINE	$60,000-80,000
Closed	
FAIR	$7500-25,000
GOOD	$25,000-40,000
FINE	$40,000-63,000

FINE SPORTS SALOON PRICE HISTORY

1982 $12,000		**1990** $75,000	
1994 $80,000		**1998** $80,000	
1982-2000 RETURN 8%			
2000-2010 5%			

1949-1955
ROLLS ROYCE SILVER DAWN

The first Rolls-Royce model ever based on a Bentley—usually it was the other way around. It shared the "standard steel" bodyshell, chassis, and all running gear with the Bentley Mark VI of these years, though engine output was rumored to be lower. Marked, of course, by the distinctive R-R grille. Unlike the Bentley, models with left-hand drive featured a steering-column gearchange. Engine displacement was increased in 1951, followed shortly afterwards by a long-tail "B7" body style. Automatic transmis-

sion was made standard beginning in 1953. Styling usually followed the British "razor edge" school, with semi-integrated headlamps; separate, sweeping fenderlines; and semi-enclosed rear wheels (covered by "spats"). As expected from Rolls, interiors were plushly outfitted with leather upholstery, wood cappings for dash and doors, and lots of detail conveniences. A good many were sent to North America, as the model was never sold in Britain.

FOR The Rolls-Royce name • Silence and refinement • Dignified styling • Many mechanical parts still available • Comfortable, well-furnished cabin • A Milestone car

AGAINST Not very fast (85-90 mph tops) • Rust-prone • Body parts extinct • Too much like a Bentley? • Milestone status

PRODUCTION

4-¼-liter 170 **4-¼-liter short tail** 110 **4-¼-liter long tail** 481

SPECIFICATIONS

Length (in.)	192.0 (1949-51),199.5 (1951-55)
Wheelbase (in.)	120.0
Weight (lbs)	4100 (average)
Price (new)	NA

ENGINES

cc/type (cid)	bhp[1]	years
4257/F I-6 (260)	NA	1949-51
4566/F I-6 (279)	NA	1951-55

[1]NA; Rolls-Royce customarily did not quote power output

PRICES

Open	
FAIR	$23,000-33,000
GOOD	$33,000-40,000
FINE	$40,000-70,000

Closed: About half the value of open models

FINE DROPHEAD PRICE HISTORY

1982 $28,000	**1990** $140,000
1994 $70,000	**1998** $70,000
1982-2000 RETURN 5%	
2000-2010 3%	

1950-56
ROLLS-ROYCE PHANTOM IV

The most exclusive of all postwar Rolls-Royce models, and not one you're apt to see any day of the week. Built on a longer Silver Wraith chassis and powered by the R-R straight six with two extra cylinders tacked on. Each Phantom IV was built to special order, and went to royalty or heads of state only. Each was fitted with a special handcrafted limousine body with wood framing, and offered seven-passenger seating capacity. In appearance, it was "British formal," with a very upright stance. Some models were fitted with freestanding headlamps; most had razor-edge styling. R-R spared no expense on the Phantoms, the pride of its fleet, and apart from the chassis and suspension they shared nothing with the more "common" Wraith and Dawn models.

FOR Tremendously scarce and desirable • Magnificent coachbuilt bodywork • Superb craftsmanship throughout • Famous first owners • A true Milestone car

1950-56 Phantom IV limousine by Mulliner

AGAINST Most mechanical and all body parts now unobtainable • Extremely costly to buy, restore, and own • Ponderous to drive

PRODUCTION

18

SPECIFICATIONS

Length (in.)	229.0 (variable)
Wheelbase (in.)	145.0
Weight (lbs)	approx. 5500
Price (new)	NA

ENGINES

cc/type (cid)	bhp[1]	years
5675/F I-8 (346)	NA	1950-56

[1]NA; Rolls-Royce customarily did not quote power or torque output.

PRICES

$80,000+ for the better models; sales reports lacking
2000-2010 RETURN 3%

1955-59
ROLLS-ROYCE SILVER CLOUD I

A near-identical twin to the Bentley S-Type (see entry) and introduced concurrently with it. Of course, it featured the distinctive, more expensive Rolls-Royce radiator and flying lady mascot. There was supposed to be a slight difference in engine power in 1955 and '56, though it would be hard to prove given R-R's nondisclosure policy. Offered as the "standard steel" four-door sedan, which is naturally the

1955-59 Silver Cloud I limousine

1956-69 Phantom V limousine

most numerous model today, as well as in long-wheelbase limousine form. Special coachbuilt bodies, mostly coupes and convertibles, were also available through Rolls-Royce's usual suppliers.

FOR As for 1955-59 Bentley S-Type, plus R-R snob appeal • Another Milestone Rolls

AGAINST As for 1955-59 Bentley S-Type

PRODUCTION
Standard body 2238 **limo** 121

SPECIFICATIONS
Length (in.)	212.0/216.0 (sdn/limo)
Wheelbase (in.)	123.0/127.0 (sdn/limo)
Weight (lbs)	4370/4650 (sdn/limo)
Price (new)	NA

ENGINES
cc/type (cid)	bhp[1]	years
4887/F I-6 (298)	NA	1955-59

[1]NA; Rolls-Royce customarily did not quote power or torque output

PRICES
Standard Steel Saloon
FAIR	$12,000-20,000
GOOD	$20,000-27,500
FINE	$27,500-35,000

(Multiply by three for Mulliner or Park Ward conv and coachbuilt cpe.)

FINE SALOON PRICE HISTORY
1982 $30,000		**1990** $60,000	
1994 $35,000		**1998** $40,000	

1982-2000 RETURN 2%
2000-2010 3%, higher for coachbuilt bodies

1959-69
ROLLS-ROYCE PHANTOM V

Successor to the Phantom IV, this massive limousine shard the chassis and running gear of the Series II Bentley S-Type/R-R Silver Cloud, but used an appropriately longer wheelbase. The chassis was the familiar, old-fashioned affair (beam rear axle, drum brakes, mechanical brake servo) that had been around for years, but was thoroughly developed and very reliable. Power was provided by the firm's new light-alloy V-8 engine with what the factory described as "adequate" output, though R-R continued to refuse stating precisely what "adequate" meant. All Phantom Vs had custom-crafted bodies by "approved suppliers," mainly Mulliner and Park Ward. Rolls-Royce built the rolling chassis only. Similar in general appearance to—but much larger than—the Silver Cloud. Almost all had seven-passenger seating, division window, and chauffeur equipment: many had air conditioning and all were equipped with a General Motors-based Hydra-matic transmission. Lofty, stately, and extremely dignified, yet capable of 100-plus mph. Produced in greater numbers than the Phantom IV, but still the ultimate in "arrival impact" for pop singers and ruling monarchs.

FOR Best of the best • Un-mistakably Rolls-Royce, with prestige to match • Enormous carrying capacity • Smooth, silent, luxurious • Active club support in U.S. and Britain • Yet another Rolls Milestone car

AGAINST Expensive • Costs a bundle to buy and run • Big and ponderous to drive, let alone park • Body parts difficult to find at the right price

PRODUCTION
793

SPECIFICATIONS
Length (in.)	238.0
Wheelbase (in.)	144.0
Weight (lbs)	5600-5800
Price (new)	NA

ENGINES
cc/type (cid)	bhp[1]	years
6230/ohv V-8 (380)	NA	1959-68

[1]NA; Rolls-Royce customarily did not quote power or torque output

PRICES
FAIR	$30,000-40,000
GOOD	$40,000-55,000
FINE	$55,000-80,000

(Add 50% for good to fine landaulette.)

FINE EXAMPLE PRICE HISTORY
1982 $50,000		**1987** $75,000	
1990 $120,000		**1994** $80,000	

1982-2000 RETURN 3%
2000-2010 3%

1959-62 Silver Cloud II sedan

1959-62
ROLLS-ROYCE SILVER CLOUD II

Essentially the original Silver Cloud with a different engine, R-R's new 6.2-liter light-alloy V-8 said to have been inspired by Cadillac's 1949 ohv unit. Identical with the companion Bentley S-Type Series II of these years except for nameplates and, of course, the Rolls-Royce radiator and mascot. As with its predecessor, most of these cars had the "standard steel" sedan body, but 299 examples were long-wheelbase limousines with division window and handcrafted coachwork. Arguably, still the "Best Car in the World" at this time, but falling behind rising standards of chassis refinement.

FOR As for 1955-56 Silver Cloud, plus more performance and smoother, quieter operation • Milestone status

AGAINST As for 1955-59 Silver Cloud

PRODUCTION

Standard body 2417 **limo** 299

SPECIFICATIONS

Length (in.)	212.0/216.0 (sdn/limo)
Wheelbase (in.)	123.0/127.0 (sdn/limo)
Weight (lbs)	4550/4650 (sdn/limo)
Price (new)	NA

ENGINES

cc/type (cid)	bhp[1]	years
6230/ohv V-8 (380)	NA	1959-62

[1]NA; Rolls-Royce customarily did not quote power or torque output

PRICES

As for 1955-59 Rolls-Royce Silver Cloud I.
2000-2010 RETURN 3%

1962-65
ROLLS-ROYCE SILVER CLOUD III

Last of the Silver Clouds, with changes both for the better and the worse. In the latter category was the styling, marked (like that of the Bentley

1962-65 Silver Cloud III sedan

S-Type Series III) by a lower hood and radiator and quad headlamps mounted in oval nacelles. Most purists thought this a shocking violation of R-R tradition at the time. One magazine went so far as to refer to the quad lights as equivalent to installing a jukebox in Winchester cathedral. Still mounted on a separate chassis, by now looking quite dated, with drum brakes and a live rear axle. In the "better" column was seven percent more power (not disclosed, but probably up to about 220 bhp net) from the aluminum 6.2-liter V-8. Again identical to its Bentley stablemate apart from the obvious grille and nameplate differences. Replaced in late 1965 by the monocoque Silver Shadow series with more modern engineering and less distinctive appearance.

⊞ FOR As for 1959-62 Silver Cloud II, including Milestone status

⊟ AGAINST As for 1959-62 Silver Cloud II, plus dubious front-end restyle

PRODUCTION
Standard body 2044 limo 253 custom body 79

SPECIFICATIONS
Length (in.)	211.0/216.0 (sdn/limo)
Wheelbase (in.)	123.0/127.0 (sdn/limo)
Weight (lbs)	4480/4650 (sdn/limo)
Price (new)	NA

ENGINES
cc/type (cid)	bhp[1]	years
6230/ohv V-8 (380)	220 (est.)	1959-62

[1]Rolls-Royce customarily did not quote power or torque output

PRICES
As for 1955-59 Rolls-Royce Silver Cloud I.
2000-2010 RETURN 3%

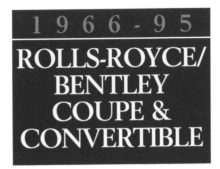

1966-95
ROLLS-ROYCE/ BENTLEY COUPE & CONVERTIBLE

Swank two-door offshoots of the 1965-vintage R-R Silver Shadow/ Bentley T-series four-doors. Sold under a confusing series of names, of which Corniche is probably the best known. The initial 1966-70 drophead and thin-pillar coupe were coachbuilt conversions chiefly by Mulliner-Park Ward, though the James Young concern managed a few coupes of near-identical design before its 1967 demise. Built in both Rolls and Bentley versions, of course, with badges and radiators the main difference, as on parent sedans. A replacement Corniche arrived in 1971 as a regular "factory" series with detail equipment and appearance changes, a larger engine, a more reliable version of Crewe's complex hydraulic suspension system, vented front-disc brakes, and

lesser assorted improvements. The original twin carbs were replaced in 1975 by a single four-barrel unit (á la Camargue). Larger, sturdier U.S.-type bumpers and a front airdam from 1977 were per that year's revised Shadow II/T2. The rear suspension was updated in 1980 to the lighter new hydro-pneumatic design of the replacement Silver Spirit/Mulsanne sedans. Coupes were dropped in 1982; two years later, the open Bentley was renamed Continental to set it further apart from the companion R-R. Specifications were again updated for 1987 "II" models with Bosch K-Jetronic fuel injection and standard antilock brakes. The last Corniche of this series was produced in 1995. The final 20 examples were turbocharged. A new Corniche was introduced in 2000, based on the Silver Seraphe, but retained the 6.75-liter turbocharged Rolls-Royce V-8.

⊞ FOR Obvious collectibles all; pre-Corniche models, coupes, and Bentley versions lead values • Quicker and more nimble than you'd think • Hushed opulence • Styling has aged better than on the sedans

⊟ AGAINST Brake, suspension, and electrical maladies common on pre-Corniche cars • Costly to buy, run, and restore • Some unique coupe trim and body panels becoming difficult • Bulky convertible top stack

PRODUCTION
R-R Silver Shadow cpe 606 (1966-70) conv

1973 Rolls-Royce Corniche convertible

1990 Rolls-Royce Corniche convertible

505 (1966-70) **Bentley cpe** 114 (1966-70) **conv** 41 (1966-70) **R-R Corniche cpe** 780 (1971-76) **conv** 1233 (1971-76) **Bentley Corniche cpe/conv** 100 (1971-76) **Corniche cpe** 53 (1977-82) **Corniche conv** 45 (1977-82) **R-R Corniche cpe est.** 300 (1977-82) **Corniche conv** est. 1300 (1977-84) **Bentley Continental/Continental II conv est.** 200 (1985-90) **R-R Corniche/Corniche II conv est.** 1000 (1985-90)

SPECIFICATIONS

Length (in.)	207.5
Wheelbase (in.)	120.5
Weight (lbs)	4820-5340
Price (new)	$59,000-265,000 in U.S.

ENGINES

cid/type	bhp	years
6230/ohv V-8 (380)	220[1]	1966-70
6750/ohv V-8 (412)	250[1]	1971-86
6750/ohv V-8[2] (412)	260[1]	1987-90
6750/ohv V-8[3] (412)	NA	1995

[1]Est. (not quoted by factory) [2]Fuel injection
[3]Turbocharged

PRICES

1968-80 Conv

FAIR	$15,000-20,000
GOOD	$20,000-35,000
FINE	$35,000-55,000

(Deduct 20% for coupe.)
In production to 1991. Top value of 1991 convertible: $125,000.
2000-2010 RETURN 3%

1 9 6 8 - 9 2
ROLLS-ROYCE PHANTOM VI

Improved evolution of the imposing Phantom V, with quad headlamps the main visual distinction. A semi-open Special Landaulette was added later and, like the closed limousine, was strictly special-order (even prices were available only by request). Befitting that status, equipment varies somewhat from car to car. The VI retained the Phantom V's chassis and running gear, but separate front and rear air conditioning units were new. A stroked version of Crewe's all-aluminum 6.2-liter V-8 arrived in early 1978; there were also various detail improvements throughout. The VI was finally discontinued in January 1992, with the last unit selling for a cool $1,000,000! Production averaged only about 20 units in most years. Bodies were handcrafted by the Rolls-owned Mulliner-Park Ward works, with final assembly at Crewe.

FOR As for 1959-68 Phantom V, but more reliable and better built

AGAINST As for 1959-68 Phantom V, but very scarce in the U.S. (and elsewhere, for that matter)

PRODUCTION

est. 450 through 1990

SPECIFICATIONS

Length (in.)	238.0
Wheelbase (in.)	145.0
Weight (lbs)	6045
Price (new)	NA, but up to $300,000 by mid-'80s

ENGINES

cc/type (cid)	bhp	years
6230/ohv V-8 (380)	220[1]	1968-78

1968-90 Phantom VI limousine

6750/ohv V-8 (412)	250[1]	1978-92	

[1]Est. (not quoted by factory)

PRICES

Early models

FAIR	$25,000-35,000
GOOD	$35,000-50,000
FINE	$50,000-80,000

2000-2010 RETURN 3%

1 9 7 5 - 8 6
ROLLS-ROYCE CAMARGUE

In its day, the costliest "Roller" in history. Born in 1969 as project "Delta," which aimed for a sportier R-R than the Silver Shadow-based two-doors then evolving into the Corniche series. Sergio Pininfarina, scion of the great Italian carrozzeria (and destined to supervise the shape of Cadillac's late-'80s Allante), penned the styling, which borrowed much from PF's Fiat 130 design but wasn't nearly so chiseled or elegant. A steel body (with aluminum hood, doors, and decklid) was welded to a modified Shadow platform. The production Shadow powertrain comprised an all-aluminum 6.7-liter V-8 and three-speed GM Turbo Hydra-Matic with Crewe's own electric shift control; switching from twin SU carbs to a single four-barrel Solex boosted power an undisclosed amount (as usual, R-R didn't quote engine outputs). The Camargue introduced the complex two-level climate control system adopted for the later Shadow II/Silver Wraith sedans and their Silver Spirit/Spur successors; it also previewed the latter's general facial look. Lavish equipment with power everything, traditional wood-and-leather cabin, and rear self-leveling were in line with a price more than twice a Shadow's. Camargue's role was the "ultimate" Rolls. It was built without regard to sales: slowly and to cost-no-object quality standards. It evolved only in details over 11 years. The final 12, all built for U.S. sale, came with silver-inlay dash veneers, compact-disc player, cellular telephone, and unique personal accessories including a silver vanity set and leather attache.

FOR Rare, distinctive modern R-R • As smooth and silent as that name implies • Opulent trim and equipment • Surprisingly competent in corners • Parts/service backup still good

AGAINST Debatable looks • Costly to buy, run, and maintain • Electricals give frequent trouble • Weak appreciator now (but holds value very well, like most R-Rs)

PRODUCTION

534

SPECIFICATIONS

Length (in.)	206.2
Wheelbase (in.)	120.1
Weight (lbs)	5175
Price (new)	$90,000-175,000

ENGINES

cid/type	bhp	years
6750/ohv V-8 (412)	220-250[1]	1975-86

[1]Est. (not quoted by factory)

PRICES

FAIR	$20,000-30,000
GOOD	$30,000-40,000
FINE	$40,000-60,000

FINE EXAMPLE PRICE HISTORY

1990 $80,000
1994 $60,000
2000-2010 RETURN 2%

1975-82 Camargue coupe

1950-64
ROVER P4 SERIES

One of postwar Britain's best known and longest running cars, and affectionately nicknamed "Aunty" Rover for its charming but dowdy appearance. It ran on a very strong separate chassis with rather heavy engines that meant a pronounced forward weight bias and consequently stodgy handling. The slab-sided styling was reportedly influenced by Raymond Loewy's 1947 Studebaker—even down to rear-hinged back doors. A characteristic square grille with vertical bars was flanked by headlamps set somewhat inboard of the fender edges. It saw various minor restyles over the years, mostly involving efforts to enlarge and smooth out the tail; the back window became progressively larger, too. Built with quality materials—wood-faced dash and doors, leather upholstery, fine carpeting—the P4 built a well-deserved reputation for reliability and longevity; in fact, many are still in daily use. Offered with six different engines during its long life span, with model designations often (but not always) reflecting rated horsepower (most commonly 60, 75, 80, 90, and 100). Automatic transmission became available in the '50s, and many cars were built with optional electric overdrive for the standard four-speed manual gearbox. In all, resolutely conservative and solid, but not widely sold or known outside the British Commonwealth. In the end, it was replaced by the similarly styled—but more modern—P5 series.

✚ FOR Solid and durable • Quality materials • Strong chassis • Wide choice of engines • Many parts still available • Cheap to buy

▬ AGAINST Stodgy handling • Heavy steering, brakes, clutch • Small-engine models sluggish • Large-engine models thirsty • Rare in U.S.

PRODUCTION

130,342

SPECIFICATIONS

Length (in.)	178.0
Wheelbase (in.)	123.0
Weight (lbs)	3050-3350
Price (new)	$2296-2562 in U.S. in 1956

ENGINES

cc/type (cid)	bhp[1]	years
1997/F I-4 (122)	60	1952-59
2103/F I-6 (128)	75	1949-54
2230/ohv I-6 (136)	80	1954-56
2286/ohv I-4 (140)	77	1959-62
2638/ohv I-6 (161)	90-108	1953-59
2625/ohv I-6 (160)	102-123	1959-64

[1]Net

PRICES

FAIR	$1000-2500
GOOD	$2500-4000
FINE	$4000-8000

FINE EXAMPLE PRICE HISTORY

1982 $3000		1990 $7500	
1994 $8000		1998 $8000	
1982-2000 RETURN 6%			
2000-2010 2%			

1959-73
ROVER P5/P5B SERIES

The second-generation postwar design from the British Rover company. All were four-door sedans featuring semi-unitized construction. A massive front subframe attached to the welded main body/floorpan structure carried the engine and transmission. Originally known as the 3-Litre, The P5 was powered by Rover's trusty F-head inline six. Rover acquired the tooling and production rights for the aluminum small-block V-8 engine first seen in the 1961 Buick Special. This engine was substituted for the 1967 model year, and the factory code designation changed to P5B. Automatic transmission was optional in all years, and power steering was made standard with the engine swap. Styling was rounded, staid, and conservative. A large square grille with vertical bars and rounded corners, split by a heavy chrome divider bearing the Rover emblem, dominated the front end. A

1950 P4 Series sedan

1967 P5B sedan

low-roof four-door sedan—oddly called "Coupe"—was also offered, and continued after introduction of the P6 series, when the standard-roof P5 models disappeared. Interiors featured lots of real wood, leather, fine-quality carpet, and traditional British fittings. More agile than its P4 predecessor, with better brakes and considerably more performance. The six-cylinder cars could reach 105 mph; with V-8 the top end was around 115 mph despite the bluff shape. A good many of these Rovers survive in their homeland today, and the model is reasonably available in the U.S. as well.

⊞ FOR Engineering integrity • Well-built • Durable • Fine furnishings • Power steering, automatic on many examples

▇ AGAINST Heavy and gas-hungry • Ponderous handling • Dubious parts supplies

PRODUCTION
NA

SPECIFICATIONS
Length (in.)	186.0
Wheelbase (in.)	110.5
Weight (lbs)	3500-3610
Price (new)	NA

ENGINES
cc/type (cid)	bhp[1]	years
2995/F I-6 (183)	105/121	1959-67
3528/ohv V-8 (215)	161	1967-73

[1]Net

PRICES
3-Litre
FAIR	$1000-2500
GOOD	$2500-4000
FINE	$4000-6000

3.5 V-8
FAIR	$2000-3500
GOOD	$3500-5000
FINE	$5000-6000

3.5 Cpe
FAIR	$3000-4000
GOOD	$4000-7500
FINE	$7500-10,000

FINE 3.5 COUPE PRICE HISTORY
1982 $4000		**1990** $10,000	
1994 $9000		**1998** $9000	
1982-2000 RETURN 5%			
2000-2010 3%			

1963-73
ROVER 2000/2000TC

Dramatically more modern than any previous Rover, the new P6-series sedans were advanced enough to continue for a decade. Construction featured a monocoque "skeleton" structure (like the Citroën DS) to which outer skin panels were bolted. This had the advantage of making body repairs easier and cheaper. Suspension was independent in front by coil springs and twin control arms; de Dion linkage was used at the rear. The 2000 was powered by a new four-cylinder overhead-cam engine with a single carburetor; the TC boasted dual carbs. Styling was a complete departure for Rover, with a subtle wedge profile, a full-width grille containing quad head-

1966-73 2000TC sedan

lamps, a squared-off decklid, and a fairly low beltline. The interior featured a "modular" instrument cluster and huge gloveboxes that doubled as crash knee pads under a full-width dash rail. On the road, the Rover delivered a soft ride, aided by super-comfortable seating, and was remarkably stable at higher speeds. Top speed was 100-plus mph in basic form; the TC (introduced in 1966) could see 110 mph. Imported to the U.S. in modest numbers, but proved fragile for North American conditions and was notoriously trouble-prone. It was succeeded in England by the more conventionally engineered, but sleeker, SD1 fastback sedan series (sold here only for 1980 as the Rover 3500).

✠ FOR
Styling • Roadability • Engineering sophistication • Comfort • Ergonomics • Quite affordable

▄ AGAINST
Rust-prone • Unrefined engine • Parts running out now • Not that many left in U.S.

PRODUCTION[1]
1963-64 NA **1965** 14,434 **1966** 18,901 **1967** 24,452 **1968** 22,528 **1969** 18,435 **1970** 25,223 **1971** 31,508 **1972** 30,035 **1973** 23,627
[1]All models

SPECIFICATIONS
Length (in.)	178.5
Wheelbase (in.)	103.4
Weight (lbs)	2770/2810 (2000/2000TC)
Price (new)	approx. $4000 U.S. in 1964; approx. $4500 for TC in 1969

ENGINES
cc/type (cid)	bhp[1]	years
1978/ohc I-4 (121)	90/114	1963-73

[1]Net, 2000/2000TC

PRICES
FAIR	$2000-3000
GOOD	$3000-4000
FINE	$4000-5000

FINE 2000TC PRICE HISTORY
1982 $2500		**1990** $5000	
1998 $5000			
1982-2000 RETURN 5%			
2000-2010 2%			

1968-75
ROVER 3500/3500S

A clever engine transplant for the Rover 2000 sedan, using the (former Buick) aluminum small-block V-8 engine. The model designation reflected engine displacement, about 3500cc—though for some reason the Brits referred to the model as the "Three Thousand Five." Except for this, the basic P6 platform was surprisingly little changed. The V-8 weighed about the same as the 2.0-liter four, so steering and suspension balance were as good as before. Performance, however, was vastly improved and top speed moved up to 120 mph. Introduced with Borg-Warner three-speed automatic transmission; later, an uprated 2000 manual gearbox was made available for the 3500S. Sold in the U.S. for a time, but Americans got a somewhat detuned engine, and very ugly wheels and triple hood scoops cluttered up the exterior. Other P6 virtues and vices remained, the main drawback being the erratic construction quality that had all but eliminated British cars as serious American market contenders by 1970. Withdrawn from the U.S. market at about that time, the Rover name wouldn't be seen here again for another decade, and then only very briefly.

✠ FOR
Effortless, high-geared performance • V-8 still in production and a known commodity here • Compact size with comfortable four-seat accommodation • Fine ride • Excellent roadability

▄ AGAINST
Rust-prone • Mechanically troublesome • Parts supply diminishing • Expensive to repair and maintain

PRODUCTION
See Rover 2000/2000TC 1963-73

SPECIFICATIONS
Length (in.)	180.0
Wheelbase (in.)	103.4
Weight (lbs)	,2865
Price (new)	approx. $5400 U.S. for 3500S in 1969

ENGINES
cc/type (cid)	bhp[1]	years
3528/ohv V-8 (215)	143	1968-75

[1]DIN; U.S. net bhp for 3500S: 184

PRICES
FAIR	$2000-3000
GOOD	$3000-4000
FINE	$4000-6500

FINE 3500S PRICE HISTORY
1982 $2500		**1990** $6000	
1994 $6000		**1998** $6000	
1982-2000 RETURN 5%			
2000-2010 2%			

1970 3500S sedan

1 9 3 0
RUXTON

Technically unique and aesthetically memorable, the Ruxton was created under the aegis of colorful and controversial promoter Archie Andrews. An early example of front-wheel drive, chosen mainly for the lower-slung looks it conferred. All models were without conventional running boards, had ultra-low fenders, and were often equipped with impractical but eye-catching Woodlite headlamps. Production ended almost as soon as it started, thus making this an early casualty of the Depression.

+ FOR Technically interesting • Important historically • Svelte, low bodywork • Always a novelty and widely admired • A CCCA Classic

- AGAINST Extremely scarce • Fairly expensive, though not as much as you'd think • Parts of all kinds impossible

PRODUCTION
Approx. 500

SPECIFICATIONS
Length (in.)	NA
Wheelbase (in.)	130.0
Weight (lbs)	4670
Price (new)	$4550 (sdn)

ENGINES
cid/type	bhp	years
268.6/sv I-8	85	1930

1962-67 GT850 coupe

PRICES
Insufficient data. Open cars up to $130,000 in top show condition; closed models to $100,000 in similar condition.

FINE PHAETON PRICE HISTORY
1982	$85,000	1994	$120,000
1998	$130,000		
1982-2000 RETURN	2%		
2000-2010	2%		

1 9 5 8 - 6 7
SAAB
GT750/GT850

The early Saab sedan in its hottest form. Introduced in 1958 with a more powerful (45 vs. 38 bhp) version of the 746cc two-stroke, three-cylinder

engine from the then-current 93 model. Styling was marked by the aerodynamic "humpback" look introduced with the original Saab 92 of the late '40s. Construction was unitized, and the very strong body/chassis had unusually good corrosion resistance. Front-wheel drive was a novelty for the day. When Saab replaced the 93 with the 96 in the early '60s, engine size went up to 841cc, and the GT version continued, again with more horsepower (57 vs. 48). Through 1960 a rather clumsy three-speed steering column gearshift was fitted, but later models had a four-speed floorshift transmission. Features on both the 750 and 850 GT (or Granturismo) were more complete instrumentation, including tachometer, plus fog lamps and special seats. Quite quick all things considered, with the engine emitting the distinctive "popcorn popper" sounds at

1930 sedan

idle characteristic of two-stroke units. Like other Saabs of the day, it was quite roomy for its size. The 850 model (known as the Sport outside the USA) was briefly marketed under the Monte Carlo name (1965-68) in recognition of the car's rally successes at the hands of driver Erik Carlsson. The GT was discontinued once Saab adopted the German Ford V-4 engine for the 95/96 models in the late '60s.

FOR Front-drive handling/roadholding • Durability • Good accommodation • Comparatively rare now • Affordable

AGAINST Noisy, smoky two-stroke engine • Parts now hard to come by • Styling sure to inspire argument

PRODUCTION

GT750 600 (546 U.S. models) **GT850** NA

SPECIFICATIONS

Length (in.)	159.0
Wheelbase (in.)	98.0
Weight (lbs)	1800-1900
Price (new)	approx. $2800 U.S. for 850GT in 1964

ENGINES

cc/type (cid)	bhp	years
748/ohv 2-stroke 3 (46)	45	1958-62
841/ohv 2-stroke 3 (51.3)	57	1962-67

PRICES

FAIR	$2000-3000
GOOD	$3000-6500
FINE	$6500-10,000

1966-70

SAAB SONETT II

A limited-production two-seat sporty coupe by Sweden's pioneer of front-wheel drive. Chassis and suspension came from the normal Saab 96 sedan, but the body was completely different. Made of fiberglass, it featured a large wraparound rear window, minimal rear overhang, a fairly long snout with a prominent hood bulge, protruding lower bumper/grille, and stubby overall proportions. The hood and front fenders were a single unit, hinged at the front to provide excellent engine access. Originally powered by the three-cylinder Saab two-stroker from the 96, but followed the sedans when the German Ford four-stroke V-4 was adopted for 1968. The sleek shape allowed the Sonett to achieve up to 100 mph while delivering good economy. However, the model was more a prestige item for Saab than a serious attempt at a volume sports car, and was replaced by the restyled Sonett III in 1970.

FOR Front-drive tenacity and traction • Peppy V-4 • Rust-free fiberglass body • Entertainment value • Rarity

AGAINST Styling • Unrefined two-stroke engine • Body hardware and trim impossible to find now • Parts for both engines becoming scarce • Not plentiful anywhere

PRODUCTION

1868

SPECIFICATIONS

Length (in.)	149.0
Wheelbase (in.)	85.0
Weight (lbs)	1565-1700
Price (new)	NA

ENGINES

cc/type (cid)	bhp[1]	years
841/2-stroke 3 (51)	60	1966-67
1498/ohv V-4 (91)	65	1968-70

[1]Net

PRICES

FAIR	$2000-3000
GOOD	$3000-5000
FINE	$5000-7500

1967 Sonett II coupe

1973 Sonett III coupe

1970-74
SAAB SONETT III

A continuation of Saab's low-volume sports two-seater, fortunately with much prettier new styling created by Sergio Coggiola of Italy. A longer, smoother nose terminated in a wide, shallow grille, with driving lights mounted behind its thin horizontal bars. Headlamps popped up from the nose. The tail was extended slightly, the Sonett II's wraparound backlight discarded, and a proper fastback roofline with lift-up hatch window substituted. Suspension and chassis still came from the Saab 96, but mounted a larger-displacement version of the German Ford V-4 engine to drive the front wheels. The body was still made of fiberglass, and featured an integral rollover bar. In all, a unique piece from Sweden. Saab's planned phaseout of the 96 (in favor of the 99) doomed the Sonett in the North American market.

FOR As for 1966-70 Sonett II, plus more handsome, practical styling • Better performance

AGAINST As for 1966-70 Sonett II, except styling

PRODUCTION
8350

SPECIFICATIONS
Length (in.)	154.0
Wheelbase (in.)	85.0
Weight (lbs)	1785
Price (new)	approx. $4000 U.S. in 1970

ENGINES
cc/type (cid)	bhp[1]	years
1699/ohv V-4 (104)	75	1970-74

[1]DIN

PRICES
As per 1966-70 Saab Sonnet II.

1965-66
SHELBY GT 350

The first—and many say the best—of Carroll Shelby's high-performance Ford Mustangs. Impetus was winning the Sports Car Club of America's B-Production road-racing title—which it did three years running, from 1965-67. Started as a specially supplied white Mustang 2+2 fastback; Shelby's small California shop then added a warmed-up 289 V-8, Borg-Warner T-10 four-speed gearbox, heftier rear axle (from Ford's big Galaxie), metallic linings for the rear drum brakes, Mustang's optional Kelsey-Hayes front-disc brakes (with metal-based pads), Koni adjustable shocks, cast-aluminum wheels, and wide rocker-panel and topside striping. A fiberglass hood with air scoop and tiedowns replaced the normal steel item, and the rear seat was omitted—a Shelby trick to qualify the GT 350 as a two-seat "sports car." A competition R-model was also developed with a

1965 GT 350 coupe

tuned-and-blueprinted Cobra 289 packing 340-360 bhp, plus an aluminum-case transmission, bumperless fiberglass nose with additional air intake, stripped interior with extra instruments and racing bucket seats, and, on a few examples, four-wheel disc brakes and flared wheelarches. No more than 30 R-models were built, all in 1965 (along with a handful of modified drag cars). Most '66 GT 350s (of which the first 250 or so were left-over '65s) came with Plexiglas side windows instead of the fastback's louvers, an optional kit that restored the back seat, revised grille, new side scoops, and more paint/stripe color choices. Five cars were fitted with a Paxton supercharger option announced at $670 factory-installed or as a $430 kit—that lifted horsepower above 400. Also, a batch of '66s—most of which were gold-on-black—was delivered to Hertz for rental at major airports; many actually went racing on weekends, and Hertz abandoned the idea as an unprofitable headache. Finally, Shelby had six '66 convertibles built as personal gifts for friends. Amazingly fast on turns and straights alike, the GT 350 remains one of the '60s greatest performance machines, but the '65 is seen as the purest, so the '66 suffers accordingly on the collector car market.

✚ FOR Huge enthusiast following (larger than ever) • History-maker • Superb performance • Strong, supportive club • Blue-chip investment, now moving up again in value • A Milestone car

▬ AGAINST Indifferent assembly quality (though Shelby components well made) • High operating costs (especially insurance) • Often hysterical asking prices • The '66 is seen as less desirable

PRODUCTION

1965 562 (incl. drag cars and 30 R-model racers) **1966** 2380 (incl. 936 Hertz GT350H, 6 prototype conv, and miscellaneous drag cars)

SPECIFICATIONS

Length (in.)	181.6
Wheelbase (in.)	108.0
Weight (lbs)	2800 (R-model: 2500)
Price (new)	$4547-5950

ENGINES

cid/type	bhp	years
289/ohv V-8	306/340/400[1]	1965-66

[1]Stock/competition (R-model)/supercharged

PRICES

1965	
FAIR	$24,000-33,000
GOOD	$33,000-40,000
FINE	$40,000-60,000
1966	
FAIR	$16,000-24,000
GOOD	$24,000-30,000
FINE	$30,000-45,000

FINE 1965 MODEL PRICE HISTORY

1982 $7000	1990 $88,000
1994 $60,000	1998 $55,000

1982-2000 RETURN 13%
2000-2010 10% ('66 7%)

1967-68
SHELBY GT 350

A continuation of Carroll Shelby's race-winning 1965-66 Mustang GT, but heavier, less technically specialized, and hardly raced at all. The '67 started with the below-the-belt restyle accorded that year's production Mustangs, but ended up more obviously different from them than were the 1965-66s. Highlights included a protruding fiberglass nose, plain "mouth" grille housing a central pair of driving lights (subsequently remounted outboard on some cars for legal reasons), scoops applied ahead of the rear wheels and on rear-roof quarters, a prominent decklid spoiler, and wide taillights. Inside, a thick padded rollbar housed inertia-reel seat/shoulder belts. Much in evidence throughout was a new Shelby emblem: a coiled cobra in anodized gold. Horsepower was nominally unchanged, but was doubtless

1967 350 GT coupe

less owing to the deletion of the previous steel-tube headers, though this contributed to a $600 price reduction. Sales remained respectable, but even more buyers preferred the new big-block GT 500 companion (see entry). The '68 moved even further away from the original GT 350: optional automatic transmission, relatively tame 302 V-8, more comfort/convenience features, and a somewhat huskier version of the '67 look. A bright spot was that Shelby offered a convertible GT 350 (featuring an integral rollover bar), though not many were asked for.

⚡ FOR As for 1965-66 GT 350, plus lower asking prices, greater refinement, appeal and rarity of '68 convertible • A Milestone car

◼ AGAINST As for 1965-66 GT-350, but not quite as "blue" a blue-chip

PRODUCTION
1967 fstbk cpe 1175 **1968 fstbk cpe** 1253 **conv** 404

SPECIFICATIONS

Length (in.)	181.6/183.6 (1967/68)
Wheelbase (in.)	108.0
Weight (lbs)	2800-3100
Price (new)	$3995-4238

ENGINES

cid/type	bhp	years
289/ohv V-8	290	1967
302/ohv V-8	250/350[1]	1968

[1]Normal/supercharged (latter production doubtful)

PRICES

Conv	
FAIR	$17,000-25,000
GOOD	$25,000-34,000
FINE	$34,000-48,000
Cpe	
FAIR	$6500-12,500

GOOD	$12,500-27,000
FINE	$27,000-33,000

FINE COUPE PRICE HISTORY

1982 $4700	**1990** $42,500
1994 $37,500	**1998** $37,500
1982-2000 RETURN 12%	
2000-2010 8%	

1 9 6 7 - 6 8
SHELBY GT 500

A typical bit of Carroll Shelby one-upmanship: a bigger big-block ponycar. When Ford made its 390 V-8 a new Mustang option for '67, Ol' Shel went further by offering his special Mustang with Dearborn's new 428 Cobra Jet engine. The result, called GT 500 (for no particular reason, as was also his wont), boasted 360 advertised horses, plus the new styling featured on that year's GT 350. Buyers responded, favoring big-block to small-block Shelbys to the tune of nearly two to one. The formula repeated for 1968 with huskier new styling—reshaped grille, wide hood nostrils as air intakes, Cougar taillamps with sequential turn signals, even more scoops, all shared with GT 350—and a new convertible alternative. Shelby went further still with the mid-sea son GT500KR models—"KR" for "King of the Road." They packed tuned 428s with big-port heads (from the racing 427) and larger intake and exhaust systems, good for an estimated 400 actual horses. Note that a few early '68 500s carried ordinary 390s, the result of a strike that limited 428 supplies. (Buyers weren't told about the substitution, which is nearly impossible to spot.) Shelby volume peaked in 1968, but the cars had already passed theirs. Ford now handled marketing and development, and 1968 models were built not at Shelby's California shop but by the A.O. Smith Company in Michigan. A great story in performance history was about to end.

⚡ FOR Staggering big-block acceleration • '67s the last Shelby-built Mustangs • Distinctive styling • Open-air appeal of '68 convertibles • Excellent parts/service support through strong national club

◼ AGAINST Staggering big-block axle tramp • More common than concurrent GT 350s (though no cheaper) • Less semi-race machine and more luxury tourer than earlier Shelbys

PRODUCTION
1967 500 fstbk cpe 2050 **1968 500 fstbk cpe** 1140 **500 conv** 402 **500KR fstbk cpe** 933 **500KR conv** 318

SPECIFICATIONS

Length (in.)	181.6/183.6 (1967/68)
Wheelbase (in.)	108.0
Weight (lbs)	3000-3200
Price (new)	$4195-4439

ENGINES

cid/type	bhp	years
428/ohv V-8	355[1]	1967
390/ohv V-8	335	1968
428/ohv V-8	360/400	1968
428/ohv V-8	400	1968

[1]Advertised; actual horsepower higher

PRICES

Conv

1968 GT 500 convertible

FAIR	$23,000-30,000
GOOD	$30,000-42,000
FINE	$42,000-63,000
Cpe	
FAIR	$11,000-20,000
GOOD	$20,000-28,000
FINE	$28,000-45,000
(Add 10% for GT 500KR conv.)	

FINE CONVERTIBLE PRICE HISTORY

1982 $6500		**1990** $78,000	
1994 $62,000		**1998** $68,000	
1982-2000 RETURN 15%			
2000-2010 8%			

1969-70
SHELBY GT 350

The final small-block Shelby-Mustangs. Built on a regular Ford line and restyled on the swoopier new bodyshells adopted for '69 stock Mustangs. The main appearance distinctions were a three-inch longer hood and reshaped front fenders (both in weight-saving fiberglass as before), large loop-style bumper/grille, the usual profusion of scoops (five NACA ducts on the hood alone), a clipped tail still bearing a spoiler and Cougar sequential turn signals, special wheel covers, and wide reflective bodyside tape stripes. The GT 350 was switched to Ford's new 351 "Windsor" V-8 with hydraulic lifters, big four-barrel carb, aluminum high-rise intake manifold, and a low-restriction exhaust system. Horsepower was the same as the previous year's 302, and the same engine was standard in the much cheaper Mustang Mach 1, one of several intramural rivals that had been steadily nibbling away at Shelby's sales. With demand fast-dwindling, Ford president Lee Iacocca agreed to terminate the Shelby GT at Carroll's request in late 1969. A handful of leftover '69s received black hoods, Boss 302-type front spoilers, and new serial numbers to become "1970" models. From 1967-69 Shelby licensed a separate company, Shelby De Mexico, to build GT 350s and sell them south of the border. These cars used some U.S.-built Shelby components, but carried the smaller 302 V-8 and lacked most of the American GT 350's unique body panels.

✚ **FOR** Last (if not the best) of a memorable breed • Macho looks • Performance still ample • Still pretty exclusive, too • Clubs welcome it as much as any Shelby or Mustang

▬ **AGAINST** Insurance and running costs muscle-car high • Less sought-after

1969 Shelby De Mexico GT 350 coupe

than earlier models • Lower dollar return, too

PRODUCTION

1969 fstbk cpe 1085 **conv** 194 **1970** 350

SPECIFICATIONS

Length (in.)	187.4
Wheelbase (in.)	108.0
Weight (lbs)	3000-3100
Price (new)	$4434-4800

ENGINES

cid/type	bhp	years
351/ohv V-8	290	1969-70

PRICES

Conv	
FAIR	$17,000-24,000
GOOD	$24,000-33,000
FINE	$33,000-46,000
Cpe	
FAIR	$9800-15,000
GOOD	$15,000-20,000
FINE	$20,000-32,000

FINE CONVERTIBLE PRICE HISTORY

1982 $5000		**1990** $55,000
1994 $40,000		**1998** $50,000

1982-2000 RETURN 14%
2000-2010 6%

1969-70
SHELBY GT 500

The big-block Shelby-Mustang in its final incarnation. Comments under 1969-70 GT 350 naturally apply here, too, except that advertised horsepower was higher than in '68, though it was doubtless lower in actuality.

✚ **FOR** As for 1969-70 GT-350

▬ **AGAINST** As for 1969-70 GT-350

PRODUCTION

1969 fstbk cpe 1536 **conv** 335 **1970** 286

SPECIFICATIONS

Length (in.)	187.4

GT 500 convertible

1986-87 GLH-S sedan with Carroll Shelby

Wheelbase (in.)	108.0
Weight (lbs)	3100-3200
Price (new)	$4709-5100

ENGINES

cid/type	bhp[1]	years
428/ohv V-8	375	1969-70

[1]Advertised

PRICES

Conv	
FAIR	$20,000-28,000
GOOD	$28,000-37,000
FINE	$37,000-66,000
Cpe	
FAIR	$11,000-18,000
GOOD	$18,000-25,000
FINE	$25,000-40,000

FINE CONVERTIBLE PRICE HISTORY

1982 $5000		**1990** $72,500	
1994 $50,000		**1998** $62,000	
1982-2000 RETURN 17%			
2000-2010 6%			

1986-87

SHELBY GLH-S

First of the limited-edition front-drive Dodges built by a reborn Shelby Automobiles Inc. in Whittier, California, but sold as a Shelby, not a Dodge (though through Dodge dealers). Chrysler had formed the firm in early 1986 as a subsidiary "skunkworks" to devise low-volume, high-performance offshoots of production Dodges, thus deepening a then four-year-old collaboration between the redoubtable Carroll Shelby and Chrysler chairman Lee Iacocca, who had previously teamed on the late-'60s Shelby-Mustangs when Iacocca was Ford president. The GLH-S was essentially a more specialized rendition of the 1983-86 Omni GLH ("Goes Like Hell"), itself a hotshot derivative of Dodge's workaday five-door subcompact. Its main distinction was a more potent, 175-horsepower version of the normal GLH's optional 146-bhp turbocharged 2.2 "Trans-4" engine. Modified plenum chamber, added air-to-air intercooler, equal-length intake runners, and other Shelby tweaks accounted for the extra power. Also standard were a manual five-speed transaxle (no automatic available), heavy-duty suspension, wide tires on multi-hole alloy wheels, tachometer, console, and somewhat snazzier cabin trim. Gloriously unrefined, almost crude in engine and chassis behavior (one tester at the time said "the accelerator pedal acts like a lane-change switch"), but fast, noisy fun. High performance plus low production and Shelby mystique suggest this as at least a minor collector's item in the not-too-distant future.

✚ FOR Fast (under 8 seconds 0-60 mph) • Fun to drive (wear earplugs, though) • Decent economy • Hatchback practical • Used-car prices still apply

▬ AGAINST Rocky ride • Unwanted turbo lag • Marked torque-steer • Mediocre fit and finish • Ultimate collectibility unclear at present

PRODUCTION

500

SPECIFICATIONS

Length (in.)	163.2
Wheelbase (in.)	99.1
Weight (lbs)	2300
Price (new)	$10,995

ENGINES

cid/type	bhp	years
135/ohc I-4¹	175	1986-87

¹Turbocharged

PRICES

FAIR	$1000-2000
GOOD	$2000-3000
FINE	$3000-5000

FINE EXAMPLE PRICE HISTORY

1990 $2000   **1994** $2000
1998 $4500
1982-2000 RETURN 4%
2000-2010 5%

1987 SHELBY CHARGER GLH-S

A "Shelbyized" edition of the L-body Dodge hatchback coupe, related to the Omni-based GLH-S in the same way that ordinary Chargers related to workaday Omnis. Not to be confused, however, with the 1982-87 Shelby Charger, a relatively low-power volume model sold as a Dodge, not a Shelby. Identical to the GLH-S five-door mechanically, and similar in chassis specs and equipment.

✚ FOR As for 1986-87 Shelby GLH-S, plus racier coupe styling

▬ AGAINST As for 1986-87 Shelby GLH-S (and alas, no more refined)

1987 Charger GLH-S fastback coupe

PRODUCTION

1000

SPECIFICATIONS

Length (in.)	174.8
Wheelbase (in.)	96.5
Weight (lbs)	2483
Price (new)	$12,995

ENGINES

cid/type	bhp	years
135/ohc I-4¹	175	1986-87

¹Turbocharged

PRICES

As for Shelby GLH-S
2000-2010 RETURN 3%

1987-88 SHELBY LANCER

A more luxurious latterday Shelby based on Dodge's H-body Lancer five-door, the division's mid-'80s midsizer and erstwhile "Eurosedan" competitor. Unlike the earlier Omni/Charger GLH-S models, this one came with power everything, offered a remote-control CD audio system and leather interior as options, and featured a Shelby signature dashboard plaque, sport steering wheel, and lacy-spoke road wheels. Also unique was a no-cost exterior "aero" package that added a front airdam, side and rear skirts, and a rear spoiler to the already smooth Lancer shape. Suspension was stiffened per Shelby practice, which meant a very hard ride but superb front-drive handling—provided you kept a rein on the 175-horsepower turbo-four engine. Carroll liked to portray this as an American answer to the Mercedes 190E 2.3-16 (see entry) and similar cars, only far more affordable. Cheaper it was, but also far less sophisticated. Again, though, production was deliberately very limited, performance and not refinement was the

1987-88 Lancer sedan

car's reason for being, and Carroll sold every Shelby Lancer his firm built.

✛ **FOR** As for 1986-87 Shelby GLH-S, plus more luxurious, better equipped, roomier, and more attractive

▬ **AGAINST** As for 1986-87 Shelby GLH-S

PRODUCTION
800

SPECIFICATIONS

Length (in.)	180.4
Wheelbase (in.)	103.1
Weight (lbs)	2895
Price (new)	$16,950-17,950

ENGINES

cid/type	bhp	years
135/ohc I-4[1]	175	1986-87

[1]Turbocharged

PRICES

As for Shelby GLH-S
2000-2010 RETURN 3%

1988-89
SHELBY CSX

1988 CSX coupe

Another Shelby Automobiles Dodge-based hotshot. The basis this time was the new-for-'87 P-body Shadow, the replacement for the L-body Omni. Introduced in '87 as an '88, the CSX was a three-door hatchback, not a five-door, and much smoother and more modern-looking. Because the production Shadow was derived from Chrysler's K-car compact like Lancer, the CSX followed the basic technical formula as the Shelby Lancer (see above) but was slightly faster owing to its smaller size and lower curb weight. It could do 0-60 in around 7.1 seconds (versus 7.7) and the standing quarter-mile in 15.1 seconds at 90 mph (versus 15.7 at 89). Top speed, however, was unchanged at 135 mph. The CSX has the distinction of being the most numerous Dodge-based Shelby special so far. Those built from 1988 on benefitted from Chrysler's VNT—Variable Nozzle Technology—turbocharging system that all but eliminated throttle lag for more responsive low- and mid-range acceleration.

✛ **FOR** As for 1986-87 Shelby GLH-S, plus more contemporary looks • Superior driveability on post-'87 production VNT models

▬ **AGAINST** As for 1986-87 Shelby GLH-S

PRODUCTION[1]

1987 750 **1988** 1000 **1989** 500
[1]Calendar year

SPECIFICATIONS

Length (in.)	171.7
Wheelbase (in.)	97.0
Weight (lbs)	2675-2790

Price (new)	$13,495-15,000

ENGINES

cid/type	bhp	years
135/ohc I-4[1]	175	1986-87

[1]Turbocharged

PRICES

FAIR	$1000-2000
GOOD	$2000-3500
FINE	$3500-6500

FINE EXAMPLE PRICE HISTORY

1990 $2000	**1994** $2000
1998 $5000	
1982-2000 RETURN 4%	
2000-2010 3%	

1999
SHELBY S.P. 360 DURANGO

Not made or designed by Carroll Shelby, the S.P. (Super Pursuit) 360 received Shelby's full blessing. Starting as a Dodge Durango, the S.P. 360 gained a Shelby-inspired blue with white stripes paint job. A more aggressive front end, hood scoops, lowered ride height, wide tires on polished alloy wheels also separated the Shelby from normal Durangos. Inside were leather quad bucket seats and carbon fiber trim accents. A video cassette player entertained back seat passengers. Suspension was modified for better agility, but ride comfort suffered. S.P. 360s could be ordered with 2WD or full-time 4WD. The most important option was the supercharged 5.9-liter V-8. Raising horsepower to 360, this engine could accelerate the two and half ton mass to 60 in less than seven seconds. Conceived by Performance

1999 S.P. 360 Durango wagon

West tuners and built by "licensed Chrylser Conversion companies", Shelby Durangos were available through Dodge dealers.

⊞ FOR Racy styling • Shelby name • Available supercharged performance

⊟ AGAINST Sport utility that loses utility • Similar paint job on Durango R/T dilutes appeal

PRODUCTION

NA

SPECIFICATIONS

Length (in.)	193.3
Weight (lbs)	4900
Wheelbase (in.)	115.9
Price (new)	$43,000-54,000 (est.)

ENGINES

cid/type	bhp	years
360/ohv V-8[1]	360	1999-00

[1]Supercharged

PRICES

Still dependent on used car market.

2000 Series 1 roadster

2000
SHELBY SERIES 1

Light weight and high horsepower is a recipe for performance that Carroll Shelby understands. The aluminum chassis and carbon fiber body keep the weight of the Series 1 roadster down to 2,650 lbs. A modified Oldsmobile Aurora V-8 puts out 320-horsepower. Shelby claims a 0-60 time of 4.4 seconds and the quarter mile in 12.8 seconds. The engine is set back behind the front suspension and the transmission is rear mounted for good weight distribution. Good balance with race-bred suspension help generate a claimed 1.0g of lateral grip. The Series 1 should generate performance similar to the AC Shelby Cobra, but with much more comfort and refinement.

⊞ FOR Cobra performance • Attractive roadster styling • Rarity and heritage

⊟ AGAINST Performance and reliability of production cars not known at time of publication • More expensive than Panoz Esperante

SPECIFICATIONS

Length (in.)	169.0
Weight (lbs)	2650
Wheelbase (in.)	96.2
Price (new)	$135,000

ENGINES

cid/type	bhp	years
244/dohc V-8	320	2000

PRICES

Market value
2000-2010 RETURN Depreciating

1931-36
SS I

The cars that marked the emergence of William Lyons' Swallow Sidecars coachbuilding company as an automaker in its own right, and historically significant as the direct ancestors of the first Jaguar. Originally offered as a closed coupe in two versions, the 2054cc Sixteen and 2552cc Twenty, both with side-valve engines and underslung chassis from Standard Motor Company. Bodies were built by Swallow to Lyons' designs. Early models had cycle-type front fenders, later ones the "clamshell" style, but all had

1934 SS I 2-door sedan

1936 SS I Tourer

long hoods. A touring convertible appeared in 1933, followed by a 2-door sedan in 1934-35. The undistinguished chassis featured beam axles at each end and cable-operated mechanical brakes. Synchromesh was added to the transmission in 1934. Long, low, and unmistakable—but not very fast as the top end was barely 80 mph. Some versions had cramped cabins and small windows. But the sexy looks, wood-and-leather interior luxury, and amazingly low prices was a winning formula. The SS I led directly to the SS100 produced under the renamed SS Jaguar marque (see entry).

FOR Historical importance • Racy styling • Reasonably priced today • Enthusiastic worldwide club interest/support

AGAINST Wood-framed—and thus rot-prone—bodies • Parts shortages makes restoration difficult • Slower than they look • Hard ride • Uncertain handling

PRODUCTION

4254

SPECIFICATIONS

Length (in.)	174.0-186.0
Wheelbase (in.)	112.0 (1931-32), 119.0 (1933-36)
Weight (lbs)	2400-3000
Price (new)	NA

ENGINES

cc/type (cid)	bhp[1]	years
2054/sv I-6 (125)	45	1931-36
2552/sv I-6 (156)	55/62	1931-36
2143/sv I-6 (131)	53/62	1933-36
2664/sv I-6 (163)	68/70	1933-36

[1]Net

PRICES

Open	
FAIR	$10,000-18,000
GOOD	$18,000-30,000
FINE	$30,000-50,000
Closed	
FAIR	$6000-15,000
GOOD	$15,000-22,000
FINE	$22,000-27,500

FINE SPORTS TOURER PRICE HISTORY

1982 $12,000	**1990** $60,000
1994 $40,000	**1998** $40,000
1982-2000 RETURN 8%	
2000-2010 5%	

1936-40
SS JAGUAR 100

Successor to the SS90—a short-wheelbase two-seater powered by the 2664cc side-valve Standard six and based on SS I chassis engineering. Only 23 SS90s were built in 1935. The SS 100 retained the 90's basic 104-inch-wheelbase platform, but mounted overhead-valve engines straight out of SS Jaguar's sedans. The initial 2.5-liter version was supplemented by a 3.5-liter unit in 1938. Though cramped even for a two-seater, the roadster styling was a sensation. Ride was hard and the steering quite vague, yet this was about the most eye-catching car on British roads and amazing value for money. The larger-engine model could do a genuine 100 mph and 0-60 in 10.4 seconds. Even more power was obtain-

1937 Jaguar 100 roadster

able via fairly simple tuning tweaks. Rare then—and even scarcer now. You'll need a bundle of bucks to put one in your garage.

➕ **FOR** Sensual, widely applauded styling • Zippy performance • Handy size • Uncommon today

➖ **AGAINST** Pricey, and becoming more so • Cramped cockpit • SS I road manners • Body parts scarce

PRODUCTION

2½ **Litre** 198 3½ **Litre** 116

SPECIFICATIONS

Length (in.)	150.0
Wheelbase (in.)	104.0
Weight (lbs)	2600
Price (new)	NA

ENGINES

cc/type (cid)	bhp[1]	years
2664/ohv I-6 (163)	105	1936-40
3485/ohv I-6 (213)	125	1938-40

[1]Gross

PRICES

2½ Litre
FAIR	$40,000-70,000
GOOD	$70,000-95,000
FINE	$95,000-120,000

3½ Litre
FAIR	$50,000-85,000
GOOD	$85,000-105,000
FINE	$105,000-125,000

FINE 3 1/2 LITRE PRICE HISTORY

1982 $60,000		**1990** $400,000	
1994 $125,000		**1998** $125,000	

1982-2000 RETURN 4%
2000-2010 5%

SS JAGUAR 2½ LITRE/ 3½ LITRE
1936-40

The four-seat running mates to the romantic SS 100 roadster, and the first cars to carry the Jaguar label. Chassis and bodywork was from SS Cars, Limited. Standard supplied transmissions and engines, the latter converted from side-valve to overhead-valve layout. Still with mechanical brakes and solid-axle front suspension, but also with great style and roomy interiors in four-door sedans and two-door convertible coupes. Massive headlamps and wire-spoke wheels handsomely set off the flowing William Lyons' lines, and cabins were trimmed in the expected wood and leather. As with the SS 100, a larger 3.5-liter engine was offered beginning in 1938, at which time bodies were switched from wood-framed to all-steel construction and wheelbase was stretched an inch. Also offered as a very similar short-wheelbase (108 inches) 1½ Litre with a 1608cc side-valve Standard four (later 1776cc ohv), but these are nowhere nearly as desirable today. Quicker than previous SS four-seaters, the rare 3.5-liter models could do at least 90 mph.

➕ **FOR** The first genuine Jags • Fleet and fleet-looking • Extra-desirable "dropheads" • Sporting sedans • Simple, easy mechanical rebuild • Ample club support and interest

➖ **AGAINST** Pre-1938 body rot • No body parts available • Marginal brakes • Old-fashioned road manners

PRODUCTION

2 ¼ **Litre** 5369 3 ½ **Litre** 1304

SPECIFICATIONS

Length (in.)	186.0
Wheelbase (in.)	119.0 (1936-37), 120.0 (1938-40)
Weight (lbs)	3500-3650
Price (new)	NA

ENGINES

cc/type (cid)	bhp[1]	years
2664/ohv I-6 (163)	105	1936-40
3485/ohv I-6 (213)	125	1938-40

[1]Gross

PRICES

Open
FAIR	$10,000-18,000
GOOD	$18,000-25,000
FINE	$25,000-35,000

Closed
FAIR	$5000-9000
GOOD	$9000-15,000
FINE	$15,000-22,500

FINE DROPHEAD PRICE HISTORY

1982 $13,000		**1990** $35,000	
1994 $30,000		**1998** $30,000	

1982-2000 RETURN 6%
2000-2010 3%

1939 Jaguar 2 ½ Litre sedan

1930-33
STUDEBAKER PRESIDENT EIGHT

Studebaker's most impressive car of the early Depression years, built between 1929 and 1933 and engineered by the legendary Delmar G. "Barney" Roos. The President turned a leisurely 2800 rpm at 60 mph, was improved in 1931 when its engine was switched from five to nine main bearings, and got more horsepower. The crankshaft, derived from the Liberty aircraft engine, was partly responsible for this powerplant's well-known durability and low-end stamina. Offered on two wheelbases for most of its life, the President listed a wide variety of handsome body styles. It was the basis for Studebaker's most successful racers in this period and probably the best overall automobile ever produced at South Bend.

FOR For years the most protested omission on the CCCA list, now a full Classic (1929-33, except the '33 Model 82) • Style and stamina

AGAINST Growing parts shortage • Open bodies not cheap • Classic status will inevitably exert upward price pressure

1932 President Eight convertible

PRODUCTION

1930 15,000 (est.) **1931** 4000 (est.) **1932** 2399
1933 1829

SPECIFICATIONS

Length (in.)	Varies
Wheelbase (in.)	125.0/135.0 (1930 and 1933); 130.0/136.0 (1931); 135.0 (1932)
Weight (lbs)	3480-4605
Price (new)	$1325-2595

ENGINES

cid/type	bhp	years
337.0/sv I-8	115-132	1930-33
250.0/sv I-8	110	1933[1]

[1]Series 82

PRICES

1930-32:
Open

FAIR	$8500-17,000
GOOD	$17,000-35,000
FINE	$35,000-60,000
Closed	
FAIR	$3000-10,000
GOOD	$10,000-23,000
FINE	$23,000-33,000

(Add 20% to closed prices for State victoria, cpe, & St. Regis brougham.)

1933:
Open

FAIR	$4000-15,000
GOOD	$15,000-25,000
FINE	$25,000-43,000
Closed	
FAIR	$2000-8000
GOOD	$8000-14,000
FINE	$14,000-20,000

(Add 25% to closed prices for cpe & St. Regis brougham.)

FINE 1932 CONVERTIBLE SEDAN PRICE HISTORY

1982 $27,000		**1990** $60,000	
1994 $50,000		**1998** $60,000	
1982-2000 RETURN 5%			
2000-2010 5%			

1930 President Eight State Sedan

1934-39

STUDEBAKER PRESIDENT EIGHT

Continuation of Studebaker's top-of-the-line series, increasingly streamlined through the late 1930s, gaining pontoon fenders and rounded grillework but retaining a crisp, individual appearance. Warner overdrive and "planar" independent front suspension came in 1935 (transverse leaf spring with upper/lower links and rotary shocks); "Hill Holder" (a device that prevented the car from rolling backwards when the clutch was depressed) in 1936. Automatic choke, vacuum-assisted brakes, rotary door latches, and all-steel bodies also arrived in late '30s. Restyled by Raymond Loewy in 1938, and from that point they just kept getting better, with a prow-front motif and flush headlamps. All Presidents in this period were powered by Studebaker's 250-cid L-head eight with up to 115 horsepower, which was more than adequate.

FOR Superb road performer • High quality and style • Huge array of bodies including the "Year Ahead" streamliners beginning July 1934

AGAINST Not nearly as widely recognized and sought after as earlier Presidents

PRODUCTION

1934 3698 **1935** 2305 **1936** 7297 **1937** 9000 **1938** 5474 **1939** 8205

SPECIFICATIONS

Length (in.)	NA
Wheelbase (in.)	123.0 (1934); 124.0 (1935); 125.0 (1936-37); 122.0 (1938-39)
Weight (lbs)	3300-3970
Price (new)	$1015-1555

ENGINES

cid/type	bhp	years
250.0/sv I-8	110-115	1934-39

PRICES

Open	
FAIR	$7500-15,000
GOOD	$15,000-27,000
FINE	$27,000-40,000
Closed	
FAIR	$2500-6000
GOOD	$6000-12,000
FINE	$12,000-18,000

FINE 1939 CONVERTIBLE SEDAN PRICE HISTORY

1982 $22,000		**1990** $32,000	
1994 $30,000		**1998** $35,000	
1982-2000 RETURN 3%			
2000-2010 3%			

1940-42

STUDEBAKER PRESIDENT

The largest and most luxurious of the Raymond Loewy-styled Studebakers in the years before World War II, priced in Buick Century and Chrysler Windsor territory. Improving finances allowed Studebaker to offer three separate trim stages in 1941-42, and nine different '42 models. The various permutations were all based on only three closed body styles. A coupe, club sedan, and four-door Cruising Sedan were offered for 1940. A sedan-coupe, Cruising Sedan, and new Land Cruiser four-door were the 1941-42 offerings. A smooth L-head straight eight delivering 110/117 bhp provided the power. Some Studes of this era sported DeLuxe-Tone bodyside two-toning, putting Studebaker in the forefront of a trend that would really take off in the '50s. The President name was dropped after World War II; it didn't return to until 1955. However, the long-wheelbase Land Cruisers were revived for the interim 1946 model year, an attempt to continue a car this size with a more economical six-cylinder engine.

1936 President Eight sedan

1941 President Skyway Cruising Sedan

✚ FOR Relative rarity • Smooth open-road performance • Quality construction

▬ AGAINST Limited body types • Unexciting styling

PRODUCTION

1940 6444 **1941** 6994 **1942** 3500

SPECIFICATIONS

Length (in.)	211.3
Wheelbase (in.)	122.0/124.5 (1940/41-42)
Weight (lbs)	3280-3540
Price (new)	$1025-1276

ENGINES

cid/type	bhp	years
250.4/sv I-8	110/117	1940-42

PRICES

FAIR	$2500-7000
GOOD	$7000-13,000

FINE	$13,000-18,500

(Add 5% for Deluxe-Tone.)

FINE EXAMPLE PRICE HISTORY

1982 $5900		**1990** $15,000	
1994 $15,000		**1998** $15,000	
1982-2000 RETURN 7%			
2000-2010 5%			

1 9 4 6
STUDEBAKER SKYWAY CHAMPION

Temporarily after the war, Studebaker built a limited number of Champions with prewar body dies and the well-proven 80-bhp L-head six. Alterations from 1942 were minimal: the upper grille molding was extended under the headlamps, side hood moldings were eliminated. As in '42, optional auxiliary lamps were available for the front fender tops. The production run was short—just 19,275 units were built—because an all-new postwar model was on the way.

✚ FOR Quite rare, especially coupes • The end of a design era • Well built

▬ AGAINST Now quite pricey for a Champion • Hard to find • Certain body parts now in short supply

PRODUCTION

3P cpe 2465 **5P cpe** 1285 **2d club sdn** 5000 **4d sdn** 10,525

SPECIFICATIONS

Length (in.)	197.8
Wheelbase (in.)	110.0
Weight (lbs)	2491-2566
Price (new)	$1002-1097

ENGINES

cid/type	bhp	years
169.6/sv I-6	80	1946

PRICES

FAIR	$1000-3000
GOOD	$3000-6000
FINE	$6000-9500

FINE EXAMPLE PRICE HISTORY

1982 $5000		**1990** $6500	
1994 $7000		**1998** $9500	
1982-1992 RETURN 4%			
2000-2010 3%			

1946 Skyway Champion coupe

1947-49
STUDEBAKER CHAMPION COUPE & CONVERTIBLE

1947 Champion Starlight coupe

The same interesting, all-new postwar styling as the 1947-49 Commander in Studebaker's lower-priced series. Rode a seven-inch-shorter wheelbase than Commander, and had a smaller 169.6-cid L-head six. Less impressive-looking and with less performance, too, but the Champion includes all the same design qualities that make Studebakers of these years so noteworthy. The Starlight coupe featured an impressively large wraparound rear window, and was truly individual-looking. Model offerings duplicate those in the Commander line, but with correspondingly lower prices then and now.

✠ FOR Trend-setting styling • Economical operation • Good parts supplies

• Both body styles are Milestone cars

▄ AGAINST As for 1947-49 Commander

PRODUCTION

1947 Starlight 5P cpe 16,731 **conv** 2251 **1948 Starlight 5P cpe** 14,481 **conv** 9996 **1949 Starlight 5P cpe** 15,746 **conv** 7035

SPECIFICATIONS

Length (in.)	190.6/191.9 (1947-48/49)
Wheelbase (in.)	112.0
Weight (lbs)	2670-2895
Price (new)	$1472-2086

ENGINES

cid/type	bhp	years
169.6/sv I-6	80	1947-49

PRICES

Conv	
FAIR	$3000-7000
GOOD	$7000-13,000
FINE	$13,000-19,000
Starlight cpe	
FAIR	$1500-3000
GOOD	$3000-6000
FINE	$6000-9800

FINE STARLIGHT COUPE PRICE HISTORY

1982 $5200		**1990** $7500	
1994 $8000		**1998** $9500	
1982-2000 RETURN 4%			
2000-2010 3% (conv 5%)			

1947 Champion convertible

STUDEBAKER COMMANDER COUPE & CONVERTIBLE

The all-new postwar Studebaker in its most glamorous (and pricey) guises. Announced well in advance of the 1947 model year in early '46, making Studebaker "First by far with a postwar car!" It was a styling sensation that, to some extent, predicted design trends not only at Studebaker, but also for the auto industry as a whole, particularly the flow-through front fenders and the low hood/deck height. The '47 was the work mainly of Loewy Associates, with input from Virgil Exner. The Starlight coupe was available in DeLuxe and Regal DeLuxe trim, but the convertible was offered only in Regal DeLuxe form. Though not as important as the Starlight, the soft top was notable for its smooth lines and jaunty top-down character.

✚ **FOR** An outstanding industrial design • Good performance • Milestone cars

▬ **AGAINST** Not cheap or easy to find anymore • Rust-prone, especially front fenders

PRODUCTION
1947 Starlight 5P cpe 13,299 **conv** 1503 **1948 Starlight 5P cpe** 14,441 **conv** 7982 **1949 Starlight 5P cpe** 8990 **conv** 1702

SPECIFICATIONS
Length (in.)	204.3/205.4 (1947-48/49)
Wheelbase (in.)	119.0
Weight (lbs)	3200-3420
Price (new)	$1755-2468

ENGINES
cid/type	bhp	years
226.2/sv I-6	94	1947-48
245.6/sv I-6	100	1949

PRICES
As per Champion, plus 10%.

STUDEBAKER COMMANDER

1951 Commander sedan

The most important collector model among 1950-51 "bullet nose" Studebakers. The main reason is that this was the first year for the firm's pioneering 232 V-8, really the first of the small-block engines (though Chevy and Ford usually get the credit). Though conventionally engineered and heavy compared to later small V-8s,

1948 Commander Regal DeLuxe convertible

this reliable powerplant could deliver surprising economy with good performance. Coupled with the Studebaker/Detroit Gear three-speed automatic announced the previous year, the V-8 made the '51 Commander very attractive, and sales were high. The most collectible models are the Starlight five-passenger coupe, the convertible, and the long-wheelbase Land Cruiser four-door. Two- and four-door sedans were also available in this year's Commander line. Nomenclature for trim levels was revised, with Regal denoting the lower coupe and sedans, while State applied to the upper-level sedans, coupe, and convertible in the Commander series. This was the next-to-last year for the 1947 "which way is it going?" design, a problem the more defined bullet-nose front helped alleviate.

✛ FOR Notable historically • Good performance/economy balance • Nicely trimmed • Solid construction

◼ AGAINST Debatable styling (especially the front) • Traditional rust problems • An oil-leaker, though not usually an oil-burner

PRODUCTION

124,329

SPECIFICATIONS

Length (in.)	197.5 (Land Cruiser: 201.5)
Wheelbase (in.)	115.0 (Land Cruiser: 119.0)
Weight (lbs)	3030-3240
Price (new)	$1997-2381

ENGINES

cid/type	bhp	years
232.6/ohv V-8	120	1951

PRICES

Conv	
FAIR	$5000-10,000
GOOD	$10,000-17,000
FINE	$17,000-25,000
Starlight cpe	
FAIR	$3000-6500
GOOD	$6500-11,000
FINE	$11,000-17,000
Others	
FAIR	$2500-5500
GOOD	$5500-9500
FINE	$9500-13,500

FINE CONVERTIBLE PRICE HISTORY

1982 $10,000		**1990** $20,000	
1994 $21,000		**1998** $22,000	
1982-2000 RETURN 6%			
2000-2010 5%			

1952
STUDEBAKER COMMANDER STATE STARLINER

A new addition to Studebaker's upper series in the last year of the 1947 body design. The bullet nose was eliminated in favor of a "shovel" snout—sometimes dubbed "clam digger"—which some designers found less appealing. (The bullet nose has received a lot of flak over the years, but somehow looks less bizarre now than it did then—could it be because of the many blunt fronts we've seen since?) The Starliner is significant in that it was Studebaker's first hardtop convertible, with a top-quality interior and pillarless roof. A companion Regal Starliner was offered in the six-cylinder Champion line as well, which had been

1952 Commander State Starliner hardtop coupe

moved up to the Commander's 115-inch wheelbase the previous year. South Bend was the last major auto manufacturer to introduce a hardtop, but in the following year would carry this body type to its ultimate.

FOR Historical interest • Good performance from small-block V-8

AGAINST Underwhelming looks • Rust susceptibility • Poor-quality chrome (an industry-wide problem during the Korean conflict)

PRODUCTION
14,548

SPECIFICATIONS
Length (in.)	197.5
Wheelbase (in.)	115.0
Weight (lbs)	3220
Price (new)	$2488

ENGINES
cid/type	bhp	years
232.6/ohv V-8	120	1952

PRICES
FAIR	$3500-8000
GOOD	$8000-14,000
FINE	$14,000-20,000

FINE EXAMPLE PRICE HISTORY
1982 $4600	1990 $9000
1994 $9500	1998 $14,000
1982-2000 RETURN 9%	
2000-2010 5%	

1953-54
STUDEBAKER CHAMPION REGAL STARLIGHT/ STARLINER

Probably the outstanding American automotive design of the '50s, certainly one of the all-time greats. The smooth Starliner hardtop and companion Starlight fixed-pillar coupe were mainly the work of Robert E. Bourke, chief of the Raymond Loewy studios at South Bend. The styling was about as perfect as it could be: nothing out of place, nothing contrived or unnatural. The Starliner is the purer of the two in styling, but the Starlight holds together better because of the extra body rigidity conferred by its fixed roof pillar. Vertical grille teeth distinguish the '54s from the toothless '53s. As in past years, the Champion versions were six-cylinder cars, identifiable externally by an S-on-a-V emblem on hood and deck in place of the V-8 emblem found on the costlier Commanders. Studebaker's side-valve six was lighter than the V-8, providing better balance and less final understeer. It was also capable of notable economy (especially with overdrive), though it offered far less performance than the V-8. The '53 Champion dashboards differed from Commander dashes, grouping instruments under a single panel instead of housing them in hooded pods.

FOR Landmark American styling • Still very affordable considering design merit • Less numerous but cheaper than Commanders • Strong appreciation potential • Both coupe and hardtop are Milestone cars

AGAINST A serious ruster • Indifferent brakes • Only fair construction quality, mainly '53s

PRODUCTION
1953 Starliner 2d htp 13,058 **Starlight 2d cpe** 25,488 **1954 Starliner 2d htp** 4302 **Starlight 2d cpe** 12,167

SPECIFICATIONS
Length (in.)	201.9
Wheelbase (in.)	120.5
Weight (lbs)	2700-2825
Price (new)	$1955-2241

ENGINES
cid/type	bhp	years
169.6/sv I-6	85	1953-54

1953 Champion Regal Starliner hardtop coupe

PRICES

Starliner

FAIR	$2800-4000
GOOD	$4000-6000
FINE	$6000-8500

Starlight

FAIR	$2000-3500
GOOD	$3500-5500
FINE	$5500-7500

FINE STARLINER HARDTOP PRICE HISTORY

1982	$4500	1990	$8500
1994	$7000	1998	$8000
1982-2000 RETURN 4%			
2000-2010 5%			

1954 Commander Starlight coupe

PRODUCTION

1953 Starliner 2d htp 19,326 **Starlight 2d cpe** 20,859 **1954 Starliner 2d htp** 5040 **Starlight 2d cpe** 6019

SPECIFICATIONS

Length (in.)	201.9
Wheelbase (in.)	120.5
Weight (lbs)	3040-3175
Price (new)	$2213-2502

ENGINES

cid/type	bhp	years
232.6/ohv V-8	120	1953-54

PRICES

Starliner

FAIR	$3500-5500
GOOD	$5500-7500
FINE	$7500-10,500

Starlight

FAIR	$2500-4000
GOOD	$4000-7000
FINE	$7000-9500

FINE STARLIGHT COUPE PRICE HISTORY

1982	$5000	1990	$8500
1994	$9000	1998	$9500
1982-2000 RETURN 4%			
2000-2010 5%			

1953-54
STUDEBAKER COMMANDER REGAL STARLIGHT/ STARLINER

The V-8 version of the daring and enduring "Loewy coupe" design, similar in most other respects to the six-cylinder Champion models. The sleek European styling was matched by equally nice interiors trimmed mainly in vinyl or (for 1954 only) cloth, both color-keyed. There was also a slightly less posh DeLuxe-trim version of the fixed pillar Starlight offered in both years. These could have been the cars that would have assured Studebaker's future, but, as the production figures suggest, they didn't. One reason was spotty assembly quality on the '53s, a result of the rush to get the design into production. Another was a flimsy frame on '53s, but improved for '54. Still another reason was the company's miscalculation about the sales of the coupes versus those of other body styles. Had Studebaker geared up to build more coupes, more would undoubtedly have been sold. As it was, the company thought the shorter wheelbase sedans and wagons, with scrunched-up lines based on the coupe styling, would sell better. Despite their greater rarity, the '54s seem to trail the '53s in value right now, but that may reverse itself in time.

✚ FOR As for 1953-54 Champion models, including Milestone status, plus good performance

◼ AGAINST As for 1953-54 Champion models, but more expensive even though more survive

1955
STUDEBAKER PRESIDENT SPEEDSTER

Studebaker's first step toward the sporty car, and forerunner to the memorable Hawks. The most expensive offering in this year's revived topline President series, this two-door hardtop featured a special interior with quilted-pattern leather and vinyl upholstery and a full complement of white-on-black instruments set into a dash with a tooled-metal appliqué. A high-performance rendition of the Studebaker small-block V-8, now bored out to 259.2 cid, was standard. The midyear Speedsters shared the heavy, more chrome-laden "fish-lip" front-end styling adopted for '55 across the line. All Speedsters wore two or

1955 President Speedster hardtop coupe

three-tone paint jobs in garish color combinations like the unforgettable "lemon and lime."

FOR Rarity • Historical interest • Excellent performance • A driver's cockpit • Equipment • Another Studebaker Milestone car

AGAINST Retrograde facelift of the clean 1953-54 • Significant rust problems • Oil leaks

PRODUCTION

2215

SPECIFICATIONS

Length (in.)	204.4
Wheelbase (in.)	120.5
Weight (lbs)	3301
Price (new)	$3253

ENGINES

cid/type	bhp	years
259.2/ohv V-8	185	1955

PRICES

FAIR	$2800-4500
GOOD	$4500-8000
FINE	$8000-15,000

FINE EXAMPLE PRICE HISTORY

1982 $8500		**1990** $13,000	
1994 $15,000		**1998** $14,000	
1982-2000 RETURN 3%			
2000-2010 4%			

1956 STUDEBAKER GOLDEN HAWK

The last Studebaker until the Avanti with styling influenced by the Loewy Studios. An evolution of the original 1953 Starliner/Starlight, distinguished by a squared-off eggcrate grille and raised trunklid. The Golden Hawk was the most luxurious, expensive, and powerful member of a four-model Hawk family for '56, and stood apart as a separate offering not directly tied to a regular series (the Flight, Power, and Sky Hawks were listed in the Champion, Commander, and President series, respectively). Available in pillarless form only, it was distinguished by grafted-on fiberglass tailfins. Standard power came from the big 352-cid Packard V-8 with 275 bhp. A heavy engine, it had a very negative effect on handling, but gave brilliant straight-line pickup. Interestingly enough, Studebaker was able to price the Golden Hawk $200 below its 1955 President Speedster predecessor because of fewer standard accessories and a correspondingly longer options list.

FOR Strong appreciation potential • Flashy looks • Impressive acceleration and high-speed cruising ability

AGAINST Thirsty • Don't take on better-balanced sports cars on a winding road

PRODUCTION

4071

SPECIFICATIONS

Length (in.)	203.9
Wheelbase (in.)	120.5
Weight (lbs)	3360
Price (new)	$3061

ENGINES

cid/type	bhp	years
352/ohv V-8	275	1956

PRICES

FAIR	$2500-4000
GOOD	$4000-8500
FINE	$8500-15,000

FINE EXAMPLE PRICE HISTORY

1982 $9000		**1990** $16,500	
1994 $17,500		**1998** $15,000	
1982-2000 RETURN 3%			

1956 Golden Hawk hardtop coupe

2000-2010 4%

1956-57
STUDEBAKER PRESIDENT CLASSIC

A luxury four-door on the longer of Studebaker's two late-'50s wheelbases, really a revival of the posh Land Cruiser after a year's absence. Actually, the '56 and similar '57 President Classics weren't so much special models as the only ones—other than Hawks—to retain the longer 120.5-inch chassis used since 1953. Inner body structure was basically '53, too, but outer panels were fully restyled to impart a more upright, "important" look, highlighted by mesh grilles (full-width on '57s) and greatly extended rear fenders. Drivers checked rate of progress with a revolving-drum "Cyclops eye" speedometer perched atop the dash directly ahead, a '30s throwback that might better have been avoided, though it was one of the few things that could be changed to make the cars seem new. Buyers evidently saw through such deceptions—or more likely feared that Studebaker was about to go under, which it was—for sales plunged in '56 and went even lower for 1957-58. The Classic is included here mainly for interest value and rarity, though we think the '56 is also one of the better-looking peri-

1956 President Classic sedan

od Studes: less ornate than the '55 and more tasteful than the '57.

⊞ FOR Strong special-interest value • Relatively rare yet inexpensive • Good performance • Lots of people and parcel space • Good club support

▦ AGAINST Uglified '57 styling • Not in high demand even among Studebaker fans • Tinworm tendencies born of so-so workmanship

PRODUCTION
1956 18,209 (all Presidents) **1957** NA

SPECIFICATIONS
Length (in.)	204.8/206.4 (1956/57)
Wheelbase (in.)	120.5
Weight (lbs)	3270-3295
Price (new)	$2489-2539

ENGINES
cid/type	bhp	years
289/ohv V-8[1]	210/225	1956

[1]Supercharged

PRICES
FAIR	$1500-2000
GOOD	$2000-4000
FINE	$4000-7500

FINE EXAMPLE PRICE HISTORY
1982 $2250	**1990** $6000
1994 $6000	**1998** $7500
1982-2000 RETURN 7%	
2000-2010 3%	

1956
STUDEBAKER SKY HAWK

A less garish relative of this year's Golden Hawk, also with hardtop styling but without the tailfins or

1956 Sky Hawk hardtop coupe

Packard engine. Part of the President series, and powered by 210- or 225-bhp versions of Studebaker's V-8, now stroked to 289 cid.

➕ FOR Good styling for the '50s • Reasonably good handling • Fine performance • Low-production appeal • Highly sought-after

➖ AGAINST Stude's usual rust and oil leak problems

PRODUCTION

3610

SPECIFICATIONS

Length (in.)	203.9
Wheelbase (in.)	120.5
Weight (lbs)	3215
Price (new)	$2477

ENGINES

cid/type	bhp	years
289/ohv V-8	225	1956

PRICES

FAIR	$1500-3500
GOOD	$3500-7000
FINE	$7000-12,500

FINE EXAMPLE PRICE HISTORY

1982 $6000	1990 $11,500
1994 $13,500	1998 $13,000
1982-2000 RETURN 5%	
2000-2010 4%	

1 9 5 7 - 5 8
STUDEBAKER GOLDEN HAWK

A continuation of the 1956 Golden Hawk, with the Packard V-8 now replaced by a Studebaker 289 fortified by a McCulloch supercharger to develop the same 275 bhp. Styling differences in these years were confined to larger concave steel fins, usually carrying the contrasting color when two-tone paint was ordered. A variation introduced in April 1957 was the 400, featuring a leather-trimmed interior, upholstered trunk, and special trim details.

➕ FOR The best Hawks of the '50s for handling and performance

➖ AGAINST As for 1956 Sky Hawk

PRODUCTION

1957 4356 **1958** 878 (figures include 400 sub-model)

SPECIFICATIONS

Length (in.)	204.0
Wheelbase (in.)	120.5
Weight (lbs)	3185/3470
Price (new)	$3182/3282

ENGINES

cid/type	bhp	years
289/ohv V-8[1]	275	1957-58

[1]Supercharged

PRICES

As per 1956 Studebaker Golden Hawk.

1 9 5 8
STUDEBAKER PRESIDENT/ COMMANDER STARLIGHT

A one-year anomaly from South Bend: hardtop coupes with a thin-section roofline and compound-curve backlight á la contemporary Chrysler products, but built from Studebaker's standard "non-Hawk" bodyshell. The Starlight name recalled Stude's first 1952 hardtop (and postwar "three-win

1957 Golden Hawk 400 hardtop coupe

1958 President Starlight hardtop coupe

dow" coupes), but 1958's lower-body facelift was clumsy and overdone: quad headlamps in grafted-on pods, equally inept tacked-on tailfins, bumps and bulges in random places. It made a compelling argument for trimming down and cleaning up—as Studebaker would do for the compact '59 Lark. The '58 Starlight came as both a top-line President with a 289 V-8 and as an only slightly less garish Commander with the smaller 259 engine. Both are equally collectible today: rare oddities from South Bend's last big crisis before it finally teetered over the brink eight years later.

✠ **FOR** Unusual even for Studebakers • Hardtop appeal • Fine small-block V-8s

▭ **AGAINST** Rust-prone, as usual • Styling certainly debatable • Not likely to yield strong dollar returns

PRODUCTION

NA

SPECIFICATIONS

Length (in.)	206.5
Wheelbase (in.)	120.5
Weight (lbs)	3355
Price (new)	$2695

ENGINES

cid/type	bhp	years
289/ohv V-8	225	1958
259/ohv V-8	180	1958

PRICES

FAIR	$1500-3500
GOOD	$3500-6000
FINE	$6000-9700

FINE EXAMPLE PRICE HISTORY

1982 $2800	**1990** $5500
1994 $6000	**1998** $8200

1982-2000 RETURN 8%
2000-2010 5%

1 9 5 9 - 6 1
STUDEBAKER LARK REGAL HARDTOP & CONVERTIBLE

The last big success before Studebaker's final fall. A pert line of compacts with trim new exterior sheetmetal

(by Duncan McRae and Bill Bonner) over the 1953-58 inner bodies and a modernized chassis (engineered by Eugene Hardig). The Lark bowed as a two-door sedan and wagon and four-door sedan in Deluxe and Regal trim, plus a pretty Regal hardtop coupe. South Bend's hoary L-head six was standard in "VI" models. Regal "VIIIs" came with a two-barrel 259 V-8 and offered a four-barrel version optionally. The '60 lineup was little changed visually, but added Deluxe-trim V-8s, four-door wagons, and six- and eight-cylinder Regal convertibles. Two feet shorter and some 200 pounds lighter than pre-1959 Studes, the Lark was lively, maneuverable, easy on gas, yet surprisingly roomy and thus perfectly timed. Sales soared, and Studebaker

1961 Lark VI convertible

made its first profit in six years. But volume eased after 1960 with the advent of Big Three compacts. The '61 Larks sold poorly despite a nice squarish restyle by Randy Faurot and many improvements including optional power steering and a modernized ohv "Skybolt Six" (which proved troublesome). The convertible and hardtop are the obvious collector choices here. But other Larks in this period, including the new-for-'61 Cruiser sedan (see entry)—though still "cheap wheels"—may show some value appreciation as Studebaker recedes further into history.

FOR Clean, tidy styling • Size still right for today • Good mileage • V-8s lively performers • Even hardtops and convertibles remain quite affordable

AGAINST Rust-prone • So-so workmanship • Hard to find in clean, original condition • Not strong value-appreciators—yet

PRODUCTION

NA; total Lark: **1959** VI 98,744 VIII 32,334 **1960** VI 70,153 VIII 57,562 **1961** VI 41,035 VIII 25,934

SPECIFICATIONS

Length (in.)	175.0
Wheelbase (in.)	108.5
Weight (lbs)	2710-3315
Price (new)	$2275-2689

ENGINES

cid/type	bhp	years
169.6/sv I-6	90	1959-60
169.6/ohv I-6	112	1961
259.2/ohv V-8	180/195	1959-61

PRICES

Conv	
FAIR	$2500-4500
GOOD	$4500-6500
FINE	$6500-9500
Htp	
FAIR	$1500-3000
GOOD	$3000-5500
FINE	$5500-8000

FINE CONVERTIBLE PRICE HISTORY

1982 $4000		**1990** $11,500	
1994 $10,000		**1998** $10,000	
1982-2000 RETURN 5%			
2000-2010 3%			

1959-61
STUDEBAKER SILVER HAWK & HAWK

Simplified successor to the Golden Hawk, a result of continued low 1957-58 sales. Listed simply as Hawk after 1959, when only a V-8 engine was offered, Studebaker's 289, in two stages of tune and without the previous supercharger. Styling became cleaner, and an optional four-speed gearbox was made available for 1961. Note that Hawks in these years were all fixed-pillar coupes, not the pillarless hard-top style.

FOR Good-looking • Lively performance • More reasonably priced than earlier "blown" models

AGAINST As for 1956 Sky Hawk • Lack of a hardtop

PRODUCTION

1959 V-8 5371 **Six** 2417 **1960** 4280 **1961** 3663 (figures do not include some 1960-61 Hawk six-cylinder export models)

SPECIFICATIONS

Length (in.)	204.0
Wheelbase (in.)	120.5
Weight (lbs)	2795-3207
Price (new)	$2360-2650

ENGINES

cid/type	bhp	years
169.6/sv I-6	90	1959
259.2/ohv V-8	180/195	1959
289/ohv V-8	210/225	1960-61

PRICES

FAIR	$2000-4000
GOOD	$4000-9000
FINE	$9000-11,500

FINE EXAMPLE PRICE HISTORY

1982 $4000		**1990** $9500	
1994 $10,000		**1998** $15,000	
1982-2000 RETURN 7%			
2000-2010 5%			

1960 Hawk coupe

1961 Lark Cruiser sedan

1961-63
STUDEBAKER LARK CRUISER

Studebaker's long-wheelbase luxury-sedan idea reborn as a Lark. Offered only as a Regal VIII with a standard two-barrel 259 V-8; a four-barrel version was optional, along with a pair of 289s from the "family sports car" Hawk. Built on the longer wagon chassis, with five extra inches of wheelbase and four-inch wider doors than on regular Lark sedans. As South Bend shifted all four-doors to the long chassis after '63, these Cruisers are the most special of the period Studebakers so named. The debut '61 bore Randy Faurot's squarish facelift of 1959-60 styling; the '62 and similar '63 shared with other Larks a major reskinning by Brooks Stevens, with longer rear fenders, revamped roofline, and square Mercedes-like grille. All were richly upholstered, the Cruiser's main selling point besides added back-seat space. Exact production is unknown but was likely quite low, so these luxury-liners are among the rarer late Studes, and all the more desirable now because of it.

[+] FOR Interesting, uncommon late-model Studebaker • Luxurious interior • Good V-8 performance • Inexpensive

[-] AGAINST More "special-interest" item than blue-chip investment • Mint examples hard to find • Indifferent workmanship • Rust-prone

PRODUCTION

NA; total Lark: **1961** 66,969 **1962** 93,004 **1963** 74,201

SPECIFICATIONS

Length (in.)	188.0
Wheelbase (in.)	113.0
Weight (lbs)	3000-3065
Price (new)	$2458-2595

ENGINES

cid/type	bhp	years
259.2/ohv V-8	180/195	1961-63
289/ohv V-8	210/225	1961-63

PRICES

FAIR	$1400-2200
GOOD	$2200-4300
FINE	$4300-6400

FINE EXAMPLE PRICE HISTORY

1982 $2000		**1990** $6500	
1994 $6500		**1998** $7000	
1982-2000 RETURN 7%			
2000-2010 3%			

1962-64
STUDEBAKER GRAN TURISMO HAWK

Updated continuation of Studebaker's four-seat sporty car, now wearing a heavy but astonishingly successful facelift by designer Brooks Stevens. Still built on the old "Loewy coupe" bodyshell and 120.5-inch wheelbase from 1953 minus the 1957-61 tailfins. Stevens added a Thunderbird-style formal roof with broad C-pillars, removed needless trim from the bodysides and outlined them in bright metal, and introduced a new three-element dash design with room enough for a big tach and clock. Studebaker's 289 V-8 in 210 and 225-bhp tune was carried over from '61 for the GT Hawk's first year. For 1963-64 it was supplemented with Avanti R-series versions packing up to 335 bhp by 1964. Despite good press and ideal packaging in the personal-car idiom, the GT Hawk was a sales disappointment, and was accordingly dropped after Studebaker consolidated production in Canada in January 1964.

1964 Gran Turismo Hawk hardtop coupe

FOR Milestone car status • Styling • Outstanding performance • Deft interior

AGAINST Rust-prone • Poor component accessibility • All-vinyl 1962 upholstery not very durable

PRODUCTION

1962 8388 **1963** 4634 **1964** 1767 (figures do not include six-cylinder export models)

SPECIFICATIONS

Length (in.)	204.0
Wheelbase (in.)	120.5
Weight (lbs)	3120-3280
Price (new)	$2966-3095

ENGINES

cid/type	bhp	years
289/ohv V-8	210-290	1962-64
289/ohv V-8[1]	290	1963-64
304.5/ohv V-8[1]	335	1964

[1]Supercharged

PRICES

FAIR	$3000-5500
GOOD	$5500-8500
FINE	$8500-13,000

(Add 10% for R1 engine, 20% for R2 engine.)

FINE EXAMPLE PRICE HISTORY

1982 $4500	**1990** $12,000
1994 $13,500	**1998** $13,500
1982-2000 RETURN 7%	
2000-2010 5%	

1 9 6 2 - 6 4
STUDEBAKER LARK DAYTONA HARDTOP & CONVERTIBLE

The sportiest models in Studebaker's aging compact line, introduced for 1962 along with a major reskinning by stylist Brooks Stevens—who again accomplished wonders for South Bend on a minimal budget. The more flowing body lines for 1962-63 were set off by a Mercedes-style square grille. For 1964, styling became more straight-edged and crisper, and a neat inverted-trapezoid grille was used. Underneath it all, however, was the basic bodyshell first seen in the 1953 Champion/Commander series. The top-line Daytona offered front bucket seats, center console, and (from 1963 on) full instrumentation.

Reclining front backrests and a floor-mounted stick shift were optional, as was an interesting folding cloth sunroof for 1962-63. Offered with both six- and eight-cylinder engines, everything from the ancient L-head six, which had been finally updated to overhead valves for 1961, to the hot R-series versions of the 289 V-8 (though very few found their way into Larks). Studebaker's declining sales volume make these models quite rare today—and they're quite good cars at that, with a useful combination of performance and economy.

FOR Economical collector-car buy • Size, character still appropriate • Ragtops' low production

1964 Lark Daytona convertible

1963 Lark Daytona hardtop coupe

PRODUCTION

1962 2d htp 8480[1] **conv** 2681 **1963 2d htp** 3763 **conv** 1015 **1964 2d htp** 2414 **conv** 703
[1]Includes Regal models

SPECIFICATIONS

Length (in.)	188.0/184.0/190.0 (1962/63/64)
Wheelbase (in.)	109.0
Weight (lbs)	2765-3320
Price (new)	$2308-2843

ENGINES

cid/type	bhp	years
169.6/ohv I-6	112	1962-64
259/ohv V-8	180/195	1962-64
289/ohv V-8	210-335	1962-64
289/ohv V-8[1]	290	1963-64
304.5/ohv V-8[1]	335	1964

[1]Supercharged

PRICES

Conv	
FAIR	$2500-5000
GOOD	$5000-7000
FINE	$7000-10,500

(Hardtop deduct 25%.)

FINE CONVERTIBLE PRICE HISTORY

1982 $5500		**1990** $11,000	
1994 $11,000		**1998** $11,000	
1982-2000 RETURN 4%			
2000-2010 3%			

1 9 6 3 - 6 4
STUDEBAKER AVANTI

Eleventh-hour attempt by Studebaker president Sherwood Egbert to rejuvenate his company's staid image. This was a four-place gran turismo with a fiberglass body styled by a team working under Raymond Loewy. The result was advanced in several ways: coke-bottle fender contours, grilleless front end, asymmetrically placed hood bulge, distinctive window shaping and large glass area, and a short, rounded tail. Inside were aircraft-like instrumentation and controls (some mounted overhead), slim-section bucket seats, and a built-in padded roll bar. Based on a shortened, modified Lark convertible chassis, with Bendix front disc brakes and anti-sway bars front and rear. Powered by a standard 240-bhp 289 V-8, but available with R-series engine options (R2: 290-bhp, R3: 335 bhp) that raised output considerably. An experimental 304.5-cid R-5 engine used twin Paxton blowers and fuel injection to develop an alleged 575 bhp. An R-3 Avanti broke 29 speed records at the Bonneville Salt Flats. But early production problems put a damper on the initial high enthusiasm for the car, and very few were actually delivered. Faltering finances caused Studebaker to consolidate its family-car operations in Canada in early 1964, which spelled the end of Avanti. But it was only temporary as the model was revived as a separate make by two Studebaker dealers in South Bend. It continued into 1991 as the Avanti II (see entry).

+ FOR A truly important postwar car with Milestone status • High performance • High desirability • Always a show stopper • No-rust body (one of the few Studebakers so blessed)

■ **AGAINST** Variable fiberglass finish • Not cheap on today's collector market • A little fuelish

PRODUCTION

1963 3834 **1964** 809

SPECIFICATIONS

Length (in.)	192.5
Wheelbase (in.)	109.0

1964 Avanti coupe

| Weight (lbs) | 3140/3195 (1963/64) |
| Price (new) | $4445 |

ENGINES

cid/type	bhp	years
289/ohv V-8	240-335	1963-64
289/ohv V-8[1]	290	1963-64
304.5/ohv V-8[1]	335	1964

[1]Supercharged

PRICES

FAIR	$7000-11,000
GOOD	$11,000-17,000
FINE	$17,000-23,000

(Add 25% for R2 engine, 60% for R3 engine.)

FINE EXAMPLE PRICE HISTORY

1982 $15,000	1990 $25,000
1994 $20,000	1998 $21,000
1982-2000 RETURN 2%	
2000-2010 3%	

1963-64
STUDEBAKER LARK DAYTONA WAGONAIRE

Another novel—and practical—styling idea by design consultant Brooks Stevens. Named for its sliding rear roof section that could be moved forward leaving unlimited "head room" for carrying tall objects. Offered in standard and Regal trim for 1963, but the sportier Daytona models in both years are more collectible today. A fixed-roof standard model came along for mid-1963 priced about $100 lower, then was made an option for '64. The Wagonaire was ostensibly continued as part of the abbreviated Studebaker line built in Hamilton, Ontario, Canada, following closure of the South Bend factory in early 1964, but the '63s are far more numerous. Listed with both six and V-8 engines, including the Avanti R-series versions of the 289, though it's likely very few (if any) were actually bolted into these wagons. Also very much worth considering from these years are the Daytona convertible and hardtop and, to a lesser extent, the Daytona Cruiser sedan.

1963 Lark Daytona Wagonaire

FOR A unique idea, never quite duplicated • Comparative rarity • Versatility

AGAINST We know of one that doesn't leak • Stude tinworm infestation

PRODUCTION

NA

SPECIFICATIONS

Length (in.)	187.0/193.0 (1963/64)
Wheelbase (in.)	113.0
Weight (lbs)	3245-3555
Price (new)	$2700-2843

ENGINES

cid/type	bhp	years
169.6/ohv I-6	112	1963-64
259.2/ohv V-8	180/195	1963-64
289/ohv V-8[1]	210-240	1963-64

[1]Supercharged

PRICES

FAIR	$1600-4000
GOOD	$4000-5500
FINE	$5500-8500

FINE EXAMPLE PRICE HISTORY

1982 $1800		1990 $6500	
1994 $6000		1998 $9000	
1982-2000 RETURN 10%			
2000-2010 5%			

1965-66 STUDEBAKER DAYTONA/ WAGONAIRE V-8

The last Studebakers, built at Hamilton, Ontario, Canada, after closure of the old South Bend plant. The '65s were essentially a carryover of the heavily revised '64 series, with the singular exception of engines—Studebaker now switched to Chevrolet power, six and V-8. In the case of the latter, it was the famous 283 small-block, mildly tuned in this application, though capable of far more. A Daytona Sport two-door sedan and sliding-roof wagon were offered with V-8 only for 1965. For 1966, a single Wagonaire and Daytona two-door were listed, but now also available with the six. Styling in Studebaker's farewell model year was marked by single headlamps instead of quads and a new grille composed of four slim rectangles. On Daytonas, air extractor vents appeared where backup lamps (now mounted lower) had been. The Wagonaire was also available in less luxurious Commander trim in these years, and a Cruiser four-door sedan was still offered as in 1961-64. A fixed-roof wagon returned for '66 after a one-year absence. None of these, however, is as collectible as the last of the sporty Daytonas and practical Wagonaires with Chevy's evergreen, lightweight V-8.

FOR They didn't make any more, and these were the best of the last • Chevy engines more durable than Stude units • Attractive package size • Fine performance

AGAINST Even da Vinci couldn't have done much with the basic styling • Some body parts almost unobtainable

PRODUCTION

NA

SPECIFICATIONS

Length (in.)	193.0
Wheelbase (in.)	109.0/113.0

1966 Daytona coupe

(Daytona/Wagonaire)
Weight (lbs)   2970-3505
Price (new) $2500-2695

ENGINES

cid/type	bhp	years
194/ohv I-6	120	1966
283/ohv V-8	195	1965-66

PRICES

FAIR	$1500-3500
GOOD	$3500-5000
FINE	$5000-8000

FINE EXAMPLE PRICE HISTORY

1982 $2500		**1990** $6000	
1994 $6000		**1998** $7000	

1982-2000 RETURN 7%
2000-2010 3%

1 9 3 2 - 3 6
STUTZ DV32

Stutz couldn't afford a multi-cylinder engine, and after experimenting with supercharging, it instead designed a new 32-valve head with double overhead cams, deleted the eight's twin ignition, and wrung 43 extra horsepower out of the 322 cubic inches. High-priced coachwork soon included the short-wheelbase Super Bearcat, initially fitted with an artificial leather Weymann body. It would do 100 mph with ease, but even sedans could cruise effortlessly at 70 and approach 90 mph. In 1932, the previous four-speed gearbox was replaced with a three-speed Muncie unit and freewheeling. This was installed on all DV32s.

✚ FOR The great name of Stutz • The heritage of a thoroughbred • Engineering exotica • Splendid coachwork • CCCA Classic status

◼ AGAINST Extremely scarce • Very expensive • Mechanically complex • Very difficult engine parts situation

PRODUCTION

Under 200

SPECIFICATIONS

Length (in.)	Variable with body style
Wheelbase (in.)	116.0/134.5/145.0
Weight (lbs)	4538-5420
Price (new)	$3795-5895

ENGINES

cid/type	bhp	years
322.0/dohc I-8[1]	161/156	1932-36

[1]4 valves per cylinder

PRICES

Bearcat
FAIR $35,000-100,000

1932 DV32 Super Bearcat convertible

GOOD	$100,000-120,000
FINE	$120,000-150,000
Open	
FAIR	$25,000-60,000
GOOD	$60,000-80,000
FINE	$80,000-120,000
Closed	
FAIR	$12,000-20,000
GOOD	$20,000-30,000
FINE	$30,000-55,000

FINE SPEEDSTER PRICE HISTORY

1982 $100,000		**1990** $200,000	
1994 $250,000		**1998** $150,000	

1982-2000 RETURN 2%
2000-2010 2%

1 9 3 2 - 3 6
STUTZ SV16

This was the less powerful of the two Stutz Eights during the final years of the company. The SV16 pumped out only 113 horsepower, but its two long chassis carried the same plush bodies as the more famous DV32, including the last of the Stutz Bearcat two-passenger speedsters. Though a twin-ignition engine like the contemporary Nash unit, it wasn't particularly lively in light of curb weights well over two tons. The bodies, however, were magnificent. All Stutzes are CCCA Classics.

✚ FOR Svelte coachwork, open and closed • The existence of a Bearcat model • Classic status

◼ AGAINST Underpowered • Mechanically complex • Parts impossible • Any left to find?

PRODUCTION

Under 300

SPECIFICATIONS

Length (in.)	Variable with body style
Wheelbase (in.)	116.0/134.5/145.0
Weight (lbs)	4488-5346
Price (new)	$1895-5095

1933 SV32 convertible (SV16 similar)

ENGINES

cid/type	bhp	years
322.0/ohc I-8	113	1932-36

PRICES

As per 1932-36 Stutz DV32, less 5%.

1992-97
SUBARU SVX

This 2+2 sporty car with full-time AWD was the most expensive Subaru ever, bowing for '92 with a $25,000 price tag (prices eventually exceeded $35K). A 3.3-liter flat six produced an impressive 230 bhp. Buff books pushed the car through the 0-60 sprint at between 7.3 and 7.6 seconds. Unfortunately, no Subaru manual trans could handle the engine's 224 pounds/feet of torque, so a 4-speed automatic was mandatory. A "smart" differential typically divided grip 60/40 front/rear, but could apportion it anywhere between 95/5 and 50/50. Window-within-a-window side glass was instantly controversial; the unusu-ally tall, hot-formed windshield and backlight made more practical sense. SVX had a lot to offer, but seemed merely interesting rather than collectible.

FOR Acceleration • AWD • Italianate styling • Novel greenhouse • Uncommon because of anemic sales

AGAINST Japanese nameplate with no history of collectibility • Mandatory automatic transmission

PRODUCTION[1]

1992 3,667 **1993** 3,859 **1994** 1,306 **1995** 1,849 **1996** 1,111 **1997** 640
[1]U.S. calendar-year sales

SPECIFICATIONS

Length (in.)	182.1
Weight (lbs)	3525-3580
Wheelbase (in.)	102.8
Price (new)	$25,000-36,245

ENGINES

cid/type	bhp	years
202/dohc flat 6	230	1992-7

PRICES

One of the few Japanese alleged collectibles to have bottomed out in appreciation early. Price range for the 1992 model $6500-10,000; more for later models which are still depreciating. **2000-2010 RETURN** 1%

1948-57
SUNBEAM-TALBOT 80

The original small-displacement edition of the Sunbeam-Talbot 90, powered by an 1185cc engine similar to that of the contemporary Hillman Minx, also made by the British Rootes Group. Offered only for two years, all 80s used the solid-axle front suspension; in other respects, it was identical to the S-T 90. Performance was predictably much less, however: no more than 70-75 mph maximum.

FOR As for 1948-57 S-T 90

AGAINST As for 1948-57 S-T 90, but much less performance

PRODUCTION

3500

SPECIFICATIONS

Length (in.)	168.0
Wheelbase (in.)	97.5
Weight (lbs)	2525
Price (new)	NA

1996 SVX coupe

1948-50 80 sedan

ENGINES

cc/type (cid)	bhp[1]	years
1185/ohv I-4 (72)	47	1948-50

[1]Gross

PRICES

FAIR	$1500-2500
GOOD	$2500-3500
FINE	$3500-6000

FINE EXAMPLE PRICE HISTORY

1982 $2000	**1990** $4000
1994 $4000	**1998** $6000

1982-2000 RETURN 6%
2000-2010 3%

1 9 4 8 - 5 7
SUNBEAM-TALBOT 90

A solid, graceful, British-built sports sedan using many Humber components. The massive separate chassis had solid-axle front suspension through the end of the 1950 model year, after which it was changed to an independent design. The body was a modern envelope in four-door sedan form, with a vertical grille, sweeping semi-integral front fenders, flush rear sides, and rounded contours. The original 1944cc overhead-valve four was enlarged to near 2.3 liters for 1951,

and its power was boosted in later years. Most cars had a column-mounted gearshift, but a floor-control conversion was offered later along with optional overdrive transmission. A product of the Rootes Group, which campaigned it very successfully on the European rally circuit in the '50s.

FOR Solid chassis engineering • Rally-winner image • Neat, inoffensive styling • Stability and road manners

AGAINST Not very fast • Parts in short supply • Seldom seen in U.S.

PRODUCTION

Mark I 4000 **Mark II** 5493 **Mark IIa** 4312 (1952, total 1952-54 approx. 15,000) **Mark III** approx. 4000

SPECIFICATIONS

Length (in.)	168.0
Wheelbase (in.)	97.5
Weight (lbs)	2725-2925
Price (new)	NA

ENGINES

cc/type (cid)	bhp[1]	years
1944/ohv I-4 (119)	64	1948-51
2267/ohv I-4 (138)	70-85	1951-57

[1]Gross

PRICES

FAIR	$1200-3000
GOOD	$3000-5000
FINE	$5000-7500

FINE EXAMPLE PRICE HISTORY

1982 $3500	**1990** $7000
1994 $6000	**1998** $7000

1982-2000 RETURN 5%
2000-2010 3%

1 9 5 3 - 5 5
SUNBEAM ALPINE

Elegant two-seat open roadster based on the Sunbeam-Talbot 90 platform. Front end styling was unchanged from the sedan's, but a long downswept tail made the Alpine look considerably more rakish, particularly with the top down. Available in 1954 with optional overdrive, which was then made standard for the 1955 models. Intended mainly for export to North America, the Alpine had a minor supporting role in the Cary Grant/Grace Kelly film *To Catch a Thief*.

FOR As for 1948-57 S-T 90, plus open-air appeal and trimmer looks

AGAINST As for 1948-57 S-T 90

PRODUCTION

approx. 3000

1953 Alpine convertible

SPECIFICATIONS

Length (in.)	168.0
Wheelbase (in.)	97.5
Weight (lbs)	2965
Price (new)	NA

ENGINES

cc/type (cid)	bhp[1]	years
2267/ohv I-4 (138)	80	1953-55

[1]Gross

PRICES

FAIR	$2000-5000
FAIR	$5000-7000
FINE	$7000-10,000

FINE EXAMPLE PRICE HISTORY

1982 $4000		**1990** $20,000	
1994 $10,000		**1998** $10,000	
1982-2000 RETURN 6%			
2000-2010 3%			

1958-67
SUNBEAM RAPIER

A British-built two-door hardtop based on the mid-'50s Hillman Minx sedan platform. It won international laurels in tough rally competition for its maker, Rootes Group, and this experience showed in improvements that came thick and fast—at least by British industry standards. The Rapier progressed from the twitchy-handling, underpowered chunky-looking 1956-58 Series I (not recommended as a collectible) to the Series II, with better styling and a larger engine, introduced for the 1959 model year. The Series III brought still-cleaner looks, a polished walnut dash, more horsepower, and standard front disc brakes. Engine displacement and power went up again for the interim Series IIIa of 1962. The Series IV received synchromesh for all gears of the standard four-speed manual gearbox. The last Series V Rapier was equipped with a larger five-main-bearing engine, but was not officially imported to the U.S. Despite its sporty character and fine rally record, the Rapier was overshadowed both here and overseas by the rakish Alpine two-seat sports car of the '60s. Nevertheless, the Rapier is an unusual collectible for British-car fans, one of the few true hardtops from England.

FOR Great rally heritage • Nicely trimmed four-seat interior • Good performance from 1.5/1.6-liter engines • Hardtop body style

AGAINST Rusts out early and easily • Chunky "transatlantic" styling

1961 Rapier Series III hardtop coupe

PRODUCTION

Mark II/Mark III 1958-59 NA **Mark III 1960**
11,643 **1961** 3850 **1962-63** 17,534 **1964-67** NA
(est. total 75,000)

SPECIFICATIONS

Length (in.)	162.5
Wheelbase (in.)	96.0
Weight (lbs)	approx. 2200
Price (new)	$2499/2649 (htp/conv) original U.S.

ENGINES

cc/type (cid)	bhp[1]	years
1390/ohv I-4 (84.8)	62-68	1956-58
1494/ohv I-4 (91)	68/78	1959-61
1592/ohv I-4 (97.1)	75-78	1962-65
1725/ohv I-4 (105.2)	85	1966-67[2]

[1]Gross [2]Series V not officially offered in U.S.

PRICES

FAIR	$1200-3500
GOOD	$3500-6000
FINE	$6000-9000

FINE EXAMPLE PRICE HISTORY

1982 $2000	**1990** $5000
1994 $5000	**1998** $5000
1982-2000 RETURN 9%	
2000-2010 3%	

1 9 5 9 - 6 8
SUNBEAM ALPINE

Rootes Group's sports car for the '60s, though it seemed more a sporty tourer to many because of its "modern" creature comforts. Included were such niceties as roll-up windows, an easily erected top, a proper heater, and fully outfitted dash. A factory bolt-on hardtop was also available for year-round weather protection. About the same size as a Triumph TR3 or MGA, the Alpine had contemporary good looks, including a broad hood that dipped low between the headlights, and upswept tailfins housing large oval vertical taillights. The fins were mercifully shorn after the 1963-64 Series III, which gained a GT model with a slightly detuned engine, walnut-trimmed dash, and a removable hardtop—but, curiously, no standard soft top. Not a great track competitor, the Alpine provided a good ride and sparkling performance for very little money, along with decent (though a bit soft) handling. U.S. imports ended after the 1968 Series V, which had a stronger, smoother five-main-bearing engine.

✚ FOR Costs less now than Triumphs and MGs • Good looks • Well-built • Well-equipped • Parts supplies still good

▬ AGAINST Monocoque-construction rust worries • Pre-1966 engines not known for longevity

PRODUCTION

1959-60 Series I 11,904 **1961-63 Series II** 19,956 **1963-64 Series III** 5863 **1964-65 Series IV** 12,406 **1966-68 Series V** 19,122

SPECIFICATIONS

Length (in.)	156.0
Wheelbase (in.)	86.0
Weight (lbs)	2255

1966 Alpine Series V roadster

Price (new) $2595 U.S.; 1963 GT $2749

ENGINES

cc/type (cid)	bhp	years
1494/ohv I-4 (91)	78	1959
1592/ohv I-4 (97.1)	77-82	1961-65
1725/ohv I-4 (105.2)	92	1966-68

PRICES

FAIR	$2000-5000
GOOD	$5000-8500
FINE	$8500-12,500

FINE EXAMPLE PRICE HISTORY

1982 $2750	1990 $8000
1994 $9500	1998 $9500

1982-2000 RETURN 10%
2000-2010 5%

1962-63
SUNBEAM LE MANS BY HARRINGTON

One of the first GT conversions of an open sports car—a Series II Alpine *sans* tailfins, with a smooth, fiberglass fastback roof running from windshield header to rear deck, where it ended in a reverse-canted "ducktail." The seams where fiberglass met the metal Alpine body toward the rear were covered by discreet "coachlines" (pin-stripes), giving the finished product a very unified look—almost as if this had been the car's original design. The engine was Rootes Group's 1592cc inline four as found in contemporary Alpines and Rapiers, but tuned to "Stage 2" specifications related to those that had won Sunbeam the Index of Thermal Efficiency at the 24 Hours of Le Mans in 1961. "Harringtons" (Sunbeam didn't use this name in the U.S.) were luxuriously trimmed in leather or vinyl (trim varied from one car to the next), and had the traditional British walnut-faced dash. Though other conversions were carried out by the Harrington firm, this was the best-selling one they did, but sales were limited because of the car's high price.

+ FOR Rare and highly sought-after • Fine styling • Good performance • Overdrive standard • Strong appreciation potential

– AGAINST Le Mans body parts now very scarce • A bit fidgety at low rpm

PRODUCTION

250

SPECIFICATIONS

Length (in.)	156.0
Wheelbase (in.)	86.0
Weight (lbs)	approx. 2300
Price (new)	$3995 U.S.

ENGINES

cc/type (cid)	bhp	years
1592/ohv I-4 (97.1)	104	1962-63

PRICES

FAIR	$2300-5000
GOOD	$5000-8500
FINE	$8500-12,500

FINE EXAMPLE PRICE HISTORY

1982 $4500	1990 $9000
1994 $11,000	1998 $11,000

1982-2000 RETURN 6%
2000-2010 5%

1964-65
SUNBEAM VENEZIA

An Anglo-Italian sports coupe based on the British Humber Sceptre sedan (some Hillman Super Minx platforms were also used in 1965), designed and constructed by the Turin coachbuilder, Superleggera. A tubular steel framework and unstressed aluminum body panels made the Venezia light, and gave it a considerable performance advantage over its Humber/Hillman parents, but high price kept sales very low. Several were imported to the U.S. by enthusiasts, though the model was never officially sold here.

+ FOR Rarity and desirability • Fine Italian styling • Plush interior

– AGAINST Body parts virtually extinct • Variable construction quality

PRODUCTION

NA, but very limited

SPECIFICATIONS

Length (in.)	177.0
Wheelbase (in.)	101.0

1962-63 Le Mans coupe by Harrington

1964-65 Venezia coupe by Superleggera

Weight (lbs) NA
Price (new) approx. $4000 (U.S. equivalent)

ENGINES

cc/type (cid)	bhp	years
1592/ohv I-4 (97.1)	88	1964-65

PRICES

As per 1963-64 Sunbeam Le Mans by Harrington plus 20%.

1964-68
SUNBEAM TIGER

An intriguing Anglo-American hybrid. The brainchild of Rootes Group's West Coast sales manager Ian Garrad, who asked Carroll Shelby to drop a small-block Ford V-8 into a suitably modified Alpine roadster. The result was electrifying enough to convince even Lord "Willy" Rootes that it should go into production. The Tiger received "good press," but never bowled the public over sales-wise. One reason was a fairly high price, not much less than a Corvette's at the time. Another was that it wasn't that obviously different from its four-cylinder sibling. Then Chrysler Corporation complicated matters by acquiring Rootes Group (and Simca in France), which put the American firm in the awkward position of selling (and providing warranty for) an engine built by its nearest competitor. And as usually happens with "captive imports," the Tiger never got the promotion it deserved in the U.S. No matter: word spread quickly among the knowledgeable that the Tiger was a terror. The car remained mostly the same throughout its rather short life. The Series I models all had the lightweight Ford 260 powerplant. On Series Ia cars, Rootes introduced pleated door panels and a new fresh-air ventilation system for top-up driving. The Series II—"Tiger II" in the U.S.—was upgraded to the 289-cid small-block and got an eggcrate grille and twin rocker panel stripes for visual distinction from the Alpine. It was a terrific performer with all the Alpine's good qualities, and widely respected in sports car circles. Unfortunately, Chrysler didn't have a substitute engine for the car and could stand the embarrassment no longer, so it halted Tiger imports after 1968. And without the lucrative U.S. market, there was little point in continuing it for British customers, so production ceased shortly afterwards.

FOR Happy on regular gas • Dynamite performance • Good construction quality • High appreciation potential • Clean styling (Series I) • Well-known Ford engine easy and cheap to maintain

AGAINST Somewhat rust-prone • Can be a handful for the uninitiated (rear traction bars a must to get power

1967 Tiger roadster

to the ground) • Retrograde Series II styling

PRODUCTION
1964 Mark I 1649 **1965-66 Mark I** 3020 **1966 Mark Ia** 1826 **1967 Series II** 421 **1968 Series II** 151

SPECIFICATIONS
Length (in.)	156.0
Wheelbase (in.)	86.0
Weight (lbs)	2550
Price (new)	$3499-3797 in the U.S.

ENGINES
cid/type	bhp	years
260/ohv V-8	164	1965-66
289/ohv V-8	200	1967-68

PRICES
FAIR	$2600-7000
GOOD	$7000-12,000
FINE	$12,000-18,000

FINE EXAMPLE PRICE HISTORY
1982 $6000		**1990** $25,000	
1994 $20,000		**1998** $18,000	

1982-2000 RETURN 7%
2000-2010 5%

1969-70
SUNBEAM ALPINE GT

A very different Alpine, this four-seat fastback coupe was sold in England as the Rapier. It was based on the chassis and running gear of Rootes Group's answer to the British Ford Cortina, the Hillman Hunter (sold here as the Sunbeam Arrow), and deadly conventional. Front suspension was by MacPherson struts, coil springs, lower transverse arms, and drag struts. The rear end was simply a live axle tied down by leaf springs. Powered by the workhorse Rootes four in its 1725cc size, it benefitted from the recent adoption of five (instead of three) main bearings. In appearance, the Alpine/Rapier resembled a scaled-down Plymouth Barracuda: slightly stubby front end (but with a horizontal bar grille and quad headlamps), pillar-less roof, and large backlight (though not one piece as on the American car). The interior featured nice high-back bucket seats, adequate space for four, a polished-walnut dash with complete instrumentation, center console, floor-shift, and full carpeting. Performance and handling were reasonably good, but construction quality was not the same as Rootes cars of yore. This, plus erratic deliveries caused by worker walk-offs, hurt the car's sales appeal (as it did the Arrow sedan's), and Chrysler began turning more strongly to its new Japanese partner, Mitsubishi, for its "captive imports." The Rapier continued in England for several more years, however, and was even offered as a hot Holbay-tuned model, the H120. A cheaper Alpine with simplified trim and equipment was also sold in the U.S., but the GT is the one to have.

FOR A bargain fastback with the respected Sunbeam name • Good mileage • Adequate performance • Nicely furnished

AGAINST Unexciting styling • Indifferent construction quality • Rust-prone • Not that numerous in the U.S. • Parts scarce outside England • Questionable appreciation potential

PRODUCTION
5000 (est. U.S. sales)

SPECIFICATIONS
Length (in.)	174.5
Wheelbase (in.)	98.5
Weight (lbs)	2360
Price (new)	$2535 U.S. list

ENGINES
cc/type (cid)	bhp	years
1725/ohv I-4 (105.2)	94	1969-70

PRICES
FAIR	$1000-2000
GOOD	$2000-3500
FINE	$3500-5500

FINE EXAMPLE PRICE HISTORY
1982 $2000		**1990** $3000	
1994 $3500		**1998** $4000	

1991-2002 RETURN 6%
2000-2010 3%

1970 Alpine GT coupe

1954-55
SWALLOW DORETTI

A short-lived attempt at a competitor for the Triumph TR2. Production was undertaken in Britain by a subsidiary of the giant Tube Investments Group. The branch was descended from the original Swallow coachworks of the '20s and '30s from which Jaguar evolved, but was not connected with the latterday Jaguar firm. The Doretti borrowed much from its intended rival, using the TR2 engine, transmission, and front suspension. Its chassis was a box-section/tubular-member affair, and was topped by a smart, two-seat roadster body. Bigger, heavier, and slower than the TR2, its top speed was nonetheless comparable at about 100 mph. However, the Doretti was very costly, and failed to sell for that reason. Production ended almost as soon as it began, marking the first—and last—attempt by this Swallow company at carmaking.

■ FOR Well-known Triumph running gear • Pleasant styling • Individual and exclusive

■ AGAINST Body and chassis parts all gone now • Extremely rare and hard to find, even in Britain

PRODUCTION
approx. 250

SPECIFICATIONS
Length (in.)	156.0
Wheelbase (in.)	95.0
Weight (lbs)	2155
Price (new)	NA

ENGINES
cc/type (cid)	bhp[1]	years
1991/ohv I-4 (122)	90	1954-55

[1]Gross

PRICES
FAIR	$5000-8000
GOOD	$8000-11,000
FINE	$11,000-15,000

FINE EXAMPLE PRICE HISTORY
1982 $5000		**1990** $16,000	
1994 $15,000		**1998** $15,000	
1982-2000 RETURN 6%			
2000-2010 3%			

1930-35
TALBOT 90/105

1932 90 tourer at Le Mans

In the mid-1920s, Swiss-born Georges Roesch began transforming British-built Talbots with a splendid series of overhead-valve sixes. By the '30s, mechanical reliability had turned into sporting prowess. The 2.3-liter "90" raced with honor at Le Mans, and the 3.0-liter "105" that followed it proved a great rally car and endurance racer.

1954-55 Doretti roadster

Both were marked by sturdy rather than advanced engineering, with simple carburetion for their deep-breathing power units. Some think of these as "vintage" cars, with a Twenties character, which is confirmed by their hard ride and lack of independent front suspension. After the French parent company went belly-up in 1935, the British subsidiary was acquired by Lord Rootes and its cars became much more pedestrian.

FOR Engine's rugged simplicity • Vintage Brit character • Reliable, sporting, and masculine

AGAINST Old-fashioned even for its day • Hard to find in ours, especially in the U.S. • Parts supplies nonexistent

PRODUCTION

1930-33 90 216 **1931-35 105** 335

SPECIFICATIONS

Length (in.)	182.0 (average)
Wheelbase (in.)	111.0/114.0 (90/105)
Weight (lbs)	3900-4100
Price (new)	NA

ENGINES

cc/type (cid)	bhp[1]	years
2276/ohv I-6 (139)	90	1930-33
2969/ohv I-6 (181)	105	1931-35

[1]Gross

PRICES

90 Open

FAIR	$10,000-15,000
GOOD	$15,000-25,000
FINE	$25,000-40,000

90 Closed

FAIR	$6000-10,000
GOOD	$10,000-20,000
FINE	$20,000-25,000

105 Open

FAIR	$20,000-30,000
GOOD	$30,000-40,000
FINE	$40,000-50,000

105 Closed

FINE	$7500-10,000
GOOD	$10,000-12,500
FINE	$12,500-15,000

FINE 105 TOURER PRICE HISTORY

1982 $12,000		**1990** $100,000	
1994 $50,000		**1998** $50,000	
1982-2000 RETURN 8%			
2000-2010 3%			

1934-37
TERRAPLANE OPEN MODELS

Replaced the Essex Terraplane as a make in its own right for four years, after which it briefly became a Hudson series before the name was retired. These years saw the most interesting styling, a major powerplant change—a new, larger six—longer wheelbases, sleeker body styling, and more performance. A 1936 sedan tested in Britain did 0-60 mph in 26.6 seconds and delivered 82 mph top speed—highly creditable for a 2800-pound car at that time. Open body styles are, as usual, the most desirable. Convertible models numbered two per year except in 1935, when there was only the DeLuxe Six convertible. A six-passenger convertible brougham was added to the DeLuxe and Super lines in 1937, independent front suspension in 1934.

FOR Handsome 1934-35 styling • Excellent performance • Strong club support

AGAINST Unlovely 1936-37 "fencer's mask" grille • Difficult to find • Increasing scarcity of body parts

PRODUCTION

Open models comprised a small fraction—perhaps 2000 per year—of total Terraplane production, which was as follows: **1934** 51,084 **1935** 51,134 **1936** 86,791 **1937** 90,253

SPECIFICATIONS

Length (in.)	NA
Wheelbase (in.)	112.0 (1934-35); 115.0 (1936); 116.0 (1934); 117.0 (1937)
Weight (lbs)	2590-2915
Price (new)	$695-845

ENGINES

cid/type	bhp	years
212.0/sv I-6	80-102	1934-37

PRICES

FAIR	$5000-11,000
GOOD	$11,000-18,000
FINE	$18,000-28,000

FINE CONVERTIBLE PRICE HISTORY

1982 $14,000		**1990** $30,000	
1994 $19,000		**1998** $28,000	
1982-2000 RETURN 4%			
2000-2010 4%			

1934 K Special convertible coupe

1965-70

TOYOTA 2000GT

An unexpected high-performance GT meant to demonstrate that Toyota was capable of something more than workaday family sedans and commercial vehicles. It began as a Yamaha prototype for Nissan that was pitched to Toyota after Nissan turned it down. The long-hood, two-seat fastback body, rendered in aluminum, was shaped by Count Albrecht Goertz of BMW 507 and later Nissan/Datsun 240Z fame. A steel box-section "backbone" chassis emulated that of the contemporary Lotus Elan, as did classic four-wheel double-wishbone suspension, rack-and-pinion steering, and all-disc brakes. Power came from a twin-cam Yamaha conversion of the single-cam 2.3-liter straight six used in Toyota's big Crown sedan. Sold only as a two-seat hatchback coupe with right-hand drive and five-speed manual gearbox, though a couple of special convertibles were built for a starring role in the 1967 James Bond film *You Only Live Twice*. Light weight and slippery shape (evocative of Jaguar's E-type) made for sub-10-second 0-60 mph times and up to 135 mph flat out. Fairly luxurious even so, with self-seeking radio, telescoping steering wheel, "rally" clock/stopwatch, full instrumentation, even a comprehensive tool kit. Racing versions ran third in the '66 Japan Grand Prix and first in that year's Suzuka 1000 Kilometers, so this was really more a testing-the-waters publicity exercise than realistic profit-maker. Still, the 2000GT was a successful low-volume warmup for the mass-market Celica sports coupes, and one of the few collectible Japanese cars built before 1970.

⊞ FOR Sexy styling • High performance • Rarity • Historic progenitor of today's Toyota Supra and Lexus SC400 • Fine investment

▬ AGAINST Cramped cockpit • Dent-prone aluminum body • Most parts impossible unless you're a Toyota executive

PRODUCTION

337

SPECIFICATIONS

Length (in.) 164.0
Wheelbase (in.) 91.7

1967-70 2000GT coupe

Weight (lbs)	2480
Price (new)	approx. $6800 equivalent U.S.

ENGINES

cc/type (cid)	bhp[1]	years
1988/dohc I-6 (121)	150	1965-70

[1]Net

PRICES

FAIR	$30,000-50,000
GOOD	$50,000-70,000
FINE	$70,000-90,000

FINE EXAMPLE PRICE HISTORY

1982 $20,000	**1990** $110,000
1994 $9500	**1998** $85,000
1982-2000 RETURN 9%	
2000-2010 3%	

1985-90

TOYOTA MR2

A mid-engine two-seat "corporate kit car" á la Fiat X1/9 and Pontiac Fiero, but more reliable and practical than either. It followed their basic formula, though: a driveline borrowed from a mass-market front-drive sedan (here, the mid-'80s Corolla) and transplanted to behind the cockpit of a unitized steel hull to drive the rear wheels. Coil-sprung MacPherson struts and disc brakes appeared at each corner; steering was unassisted rack-and-pinion. Offered at first only with a five-speed manual transaxle, but an optional four-speed overdrive automatic was added for '86, when a new T-bar roof option and add-on "aero" body kit were offered. A supercharged version with Roots-type blower, air-to-air intercooler, and a suitably fortified drivetrain arrived for 1988 with 30 percent more horsepower and 45 percent more torque. For 1991, the square-lined first-generation models were replaced by an all-new Ferrari-esque design with 2.2-liter powerplants in normal and supercharged guise. Early "Mister Twos" are still too new and numerous to be high-return investments, but they're definitely high-fun "cheap

1985 MR2 coupe

wheels" that may pay dividends some distant day depending on survival rates and ultimate collector opinion.

FOR Loads of driving fun, town and country alike • Good go (especially Supercharged model) • Fair interior space for exterior size • Near-bullet-proof Japanese reliability • Well-built • Parts/service still readily available • Affordable

AGAINST Anti-Japan bias among some collectors • Won't command significant attention for a long time (if ever) • Tail-heavy, so prone to trailing-throttle oversteer • Many examples likely hard-driven

PRODUCTION

NA

SPECIFICATIONS

Length (in.)	155.5
Wheelbase (in.)	91.3
Weight (lbs)	2290-2620
Price (new)	$11,000-17,500

ENGINES

cid/type	bhp[1]	years
97/dohc I-4	112-115	1985-90
97/dohc I-4[2]	145	1988-90

[1]SAE net for U.S. model [2]Supercharged

PRICES

Price range in 2000 for the 1989 supercharged version was $1700-5450.
2000-2010 RETURN 1%

1988-93
TOYOTA CELICA GT AWD

Toyota did more than just add all-wheel-drive to its Celica sport coupe to make it an All-Trac. The All-Trac was a sturdier car than other Celicas. The body was beefed-up not only to handle the new drive-train, but also to cut noise and vibration. Turbocharging boosted the power of the 16-valve four from 135-horsepower to 190. The car needed that extra power. The transition to All-Trac added 550 pounds. Acceleration dropped below eight seconds and top speed rose above 130 in spite of the extra weight. Handling was sure and predictable under any road condition, but the price for the added weight was a loss of agility.

FOR Fast, stable, refined • All-weather capability • Comfortable driver seat

AGAINST Slower on twisty roads than fwd Celicas • Cramped back seat

PRODUCTION

NA

SPECIFICATIONS

Length (in.)	171.9
Weight (lbs)	3270
Wheelbase (in.)	99.4
Price (new)	$20,498-28,298

ENGINES

cid/type	bhp	years
122/dohc I-4[1]	190	1988-93

[1]Turbocharged

PRICES

Price range in 2000 was between $3000 and $9000 depending on model year.
2000-2010 RETURN Depreciating

1989 Celica GT AWD coupe

1991-95

TOYOTA MR2

Second-generation, 2-place, rear-drive "Mister Two" sports car was smooth, quick, and solidly assembled, with the added fillip of a mid-engine layout. Base motor was a 2.2-liter four with 130 bhp; an optional 2.0-liter Turbo intercooled four produced a rousing 200 horses—more than the steering setup could easily handle on early models. By the end of the car's run, prices for the top Turbo had ballooned to $30,000—far too much in a market with more affordable alternatives. U.S. sales, never robust, declined precipitously.

➕ FOR Acceleration • Handling (1993-95) • Relative rarity

➖ AGAINST Oversteer (1991-92) • Squirrely handling (1991-92) • Polished but passionless • Japanese origins

PRODUCTION

78,997

SPECIFICATIONS

Length (in.)	164.2
Weight (lbs)	2559-2657
Wheelbase (in.)	94.5
Price (new)	$15,148-29,238

1993 MR2 coupe

ENGINES

cid/type	bhp	years
132/dohc I-4	130/135	1991-5
122/dohc I-4[1]	200	1991-5

[1]Turbocharged

PRICES

Used car market.
2000-2010 RETURN Depreciating.

1993-98

TOYOTA SUPRA

Toyota's fourth generation Supra appeared just as the market for big-buck Japanese sport coupes collapsed. Sales were never high for this, the best of the Supra line. The Toyota shared its dohc in-line six and rear-drive platform with the Lexus SC 300 luxury coupe. The Supra was definitely a sport coupe with firm suspension and short wheelbase. The smooth six gave spirited performance in base version and searing acceleration in the Turbo coupe. Only Ferraris and such could beat the Supra Turbo to sixty. Steering, handling, and brakes were in keeping with performance.

➕ FOR Acceleration • Strong brakes • Precise steering and handling

➖ AGAINST Stiff ride • Austere interior • Back seat useless even for a 2+2 • Turbo's optional boy-racer spoiler

PRODUCTION

43,015 (including Turbos)

1993 Supra coupe

SPECIFICATIONS

Length (in.)	177.7
Weight (lbs)	3320-3480
Wheelbase (in.)	100.4
Price (new)	$29,500-47,500

ENGINES

cid/type	bhp	years
183/dohc I-6	220-225	1993-98
183/dohc I-6[1]	320	1993-98

[1]Turbocharged

PRICES

Used car market.
2000-2010 RETURN Depreciating

1936-39
TRIUMPH DOLOMITE

As an independent company, Triumph's finances sagged in the Thirties, yet its cars became more and more elegant. For 1937, its stylists took a long look at the SS Jaguars being built only hundreds of yards away, adopted similar lines, then grafted on a Hudson-like waterfall grille

sometimes unflatteringly referred to as the "fencer's mask." Lifting the Dolomite name from its Alfa-inspired supercharged straight-eight roadster of 1935, the firm offered a choice of four- or six-cylinder engines and three different wheelbases on these successors to the previous Gloria and Vitesse models, which were similar in engine and chassis design. They boasted all the middle-class British virtues, including wire-spoke wheels, "tasteful" interiors, and—at last—gearbox synchronization. On the other hand, they lacked independent front suspension, typical of the UK in this period. Body styles included the Foursome convertible coupe with a three-position folding top, and the rumble-seat Roadster Coupe, plus various close-coupled sedans. The Roadster was a fine rally car, and all Dolomites could be considered useful alternatives to equivalent Rileys and SS Jaguars. Alas, Triumph went broke in mid-1939. The company was revived after the war, but not these cars.

FOR A famous name in its heyday • Real British elegance • Handsome styling • Simple engineering

AGAINST Limited performance • Rot-prone coachbuilt bodies • Parts almost impossible to find

PRODUCTION

1000 (est.)

SPECIFICATIONS

Length (in.)	168.0-181.5
Wheelbase (in.)	108.0/110.0/116.0
Weight (lbs)	2800-3300
Price (new)	NA

ENGINES

cc/type (cid)	bhp[1]	years
1496/ohv I-4 (91)	50	1938-39
1767/ohv I-4 (108)	60/65	1936-39
1991/ohv I-6 (122)	72/75	1936-39

[1]Gross

PRICES

Open	
FAIR	$6000-10,000
GOOD	$10,000-15,000
FINE	$15,000-20,000

(Deduct 60% for closed models.)

FINE ROADSTER-COUPE PRICE HISTORY

1982 $7500	1990 $35,000
1994 $20,000	1998 $20,000

1982-2000 RETURN 8%
2000-2010 3%

1936-39 Dolomite convertible

510

1946 1800 Town & Country sedan

1 9 4 6 - 4 9
TRIUMPH 1800 TOWN & COUNTRY SALOON

The only prominent postwar make apart from Rolls-Royce to offer sedans with "knife-edged" styling, Triumph built the Town & Country (also known as the 1800 Saloon) to a beautiful design by Walter Belgrove. A luxurious leather and walnut interior and big, freestanding Lucas headlamps distinguished this attractive four door. Front suspension was independent with a transverse leaf spring; the chassis was made up of steel tubes. The engine was built by Standard, hooked to a four-speed gearbox with column shift.

➕ FOR Often mistaken for a Rolls, which doesn't hurt • Fine construction quality • Classy looks

➖ AGAINST Wood-framed body tends to rot • All have right-hand drive

PRODUCTION

approx. 4000

SPECIFICATIONS

Length (in.)	175.0
Wheelbase (in.)	108.0
Weight (lbs)	2828
Price (new)	$3150

ENGINES

cc/type (cid)	bhp[1]	years
1776/ohv I-4 (107)	63	1946-49

[1]Net

PRICES

FAIR	$2000-3000
GOOD	$3000-5500
FINE	$5500-7500

FINE EXAMPLE PRICE HISTORY

1982 $7000		**1990** $8500	
1994 $7500		**1998** $7500	
1982-2000 RETURN 0%			
2000-2010 2%			

1 9 4 6 - 4 8
TRIUMPH 1800 ROADSTER

Triumph's Sir John Black was determined to compete with Jaguar with this car, but he didn't know about the forthcoming XK-120. A Jaguar it was not, though it did have its own appeal. The bizarre styling was the work of two different designers (the ideas meet at the cowl), and included a rumble seat with a flip-up windshield. Mechanically identical with the 1800 sedan, it was stylistically unique, with freestanding Lucas lights and bulging front fenders engulfing the Triumph radiator.

➕ FOR Few open British cars of the early postwar years can be had for its price • Definitely unique looks • Good construction quality

➖ AGAINST Hardly a classic piece of styling, though more appealing now than then • Aluminum bodywork subject to corrosion • Some rot may beset body's wooden framing

1946 1800 roadster

PRODUCTION

2501

SPECIFICATIONS

Length (in.)	168.1
Wheelbase (in.)	108.0
Weight (lbs)	2541
Price (new)	$3025 original U.S. equivalent

ENGINES

cc/type (cid)	bhp[1]	years
1776/ohv I-4 (107)	63	1946-48

[1]Net

PRICES

FAIR	$4000-8000
GOOD	$8000-13,000
FINE	$13,000-18,000

FINE EXAMPLE PRICE HISTORY

1982 $5500		**1990** $19,500	
1994 $18,000		**1998** $18,000	
1982-2000 RETURN 7%			
2000-2010 3%			

1949-53
TRIUMPH MAYFLOWER

Triumph's managing director, Sir John Black, liked the looks of his 1800/2000 sedans, and ordered his designers to apply the same razor-edge lines to a smaller economy model. As General Motors' former styling chief, William L. Mitchell, might say, this was like trying to tailor a dwarf. The result was named Mayflower to appeal to Americans, to whom it was aimed. Alas, it didn't appeal in the U.S. It was cute, though hardly elegant: the scale and proportions were all wrong. Nonetheless, the boxy body did offer an incredible amount of space for its overall size. Today, it's invariably a cause for smiles, and amusing to the collector with a sense of humor. It's a winsome little car that will grow on you, and it doesn't cost a mint to buy or restore.

FOR Nothing quite like it • Big interior for its tiny size • Active club interest • "The Watch-Charm Rolls"

AGAINST No power • Tricky aluminum-head engine • Many parts now scarce

PRODUCTION

2d sdn 34,990 **conv** 10

SPECIFICATIONS

Length (in.)	154.0
Wheelbase (in.)	84.0
Weight (lbs)	2016
Price (new)	$1695 (U.S. equivalent)

ENGINES

cc/type (cid)	bhp[1]	years
1247/sv I-4 (76)	38	1949-53

[1]Net

PRICES[1]

FAIR	$1000-2000
GOOD	$2000-3000
FINE	$3000-6000

[1]If found, one of the 10 original dropheads (convertibles) would add 200% to the above prices.

FINE EXAMPLE PRICE HISTORY

1982 $2000		**1990** $5500	
1994 $4000		**1998** $6000	
1982-2000 RETURN 7%			
2000-2010 3%			

1949
TRIUMPH 2000 SALOON

Successor to the 1946-48 1800 sedan, and unchanged in appearance. Specifications were identical also, except that a relaxation in British horsepower tax encouraged Triumph to install the 2.0-liter engine and gearbox from Standard's Vanguard series. Unfortunately, the 2000 used a three- instead of four-speed transmission (although fully synchronized), and the shifter was still mounted on the steering column rather than on the floor.

FOR As for 1946-48 1800 Town & Country

1953 Mayflower 2-door sedan

■ **AGAINST** As for 1946-48 1800 Town & Country, plus less flexible gearbox

PRODUCTION

2000

SPECIFICATIONS

Length (in.)	175.0
Wheelbase (in.)	108.0
Weight (lbs)	2828
Price (new)	$2950 original U.S. equivalent

ENGINES

cc/type (cid)	bhp[1]	years
2088/ohv I-4 (128)	68	1949

[1]Net

PRICES

As per 1946-49 Triumph 1800 Town & Country saloon.

1949

TRIUMPH 2000 ROADSTER

Continuation of the 1800 Roadster, still on a tubular-steel chassis. Like its 2000 sedan counterpart, it adopted the drivetrain from the Standard Vanguard. With a high price and mediocre performance, this Roadster was outflanked by MG on one side and Jaguar on the other. By 1950, Standard-Triumph would drop this model and concentrate its attention on a brand-new and faster sports car to be known as the TR2.

✚ **FOR** As for 1946-48 1800 Roadster

■ **AGAINST** As for 1946-48 1800 Roadster

PRODUCTION

2000

SPECIFICATIONS

Length (in.)	168.1
Wheelbase (in.)	108.0
Weight (lbs)	2540
Price (new)	$2950 original U.S. equivalent

ENGINES

cc/type (cid)	bhp[1]	years
2088/ohv I-4 (128)	68	1949

[1]Net

PRICES

As per 1946-48 Triumph roadster.

1950-54

TRIUMPH RENOWN

The final development of the razor-edge Triumph 1800/2000, now based on the Standard Vanguard pressed-steel chassis and coil-spring independent front suspension. In late 1951, a limousine with a division window was produced on a three-inch longer wheelbase, and beginning in 1952 all models adopted the longer chassis. While the Renown sedan is the most available razor-edge Triumph, the low-production limo is

---

1952-54 Renown limousine

conversely the hardest to come by—extremely rare and desirable.

✚ **FOR** Optional overdrive worth looking for • Same well-balanced styling as on the 1800/2000 • More up-to-date layout • Quality materials and assembly

■ **AGAINST** As for 1946-48 1800 and 1949 2000, plus likely high asking prices for the limousine version

PRODUCTION

4d sdn (108-inch wb) 6501 **4d sdn** (111-inch wb) 2800 **limo** (111-inch wb) 190

SPECIFICATIONS

Length (in.)	175.0 (1950-52), 181 (1952-54)
Wheelbase (in.)	108.0 (1950-52), 111.0 (limo and 1952-54)
Weight (lbs)	2800-3024
Price (new)	$3150/3400 (sdn/limo) U.S. equivalent

ENGINES

cc/type (cid)	bhp[1]	years
2088/ohv I-4 (128)	68	1950-54

[1]Net

1949 2000 roadster

PRICES

Saloon	
FAIR	$2000-3000
GOOD	$3000-4000
FINE	$4000-6000
Limo	
FAIR	$2500-3500
GOOD	$3500-5000
FINE	$5000-8000

FINE EXAMPLE PRICE HISTORY

1982 $7500	**1990** $9000
1994 $8000	**1998** $9000
1982-2000 RETURN 0%	
2000-2010 2%	

1953-55
TRIUMPH TR2

First in the long-lived series of post-war Triumph sports cars, the TR2 was developed from the 20TS or "TR1" prototype first shown at the Earls Court auto show, and evolved into a rapid machine selling at an attractive price. Body design by Triumph's Walter Belgrove, featured a grilleless radiator opening (one of the many tricks used to keep the price down), cutaway doors, flowing fenders integral with the body, and a relatively roomy trunk—the area where the production car differed most from the prototype. TR2s quickly began winning rallies and races, beginning a victory streak that would make TRs famous and respected. From the very beginning, 100-mph performance was available from the four-cylinder engine (with "wet" cylinder liners), a virtually unbreakable powerplant if you observed the redline. A classic British sports car that, for just a little more money, outperformed the MGs of the day.

✚ FOR Rugged construction • Strong

1953 TR2 roadster

engine • Large following • Plentiful new and old-stock and remanufactured parts • A Milestone car

◼ AGAINST Dumpy though appealing styling • Rusts easily • A hundred rain leaks • Some poor-quality interior trim

PRODUCTION

8628

SPECIFICATIONS

Length (in.)	151.0
Wheelbase (in.)	88.0
Weight (lbs)	1848
Price (new)	$2499 in the U.S.

ENGINES

cc/type (cid)	bhp[1]	years
1991/ohv I-4 (121.5)	90	1953-55

[1]Gross

PRICES[1]

FAIR	$4000-6000
GOOD	$6000-9000
FINE	$9000-14,000

[1]Prices are for long-door early versions (bottom of door covers the rocket panel). Deduct 10% for short-door, add 10% for hardtop.

FINE EXAMPLE PRICE HISTORY

1982 $5000	**1990** $13,000
1994 $14,000	**1998** $14,000
1982-2000 RETURN 6%	
2000-2010 5%	

1955-57
TRIUMPH TR3

A mildly restyled successor to the TR2, easily distinguished by a proper grille with large eggcrates built into the front air intake. There were no major dimensional or mechanical changes except for introduction of front disc brakes early in the production run. Introduced with a small horsepower gain over the TR2, though this was later increased to an even 100 bhp. Remarkably, the TR3—like the TR2— doesn't enjoy the huge following of the "wide-mouth" TR3A. This translates into a lower price despite its greater rarity.

✚ FOR Costs less than TR3A, yet is scarcer • Others as for 1953-55 TR2, including Milestone status

◼ AGAINST As for 1953-55 TR2

PRODUCTION

13,377

SPECIFICATIONS

Length (in.)	151.0
Wheelbase (in.)	88.0
Weight (lbs)	1988
Price (new)	$2625 original U.S. list

ENGINES

cc/type (cid)	bhp[1]	years

1957 TR3 roadster

1991/ohv I-4 (121.5)	95/100	1955-57

[1]Net

PRICES

FAIR	$4000-6000
GOOD	$6000-9000
GOOD	$9000-14,000

Add 10% for hardtop.

FINE EXAMPLE PRICE HISTORY

1982 $5000	1990 $12,500
1994 $14,000	1998 $14,000

1982-2000 RETURN 6%
2000-2010 5%

1958-62

TRIUMPH TR3A

Continuation of the TR3, and one of the most ubiquitous sports cars of the late '50s/early '60s. It was more civilized than its prede-cessors thanks to better seats, proper door handles, and other interior refinements. Marked by a full-width stamped grille, it earned the name "wide mouth," this in contrast to the "small mouth" TR3. The TR3A offered sparkling performance, unsophisticated handling (particularly on wet roads), and jaunty if slightly chubby styling, all at a highly competitive price. It enjoyed a long production run, and people continued clamoring for it even after the TR4 arrived. A long string of competition successes and its thoroughly British character helped win it an avid following that continues to this day.

+ FOR Right now, your best TR investment • Greater comfort, refinement than TR2/3 • Others as for 1953-55 TR2 • Another Triumph Milestone car

– AGAINST As for 1953-55 TR2, and still a devil in the wet

PRODUCTION

58,236

SPECIFICATIONS

Length (in.)	152.0
Wheelbase (in.)	88.0
Weight (lbs)	2050
Price (new)	$2675 original U.S. list

ENGINES

cc/type (cid)	bhp[1]	years
1991/ohv I-4 (121.5)	100	1958-62

[1]Net

PRICES

FAIR	$3000-6500
GOOD	$6500-10,000
FINE	$10,000-14,000

(Add 10% for hardtop.)

FINE EXAMPLE PRICE HISTORY

1982 $6000	1990 $14,000
1994 $14,000	1998 $14,000

1982-2000 RETURN 6%
2000-2010 5%

1961 TR3A roadster

1 9 6 2 - 6 3

TRIUMPH TR3B

Not an official "factory" model and produced only for the U.S. market. What Triumph referred to as the "3B" comprised leftover TR3As, some equipped with the 2138cc engine and all-synchro gearbox from the successor TR4. Later 3Bs could be distinguished by a vinyl-covered central instrument panel, but were otherwise identical in looks to the TR3A.

✚ **FOR** As for 1953-55 TR2 and 1958-62 TR3A, plus low-production appeal • Still a Milestone car

▬ **AGAINST** As for 1953-55 TR2

PRODUCTION

3331

SPECIFICATIONS

Length (in.)	152.0
Wheelbase (in.)	88.0
Weight (lbs)	2100
Price (new)	$2365 original U.S. list

ENGINES

cc/type (cid)	bhp	years
1991/ohv I-4 (121.5)	100	1962
2138/ohv I-4 (130.4)	100	1963

1963 TR3B roadster

PRICES

As per 1958-62 Triumph TR3A plus 10%.
2000-2010 RETURN 6%

1 9 6 1 - 6 7

TRIUMPH TR4/TR4A

Triumph's new-generation sports car with body design by Italy's Giovanni Michelotti. Originally based on the TR3A chassis and running gear with a larger engine (though the

1991cc unit was available optionally to qualify for 2.0-liter class racing) and a new all-synchromesh gearbox. The TR4A brought a tubular grille to replace the rather cheap stamped original item, and you could have independent rear suspension—by coil springs and semi-trailing arms—at extra cost. The TR4A also had a "quick-erect" top, whereas the TR4's roof came off altogether, although it was not as tedious to button up as the TR3's. Also, the folded 4A top took up most of the space behind the rear seats. Michelotti's styling was contemporary and good-looking, with a squared tail and a curvaceous nose featuring high-set

1966 TR4A roadster

headlamps with "eyelids" formed by humps in the hood. A "power blister" offset to the right on the hood provided clearance for the air cleaners/carburetors (even after Triumph switched carbs and the bulge was unnecessary).

➕ FOR Styling seems to look better as time passes • Very soundly built • Plush leather buckets and glossy walnut dash in all but very early models

➖ AGAINST Rust a continuing worry • IRS TR4As sometimes require costly suspension work • Not going anywhere fast in value

PRODUCTION

1962-64 TR4 40,253 **1965-67 TR4A** 28,465

SPECIFICATIONS

Length (in.)	153.6
Wheelbase (in.)	88.0
Weight (lbs)	2128/2240 (TR4/TR4A)
Price (new)	$2849 original U.S. list

ENGINES

cc/type (cid)	bhp[1]	years
2138/ohv I-4 (130.4)	100/104	1961-67
1991/ohv I-4 (121.5)	100	1961-67

[1]Net, TR4/TR4A

PRICES

FAIR	$3000-5500
GOOD	$5500-8000
FINE	$8000-12,000

(Add 20% for surrey top model.)

FINE EXAMPLE PRICE HISTORY

1982 $5000		1990 $10,500	
1994 $11,500		1998 $12,000	

1982-2000 RETURN 5%
2000-2010 3%

TRIUMPH SPITFIRE MARK I & II

Triumph's reply to the Austin-Healey Sprite and MG Midget: a "budget" sports car companion for the "big" new TR4 (see entry). Really a return to the original TR concept in size, price, and power. The basic running gear and all-independent suspension with rear swing axles came from Triumph's small Herald family sedan, but the Spitfire's engine was tuned for an extra 12 horsepower, and its chassis was a new backbone type topped by a separate fully welded steel body (the Herald shell was bolted together). Also like the Herald—and the original "bug-eye" Sprite—the hood and front fenders were a single hinged unit that tilted forward for superb engine access. Styling was by Giovanni Michelotti, then Triumph's favored "contract" designer. Instantly popular despite limited performance and alarming lift-throttle swing-axle oversteer, the Spitfire was made more attractive in '63 with three options: electric overdrive (effective on the top two ratios of the normal four-speed manual gearbox), center-lock wire wheels, and detachable steel hardtop. A Mark II evolution arrived in 1964 with four more horses, better

seats, a vinyl-covered dash (replacing painted metal), and floor carpeting (versus rubber mats). It became a fast favorite with weekend racers, who could order various factory kits offering extra carbs, wilder cams, and freer-breathing manifolds. Simple, fun and, above all, charming, though some of that charm would be sacrificed in later editions.

➕ FOR Open-air appeal • Fix-it-yourself simplicity • Still plentiful and cheap • Many parts in good supply • Avid club support

➖ AGAINST Rusts with merry abandon • Not much go • Very low, snug cockpit • Few amenities

PRODUCTION

Mark I 45,573 (1962-64) **Mark II** 37,409 (1964-67)

SPECIFICATIONS

Length (in.)	145.0
Wheelbase (in.)	83.0
Weight (lbs)	1570
Price (new)	approx. $1800-2250 in U.S.

ENGINES

cc/type (cid)	bhp[1]	years
1147/ohv I-4 (70)	63	1962-64
1147/ohv I-4 (70)	67	1964-67

[1]Net

PRICES

FAIR	$1500-2500
GOOD	$2500-3500
FINE	$3500-6000

FINE EXAMPLE PRICE HISTORY

1982 $2500	1990 $4500
1994 $5000	1998 $8000

1982-2000 RETURN 5%
2000-2010 3%

1963 Spitfire Mark I roadster

1966-73

TRIUMPH GT6

Smooth "fasthatch" coupe derived from the Spitfire. It shared the roadster's lower-body styling, tilt-up hood/front fenders, and instrument panel, but carried a small straight six (from Triumph's contemporary 2000 sedan) instead of a pedestrian four. Better equipped and more nicely trimmed than the Spitfire, it was a more able highway cruiser thanks to the quieter, easier-revving engine and long-legged gearing (via a four-speed manual gearbox with Laycock de Normanville electric overdrive). Alas, it inherited the Spitfire's tricky rear swing axles, making it prone to sudden oversteer and rear-end "jacking." But Triumph cured this from late '68 by substituting the double-jointed half-shafts (with A-arms below and a transverse leaf spring above) developed for the Spit, which brought the bonus of a slightly wider rear track. This plus the new "bone in mouth" Spitfire grille were the main changes for what was sold as the GT6+ in America and the Mark II everywhere else. Other changes involved standard mag-look wheel covers, rear-quarter roof air vents for a new flow-through ventilation system, and more horsepower for non-U.S. models (up from 95 to 104) via a new cylinder head, reprofiled camshaft, and freer-breathing manifolds. Late 1970 brought a further-improved replacement, called Mark III in all markets, with the smoother bumpers, modestly flared wheelarches, and crisp new tail styling applied to the Spitfire Mark IV, plus recessed exterior door handles, swept-back rear side windows, and a tidier dash. Unhappily, the U.S. version was progressively detuned for tighter yearly emissions standards and dropped from 95 to a miserable 79 bhp by 1973, when the first energy crisis and declining U.S. demand prompted Triumph to end the model worldwide.

➕ **FOR** One of the sweetest small sixes ever • Good looks • Hatchback convenience • Comfy long-haul tourer • Super engine access • Nicely equipped • Still not widely collected and thus cheap

➖ **AGAINST** Pretty small inside and out • Indifferent construction quality • A fierce ruster • Styling suffers after Mark I

1969 GT6 Mark II coupe

PRODUCTION

Mark I 15,818 (1966-68) **Mark II/GT6+** 12,066 (1969-70) **Mark III** 13,042 (1971-73)

SPECIFICATIONS

Length (in.)	145.1 (147.0 U.S. Mark III)
Wheelbase (in.)	83.0
Weight (lbs)	1905-2030
Price (new)	$2895-3045 in U.S.

ENGINES

cc/type (cid)	bhp	years
1998/ohv I-6 (121.9)	95/104[1]	1966-73
1998/ohv I-6 (121.9)	95/90/79[2]	1966-73

[1]Net for European models [2]SAE net for U.S. models

PRICES

FAIR	$1500-2500
GOOD	$2500-3500
FINE	$3500-6000

FINE EXAMPLE PRICE HISTORY

1982 $2500		**1990** $5000	
1994 $6000		**1998** $6000	
1982-2000 RETURN 5%			
2000-2010 3%			

1967-70

TRIUMPH SPITFIRE MARK III

A continuation of Triumph's junior sports car with several improvements. The main one was substituting a newer, larger, and more powerful eight-port engine for the previous siamesed-port unit, plus a beefed-up clutch and front-disc brakes to match. The brakes were welcome, as the Mark III was the fastest Spitfire yet—near 100 mph all out—and, as events would prove, the fastest ever. Other changes included a more convenient, permanently affixed soft top (replacing

1967-70 Spitfire Mark III roadster

the detachable Erector-set affair of old), wood-veneer dash trim and, the most noticeable, a higher-set "bone in mouth" front bumper, a change made in anticipation of U.S. safety standards. Further improvements involved an instrument cluster moved from the center of the dash to directly ahead of the wheel on 1969 U.S. models, plus wider wheels and improved cockpit padding for the final 1970 versions. Replaced by a more heavily modified model, the Mark IV (see entry).

FOR As for 1962-67 Mark I and II, plus better performance and more convenient top • Fun to drive

AGAINST As for 1962-67 Mark I and II

PRODUCTION
65,320

SPECIFICATIONS

Length (in.)	145.0
Wheelbase (in.)	83.0
Weight (lbs)	1570
Price (new)	$2295 U.S. in 1969

ENGINES

cc/type (cid)	bhp[1]	years
1296/ohv I-4 (79)	75	1967-70

[1]Net

PRICES
As per 1962-67 Triumph Spitfire Mark I/II.

1967-68
TRIUMPH TR5 PI & TR250

Interim versions of Triumph's big '60s sports car, a reply to the Austin-Healey Six/3000. These were the first postwar Triumph sports cars with a six, derived from the late-'50s-vintage Herald/Spitfire four to replace the TR's rugged old wet-liner four. TR5 PI boasted Lucas mechanical petrol (fuel) injection (hence that suffix), the basic system used by the contemporary Maserati 3500GTI. But this 150-horsepower engine wasn't amenable to new U.S. emissions standards, so Triumph created the TR250, essentially a detoxed TR5 with 104 bhp via twin Zenith-Stromberg carburetors. Both models were otherwise like the TR4/4A save badges, detail trim, "mag-look" wheel covers (genuine wires were optional), vinyl instead of leather seats, and imitation instead of genuine wood dash trim. TR250s went further with gaudy transverse nose stripes (some say the stripes were a post-production option) and reflective tape around side and rear windows for better nighttime safety. Chassis specs were unchanged save standard radial tires, numerically lower final-drive ratios to suit the torquier engines, and no more solid-rear-axle option as on U.S. TR4As. The 250 had no more horsepower than a 4A and was thus no faster, but the TR5 could wind to an easy 6000 rpm and near 120 mph while cutting no less than 20 seconds from the 4A's 0-100 mph time. Still, these were old bottles with new wine, though Triumph would correct that after 18 months with one fully restyled successor, the TR6 (see entry).

FOR Smooth, willing performance (especially TR5) • Not fiercely coveted by TR types, so prices still reasonable • Others as for 1961-67 TR4/4A

AGAINST As for 1961-67 TR4/4A, but prices trending upward now • Some parts supplies short • Less soundly built than TR4/4A • TR5 not common in U.S.

PRODUCTION
TR5 PI 2947 TR250 8484

SPECIFICATIONS

Length (in.)	153.5
Wheelbase (in.)	88.0
Weight (lbs)	2270

1968 TR250 roadster

Price (new) $3175 (TR250)

ENGINES

cc/type (cid)	bhp	years
2498/ohv I-6[1] (152.4)	104/150[2]	1967-68

[1]Fuel injected on TR5 [2]Net TR5/TR250

PRICES

TR5 PI[1]
FAIR	$3500-6000
GOOD	$6000-10,000
FINE	$10,000-18,000

[1]TR5 PI prices are from UK market, which is substantially higher for TRs; the TR5 PI was not officially imported into the USA.

TR250
FAIR	$2500-4500
GOOD	$4500-6500
FINE	$6500-9000

FINE TR250 PRICE HISTORY

1982 $3000		1990 $9000	
1994 $10,000		1998 $9000	

1982-2000 RETURN 6%
2000-2010 3%

1969-76
TRIUMPH TR6

The smoothly redesigned successor to the TR5/250, facelifted by Karmann of Osnabruck, the German coachbuilders. Essentially, the rework involved only the front and rear ends. The former had headlights moved outboard to the fender tips and a neat new grille. The rear was lengthened and squared off, adopting a Kamm-style chop and wraparound horizontal taillights. While these cosmetic changes gave the car a new lease on life, there was still no gain in performance, and the American version remained much less lively than its British counterpart. The TR6 continued in production through 1975, with U.S. sales extending into 1976 (mostly leftovers already in the export pipeline). Replaced by the four-cylinder TR7 coupe as Triumph's sporting two-seater in 1975. As with so many other cars of the '70s, bumpers became uglier and engines weaker on later TR6s. While it's a bit early to assess the TR6's ultimate value as a collectible, the demise of Triumph sports cars (and the TR6's acceptance among enthusiasts as a "true" TR) suggests it has potential.

FOR   As for 1968 TR250, plus better looks

AGAINST   Still a ruster • Others as for 1968 TR250

PRODUCTION

94,619

SPECIFICATIONS

Length (in.)	156.0 (1969-72), 162.1 (1973-74), 163.6 (1975-76)
Wheelbase (in.)	88.0
Weight (lbs.)	2390 (1971-74), 2438 (1975-76)
Price (new)	$3275 original U.S. list; $6050 in 1976

ENGINES

cc/type (cid)	bhp[1]	years
2498/ohv I-6 (152.4)	104-106/150[2]	1969-76

[1]net [2]U.S./European

PRICES

FAIR	$2750-4500
GOOD	$4500-7000
FINE	$7000-12,500

FINE EXAMPLE PRICE HISTORY

1982 $4500		1990 $10,000	
1994 $10,000		1998 $11,000	

1982-2000 RETURN 6%
2000-2010 5%

1970-80
TRIUMPH SPITFIRE MARK IV/1500

Triumph's winsome little sports car in the final 10 of its total 18 years. Mark IV was essentially a Mark III with larger grille opening, modified front bumper, one-piece front fenders, and a clipped TR6-type tail, all courtesy of Italian stylist Michelotti. Distinct side-marker lights adorned U.S. models, but all IVs sported the more logically ordered dash of the Mark 3 GT6, which also donated an all-synchromesh four-speed gearbox to replace the outmoded Spitfire transmission with non-synchronized "crash" first gear. But the most welcome change was "swing spring" rear suspension geometry in which the transverse leaf spring was free to pivot atop the differential. The new setup looked just like the old, but eliminated the severe rear-wheel jacking and snap oversteer that had made Spitfires so treacherous in hard cornering. It also brought a slightly wider

1974 TR6 roadster (with hardtop)

1978 Spitfire 1500 roadster

track, which also helped handling. By 1974, power losses to interim U.S. emissions standards prompted stroking the existing 1296cc engine to 1493cc for the Spitfire 1500. This engine was also destined for the MG Midget to simplify emissions certification for parent company British Leyland. U.S. horsepower kept withering, though, and "Federal" cars further suffered big black "safety" bumpers that could ward off five-mph shunts, but looked awful and added weight. Non-American 1500s packed a healthy 71 DIN horsepower, however, and could do upwards of 100 mph—about equal to the Mark 3's best. But the Spitfire was doomed by then as an assembly-line "orphan" with no more relatives to help defray tooling costs,

which BL was increasingly unable to afford. Production thus ended in August 1980, after which BL gave up on sports cars altogether in another of its many unsuccessful gropes toward profitability.

⊞ FOR As for 1967-70 Mark 3, plus nicer cockpit trim and furnishings

⊟ AGAINST As for 1967-70 Mark 3, but U.S. models much poorer performers

PRODUCTION

Mark IV 70,021 (1970-74) **1500** 95,829 (1974-80)

SPECIFICATIONS

Length (in.)	149.0 (156.3 for U.S. 1500)
Wheelbase (in.)	83.0
Weight (lbs)	1720-1750
Price (new)	$7365 U.S. in 19800

ENGINES

cc/type (cid)	bhp	years
1296/ohv I-4 (79)	63[1]	1970-74
1296/ohv I-4 (79)	58/82[2]	1970-74
1493/ohv I-4 (91.1)	71[1]	1974-80
1493/ohv I-4 (91.1)	57[2]	1975-80

[1]DIN for European models [2]SAE net for U.S. models

PRICES

As per 1962-70 Triumph Spitfire Mark I/II/3.

1975-81

TRIUMPH TR7

The last new-design TR, and sadly one of the worst. It bowed as a four-cylinder coupe, which seemed unrelated to previous six-cylinder roadsters. The cartoonish "flying doorstop" styling taken from an offhand doodle by Harris Mann. Unit construction was new for a Triumph sports car, but parent British Leyland production economics and internal politics meant "parts bin" engineering. Thus the conventional all-coil suspension with front MacPherson struts and a live rear axle, rack-and-pinion steering, and front-disc/rear-drum brakes. The engine was an enlargement of the 1.7-liter Triumph-designed four then also used by Saab (which greatly evolved it), linked to a four-speed manual gearbox, optional overdrive five-speed (from the big Rover SD1 sedans), or extra-cost three-speed automatic.

1978 TR7 coupe

Assembled first at BL's new Speke factory near Liverpool, but many serious quality problems there forced a transfer to Triumph's Canley plant, near Coventry, in late 1978, resulting in a six-month gap. Two years later, the TR7 was shifted to Rover's Solihull facility in the face of BL's continuing cash shortfalls and need to economize. A companion convertible was announced soon afterwards and looked miles better. But it did nothing for sales, especially in the ever critical U.S. market, and the arrival of new managers opposed to sports cars sent the TR7 to its grave in October '81. Better-built non-Speke cars, identified by "wreath" nose badges, are greatly preferred, as are convertibles, especially the late, low-volume Spider and "Victory Edition" special-trim models.

FOR Not widely saved yet, so even convertibles are dirt cheap • Great handling • Fairly roomy cockpit • Decent two-seater trunk space

AGAINST Engine blows head gaskets regularly • Troublesome electrics and pop-up headlamps • Weak four-speed gearbox • Build quality not that great even on non-Speke cars

• Convertible structure rather wobbly
• Some "soft trim" already in short supply

PRODUCTION
112,368

SPECIFICATIONS

Length (in.)	160.1/165.4
	(European/U.S. versions)
Wheelbase (in.)	85.0
Weight (lbs)	2205-2470
Price (new)	$8645 U.S. in 1980

ENGINES

cid/type	bhp	years
1998/sohc I-4 (122)	105[1]	1975-81
1998/sohc I-4 (122)	86-90[2]	1975-81

[1]DIN for European models [2]SAE net for U.S. models

PRICES

Cpe	
FAIR	$1500-2250
GOOD	$2250-3000
FINE	$3000-6000
Conv	
FAIR	$2500-3000
GOOD	$3000-4000
FINE	$4000-7500

(Add 10% for Spider.)

FINE CONVERTIBLE PRICE HISTORY

1990 $5000	1994 $5000
1998 $8000	
1990-2000 RETURN 4%	
2000-2010 2%	

Triumph's very last TR, but also the quickest. Essentially the four-cylinder TR7 fitted with the small V-8 it was also designed to accept. This was the all-aluminum engine that Rover had acquired from General Motors (where it powered the early-'60s Buick Special/Olds F-85 compacts) and passed on to successor British Leyland. Most TR8s were convertibles built for U.S. sale with three-speed automatic transmission, though the TR7's manual five-speed was standard and some 202 American-spec coupes were sent over for preliminary evaluation in 1978-79 before being privately sold by importer Jaguar-Rover-Triumph. For emissions reasons, California cars always had Bosch L-Jetronic fuel injection; this substituted for twin Stromberg carbs on all swan-song '81 models, though it did little for power or torque. Other differ-

1981 TR8 roadster

ences from the TR7 included rangier final-drive ratios, the obligatory stiffening of springs and shocks, larger front brake pads, and faster steering with standard power assist. Tinted glass, AM/FM stereo, and metallic paint were also included; air conditioning was the lone factory option. Though the TR8 added spirited performance to the TR7's fine handling and relatively practical two-seat package, it wasn't built any better—certainly not enough to satisfy increasingly picky Yanks. But it was a last gasp anyway, and it disappeared along with BL's other sports cars in a British-government takeover of the ailing automaker. Surely the most collectible late TR for obvious reasons, but not likely to yield high dollar return for some time.

FOR As for 1975-81 TR7, plus greater rarity, more comprehensive equipment, and better performance (0-60 in about 8.5 seconds, 135 mph all out)

AGAINST As for 1975-81 TR7

PRODUCTION
2497 (incl. 2308 U.S. models)

SPECIFICATIONS
Length (in.)	165.5
Wheelbase (in.)	85.0
Weight (lbs)	2655
Price (new)	$11,150 (cpe) and $11,900 (conv) in U.S. in 1981

ENGINES
cid/type	bhp	years
3528/ohv V-8 (215)	133/137[1]	1980-81

[1]SAE net for carbureted/fuel injected U.S. models

PRICES
FAIR	$6000-8000
GOOD	$8000-11,000
FINE	$11,000-14,000

FINE EXAMPLE PRICE HISTORY
1990 $10,000	1994 $14,000
1998 $14,000	
1990-2000 RETURN 3%	
2000-2010 5%	

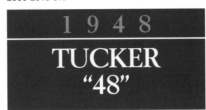

1948
TUCKER "48"

The most futuristic of the many advanced cars promised for the immediate postwar period, now almost legendary. Contrary to what you may have heard, Tucker was not done in by General Motors or Michigan's congressional delegation. Preston Tucker hired noted stylist Alex Tremulis to design this "torpedo" four-door sedan. Power was supplied by an unusual 335-cid aluminum-alloy flat six (a helicopter engine), mounted at the rear for a claimed benefit to weight distribution. Four-wheel independent suspension, a central headlight that pivoted in the same direction as the front wheels, and a padded safety dash were other uncommon features trumpeted in Tucker advertising. Performance put everyone else in Detroit to shame: 0-60 mph in 10 seconds, a top speed of about 120 mph.

FOR An intriguing concept with an interesting history • Good appreciation potential • Outstanding performance • A Milestone car

AGAINST Forbiddingly expensive today • Scarce parts • Very few left on the market

PRODUCTION
51 (including prototype)

SPECIFICATIONS
Length (in.)	219.0
Wheelbase (in.)	128.0
Weight (lbs)	NA
Price (new)	$2450 (projected)

ENGINES
cid/type	bhp	years
335/ohv flat 6	166	1948

PRICES
FAIR	$50,000-125,000
GOOD	$125,000-180,000
FINE	$180,000-275,000

FINE EXAMPLE PRICE HISTORY
1982 $50,000	1990 $175,000
1994 $250,000	1998 $200,000
1982-2000 RETURN 11%	
2000-2010 10%	

1948 "48" sedan

1958-61 Grantura coupe

1958-67

TVR GRANTURA

This was a fastback, fiberglass-body two-seat sports car built by the Blackpool, England, firm started by Trevor Wilkinson—hence the initials TVR. Sold both as a kit and fully assembled, the TVR was powered by a variety of proprietary engines. The most familiar of these was the BMC (British Motor Corporation) 1.8-liter B-series four as used in the MGB. All TVRs were built on a short-wheelbase tubular backbone chassis. The Mark I through Mark IIA models had an all-trailing-link, VW Beetle-type suspension. This was replaced by a more up-to-date coil-spring-and-wishbone arrangement derived from Triumph Herald components. These early TVRs bear some styling resemblance to the Lotus Elite. The 1800S, introduced initially as the Mark III in 1962, had a much larger rear window and a severely chopped tail that gave it a stubby, truncated look. Very light and built low to the ground, these were hard-riding sports machines with excellent roadholding. Equipment levels were pretty complete, too, and included wind-up door windows. As one of Britain's numerous "cottage industry" specialist makers, TVR was a small firm that went through several management changes in its early years, so it's difficult to pinpoint precise model changes; improvements were usually instituted as needed, without regard for the calendar. The Grantura was a relation to the Ford V-8-powered Griffiths.

FOR Light, rust-free fiberglass body • Fierce handling/roadholding • Many parts still stocked • Good appreciation potential

AGAINST Fragile construction quality • Cramped interior

PRODUCTION

1958 Mark I 100 **1959-62 Mark II/IIA** 400 **1962-65 Mark III** 90 **1800S** 206

SPECIFICATIONS

Length (in.)	138.0
Wheelbase (in.)	84.0/85.5
Weight (lbs)	1455-1790
Price (new)	NA

ENGINES

cc/type (cid)	bhp	years
1172/F I-4 (71.5)	36	1958-59
1098/ohc I-4 (67)	85	1958-59
1588/ohv I-4 (97)	80	1959-62
1216/ohc I-4 (74.2)	83	1959-63
1622/ohv I-4 (99)	90	1962-63
1340/ohv I-4 (81.8)	54	1962-63
1798/ohv I-4 (109.7)	88/95	1963-67

PRICES

FAIR	$8000-12,000
GOOD	$12,000-16,000

FINE	$16,000-22,000

FINE EXAMPLE PRICE HISTORY

1982 $6000		**1990** $10,000	
1994 $15,000		**1998** $20,000	
1982-1992 RETURN 6%			
2000-2010 5%			

1963-65

TVR GRIFFITH

A Grantura derivative with American Ford 289 V-8 power and four-speed manual gearbox, basically the Shelby-Cobra drivetrain installed Stateside by Griffith Motors. Proprietor Jack Griffith had cared for a Cobra and an MGA-powered Grantura from Sebring 1962. His mechanics found that the Cobra drivetrain fit the Grantura, and the TVR Griffith 200 was announced the following year. Save for a pronounced hood bulge to clear the V-8, it was identical in appearance with the Mark 3/1800S Grantura, including stubby tail and large wrapped rear window (though the first few cars differed slightly). Supplied in 195-horsepower stock and 271-bhp "Hi Performance" versions, as per Ford. Severe overheating problems and spotty workmanship were addressed by a replacement Griffith 400 in 1964 with an enlarged radiator, Kenlowe thermostatic cool-

1965 Griffith 200 coupe

ing fans, and somewhat better assembly. There were detail appearance changes, too, including a larger rear window, more sharply truncated tail, and "pie-plate" tail-lamps lifted from the British Ford Cortina family sedan. All Griffiths offered shattering performance (up to 155 mph flat out), nimble handling, and tenacious road-holding—and a bone-jarring ride, cramped seating, and no luggage space. TVR supplied engineless cars, but continuing quality problems and a prolonged dock workers strike forced Jack Griffith to abandon the venture, which in turn forced a 1965 reorganization of TVR, its fourth since 1956. Replaced by the re-engineered Tuscan V-8 with Ford 302 small-block power.

⚍ FOR As for 1958-67 Grantura, plus much greater performance from easily serviced, well-known Ford 289 V-8

▭ AGAINST As for 1958-67 Grantura

PRODUCTION
300

SPECIFICATIONS

Length (in.)	138.0
Wheelbase (in.)	85.5
Weight (lbs)	1905
Price (new)	NA

ENGINES

cid/type	bhp[1]	years
289/ohv V-8	195/271	1963-67

[1]SAE gross

PRICES

FAIR	$8000-15,000
GOOD	$15,000-22,000
FINE	$22,000-30,000

FINE EXAMPLE PRICE HISTORY

1982 $8000	**1990** $15,000
1994 $22,000	**1998** $25,000
1982-1992 RETURN 6%	
2000-2010 5%	

1 9 6 7 - 7 1
TVR TUSCAN

Further developments of the Grantura/Griffith under the auspices of Martin Lilley, who took over TVR in 1965 and renamed it TVR Engineering, Ltd. The Tuscan, introduced in 1967, was essentially a revival of the Griffith 400 based on the better-built interim Grantura "Mark IV," still with a fiberglass body atop a multi-tube steel backbone chassis with four-wheel double-wishbone suspension. Most carried 195-horsepower Ford 289 V-8s, a few the 271-bhp "Hi-Po" version. Only 28 were built. Later in '67 came a Tuscan SE with a stretched 90-inch wheelbase, different taillamps (from the British Cortina Mark II), and a revised hood; just 24 were called for. A facelifted SE was announced in 1968 with Ford's 302 V-8 and somewhat wider and smoother bodywork, but it saw just 21 copies (including two with right-hand drive) through August 1970, at which point TVR abandoned Ford V-8 power. The most successful Tuscan was the V-6, introduced in 1969 with the 3.0-liter "Essex" engine and four-speed gearbox from Ford Britain's Capri "ponycar" and Zephyr/Zodiac sedans (a drivetrain also found in the Reliant Scimitar GTE Sportwagon and odd-looking Marcos GT). Exactly 101 were built through early 1971. V-6s were not officially sold in the U.S. due to the cost and difficul-

1967 Tuscan coupe

ty of certifying that engine for American emissions standards. Tuscan V-8s, though, were imported, mostly by the Gerry Sagerman organization. Numbers were small, so they were exempt from federal safety standards, and the engines were detoxed with help from Dearborn. Tuscans had nicer fittings than any Grantura or Griffith, including polished wood dash trim. All versions were swept away after '71 in favor of a more modern TVR, the M-series.

⊞ FOR Performance (V-8) • Better styling • Equipment • Others as for 1958-67 Griffith/Grantura

⊟ AGAINST As for 1963-67 Griffith/Grantura, but overshadowed by superior M-series successors

PRODUCTION
V-8 28 (1967) **SE V-8** 24 (1967-68) **"Wide-Body" V-8** 21 (1968-70) **V-6** 101 (1969-71)

SPECIFICATIONS
Length (in.)	138.0/145.0 (early V-8/others)
Wheelbase (in.)	85.5/90.0 (early V-8/others)
Weight (lbs)	1905-2240
Price (new)	$6250 in U.S. in 1969

ENGINES
cc/type (cid)	bhp	years
2994/ohv V-6 (182.7)	136	1969-71
4727/ohv V-8 (289)	195/271	1967
4949/ohv V-8 (302)	220	1968-71

PRICES
As per 1963-65 TVR Griffith.

1972-77
TVR 2500M/3000M

Replacement for the Tuscan series, again from the Martin Lilley regime, but much like it in appearance and concept. All-round double-wishbone suspension, front-disc/rear-drum brakes, rack-and-pinion steering, 90-inch wheelbase, and central "backbone" were retained for an all-new chassis—the first since 1962 and only the third in TVR history—which went from a tubular platform design to a "space frame" type with square- and round-section tubing and wider tracks (53.75 inches front and rear). As ever with TVR, this chassis was designed to accept a variety of "bought-in" engines, including the 1.3-liter Triumph Spitfire four and British Ford 1.6 cross-flow "Kent" four-cylinder. Our focus is the 2500M with the Triumph TR6 inline six and the 3000M with the British Ford "Essex" V-6 (as in the 1969-71 Tuscan V-6). The former weighed about as much as a TR6 and thus had similar performance: about 110 mph all out. The 3000M could reach 115 mph. Just to confuse matters, TVR built 289 Tuscan-based 2500 models with American-spec TR6 power, all in 1971, along with 96 Tuscans on M-series chassis. The definitive 2500M, sold in America and elsewhere, was dropped in 1977 once TR6 engine supplies dried up. The 3000M took over for it in the U.S. But though sales continued into 1979, they were mostly leftovers, the model having been replaced by a modernized evolution, the Taimar (see entry). TVR converted a few late 3000Ms to turbocharging, and continued the practice with the Taimar, but only 63 such cars would be built.

⊞ FOR Fine performance (especially Turbo) • Good road car • Distinctive looks • All versions rare, especially in U.S. • Most engine parts still in good supply • Rot-free, easily repaired fiberglass bodies

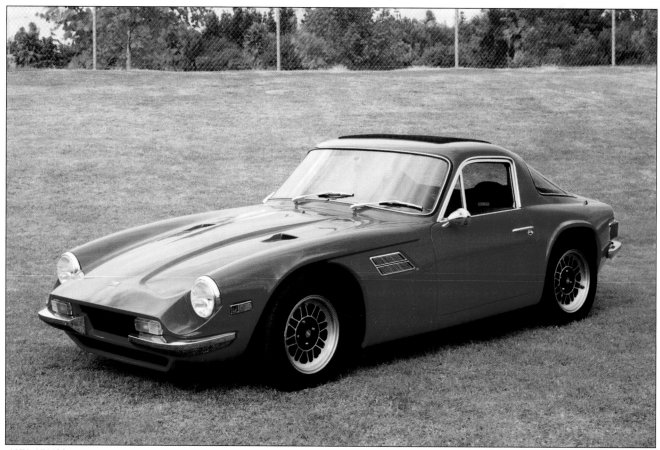

1973 2500M coupe

■ **AGAINST** TVR's usual cramped cockpit and meager cargo space • Workmanship highly variable • Scant U.S. following and parts/service support

PRODUCTION

2500M 947 (1972-77) **3000M** 654 (1972-77)

SPECIFICATIONS

Length (in.)	154.0
Wheelbase (in.)	90.0
Weight (lbs)	2240-2300
Price (new)	$5200-8900 in U.S.

ENGINES

cc/type (cid)	bhp	years
2498/ohv I-6 (152.4)	106[1]	1972-77
2994/ohv V-6 (182.7)	138/142[2]	1972-77
2994/ohv V-6[3] (182.7)	230[4]	1976-77

[1]Net [2]DIN/SAE net (European/U.S. models)
[3]Turbocharged [4]DIN

PRICES

FAIR	$4000-6000
GOOD	$6000-8000
FINE	$8000-9000

FINE EXAMPLE PRICE HISTORY

1982 $8000		**1990** $12,000	
1994 $10,000		**1998** $9000	
1982-2000 RETURN 1%			
2000-2010 3%			

1976-79
TVR
TAIMAR

The last but arguably best variation of the original TVR concept.

Unveiled at the London Motor Show in late 1976, still a stub-tail coupe, but with a more pleasingly shaped nose, a rear window that finally functioned as a hatch, and a revised interior catering to modern safety and ergonomic needs. An open version, a first for TVR, followed two years later. Prosaically named Convertible, it was actually a roadster, with side curtains instead of roll-down door glass, though the top was permanently affixed (and fairly easy to operate). Ever a tiny producer, TVR managed a waiver on meeting U.S. smog laws, and Taimars came Stateside with the same 3.0-liter British Ford V-6 offered in their native land. A few were turbocharged á la late 3000Ms.

■ **FOR** As for 1972-77 2500M/3000M, plus somewhat better workmanship and all-round performance • Convertible's open-air allure

■ **AGAINST** As for 1972-77 2500M/3000M

PRODUCTION

Taimar 395 (1976-79) **Convertible** 258 (1978-79)

SPECIFICATIONS

Length (in.)	154.0
Wheelbase (in.)	90.0
Weight (lbs)	2300-2335
Price (new)	$15,900 original U.S list

ENGINES

cc/type (cid)	bhp	years
2994/ohv V-6 (182.7)	138/142[1]	1976-79
2994/ohv V-6[2] (182.7)	230[3]	1976-79

[1]DIN/SAE net (European/U.S. models)
[2]Turbocharged [3]DIN

PRICES

Conv	
FAIR	$7000-9000
GOOD	$9000-10,000
FINE	$10,000-13,500
Cpe	
FAIR	$3000-5000
GOOD	$5000-6000
FINE	$6000-8000

FINE ROADSTER PRICE HISTORY

1982 $9000		**1990** $12,000	
1994 $19,000		**1998** $15,000	
1982-2000 RETURN 3%			
2000-2010 3%			

1980-90
TVR
TASMIN SERIES

TVR's mainstay for much of the '80s, and its most successful model line to date, but not a permanent replacement for the traditional TVR (which returned after a six-year absence as a much-modified Taimar Convertible called TVR S). Tasmin bowed as a wedgy two-seat fastback coupe with a distinctive "anteater" nose. A derivative two-seat convertible and 2+2 coupe appeared within a year on the same new 93.9-inch wheelbase. All followed customary TVR concepts save disc instead of drum rear brakes and roomier, more ergonomic cockpits. Proprietary drivetrains were featured as before, with the German Ford 2.8-liter V-6 the principal engine through

1976-79 Taimar coupe

out. The Tasmin was renamed 280i in 1984, reflecting the 1981-82 takeover of TVR by Peter Wheeler, who began offering new variants powered by Rover's ex-GM all-aluminum V-8. First was the 190-horsepower 350i with the original 3.5-liter displacement. A bored-out 3.9-liter 275-bhp 390SE arrived in late '84, followed by a 4.2-liter 420SEAC with 300 bhp, plus swoopy rocker-panel skirting and a full color-matched interior. The two largest V-8s were further enlarged in 1989 for replacement 4.3-liter 400SE and 4.5-liter 450SE models. There were few other changes save slightly smoother styling from 1986, plus suitable suspension retuning and equipment juggling. Limited U.S. sales began in 1983, but most of these TVRs were delivered to British and Continental customers.

FOR Unmistakable looks • Uncommon sights all • Great V-8 go (up to 150 mph and 5.6 seconds 0-60) • Ready parts/service backup • Fiberglass bodies don't rust

AGAINST Steel chassis do rust • Parts/service exist mainly in UK • V-6s not that fast (11.8 seconds 0-60, about 108 mph maximum) • Little known in U.S. • Ultimate collectibility unclear

PRODUCTION

NA

SPECIFICATIONS

Length (in.)	158.0
Wheelbase (in.)	93.9
Weight (lbs)	2365-2535
Price (new)	approx. $27,700-50,000

ENGINES

cc/type (cid)	bhp[1]	years
2792/ohv V-6 (170)	145/160[2]	1980-87
3528/ohv V-8 (215)	190	1984-90
3905/ohv V-8 (238.3)	275	1984-88
4228/ohv V-8 (258)	300	1984-88
4282/ohv V-8 (261.3)	275	1989-90
4441/ohv V-8 (271)	319	1989-90

[1]DIN [2]U.S./European models

PRICES

Prices in 2000 ranged from $5300 to $8700 for 1983 models.
2000-2010 RETURN 0%

1959-64
VANDEN PLAS PRINCESS 3 LITRE

1959-64 Princess 3 Litre sedan

A carefully reworked, upper-crust version of a mass-market sedan, the familiar British Motor Corporation (BMC) mid-range series introduced in 1958 and styled by Pinin Farina. Like the cheaper Austin A99/A110 varia-

1984 Tasmin 280i coupe

tions, the V-P featured prominent fins and rather boxy overall contours, but the front had a distinctive square grille with vertical bars. Construction was monocoque, and the rear suspension was a simple beam-axle affair. It was powered by BMC's old but sturdy 3.0-liter overhead-valve straight six, which gave moderately good performance—around 100 mph tops. Unlike its corporate relatives, the Princess was trimmed at the Vanden Plas works, which installed plush carpeting, walnut-covered dash, a good deal of extra sound deadening, and other equipment to set this model apart. All in all, it was rather like what GM would do two decades later when it offered the J-car both as a Chevrolet Cavalier and a Cadillac Cimmaron.

✚ **FOR** Quality trim and furnishings • Mechanically simple • British-traditional appeal • Vanden Plas name a plus for some • Good appreciator

▬ **AGAINST** Indifferent road manners • Modest performance • Many parts no longer available

PRODUCTION

Mark I 4719 **Mark II** 7984

SPECIFICATIONS

Length (in.)　　　　188.0

Wheelbase (in.)　　108.0/110.0
Weight (lbs)　　　　3480-3540
Price (new)　　　　NA

ENGINES

cc/type (cid)	bhp[1]	years
2912/ohv I-6 (178)	105/120	1959-64

[1]Net

PRICES

FAIR	$2000-3000
GOOD	$3000-4500
FINE	$4500-7500

FINE EXAMPLE PRICE HISTORY

1982	$3000	1990	$7500
1994	$6000	1998	$6000

1982-2000 RETURN 5%
2000-2010 2%

1963-75
VANDEN PLAS PRINCESS 1100/1300

Another "badge engineering" job from BMC, in this case the plushest and most expensive derivative of the front-drive 1100/1300 series designed by Alex Issigonis along the lines of his trend-setting Mini. Like the larger Farina-based Princess models, final assembly and trim application was carried out by Vanden Plas, but there was little difference in appearance or mechanical specifications from those of the down-market models. Features included all-independent suspension by BMC's innovative—and troublesome—"Hydrolastic" gas "springs," interconnected front-to-rear on each side, plus a transversely mounted A-series four-cylinder engine and space-saving front-drive body design. Small but roomy for its size, and nicely equipped in this form with a walnut veneer dash, leather upholstery, and full equipment. As expected, this Princess was marked by the traditional V-P stand-up vertical bar grille. It was even sold briefly in the U.S., but most of the emphasis was given to an MG version here. Later, the same basic car was sold here as the Austin America. Though the 1100/1300 series was extremely successful in Britain, it bombed in the States, and imports effectively ended after 1969.

✚ **FOR** Quality furnishings • Nimbleness • A certain cuteness • Good economy

▬ **AGAINST** Meager performance and an engine-killing final drive ratio • A bit small for some • A rare bird in the U.S. • Parts very difficult to obtain

1963-67 Princess 1100 sedan

• Unreliable suspension • Rust-prone

PRODUCTION

approx. 39,000

SPECIFICATIONS

Length (in.)	147.0
Wheelbase (in.)	93.5
Weight (lbs)	approx. 2000
Price (new)	NA

ENGINES

cc/type (cid)	bhp[1]	years
1098/ohv I-4 (67)	55/58	1963-67
1275/ohv I-4 (78)	65	1968-75

[1]Net

PRICES

FAIR	$1500-2500
GOOD	$2500-3000
FINE	$3000-5000

FINE EXAMPLE PRICE HISTORY

1982	$2500	1990	$4000
1994	$4500	1998	$5000
1982-2000 RETURN 4%			
2000-2010 2%			

1964-68
VANDEN PLAS PRINCESS 4 LITRE R

This was a reworked replacement for BMC's prestige medium-size sedan. The "R" in the designation stood for Rolls-Royce, which supplied the light-alloy F-head six-cylinder engine, a relative of the Silver Cloud unit. Borg-Warner automatic transmission was standard, and all the luxury touches from the previous BMC-engined Princess 3 Litre were retained. By now, the trendy mid-'50s fins of the original Farina body were becoming dated, so they were sheared off. Other spotter's points included horizontal taillamps and smaller-diameter wheels. Not widely seen in the U.S.—even before the advent of federal regulations—and only a modest seller at home, so finding one will be a challenge.

✚ FOR As for the 1959-64 Princess 3 Litre, plus slightly better performance (top speed up to 106 mph) and Rolls-Royce engine snob appeal

▬ AGAINST Engine costly to maintain • The same crashing boredom of the Princess 3 Litre

PRODUCTION

7087

SPECIFICATIONS

Length (in.)	188.0
Wheelbase (in.)	110.0
Weight (lbs)	3570
Price (new)	NA

ENGINES

cc/type (cid)	bhp[1]	years
3909/F I-6 (239)	175	1964-68

[1]Gross

PRICES

FAIR	$2500-3500
GOOD	$3500-5500
FINE	$5500-8500

FINE EXAMPLE PRICE HISTORY

1982	$5000	1990	$9500
1994	$8500	1998	$8000
1982-2000 RETURN 3%			
2000-2010 3%			

1996-97
VECTOR M12

Mid-engine supercar descended from the Vector W2 ("W" for founder Gerald Wiegart) announced in 1977. Only a single prototype was produced from 1977-87, followed by about 18 production cars (by now called W8) during 1987-93. Tangles with his Indonesian partners and the Vector board put Wiegart on the street in 1993. The Indonesian group (which later purchased Lamborghini) built just two cars (dubbed Avtech WX3/Avtech SC) during 1993-94, and introduced the M12 early in 1996. A 5.7-liter Lamborghini V-12 mated to a 5-speed manual ZF transaxle cranked out a vein-popping 490 horsepower, good for a top speed of 190 mph and 0-60 times below 4.5 seconds. More money troubles followed, and the company

1964 Princess 4 Litre R sedan

was bailed out by a Bahamas-based group in 1997. All told, at least eight Vector M12s have been produced. The most recent per-unit factory price was $189,000.

➕ **FOR** Extreme exclusivity • Acceleration • Supercar cachet

➖ **AGAINST** Examples are likely to change hands privately, or for inflated prices at auction • Forget concept of "dealer support" • Is this a car or a soap opera?

PRODUCTION

Appox. 8

SPECIFICATIONS

Length (in.)	188.2
Weight (lbs)	3600 (est)
Wheelbase (in.)	108.0
Price (new)	$189,000

ENGINES

cid/type	bhp	years
348/dohc V-12	490	1996-97

PRICES

Used car market.
2000-2010 RETURN Depreciating

1 9 4 6 - 5 2
VOLKSWAGEN BEETLE SPLIT-WINDOW

The phenomenal "People's Car," designed by Dr. Ferdinand Porsche

1949 Beetle Standard coupe

before World War II, though serious production began only gradually in a ravaged postwar Germany. By now, everyone is familiar with the formula: steel platform chassis with all-independent torsion-bar suspension and an understressed, air-cooled alloy flat four mounted at the rear. Styling needs no description—it's what earned the Type I the "Bug" or "Beetle" nickname in the U.S., where Volkswagen almost singlehandedly put imports on the map to stay. The early Beetle's future as a collectible is assured. In time, the only car to exceed the Model T in production volume will be as ubiquitous—and prized—as the Tin Lizzy. For now, the pre-1953 models with the split rear window are clearly the ones to look for. Model years were not formally

observed until 1955, with detail changes being made almost continuously. The last split-window Beetles of 1952 received synchromesh on the upper gears, plus door vent wing windows, twin taillights, wider tires, and the famous (or infamous) rotary heater knob. And don't forget the semiphore directional signals that persisted through the mid-Fifties—they're always a nice talking point. Though the Beetle remains in production today in Mexico (and is the best-selling car there), the Bug was changed so much through the '50s, '60s, and '70s that virtually nothing was interchangeable between early and late models. Perhaps the things that haven't changed are the Bug's virtues and vices. It has strange oversteer han-

1996-97 M12 coupe

dling characteristics, it's far from quick (especially these early cars), cross-wind stability leaves a lot to be desired, and creature comforts are notable by their absence. On the other hand, traction is terrific, steering light, the engine reliable (but not so much so for the early models), and the general charm irresistible. Except for convertibles, it's too early to predict the exact course of later Beetles as collector's items, though there's evidence some upward movement in interest and prices has already begun.

➕ FOR Landmark historical importance • Great nostalgia car • Low-mileage originals have high appreciation potential

➖ AGAINST Underpowered • Tricky handling • Meager trunk space • Feeble heater • Older-model parts not as easy to obtain as you might think

PRODUCTION

1946-48 91,921 **1949** 43,633 **1950** 81,917 **1951** 93,358 **1952** 114,327 (calendar year)

SPECIFICATIONS

Length (in.)	160.0
Wheelbase (in.)	94.5
Weight (lbs)	approx. 1700
Price (new)	$1280 original 1949 U.S. list price

ENGINES

cc/type (cid)	bhp	years
1131/ohv flat 4 (69)	27.5-30	1946-52

PRICES

FAIR	$3500-6000
GOOD	$6000-9000
FINE	$9000-12,000

FINE EXAMPLE PRICE HISTORY

1982 $2500		**1990** $9000	
1994 $9000		**1998** $12,000	
1982-2000 RETURN 10%			
2000-2010 5%			

1953-79 VOLKSWAGEN BEETLE CONVERTIBLE

In light of the current "retro-look" (including a retro Beetle), it's impossible to overlook Volkswagen's Type 1 cabriolet as a collectible. After all, Beetle ragtops of all years are in strong demand, and have been for some time. Karmann of Osnabruck carried out the assembly work, including installation of the typically Teutonic folding top. When buttoned up, the convertible was as tight and quiet as the sedan thanks to its thick "sandwich" top construction and glass (not plastic) rear window. When folded down, however, the top created an enormous "bustle," giving the car a look like that of no other. Styling and mechanical refinements followed those made to sedan models over the years, so let your taste and pocketbook be your guide. The parts situation naturally gets progressively better the newer the model you're talking about. The last Beetle convertibles were built in 1979, and by that time had become quite expensive in the U.S. owing to inflation and the relative value of the dollar versus the deutsche mark. These will no doubt command the highest collector prices as time goes on as "last of the line" models. In all, the VW ragtop is an automobile with permanent appeal, a piece of history that you can still drive every day.

➕ FOR Strong appreciation • A coast-to-coast network of dealers still happy to provide service • High-quality materials and finish • Beetle reliability, simplicity

➖ AGAINST All the Beetle's well-known infuriations, plus somewhat greater rust susceptibility and high rebuild costs for the soft top

PRODUCTION

20,000 per year (est. average)

SPECIFICATIONS

Length (in.)	160.0 (1953-71), 165.0 (1972-79)
Wheelbase (in.)	94.5 (1953-72), 95.3 (1973-79)
Weight (lbs)	2000 (average)
Price (new)	$1995 (1953), $6800 (1979) in U.S.

ENGINES

cc/type (cid)	bhp[1]	years

1957 Beetle convertible

1958 Karmann-Ghia coupe

1192/ohv flat 4 (72.7)	36/40	1953-65
1289/ohv flat 4 (78.4)	50	1966
1493/ohv flat 4 (91.1)	53-57	1967-79
1583/ohv flat 4 (96.6)	60[2]	1971

[1]Gross [2]46-48 net

PRICES

FAIR	$4000-7000
GOOD	$7000-10,000
FINE	$10,000-15,000

FINE EXAMPLE PRICE HISTORY

1990 $15,000	**1994** $8000
1998 $14,000	
1990-2000 RETURN 0%	
2000-2010 5%	

1956-74
VOLKSWAGEN KARMANN-GHIA

Volkswagen's sporty, two-seat alternative to the Beetle. It was based on the stock Type 1 Beetle platform with a specially crafted body built by the Karmann coachworks of Osnabruck, West Germany. Styling was the work of Luigi Segre of the Ghia studios in Italy, and was patterned closely after the Chrysler d'Elegance show car by Virgil Exner, though obviously in 3/4 size. The combination of swoopy, rounded looks, impeccable construction, and the ordinary but sturdy and economical Beetle drivetrain proved irresistible, and led to a long production run and many admirers for the K-G. The new body also brought two beneficial side effects: slightly better crosswind resistance on the highway and a bit better cornering ability compared to the Beetle. The convertible model's top was constructed similarly to that of the Beetle cabriolet: several layers of top material and insulation and a glass (not plastic) rear window. The K-G ragtop was great for sunny days, but the very wide rear quarters made for hellish visibility with the top up. But compared to contemporary British roadsters, converting the K-G cabriolet from open to closed (or vice-versa) was simplicity itself. VW advertising made much about Karmann's almost hand construction methods, which included filling, filing, and sanding all seams before painting. It was great for appearance, but made for costly repairs if you ever had to replace a panel. In all, a very pleasant little tourer, and so numerous that finding one even now presents no problem. Most mechanical parts are still available, too, through the large chain of VW dealers that helped make this marque so successful in the U.S. Of all the models, the 1500cc 1967 version is probably the most desirable as the peppiest. It was also the last K-G unaffected by U.S. safety and emissions rules.

FOR Superb styling for its day, and aging gracefully • Fine construction quality • No mechanical parts shortages • Thrifty

AGAINST Extremely rust-prone, especially the front fenders (even worse than the postwar Studebakers!) • Early body parts becoming scarce • Not as fast as it ought to be • Only two-passenger accommodation • Post-1967 models suffer from U.S. safety/emissions equipment

PRODUCTION

1956 2452 **1957** 4130 **1958** cpe 4700 **conv** 1325 **1959** cpe 6265 **conv** 1770 **1960** cpe 7247 **conv** 2044 **1961** cpe 6706 **conv** 1891 **1962** cpe 9656 **conv** 2723 **1963** cpe 12,010 **conv** 3387 **1964** cpe 13,084 **conv** 3691 **1965** cpe 14,191 **conv** 4003 **1966** cpe 17,112 **conv** 4827 **1967** cpe 16,107 **conv** 3174 **1968** cpe 19,177 **conv** 4157 **1969** cpe 21,100 **conv** 4584 **1970** cpe 32,952 **conv** 5873 **1971** cpe 17,816 **conv** 5567 **1972** cpe 11,208 **conv** 3076 **1973** cpe 10,271 **conv** 2650 **1974** cpe 5779 **conv** 1926 (U.S. sales; 1958-66 breakdowns est.)

SPECIFICATIONS

Length (in.)	163.0
Wheelbase (in.)	94.5
Weight (lbs)	approx. 2300
Price (new)	$2395 (1956), $2725 (1958 conv), $3500-4000 by 1974 (U.S. list prices)

ENGINES

cc/type (cid)	bhp[1]	years
1192/ohv flat 4 (72.7)	36/40	1956-65
1289/ohv flat 4 (78.4)	50	1966
1493/ohv flat 4 (91.1)	53-57	1967-70
1583/ohv flat 4 (96.6)	60[2]	1970-74

[1]Gross [2]45-48 bhp net

PRICES

Conv	
FAIR	$2200-4500
GOOD	$4500-7500
FINE	$7500-9000
Cpe	
FAIR	$2000-4000

GOOD	$4000-7000
FINE	$7000-8000

(Deduct 10% for heavy-bumper 1973-74 models.)

FINE 1967 CONVERTIBLE PRICE HISTORY

1982 $2500		1990 $7500	
1994 $6000		1998 $11,000	
1982-2000 RETURN 8%			
2000-2010 5%			

1962-67

VOLKSWAGEN KARMANN-GHIA TYPE 3 1500/1600

This was the less-than-successful Karmann-Ghia idea applied to Volkswagen's boxy, new-generation design of the early '60s, the Type 3. Although Type 3s were sold here as the Fastback and Squareback (three-door wagon) "sedans," the Karmann-Ghia models were never officially imported to the U.S. Those few that did seep in did so privately, some through Canada, others from abroad directly, all well before the Type 3's formal U.S. introduction. The styling was not nearly as successful as on the Type 1 Karmann-Ghia, with rather angular lines and an awkwardly shaped front end with sheetmetal creases curling around the headlamps. Virtually all those built were coupes, but a few convertibles were also constructed. Though the Type 3 was superficially similar in layout to the Type 1, its engine was completely different, having a flatter "pancake" block and initially more displacement. The Type 3s first brought into the U.S. all used the 1600cc version of this engine instead of the original 1500cc size. Like the Type 1, the Type 3 mounted its air-cooled engine in the rear of a steel platform chassis with all-independent torsion bar suspension.

FOR Uniqueness • Roomier than Type 1 Karmann-Ghia • Marginally better performance

AGAINST Nobody, it seems, liked the styling • Parts scarce • Suspect construction quality, including the usual K-G rust problems • Low appreciation potential

PRODUCTION

NA

SPECIFICATIONS

Length (in.)	168.5
Wheelbase (in.)	94.5
Weight (lbs)	approx. 2200
Price (new)	$2875 (cpe), $3300 (conv) U.S. equivalent

ENGINES

cc/type (cid)	bhp	years
1493/ohv flat 4 (91.1)	53	1962-65
1583/ohv flat 4 (96.6)	60	1966-67

PRICES

Cpe	
FAIR	$2000-4000
GOOD	$4000-7000
FINE	$7000-8000

FINE EXAMPLE PRICE HISTORY

1982 $2000		1990 $4050	
1994 $6000		1998 $7000	
1982-2000 RETURN 8%			
2000-2010 5%			

1964 Karmann-Ghia Type 3 coupe

1990-92
VOLKSWAGEN CORRADO G60

Credible attempt by VW to produce its first high-performance car, based on the second-generation Golf GTI. A G-shaped, intercooled supercharger (G-Lader in Deutsche) wrung 158 horses from a 1.8-liter 4. VW claimed 0-60 times in the 7.5-second range, an almost certain overstatement; 9 seconds was more likely. An "active" rear spoiler deployed automatically above 45 mph, ostensibly hindering lift and definitely blocking one's rearward vision. The spoiler returned to rest at 25 mph. The G60 was a modest breakthrough for VW, but despite its competence, sales in the U.S. were poor.

FOR Interesting engineering • Handling and roadholding • Steering • Scarce on these shores • VW dealer network

AGAINST Not as stirring as it wanted to be • Balky, cable-operated 5-speed shifter

PRODUCTION

1990 21,893 **1991** 17,058 **1992** 16,085

SPECIFICATIONS

Length (in.)	159.4
Weight (lbs)	2660-2675
Wheelbase (in.)	97.3
Price (new)	$17,900-19,860

1990 Corrado coupe

ENGINES

cid/type	bhp	years
109/ohc I-4[1]	158	1990-92

[1]Supercharged

PRICES

FAIR	$2000-5000
GOOD	$5000-7000
FINE	$7000-10,000
2000-2010 RETURN Depreciating	

1998-2000
VOLKSWAGEN NEW BEETLE

No car turned more heads than the Volkswagen New Beetle at the time of its release. The retro styling not only recalled the original Beetle, but was good looking in its own right. The interior combined retro with modern industrial design. Front seat comfort was excellent. Back seat passengers, with their heads against the rear window, paid the price of fashion. Other than styling, there were more differences than similarities between the old and New Beetles. The rear engine/rear drive setup of the original was replaced by the front engine/front drive chassis of the VW Golf. Thanks to the Golf components, the New Beetle was not only fun to look at, but fun to drive as well. The standard and diesel engines provided adequate performance. The turbocharged engine added in '99 was faster, but still no pocket rocket.

FOR Likeable styling that stands

1999 New Beetle coupe

1963 PV544 coupe

out in a crowd • Even base models are well equipped • Fun and practical

■ AGAINST Uncomfortable back seat • High sales will make less collectible

PRODUCTION

1998 107,090 **1999** 159,000

SPECIFICATIONS

Length (in.)	161.1
Weight (lbs)	2800
Wheelbase (in.)	98.9
Price (new)	$15,200-21,075

ENGINES

cid/type	bhp	years
121/ohc I-4	115	1998-00
116/ohc I-4[1]	90	1998-00
109/dohc I-4[2]	150	1999-00
[1]Diesel [2]Turbocharged		

PRICES

Used car market but can be volatile.
2000-2010 RETURN Depreciation will cease if they cut off production early, but so far they sell like hotcakes.

1·9·5·8 - 6·5

VOLVO PV544

This was the final version of the first postwar design by Sweden's long-time automaker, first introduced as the PV444 in 1944. The PV544 was also the first Volvo to have any significant impact on the American market, differing from the PV444 in having a one-piece (instead of divided) windshield, a larger rear window, revised interior, and minor trim changes. In appearance, however, the car remained nothing so much as a scaled-down version of the 1946 Ford (both Henry and Edsel would have been flattered), with a rounded fastback two-door-sedan body, tapering hood, distinct front and rear fenderlines, rectangular grille, and low-mounted integral headlamps. Powered by Volvo's own (and excellent) four-cylinder engine, it was available in standard and more powerful "S" tune. Built to last indefinitely and reliably even in severe climates, the PV544 established Volvo's reputation for sturdiness and solid construction, which exists to this day. This model was also surprisingly quick in its time, and saw sporadic competition successes in the U.S. Ultimately, it was succeeded by the more stylish (but still very upright) Amazon/120 series notchbacks, which borrowed much from it mechanically. The two lines ran side by side for several years, proof enough of the 544's staying power.

✚ FOR Rugged Swedish reliability • Good handling and performance • Adequately roomy • Me-too styling

that's somehow still appealing to many
• Some parts still available

■ **AGAINST** That same styling • Not
numerous any more

PRODUCTION

243,995

SPECIFICATIONS

Length (in.)	177.0
Wheelbase (in.)	102.5
Weight (lbs)	2100-2200
Price (new)	NA

ENGINES

cc/type (cid)	bhp[1]	years
1583/ohv I-4 (97)	60/75	1958-60
1778/ohv I-4 (109)	90/95	1961-65

[1]Gross

PRICES

FAIR	$1750-3000
GOOD	$3000-4500
FINE	$4500-6000

FINE EXAMPLE PRICE HISTORY

1982	$2500	1990	$4500
1994	$4500	1998	$5500

1982-2000 RETURN 5%
2000-2010 3%

1962-73
VOLVO P1800/1800S/ 1800E/1800ES

V olvo's "sports car," a rakish 2+2 sports coupe introduced as a 1962 model in late '61. Bodies were initially supplied by Jensen in England, which also assembled the first cars, designated P1800. Production was transferred to Sweden in late 1964, and the designation changed to P1800S. For the 1969 model year, the original 1.8-liter four-cylinder engine got a displacement boost to a full 2.0 liters plus Bosch fuel injection to become the 1800E. All these cars used the chassis and running gear of Volvo's 120/ Amazon sedans of the mid-'50s to mid-'60s, clothed in styling that was rather dated by the time the 1800 was announced. The lines were curvy,

marked by a jutting nose carrying an oval eggcrate grille. Out back were modest little fins and bullet-shaped pod taillights. The roof was quite low, and so was the driving position, which gave a real bathtub effect. The rear seat was virtually useless for anyone larger than kids, but the 1800 shone as a two-seater with ample luggage space for a sporty car. For 1973, Volvo re-roofed the basic bodyshell to convert it into the 1800ES, a sports/GT wagon with a deep frameless glass hatch. The coupe was discontinued, and the 1800ES continued for a short while before Volvo decided to abandon the market. Not very fast or terribly refined, but a good-handling car offering comfortable accommodations (Volvo's orthopedically designed seats were famous by now) and great durability. The injected 1800E and ES are probably the most desirable models in this bunch, having four wheel disc brakes, aluminum alloy wheels, a beefed-up gearbox, and nicer furnishings than earlier models. A good many 1800s were equipped with a manual

1966 P1800S coupe

four-speed transmission with electric overdrive effective on top gear.

➕ **FOR** Pleasant touring car • Good mileage • Nicely equipped • Robust Volvo construction • 1800ES a kind of Swedish Chevy Nomad • Models through 1967 are Milestone cars

➖ **AGAINST** Bathtub driving position • Crowded interior—no head room • Body parts now difficult to find • Somewhat rust-prone • Throbby engine

PRODUCTION

1962-63 P1800 6000 **1963-68 1800S** 23,993
1969-72 1800E 9414 **1973-74 1800ES** 8078

SPECIFICATIONS

Length (in.)	172.6
Wheelbase (in.)	96.5
Weight (lbs)	2400-3000
Price (new)	$6000 U.S. for '72 1800ES

ENGINES

cc/type (cid)	bhp[1]	years
1778/ohv I-4 (109)	100-115	1962-68
1986/ohv I-4 (121)	118-135	1969-73

[1]Gross

PRICES

FAIR	$2500-3500
GOOD	$3500-5500
FINE	$5500-9200

FINE 1800ES PRICE HISTORY

1982 $4000	**1990** $9500
1994 $7500	**1998** $8500
1982-2000 RETURN 5%	
2000-2010 5%	

1972 1800ES wagon

1941-42
WILLYS AMERICAR

Ordinary but well-built compact passenger cars produced under the presidency of Joseph W. Frazer (later of Kaiser-Frazer) and engineered by Barney Roos. The L-head four-cylinder engine and ladder chassis were conventional, while the sharp-nosed body styling owed a little to previous Hudsons and Nashes. Prices as low as $634 made the lightweight American competitive, but production had hardly begun when the company regrouped to build the immortal Jeep. Three variations—Speedway, DeLuxe and Plainsman—were offered, each with a coupe and sedan, plus a DeLuxe four-door woody wagon. Production did not resume after the war.

➕ **FOR** Inexpensive now • Economical and nimble • The last Willys cars until 1952

➖ **AGAINST** Styling • Conventional specs • Body parts scarce now • Slow to appreciate

PRODUCTION

1941 approx. 22,000 **1942** approx. 7000

SPECIFICATIONS

Length (in.)	170.0
Wheelbase (in.)	104.0

1941 Americar coupe

| Weight (lbs) | 2116-2512 |
| Price (new) | $634-978 |

ENGINES

cid/type	bhp	years
134.2/sv I-4	63	1941-42

PRICES

Wgn

FAIR	$3000-7500
GOOD	$7500-10,000
FINE	$10,000-16,000

Others

FAIR	$1500-2500
GOOD	$2500-5500
FINE	$5500-9000

FINE STATION WAGON PRICE HISTORY

1982 $6250	1990 $10,000
1994 $9000	1998 $16,000
1982-2000 RETURN 5%	
2000-2010 3%	

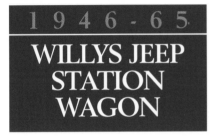

1946-65
WILLYS JEEP STATION WAGON

A high, boxy Jeep-inspired wagon that outlived Willys, which expired in 1955 after a short-lived postwar stab at the auto business. Regarded by some as more truck than car, though still called a "Station Sedan" (as Willys once did) and can lay fair claim as America's first all-steel wagon by at least three years. Practical two-door styling by Brooks Stevens, but front end still managed to evoke the beloved wartime Jeep. Engineering was strictly prewar Willys passenger car, including the odd, semi-independent "Planadyne" front suspension and sturdy but old L-head four. Always rather costly against "Low-Priced Three" competitors and thus never a big seller, but it would last almost 20 years with numerous interim changes minor and major. Among the latter were optional six-cylinder power from 1948, a four-wheel-drive option and modernized F-head engines in 1949, and increasingly deluxe trim/color choices. The original flat-face grille turned pointy for 1950 (when the rear bumper was wrapped), then went from five to three horizontal bars for 1954. A one-piece windshield appeared in '58, and 1959 brought colorfully two-toned Maverick and Harlequin models, the latter with rocket-like chrome side trim. Two-piece tailgate throughout. Production figures are hard to come by, but '59 was probably the peak sales year. Ultimately replaced by the new-for-'63 Jeep Wagoneer (another Stevens creation), but sold in diminishing numbers through 1965. Though outside the scope of this book, a companion pickup has also lately attracted collector interest.

✚ **FOR** Rugged, practical design • Just uncommon enough to attract attention • Low demand, so low priced • Lots of variations, plain to fancy • Many parts still available

▬ **AGAINST** Values won't rise much, if at all • More truck than car to drive • Two doors, so wagon utility not the best • Rust-prone • Clean originals hard to find

PRODUCTION

1946 6533 **1947** 33,214 **1955** 12,265 **1959** 30,778 **Other years** NA

SPECIFICATIONS

Length (in.)	176.3
Wheelbase (in.)	104.0/104.5 (2WD/4WD)
Weight (lbs)	2800-2995
Price (new)	$1495-2357

ENGINES

cid/type	bhp	years
134.3/sv I-4	63	1946-49
134.3/ohv I-4	72	1949-65
148.5/F I-6	72	1948-49
161/ohv I-6	90/115	1949-65

PRICES

FAIR	$2000-3000
GOOD	$3000-6000
FINE	$6000-8000

1948 Jeep station wagon

1948 Jeepster convertible

FINE EXAMPLE PRICE HISTORY

1982 $3000   **1990** $6500
1994 $6700   **1998** $7200
1982-2000 RETURN 6%
2000-2010 3%

1 9 4 8 - 5 1
WILLYS JEEPSTER

A sprightly touring car with styling by Brooks Stevens in the World War II Jeep vein. It could have had tremendous appeal in the early postwar years, but proved uncomfortable and clumsy to drive, and too expensive. It was accordingly dropped as Willys' "passenger car." Engines were converted to an overhead-valve configuration in mid-1949. The 1948-49 Jeepsters, with upright instead of eggcrate grilles, were finished to a higher standard than the later models. Though unsuccessful in these years, the Jeepster concept was revived about 15 years later for the Commando line of jaunty Jeep-based recreational vehicles.

+ FOR Fair collector following • Many parts still available • Interesting styling and concept • Milestone car status • Active club

– AGAINST Slow appreciation • Noisy • Uncomfortable

PRODUCTION

1948 4-cylinder 10,326 **1949 4-cylinder** 2307 **6-cylinder** 653 **1950-51 4-cylinder** 4066 **6-cylinder** 1778

SPECIFICATIONS

Length (in.)	174.8
Wheelbase (in.)	104.0
Weight (lbs)	2392-2485
Price (new)	$1390-1765

ENGINES

cid/type	bhp	years
134.3/sv I-4	63	1948-49
134.3/ohv I-4	72	1949-51
148.5/sv I-6	72	1949-50
161/ohv I-6	75	1950-51

PRICES

FAIR	$3000-4500
GOOD	$4500-7000
FINE	$7000-11,000

FINE EXAMPLE PRICE HISTORY

1982 $4000   **1990** $9500
1994 $10,000   **1998** $10,000
1982-2000 RETURN 6%
2000-2010 5%

1 9 5 2 - 5 4
WILLYS AERO-EAGLE

Willys' return to a "proper" passenger car, engineered by Clyde Paton and styled by Phil Wright. Built with monocoque construction, the clean-lined Aero Willys was practical in size and one of the best-riding compacts of the early '50s. Unfortunately, the price was too high to wean many buyers away from Ford, Chevy, and Plymouth models, even the cheaper ones. The Aero-Eagle two-door hardtop was the costliest and most luxurious of the various models offered, which also included Wing, Lark, Ace, and Falcon two- and four-door sedans. Kaiser acquired Willys in 1954, and the 226-cid Kaiser six was offered as an optional alternative to the Willys F-head four and 161-cid six. The Custom designation was introduced that year to denote an exterior or "continental" style spare tire mount.

+ FOR Nice looks • Fine ride/handling combination • 226-cid models have

1954 Aero-Eagle hardtop coupe

good performance • Reasonable economy even today

■ **AGAINST** Slow appreciation • Early rust-out threat • Body parts scarce

PRODUCTION

1952 2364 **1953** 7018 **1954 226-cid** 973 (incl. 11 Customs) **161-cid** 583 (incl. 499 Customs)

SPECIFICATIONS

Length (in.)	180.9/183.0 (1952-53/1954)
Wheelbase (in.)	108.0
Weight (lbs)	2575-2847
Price (new)	$2155-2904

ENGINES

cid/type	bhp	years
134.2/F I-4	72	1953-54
161/F I-6	75	1952-54
226.2/sv I-6	115	1954

PRICES

FAIR	$1500-2500
GOOD	$2500-4000
FINE	$4000-6000

FINE EXAMPLE PRICE HISTORY

1982 $3000	**1994** $5500
1998 $6000	
1982-2000 RETURN 4%	
2000-2010 3%	

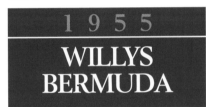

1 9 5 5
WILLYS BERMUDA

Renamed successor to the Aero-Eagle hardtop, a last-ditch attempt to improve its meager sales. A modest facelift on the Aero-Willys body included a vertical-bar grille, bodyside two-toning, and new ornamentation and taillights. Hardtop prices were cut to just below the $2000 level in an effort to stimulate showroom traffic. But it wasn't enough, and only a few Bermudas were produced, along with an equally modest number of Ace and Custom sedans. Rarity, top-line status, and the marque's final model year make the Bermuda the most collectible of all the Aero-Willys models. Willys passenger cars continued to be built for several years in Brazil following the end of Kaiser-Willys' U.S. operations.

✚ **FOR** Scarcity • Others as for 1952-54 Aero-Eagle

■ **AGAINST** Styling • Others as for 1952-54 Aero-Eagle

PRODUCTION

226-cid 2156 **161-cid** 59

SPECIFICATIONS

Length (in.)	189.9
Wheelbase (in.)	108.0
Weight (lbs)	2831
Price (new)	$1997

ENGINES

cid/type	bhp	years
161/ohv I-6	90	1955
226.2/sv I-6	115	1955

PRICES

FAIR	$2000-3500
GOOD	$3500-5000
FINE	$5000-6500

FINE EXAMPLE PRICE HISTORY

1982 $3250	**1990** $7000
1994 $6500	**1998** $6500
1982-2000 RETURN 4%	
2000-2010 3%	

1955 Bermuda hardtop coupe

MINOR MAKES

NOTES TO THE READER

What follows is a compilation of 1940-70 minor American-built automobiles not listed in the main body of the book. The vast majority of these saw very limited production; some never proceeded beyond the prototype stage; a rare few were sold for several years. A number of prototypes are included because there was evidence of serious intent to manufacture in complete form. Vehicles sold as kits ("kit cars") are included only where fully assembled models were available from the manufacturer or a dealer. The facts about some of them are, unfortunately, completely elusive, or at best sketchy.

Each entry is dated as accurately as possible, and builder or factory locations are stated where known. Where only one year is shown (1965-?) the editors were unable to determine exactly when "production" ceased. When "c." (circa) is shown, it was not possible to determine the precise date production started and/or terminated.

The cars in this section were rare when new. Today there may be few, if any, survivors. Pricing would be inaccurate, if not impossible, and has not been attempted.

AEROCAR (1948-c.1970)

Aerocar Inc. of Longview, Washington had been building combination car/planes since 1948, but only seven had been constructed through 1970. Moulton P. Taylor developed the Aerocar; airworthiness certification was first received from the Civil Aeronautics Authority in 1954. The earliest models used a 100-bhp Franklin engine for both ground and air propulsion. Top speed on the ground was 50 mph, 110 in the air. As a plane, the Aerocar had a 300-mile range. It needed 655 feet for take-off and only 300 feet for landing. At least one prototype had semi-retractable landing gear. Conversion from car to airplane or

vice-versa took just five minutes for one person with a wrench. In car form, the wings and propeller assembly were carried in a 14-foot trailer. The main section measured 124 inches long overall, and wheelbase was 78 inches. Gross flying weight was 1750 pounds. Aerocar was to have been priced starting at $3995, but listed for $7500 in 1954. By the early 1970s its price was well into five figures.

An Aerocar International Corp. of Fort Worth, Texas reportedly planned production in 1961. Sufficient orders were apparently on hand to make this feasible, but the effort failed. It is unknown whether any were built, but it seems unlikely. The relationship of this firm to Aerocar Inc. is also a mystery. It is not clear whether it was an independent contractor or a subsidiary of the Washington firm.

AEROMOBILE (1958)

Aeromobile was built in 1958 by Waldo Dean Waterman of San Diego, California. It was a car/plane, but little information about it is available. It was reported to have had no tail.

AIRCAR (1970-c.1973)

The Aircar, from Advanced Vehicle Engineers of Van Nuys, California, revived the "flying auto" idea in a somewhat different form. Instead of being purposely designed, the Aircar was an aeronautical conversion. Control surfaces from a Cessna Skymaster were attached to an ordinary production car. Pontiac Firebirds were most commonly used, but some heavier cars were also given wings and used more powerful turboprop engines. Development continued until at least 1973, at which time a Pinto was being test-flown under the name Mizar.

AIRPHIBIAN (1946-52)

Mass production of flying autos never got off the ground, but it wasn't because nobody tried. Robert E. Fulton, Jr. was one of

many who saw great possibilities for the car/plane in the postwar market. His Airphibian was first shown in 1946, under the aegis of Continental, Inc., Danbury, Connecticut, of which Fulton was president. The Airphibian's passenger compartment (or cockpit) was made of aluminum. As a plane, it could be converted to a two-passenger, four-wheeled car by detaching wings, propeller, and fuselage (a five-minute exercise). In the air it could reach 120 mph. Top speed on the highway was a modest 45 mph. A six-cylinder, 150-horsepower, aircooled engine provided the power. When ready for flying, the Airphibian weighed 2200 pounds and could travel 400 miles on 30 gallons of gasoline. Highway mileage was 25 mpg. In 1952, Fulton was still trying to get production started.

AIRSCOOT (1947)

You've just arrived at your local airport in your private plane. How do you get home? Simply pull your folded-up Airscoot out of the baggage compartment and prepare it for the road. After you've unfolded this vehicle's two seats and two-suitcase luggage rack (in front of the seats), you fire up the one-cylinder, 2.6-horsepower engine and drive away at speeds up to 25 mph.

The three-wheeled Airscoot was made of lightweight tubing, which accounts for the toteable weight of only 72 pounds. The gas tank on this midget commuter held only three-tenths of a gallon; a full gallon would take you 60 miles. Overall length was 37 inches. Aircraft Products Company of Wichita, Kansas apparently was never able to get their unique little folding auto into production.

AIRWAY (1948-50)

At least two Airway "vicinity car" prototypes were built, but they were not very similar in appearance. The 1948-49 version had a very plain fastback two-door sedan body. The 1950 Airway was a notchback-style coupe. Under the skin, the cars were much more alike. A 10-horsepower air-cooled aluminum engine transmitted power through a fluid drive. Both cars were 2- to 3-seaters, and had space for packages behind the single seat. The first prototype weighed 600 pounds and had an aluminum body. The 1950 car weighed 775 pounds with its body-of aluminum alloy and plastic. Wheelbase on both was 100 inches. Top speed was 45-50 mph.

The T. P. Hall Engineering Corporation of San Diego developed the designs and licensed Airway Motors, Inc. to manufacture them. Prices were expected to be in the $500-$750 range. It is doubtful any were sold.

AMITRON (1967-?)

Amitron was a co-operative effort by Gulton Industries of Metuchen, New Jersey and American Motors in Detroit. It was a three-passenger electric car, powered by lithium-nickel fluoride batteries, which are about 10 times more powerful than the lead-acid type. Two batteries weighing 75 pounds each were used along with two nickel-cadmium batteries. The car could accelerate from 0 to 50 mph in about 20 seconds. Range was some 150 miles, even at speeds up to 50 mph. The wedge-shaped Amitron featured vinyl bumpers in an off-white color.

APACHE (1966-?)

Apache was similar to European economy cars in overall size, engine displacement, and seating, although further details about it are unavailable. Its most unusual feature was a collapsible roof, which transformed it from a fastback coupe to an open convertible. Production of 500 to 1000 cars a year was predicted in 1966 by John G. Zullo, president of Interco Development Corporation of New York City. Volume never reached that figure though.

ARGONAUT (1959-63)

A large and very ambitiously designed luxury car, the Argonaut appeared in 1959. It was made by the Argonaut Motor Machine Co. of Cleveland, Ohio. There were seven models planned, ranging from a two-passenger sports coupe, sometimes referred to as the Steed, to a limousine. Another model was dubbed Smoke.

Frames were made of five-inch seamless steel tubing. Wheelbases were 126½ to 154 inches, while total length ran from 218 to 258 inches. The aluminum bodies were made in the United States or Italy. Interiors were trimmed to owner specifications.

An air-cooled, overhead-cam, aluminum V-12 was used. This was thought to be a military engine. After some hesitation, the company revealed this powerplant developed an astonishing 1020 horsepower. Yet fuel consumption was a surprisingly good 13 mpg. A top speed in excess of 240 mph was claimed. A manual transmission with overdrive was standard, but a three-speed automatic was optional.

Prices were targeted at $25,150 and up to $36,000. The cars would have been sold directly from the factory, and servicing would be done either at factory depots or the owner's home. Twice-a-year inspection by factory engineers was also planned. Production ended by 1963.

ARNOLT-MG (1952-63)

S. H. "Wacky" Arnolt was a sportsman from Warsaw, Indiana and first made money by building marine engines during World War II. After the war, he expanded into other industries. Because he liked automobiles, one of his early interests was a foreign car dealership in Chicago.

His first creation was the Arnolt-MG. He later built the Arnolt-Bristol. Arnolt had found a Bertone body at the Turin Auto Show in 1952. He contracted to buy 100 copies, and went to MG for mechanicals. The $3195 Arnolt-MG resembled contemporary MGs only in its narrow, upright grille. The price, and the fact that the Arnolt was no faster than a standard MG, kept sales low (65 copies) in spite of attractive styling.

When Mr. Arnolt died of a heart attack in 1963, the Arnolt-MG died with him.

ARROWBILE (c. 1937- c.1958)

Initially known as Arrowbile, and later Aerobile, this series of flying autos by Waldo D. Waterman was perhaps this country's first serious attempt to get such a vehicle into production. A 1937 effort using a Studebaker Commander six-cylinder engine almost reached full production: five or six vehicles were built in Santa Monica, California. Studebaker was to sell the Arrowbile through selected dealers, but backed out because of a downturn in the economy.

A report in December 1940 showed a drawing of an Aerobile three-wheeled "torpedo-shaped" car with detachable wings, by a Dayton, Ohio inventor and manufacturer. The final Aerobile was apparently put together in San Diego during the '50s. It was powered by a horizontally opposed, water-cooled Franklin six-cylinder engine.

ASARDO (1959)

The name Asardo stems from the initials of its builder, the American Special Automotive Research & Design Organization, in North Bergen, New Jersey. The car had a tubular space-frame with an 88-inch wheelbase. A 195-pound fiberglass sport coupe body was used, as well as an aluminum belly pan. Overall length was 150 inches, and total weight was some 1350 pounds.

The engine was a four-cylinder 91.3 cubic-inch Alfa Romeo unit, tuned to develop 135 horsepower. A four-speed transmission was standard. The car's 0-60 mph acceleration time averaged 6.4 seconds, and a top speed of 135 mph was claimed. The price, including Borrani wire wheels, was $5875.

ASCOT (1955)

Ascot was made by the Glasspar Co. of Santa Ana, California. Not surprisingly, its roadster body was made of fiberglass. It had butterfly-type fenders. free-standing headlights, a square grille, and external deck-mounted spare tire. Originally, the car was designed for a 172 cubic-inch Ford industrial engine, but various other units were tried, including a Studebaker six. Wheelbase for this 1770 pound car was 94 inches. Height with the top up was just 48 inches. Production apparently took place only during 1955.

ASTRO-GNOME (1956)

Astro-Gnome, designed by the Richard Arbib Co. Inc. in New York, was a futuristic prototype. (Richard Arbib had a hand in the facelift for the 1956 Hudson, and also created the 1952 Packard Pan American.) Andrew Mazzard carried out the custom body work. The AstroGnome's side panels were made of ribbed anodized aluminum, offered in a choice of colors. They were easily replaceable. The car's bubble top provided unobstructed vision and was high enough so passengers could walk in. Leather was used for the upholstery, interior trim, and floor. Matching leather luggage was also supplied. The Astro-Gnome was only 13½ feet long, but comparatively wide at six feet. The unusual styling also featured an integrated full-perimeter bumper.

AUBURN (1967-?)

In 1966, Glenn Pray left the Cord Automobile Company he had formed several years earlier. He had made some mistakes, but had learned a great deal about making replicas of classic automobiles.

Now it was time to start a new venture. This time it would be a revival of the Auburn 851/852 Speedster of 1935-36. The new model would be known as the 866. Unlike the 8/10-scale Cord, the 866 was a full-size replicar. The 127 inch wheelbase of its modified Ford Galaxie frame was identical to the original's. Overall weight was considerably less, however: 3100 pounds versus the 851's 3850. The big 428 cubic-inch Thunderbird V-8 engine turned out 365 horsepower. The body was made of fiberglass, like those of most other revivals. Some of the hardware was reported to be new old stock from the original Auburn factory. Top speed was estimated to be in the neighborhood of 130 mph. Many sto-

ries were told about vintage-car enthusiasts being fooled into believing the 866 was an original. Pray had obviously done his homework well. And the price of $8450 was certainly less than you would expect to pay for a mint-condition original—if you could find one. The only options were the customer's choice of upholstery materials and paint colors.

Other Auburn replicas would follow from Pray's company and a spate of others. The 866 was later joined by Model 874, a dual-cowl phaeton that was an interesting variation, even though it had no counterpart in the '30s. These cars continued in limited production through the early 1980s.

AURORA (1954)

Aurora was a one-off safety car prototype designed by Father Alfred A. Juliano of Branford, Connecticut. It was based on a 1954 Buick Roadmaster chassis, but could accommodate Cadillac, Lincoln, or Chrysler engines. The fiberglass body was topped by a transparent plastic roof. Its bubble-shaped windshield was raked forward.

Only one prototype was built at a cost of $30,000. It was hoped that interest in the design would be high enough to make limited production commercially feasible, in which case the car would have cost an estimated $15,000. Sales profits would have been used for further research in car safety.

AUTO CUB (1956)

Auto Cub was the creation of Randall Products of Hampton, New Hampshire. It was a small, single-passenger runabout with tiller steering, and was only 51 inches long. The car reached a top speed of 15 mph with a 1.6-horsepower Briggs & Stratton or Clinton engine mounted at the rear. Fuel consumption for this 115-pound mite was 75 mpg. Its price was $169.50 complete. The Auto Cub appears to have been the economy mate to the Daytona.

AUTOETTE (1952-57)

Autoette was produced for approximately five years beginning in 1952 by Autoette Electric Car Co., Long Beach, California. A small, electric shopping-type car for two passengers, it was a threewheeler with a sin-

gle wheel at the front. The body was made of steel. A set of four heavy-duty 6-volt batteries supplied power to a 24-volt DC motor. Prices ranged from $775 to $950 in 1954 and three models were available.

BASSONS STAR (1956)

One wheel in front, two in the rear, a low-slung two-passenger open fiberglass body, and a single-cylinder, two-cycle engine—that was the Bassons Star. Gil D'Andrea designed it for Bassons Industries Corporation of Bronx, New York. Bassons intended their creation for use as a low-cost, short-haul delivery car. Other suggested customers for this $1000 vehicle were commuters, farmers, and families needing an economical second car. The unenclosed storage space over the rear wheels could carry up to 500 pounds. The 10-horsepower, one-cylinder, two-cycle German J.L.O. engine was mounted between the passengers and the storage area. The Star could cruise at 40 mph, top speed was 70. The entire vehicle weighed only 400 pounds. It was 33 inches high, 49 inches wide, and 125 inches long.

Bassons also showed an enclosed reinforced plastic bodied delivery van called Stationette in 1955. This was an update of the earlier wooden-bodied Stationette. Both of these three-wheelers were designed by James V. Martin (see Martinette).

BAYMONT (1955)

Simple, safe, convenient transportation at an operating cost of 3 cents a day-average operating costs of less than $1.00 a month. What else but an electric car? This one was made by Baymont Company in Redwood City, California. Most of the electrics in the 1950s were golf carts modified for local running on city streets. The Baymont Suburban Model 240 was no exception. It had sufficient space for two passengers, and room in the rear for several bags of groceries. Factory equipment included a single headlight, taillight, and horn. Six color choices were available. For a few extra dollars, the customer could add a windshield or a top. The company claimed the Suburban had sufficient power under full load to climb any paved road in

America. Speeds up to 20 mph were said to be easy to achieve. The driving range was as high as 60 miles per day.

BEARCAT (1956)

Bearcat was an unusual little car, built by the American Buckboard Corp. of Los Angeles. It had five wheels: the extra one, located at the rear, was connected by chain to the rear-mounted two-cylinder engine and served as the drive wheel.

Wheelbase, excluding the fifth wheel, was only 70 inches, and the car was just 120 inches long overall. Its fiberglass sports body was formed in one piece. A claimed 50 mpg was achievable by this $1000 vehicle.

BEECHCRAFT PLAINSMAN (1948)

The Plainsman was a prototype for a possible venture into the automobile business by the Beech Aircraft Co. of Wichita, Kansas. Unit construction was used with an aluminum frame and body panels. For better visibility and entry/exit, the windshield and door openings were cut into the roof.

The Plainsman's drive system was quite unorthodox. A four-cylinder Franklin air-cooled engine was used to drive an electric generator which, in turn, drove four electric motors—one at each wheel. Although the gas-electric system was never installed in this four-wheel-drive car, it was successfully tested in some military trucks. The Plainsman had a very large six-passenger body. Riding comfort was enhanced by an all independent suspension system featuring a rubber air bag and an air-filled shock absorber at each wheel.

The price was optimistically pegged at $5000, but the car certainly would have cost more than that to produce.

BERGERMOBILE (1949)

Bergermobile, named after its inventor Joseph M. Berger, was a prototype built by the Berger Air Turbine Car Co. of Mount Vernon, New York. Basically, it was a converted Chevrolet. The engine was removed and replaced by a 30-gallon air tank and an Ingersoll-Rand air turbine. A 24-volt airplane-type storage battery supplied electrical power to

drive the compressed-air turbine and also powered the electrical system. A simple forward/reverse lever controlled both speed and drive direction.

B. M. C. (1952)

1952 BMC

B. M. C. Sports got its name from the British Motor Car Co. of San Francisco, which built it in 1952. BMCC president, Kjell H. Quale, was one of its designers. The vehicle had no connection with the British Motor Corporation, and in fact used components from the rival Rootes Group of Britain. The car was designed around the chassis and engine of the production Singer 1500. The B. M. C. used a one-piece fiberglass body with much different styling, however. The project was terminated after only a few months, despite plans to produce 400 units a year.

BOBBI-KAR (1945-47)

1946 Bobbi-Kar

S. A. Williams was a shrewd promoter who began as a dishwasher in 1936 and ultimately found prosperity in the restaurant business. Attracted by a car-hungry market at the end of World War II, he bankrolled the Bobbi Motor Car Corporation in San Diego. The resulting "aero-engineered" lightweight was named Bobbi-Kar, after Williams' son. The original prototype, affectionately dubbed the "Iron Monster," had a four-cylinder, 25-horsepower rear engine. Top

speed was an unspectacular 55 miles an hour. Overall length was 132 inches; wheelbase was 80 inches. Projected price for the tiny two-place roadster was around $500. A plastic body and four-wheel independent "Torsilastic" suspension were publicized features. The suspension was developed by B. F. Goodrich. It used the torsion-bar principle with rubber bushings bonded to steel at the control points.

Subsequent convertible and station wagon prototypes were much larger than the original, although they retained the same styling themes. Length was now up to 152 inches and the wheelbase became 92 inches. Optimistic advertising brochures showed sketches of other proposed body styles; sedan, urban sedan (a wood-bodied two-door), coupe, and the Bobbi-Wagon package car (without doors). The grand plan called for production in an unused Consolidated Vultee aircraft plant.

Following investigations of his stock-selling schemes, revelation of his prison record, and a hasty move of operations to Birmingham, Alabama, Williams sold out and returned to California. He later became involved in at least two more automobile ventures, the Towne Shopper and the Elektrakar. The Bobbi-Kar became the Keller, and the story continues under that heading.

BOLIDE (1969-?)

Bolide came from the Bolide Motor Car Corp. of Huntington, New York, but the name graced two quite different models. Both were built by Andrew J. Griffith, Jr. who was associated earlier with the Griffith operation. The fiberglass-bodied Can-Am 2 was designed for use on street or track. It had a wheelbase of 105 inches, and used a Ford 351 V-8 located amidships. This model was priced at $3500.

Another model called XJ002 was a four-wheel-drive, Jeep-style two-passenger sports car. Designed for on- or off-road use, it was powered by a 225 cubic-inch 160-bhp V-6.

BOSLEY (1955-66)

1966 Bosley Mark II Interstate

Richard Bosley of Mentor, Ohio spent nearly three years and $9000 building his first car, the Bosley Mark I. The attractive fiberglass-bodied sports coupe could easily have come from Torino. The specially built frame supported a 1952 Chrysler V-8 with a Cunningham intake manifold. With the 225 horsepower produced by this combination, the car could reach a top speed of 160 mph. With long-distance races in mind, Bosley installed a 55-gallon fuel tank.

In late 1966, a second car was shown, the Bosley Mark II Interstate. Again, the styling had a distinct Italian flavor. This time, power was provided by a 345-bhp Pontiac V-8. The fiberglass body rested on a reinforced Corvette chassis with a 102-inch wheelbase. Gas tank capacity was now a mere 35 gallons.

BROGAN (1946-50)

Brogan was one of several small-car designs from the B & B Specialty Co. of Rossmoyne, Ohio. Some models were also known as Broganette and the B & B Three Wheel.

A three-wheeler with a single wheel in front, this car had a 60-inch wheelbase. The top of its windshield stood less than four feet above ground. Total weight was a mere 450 pounds. Its air-cooled two-cylinder engine produced 10 horsepower and was rear-mounted. No clutch was required. Mileage claims of 65-70 mpg were made, and top speed was 45 mph. The smaller Broganette scored up to 85 mpg, but its top speed was scarcely 40 mph.

By 1951, the Brogan name was

phased out and considerable changes were made to the Broganette. It was still a three-wheeler, but the lone wheel was moved to the rear. Overall length was now about 10 feet, but width was a narrow 52 inches. A roof was provided on the deluxe version of this two-seat design.

With its air-cooled 10-bhp Onan engine and three-speed transmission, the Broganette could reach 50 mph. Fuel consumption was in the 55-60 mpg range. Price was $550.

Some models in 1947 were apparently sold under the name B & B Three Wheel. However, not more than 30 of them were built.

BRYAN (1949-72)

Leland (Dewey) Bryan, a General Motors Proving Grounds employee, built at least three flying automobiles. Several different names for his vehicles have been reported by the press: Bryan, BryCar, and Roadaplane. Bryan's design differed from most others by utilizing permanently attached folding wings rather than detachable wings. The third version (Bryan 111, 1972) had wings that folded electrically in 35 seconds. The unusual craft was licensed as an automobile by the state of Michigan. All Bryan's inventions used pusher props mounted at the rear of the fuselage. Maximum road speed of the several versions varied from 50 to 70 mph; top air speed ranged from 60 to 80 mph. The second version had a 75-horsepower A-75 Continental engine.

BUCKAROO (1957)

Buckaroo was built in Cleveland, Ohio by an unidentified manufacturer. It was very small, and its air-cooled engine was capable of providing a top speed of only 18 mph. Very little else is known about this $400 vehicle.

BUCKBOARD (1956)

An Ariel "Square-4" motorcycle engine, mounted amidships on a Renault 4CV frame, powered this modern cycle car by Don Bruce of Bronx, New York. Bruce first displayed the car at an auto show in

Hartford, Connecticut, and offered construction plans for do-it-yourselfers. It is not known if he built more than the one car.

The unusual body was constructed of $3/8$-inch marine plywood with oak stringers and mahogany strips. The light weight of 738 pounds combined with the 43- (later reported as 61-) horsepower engine enabled the Buckboard to reach speeds in excess of 90 mph. It had retractable headlights controlled from the driver's seat (the right headlight turned with the wheels). The car was 143 inches long overall, and had a 94-inch wheelbase.

BUGETTA (c.1968-?)

Bugetta was made by Bugetta Inc. of Costa Mesa, California. Its fiberglass body would seat two to four passengers. A fiberglass or fabric top was available. It was a mid-engine design powered by a Ford 302 V-8. Prices started at $3695. Some off-road type vehicles were also made.

BUSHMASTER (1968-?)

Bushmaster was built by the Bushmaster Co. of Austin, Texas. Production began in 1968 and apparently lasted into the early '70s.

CALIFORNIAN (1945-46)

1946 Californian

This three-wheeler was the predecessor of the Davis. The prototype was built by Frank Kurtis. Although its size and general shape were similar to the Davis, the Californian differed in several respects. Its grille was in front, with the headlights mounted behind it. The Davis had hidden lights and no grille. It also used separate rear fenders, while the Davis had flush side panels. And the Californian was a convertible; the production

Davis was a hardtop. The Californian's 58-horsepower engine helped it reach a 100-mph hour top speed while returning 40 mpg.

In 1945, publicity referred to Warner Manufacturing Company of Glendale, California, but 1946 reports indicated the maker as Californian Motor Car Company of Los Angeles.

CANNON (1955)

Cannon was a product of Cannon Engineering Co., North Hollywood, California. Although it definitely existed, its design details have been lost to researchers.

CHADWICK (1960)

Chadwick was an open shopper from the Chadwick Engineering Works, Pottstown, Pennsylvania. A 58-inch wheelbase tubular-chassis was used, with independent suspension at the front and quarter-elliptic leaf springs at the rear. Four-wheel hydraulic brakes were featured. A single-cylinder 13-horsepower air-cooled BMW engine was connected to a four-speed BMW transmission with enclosed chain drive. Overall length was 87 inches and weight was only 680 pounds. Radio, headlights, fixed windshield and top, and a speedometer were available as options. The Chadwick was built only in 1960.

CHARLES TOWN-ABOUT (1958-59)

Charles Town-About was a product of the Stinson Aircraft Tool & Engineering Corporation of San Diego, California. Stinson's vice president, Dr. Charles H. Graves, was responsible for the design as well as the name.

The vehicle was an electric, using two 3.2-horsepower motors, one for each rear wheel. A 48-volt electrical system was used. The car had a 77-mile range between charges, and a top speed of 58 mph.

The Town-About used a modified VW Karmann-Ghia body. Behind its tubular loop front bumper was a dummy grille. At the back, DeSoto fins and taillights were grafted on. Suspension was by tor-sion bars. Despite the heavy batteries, the car weighed just 90 pounds more than a standard Karmann-Ghia.

Van-About was Graves' name for his utility model. At the back, it had a protruding cargo box, like the coupe-pickups of the 1930s. Production of both models was limited to 1958 and 1959.

CHICAGOAN (1952-54)

The Chicagoan came from Triplex Industries Ltd. of Blue Island, Illinois. A two-passenger fiberglass sports car, it used a six-cylinder Willys engine. It's likely no more than 15 cars were built from 1952 to 1954, and the name was probably changed to Triplex around 1954.

COLT (1958)

According to one source, the Colt was made by Colt Manufacturing Company of Milwaukee. But a catalog names the Colt Motors Corporation of Boston as the maker. A change in location and manufacturer might explain this discrepancy.

The Colt was a small, 700-pound, two-passenger economy model. Its single-cylinder four-cycle engine was a 23 cubic-inch Wisconsin air-cooled unit capable of 60 mpg, even with automatic transmission, which was standard. The fiberglass Colt had a top speed of 50 mph, and its price was $995.

COMET (i) (c.1946-48)

Comet (i) was built by General Developing Company of Ridgewood, New York. A three-wheeler with a tubular frame and plastic body, it measured only 114 inches in length. The single wheel was mounted at the front while the engine was located at the rear. With a modest 4.5 horsepower, the Comet's fuel economy was a claimed 100 mpg.

COMET (ii) (1951-55)

Micro-midget race cars were the mainstay of Comet Manufacturing Company's production in the early '50s. In 1951, however, it advertised a special roadster that could be assembled by the buyer, or bought fully assembled and ready to drive. The Sacramento, California firm claimed its Comet Roadster was the world's lowest-priced transportation, and could be driven for 50 cents a week. The sleek little open two-seater came equipped with a 6-horsepower engine, automatic drive, heavy-duty brakes, and oversize balloon tires. Ratings of 60 mpg and 40 mph were touted.

CONVAIRCAR (1941-48)

Convaircar, occasionally spelled ConVaircar or ConvAircar, was a car/plane made by the Consolidated-Vultee Aircraft Corporation of San Diego. The prolific Ted Hall headed the Convaircar project after he had designed the Roadable.

For road use, the vehicle got its power from a 26.5-horsepower Crosley engine. It had a second engine for flying, a 190-bhp Lycoming. The Convaircar had a four-seat fiberglass body, with a long sloping back and considerable rear overhang. The airframe, with its 34½ foot wing span, was attached to the roof at three points. Portable aluminum jacks supported the airframe section during attachment.

The Convaircar had made three successful trial flights before it ran out of fuel and crashed in late 1947. Development work continued, however, and by 1950 the car was known as the Hall Flying Auto, with a price tag of $20,000.

CORD (1964-66; 1968-70)

This mid-'60s replicar revived one of the all-time greats: the 1936-37 Cord 810/812. It was built by the Cord Automobile Co. of Tulsa, Oklahoma (registered as a Delaware corporation) under the aegis of Glenn Pray, a former school teacher. Gordon Buehrig, who had designed the original, styled the revival too, and kept its lines faithful to the original's. Pray's car was about 80 percent of the 1936-37 model in size, so it was designated the Cord 8/10.

U.S. Rubber, now Uniroyal, had developed a plastic material in the early '60s called Royalex, and this was chosen for the 8/10 body.

Maintaining tradition, the new Cord retained front-wheel drive. Power came from the Chevrolet Corvair air-cooled flat six that developed 110 horsepower from 164 cubic inches.

Available only as a two-passenger convertible, the Cord 8/10 was priced at $4000 in 1964. This rose to nearly $6000 by the time production ended in 1966. A total of 91 Cords were built, excluding prototypes.

Despite several attempts by company president Wayne McKinley to keep the firm solvent, the Cord Automobile Company went into receivership. (Glenn Pray was no longer part of the organization by then.) A bankruptcy sale was held in March 1967.

In 1967-68, the firm was owned briefly by Elfman Motors Inc. of Philadelphia. Exactly what took place during that time is hazy, though it seems certain no cars were produced during the Elfman regime. Then in 1968, the car was taken over by the Sports Automobile Manufacturing Company of Mannford, Oklahoma.

SAMCO, as the company was more commonly known, produced a much different car than the previous version. Since the Corvair was being phased out, a new powerplant was sought and two were finally adopted. The Ford 302-cid V-8 was selected as the standard engine and Chrysler's 440 Magnum V-8 was offered optionally. SAMCO phased out Royalex and reverted to conventional fiberglass body construction. The styling was also revised. Its retractable headlights were now fixed in the open position and front-wheel drive gave way to rear drive.

Two models were offered: the Warrior, on a 108-inch wheelbase, and the Royal, on a 113-inch wheelbase. (The original Cord's wheelbase was 125 inches and that of Pray's revival was 100 inches.) SAMCO prices were $7300 and up. Production ended in the spring of 1970.

CORTEZ (c.1947-c.1950)

Though the Cortez does not appear to have reached produc-

tion, this full-size car was intended for volume sale at $1000 a copy. An October 1950 news clipping indicated that a new $40 million corporation was to introduce a new light car to the public "next year, providing military production does not interfere." The company, North American Motors, Inc., was located in Dallas, Longview, or Grand Prairie, Texas, depending upon which report you read. Perhaps the company moved frequently during its short life span. Various reports were consistent, however, in stating that well-known automotive designer John Tjaarda (of Lincoln-Zephyr fame) was involved in the Cortez project. A wheelbase of 100 inches, weight of about 1000 pounds less than a standard car, and fuel consumption of 45 miles per gallon were all part of the grand plan.

CROFTON (1959-61)

1960 Crofton Bug

The Crofton, or Crofton Bug, was built by Crofton Marine Engine Company of San Diego. Crofton acquired the rights to the Crosley engine after that car went out of production. A 35-horsepower version of this engine went into a Jeep-style vehicle, an on- or off-road machine that weighed 1100 pounds. Wheelbase was 63 inches, overall length 111 inches.

Crofton's price was $1350, but for an extra $450 a "Brawny Kit" was available. This consisted of a six-speed transmission, limited-slip differential, crash pan, 9.00x10 tires (5.30x12s were standard), and deluxe seats.

Approximately 200 Croftons were built from 1959 until production terminated in 1961.

CRUE-CUT (1966-?)

Missouri (Sugar Creek and Kansas City) and later Kansas

(Gardner) have been the home for hundreds of half-scale cars made by Crue-Cut Manufacturing Company since 1966. Starting with the Tin Lizzie formerly made by McDonough Power Equipment, Inc., this firm has added Ford Lotus, Stutz Bulldog, GM touring car, and Chrysler replicas to its line over the years. The Model T roadster also provided the basis for a fire engine version with "real wood ladders." These "magnificent minis" apparently serve well in sales promotions, fundraising events, and advertising. All are powered by 3-horsepower engines that can take them up to 12 mph.

CUBSTER (1949)

Osborn Wheel Company of Doylestown, Pennsylvania wasn't content to sell just wheels. In 1946, you could buy its Model A racer chassis (with a 12-inch steering wheel and 10x0.175 Goodyear semi-pneumatic tires) mounted on, of course, Osborn ball-bearing steel wheels. Customers added a body and engine to suit. In 1949, the Model D chassis was available for $299.50, complete with 6.6-horsepower engine, or $159.50 without engine. Osborn now offered a kit for its Cubster body that fit nicely on the Model D chassis. Company advertising made no mention of what material was used for the body, but it was a 118-inch long, two-passenger ("any age") roadster of modern fenderless style. The ads did claim 35 mph was attainable.

CURTISS-WRIGHT AIR-CAR (1959-60)

Curtiss-Wright introduced their own car in 1959, and it was unlike any other. This one had no wheels. The Air-Car traveled on a cushion of low-pressure, low-velocity air at a height of 6 to 12 inches over land, water, swamps, or mud. Production of the 300-horsepower Model 2500 Air-Car was scheduled for November 1959 in South Bend, Indiana. The odd-looking, four-passenger vehicle was said to have a top speed of about 60 mph. A January 1960 press photo showed an Air-Car on display in

New York's Rockefeller Plaza with the caption stating production was then underway. How many were produced is not known. Other versions planned were an Air-Bus and Air-Car pickups and trucks.

CUSHMAN (1945-?)

1960 Cushman

Cushman was a shopper-type car from Cushman Motor Works Inc. of Lincoln, Nebraska. Cushman is best known for its motor scooters and golf carts, but it has made some carlike runabouts over the years. With a low-power, one-cylinder, air-cooled engine, the Cushman was small and very economical. Electric models had also been occasionally available. Around 1969, the Town & Fairway model was offered. It could be converted from a four-passenger minicar to a golf cart or carry-all.

CUSTER (1959-60)

The Custer Specialty Company of Dayton, Ohio entered the automobile business earlier than most. Custer had built an electric car in 1898 or 1899. It again offered cars from 1920 to 1946, and in 1959 made another try at the business.

This latest effort was a two-passenger "buckboard" vehicle, with either a Custer Special electric motor, or a 6-horsepower four-cycle gasoline engine. The electric motor had two forward and two reverse speeds, and gave a top speed of 18 mph. The gas model could reach 40 mph. Wheelbase of either model was 70 inches, and overall length was 93 inches. Custer left the automobile business permanently in 1960.

DARRIN (1946-47)

A prewar designer of custom coachwork, Howard A. "Dutch"

Darrin made a bid for the volume market with an intriguing convertible in 1946. One of the first cars designed expressly for fiberglass body construction, this five-seater was vaguely reminiscent of Darrin's styling for the production 1947 Kaiser and Frazer: the grille was horizontal like the Frazer's, and the overall look was rounded with slab sides. But there the similarities ended: mechanically, the Darrin was unique. An elaborate hydraulic system provided power for the car's convertible top, power front seat, four-wheel jacking system, and hood-raising mechanism. The Darrin's hood and front fenders pivoted up as a unit to expose the entire engine and front suspension. The rectangular frame was of box-section steel. Wheelbase was 115 inches, overall length 185 inches. Power was derived from a 100-bhp Kaiser six of 226 cubic inches.

Darrin hoped to build up to 30,000 of these cars a year. After constructing a running prototype, he attempted to interest financial backers in production. The most promising opportunity appeared in the form of Lehman Brothers, the New York financial house, which had simultaneously been approached by Kaiser interests to help underwrite K-F. Possibly because of Lehman's inability to reach a deal with Kaiser and because of Darrin's association with K-F, neither arrangement ever materialized.

DAVIS (1947-49)

1948 Davis

The Davis is perhaps the best known postwar three-wheeler made in the U.S. Its maker was the Davis Motor Co. of Van Nuys, California, headed by Glenn Gordon "Gary" Davis. It is said his

idea for a "tricycle" car came from none other than Howard Hughes.

A seven-passenger sedan and an 11-passenger station wagon were planned, but only a four-place, single-seat coupe was actually built. Its 64-inch bench seat was supposed to hold four people.

The body consisted of nine aluminum panels, each attached by twist bolts for easy removal or replacement. The metal top was detachable. Doors opened by means of external push buttons instead of conventional handles. Styling was simple and sleek. A single wheel was mounted at the front, the prow was quite pointed, and the headlights were hidden.

A Continental engine was used in the first few cars built, but most had a four-cylinder, 133 cubic inch 60-horsepower Hercules unit. A top speed of 116 mph was claimed. If true, that would make the Davis the fastest U.S. car of 1947.

The Davis was intended to sell for $995, and production of 40,000 units was anticipated for 1949. Actually, just 17 cars were completed, all prototypes, which were never formally sold. Gary Davis was convicted of fraud in the financing of his firm, though he claimed innocence.

DAYTONA (1956)

Daytona was made by Randall Products of Hampton, New Hampshire. Priced at $495, this was the rich-man's version of the Auto Cub. The Daytona was bigger, heavier, and more substantial. It was 72 inches long and weighed 235 pounds. A steel chassis was used for this two-passenger runabout. Unusually, body panels were made of Formica. A rear-mounted 2-horsepower Briggs & Stratton engine gave the car a top speed of 18 mph and fuel economy of 75 mpg.

DEBONNAIRE (1955)

Although contemporary accounts of the Debonnaire indicated it was available with top for about $1800, it is unclear whether this was a complete car or just a body kit ready to mount on the chassis of your choice. It is clear, however, that the fiberglass body was designed for the 1941-48 Ford platform. Replac Corporation of Euclid, Ohio was the maker.

DELCAR (1947-49)

Delcar was produced by American Motors Inc. of Troy, New York. The company's name is coincidentally similar to that of the Wisconsin automaker formed by the Nash/Hudson merger a few years later.

Delcars were built from 1947 to 1949. Most were small delivery trucks, but at least one station wagon was built. It was a very boxy vehicle with no hood. The front-mounted four-cylinder engine was situated under the front floor. The station wagon was roomy enough for six people, yet it had a very short 60-inch wheelbase, a 102-inch overall length, and stood 78 inches tall.

DEL MAR (1949)

Del Mar Motors Inc. of San Diego completed only a few prototypes of a neat-looking subcompact. The engine was a four-cylinder, 160 cubic-inch, 63-horsepower Continental. With its three-speed Warner transmission, 80 mph was possible. Fuel consumption was as high as 30 mpg. Wheelbases varied between 100 and 104 inches. The suspension used Ford transverse leaf springs front and rear, although some examples had semi-elliptic rear springs. Monroe aircraft-type rubber-filled shock absorbers were installed.

The body was a combination of aluminum, plastic, and steel. Styling was not unlike that of the British Hillman introduced at about the same time. The Del Mar's projected price was around $1200, and production of two-door sedans, business coupes, and convertibles was planned at the rate of 600 per day.

DEVIN (1957-64)

1957 Devin SS

Bill Devin owned Devin Motors in Los Angeles, California where he and partner Ernie McAfee sold exotic cars like Siatas and Ferraris to wealthy racers. Devin received a particularly pretty Ermini 1100 that he sold to racer Jim Orr. But before he did, he made a fiberglass mold of the Ermini's aluminum Scaglietti body. Devin then invented a system of modular molds that would enable him to alter the dimensions of the Scaglietti design to fit a wide variety of chassis and drivetrains.

Soon after Devin got into the kit-car business, he received an intriguing order from an Irish engineer named Malcolm MacGregor. MacGregor wanted a body kit to fit a chassis he was building around the Corvette V-8.

MacGregor's chassis was state of the art in 1957. Steel tubing, three inches in diameter, was formed into a ladder-type frame with tubular loops at the cowl and behind the seats. Rear suspension was fully independent, including De Dion tube, coil springs, dual parallel trailing arms, and huge 11-inch Girling disc brakes mounted inboard next to the differential. At the front were parallel A-arms with coil springs and tubular shock absorbers, along with another pair of Girling discs. The Devin chassis was one of the first to offer all independent suspension and four-wheel disc brakes.

Rolling chassis were shipped to El Monte, California where Devin and his crew completed assembly. A stock Corvette 283-cid V8, fitted with a special low-profile manifold and carburetor so it would fit under the low hood, was bolted in along with the Corvette's BorgWarner T10 four-speed transmission. The result was dubbed Devin SS. It could run 0 to 60 mph in 4.8 seconds, and 0 to 100 in 12 seconds. Top speed was over 140 mph.

Yet the cars didn't sell. Production lasted from early 1958 through the end of '61, during which time exactly 15 were sold.

Devin had other irons in the fire. In 1959, he restyled his original body, giving it a high trunk into which a Volkswagen engine fit like

hand in glove. He built a frame of square tubing and bonded it to a fiberglass undertray. This was planned to take stock VW suspension components. The interior was fitted with bucket seats. The car, called the Devin D, was available as a kit for only $1495 or completely assembled for just $2950. It was pretty, reliable, and surprisingly sophisticated. Hundreds were sold along with a derivative Devin C—the same chassis but with a Chevy Corvair powerplant.

Unfortunately for Devin, that smooth, Scaglietti-styled body for which his cars were famous had come to look old fashioned by the mid-1960s. His kits had been fairly profitable in their day, but the SS, C, and D were too costly to produce for their limited market. Eventually, Devin got out of the car business completely.

DIEHLMOBILE (1962-64)

The Diehlmobile three-wheeler was made by the H. L. Diehl Co. of South Willington, Connecticut. Its unique feature was that it could be folded up flat, and fit into the trunk of a normal car, With wire wheels and 3-horsepower Briggs & Stratton engine, it weighed 225 pounds. Its price was only $299.50.

DIE VALKYRIE (1952)

In 1952, Brooks Stevens was commissioned by a Cleveland syndicate to create a low-volume, special-order car on a contemporary Cadillac chassis. The Die Valkyrie show prototype, built by the Spohn bodyworks of Ravensburg, West Germany, was the result. It created some interest at that year's Paris Auto Salon, but production did not materialize.

Stevens emphasized the car's V-8 power by a strong V frontal motif. The long-hood/short-deck body configuration prefigured that of several forthcoming luxury cars, notably the Continental Mark II. Die Valkyrie also evidenced Stevens' first use of what he called the "Washington coach door line." This allowed rear seat entry and exit in a two-door without materially disturbing the front passengers.

This feature later appeared on the Gaylord.

DOUGHERTY (1955-56)

Dougherty was made by Frazer Dougherty of Sierra Madre, California in 1955 and 1956. No information about its design is available.

DOW ELECTRIC (1960)

Dow Electric came from the Dow Testing Laboratory Inc. of Detroit. It's possible this is another name for a car called the D.T.L. made by Detroit Testing Laboratory Inc. at about the same time.

Douglas Dow, former research chief of the Detroit Edison Co., designed this two-passenger electric. Two 0.3-horsepower motors were used. Power came from three 12-volt and four 2-volt batteries. Top speed was about 15 to 20 mph and the range was 30 miles. Operating costs of $1/4$ cent to $1/2$ cent per mile were claimed. Rear disc brakes were a feature of this 447 pound, 74-inch-long vehicle.

Dow tried to get his electric car produced but couldn't find a company willing to take it on. If it had been produced, the Dow car was expected to sell for around $500 to $800.

DUESENBERG (i) (1959)

Duesenberg (i) was a hybrid built by Mike Kollins of Detroit. Based on a 1950 Packard chassis, it was powered by the famous Duesenberg straight eight, rebored to yield a displacement of 435 cubic inches and 400 horsepower. The steel and aluminum roadster body was hand-formed. Only one example is believed to have been built.

DUESENBERG (ii) (1966)

1966 Duesenberg 4-door prototype

Duesenberg (ii) was one of several attempts made in the '60s to revive famous nameplates of the past. The Duesenberg Corp. of Indianapolis was formed with Fred "Fritz" Duesenberg as chairman of the board. Fritz was the son of August and a nephew of Fred, the famous brothers who built the original Duesenbergs.

The revived Duesenberg was not a replica of the classic 1930s model, but rather an all-new super-luxury sedan—a latter-day Duesie in the modern idiom. Its styling was the work of Virgil Exner, former styling chief at Chrysler Corp. The body was made by Ghia in Italy.

Naturally, it had to be big. The wheelbase was $137^{1}/2$ inches and overall length was 245 inches. That was a half an inch more than a contemporary Cadillac limousine. Legroom was a generous $42^{1}/2$ inches in front, and 44 inches in back. The hood was a massive 80 inches long. Under it was a 440 cubic-inch, 425-horsepower Chrysler V-8.

Production never progressed beyond one prototype. But the Duesenberg's general design was adopted in 1970 for a similar Stutz revival.

DYNAMO JR. (1959)

Dynamo Jr. was an electric from Dynamo Electric Co. of Los Angeles. It was little more than a fiberglass-bodied golf and shopping cart.

EDWARDS (1949-55)

1954 Edwards AMG/LXA coupe

Sterling H. Edwards built this car under the auspices of his Edwards Engineering Co., in South San Francisco, California. The first Edwards Special appeared in 1949 as a four-seat convertible with hardtop and windshield that could be quickly removed for racing.

Edwards' "production" car, the America, was announced in late 1953. A slab-sided, good-looking four-seat convertible, it had a large rectangular eggcrate grille and 1952 Mercury taillights. Greater rigidity was provided by a Mercury station wagon chassis, sectioned to a wheelbase of 107 inches.

By 1955, an Edwards cost over $7800. All models came standard with electric window lifts, HydraMatic transmission, and Kelsey-Hayes wire wheels. The high price kept demand extremely low.

ELECTRA KING (1961-?)

Electra King is made by the B & Z Electric Car Co. in Long Beach, California. The firm was founded by Messrs. Billard and Zarpe in 1961. Zarpe withdrew shortly after the company was founded, while Billard sold out in 1972 because of poor health. The next owner was Robert E. McCoy, who had a background in electrical engineering.

Originally, a 1-horsepower DC electric motor was used and gave the car a 45-mile range. A modest cruising speed of 18 mph was advertised. Usually, five 6-volt batteries were provided, but some examples had 24-, 30-, and 36-volt electrical systems. A two-passenger car only 88 inches long, the Electra King was available with either three or four wheels. The single wheel is at the front of the tricycle model. Tire size is 4.00x8. With a fiberglass top, total weight is only 675 pounds. The interior was carpeted, as was the seven cubic-foot trunk.

Electra King later had a choice of four motors, ranging from 1 to 3.5 horsepower. Several types of battery packs were also offered, so performance and range varied depending on the motor/battery selection. Speeds ran from 16 to 29 mph, and range from 18 to 36 miles between charges.

Styling did not change greatly over the years, but prices rose. The 1974 models sold for $2270 to $2900.

ELECTRICAR (1950-c.1966)

Electricar was made by the Boulevard Machine Works of North Hollywood, California. Established in 1949, this firm made a vehicle known by its initials, B.M.W. But in 1950, the firm moved to North Hollywood, and its product was renamed Electricar. Three models were announced, each a small open runabout.

The Boulevard model was a two-seater, 106 inches long. It had four 1/6-horsepower electric motors, one to drive each wheel. The Cutie, a single-passenger version, had two such motors, one driving a front wheel and the other a rear wheel. Its top speed was 25 mph. The Cutie Junior had just one motor, and its top speed was only 10 mph.

How long production continued is uncertain. There were reports of a 1966 model that could reach 70 mph.

ELECTRIC SHOPPER (c.1956-?)

1960 Electric Shopper

Made by the Electric Car Co. of Long Beach, California, this vehicle was just what its name implied: an electrically powered shopping car. Its lifespan is open to question, however. One source says the car was built from about 1960 to 1973, while another lists the period as 1956 to 1962. All agree that it was a fiberglass three-wheeler, 86 inches long on a wheelbase of 61 inches. The price was $945, although a metal bodied model was also sold for $750. The motor was a 24-volt DC series-wound unit, rated at just 1.5 horsepower. The car could reach speeds up to 18 mph in either forward or reverse. Range was 30-35 miles between charges.

ELECTRO MASTER (1962-?)

Electro Master, from Nepa Manufacturing Co. of Pasadena, was an electric shopping car with a fiberglass body. Its 2-horsepower motor was connected to six 6-volt batteries. Top speed was 20 mph and range was 40 miles. Weight

was just 680 pounds. Production began in 1962 and reportedly ended in 1964, but may have continued longer.

ELECTROBILE (1951)

Two enterprising gentlemen from Chicago thought they had the answer to burgeoning suburban transportation problems. Their Electrobile design was a three-wheeled fiberglass-bodied runabout for shopping and running errands. This 300-pound electric was expected to travel 25-35 miles on a recharge. A high-speed DC motor and a built in charger were included in the proposed price of $350. The fiberglass body consisted of several molded sections mounted over an aluminum frame. Press releases showed only sketches of the Electrobile. It is doubtful even a prototype was ever built.

ELECTRONIC (1955)

Electronic was an unusual car planned in 1955 by the Electronic Motor Car Corp. of Salt Lake City, Utah, A sedan, station wagon, and panel truck were proposed, as well as a sports car to be available with or without a hardtop. Overall length was 210 inches, and wheelbase was 110 inches.

A gasoline or diesel engine provided power to an 80-cell battery pack, which was connected to a "Dual-Torque" electric motor located within the rear axle housing. Also incorporated was the "Electro-Magnetic Differential," an electric device that was supposed to act like a limited-slip differential.

Only the prototype Electronic was built. Production had been planned for either Detroit or Oxford, Michigan.

EL MOROCCO (1956-57)

El Morocco was a Chevrolet conversion designed by Reuben Allenden of Detroit. The car was basically a 1956 or 1957 Chevrolet hardtop or convertible with somewhat altered styling. Revisions were made to the grille, bumpers, side trim, and fins. The result looked very much like the contemporary Cadillac Eldorado. In spite of all the work involved, the con-

verted car cost about as much as a standard Chevrolet. It is believed that about 30 El Moroccos were built over a two-year period.

ESHELMAN (c.1954-date)

Cheston L. Eshelman of Baltimore, Maryland and now Miami, Florida has built quite a variety of vehicles over the years. All of his early cars were very tiny ones for children, and slightly larger ones for one or two adults.

In the mid-to-late '60s, Eshelman began selling franchises for his Golden Eagle line of automobiles. These were various Chevrolet models with large Eagle emblems and nameplates in place of the standard badges. Apparently there were no other modifications. At this writing, Eshelman sells Golden Eagle Prestige Car accessory kits (emblems and nameplates) and experimental rights to his electric car and/or his 30-mph crash absorber.

FERGUS (1949)

Fergus, from Fergus Motors Inc. of New York City, was that firm's second attempt at car making. Its first effort lasted from 1915 to 1922. The second endeavor was a car based on the Austin A40 from Britain. It used the A40 engine and its styling somewhat resembled that of the relatively uncommon Austin A40 Sports. Development did not progress beyond the prototype stage, however.

FERRER (1966)

The Ferrer GT was made by Ferrer Motors Corp. of Miami, although one source names the manufacturer as Bottier Engineering of Camden, New Jersey. This car had a sleek steel-reinforced fiberglass body, similar in appearance to Ford's GT of the mid-'60s. The ubiquitous Volkswagen Beetle provided the chassis, with a wheelbase of 94.5 inches. Overall, the Ferrer was 158 inches long, 60 inches wide, and 42 inches high. It was sold as a basic kit for $990 and as a more complete deluxe kit for $1750. However, the buyer could have a fully assembled car with 50-horsepower engine for $2950. An optional VW engine reworked to put out 70 bhp could boost price to $3800.

Ferrer claimed their standard model would cruise at a 90-mph top speed, and was capable of 29 mpg at a steady 68 mph. The 0-60 mph run could be accomplished in 12.5 seconds.

FINA (1953-c.1955)

Perry Fina, a New York City importer of European cars and a connoisseur of fine automobiles, backed development of the Fine Sport. Based on a 115-inch wheelbase Ford chassis, its overall length was 188 inches. The bodies, convertible or hardtop were built by Vignale of Italy. A floating U-bar was the main feature of the grille design. Standard engine was the contemporary 210-horsepower Cadillac V-8, but a hopped-up version with 300 bhp was also available. The car could be fitted with any other V-8 to special order. The transmission was a General Motors Dual-Range Hydra-Matic.

Despite the high $10,000 price, Fina deliveries were said to be running about five months behind at one point. Evidently, the market was quickly saturated.

FITCH (1949; 1961-69)

The first car called Fitch was made by Sports and Utility Motors Inc. of White Plains, New York. It was designed for both competition and general road use, but the emphasis was largely on the sports side. Its originator was John Fitch, a famous race driver, sports-car promoter/builder, and safety expert. Only one prototype was built in 1949.

The Fitch Type B (the prototype was Type A), used the 96-inch-wheelbase Fiat 1100 chassis. Its engine was the small 60-horsepower Ford V-8, souped up to yield 105 bhp. This was wrapped in a greatly modified Crosley Hot Shot body. Dry weight was only 1520 pounds. This excellent power-to-weight ratio gave the Fitch a 0-50 mph acceleration time of 6.3 seconds. Top speed was 120 mph.

John Fitch and Co. Inc. at Falls Village, Connecticut started turning out customized Corvairs bearing the name Fitch Sprint beginning in 1961. Performance, handling, and appearance alterations turned the standard 1960-64 Corvair coupe into an outstanding GT. The modifications could be carried out on an existing car or on a brand-new one ordered through Fitch.

The engine kit, costing only $29.00 installed, raised output of the Corvair flat six to 155 bhp. That was good enough for a 0-60 mph time of only 9.5 seconds. Other modifications were available for suspension and steering.

On 1965 and later Corvairs, the Sprint package included a "tunnel" fastback roof, created by attaching a "blade" on each side of the rear window.

An entirely different concept was the Fitch Phoenix, which appeared in 1966. Illustrator Coby Whitmore helped design the body, which has been described as "wickedly beautiful." Body construction was done in Turin, Italy by Frank Reisner's Intermeccanica company. The Phoenix used Corvair running gear, and featured an integrated "targa" rollbar. The front part of the roof was removable. A spare tire was mounted in each front fender, which was humped to clear it. Two spares were needed because the car used two different tire sizes: the fronts were 175x14 while the rears were 185x14. Flying-buttress roof styling was used, although the Phoenix was really a notchback. Its reverse-slant rear window could be raised or lowered electrically.

The Phoenix's 2150-pound weight was about 300 pounds lighter than the comparable Corvair. Its wheelbase was 95 inches, total length 174 inches. A modified Corvair engine was used and produced 170 bhp. The car could cruise at 100 mph, but top speed was in excess of 130 mph. Acceleration from 0 to 60 mph took only 7.5 seconds.

A production run of 500 was planned, but the Phoenix project was halted because of the expense involved in meeting federal safety standards, which went into effect for 1968. Only one prototype was built.

FLETCHER (1954)

The Fletcher Flair was built by Fletcher Aviation Corp. of Rosemead, California. It was a four-wheel-drive, Jeep-type vehicle with an unlikely powerplant—a Porsche 1500cc engine. Riding a 78-inch wheelbase, the Fletcher had an overall length of 126 inches, which could be shortened to 115 by body alterations.

FLINTRIDGE-DARRIN (1957)

This car, sometimes known as Flintridge Darrin-DKW or Flintridge-DKW, was made by the Flintridge Motor Manufacturing Corp. of Los Angeles. Howard "Dutch" Darrin, who had designed the 1946 Darrin and the Kaiser-Frazer cars, did the styling.

The Flintridge-Darrin was based on the chassis of a German D.K.W. four-door sedan. Darrin's rear-end treatment was unique: concave, with a scalloped decklid lip. The body, supplied by Woodill, was made of fiberglass and made the Flintridge 10 inches longer and 6.5 inches lower than the D.K.W. It weighed 1870 pounds, about 200 pounds less than the D.K.W. Its price was $3195, compared to $2275 for the D.K.W. sedan. Some 15 of these cars had been made when problems at Woodill cut off delivery of the bodies.

FORD 1901 REPLICA (1968)

The Ford 1901 Replica was built by the Horseless Carriage Corp. of Ft. Lauderdale, Florida. It was said to be "a ³/₄-scale replica of a 1901 Ford," but since the first production Ford wasn't built until 1903, this description was obviously inaccurate. Specifications of this replicar, including the engine it used, are not known. Production lasted only a few months.

FORMACAR (c. 1968)

Marbon Division of BorgWarner Corp., Washington, West Virginia, built this prototype to demonstrate a new lightweight plastic material called Cycoloc for automotive use. The Formacar's total weight was 2200 pounds. Its 290 cubic-inch, 198-horsepower V-8 and transmission accounted for over a third of that. The GT-type body design had a 90-inch wheelbase and a 162-inch overall length. Formacar never reached production.

FRICK (1955)

The Frick, sometimes called Frick Special, was one of several cars built by Bill Frick Motors of Rockville Centre, New York. Already established as an expert in dropping Cadillac motors into various production cars (see Studillac), Frick decided to build a complete car from the ground up. For it, he devised a box-channel chassis with a 110-inch wheelbase. The independent front suspension consisted of coil springs with unequal-length wishbones. At the rear, semi-elliptic leaf springs were used. Not surprisingly, the engine was a Cadillac and a supercharger was planned. Dual-Range Hydra-Matic transmission completed the drivetrain. The coupe body, not unlike a Ferrari in appearance, was made by Vignale in Italy. The car's all up weight was 3000 pounds.

GADABOUT (1945)

The Gadabout was designed and built by industrial designer Ray Russell in his Grosse Pointe Park, Michigan home workshop. The relatively small three-passenger roadster had a wheelbase of only 80 inches. His prototype consisted of a modern-style "duraluminum" body mounted on an MG chassis and powered by the original British four-cylinder engine. This accounted for its right-hand drive, though production models were to have conventional left-hand drive. An unobtrusive steel tube surrounded the body at bumper height as a crash protection measure. Front or rear engine placement was to be at the customer's option. The lightweight body helped keep the total weight to 1100 pounds, which contributed to claimed mileage of 50 mpg. Maximum speed was 50 mph. The car probably never got beyond the prototype stage.

GASLIGHT (1960-61)

From Gaslight Motors Corp. of Detroit came this replica of the 1902 Rambler. Weighing 640 pounds, the car had a 77-inch wheelbase. Power was provided by a single-cylinder, 4-horsepower, air-cooled engine. The price was about $1495. Production is believed to have ended sometime around 1961. The Gaslight may have been a successor to the 1902 Rambler Replica.

GAYLORD (1955-57)

Gaylord

Gaylord Cars Ltd., Chicago, Illinois, was founded by Edward and Jim Gaylord to build an exclusive luxury two-seater. Brooks Stevens of Milwaukee was hired to create the design. Jim Gaylord's concept involved a modern envelope body with classic overtones. Stevens suggested the body be built by his associates at the Spohn Company in Ravensburg, Germany. The Gaylords hoped to introduce a finished prototype at the 1955 Paris Salon.

The Gaylord's retractable roof was ingenious. With the push of just one button, the decklid lifted on a pair of electric supports, then the top was pulled back into the trunk by a chain drive. The roof itself contained a recessed rear window and extractor vents for stale air. Ford stylists took many photos of this system, but the later Ford retractable was much more complicated than the Gaylord.

Jim Gaylord designed the very strong chrome-molybdenum tubular chassis, using coil springs and A-arms for the front suspension and a beam axle with leaf springs at the rear. The suspension made extensive use of rubber; the passenger compartment was absolutely impervious to shock over rough surfaces. The original engine was a 365-cid Chrysler Hemi V-8. Although it scaled close to 4000 pounds, the Gaylord behaved like a 2000-pound sports car. Runs from 0 to 60 mph averaged about eight seconds. Top speed was an easy 120 mph.

Yet the Gaylord failed. It was extremely expensive—the target production price was $17,500, but that wasn't the real problem. Jim Gaylord was a perfectionist, and drove himself to a breakdown during the car's production engineering phase. Gaylord Motors also got into a dispute over quality control with the firm that was to build production models, Luftschiffbau Zeppelin in Freidreichshaven, West Germany. By 1957, the project had been abandoned. Three production chassis were built. Two of them are on display at the Early American Museum in Orlando, Florida.

GLASCAR (1956)

Glascar was built by Bob Tucker of Richmond, Indiana. The fiberglass body panel molds were made from altered Corvette panels. The grille was different from the Corvette's and incorporated the headlights. A vee'd windshield was used, and there were fins at the rear. The prototype carried an Oldsmobile V-8, but a modified flathead Ford V-8 was planned for production models. With a 100-inch wheelbase, the Glascar was to have sold for $2500. Whether actual production ever took place is not clear.

GLASSIC (1966-75)

Jack Faircloth and his son Joel began Glassic Industries Inc. in West Palm Beach, Florida by building fiberglass-bodied cars on International Scout chassis. The Scout's 93.5-horsepower four was retained. Styling was deliberately in the image of the Model A Ford phaeton. Later, a Model A styled roadster with rumble seat was also offered. Price was around $3800 when the car first appeared in 1966. However, this rose considerably, reaching $10,000 by the time production ended. In 1967, the Glassic was sold by the famous New York department store of Abercrombie and Fitch under the name Abercrombie Runabout, priced at $5200.

In 1972, Fred Pro bought the business and moved it to larger facilities. The firm's name changed to Glassic Motor Car Co. Changes were made to the cars as well. They switched to the 210-bhp Ford 302 V-8 and were available with Ford automatic transmission. Cruising speed was increased to 70 mph. Sometime in 1976 or 1977 the name was changed to Replicar.

GOFF (1956)

Charles Goff of Texarkana, Texas offered this $600 kit car—a five-passenger sports model. It used a stock 1939 Ford engine, and a rebuilt '39 Ford chassis. The body consisted of five fiberglass panels. A plastic top was also available. Fully assembled, the car cost $1500. Other engines could be installed at extra charge.

GORDON (c.1947-48)

Gordon Diamond was a very unusual car built by H. Gordon Hansen of San Lorenzo, California. The name "Diamond" refers to the car's wheel placement: a diamond pattern with one wheel at the front, one at the back, and one on each side. Wheelbase between the front and back wheels was 156 inches, with the side wheels situated halfway in between.

Several advantages were claimed for this unorthodox arrangement. The middle wheels created a smoother ride." Because the front and rear wheels steered, the Gordon could be pivoted on its middle wheels, resulting in a 12-foot turning circle, extremely short for the car's 214inch overall length. Whether it managed to stay upright on twisty roads is not known, but a tubular body cage provided protection in case of rollover. A 100-horsepower Ford truck V-8 located just ahead of the rear wheel provided power to the middle wheels. The car was capable of 95 mph, which was good for a 3750-pound car and was undoubtedly exciting given the unusual chassis.

Hansen sought financial backing for regular production. Although some interest was expressed, no firm commitment was ever secured.

GRAHAM (1967)

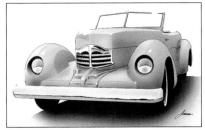
1967 Graham

This replicar effort was intended to bring the 1940 Graham Hollywood back to life. However, it appears the project died soon after the prototype was built. The prototype was shown at a Fort Wayne, Indiana shopping center and, according to maker Bob Gerig, hundreds of inquiries and scores of orders resulted. Even a price was established: $5200 at the factory.

The original Graham Hollywood was made from modified 1937 Cord dies. As is true of many replicars, the new Graham took a bit of license with the original design. Although all production Hollywoods were sedans, the revival was the convertible Graham and Hupp originally hoped to build, but didn't. The revival's body was made of fiberglass and mounted on a Kaiser Jeep chassis. The former freestanding headlight pods were sunk into the fenders, but were not covered as on the original Cord. The grille was from a 1948-50 Packard. The powerplant was a 160-horsepower V-6. A removable top was standard equipment.

GREEN MINI BUG (1968)

Green Mini Bug was made by the Green Leaf Cycle Co., and also by Green Motors Inc., of Livonia, Michigan for a short time in 1968. No description of this car is available.

GREGORY (1948; 1952-?)

1949 Gregory front-drive

Ben F. Gregory of Kansas City, an avid fan of front-wheel drive, had designed and built cars with this layout between 1918 and 1922. Interestingly, his 1948 design had a rear-mounted engine.

The Gregory was quite small, just 153 inches in overall length. Wheelbase was 94 inches, weight 1800 pounds.

The Gregory's engine was a flat-four Continental rated at 40 horsepower. It was removable by one man in an hour, the company claimed. Only one prototype of this unusual car was built, but Gregory made another try in 1952. This one was a sports car built on a contemporary Porsche chassis and using its 1600-cc, 70-bhp engine. Gregory now transplanted the engine to the front of the car, to drive the front wheels. Weight was 1925 pounds, wheelbase 80 inches. The body on production models would have been made of either aluminum or fiberglass.

HENNEY (1960-1980)

The Henney Kilowatt was an electric car made by the Henney Motor Co. of Canastota, New York. It was designed by C. Russell Feldman. Feldman had become chairman of the board and president of National Union Electric Corp., which made Exide batteries. The Henney Motor Co., a division of National Union, was well-respected for its custom limousines and funeral coaches.

The Kilowatt was a very different sort of vehicle. Its body was that of the French-built Renault Dauphine, outfitted with 12 6-volt batteries that powered a 7-horsepower electric motor. A normal 12-volt battery provided power for lights, horn, and windshield wipers. The Kilowatt ran at up to 40 mph, though 30 mph was recommended in order to extend range to 40 miles. The batteries could be charged in eight hours from a conventional 115-volt 30-amp source. Curb weight was 2250 pounds, some 750 pounds heavier than the regular Dauphine, and didn't promise much performance. By the end of 1961, some 47 Kilowatts had been sold, mainly to utility companies across the country. Further development, testing, and production continued until around

1964. Although Henney had ordered 100 Renault bodies, the number of cars it actually built is not known. It seems safe to assume that more Kilowatts were made than any other single U.S. electric car since the first electrics of the early 1900s. Interestingly, they were still available in 1980 from Robert Steven Witkoff of Glen Cove, New York for $5995. These were believed to be leftovers from the Henney production run.

HONEY BEE (1959)

Honey Bee was made by the Swift Manufacturing Company of El Cajon, California. The same company made several mini-replicars under the name Swift. The Honey Bee was a very small three-wheeler, with one wheel in front and four-cycle Briggs & Stratton 1½-horsepower engine in the rear. The fiberglass body had a teardrop shape, with a low, rounded nose and an open cockpit. Priced at $195 ready to run, the Honey Bee was advertised as "designed for kids between 7 and 77."

HOPPENSTAND (1948-49)

Hoppenstand Motors Inc. of Greenville, Pennsylvania built this rather odd-looking, two passenger open economy car. A coupe and convertible were also proposed. The design featured a 90-inch wheelbase, with all-independent coil suspension, and an overall length of 162 inches. The car's aluminum body kept weight to just 684 pounds.

The Hoppenstand "Firebug" engine was an air-cooled flat twin. Displacement was 21.4 cubic inches for an output of 8.5 horsepower. It was located in the chassis just ahead of the rear axle. An automatic torque converter was also included. The Hoppenstand's base price was around $1000. Top speed was 50 mph, but fuel economy was said to be 35 mpg.

HUMMINGBIRD (1946)

Hummingbird was the name Talmadge Judd of Kingsport, Tennessee gave to the small car he designed and built in 1946. Only 85 inches long, his two-pas-senger convertible weighed just 1350 pounds. The body was made of 8-gauge steel, instead of the usual 20-gauge. The four-cylinder engine gave up to 50 mpg and provided a top speed of 70 mph. Despite Judd's ambitious efforts to interest backers in regular production, only the prototype was built.

HYDRAMOTIVE (c. 1960)

The novel Hydramotive was built by the Hydramotive Corp. of Charlotte, North Carolina, and designed by Durward Willis of that city. The car was the crux of a stock fraud investigation involving more than a million shares. In 1961, the Securities and Exchange Commission uncovered a prototype as part of its investigation. It had no transmission, universal joints, driveshaft, differential, axles, or brakes. These had been promoted as features the Hydramotive would not need. The car did have a diesel engine and was supposed to sell for $1200, but production never got going.

HYDRO-IMP (1948)

The Hydro-Imp was a buck-board-type vehicle from Center-scope Products Inc. of Glendale, California. A description of this car is lacking. There is a possibility this car is related to the Imp.

IMP (1948-51)

Although many new small cars were introduced in the late '40s, few were as tiny as the Imp. Several different models were produced over a span of four years, but all held to the original concept of a midget convertible. International Motor Products (whose initials apparently inspired the name) of Glendale, California intended this little car as transportation for teenagers or as a second car for the family. R. Stanley Griffin, the firm's president, hoped to sell it for $500.

The production prototype of 1949 was powered by a 7½-horsepower Gladden 75 engine, mounted at the rear of the 63-inch wheelbase chassis. The open, doorless fiberglass-laminate body was supported by a tubular-steel frame.

The whole thing weighed only 475 pounds, and was 120 inches long overall. The 3-gallon gas tank provided a range of 180-240 miles. Maximum speed was 35 mph. A tubular bumper completely encircled the car. The 1951 version was even smaller, with a 108-inch overall length. Although styling differed from earlier models, the Imp remained a two-passenger car, using the same powerplant as the 1949 prototype. The price, however, did change—it was now $795.

INMAN (1946)

Inman was made by Frank Inman of Goose Creek, Texas. Details on this car are not available.

JETMOBILE (1952)

Jetmobile was an eye-catching three-wheeler, a flight of fancy of Richard Harp in Frederick, Maryland. It was a missile-shaped, single-passenger car made out of an aircraft fuel tank. The odd wheel was at the front, and the engine was at the rear. Originally, a 75-horsepower Lycoming engine provided the Jetmobile with a 110-mph top speed, but later a 60-bhp Ford V-8 was used. The builder had plans to add folding rotors so the Jetmobile could become airborne, but that idea (like the car itself) never got off the ground.

JOHNSONMOBILE (1959)

The Johnsonmobile was a product of Horton Johnson Inc. in the Chicago suburb of Highland Park. A replica of an antique car circa 1904, it had a two-passenger body made of plywood. Only one prototype was built. It was powered by an air-cooled 3-horsepower Clinton engine.

JOMAR (c.1954-60)

The Jomar appeared about 1954 from the Manchester, New Hampshire firm of Saidell Sports Racing Cars, headed by racing enthusiast Ray Saidell. This was basically a marriage of the British-made TVR chassis and a specially designed aluminum body (the TVR body was fiberglass). The standard engine was the 71.5 cubic-inch Ford Anglia four-cylinder unit. Various optional engines were offered, including a supercharged version of the Anglia engine and at least three different Coventry-Climax powerplants. Depending on the engine selected, prices ranged from $2995 to $4595.

KEEN STEAMLINER (c.1955-c.1968)

1968 Keen Steamliner

The original Keen Steamliner was a shortened, modified Plymouth of 1946-48 vintage, converted to steam power. It was the brainchild of Charles F. Keen of Madison, Wisconsin.

Sometime between 1955 and 1968, Keen produced a second car, this one with a modern fiberglass convertible body. In fact, it was the same Victress bodyshell as used for the Williams steamer, often leading to the mistaken belief that they were one and the same. The Keen car had its engine in the rear and the boiler up front, just the reverse of the Williams brothers' design. It also had different style bumpers. The second Steamliner could build up sufficient steam from a cold start for a smooth, powerful takeoff in less than 30 seconds. Conflicting reports mentioned top speeds of 60 mph and 100 mph. The rear-mounted engine was a V-4 of unknown origin, and reportedly operated on any distillate fuel, such as kerosene.

By 1968, Thermal Kinetics Corporation of Rochester, New York had acquired Keen's interests. It is unlikely any additional cars were produced by that firm.

KELLER (1948-50)

Bobbi Motor Car Corporation was reorganized as the Dixie Motor Car Corp. in July 1947. It was at this point that George D. Keller took over. Keller was a respected former general sales manager for Studebaker. The company was reorganized again in November 1947 as Keller Motors Corp. It moved to Huntsville, Alabama, and the car's name was changed to Keller.

The Keller retained the Bobbi-Kar's front-end styling with its low horizontal grille, along with its Torsilastic suspension. Overall length for both convertible and station wagon models was now 171 inches. A choice of a fabric or metal top was offered for the convertible. The Keller featured more powerful engines than the Bobbi-Kar. A 133-cid 47-bhp Hercules unit or a 162-cid 58-bhp Continental could be ordered. Both body types were offered in two series—the Chief, and the more deluxe Super Chief. The Hercules engine powered the Chief; the Super Chief used the Continental, Fuel consumption of 35.6 mpg was claimed. The three-passenger convertible was available either front- or rear-engined, but the station wagon had its powerplant up front. The wagon was a two-door model, and weighed 2100 pounds. The convertible was 300 pounds lighter. Plastic-fabric upholstery material was used. Base prices started at $895 for the Chief convertible. A double bed was optional for the station wagon.

In 1948, Keller claimed to have a dealer network totaling 1150. Production was supposed to reach an annual rate of 150,000-volume almost as high as Mercury's at the time. But a mere 18 cars had been built by 1949, and the company went bankrupt in the spring of 1950. That was the end of Keller in the United States, although there was an attempt in the early '50s to build a restyled version in Belgium.

KING MIDGET (1946-69)

1953 King Midget Deluxe roadster

Midget Motors Supply Co. later changed its name to Midget Motors Corp. of Athens, Ohio. Its King Midget was one of the more successful new American makes introduced in the postwar period. This tiny economy model was developed by Claud Dry and Dale Orcutt. The earliest 1946 versions were available only as kits. When assembled, the King Midget looked like a slightly modernized buckboard. At first, a manual transmission was used, but Dry and Orcutt soon produced their own automatic transmission, which then became standard.

In 1951, a redesigned King Midget was offered. Its appearance was more carlike than the original model, and its two-passenger carrying capacity was 100 percent greater. The second-generation model continued through early 1957. A third series was then introduced, and it looked even more conventional.

Until 1966, Wisconsin one-cylinder engines powered the King Midget, rated at 7.3 to 8.5 horsepower. After that, Kohler engines of 9.3 to 12 bhp were fitted. Throughout its history, fuel economy was the King Midget's strongest selling point: it could get up to 60 mpg.

Like Detroit cars, the King Midget grew over the years. Overall length stretched from 96 inches to 117. Yet, the wheelbase was still only 76.5 inches for the third series, which was the largest model. The King Midget also put on weight as it grew older, from around 400 pounds to almost 700. Naturally, prices kept pace—from a low of near $350, rising to just over $1000.

The King Midget came to an end in 1969 after 23 years, a phenomenal run for such a car in the American auto industry. Production over the years amounted to approximately 5000 units.

KNUDSEN (1948)

The Knudsen was a prototype made by the Knudsen Manufacturing & Design Co. Inc. of Buffalo, New York. Descriptive details are unavailable.

KRIM-GHIA (1966)

Krim-Ghia originated at the Krim Car Import Co. of Detroit. Krim designed two different models. Bodies for both were supplied by the famous Ghia coachbuilding house of Italy. A sports model, the 1500 GT was based on the Fiat 1500 and used its 86-horsepower four-cylinder engine. The other model was a roadster based on the Plymouth Barracuda chassis, powered by a 245-bhp Plymouth V-8. Production lasted only a few months in 1966.

KRUEGER (1947)

In 1947, you could order a new Krueger for $15,000 if production had gotten underway as planned. Although that was a whopping sum of money then, consider what you might have had: a sleek, low slung, boattail roadster with a classic upright grille, rakish windshield, full fender skirts, and a 225-horsepower Marmon V-16 powerplant. The chassis was Duesenberg, with a wheelbase of 106 inches. Top speed was said to be 140 miles per hour.

The car began life in 1933-34 in the Los Angeles area, with a Duesenberg Model A straight-eight engine. Some of the other parts were from production cars of that era. It appears Mr. Krueger acquired the car during or after the war and, following a few modifications, had thoughts about selling duplicates of it. It is doubtful any additional cars were produced.

LAHER (1960-1963)

The Laher was made by the Laher Spring & Electric Car Corp. of Oakland, California and Memphis, Tennessee. It was a two-passenger, three-wheeled, open electric with a single front-mounted wheel. It was little more than a golf cart.

LARSON (1966-?)

Larson was built by the Larson Boat Works, of Little Falls, Minnesota. Although limited production began in 1966, the car reportedly continued into the '70s. There is little other available information about it.

LA SAETTA (1955)

During the '50s, there were many cars with bodies made of that new wonder material, fiberglass. The Testaguzza brothers of Detroit joined the parade with their La Saetta (The Thunderbolt). Typical of most fiberglass-bodied cars, it was basically a two-passenger roadster. At least 15 were built, but no two were alike. They differed in engines (primarily Olds 88 and Hudson), windshields, grilles, taillights, dashboards, and other components. Wheelbase was around 110 inches; overall length ranged from 200 to 210 inches. Late in 1955 a linkup was formed with Electronic Motor Car Corporation of Salt Lake City. The result was a turbo-electric called Electronic.

LAWLER (1948-50)

James H. Lawler of Huntington Park, California was the inventor of this steam-powered conversion of a 1938 Terraplane. There is some indication he carried out similar conversions of other cars at nearby South Gate. Whatever base was used, all conversions were dubbed Lawler Steamobile.

LOST CAUSE (1963-64)

Lost Cause was the unlikely name of what was actually a Corvair modified by the famous Derham Body Co. of Rosemont, Pennsylvania. It was sold by Charles Farnsley, former mayor of Louisville, Kentucky, and proprietor of Lost Cause Motors.

The car's roof and seats were covered with black leather, and wire wheels were fitted. Most of the special equipment was found inside. The dash panel included an altimeter, compass, and clock, as well as a full complement of rally and racing instruments. The dash, steering wheel, and door panels were finished in hand-rubbed Kentucky burl walnut. Other items included lap robes, fitted luggage, and a picnic hamper. Proclaimed as "the world's most expensive small car," the Lost Cause carried a $23,200 price tag. The only option was an engine modified by John Fitch (see Fitch), which lifted

top speed to nearly 120 mph.

LUPEAR (1963)

George Lupear from Walled Lake, Michigan was formerly with the Ford Motor Company. He had invented jet-propelled water skis and a portable magnetic drill press. His car, an 8-passenger utility vehicle, was constructed with the assistance of Rocco Pugliese. A 6000-pound winch was one of its features. Top speed was 60 mph, and it could get a claimed 40 mpg.

MK III (1968)

MK III seems to be Fiberfab's Valkyrie with some variations. The Portland, Oregon firm of Auto Craft Northwest marketed this car with either a mid- or rear-engine setup. The buyer had a choice between Chevrolet 327 or 427 cubic inch V-8s for the mid-engine model. The rear-engine version mounted the 164-cid Corvair flat six. Prices were $4600 (rear-engine), $7500 (327 V-8), and $12,500 (427 V-8). MK III was offered as a limited-production sports car personally built to owner specifications. The interior featured full instrumentation and naugahyde bucket seats flanking a center console. Leather upholstery was an option. MK IIIs were also available in a variety of kits at prices ranging from $895 to $4850.

MARKETEER (1954-?)

Marketeer was a two-passenger shopping car from Electric Marketeer Manufacturing Co. of Redlands, California. As the name suggests, it was powered by six 6-volt batteries that ran a 3-horsepower electric motor. A range of 30-35 miles between charges was normal. This was a three-wheeler with its single wheel at the front. The top was made of fiberglass. Operating costs of only $1 per month were claimed by the manufacturer. A 1956 Californian model sold for $735.

MARKETOUR (1964)

Marketour was built in Long Beach, California by Marketour Electric Cars. It was a two-passenger, three-wheel electric with the single wheel at the front. Six heavy-duty batteries, specially engineered for electric cars, provided power for its 36-volt motor. The car had four forward speeds and one reverse. Operating range was 35-40 miles on a single charge. This boxy vehicle had a steel body with a removable leatherette-covered top. Overall length was 84 inches, wheelbase 64 inches. A 1/4-ton pickup model was also built.

MARKETTE (1967-68)

1967 Markette

Westinghouse Electric Corp. built this boxy electric. It was 116 inches long and had a 45-horsepower motor. Twelve 6-volt batteries accounted for about half the 1730-pound curb weight. A retractable electric cord for battery recharging was supplied. The batteries were good for at least two years, and could be replaced for about $300. Range was 50 miles, and top speed was 25 mph. Although this was a prototype, production cars were planned to sell for less than $2000. It is believed production did not actually get underway, probably due to lack of buyer interest. The Markette is sometimes confused with the Marketeer because it was made by the Marketeer Division of Westinghouse.

MARQUIS (1954)

The chassis of this two-door fastback sports coupe was a Renault, presumably the 4CV model. Marquis was to be a rather luxurious small car with a proposed selling price of $3100. The prototype's body was made of aluminum, but production models were to be of "plastic," perhaps fiberglass. The developer was Plasticar of Doylestown, Pennsylvania. The name Plasticar has erroneously been applied to this car.

MARS II (1966-c.1970)

Mars II, from Electric Fuel Propulsion Inc. of Ferndale, Michigan, was an electric car based on the Renault 10 body.

Power was provided by four 3-volt battery packs, each consisting of five lead-cobalt batteries. The battery packs alone weighed 1900 pounds, accounting for almost half the car's 4160-pound weight. Dynamic braking charged the batteries during coasting and braking, so the driving range was 60-120 miles between charges. Five-year or 50,000-mile battery life was claimed. Replacement cost for the power packs was around $600. This electric had a top speed of 68 mph, but cruising speed was around 45 to 55 mph. It took just 12 seconds to accelerate from 0 to 40 mph.

MARTINETTE (1954)

Martinette was built by Martin Development Laboratories in Rochelle Park, New York. James Vernon Martin, an innovative designer, sketched out a three-wheeler in 1932. After many experiments, false-starts, and revisions, a prototype was completed in 1948.

By 1954, Martin's company had been reorganized as the Commonwealth Research Corp. of New York City. Under Commonwealth's auspices a few cars were produced. Like the prototype, they were two- or three-passenger vehicles of teardrop shape, all three-wheelers with the single wheel at the rear. The body was 114 inches long and made by Biehl Autobody. It had wood paneling like a station wagon, hence the new name Stationette (or sometimes, Martin Stationette). Suspended on rubber, the Stationette used no springs, shock absorbers, axles, driveshaft, universal joints, or differential. Its magnetic fluid drive made a clutch unnecessary. The rear-mounted engine was a 24-bhp Hercules four. Maximum speed was between 40 and 45 mph, fuel consumption 60 to 70 mpg. An unknown number of Stationettes were built and sold for $1000 each. One was a panel delivery pro-

duced in 1955 based on Martin's designs. The designer sold his business to Bassons Industries Corp. sometime around 1955 or '56. His car was then renamed the Bassons Star.

MAVERICK (1953-55)

1955 Maverick

This Maverick was not connected with the Ford Motor Company. Rather, it was made by Maverick Motors of Mountain View, California.

For a three-passenger car, it was quite large. Mounted on a Cadillac chassis, it had a wheelbase of 122 to 128 inches, and its length was 16 feet. The sleek fiberglass body was available with one, two, or no doors.

A spun-copper instrument panel incorporated a Stewart-Warner vacuum gauge, tachometer, and 160-mph speedometer, among others. Plastic was used for the upholstery. Although the floor was made of half-inch marine plywood, it was impregnated with special resin, then coated with sound-deadening material. A Cadillac engine with Borg-Warner overdrive was used. Only about seven cars had been completed when production came to an end in 1955.

McDONOUGH (1959-65)

McDonough, Georgia was the home of the Tin Lizzie and the Buckboard, small cars made primarily for youngsters by McDonough Power Equipment, Inc. The Tin Lizzie Model T-10 Torpedo was a half-scale replica of a 1910 Ford Model T. A 3-horsepower engine propelled the fiberglass-and-steel-bodied car up to 10 miles per hour on driveways, parks, etc. (it was not intended for road use). Although built for youngsters, it had "ample power and strength for hauling two adults."

Fully assembled, the Tin Lizzie sold for $353.00; in kit form, minus engine, the price was $249.50.

MERCURY SPECIAL (1946)

Mercury Special was built by Paul Omohundro of Los Angeles, who put an aluminum sports-car body on a Mercury chassis. Though Omohundro contemplated using Cadillac power, the original Mercury engine was retained. Hopes of getting this car into production were dashed by postwar material shortages.

MERRY OLDS (1958-62)

Merry Olds was billed as the car with "the backward look" (contrasting with Chrysler Corporation's "forward look" slogan of that time). It emulated the original curved-dash Olds of 1903 and was built by American Air Products, a Fort Lauderdale, Florida firm. Construction was of plywood and steel. Power came from a Clinton 4-horsepower air-cooled single, which drove the left rear wheel by chain. The car had two forward speeds and one reverse, plus an automatic clutch. Top speed was 35 mph, fuel economy an astonishing 67 mpg.

MERRY RUNABOUT (C.1960)

The Merry Runabout, from Greg-San Klassic Kars of Glendale, California, was a half-scale replica of the curved-dash 1903 Olds. A Lawson 2.5-horsepower four-cycle engine was used. Top speed was 15 mph. A two-passenger novelty vehicle, it was only 65 inches long and weighed a mere 190 pounds.

MIDGET (date unknown)

Midget was built by Greenfield-Lippman in Buffalo, New York and may be related to the Playboy. However, no other information about this car is available.

MIGHTY MITE (1953)

Once again, front-wheel drive advocate Ben F. Gregory presented a new vehicle design. This time, however, it was a full-time four-wheel-drive Jeep-like vehicle. Mid-America Research Corporation of Wheatland, Pennsylvania had great hopes for getting this small, versatile vehicle into production with a wide range of body types. The combination of a light engine, aluminum body, and small size (64-inch wheelbase, 96-inch length) made this lightweight (1496-pound) vehicle ideal for the Marines as a transport vehicle for airborne assaults. The prototype's air-cooled Porsche engine was to be replaced in production versions by a modified Lycoming 65-horse-power aircraft engine.

MINICAR (1969)

Minicars Inc. of Goleta, California designed this small three-passenger machine with big-car features like automatic transmission and air conditioning. In spite of its short dimensions, it had 40 inches of legroom. Overall length was a modest 108 inches. A 164-cid air-cooled six was used. The anticipated price of $2500 was based on production volume of 25,000 units annually, but it's doubtful the project ever went beyond the 1969 prototype.

MOBILETTE (c.1965)

The Mobilette was made by Mobilette Electric Cars, Long Beach, California. There is no description of this car available, other than the fact that it was an electric runabout.

MOHS (1967-78)

The first Mohs car was not built until 1967, though Bruce Baldwin Mohs' Madison, Wisconsin company dates back to 1948.

The monstrous Ostentatienne Opera Coupe tipped the scales at 5740 pounds, and measured 246 inches long and 69 inches high. Overhang was considerable, since the wheelbase was only 119 inches.

International Harvester supplied the chassis to Mohs' specifications, as well as a 304-cubic-inch V-8 with 193 horsepower. Optional were a huge 549-cid V-8, which developed 250 bhp, and a five-speed manual transmission. The larger engine was claimed to give the car a top speed of 115 mph; with the smaller engine, 100 mph was the maximum.

Here are just a few items from the Ostentatienne's long list of equipment: quartz-iodine headlights, sealed-beam taillights, wide whitewall 7.50x20 tires by Denman (the inner tubes filled with pure nitrogen), water-cooled automatic transmission, removable skylight, butane furnace-heater, 24-karat gold inlaid walnut-covered instrument panel, $3/4$-inch Ming Dynasty-style carpet with $3/8$-inch pad, and velvet

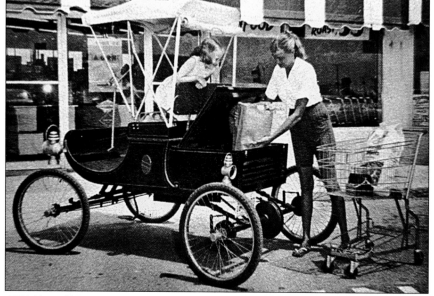

1959 Merry Olds

upholstery. All this cost $19,600 in the late '60s, with the 549 V-8 priced at $25,600.

Understandably, the demand for such an expensive, unorthodox package was extremely limited, and production generally ran to about three or four cars per year. Nevertheless, the model was ostensibly in production through 1978, at least. An additional model, the Safarikar, was introduced in 1971. It was described as a dual-cowl phaeton with metal top, and sold for $14,500.

MOTA (1953)
Mota came from Banning Electric Products Corp. Automotive Division of New York City. It had a fiberglass body and was a gas/electric hybrid.

MOTORETTE (1947-48)
At first glance, it appeared to be a motor scooter. Its two-passenger capacity and three wheels, however, took it out of the scooter class—barely. Raising the rear hood exposed a 4.1-horsepower, one-cylinder air-cooled engine. Power was transmitted to the left rear wheel by chain drive. Luggage was stored under the bench seat or in a front storage compartment under a tiny hinged lid. In place of a steering wheel was a sort of handlebar. Total weight was 380 pounds. Overall length was only 90 inches, and wheelbase was just 60 inches. Tires were 4.00x8. Motorette Corporation of Buffalo, New York sold it complete with push button starter, horn, lights, mechanical brakes, and 6-volt battery for only $495. The company is said to have gone bankrupt in 1948.

MULTIPLEX (1952-54)

1952 Multiplex

Multiplex was built by the Multiplex Manufacturing Co. of Berwick, Pennsylvania. From 1912 to 1915, this firm built a very good car, but production was limited to scarcely more than a dozen units. Multiplex tried for a second time after World War II (its primary business was the manufacture of Crispin air valves).

The postwar Multiplex was a two-passenger sports model made from proprietary components. Willys F-head four- and six-cylinder engines were used, modified to develop 87 and 124 horsepower, respectively. The car's frame was a tubular truss-type. A transverse spring and wishbones made up the independent front suspension.

Only three cars were built from 1952 to 1954.

MURENA (1969-70)
The Murena was a luxury 2-door sports station wagon conceived by Joseph Vos, an importer of British cars for Murena Motors Ltd. of New York City. The cars were built by Intermeccanica of Turin, Italy. A 360-horsepower, 429 cubic-inch Ford V-8 provided the power. The vehicle was 205 inches long on a 118-inch wheelbase. Weight was approximately 3770 pounds. An indication of the car's luxury was its $14,950 price.

MUSTANG (1948)
The Mustang was designed by Roy C. McCarty of the Mustang Engineering Corp. in Seattle. Earlier, McCarty had been service manager of the Ford Motor Company's Lincoln Division. With its flat front, the Mustang looked much like a bus in the head on view. It also had a sloping rear end.

The 59-horsepower rear-mounted Hercules four was accessible by a door on the left side. A tubular-steel frame with a 102-inch wheelbase was used, and the body was aluminum. The Mustang had room for six people: two in front and four in the back. It was expected this unusual car would sell for $1235, but volume production was not achieved.

NAVAJO (c.1954)
The Navajo was made by Navajo Motor Car Co. of New York City. One source names the maker as Jim Craig of Rumson, New York.

The Navajo was a three-passenger sports car. Bucket seats had not yet made much impression on Americans, so it had a simple bench seat. A Mercury flathead V-8 tweaked up to 130 horsepower was used. A 0-60 mph acceleration time of 7.8 seconds was quoted. The car's most striking feature was its styling, a close copy of the Jaguar XK-120.

NORVELL (1946)
The Norvell was named for its builder, Jack Norvell of Los Angeles. A description of this car

1954 Navajo

is not currently available.

NU-KLEA (1959-60)

Despite its name, the Nu-Klea, from Nu-Klea Automobile Corp. of Lansing, Michigan, was a small electric, not an atomic-powered, car. Each rear wheel was driven by a separate motor. The steel chassis carried a fiberglass body in either convertible or hardtop style. A range of 75-85 miles per charge was claimed. This two-passenger car was suspended by leaf springs at the rear and coil springs in front.

OLDS 1901 REPLICA (1968)

The Olds 1901 Replica came from the Horseless Carriage Corp. of Fort Lauderdale, Florida. It was a 3/4-scale facsimile of the early curved-dash Olds runabout.

OMEGA (1967-68)

A stillborn 1966 prototype from the builder of the TVR Griffith was given new life in 1967 as the Omega. The car was taken over by Suspensions International Corporation of Manhasset, New York, though actual construction was carried out by Holman and Moody of Charlotte, North Carolina. Steve Wilder, former technical editor of *Car and Driver* magazine, was the head of Suspensions International. A Ford 289 V-8 engine and driveline were used. The price was $8250. For 1968, the 302 Ford V-8 was listed as a factory-installed option for $400. Base price had now risen to $8950. Steel bodies were made by Intermeccanica in Turin, Italy.

After this point, the car continued in production for several years as the Torino, Italia, and IMX. All were presumably assembled by Intermeccanica.

PANDA (1955-56)

The Panda, from Small Cars Inc. of Kansas City, was a $1000, two-passenger vehicle built on a 70-inch wheelbase. A fiberglass roadster body styled like a child's pedal car was mounted on a frame of the manufacturer's own design. The top was a two-piece plastic affair, which could be stored in the trunk. A choice of a 44 cubic-inch Aerojet four-cylinder engine or a 67-cid Kohler flat twin was announced for 1956 (the 1955 prototype sported a Crosley engine).

PANKOTAN (1940)

Paul Pankotan of Miami, Florida is the only reference to this vehicle, aside from a 1940 build date. Specifications are not currently available.

PANTHER (1962-c.1963)

1962 Panther

The Panther Automobile Co. in Bedford Hills, New York made this two-passenger fiberglass sports car of very sleek appearance. Two models were available, each using a 157.4 cubic-inch Daimler V-8 that developed 145 horsepower. In the deluxe model M, higher compression and twin carburetors raised output to 190 bhp. The M could hit 150 mph, and the standard model 130 mph.

Coil springs were used for the independent front suspension, while semi-elliptic leaf springs and radius rods were employed at the rear. The Bendix brakes were self-adjusting. A 94-inch wheelbase was used for both models. Prices were $4250 for the standard version and $4995 for the M.

PAXTON (1951-54)

Sometimes known as the Paxton Phoenix, this was a five-passenger car from Paxton Engineering Co. of Los Angeles. This was the same firm that supplied superchargers to Studebaker in the early '60s. Brooks Stevens did the styling for the fiberglass hardtop body. The top was designed to open and close electrically: when open, it moved backwards and rested on the rear deck. A "torque-box" frame weighing 160 pounds was used. Wheelbase was 118 inches.

At least two possible engines were considered. The more interesting of these was a 120-horsepower three-cylinder steamer. A compound six-cylinder steam engine was also under development. Much of this engine work

was done by none other than Abner Doble, who had created the advanced Doble steam cars of 1914-1931.

Despite the Paxton's top-notch technical backing, it ultimately did not run on steam. A rear-mounted Porsche 1500 engine was fitted instead. Production costs convinced builder Robert Paxton McCulloch not to pursue the program, which ended in 1954.

PECO BUCKAROO (1957)

Another of the "buckboard" type vehicles, the Buckaroo was produced by Production Engineering Company (PECO) of Austell, Georgia. This small, inexpensive off-road "fun" car was powered by a 3-horsepower rear-mounted engine. The basic white ash frame, steel fenders, and fiberglass cowling (with the "smart continental look") rode on 12-inch wheels, and a 57-inch wheelbase. A top speed of 18 miles per hour was attainable in this 185-pound car.

PERRYMOBILE (1942-45)

The Perrymobile Company of Los Angeles and a build date of 1942-45 are the only pieces of information currently available about this vehicle. The time span would suggest a small runabout designed to run on miniscule quantities of rationed gasoline, or powered by electricity.

PIONEER (1959-c.1960)

Pioneer, Lippencott Pioneer, and Nic-L-Silver are names that have been variously applied to this electric model made by the Nic-L-Silver Battery Co. of Santa Ana, California. Whatever the name, the design featured twin motors to drive the rear wheels. By flipping a simple toggle switch, the driver could put the car in forward or reverse. Depending on driving conditions, load, and speed, range was 40-100 miles between battery charges. The batteries could be charged overnight from 110- or 220-volt outlets.

Offered in sport coupe, hardtop, and station wagon styles, the Pioneer used fiberglass body construction. Proprietary production car wheels, axles, and brakes were incorporated. Suspension was of the trailing-arm, torsion-bar type. Overall length was 157 inches and curb weight was 1800 pounds. Production ended in late 1959 or early 1960.

PIRANHA (1967)

Piranha was made by AMT Corp. of Phoenix, Arizona with essentially the same lower body styling as the 1964 experimental CRV. Cycolac plastic was used for the body, which had hidden headlights and gullwing doors. A tilt-type steering wheel was also featured. By mid 1967, only five or six cars had been constructed. The project ended shortly thereafter. Price for this two-passenger car was to have been around $6000.

PLAYBOY (1947-51)

1948 Playboy

Playboy was the much-publicized minicar of the Playboy Motor Car Corp. of Buffalo, New York.

Former Packard salesman Louis Horowitz was president of the Playboy company. The vice-president was Charles D. Thomas, formerly of Pontiac. Experimental work on the car had begun before U.S. entry into World War II. A prototype appeared as early as 1940. Although Horowitz expected production to reach 100,000 cars annually, just 90-97 were built over the make's short four-year lifetime.

The Playboy was a three-passenger convertible, with a factory undercoated unit body. A normal fabric top was found on some of the very first examples, but the famous folding steel top soon became a Playboy trademark. It could be opened or closed by hand from within the car.

A Hercules 40-horsepower four was used in most Playboys, although some had a Continental engine of similar displacement. The manufacturer claimed fuel consumption of 25 mpg for city driving, and 30 mpg for

the country. Two of the car's more noteworthy mechanical features were a three-speed Warner Gear automatic transmission and self-adjusting brakes. On a 90-inch wheelbase, the 2035-pound Playboy had an overall length of 155 inches.

POWELL (1954-56)

1955 Powell Sport Wagon

The Powell Sport Wagon was unusual in several ways. Although registered and sold as new, it incorporated remanufactured Plymouth parts. It was a full-sized model, selling initially for only $998. The Powell concept of a relatively low-slung pickup on a passenger-car chassis was later popularized by Ford's Ranchero and Chevrolet's El Camino. Though not unattractive, the Sport Wagon's appearance was rather boxy and plain, contributing to the ease and low cost of building it. The body was steel, except for a fiberglass nose panel. The rebuilt chassis and 90-horsepower engine were from Plymouths of the '40s and '50s. Overall length was 14 feet 9 inches, wheelbase was 117 inches, height was 5 feet 8 inches.

Powell Manufacturing Company (brothers Channing and Hayward) of Compton, California had been a motor scooter manufacturer before switching to larger vehicles. By 1956, the price of the Sport Wagon (pickup) had reached $1195 (standard) and $1295 (deluxe), and a station wagon ($1525) had been added to the line. Approximately 2200 pickups and 200 station wagons were sold through a very limited dealer network.

POWER CAR (1953-67)

Although designed mainly for children, some of these little vehicles were promoted as adult fun cars. The 1953 Power Car Jr. was powered by a modified starter motor from a Ford V-8. In appear-

ance it resembled a miniature tractor with wheels. The distributor was Mystic River Sales Company of Mystic, Connecticut. The Power Car Company, also of Mystic, was the maker of the electric powered Thunderbird Jr. from 1955 to 1957. The 1957 version and a miniature '57 Mercury (Big M Junior) were available with a 2-cycle, 2-horsepower gasoline engine at extra cost. In 1965, the Thunderbird Jr. and Mustang Jr. were available in children's models with electric power, or with either 20-mph gasoline engines or 5-mph electric motors for "adult fun."

PUBLIX (1947-48)

The Publix was announced in 1947 by the Publix Motor Car Co, which claimed to have factories in Buffalo, New York, and across the river in Canada at Fort Erie, Ontario. It was a two-passenger three-wheeler with a choice of fabric or plexiglass top. The single wheel was at the front. An aluminum tube frame was used, along with an aluminum body. Aluminum engines ranging from 1.7 to 10.4 horsepower were considered. A feather-light vehicle, Publix weighed only 150 to 250 pounds. On a 50-inch wheelbase, its overall length was 72 inches.

The steering wheel could be positioned for driving on either side of the car. The starter was the simple pull-type and a belt-drive transmission was used. Speeds of 40-60 mph were attainable, depending on the engine, and claimed fuel economy was in the 70-90 mpg range.

One B. de H. McCloskey designed the Publix, and planned to build 1000 a week, mostly for export. However, there's reason to believe not everything was right about the company. Company offices were said to be located in Newark, New Jersey and Wilmington, Delaware, but the Newark address was nothing more than a mailbox.

PUP (1948-49)

Two quite differently styled cars were proposed under the Pup nameplate. One was a very basic open two-seat roadster with four separate fenders and no doors or top. The other, presumably a later design, was an enclosed coupe with slab-sided styling. Features included side curtains and a full perimeter rubber bumper. Both models were to be available with an automatic clutch and choice of a 7.5-horsepower single-cylinder Briggs & Stratton engine, or a 10-bhp two-cylinder unit. The bodies of both were of wood; varying reports indicated plywood or pressed-wood construction. Fuel consumption was in the 50-60 mpg range, top speed was 35-40 mph, and prices were $500-$600. The maker was Pup Motor Car Company of Spencer, Wisconsin.

QUANTUM (1962-63)

1963 Quantum

The Quantum was a rebodied Saab, built by Quantum Corp. of Rockland, Massachusetts. Mechanical components, including the 42-horsepower, three-cylinder, two-stroke engine and front-wheel drive, were naturally of Saab origin. The Quantum was 150 inches long, eight inches less than the Saab; its 85-inch wheelbase was a foot shorter. Curb weight was a light 900 pounds. The car was distributed through individual Saab dealers in the U.S.

RAMBLER 1902 REPLICA (c.1959-60)

The Rambler 1902 Replica was another old-time revival of American Air Products of Fort Lauderdale, Florida (see Merry Olds). In 1960, production was taken over by Gaslight Motors Corp. of Lethrup Village, Michigan. In view of this, it seems reasonable to assume the Rambler Replica was a predecessor of the 1960

Gaslight.

RIK-MOBILE (1948)

Rik as in rickshaw, mobile as in motorized transportation tells the story. China Engineering Corporation of San Francisco must have seen a market for a three-place, three-wheeled motor scooter to replace the venerable rickshaw. The first model was shipped to China for demonstration purposes. Steering was controlled by handlebars, the throttle by a right hand grip. Clutch and brake pedals were conventionally positioned on the floorboard. Top speed was only 35 miles per hour.

Fuel consumption was a thrifty 80 miles per gallon.

ROADABLE (1946)

Roadable, from the Southern Aircraft Division, Portable Products Corp. of Garland, Texas was a car/plane combination designed and built by Ted Hall. Only one example is thought to have been constructed.

A three-wheel design, the Roadable had its single wheel mounted at the front. The two rear wheels and the propeller aided in take-off. When airborne, the wheels disengaged from the drive, and ailerons and elevators were controlled by the steering wheel. A Franklin 130-horsepower engine powered this machine, which could cruise at about 110 mph in the air with a range of 600 miles. Only five minutes were required to remove the wings, twin-boom tail section, and propeller in converting the vehicle for road use. Such items might then, presumably, be left at the airport. On the highway, the Roadable could travel at speeds up to 60 mph.

ROADPLANE (1945)

Roadplane was designed by Norman Davidson, an engineer with Consolidated Aircraft Co. in San Diego. Consolidated was not involved with this project, although as the name implies this vehicle could be driven as a car or flown as a plane. The 36-foot wings and other airplane controls were detachable. A 75-bph, air-cooled engine powered this three-wheeler.

There is some indication the prototype may not have been completed.

ROAD RUNNER (1963)

Road Runner was made by the Cyclone Sales Co. of Los Angeles. No further description is obtainable at present.

ROCKEFELLER YANKEE (1953)

A tough, durable body of fiberglass and Vibrin was the main feature of this four-passenger sports car. Designer Warren Shiber had a liking for Ford products, hence the Ford V-8 engine, clutch, gearbox, rear end, and springs. Even the frame was modified Ford. For $2500 you would get a 2000-pound car that could do 100 miles per hour tops, and 0 to 60 mph in 12 seconds. And if you should damage the body (molded by Lunn Laminates of Long Island) a repair kit was provided so you could fix it up in a hurry. Dimensionally, the car had a 100-inch wheelbase, 66-inch width, and 14-foot overall length. The Yankee featured full Stewart-Warner instrumentation, including a tachometer. Rockefeller Sports Car Corp. of Rockville Centre, New York expected this car to get 25 miles or more per gallon.

ROCKET (1948)

The Rocket car, from Hewson Pacific Corp. of Los Angeles, was a three-passenger model riding a 106-inch wheelbase, with a 161-inch overall length. Two engines were available, either a 65-horsepower four or a 95-bhp six. With either engine, a torque-converter automatic transmission was standard. Top speed was 75 mph for the four and 95 mph for the six. The body consisted of ten aluminum panels, and the styling was simple and attractive. Price was around $1500. Very few of these cars were made.

ROLLSMOBILE (1958-c.1961)

Rollsmobile was a replicar from Fort Lauderdale, Florida. It was made by Starts Manufacturing Co. from 1958 to around 1960, then by the Horseless Carriage Corp. for a short time. Two models were offered, each slightly smaller than the original that inspired them. One was based on the 1901 Olds, the other on the "1901" Ford. (Since the first production Ford appeared in 1903, the latter designation is incorrect.) Power came from an air-cooled, 3-horsepower Continental engine, and top speed was 30 mph. Gas consumption was a commendable 100 mpg.

ROWAN (1967-69)

1967 Rowan electric

The tiny Rowan electric was built by Rowan Controller Co. of Westminster, Maryland, and/or Oceanport, New York. It was a closed electric runabout with a pleasant-looking Ghia body. Some of its mechanical parts were from DeTomaso. The car used the dynamic-braking method of generating power during coasting and deceleration. Its range was a remarkable 200 miles between charges.

RSL (c. 1969-?)

The RSL came from RSL Corporation of Cleveland. Although it seems to have been made for a number of years starting in 1969, there is no available data on the car's specifications.

RUGER (1969-c.1972)

The Ruger was built by gun maker Sturm Ruger & Co. Inc. of Southport, Connecticut. A replica, it was inspired by the 4.5-liter Bentley tourer. The Ruger used fiberglass body panels covered with naugahyde to imitate the leather-covered Bentley body. Semi-elliptic leaf springs were used all around. The wheelbase was 131 inches, overall length was 186 inches. The engine was a 427-cid, 425-horsepower Ford V-8, which gave 0-60 mph acceleration of about 7.7 seconds—very good for a 3535-pound car. A maximum speed of 110 mph was claimed. The price was

$13,000. Production continued into the early 1970s.

RUSSELL (1946)

Raymond Russell of Detroit, a former Ford Motor Co. employee, was behind this mechanically unusual car. It used hydraulic four-wheel drive: the main engine pumped oil through a motor at each wheel. There were seven to 15 forward speeds. The car was claimed to be smoother-running than a steamer, and to have more power in low gear than any other car. Braking was accomplished by slowing the oil flow, or reversing it. There was no need for a transmission or driveshaft. A plywood body on an experimental chassis helped keep total weight to around 2000 pounds. A year earlier, Russell had built the Gadabout.

SAVAGE (1968-69)

If you had a yen for a Plymouth Barracuda but wanted something hotter than the factory could provide, and perhaps a customized appearance as well, Auto Craft Company was happy to oblige. The Fond du Lac, Wisconsin company equipped convertibles or coupes with 340-, 383-, or 440-Magnum engines with carburetor and manifold modifications. The suspension was stiffened up a bit. The GT image was aided by the addition of custom aluminum wire wheels, special grille, custom fiberglass hood and decklid (with integral spoiler), and exposed chrome exhausts below the rocker panels. The interior was not overlooked, either. The real wood dashboard contained full instrumentation, and the steering wheel was also wood. An all-vinyl bucketseat interior was standard, complete with wall-to-wall loop-pile carpeting.

SAVIANO (1960)

Saviano Scat was built by Saviano Vehicles Inc. in Warren, Michigan. "Scat" was an acronym for Saviano Cargo and Touring, and was apt for this vehicle, a go anywhere two-door, four-passenger Jeep-type car. The rear seats could be folded down for additional cargo space. The frame was made of welded rectangular tubing. The

body used 16-gauge steel, twice the thickness of that commonly used. The doors were easily removable. Steel or canvas tops were optional, and could also be removed. The engine was an air-cooled, 25-horsepower Kohler unit teamed with a three-speed Borg-Warner transmission. This 1700-pound vehicle had an 80-inch wheelbase, and was priced at $1395.

SCOOTER CAR (1947)

The Scooter Car, the product of an unknown manufacturer, was a two-passenger vehicle available in several forms. One 5-horsepower model lacked a conventional body and was fitted only with angular mud guards. A 7.5-bhp model had a full body, while a third variation had only front-end body panels. Production lasted only a few months.

SCOOTMOBILE (c.1946-1952)

Scootmobile was the result of efforts by three Corunna, Michigan men: Norman Anderson, Vernon Servoss, and Lester Sworthwood. Their car made use of many aircraft parts. The body was a modified auxiliary fuel tank that rolled on airplane wheels, two in front and one at the rear. Top speed was a moderate 40 mph, although 70 mph was claimed. Production plans for this $350 car, which included automatic transmission, never materialized.

Anderson moved to Owasso, Michigan, and made another Scootmobile in 1952. Like the first version, this was a three-wheeler with the lone wheel at the back. A 12-horsepower two-cycle engine was also rear-mounted. Overall length of this torpedo-shaped roadster was about 108 inches.

SEAGRAVE (1960)

1960 Seagrave

Seagrave was a stab at the growing compact-car market, made by Seagrave Fire Apparatus Co. in Columbus, Ohio. Three prototypes were built, all on a 93-inch wheelbase. Two had fiberglass bodies, while the third was made of aluminum. A four-cylinder Continental engine gave the 1700-pound car a top speed of 75-80 mph. Seagrave hoped to sell it for under $3000, but the car never saw production.

SKORPION (1952-54)

1952 Skorpion

The Skorpion, made by the Wilro Co. of Pasadena, California, was a pleasant looking, low priced, fiberglass sporty car that received rather wide publicity in its day. It was sold as a kit for just $445, or fully assembled for $1200. The Skorpion was designed to accept several different chassis and engines. The best combination was the Crosley Hot Shot chassis and the Ford flathead V-8. On this 80-inch wheelbase, the little car tipped the scales at just over 1000 pounds. A Super Skorpion with opening doors instead of cutdown sides was advertised for $640.

SKYLINE (c.1953)

Skyline was produced by Skyline Inc. of Jamaica, New York. Skyline was a two-passenger hardtop-convertible. Its L-head, 85-horsepower six, along with its chassis and most lower body panels, were shared with the Henry J. The grille resembled that of the 1951 Nash. At the push of a button, the top swung completely out of sight. Many safety features were incorporated. The instrument panel was leather-covered, and all knobs and switches were located on a console between the seats. High-back seats, and safety belts with shoulder harnesses were standard. The Skyline was intended to sell for less than $3000.

SPOOK ELECTRIC (1968)

1968 Spook electric

"Charge Now—Drive Later" was Dynamic Development's advertising slogan for its version of the small electric town car. The Pasadena, California firm touted it as the first modern production electric. It was, in fact, typical of many such designs that did not succeed. A 36-volt DC ball-bearing motor was connected to the rear wheels by a chain drive. Six 6-volt batteries completed the power package. The steel and fiberglass body rested on a steel channel frame. The car weighed only 750 pounds, and was 99 inches long and 41 inches high. The suspen-

1967 Valkyrie

sion was by coil springs, with all four wheels independently sprung.

STAR DUST (1953)

Star Dust was made in Los Angeles, presumably by the Grantham Motor Car Co. There was a close connection between the Grantham kit car and the Star Dust. The latter was possibly the assembled version. Star Dust used an altered Ford chassis with a 110-inch wheelbase. The engine was also Ford, but located five inches lower and 19 inches farther back in the chassis than normal. Weight was 2650 pounds. Estimated price was $3750.

STARLITE (c.1959-?)

Starlite, manufactured by Kish Industries Inc. of Lansing, Michigan, may also have been known as the Kish. It was an electric sports model, with an 82-inch wheelbase and an overall length of 148 inches. A soft-top version was produced, and a clear-plastic hard-top model was planned. Prices were around $3000.

STORM (1954)

Storm was a short-lived product of Sports Car Development Corp. in Detroit. Details are quite sketchy. It had a two-passenger Bertone body and 250-horsepower Dodge V-8, but little other information about it is available.

STORY (1950)

The Story was constructed by Tom Story of Portland, Oregon. It was a sports model, based on a frame made of 10-gauge Chrome Moly channel steel, to which Willys front suspension, rear axle, and springs were attached. The steering gear was from a Mercury.

The engine was basically a Ford V-8 but with Offenhauser 10.5:1 compression heads, twin carburetors, and dual manifolds, which boosted output to 113-bph. Top speed was 105 mph. To give good balance and improve rear traction, the engine was located 16 inches farther back than normal. Wheelbase was 97 inches, and the car weighed 2080 pounds. Probably only one car was made, though Story intended to produce more copies for sale at about $3500 apiece.

STOUT PROJECT Y (1946)

Beginning in 1936, the brilliant inventor-engineer William B. Stout produced unique streamlined cars called Scarabs, in his Detroit factory. The design was taken largely from John Tjaarda's experimental Sterkenbergs, which had themselves evolved into the prewar Lincoln-Zephyr. Stout quoted a price of $5000 for his rear-engined fastbacks, and a handful were built through 1941. In June 1945, Graham-Paige President Joseph W. Frazer acquired Stout's services to develop a proposal for the postwar car he hoped to build. After Frazer joined with Henry Kaiser to form Kaiser-Frazer Corporation, Stout continued to experiment at K-F's factory in Willow Run, Michigan.

Stout's prototype was called "Project Y," and differed in detail from his prewar Scarabs. Instead of a Ford V-8, the new design used a 95-bhp Mercury V-8—though this would have obviously been replaced by a K-F engine on production models. The body was fiberglass—along with the 1946 Darrin, one of the first uses of this material for body construction. Like the Scarabs, Project Y featured a vast open space behind the front seat in which a 74-inch-wide rear seat, cargo platform, or even a small desk might be installed at the owner's whim.

K-F abandoned Project Y in late 1946 because it was too radical and too expensive. The price was also forbidding: Stout estimated a production version might cost $10,000. Project Y was fortunately saved for posterity, and may be seen today at the Detroit Historical Museum.

STUART (1962)

1962 Stuart Electric

The Stuart was a two-passenger fiberglass-bodied electric made by Stuart Motors in Kalamazoo, Michigan. Overall length was 115 inches, width 64 inches, height 56 inches. Eight 6-volt batteries supplied current to the 4-horsepower motor. The Stuart had a 40-mile range when driven at 35 mph. The 1200-pound vehicle was available in a passenger version for $1600, or as a commercial for $1500.

The six-year-old company had produced a predecessor in 1960, the Voltaram electric. Neither car seems to have gotten beyond the prototype stage, however.

STUDILLAC (1953-55)

The Studillac conversion was built by Bill Frick Motors of Rockville Centre, New York. Around 1953, Frick began installing Cadillac engines in Studebaker hardtops. This was a great combination: a production body of outstanding beauty coupled with a high-performance Cadillac V-8. Acceleration from 0 to 60 mph took just 8.5 seconds, and top speed was 125 mph. The Studillac conversion added some $1500 to the Studebaker's cost, so the total package price in 1954 was $3695 with three-speed manual transmission, or $4195 with Dual-Range Hydra-Matic.

STUTZ (1969-?)

The Stutz, built by Stutz Motor Car of America Inc., New York City, is another revival, but in name only. The car itself is modern, quite similar in appearance to the 1966 Duesenberg (ii). Indeed, Virgil Exner styled both cars.

Based on the Pontiac Grand Prix chassis with a 116-inch wheelbase, Stutz offered two-door hardtop, convertible, and limousine body styles, and, briefly, a ceremonial parade car. The bodies were supplied by Carrozzeria Padana of Italy. The Pontiac 400-cid V-8 was used originally; later a 455-cid V-8 was installed, followed by a 403 V-8. Prices, depending on model, have ranged from $22,500 to over $100,000.

STUTZ BEARCAT (1969)

The legendary Stutz Bearcat was considered the sports car of its day. Howard D. Williams of

Tulsa, Oklahoma was certain its name and image still spelled magic in 1968. Late that year he began road testing a bright yellow prototype of a new Bearcat. Williams, a member of the Oklahoma House of Representatives, had chosen the chassis and engine of the International Scout as the basis for his replicar. The standard 198-cid four-cylinder Scout engine produced 111 horsepower—enough to move the new car at speeds up to 100 mph. The transmission was a three-speed manual. Included in the $4950 price were a "monocle" (round) windshield, a temperature gauge on the radiator cap, and a choice of wire-spoked or disc wheels.

SUPER KAR (1946)

The Super Kar prototype was created by Louis R. Elrod of Cleveland, Ohio. Information about it is limited. It was a three-wheeler powered by an air-cooled 15-horsepower engine.

SUPER STATION WAGON (1954)

The Super Station Wagon was a conversion by the Henney Motor Co. of Freeport, Illinois. It was based on the contemporary 1954 Packard Cavalier sedan. A 12-passenger station wagon, it featured an observation lounge arrangement with a three-passenger curved rear seat and a table. Packard's 359-cid, 212-horsepower straight-eight engine was retained. Though production was intended, the car's price of around $7500 precluded many orders.

SURREY (c.1960)

The Surrey, made by the E. W. Bliss Co. of Canton, Ohio, was an antique replica, duplicating the appearance of the early curved dash Olds. The standard engine was rated at 4.8-bhp, but an 8-bhp air-cooled Cushman unit was optional. Other mechanical features were semi-automatic clutch and chain drive. The car rode on 12-spoke wooden wheels. Top speed was 35 mph and mileage was a claimed 65 mpg. The base model was priced at $1045; the

DeLuxe model was $100 more. The Surrey was also available in kit form for $895.

SWIFT (1959)

The Swift was first built by Swift Manufacturing Co. in El Cajon, California, then by W. M. Manufacturing Co. in San Diego. Three different $5/8$th-scale replica models were offered. All used the same basics—a single-cylinder air-cooled Clinton engine and belt drive. The Swift-T looked like a 1910 Model T Ford. The Stutz Bearcat was mirrored by the SwiftCat, while the Swifter was similar to the first 1903 Cadillac. Top speed was hardly swift at 27 mph. Prices were in the vicinity of $795. (See also Honey Bee.)

TASCO (1948)

Tasco is an acronym for The American Sports Car Company based in Hartford, Connecticut. It was organized by members of the Sports Car Club of America (SCCA) to build an American sports car. Designed by Gordon Buehrig (see Cord 810/812) the prototype was constructed by the Derham Body Co. of Rosemont Pennsylvania, a firm well-known for its custom bodywork of the 1930s. The Tasco has been described as "a wingless cockpit on wheels." The front as well as the rear wheels were enclosed by cycle-type fenders. The front fenders turned with the wheels as the car was steered. Removable plastic roof panels prefigured a popular feature adopted by the industry some 25 years later. The engine was a modified Mercury V-8. Had it been produced, the Tasco would have cost $7500, too high to attract many buyers in 1948.

TAYLOR-DUNN (1949-68)

Taylor-Dunn was an electric built by the Taylor-Dunn Manufacturing Co. of Anaheim, California. Taylor and his son-in-law Dunn left Pacific Telephone and Telegraph to produce electric industrial trucks. Some cars were produced over the years as well.

The cars were built with three

or four wheels. The three-wheelers had a 98-inch wheelbase, while four-wheelers had an inch-longer wheelbase and were three inches longer overall. Passenger capacity varied from two to four, depending on model. These electrics could reach a speed of 12 mph and had a range of 30 miles between charges.

The company began building electric cars in 1949. Around 1959 or 1960, they were sold under the name Trident.

THORNE (1945)

The Thorne Tiger came from Thorne Engineering Co. in Los Angeles. Not much is known about this car, except that it was designed by Art Sparkes. Apparently, it was a forerunner of the Californian.

THRIF-T (1947-55)

Tri-Wheel Motor Corporation of Oxford, North Carolina (later Springfield, Massachusetts) tried for several years to get their three-wheel delivery vehicles into serious production. Body types included a pickup, an enclosed delivery, and an open utility model. The power source was a 10-horsepower, 62.6-cid Onan flat twin. The most notable feature of the $800 Thrif-T was that its powerplant was mounted on a detachable cradle under the rear deck. The entire unit could be detached and rolled away on the rear wheels in about 30 minutes. The idea, of course, was to speed engine repairs or replacement. Curb weight was about 900 pounds, and payload was 500 pounds. Top speed was 35-40 miles per hour. The wheelbase was a very compact 85 inches, and overall length a mere 126 inches. The company optimistically expected to produce 500 vehicles per month, although it indicated a more modest 50 units monthly in the early stages of production. It is doubtful even that rate was ever achieved.

TOWNE SHOPPER (1948)

The Towne Shopper was developed by the International

Motor Car Company of San Diego. It was a tiny two-passenger model designed for shopping and urban use. Overall length of the prototype was only 116 inches, wheelbase was 63 inches. Considerable use was made of aluminum in the car's construction, helping to keep weight down to 600 pounds. The car's most unique mechanical feature was a combination starter-generator-flywheel. A two-cylinder Onan 10.5-horsepower engine gave a top speed of 50 mph and fuel consumption of 50 mpg. The announced price was $595, based on planned production of 100 units per day. The company collapsed in 1948, however.

In September 1948, the Carter Motor Corporation issued publicity sheets on a Town Shopper (note the different spelling of Town) with considerably different specifications. Overall length was now 130 inches and wheelbase 79 inches. Weight was listed as 1000 pounds. The body and frame were to be made of steel. It is not known whether this was a revised design by a reorganized company, or a totally different car by a different company.

TRI-CAR (1955)

The Tri-Car was a three-wheeler with two wheels in front and one in the rear. Sources disagree on who manufactured it: either Lycoming Division of the Avco Corp. in Williamsport, Pennsylvania or the Tri-Car Co. in Wheatland, Pennsylvania.

The Tri-car used a closed three-passenger fiberglass body mounted on Goodrich rubber suspension. A Lycoming vertical twin connected to a Westinghouse-Schneider torque converter drove the single rear wheel. Top speed was said to be 65 mph, and fuel consumption of 41.5 mpg was reported. Overall length of this rear-engined shorty was just 117 inches.

TRIPLEX (c.1954-55)

Triplex was a product of Ketchem's Automotive Corp. of Chicago. It was a two-passenger sports car with a one-piece fiberglass body and a box-section frame. Almost any American engine could be used, but the chassis was primarily designed to accept a contemporary Ford V-8. Sometimes referred to as the Triplex Lightning, this car was derived from the earlier Chicagoan.

U.S. MARK II (1956)

The U.S. Mark II was built by the U.S. Fiberglass Co. of Norwood, New Jersey. Its fiberglass convertible body spanned a wheelbase of 110 to 118 inches. The car was available in kit form or completely assembled. It is not known how long production continued.

VALKYRIE (1967-69)

1967 Valkyrie coupe

For years, Fiberfab has been one of the best-known producers of fiberglass bodies, mostly designed for the Volkswagen Beetle chassis. One of these designs, the Valkyrie, was available for a time fully assembled for the rather outlandish price of $12,500. This sum bought the Valkyrie body wrapped around a Chevrolet 427 V-8 mounted at the rear of a special ladder-type chassis. The 450-bhp engine and five-speed ZF transaxle resulted in a claimed 0-60 mph time of 3.9 seconds. Top speed was said to be in excess of 180 mph. Conspicuously a drag chute was provided.

VIKING (1966)

The Viking, produced by the Viking Corp. of Miami, had a brief existence in 1966. Details about its design are unavailable.

VOLTRA (c 1962)

Voltra Inc. of New York City built this electric car powered by a General Electric DC motor. With a wheelbase of 106 inches, the Voltra was 170 inches long and weighed 1600 pounds, which was quite light for an electric. Maximum speed was about 45 mph.

WAGON DE VILLE (1965)

Wagon De Ville was a conversion from Cadillac Wagons Limited of Linden, New Jersey. On the contemporary Cadillac body and chassis, the Wagon De Ville could seat up to nine passengers. It featured an electrically operated sunroof and a rooftop luggage rack. Its price was $14,950.

WARRIOR (1964)

1964 Warrior I

The Warrior I was built by Vanguard Products Inc., a maker of air conditioners in Dallas. It was a two-passenger sports car featuring a removable one-piece roof panel. When in place, the panel fastened to the windshield and a built-in rollbar. With the panel removed, the car had an appearance much like the open "T-bar" roofs of a decade later, but without that design's longitudinal brace. The fiberglass body was mounted on a 94-inch-wheelbase chassis made up of rectangular tubing. Power came from a rear-mounted V-4 engine from Ford of Germany.

There was no connection beween the builders of this car and Vanguard Motors Inc., producers of the Vetta Ventura, although both firms were building cars in Dallas at about the same time.

WILLIAMS (1957-68)

1968 Williams

Williams was a steam car from the Williams Engine Co. Inc. of Ambler, Pennsylvania. Since the early 1940s, Calvin Williams and his sons had been trying to develop a practical steam-powered car. Eventually, they entered the market in 1957. Most of these cars used conventional gasoline engines converted to steam operation. A 1963 model had an S-4 body from Victress, the kit-car manufacturer, and sold for $7000.

Another model—a converted 1966 Chevrolet Chevelle—carried a $10,250 price tag. The high cost of maintaining such low-volume production forced the firm to abandon car making in 1968.

WOODILL (1952-56)

Woodill Motor Company of Downey, California gets credit for the first production fiberglass sports car. Its Wildfire arrived in 1952, a year or so before the Corvette and Kaiser-Darrin. But only a few were sold as complete cars off the floor; most were kits.

The Wildfire was conceived by B. R. "Woody" Woodill, a Downey Dodge-Willys dealer, and most were built around Aero Willys components.

The Wildfire frame was constructed on a 101-inch wheelbase by hot rodder Shorty Post. It featured a very low driveshaft tunnel and a passenger compartment/firewall built into the frame. The Willys engine produced 90 horsepower and came with three-speed overdrive transmission as standard. Woodill offered no fewer than nine rear axle ratios, ranging from

a stump-pulling 5.88 to a less frantic 3.88:1. Post reduced the steering ratio to only 2.5 turns lock-to-lock. The price of the assembled car was $2900, and Woodill recruited a network of Willys dealers to sell the Wildfire across the nation.

Woodill was market-wise, and soon realized the conservative little Willys six would not be enough for some drivers. So he had Post redesign the frame to accept the Ford V-8 drivetrain. The V-8 version was apparently not considered a Wildfire.

Glasspar's body was the Wildfire's best feature. It had a low, crouching silhouette, and a large oval radiator opening that accepted various grilles.

The Woodill Wildfire received tremendous publicity. The car came close to volume production. Willys-Overland was interested, and negotiations were well along when Kaiser-Frazer bought Willys. K-F went on to build the Darrin, and Woody Woodill went on selling Wildfires himself—assembled and in kit form. Prices for the fully assembled cars rose to $3263, and finally to $4500. Between 1953 and '56, Woodill says he produced 300 cars, of which only 15 were "factory assembled."

WORTHINGTON (1957)

The Worthington was made by Worthington Motor Co., Stroudsburg, Pennsylvania. Little information survives as to its design or production history.

X-RAY SPECIAL (1955)

The X-Ray Special was built by X-Ray Inc. of Highland Park, Michigan. Details about the car are not available.

YANK (1950)

The Yank, from Custom Auto Works of San Diego, was a two-passenger, aluminum-bodied sports car with a 100-inch wheelbase. A top speed of 78 mph was claimed for its Willys four-cylinder engine. The price was $1000.

YANKEE CLIPPER (1953-54)

The Yankee Clipper was produced by the Strassberger Motor Co., Menlo Park, California. The firm used a lightweight, 101-inch wheelbase chassis of its own design, fitted with a Glasspar G-2 body (see Woodill). A completely assembled car, it stood only 37 inches tall and weighed 1900 pounds. Many 1954 Ford Components were used, including a 130-horsepower V-8 engine. Early plans called for production of 40 units per month and a selling price of $3400.

YENKO (1965-69)

1967 Corvair Monza Yenko

Yenko Sportscars Inc. of Cannonsburg, Pennsylvania, was operated by Don Yenko, a Chevrolet dealer. In essence, Yenkos were Corvair coupes modified for high-performance work, mainly racing. Five Yenko "Stinger" models were offered, ranging in horsepower from 160 to 240 bhp. All used the 164-cid Corvair flat six, except the 240-bhp version, which had a slightly overbored 176-cid powerplant with 1.36-bhp per cubic inch. The Yenko won the D production national championship in Sports Car Club of America (SCCA) competition in 1967.

Two Camaro-based Yenko models were listed for 1969, with engines of 435 and 450 bhp. Production ended in 1969, after 185 Yenko conversions had been completed, including both Corvair- and Camaro-based models. In 1971, Yenko announced his Turbo Stinger, a turbocharged version of the Vega, to be available through selected Chevrolet dealers. It is not known how many of these were produced if, indeed, the project ever got past the prototype stage.

CLASSIC CAR CLUB OF AMERICA
APPROVED LIST OF CLASSIC CARS 1925-48

Founded in 1952, the Classic Car Club of America is for "persons who own or are interested in fine or unusual foreign or domestic motor cars built between and including years 1925 and 1948, and distinguished for their respective fine design, high engineering standards and superior workmanship." Cars recognized by the CCCA as "Classic" were usually high priced and built in small quantities. Owners of cars listed "Application Considered" may apply to the CCCA to have their car recognized as a classic.

Classic Car Club of America
2300 E. Devon Avenue,
Suite 126
Des Plaines, IL 60018
847/390-0443

AC—All
Adler—Application Considered
Alfa Romeo—All
Alvis—Speed 20, Speed 25, and 4.3-liter
Amilcar—Application Considered
Armstrong Siddeley—Application Considered
Aston-Martin—All 1927-39
Auburn—All 8- and 12-cylinder

1933 Auburn 8-101A

Austro-Daimler—All
Ballot—Application Considered
Bentley—All

1936-39 Bentley 4¹/₄ litre

Benz—Application Considered
Blackhawk—All
B.M.W—327, 328, 327/318, and 335
Brewster—1934-36 All Heart Front Grilles
Brough Superior—Application Considered
Bucciali—TAV 8, TAV 30, TAV 12, and Double Hiut
Bugatti—All except Type 52

1931 Bugatti Royale

Buick—1931-42 90 Series and Limited
Cadillac—All 1925-35, All

1939 Cadillac 60 Special

Twelves and Sixteens
  1936-48—All 63, 65, 67, 70, 72, 75, 80, 85, 90 Series
  1938-47—60 Special
  1940-47—All 62 Series
Chenard-Walcker—Application Considered
Chrysler—1926-30 Imperial 80,

80L, 1929 Imperial L, 1931-37 Imperial Series CG, CH, CL, and CW.
Newports and Thunderbolts
1934 CX
1935 C-3
1936 C-11
1937-48 Custom Imperial, Crown Imperial,
Series C-15, C-20, C-24, C-27, C-33, C-37, C-40
Cord—All

1930 Cord L-29 speedster

Cunningham—Series V6, V7, V8, V9
Dagmar—6-80
Daimler—All 8- and 12-cylinder
Darracq—8-cylinder and 4-liter 6-cylinder
Delage—Model D-8
Delahaye—Series 135, 145, 165
Delaunay Belleville—6-cylinder
Doble—All
Dorris—All
Duesenberg—All

1930 Duesenberg J Series

duPont—All
Excelsior—Application Considered
Farman—1925-31
Fiat—Application Considered
FN—Application Considered

Franklin—All models except
    1933-34 Olympic
Frazer Nash—Application
    Considered
Georges Irat—Application
    Considered
Graham—1930-31 Series 137
Graham-Paige—1929-30
    Series 837
Hispano-Suisa—All French
    models
Spanish models T56, T56BIS,
    T64
Horch—All
Hotchkiss—Application
    Considered
Hudson—1929 Series L
Humber—Application
    Considered
Invicta—All
Isotta Fraschini—All
Itala—All
Jaguar—1946-48 2¹⁄₂ liter,

1946 Jaguar 1¹⁄₂ Mark IV (2¹⁄₂ similar)

3¹⁄₂ liter (Mark IV)
Jensen—Application
    Considered
Jordan—Speedway Series Z
Julian—All
Kissel—1925-26, 1927 8-75,
    1928 8-90 and 8-90 White
    Eagle, 1929-31 8-126
Lagonda—All models except
    1933-40 Rapier
Lanchester—Application
    Considered
Lancia—Application
    Considered
LaSalle—1927-33
Lincoln—All L, KA, KB, and K,
    1941 168H, 1942 268H
Lincoln Continental—All

1934 Lincoln Series KB convertible

Locomobile—All models 48
    and 90, 1927-29 Model 8-80,
    1929 8-88
Marmon—All 12- and 16-cylin-
    der, 1925-26 74, 1927 75,
    1928 E75,
    1930 Big 8, 1931 88 and
    Big 8
Maserati—Application
    Considered
Maybach—All
McFarlan—TV6 and 8
Mercedes—All
Mercedes-Benz—All 230 and
    up, K, S, SS, SSK, SSKL,
    Grosser and Mannheim
Mercer—All
M.G.—1935-39 SA, 1938-39
    WA
Minerva—All except 4-cylinder
N.A.G.—Application
    Considered
Nash—1931 Series 8-90, 1932

1933 Nash Ambassador 8 Cvt. sedan

Series 9-90, Advanced 8, and
    Ambassador 8, 1933-34
    Ambassador 8
Packard—All 6- and 8-cylinder

1939 Packard Super 8 sedan

1925-34
    All 12-cylinder models
    1935 Models 1200 through
    1205, 1207 and 1208
    1936 Models1400 through
    1405, 1407 and 1408
    1937 Models 1500 through
    1502 and 1506 through 1508
    1938 Models 1603 through
    1605, 1607 and 1608
    1939 Models 1703, 1705,
    1707, and 1708
    1940 Models 1803, 1804,
    1805, 1806, 1807 and 1808
    1941 Models 1903, 1904,
    1905, 1906, 1907, and 1908
    1942 Models 2023, 2003,
    2004, 2005, 2055, 2006,
    2007, and 2008
    1946-47 Models 2103, 2106,
    and 2126
    All Darrin-bodied
Peerless—1925 Series 67,
    1926-28 Series 69, 1930-31

1940 Packard Custom Super 8 sedan

Custom 8,
    1932 Deluxe Custom 8
Peugeot—Application
    Considered
Pierce-Arrow—All

1934 Pierce-Arrow Silver Arrow

Railton—Application
    Considered
Raymond Mays—Application
    Considered
Renault—40 and 45 HP
Reo—1931-34, Royale 8-cylin-
    der

1931 Reo Royale

Revere—All
Riley—Application Considered
Roamer—1925 8-88, 6-54e,
    4-75, and 4-85e, 1926 4-
    75e, 4-85e, and 8-88, 1927-
    29 8-88, 1929-30 8-120
Rochet Schneider—Application
    Considered
Rohr—Application Considered
Rolls-Royce—All

Rolls-Royce Phantom II

Ruxton—All
Squire—All

S.S. and SS Jaguar—1932-40
    S.S.I, S.S. 90, SS Jaguar
    and SS Jaguar 100
Stearns Knight—All
Stevens Duryea—All
Steyr—Application Considered
Studebaker—1929-33

1931 Studebaker President 80 roadster

President except Model 82
Stutz—All
Sunbeam—8-cylinder and 3-
    liter twin cam

Talbot—105C and 110C
Talbot Lago—150C
Tatra—Application Considered
Triumph—Dolomite 8 and
    Gloria 6

Triumph Dolomite Straight 8 supercharger

Vauxhall—25-70 and 30-98
Voisin—All
Wills-Sainte Claire—All
Willy-Knight— Series 66, 66A,
    66B—Custom Bodied only—
    Application Considered

THE MILESTONE CAR SOCIETY
CERTIFIED MILESTONE CARS 1945-72

The Milestone Car Society was founded in 1971 to recognize post-war cars (1945-72) of historical significance. The Milestone Society judges cars in five categories: styling, engineering, roadability and performance, innovation, and craftsmanship. A Milestone car must be superior to its contemporaries in at least two categories.

AC Ace 1954-61
AC Aceca 1955-61
AC Buckland Open Tourer 1949
AC (Shelby) Cobra 1962-67
Alfa Romeo Giulietta Spider 1956-64
Alfa Romeo Giulietta/Guilia Sprint Speciale 1959-61
Alfa Romeo 6C 2500 Super Sport 1949
Allard Series J2, K2, K3 1946-56

1952 Allard J2-X

AMX, two-seater 1968-70
Apollo 1963-66
Arnolt Bristol 1952-62

Arnolt Bristol roadster

Aston Martin 1948-63
Aston Martin DB4, DB5, DB6 (all) 1964-67

Austin-Healy 100/100M 1953-56
Austin-Healy 100-6 1956-59
Austin-Healy 3000 1959-67

1958 Austin-Healey 100/6 roadster

Austin/Morris Mini 1959-70
Bentley (all) 1946-69

Benley S-type Continental Flying Spur

BMW 507 1957-59
BMW 2800 CS 1968-71
Bugatti Type 101 1951
Buick Riviera 1949 and 1963-70

1963 Buick Riviera 2-door hardtop

Buick Skylark 1953-54
Buick Stage I coupe and conv. 1970-72
Cadillac Eldorado 1953-58
Cadillac Eldorado 1967-70
Cadillac Eldorado Brougham 1957-58
Cadillac 60 Special 1948-49
Cadillac 61 coupe (fastback) 1948-49

Cadillac 62 Sedanet Coupe 1946-47

1956 Cadillac Eldorado Biarritz

Cadillac 62 Sedanet, convertible, Coupe de Ville 1948-49
Cadillac 75 sedan/limousine 1946-70
Chevrolet Bel Air V-8 hardtop 1955-57
Chevrolet Bel Air V-8 convertible 1955-57
Chevrolet Impala Sport coupe and convertible 1958
Chevrolet Camaro SS/RS V-8 and Z-28 1967-69
Chevrolet Camaro Z28 RS 1970-72

1963 Chevrolet Corvette Sting Ray conv.

Chevrolet Corvette 1953-72
Chevrolet Nomad 1955-57

1955 Chevrolet Nomad station wagon

Chrysler 300 Letter Series 1955-65
Chrysler 300 Hurst 1970

Chrysler Town & Country
1946-50

1947 Chrysler Town & Country convertible

Cisitalia Type 202 Gran Sport
(Pinin Farina) 1946-49
Citroën DS and ID 19 1955-64
Citroën Chapron (DS and ID)
1960-70
Citroën SM 1970-72

Citroën SM

Continental convertible
1958-60
Continental Mark II 1956-57
Continental Mark III 1969-71
Corvair Monza 1960-64
Corvair Monza Spyder 1962-64
Corvair Monza and Corsa
1965-69
Crosley Hotshot/SS 1950-52
Cunningham 1951-55
Daimler DE-36 (custom-built)
1949-53
Daimler 2.5 Special Sport
convertible 1949-53
Delage D6 sedan 1946-49
Delahaye Type 135, 175,180
1946-51
DeSoto Adventurer 1956-58
Deutsch Bonnet GT Panhard
engined 1950-61
Devin S/S 1958-62
Dodge Coronet R/T 1967-70
Dodge Charger R/T and
Daytona 1968-70
Dual Ghia 1956-58
Excalibur II Series I 1965-69
Facel Vega V-8 1954-64

1964 Facel Vega III

Ferrari V-12 (all front-engined)
1947-72
Ford Mustnag GT/GTA V-8
1965-67
Ford Mustang Boss 302/Mach
I 1969-70
Ford Crestline Skyliner 1954
Ford Skyliner Retractable
1957-59
Ford Crown Victoria Skyliner
1955-56
Ford Sportsman 1946-48
Ford Thunderbird 1955-60

1960 Ford Thunderbird coupe

Ford Thunderbird Sports
Roadster 1962-63

1963 Ford Thunderbird

Frazer Manhattan 1947-50
Gaylord 1955-58
Healy Silverstone 1949-50
Hudson (all) 1948-49

1948 Hudson Commodore sedan

Hudson Hornet 1951-54
Imperial 1955-56
Jaguar XK120 1948-54
Jaguar Mark V drophead 1951
Jaguar Mark VII 1951-54

1953 Jaguar Mark VII Saloon

Jagaur Mark VIIM 1954
Jaguar XK140 1954-57
Jaguar Mark VIII 1956-57
Jaguar Mark IX 1958-61
Jaguar Mark X 1962-64
Jaguar XK150 1958-61
Jaguar 3.4 and 3.8 sedans
1957-64
Jaguar E-Type 1961-71
Jowett Javelin saloon 1947-53
Jowett Jupiter 1, 1A, R1, R4
1950-54
Kaiser Darrin 161 1954
Kaiser DeLuxe and DeLuxe
Virginian 1951-52
Kaiser Dragon 1951-53
Kaiser Manhattan 1954-55
Kaiser Vagabond 1949-50
Kaiser Virginian (hardtop)
1949-50
Kurtis sports car KSC 1949
Kurtis sports car 500S, 500KK
1953-55
Kurtis sports car 500M, 500X
1953-55
Lagonda V-12 1948-49
Lagonda 2.5-liter drophead
coupe 1949-53
Lamborghini Espada/4000GT
1967-72
Lamborghini Miura P400 S, SV

coupe and targa 1967-72
Lancia Flaminia Zagato 1959-64
Lancia Flaminia GT two-passenger coupe and convertible 1961-63
Lancia Aurelia B.20 and B.20 coupe 1951-59
Lancia Aurelia B.24 Spyder and convertible 1953-59
Lancia Flavia coupe 1962-66
Lea-Francis 2.5-liter Eighteen Sports 1950-54
Lincoln Capri 1952-54
Lincoln Continental 1946-48

1948 Lincoln Continental convertible

Lincoln Continental 1961-67
Lincoln Continental custom limousines (Lehmann-Perterson) 1963-67
Lotus Elite 1958-63
Maserati A-6/1500, A6G/2000, A6GCS Berlinetta 1946-57
Maserati 3500/3700 GT 1957-64
Maserati Ghibli, Mexico, Indy, 500GT 1959-72
Maserati Quattroporte 1963-69
Maserati Sebring, Mistral 1965-70
MG Type TC 1946-49
MG Type TD 1950-53
MG TF/TF 1500 1954-55
MGA Twin Cam 1958-62
MGB GT V-8 1972
Mercedes-Benz 190SL 1955-63
Mercedes-Benz 220 coupe and convertible 1951-55
Mercedes-Benz 220S/SE coupe and convertible 1956-60
Mercedes-Benz 220/250/280/300, 3.5 SE coupe and convertible 1960-71
Mercedes-Benz 230/250/280

SL 1963-71
Mercedes-Benz 300 non-unitized body (all models) 1951-63

1964 Mercedes-Benz 300 SE Cabrio

Mercedes-Benz SEL 6.3 1967-72
Mercedes-Benz 600 (all) 1963-72
Mercury Cougar XR-7 1967-68
Mercury Sportsman 1946
Mercury Sun Valley 1954-55
Morgan 4/4 1955-70
Morgan Plus 4 1950-64

1959 Morgan Plus 4 roadster

Morris Mini/Austin 1959-70
Muntz Jet 1950-54
Nash-Healey 1951-54
NSU Wankel Spyder 1964
OSCA MT-4 1948-56
Oldsmobile 88 (Holiay coupe and convertible) 1949-50
Oldsmobile 98 Holiday hardtop 1949
Oldsmobile Fiesta 1953
Oldsmobile 4-4-2 1964-71
Oldsmobile Toronado 1966-67
Packard Caribbean 1953-56
Packard Custom Super Clipper 1946-47
Packard Custom 8 1948-50
Packard Pacific/convertible 1954
Packard Panther Daytona 1954
Packard Patrician/400 1951-56
Panhard Dyna 1946-67
Pantera 1971-72

Pegaso (all) 1951-58
Plymouth Fury 1956-58
Plymouth Satellite SS and GTX 1965-70
Plymouth Barracuda Formula S 1965-69
Plymouth Road Runner and Superbird 1968-70
Pontiac Safari 1955-57

1957 Pontiac Safari wagon

Pontiac GTO 1964-69
Porsche Series 356 (all) 1949-65
Posche 911 L, T, E, S coupe, and Targa 1964-72
Riley 2.5 (RMA, RME) 1945-55
Rolls-Royce (all) 1947-69
Rover 2000/2000TC
Shelby 350 GT and 500 GT 1965-70
Sunbeam Tiger convertible 1965-67
Studebaker Avanti 1964-64
Studebaker Gran Turismo Hawk 1962-64
Studebaker Starlight coupe (all) 1947-49
Studebaker convertible 1947-49
Studebaker Starlight coupe (6 and V-8) 1953-54
Studebaker Starliner hardtop (6 and V-8)
Studebaker President Speedster 1955
Talbot Lago 4.5 (all) 1946-54
Toyota 2000 GT 1966-70
Triumph TR2/TR3 1953-63
Tucker 1948
Volkswagen Karmann Ghia 1956-72
Volvo P, S, E, ES 1800 Series 1961-72
Willys Overland Jeepster
Woodill Wildfire 1952-58